CW01496773

ISBN 978-0-260-03062-7
PIBN 10923437

State of Connecticut.

TWELFTH ANNUAL REPORT

OF THE

INSPECTOR OF FACTORIES

OF THE

STATE OF CONNECTICUT,

FOR THE

YEAR ENDING SEPTEMBER 30, 1898.

ORDERED PRINTED BY THE LEGISLATURE.

MERIDEN, CONN.:
PRESS OF THE REPUBLICAN PUBLISHING CO.
1898.

𝕾tate of Connecticut.

OFFICE INSPECTOR OF FACTORIES,

HARTFORD, CONN., November 30, 1898.

To His Excellency LORRIN A. COOKE, *Governor of the State of Connecticut.*

SIR—I have the honor to submit herewith my report for the year ending September 30, 1898.

Very respectfully yours,

GEO. L. McLEAN,

Inspector of Factories.

State of Connecticut.

REPORT

OF THE

FACTORY INSPECTOR.

OFFICE OF THE INSPECTOR OF FACTORIES,

HARTFORD, CONN., November 30, 1898.

To His Excellency LORRIN A. COOKE, *Governor of the State of Connecticut.*

SIR — In accordance with the law under which this office is organized, the Inspector of Factories herewith submits his report of the conditions as respects safety to life and health of the employes in factories and bakeshops visited, together with a detailed statement of inspections made and orders issued by this office during the year ending September 30, 1898.

In submitting the twelfth annual report of this department, it gives me pleasure to state that the orders given for improvements in ventilation, sanitary conditions, and guarding of dangerous machinery, have in most cases been promptly complied with, and the inspector courteously received.

During the fiscal year ending September 30, 1,425 factories and 211 bakeshops have been visited, and their conditions are reported in the printed tables.

FACTORY INSPECTION.

Factory inspection was first begun in Connecticut in the year 1887. The first inspection was made on November 23, of that year.

Much good was accomplished under the original law, but greater scope was given to the department by the Legislatures of 1889, 1893 and 1895.

The question is sometimes asked, What good has been accom-

plished by the factory laws of this State? In reply I would state
that dangerous machinery has been guarded, elevators examined, better ventilation and sanitary conditions provided in the
factories of the State.

A careful investigation of the reports of accidents which have
occurred in the factories during the past four years shows that in
some cases these accidents would never have occurred if certain
precautions had been taken. In one instance an order was given
to a manufacturing concern to provide safety appliances for an
elevator. A report of this office certifies that the superintendent
stated in writing that the change had been made. A short time
after this he was killed by this elevator falling. An investigation
showed that the change ordered by the Inspector had never been
made. Had the order been obeyed the accident would not have
happened.

In another instance, safety appliances were recommended by
the Inspector, for an elevator. He was told that there had been
no accident on that elevator for over thirty years, and the owner
of the plant could not be convinced that there was any necessity
for safety catches. Only a few days after, the Inspector called
again, with a written order, and was shown a press copy of a
letter ordering safety appliances for the elevator ; and it was also
stated by the manufacturer that only two days after the first
inspection an accident had occurred, and that if he had realized
the danger he would never have argued against the necessity of
the change.

The attention of one of our large railroad corporations was
called to the necessity of procuring a guard for a certain machine.
The master mechanic saw its necessity, and was willing to provide one. The operator, who had been working on the machine
for over fourteen years, did not think the guard was needed,
although he would used it if provided. Several days afterwards,
and before the guard could be procured, he had the fingers of his
hand torn off. The company was allowed one month to make
the change suggested, but the master mechanic reproached himself because he did not do it immediately, and thus avoid the
accident.

These are a few of the many instances that show the practicability of factory inspection.

The following table will show the number of factories inspected, and also the number of operatives employed, from the

year 1889 until 1898, inclusive, and will give the general public
an idea of the increased work done by this department :

	No. of Factories Inspected.	No. of Operatives in Places Inspected.
1889 (5 months),	255	42,089
1890 (1 year),	489	63,140
1891 "	435	55,922
1892 "	414	51,966
1893 '	476	68,098
1894 "	1,154	93,428
1895 (10 months),	1,091	93,467
1896 (1 year),	1,461	135,909
1897 "	1,426	131,700
1898 "	1,425	132,180

Number of males employed in factories visited in 1898, 93,277 ;
number of females, 38,903 ; total, 132,180.

BAKESHOPS.

Number of bakeshops visited :

1897,	- - - - - -	254
1898,	- - - - - -	211

COMFORT AND CONVENIENCE OF EMPLOYES.

There are employers of labor in this State who have expended
large sums of money in bettering the social and moral conditions
of their help. In some places, restaurants are connected with
the factory, where lunch is served to the employes at cost; also
reading rooms, where instructive and entertaining books can be
had during the noon hour.

The Seaside Institute of Bridgeport, Conn., of which a cut is
shown on the opposite page, was built by the Warner Brothers
Company, in 1887, for the use of their employes.

This building contains a large restaurant, free reading room,
library, bath rooms, and a large public hall, and rooms for evening classes. The plans of this institution have been carried out
according to the original idea. Practically every department is
being used and managed exactly as during the first year. Everything is free to the employes except the restaurant, in which
meals and lunches are served practically at cost.

Such an outlay of money for bettering the condition of the
laboring classes is worthy of commendation, but can be accomplished in but a few instances.

VENTILATION.

The subject of proper ventilation in factories has engrossed the attention of many manufacturers and engineers within the past few years. Great improvements have been made through natural and mechanical means. Exhaust systems for removing injurious dust and poisonous gases from the workrooms have come into general use. These exhaust systems, no doubt, have been the means of preserving many lives.

It is not generally realized that impure ventilation is the cause of more deaths than have ever occurred through machinery. There are some occupations, which, by their nature, are necessarily unhealthful, and no means now known can wholly do away with the danger, although great improvement has been made in recent years.

ELEVATORS.

All factory elevators have been carefully examined during the year, and, if the cables were found crystalized or weak, new ones to replace them have been ordered. Safety appliances have been provided, and within the last two years there has been no knowledge of the occurrence of any fatal accident in the factories, while Hartford alone, in the mercantile buildings and storehouses, there have occurred two fatal accidents.

GUARDING ELEVATOR OPENINGS.

Automatic hatches, which are operated by the movement of the elevator car, have proved satisfactory, as the elevator shaft is kept covered when the car is passed the different landings, thereby removing the danger of a person falling to the bottom of the shaft, and causing instant death. The construction of some factories is such that hatches are not practical, and in such cases self-closing gates are recommended. There are many ingenious devices used to make such gates automatic in their closing, and at the same time so perfect in their mechanism as to require little care and repairing.

Many manufacturers are looking for an automatic elevator gate so constructed that it will not be continually out of working order. They also wish for a detailed plan showing some device which is not patented, and can be constructed and applied by any ordinary mechanic. The cut on the opposite page, showing a gate which for the past two years has proved satisfactory, and of which a blue print plan can be had free by applying at this office, is hereby submitted.

This illustration represents details of fixtures of automatic gates with weights made of two-inch iron pipes, about eighteen inches long, with a cap screwed on at each end. The pipe is loaded on the inside with lead washers, with a take-up weight of iron three and one-half inches in diameter, made as represented, with a rubber packing between the take-up weight and the weight.

The point of excellence claimed for this plan is, that after the gate, which is counterweighted in the usual manner, reaches a certain point in its descent, the velocity of the gate increases, and it is likely to strike the bottom of the floor and slack the counterweight cords, which are likely to run off from the pulleys and get out of order. Many gates have been seen which were out of repair, and for this reason have sometimes been nailed up. This, of course, does not make any protection whatever for the elevator opening.

On the plan submitted, the gate, as it descends, picks up in the pocket on the side, the extra counterweight at the place most needed, and the gate does not strike the floor with force enough to slack the counterweight rope.

FIRE ESCAPES.

Fire escapes are required by law to be placed in factory and mercantile buildings in this State. The enforcement of this law is placed in the hands of the building inspector of each city, the warden of each borough not having a building inspector, or the first selectman of each town. They are required to visit such places at least once each year, between April and October, and see that the law is properly observed. Many violations of the law have been reported, from time to time, to the authorities, and in most instances proper egress has been provided. In other cases, nothing has been done. In one four-story building, which was reported by the Factory Inspector to the local authorities, no permanent fire escape or additional stairway has been provided, but in lieu of this a canvas chute has been placed in position. It is doubted whether in case of fire or panic in this building, the many employes on the upper floors would use this means for escaping.

GUARDING OF DANGEROUS MACHINERY.

In the past few years special attention has been given, by the makers of machinery, to the guarding of dangerous and exposed parts. This, of course, can be accomplished more easily at the places where the machinery is made than at the factories where it is run. In countries where the factory laws are extremely strict, all machinery is guarded where practical, so there is but little danger of an operative becoming injured in the ordinary course of his duties. There can be no means devised to prevent accidents where people are needlessly careless.

PROJECTING SET SCREWS AND BOLT HEADS IN COLLARS AND COUPLINGS OF SHAFTING.

Projecting set screws are generally recognized as a source of danger, either in oiling or tightening hangers, and they are generally found covered or sunk flush. During the past few years many fatal accidents have occurred by workmen being caught on set screws and wound around the shafting. One accident occurred during the last year, whereby the master mechanic of a factory was caught while tightening a hanger, and was thrown around the shafting. An order was given to the owners of the factory to cover or sink flush all projecting set screws in collars on shafting. The order was referred to this man, and he was directed to make the necessary changes, which, no doubt, he did at once.

PROPER WATER-CLOSET ACCOMMODATIONS IN FACTORIES.

Section 2,267 of the General Statutes requires every person owning or operating any factory employing more than five persons to provide suitable water-closet accommodations for the use of the employes, and it also says that they shall be kept in good sanitary condition. This is a vexatious problem for many manufacturers, who have provided good flush closets, and have found them within a short time broken. In many places there are no sewer systems, and earth closets are provided, which, if not properly cared for, are found in an unsanitary condition. The extension of the sewerage systems in our large cities has been the means of doing away with many earth closets and replacing them by good flush water-closets.

WELL LIGHTED WORK ROOMS.

Several complaints have been make to the Inspector, during the past year, in regard to insufficient light in work rooms, but there is no clause in the factory laws of Connecticut requiring proper light. In the factory laws of other States all work rooms are required to be properly lighted, as well as ventilated. These complaints were investigated, and there is no doubt in the minds of the Inspector, and the expert oculist employed, that there were just grounds for complaint, but there is no way, under the present law, whereby the owners can be compelled to make any improvement. The Inspector would recommend, therefore, the changing of our factory laws so as to conform with the laws of other States in regard to the lighting of work rooms.

Respectfully submitted,

GEO. L. McLEAN,

Inspector of Factories.

LAWS

Factories and Factory Inspectors

CONNECTICUT.

(General Statutes.)

CHAPTER CXLV.

SECTION 2264. The inspector of factories shall, as often as practicable, carefully examine all buildings and places where machinery shall be used, and shall have authority to enter such buildings and places at all proper times for the purposes of such inspection.

SEC. 2265. All factories and buildings where machinery shall be used shall be well ventilated, and kept as clean as the nature of the business will permit. The belting, shafting, gearing, machinery, and drums of all factories and buildings where machinery shall be used, when so placed as, in the opinion of the inspector, to be dangerous to the persons employed therein while engaged in their ordinary duties, shall, as far as practicable, be securely guarded. No machinery other than steam engines in a factory shall be cleaned while running, after notice forbidding the same is given by the inspector to the owners or operators of the factory.

SEC. 2266. The inspector may order the opening of all hoist-ways, hatchways, elevator-wells, and wheel-holes, upon every floor of any factory or other building where machinery shall be used, to be protected by good trap-doors, self-closing hatches, and safety-catches, or other safeguards, such as will insure the safety of the employes in such factory or other buildings where machinery shall be used, and all due dilligence shall be used to keep such trap-doors closed at all times, except when in actual use by an occupant of the building having the use and control of the same.

(Amended by Chap. CXVIII, Public Acts, 1893.)

SEC. 2267. Every person or corporation managing or operating any factory, or owning or controling the use of any other building where more than five persons shall be employed at labor, shall provide suitable water-closet accommodations for the use of the persons employed, and shall keep the same in good sanitary condition.

SEC. 2268. It shall be the duty of the inspector to enforce the provisions of this chapter by giving proper orders or notices to the persons or corporations owning, operating or managing the factories or buildings inspected by him, and also to make complaint to the state's attorney in the several counties respectively of all violations of this chapter.

SEC. 2269. Any person, firm, or corporation being the owner, lessee, or occupant of any factory or building included within the provisions of this chapter, or owning or controlling the use of any room in such building, shall, for the violation of any provisions of sections 2265, 2266, or 2267, forfeit to the use of the state not less than fifty nor more than five hundred dollars, and shall also be liable to any employe for all damages suffered by him by reason of such violation. It shall be the duty of the state's attorneys in the several counties to collect forfeitures under this chapter, but no suit shall be brought for any such violation, either in behalf of any person or the state, until four weeks after notice has been given by the inspector to such person, firm, or corporation of any changes necessary to be made to comply with the provisions of said sections, and not then, if, in the meantime, such changes have been made in accordance with such notification. Nothing herein shall be construed as limiting in any way the right of a person injured to bring an action to recover damages for the same, as though this chapter had not been enacted.

(Amended by Chapter CCXXV, Public Acts, 1889.) ·

SEC. 2270. The orders and notices given by the inspector under this chapter shall be written or printed, and signed by him officially, and may be served by himself or any proper officer or indifferent person, by leaving an attested copy thereof with or at the usual place of abode of the person upon whom service is to be made; and the notice, properly endorsed with the doings of the persons or officer serving the same, shall be returned to the office of the town clerk of the town in which is located the factory, building, or business to which such notice appertains, where it shall be kept on file. Such notice, and copies thereof, duly certified by the town clerk, shall be *prima facie* evidence that notice was given as therein appears. Notice to one member of a firm shall be notice to every member thereof, and notice to the president, secretary, or treasury of a corporation shall be notice to such corporation. The fees for serving such orders and notices, unless served by the inspector, shall be the same as for the service of process in civil action, and shall be included in the necessary expenses of the inspector and paid by the state.

SEC. 2271. It shall be the duty of the comptroller to provide

suitable rooms in the capitol at Hartford for the use of the inspector, and to furnish him blank forms for the purpose of giving
notices and orders required by this chapter, and for annual reports
to be made to the governor. The inspector shall keep, in books
provided for the comptroller for that purpose, copies of all notices
and orders given by him, and a record of all inspections and examinations made, and upon the expiration of his term of office shall
file his books of record with the secretary of state.

SEC. 2272. The inspector may from time to time employ
special agents to assist him in his inspections and examinations,
who shall receive compensation for the time actually employed in
such service only. The total amount expended under this section
shall not exceed in any one year the sum of fifteen hundred dollars,
which shall be paid by the state upon proper vouchers by the special
agents, which shall be signed by the inspector.

(Amended by Chapter CCVI, Public Acts, 1893.)

(Public Acts of 1889.)

CHAPTER CLXXIII.

An Act concerning Printing of Reports of the Inspector of
Factories.

*Be it enacted by the Senate and House of Representatives in General
Assembly convened:*

SECTION 1. The comptroller shall annually cause to be printed,
at the expense of the state, five thousand copies of the report of
the inspector of factories.

SEC. 2. This act shall take effect upon its passage.

Approved, June 4, 1889.

(Public Acts of 1889.)

CHAPTER CCXXV.

An Act Relating to Factories.

*Be it enacted by the Senate and House of Representatives in General
Assembly convened:*

Section 2269 of the general statutes is hereby amended by in-
serting between the words ''sections'' and the figures ''2265'' in
the fifth line thereof, the figures '' 2264,'' so that the first sentence
of said section as amended shall read as follows : Any person,
firm, or corporation being the owner, or lessee, or occupant of
any factory or building included within the provisions of this
chapter, or owning or controlling the use of any room in such
building, shall, for a violation of any provisions of sections 2264,
2265, 2266, 2267, forfeit to the use of the state not less than fifty

nor more than five hundred dollars, and shall also be liable to any employe for all damages suffered by him by reason of such violation.

Approved June 19, 1889.

(Amended by Chapter CCVI, Public Acts, 1895.)

(Public Acts of 1893.)

CHAPTER LIX.

An Act concerning the Employment of Custodians of Elevators.

Be it enacted by the Senate and House of Representatives in General Assembly convened:

SECTION 1. No person, partnership or corporation shall permit or employ any person under the age of sixteen years to have the care, custody, operation, or management of any elevator.

SEC. 2. Any person, partnership, or corporation violating the provisions of this act shall be punished by a fine of not less than five nor more than twenty-five dollars for each offense.

Approved, April 19, 1893.

(Public Acts of 1893.)

CHAPTER LXXVII.

An Act concerning Seats for Female Operatives.

Be it enacted by the Senate and House of Representatives in General Assembly convened:

SECTION 1. Every person, partnership or corporation employing females, in any mercantile, mechanical or manufacturing establishment in this state, shall furnish and provide suitable seats for the use of all females so employed, and shall permit the use of such seats by said females when they are not necessarily engaged in the active duties for which they are employed.

SEC. 2. Any person, partnership, or corporation violating any of the provisions of this act shall be punished by a fine of not less than five dollars nor more than fifty dollars for each and every offense.

Approved, April 19, 1893.

(Public Acts of 1893.)

CHAPTER CXVIII.

An Act concerning Elevators.

Be it enacted by the Senate and House of Representatives in General Assembly convened:

Section 2266 of the general statutes is hereby amended to read as follows: The inspector of factories may order the opening of all hoistways, hatchways, elevator-wells, and well-holes, upon every floor of every factory, mercantile establishment, or other building where machinery shall be used, to be protected by good trap-doors, self-closing hatches, and safety-catches or other safeguards, such as will ensure the safety of the employes in such factory, mercantile establishment or other building where machinery shall be used, and all due dilligence shall be used to keep such trap-doors closed at all times, except when in actual use by an occupant of the building having the use and control of the same. All elevator cabs or cars, whether used for freight or passengers, shall be provided with some suitable mechanical devices, if considered necessary by the said inspector, whereby the cab or car will be securely held in the event of an accident to the shipper-rope or hoisting machinery, or from any similar cause, and said mechanical device shall at all times be kept in good working order.

Approved, May 18, 1893.

(Public Acts of 1893.)

CHAPTER CCIV.

An Act for the Preservation of the Health of Factory Employes.

Be it enacted by the Senate and House of Representatives in General Assembly convened:

SECTION 1.   Whenever the inspector of factories, on the complaint of any person, after due investigation, shall find it necessary for the preservation of the health of the employes in any manufacturing establishment, factory, or mill in which is carried on the business of buffing, polishing, or grinding metal, or any operations in which an excessive amount of dust is generated, that the excessive dust resulting from said operations should be removed from the atmosphere of the rooms or apartments used for that purpose, he shall, in writing, direct the person or persons or corporation owning or occupying said premises, or carrying on business in such premises, within three months from the date of said order, to introduce and operate such appliances and devices as may be necessary to remove, so far as the nature of the business will permit, such excessive dust or foreign matter from the atmosphere of such mill, factory, or apartment used for the purposes aforesaid ; provided such appliances or devices do not restrict or interfere with the aforesaid business or operations.

SEC. 2. Any violation of any proper order made or given by the inspector of factories, under the provisions of the preceding section, shall be punished in the manner provided in section 2269 of the general statutes.

Approved, June 14, 1893.

(Public Acts of 1893.)

CHAPTER CCVI.

An Act relating to Duties of the Inspector of Factories.

Be it enacted by the Senate and House of Representatives in General Assembly convened:

Section 2272 of the general statutes is hereby amended to read as follows : The inspector may from time to time employ special agents to assist him in the performance of the duties of his office. Such special agents while so employed shall have the same power and authority as the inspector, subject to his approval. The total amount expended under this section shall not exceed in any one year the sum of three thousand dollars, which shall be paid in the same manner as the expenses of other departments of the state government, upon proper vouchers by the special agents, signed by the inspector.

Approved, June 14, 1893.

(Substitute for House Bill No. 263.)

Public Ats of 1895.

CHAPTER CCVI.

An Act concerning Inspection of Factories.

Be it enacted by the Senate and House of Representatives in General Assembly convened:

SECTION I. Section 2269 of the general statutes is hereby amended to read as follows: Any person, firm, or corporation, being the owner, lessee, or occupant of any factory or building included within the provisions of this chapter, or owning or controlling the use of any room in such building, shall, for any violations of sections 2265, 2266, or 2267 of the general statutes, or for obstructing or hindering the inspector of factories in carrying out the duties of his office, forfeit to the use of the state not more than fifty dollars. It shall be the duty of the state's attorneys in the several counties to collect forfeitures under this chapter, but no suit shall be brought for any such violation until four weeks after notice has been give by the inspector to such person, firm, or corporation of any changes necessary to be made to comply with the provisions of said sections, and not then if, in the meantime, such changes have been made in accordance with such notification. Nothing herein shall be construed as limiting in any way the right of a person injured to bring an action to recover damages for the same, as though this chapter had not been enacted.

SEC. 2.. Any person, firm, or corporation aggrieved by any order of an inspector of factories may appeal to the superior court in the county where the person, firm or corporation owns, leases, or occupies the factory or building in relation to which said order relates, within four weeks after notice of such order shall be given. Said appeal shall operate as a supersedeas, shall be made in writing, and shall contain a brief statement of the facts and reasons of appeal and a citation to the inspector of factories to appear before said court, and said court or any judge thereof may direct the time of appearance and the manner of service. Said court may review the doings of the factory inspector, may examine the questions in issue, and may confirm, change, or set aside the doings of the factory inspeetor, and may make such orders in the premises, including orders as to costs, as it may find to be proper and equitable.

SEC. 3. All acts and parts of acts inconsistent herewith are hereby repealed.

Approved, July 9, 1895.

(House Bill No. 269.)
CHAPTER CCXCIV.
An Act concerning Department Reports.

Be it enacted by the Senate and House of Representatives in General Assembly convened :

SECTION 1. All reports heretofore or hereafter required to be made by state departments, institutions, commissions, boards, or any recipients of state money shall, from and after the passage of this act, be made to the governer and by him transmitted to the general assembly.

SEC. 2. All reports above referred to shall be made to and including the thirtieth of September, 1895, and annually thereafter, and shall be published on or before the thirty-first day of December following ; provided, however, that the reports of the insurance commissioner and the state board of education may be made at times and for the periods now required by law, and the reports of the state board of agriculture and of the agricultural experiment stations may be made as heretofore.

SEC. 3. All acts and parts of acts inconsistent herewith are hereby repealed.

SEC. 4. This act shall take effect from its passage.

Approved, July 4, 1895.

RECORD OF INSPECTION

OF

FACTORIES.

Inspection and Orders from October 1, 1897, to September 30, 1898.

Order No.	Goods Manufactured.	No. of Employes. M.	F.	Orders Given.	Compliances.
1	Job Printing,	2	3	No orders.	
2	Newspapers,	22		No orders.	
3	Newspapers and Printing,	20	5	No orders.	
4	Job Printing,	7		No orders.	
5	Brass Castings, Bees	12		No orders.	
6	Lithographic . and Lathes,	32		No orders.	
7	Pianos,	25	15	No orders.	
8	Ladies' Fur Hats,	60		No orders.	
9	Illuminating Gas,	7		No orders.	
10	Hatters' Furs, ...y,	125	50	No orders.	
11	Special ...y,	10		No orders.	
12	Dye Wds & Licorice	250		No orders.	
13	Roller Covering,	5		No orders.	
14	Bleaching, Dyeing and Finishing,	256	46	(1) Provide better ventilation in singeing room. (2) ...he up...de posts of large elevator in printing room. (3) Guard ...ge gears ...t ...mn 5-roll calender in calender room.	Complied.
15	Cotton Cloth,	165	175	Provide ...ter ventilation in ...s for ...we room, brick mill, ...nd keep the ...me in good sanitary condition.	Complied.
16	Cotton Yarn,	4	16	No orders.	
17	Fancy Cotton Goods,	331	196	Provide ...w ...able for el...vaor in ...ock room.	Complied-
18	Laundry,	1	9	No orders.	

19	Guns, Pistols and Bicycles,	100	90	Provide new ☐ and belt to new ... able to main elevator. ☐ or railing fly ... ☐ by ☐	Complied.
20	Monumental Work,	8		No orders.	
21	Bicycle Chains,	12		No orders.	
22	General Wood Work,	8		No orders.	
23	Iron Castings,	30		No ☐.	
24	Cotton Yarn,	90	90	(1) Provide new ☐ by ☐ engine ☐ ☐ (2) No ☐ ☐ is ☐.	
25	☐ ☐,	25	25	No orders.	
26	Cotton Yarn,	25	25	No orders.	
27	☐ Yarn,	20	20	No orders.	
28	Cork Stopples,	20	20	No orders.	
29	Plumbing Supplies,	10		No orders.	
30	Fancy Cords & Braids	5	35	No orders.	
31	Belting and Straps,	30	10	No orders.	
32	Bicycle Chains,	20		No orders.	
33	Firearms,	50	13	No ☐.	
34	Laundry,	8	10	No orders.	
35	☐ ☐ry,	2		No orders.	
36	Cabinet Work, ☐	8		No ☐.	
37	Steam and Hot Heaters,	70	15	Repair pipe ☐ with ☐-pipe in prevent water from running on floor.	Complied.
38	Button Backs,	15	57	No orders.	
39	Paper Boxes,	15	1	No orders.	
40	Steam & Gas Pipes,	35		No orders.	
41	Printing,	13		No orders.	
42	☐ Traps,	10		☐-closet to No orders.	Complied.
43	Soda ☐,	7		No orders.	
44	☐ and Cyclometers,	220	230	Provide new cable for elevator.	
45	Buttons & Novel ties,	125	140	No orders.	
46	Machinery,	75	2	No orders.	
47	Clock ☐s,	125	10	No orders.	
48	Bl ☐ Books,	18	4	No orders.	

REPORT OF INSPECTIONS.— CONTINUED.

Order No.	Goods Manufactured.	No. of Employes. M.	F.	Orders Given.	Compliances.
49	Silk Thread,	1		No orders.	
50	Elastic Webbing,	40	58	Guard by secure railing main belt ... img water- wel shaft.	Complied.
51	Brass Goods,	150	160	N orders.	
52	Wood Work,	15	50	Box l elt running ... l sw on s ... nd flor at l ... at three feet hgh.	Complied.
53	Buckles,	200	200	No orders.	
54	Clocks and Watches,	638	318	No orders.	
55	Brass Goods,	400	200	No orders.	
56	Electric Power Station,	30		No orders.	
57	Wood Work,	20		No orders.	
58	Machinery and Tacks,	20	20	(1) ...ly cl an nd dis ... ict water-closets and keep ... he me in gd ... y con dion. (2) Repair ... dble water-cl set.	Complied.
59	Silver Plated Ware,	100	20	No orders.	
60	Heavy Paper,	50		No orders.	
61	Carpet Linings,	4		No orders.	
62	Table Cutlery,	65	2	No orders.	
63	Stoves and Hot Water Heaters,	150		No orders.	
64	Woolen Goods,	22	8	(1) Provide hangers for lo ... se ... lit in ... her room. (2) ...r or ... sik flush pr ... g et ... sw in collar on main ... lit, ar ... th.	Complied.
65	Monuments,	10		No orders.	
66	Book and Lithograph Paper,	125	45	(1) Guard ... dig on main ... lit nar prt ... on in he ... her room. (2) Cover or sik ... th all proj ... ig et screws in collars on ... y to ol ... ne hte in not on. shafting, where	Complied.

		430	70	(1) (2) (3)	Complied.
67	Dyeing, Bleaching and Printing,				Complied.
68	Colored Cover Papers	35	9	No ers.	
69	Silk Ribbons,	12	50	No orders.	
70	Woolen Goods,	95	30	No orders.	
71	Denims & Tickings.	150	350	No orders.	
72	Tanning & Finishing,	45		No ers.	
73	Woolen Goods,	15	10	No	
74		28		No	
75	El	6		No orders.	
76	Work,	5		No orders.	
77	General	8		No orders.	
78	Work,	35		No orders	
79		12		No orders	
80	N	35	25	No orders.	
81	Quilts,	100	40	No orders.	
82		60	2	No ers.	
83		18		No orders.	
84	ay Wall Paper,	8	18	No ers.	
85	Paper Boxes.	22		No orders.	
86	Heavy Paper,	16		No orders.	
87	Heavy Paper,	10		No orders.	
88	Wood Working Ma-			No orders.	
89	Silk	40		No orders.	
90	Dye W	20		No orders.	
		18			

REPORT OF INSPECTIONS.— CONTINUED.

Order No.	Goods Manufactured.	No. of Employes. M.	No. of Employes. F.	Orders Given.	Compliances.
91	Denims,	100	80	No ords.	
92	Fancy Cotton Goods,	65	100	(1) Provide new cable to elevator in stone mill. (2) Guard large belt in the basement of stone mill ext to ... (3) Thoroughly clean and ... water- ... for ... the mill, and keep the same in good sanitary ...	Complied.
93	Woolen Goods,	80	35	(1) Provide hangers for all ... running lose on shafting. (2) Introduce and ... within three months from the ate of his ... such appliances as may be necessary to provide ... ventilation as will ... the excessive steam generated in the gig ron.	Complied.
94	Woolen Goods,	1 0	50	No orders.	
95	Doors, Sash & Blinds,	30		No orders.	
96	Rasps and ...,	20		No ords.	
97	... Goods,	40	10	No ords.	
98	... ...,	500	950	No ords.	
99	... Power Station,			No	
100	Cotton Cloth,	8	50	No orders. (1) Replace and put in proper working order safety ... on elevator in ... (2) Remove ... roping and all other obstructions from the ... leading to ... (3) ... and keep ... same in good sanitary condition.	Complied.
101	Furniture Paper,	8		No orders.	
102	Heavy Paper,	8		No orders.	
103	Rope & Manila Paper,	10		No orders.	
104	Bicycles,	35		No orders.	

No.	Industry			Orders	Status
105	Repairing and Electric Power,	15		No orders.	
D6	Crackers & Biscuits,	100	50	No orders.	
D7	Acids, etc.,	10		No orders.	
108	Lager Beer,	15		No orders.	
109	Silver Plated Ware,	150	50	No orders.	
110	Brass Goods.	110	20	Box two belts running through floor of sawing room, near brass-turning room, on second floor.	
111	Knit Underwear,	30	125	Box driving belt to press in spinning room at last three feet high. (1) Box belt in cuff room near door. (2) Cover or sink flush all projecting set screws in collars on shafting. (3)	Complied.
112	Pins & Brass Goods,	200	100	Provide new cable for elevator.	Complied.
113	Cutlery,	70	6	No orders.	
114	Carriages,	.5		(1) Cover or sink flush projecting set screws in collars on main shafting in basement. (2) Cover main belt running engine in basement.	Complied.
115	Sheet Brass,	17		No orders.	
116	Buttons & Novelties,	25	30	Cover or sink flush projecting set screws in collars on shafting in the weave and buffing rooms.	Complied.
117	Job Ptg;	8	4	No orders.	
118	Silk Ptg;	50	117	No orders.	
119	Body Silk,	5	11	No cuts.	
120	Bed Quilts and Carpet Lining,	100	50	Guard fly wheel to engine as suggested.	Complied.
121	Shirtings & Suitings,	50	30	No orders.	
122	Doors, Sash & Blinds,	15		No orders.	
123	Boilers,	30		No orders.	
124	Car Repairing,	30		No orders.	
125	Laundry Wk,	8	5	No orders.	
126	Paper Boxes,	10	30	No orders.	
127	Cotton Gins and Printing Presses,	200	3	No orders.	
128	Wood Sawing and Planing,	15		No orders.	

REPORT OF INSPECTIONS.—CONTINUED.

Order No.	Goods Manufactured.	No. of Employes. M.	F.	Orders Given.	Compliances.
129	Laundry Work, Clks and Drills, Cor dts,	8		No orders.	
130	Ship ilg ad Repairing.	70	3	Guard pulley and belt to dynamo in engine room.	Complied.
131	Steam Engines and Boilers,	10		No orders.	
132		60		Cover or sink flush all projecting set screws in collars on shag.	
133	Laundry Wk,	12	2	No orders.	
134	Radiators and Gray Iron Castings,	60		No orders.	
135	Monuments,	16		No orders.	
136	Electric Power,	5		No orders	
137	Bicycles,	15		No eds.	
138	Iron Vises.	20		No orders.	
139	Monuments,	8		No orders.	
140	Bed Quilts,	80	75	No orders.	
141	Toilet Paper,	7	8	No eds.	
142	Denims, Shirtings and Fancy Cotton Goods,	225	275	Put in proper working order sliding floor in carding room, second floor.	Complied.
143	Sp b Silk ad Dress Gs,	100	350	No orders.	
144	Castings,	6		No orders.	
145	Velvet, ilg,	90	40	No orders.	
146	l	15		No orders.	
147	Silk Mry,	153		No orders.	
148	Silox,	15		No orders.	
149	Spools,	28		No eds.	

No.				Orders
150	Soap.	8	18	No orders.
151	Paper Machinery,	40		No orders.
152	Globes and School Materials,	2	3	No orders.
153	Woolen Goods,	50	10	No orders.
154	Rope and Twine,	4	3	No orders.
155	Satinets,	70	30	(1) Provide new rope for elevator. (2) Keep ⬚s to elev ⬚or openings closed when el ⬚ator is away ⬚⬚n ⬚d openings. (3) Prohibit persons from riding on elevator unless the car is provided ⬚h some ⬚ ⬚e. — Complied.
156	Fertilizer,	15		No orders.
157	Rope and Twine,	5		N orders.
158	Ship Building and Repairing,			No orders.
159	Woolen Goods,	400	75	(1) ⬚ir ⬚d thoroughly cl ⬚n water-cl ⬚ts for ⬚⬚h ⬚ale ⬚d ⬚ale 1 ⬚ ⬚ts ⬚d keep ⬚m in good sanitary ⬚n. (2) Provide sufficient ⬚er ⬚d some ⬚s ⬚ere by ⬚e same ⬚n be properly ⬚⬚d ⬚n ⬚d. (3) ⬚ ⬚e ⬚ts to be ⬚d by ⬚s, ⬚d prohibit ⬚e ⬚s ⬚m ⬚sg ⬚e same. (4) ⬚e some m ⬚ as for removing ⬚e ⬚n f ⬚n ⬚e dye house. — ⬚plied.
		100		
160	⬚ted Wire and ⬚s,	37		No ⬚ts.
161	Pins,	5	7	No ⬚ts.
162	⬚s,	50	3	N o ⬚ts.
163	⬚ss Goods,	225	150	N orders.
164	⬚se ⬚e Nails,	50	20	No ⬚ts.
165	⬚r.	6		No orders.
166	Small Lathes,	6		No ⬚ts.
167	⬚ ⬚s ⬚d Augers,	8		N o ⬚ts.
168	⬚d ⬚er Goods,	35		No orders.
169	⬚n ⬚h,	16	13	No orders.
170	Doors, Sash & Bl'ds.	12	12	No ⬚ts.

REPORT OF INSPECTIONS. — CONTINUED.

Order No.	Goods Manufactured.	No. of Employes. M.	No. of Employes. F.	Orders Given.	Compliances.
171	●● ●●, ●●s	5		No orders.	
172	Fancy Cotton ●● Cl ●●,	200	250	No orders.	
173	●●, Thread ●● Yarn,	125	225	No orders.	
174	●● Presses,	300		No orders.	
175	●● & Repairs,	6		No orders.	
176	●● Wicking ●●			No orders.	
177	Cord,	5	4	No ●●s.	
178	Woof, Stg,	10		No ●●ers.	
179	Wolen ●●s,	80	25	No ●●s.	
180	●●,	190		No ●●s.	
181	Insulated Wire,	15	40	No ●●s.	
182	Lamps & Bedsteads,	150	30	No ●●s.	
183	●● & Repairs,	7		No ●●rs.	
184	Brass ●●s,	16	6	No ●●rs.	
185	Printing,	20		No ●●s.	
186	Clock Trimmings,	60	15	●● ●●side ●●er-closets so t●●t t ●●e will be enough ●●w of ●● to properly ●●h ●●e ●●e.	Complied.
187	Gem Nail Clippers, Electrical Supplies,	8	70	No ●●s. ●●er or ●●t l●●h projecting ●●t ●●ws in collars on shafting in finishing ●● on first floor.	Complied.
188	Webbing,	40	250	No orders.	
189	Augers and Bits,	50		No ●●rs.	
190	Augers and Bits,	30	2	No ●●s.	
191	Drawing Knives,	40	1	No ●●s.	
192	Stove Trimmings and Bicycle Parts,	30		No orders.	
193	Roll Covering,	5		No orders.	

No.	Description				Remarks
194		1			ds.
195	Gn Cl dn, Wood Work, Oper	300	15	No	ds.
196	Cal Wood Work,	10	450	No	ds.
197	Bt Brass & Oper	350		No	ds.
198	My, Or,	550		No	orders.
199	Brass ad Or,	375	15	No	orders.
200	Ns,	60		No	ds.
201		75		No	ds.
202	Dress Stys,	8	14	No	ds.
203	Gt s, &c ,	10	45	No	ds.
204	Thread ad Sk,	35	100	No	ds.
205	Bells, ad	50		No	ds.
206	Bells, ad Bicycle Specialties,	90	10	No	orders.
207	Gn & Iron Nets,	1	8	No	orders.
208	Brass Gs, and	18		No	orders.
209	Nickel Bag and Buffing,	6		No	orders.
210	Bells, ad Bolt Machinery,	20		No	orders.
211	Nut ad Bolt Machinery,	5		No	orders.
212	Bls ad El Toys,	27		No	ds.
213	Bell Bs ad cle	12		No	ds.
214	Sundries,	75	12	No	ds.
215	Bells,	2	3	No	ds.
216	Paper Boxes,	6		No	ders.
217	Be Bries,	275		No	ders.
218	Bs & er Wire, Bs, ir ad pt in hine dp. ir ad safety catches on elevator in ds.	150		No	Complied.
219	Bicycles,	107			
220	Electric Light and Power, Guard by secure casing or railing fly wheels on Fitchburg engine and balance wheel of Ball engine.	11		No orders.	Complied.
221	Pins,	15	15		

REPORT OF INSPECTIONS.— CONTINUED.

Order No.	Goods Manufactured.	No. of Employes. M.	F.	Orders Given.	Compliances.
222	Bicycles,	150	25	...g or ...ling fly wheel and belt of engine	In process
223	Dress Silk,	3	12	...g or railing fly wheel, crank and belt	Complied.
224	Combs, Pins, etc.,	25	6	No ...	
225	Toys, ...	8		No ...	
226	Cut ... Work,	15		No orders.	
227	... Sawing and	6		No orders.	
228	Band Sawing and	7		No orders.	
229	Laundry ...	8	8	No orders	
230	Dress ...	12	26	No orders	
231	...	6		No orders.	
232	...	300		No orders.	
233	...	10		No orders.	
234	...	20	200	No orders.	
235	Dress ... and			No ...	
236	Dress ...	14	40	No ...	
237	...	60		No ...	
238	... Weaving,	115	100	...ders.	
239	Suspender Webbing,	25	75	No ...	
240	Suspender Weaving,	50	50	No ...	
241	...	7		Repair ... pt in pro ... working order safety catches on	Complied
	...	125	300	... in ...com.	
242	Writing Machines,	90	20	No orders.	
243	Bolts,	35		No ... es.	pt in ... ...g ... safety	
244	Planes,	f0		... ... safety ... ...s on	Complied.

No.	Establishment			Remarks	
245	Suspender Straps and Hangers,	20 12	No ds. No ds.		Complied.
246	Soap,	15	The new cable for elevator.		
247	Machine Twist,	40	No ds.		
248	Cotton Yarn,	28	No ds.		
249	Hardware,	230	(1)	Cover or ... ... was in coll as on ...	Complied.
250	Iron and Tin Ware.		(2)	... ... pt in good sanitary ... in wa. t-closet	
			(3)	... ... le water-cl et ... as for males.	
251	Steam Engine Governors,	55	No ds.		
252	Silver Plated Ware,	125	No ds.		
253	Enameled Ware,	240	(1)	Good ... ping to ... by on ... dr of blue ...	Complied.
			(2)	... ... high to ...	
			(3)	... ... by the males.	
254	Carriages & Wagons,	8	No	No ds.	
255	Rubber Boots and Shoes,	130	65	No orders.	
256	Heavy Machinery,	150		No orders.	
257	Electricity,	22		No orders.	
258	General Wood Work,	30		No orders.	
259	Silver Plated Ware,	225	12	Thoroughly clean earth-closet and keep the same in good sanitary condition.	Complied.
260	Castings, Hardware and Iron ?s,	65 3	4	No orders. No orders.	
261	Hammers, ?				
262	Sawing and Dressing S?,	8 8	7	No orders. No orders.	
263	Tin Ware & Buckles,	5		No orders.	
264	Hammers,	70		No orders.	
265	Stone Quarrying,				

REPORT OF INSPECTIONS.— CONTINUED.

Order No.	Goods Manufactured.	No. of Employes. M.	F.	Orders Given.	Compliances.
266	Tin Ware,	24		No orders.	
267	Gun Sights,	18	2	No orders.	
268	Cotton Yarn,	20	24	No orders.	
269	Ivory & Bone Goods,	32	18	No orders.	
270	Spirit Levels and Nippers,	10		No orders.	
271	Printing,	8	2	No orders.	
272	Electricity,	5		No orders.	
273	Extension Tables and Piano Stools,	10		No orders.	
274	Brass Goods,	100	50	No orders.	
275	Laundry Work,	5	8	Provide suitable means to flush closet used by females.	Complied.
276	Novelties,	20	15	No orders.	
277	Woolen Goods,	60	20	No orders.	
278	Needles, etc.,	375	200	No orders.	
279	Hardware,	400	12	No orders.	
280	General Wood Work,	75		No orders.	
281	Machinery,	250		No orders.	
282	Bicycles,	325	6	No orders.	
283	Bone Goods and Fertilizers,	55	20	Provide new cable to small elevator.	Complied.
284	Files,	8		No orders.	
285	Padlocks,	80	4	No orders.	
286	Ornamental Iron Work,	8		No orders.	
287	Hammocks, Linings and Netting,	75	70	No orders.	
288	Bicycle Bells,	8		Guard by iron railing balance wheel of engine next to stairway.	Complied.
289	Paper Boxes,	1	10	No orders.	

No.	Article			Remarks	Result
290	Horse Blankets,	33	13	No orders.	
291	Turning and General Wood Work,	8	80	No orders.	
292	Rubber Webbing,	40	16	No orders.	
293	Cotton Yarn,	18	9	No orders.	
294	Twine and Cord,	11	18	No orders.	
295	Twine,	14	18	Provide better water-closet accommodations for male employes.	Complied.
296	Work,	5	5	No orders.	
297	Y as ad Ducking,	8	10	No orders.	
298	T,	10	5	No orders.	
299	We,	10	14	No orders.	
300	Netting ad Twine,	15	8	No orders.	
301	We ad Yarn,	5		No orders.	
302	Drop Forgings ad	6	2	ds.	
303	Flat We,	9	1	ds.	
304	lsr d Ware,	9	6	ds.	
305	We ad Gd,	10	4	ode r	
306	We ad Gd,	5		ds.	
307	Hs,	2	9	ds.	
308	Hs,	15		de	
309	He,	15		ds.	
310	Hs,	75	75	No	Rail to stairs leading to second floor. Complied.
311	Newspapers and g,	6	5	No orders.	
312	Brass, a Trimmings	900	14	No orders.	
313	Sk Tread,	48	40	No orders.	
314	Silk d,	19	140	No orders.	
315	Machinery, r ad	50		No orders.	
316	Sheet	5		No orders.	
317	Augers,	85		No orders.	
318	Ss ad	10		No orders.	

REPORT OF INSPECTIONS.—CONTINUED.

Order No.	Goods Manufactured.	No. of Employes. M.	F.	Orders Given.	Compliances.
319	Screen and Cotton Cloth,	5	4	No orders.	
320	Woolen Goods,	90	60	No orders.	
321	Piano and Organ Keys and Actions,	200	50	No orders.	
322	Piano Keys.	22		No orders.	
323	Piano Brackets,	6		No orders.	
324	Auger Bits,	28		No orders.	
325	Malleable Iron Castings.	100		No orders.	
326	Wood Work,	8		Guard by boxing or railing driving belt to sewing machine in turning room.	Complied.
327	Locks,	300	75	No orders.	
328	Organ Stops & Knobs	4	2	No orders.	
329	Fancy Wood Turning	80		No orders.	
330	Paints,	5		No orders.	
331	Steel and Bone Novelties,	12		No orders.	
332	Wire Novelties,	40	3	Provide some suitable mechanical device whereby the elevator car will be securely held in event of accident to hoisting machinery or shipping rope.	In process
333	Ivory Combs and Piano Keys,	22	5	No orders.	
334	Auger Bits,	6		No orders.	
335	Auger Bits,	10		No orders.	
336	Organ and Piano Keyboards,	215	15	No orders.	
337	Wood Turning,	15		No orders.	
338	Cut Glass,	6		No orders.	

No.	Article				Remarks
339	Auger Bits.	40			Complied.
340	Clocks and Watches,	250	1 D	No	
341	Clocks and Watches,	240	25	No	
342	Clock Cases,	110	30	No	
343	Pocket Cutlery,	18	2	No	
344	Brass Goods,	325		No	...ailing or casing large driving belt to ... rolling
845	Pocket Cutlery,	40	3	No	
346	Pocket Knives,	18	3	No	
347	Pocket Knives,	17		No	
348	Woolen Goods,	30	5	No	orders.
349	Shears,	115	10	No	Complied.
350	... Bits,	170	10	No	
351	Auger & ... Bits,	18		No	
352	... Bits, ...	6		orders	
353	...y Bone ... Wire	8	4	No	
354	Bright ...	20	20	No orders.	
355	Axe & ... Handles,	5		No orders.	
356	...d Brushes,	7	2	No orders.	
357	...	25	35	No orders.	
358	Agricultural ...	75		No orders.	
359	Planters' ...	15			Cover or sink flush all projecting set screws in collars on shafting.
360	Planters' Hoes and Drop Forgings,	20			Cover or sink flush all projecting set screws in collars on shafting. No orders.
361	Gimlets & Novelties,	5			
362	Planters' Hoes and Grinding Shop,	25			Cover or sink flush all projecting set screws in collars on shafting.

REPORT OF INSPECTIONS.—CONTINUED.

Order No.	Goods Manufactured.	No. of Employes. M.	No. of Employes. F.	Orders Given.	Compliances.
363	Planters' Hoes and Forge Shop.	60		(1) Cover or sik th all je g et ves in coll as on main fg in all the mills. (2) Box at at dr t lh. t g to vr vl in wr forging ad l . e belts ming g ad d by g or s.	In process
364	Hats in the Rough,	80		d r s of g g sewing s.	Complied. Complied.
65	Fur Hats,	75	25	No orders.	
66	Fur Hats,	50	20	No rs.	
67	Hatters' Furs,	70	7	No rs.	
68	Fur Hats,	75	45	No s.	
69	Fur Hats,	90		No s.	
70	Shoes,	90	50	No s.	
71	Hatters' Furs,	60	10	r or sik th ge et s ew in collar on shafting g poler e on t dr.	Complied.
72	Silk Ribbons,	40	12	No rs.	
373	Fur Hats,	90	90	No rs.	
374	Straw Hats,	25	60	No s.	
25	Machinery,	5		No rs.	
376	Metal Bedsteads,	00	15	No rs.	
377	Sheet Brass, Copper and Lamps,	200	60	(1) Cover or sink flush all projecting set screws in collars on shafting. (2) Cover or guard projecting bolt-heads in couplings on shaftings where near pulleys or hangers. (3) Repair automatic hatches to elevators in south mill, or replace same by new.	Complied.
378	Laundry Work,	4	6	No orders.	

No.				Orders / Remarks	
379	Steam Heaters and Furnaces,	45		Cover or ... all projec... set screws in collars on ...	Complied.
80	Hardware,	60	2	No ...	
81	Hatters' Tools,	6		No ...	
82	Packing Cases,	12		No ...	
83	Paper Boxes,	25	51	No orders.	
384	Paper Boxes,	50	60	... ten years of age from having the ... elevator.	Complied.
85	...	25		No ...	
86	...		3	No orders.	
387	Bolts, ...	22		No orders.	
88	... Cutlery,	40	7	No orders.	
89	Rubber ...	170	2	No orders.	
90	...	93		No orders.	
91	...	75	4	No orders.	
392	Hoo...	10		No ...	
393	Paper,	24	80	... rail driving ...	Mill closed
		75	4	(1) ... (2) ... (3) ... (4) ... remove the ...	
394	Printing Presses,	66	43	No ...	
395	Horn Buttons,	18		No ...	
396	Drop Forgings,	64		No ...	
397	Mosquito Netting and Dress Goods,	103	100	(1) Provide new cable to elevator in finishing mill. (2) Repair hatches to elevator shafts in both factories so that they will be closed when elevator cars are away from opening. (3) Prohibit any person under the age of sixteen years to have the care, custody or operating of any elevator.	Complied.

REPORT OF INSPECTIONS.— CONTINUED.

Order No.	Goods Manufactured.	No. of Employes. M.	F.	Orders Given.	Compliances.
398	Hosiery and Men's Underwear,	4	110	No ds.	
399	Carriage Bolts,	30	1	No ds.	
400	Harness Snaps,	6		No orders.	
401	Hats,	40		the operatives so ...	Complied.
402	Hats,	30	25		Complied.
403	Hat Forms,	20		No ds.	
04	Wd k,	5		No ds.	
405		140		No ders.	
406	s, Sash & Blinds,	12		No ders.	
07	Electricity,	7		No ds.	
408	El tic Webbing,	20	15	No ds.	
409	Straw Hats,	40	10	No	
410	s,	75	700	railing large belt of electric machine in room.	Complied.
411	Shirts,	25	200	No ds.	
412	Monuments,	15		No ds.	
413	Castings,	30		bxing at 1 t high.	Complied.
414	Castings,	55		No ds.	
415	Typewriters' Supplies,	25		No orders	Complied.
416	Tissue Paper,	8	3	Repair and put in proper working order safety device on elevator to prevent accident in case of cable breaking or disarrangement of hoisting machinery.	Complied.

417	Overcoatings,	100	80	Guard by railing main belt in wheel room.	Complied.
418	Felt Goods,	50	15	No orders.	
419	Ice Tools,	6		No orders.	
420	Soap,	12	8	Guard large belt to engine on both sides.	Complied.
421	Wire Cloth,	150	1	No orders.	
422	Curled Hair,	7		No orders.	
423	Silox,	15		No orders.	
424	Woolen Goods,	150	150	Repair supply pipe to water-closet for men in card room No. 1.	Complied.
425	Bolts and Nuts,	350	50	No orders.	
426	Telephones and Gas Engines,	40		Guard by boxing two large belts running through floor of machine room at least three feet high.	Complied.
427	Street Railway Supplies,	20		No orders.	
428	Plush Goods,	50	15	(1) Guard driving belt to drying machine on first floor. (2) Repair and put in proper working order automatic hatch to elevator opening on second floor.	Complied.
429	Table Cutlery,	360	30	(1) Repair and put in working order safety device to elevator in office flg. (2) Put in proper working order gate to elevator openings on second ds of main factory. (3) Cover or sink wth projecting set screws in collars on shafting on third fl to	Complied.
430	Kitchen Hardware,	180	28	Provide guard on automatic hatch to elevator on second floor to prevent persons crossing same.	Complied.
431	Coffin Hardware and Machine Screws,	75	3	No orders.	
432	Builders' Hardware and Chucks,	175	35	No orders.	
433	Paper Boxes,	15		No orders.	
434	sity for Light and Power,	9		No orders.	
435	General Wood Wk,	36		No orders.	
436	Carpenter Tools,	380	20	No orders.	

REPORT OF INSPECTIONS.— CONTINUED.

Order No.	Goods Manufactured.	No. of Employes. M.	No. of Employes. F.	Orders Given.	Compliances.
437	Men's Underwear,	75	225	I ... and operate within three months from the date of this order ... use appliances or devices as may be necessary to ... the excessive steam in dye house.	1 paid.
438	Underwear,	127	329	No orders.	
439	Special ; My,	35		No orders.	
440	Cereal Grinding,	7		No orders.	
441	... oaks,	135	15	No orders.	
442	... Hardware,	1200	200	No orders.	
443	Builders' Hardware and Paper Boxes,	550	200	Provide better system of ventilation in lacquer room.	Complied.
444	N ds,	5		No orders.	
445	... Specialties,	5		No orders.	
446	Turning & Moulding,	10		No orders.	
447	Electric Light Holders,	2	3	No orders.	
448	Brass Valves and Faucets,	23		Introduce and operate within three months from the date of this order ... use appliances or devices as may be necessary to remove the dust generated in polishing and buffing room.	In process of completion.
449	Brass Goods,	4	5	No orders.	
450	Rubber Shoes,	150		No orders.	
451	Metal Specialties,	7		No orders.	
452	Rubbers and Shoes,	800	400	No orders.	
453	Electricity,	5		No orders.	
454	Paper Boxes,	8	35	No orders.	
455	Rubber Boots & Shoes	718	607	... cleanse and disinfect water-closet in black mixing room of b... to and shoe factory and keep the same in good sanitary condition.	
456	Reclaimed Rubber.	100		No orders.	Complied.

No.				Orders	
457	Screws,	250	125	Provide new cable for elevator in packing room of screw shop.	Complied.
458	Builder's Hardware,	550	50	Guard side of fly wheel of engine near pump room by casing or iron railing at least three feet high.	Complied.
459	Saddlery Hardware,	250	125	(1) Guard fly wheel of new engine by iron railing extending from brick wall to engine.	Complied.
				(2) Guard gears to stamping machine where passage-way is used between machines.	Complied.
460	Metal Suspender Trimmings,	125	250	(1) Guard fly wheel of Fitchburg engine by railing, or casing same to a height of three and one-half feet.	Complied.
				(2) Provide some means whereby lacquer room can be better ventilated.	
461	Thimbles,	5	5	No orders.	
462	Buttons,	15	30	No orders.	
463	Buttons.	8	2	No orders.	
464	Malleable Iron Castings,	300		No orders.	
465	Safety Pins, etc.,	7	10	No orders.	
466	Nails,	30		No orders.	
467	Knitting Machine,	6		No orders.	
468	Brass Foundry,	7		No orders.	
469	Malleable Iron Castings,	125		No orders.	
470	Grinding Wheels,	5	60	No orders.	
471	Paper Boxes,	15	16	No orders.	
472	Shirts, Collars & Cuffs	7	1	No orders.	
473	Hardware Specialties	15		No orders.	
474	Wire Mattresses and Bedsteads,	8		No orders.	
475	Pocket and Sheffield Hardware	100	25	No orders.	
		18	2	No orders.	
476	Job Printing,	80	6	No orders.	
477	Malleable Iron Castings,	2	13	No orders.	
478	Laundry Work,			No orders.	

REPORT OF INSPECTIONS.—CONTINUED.

Order No.	Goods Manufactured.	No. of Employes. M.	F.	Orders Given.	Compliances.
479	Job Printing,	12		No orders.	
480	Job Printing,	22		No orders.	
481	Hosiery,	45	90	No orders.	
482	Brass and Bronze Goods,	12	3	No orders.	
483	Bits,	175		No orders.	
484	Hack Saws,	5		No orders.	
485	Buckles,	8	30	No orders.	
486	Key Blanks,	30		No orders.	
487	Printing,	5		No orders.	
488	Electric Power,	7		No orders.	
489	Structural Iron Work	45		No orders.	
490	Bits,	30		No orders.	
491	Water Pipes,	15	40	No orders.	
492	Castings and Machinery,	5		No orders.	Mill closed
493	Woolen Goods,	74	26	No orders.	
494	Woolen Goods,	45	14	(1) Guard fly wheel to engine by iron railing or by boxing same at least three feet high. (2) Introduce and operate within three months from the date of this order such appliances or devices as may be necessary to provide such ventilation as will remove the excessive steam generated in the dye house. (3) Cover or sink flush projecting set screws in coupling on shafting in same room. (4) Repair and put in good sanitary condition water-closet for male operatives.	
495	Woolen Goods,	65	25	Thoroughly clean and disinfect closet used by male operatives and keep the same in good sanitary condition.	Complied.

No.	Goods			Orders	
496	Woolen Goods,	30	6	(1) Provide water-closet for the female operatives. (2) Provide suitable water-closet for the male operatives.	Complied.
497	Woolen Goods,	40	20	No orders.	
498	Woolen Goods,	35	15	No orders.	
499	Turbine Water Wheels,	8		No orders.	
500	Thread,	11	4	Box or screw belt on and floor at least three feet high.	Complied.
501	Shoes,	20	10	der or sink fish all projecting set screws in couplings and collars on main shaft on third floor.	
502	Kerseys,	30	12	No orders	
503	Thread,	80	60	No orders	
504	Flocks,	20	6	Provide new bale of elevator.	Complied.
505	Woolen Goods,	50	40	Guard fly wheel to engine by extra iron railing at least three feet in height.	Complied.
506	Shoddy,	20		No orders.	
507	Woolen Goods,	100	50	Provide with water-closet for employes of wood mill to replace dry sy tem with soil pipes.	Complied.
508	Woolen Goods,	60	30	No orders.	
509	Worsted Yarns,	50	60	No orders.	
510	Shoddy and Extracts,	15		No orders.	
511	Woolen Goods,	70	30	No orders.	
512	Denims,	45	30	(1) Guard front side of main belt in power use by secure wood or iron railing. (2) Guard by main iron railing fly wheel, crank and driving rod to engine. (3) Guard main belt in weave room by boxing same at least three feet high. (4) and belt in lapper room and ng room by boxing same at least three feet high.	Complied.
513	Woolen Goods,	60	30	No orders	
514	Carriage Hardware,	55	20	No orders	
515	Bolts,	30	9	No orders.	
516	Hat Braid,	3		No orders.	
517	Axles,	50		No orders.	
518	Lincrusta & Bronze,	30		No orders.	
519	House Trimmings,	1 0		No orders.	

REPORT OF INSPECTIONS.—CONTINUED.

Order No.	Goods Manufactured.	No. of Employes. M.	F.	Orders Given.	Compliances.
520	Wood Work,	8		Guard by ; use railing fly wheel and driving belt to engine in engine room.	Complied.
521	Cereal Mfg,	5		No orders.	
522	Shoes,	45	25	No orders.	
523	Bed,	10	30	Guard by secure railing fly belt to engine.	Complied.
524	Typewriters,	160	15	No ords.	
525	Locks.	700	100	No ords.	
526	Fur Hats,	15	10	No orders.	
527	Hat Mfs,	5		Guard by railing fly wheel to Otto gas engine.	Complied.
528	Hatters' Machinery,	21		No orders.	
529	Hat , Mfy,	8		No orders.	
530	Hatters' Furs,	50		No orders.	
531	Soft Hats,	150	50	Cover or sink flush all projecting set screws in collars on alfg. No orders.	Complied.
532	Fur Hats,	100	50	No orders.	
533	Machinery and Hat Bands,	16	4		Complied.
534	Fur Hats,	175	75	(1) Provide porcelain urinals, with water to ush sme, to ake plce of zinc oes. (2) Provide pull for at clset in pcking rom. No orders.	
535	Silk Braid & Bands,	5	52	No orders.	
536	Fur Hts,	225	100	No ods.	
537	Machinery,	5		No orders.	
538	Fur Hats,	80	40	No orders.	
539	Silver Pted Novelties,	50	15	Connect buffing lathes with exhaust system.	Complied.
540	Fur Hts,	150	50	No orders.	
541	Fur Hts,	75	60	No orders.	

No.	Establishment			Order	Remarks
542	Hatters' Machinery,	42		Cover or sink with all projecting set screws in collars on shafting.	Complied.
543	Fur Hats,	6		Guard stairway opening by secure railing on side.	Complied.
544	General Wood Work,	20		No ems.	
545	Fur Hats,	20	14	Repair, thoroughly clean and disinfect wat-closet.	Complied.
546	Fur Hats,	18	16	No orders.	
547	Fur Hats,	175	50	No orders.	
548	Fur Hats,	100	55	(1) Guard by ...g belt running through ...for in finishing ron. (2) Cover or sink with all projecting set ...ws in collars on shafting.	Complied
549	Gas and Electric Lighting,	7		Guard by covering projecting keys in main shaft of gas engines ...re passage-way between ...ges is ...d.	
550	Fur Hats,	175	100	(1) Guard by casing driving belt running from forming to stiffening and ...ig room. (2) ...or sink flush all projecting set screws in collars on shafting.	Complied.
551	Hats in the Rough,	5	4	Guard fly wheel to engine by casing or ...g.	Complied.
552	Fur Hats,	100	45	Cover or sink flush all projecting set ...ws in collars on shafting.	
553	Paper Boxes and Hat Cases,	80	20	No orders.	
554	Printing,	12	12	No orders.	
555	Hatters' Furs,	50	6	No orders.	
556	Hatters' Furs,	12		No orders.	
557	Bicycles,	6		No orders.	
558	Soft & Stiff Fur Hats,	30	12	(1) Cover or sink with all projecting set screws in collars on ...ng. (2) Thoroughly clean and disinfect outside earth-closets.	Complied.
559	Book Paper,	120	80	No orders.	
560	Chucks and Drills,	26		No orders.	
561	Paper Machinery,	6		No orders.	
562	Cotton Warps . and Yarns,	100		No orders.	
563	Gin,	7	125	No orders.	

REPORT OF INSPECTIONS.—CONTINUED.

Order No.	Goods Manufactured.	No. of Employes. M.	F.	Orders Given.	Compliances.
564	Sewing Silk and Thread,	30	70	No orders.	
565	Tissue Paper,	29	6	Provide new cable for large elevator.	Complied.
566	Fine Underwear,	50	125	No orders.	
567	Trucks and Exhaust Fans,	17		No orders.	
568	Paper Boxes,	67	11	(1) Guard passage-way over low shafting near pulley by boxing same. (2) Guard upright shaft to water wheel by boxing same to a height of four feet.	Complied.
569	Sewing Silk,	10	45	Provide some means to remove the excessive steam in dye room.	Millclosed
570	Rag and White Tissue Paper,	25	5	No orders.	
571	Novelty Yarns,	25	35	No orders.	
572	Artificial Ice,	15		No orders.	
573	Mineral Grinding,	25		No orders.	
574	Electricity,	6		No orders.	
575	Hatters' Furs,	160	35	No orders.	
576	Builno Hardware,	200		No orders.	
577	Chemicals,	24		No orders.	
578	Dyes,	275	8	No orders.	
579	Iron Castings,	48		No orders.	
580	Rus,	25		Guard by rbg lower part of band saw.	Complied.
581	Hardware Specialties	6		No orders.	
582	Electro Mfg,	7		No orders.	
583	Fish Hooks,	9	4	No orders.	
584	Sig Beds,	12		No orders.	

No.	Description			Remarks	Status
585	Ste am Fitters' Sup-plies.	10		No oders.	
586	Electric Power, iet Wk,	11		No ets.	
587	Electric Power,	20		Guard by casing belt running counter shaft on second floor.	Complied.
588		11	25	No orders.	
589	Hosiery,	4		No orders.	
590	Wood Wk,	8		No orders.	
591	Wd Wk,	8		No orders.	
592	Machinery,	8		No orders.	
593	Ion Castings,	40		No orders.	
594	Machinery,	15		No orders.	
595	My,	10		No orders.	
596	Wood Wk,	15	20	No orders.	
597	Wal Cs,	25	45	No orders.	
598	Writing Paper,	30		No orders.	
599	Mla Paper,	25		No orders.	
600	Me dy,	130	5	Provide Ner to pipes for polishing room in the finishing department.	Complied.
601	Cotton Batting and Yarn,	20		No orders.	
602	Bolts, Nuts & Rules,	35	45	(1) Provide new cable for elevator in cutting department. (2) Replace covering to set screws in collars on main shafting.	Complied.
602	Binders' Board,	10		Repair and put in proper working order automatic hatches to elevator opening on first floor.	Complied.
604	Nut Machinery and Finished Nts,	7		No orders.	
605	Wd Turning aud Mse Traps,	8	6	No orders.	
606	Press Work and Bi-cyle Bells,	15		No orders.	
607	Glass Gtters and Stencils,	6		Guard fly wheel upon the back side where necessary to go to oil bearings.	Complied.
608	Hardware and Paper Boxes,	3	8	No orders.	
609	Manila Paper,	20	5	No orders.	

REPORT OF INSPECTIONS.—Continued.

Order No.	Goods Manufactured.	No. of Employes. M.	F.	Orders Given.	Compliances.
610	Tissue Paper,	18	10	No orders.	
611	Colored Paper,	16	3	No orders.	
612	M's Fine Under-wear,	6		No orders.	
613	Wool Yarns,	15	12	No orders.	
614	Book Paper,	30	15	No orders.	
615	Carpet and Rugs,	500	12	No orders.	
616	Casket Hardware,	40	462	No ers.	
617	Bicycle arts,	184	5	No ers.	
618	Hardware Specialties	35	52	No orders.	
619	Hydraulic Presses,	40		No orders.	
620	Dynamos and ...,			No oders.	
621	Machine Screws,	130	15	No orders.	
622	Machinery & ...,	23	2	No orders.	
623	Printing,	5		No orders.	
624	Special Machinery,	12		No orders.	
625	Gin Implements,	18	1	No orders.	
626	Small Hardware,	13	5	No orders.	
627	Bicycle Wrenches,	35		No orders.	
		30		Introduce and ... within three months ... the ... dust generated in the polishing room.	Complied.
628	Wheel Spokes and Picker Sticks,	6		No orders.	
629	Woolen Goods,	40	10	Guard belt running from engine near lathe by iron railing. (1) Cover or sink flush two projecting set screws in collars on shafting near hangers.	Complied.
630	Shoddy,	5		(2) Guard flange coupling so as to cover projecting bolts and nuts, same line of shafting.	Complied.

No.	Article			Order	Result
631	Paper Boxes,	7	6	No orders.	
632	Sewing Silk and Machine Twist,	12	42	No orders.	
633	Cotton Cloth,	50	50	No orders.	
634	Bicycles,	28	2	No orders.	
635	Church Organ Wool Pipes,	5	14	No orders.	
636	Silk,	2	16	No orders.	
637	Sewing Silk,	4		No orders.	
638	Shoddy,	20		No orders.	
639	Salted Meats and Provisions,	165		Repair and put in proper working order safety device on elevator running from cutting to pickling room:	Complied.
640	Salted Meats and Provisions,	21	6	No orders.	
641	Machinery,	18	50	Repair and put in proper working order elevator in south building so that the safety appliance will work properly.	Complied.
642	Underwear,	7		No orders.	
643	Dressed Beef,	25		No orders.	
644	Dressed Beef,	18		No orders.	
645	Colophite,			(1) Guard by railing belt and wheel of hydraulic pump. (2) Guard by casing driving belt running through floor of shipping room to a height of at least three feet.	Complied.
646	Brass Goods,	250	60	No orders.	
647	Carriages,	30		No orders.	
648	Carriages,	25		No orders.	
649	Carriages,	20		No orders.	
650	Wood Work,	20		No orders.	
651	Horse Collars,	15		No orders.	
652	Sheet Metal,	75	2	No orders.	
653	Bit Braces and Press Drills,	5	2	No orders.	
654	Clocks,	60	10	No orders.	
655	HardwareSpecialties	14	9	No orders.	
656	Lamps,	80	84	Repair and put in working order exhaust system in buffing room so that it will more effectually remove the dust.	In process

REPORT OF INSPECTIONS.—CONTINUED.

Order No.	Goods Manufactured.	No. of Employes. M.	F.	Orders Given.	Compliances.
657	Clocks,	64	25	No orders.	
658	Screw ...le Work	5		Guard belt to engine by iron railing or by boxing same.	Complied.
659	Saws, ...le e?s,	12		No orders.	
660	...le e?s,	73	16	No orders.	
661	Spoons ad Forks, Mn's	105	25	No orders.	
662	Women's ad Underwear,	90	75	Pr... de hand-railing to stairway leading to second floor, ...st factory.	Complied.
663	Shears and Bells,	44	6	No orders.	
664	Sall Springs,	10	5	N oorders.	
665	Paper Boxes,	5		No orders.	
666	Arm Bands,	3	12	No orders.	
667	Steel Glass ...ds,	7		No orders.	
668	Clock ...ds & ...s,	9	1	No orders.	
669	Electric Light and Power,	6		No orders.	
670	Steel Fishing Rods,	27	3	No orders.	
671	Cereal Grinding,	5		No orders.	
672	Laundry Work,	2	4	No orders.	
673	Clock Machinery,	7		No orders.	
674	Sm...l Springs,	48	19	No orders.	
675	Clocks, Movements and Gas ...s,	12	6	No orders.	
676	Wd and Steel Enameling and Japanning,			No orders.	
677.	Clock Dals,	45		No orders.	
678	Clock Movements,	11	2	No orders.	
679	Cks (Marine),	95	25	No orders.	
		7	10	No orders.	

No.	Article			Orders	Remarks
680	Clock ads.	280		20	No orders.
681	Suspender Buckles,	80		60	No orders.
682	Soda Water and Bot- tid ros,	5		15	Guard by railing or casing belt and balance wheel of engine. Complied.
683	Wine N das, Photographic Appa-	20			No orders. Complied.
684	r tus,&	55		10	Cover or sink flush set screws in collars on main shafting.
685	Fire Brick Goods,	25			No orders.
686	Bent Carriage Wood Wk,	50		5	No orders.
687	Wire,	125			No orders.
688	Bar Ion,	250			(1) Guard by substantial iron railing belt of dynamo engine. Complied. (2) Gu rd fly wheel of engine in machine shop by railing or ang.
689	Boilers,	125			No orders.
690	Drop Forgings,	17			No orders.
691	Kegs, Tubs, etc.,	20			No orders.
692	Machinery,	15			No orders.
693	Sawed or Dressed Lumber,	20		20	Guard by railing or casing large belt running small saw on first floor. Complied.
694	ach Lamps,	8			No orders.
695	Bent Steel Coils and fg,	30			No orders.
696	ware,	3		10	No orders.
697	Hardware,	45			No orders.
698	Wrapping and Hard- ware Papers,	15			No orders.
699	Hatters' Furs,	8			Cover or sink with all projecting set screws in collars on fg. Complied.
700	Fur Hats,	80		30	(1) Guard fly wheel of engine by casing or railing. (2) Cover or sink with all projecting set screws in collars on shafting. Complied.
701	Fur Hats,	40		20	(1) and fly wheel and belt of engine by railing or casing. Complied. (2) Cover or sink flush all projecting set rews in collars on shafting. Complied.

REPORT OF INSPECTIONS.—CONTINUED.

Order No.	Goods Manufactured.	No. of Employes. M.	F.	Orders Given.	Compliances.
702	Fur Hats,	50	35	Cover or sink flush all projecting set screws in collars on shafting.	Complied.
703	Twist Drills,	75		Cover or sink flush all projecting set screws in collars on shafting.	
704	Hatting Machinery,	5		No orders.	
705	Soft Fur Hats,	160	40	No orders.	
706	Fur Hats,	160	84	No orders.	
707	Fur Hats,	123	41	No orders.	
708	Fur Hats,	40	20	No orders.	
709	Fur Hats,	75	40	No orders	
710	Fur Hats,	125	65	No orders.	
711	Coal Wood Work,	5		No orders.	
712	Belting,	12		No orders.	
713	Saddlery Hardware,	125		No orders.	
714	Carriage Wd Work	35	10	No orders.	
715	Drop Presses,	12		No orders.	
716	ParallelPliers&Hardware Specialties,	85		No orders.	
717	Carriages,	35	2	No orders.	
718	Indian Medicines,	7	8	Guard opening through which elevator weight runs by wire screening or boards.	Complied.
719	Trunk Hardware and Furniture Trimmings,	48	2	No orders.	
720	Bicycle Grips and Wood Turning,	15		No orders.	
721	Furniture Castings and Rivets,	25	5	No orders.	

No.				
722	Bicycle ... and ... Keys,	28		No orders.
723	Bit Braces,	8		No orders.
724	Hot Air Furnaces,	5		No orders.
725	...le & Door Bells,	250	75	No orders.
726	...s and Children's Underwear,	25	75	No orders.
727	...y Iron Castings, Special	325		No orders.
728	Special ; ...,	6		No orders.
729	...'s and Children's Underwear,	50	100	No orders.
730	...s and Special ...,	14		No orders.
731	Saddlery ...,	40		No orders.
732	Brass and Bronze Castings,	13		No orders.
733	Edged Tools and Agricultural Imple-...s,	625	40	No orders.
734	Cotton ...,	36	7	No orders.
735	Cotton Cloth,	8	4	No orders.
736	Cotton ...n,	13	6	No orders.
737	...n Goods,	24	3	No orders.
738	Repeating Rifles, etc.	150	4	No orders.
739	Dyeing & Cleaning,	11		No orders.
740	... ...y & Screws,	12		No orders.
741	Beer,	37		No orders.
742	Hardware and Ma-...ry,	31	1	No orders.
743	Iron Castings,	60		No orders.
744	Br...s,	10		No orders.
745	...ial Ice,	18		No orders.
746	Rubber Foot Wear,	750	750	Provide hand-rail on left side of stairs in midway packing room. Complied.
747	Pianos.	100	2	No ...ers.

REPORT OF INSPECTIONS.— CONTINUED.

Order No.	Goods Manufactured.	No. of Employes. M.	F.	Orders Given.	Compliances.
748	Ca ats,	35	9	No orders.	
749	Boilers,	25		No orders.	
750	ng Wood,	10		No orders.	
751	Printing,	55	10	No orders.	
752	Carriages,	200	2	No orders.	
753	Paper Boxes,	7	42	No orders.	
754	Silk Thread,	10	50	No orders.	
755	ny Work,	2	10	No orders.	
756	Rattan Goods.	20	3	No orders.	
757	Tinners' Machine s,	125	3	Guard passage-ways under elevators on first floor by strips of leathers as a tell-tale.	Complied.
758	Edge Tols,	65		No orders.	
759	Steam Fitters' and Plumbers' Supplies	14	1	No orders.	
760	Paper Bags,	16	38	No orders.	
761	Carriage Hardware,	20		No orders.	
762	Builders' Hardware,	5	1	No orders.	
763	House Furnishings and al Hard- ware,	280	20	Repair or build new water-closet to take the place of the west closet.	Complied.
764	Rolled Metal, Nuts and Washers,	90		No orders.	
765	Ceiling and Floor Plates,	7		No orders.	
766	Pocket Cutlery and Bicycle Parts,	110	50	No orders.	

No.	Business			Orders	Result
767	...al Grinding and Wood Sawing,	5		No orders.	
768	Electric Light and Power,	5		No orders.	
769	Bolts,	80		No orders.	
770	Bicycle Parts,	6		No orders.	
771	Bolts,	50	5	No orders.	
772	Carriage and Bicycle Forgings,	100		No orders.	
773	Carriage Hardware, ...	60		No orders.	
774	Carriage Hardware, ...	250	75	Provide some means for the proper ventilation of the water-closets in the brick mill.	Complied.
775	...al Grinding and Boxes,	20		No orders.	
776	Shoddy,	42	8	No orders.	
777	Wrapping Paper,	12		No orders.	
778	Woolen ...,	196	100	No orders.	
779	Gin,	8		No orders.	
780	Saddlery and Basket Hardware,	15	10	No orders.	
781	Electrotyping,	15	1	No orders.	
782	Steam ...,	25		No orders.	
783	Cr c ers,	35	3	No orders.	
784	...,	30	300	No orders.	
785	Buttons,	2	10	No orders.	
786	Paper Boxes & Paste,	10	50	No orders.	
787	Screws,	75	15	No orders.	
788	...	25	Box belt ... No ...	...ing main shaft on first floor in planing room.	Complied.
789	Carriages,	50	4	No orders.	
790	Saddlery Hardware,	215		No orders.	
791	Buttons,	8	20	No orders.	
792	Builders' Hardware,	300	8	(1). Guard by railing belt and wheel to engine, west side. (2) Cover or sink flush all projecting set screws in collars on shafting in padlock room.	Complied.
793	Wood Work,	6		No orders.	

REPORT OF INSPECTIONS.— CONTINUED.

Order No.	Goods Manufactured.	No. of Employes. M.	F.	Orders Given.	Compliances.
794	Sash, Doors & Blinds,	50	12	Box belt running bl wer in planing mill.	Complied.
795	Hardware Specialties &h ffs,	12		No orders.	
796		6		No orders.	
797	HardwareSpecialties	15		No orders.	
798	Mouldings,	18		No ers.	
799	Mouldings,	25		And large wheel and belt of engine in saw room.	Complied.
800	Stairs,	12		No orders.	
801	Printing,	12		No orders.	
802	Printing,	48	2	No orders.	
803	Hardware,	75		No orders.	
804	Carriages,	77	2	No orders.	
805	Hardware and Carriages,	55	12	No orders.	
806	Printing,	80	30	No orders.	
807	Ss,	30	15	No orders.	
808	Paper Boxes,	5	30	No orders.	
809	Leather ilg,	7		No ers.	
810	Car Registers,	15	3	No orders.	
811	Mantels, etc.,	25		No orders.	
812	Paper,	30	7	No orders.	
813	Special Machinery,	50		No orders.	
814	Castings,	50		No orders.	
815	Castings,	35		No ers.	
816	Sewing Machine Attachments,	130	10	Guard driving belt to polishing shaft near door by rail or boxing.	Complied.
817	Cleaning and Dyeing,	35	55	No orders.	
818	Drop Forgings,	25		No orders.	

No.	Description				Complied.
819	Picker Sticks, Axes and Pick Handles,	8		No orders.	
820	Hosiery Yarn,	8	1	No orders.	
821	Newspapers,	20		No orders.	
822	Carriages,	18		No orders.	
823	Machine Tools,	100		No orders.	
824	Newspapers,	40		No orders.	
825	Bird Cages,	110		No orders.	
826	Match Machinery,	35		No orders.	
827	Special Machinery,	68	30	No orders.	
828	Patterns and Models,	9		No orders.	
829	Laundry Work,	5	7	No orders.	
830	Special Machinery and Small Tools,	1000		No orders.	
831	Dyeing and Carpet Clearing,		6	Put in proper working order gates to elevator in No. 3 building so that they will be closed when elevator is away from same.	Complied.
832	Special Machinery and Jobbing,	18	22	No orders.	
833	Patterns,	5		No orders.	
834	Incandescent Lamps,	12		No orders.	
835	Cereal Grinding,	6		No orders.	
836	Carriages,	8		No orders.	
837	Special Machinery,	20		No orders.	
838	Corsets,	12		No orders.	
839	Carriage Wheels,	125	900	No orders.	
840	Printing,	40		No orders.	
841	Hardware Specialties	50	20	No orders.	
842	Carriage Lamps,	65		No orders.	
843	Caskets,	20		No orders.	
844	Doors, Sash & Blinds,	15		No orders.	
845	Machinery and Elevators.	8		No orders.	
846	Electricity,	22		No orders.	
		17		No orders.	

REPORT OF INSPECTIONS.—CONTINUED.

Order No.	Goods Manufactured.	No. of Employes. M.	F.	Orders Given.	Compliances.
847	Clocks and Watches,	500	100	Box belt and gearing of embossing machine in case depart-ment.	Complied.
848	Cigar Boxes,	6	9	No orders.	
849	Printing Presses and Screw Machines,				
850	Special Machinery,	35		No orders.	
851	Bicycle Spokes and Nipples.	30		No orders.	
852	Wood Work,	30		No orders.	
853	Ale and	7		No orders.	
854	chair	11		No orders.	
855	Cabinet Work,	5		No orders.	
856	Electrical Supplies,	20		No orders.	
857	Cabinet Work and	45	120	...ed by railing both sides of driving belt of engine.	Complied.
858	Shoe Nails,	20		No orders.	
859	Cabinet Work and Mouldings.	125		No orders.	
860	Mouldings,	15		No orders.	
861	Screws, Pin-ing Mill,	28		No orders.	
862		16		No orders.	
		20		No orders.	
863	Drop Forgings,	5		No orders.	
864	Electrotypes,	16		No orders.	
865	Novel-		10	No or ods.	
866	Shirts,	3	3	No or ods.	
867	Printing,	2	6	No ods.	
		10	5	No or ods.	

No.	Description			Remarks
868	Perfumery,	.5	10	No orders.
869	Steam Heating Appliances,	20		No orders.
870	Binding & Printing,	9	3	No orders.
871	Gun Parts,	30		No orders.
872	Saws and Sewing Machinery,	18		No eds.
873	Carriage Wk,	6		No eds.
874	Carriage Tops,	6		No eds.
875	Web Goods,	100	100	Guard by lag or railing pulley and belt running buzz saw in ßw shop. Complied.
876	Electric Supplies,	7		No orders.
877	Silk Mittens,	1	20	No orders.
878	Special Machinery,	5		No eds.
879	ßg and Booking,	8	10	No orders.
880	Pocket Books and Diaries,	8	16	No orders.
881	Knit Goods,	1	6	No orders.
882	Printing and B ßg,	6	6	No orders.
883	General Wood Work,	6		No orders.
884	Printing Machinery and Foundry,	135		No orders.
885	Gas for Lighting,	40		No orders.
886	Cabinet Wk,	23		No orders.
887	Mouldings,	12		No orders.
888	General Wd Wk,	14		No orders.
889	Dyestuffs and Chemßs,	5		No orders.
890	Electric Supplies,	28		No orders.
891	Printing and Wood Engraving,	40	20	No orders.
892	Overalls, ɪ ßers	2	28	No orders.
893	and Shirts, ßs,	20	175	No orders.

REPORT OF INSPECTIONS.—Continued.

Order No.	Goods Manufactured.	No. of Employes. M.	F.	Orders Given.	Compliances.
894	Shelf Hardware,	1300	150	No orders.	
895	Firearms, Printing Presses & Engines,	502	2	No orders.	
896	Machinery & Tools,	30		No orders.	
897	Machine Tools and Machinery,	85	50	No orders.	
898	Wd Screws,	22	22	No orders.	
899	Doors, Sash & Blinds,	24		No orders.	
900	General Wood Work,	7		No orders.	
901	d,	16		No orders.	
902	Wr Meters,	22		No orders.	
903	Laundry Work,	5	6	No orders.	
904	Envelopes,	50	215	No orders.	
905	General Wood Work,	5		No orders.	
906	Leather g,	138	2	No orders.	
907	Pins,	14	12	No orders.	
908	Gaiters and Leggins,	25	75	Remove boxes from passage-way to fire escape on second and third floors so that as to same may be had at all times.	Complied.
909	s,	55		No ds.	
910	Carriages,	65		No orders.	
911	Carriage Repairing,	6		No orders.	
912	s,	11		No orders.	
913	Electro Plating,	8		No orders.	
914	General Wd Work,	9		No orders.	
915	Gas s,	15		No orders.	
916	Hardware Specialties	50	2	No orders.	
917	Butter,	15		No ders.	
918	Paper Boxes,	60	90	No orders.	
919	Starch,	20	3	No orders.	

920	Wire Cloth,	9		No orders.
921	Printing,	22		No orders.
922	Paper Boxes,	3	3	No orders.
923	Special Machinery and Repairing,	8	15	Repair and put in good sanitary condition water-closet, on lower floor, in three-story brick building. Complied.
924	Lithographing	10		No orders.
925	Automatic Time Stamps,	5		
926	Pay Station Boxes,	8		No orders.
927	Ptg & Bin idg,	25	5	No orders.
928	Plaster of Paris goods,	12		No orders.
929	Laundry Work,	5		No orders.
930	Heavy Trucks and Wagons,	25	25	No orders.
931	Special Machinery and Repairing, etc.,	8		No orders.
932		16		No orders.
933	Bicycle Handles and Insulators,	20	15	No orders.
934	Horse Shoes,	20		No orders.
935	Steam Boilers,	20		No orders.
936	Electric Power,	33		No orders.
937	Signal Machinery,	30		No orders.
938	Iron Railings & Gates	5		No orders.
939	Car Repairing,	150		No orders.
940	Lager Beer,	20		No orders.
941	Laundry Wk,	12	12	Provide separate water-closet accommodations for female hands of laundry. Complied.
942	Laundry,	18	20	No orders.
943	Steam Stone Cutting	20	1	No orders.
944	Cereal Grinding,	15		No orders.
945	Mouldings and General Wood Work,	20		No orders.

REPORT OF INSPECTIONS.—CONTINUED.

Order No.	Goods Manufactured.	No. of Employes. M.	F.	Orders Given.	Compliances.
946	Packing Boxes and Pumps,	6		No orders.	
947	Plumbers' Supplies,	6		No orders.	
948	Castings,	20		No orders.	
949	Brass Castings,	10		No orders.	
950	Paper Boxes,	3	17	No orders.	
951	Machinery & Repairs,	5		No orders.	
952	Boilers,	5		No orders.	
953	Steam, Boilers and Engines,	25		No orders.	
954	Soap,	5		No orders.	
955	Silver Plated Ware,	125	15	Put gate to elevator in north wing in order so that it will close when elevator is away from opening.	Complied.
956	Sterling and Silver Plated Ware,	80	70	No orders.	
957	Mattresses, and Spring Beds,	15	3	No orders.	
958	German Silver Castings,	7		No orders.	
959	Engines and Cars,	650		No orders.	
960	Mechanical Toys,	10		No orders.	
961	Confectionery,	27		No orders.	
962	Knit Goods,	2	8	No orders.	
963	Lager Beer,	21	45	No orders.	
964	Drop Forgings and Machine Tools,	200		No orders.	
965	Machine Screws and Machinery,	375	60	No orders.	

966	Experimental Ma-ly,	12		No orders.	
967		37	16	No orders.	
968	Brass Goods,	12	6	No orders.	
969	Paper Boxes,	140	150	No orders.	
970	Brass ...s,	11		No orders.	
971	...e and Bicycle Hardware,	55		No orders.	
972	Firearms,	1400	800	Repair ...d put in ...per w...rking order water-cl...ets on ...d, third ...d fourth floors in buil...ing No. 4 and keep ...he ...se in good sanitary con...din.	Complied.
973	Iron & Steel Tubing,	200		No orders.	
974	Rubber Tires,	466	82	No orders.	
975	Motor Carriages,	60		No orders.	
976	Bicycle,	1100	50	No orders.	
977	Typewriters,	40	15	(1) Box pulleys to dynamo where ...se ...re 1 ...se first and ...nd floors.	Complied.
978	Asbestos Goods,	50		(2) P...ce ...ble guard around ...dyno on first floor.	
979	Special Machinery,	90		No ...ers.	
980	Steam and Water Valves,	249		No orders. (1) Provide new cable to No. 1 elevator. (2) Repair and put in proper working order safety device to No. 1 elevator.	Complied.
981	Harness ...d Horse Goods,	185	15	No orders.	
982	...l ...h,	20	5	Guard fly wheel to engine by boxing same or by iron railing.	Complied.
983	...s, ...s,	100		No orders.	
984	...m ...d ...er Heaters,	25		No orders.	
985	Wire ...s ...d Iron Beds,	120	5	No orders.	
986	...le Switches ...d Incandescent Lamps,	50	75	No orders.	

REPORT OF INSPECTIONS. — CONTINUED.

Order No.	Goods Manufactured.	No. of Employes. M.	F.	Orders Given.	Compliances.
987	Typesetting Mn-ey,	30		No orders.	
988	Bicycles,	377	35	No orders.	
989	Printing ad Book-(llg,	165	1	No orders.	
990	Lithographing,	40		No orders.	
991	Electrotyping,	7		No orders.	
992	Nl Plating,	6		No orders.	
993	Gd Leaf,	5		No orders.	
994	Stationery, Envel-ps ad Printing,	100	200	Provide new cable for small freight elevator.	Complied.
995	Electric lgs,	12	2	No orders.	
996	Bicycle Supplies,	6	2	No orders.	
997	llg,	6		No orders.	
998	Printing ad Book-binding,	8		No·orders.	
999	Printing ad B k-o ldg,	5	5	No orders.	
1000	Printing, ldg,	8		No orders.	
1001	Sm Engine Re-ag,	12		No orders.	
1002	Gt Hardware,	10		No orders.	
1003	Brass Castings,	5		No orders.	
1004	Brass gs,	6		No orders.	
1005	Cl Wd Work,	6		No orders.	
1006	Kindling Wd,	5		No orders.	
1007	Ms' fhrt Waists ad M.	4	25	No orders.	

					Complied.
1008	Ladies' Shirt Waists and Wrappers,	1		No orders.	
1009	General Wood Work,	25	5	No orders.	
1010	Cyclometers,	20		No orders.	
1011	Engine and Car Re-ing,	71	80	No orders.	
1012	General Wood Work,	20		No orders.	
1013	Cornices & Skylights,	6		No orders.	
1014	Brushes,	7		No orders.	
1015	General Wood Work,	12		No orders.	
1016	Laundry Work,	8	14	No orders.	
1017	Car Hardware,	25		No orders.	
1018	Thread Finishing and Winding,	8	32	No orders.	
1019	Silk Ribbons,	20	90	No orders.	
1020	Wire & Doors Screens	10		No orders.	
1021	Chemical Extracts,	8	6	No orders.	
1022	Electric Power,	8		No orders.	
1023	Repairing Cars,	35		No orders.	
1024	Chairs, Settees and Ladders,	6		No orders.	
1025	Lager Beer,	21		No orders.	
1026	Plumbers' Supplies,	15		No orders.	
1027	Ale and Lager Beer,	50		No orders.	
1028	Biscuits & Crackers,	25		No orders.	
1029	Flour and Feed,	20		Cover or sink flush projecting set screws in collars on main shafting.	Complied.
1030	Engine and Car Re-pairing,	200		No orders.	
1031	Engine and Car Re-pairing,	200		No orders.	
1032	Printing,	6		No orders.	
1033	Lithographing and Wood Engraving,	36		No orders.	
1034	Printing,	6		No orders.	

REPORT OF INSPECTIONS.—CONTINUED.

Order No.	Goods Manufactured.	No. of Employes. M.	No. of Employes. F.	Orders Given.	Compliances.
1035	＆n ＆d Worsted	190	60	No orders.	
1036	＆n Yarns and Knit ＆s,	125	75	No orders.	
1037	＆d ＆s, ＆ly for ＆t-	240	70	No orders.	
1038	ing,			No orders.	
1039		5		No orders.	
1040	＆d ＆d Woolen	50	100	No orders.	
1041	＆s, ＆d Woolen	250	100	No orders.	
1042	＆s, Worsted Goods,	280	90	No orders.	
1043	＆n ＆d Worsted	62	7	No orders.	
1044	＆s, ＆n Yarn,	165	60	No orders.	
1045	＆n Yarn,	7	16	No orders.	
1046	＆e Linings ＆d	28	26	Thoroughly clean and disinfect outside closets for wood mill.	Complied.
1047	＆r ＆n, ＆t ＆d ＆e	35	30	No orders.	
1048	Card Paper, ＆ Silk,	75	225	No orders.	
1049	Bon ＆ Soap,	6	2	No orders.	
1050	Straw Board,	20	5	No orders.	
1051	＆g Paper,	7		No orders.	
1052	＆d ＆,	7		No orders.	
1053	＆s ＆r, ＆	15	35	No orders	
1054	＆g ＆d ＆	6	4	No orders.	

No.	Description			Remarks	Complied.
1055	...n Warps and ...e Yarns,	12	9	No orders.	
1056	Woolen ...,	40	25	Guard ... to ... ...r as suggested by	Complied.
1057	Binders' Board,	12	30	No orders.	
1058	Woolen Goods,	60	15	No orders.	
1059	Wg ...r,	45	36	No orders.	
1060	...n Goods,	150	25	No orders.	
1061	...e Writing Paper,	25	34	No orders.	
1062	Book ...r,	42		No orders.	
1063	Ma ...,	45		No orders.	
1064	...n ...g,	10	20	No orders.	
1065	Straw ...d Sheathing Board,	6		No orders.	
1066	...n Thread,	20	30	No orders.	
1067	e...g Silk and ...a- ...e Twist,	8	10	No orders.	
1068	Binders' ...d Al ...m Board,	18		No orders.	
1069	Press ...,	43		No orders.	
1070	Press ...r,	12		No orders.	
1071	Press ...r,	12		No orders.	
1072	Silk ...ins,	25	50	Box belt that comes up through floor near spinning frame on first floor.	Complied.
1073	...et ...g and Throwing,	557	450	No orders.	
1074	Spinning and Dressing ...,	200	267	No orders.	
1075	Paper & W ...Boxes,	77	4	No orders.	
1076	Dyeing and Finishing ...s,	215	190	No orders.	
1077	Plumbing,	10		No orders.	
1078	Lager Beer, ...,	15		No orders.	
1079	...r	75	75	No orders.	
1080	Brooms,	5		No orders.	
1081	Mills & Burr Stones,	6		No orders.	
1082	Wood Work,	10		No orders.	

REPORT OF INSPECTIONS.—Continued.

Order No.	Goods Manufactured.	No. of Employes. M.	F.	Orders Given.	Compliances.
1083	Newspapers and ▪▪ing,	8		No orde s.	
1084	N▪▪ ▪ers,	40	7	No orders.	
1085	N▪▪ ▪ers,	20		No orders.	
1086	N▪▪ ▪ers,	50	4	No orders.	
1087	Daily N▪▪ ▪s,	21		No orde s.	
1088	▪ly & Flat Wire,	75	15	N o orders.	
1089	Soaps,	60	10	No orders.	
1090	Ground ▪ ▪r,	13		No orders.	
1091	Bin ▪ Board,	10		No orders.	
1092	L▪c▪▪s & Hardware,	225	25	(1) Provide suitable w▪closet ▪ ▪ations of male ▪p. ▪ (2) Repair exhaust ▪▪n in buffing ron so as to remove the ▪▪t more ▪ ▪y. (3) Provide nw ▪▪ds over jars ▪ ▪▪g ▪▪d dips so ▪▪t the gases ▪all ▪e ▪▪n close to ▪e jars.	Complied.
1093	Malleable Iron Castings,	330	45	No orders.	
1094	Corsets and Waists,	4	7	N▪ orde s.	
1095	Fur Hats,	20	10	Cover or sink ▪▪g dr ▪ ▪s in ▪ ▪g bolt ▪s in ▪ ▪s on l ow ▪g room.	Complied.
1096	Fur Hats,	90	45	No orders.	
1097	Hats,	50	20	No ▪▪ds.	
1098	Hats,	79	44	Cover or ▪ ▪k ▪h bolt ▪s ▪ ▪pling ▪n line shaft on ▪t l▪or near ▪ger.	Complied.
1099	Hat Forms,	18	6	No ▪▪ts.	
1100	Paper Boxes and Hat Cases,	4	7	No orders.	

No.	Establishment			Order	Disposition
1101	apeB Boxes and Hat Cases,	5	8	No orders.	
1102	Paper Boxes and Hat Cases,	5	7	No orders.	
1103	Organs,	135	1	No orders.	
1104	Æolian Organs and Music,			No orders.	
1105	Bid Ces,	100	12	No orders.	
1106	Harness Trimmings,	75	23	No orders.	
1107	Machinery,	65	10	No orders.	
1108	Mal Goods,	13	250	No orders.	
1109	Metal Spoons,	300	50	No orders.	
1110	Electro Plating and Bhel Ware,	35		No orders.	
1111	Curtains,	20	4	No orders.	
1112	Curtains,	40	10	No orders.	
1113	Decorated Glass and China Ware,	125	125	No orders.	
1114	Clocks,	25	70	No orders.	
1115	ons and Machinery,	40	20	Thoroughly clean and disinfect earth-closet and keep the same in good sanitary condition.	Complied.
1116	Piano Stools,	18	3	No orders.	
1117	Laundry Work,	3	6	No orders.	
1118	Brass and Art Metal Goods,	600	60	No orders.	
1119	Electric Power,	5		No orders.	
1120	Printing Presses,	.10	1	Box belt on sad floor running press on third flor at least four feet high.	Complied.
1121	Lager Beer,	25	5	No orders.	
1122	Telephones, etc.,	17	5	No cars.	
1123	Iron Goods,	125		(1) Introduce and operate within three mths from the date of this order uch appliances or ades as may be necessary to ave the me dst generated in the lng rom. (2) Repair doors to elevator openings in polishing room.	Partially Compl'd.

REPORT OF INSPECTIONS.—CONTINUED.

Order No.	Goods Manufactured.	No. of Employes. M.	F.	Orders Given.	Compliances.
1124	Silver Ware and Cut Glass,	200	10	No orders.	
1125	Hardware Specialties	6		No orders.	
1126	Paper Boxes,	12	10	No orders.	
1127	..h Goods,	75	75	Repair water-closet and urinal used by men in weaving r..m.	Complied.
1128	..pl, etc.,	125	10	No ods.	
1129	Silverware,	200	10	No orders.	
1130	Hardware Specialties	12		No orders.	
1131	Casters, &c.,	25	4	No orders.	
1132	Hardware,	8		No ods.	
1133	Ct Glass Ware,	40	30	No ods.	
1134	Mch' .ry,	16		No ods.	
1135	Machinery,	5		No orders.	
1136	Pearl .. ods,	80	10	No orders.	
1137	Wood Trimmings,	25		No orders.	
1138	Silver Pl .d Ware,	200	50	Guard elevator opening which is used as a passage-way between machine room and plating room by this or age to prevent persons from passing under elevator.	Complied.
1139	Silver Plated Ware,	25		No orders.	
1140	Printing,	40	6	No orders.	
1141	Decorated Glass Ware,	20	10	No orders.	
1142	Paper Boxes,	12	20	Provide separate water-closet accommodations for female employes.	Complied.
1143	Wood Work,	5		(1) Box large belts running through second floor in both front and rear rooms. (2) Put up bar across open door on second floor north front building.	Complied. Complied.
1144	Silverware,	700	200	No orders.	

				...ions for employes	Complied.
1145	Wrought Iron Work,	6		No orders.	
1146	Laundry Wk,	3	5	No orders.	
1147	Satinet,	50	40	No orders.	
1148	Sh eso	65	15	No orders.	
1149	General Wood Work,	15		No orders.	
1150	...n Goods,	40	10	No orders.	
1151	Cotton Cloth,	90	100	No ers.	
1152	Cotton Cloth,	100	70	No orders.	
1153	Castings,	7		No orders.	
1154	Cotton Cloth,	150	100	No orders.	
1155	Dyeing & Bleaching,	160	15	No orders.	
1156	Underwear,	40	70	No orders.	
1157	Wood & Paper Boxes,	3	4	No ers	
1158	Shoes,	28	4	No orders.	
1159	Sewing & Spool Silk,	18	45	No orders	
1160	Cotton Cloth,	70	50	No orders.	
1161	Cotton Cloth,	175	150	No orders.	
1162	...,	10		No orders.	
1163	Slippers,	5	2	No orders.	
1164	...,	6		No orders.	
1165	Wood Wk,	7		No orders.	
1166	... Beer,	35		No orders.	
1167	Lager Beer,	22		No orders.	
1168	Ale, Porter and Weiss Beer,	7		No orders.	
1169	Leather Belting,	10		No orders.	
1170	Electric Power,	9		No oders.	
1171	Bit Brace & Tool Sets,	60	2	No orders.	
1172	... Ware,	190	35	No orders.	
1173	Furniture Springs,	6		No orders.	
1174	Cloakings,	120	30	No orders.	
1175	Binders' Board,	16		No orders.	
1176	Woolen Goods,	78	25	No orders.	
1177	Underwear,	25	45	Provide suitable water-closet of knitting room in mill No. 1.	
1178	Knit Goods,	25	46	No orders.	

REPORT OF INSPECTIONS.— CONTINUED.

Order No.	Goods Manufactured.	No. of Employes. M.	F.	Orders Given.	Compliances.
1179	Silk Plushes and Velvets,	300	210	No orders.	
1180	Electro Plating,	8		No orders.	
1181	Crucibles,	40		No orders.	
1182	General Wood Work,	11		No orders	
1183	Corsets,	30	350	(1) Guard main belt in engine room by continuing railing from fly wheel to partition. (2) Cover couplings on shafting to stitching ...	Complied.
1184	Pocket Cutlery,	80	4	No orders.	
1185	Car Springs,	45		No orders.	
1186	Cereal Grinding and Kindling Wood,	10		No orders.	
1187	Shears,	50	10	(1) Guard by ... or railing fly wheel driving rod or crank of engine. (2) Cover or sink ... set ... in collars on ... in ... room. (3) Remove outlet pipe for exhaust ... from any ... tion with soil pipe of closet near office. Provide ... of ventilating ... closet of office bldg.	Complied.
1188	Emery Wheels,	20	2	No orders.	
1189	S ... er Webbings ad ...,	50	60	No orders.	
1190	Metal Novelties and Dies,	6		No orders.	
1191	General Wood Work,	54		No orders.	
1192	Shears and Sp ons,o	30	20	No orders.	
1193	Motors,	10		No orders.	
1194	Optical Goods,	16	3	No orders.	

No.	Business			Remarks
1195	Wood Novelties and Cork Handles,	30	3	No orders.
1196	Knives,	70	6	No orders.
1197	Leather,	8		No ords.
1198	Leather,	18		No orders.
1199	General Wood Wk,	85		No orders.
1200	Wd Mantels,	6		No orders.
1201	Shells & Cartridges,	800	550	No orders.
1202	Heavy Guns & Shells,	350		No orders.
1203	Steam Boilers and Engines,	112		No orders.
1204	Power,	8		No orders.
1205	Gas,	25	125	No orders.
1206		6		No orders.
1207	Dies, Refrigerator Machines,	15		No orders.
1208	Boilers,	20		No orders.
1209	Special Machinery,	71		No orders.
1210	Plumbers' Brass Goods,	8		No orders.
1211	Hats,	6	6	No orders.
1212	Job Printing,	20	6	No orders.
1213	Boiler and Pipe Cork Coverings,	70	10	(1) Box driving shfts to two circular saws on 2nd floor. (2) Guard belt in engine room by ...ing same or by secure railing three feet high. (3) Guard el...or ...ings in ...ain f c ...ry by gates, bars or ...ihs.	Complied. Complied.
1214	Castings,	90		No orders.
1215	Illuminating Gas,	30		No orders.
1216	Sewing Machines,	761		No orders.
1217	Cabinet Work,	300		No orders.
1218	Soap,	40		No rders.o
1219	Sewing Machine N ls,			
1220	Lager Beer,	55	40	No orders.
		15		No orders.

REPORT OF INSPECTIONS.—CONTINUED.

Order No.	Goods Manufactured.	No. of Employes. M.	F.	Orders Given.	Compliances.
1221	Laundry Work,	10	45	Guard fly wheel and belt to engine as suggested.	Complied.
1222	Bolts, etc.,	60	7	No orders.	
1223	Metal Specialties.	25	15	No orders.	
1224	Scythes,	24		No orders.	
1225	Laundry Work,	10	11	No orders.	
1226	Yarn,	12		No orders.	
1227	Hardware and Fancy Brass Goods,	80	30	No orders.	
1228	Printing,	50	10	No orders.	
1229	Edged Tools,	80		(1) Introduce and operate within three months from the date of his order such appliances or devices as may be necessary to ore the excessive dust generated in polishing r m.o (2) Put up guard the entire gth of large belt and wheels running large grinding stone in auger department near stairs.	Complied.
1230	Cutlery Ware,	170	8	No orders.	
1231	Soes,	25	25	No orders.	
1232	Hosiery,	35	135	No orders.	
1233	Printing,	8	2	No orders.	
1234	Clocks,	200	50	No orders.	
1235	Pins & Paper Boxes,	40	50	No orders.	
1236	Machinery,	7		No orders	
1237	Wood Turning,	5		No orders.	
1238	Edged Tools,	50		No orders.	
1239	Silk Thread,	21	84	No rders.o	
1240	Undertakers' Goods,	90	12	No orders.	
1241	Steam and Water Gauges,	160		No orders.	

No.	Business			Orders	
1242	Razors,	30	2	No orders.	
1243	Special Machinery,	7		No ods.	
1244	Paper Boxes,	20	80	Repair and put in proper working order gates to elevator openings.	Complied.
1245	Coffin Tri...ngs,	35	5	No orders.	
1246	...M's Underwear,	40	90	No orders.	
1247	...on Cloth.	75	75	No rders.o	
1248	Hot W...he Heaters,	30		No days.	
1249	Silk,	35	130	No...ders.	
1250	Cotton Cl...h,	430	550	No orders.	
1251	Straw r...,	22		No orders.	
1252	Ale and Porter,	5		No rders.o	
1253	Lager Beer,	13		No rders.o	
1254	Copper and Brass Goods,	700	50	Place hoods in their proper place and put exhaust fan in good working order, so that the injurious gases may be carried off more effectually from the dip room.	Complied.
1255	Bicycles,	250		No orders.	
1256	Bronze and Brass Castings,	19			
1257	Machinery and Castings.			No orders.	
1258	Brass Clips & Rules,	70		No orders.	
1259	Packing r...,	5		No orders.	
1260	Shirts,	20		No orders.	
1261	Electro Plating,	12	8	Clean out all small pipes connected to buffing wheels and keep them clean from obstructions at all times, so that the exhaust fan can exercise its functions properly.	Complied.
1262	Dress Stays and Paper Boxes,	50	200	(1) Cover or sink flush projecting set screws in old style coupling on shafting in buffing room. (2) Introduce and operate within three months from the date of this order such appliances or devices as may be necessary to remove the dust generated in buffing room in basement.	Partially Complied.
1263	Paper Boxes,	7	20	No orders.	

REPORT OF INSPECTIONS.—CONTINUED.

Order No.	Goods Manufactured.	No. of Employes. M.	No. of Employes. F.	Orders Given.	Compliances.
1264	Infants' Underwear,	10	30	No orders.	
1265	Light Metal Goods,	12	3	No orders.	
1266	Cold Rolled Steel,	250	.	Provide some means whereby wate lots used by the employes in the rolling polishing, buffing and pickling rooms shall be flushed often enough to keep them in g sanitary condition.	Complied.
1267	Fuse,	39	47	No orders.	
1268	Jute,	9	9	No orders.	
1269	Horse Shoe Nails,	87		Provide suitable light for employes on ground floor of factory.	
1270	Hot Rolled Steel,	150		No rders.	
1271	Refined Copper,			No orders.	
1272	Wrought Iron Shafting,	75		No orders.	
1273	Iron & Bronze Wk,	15		No orders.	
1274	Machinery & Tools,	25		No orders.	
1275	Piano and Organ Hardware,	44		Guard fly wheel, crank and driving rod to engine.	Complied.
1 76	Organs,	40		No orders.	
1277	Novelties,	50		No orders.	
1278	Silk Dress Goods,	150	125	No orders.	
1279	Fuel Gas,	9		No orders.	
1280	Embroidered Flannel and Lace,	6	12	No orders.	
1281	White Metal Monuments,	40		No orders.	
1282	Carriages & Wagons,	125		No orders.	
1283	Laundry Wk,	5	18	Repair and put in proper working order exhaust fan in basement.	Complied.

1284	Printing and Book-binding,	21	2	No orders.	
1285	B & Job Printing,	20		No orders.	
1286	Electric Supplies,	150	15	No orders.	
1287	Electric Supplies,	15		No orders.	
1288	Wheels & Cycle Bars,	25	4	No orders.	
1289	Spoons and Forks,	75	125	No orders.	
1290	Silverware,	475		No orders.	
1291	Rubber Goods,	32		No orders.	
1292	Toy Caps,	40	40	No orders.	
1293	Sterling Silver and Plated Ware,	200	3	Provide new cable to show-room elevator.	Complied.
1294	Iron & Brass Goods.	350	150	No orders.	
1295	Ser Plated Hollow-Ware,	38	5	No orders.	
1296	nd Wire,	91	16	No orders.	
1297	Silverware,	18	1	No orders.	
1298	Silver Flat Ware,	70	2	No orders.	
1299	Brass Goods,	40	20	No orders.	
1300	Silver Plated Ware,	125	3	No orders.	
1301	Carriages & Wagon Wheels,	10		No orders.	
1302	r sBIronCastings,	60		No orders.	
1303	Cards,	2	6	No orders.	
1304	Spoons,	25	5	No orders.	
1305	Scales,	12		No orders.	
1306	Mattresses,	7	1	No orders.	
1307	Buttons,	25	18	No orders.	
1308	g Bags,	21	9	No orders	
1309	Planes,	7		No orders.	
1310	Leather,	28	5	No orders.	
1311	Paper,	25		(1) d fly-wheel of engine. (2) Put up gu r in front of large wheel running paper machine No. 1, on st side.	Complied.
1312	Twine,	12	18	No orders.	

REPORT OF INSPECTIONS.— CONTINUED.

Order No.	Goods Manufactured.	No. of Employes. M.	F.	Orders Given.	Compliances.
1313	Starch,	15		Box belt running through flor on fourth floor at end of main shafting.	Complied.
1314	...e Linings,	2	5	No orders.	
1315	Flour and ...d,	7		No orders.	
1316	Underwear,	3	40	No orders.	
1317	Edged Tols,	30		No o...	
1318	Cotton Yarn,	20	20	No orders.	
1319	Shoddy,	5		No o...	
1320	Jewelry,	10	12	No orders.	
1321	Silk Braid,	2	3	No orders.	
1322	General Wood Work,	12		No orders.	
1323	...				
1324	Sewing Silk,	20	130	No orders.	
1325	Brass ...,	250	250	No orders.	
	Brass ...,	400	250	...er or sink fish all projecting set screws in collars on shafting in stringing r m.o	Complied.
1326	Machinery,	300		No o...	
1327	...l Cornices,	17		No orders.	
1328	...s,	4	1	No orders	
1329	Silver ...d Ware,	54	6	No o...	
1330	Corsets,	3	30	No orders.	
1331	Flour and Feed,	7		No orders.	
1332	Enameled ...d Collar Buttons,	3	2	No orders.	
1333	General Wood ...,	5		No orders.	
1334	...le Fittings,	15		No orders.	
1335	I ...ic Grinding Machines,	15		No orders.	
1336	Buckles,	20	30	No orders.	

No.	Description			Remarks
1337	Special Brass Goods,	20		No orders.
1338	White Metal Goods,	10		No orders.
1339	Brass and Iron Steam Fittings,	765	20	No orders.
1340	Steam Fittings,	60		No orders.
1341	Engine and Repairing,	30		No orders.
1342	Boring and Turning Machinery,	200		No orders.
1343	Hardware Specialties	120		No orders.
1344	Brass Castings,	15		No orders.
1345	Furniture Hardware,	170		No orders.
1346	Plumbers Supplies & Rubber Specialties,	25	15	No orders.
1347	Dress Shields and	20	12	No orders.
1348	Belting, etc.,	200	30	No rders.o
1349	Horn	6	5	No rders.o
1350	Bar,	23	3	No orders.
1351	Printing,	5		No orders.
1352	Electrical Supplies,	34	3	No rders.o
1353	Str Hats,	30	3	No orders.
1354	Machinery,	20	60	No rders.o
1355	Electric Power,	22		No rders.o
1356	Carriages,	15		No orders.
1357	Brass & Brass Goods,	650	200	Box belts running through part of covered wire department on third floor. Complied.
1358	Wood Work,	25		No orders.
1359	Sash, Doors & Blinds,	25		No orders.
1360	Band Saws,	10		No orders.
1361	Paper Boxes & Printing,	30	75	No orders.
1362	Paper Bags and Envelopes,	30		No orders.
1363	Saddlery Hardware,	5	50	Guard pulley in doorway in basement by casing. Complied.

REPORT OF INSPECTIONS.— CONTINUED.

Order No.	Goods Manufactured.	No. of Employes. M.	F.	Orders Given.	Compliances.
1364	Silex, Paint & Wood Filler,	35		No orders.	
1365	Pottery Ware,	21	9	No orders.	
1366	Couches and Chairs,	33	1	No orders.	
1367	Car Wheels, Machinery and Castings,	90		No orders.	
1368	Shears,	20	1	Introduce and operate within three months from the date of this order such appliances or devices as may be necessary to remove the excessive dust generated from dry polishing and buffing wheels.	In process
1369	General Wood Work,	5		No orders.	
1370	Pig Iron,	28		No orders.	
1371	Castings and Small Hardware,	30	1	No orders.	
1372	Fertilizers, Tallow & Soap,	7		(1) Guard elevator openings on 2d and 3d floors by gate, bars or chains. (2) Guard by casing or railing large belts running through 2d floor. (3) Cover or sink flush all projecting set screws in collars on main shafting.	Complied.
1373	Drop Forgings,	15		No orders.	
1374	Belting and Mill Supplies,	20		No orders.	
1375	Special Machinery,	8		No orders.	
1376	Heavy Trucks and Wagons,	34		No orders.	
1377	Coach Lace,	10	14	No orders.	
1378	Paper Boxes,	4	10	No orders.	

No.	Industry			Orders
1379	Elastic ...g,	60	30	No orders.
1380	Carriage Springs,	50		No orders.
1381	General Wood Work,	6		No orders.
1382	...s,	75		No orders.
1383	Brass & Copper Cast-ings,	30	525	No orders.
1384	Pipe, Cutting and Threading ...Min-ery,	28		No orders.
1385	Car Couplings,	15		No orders.
1386	Hardware Special-ties,	40		No orders.
1387	Automatic Machin-ery,	12		No orders.
1388	General Wood Ma-...ry,	15		No orders.
1389	...d,	7	7	No rders.o
1390	...ight,	8		No orders.
1391	...el Stock,	22		No orders.
1392	Carriage Trimmings,	45		No orders.
1393	Suits and Cloaks,	50		No orders.
1394	...d Patterns,	15		No orders.
1395	Patent Leather, ...Wk	35		No orders.
1396	General Wood and Carving, ...d	10	130	Guard belt to new engine by railing from post to brick wall. Complied.
1397	...d Turning and Mouldings.	10		No orders.
1398	Typewriters,	350	50	No orders.
1399	Graphophones,	750	110	Provide hood over plating and dip r... jars and potash kettles in... same through piping with chimney or... to carry off injurious gases generated in...
1400	Job Printing,	10		No ...
1401	Toys and Novelties,	50	10	Box main belt at least three feet high on top floor. Complied.
1402	Newspapers,	80	6	No orders.

REPORT OF INSPECTIONS.—CONTINUED.

Order No.	Goods Manufactured.	No. of Employes. M.	F.	Orders Given.	Compliances.
1403	Malleable Iron Castings,	450		No orders.	
1404	Corsets,	8	100	No orders.	
1405	Light Hardware,	40	10	No orders.	
1406	Men's Shirts,	75	350	No orders.	
1407	Small Tools and Bicycle Fittings,	175	7	Introduce and operate within three months from the date of this order such appliances or devices as may be necessary to provide such ventilation as will remove the injurious gases generated in dip room.	
1408	Corsets and Paper Boxes,	250	1150	No orders.	
1409	Mantles and Scroll Work,	5		No orders.	
1410	Oyster dry & Tools,	25		No orders.	
1411	Blank Books & Binding,	5	5	No orders.	
1412	Harnesses,	25		No orders.	
1413	Organ Springs,	7		No orders.	
1414	Machinery,	80		No orders.	
1415	Sheet Brass,	400	26	No orders.	
1416	Machinery,	12		No orders.	
1417	Brass Goods,	50	40	No orders.	
1418	Machinery,	50		No orders.	
1419	Buttons,	30	100	No orders.	
1420		31	30	No orders.	
1421	Metal dd,	200	100	No orders.	
1422	Printing,	8	3	No orders.	
1423	Piano Hardware,	30	12	No orders.	
1424	Brass Novelties,	8	10	No orders.	
1425	Printing,	7		No orders.	

SYNOPSIS OF INSPECTION LAWS

OF OTHER STATES AND PROVINCES,

AS REPORTED TO THE

11th Annual Convention of Factory Inspectors.

MAINE.

No child under 12 years of age shall be employed in any manufacturing or mechanical establishment, nor any child under 15 years of age except during vacation of the public schools, unless such child has attended school sixteen weeks of each year preceding its 16th year. To secure employment every child must procure a certificate from the school authorities to the effect that the school laws are complied with, and it shall contain the age and birth-place of such child, and be kept on file for reference by the employer.

No female under 18 years of age and no male under 16 years of age shall work more than ten hours per day or sixty hours per week. Male minors over 16 years of age, with consent of parents, may contract to work longer hours, otherwise ten hours is a legal day's work for such minors. The same rule applies to women over 18 years of age, with the provision that the limit of overtime for women shall not exceed six hours in any one week or sixty hours in one year. Employers must post in every room where minors and women are employed a notice in large type regulating the hours of labor for such persons.

The inspector must enforce a law requiring the proper swinging of doors in factories and workshops.

Whatever is discovered by the inspector which endangers the life or health of employes in factory, workshop, mine or quarry must be reported to the local board of health, who must investigate.

Every firm and corporation, including municipal corporations and excluding railroad corporations. employing more than ten persons, must pay fortnightly all wages earned by employes.

MASSACHUSETTS.

Children under 13 years of age cannot be employed in any factory, workshop or mercantile establishment. A sworn statement of the age of all minors under 16 years of age must be obtained and kept by employers. Children under 14 years of age, applying for employment, must produce a certificate of school attendance of thirty weeks during the year preceding employment. In cities where manual training is conducted, school attendance is required to the age of 15 years. No child under 14 years of age shall clean machinery operated by mechanical power, and the chief of the department of inspection, with the approval of the Governor, may designate what employments are injurious to the health of children under 14 years of age, and prevent their employment thereat. No child under 15 years of age shall operate or have charge over any elevator, nor any minor under 18 years of age shall operate or have charge over any elevator running over 200 feet per minute. Children under 15 years are prohibited from appearing in any circus or theatrical exhibition.

Minors under 18 years of age and all women employed in manufacturing establishments are prohibited from working more than fifty-eight hours in one week, and more than ten hours in one day. No minor under 18 years of age can be employed more than sixty hours in one week. Legal day's work for both sexes employed by the State is nine hours, whether employed by the State directly or by contract for the State. No child under 14 years of age can be employed in any establishment before 6 A. M. or later than 7 P. M., nor any minor or woman in any manufacturing establishment between the hours of 10 P. M. and 6 A. M.

All factories must be kept clean and well ventilated; and in factories employing five or more persons, and in workshops employing five or more children, young persons or women, inspectors may make such changes, and compel the application and use of any mechanical means, without incurring unreasonable cost, which in their judgement is necessary to secure proper ventilation. Public buildings and school-rooms come under the factory laws providing for sanitation and ventilation. Sweat shops are regulated by license laws requiring cleanliness in and about the tenement house so used, and a tag upon all clothing made under the system, guaranteeing that it is free from vermin and all infectious or contagious matter.

Belting, shafting, gearing and drums in factories must be securely guarded. Wherever manufacturing machinery is propelled by steam, suitable communication must be provided between each room where such machinery is placed and the engine room, in order to control the motive power in case of accident. Machinery other than steam engines must not be cleaned while running if objected to by an inspector. The openings for hoistways, hatchways, wellholes and elevators in all buildings must be protected in such manner as inspectors may direct, and any elevater deemed dangerous or unsafe by an inspector shall be placarded as such, and its use prohibited until made safe.

Inspectors may order fire escapes, safe stairways inside or outside of buildings and the altering of doors and windows suitable for speedy egress in all public buildings, and in all factories, workshops, mercantile establishments, hotels, tenements, etc., having at any time more than ten persons, or any floor above the second, and all such floors shall require suitable means for extinguishing fire.

Six special inspectors are appointed to inspect all uninsured steam boilers of a certain capacity and used in connection with stationary engines, or for heating public buildings, and to examine engineers and firemen as to their competency to have charge over such steam plants.

Engineer or fireman operating boiler must have license; license must be renewed at end of three years. License fee, $1.

Manufacturers and mercantile establishments must report "forthwith" all accidents resulting in the death of an employe, or which prevents his return to work within four days after the occurrence.

The chief inspector can compel all persons and corporations employing twenty-five or more persons to pay employes their wages weekly, excepting when the railroad commissioners shall exempt any railroad corporation from the provisions of this act, if, in their opinion, any of the employes of said corporation wish less frequent payment.

The system of grading work now or at any time hereafter used by the manufacturers shall in no way effect the wages of a weaver except for imperfections in his own work, and in no case shall the wages of those engaged in weaving be affected by fines or otherwise, unless the imperfections complained of are first exhibited and pointed out by the person or persons whose wages are to be affected, and no fine shall be imposed upon any person for imperfect weaving, unless the provisions of this act are first complied with and the amount of the fines agreed upon by both parties.

RHODE ISLAND.

No child under 12 years of age can be employed in any manufacturing or mercantile establishment. Employers must keep office register of all minors under 16 years of age. Minors under 16 are not allowed to clean machinery while in motion.

Hours of labor for women and minors are limited by law to sixty hours per week, but this is not included in factory act.

Separate closets for sexes are required, and wash and dressing rooms for females; to be located to meet the demands of health and propriety.

Belting, shafting, gearing, drums and other dangerous machinery, and all vats, pans and other structures filled with molten metal or hot liquid, must be properly and securely guarded, and all hoisting shafts and wellholes be properly secured, and elevators to be provided with traps, automatic doors or railings.

Inspectors are empowered to provide and direct improvements in means of egress in case of fire.

Fatal accidents must be reported within forty-eight hours, and all serious accidents within three weeks from time of occurrence.*

NEW YORK.

No child under 14 years of age can be employed in any factory or workshop, and all minors between 14 and 16 years of age are required to furnish a health ward certificate as to age, etc., before obtaining employment, and a record of the names, etc., of same is kept in the office. Children between the age 14 and 16 years are required to be able to read and write simple sentences in the

---

*NOTE—The factory act applies to all establishments where five or more women or minors are employed.

English language, otherwise they can be employed only during vacation times of the public schools. No minor under 15 years of age shall have charge over or operate an elevator running at a speed of more than 200 feet per minute, nor shall he be allowed to clean machinery while in motion, and any person is forbidden to remove guards from machinery unless for immediate repairs.

No minor under 18 years nor woman under 21 years of age is allowed to work more than ten hours in any one day, unless for the purpose of making a shorter work-day on Saturday, and minors shall not work more than sixty hours in one week, and no minor under 18 years of age and a woman under 21 years of age can commence working any day before 6 A. M. nor be employed after 9 P. M.

In all factories and workshops between the hours of 6 A. M. and 6 P. M. 250 cubic feet of air space is required for each employe, and 400 cubic feet from 6 P. M. to 6 A. M., but inspectors may grant less air space where rooms are lighted at night-time by electricity. All work rooms are required to be kept in clean condition, and exhaust fans and other means of ventilation may be required in work-rooms in order to carry away dust or other impurities. In all establishments separate closets must be provided for the sexes — with suitable wash and dress rooms for females. Rooms, ceilings and walls must be whitewashed or painted by direction of the inspectors. Sweatshops are controlled by license laws requiring cleanliness and thorough disinfection of premises, and restricting the work done in each tenement workshop to the members of the family dwelling therein. A tag is to be placed upon all sweater-made clothing, etc., manufactured in violation of the provisions of the act or made under unclean or unhealthy conditions. The sanitary regulations of bakeries is provided for by special enactment. Six (6) inspectors are appointed to carry out requirements of the law.

Elevator openings, hoisting-shafts and well-holes must be inclosed with railing or casing, and be provided with properly adjusted trap or automatic doors and gates. Cables, gearing, shafting and other machinery or apparatus must be guarded and kept in safe condition. Handrails must be provided on all stairways, and stairs screened where females are employed, and when deemed necessary stairs must be covered with rubber covers.

Buildings of three or more stories, with employes on or above the third story, must be provided with suitable fire-escapes, easy of access, and free from draft from any hoistway, stairs or other floor openings. Doors must open outwardly and be kept unfastened during work hours.

Every case of accident or injury to any employe must be reported with full details within forty-eight hours after its occurrence.

Every corporation, excepting steam surface railway corporations, is required to make weekly payment of wages to employes.

Inspection of mines is placed under the factory inspection department in New York.

NEW JERSEY.

Boys under 12 years of age and girls under 14 years of age are prohibited from working in any manufacturing establishment. Children between the age of 12 and 15 years must produce school certificate of school attendance for twelve weeks during the year immediately preceding date of employment. No minor under the age of 16 years shall be employed at work dangerous to health and without certificate from physician, and no minor shall clean machinery in motion or be employed between the traversing parts.

The hours of labor for minors of both sexes is limited to fifty-five per week.

Inspectors have power to regulate heating, lighting and other sanitary conditions. They can prohibit the overcrowding of factories and workshops, and to produce proper ventilation in factories where dust is created they can have suitable mechanical means applied, and in all establishments where women are employed suitable and separate closets for the sexes must be provided, with wash and dress rooms for females. Factories where dusty work is performed and wherein women and children are employed shall be white-washed or painted once in twelve months. Bakeries must be thoroughly ventilated and be provided with proper plumbing connections, and must have no connection within or without the room with any water-closet, earth-closet, ash-pit or other nuisance. Employes must have sleeping quarters separate from bake-rooms.

Belting, shafting, gearing, drums and other machinery of a dangerous character, and all vats, pans and other structures containing molten metal or hot liquid must be suitably protected. All floor openings for hatchways, hoistways, well-holes and elevators must be provided with automatic or trap doors and otherwise be guarded with a railing three feet high. Stairs in use by females must be screened, and no female must be allowed to clean machinery in operation or to work between its traversing parts.

Explosives or inflammable matter must not be placed or used in such manner as to obstruct egress or to endanger life in case of fire. Upon all buildings for manufacturing purposes two or three stories in height, where thirty or more persons are employed above the first floor, one or more fire escapes may be ordered by the inspectors, and suitable means for extinguishing fire provided for each floor.

Accidents resulting in death must be reported within twenty-four hours after, and those which prevent the return to work of the injured person within two weeks must be reported to an inspector within twenty-four hours after expiration of said two weeks.

PENNSYLVANIA.

Children under 13 years of age cannot be employed in any manufacturing or mercantile establishment. Sworn statement is required of child's age from parents or guardians, and wall record in each room where children are employed, and office register must be kept of all minors under 16 years of age. No boy under 14 years is allowed to run an elevator, and no minor under 16 years to clean machinery while in motion.

Minors must not be employed in any one day longer than twelve hours nor in any one week more than sixty hours.

Heating, lighting, ventilation and other sanitary conditions come under the regulation of inspectors. Suitable and separate water-closets and wash and dress rooms must be provided for females; they must not adjoin closets for males, and shall be kept clean, properly screened and ventilated. Special enactment regulates the sweatshop system.

All floor openings for elevators must be properly guarded and provided with automatic traps or doors. Belting, shafting, gearing, drums, and other dangerous machinery must be sufficiently guarded, and all vats, pans and structures containing molten metal or hot liquid must be surrounded with proper safeguards. Shifting belts and pulleys must be provided with shifters.

Inspectors can order all buildings more than two stories high provided with one or more fire-escapes, after a certain model designated by statute, and with life-ropes and chains, as any such building may require.

OHIO.

The age at which children may be employed in manufacturing establishments is 14 years, with the provision that children more than 12 years of age may be employed at non-dangerous employment during the time they are not required by law to attend school. The school law requires that all children under 14 years of age and over 8 years must attend school during the school term. This law is not enforced by factory inspectors, but by truant officers, one or more, in all school districts. Office record must be kept by employers of all minors under 18 years of age, giving name, date, and place of birth, with residence of parents or guardians. No minor under 16 years of age shall work at any employment whereby his life or limb is endangered, or his health is likely to be impaired, or his morals may be depraved.

No minor under the age of 18 years shall be employed in any manufacturing establishment more than ten hours in one day, nor more than sixty hours in one week. Notices containing the law must be posted by manufacturers in a conspicuous place in every room where minors are employed, the chief inspector of factories to furnish such notices.

Heating, lighting, ventilation and other sanitary requirements in factories, workshops and mercantile establishments are under the inspector's supervision, and to secure such he may cut through walls, floors, roofs and ceilings, or make changes in sewerages and plumbing, and require proper closet arrangements, and may demand separate closets for the sexes, with toilet and dressing rooms for females on the floors on which they work, and seats for females to be used by them when not actively engaged. Special bakeshop and sweatshop laws.

Inspectors must order guards for belting, shafting, gearing, elevators and other machinery; also for vats, pans and other structures filled with molten metal or hot liquid; also efficient safety gates for elevator openings, guarding of hatchways and hoisting apparatus in floors or outside of buildings, the repair of all elevators and all gearing, and of defective walls, roofs, ceilings, stairways and doors, and all other improvements necessary to secure the safety of employes. Blowers may be required where dust-creating machinery is used.

Inspectors have power to examine all buildings as to their

safety, and to order all necessary alterations to obtain the same ; also to provide for stairways and fire-escapes and other efficient means of egress, and hand rails on all stairways, and may require in all halls and other buildings for public assemblage means of extinguishing fire on all floors above the the first and that all doors in such buildings shall open outward.

Employers must report all accidents upon blanks furnished by inspectors ; those resulting in death within seven days after, and those in bodily injury, necessitating six days consecutive loss of time, within thirty days after.

Stated wages, beforehand agreed upon between employer and employe, must be paid to all minors, and the retention of such by fines or upon any other pretext is absolutely prohibited. No change of wages must occur without a written notice being given to each minor affected twenty-four hours before such change shall take place.

ILLINOIS.

Children under 14 years of age cannot be employed in any factory or workshop, and minors must produce sworn statements as to age. Office register of minors must be kept by employers and a record of names and ages of minors posted in rooms where they are employed. Physician's certificates as to the physical ability of any minor to perform certain labor may be demanded by inspectors.

Inspectors have access to every place where articles of clothing are manufactured for sale ; with power to condemn and order destroyed garments found infectious or infested with vermin, and to prohibit the employment in any dwelling rooms of any person not member of the family living therein.

MICHIGAN.

Children under 14 years of age cannot be employed in any factory or workshop. Sworn statement as to the age of miners under 16 years must be furnished to employers, who must keep office register of such and post a record thereof on the walls of workrooms. Female minors under 21 and male minors under 18 years of age must not be allowed to clean machinery while in motion.

Males under 18 years and females under 21 years of age, cannot work more than ten hours in one day, unless to make a shorter workday on Saturday, and not more than sixty hours in one week.

Means must be provided to carry dust from all dust-creating machinery ; separate closets must be provided for each sex, and wash and dress rooms for all females, and such closets and dress rooms must be kept in clean condition.

Elevators, hoisting shafts or well-holes must be secured and equipped with trap or automatic doors, and all gearing, shafting and other apparatus kept in safe condition. Hand-rails must be provided on stairways, and stairs screened, and, when necessary, stair steps must be provided with rubber covers.

Factory buildings of three or more stories must be provided with fire-escapes ; easy of access and free from draft of hoistway or stairway. Doors must be properly hung and open outwardly, and not fastened during working hours.*

MISSOURI.

No minor shall be required to clean machinery or to work between its traversing parts while it is in motion.

Inspectors have power to prevent overcrowding in all establishments where labor is employed, and can regulate heating, lighting, ventilating and other sanitary arrangements, and may order suitable mechanical means for carrying away dust and other impurities generated by manufacturing. And where females are employed at unclean work, wash and dress rooms must be provided, and stairs used by females must be properly screened, seats must be provided and conveniently located so that females can use them when not required to be on their feet, and where both sexes are employed separate and distinct water-closets must be provided for each sex.

Belting, shafting, gearing and drums in all establishments must be safely and securely guarded, and all vats, pans, ladles or structures filled with molten metal or hot liquid, or any furnace, must be surrounded with safe-guards, and all platforms, passage-ways and other arrangements about railroad yards must be made comparatively safe. The openings of hatchways, elevators and well-holes must be protected by trap-doors, self-closing hatches or safety catches, or railing three feet high. Where guards are not practicable, notice of danger must be posted.

Establishments two or more stories high, in which twenty or

---

* Note.— All places where goods, wares or produce are manufactured, repaired, cleaned or stored in cities and all such places outside of cities employing five or more persons, come within the provisions of the factory law.

more persons are employed above first floor, must be provided with fire-escapes, and in addition for every twenty persons employed above the second floor, one rope or other portable fire-escape; and each floor must be supplied with means for extinguishing fire. All doors must open outwardly, and must not be locked or bolted during labor hours. In any building or any part thereof supposed to be unsafe, or means of egress insufficient, the inspector may order necessary changes.

Any accident resulting in death, or which prevents an employe's returning to work within two weeks, must be reported.*

MINNESOTA.

The law forbids any parent or guardian to let or hire any minor under 21 years of age, nor must any person willfully permit any child under 14 years to work at any employment injurious to health, dangerous to life and limb, or likely to deprave its morals.

Children under 16 years of age must not be permitted, nor must any woman be compelled to work more than ten hours in one day, or to work earlier than 7 A. M. nor later than 6 P. M. of any one day.

All workrooms must be well lighted, heated and ventilated and kept in clean condition. Exhaust fans must be adjusted for carrying dust from emery wheels and grindstones. Separate closets for the sexes must be provided, and wash and dress rooms where females are employed, and seats for their use in mercantile establishments. Bakeries, including hotel and restaurant kitchens, must have no connection within or without the room with any water-closet, earth-closet, ash-pit or other nuisance, and employes or others are not to be permitted to live or sleep in bakeries.

The law is specific in authority and includes almost the whole range of machinery employed in industrial operations. It provides that saws, planers, wood-shapers, jointers, sandpapering machines, ironing mangles, set-screws, drums, belts, shafting, cables, flywheels, dynamos and other electrical apparatus and appliance, vats, pans and such other structures, and all dangerous places in and about factories and other works must be

---

* NOTE. — All factories employing five or more persons, and all workshops where children, young persons or women are employed, come under the inspector's authority so far as sanitary provisions are required, while the factory or inspection whole apply to establishments in general employing ten or more person.

guarded. Loose pulleys must be adjusted where practicable, and shift-belts provided with shifters. All elevaters and other floor openings must be fenced or otherwise protected, and all elevators supplied with safety devices.

In all factory and other buildings in which people are employed more than one means of egress must be provided. Doors leading therefrom must open outward, and be kept unfastened and unobstructed during working hours. Handrails on stairways must be provided, and stairs properly screened when used by females. One or more fire-escapes shall be placed upon all factory and other such buildings if three or more stories in height. Plan of escape is defined by enactment.

Steam boilers are inspected by a separate state department constituted of five inspectors.

Accidents to employes requiring the aid of a surgeon or resulting in death must be reported by employer within ten days after occurring.

ONTARIO.

No child under 14 years of age can be employed in any factory except in canning and dessicating fruit and vegetables.

No child under 14 years, and no girl or woman can be employed for more than ten hours in one day or sixty hours in one week, except when employed in factories for canning and dessicating fruit and vegetables. In these, females under 18 years may be employed for as many as thirty-six nights in twelve months until 9 P. M.; and women over 18 years may be required to labor "until the work is finished" twenty nights in twelve months.

Every factory must be kept clean and not overcrowded, and must be ventilated so as to render harmless, as far as practicable, all unwholesome effluvia, and to take away dust and other injurious impurities generated by manufacturing machinery. Separate closets must be provided for the sexes, each sex to have separate approaches, and to be kept clean and well ventilated at all times. Special act governing sanitation, etc., in bakeshops.

Belting, shafting, gearing, fly-wheels, drums and other moving parts of machinery, vats, pans, cauldrons, reservoirs, wheel-races, flumes, water channels, doors, openings in floors or walls, bridges and all dangerous structures must be, as far as practicable, securely guarded. Hoistways, hatchways, elevators and well-holes must be protected by such automatic appliances as the Inspector may desire, and all elevator cabs and cars must be provided, to the satisfaction of the Inspector, with suitable safety attachments. No machinery other than steam engines must be cleaned while in motion, if Inspector so orders, and no woman must be allowed to clean mill gearing while in motion nor to work between the traversing parts of machinery.

Factories three or more stories high must be provided with fire-escapes, unless supplied with sufficient tower stairways protected with iron doors. All inside and outside doors must open outwardly, and all doors entering stairway towers or leading to fire-escapes must be kept unlocked and unbolted during working hours. In every factory there must be provided such means for extinguishing fire as the inspector may direct.

Accidents resulting in bodily injury to an employe must be reported by the employer within six days after, and if accident shall prove fatal, within twenty-four hours from time of its occurrence.*

QUÉBEC.

No boy under 12 years and no girl under 14 years of age can be émployed in any factory, work-shop, work-yard or mill of any kind. In establishments classified as "dangerous, unwholesome or inconvenient," the age of employes shall not be under 16 years for boys and 18 years for girls. Age certificate may be required of parent or guardian. Children discharged if pronounced physically unfit for work by sanitary or other physician. Employer must keep register containing names and ages of boys, girls and women employed, the period of each day and week they are employed, and the hour at which they begin and finish work.

No boy under 18 years of age and no girl or woman shall be employed more than ten hours in any one day and sixty hours in any one week. The day shall not commence before 6 o'clock in the morning nor end after 9 o'clock at night. In certain exigencies the inspector may extend the working day to twelve hours for a period not exceeding six weeks.

Establishments must be kept clean, well lighted, well ventilated ; must be provided with apparatus for expelling dust and gases, and employers must furnish inspector with certificate from

*NOTE.—The word "factory" includes manufacturing establishments and work-shops where six or more persons are employed.

health officers that establishment fulfills sanitary conditions imposed by factory act and by regulations of Board of Health of Province.

Platforms and elevated passageways must be provided with guards; belting, cables and shafts must be closed in to a height of six feet; pits, cells, wells, traps and vats must be covered or fenced in; warning placards must be posted near tanks of corrosive or burning liquids. Hoist, elevator and lift shafts must be closed in with self-closing doors and shall be examined every six months. Machinery of all kinds must be guarded, and may not be oiled, cleaned or repaired while in motion.

Owner, tenant and occupant of property on which establishment is built are jointly and severally responsible for construction and repair of fire-escapes. Doors of egress must open outward, must be left free during working hours, must close by means of weights or spring only. In buildings three stories or more high, inspectors may require additional exits and outside iron fire-escape stairs, these exits to consist of doors or windows opening out upon balcony or gallery. Receptacles for oil and petroleum must be kept in special closed room. Gas works must be separated from workshop and in charge of men over 18 years of age. Places in which explosive or inflammable gases are produced or kept must be lighted only from the outside and visited only with safety lamps.

In new establishments steam boilers and moters must, if possible be placed outside of main building. In older establishments may be closed in on side where work is done, and accessible only to the workman in charge. Every boiler must be provided with not less than two safety valves, a steam guage and two independent water guages.

Employer must send to inspector a written notice of any accident whereby a workman has been killed or so seriously injured as to prevent his continuing at work. The notice must be sent within forty-eight hours of time of accident, and must state where the person injured or killed has place of residence, or the place to which he has been removed. The inspectors may be present at coroner's inquests and at inquiries by fire marshals. The inspectors may hold such inquiries as they deem proper, may examine any person employed, summon witnesses and administer the oath to them.

Public buildings, as well as industrial establishments, are inspected under these laws.

INSPECTION OF BAKESHOPS.

During the year ending September 30, 1898, two hundred and eleven bakeshops have been visited by the Inspectors, and their condition if found unsanitary has been reported to the local health officers.

A marked improvement has been noticed within the past year. Some shops that were found in a very filthy condition the previous year have been thoroughly renovated. Proprietors of places which were in an unsanitary locality have moved to better quarters, and seem proud of the improvements they have made.

There has been about one-half as many complaints made to the health officers this year as in the previous year. This plainly shows that improvement has been made.

The causes which produced the former conditions are found to be as follows:

Underground shops situated in the densely populated portions of our large cities, and which were not properly drained, and located so that at high tide the water would set back into the bakeries, causing damp and mouldy floors and side walls, and creating unhealthful conditions under which to work.

Height of some shops, which in some instances were found to be only five and one-half feet high, with no means of ventilation except a small hatchway or window, the gases rising from the oven rendering the atmosphere particularly unhealthful.

The plumbing connections of closets or sinks made with a covered cesspool or sewer and not being trapped. Leaky soil-pipes from closets, and leaky sink pipes.

Personal habits of men employed, whose clothing was found very dirty.

Instances where owners of buildings rented as bakeries were unwilling to make necessary repairs to keep their buildings in proper sanitary condition, claiming that it was the tenants' duty to make such repairs, though no written lease could be found requiring it.

Bakeries in which night and day bakers were employed, each shift claiming that it was the duty of the other shift to keep the shop clean and remove the refuse. This generally resulted in the shop being rarely clean. Complaints have been made to the Inspector in some places by the bakers that they were required to work from fourteen to sixteen hours per day and had no time to keep the shop clean.

I wish also to thank the local health officers, who have rendered all the assistance possible in enforcing the law.

The following personal letter was sent to the different health officers :

Dear Sir : — The twelfth annual report of the Department of Factory Inspection is nearly ready for the press. As this report is to contain a summary of the inspections made of the bakeshops of the State, the opinions of the health officers who have assisted the department in enforcing the law concerning the sanitary conditions of the bakeshops would, it is believed, be of value to the general public, and would go far to show the necessity of the existing law. Would you, therefore, kindly state briefly your opinion as to the value to the public of the present law, and how far, in your judgment, under its operation former conditions have been improved.

Yours truly,
GEORGE L. McLEAN,
Factory Inspector.

The following letters are some of the replies received :

GEORGE L. McLEAN, Esq.,

My Dear Sir : I believe the law regarding the inspection of bakeshops is a very important one, for it touches on a subject which concerns the whole public.

So far as my observation goes, this inspection has been the means of improving the sanitary condition of many shops, and raising the standard of their output.   Yours truly.

E. E. STARK, M. D.,
Norwich, Conn.

G. L. McLEAN, Factory Inspector,

Dear Sir : The law in regard to the inspection of bakeshops is a good one, and has been the means of working great improvement in the sanitary conditions of these places in New Haven. I would suggest that the law be amended so as to apply to the owners of buildings rented for bakeshops. Often the baker is willing to make improvements, but the owner of the building will do nothing.

Yours truly,
FRANK W. WRIGHT, <i>Health Officer,</i>
New Haven, Conn.

Mr. GEORGE L. McLEAN, State Inspector, Hartford, Conn.,

My Dear Sir : I wish to express my appreciation of the work that you have done in the inspection of bakeshops, and in assisting in bringing about better sanitary conditions in these places. Your efforts, with the authority of the State behind you, have accomplished more in this one year than local efforts could have done in a much longer period.

There is still work to be done, and I trust that we shall continue to have your co-operation and efforts along this line.

Very truly yours,

E. A. McLELLAN, Health Officer,

Bridgeport, Conn.

GEORGE L. McLEAN, Inspector of Factories of State of Connecticut,

Dear Sir : From an intimate knowledge of the workings of the law concerning bakeshops incorporated in " An Act concerning the Regulation of the Manufacture of Flour and Meal from Cereals into Food." I consider that it has been of incalculable value to the public. The improvement in surroundings and cleanliness, as well as in ventilation and plumbing has been great.

In every instance the changes ordered by the Inspector were fulfilled to the letter. Only those who have had opportunity can realize the conditions that obtained in certain quarters, but which now are so happily changed under the new regime.

Trusting that the work now so well undertaken may be continued, I am   Yours very truly,

C. W. S. FROST, M. D., Health Officer,

Waterbury, Conn.

A careful examination of one of the above letters will show that many times the conditions found in the bakeshops are due to the negligence of the owners of the buildings, who will not make the necessary repairs in the plumbing and ventilation. I would, therefore, recommend a changing of the factory laws in regard to bakeshops, making it the duty of the owners of the buildings, except when written leases exist to the contrary, to make all necessary repairs in plumbing and ventilation.

The Inspector further recommends a gradual abolishment of the low cellar shops. This can be brought about by requiring all new shops to be at least eight feet in height, and to be situated so that they can be properly ventilated and drained.

BAKESHOP LAW OF CONNECTICUT.

An Act concerning the Regulation of the Manufacture of Flour
and Meal from Cereals into Food.

*Be it enacted by the Senate and House of Representatives in General
Assembly Convened :*

SECTION 1.   Every building, room, or place used in or in
connection with the manufacture for sale of any article of food
composed wholly or in part of flour or meal from cereals, shall
be known under this act as a "bakeshop."

SEC. 2.   Every bakeshop shall be properly drained, plumbed,
ventilated, and kept in a clean and sanitary condition, and conducted with proper regard to the health of the operatives and the
production of wholesome food.

SEC. 3.   Every bakeshop shall be provided with a proper
wash-room and water-closet or closets, apart from the bakeroom
or rooms where the manufacturing of such food products is conducted, and no water-closet, earth closet, or privy shall be within
the bakeroom of any bakery.

SEC. 4.   The sleeping places for persons employed in a bakeshop shall be kept separate from the room or rooms where flour
or meal food products are manufactured or stored.

SEC. 5.   The factory inspector shall examine all bakeshops as
frequently as may be necessary, to ascertain whether they are
kept and conducted in the manner herein provided ; and shall, in
addition to such regulation as the factory inspector is by law now
authorized to make, report in writing to the local health officer of
any town, city, or borough, every bakeshop located within such
jurisdiction found not kept and conducted as herein provided ;
and such health officer shall thereupon investigate, or cause to be
investigated, by other health officer or officers, such unsanitary
conditions so reported to him, and if found to exist, shall cause
the same to be removed in the manner now provided by the laws
relating to public health, as provided in section 2592 of the
general statutes.

Approved May 25, 1897.

THE NEW YORK LAW.
[Passed May 2, 1895 ; amended May 14, 1896 ; took effect July 1, 1896.]

SECTION 1.   No employe shall be required, permitted or suffered to work in a biscuit, bread or cake bakery or confectionery

establishment more than sixty hours in any one week, or more than ten hours in any one day, unless for the purpose of making a shorter workday on the last day of the week, nor more hours in any one week than will make an average of ten hours per day for the whole number of days in which such person shall so work during such week.

SEC. 2.   All buildings or rooms occupied as biscuit, bread, pie or cake bakeries shall be drained and plumbed in a manner to conduce to the proper and healthful sanitary condition thereof, and constructed with air shafts, windows or ventilating pipes sufficient to insure ventilation, as the factory inspector or any of his deputies shall direct.   No cellar or basement not now used as a bakery shall hereafter be occupied and used as a bakery unless the proprietor shall have previously complied with the sanitary provisions of this act.

SEC. 3.   Every room used for the manufacture of flour or meal food products shall be at least eight feet in height and shall have, if deemed necessary by the factory inspector, an impermeable floor constructed of cement or of tiles laid in cement, with an additional flooring, or* of wood properly saturated with linseed oil. The side walls of such rooms shall be plastered or wainscoted, and if required by the factory inspector or a deputy factory inspector, the side walls and ceiling shall be whitewashed at least once in three months, and the woodwork of such walls shall be painted when required by such inspector or deputy.   The furniture and utensils in such rooms shall be so arranged that the furniture and floor may at all times be kept in a proper and healthful sanitary and clean condition.   No domestic animal, except cats, shall be allowed to remain in a room used as a biscuit, bread, pie or cake bakery, or any room in such bakery where flour or meal food products are stored.

SEC. 4.   The manufactured flour or meal food products shall be kept in perfectly dry and airy rooms, so arranged that the floors, shelves and all other facilities for storing the same can be easily and perfectly cleaned.

SEC. 5.   Every such bakery shall be provided with a proper wash-room and water-closet or closets, apart from the bakeroom or rooms where the manufacturing of such food products is conducted ; and no water-closet, earth-closet, privy or ash-pit shall

---

* So in original.

be within, or communicate directly with, the bakeroom of any bakery, hotel or public restaurant.

SEC. 6. The sleeping places for the persons employed in the bakery shall be kept separate from the room or rooms where flour or meal food products are manufactured or stored, and the factory inspector or a deputy factory inspector may inspect such sleeping places if they are on the floor as the bakery, and order them cleaned or changed in compliance with sanitary principles.

SEC. 7. Any person who violates any of the provisions of this act, or refuses to comply with any requirement of the factory inspector or a deputy factory inspector, as provided herein, shall be guilty of a misdemeanor, and on conviction shall be punished by a fine of not less than $20 nor more than $50 for a first offense, and not less than $50 nor more than $100 for a second offense, or imprisonment for not more than ten days, and for a third offense by a fine of not less than $250 and not more than thirty days' imprisonment.

SEC. 8. For the purpose of enforcing this act and of Chapter 409 of the laws of 1886 and acts amendatory thereof, the factory inspector may appoint six deputies, each of whom shall receive an annual salary of $1,200, together with his necessary traveling and other expenses incurred in his discharging the duties of his office, payable monthly by the Treasurer on the warrant of the Comptroller, upon proper vouchers approved by the factory inspector. Under the direction of the factory inspector such deputies shall inspect all bakeries and see that the provisions of this act and of Chapter 409 of the laws of 1886, and the acts amendatory thereof, are observed therein. Such deputies shall have all the powers and duties of the deputy inspectors and shall be amenable to the supervision and control of the factory inspector the same as the deputy factory inspectors appointed under Chapter 409 of the laws of 1886 and the acts amendatory thereof. The factory inspector, or a deputy factory inspector authorized by him, shall issue a certificate to a person conducting a bakery where such bakery is conducted in compliance with all the provisions of this act.

SEC. 9. The owner, agent or lessee of any property affected by the provisions of Sections 2, 3 or 5 of this act shall, within sixty days after the service of a notice requiring any alterations to be made in or upon such premises, comply therewith, and such notice shall be in writing and may be served upon such owner, agent or lessee, either personally or by mail, and a notice mailed to the last known address of such owner, agent or lessee shall be deemed sufficient for the purposes of this act.

OHIO BAKESHOP LAW.

[Passed April 27, 1896.]

SECTION 1. *Be it enacted, etc.,* That no employe shall be required, permitted or suffered to work in a biscuit, bread or cake bakery or confectionery establishment more than sixty hours in one week, or more than ten hours in one day, unless for the purpose of making a shorter workday on the last day of the week, nor more hours in one week than will average ten hours per day for the whole number of days in which such person shall so work during the week; and the working time shall begin by entering the shop and be concluded ten hours thereafter. No employe in any biscuit, bread or cake bakery shall be discharged by his employer for having made any truthful statement as a witness in a court, or to the factory inspector, in pursuance of this act.

SEC. 2. The manufactured flour [or] meal food products shall be kept in perfectly dry and airy rooms, so arranged that the floors, shelves and all other facilities for storing the same can be easily and perfectly cleaned.

SEC. 3. Every such bakery shall be provided with a proper wash room and water-closet or closets, apart from the bake-room or rooms where the manufacturing of such food products is conducted; and no water-closet, earth-closet, privy or ash-pit shall be within or communicate directly with the bake-room of any bakery, hotel or public restaurant.

SEC. 4. All buildings or rooms occupied as biscuit, bread or cake bakeries shall be drained and plumbed in a manner to conduce to the proper healthful and sanitary condition thereof, and constructed with air-shafts, windows or ventilating pipes sufficient to insure ventilation, as a factory inspector or any of his deputies shall direct. No cellar or basement not now used as a bakery shall be hereafter used and occupied as a bakery, and a cellar heretofore occupied shall, when once closed, not be reopened unless the proprietor shall have previously complied with the provisions of this act.

SEC. 5. Every room used for the manufacture of flour or meal food shall be at least nine feet in height. The side walls and ceilings of such rooms shall be plastered or wainscoted, and, if required by the factory inspector, shall be whitewashed at least once in three months. The furniture and utensils of such rooms shall be so arranged that the furniture and floor may at all times be kept in a proper healthful sanitary condition. No domestic animals, except cats, shall be allowed to remain in a room used as a biscuit, bread or cake bakery, or for the storage of flour and meal food products.

SEC. 6. The sleeping places for persons employed in a bakery shall be kept separate from the room or rooms where flour or meal food products are manufactured or stored, and the factory inspector or deputy factory inspector may inspect such sleeping places, if they are on the same premises as the bakery, and order them cleaned or changed in compliance with sanitary principles.

SEC. 7. For the purpose of enforcing this act, the chief inspector of workshops and factories shall appoint two additional district inspectors who shall be appointed in the same manner and possess the same qualifications, and whose term of office shall be the same and on the same conditions, and receive the same compensation as the district inspector authorized by Section 2572a, including Sections 2 and 3 and Section 2573a-2 revised statutes. After the inspection of a bakery has been made, and it is found to conform to this act, the chief inspector may issue a certificate to the owner or operator of such bakery, that it is conducted in compliance with all the provisions of this act; but where orders are issued by the inspector to improve the condition of a bakery no such certificate shall be issued until such order and the provisions of this act shall have been compled with.

SEC. 8. The owner, agent or lessee of any property affected by the provisions of Sections 2, 3 or 5 of this act shall, within thirty days after the service of a notice requiring any alterations to be made in or upon such premises, comply therewith, and such notice shall be in writing and may be served upon such owner, agent or lessee either personally or by mail, and a notice mailed to the last known address of such owner, agent or lessee shall be deemed sufficient for the purposes of this act.

SEC. 9. Any person who violates the provisions of this act or refuses to comply with any requirement of the factory inspector or deputy factory inspector, as provided herein, shall be guilty of a misdemeanor, and on conviction shall be punished by a fine of not less than $20 or more than $50 for the first offense, and not less than $50 or more than $100 for the second offense, or imprisonment for not more than ten days, and for the third offense by a fine of not less than $250 and not more than thirty days imprisonment.

PENNSYLVANIA LAW.

An Act to regulate the Manufacture of Flour and Meal Food Products.

SECTION 1. *Be it enacted, etc.*, That no employe shall be required, permitted or suffered to work in a biscuit, bread or cake bakery, confectionery establishment more than six (6) days in any one week, said week to commence on Sunday not before six o'clock post meridian, and to terminate at the corresponding time on Saturday of the same week. No person under the age of eighteen (18) years shall be employed in any bakehouse between the hours of nine (9) o'clock at night and five (5) o'clock in the morning. Excepted from this rule shall be the time on Sunday for setting the sponges for the night's work following.

SEC 2. All buildings or rooms occupied as a biscuit, bread, pretzel, pie or cake bakery, or macaroni establishment, shall be drained and plumbed in the manner directed by the rules and regulations governing the house drainage and plumbing as prescribed by law, and all rooms used for the purpose aforesaid shall be ventilated by means of air shafts, windows or ventilating pipes, so as to insure a free circulation of fresh air. No cellar or basement, not now used for a bakery, shall hereafter be occupied and used as a bakery, unless the proprietor shall have previously complied with the sanitary provisions of this act.

SEC. 3. Every room used for the manufacture of flour or meal food products shall have an impervious floor, constructed of cement or of tiles laid in cement, or of wood which all the crevices shall be filled in with putty, and the whole surface ated with oil varnish. The inside walls and ceilings shall be plastered and either be painted with oil paint, three (3) coats, or be limewashed, or the side walls plastered and wainscoted to the height of six (6) feet from the floor, and painted or oiled; when painted, shall be renewed at least once in every five (5) years, and shall be washed with hot water and soap at least once in every three (3) months; when limewashed the lime washing shall be renewed at least once in every three (3) months. The furniture and utensils in such room shall be so arranged that the furniture and floor may at all times be kept in a thoroughly sanitary and clean condition. No domestic or pet animal shall be allowed in a room used as a biscuit, bread, pie or cake bakery, or in any room in such bakery where flour or meal products are stored.

SEC. 4.   The manufactured flour and meal food products shall be kept in perfectly dry and airy rooms, so arranged that the floors, shelves and all other places for storing the same can be easily and perfectly cleaned.

SEC. 5.   Every such bakery shall be provided with a proper wash-room and water-closet or closets, apart from the bakeroom or rooms where the manufacture of such food products is conducted, and no water-closet, earth-closet, privy or ash pit shall be within or communicate directly with the bakeroom of any bakery, hotel or public restaurant.

SEC. 6.   Every sleeping room for persons employed in every bakery shall be kept separate from the room or rooms where flour or meal products are manufactured or stored, and shall be provided with one or more external glazed windows, each of which shall be at least nine (9) superficial feet in area, of which at least four and one-half (4½) superficial feet shall be made to open for ventilation ; and such sleeping places, when they are on the same floor as the bakery, shall be inspected in order to maintain them in a condition of cleanliness.

SEC. 7.   No employer shall knowingly require, permit or suffer any person to work in his bakeshop who is affected with consumption of the lungs, or with scrofulous diseases, or with· any venerial diseases, or with any communicable skin affection, and every employer is hereby required to maintain himself and his employes in a clean condition while engaged in the manufacture, handling or sale of such food products, and it is hereby made the duty of the Board of Health to enforce the provisions of this section.

SEC. 8.   Any person who violates any of the provisions of this act, or refuses to comply with any requirements as provided herein of the factory inspector or his deputy, who are hereby charged with the enforcement of this act, excepting section seven, shall be guilty of a misdemeanor, and on conviction shall be punished by a fine not less than twenty (20) nor more than fifty (50) dollars for a first offense, and not less than fifty (50) nor more than one hundred (100) dollars for a second offense, or imprisonment for not more than ten (10) days ; and for a third offense,

by a fine of not less than two hundred and fifty (250) dollars and
more than thirty (30) days' imprisonment.

SEC. 9. The factory inspector is authorized to issue a certificate of satisfactory inspection to a person conducting a bakery
where such bakery is conducted in compliance with all the provisions of this act.

SEC. 10. The owner, agent or lessee of any property affected
by the provisions of sections 2, 3 and 5 of this act, shall, within
thirty (30) days after the service of a notice requiring any alterations to be made in or upon such premises, comply therewith,
and such notices shall be in writing and may be served upon such
owner, agent, or lessee, either personally or by mail, and notice
to the last known address of such owner, agent or lessee shall be
deemed sufficient for the purposes of this act.

SEC. 11. A copy of this act shall be conspicuously posted
and kept posted in each workroom of every bread, cake or pie
bakery, or confectionery establishment in this State.

SEC. 12. This act shall take effect thirty (30) days after the
same shall have been approved and signed by the Governor of
this Commonwealth.

Approved the 27th day of May, 1897.

BAKESHOP LAW IN NEW JERSEY.

[Approved April 16, 1896]

SECTION 1. *Be it enacted, etc.* No employe shall be required,
permitted or suffered to work in a biscuit, bread or cake bakery
or confectionery establishment more than sixty hours in any one
week or more than ten hours in any one day unless for the purpose of making a shorter workday on the last day of the week,
nor more hours in any one week than will make an average of
ten hours per day for the whole number of days in which such
person shall so work during such week ; but it shall be lawful, in
cases of emergency, for employers to permit any employe and for
the latter to work an additional time not exceeding two hours per
day, such extra work to be remunerated at the current rate of the
weekly wages paid to such employe for his weekly work of sixty
hours ; no employe in any biscuit, bread or cake bakery shall be
discharged by his employer for having made any truthful statement
as a witness in court or to the factory inspector or a deputy factory
inspector in pursuance of this act.

SEC. 2. All buildings or rooms occupied as biscuit, bread or cake bakeries shall be drained and plumbed in a manner to conduce to the proper and healthful sanitary condition thereof, and constructed with air shafts, windows or ventilating pipes sufficient to insure ventilation, as the factory inspector or any of his deputies shall direct; no cellar or basement not now occupied as a bakery shall hereafter be occupied and used as a bakery, and a cellar bakery heretofore occupied, when once closed shall not be reopened, unless the proprietor shall have previously complied with the provisions of this act.

SEC. 3. Every room used for the manufacture of flour or meal food products shall be at least eight feet in height and shall have, if deemed necessary by the factory inspector, an impermeable floor, constructed of cement or of wood properly saturated with linseed oil; the side walls of such rooms shall be plastered or wainscoted, except where brick walls are shown, and, if required by the factory inspector, shall be whitewashed at least once in three months; the furniture and utensils in such rooms shall be so arranged that the furniture and floor may at all times be kept in a proper and healthful, sanitary and clean condition; no domestic animal, except cats, shall be allowed to remain in a room used as a biscuit, bread or cake bakery, or for storage of flour or meal food products.

SEC. 4. The manufactured flour or meal products shall be kept in perfectly dry and airy rooms, so arranged that the floors, shelves and all other facilities for storing the same can be easily and perfectly cleaned.

SEC. 5. Every such bakery shall be provided with a proper washroom and water-closet or closets apart from the bakeroom or rooms where the manufacturing of such food products is conducted; and no water-closet, earth-closet or privy shall be within or communicate directly with the bakeroom of any bakery, hotel or public restaurant.

SEC. 6. The sleeping places for the persons employed in a bakery shall be kept separate from the room or rooms where flour or meal food products are manufactured or stored, and the factory inspector or a deputy factory inspector may inspect such sleeping places, if they are on the same premises as the bakery, and order them cleaned or changed in compliance with sanitary principles.

SEC. 7. Any person who violates any of the provisions of this act or refuses to comply with any requirement of the factory inspector or deputy factory inspector, as provided herein, shall be guilty of a misdemeanor, and on conviction shall be punished by a fine of not less than $20 nor more than $50 for the first offense, and not less than $50 nor more than $100 for a second offense, or imprisonment for not more than ten days, and for a third offense by a fine of not less than $250 and not more than thirty days' imprisonment.

THE ONTARIO BAKESHOP ACT.

[Assented to April 7, 1896.]

1.   This act may be cited as the bakeshops act, 1896.

2.   In the construction of this act the following words shall have the meanings hereinafter expressed unless a contrary intention appears :

(1) The word "bakeshop" shall mean any building, premises, workshop, structure, room or place wherein is carried on the manufacture, for sale, of confectionery or of bread, biscuits, cakes or any other food product made from flour or from meal, or from both, in whole or in part, and the said bakeshop shall include also any room or rooms used for storing the flour or meal, and also any room or rooms used for storing the confectionery, bread, cakes, biscuits and other food products.

(2) The word "inspector" shall mean any inspector appointed by order of the Lieutenant-Governor in Council under the provisions of the Ontario factories act, or any inspector appointed by order of the Lieutenant-Governor in Council for the enforcement of this act.

(3) The word "employer" shall mean any person who, in his own behalf or as the manager, superintendent, overseer or agent of any person, firm, company or corporation, has charge of any bakeshop or employs any person or persons therein.

(4) The word "week" shall mean the period between midnight on Sunday night and midnight on the succeeding Saturday night.

3.   All bakeshops to which this act applies shall be constructed as to lighting, heating, ventilating and draining in such a manner as not to be detrimental or injurious to the health of

any person working therein, and shall also be kept, at all times, in a clean and sanitary condition, so as to secure the production and preservation of all the food products thereof in a good, wholesome condition.

4. Every bakeshop shall be provided with a proper washroom, closet and other conveniences necessary for the health and comfort of the persons employed therein, the wash-room, closet and other conveniences to be separate from the bakeshop; and such wash-room, closet and other conveniences shall be kept clean and in a sanitary condition.

5. The sleeping place or places of the employes of every bakeshop shall be entirely separate from the bakeshop, and no person shall be allowed to sleep in such bakeshop.

6. Every bakeshop shall be provided with proper means and facilities of escape in case of fire, such means or facilities to be to the satisfaction of the inspector empowered by this act to inspect such bakeshops.

7. No employer shall require, permit or suffer any employe in any bakeshop to work more than sixty hours in any one week, except by permission of the inspector, given in writing to the employer.

8. No employer shall knowingly require, permit or suffer any person to work in his bakeshop who is affected with consumption of the lungs, or with scrofula, or with any venereal disease, or with any communicable skin disease, and every employer is hereby required to maintain himself and his employes in a clean and healthy condition while engaged in the manufacture, handling or sale of such food products.

9. The inspectors appointed under the Ontario Factories act are hereby appointed inspectors under this act, for the purpose of enforcing it, and the Lieutenant-Governor in Council may, in addition, appoint one or more persons as inspectors under this act for the purpose of enforcing it, and these inspectors shall have full powers at all times to enter and inspect all bakeshops, and to institute proceedings at law for the enforcement of this act.

10. Any employer who violates any section of this act, or who refuses the inspector admittance to his bakeshop, or who neglects or refuses to comply with any lawful requirement of the

inspector in connection with the enforcement of this act shall, for the first offense, on conviction thereof, forfeit and pay a penalty of not less than $20 besides costs and not more than $40, besides costs ; and for the second offense, on conviction thereof, such person shall forfeit and pay a penalty of not less than $50, besides costs, and not more than $100, besides costs, and in default of payment thereof he shall be imprisoned in the county gaol of the county in which the offense is committed for a period not exceeding thirty days, and to be kept at hard labor at the discretion of the convicting magistrate ; and for the third or subsequent offense, on conviction thereof, such person shall be imprisoned in such gaol for a period not exceeding six months, to be kept at hard labor in the discretion of the convicting magistrate.

RECORD OF INSPECTION

OF

BAKERIES.

Bakeries Inspected and Complaints Made

— TO —

LOCAL HEALTH OFFICERS.

Order No.	Location of Shop.	COMPLAINTS.
1	First floor,	Sink has no outlet pipe and the water is caught in pails.
2	Basement,	Closet in one corner of bake-room not closed in tight and ventilates into a room.
3	First floor,	No complaint.
4	Basement,	No complaint.
5	First floor,	No complaint.
6	First floor,	No complaint.
7	Cellar,	No complaint.
8	Basement,	No complaint.
9	First floor,	No complaint.
10	First floor,	The sink is not trapped, pipe goes through floor, cannot tell where it empties, but find the sewage standing under the floor in a quantity. No cellar, cannot tell what surface it covers.
11	First floor,	No complaint.
12	2d & 3d floors	No complaint.
13	First floor,	No complaint.
14	First floor,	No complaint.
15	Basement,	No complaint.
16	First floor,	No complaint.
17	First floor.	No complaint.
18	First floor,	No complaint.
19	Basement,	No complaint.
20	Basement,	No complaint.
21	Basement,	No complaint.
22	Basement,	No complaint.
23	First floor.	No complaint.
24	First floor,	No complaint.
25	First floor,	No complaint.
26	Basement,	No complaint.
27	First floor,	No complaint.
28	First floor,	Closet has no means of ventilation except into the cellar where goods are stored.
29	First floor,	No complaint.
30	Basement,	Bakery needs cleaning and whitewashing. A hood over the ovens is also needed.

BAKERIES INSPECTED.— Continued.

Order No.	Location of Shop.	COMPLAINTS.
31	Basement,	Walls and floors very dirty. Very poor floor. Rooms should be thoroughly cleaned and whitewashed. New floor laid in places. Better ventilation.
32	First floor,	Bakery should be cleaned and floors kept in healthful condition.
33	Basement,	Bakery should be cleaned, walls and ceiling whitewashed.
34	Cellar,	Egg shells and refuse matter need to be removed, floor and walls cleaned and ceiling and walls whitewashed, and some means provided to give better ventilation.
35	Basement,	Horse barn is near bakery and with doors open next to it must get the stench from the same.
36	Basement,	No complaint.
37	First floor,	No complaint.
38	Basement,	No complaint.
39	Basement,	Pipes under sink leak badly, water from sink and Chinese laundry next door run upon the cement floor.
40	First floor,	This place needs whitewashing on walls and ceiling.
41	Basement,	Sink pipe leaks on floor. Owner engaged plumber to fix it at once.
42	Basement,	Water barrel leaks on floor so that there is water standing on the floor all the time. Walls and ceiling very dirty, should be cleaned, whitewashed and painted. Tank for water should be repaired or a new one provided.
43	Basement,	No complaint.
44	Basement.	No complaint.
45	First floor,	No complaint.
46	Basement,	No complaint.
47	First floor,	Floor rotten and very dirty, ceiling falling down and very dirty.
48	Basement,	No complaint.
49	First floor,	No complaint.
50	First floor,	No complaint.
51	First floor,	No complaint.
52	First floor.	No complaint.
53	Basement.	No complaint.
54	Basement,	No complaint.
55	First floor.	No complaint.
56	First floor.	No complaint.
57	First floor,	No complaint.
58	First floor,	Sink is not trapped, drain goes into a cesspool, rooms should be cleaned and whitewashed.
59	First floor,	The sink runs into a cesspool and is not trapped.
60	Basement,	No complaint.
61	First floor,	No complaint.
62	Basement,	No complaint.
63	Basement.	No complaint.
64	Basement,	No complaint.

BAKERIES INSPECTED.— Continued.

Order No.	Location of Shop.	COMPLAINTS.
65	Basement,	No complaint.
66	Basement,	No complaint.
67	Basement,	No complaint.
68	Basement,	No complaint.
69	Basement,	No complaint.
70	Basement,	No complaint.
71	Basement,	No complaint.
72	Basement,	Closet in bakeroom partly inclosed.
73	First floor,	No complaint.
74	First floor,	No complaint.
75	Basement,	No complaint.
76	First floor,	No complaint.
77	First floor,	No complaint.
78	Cellar,	No complaint.
79	First floor,	No complaint,
80	Basement,	No complaint.
81	Basement,	No complaint.
82	First floor,	Water-closet does not flush and seat is broken. Place very foul and should be attended to at once.
83	Basement,	No complaint.
84	First floor,	The bakery is very dirty and filthy. It should be thoroughly cleaned and the walls whitewashed.
85	First floor,	Bakery should be thoroughly cleaned and the walls whitewashed and new floor laid.
86	First floor,	The bakery should be thoroughly cleaned, the walls whitewashed and new floor laid in part of room. Present occupants are going to move June 1st. This place should be thoroughly overhauled before new tenant moves in.
87	First floor,	This place should have the walls whitened and a new floor laid in the front part before new tenant moves in.
88	First floor,	Walls need whitening.
89	Basement,	Thoroughly clean bakery and whiten walls.
90	Basement,	Bakery is small and low, not properly ventilated and is very dirty.
91	First floor,	Bakery should be thoroughly cleaned and walls whitened. Supply cellar should be cleaned out.
92	First floor,	No complaint.
93	Basement,	The water-closet is a good flush one, but it is not cased in at the top next to the bakeroom. Walls need whitening.
94	First floor,	The bakery is in a very filthy condition, and although it is on the first floor it is poorly ventilated. The plastering is off the walls in places and the floor is poor.
95	First floor,	Walls of bakery need whitening and cellar cleaned out where supplies are kept, otherwise in good shape.
96	First floor,	No complaint.

BAKERIES INSPECTED.-- CONTINUED.

Order No.	Location of , Shop.	COMPLAINTS.
97	Basement,	Bakery needs new floor, walls need whitening, and ventilation given for closet in storeroom otherwise than into room. This place has just been opened, and the lessee intends to make the above changes within one month.
98	First floor,	No complaint.
99	Basement,	The bakery is in a very filthy condition. Horse stable in the rear makes it very unhealthful for a bakery to be located there.
100	First floor,	No complaint.
101	Basement,	No complaint.
102	Basement,	No complaint.
103	Basement,	No complaint.
104	First floor,	The closet is situated in the bakeroom, and while inclosed there should be some ventilation. It is a dark place and no means of ventilation except into bakeroom.
105	Basement,	Ought to be whitewashed.
106	Basement,	No complaint.
107	First floor,	No complaint.
108	First floor,	No complaint.
109	First floor,	No complaint.
110	Basement,	No complaint.
111	Basement,	Bakery needs whitewashing.
112	First floor,	No complaint.
113	First floor,	No complaint.
114	Basement,	No complaint.
115	First floor,	No complaint.
116	First floor,	There is much filth in the bakery, sink is not trapped, sewer gas is strong, closet is in the building where the horse power is and no means of cleaning it out except from the inside.
117	First floor,	Sink is not trapped, empties into cesspool, not ventilated. Bakery should be cleaned out and whitewashed.
118	First floor,	Bakery should be cleaned out and whitewashed.
119	First floor,	No complaint.
120	First floor,	No complaint.
121	Basement,	No complaint.
122	Basement,	No complaint.
123	Basement,	Walls need whitewashing and the place cleaned up.
124	Basement,	No complaint.
125	Basement,	No complaint.
126	Basement,	No complaint.
127	Basement,	No complaint.
128	Basement,	Refuse from shop allowed to accumulate and should be cleaned out.
129	Basement,	No complaint.
130	Basement,	No complaint.
131	Basement,	No complaint.
132	Basement,	No complaint.
133	First floor,	No complaint.

BAKERIES INSPECTED.— CONTINUED.

Order No.	Location of Shop.	COMPLAINTS.
134	First floor,	No complaint.
135	Basement,	No complaint.
136	Basement,	No complaint.
137	Basement,	Plumbing of water-closet out of order.
138	First floor,	No complaint.
139	Basement,	No complaint.
140	Basement,	No complaint.
141	Cellar,	No complaint.
142	First floor,	No complaint.
143	Basement,	No complaint.
144	Basement,	No complaint.
145	First floor,	No complaint.
146	First floor,	No complaint.
147	First floor,	No complaint.
148	Cellar,	Floor dirty and needs cleaning, ceiling needs white-washing, and a new floor should be laid in part.
149	First floor,	Ceilings need scraping and painting, ventilation is bad, caused by the smoke from cruller kettles, which are used much and need a hood over them and connected with an unused chimney flue by a metal pipe, or else by a pipe running through the building out doors. The place needs a new floor in part, as the old one is broken in places and cannot be kept clean.
150	First floor,	Floor needs scraping and trap of sink repaired, and new woodwork around bowl.
151	First floor,	No complaint.
152	First floor,	No complaint.
153	First floor,	No complaint
154	Cellar,	This place has no floor except the cellar bottom. The sink needs to be replaced by a new sink, and a trap provided. Barrels of refuse should be removed and ceilings and walls whitened. There is one small window in the street side and one in the rear. There should be another window cut through the front wall, so that the workmen can have more air and light.
155	First floor,	Cap should be provided for end of soil pipe to sink. Floors need cleaning, and the whole shop should be thoroughly cleaned.
156	Cellar,	Floors should be cleaned and the walls white-washed.
157	First floor,	No complaint.
158	Basement,	Sink is not trapped in bakery, otherwise in good order.
159	Basement,	The floor is in bad condition, and bakery and storeroom should be cleaned and walls whitened. The closet is inclosed in one end of the bakery. The whole place is very unwholesome in appearance.
160	Basement,	Bakery should be thoroughly cleaned and walls whitened. Closet, while outside of bakery, is very filthy and does not flush properly.

BAKERIES INSPFCTED.— CONTINUED:

Order No.	Location of Shop.	COMPLAINTS.
161	Basement,	No complaint.
162	Basement,	No complaint.
163	First floor.	No complaint.
164	First floor,	No complaint.
165	Basement.	Bakery should be cleaned and walls and ceiling whitewashed. Barn and hennery in the rear. and much filth both inside and outside of bakery. Is very unwholesome. Could be made a very good bakery if properly taken care of.
166	First floor,	Bakery should be cleaned and whitewashed. There is much filth in the bakery. Sink not properly taken care of.
167	Basement,	No complaint.
168	Basement,	No complaint.
169	Basement,	No complaint.
170	Basement,	No complaint.
171	Basement,	No complaint.
172	Basement,	No complaint.
173	Basement,	There should be a new floor laid. Closet should be provided for the use of employes. Bakery and storeroom should be thoroughly cleaned and wall whitewashed. The ventilation is poor and could be remedied by use of a ventilator.
174	First floor,	No complaint.
175	First floor,	No complaint.
176	Basement,	No complaint.
177	Basement.	No complaint.
178	First floor,	No complaint.
179	Basement,	No complaint.
180	Basement,	No complaint.
181	Basement,	No complaint.
182	First floor,	No complaint.
183	Basement,	No complaint.
184	Basement,	No complaint.
185	Cellar,	The bakeshop is in a cellar poorly ventilated and very filthy. Barn and hennery in the rear close by and yard very filthy. Closet, while outside, in a very filthy condition.
186	Basement,	Much surface water comes into the cellar. Find cockroaches. Walls need whitewashing.
187	Cellar.	This bakery is in cellar. No means of ventilation except from the outside door. Very damp and filthy. I find a bed and change of clothing there, and believe he eats, sleeps and lives there, together with boy who has scrofulous affection on his face.
188	First floor,	The closet is so situated that it should be ventilated overhead, and a spring put on the door to keep it closed. The old bakeroom, 20 x 30, is very dirty; walls and ceiling should be whitewashed. Floor around sink is very dirty. The help are as clean in their dress as in other bakeries.

BAKERIES INSPECTED.— Continued.

Order No.	Location of Shop.	COMPLAINTS.
189	Basement,	No complant.
190	Basement,	No complant.
191	Basement,	No complant.
192	Basement,	No complant.
193	First floor,	No complant.
194	First floor,	No complant.
195	First floor,	No complant.
196	Basement,	The bakery should be cleaned and the wall and ceiling whitened.
197	Basement,	Bakery should be cleaned and walls and ceiling whitened.
198	Basement,	No complaint.
199	First floor,	Sink does not appear to be trapped. Walls and ceiling should be cleaned and whitened.
200	Basement,	No complaint.
201	Basement,	No complaint.
202	Basement,	No complaint.
203	First floor,	No complaint.
204	First floor,	No complaint.
205	First floor,	No complaint.
206	First floor,	No complaint.
207	Basement,	No complaint.
208	First floor,	No complaint.
209	First floor,	No complaint.
210	Basement,	No complaint.
211	First floor,	No complaint.

CONTENTS.

SEWAGE DISPOSAL IN CONNECTICUT

REPORT

OF THE

SEWAGE COMMISSION

TO THE

GENERAL ASSEMBLY

OF THE

State of Connecticut

January Session of 1899

———•◦•———

HARTFORD, CONN.

PRESS OF THE CASE, LOCKWOOD & BRAINARD COMPANY

1899

MEMBERS OF THE COMMISSION.

EDWARD H. JENKINS, Ph.D., *Chairman*, New Haven.
ROBERT A. CAIRNS, C. E., *Secretary*, Waterbury.
JOHN S. CHENEY, South Manchester.
JOHN N. WOODRUFF, M.D., Sherman.
FAYETTE L. WRIGHT, Pomfret Center.

TABLE OF CONTENTS.

TABLE OF CONTENTS.

REPORT OF THE COMMISSION.

To the General Assembly of the State of Connecticut:

The Sewage Commission herewith respectfully presents a Report, as required by law.

The General Assembly, at the January Session of 1897, passed the following:

APPOINTING A SEWAGE COMMISSION.

Resolved by this Assembly:

Section 1. That the Governor be and he hereby is empowered to appoint five suitable persons as a commission, who shall serve without pay, except for their expenses, and shall investigate the subject of sewage disposal of the cities, boroughs, and towns of Connecticut.

Sec. 2. Said Commission shall have power to summon witnesses before it, with books, papers, and maps, and, at the conclusion of its investigation, shall formulate a report and submit the same to the next General Assembly.

Sec. 3. Any town, city, or borough may consult said Commission, and obtain its advice concerning sewage systems, methods of sewage disposal, and operations relating thereto, and shall pay to said Commission all expenses incurred by it in any service rendered to such town, city, or borough.

Sec. 4. Except as provided in Section 3, the expenses of said Commission, approved by the Governor, shall be paid by the State to an amount not exceeding one thousand dollars in any one year.

This resolution was approved by the Governor on June 12, 1897, and on September 17, 1897, the following were appointed members of the Commission:

ROBERT A. CAIRNS, C.E., Waterbury.
JOHN S. CHENEY, South Manchester.
EDWARD H. JENKINS, Ph.D., New Haven.
JOHN N. WOODRUFF, M.D., Sherman.
FAYETTE L. WRIGHT, Pomfret Center.

The work of the Commission is summarized in the following

REPORT OF THE SECRETARY.

In accordance with notice sent to each member by Dr.
Jenkins, the Commissioners met at Hartford on the 5th day
of October, 1897.   Organization was effected by the election
of Edward H. Jenkins, Ph.D., as Chairman, John N. Woodruff, M.D., Vice-Chairman, and Robert A. Cairns, C.E., Secretary.

On the first day of November of the same year, the Commission met at the Capitol by appointment with Governor
Cooke, for the purpose of hearing his suggestions and recommendations in regard to the best course to be pursued in attempting with limited means to secure the results aimed at in
the creation of the Commission.

November 15th and 16th were devoted to visiting the
sewage disposal works in successful operation at Danbury,
Bristol, and Meriden.   The Commissioners were given every
opportunity to thoroughly examine the workings of each system.   The process at each of these works is essentially that
defined as intermittent filtration.

December 3d a visit was made to Worcester, Massachusetts.
The Commission was met by the Mayor and other city officials
and taken in carriages to the Chemical Precipitation Works, at
which some eighteen millions of gallons of sewage daily were
undergoing the typical chemical process of purification.   These
works are credited with being in many respects as efficiently
managed as any similar works in the world, and the members,
as a result of the full explanation of every detail, made by the
officers in charge, felt satisfied that they had seen the latest and
best phases of this form of treatment.

At a meeting held in New Haven on January 30, 1898,
a letter was presented from the engineer employed by New
Britain, which asked the Commission to state its probable attitude toward a proposition to discharge the untreated sewage
of that city into the Connecticut.   As the request did not
come from the city itself, the Commission could not consider
it in the manner provided for in the act authorizing its appointment, and not having at its command the necessary data
upon which a just opinion could be based, the secretary was instructed to make the following reply:

WATERBURY, CONN., January 20, 1898.
Samuel M. Gray, Esq.,
174 Weybossett Street,
Providence, R. I.

DEAR SIR: — At a meeting of the State Sewage Commission held to-day, your letter of December 24th, regarding the disposal of New Britain's sewage, was fully discussed.

This Commission cannot give an opinion on the subject without such information regarding the special conditions existing there as you are now gathering.

If a thorough study of the whole subject is made by you, and the results are submitted to us by the authorities of New Britain, we will then give the matter careful consideration.

The Commission is not provided with means for making such investigation itself.

Very respectfully,
R. A. CAIRNS, *Secretary.*

April 22, 1898, at Meriden, the principal subject for discussion was a request that the Commission visit Norfolk and give advice in regard to sewers and sewage disposal. It was decided to go there on April 28th. This was done, and the day was spent in a general examination of the locality, more particularly as to the best place and methods for disposal.

· On May 5th the Commission met at Bridgeport and adopted the following report:

" The Norfolk Sewer District Committee, Norfolk, Conn.:

" GENTLEMEN: — The State Sewage Commission, after examining . the local conditions in Norfolk, and carefully considering the problem of sewerage and sewage disposal there, would respectfully advise you as follows:

" That the welfare of the community and the continuance of the town's attractiveness imperatively demand the immediate construction of proper sanitary drains by which all the sewage of that portion of the town included within the limits of the sewer district shall be conveyed outside the district. When this has been done, all those open drains and hidden cesspools, which at present so greatly detract from the beauty and threaten the healthfulness of the village, should be disinfected and filled up. The sanitary drains or sewers should be constructed in accordance with the best sanitary principles, nothing essential to their effectiveness being omitted through too great desire for economy. In this connection it should be observed that the employment of an expert sanitary engineer to prepare the general plan and give advice as to material and methods of construction will be found to be a wise investment.

" All storm water should be rigidly excluded from the sewers, and these should be so built as to keep out ground water, so far as possible. Steps should be taken to restrain all unnecessary or extravagant use of water from the Water Company's mains, so far as its use will increase the quantity to be provided for in the sewers and at the disposal plant. These precautions taken at the outset will result in the avoidance of much unnecessary expense and will enable you to accomplish better results with the means at your command.

" In regard to the disposal of the sewage so collected and conveyed to a point beyond the limits of the district, the Commission
would advise you that, although a carefully managed disposal works
is not necessarily a cause of offense to persons living at a distance of
a few hundred feet, yet its location should preferably be somewhat
removed from the neighborhood of dwellings.

" Simple subsidence in tanks, proposed as a means of clarifying
sewage, does not remove any considerable part of its noxious elements, and is not to be considered for a moment as a method of preparing sewage for discharge into a stream.

" Various patent processes of sterilizing sewage are ineffectual,
because, at best, they simply remove from it the germs of putrefaction, but do not destroy the putrescible matter of the sewage. which
is speedily inoculated again with the germs in the rivers into which
it is discharged.

" The only methods about which enough is known to pass judgment on their merits for any given place are dilution, chemical precipitation, and land filtration.

The first method, — i. e., discharge of the crude sewage into Black-
berry River — we believe is not advisable, because of the objection of
riparian owners below, who could, moreover, if a nuisance should
be proved. stop the discharge of sewage into the stream, by injunction. If this system were adopted, it would be regarded as being
probably only a temporary make-shift.

" Chemical precipitation, while not as effectual as land filtration,
clarifies and considerably purifies the sewage, and, if properly done,
would give an effluent quite unobjectionable, at present, to discharge
into the stream. This system is practiced on a small scale in the
town of New Rochelle, and we would suggest that some investigation
of it by your committee might be desirable.

" Land filtration is, unquestionably, the most satisfactory system
of disposal known at present, because, when properly managed, the
foul matter of the sewage is destroyed within the pores of the filter
itself. Unfortunately, it cannot be used in all cases, because sand
of a certain grain is necessary in considerable quantity for the
preparation of the filtration areas.

" We believe that the land of which your commission now have
the refusal might be quite suitable for precipitation tanks, but we do
not think it is well suited for filtration beds. The place which was
shown to us further down the stream on a sandy ridge covered with
white birches appears to be very suitable for sand filtration and
irrigation.

" Collection of the sewage of Norfolk by the ' separate ' system,
so-called, its conveyance below the village to a point on the sandy
ridge above mentioned, and its disposal there by intermittent filtration through prepared beds of sand, or by broad irrigation, would
seem to this Commission to be one very suitable solution of your local
problem.

" The final choice as to which of the methods named should be
adopted and the special form of the disposal work should be made
after consultation with an engineer who is conversant with the details of both systems, and after a careful estimate of the cost of construction and maintenance.

" Allow us to express the hope that your people will proceed with
the work of providing sanitary sewerage for your village, and not
permit a locality for which nature has done so much to be deprived
of its remarkable advantages because of a distrust of its healthful-

ness; a distrust which will surely spring up unless the present conditions are speedily remedied."

Very respectfully,

R. A. CAIRNS, *Secretary.*

At the Bridgeport meeting it was also decided that the Commission should spend two days in viewing works at various points in New York, New Jersey, and Pennsylvania. In accordance with this decision, the Commissioners met at New Rochelle, New York, on June 7th, and were shown the chemical precipitation process used there on a small scale. It appeared to be quite successful as a preparation for discharge into the waters of the Sound, where extensive dilution immediately takes place.

On June 8th the sand filtration beds at Plainfield, New Jersey, and the works at Wayne, Pennsylvania, were studied. The latter process is an interesting illustration of the utilization of a heavy, impervious, and generally unsuitable soil. By pumping the sewage to the top of a considerable slope, and allowing it to flow down through barriers of broken stone and tracts of grass land, considerable purification seems to be effected.

October 19th the Commission met at New Haven, the time being largely devoted to discussion of the report to be made to the General Assembly. It was decided to make a thorough examination of the Naugatuck Valley.

November 2d was spent in viewing the conditions at Derby, Ansonia, and Waterbury.

November 3d the river was examined for some distance below the sewer outlets at Torrington. The filtration fields at Litchfield were visited, and some time was spent in Winsted. The latter place has no system of sewerage.

November 29th the Commission met at Waterbury to consider the report and incidentally to learn something of the progress of the suit then being tried, involving an application for an injunction to restrain the city of Waterbury from discharging sewage into the Naugatuck River.

Upon invitation, the Commission met the Rivers Pollution Commission of New Jersey at the Lawyers' Club, New York city, on January 5, 1899, for the purpose of conference and a general interchange of views on subjects of common interest. We found that the New Jersey Commission was chiefly concerned with the Valley of the Passaic, and was studying the question of how best to divert the sewage which now makes that river very offensive. In a published report a similar commission, previously appointed, recommended a trunk sewer running through the valley, intercepting the sewage of the several cities, and discharging it into Newark Bay. As this body of water is shallow, fears are expressed lest the sewage so discharged should become a nuisance to the communities along its shores. The discussion touched upon the engineering questions involved in sewage disposal, as well as upon the legal and economic features of the problem, and the whole conference proved to be most interesting and instructive.

At a meeting held subsequently on the same day several hours were devoted to formulating the conclusions and recommendations to be presented to the General Assembly as a part of the report.

R. A. CAIRNS, Secretary.

In addition to the work noticed in the secretary's report, the members of the Commission have also acquainted themselves as far as possible with recent work on the general subject of sewage disposal, and have endeavored to learn from personal inspection and all other available sources the present condition and needs of our own State in this regard and the possibilities of improvement.

The Commission has confined its report to a statement of the general system of sewage disposal now in use in this State, a discussion of its merits and its dangers, its effects on the waters of our rivers and harbors, a description of the only methods of disposal which can be substituted for the present one, with suggestions as to the general policy of the State with regard to the sewage disposal of cities.

It will be a disappointment to some that this report does not take up in detail the local problems which confront certain cities, districts, and river valleys of the State, and indicate what should be done for their relief.

Such a work, however, was a physical impossibility in view of the time and means at our disposal. Every city and town presents special problems and engineering difficulties not to be settled offhand by a State Commission, but by the careful surveys, plans, and estimates of a competent civil engineer. No one system of disposal is equally suited to all. The topography of the place, its present size and probable rate of growth, its financial condition and its position with regard to other large places, all have to be carefully considered before recommending a great outlay for sewage disposal. It can hardly be done gratuitously.

It may not be inappropriate to add that the members of this Commission undertook their duties and have done this work fully realizing the disadvantages under which they labored, and the inadequacy of the means provided by the Legislature to the end sought by it, but with the conviction that something ought to be immediately done, and that such a report as has been outlined above will be helpful, as a matter of general information, and in guiding legislation on the subject when it becomes necessary.

As provided in the joint resolution, the services of the Commissioners have been gratuitously rendered. Of the two thousand dollars provided by the State for necessary expenses, there were spent, up to January, 1899, less than $800.

NATURE OF SEWAGE.

Sewage is the water-borne waste of a family or of a community. Besides the mineral matters or salts, which are of small importance from a sanitary point of view, household waste contains a great variety of animal and vegetable remains which come from the food, the bathing, washing, and excreta of the household.

The different kinds of domestic waste which go into sewage become about equally offensive and all become dangerous to health if not promptly destroyed. The contents of water-closets may, to be sure, at certain times contain the special germs of typhoid or diarrhœal diseases, but these germs can also live for a time in any household waste water.

Where such diseases exist the excreta of the patient should be burned or all the bacterial life in them absolutely destroyed by disinfection before discharge into the other sewage. Nothing, however, is to be gained by attempting to make any separate disposal of the kitchen water and the excreta.

In any large community, factory wastes of the most varied character form a part of its sewage. To give a single example: Dr. Williston, in a valuable paper on Rivers Pollution (Conn. State Board of Health Report, 1887, p. 175), after thorough study of the matter, estimated that there are annually discharged into Piper's Brook — a tributary of Park River, which receives the larger part of the sewage of New Britain — the following materials from manufacturing establishments in New Britain, which at that time employed 3,000 men out of a total population of 18,000:

Metal salts,	.	.	.	.	700,000 pounds
Free acids, .	.	.	.	.	100,000 "
Lime salts, .	.	.	.	.	35,000 "
Alkali salts, .	.	.	.	.	100,000 "
Soap, .	.	.	.	.	25,000
Fatty matters,	.	.	.	.	100,000 "
Vegetable refuse (from cotton, etc.),	.			.	20,000 "

$$1,080,000$$

"The volume of sewage turned out daily by one manufacturing plant is often as great as the sewage of a village of considerable population, and the organic matters contained in manufacturing sewage are often much greater than in the same volume of town sewage." (Mass. State Board Health Report, 1896, p. 428.) Some factory wastes—from tanneries, wool scouring establishments, and paper mills — greatly increase the difficulty of purifying the sewage into which they are discharged.

The washings of streets and storm water also, which are quite generally led into sewers, largely increase the volume of their flow.

A part of this water-borne waste is solid material, merely suspended in the water, shreds of meat, fragments of vegetables and paper, straw, grease, excrement, etc., which could be removed from the sewage by skimming or filtering. A considerable part of the waste — and by far the more dangerous part from a sanitary point of view — is, unfortunately, dissolved in the water, just as sugar or salt are dissolved, and cannot be removed by any mechanical means. Such things are extracts of meat and vegetables, soap, urine, etc.

It is hardly necessary here to attempt any statement of the chemical composition of sewage. It never has the same composition in any two cities, and in any given sewer the character of the sewage varies with the hour of the day, the season of the year, and the state of the weather. Sufficient for our purpose is the statement of Mr. H. F. Mills, engineer of the Massachusetts State Board of Health, that sewage stronger than the average from American towns contains about 998 parts of water, one of mineral matter, and one of organic matter.

DECOMPOSITION OR DECAY OF SEWAGE.

Fresh sewage, while unsightly, is nearly or quite free from bad odor; but, either standing or flowing, it soon gets an evil smell, which is the sign of putrefactive decay. If left by itself the odor becomes very offensive; if largely diluted the smell is less and may be unnoticeable. If the sewage is distributed over a tract of land no odor may arise from it. Yet, whatever is done with it, the organic matters of the sewage sooner or later decompose and are prepared for assimilation by animals and plants.

This prompt decomposition or decay of sewage is inevitable. Attempts to prevent decay by sterilization with antiseptics must prove abortive. They may retard it, but by so doing only complicate the process and introduce new dangers, which then can be less easily overcome. Besides being inevitable, prompt decomposition is desirable, because by this means only can the wastes of life be so transformed as to become again useful in the economy of nature.

Moreover, the decomposition of liquid sewage does not necessarily involve the giving off of noxious vapors or a powerful stench. It may be done, as will appear later, without noxious odors of any kind.

Nature of the Decomposition. — The decomposition of sewage consists in breaking up the very complex bodies that compose it into comparatively simple bodies which do not putrefy, are not dangerous to the community, and are taken up as food by plants and animals. To illustrate: Urine is a highly complex body, useless in its fresh state, and a source of trouble and nuisance because subject to putrefactive decay. But when poured over the ground it is decomposed within it, yielding carbonic acid, ammonia, and afterwards nitric acid, water, and some mineral matters, all of them innocuous and at once available to plant life. If left to stand by itself, or diluted with water, urine likewise decomposes, and if it stands long enough may come to the same thing in the end: water, carbonic acid, and nitrates; but it will reach this end by a slow and roundabout course of chemical changes, forming intermediate products which are an offense to the whole neighborhood. Here are two kinds of decomposition which at last reach the same end and destroy the sewage material; but one of them is rapid, odorless, and safe; the other is slow, offensive, unsafe.

Cause of the Decomposition of Sewage. — It is well understood that the decomposition or decay of animal and vegetable
(" organic ") matters is due to the agency of micro-organisms,
variously called microbes, bacteria, or germs.   These are the
most minute living things which we know, visible only under
a powerful microscope, exceedingly simple in structure, amaz-
ingly prolific and capable of intense activity.   There are different kinds or species of bacteria, requiring different media
and environment in which to grow, different kinds of food for
their support, and yielding different products of their activity.
Conditions which favor one kind are deadly to certain other
kinds.   For example: The species which convert ammonia
into nitrous and nitric acids, and which are specially useful in
the safe destruction of sewage, require abundance of atmospheric air for their activity.   If the air supply is limited they
become inactive; if it is cut off, they die.   On the other hand,
the several species of microbe which cause meat or broth to
putrefy cannot be active where much air is present.   Perfect
aeration, either directly or indirectly, destroys them.

In these days of microbiphobia it needs to be said that the
existence of higher forms of life on the globe is dependent on
the life and work of microbes; and that the larger number of
kinds, so far as we know, are perfectly innocuous as well as indispensable to us.   Microbes are much like people, good and
bad, but for the most part passively good and not actively bad.
The microbes which cause specific diseases belong, of course,
to the " criminal classes."   But the microbes which silently,
rapidly, and without offense make plant food out of sewage,
and bear the burden of the world's work without proclamation
or protest, correspond to the " forgotten man."   But most of
the talk is of the criminal microbes and their misdeeds, and
most of the effort of sanitarians is to avoid injury from them,
and many come to regard the whole community of microbes
as against us, which is as irrational as to judge of the character
of the citizens of Connecticut by observations at the state
prison.

Fresh sewage contains a countless host of microbes belonging to a vast number of species, of the most diverse character,
and capable of working the most diverse effects on the organic
materials in which they live.   But the kind of decomposition
which sewage undergoes is determined by the kind of microbes
which can freely develop and remain active in sewage; and the

kind of microbes which can develop and remain active is, in turn, determined by the access or exclusion of air and light, by temperature and by the chemical reaction of the whole.

These facts are of prime importance, for they furnish the basis of all good systems of sewage disposal. The prompt destruction of sewage, i. e., the conversion of its organic matters into forms which are harmless and can be immediately appropriated by living animals or plants, is the end and aim of any rational system of sewage disposal. This can only be done practically by the work of microbes. Putrefactive processes are slow, a source of annoyance and discomfort, and often a menace to the health of a family or neighborhood. Processes of oxidation are more rapid and complete and are entirely inoffensive. By following certain well-ascertained laws, it is possible to elect which of these processes shall go on, what kind of microbe life shall do the work, and whether it shall proceed harmlessly and unobserved, or dangerously and with an all-pervading stench.

THE HISTORY OF SEWAGE DISPOSAL.

The history of sewage disposal has been much the same in all New England communities. In any new settlement the wastes of the house were used in the garden patch, about favorite fruit trees and shrubs, and over the bit of lawn. The waste water was thus well spread on the surface of the ground, intermittently and in moderate quantity. It was the safest disposal possible; and to this system, in greatly modified form, sanitary science is leading us back as the best system for cleansing the sewage of some of our large cities.

The next step — and in the wrong direction — was to use a sink drain, which ran the kitchen waste, the most evil kind of sewage, on to the land continually in one place and in too large amount for safety. Coarse grasses soon marked the spot, and in summer it was often an offense to the nostrils.

As population became more dense and water was used in large quantity, the cesspool was devised, and the whole dreadful mess was run into it. The cesspool was generally made with no bottom, so the filthy liquids drained off into the soil, while the solid matter was taken out when necessary: the most noisome job that ever fell to the lot of man, and one which stirred the whole neighborhood.

When the straggling village became a closely-built town — and often before then — wells, cesspools, and privies were not always far apart. The ground between them became charged with more filth than it could cleanse, and deodorized sewage and excreta crept into the wells. Then followed typhoid and other ailments. But the well was formerly the last thing to suspect. The well was almost like one of the family. Did not our parents and grandparents, from a " time whereof the memory of man runneth not to the contrary," drink from it? Though the old oaken bucket had given place to the punky pump log, and that in turn to some clanking modern monstrosity, surely the morals of the well itself could not have changed.

Sooner or later, however, enforced by village tragedies, conviction became general that the wells were fouled; and then their owners turned against them, and the *wells* were given up — not the cesspools. A water supply from some stream or lake was introduced, and peace reigned again. The quantity of sewage, however, is greatly increased with the introduction of a water supply which flows instead of needing to be pumped, and so the house drainage sometimes overtaxed not only the cleansing, but even the absorptive power of the soil. Gradually, too, it came to be understood that even where drinking water was not fouled, the discharge of liquid filth into the soil of a thickly-settled place may be dangerous to the public health; that people within city limits as a rule cannot cleanse their waste water on their own premises, nor can they be trusted to carry it off in a way which is unobjectionable. Hence the municipality, in the public interest, undertook this work, and built a sewer system to secure perfect drainage for houses, and generally for streets as well.

This sketch marks in a general way, and with the inherent defects of any mere diagram, the general course of things up to the present time. Many still fondly cling to the cesspool, some even make a cesspool of the disused well, and, if not stopped by the health board, will run the liquid waste from their houses into it, only connecting its *overflow* with the sewer.

In any thickly-settled community a sewerage system is at present a necessity, being the only practicable means of gathering and removing sewage before it becomes putrid and intolerable.

SEWAGE DISPOSAL IN CONNECTICUT.

There are in this State eighteen cities, which, according to the estimates of the State Board of Health (derived from the school census) had a population in 1896 of 481,000 (in some cases this includes the town, the boundaries of which include more than the incorporated city), being more than half the total population of the state (816,712). All of these cities have water supplies, and all, excepting Putnam, sewerage systems. The cities of Meriden and Danbury purify their sewage by land filtration. All the other cities discharge their sewage into water-ways; — " water carriage and dilution."

There are twenty-two boroughs in Connecticut, seventeen of which have a water supply, and eight have a sewerage system or at least some sewers. Of these Bristol and Litchfield purify their sewage by land filtration. In other places the sewers discharge either into swamps or water-ways. In addition to these, seven towns have a water supply and some sanitary sewers, which discharge crude sewage.

There are twenty-one other towns which have a water supply but no considerable number of sewers. The particulars regarding these cities, boroughs, and towns appear in following tables, pages 18 to 20, which have been compiled from data given in Baker's Manual of American Water-works, 1897, and in Connecticut Board of Health Report, 1896, p. 341, with some additional details obtained by correspondence.

2

WATER SUPPLY AND SEWAGE DISPOSAL OF CONNECTICUT CITIES.

City or Town.	Population.	Source of Water Supply.	Sewer System.	Means of Sewage Disposal.
Ansonia, ...	18,000	Beaver brook and springs,	Sanitary and storm,	Naugatuck River.
Bridgeport,*	65,000	Poquonnock, Mill, and Horse Tavern Rivers,	" "	River and Harbor.
Danbury, ...	19,473§	Surface water, impounding reservoir,	" "	Land Filtration.
Derby, ...	8,500	Springs, small streams, impounding reservoir,	" "	Housatonic River.
Hartford, ...	65,000	Brooks, impounding reservoirs,	" "	Connecticut River.
Meriden, ...	30,000	Surface water, pumped,	Sanitary,	Land Filtration.
Middletown, ...	18,000	Laural Brook, and stream from Higby mountain, impounding reservoir,	Sanitary and storm,	Connecticut River.
New Britain, ..	25,000	Shuttle Meadow Lake, Roaring Brook & springs,	" "	Piper's Brk via Park River to Conn. River.
New Haven, ..	96,000	Lakes, impounding reservoir,	" "	Rivers and Harbor.
New London,..	15,500	Lake Konomoc,	Sanitary only,	Thames River.
Norwalk,†	10,000	Silver Mine Brook and impounding reservoir,	Sanitary and storm,	Norwalk River.
Norwich, ...	23,000	Brooks, springs, impounding reservoir,	Sanitary,	Thames River.
Putnam, ...	6,884	Roseland Lake, Little River,	Storm drains only,	Quin'g River to Thames Riv.
Rockville, ...	9,000	Schenipsit Lake,	Sani'y sep'ate system,	Hockanum River.
So. Norwalk,‡	7,000	Brooks, surface water, impounding reservoir,	Sanitary,	Norwalk River and So. Norwalk Harbor.
Stamford,......	18,000	Mill River, impounding reservoir,	Sanitary and storm,	Mill River (?.
Waterbury,....	40,000	E. Mount. & Mad Riv's, west br'ch Naugatuck,	" partial storm,	Naugatuck River.
Willimantic, ...	10,000	Natchaug River,	Sanitary and storm,	Willimantic River.]
	481,357			

* Also supplies Easton.
† Also supplies Winnepauk and part of South Norwalk.
‡ Also supplies East Norwalk.
§ Census of 1890.

WATER SUPPLY AND SEWAGE DISPOSAL OF CONNECTICUT BOROUGHS.

Borough.	Source of Water Supply.	Public Sewer System.	Sewage Disposal.
Bethel,.........	Surface water, impounding reservoir, filter,	Sanitary and storm,	Saugatuck River.
Branford,.......	Water-works under construction,	None,	Land Filtration.
Bristol,.........	Springs, surface water, and Poland River,	Sanitary and partial storm,	
Colchester,.....	None,	None,	
Danielson,......	Higgins Brook,	None,	
Fair Haven East,	Same as City of New Haven,	None,	Private drains to Quin'piac Riv.
Greenwich,*....	Streams, impounding reservoir, mechanical filter,	Sanitary,	Long Island Sound.
Guilford,.......	None,	None,	
Jewett City,....	Impounding and storage reservoir,	Sanitary,	
Litchfield,......	Griswold Brook, driven wells,	Sanitary,	Land Filtration.
Naugatuck,.....	Straitville Brook,	Partial sanitary and storm,	Naugatuck River.
New Canaan,...	Springs and Five-Mile River,	None,	
Newtown,......	None,	None,	—
Ridgefield,.....	None,	None,	
Shelton,........	Surface water, Curtis Brook,	Sanitary and storm,	Housatonic River.
Southington,†..	Humiston's Brook, impounding reservoir,	None,	
Stafford Springs,.	Roaring Brook, impounding reservoir,	Partially sewered,	Willimantic River.
Stonington,‡...	Mistuxet Brook,	None,	
Torrington,.....	Surface water, impounding reservoir,	Sanitary,	Naugatuck River.
Wallingford,....	Lake Pistapaug,	Sewers,	Quinnipiac River.
West Haven,....	Springs, pumped to reservoir,	None,	
Winsted,........	Mad River, Rugg Brook, Highland Lake,	None,	—

* Port Chester and a part of Rye and Belle Haven also supplied.　　‡ Groton and Mystic also supplied.
† Plantsville also supplied.

The following towns also have some sewers:

Town.	Water Supply.	System of Sewers.
East Hartford,..	Springs, Salem Br'k, impounding reservoir,	Partial sanitary and storm.
Farmington, ...	Springs,	Sanitary, separate system.
New Milford,..	Surface water, tributary of Great Brook,	Sanitary and storm.
Norfolk,.......	Lake Wangum,	Separate system.
So. Manchester,	Small brooks and springs,	Sanitary and partial storm.
Thomaston, ...	Springs and small brook,	Partial sanitary and storm.
Thompsonville,	Springs and distributing tank,	Sanitary.
Unionville,.....	Springs and stream,	Storm sewers.
Westport,.	Wells and stand pipe,	Partial storm.
Windsor, ...	Springs,	Sewers.

The following towns have a partial water supply:

Town.	Water Supply.	Town.	Water Supply.
Canaan, ...	Springs and impounding reservoir.	Plainville, ...	Crescent Lake, surf'ce water.
Durham,......	Cold Spring.	Portland,.	Somasic Br'k and impounding reservoir.
Granby,......	Salmon Brook.		
Hazardville, ..	Springs, pumped to tank.	Preston,.......	Spring.
		Sharon,.......	Springs and Beardsley Pond.
Kent,........	Br'k & small springs.		
Lakeville,.....	Mountain stream.	Simsbury, ...	Surf'e water of str'ms, spr'gs & imp. res'r.
Newington,...	Springs and stream.		
Manchester,...	Ponds and streams.	Terryville,....	Springs.
New Hartford,	South Mt. Brook.		
North Canaan,	Springs and impounding reservoir.	Winds'r Locks,	Spring & stand pipe.
No.Manch'st'r,	White's Br'k and impounding reservoir	Woodbury,....	Brooks and springs, imp'ding reservoir.

To recapitulate: All of our cities have a water supply, all but one are sewered, and with two exceptions all are discharging their sewage into water-ways. Of our twenty-two boroughs, next to our cities the most thickly-settled districts, while seventeen have water supplies, only eight have any sewers, and six of these do not cleanse their sewage. The construction of sewers will be taken up by these boroughs as population increases, in a more or less haphazard way; and, if conditions continue as they are now, their sewage will probably be disposed of by water carriage for the most part. Sewers will be built, because when a water supply has been introduced, as we have explained before, the evils arising from cesspools and drains are aggravated, and it becomes in time a necessity to remove the sewage from the neighborhood, increased in quantity by the introduction of a water supply. Passing from the boroughs to the towns, we find ten which have both sewers and a water supply, and all discharge sewage into water-ways. Nineteen other towns have a water supply but no sewers. In these places, no doubt, a considerable amount of sewage finds its way into streams, and the amount will increase rapidly with the growth of the towns and the inevitable introduction of sewers.

It is not necessary to make any estimate of the quantity of sewage daily or yearly poured into our streams, nor of the precise number of population which contributes to this discharge. It is probably true that the sewage of half of our population is poured uncleansed into our water-ways, and that the gross amount of sewage, as well as the proportion of population contributing to this pollution of our streams will increase in the ordinary course of things with the growth of our centers of population and the introduction of water-works and sewerage systems.

THE ULTIMATE DISPOSAL OF WATER-BORNE SEWAGE.

As most of our sewage is poured into streams or bays, we must follow it further to find out what finally becomes of it. If sewage is simply taken away from under our own sight and noses, to decompose under the sight and noses of another community, however remote from us, or to be put where it will accumulate and in time create a nuisance, it is neither good morals, good law, nor common sense to regard this as a " disposal." It is, therefore, necessary to inquire whether the ocean and our large streams which receive our sewage discharge can destroy or, rather, so transform its elements as to render them quite harmless and available as food to animal and vegetable life.

SEWAGE DISPOSAL IN THE OCEAN.

The ocean is not simply a great sink or cesspool to receive the offscouring of the nations and hide it. Nature has no cesspools.

As soon as sewage meets salt water the clay or mud flocks

together and begins to sink.   Sea birds gather what food they can from the solid parts of the sewage and fishes also feed upon it.   With the fishes are included all the lower forms of animal life, some of them almost microscopic, which abound in sea water and feed wholly upon the solid matter suspended in it. These all are the ocean scavengers.

But the most dangerous and elusive things in sewage, those which are the hardest to manage in any system of treatment, are the nitrogenous matters, animal and vegetable, which are not suspended but are dissolved in the water, and are thus beyond the reach of birds or fish or any kind of animal life.

The algae and other higher forms of aquatic vegetation cannot live in concentrated sewage, but when it is sufficiently diluted they feed upon its dissolved elements, take them into their structure and assimilate them, thus making them innocuous.   It is stated that under suitable conditions the algae can decompose volatile fatty acids, indol, skatol, and other offensive soluble matters of sewage.   (Bokorny, Archiv. Hyg., 1894, **20**, p. 281, ref. Jahresber. Ag. Chem., XVII, p. 49.)

But the soluble elements of sewage, whether concentrated or diluted, are undoubtedly decomposed and returned to living forms by the agency of bacteria living in the sea.   The studies of Russell (*Botanical Gazette*, 1892, XVII, p. 312, and 1893, XVIII, pp. 411 and 439) indicate that while the microbes of sewage and of fresh water soon perish in sea water, species of bacteria peculiar to the ocean are found at all depths. Thus, in Mediterranean sea water, from surface to bottom, 3,200 feet, bacteria abound in nearly the same proportion at all depths, below the limit of constant temperature, 280 to 4,200 individuals per fluid ounce, from 10 to 150 per cubic centimeter.   The sea bottom is inhabited by active bacteria in vastly greater numbers than the water.   This bacterial life is indigenous there, being different in kind from that of the water above.   Now this bacterial life is believed to depend for its existence on the soluble nitrogenous matter in the sea water, taking energy from the polluted matter and breaking it up into simpler and harmless forms.

Much remains to be learned regarding the various forms of marine life in their relation to sewage disposal, but we know enough to convince us that the sea is not a mere diluent of sewage; it is no cesspool.   It gathers up the wastes of human

life, restores energy to them, and returns them to us clean and
wholesome.

> "Ever at toil, it brings to loveliness
> All ancient wrath and wreck."

Much has been said by some writers of the enormous
waste of fertilizing material which is annually poured into the
sea in sewage, and attempts are continually made to extract
from the filth, which goes to make up sewage, some valuable
fertilizer for land. It would be an economy if this could be
done without offense or danger to public health, and by suitable arrangements it is possible under some conditions to use
sewage directly as a fertilizer, thus cleansing it and securing
its fertilizing elements at the same time. But it needs also to
be remembered that fertilizers poured into the sea are not forever wasted; that to a large extent — we cannot judge how
large at present — they are again converted into human food,
in part directly, without the intervention of vegetation, and
are given back to us by our fisheries. Huxley estimated that
the annual product of an acre of arable land is the equivalent of
one ton of grain or 200 to 300 pounds of meat or cheese,
"while an acre of sea-bottom, in the *best fishing ground*,
yields a greater weight of fish every week in the year."

SEWAGE IN STREAMS, " SELF-PURIFICATION " OF FLOWING WATER.

More immediately important is the inquiry whether our
inland waters, the small streams and large rivers of our State,
can purify sewage which is poured into them. Is sewage
actually destroyed in considerable amount in our streams, or
are its putrescible matters resolved into harmless forms?

That streams which receive moderate quantities of sewage
do, in some cases, become purer after flowing for even quite
moderate distances is certain. There is still wide difference of
opinion as to the possible limits of this self-purification, and the
practical effect of it in making a stream, once polluted, again
suitable for domestic use and in preventing nuisance to riparian
property-owners. There is, however, practical agreement as
to the fact of some purification and as to the purifying agencies
in streams. The means of self-purification are sedimentation,
dilution, chemical oxidation, biological oxidation caused by
microbes, and the agency of animal and vegetable life.

Sedimentation. — The amount of sedimentation depends
on the rate of flow of the stream and the character of the

sewage.   If either carries with it much sand, silt, or clay, the
deposit of organic matter from the sewage will be much larger
than otherwise when the river flow is slow enough to permit
deposit at all.   The matter deposited from sewage on the bottom of a river does not decay very rapidly; it silts up the river
bed; as in the Thames near London, where it is stated that
the sewage deposits are deeper than the waters of the river.
When exposed by subsidence of the stream in summer it may
cause a nuisance by putrefactive decay; in spring freshets it
may be scoured away by the flood, and either borne out to sea,
left on flowed meadows, or deposited in the river bed further
down.   While at any time such deposits would menace a water
supply taken from the stream below them, and while, as shown
by the observations of MacAdam (Jour. Roy. Micr. Soc., 2d
Ser., Vol. IV, Feb., 1884, p. 1, ref. Rafter, Sew. Disp. in
U. S., p. 94) the organic constituents of human excrement can
be identified, even in muds which have been deposited a considerable time, it seems likely that some slow putrefactive decomposition goes on in a sewage mud, yielding gases which rise
to the surface, and a residuum which is somewhat less rapidly
putrescible when again mixed with the waters of the stream.
But the real purification effected by sedimentation is surely
very uncertain and insignificant.

Dilution of sewage makes the pollution less evident and
tends to absorb evil odors, preventing their rapid escape into
the air.   But the purifying effect of dilution is due solely to
the additional oxygen thus supplied to forms of animal and
vegetable life which prey upon the solid and dissolved elements
of the sewage, as will be noticed later.

Chemical Oxidation. — The slow oxidation of some kinds
of dead organic matter was formerly thought to go on even at
moderate temperatures by the union of the free oxygen of the
air, either directly or by means of some " carrying agent," with
combustible material, just as wood oxidizes or burns in a stove;
the visible effects — smoke, heat, and light — being masked in
the former case by the slowness of the process.   Recent study
has shown that in the cases under experiment this oxidation
took place actively in the presence of microbic, bacterial life,
less actively when this life was for any reason less active, and
that it ceased altogether whenever microbe life was excluded,
though all other conditions remained unchanged.   The conclusion is justified that this microbe life is an efficient, if not

the sole, cause of the oxidation. Hence investigators have come to regard chemical oxidation of organic matter as of minor importance in flowing streams, some questioning whether it has the slightest practical effect, and to ascribe the disappearance of organic matters to the agencies named below.

Biological Oxidation. — By this is meant the oxidation (burning) of organic matter through the activity of living micro-organisms (microbes, bacteria). We have elsewhere noticed the nature and work of these organisms and here only call attention to the oxygen of the air as related to them. Air is inimical to that kind of bacterial action which causes putrefactive decay and the foul odors always attending it. On the other hand, air — or rather the oxygen which makes up onefifth of its volume — is essential to the bacterial action which oxidizes or burns the elements of sewage, without giving off foul odors. To expose sewage freely and fully to the air in the presence of these bacteria under suitable conditions of heat and moisture is to ensure its destruction quietly and without offense. Now water dissolves air, and nearly 35 per cent. of the dissolved air consists of free oxygen. (Roscoe & Schorlemmer, Treatise on Chem., Vol. I, p. 244.)

The following table shows the amount of dissolved gases contained in Thames water taken at different points. (R. & S., *loc. cit.*):

DISSOLVED GASES IN WATER OF THE THAMES RIVER (ENG.) AT THE PLACES NAMED.

	Kingston, cubic centimeters.	Hammersmith, cubic centimeters.	Somerset House, cubic centimeters.	Greenwich, cubic centimeters.	Woolwich, cubic centimeters.	Erith, cubic centimeters.
Total volume of gas per litre, .	52.7	....	62 9	71 25	63.05	74.3
Carbonic acid, · ·	30.3	....	45 2	55 6	4$ 3	57.
Oxygen, ...	7.4	4.1	1.5	0 25	0.25	1.8
Nitrogen, . . .	15.0	15.1	16 2	15.4	14 5	15.5
Ratio of Oxygen to Nitrogen, .	1:2	1:3.7	1:10.8	1.6	1:58	1:8.6

The sample at Kingston is tolerably pure river water; the others are contaminated and mark the increasing pollution of

the stream as it flows to the sea.   The pure water contains 7.4
parts or quarts of oxygen dissolved in 1,000 quarts of water.
In some way, entirely unknown to us, the microbes everywhere present in the water attack the organic matter, a small
quantity of sewage, for example, and *with the help of the dissolved oxygen* burn the carbon to carbonic acid, and, if the
operation is completed, leave the nitrogen combined with
hydrogen to form ammonia.   This in turn is oxidized to
nitrous acid, and lastly to nitric acid, which is combined with
mineral matter to form a nitrate.   The end products are carbonic acid, ammonia, nitrates, all of them perfectly innocuous
in the stream and all readily available to plant life.   This, in
brief outline, is the present belief regarding sewage disposal by
oxidation.

It can only be done where oxygen is constantly and abun-
dantly present.   If the supply is limited, carbon in the sewage
will be destroyed as far as it can be, but there will be no nitrification (oxidization) of ammonia, and as the supply of oxygen
decreases, less of the carbon is destroyed.   When the oxygen
is used up, all purification by this means ceases, the oxidizing
bacteria cease to work, and the bacteria of putrefaction begin.
The oxygen removed from water by these processes is replaced
in time from the air, but not quickly enough, probably, to keep
pace with rapid oxidation induced by bacteria, at least to any
distance below the surface.

The more sewage is poured into a stream the greater the
demand for oxygen and the less is present to meet this demand.
The table above given shows this.

At Kingston, where the water was pure and no demands
for free oxygen in it, there were 7.4 quarts of oxygen in every
1,000 quarts of water.   At Hammersmith, where the stream
contained sewage and " self-purification " was called for — and
doubtless taking place — only 4.1 quarts; at Somerset House,
1.5 quarts; at Greenwich — a grossly polluted part of the
river — half a pint of oxygen, only 1-30 the amount which
the pure river water had.

When a clean tributary empties into the foul stream it
brings with it free oxygen, and in this way dilution assists
purification.   As long as an abundance of free oxygen is present, self-purification may go on in rivers.   Sewage itself contains none of it, and every addition of sewage reduces the supply
of oxygen in the stream.   Oxygen is dissolved constantly from

the air by the stream, but by no means fast enough to supply the needs of the bacterial life in strongly polluted waters.

Pouring filth into flowing water is a very slow and dangerous way of destroying filth, but a short and easy way to destroy pure water.

The Agency of Animal and Vegetable Life. — This has already been alluded to in the discussion of sewage purification in the ocean, but we return to it here because we have somewhat more definite information regarding the animal life in sewage-polluted streams.

Among microscopic or extremely minute forms of animal life are certain kinds which are found in the greatest abundance in filthy water, and devour the solid matter in sewage, however finely divided it is. There is no evidence that the dissolved matter is used by them.

A very interesting account of them is given by Rafter in the Trans. Am. Soc. C. E., Vol. XXIV, pp. 70-76, from which some of the following statements are taken: As common representatives are (1) certain filth infusoria,* (2) certain hydroids, (3) certain rotifers, (4) numerous species of entomostracans which are probably the animals which do most service, (5) the fresh water shrimp, (6) the larvae of water insects. All of these forms multiply with prodigious rapidity under favoring conditions. The definite action of the entomostracans has been studied by Dr. H. C. Sorby (Jour. Roy. Micr. Soc., 1884, pp. 988-991). He says:

"It is known that entomostraca will eat dead animal matter, though probably not entirely dependent on it. I have myself proved that they may be kept alive for many months by feeding them on human excrement, though they soon died without it. In stagnant, muddy pools, where food abounds, I have found an average of 200

---

* It is not easy to give a description of the low forms of life here referred to, which will be clear to those who are wholly unacquainted with them.

The *protozoa* are animals of the simplest form consisting of a single cell or having several cells alike in structure and use.

The *infusoria* are protozoans, mostly microscopic in size, aquatic and free-swimming by means of motile fibers.

The *hydroids* are animals, plant-like in form, very simple in structure, soft and gelatinous.

The *rotifers* are microscopic animals, having a head with circles of motile fibers about it, which, under the microscope appear-like revolving wheels, hence the name. They have an intestinal tract. The tail is well marked and variously modified for swimming, skipping, creeping, or rooting.

The *entomostraca* are much higher in the order of being than the classes named above, and may be well described as minute animals much resembling shrimps.

The *algae* are water plants varying greatly in shape from the delicately branched seaweeds to shapeless jelly like masses.

The *confervoid algae* are many celled green, thread-like plants, which form a green "scum" in stagnant pools.

The *diatoms* and *desmids* are single-celled microscopic algae, the former distinguished by their silicious coating.

per gallon. In the case of fairly pure rivers, the total of free swimming animals (not small enough to pass a sieve with meshes 1-250
in. in diameter) is not more than one per gallon. I found, however,
that where what may be called sewage was discharged into such
water, the number per gallon rose to 27, and the percentage rela-
tionships between the different groups of entomostraca were greatly
changed.

"There is, however, a very decided limit to the increase of entro-
mostraca when the water of a river is rendered very impure by the
discharge of too much sewage, probably because oxygen is deficient,
and free sulphide of hydrogen present.

"We thus appear to be led to the conclusion that when the
amount of sewage discharged into a river is not too great, it furnishes food for a vast number of animals, which perform a most
important part in removing it. On the contrary, if the discharge
be too great, it may be injurious to them, and this process of purification may cease. Possibly this explains why in certain cases
a river which is usually unobjectionable may occasionally become
offensive. It also seems to make it clear that the discharge of rather
too much sewage may produce relatively very great and objectionable results."

Dr. Sorby suggests the possibility of the destruction of
disease germs by minute infusoria as a fruitful field for further
study. He also alludes to the vegetable life in polluted water,
diatoms, desmids, and confervoid germs, and to the important
office they may perform in decomposing carbonic acid — only
in presence of light — and thus freeing oxygen for the use of
animal life and counteracting putrefactive decay.

Regarding the fate of these low forms of life which appropriate sewage in polluted water, Prof. S. A. Forbes of the
Illinois State Laboratory of National History has made important observations.

He finds " that the earliest food of the whitefish consists almost wholly of the smaller species of entomostraca "; " that the
young *cyprinidae* (minnows) draw almost indiscriminately for
their food supply upon protozoa, algae, and entomostraca."
Entomostraca furnish 92 per cent. of the food of young perch,
and from 50 to 70 per cent. of that of young bass, sunfishes,
and pickerel. "I find that, taking together the young of all
the genera studied, considering each genus as a unit, and combining the minute dipterous larvae with the entomostraca as
having essentially the same relation, about 75 per cent. of the
food taken by young fishes of all descriptions is made up of
these elements."

Our knowledge of the food supply of the lower orders of
animal life is still very meager, but enough is known to show

the interdependence of all forms of animal life and that individual death and decay are not the end, but merely an incident, of the world's life and growth.

It may be asked, if the elements of sewage are noisome and contain the germs of disease, can the fish which feed upon these things be wholesome? They can. Fish are so organized that they can take with impunity, and digest and thus convert into their tissue, things which would be repulsive, indigestible, and unhealthful to man. And, after this making over, the product — fish food — is easily digestible and healthful to man. The disease germs of the sewage are very likely destroyed in the digestive tract of the fish; if not, they leave the body in the excrement. Certainly they do not continue to live in the tissue of the healthy fish. Even were that true, they would be destroyed in the cooking which fish always receive.

The sewage destroyed by animal life in our rivers is limited to the solid matter which is in suspension in water. Animals do not, as far as we know, utilize the dissolved matter.

Such are the means by which nature strives to prevent putrefaction in streams, and to take up promptly into new life the wastes of other life. Obviously, large quantities of foul matters may be disposed of in the ways just indicated. The vital questions are: How much can thus be cleansed? What is the precise relation between the volume of sewage and the volume of water necessary for its cleansing? What amount of time or distance of flow is required? No definite answer can be given, and there is very great discrepancy of opinion.

One of the most satisfactory series of observations on the self-purification of streams which has been noted by the Commission is found in Illinois State Board of Health, Ninth Report (referred to by Rafter, Sewage Disposal in U. S., p. 66.)

At Bridgeport, the sewage-polluted water of the South Branch is pumped into the Illinois and Michigan canal and flows through it past Lockport, twenty-nine miles below. Between these points the canal receives nothing but the rainfall and some slight infiltration, stated to amount to nothing. When the tests to be referred to were made, summer of 1888, the pumps at Bridgeport, in continual action, discharged into the canal 50,000 cubic feet per minute, an amount on an average for each whole day about seven times in excess of the total of sewage flowing into the river from all sources. No water plants grow in the canal, the frequent passage of boats stirs up the canal to the bottom, the current itself prevents sedimentation, and frequent dredgings prove that there is no deposit of sewage. The place would seem an ideal one to study the joint effects of chemical and biological oxidation, and possibly of the destruction of sewage by minute animal and vegetable life; in other words, the self-purification of an ordinary stream receiving a large quantity of moderately dilute sewage, where the effects of subsidence, dilution, and conspicuous marine vegetation were eliminated.

Between May 1st and November 15th Professor J. H. Long made 750 analyses of water collected at the two points named, to determine how much sewage matter was destroyed between Bridgeport and Lockport. The average of all analyses from May to October, inclusive, is shown in the following table.

ANALYSES OF THE WATER OF THE ILLINOIS AND MICHI-
GAN CANAL.

Parts per 100,000.

	Total Solids.	Matters in Suspension.	Nitrogen in Nitrates.	Chlorine.	Hardness. Ca CO₃.	Free Ammonia.	Albuminoid Ammonia.	Oxygen Consumed.
Bridgeport, . .	47 12	12.92	0.0	4.68	20.13	1.23	0 26	2.21
Lockport, . .	43 12	6 98	0 0	4.61	20.77	1.08	0.20	1.62
Difference, . .	4.00	5.94	0.0	0.01	0.64	0.15	0.06	0.59
Percentage decrease,	8.5	46.0	....	....	.....	12.2	23.1	26.7

Assuming that the total solids include matters in suspension, it would appear that at Lockport, while the total solid matter has been reduced by some 8½ per cent., *the solid matter in solution* has increased by 5.6 per cent.; that is, a considerable amount of suspended matter has been dissolved by the canal water between Bridgeport and Lockport. The "free ammonia" has been reduced by 12 per cent., and the "albu-

minoid ammonia " — our best measure of the nitrogenous organic matter — by 23.1 per cent.

At this same rate of purification, supposing no tributaries
enter the stream, it would require a flow of 125 miles to clean
the water as perfectly as it is ordinarily done by sand filtration
(90 per cent.); but the same rate of purification could not be
maintained.

Prof. W. P. Mason states (Rafter and Baker, Sewage Disposal in the U. S., p. 69) " that the rate of purification varies
directly as the amount of sewage contamination," and that
" given a stream with a certain amount of pollution, the per
cent. of such pollution which must disappear per mile of flow
will continually decrease as the stream flows on."   But without further discussion it is evident to the layman that the removal of 23 per cent. of the putrescible matter in polluted
streams, in a flow of twenty-nine miles, is not a " purification "
which can be of great practical account in the rivers of this
State.

A somewhat careful study of the observations made on the
self-purifying power of streams convinces us that, while the
causes which effect this cleansing are probably understood, it
has not been possible to measure their quantitative effects in
water polluted with so nondescript and varying a material as
sewage; that the self-cleansing must vary daily with temperature, flow of stream, quantity of sewage, and many other conditions, and that the statements as to the quantity of sewage
which can safely be turned into a given stream are nothing
more than the guesses of intelligent people with quite different
ideas as to what constitutes " safety."

Streams undoubtedly have some self-purifying power.
But as the free oxygen in a stream is diminished, the self-
purifying power of the stream is diminished, and at the very
time when the need for it is increased.

The question of how much sewage is permissible in the
smaller streams of this State is specially difficult to answer,
because the volume of water varies so enormously with the
season.   What is a raging torrent in spring becomes a very
tame rivulet in August.   In April certain streams could carry
much more sewage than is run into them without creating any
nuisance.   In July and August the same streams would
scarcely flow at all but for the sewage that makes them foul
and offensive.   The capacity of a stream for safe sewage dis-

posal is its capacity measured when the natural waters of the stream are at their lowest, and conditions favor active putrefaction.

THE SYSTEM OF WATER CARRIAGE AND DILUTION.

When sewage can be carried to the ocean by a natural stream without injury to any riparian owners or the defilement of any water supply, this is unquestionably in most cases the cheapest and best method of disposal. New York is the most favorably situated of all our cities in this respect. The strong tides on both sides, twice daily, sweep out the city sewage into the deep waters of the sound and ocean, and as yet there is no evidence of any objectionable feature in this. It was the garbage, not the sewage, of New York which formerly made trouble along the shores of the lower bay and beyond.

The city of Boston, not so favorably situated as New York, pumps sewage into a receiving basin on Moon Island several miles below the city, near the harbor mouth, from which it is discharged twice daily into the young ebb tide. (See Mass. Board Health, 1889.) From this basin alone 15,000,000 gallons are discharged in this way within forty minutes. Careful observations made by the board show that two hours after it leaves the sewer no evidence of sewage is to be found in the tidal current into which it enters.

As this sewage enters the sea it rises to the surface and spreads till it has a depth of less than a foot. Half an hour after discharge has begun the sewage covers an area about half a mile in diameter. " In this condition the sewage, already considerably diluted, moves outward with the current, and further dilution takes place, the process going on most rapidly at the bottom of the layer of sewage.

" Up to a certain stage in the progress of this dilution, the surface of the sewage contains enough greasy matter to prevent waves, except when the wind blows very hard. When the dilution of the sewage has progressed so far that waves begin to form and its specific gravity has approached that of the sea water, it rapidly becomes mixed with water from greater depths, and very soon cannot be distinguished by the eye or nose from unpolluted sea water. The last change here described takes place in less than an hour and a half after the sewage is discharged, and at a distance from the outlet not exceeding two miles."

Not one of our Connecticut coast cities discharges its sewage directly into the deep waters of Long Island Sound. The sewage of New London, New Haven, Bridgeport, South Norwalk, and Stamford is discharged into a river or bay or arm of the sea, where it tarries for no one knows how long, and is in some cases an offense. New Haven's sewage, for example, is borne up and down the harbor and river with the ebb and flow of the tide, a part of it being left on the mud flats at low water. On quiet nights during the summer the odor of decaying sewage is very evident and extremely disagreeable in those streets which are near the water. This state of things will continue and become worse until the city is willing to complete the work contemplated in the original design, and build an intercepting sewer to receive and carry all the sewage much further down the harbor or beyond it.

A somewhat similar state of things was noted in Bridgeport in 1888, Connecticut State Board of Health Report, 1888, p. 337: "There are at least ten public sewer outlets on the east side and eighteen on the west side of the harbor, besides numerous private ones, emptying their foul contents in most instances upon the flats, which are uncovered except during high tide, and in some instances beneath the windows of habitations which have to be closed on hot summer nights, and under the noses of passers on the bridges, who, with averted faces, hasten on." Since then, as we are informed by a city official of Bridgeport, many of the sewers have been extended to active tide water.

These cases are cited as illustrations of the fact that even in places situated on tide water, the present method of " disposal " by water carriage is often so badly managed as to cause a public nuisance. Sewage discharged continuously into the tide water of a harbor is not promptly and completely removed, but hovers about, being carried back and forth by the set of the tide. If discharged only on the young ebb tide, in the channel and near enough to the open sea, there is a strong probability of its being completely and permanently removed. Such a plan, however, requires the construction of tanks large enough to hold the sewage delivered during eleven hours, and in most cases, if not all, the pumping of this sewage from the sewer outlets to these tanks.

3

But most of our Connecticut cities and large towns discharge their sewage not into the sea or an arm of the sea, but into streams — the Thames, Connecticut, Quinnipiac, Naugatuck, Housatonic, and their several tributaries, which are regarded as the " natural " outlets for sewage.

The system of these cities and towns is called " water carriage and dilution," and consists in pouring all of their sewage into the nearest available stream and let what will come of it. They trust it will hurt no one down stream, but at any rate they are rid of it.

" How if a' will not stan'? " asks the watch. " Why, then," replies Dogberry, " take no note of him, but let him go; and presently call the rest of the watch together, and thank God you are rid of a knave."

This apparent disregard of the rights of riparian owners below is not, however, deliberate. In the construction of works necessary for the public good, but unproductive of revenue, every effort to avoid expenditure is made, and rightly made, by temporary arrangements as to sewer construction and the discharge of sewage, till the requirements of public health and the growth and development of the special industries of the city or borough shall make a more complete system necessary and the means for its construction possible. (Kiersted, Sewage Disposal, 1894, p. 7.)

While this method has been so generally adopted without regard for the rights or comfort of riparian owners below, or in entire ignorance of its effects upon them, but solely because it was the cheapest and most convenient way of handling sewage, it is, nevertheless, true that in some cases it is a safe and unobjectionable way, at least so far as our present knowledge goes. We have already discussed the several purifying agencies which are at work in streams, and it is clear that a stream which is only moderately polluted may create no nuisance and may to some extent clean itself as it flows. If the quantity of sewage is relatively small, if the stream is rapid enough to keep its bed scoured and prevent the deposit of solid matter either on the bottom or on the banks, if it does not foul the water supply of any town or city, if the sewage does not make the water unfit for manufacturing uses, if it does not kill the fish in the streams, or taint the air about it, then little or no objection can be raised to the practice.

But to name these things is to catalogue the evils from

which a considerable number of communities in this State are already suffering, and from which they will suffer much more until some of our large cities purify their crude sewage before sending it into our inland waters.   Our cities are growing all the time, the quantity of sewage discharged into streams is thereby increased, and the practice which twenty years ago may have been unobjectionable has in many cases become unbearable.

. An impression has become general that our water-ways were designed by nature to carry all our sewage, and that centers of population have a prescriptive right to them for that purpose, but the fact that the riparian owner has a right to the waters of the stream, unpolluted by sewage, seems to have been in some quarters entirely forgotten.

THE PRESENT EVILS OF THE SYSTEM OF WATER CARRIAGE IN CONNECTICUT.

These are all summed up in the statement that the carrying and cleansing capacity of some of our streams for sewage is overtaxed.   The first of these evils is

Contamination of water and ice supplies.   According to modern sanitary ideas, supported by convincing, if not irrefragible proof, water taken from a river at any point below the outfall of the sewers of a community of any size, is unfit for drinking unless filtered through sand, and will be the cause of a considerable amount of sickness and death yearly, even though no epidemics call attention to the matter, and the " annual death rate " is not exceptionally high.   Wherever a city which has been using water from a sewage-polluted stream for a term of years puts in sand filtration works and filters the whole water supply through it, the death rate, particularly the death rate from typhoid and diarrhœal troubles, immediately falls.

Very striking was an epidemic of diarrhœal troubles in Hartford in 1878, which followed the use of river water to supplement the reservoir supply in a season of drought. (Conn. Bd. Health Rep., 1878, p. 87.)   The onset of the disease was sudden, severe, and extensive, but limited to the region supplied with river water.   In many cases recovery was slow, and in the next month there were an unusual number of cases of typho-malarial and typhoid fever, with a larger rate of mortality from typhoid than had been reported in eighteen years. Nearly every family in the affected district had one or more cases of disease, and in many none escaped. Investigation showed that a large sewer discharged 50 feet down stream from the intake, and the tide, which rises 18 inches at that point, though the water is not brackish, made an eddy at high water and sent some sewage back into the water supply. An outbreak of typhoid in Hartford in 1891-2 is also attributed to water pollution. (Conn. Bd. Health Rep., 1892, p. 206.)

We may cite one other illustration, even more striking, where the cause of sewage contamination was not so near at hand. (Mass. Bd. Health Rep., 1896, p. 568.)

The city of Lawrence, Mass., had for twenty years used for its supply the water of the Merrimac River, which above Lawrence received the sewage of Lowell and other places. The impression seemed to prevail that direct poisoning of the supply was not possible by the sewage of Lowell, nine miles above, with a fall of ten feet through a rapid a mile long on the way, which fall offered a fine chance for self-purification of the water by oxidation. The thought of drinking water from a river into which the sewage of 70,000 people had been poured only eight hours before was not, to be sure, appetizing. Every year the river grew more foul and the death rate from typhoid fever every year increased till, early in 1891, the Board of Health warned the people of Lawrence of their danger, and advised them to boil all drinking water until some permanent relief could be secured. The public took the alarm, and the typhoid death rate began to fall.

A sand filter was built to purify the whole city supply, and was first operated in September of 1893. What followed is shown by the figures in the following table, which gives the deaths from typhoid fever alone, per 10,000 inhabitants, for eleven years. The death rate crept up with increasing pollution of the water supply from 4.2 in 1885 to 13.75 in 1889 and 13.33 in 1890. In 1891 and 1892, after the warning given by the Board of Health, it fell to 11.11. In 1893, with the filter in use for four months, it was cut down to 8.66, and in 1896, the last year for which we have returns, to 1.86. More than one-half of the people who died of typhoid in 1896 used unfiltered water and not the city supply.

MORTALITY FROM TYPHOID FEVER IN LAWRENCE, MASS.

(Mass. State Bd. Health Rep., 1896, p. 568.)

Year.		Deaths from Typhoid per 10,000 Inhabitants.	Total No. of Deaths.
1885,		4.2	17
1886,		5.75	23
1887,		11.75	47
1888,		12.00	48
1889,		13.75	55
1890,		13.33	60
1891,	Warning by Board of Health,	12.20	55
1892,		11.11	50
1893,	Filter operated for 4 months,	8.66	39
1894,	Filtration continues,	5.00	24
1895,	" "	3.07	16
1896,	" "	1.86	10.

· But at present none of our Connecticut rivers furnishes a water supply below the points at which they receive any large amount of sewage (see description of Conn. Water Supplies, Conn. State Board Health Rep., 1896, pp. 289 and 344), and the water of those which are now polluted can never be brought into condition again to meet the requirements for a city water supply, according to modern ideas of sanitation, without sand filtration. The water in those rivers or parts of rivers which are now somewhat, but not grossly polluted by sewage could, no doubt, be safely used for city water supplies, if it were necessary, by filtering it through suitably prepared and managed sand filters. The pollution by sewage of ponds from which ice is cut is not so serious a matter as the pollution of water supplies, because ice is not so universally used, and because the impurities tend to separate and remain in the water rather than in the ice. For this reason ice has often been gathered where drinking water would not have been taken. It is certain, however, that not only organic impurities but also bacteria in dormant condition may be included in ice taken from contaminated ponds or rivers, and ice should never be cut from bodies of water which would be deemed unfit for drinking — if the ice is to be used in contact with food or drink, or in family refrigerators.

Another evil of the present prevalent system of water carriage and dilution of sewage is stated to be

The destruction of fish. The effect of factory wastes has

been studied by a number of investigators. Thus, Penny and Adams, Fourth Report Rivers Pollution Com., Vol. II, p. 377, found that one part of the several chemicals and wastes dissolved (or, in some cases, suspended) in the number of parts of water given below was soon fatal to minnows and goldfish, while in double the quantity of water both lived during the period of observation.

DESTRUCTION OF FISH.

	Fatal to Minnows.				Fatal to Goldfish.		
Nitric or sulphuric acids,	.	1 part in	50,000	water,	1 part in		......
Tannic acid, . . .	.	1	"	14,000	"	1	" 7,000
Gallic acid, . . .	.	1	"	7,000	"	1	" 7,000
Acetic acid . . .	.	1	"	8,750	"	1	" ......
Carbolic acid, .	.	1	"	70,000	"	1	" 3,000
Copper sulphate, . .	.	1	"	100,000	"	1	" 100,000
Sugar of lead; alum, salts of iron and potash,	.	1	"	4,000	"	1	" 4,000
Carbonate of soda,	.	1	"	17,500	"	1	" ......
Saturated solution of bleaching powder,	.	1	"	16,000	"	1	" ......
Iodine and bromine,	.	1	"	35,000	"	1	" ......
Caustic potash,	.	1	"	35,000	"	1	" 7.000
Galls, . . .	.	1	"	2,808	"	1	" 936
Sumac and madder solutions,	1	"	7,000	"	1	"	......
Crude soap, . . .	.	1	"	......	"	1	" 4,375
Ashes and furnace cinders,	.	1	"	140	"	1	" 140
Coal tar, . . .	.	1	'	......	"	1	" 8,750
Heavy pitch oil, . .	.	1	"	35,000	"	1	" 35,000

The bicarbonate and yellow and red prussiates of potash were comparatively harmless. In water containing one part of a saturated solution of chlorine to 2,000 of water, minnows and goldfish both lived. Linseed oil appeared to be innocuous. More extended and critical observations on the effects of factory wastes on fish life are now being carried out by König and Haselhoff, the first results of which are given in Landw. Jahrbücher, Bd. XXVI, 1897, p. 75.

Saare and Schwab (Archiv. fur Hygeine, Vol. 3, Part I, p. 81), experimenting with tench and trout, found that from 0.04 to 0.005 per cent. of bleaching solution killed tench, and that 0.0008 per cent. killed trout. Copper sulphate in 0.1 and potassium cyanide in 0.01 to 0.005 per cent. were also fatal to trout.

These tests, no doubt, show the maximum limit of concentration. It is reasonable to suppose that an amount of chemicals which a sound adult fish could endure during the period of observation would be very considerably greater than would suffice to kill the eggs or young of the fish or its food supply, or to render the water so distasteful that the fish would leave it. The effects on fish life of factory refuse and chemicals, and also of sawdust, which has been discharged into streams in lumbering regions in enormous quantities, have been more carefully studied than the effects of ordinary household sewage. There is an abundance of testimony regarding the disappearance of fish from streams into which sewage is discharged, but no clear demonstration of the effects of sewage alone, apart from all other causes. König and Haselhoff (Land. Jahrbücher, Bd. XXVI, 1897, p. 75) assert that ordinary sewage, *in its fresh state*, is not injurious to fish, unless the suspended matter—paper or wood-fiber—interferes with their gills. The observed poisoning of fish usually comes in the summer when putrefaction is rapid, and is caused by poisonous products given off during sewage decay. The sudden dying of fish in large numbers usually occurs in summer immediately after a rise in temperature attending a heavy downpour of rain. The rain sweeps a large amount of filth into the stream, and rapid putrefaction follows the rise in temperature. We believe, however, that the disappearance of fish in polluted streams is more often due to the presence in the water of waste chemicals than to the effects of house sewage.

C. Duncan and F. Hoppe-Seyler (Zeitschr für Physiol. Chem., 1893, Bd. 17, p. 165) have shown that tench and trout can live in running water which contains only about one-third the normal quantity of dissolved oxygen. But as sewage contains no dissolved oxygen and quickly takes up oxygen brought into contact with it, it is clear that the discharge of much sewage into a stream may reduce the amount of oxygen in it far below the limit which is required for fish life, while at the same time putrefaction of the sewage liberates products which are distinctly poisonous to fish life.

Charles A. Cameron (Chem. News, Vol. 44, No. 1131, p. 52) states that oysters are brought from the coast of Wexford and laid down in Dublin Bay to finish their growth. Formerly they did well, but with the growth of Dublin the harbor and river have become increasingly fouled, until now a large percentage of the oysters die soon after transplanting. At ebb tide the water around them smells of sewage, and analysis shows that it contains much nitrogenous matter. The oysters themselves have an evil odor, and the water in them abounds with the same organisms which occur in the sewage.   Many cases of illness, which have followed the eating of these oysters, are attributed to the effects of sewage contamination.

The United States Commissioner of Fish and Fisheries, Hon. George M. Bowers (Report on the Pollution of Rivers, by Henry Talbot, Washington, 1898, p. 17), says:

"The data are sufficient to clearly establish the point that river pollution is both directly and indirectly most injurious to fish and fisheries by destroying fish and fish eggs, by driving fish away, by interfering with the fishing apparatus, and by killing or impairing the supply of minute animals and plants which are the basis of fish life."

The infection of oysters by sewage, noted by Cameron, has again been illustrated, in this state.   The cause of an epidemic of typhoid at Middletown in 1894 was clearly traced to oysters which had been laid down to "fatten" in the Quinnipiac River, about 100 feet from a private sewer, which at the time carried the dejections of two persons who had the disease.   None of the persons who ate these oysters *stewed* had typhoid, but at certain social gatherings, where they were eaten raw, twenty-four persons, about 25 per cent. of the guests who ate, took the disease.   A full account of the epidemic is given in the Seventeenth Report, Conn. State Board of Health for 1894, p. 243.

These facts do not indicate that fish which have fed on particles of sewage are dangerous as food.   (See p. 29.)   In the case cited, the oysters were surrounded with water charged with the specific typhoid germ, which, of course, entered their shells and lodged on the edible portion.   Even then subsequent cooking destroyed the germs.

But the evils already named, which are tangible, easily described, and which can perhaps be measured to determine their effects and the damage wrought by them to riparian owners, are not, after all, the chief cause of the present distrust of the safety of our sewage disposal and of the call for more careful attention to the subject on the part of the public and the legislature.

There is a widespread conviction that the unlimited discharge of sewage into our rivers is rendering them more and more unwholesome to those who live near them; that a sewage-polluted stream is indirectly at least a cause of ill-health, if not of active disease, to the community living on its banks; and that until the present method of "disposing" of sewage is reformed, these evils will continue and increase.

Renewed attention is called to the right of the riparian owner to the water of the stream in its natural purity, undetained and not unnecessarily polluted, and to the fact that it has been ruled by our courts that the discharge of sewage into a stream is an unnecessary pollution.

Unsightly appearance. Still further, there is the objection, lightly waved aside by some as "purely sentimental," that the unlimited discharge of sewage into our water-ways makes them dark, murky, and disgusting in their appearance. What should be a delight, a rest to the eye and the spirit, serving much the same purpose as a public park or forest reservation, can only be looked upon now as an open sewer, a sluiceway for all the disgusting filth of neighbors who cannot or will not clean their own premises except by casting their filth into the highway.

Much of the unsightliness of rivers, and especially of their banks, is due to things not included in sewage, which are heedlessly cast into the stream by those whose sense of decency is small. Barrels and boxes, waste lumber and paper, dead animals, and many other kinds of refuse greet the eye in our streams and on their banks. The discharge from dye-works, tanneries, and certain other factories, either alone or when mixed with other wastes, greatly discolors the stream, and in some cases makes it inky black, so that its waters are in fact a pale ink. We believe the time will come when such unnecessary untidiness will be forbidden by law as well as by public sentiment. But when the water is low, and at the time of year when putrefaction is most active, solid animal and vegetable matters coming from the sewage itself frequently lodge on river banks and make them unattractive and even repulsive.

Regarding this last objection it is to be said that, if "purely sentimental," it is, nevertheless, real and cannot be fairly met or brushed aside by calling it names. Sentiment is a fact, as real as sewage. Its reality is demonstrated to the most "practical" of men, who prides himself on his freedom from sentiment, by the fact that it has a market value, it can be measured in dollars and cents. A beautiful view, a fine shade tree, a clear stream of water, and agreeable neighbors enhance the value of a piece of real estate. Uncongenial surroundings, unkempt premises, a stream which rolls along the filth of a community or the

refuse dye-stuffs of a factory are perfectly well recognized as a
distinct damage to the value and the selling price of a piece of
property.   And the damage may be purely " sentimental," for
no " nuisance " is established which would for a moment be
considered by the courts.

We believe, too, that clean streams, like clean streets, clean
houses, and clean places of amusement, have a great beneficial
effect on the general moral and physical tone and well-being
of the whole community, quite apart from any direct effect
which is recognized by the sanitarian.   Physical and moral
cleanliness are closely associated, and either one promotes the
other.

Danger to Health.   Leaving now the " sentimental " objection to grossly polluted streams, we come to notice the second
which has been named, *i. e.*, a widespread conviction that the
unlimited discharge of sewage into our streams is rendering
them generally unwholesome and indirectly at least a cause
of ill health to the community living on their banks.

With reference to this objection it may be granted that no
facts have fully demonstrated that illness, sporadic or epidemic, has ever been caused by proximity to a polluted stream
except where specific poisons have been introduced into the
system through drinking its water.   It must also be said, however, that from the nature of the case such demonstration is
quite impossible.   In very few cases can a physician go further
than to name the probable cause of any illness.   There is always a variety of possible causes for a sickness, several of which
may have operated together, and to no one of which the whole
effect can be ascribed with absolute certainty.

If a person lived on the bank of a grossly polluted, evil-
smelling stream, amid surroundings otherwise healthful, his
physician would surely attribute any general debility and resulting illness to the proximity of this filthy stream, and the
common sense of the neighborhood would unanimously endorse
his opinion.   Yet *proof* of his view would be entirely wanting
and impossible to secure.   The further the person named lived
from the noisome stream, or the smaller the amount of obvious
filth in the stream, the less unanimous would be the opinion of
the neighborhood; and if the question of the cause of illness
involved the cleaning of the stream at the expense of the community, a part of the public, at least, would be honestly convinced that the stream's pollution had absolutely nothing to do

with the case, and medical experts would be found who would share this view.

The really important question in this State is, however, this: Can a stream, which is not so strongly charged with sewage as to make it a public nuisance, be indirectly a cause of ill health to individuals or communities living on its banks?

We believe the general opinion of sanitarians and physicians is that a moderate amount of sewage in the stream would probably not at all affect the health of riparian proprietors. In proportion, however, to the increase of sewage in the stream, is increased the possibility and probability of injury to the public health by a general depression of the tone of the system, and so of the disease-resisting power. The danger from this cause is all the greater because insidious and slow in its effects.

Legal rights of the riparian owners. We come now to the third element in the present agitation regarding sewage disposal, viz., the legal rights of the riparian owner to the water of the stream as it was wont to flow. The principles of law bearing on the matter have recently been clearly stated by Judge G. W. Wheeler in a decision rendered in the Superior Court, Fairfield County, August 1, 1895, in the case of Morgan *et al.* vs. the City of Danbury. The complaint of Morgan was substantially this: The city has rendered the stream filthy, noxious, and unclean by its sewage, and intends to increase the pollution by building new sewers. By this action the plaintiff has been largely deprived of the use of the waters of the river at his mill and water privilege; he and his workmen have been injuriously exposed to noxious and unhealthy odors; the air in the neighborhood has been corrupted and poisoned, endangering health; he has been unable to use or sell his mill and building lots; his dam has been partly filled up with filth; the value of his lands and water privilege have been greatly diminished, and will ultimately be wholly destroyed if the defendant is not enjoined.

We cannot do better than quote Judge Wheeler's decision in full as far as it relates to the rights of a riparian owner:

."Before considering the case as presented on the evidence let us first ascertain the rights under the law of a riparian proprietor (as is this plaintiff) in the waters of a running stream.

" In discussing the right of the riparian proprietor in the waters of a running stream, Butler, C. J., in Agawam Canal Co. vs. Edwards, 36 Ct., 497, says: ' But it is not a title to the waters; it is a usufruct merely; a right to use it while passing over the land. The same right pertains to the land of every other riparian proprietor on the same stream and its tributaries; and as each has a similar and equal usu-fructuary right, the common interest requires that the right should be exercised and enjoyed by each in such a reasonable manner as not to injure unnecessarily the rights of any other owner above or below. Each is therefore required by law to let the water flow as it has been wont to flow, that all may receive and enjoy it on their lands; and no one can divert or detain it unnecessarily without doing an injury to the usufructuary right of others below him.'

"Id. Harding vs. Stamford Water Co., 41 Ct., 92.
Wadsworth vs. Tillotson, 15 Ct., 373.

"While the riparian proprietor has a right to the use of the water in its natural state, subject to the equal right of other riparian pro-prietors, it is to be remembered that 'all running streams are to a certain extent polluted: and especially are they so when they flow through populous regions or country, and the waters are utilized for mechanical and manufacturing purposes. The washings of the manured and cultivated fields, and the natural drainage of the country, of necessity bring many impurities to the stream, but these and the like sources of pollution cannot, ordinarily, be restrained by the Court.'

"Wood vs. Sutcliffe, 2 Sim. (N. S.), 163.

"Therefore, when we speak of the right of each riparian pro-prietor to have the water of an actual stream flow through his land in its natural purity, those descriptive terms must be understood in a comparative sense; as no proprietor does receive, nor can be reason-ably expected to receive, the water in a state of entire purity.

"What, then, is a reasonable use of the water of a stream by a riparian proprietor? It is such a use as will not unnecessarily injure the right of any other riparian owner. Each case must determine the reasonableness of the use after a consideration of all the facts involved. It is settled law that a question of this kind is one of fact, to be decided upon all the circumstances of each particular case.

"Keeny vs. Wood Mfg. Co., etc., 39 Ct., 581.

"And further, 'The question of reasonable use is to be deter-mined in view of the rights of others.'

"Hurlbut vs. McKane, 55 Ct., 42.
Id. Mason vs. Hoyle, 56 Ct., 255.

"At the time the sewer system of Danbury was adopted the waters of the stream at Morgan's pond were used for mill purposes and not for drinking. Assuming that the stream at this point was a non-potable one and given over to secondary uses, as the defendant claims, what rights are reserved to the riparian proprietors (as is this plaintiff) in this non-potable stream? The plaintiff as riparian proprietor upon Still river is entitled to the primary and secondary uses of the waters of that stream. No matter what servitude be im-posed upon that use, no additional and material servitude can be imposed unless it be acquired by grant or prescription. The condi-tions of the stream may be unfit for domestic uses and given over to secondary uses, but that cannot give this defendant the right to further pollute the stream in a material manner. Because others have polluted the stream is no reason why riparian proprietors should be compelled to suffer this defendant to further pollute the stream.

"In Indianapolis Water Co. vs. American Strawboard Co., 57 Fed. R., 1003, Baker, J., said: 'It is claimed that the people living along the river pollute the water by draining into it the filth and other refuse matter which accumulate on their premises. But it is no answer to a suit for creating and maintaining a nuisance that others, however many, are committing similar acts. Each one is liable to a separate suit and may be restrained.' In the well-considered case of Mayor, etc., of Baltimore, vs. Warren Mfg. Co. *et al.*, 51 Md., 105, the Court said: ' It is distinctly alleged that the filth and excrement from those erections are discharged into the stream whereby the water flowing into the lake is greatly polluted. This source of pollution should be restrained, and even though there be other sources of pollution, or that many other persons are committing the same sort of nuisance, forms no reason why this particular cause or source of pollution should not be restrained.' What then is the remedy for the riparian proprietor whose rights in a stream have been invaded?

" Id. Ferguson vs. Firmenich Mfg. Co., 77 Ia., 578.

" In Wood vs. Sutcliffe, 42 Eng. Ch. R. (2 Sim. N. S.) 164, the Court says, ' if the granting of an injunction will restore, or tend to restore those parties to the position in which they previously stood, etc., and if the injury cannot be compensated in damages, and if they use diligence, they have a right in general to come to a Court of equity and say: " Do not leave us to bring action after action for the purpose of recovering damages; but interfere with a strong hand, and prevent the continuance of the acts we complain of," etc. I say, in general, because the Court must regard not only the dry strict right, but the surrounding circumstances. I say seriously obstruct, because if the damage be small but continuous, it is serious. . . . . I say restore or tend to restore, because I conceive it is no answer to an application of this sort, for the defendant to say that other persons as well as he are polluting the stream, and that, therefore, the injunction will not restore the plaintiff to the enjoyment of his legal right, inasmuch as it will not prevent those other persons from continuing to pollute the water; for the plaintiff must sue each of the wrong-doers separately; unless, indeed, they are acting in partnership or in concert together, and the obtaining of an injunction against any one of the wrong-doers, though it may not actually restore, does tend to restore, the plaintiff to the enjoyment of his rights, as it is a step towards obtaining an injunction against each of them.'

" Id. Atty.-Gen'l vs. Leeds Corporation, 5 Ch. App. Cas. L. R., 595.

Id. Atty.-Gen'l vs. Prop'rs of Bradford Canal, 2 Eq. Cas. (L. R. 79).

Crossley vs. Lightowler, L. R., 3 Eq. Cas., 279.

Clowes vs. Staffordshire. P. Co. 8 Ch. App. Cas., 125.

Chipman vs. Palmer, 77 N. Y., 51.

Schiever vs. Village of Johnstown, 71 Hun., 233.

Wood on Nuisances, p. 582, Sect's 439, 440.

" That the sewers were built by the defendant for a public purpose under authority of law and in the exercise by it of a governmental duty is of no importance. Its use of the stream (to the material injury of the plaintiff) under its charter without obtaining the right to the use of the stream by grant or prescription and without compensation, is an illegal use.

" Kellogg vs. New Britain, 62 Ct., 239.

" That the sewage system was constructed under competent engineers and with due care, is no justification for causing material injury to the plaintiff without right.

" In Indianapolis Water Co.-vs. American Strawboard Co., 57 Fed. R., 1003, the Court said: ' It is urged that the defendant is prosecuting a business useful in its character, beneficial to the public, and furnishing employment to a large number of men, and that it is conducted with skill and prudence, and with the most improved machinery, and, if damages result, it arises from no fault of the defendant; and that in such cases the ancient rigor of the law has been modified in furtherance of industrial progress and development. This contention finds no support, either in principle or authority. It is rudimentary that no man can be· deprived of life, liberty, or property but by due process of law, nor can private property be taken, even for a public use, without just compensation first having been made or received; and under no form of government having regard for man's inalienable rights can one be permitted to deprive another of his property without his consent and without compensation, on the plea that the injury to the one would be small, and the advantage to the other, or even to the public, would be great.'

" Id. Gladfelter vs. Walker, 40 Md., 11.
        Bennoyer vs. Allen, et al., 56 Wisc., 503.

" That the sewer was constructed at great expense and without protest on the part of the plaintiff cannot raise an estoppel against his prosecution of this action.

" The defendant knew better than the plaintiff whether the construction of the sewer would prove injurious to the plaintiff. Until the plaintiff's rights were interfered with it was natural for him to submit without protest rather than embark in long and tedious litigation. The sewer might or might not become a nuisance to him; he must know the method of its use and the results of that use, before he can be charged with notice of its results. But the acts done by the defendant were done, it is claimed, with legislative sanction, and no presumption could arise that the acts to be done were to create a nuisance. The presumption was, and the plaintiff had a right to rely upon it, that the construction of the sewer would be in such a way as not to create a nuisance.

Indianapolis Water Co. vs. American Strawboard Co., *supra*.

" In Village of Dwight vs. Hayes, 150 Ill., 273, the Court says: ' So far as the village expended money or incurred liability in the matter of constructing a proposed sewer, it must be held to have done so with full knowledge of the fact that the complainant had in no way obligated himself to allow the sewage to be discharged into the creek by any binding act or instrument, and that he was at liberty at any time to recall the consent which he had already given. And if under such circumstances, and without seeking to obtain from him any grant of the right of way over his land· or the execution by him of any other binding obligation in the premises, the village authority saw fit to take steps towards the construction of the sewers, they are hardly in a position to invoke the doctrine of estoppel for the purpose of precluding the complainant from the assertion of his legal or equitable right in the premises.'

Id. Atty.-Gen'l vs. Leeds Corporation L. R., 5 Ch. App. Cas., 595.
    " Woodyear vs. Schaefer, 57 Md., 1.
        Snow vs. Williams. 16 Hun., 471.

" That the river is the only outlet for the drainage of the city and public necessity requires its use, is no justification for such use. The lower proprietor has certain rights in the stream which can only be lost by his voluntary grant or by prescriptive use. It may be of advantage to his neighbor to invade those rights as it may be of advantage for a community to invade those rights; but he is protected by the law in his possession equally against each. They cannot be taken from him against his wish, save by condemnation, and if the necessity of the community requires that he give them up, it is for the community to secure authority from the legislative body, and that will be granted only upon compensation, if the grant is to be held valid. To take without compensation and against consent is to confiscate.

"This question has been before passed upon by the courts, and the doctrine of the law well stated in Wood on Nuisances, Sec. 434, to be, 'The fact that the public convenience, or that of the preservation of public health even, requires that the sewage of a town shall be removed, and that there is no other method by which it can be disposed of except to discharge it into a running stream, will not justify the discharge there to the injury of riparian owners, and the fact that the population of the town is large, and the number of persons to be affected by the nuisance few, makes no difference.'

"Id. Atty.-Gen'l vs. Colney Hatch Lunatic Asylum, (L. R.) 4 Ch. App. Cas., 154.
Atty.-Gen'l vs. Leeds, 5 Ch. (L. R.), 589."

In the case cited the city was enjoined from discharging sewage after a given date into the stream named in the complaint.

The case went on appeal to the Supreme Court (67 Conn., p. 484), which found no error.

The judges say, in their decision: "The discharge of sewage and other noxious matter into an inland stream, to the injury of a riparian proprietor below, has been held to be an unlawful invasion of the rights of said proprietor, remediable by injunction, by the courts of nearly every state, by the federal courts, and by the courts of England." There follows the citation of numerous references.

In the case of Patrick Nolan vs. the City of New Britain, a verdict for $2,000 damages was awarded by a jury in 1897 on account of the pollution by sewage of a stream passing through his land, Piper's Brook — a tributary of Park River — and New Britain is now arranging for some change in its method of disposal. The Supreme Court of Errors, to which the case went on appeal (Patrick Nolan vs. New Britain, 69 Conn., p. 668), held that the pollution of a water-course with the sewage of a city, unless authorized by law, constitutes a public nuisance and renders the city liable in damages to a lower riparian proprietor who is specially injured thereby. No right to commit a public nuisance can be acquired by prescription nor to commit the acts which constitute such a nuisance as against a plaintiff who suffers a special injury thereby.

That this method of stopping the gross pollution of a
stream by private suit against the municipality is likely to be
adopted only after the nuisance has been long continued, is
seen by the facts stated in letters to one of the members of this
Commission, which were written by residents of Newington
eleven years ago. In May, 1887, one of them wrote as follows:

"The following facts can be proved in court: (1) That
before New Britain drained its sewage into the stream it was a
clear, pure stream.   Since then it looks dirty.   (2) Fish were
abundant in the stream, lamprey and silver eels, roach, suckers,
etc.   Now there are but few fish there, and fish have sometimes been seen to die in large numbers.   (3) People used to
cut and secure ice from the stream; now it is never done.   (4)
It stinks most vilely in the summer time when the water is
low."

Another correspondent, in February of the same year,
writes: "Hay cut along the banks has an unpleasant odor; the
grass receiving the sediment of the overflow, or upon which
the fogs rising from the stream settle, has the same odor which
we perceive when passing through the fog.   Cattle do not like
the water.   The Elmwood Creamery of West Hartford gives
notice that they will not receive milk from cows which have to
drink at the stream which runs from New Britain."

But it was ten years after this state of things obtained
before it had become so aggravated that it was morally certain
that a jury would give a verdict in favor of the rights of a
single person as against the convenience, comfort, and financial
status of a city.   Only when this point had been reached was
it safe for an individual to undertake the expense necessary
for a legal tournament.

From what goes before it appears that:

(1)   The system of water carriage and dilution is almost
universally employed in Connecticut for sewage disposal.

(2)   This system is the most economical one, and is apparently safe when the volume of sewage compared with the
volume of the stream is relatively small at all seasons of the
year, and where no town or city water supply is polluted.

(3)   In some places the volume of sewage which the river
can safely carry has already been exceeded, resulting in a
public nuisance.

(4)   If there is no change in our laws or in public opinion
on the subject, with increasing population those inland waters

of our State into which sewage is now discharged will become more and more polluted, and other smaller streams which are now clear of sewage will be used by towns and boroughs as outlets for their sewage.

(5) When the pollution of any given stream has gone so far as to create an intolerable nuisance, which can be established in a court, any and every riparian owner can bring suit against any and every city or borough contributing to such pollution, which must result in an injunction, stopping further discharge of crude sewage into the stream. While pollution so great as to secure the intervention of the courts may be very remote in the case of our largest rivers, the Connecticut and the Thames, such a condition is imminent or already exists in some of the smaller streams.

(6) When the discharge of sewage into a stream has been forbidden, the city or town so enjoined must change the whole system and partially or completely destroy its own wastes on its own premises.

It remains to inquire what means can be used to do this. It is not our purpose to describe these in great detail, but to call attention to the general principle involved, and to give some examples of their efficiency.

THE STERILIZATION OF SEWAGE.

It has been proposed to sterilize sewage before its discharge into water-ways, thus destroying its odor, and partially or completely destroying that microbe life in it which causes putrefaction, incidentally, no doubt, destroying a small portion of the organic matter of the sewage itself. Such a process is utterly worthless as a means of disposal. Sterilization is merely a postponement of decomposition. As soon as the sterilized sewage falls into a river, the antiseptic or disinfectant loses its power, by dilution, evaporation, and chemical reaction, the sewage is immediately inoculated with the germs of decay, and decomposition begins.

Colonel Waring, a recognized authority, says (Proper Disposal of Sewage, Yale Med. Jour., Nov., 1896): "There can be no proper disposal that does not secure rapid resolution into elements. In fact, no other result is admissible from the point of view of the sanitarian. Disinfection, as by the use of chlorides and of other germicide methods, simply arrests the

4

necessary process, with a certainty that whenever and wherever the power of the germicide shall cease, whether from dilution in a stream of water, from evaporation, or from whatever cause, the processes of decomposition or putrefaction must inevitably begin."

SEDIMENTATION OF SEWAGE.

This method consists in holding the sewage in large settling tanks till all the lighter material has risen to the surface and the heavier solid sewage particles, sand, etc., have fallen to the bottom.

By skimming the surface and leaving the settlings, the sewage can be discharged into the stream somewhat clarified and so a little better in its appearance. As a means of *purification* by itself, however, sedimentation is worthless. As we have seen, the most dangerous, because the most putrescible, portion of sewage is in solution and therefore is not removed by resting in a tank. The sewage is decidedly worse for the " treatment," because nothing could be devised more favorable to putrefactive decay, the very thing which it is sought to avoid.

In some cases, however, sedimentation may be useful, but only as a preliminary to further treatment.

CHEMICAL PRECIPITATION AND PURIFICATION.

By this process the stream of sewage at its outfall is continually dosed and thoroughly mixed with certain chemicals in solution or suspension in water (copperas and milk of lime are most commonly employed), and passes on to large settling tanks. By this reaction of the chemicals with each other, and with the matters suspended and dissolved in the sewage, a flocculent, bulky precipitate is formed and falls to the bottom of the tanks, leaving the sewage quite clear and much less foul than before. The process is sedimentation, hastened and made more complete by chemical reaction.

Often the sewage passes through the tanks continuously, slowly enough to deposit its sludge, and so off over a weir. In other works, a tank is filled with the sewage, which stands long enough to deposit and is then drawn off. In all cases the tanks are periodically cleared, the semi-fluid sludge being pumped out and allowed to drain till dry enough to handle or put through hydraulic presses and made into cakes, which are sold or given away to farmers or buried at the works.

Much has been said of the valuable fertilizing materials thus saved from sewage, but facts do not bear out the claims. The most available part of the nitrogen and potash in the sewage is not thrown down by the precipitation process, and the large amount of water in the sludge, even after pressing, makes the cost of freight on the fertilizing matter in it very high.

The average composition of pressed sewage sludge from the London works at Crossness is stated by Dibdin (Purification of Sewage and Water, p. 39) to be as follows:

		Per Cent.
Moisture,	. . . . .	58.06
Organic Matter,	. . . .	16.69
Mineral, "	. . . .	25.25
		100.00

The organic matter contains:

	Per Cent. on Pressed Sludge.	Per Cent. Nitrogen.
Saline Ammonia, ...	0.035	
Organic Nitrogen, calculated as		0.87
Ammonia, ...	1.025	

The mineral matter contains:

		Per Cent.
Carbonate Lime,	. . . .	7.94
Free Lime,	. . . .	2.45
Silica,	. . . .	8.08
Oxide of Iron,	. . . .	0.97
Oxide of Alumina, .	. . . .	3.39
Phosphoric Acid (phosphate of lime, 1.44),	. . . . .	0.658
Magnesia,	. . . .	trace.

Three dollars a ton, *delivered*, would be a high valuation for such material, considered as fertilizer.

On this point Shaw (Municipal Government in Great Britain, p. 124) says, describing the sewage disposal in Glasgow: " No very profitable use can be made of the sludge cakes, but it is calculated that they will at least pay for the cost of their removal to farming lands."

In Birmingham (Ib., p. 183) trouble was had with the sludge at first, but now it is spaded into shallow trenches, covered with fresh soil, and so absorbed by the land as a fertilizer.

Speaking of the disposal of London sewage, he says (Ib., p. 270): "There is a fleet of six great sludge steamers that carry the soft mud from the precipitation tanks out to the deep sea. It has been demonstrated that no successful use of the sludge can at present be made for agricultural purposes." Its use "was found to pay only a fraction of the expense of compression and transportation."

In Worcester, Mass., as the Commission is informed by the manager of the works, the sludge, after draining and drying, may contain 90 per cent. of moisture, and is given away, more than 10,000 two-horse loads being annually taken. By the presses, 3,500 gallons of sludge can be compressed into $1\frac{1}{2}$ cubic yards of cake, containing 50 to 60 per cent. of moisture.

But the main question is, How far does this chemical treatment purify sewage? It makes the sewage clear and nearly or quite colorless, but never pure enough to permit of its discharge into a potable stream. Careful experiments on chemical precipitation have been made by the Massachusetts State Board of Health at their Experiment Station at Lawrence, Mass., under the direction of Mr. Allan Hazen, which are described in the Massachusetts State Board Health Report, 1890, pp. 735-791. These experiments, made with a variety of chemicals which have been used in various works for the purpose, are thus summarized (loc. cit., p. 668):

"The best results that we have obtained — and we know of no others that are so good — leave as much as one-third of the nitrogenous organic matter of the sewage in the effluent; this is an abundant food supply for the unlimited growth of the large number of bacteria that remain. The number is called large, because five per cent. of 700,000, or 35,000, in a thimbleful, is a large number; and, if any of these are disease-producing germs, there would be no safety in turning such a liquid into a drinking-water stream; and whether it would be admissible to turn a liquid containing from one-third to one-half as much nitrogenous organic matter as sewage, with abundant bacteria, into any other stream, would depend upon nearly the same conditions that would attend discharging a less amount of sewage into the same stream. There would, however, be this difference, and it is an important one — the objectionable appearance would have been removed, and would not come again, unless, collecting in pools or in eddies or on flats, or rising to the surface on a liquid having greater specific gravity, putrefaction of the remaining organic matter should follow. The remaining organic matter would probably not putrefy as readily as the original sewage diluted to the same extent; but that it is not so stable a compound that it will not readily decompose under favorable conditions, is shown by the fact that five-sixths of it may be nitrified while moving slowly for one day over gravel stones in intermittent filtration.

"Such an effluent as may be obtained from chemical precipitation of sewage, turned into a large and rapidly-flowing stream, or into a tidal current that would soon take it to sea, would be disposed of without making a nuisance, when crude sewage might be very objectionable. Under such circumstances, and there may be others where the conditions for intermittent filtration are unfavorable, the partial purification of sewage by chemical precipitation may be the best practicable way to avoid a nuisance. But the incompleteness of the purification and the cost of 30† cents per inhabitant yearly for chemicals, together with the additional expense of manipulation and disposing of the sludge, will be likely to confine the application of chemical precipitation in the purification of sewage to narrow limits."

The remaining methods of sewage disposal which we shall notice may be classed together under the heading of purification by biological processes.

PURIFICATION BY BIOLOGICAL PROCESSES.

While very various in the size and equipment of the disposal works which these systems require, they are all alike in the general principle involved — all use the same purifying agent. This agent is microbe life of several different kinds, which in one way or another decomposes the putrescible matters of sewage, changing them into forms which are invisible and odorless, and which do not create a nuisance or defile the waters in which they are carried. These biological methods of sewage disposal are the ones to which modern sanitary science is leading us back. They have so far passed the experimental stage that experts are convinced that they are correct in principle and are practicable for use on an extensive scale. It is probable that by further experiment and experience they will be greatly improved both in efficiency, initial cost, and cost of maintenance.

It would carry us too far to discuss in detail the many engineering devices used in the systems to be described, the special conditions which each system is best suited to meet, the expense involved in establishing and in maintaining the plant. We can only describe in a general way these systems of disposal, enough to show the principle involved, and their efficiency in cleansing sewage. The first which we shall notice is

† At Worcester it is reported that the total cost of chemicals, labor, and expenses of operating the plant amounts to 29 cents per capita yearly. The expense per capita will naturally be larger where the amount of sewage handled is small.

BROAD IRRIGATION.

By this method sewage is run over land occupied by growing crops and supplies them with both water and plant food,
the cleaned water, so far as it is not evaporated through the
plants, filtering through to the subsoil, where it passes into the
ground water. The special arrangements for securing this
flow depend on the nature of the soil and the topography of the
irrigated district. The essentials are that the flow must not
be continuous, but intermittent, and that the quantity of sewage used must not be in excess of the requirements of the crop.
At certain times, as during harvest, the sewage must be entirely withheld from the fields, and, of course, during cold
weather, when there is little or no growing vegetation, a given
area will take care of much less sewage than when the weather
is warm and the crops are growing, and, consequently, evapo-
rating water rapidly.

The general application of this system of sewage disposal
is greatly limited by the fact that the sewage must be taken
care of every day in the year, while successful sewage farming
requires that the sewage should be withheld from the land at
certain times, and that in rainy weather, when the volume of
sewage is much larger, the crops need it least and the land can
take up less of it.

It has been well known for many decades that impure and
putrid water could be deodorized and cleaned by filtering it
through even a shallow layer of earth. The full explanation
of this well-known fact has only recently become known. We
shall refer to this more in detail further on, in describing the
system of "intermittent filtration." It will suffice here to say
that, when properly managed, sewage may be cleansed very
effectively by broad irrigation as above described; its dangerous elements are broken up, converted into plant food, and
pass into the vegetation, while the effluent water, clear and
sparkling, is either pure enough for drinking, or at least contains nothing putrescible and may safely be discharged into
water-ways. Many sewage farms are now in successful operation in England and on the continent of Europe, the most
widely known perhaps being those at Gennevilliers, near Paris,
where a small portion of the sewage of Paris is treated, and the
sewage farms near Berlin. The question is naturally raised by
those who are unfamiliar with these sewage farms whether

they are not noisome and offensive, whether those working on them are not poisoned, or at least injured in health by their occupation, and whether the crops raised with the help of sewage irrigation are not likely to be a source of infectious disease, like typhoid.

Dr. Alfred Carpenter, who lived in the neighborhood and had for years been familiar with the Beddington sewage farm, in a paper read to the British Medical Association in 1888, concludes (cited by Rafter, Sewage Disposal in the U. S., p. 251):

"(1) That the application of the sewage of a water-closet town to land in close proximity to dwelling houses is not injurious to the health of the inhabitants of those houses provided the sewage be fresh; that it be applied in an intermittent manner, and the effluent be capable of rapid removal from the irrigated fields. (2) The judicious application of sewage to soil of almost any kind, if it (the soil) be mainly inorganic, will satisfactorily cleanse the effluent water, and fit it for discharge into any ordinary stream, provided the area treated is not less than an acre of land for each 250 persons.* (3) That vegetable products grown upon fields irrigated by sewage are satisfactory and safe as articles of food for both animals and man. (4) That sewage farms, if properly managed, do not set up either parasitic or epidemic disease among those working on the farms or among the cattle fed upon its produce." . . .

(6) That sewage farms may be carried on in perfect safety close to populations. It is not, however, argued that the effluent water is safe to use for dietetic purposes. . . .

In the neighborhood of Berlin 17,000 acres of land are used for sewage irrigation, the works having been in use, in part, since 1876. During the five-year period from 1885 to 1890, the average annual population, as given by Mr. Roechling (Proc. Inst. C. E., Vol. CIX, Sess. 1891-92, Part III) was 1,598, — 986 men (most of them under sentence for misdemeanors), 285 women, and 327 persons under 15 years of age. Since the larger part of the population consists of paupers and incipient criminals, ill-health and a large death rate might be anticipated. But the annual death rates for the five-year period were 11.24, 9.22, 14.83, 6.79, and 4.81, a mean of 9.75. The mean death rate from zymotic diseases was 2.53. The only source of drinking water is wells, but in only one case has there been trouble from a well. No disease in cattle has resulted on the sewage farms or those adjoining. Further evidence could be given, all of which goes to show that sewage

---

* The sewage population which can be served by an acre of land must depend on the volume of the sewage. The larger the volume of sewage, per capita, other things being equal, the smaller the sewage population which an acre of land will care for. In this country as a rule the volume of sewage per inhabitant is larger than in England.

farms, properly managed, have not been a source of annoyance or disease.

It is stated that the sewage farms of Berlin began with the proportion of one acre to 250 sewage population. This was reduced to 100 in a few years, and the director hopes to reduce it to 75 and even 50, and thus to make a slight profit as well as to get rid of all evil odors, and to avoid an alleged increasing pollution of the ground water.

It seems that sewage farming as a means of complete sewage disposal is impracticable for most large cities, but as an incident and help to sewage disposal it is very valuable and may in some cases greatly lessen the expense of disposal.

The system is especially adapted for the use of isolated public institutions, schools, hospitals, asylums, and prisons, in which the amount of sewage is comparatively small, where storm water is excluded, and where there is a large area of grass land controlled by the institution.

INTERMITTENT FILTRATION.

To this process we wish to call special attention because it is more effective than any other in destroying the putrescible matters of sewage, as well as the bacteria which cause putrefaction; it is being operated successfully in many cities and villages in this country; three of our Connecticut cities have adopted it and it seems likely to be commonly adopted where sewerage systems are for the first time introduced, or to be substituted for dilution when the latter system has to be abandoned.

The process is, in brief, this: Sewage is made to flow over prepared filter beds of fine material, sand, coke, or cinders, till the material is saturated at the surface; the stream is then turned to a second bed, while the sewage sinks slowly through the saturated bed to the underdrains, and the effluent water passes off through them to some water-way. After draining and resting a while, the first bed is ready to receive sewage again, and the process is repeated.

Nature of the Process. Let us notice this more in detail. Here is a bed, newly built, consisting of an acre of level sand, like that of the Wallingford plains, for instance, four feet or more in depth, the whole area bounded by an embankment, having sewer outfalls at the corners. The gates are opened and 15,000 gallons of crude sewage are quickly discharged over the surface, so that the whole is covered to the depth of half an inch or more, when the gates are closed. The sewage disappears rapidly into the sand. The next day the surface of the bed is quite dry and generally ready to be flowed again with sewage, and so on.

After several applications of sewage to the surface, water begins to flow out from the underdrains. It may be clear or only slightly cloudy, without any smell, but when allowed to stand in a warm place for some time it becomes turbid and offensive. Chemical tests of this drainage water, or effluent, show that it is polluted, but less so than the sewage which went on to the surface above. But examinations of the effluent made day after day show that it is all the while becoming cleaner; it putrefies less rapidly on standing. Within a few days or weeks, the time depending on a variety of conditions, the effluent will not putrefy on standing. Fish will live in it indefinitely and chemical analysis shows that it is as pure, so far as organic contamination goes, as most well waters are, and that 90 per cent. or more of the soluble organic matter of the sewage has disappeared. Bacteriological tests show that from 90 to 99 per cent. of the bacterial life of the sewage has also gone. Next the quantity of sewage applied is gradually increased to 60,000 gallons daily, and still it is almost completely purified in passing through the sand " filter."

What has become of the foul matter? The first thought is that it has been retained by the " filter " and is gradually polluting it so that shortly it will become clogged and putrid and will let the sewage through uncleansed. But this is not true. There are filters at the Lawrence Experiment Station and also large filter areas in other places which have been purifying city sewage continuously for eight years without clogging, or becoming putrid and which do better work to-day than in the months immediately following their construction. Moreover, examination of the sand in the interior of these filters shows that it has no bad odor and is almost as clear of organic matter as when it was first put in. The enormous quantity of filth poured into the sand during a term of years has not evaporated, it has not gone through, it has not staid in the filter. The only other thing possible has happened to it — it has been burned up.

It is beside our purpose to follow the history of those observations and investigations, from the time of Way down to the present, which have made clear the nature of the work which goes on within the " filter " or to present the proof in detail of the facts regarding its operation.   We here state only what has been well established regarding the action of the filter and the conditions of its activity.

We have before referred to the work of microbes or bacteria in decomposing sewage.

Let us notice now, briefly, what goes on in the sand filter. About half the space in the filter, the chinks between the particles, is filled with air.   The sewage flowing down over the sand particles is thus spread in a thin sheet in contact with this air.   Those microbes or bacteria which oxidize or burn nitrogenous organic matters are thus well supplied with food, and with the air (oxygen) which is essential to their life and growth. They immediately multiply rapidly and begin to decompose the organic matter *by oxidation* (burning), changing its complex elements into carbonic acid, water, ammonia, nitrates, and nitrates.   On the other hand, the sorts of bacteria which cause putrefactive decomposition, while well supplied with food, cannot thrive in the presence of air, and so do not multiply rapidly. The oxidizing bacteria begin to get the upper hand, the bacteria of putrefaction are in the minority, the effluent begins to show less foulness than the sewage.

If the sewage were continually poured on the sand, the oxygen within the filter would be speedily exhausted or expelled by the foul water, and then the tables be turned in favor of the putrefying forces.   Instead, the flow of sewage is discontinued for a time, and as that which was first put on sinks through the sand, it draws after it a fresh supply of air, and after the period of rest leaves the sand fully aerated, and having a much larger population of oxidizing bacteria and a much smaller population of bacteria of putrefaction than at the beginning.   The oxidizing bacteria appear to attach themselves to the surface of the sand grains in a jelly-like mass of extreme thinness.   The next flowage of sewage, as a result of this increased number of oxidizing bacteria, is purified more than the last, a larger part of its organic matter is destroyed, and nitrates, the " ashes " or harmless end product of the burning of the nitrogen of animal and vegetable waste, appear in the effluent.

And so the process goes on, constantly increasing in efficiency, under proper management, up to the point of maximum work of microbe life in the filter. The dead organic matter of the sewage is not the only thing which is destroyed. The bacteria of putrefaction, which the sewage brought, are also destroyed within the filter in as great, and even greater, proportion than the organic matter.

"The cause of the death of the ordinary sewage bacteria in the tanks, especially during nitrification, is not yet entirely clear. It may be that the activity of the nitrifying organisms is of itself inimical to the ordinary bacteria; but further experiments will be necessary in order to explain all the facts in our possession." — Massachusetts State Board of Health, Part II, Report on Water Supply and Sewerage, 1888-1890, p. 847.

We speak of the process as "intermittent filtration," but it is clear that mechanical filtration is a very subordinate part of it. Simple as this operation appears at first sight, it depends for success on the most extraordinary and interesting biological processes. The filter bed is a farm where certain species of micro-organisms are grown by the acre, to the exclusion of hurtful species. Inadequate as the simple means seem to the end desired, these filter beds, properly managed, can pick out and burn up the one or two parts of dissolved organic matter from each thousand parts of water, they can change the foul sewage which lies on their surface into good drinking water at a depth of five feet, and can do this continuously year after year without any considerable fouling of the filtering sand, except within a few inches of the surface. The principle involved in intermittent filtration is the same which governs the purification of sewage by broad irrigation, previously described. The process can, of course, be much more readily observed and studied in the sand filters than on larger areas covered with farm crops.

Materials which are suitable for filter beds. In general, any coarse or fine gravel or sand, as well as coke and cinder, can be used for the purpose, and either, under proper management, will cleanse sewage effectively. Thus at the Lawrence Station, 97 per cent. of the organic nitrogenous matter of sewage and 99 per cent. of the bacteria were removed from it by "filtration" through a bed of pebbles, which were as large as robin's eggs, and this process was continued for some

months.   (Mass. State Bd. Health Rep., 1890, p. 578.)   On
the other hand, the filtration of sewage through river silt, which
was mostly a very fine sand; yielded clear effluents as pure as
the other.   But convenience of management, as well as the
amount of sewage which can be daily cleansed on a given area,
depend very much on the fineness — the mechanical condition
— of the filter material.   If the material is very coarse, great
care is needed to evenly distribute the sewage over the whole
surface, and it must be run on the bed very slowly, as otherwise it will pass through the filter too quickly without giving
time for oxidation or cleansing.   If the material, on the other
hand, is too fine, it holds the sewage so strongly by capillary
attraction that its passage through the filter is greatly retarded,
and the necessary time allowed for drainage and aeration is so
great that the quantity of sewage purified in a given time is
very limited.   Peat cannot under any circumstances be used
as a filtering medium for sewage; good arable soil is also unsuitable for the purpose.   The light, leachy soils of this State,
such as are found at Wallingford, Meriden, and many other
places, are admirable materials for making sewage filters.

Efficiency of Sand Filters.   In a following table are given
data showing, in the last three columns, the percentage purification effected by experiment filters at the Lawrence Station,
for the year 1895, each filter having an area of 1/200 acre
(Mass. State Bd. Health, Rep. 1895, p. 461), as measured by
the percentage removal of albuminoid ammonia (putrescible
nitrogenous matter) and bacteria, and by the percentage reduction of " oxygen consumed."

EFFICIENCY OF LAND FILTERS.

No. of Filter.	Depth of Sand, inches.	SIZE OF SAND.		In Operation Since	Av. Rate of Filtration Gals. per Acre, Daily.	AVERAGE PER CENT. REMOVED OF		
		Effective Size* (Millimeters), 10 per cent. finer than,	Uniformity** Coefficient.			Albuminoid Ammonia.	Oxygen Consumed.	Bacteria.
1	63	0.48	2.4	Jan. 10, 1888,	67,000	89	86	97.55
2	60	0.08	2.0	Dec. 19, 1887,	34,000	97	95	99.98
4	60	0.04	2.7	Dec. 19, 1887,	15,000	98	96	99.99
5a	63	1.40	2.4	Sept. 14, 1891,	66,000	85	83	94.50
6	44	0.35	7.8	Jan. 12, 1888,	56,000	90	89	99.10
9a	60	0.17	2.0	Nov. 18, 1890,	66,000	90	89	98.70
10	60	0.35	7.8	July 18, 1894,	30,000	94	90	99.50

* The "effective size" of a sample of sand is such a size that ten per cent. of the material is of smaller grains and ninety per cent. of larger grains than the size given. The results obtained at Lawrence indicate that the finer ten per cent. have as much influence upon the action of a material in filtration as the coarser ninety per cent
** The "uniformity coefficient" designates the ratio of the size of grain which has sixty per cent. finer than itself to the size which has ten per cent. finer than itself.
For discussion of the physical properties of sands and gravels, with reference to their use for filtration, see Mass. State B'd Health Rep't, 1892, p. 541.

Here are filters, some of which have been in continuous use for eight years, disposing of from 15,000 to 66,000 gallons per acre of sewage daily, and removing from 83 to 96 per cent. of the putrescible nitrogenous matter, and from 94½ to 99.99 per cent. of bacteria.

These results show that with skillful management, from 30,000 to 70,000 gallons of sewage may be purified every twenty-four hours on an acre of filter bed. Other experiments indicate that an acre of land will purify 100,000 gallons of crude sewage per day *during the spring, summer, and fall,* but the amount which can be purified per acre *in winter,* in this latitude, is very much less.

Professor L. P. Kinnicutt (Jour. Am. Chem. Soc., Vol. XX, No. 3, Mar., 1898, p. 187) states that from observations made at several disposal works in Massachusetts, he believes that twice, at least, and possibly four times, as much area is required in winter as in summer. If less skill is used in management, the amount purified will be smaller or else the degree of purification will be lower both summer and winter. Much larger quantities of sewage could have been handled on these beds if

those operating them had been content with a less thorough
purification.   Under ordinary conditions and working on a
large scale, it is quite probable that the degree of purification
would be considerably lower than in the Lawrence experiment.

Odor from the beds.   It is often stated that these filtration
beds are odorless.   It is true that at some seasons no odor can
be noticed even in their immediate neighborhood.   But it is
not true that they are always free from odor, even when properly managed.   On warm days in March, when the frost is
coming out of the ground, and on close " muggy " days in summer, there is a distinct sewage smell noticeable at a short distance from the beds.   This comes largely from the moist
sludge, the solid matter in the sewage, which remains on the
surface until raked up.   The odor is not intense, it is not widespread, but it is certainly there.   It would not be wise to use
for sewage disposal a small tract of land, close to a popular
highway or in a thickly-populated district.   The city should
own enough land, unsettled, to make the odors unnoticeable
in dwelling houses.   A well-managed sewage farm ought not
to be as offensive to the public as a well-managed rendering
establishment, but neither of them should be installed in a
thickly-settled place.

Permanency of the filter beds.   After six years of careful
experiment at the Lawrence Station, these conclusions have
been reached (Mass. State Bd. Health, Rep't 1894, p. 490):
" (1) With the same main body of sand, sewage filters may
continue to purify sewage for an indefinite time, provided they
receive proper treatment to insure sufficient ventilation for the
oxidation and nitrification of the applied organic matters.   (2)
That the permanency of sewage filters is independent of the
size of the filtering material, and is directly dependent upon
the treatment which they receive."

Two years later (Mass. State Bd. Health, Rep't 1896, p.
471) the Board reports: " There are now at the Station six
filters, 1/200 of an acre in area and containing different
grades of filtering material, which have been in operation for
periods varying from five to nine years. . . .   Since 1893 there
has been no removal of filtering material from any of the large
experimental filters, and the removal or destruction of the
large amount of organic matters of the sewage has been accomplished without impairing the action or shortening the life of
the filter.   That is to say, this organic matter has either passed

from the filters into the air in gaseous forms of carbon and nitrogen, or has united with a base and passed away in the effluent in the form of mineral salts in solution."

Effects of frost. On this point the observations made by the Massachusetts Board of Health and the experience of the Massachusetts Municipal Sewage Disposal Works have special value, as they apply directly to our conditions. Our winters are not more rigorous than theirs. The Massachusetts State Board of Health, Report 1894, p. 530, sums up the present knowledge on the subject as follows:

" (1) In Massachusetts the qualitative efficiency of sewage filters may be less in winter, owing chiefly to inactivity of micro-organisms caused by exposure to low temperature; and from our present knowledge it does not seem advisable to allow filters exposed to the weather to rest in winter, even for limited periods. . . . (2) Qualitative deterioration is a serious matter in winter, because when a period of biological reconstruction is necessary, nitrification cannot be promptly re-established, as is the case in summer, but requires a period of several weeks and possibly months. (3) While nitrification cannot be readily re-established in winter, it has been learned that in those cases where this process was in a satisfactory state at the beginning of the winter it could, by proper treatment, be preserved during the cold season. . ʻ. . (6) The less exposure to cold winter weather which the surface of the filter undergoes, the greater the number of heat units saved, and the better will be the results, both quantitatively and qualitatively. (7) The application of sewage to limited portions, such as trenches, in the case of filters of fine materials, concentrates the heat, thereby aiding in preserving the biological processes and in maintaining the qualitative efficiency. . . . (9) The composition of sewage, and particularly the amount of sludge applied to filters, is a much more marked factor in winter than in summer, even in the case of experimental filters where especial lines of treatment to keep the filters in operation are feasible."

In this connection we may cite an experience of the Framingham Sewer Committee (Rep. Sewer Com., Framingham, Mass., 1893, p. 120):

" Much apprehension was felt by many of our citizens, when this system was first recommended to the town, that, during extreme cold weather, much difficulty would be encountered in disposing of the sewage. During the last winter, which has been the coldest known for years, several practical tests were made, to determine exactly how long it would take to remove the frost from the soil. These tests were made at the suggestion of representatives of the State Board of Health, and were successful far beyond our most sanguine expectations. They were as follows:
" January 9, 18 inches frost. 10 inches snow; temperature 6 degrees below zero; pumped 300,000 gallons sewage; January 10, pumped on same bed 150,000 gallons sewage; underdrain started in six hours; January 11, frost entirely out in some places; January 12, frost almost entirely gone, and sewage all disappeared; tempera-

ture of sewage 50 Fahrenheit; area of bed, seven-eighths acre. No sewage matter has been pumped on the bed since September.

"On January 16th, another test was made on bed of one acre. Pumped 500,000 gallons sewage, temperature 49 Fahrenheit; January 17, pumped 175,000 gallons. On this bed there was fifteen inches of snow and from twenty to thirty inches of frost. Temperature of weather January 16th, 6 below; 17th, 20 below; 18th, 4 below zero. Underdrain started in 7 hours from commencement of pumping. January 18, frost all gone in some places; 19th, frost nearly all disappeared and sewage had entirely disappeared. Not more than ten inches of frost has been encountered there previous to this year."

Practical experience in sand filtration of sewage. More convincing, perhaps, to some, than the results obtained with small experimental filters under the management of chemists and bacteriologists will be the actual results of the work of sewage disposal works in cities and boroughs, managed by practical men, on the general plan suggested by the experiments of investigators. South Framingham excludes storm water from its sewers, and in 1889 began to purify its sewage by intermittent filtration. A full description of the plant, with a plan of the beds, is found in Massachusetts State Board Health, Report 1892, p. 560. There are seventy acres of land owned by the town, of which twelve acres are prepared for filtration beds. On a large part of these, crops have been raised with favorable effect on the purification of the sewage. The following extracts from the town reports will show what the actual working of the beds has been for eight years.

Report of 1890. "At the irrigation field the sewage has been disposed of on an area not exceeding one and a half acres. Most of the sewage during the winter has been directed by means of shallow ditches to flow over stump land. The surplus, — a comparatively small quantity, — was turned into the beds. Both beds and unprepared land have worked very satisfactorily. The greatest depth of frost at the farm over which the sewage flowed was three inches; this, in five hours after commencement of pumping, had completely disappeared. No sewage is to be seen outside of the ditches forty-five minutes after the pumps have stopped."

Report of 1891. "At the sewage field no trouble has been experienced in disposing of the sewage. In the summer season nearly all has been allowed to flow on the stubble land; during the last three months two of the filtration beds have been used. No trouble from frost has been experienced in either method of disposal. No complaint has been made to us of any offensive odors arising from the sewage fields and we do not anticipate any difficulty from that source."

Report of 1892. "At the sewage farm no trouble has been experienced in disposing of the sewage, and its treatment has met the approval of the State Board of Health, who, in their last report, commented favorably on the disposition of sewage at the Framingham sewage farm. Some experiments have been made the past year in raising crops at the irrigation field, and enough has been accomplished to convince your Committee that quite an income can be derived by the town from this means; and your Committee believes that the raising of crops should be increased from year to year as the condition of the ground will admit of it. This can be done with little or no extra expense."

Report of 1894. "At the sewer farm everything is in a most satisfactory condition. No trouble has been experienced in disposing of the sewage, and an analysis made by the State Board of Health, samples being taken every two (2) weeks during the entire year, shows that ninety-eight (98) per cent. of the impurities have been removed from the sewage. . . . There were raised on the filter beds the past year, a large quantity of field corn, squash, beans, potatoes, and cabbage, which, owing to Section 17 of the town's by-laws, we are obliged to sell at public auction, selling much below their value, by reason of the uncertainty of just how much each bed would yield. . . . Your Committee believe that in a few years the sewer farm will, if properly managed, become self-sustaining."

Report of 1896. "At the sewer farm everything is in a most satisfactory condition. During the year three (3) new beds have been constructed and all the banks have been levelled up and the appearance of the whole farm has been very much improved. The crops which have been raised, mostly field corn, were fully as abundant as formerly, but, owing to the low price of Western corn, we were unable to obtain as high a price as the year previous, but the amount sold netted the town three hundred and seven dollars and eighty-five cents ($307.85). The analysis of the effluent at the sewer farm, by the State Board of Health," shows satisfactory purification.

Report of 1897. "We have also been obliged to make over three of the filter beds, the surfaces of which had become *quite uneven*, so that their efficiency had become impaired to quite an extent. . . . The amount of sewage continues to increase, the average daily amount now being about 400,000 gallons."

Report of 1898. "The buildings and grounds at the pumping station are in good order, and the plant is operated at a very small expense for labor. The sewer farm is in a satisfactory condition, the filter beds are doing their work well, as is shown by the analysis of the effluent water made at intervals by the State Board of Health. The crop of corn raised the past season sold at auction for $290.50."

Late in October, 1898, in reply to letters of inquiry addressed to the managers of all sewage filtration works in Massachusetts, we received the following information regarding the practical working of the beds:

Medfield. (System introduced in 1886.) "No trouble with odor from the beds, nor with freezing in winter, nor with clogging of the beds."

Gardner, Mass. (System introduced in 1891.) "No trouble with odors. Owing to scarcity of suitable filter material, our filter beds having an area of only about two and one-half acres, and to the formation of ice, we cannot scrape

5

and clean the surface of the beds in winter, so that they become somewhat clogged during the extreme cold weather. We do not notice any decrease in efficiency of the beds from year to year. Each spring, after the ice is gone, we plow the surface deeply, after cleaning off the winter's deposit, then harrow and smooth the beds, and they work just as well as ever. Our minimum flow of sewage is about 225,000 gallons daily."

Westboro, Mass. (System introduced in 1893.) "We have no reason for complaint of odors; the sludge hole near the gatehouse is the only thing that ever smells, and twenty rods from that you would not know it was in existence. The beds never freeze. We have one hundred and fifty thousand gallons of spring water a day through the winter months, so we can cover the beds, that the soil of the beds does not freeze, so they filter all winter. The decrease in efficiency is very slight, if any. We plant the beds to corn every year, which helps to remove the foul matter. I might say the beds are working very satisfactorily.

Brockton, Mass. (System introduced in 1894.) "There is no serious trouble at any time from odor from the filter beds. Odor is most noticeable during the months of March and April, when the frost is coming out of the ground. The nearest dwelling is one-half mile distant from the beds, except the house occupied by the man in charge, who, together with his wife and children, live there throughout the year."

"During the first winter after the beds were put in operation there was trouble with frost. The next winter all the beds were furrowed. Flowing in these furrows the sewage exposes less surface to the air and hence holds its heat better. Subsidence cannot take place till the sewage has thawed the sand below, and meantime a thin sheet of ice forms over the surface. Subsidence of the liquid sewage follows, but the thin ice sheet spanning the trenches protects them in great measure from further freezing. In time, however, an impervious layer of sludge forms in the bottom of the trenches, which impairs the rapidity of the filter. The objectionable feature of furrows is the increased difficulty of cleaning them in the spring. As long as the sludge deposit remains frozen, no odor results; but when spring comes the odors are manifest, though not constituting a nuisance by any means. The deposits were removed early in April, since which time no odor sufficient to be called objectionable by the most sensitive has been apparent."

Regarding the permanence of the beds, the engineer says: " The clogging of sand usually extends but a few inches below the surface, so that the bed, after being raked and allowed to rest for a short time, is as efficient as before. I would say in addition that we have twenty-three beds of one acre each, and we use from six to eight beds daily.

Natick, Mass. (System introduced in 1896.) " Our filter beds are two miles from the center of the town — nearest farmhouses about half a mile distant. Our system is just entering on its third year; only 250 connections; very much ground water enters the system which assists the filtration, and no large amount of organic matter remains on the surface, which is frequently scraped. There is an odor noticeable in the vicinity at times, but not continuous. On account of the small number of connections and the large amount of ground water entering the system (two-thirds of entire pumping of 250,000 gallons per day), and the short time in use, we have had no difficulty as yet with clogging of the beds. By watching gates and changing twice or more times a day, what freezes on the beds in winter will thaw out soon after the introduction of sewage the next morning. We are working six beds, each a square acre. In the summer and fall one bed will handle the pumping of two days without change, while in the winter and early spring three beds are often employed in one day. Heavy snowfalls also cause some trouble."

The first works for the disposal of town sewage by intermittent filtration in Massachusetts were built at Lenox in 1876. Amherst followed in 1881, Medfield in 1886, Framingham in 1889, Gardner and Marlborough in 1891, Westborough in 1893, Brockton 1894, Leicester and Natick in 1896. Brief descriptions of these several plants and analyses of their sewage and effluent waters will be found in the Reports of Massachusetts State Board of Health, 1893, pp. 563-594; 1895, pp. 601-635; 1896, pp. 581-597.

In our own State the system of sewage disposal by sand filtration was adopted in Meriden and Litchfield in 1892, in Bristol in 1895, and in Danbury in 1897. In all these places in Massachusetts and Connecticut the system is to-day in successful operation. It is also in use in many other places, chiefly in this latitude or to the south of it, but these are named because they are in our immediate neighborhood.

Need of strict regimen in management. A study of the

means by which sewage is cleansed in the sand filters, as well
as of the experience of those who have practically operated
them, makes it clear that they require constant care and great
regularity in their treatment.   The sand filters are not dead,
they are teeming with active life, and this life depends on certain things: food supply, air, heat, etc., and on regularity in
the supply of these things.   To leave the sewage running on a
bed for twelve hours beyond the prescribed time, because of a
severe storm or a circus in the next town, is as culpable as to
leave a herd of cows or a barn full of horses without food or
drink for the same length of time, and may be vastly more
harmful to the property and health of the community.   If
sewage stands too long on a filter, the air supply is reduced
below the normal, the nitrifying microbes are checked in their
work, perhaps destroyed in part, and thus the filter is made less
efficient, not for a single day only, but for a considerable period
of convalescence. If excessive quantities of sewage are poured
on, the whole filter may become foul and require weeks to
clear itself.   " It becomes evident that the efficiency of a filter
depends much upon steadily following a course of action, and
requiring every part of it to accomplish the same work at regular intervals of time.   The filter becomes a delicate organization, adapted to what is required of it, if its possibilities are
not exceeded; but any change from the requirements is likely
to render necessary weeks of time before the filter can become
adapted to the changed conditions."   (Mass. State Bd. Health,
Part II, Report on Water Supply and Sewerage, 1888-1890,
p. 25.)   No chemical or bacteriological skill is necessary for the detail of management on the sewage field,
but there is needed a man who is absolutely faithful in carrying out the directions of the city engineer or selectmen, who
is intelligent, and who has acquired experience in meeting all
the vicissitudes of weather and knows the individual peculiarities of the beds.   The Commission have had occasion to observe the havoc wrought by a field superintendent without
these qualifications, and to see a disposal field which had been
working perfectly, made inefficient and a menace to health because of a city election.   A superintendent, who was faithful
and competent but incapacitated from further work, presumably, because of his views on questions of national finance or
legislative representation, was replaced by a man utterly without experience in managing a sewage field.   But the new man

had these qualifications: he was presumably sound in his views on national finance; he had great influence in his end of the ward; he had worked for the ticket and therefore he had earned the patriot's reward—steady light work and sure pay from the public funds. As well might a city overturn its fire and engineering departments, or its police force, after an election, as the management of its sewage disposal works. " Offensive partisanship " gets a new meaning and illustration when, in the way just referred to, the sewage disposal works of a city are neglected or mismanaged. The same trouble has been experienced in England. " There cannot be too plain speaking upon this matter. It has for years been a standing evil, and many who have had to do with sewage treatment have keenly felt the disadvantages they have been laboring under when they see a delicately worked-out process handed over to the fumbling of a farm laborer, or superannuated foreman, or an engine driver, without the slightest knowledge of the real engine which he has to drive, namely, the process entrusted to his charge." (Purification of Sewage and Water, Dibdin, p. 82.)

The data which have been given above make it clear that where land and suitable filtering material are available, the system of intermittent filtration will thoroughly cleanse sewage so that the effluent from it may safely be discharged into any water-way not used as a water supply, and that this effluent can neither putrefy by itself nor induce putrefaction in other waters. There may be cases where, for various reasons, this method is inapplicable and some other way must be found. But where suitable filter beds can be made, near at hand, and the sewage delivered to them at any reasonable cost, filtration with auxiliary sewage farming seems to offer the best solution of the question of sewage disposal for our larger towns and cities.

Thus we come back again to the old farm way of getting rid of dish water! Throw it on the surface, not always in one place, never in a steady stream, but always intermittently. The housekeeper of fifty years ago unwittingly cultivated nitrifying microbes and cleansed her waste water by their help, without offense to any one. The modern city, with modern knowledge, may, and in some cases must, do the same thing for its sewage. Smaller cities and boroughs which have not yet provided themselves with a sewer system would do

well at the outset to get a sewage disposal field, if possible
near at hand, in an unsettled neighborhood, before the growth
of the place has made such property hard to secure.   A few
acres can then be prepared to take care of the present flow of
sewage, and more can be put in order as the growth of the
place makes it necessary.

It sometimes happens that a village grows in such a way
that there is immediate need of a system of sewers and provision for sewage disposal, with due allowance for subsequent
enlargement, long before the village has a population large
enough to bear the initial expense of such an undertaking.   It
is suggested that in such cases a wealthy citizen, who wishes
to leave some memorial of himself in his native town, could do
nothing which would contribute more to the health and comfort of its inhabitants than to establish and equip a tract of land
for sewage disposal by filtration with or without farm irrigation.   While such a place might not gratify the æsthetic sense,
perhaps, as a watering-trough, with a verse of Scripture, or a
chime of bells, or a stained-glass window might gratify it, it
would yet teach a daily lesson of cleanliness, and it would protect the community from much preventable sickness and death.
In itself it would be far from unsightly, which is more than
can be said of very many " memorial " atrocities.

DIBDEN'S METHOD OF SEWAGE FILTRATION.

In England, where sand suitable for making sewage filters
is not as common as in this part of the United States, certain
porous materials, especially coke, cinders, clinker, burned clay,
etc., have been substituted.   Mr. W. J. Dibden, a chemist of
experience, as the outcome of experiments made with London
sewage, has devised a filtration system, differing in construction and management from that already described, but similar
in principle, i. e., the organic matter of the sewage is destroyed
by microbe action.   This system, at first applied to the effluents
from chemical precipitation works, has now been used successfully for crude sewage and also for factory wastes.   Sutton, England, was the first town to introduce the system, which
is thus described by Professor L. P. Kinnicutt (Jour. Am.
Chem. Soc., Vol. XX, No. 3, Mar., 1898, p. 189):

" The population draining into the sewers is about 13,000, and
the dry weather flow equals about 400,000 gallons per day. The
sewage system is on the ' separate ' plan, rainfall being excluded,

yet during wet weather a large volume of subsoil water gains access to the sewers. The town contains few, if any, manufacturing establishments, and the sewage may be considered as a strong domestic sewage.

"Sutton formerly purified its sewage by the use of chemicals, and one of the precipitating tanks was utilized for the construction of a (Dibden) filter. On the floor of the tank, whose area was 183 square yards, was laid a six-inch drain, connected with nineteen lateral drains three inches in diameter. The main drain was provided with a six-inch valve so that the filter could be emptied or filled at will. The pipes were covered with very coarse, burnt clay, and upon this was placed a layer of burnt clay three feet deep, the smallest pieces of which could not pass through a half-inch mesh. The total capacity of this filter was 218 cubic yards, and when filled with burnt clay it would hold 13,500 gallons.

"The crude sewage, after passing through iron screens to intercept large pieces of paper, is carried directly to the filter, the flow being stopped as soon as the sewage level reaches within an inch or so of the burnt clay. The time required for filling the filter is about one hour. The filter is allowed to remain full for about two hours, and then emptied, the time occupied in emptying it being one and one-half hours. The filter is then allowed to rest for two hours, after which it is again charged. The effluent obtained is clear and without any strong odor, and appears to the eye equal to the best effluent obtained by the chemical precipitation process. From analyses made three or four times each month, from November, 1896, to June, 1897, and published in the *Surveyor* for July 9, 1897, the amount of purification, as calculated from the albuminoid ammonia, equals about fifty-eight per cent., while the amount of suspended matter is reduced from fifty to two and three-tenths grains per gallon.

"The work of the filter compares favorably with the results obtained by many of the chemical precipitation processes, and, though twelve months is possibly too short a period from which to draw conclusions, the city is now constructing three more bacteria filters, and there seems to be no question that the above method leads one to entertain the view that, with domestic sewage, a purification equal to that obtained by chemical precipitation is possible with comparatively small, artificially prepared filters: and from experiments which are now being made, it seems possible that some similar plan can be used with the sewage of a manufacturing city.

"The effluent obtained by the bacteria filter when running at the rate of 1,000,000 gallons per acre, is not sufficiently pure to drain into a water-course, whose volume only equals or is less than the volume of the effluent; and when the stream runs through a thickly populated district as is the case in Sutton, the first effluent must be run through another filter of the same size and construction, filled, however, with burnt clay, all of which is small enough to pass through a half-inch mesh. The effluent from this second filter, at the time of my visit, was bright, clear, and without odor. The average amount of albuminoid ammonia in this effluent, during the seven months from November to June, was 0.243 part in 100,000 parts, the original sewage containing 1.130 parts, and the amount of suspended matter was reduced to 0.703 grain per gallon."

In the Jour. Soc. Chem. Ind., 1898, April, p. 315, Dibden gives the results of the operation of the Sutton filters

for eighteen months, on crude sewage. The degree of purification is measured by the oxygen consumed, reduction of
albuminoid ammonia, increase of nitrites, etc. From February, 1897, to March, 1898, inclusive, the average monthly
purification ranged from 48 to 90 per cent. of the albuminoid
ammonia contained in the crude sewage, the average of all
being 77 per cent. The Dibden system is stated to have also
worked successfully with sewage strongly polluted with some
special factory waste. It is stated that at Leeds during six
months 200,000 gallons per day have been successfully purified, the effluents being bright, odorless, save for a slight earthy
smell at times, and absolutely non-putrescible. Fish have
lived and thrived in them for three months.

The town of Oswestry, England, population 10,000, has
adopted this system after experiments lasting nearly a year,
during which 15,000 gallons of crude sewage were daily
treated, removing about 95 per cent. of the organic matters on
the average. The following brief description of the experimental works is taken from the Oswestry and Border Counties
Advertiser, kindly sent to us by Mr. R. O. Wynne-Roberts,
the borough surveyor and engineer:

"Some £30 were spent in the making of the necessary tanks. .
. . A stream of the partially separated sewage flows into a gauge
tank. It then passes over a two-inch notch, by which 15,000 gallons per day are dealt with, and along wooden troughs on to beds
of riddled cinders, taken from the rubbish heaps. There are four
of these beds, each 16 yards in superficial area, and having a depth
of 4 feet 6 inches. During its passage through the cinders the
sewage, which contains the germs of its own destruction, is purified
by the bacteria which are cultivated. In the filter beds these
creatures live on the filth, and while the tank stands full, purify
the liquid. . . . The four beds are used alternately, and Mr.
Roberts, by an ingenious and simple contrivance, has devised an
arrangement by which they are controlled automatically. The sewage from the gauging tank is received in a center basin, and flows
thence by a valve on to one of the beds. When the water reaches
a certain level it overflows along a pipe into a tumbling basin which,
when partially full, tips over, and in doing so closes the valve of
bed No. 1, and opens that of No. 2, which is the next to receive the
sewage. Two hours are taken to fill a tank, and in that time it is
stated by experts the bacteria have had ample time to do their work.
Bed No. 2 next overflows and automatically closes its own valve,
and opens that of No. 3, at the same time discharging the sewage
of No. 1, which has been standing full. This discharge takes ten
or fifteen minutes, after which the bed remains empty for some
hours, and the bacteria in the filters get their necessary supply of
air. Though this treatment is continually going on, there is no filth
left in the cinders, the millions of microbes having destroyed all

trace of it. From these beds the effluent, which is of the usual light gray color when leaving bacteria-filters, passes on to another bed made of screenings from the rubbish heap, through which it percolates. This is the end of the treatment, and the final effluent is remarkably good, both in appearance and taste. In looks it is little different from spring water, and it has absolutely no smell."

A description of the works for treating all the sewage of Oswestry, communicated to us by Mr. Wynne-Roberts, is as follows:

"The Town Council were so satisfied with the results of the experiments that they voted £200 to construct large filter beds; to this sum they have already added £620, making a total of £820, spent out of revenue. The large beds are arranged in two series, called for distinction the Primary and Secondary Beds. The Primary Beds are nine in number, each measuring 60 feet by 60 feet by 4½ feet deep. The Secondary Beds, also nine in number, measure 60 feet by 50 feet by 4 feet deep. The primary bed takes about 1½ hours to fill, and will stand full for about 3 hours, during which time the bacteria perform their purifying functions. The whole of the beds are made of simple earth embankments with the usual slopes, no concrete or brickwork used whatever. The beds are underdrained by means of 4-inch agricultural drain pipes, laid in parallel rows three feet apart, connecting to the main collecting channel and thence to the center valve. The center valve was designed by our surveyor and is automatic in action. The sewage flows through a trough on the top and is distributed to the various beds in their turn. At the same time the outlet pipes are opened according to the time the beds have been standing full. By means of these center valves manual labor, superintending the working of the beds, is reduced in day time to a minimum, while it dispenses with night and Sunday labor entirely. The cost of the complete series of beds will be about £1,500, the land cost £1,000, making a total of £2,500. The annual burden will be about £100."

Dibden's system of filtration is well worth further study, as it may possibly be suited for places which cannot get access to suitable filtration areas of sufficient size. An acre of filter surface, arranged on Dibden's plan, will apparently take care of vastly more sewage per day than an acre of sand filter, though the degree of purification effected, where large quantities of sewage are treated, is not so great.

Roscoe, in a report on the effluents from disposal works (Jour. Soc. Chem. Ind., 1896, p. 916), says: "So far as chemical results are concerned, land filtration far excels the results of either coke or cinder filtration"; but it is pointed out that the volume of effluent which can be treated permanently on land is limited, as compared with the volume which can be treated by artificial filters.

THE SEPTIC TANK.

The last method of treating sewage which we shall notice
is the so-called septic tank. This is rather to be regarded as
a method of preparing sewage for intermittent filtration than
a system complete in itself. We have already spoken of the
two great classes of microbes, those which live only where air
(oxygen) is absent, or its supply very limited, and those which
require abundance of air. In the first class are the microbes
of putrefaction which decompose the organic matters of sewage, yielding gaseous and solid products which have an offensive odor. The septic tank is a device for decomposing sewage
by the microbes of putrefaction, with exclusion of air. One
has recently been installed at Exeter, England, planned by
Mr. Cameron, and thus described by Professor Kinnicutt
(Jour. Am. Chem. Soc., Vol. XX, No. 3, March, 1898, p.
192):

"The plant consists of the so-called septic tank, which is an
underground tank built of cement concrete, sixty-four feet long,
eighteen feet wide, and of an average depth of seven feet, having
a capacity of about 53,000 gallons, and of five filters made of coke
breeze and furnace clinkers, about five feet in depth and covering
all together an area of 400 square yards, having a capacity of 695
cubic yards. The crude sewage, as it arrives at the plant, passes
through a railing to prevent large objects from entering the tank,
while all small particles and solids in suspension pass freely to a
grit chamber, which is divided in two, each part having an inlet
into the tank. The inlets are close to the bottom of the tank, and
the aperture of the inlet pipes is smaller on the tank side than on
the sewer side, so that the sewage enters the tank with considerable force. The outlets are also underneath the surface of the
water so as not to admit air or light, and so arranged that the water
at the middle depth alone escapes. They are gauged so that the
rate of flow may be measured; usually it is about 3,000 gallons per
hour. The sewage from the septic tank is discharged simultan-
eously on two of the bacteria filters, arranged according to Dibden's
method. When these two filters are full they are emptied of their
contents, and, while being emptied, the sewage from the tank
passes on to others. The fifth filter remains idle one week, when it
takes the place of the one that has longest been in use. Thus each
filter remains idle one week out of every four. The filling and
emptying of these filters is done automatically by an ingenious arrangement patented by Mr. Cameron and is said to be most satisfactory.

"The action inside the tank is essentially of a putrefactive
nature, no nitrates being formed. The organic matter is decomposed, or rather broken up into simpler forms, a large amount being
rendered soluble, while at the same time ammonia and, I believe,
free nitrogen, are being formed. According to analyses made by
Dibden, the amount of oxidizable organic matter in solution is reduced about 30.8 per cent., the free ammonia about 26.9 per cent..

the albuminoid ammonia about 17 per cent., and the suspended solids about 55 per cent. Pearmain and Moor, who have made a report on the process, state that there is no accumulation of sludge in the tank beyond a small amount of thin black sediment, which they report is so slight that a year's accumulation would scarcely be worth the trouble of removing. F. J. Commin, in a report on the process, published in the *Lancet* for December, 1896, says that the deposit is very fine and inorganic, and that in a small tank, after seven months' continual working, and after quite 2,000,000 gallons of sewage had passed through the tank, the deposit was less than four inches over a surface of twenty-four feet by nine feet.

".On top of the liquid in the tank there is a layer of flocculent matter from two to two and one-half inches in thickness, and from all accounts this seems to have been formed during the first few weeks that the tank was used and not to have increased much in thickness since that time. It appears to be composed of organic matter, formed, I believe, from the suspended matter in the sewage; and from all the information I have been able to obtain, it seems as though the organic matter in this flocculent layer was at first partially decomposed by the putrefactive organisms. Portions of it then sank to the bottom of the tank, where further action took place. Bubbles of gas collected around the fragments that had been carried down, causing them to rise to the surface, and this process went on till the residue that remained at the bottom contained very little organic decomposable matter. . . .

" According to Dibden the liquid that comes from the tank is of a brownish yellow color, offensive, and contains 2.73 grains per gallon of free ammonia, 0.175 grain of albuminoid ammonia, and the amount of oxygen absorbed from potassium permanganate in four hours is 1.405 grains per gallon. It contains no nitrates nor nitrites. The original sewage contained at the same time 3.778 grains free ammonia, 0.212 grain albuminoid ammonia, and the oxygen absorbed from the potassium permanganate was 2.028 grains per gallon. This liquid is passed upon the filters as has been described, and the effluent from these filters contains 1.705 grains free ammonia, 0.078 grain albuminoid ammonia, 0.253 grain nitrogen as nitrites, 0.353 grain nitrogen as nitrates, no suspended matter, and the absorbed oxygen from the potassium permanganate in four hours is only 0.388 grain per gallon.

" The great advantage of the septic tank process, if it does what it appears to do, is that so large an amount of suspended matter is removed from the sewage that there will be very much less trouble with the clogging up of the surface of filter beds in winter, and consequently an area that is large enough for the purification in summer will be more nearly, or possibly quite, sufficient for the work during the winter months.

" It is also claimed that a large amount of the organic matter in solution is removed in the septic tank; and if this is so, which appears probable from the analyses that have been made, it may not be too much to hope that future developments in this direction, taken in connection with the using of the cubical capacity of a bacteria filter, may so reduce the area required for purification, that filter beds may, without too great expense, be protected from snow and ice."

Sailors are familiar with the fact that impure and even foul water, if barrelled up, will in time " work itself clear," so that it makes excellent drinking water. The process which goes on in the water barrel is in its nature like what goes on in this septic tank.

The use of the septic tank is still in the experimental stage. We cannot regard the efficiency of the Dibden system of rapid filtration through coarse coke breeze or cinder as yet fully determined, but the accounts of its operation so far make it seem probable that it will greatly increase the working capacity of a given area of filter surface, and thus reduce the cost of sewage disposal by filtration for large cities.

The system of chemical precipitation has been fully tested, so that its possibilities and limitations are thoroughly understood.

Chemical precipitation, the septic tank, and Dibden's coke breeze filters dispose of most of the sludge, which greatly limits the filtering capacity of sand filters, but these systems, where full sewage purification is desired, must be regarded, not as independent, but rather as auxiliary to the system of sand filtration. It is possible that further study will prove that large sand areas can be economically replaced by more artificial construction and filtering material, which will make bacterial action more intense, and thus make it possible to handle a given quantity of sewage in less time, on a much smaller area, and at a smaller outlay than under the present system of sand filtration.

SUMMARY.

With four or five exceptions all the cities, towns, and boroughs in Connecticut which have public sewers discharge their sewage into streams or harbors. Many private sewers and drains from factories and dwellings discharge in.the same way.

Considerably more than one-half of the inhabitants of the State live in sewered cities or towns, and the dwellings of a majority of these inhabitants contribute to the sewage discharge.

With the increase of population and its concentration in cities and large towns, the relative portion of population contributing to the pollution of our streams, as well as the total amount of pollution, is rapidly increasing.

Strongly polluted streams cannot sufficiently purify themselves.

All the larger streams in the State are so far polluted as to be non-portable and their waters can never be used for domestic water supply unless filtered through sand.

While the largest rivers are not so seriously polluted as to make them a public nuisance, other streams like the Naugatuck, Park River, and the Hockanum have either reached the limit of permissible pollution or have passed it, so that suits are being brought for nuisance and will probably be brought in increasing numbers.

The complaints made in these suits are chiefly of deposits of filth in mill ponds, injury to health by noxious odors and resulting damage to land values.

The courts have found for the plaintiffs in every case that has come to our knowledge, and have rendered decisions strongly upholding the rights of a single riparian owner as against the convenience and financial interests of a large community.

The evils which result from the present excessive pollution of our streams and harbors are (in addition to the invasion of legal rights of riparian owners) possible contamination of water and of ice supply, destruction of fish, general unsightly appearance of the streams, and damage to the public health.

There are only three methods of sewage disposal which are at all permissible as substitutes for water-carriage and dilution, viz:

1. Chemical Precipitation.
2. Broad Irrigation.
3. Intermittent Filtration.

Of these the first cannot be regarded as in itself complete. It removes all suspended matter and from 30 to 50 per cent. of the putrescible matter of sewage and gives a clear or nearly clear effluent which may safely be discharged into streams under some conditions, but under other conditions filtration of the effluent will be necessary.

The second method, Broad Irrigation, requires a relatively large area of land and may profitably be combined in some cases with the third method, Intermittent Filtration.

This third method, properly managed, secures the almost complete destruction of the dangerous organic matters and bacteria of sewage, and having been in successful operation in this climate for a term of years may be regarded as no

longer an experiment, but as a well established and most effective method of destroying sewage.

Unfortunately, some cities are so situated that their sewage
can only be brought to land suitable for filters at very large
expense.

In conclusion, the Commission offers the following expression of opinion, based on its study of sewage disposal in this
State:

1. The disposal of sewage without nuisance is a duty
which each community owes to the public.

It is a problem to be settled by each community for itself,
with such state supervision and control as is necessary in the
public interest.

In some cases, however, several communities, lying in the
same topographical district, may profitably unite in the construction and operation of common outfall sewers or of disposal works.

2. No city, borough, or town, which has not now a sewerage system, should be allowed hereafter to build one which will
discharge sewage or polluted water into any stream, whether
such stream at the time is used by others for sewage disposal
or not, nor should private corporations or individuals be
allowed to discharge house sewage or excreta into any streams
or rivers.

3. To insure sewerage construction and methods of
sewage disposal which will be permanently satisfactory, the
General Assembly should not grant to any corporation authority to issue bonds for building, or to condemn land for
building, or to build any sewers, or system of sewers, until an
accurate topographical survey of the region to be sewered has
been made, and together with plans for effective sewage purification before discharging the effluent into any stream, has been
submitted to, and approved by, some competent state authority.

4. Provision should also be made by which cities and
boroughs now having sewage disposal works, or which may
hereafter build them, may be compelled by the State to so
manage them that the sewage shall at all times be effectively
purified before its discharge into rivers.

The State is now at the parting of the ways.

It may leave the whole matter to drift as it will. Our
smaller streams will then become more and more polluted,

and at last will be so foul during the summer months that private individuals, plagued beyond endurance, will undertake the expense and wearisome delay of lawsuits, and after years of litigation, it may be, will at last succeed in holding up those cities which have most contributed to the defilement and force them to discontinue it and. spend hundreds of thousands of dollars in changing their system of disposal. This is what is going on in this State to-day.

Or the State may take up the matter and seek, without unduly interfering with municipalities or manufacturing industry, to stop further pollution of our streams and reduce the present amount of it in the interest of public comfort and health.

Such a policy will need to be framed and executed with great judgment so as always to have behind it the force of public opinion, to be consistent and continuous in its operation, and to be administered with strict impartiality.

This course, we believe, the State should adopt.

RECOMMENDATIONS.

If this commends itself to the General Assembly, we recommend that an act be passed embodying the points covered by Sections 2, 3, and 4, just given. This will check the increase in the fouling of our streams, and will be an advance in the right direction.

We also recommend that the study of sewage disposal in this State be continued by a Sewage Commission. The foregoing report, as already intimated, is of necessity merely preliminary.

There are questions pressing for solution which cannot be immediately answered, but should have careful and intelligent study before any legislative action is taken. Ill-advised legislation, or injunctions of the courts, which will surely follow neglect of these questions by the public, are likely to inflict most serious injury on municipalities and on manufacturing interests.

As examples of these questions we may cite the following:

Are there any means, the value of which has been proved, by which the suspended matters in sewage may be separated and destroyed, by bacterial or other action, so as to greatly increase the quantitative efficiency of sand filtration, with a proportionately large reduction of the area and expense in-

volved in sewage disposal? A most important question where
suitable land is scarce or high in price.

Is it practicable or advisable to classify the rivers of our
State, or to divide certain streams into sections, a part of which
shall be given over to the carriage of sewage, in quantity not
sufficient to create a nuisance, and a part of which shall be
protected in every possible way from pollution?

Are there certain topographical sections of the State the
inhabitants of which, in the interests of economy and public
welfare, should be recommended or required to join in the construction of outfall sewers or disposal fields?

Are there factory wastes now discharged into streams
which by proper treatment can be purified, made entirely unobjectionable, and the cost of the treatment largely, if not
wholly, met by the value of products recovered from those
wastes?

There are other equally important questions awaiting
study and intelligent decision.

All which is respectfully submitted.

APPENDIX.

A

TWO REPORTS ON SEWAGE DISPOSAL.

As affording some idea of the serious nature of the burden which the necessity for sewage disposal, as at present understood and practiced, may impose upon Connecticut municipalities, we have made the following extracts from reports recently submitted to the cities of New Britain and Waterbury.

WATERBURY.

The report to Waterbury is dated August, 1896, and is made by Rudolph Hering, Esq., of New York, who is recognized as probably the leading sanitary engineer in this country. His finding of facts, discussion, and conclusions may be gathered from the following abstracts:

"The system of sewerage which has been built in your city collects the sewage and discharges it into the Naugatuck river. In the report accompanying the original design for the system (1882), it is stated that the river is sufficiently large to receive the sewage that would be discharged into it then 'without dangerous effects to the towns below. Yet it is not so large that this condition would not change within a reasonable number of years. As soon as the pollution of the river is objected to by other towns the city will be compelled to purify the sewage.' . . . .

"In view of the progress that has been made in the art of sewage disposal since the above was written (1883), you desire that this question now be studied in detail. To do this has required the general inspection of the Naugatuck valley, from Waterbury to the Sound, the making of surveys as far down as Beacon Falls, the examination of sites and soil, where filtration was thought to be practicable, and the collection of other data. All known means of sewage treatment were considered more or less in detail with reference to their application to your city. . . . .

"The population of Waterbury is now estimated at about 35,000. Any works for the disposal of its sewage should now take into consideration a population of at least 75,000 persons.

"While it is proper, when considering the dilution of sewage in a stream, to use the population as a basis and not the quantity of sewage, it is not proper to use the same basis when considering other methods of sewage purification. When dealing with the sewage itself, the size of the sewers, the area of land, the tanks and whatever apparatus may be required, must all be large enough to take the actual quantity delivered, which consists usually of the waste water from houses, of the sub-soil water, and of some rain-water. The great length of an out-fall sewer for the Waterbury sewage renders it important that this quantity should be determined with care and also that it should be kept as small as possible.

"To resume, therefore, it is advisable to calculate at least for the sewage of 75,000 persons at 85 gallons per head, or 6,375,000 gallons per day. This quantity being the average per day, a suitable addition should be made for the maximum flow, which in the case of a long outfall sewer can be estimated at 25 per cent., and represents one-half of the daily sewage running off in about ten hours, or at the rate of 8,000,000 gallons per day. . . . .

"I have assumed, further, that the subsoil water reaching the outfall sewer may be kept down to a flow of 500,000 gallons per day.

"Finally, the rain-water or flushing water which is allowed to enter, I have assumed as being equal to the maximum flow of sewage and sub-soil water combined, or at the rate of 8,500,000 gallons per day. . . . .

"Therefore, the total maximum quantity of water to be provided for is assumed at 17,000,000 gallons per day, or 26.3 cubic feet per second. The outfall sewer must be large enough to carry at least this quantity. The disposal works must be sufficiently large to purify the daily flow of sewage, also to receive the ground water and a certain quantity of rain-water. The daily flow of sewage and ground water are together assumed at 6,875,000 gallons. The rain-water is a variable quantity and is contributed only occasionally.

Purification of Sewage.

"Besides the method of disposal in the Naugatuck river as used at present, there are in vogue two other practicable methods of rendering sewage inoffensive. One is filtration through porous soil, the other is precipitation and removal of the suspended and some of the dissolved organic matter contained in the sewage.

"There is, however, still another method, and in the distant future possibly the preferable one, and that is the collection of the sewage of the Naugatuck valley in a common outfall sewer, and its discharge into the Sound, in a manner to cause it to be diluted and dispersed by the tidal flow.

"A trip was made down the river, the line located in a general way, and an outlet found. The length of the outfall sewer would be about 31 miles and its cost, if large enough for Waterbury alone and on the economical assumptions made above, would not be less than $1,500,000. To make such a sewer a practicable undertaking would necessitate the co-operation of all the larger towns along the river, which it would be difficult to obtain. But even if it could be obtained, the cost for the city of Waterbury would not be proportioned much below the above figure, and therefore be too high to allow of a serious consideration of the project at the present time. In view of these facts, the details of the plan were not worked out.

"The importance of the problem led to the consideration of still other methods, tried and untried, in order to discover the best solution. But, either the great expense, or the undoubted failure of one or the other to provide the necessary relief to the city and the residents of the Naugatuck valley below, led to their abandonment.

. . . .

"In the present case it is not necessary to obtain a high degree of purity, as the Naugatuck river, into which the treated sewage would return, is not used for drinking or other potable purposes. .

. . .

"Among the two available tracts the one at Beacon Falls is alone sufficiently large to filter the crude sewage of a city of 75,000 persons. There are about 100 acres available, which happens to be the minimum area required.

"The Platt's Mills tract contains only 33 acres. It can therefore be utilized for the above population only after the sewage has been previously treated and freed of suspended matter, which allows a larger quantity to be discharged upon it per acre, than when in a crude state.

"The Beacon Falls tract requires an outfall sewer nine miles long and it (the sewer) will be high enough to deliver the sewage entirely by gravity. The Platt's Mills tract requires an outfall sewer 1.4 miles long, and a lifting of the sewage some 65 feet. . . . .

"Precipitation of the suspended matter contained in the sewage, or a clarification of the same, is a method of purification which has been frequently resorted to where sufficient land was not available for filtration. . . . .

"If the effluent sewage from these works can subsequently be filtered through land, the method is valuable, because, while an acre of porous soil under the conditions I have above assumed, may receive as much as 166,000 gallons of crude sewage per day, it may receive 500,000 gallons of clarified sewage per day, and thus require respectively a much smaller area of land for the same quantity of sewage. For a total flow of 17,000,000 gallons the area would be about 33 acres. . . . .

"The 33 acres of porous land west of Platt's Mills, above mentioned, are not sufficient to purify the crude sewage, even at the present time, by filtration alone. But they are quite sufficient to be used conjointly with the precipitation process, which first clarifies it, and may be sufficient until the assumed population of 75,000 is reached.

"It has been stated that the outfall sewer should be large enough to carry a maximum flow of at least 17,000,000 gallons per day, or 26.3 cubic feet per second. It is therefore assumed for purposes of estimate at 40 inches in diameter.

"If the additional expense for a larger outfall is not a serious objection to your community, it would be well at once to build it 48 inches in diameter, which would increase its capacity to 28,500,000 gallons per day, or 44 cubic feet per second. . . . .

Estimate of Cost and Conclusions.

"The investigation has narrowed the projects down to two that are practicable, and either would render the river free from nuisance. . . . .

"From a sanitary point of view, there is practically no difference between the two projects. A nuisance need not occur in either case. The preference, therefore, must rest upon the question of economy.
. . . . .

"I have given an estimate for the present as well as for the future needs, the former representing the immediate outlay. I have also given the present and future actual annual outlay, in the way of interest, repairs, renewals, and operation, because it furnishes the best means of making a comparison between the two projects.

"A condensed statement is as follows:

	I BEACON FALLS.		II PLATT'S MILLS.	
	Present.	Future.	Present.	Future.
Total investment,	$609,730	$767,580	$138,380	$336,270
Annual cost,	28,489	40,003	21,335	59,569
Average,	$34,246		$40,452	

"In conclusion it may be recapitulated:

"That there are only two ways of solving the problem of sewage purification in your city, with the certain prospect of accomplishing satisfactory results, viz.: by land filtration alone, as, for instance, near Beacon Falls, and by combined chemical precipitation and land filtration, as, for instance, near Platt's Mills. Other known ways are either less efficient or more costly. Nor is any process that has been suggested, but is as yet untried, sufficiently promising in the light of modern knowledge, to warrant the expenditure for an experiment.

"On account of their expense, both of the available processes would require the prevention of waste in the use of water, a requirement that entails no real hardship nor evils of any kind. Both processes would also require a restriction regarding the free entrance of rain-water into the sewer system, a demand that is not difficult to enforce.

"Of the two processes, the one contemplating a preliminary precipitation, is not only more complicated, but also more costly to operate; *ceteris paribus*, it is not as advantageous as filtration alone. Unless other than engineering facts enter the problem, the latter process, with the fields at Beacon Falls, should therefore be preferred."

Thus we see that in the opinion of this very eminent engineer, the wisest plan for Waterbury to adopt, if compelled to dispose of its sewage otherwise than by discharging it into the Naugatuck river, would be to carry it to sand filtration fields at Beacon Falls, at a cost of from $600,000 to $770,000, and an annual burden beginning at $28,000 and growing to $40,000 by the year 1915. These figures for annual charges do not include any sinking fund payments.

NEW BRITAIN.

The New Britain report is dated January 25, 1898. It is written by Samuel M. Gray, Esq., of Providence, Rhode Island, formerly city engineer of that city, and author of an extensive report on European sewerage practice.

"New Britain is situated about eight miles west of the Connecticut river and covers an area of about 2,250 acres, and has a population approximating 26,000.

"On the north and east of the city, and also on the southwest, is additional territory, approximating 750 acres, which may and probably will, become a part of the city in the near future, making a total area of 3,000 acres.

"The topography of the city is considerably broken up into ridges and valleys. Its elevation is for the most part between 100 and 300 feet above tide-water, affording good surface drainage by two comparatively small water courses; Piper brook and Shuttle Meadow brook, the former flowing northeasterly through Newington to Hartford, where it empties into Park river; and the latter flowing south easterly, emptying into the Sebethe river, and finally into the Connecticut river just above Middletown.

"At present there are said to be approximately forty-five miles of streets in the city, and 26.6 miles of sewers, including the southwest district now under construction, all of which, excepting the latter district, were constructed on the combined system. . . . .

"The discharging of the crude sewage into these small water courses and into Piper brook, has been the cause of considerable complaint and litigation against the city, resulting in the city having to pay more or less damages. . . . .

" In considering this question of sewage disposal it will be necessary to take into account the probable future requirements as well as the present needs. . . . .

" It has been thought best to allow for an area of 3,000 acres, and a population of 110,000 for future needs, or in the year 1925, and for the present needs, for a population of 30,000. . . . .

Methods of Sewage Disposal.

" The methods of sewage disposal commonly adopted, may be spoken of as Crude Disposal, Disposal by Irrigation or Filtration, and Disposal by Chemical Precipitation. . . . .

Crude Disposal Into Connecticut River.

" The estimate of cost for disposing of the sewage into the Connecticut river is as follows:

Sewers, rights of way, etc., necessary to take the sewage from New Britain to the Connecticut river, above Middletown. First cost for present and future needs,	$225,600.00
Annual cost of operating, exclusive of interest on the first cost, $3,356.00, capitalized at 5 per cent.,	$67,120.00
Added to the first cost makes, ...	$292,720.00
To discharge the sewage into the river below Middletown first cost for present and future needs,	$313,070.00
Annual cost of operating, exclusive of interest on first cost, $4,810.70, capitalized at 5 per cent.,	96,214.00
Added to the first cost makes, ...	$409,284.00

Filtration at Plainville.

" The estimate of cost for disposing of the sewage by filtration at Plainville is as follows:

Pumping station, force-main, land, right of way, construction of filter beds, etc., necessary to dispose of the sewage by filtration at Plainville. First cost for present needs,	$190,000.00
Annual cost of operating, exclusive of interest on first cost, $14,356.00, capitalized at 5 per cent.,	287,120.00
Added to first cost makes, ...	$477,120.00
That for future needs. First cost, . . .	367,160.00
Annual cost of operating the same, $28,203.60, capitalized at 5 per cent.,	564,072.00
Added to first cost makes, ...	$931,232.00

Filtration on Artificial Beds.

" The estimated cost of disposing of the sewage by filtration on artificial beds, to be built near the city of New Britain, upon tracts of land before referred to, and indicated on the accompanying plan, are as follows:

For present needs. First cost, ...	$679,460.00
Annual cost of operating $8,994.60, capitalized at 5 per cent.,	179,892.00
Added to first cost makes, ...	$859,352.00

For future needs. First cost, ... $1,698,650.00
Annual operating expenses $20,736.50, capitalized at 5
  per cent., ... 414,730.00

Added to first cost makes, . . . $2,113,380.00
"By these estimates it will be seen that the project of disposing of the sewage by filtration at Plainville is less expensive than to build filter beds near the city of New Britain.

Chemical Precipitation.

"The following is the estimated cost of chemical precipitation, without subsequent filtration of the effluent:
For present needs. First cost of work, . . . $78,967.00
Annual cost, including labor, cost of chemicals, etc., $14,-
  161.67, capitalized at 5 per cent., . . . 283,233.00

Added to first cost makes, ... $362,200.00
For future needs. First cost of work, . . $180,332.00
Annual cost of operating as above, $31,609.37, capitalized
  at 5 per cent., ... 632,187.00

Added to first cost makes, ... $812,519.00

"The following is the estimated cost of chemical precipitation with subsequent filtration through sand:
For present needs. First cost of works, . . $172,153.00
Annual cost maintenance $8,541.53, capitalized at 5 per
  cent., ... 170,830.00

Added to first cost makes, ... $342,983.00
For future needs. First cost of works, . . . $413,297.00
Annual cost of operating $22,456.37, capitalized at 5 per
  cent., ... 449,127.00

Added to first cost makes, ... $862,424.00

"By the estimates it will be seen that the first cost of the chemical precipitation project is less than any other method so far considered, but it will also be seen that the cost of operating capitalized makes it more expensive than the method of chemical precipitation and filtration combined.

"The reason for this is, that the chemical treatment will not need to be quite so thorough by this method as in the former, thereby reducing the annual cost of operating.

"Recapitulation of the estimates of cost of the projects thus far considered:

Crude Disposal Into Connecticut River.

Above Middletown, present and future first cost, $225,600.00; capitalized cost, $292,720.00.
Below Middletown, present and future first cost, $313,070.00; capitalized cost, $409,284.00.

Filtration at Plainville.

Present needs, first cost, $190,000.00; capitalized cost, $477,120.00.
Future needs, first cost, $367,160.00; capitalized cost, $831,232.00.

Filtration on Artificial Beds.

Present needs, first cost, $679,460.00; capitalized cost, $859,352.00.
Future needs, first cost, $1,698,650.00; capitalized cost, $2,113,-
380.00.

Chemical Precipitation Without Subsequent Filtration.

Present needs, first cost, $78,967.00; capitalized cost, $362,200.00.
Future needs, first cost, $180,332.00; capitalized cost, $812,519.00.

Chemical Precipitation and Filtration Combined.

Present needs. first cost, $172,153.00; capitalized cost, $342,983.00.
Future needs, first cost, $413,297.00; capitalized cost, $862,424.00."

In further discussion of the subject Mr. Gray recommends either
chemical precipitation, with subsequent rapid filtration, or filtration
at Plainville, as being better adapted to that locality than any of the
other of the well-established methods. The first he estimates, on
the basis of works sufficient for the city needs at the present time,
will cost over $172,000.00 to build and $17,150.00 annual charges.
For 1925, $413,300.00 to build and $43,120.00 annual charges.

The second plan he estimates in a similar manner at $190,000.00
first cost and $23,856.00 annual charges for present needs, and $367,-
160.00 first cost and $46,560.00 annual charges for 1925. (Annual
charges do not include any provision for a sinking fund to take up
the bonds, but in all cases include interest at 5 per cent. on the first
cost.)

B

THE SEWERAGE SYSTEM AND DISPOSAL FIELDS OF MERIDEN.

In contrast with the very heavy financial burdens which will be
imposed on Waterbury and New Britain by a change in their method
of sewage disposal may be cited the experience of the city of Meriden, which arranged for sewage disposal by filtration at the same
time that a sewerage system was introduced.

Being prevented by legislative action from adopting a plan which
discharged the sewage into the Quinnipiac River, the city secured a
tract of land of 145½ acres, its center being 17,500 feet from the
center of the city, at a cost of $7.148, and built four beds, each having
an area of one acre, for the intermittent filtration of sewage. The
work was begun in 1891, and at present there are fourteen of these
beds in operation. A following diagram shows the topography of the
field and the arrangement of the beds.

The city has a population of about 30,000 and an area of 2,414
acres. A water supply was introduced in 1869. The sewer-pipe
system is designed for a population of 70,000, discharging 100 gallons of sewage proper per capita daily, with a maximum hourly
discharge of 5 gallons per capita. The daily capacity of the outfall
is 11,016,000 gallons.

The soil of the disposal field consists of three feet of fine material, underlaid by sand and gravel of unknown depth, admirably
suited for sand filtration. The ground water is 18 feet below the
surface. It has been found advisable to remove most of the fine
material from the surface. Underdrains to receive the effluent have
proved to be unnecessary.

Each sewer outlet on the beds has a sort of low fence screen, shown in the pictures which follow.   The screen is of galvanized iron wire netting, ¾-inch mesh.

This holds back the coarser part of the sludge, which is removed, and composted after each sewage discharge.

After removing the fine material from the surface of the beds first made, and providing for suitable supervision, the disposal field has worked very successfully, without nuisance, purifying the sewage perfectly.

At present about 391,600,000 gallons of sewage are annually treated at the field, or an average of 1,983,000 gallons per day.

The large beds receive from 900,000 to 1,000,000 gallons of sewage per day *on those days when they are in use.*

The accompanying pictures give a good idea of the appearance and equipment of the filtration beds.

The annual burden for care and maintenance of the filtration beds and that portion of the sewer which is within the filtration field is $3,000, five men and one team being employed.

The following table gives the cost of the *whole sewerage system,* including the disposal field, from the time when the plans were first made:

Appropriations.		Expenditures.		Realized from Bonds, Taxes, and Assessments.		
1890,	$500.00	. . . .		1890,	Tax,	$500.00
1891,	95,000.00	1891,	$471.80	1891,	Bonds,	85,000.00
1892,	60,800.00	1892,	104,922.16	1892,	Bonds,	50,000 00
				1892,	Tax,	10,800.00
1893,	110,000.00	1893,	98,722.34	1893,	Tax,	5,000.00
				1893,	Assessment,	49,993.86
1894,	49,700.00	1894,	50,390 28	1894,	Tax,	9,700.00
				1894,	Assessment,	33,448 00
1895,	60,000.00	1895,	49,669.74	1895,	Tax,	10,000.00
				1895,	Assessment,	28,920.00
1896,	60,000.00	1896,	55,143.34	1896,	Tax,	10,000.00
				1896,	Assessment,	32,100.00
1897,	59,000.00	1897,	32,210.59	1897,	Tax,	9,000.00
				1897,	Assessment,	18,255.00
. . . .		1898,	45,896.19	. . . . . .		. . . .
	$495,000.00		$437,426.44			$347,716.86

It appears that up to December, 1898, the total cost had been $437,426.44, which had been raised by:

Bonds,	.	.	.	$135,000.00
Assessments,	.	.	.	157,716.86
Taxation,	.	.	.	144,709.58
Total,		.	.	$437,426.44

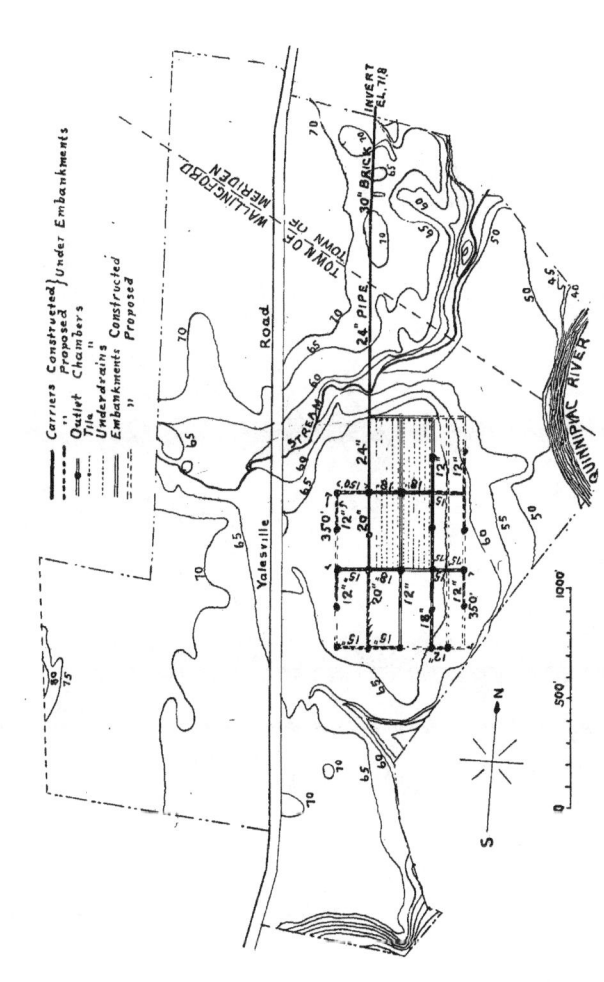

SEWAGE DISPOSAL AREA AT MERIDEN, CONN.

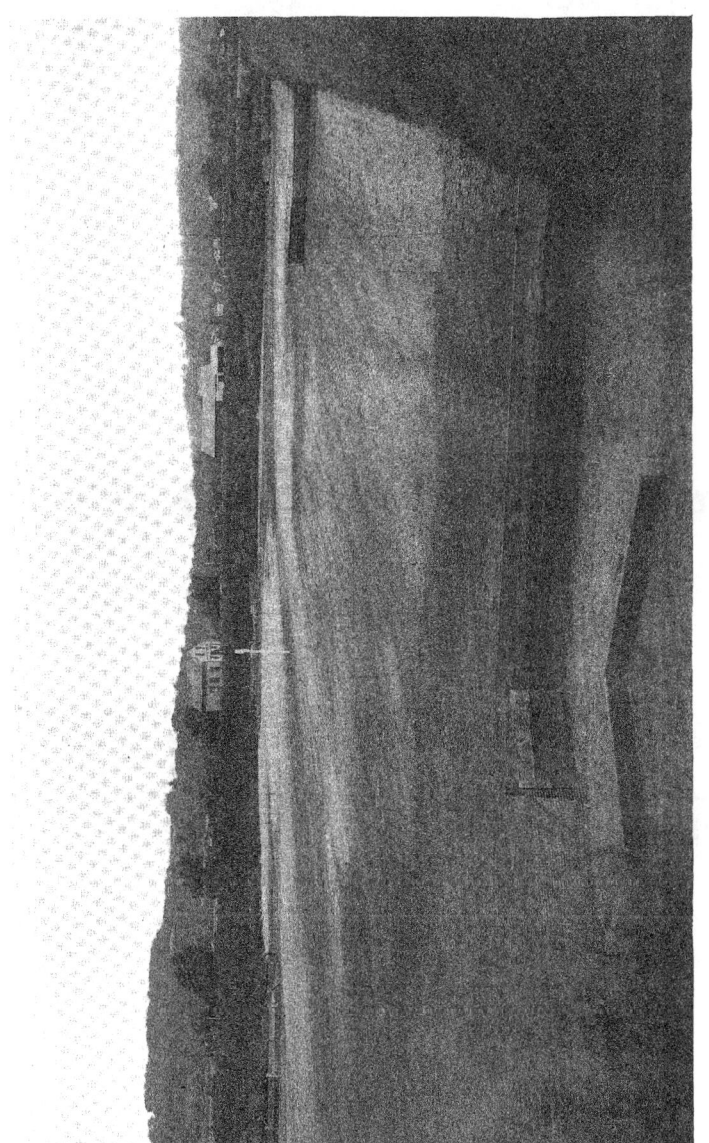

FILTRATION BED, MERIDEN.

Ready to receive sewage.

FILTRATION BED, MERIDEN.
Discharging sewage on the filter.

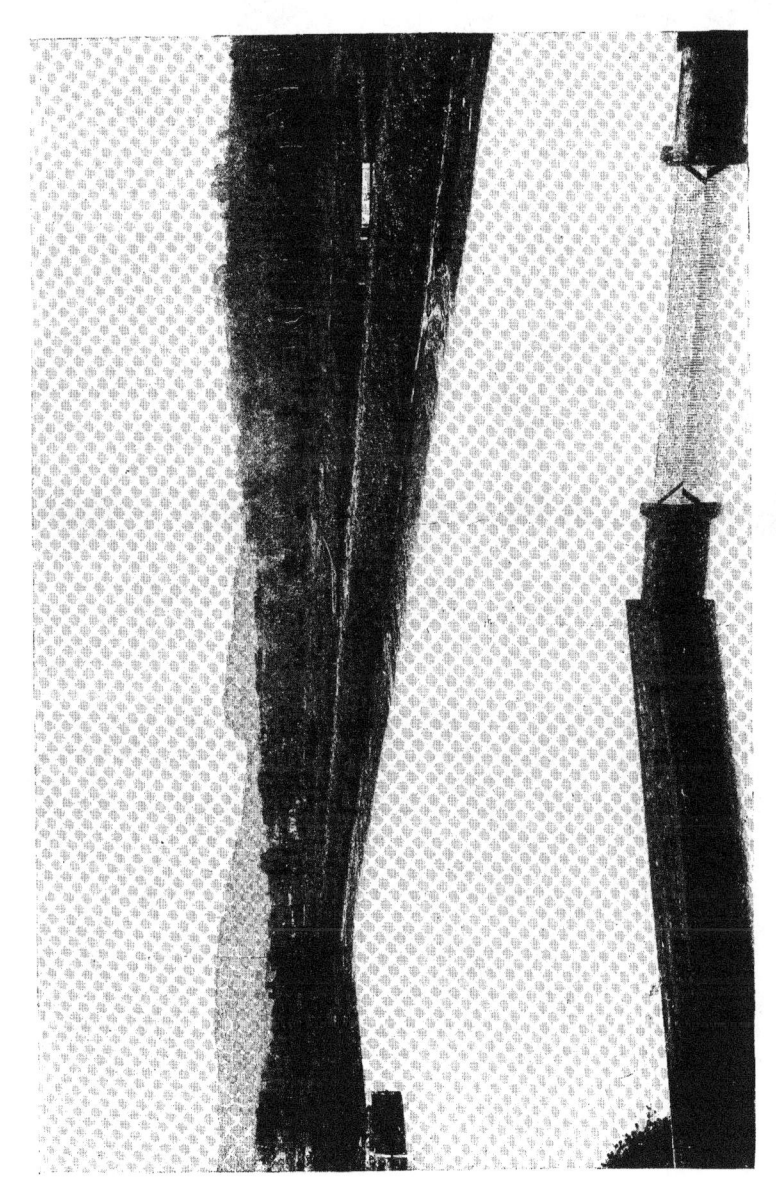

FILTRATION BED, MERIDEN.
Bed flooded with sewage.

FOURTEENTH ANNUAL REPORT

OF THE

BUREAU OF LABOR STATISTICS

OF THE

STATE OF CONNECTICUT,

FOR THE

YEAR ENDING NOVEMBER 30, 1898.

PRINTED BY ORDER OF THE GENERAL ASSEMBLY.

NORWICH, CONN. :
PRESS OF THE BULLETIN COMPANY,
1898.

CONTENTS.

(3)

LETTER OF TRANSMITTAL.

STATE OF CONNECTICUT,
OFFICE OF THE COMMISSIONER OF BUREAU OF
LABOR STATISTICS.

HARTFORD, December 1, 1898.

To His Excellency, LORRIN A. COOKE,
Governor of Connecticut:

SIR: I have the honor to transmit herewith the Fourteenth Annual Report of the Bureau of Labor Statistics.

Very respectfully,

SAMUEL B. HORNE, *Commissioner.*

WILLIAM W. IVES, *Clerk.*

INTRODUCTION.

In presenting the Fourteenth Annual Report of the Bureau it is essential that the subjects investigated by it and the results attained, be briefly explained as a preliminary to the exposition contained in the tabulated statements to be found in the following chapters.

Much time and labor has been expended in the work of gathering and compiling the material contained in this report, and it is a source of much gratification that, as the purposes of the Bureau become better understood, the people with whom its representatives come in contact willingly render them invaluable aid in securing the necessary data for its publications. This cannot be too highly commended, and a continuance of the existing most friendly relations between all persons and the officials of the Bureau is confidently anticipated.

CURRENT WORK OF THE BUREAU.

The current work of the Bureau covered by this report includes an investigation as to the conditions of the textile industries of the State, an exhaustive statement as to organized labor and trades unions, a complete tabulated statement of the conditions of manufactures, and an abstract of recent labor legislation in this and other countries.

TEXTILES.

Part I. of the report is devoted to the subject of textiles, it being deemed a proper investigation to be undertaken when the comparative conditions of the industry are considered. The difficulties attending the gathering of the necessary material were overcome, and the tables showing the results of the investigation will be found of interest and easy of solution. When it is understood that the manufacturers of textiles, particularly of cotton

(7)

goods, have been, and are in close and direct competition with producers of similar goods in the Southern States, where the prevailing conditions as to hours of labor, rates of wages, and employment of children, are so dissimilar and disadvantageous to the manufacturers of the North, it would seem that some universal plan should be devised whereby the sections of the South employing children of a tender age, and running their manufactories a longer number of hours daily than is lawful in the North, should be brought to the same standard of belief concerning the matters pertaining to the bettering of the conditions of the working men and women, as prevails in the States of New England, the textile manufacturers of which are particularly and so peculiarly affected by Southern competition which has been so forcibly shown, and has so rapidly grown in the past few years, as to seriously threaten the prosperity of such a large portion of the manufacturing and laboring classes as are affected by it. '

It should be mentioned here, that the condition of affairs as above outlined, has become a matter of such great importance, and public knowledge, that movements are at this time under way, advocated and supported by manufacturers and textile workers as well, looking to the formulation and enactment of National legislation for the relief of the manufacturers of cotton and other fabrics who suffer from competition, the character of which is such as can be regulated by legislation, requiring that the same number of hours shall constitute a day's work in all sections alike.

ORGANIZED LABOR.

Part II. consists of a complete statement of the condition of organized labor in the State, the form, scope and purpose of each particular trade having a distinct organization, the hours of labor which prevail in the different trades considered, together with a statement concerning the rates of wages paid and the benefits derived from membership in trades unions and kindred organizations.

The toilers or wage-earners, as distinguished from the employers or capitalists, constitute so large a portion of the body politic as to entitle them to the special consideration of the State, and such laws as are necessary to the fullest safe-guarding of their interests should be enacted and enforced, care being taken.

to avoid, as far as possible, any curtailment or infringement of the absolute rights of others. An excess of zeal may, in some cases, result in the enactment of laws, ostensibly favoring the working-man, which would have the effect to hurt rather than help him, in that they might, perhaps, cause the transfer of capital and industries to other States.

Labor organizations are made necessary by the growing tendency of capital towards concentration, a condition not entirely free from danger to the interests of labor, and such organizations should have the countenance and support of the State in every legitimate effort to protect and elevate labor. It is to be regretted that sometimes the wisest counsels do not prevail in shaping the policy or directing the action of the organizations. Labor and capital should find no insurmountable difficulties in the way of harmonious and mutually profitable employment. The greatest obstacle to such a condition is found to be the unwise course of demagogues, whose counsel is, in many instances, prompted by some motive less praiseworthy than an unselfish regard for the interest of those who follow.

One fact has been impressed upon the minds of those whose official duties or business interests have brought them in close connection with the wage-earners generally, and that is, that in the great centers of population there is, in almost every branch or trade, a surplus of willing hands, and in such branches as do not require a high degree of skill and intelligence this condition is especially noticeable; in other words, the labor market is over-stocked, and the demand for subsistence leads to a willingness to work at rates which often barely suffice for the actual necessaries of life. How to ameliorate this condition is a problem, the solution of which calls for the exercise of the highest degree of political wisdom.

Of the numberless questions involved in the relations between employer and employe, that of wages is the one which most frequently cause differences and disturbances of the amicable relations so essential to the best interests of both parties. The skill and muscle of the artisan are as much his capital and stock in trade as are the goods of the merchant or the money of the capitalist theirs, and he may ask such price for what he has to exchange for money as he estimates his services to be worth. The value of that which he offers is, however, fixed by the law of supply and demand, just as is the value of the merchant's goods,

The State may not, of right, interfere in any manner concerning the rate of pay at which one shall give his services and
another receive them, but the conditions under which one shall
work and receive his pay are fair subjects for the care and attention of the State, to the end that right and justice shall char-
acterize the dealings of citizens, one with the other.

MANUFACTURES.

Part III. has reference to the conditions of manufactures as
found to exist in the State during the current year, and closely
follows the form of investigation adopted by the Bureau and published in its annual reports for the past four years. The system
thus instituted has met with approval, and if continued will be of
much value to statisticians in future years. Comparisons made
with the facts shown in these reports from year to year are becoming an important factor in the solution of many questions
arising from the constantly changing industrial conditions.

LABOR LEGISLATION.

Part IV. contains an abstract of all laws relating to labor
which have become operative in this and other countries since
the publication of the last report of the Bureau, and will be found
of interest to legislators and others who are interested in the advancement of and improvement in the condition of the wage-
earner. Many of the laws, it will be noticed, bear close relation
one to the other, showing conclusively that each State is progressing toward uniformity in legislation, which accentuates the
contention of many economists that uniform or universal labor
laws would work the greatest measure of good for all classes.

WORK OF BUREAUS OF LABOR STATISTICS DURING 1897-8.

The following explains the work of the National Department
of Labor, and the State Bureaus of Labor and Industrial Statistics, as well as that of Foreign Bureaus, which has been accomplished or was in progress during the current year. As will be
seen the range of subjects investigated is wide, and the scope
unlimited. The increasing number of States instituting depart-

ments of labor is sufficient evidence that the work done and good accomplished is becoming of recognized value among legislators who deem the matter of statistical knowledge worthy of consideration.

UNITED STATES BUREAU OF LABOR.—

Economic aspects of the liquor traffic (By direction of Congress). Municipal and private ownership of gas, electric light and water plants.

CALIFORNIA.—

Free employment agencies. Collection of wages. Time check system. Eight-hour day. Japanese labor. Bake-shops. Sweat-shops. Trade unions.

COLORADO.—

Industrial conditions. Labor organizations. Cost of living. Strikes and lockouts.

ILLINOIS.—

Franchises and taxation. Mine inspection. Private and municipal ownership of gas, electric light and water plants.

INDIANA.—

Industrial statistics. Mortgages and satisfactions. Railroad statistics.

IOWA.—

Employment statistics. Railroad employes' wages. Manual training schools.

KANSAS.—

Milling industry. Creamery industry. Poultry industry. General manufactures. Labor unions. Cigar industry. Packing industry. Lead and zinc mines.

KENTUCKY.—

Mineral and agricultural resources of the State. Farm products and cost of production. Coal miners' strikes.

MARYLAND.—

Industrial statistics. Iron industry. Street railways. Female labor. Sweat-shops. Employment agencies. Convict labor. Strikes and compulsory arbitration.

MAINE.—

Manufacturing statistics. Summer resorts of Maine. Manufactures in wood novelties.

MASSACHUSETTS.—

Graded weekly wages. Statistics of manufactures. Relation of intemperance to crime, pauperism and insanity. Labor chronology.

MICHIGAN.—

Manufacture of vehicles. Eight-hour workday. Penal and reformatory institutions. Strikes and lockouts.

MINNESOTA.—

Purchasing power of gold.

MISSOURI.—

Street railway franchises. Taxation of real estate. Farm mortgages. Factory inspection.

MONTANA.—

Railroad wages and traffic. Labor and employment.

NEBRASKA.—

Resources of Nebraska. Farm and industrial statistics. Mortgage indebtedness.

NEW HAMPSHIRE.—

Manufacturers' statistics. Shoe industry. Retail prices of food and fuel. Strikes and lockouts.

NEW JERSEY.—

Statistics of manufacturers. Building and loan associations. Labor legislation.

NEW YORK.—

Condition of organized labor. Progress of business in the productive industries of the State for five years. Wholesale and retail prices of meats and groceries for five years. Private and municipal ownership of gas, electric light and water plants. Wages, condition and treatment of unorganized workmen in New York City.

NORTH CAROLINA.—

Agricultural statistics. Cotton and woolen mills. Tobacco factories.

OHIO.—

Employment agencies. Clay-working industries. Coal mining statistics. Manufacturers' statistics.

PENNSYLVANIA.—

Statistics of manufacturers. Tin-plate mills in the State. Industrial time and earnings. Strikes and lockouts. Prison labor.

RHODE ISLAND.—

Statistics of manufacturers. Textile industries. Occupation by sex.

TENNESSEE.—

Mines and mine inspection. Mine wages and regulations. General labor conditions. Phosphate industry. Marble industry. Petroleum fields.

WISCONSIN.—

Cost of grain production and the relation of this cost to the value of the product. Manufacturers' statistics. Factory inspection.

FOREIGN BUREAUS.

AUSTRIA.—

Strikes by industries, percentage of strikers and days lost.

BELGIUM.—

Wages and cost of living.

FRANCE.—

Minimum wages paid to employes on public works in England, Belgium, Holland, Switzerland, United States and France.

GERMANY.—

Labor conditions of garment workers. Hours of labor, wages, health and morals.

GREAT BRITAIN.—

Trades unions in Great Britain and Ireland. Price lists and sliding scales. Changes in wages and hours of labor.

ITALY.—

Strikes and lockouts. Causes and results.

NEW ZEALAND.—

Account of accidents and legal decisions under the Factory Act. Condition of the labor market. Conciliation and arbitration. Hours of labor and wages. Report on factory inspection.

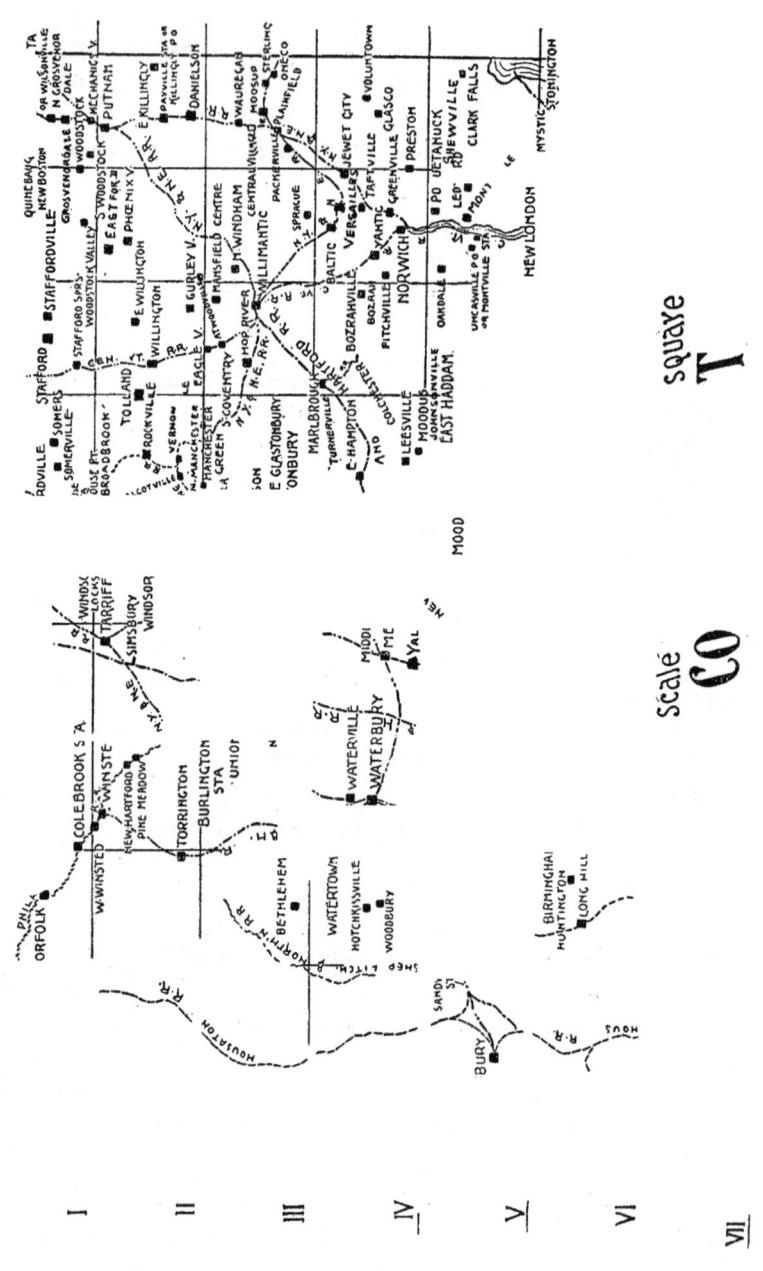

PART I.

TEXTILE INDUSTRIES OF CONNECTICUT.

---

1. COTTON.

2. WOOLEN.

3. KNIT GOODS.

4. SILK.

5. CAPITAL.

6. NUMBER EMPLOYED.

7. WAGES.

8. LOOMS AND SPINDLES.

9. VALUE OF PRODUCT.

10. ASSESSMENTS AND TAXES.

TEXTILE INDUSTRIES OF CONNECTICUT.

COTTON.

THE depression which has prevailed throughout the country for the past five years, has most materially affected the Textile manufacturing industries of Connecticut, and it is the purpose of the Bureau to give, in this chapter of the report, as complete and exhaustive a statement of the actual condition of the manufacturing establishments of the State which are engaged in the cotton, woolen, knit goods and silk industries, as has been possible to secure.

The tables have been prepared and arranged with a view to simplicity in detail, and the results obtained will show that the desire of the Bureau for accuracy and completeness has been gratified.

The collecting of the material for this portion of the report necessitated the performance of an immense amount of labor, in order that the data secured should be of the utmost reliability, and that this has been attained is unquestionable. Much of this labor might have been saved had more of the manufacturers complied with the requests made by the Bureau, and made the returns on the blank schedules which were prepared and mailed to every manufacturer of Textiles in the State. This reluctance, on the part of the proprietors of many establishments, rendered personal visits necessary, and in some instances the special agent engaged in this work was compelled to make numerous calls and earnest solicitation in order to secure the statements required.

Some little objection was made by the proprietors of a few establishments to furnish the Bureau with a statement of the amount paid in wages, obviously fearing exposure of labor cost of product. When assured, however, that in no event was the identity of the establishment to be disclosed, the figures were obtained, and it should be here stated that the assurances thus given have been fully complied with, and the wage account as rendered does not appear separately, but in the aggregate only.

Reference should be made to the fact that the amounts given in the tables as "capital invested" is hardly a just statement, as in many cases the statements of manufacturers concerning this point was to the effect that the amount so given was "capital stock of corporation" or "original capital," and in a few cases only were the figures given stated to have included "capital and surplus". It is, therefore, safe to assume that the amount of capital actually invested in the manufacture of Textiles in Connecticut is largely in excess of the amount given in the tables as total capital invested.

The table showing the total number of spindles in operation in 1897, exhibits most accurately the capacity of the cotton mills of the State, for, while the number of working spindles is by no means an exact measure of capacity, it is most certainly the best measure. Either this, or the quantity of raw material used must be taken as a measure of capacity. Should the quantity of raw material, that is of cotton, or the superficial area or weight of the product be taken as such measure, either would be open to the fatal objection that the cheapest goods are those in the making of which the largest amount of cotton is consumed. The same fatal objection would also apply to all other manufactures of Textiles. It would appear, therefore, that the capacity for production can be most accurately determined on the basis of the number of spindles in operation.

Comparisons made with the United States Census report of 1890 develops the fact that there were 934,155 spindles in active operation in the cotton mills of Connecticut at that time. The number found to be in operation in the sixty establishments represented in the tables as manufacturers of cotton cloths, warps, webs, threads and yarns in 1897 was 1,038,020, an increase in number of spindles of 103,865, or 11 per cent.

The number of idle spindles in the State in 1890, as given in the same report, was 16,852, while in 1897 there were reported 56,048 as being idle, an increase in number of idle spindles of 39,196, or 233 per cent. The total spindle capacity in the

State, however, was in 1897, 1,094,068 (idle spindles included), while by the census figures of 1890 there were 951,007 (idle spindles included), an increase in 1897 over 1890 of 143,061, or 15 per cent.

Reference to the tables which follow this analysis will show that, as stated in the preceding paragraph, the number of spindles in operation in 1897 was 1,038,020; the number of persons employed in the sixty establishments engaged in the manufacture of cotton cloths, warps, webs, threads and yarns being 15,637, and the amount paid in wages, exclusive of salaries, $4,830,023.37. The labor cost per spindle, therefore, being $4.65, and the number of spindles operated per employe 66.38.

The number of pounds of cotton consumed in the same establishments in 1897 was 53,104,000, the consumption, therefore, being 51.16 pounds per spindle.

The thirty-one establishments represented in the tables as manufacturing cotton cloths, by which term it is intended to cover manufacturers of cotton cloths, prints, crinolines, tarletans, denims, ticks, ducks, ginghams, cambrics and satines, produced 162,067,993 yards of goods in 1897. The total value of product is stated to have been $8,487,664.51, or 5.24 per yard. The amount paid in wages, exclusive of salaries, was $3,204,131.94, or 37.8 per cent. of product value.

The per cent. of product value paid for wages in the sixty establishments referred to in the tables, when placed in comparison with the figures given in the United States Census of 1890, are interesting and instructive, for in these establishments in 1897 the total value of product, as will be seen by reference to the tables, was $15,540,534.42, and the total amount paid in wages by the same establishments for the period named was $4,830,023.37. The wages paid, therefore, being 31.1 per cent. of product value. By the use of the same method in the data drawn from the Census report, it is found that in the cotton industries of Connecticut in 1860, the per cent. wages paid of product value was 19.6; in 1870, 23.1 per cent.; in 1880, 22.6 per cent.; and in 1890, 29.4 per cent. It is obvious then, that the contention of some economists that labor is gradually but surely increasing the portion secured by it of the value of its productions, is substantiated.

As before stated, the number employed in the sixty establishments referred to in the tables as manufacturers of cotton cloths, warps, webs, threads and yarns was, in 1897, 15,637, which sub-divided, comprised 6,950 men, 7,135 women, 817 boys and 735 girls—the two latter named classes being under 16 years of age, showing that of the total number employed in these industries 9.9 per cent. were children.

In respect to the above, it might be well to compare this condition with that which exists in North Carolina, where, according to the report of the Bureau of Labor Statistics of that State, issued in 1897, there were employed in all the mills 23,435 persons, 6,046, or 25.8 per cent. of which were classified as children.

The tables which follow have been compiled with great care and the accompanying explanations will render them of much interest and value.

COTTON CLOTHS.

TABLE No. 1.— Capacity for Production.

Number of Establishment.	Capital invested.	Horse power.	Looms in operation.	Spindles in operation.	Bales of cotton used in 1897.	Average number employed during 1897.				
						Men.	Women.	Boys.	Girls.	Total.
1	$150,000	300	307	14,640	1,561	65	38	11	12	126
2	600,000	1,800	1,464	59,616	4,429	408	231	22	10	671
3	135,000	275	282	15,296	487	88	52	10	7	157
4	175,000	400	451	21,080	1,703	108	78	3	1	190
5	2,000,000	2,100	2,775	118,938	2,500	500	700	160	140	1,500
6	100,000	150	172	10,704	900	45	20	18	16	99
7	100,000	300	224	7,500	3,454	100	80	6	6	192
8	100,000	250	300	13,280	1,423	62	56	15	9	142
.9	200,000	650	648	23,640	2,784	170	95	3	6	274
10	150,000	400	465	20,000	1,811	85	68	27	27	207
11	150,000	250	358	11,696	1,250	83	52	36	18	189
12	90,000	200	235	12,000	1,000	45	50	5	3	103
13	500,000	900	742	20,892	8,066	195	270	15	20	500
14	300,000	400	451	19,348	2,217	75	60	20	18	173
15	300,000	1,200	a432	b20,756	2,080	90	104	25	6	225
16	600,000	1,075	1,074	53,982	4,067	130	260	55	70	515
17	500,000	700	711	22,900	6,200	270	185	13	18	486
18	500,000	1,950	1,514	59,864	7,055	353	281	16	24	674
19	150,000	300	308	13,520	1,584	55	40	13	12	120
20	100,000	350	124	16,500	1,900	65	35	30	22	152
21	20,000	600	42	8,200	249	30	14	4	3	51
22	300,000	1,500	450	19,000	10,000	280	350	30	25	685
23	200,000	400	420	12,500	1,200	154	111	8	·5	278

a Increased to 850 in 1898.   b Increased to 35,800 in 1898.

COTTON CLOTHS — *Concluded.*

TABLE No. 1. — Capacity for Production — *Concluded.*

Number of Establishment.	Capital invested.	Horse power.	Looms in operation.	Spindles in operation.	Bales of cotton used in 1897.	Average number employed during 1897.				
						Men.	Women.	Boys.	Girls.	Total.
24	$10,000	99	15	1,400	250	10	4	.....	.....	14
25	2,500	25	24	....	*......	5	2	.....	1	8
26	1,000,000	800	754	19,976	2,879	348	169	17	13	547
27	200,000	75	150	8,200	636	30	36	4	.....	70
28	400,000	650	690	25,000	1,663	152	85	16	13	266
29	400,000	2,000	2,947	110,896	10,809	620	700	40	37	1,397
30	150,000	380	508	20,656	2,000	113	65	16	8	202
31	200,000	600	700	30,000	1,276	153	153	22	22	350
Total	$9,782,500	21,079	19,737	806,980	87,383	4,887	4,444	660	572	10,563

*Cotton yarns purchased.

COTTON WARPS, WEBS, THREADS AND YARNS.

TABLE No. 1.—Capacity for Production.

Number of Establishment.	Capital invested.	Horse power.	Looms in operation.	Spindles in operation.	Bales of cotton used in 1897.	Average number employed during 1897.				
						Men.	Women.	Boys.	Girls.	Total.
32	$1,000,000	750	550	15,000	3,000	215	496	50	75	836
33	50,000	150	....	3,000	420	33	28	2	2	65
34	20,000	100	....	980	400	8	2	1	1	12
35	300,000	500	....	17,000	1,325	80	56	16	20	172
36	40,000	90	....	4,500	500	19	13	3	5	40
37	40,000	80	....	3,200	439	20	12	.....	.....	32
38	80,000	100	....	1,500	1,584	20	.....	5	3	28
39	20,000	100	....	552	100	20	.....	.....	.....	20
40	30,000	30	....,....	600	250	4	4	.....	.....	8
41	40,000	50	....	3,500	477	31	13	5	1	50
42	175,000	200	....	2,912	535	26	30	3	3	62
43	125,000	40	100	....	*......	75	50	4	6	135
44	100,000	125	150	....	*......	25	275	.....	.....	300
45	50,000	85	43	....	*......	110	40	.....	.....	150
46	15,000	30	38	....	*......	12	13	.....	.....	25
47	50,000	40	35	....	*......	12	10	3	.....	25
48	75,000	100	140	....	*......	50	175	.....	.....	225
49	60,000	800	157	....	*......	175	75	.....	.....	250
50	594,200	900	....	39,000	1,360	100	200	25	25	350
51	50,000	20	....	3,000	*......	5	20	.....	.....	25
52	50,000	75	....	3,000	*......	10	18	2	3	33
53	60,000	130	....	5,000	500	40	50	10	.....	100
54	40,000	265	....	5,200	400	20	7	3	4	34

*Cotton yarns purchased.

COTTON WARPS, WEBS, THREADS AND YARNS—*Con'd.*

TABLE No. 1.— Capacity for Production — *Concluded.*

Number of Establishment.	Capital invested.	Horse Power.	Looms in operation.	Spindles in operation.	Bales of cotton used in 1897.	Average number employed during 1897.				
						Men.	Women.	Boys.	Girls.	Total.
55	$250,000	250	130	....	*......	75	75	.....	....	150
56	350,000	500	....	14,000	1,500	125	160	.....	.....	285
57	25,000	160	....	2,800	320	12	13	8	4	37
58	2,000,000	3,500	....	87,000	5,000	700	800	15	10	1,525
59	200,000	100	....	15,000	*160	19	46	1	.....	66
60	50,000	150	....	4,296	555	22	10	1	1	34
Total	$5,889,200	9,420	1,343	231,040	18,825	2,063	2,691	157	163	5,074

*Cotton yarns purchased.

ASSESSMENTS AND TAXES.

The commercial importance of the Textile industries to the State and to the towns can be no more clearly shown than by exhibiting in figures the amount assessed against the several establishments, for purposes of taxation, together with the amounts paid by them in taxes to the towns in which they are located. The following table shows the assessments and taxes paid by the thirty-one establishments represented in the table as engaged in the manufacture of cotton cloth.

COTTON CLOTHS.

Assessments and Taxes Paid, Divided by Towns.

Town.	Assessment on Grand List, 1897.	Amount paid in taxes, 1897.
Putnam	$742,700	$14,111.29
Plainfield	793,115	9,517.38
Brooklyn	542,142	5,692.50
Norwich	2,117,734	19,534.57
Killingly	544,807	8,171.10
Sprague	290,000	4,350.00
Mansfield	28,425	326.37
Montville	256,541	4,104.66
Windham	200,675	4,605.52
Huntington	140,000	2,100.00
Voluntown	75,000	1,350.00
New Hartford	326,040	3,912.48
Stonington	70,000	1,225.00
East Haddam	3,000	37.50
Canterbury	2,050	24.60
Griswold	645,000	6,450.00
Thompson	745,696	8,948.35
Total	$7,522,925	$94,461.32

ASSESSMENTS PER SPINDLE.

The same reference as in the foregoing can be made concerning the comparative assessments per spindle. It has been asserted that the methods of assessments of cotton mills in some States is made on a basis of spindles in use, and that Connecticut manufacturers suffer in comparison with these, by reason of the fact, which has been stated as being true, that the assessments made by the towns against Connecticut mills, when considered on the basis of spindle power, is excessive; how far or to what extent this contention can be borne out by the facts adduced, the following table will show. Certain it is, however, that the rate of assessment per spindle shows great irregularity in the systems of making assessments in the various towns.

It must be remembered in comparing the preceding with the table which follows, that while the total amount assessed is the same in each, yet the division by towns in the latter table show different amounts. This was rendered necessary by reason of the fact that some establishments were assessed in two or more towns, and therefore, in order to obtain accurately the rate of assessment per spindle, the total assessment should be used as a basis for the computation.

COTTON CLOTHS.

Assessment per Spindle by Towns.

Town.	Total assessment.	Number of spindles.	Rate of assessment per spindle.
Putnam	$742,700	81,544	$9.11
Plainfield	793,115	101,616	7.81
Norwich	*2,877,734	178,026	13.36
Killingly	*1,253,490	166,766	7.52
Thompson	745,696	110,896	6.72
Mansfield	28,425	10,704	2.66
Montville	†120,000	7,500	16.00
Windham	200,675	40,656	4.94
Canterbury	*2,050	....	....
Griswold	645,000	44,976	14.34
Huntington	140,000	11,696	11.97
Voluntown	75,000	16,500	4.55
New Hartford	326,040	22,300	14.69
Stonington	70,000	12,500	5.60
East Haddam	3,000	1,400	2.14
Less Canterbury (No spindles in use)	$7,522,925 2,050	806,980	Average...$9.32
Total	$7,520,875		

*Assessment in other towns added.
†Amount deducted for assessment in other towns.

COTTON WARPS, WEBS, THREADS AND YARNS.

Assessments and Taxes Paid, Divided by Towns.

Town.	Assessment on Grand List, 1897.	Amount paid in taxes, 1897.
Middletown	$352,910	$5,791.10
Middlefield	40,600	730.80
Haddam	39,000	663.00
Vernon	106,650	713.25
Plainfield	44,655	535.86
Griswold	93,850	938.50
Windham	1,194,070	27,463.61
East Haddam	104,152	1,301.40
Montville	10,000	160.00
Farmington	11,587	139.04
East Lyme	6,200	74.40
Bridgeport	78,000	936.00
Ansonia	38,000	836.00
Columbia	18,460	276.90
Norwalk	21,360	427.20
Waterbury	75,000	2,475.00
Hamden	64,950	974.25
Stonington	110,350	2,482.88
Westport	17,500	175.00
Killingly	14,190	212.85
Windsor Locks	112,150	1,121.50
Mansfield	24,795	371.92
Total	$2,578,429	$48,800.46

COTTON CLOTHS.

TABLE No. 2. — Capacity for Production.

Number of Establishment.	Pounds of cotton used during 1897.	Yards of goods produced during 1897.	Value of product manufactured.	Value per yard.	Per cent. production of full capacity.	Value of product, full capacity.
1	780,500	2,663,505	$99,000.00	3.7	95	$104,210.53
2	2,214,500	7,990,515	485,000.00	6.1	90	538,222.22
3	243,500	1,500,000	115,000.00	7.7	88	130,681.82
4	851,500	3,871,165	120,870.27	3.1	85	142,200.32
5	1,250,000	24,000,000	1,200,000.00	5.	100	1,200,000.00
6	450,000	1,650,000	75,865.86	4.6	95	79,858.80
7	1,727,000	3,920,700	291,180.11	7.4	100	291,180.11
8	711,500	2,556,580	128,791.61	5.	95	135,570.12
9	1,392,000	3,723,535	222,315.30	6.	94	236,505.64
10	905,500	2,976,000	116,641.44	3.9	87	134,070.28
11	625,000	5,124,641	168,809.32	3.3	95	177,694.02
12	500,000	3,000,000	70,000.00	2.3	75	93,333.33
13	4,033,000	10,081,608	604,895.00	6.	96	630,098.96
14	1,108,500	3,833,814	142,000.00	3.7	95	149,473.68
15	1,040,000	4,250,000	180,000.00	4.2	100	180,000.00
16	2,033,500	10,861,457	405,190.75	3.7	88	460,444.03
17	3,100,000	8,129,000	482,764.91	5.9	90	536,405.46
18	3,527,500	11,418,444	480,000.00	4.2	88	545,454.55
19	767,000	2,556,946	97,000.00	3.8	95	102,105.26
20	950,000	1,290,000	60,000.00	4.7	95	63,157.89
21	124,500	135,535	18,000.00	14.	67	26,865.67
22	5,000,000	4,221,410	522,034.09	12.3	100	522,034.09
23	600,000	4,000,000	307,000.00	7.7	100	307,000.00

COTTON CLOTHS — *Concluded.*

TABLE No. 2.—Capacity for Production — *Concluded.*

Number of Establishment.	Pounds of cotton used during 1897.	Yards of goods produced during 1897.	Value of product manufactured.	Value per yard.	Per cent. production of full capacity.	Value of product, full capacity.
24	125,000	107,210	$10,000.00	9.3	60	$16,666.67
25	*...........	133,380	9,000.00	6.7	50	18,000.00
26	1,439,500	5,070,106	391,355.72	7.7	80	489,194.65
27	*318,000	1,260,000	50,000.00	4.	80	60,250.00
28	831,500	2,827,080	189,960.79	6.7	82	231,659.50
29	5,404,500	19,323,087	1,040,000.00	5.4	100	1,040,000.00
30	1,000,000	3,537,496	126,934.08	3.6	100	126,934.08
31	638,000	6,054,779	278,055.26	4.6	100	278,055.26
Total	43,691,500	162,067,993	$8,487,664.51	5.2	†94	$9,047,326.94

.*Cotton yarns purchased.   †Average.

COTTON WARPS, WEBS, THREADS AND YARNS.

TABLE No. 2.—Capacity for Production.

Number of Establishment.	Pounds of cotton used during 1897.	Pounds of goods produced during 1897.	Yards of goods produced during 1897.	Dozens of goods produced during 1897.	Value of product manufactured.	Per cent. production of full capacity.	Value of product, full capacity.
32	*1,500,000	1,100,000	23,000,000	....	$852,000.00	100	$852,000.00
33	210,000	175,000	....	....	40,000.00	90	44,444.44
34	200,000	115,000	....	....	7,500.00	100	7,500.00
35	662,500	539,000	....	....	190,000.00	67	283,582.09
36	250,000	166,000	....	....	35,000.00	100	35,000.00
37	219,500	193,766	....	....	29,064.90	100	29,064.90
38	792,000	632,495	....	....	24,500.00	100	24,500.00
39	†50,000	†48,852	....	....	†80,000.00	90	88,888.89
40	125,000	100,000	....	....	10,000.00	33	30,303.03
41	238,500	180,793	....	....	39,505.01	50	79,010.02
42	267,500	218,277	....	....	35,800.00	60	59,666.67
43	‡.........	....	1,000,000	....	230,000.00	50	460,000.00
44	‡.........	....	4,000,000	....	400,000.00	100	400,000.00
45	‡.........	....	2,147,065	....	160,000.00	100	160,000.00
46	‡.........	....	....	286,532	28,000.00	100	28,000.00
47	‡.........	....	955,000	....	40,000.00	30	133,333.33
48	‡.........	....	4,294,120	....	300,000.00	75	400,000.00
49	‡.........	....	4,500,000	....	362,000.00	100	362,000.00
50	680,000	....	....	1,200,000	400,000.00	85	470,588.24
51	‡.........	112,000	....	....	75,000.00	75	100,000.00
52	‡.........	639,000	....	....	100,000.00	100	100,000.00
53	250,000	163,000	....	....	75,000.00	75	100,000.00
54	200,000	138,000	....	....	22,000.00	50	44,000.00

* 5,000 pounds other material used.   † Other stock purchased and sold.
‡ Cotton yarns purchased.

COTTON WARPS, WEBS, THREADS AND YARNS—*Con'd.*

TABLE No. 2.— Capacity for Production—*Concluded.*

Number of Establishment.	Pounds of cotton used during 1897.	Pounds of goods produced during 1897.	Yards of goods produced during 1897.	Dozens of goods produced during 1897.	Value of product manufactured.	Per cent. pro-duction of full capacity.	Value of product, full capacity.
55	‡.........	....	2,250,000	....	$275,000.00	70	$392,857.14
56	750,000	637,500	....	....	320,000.00	80	400,000.00
57	160,000	116,000	....	....	27,500.00	100	27,500.00
58	2,500,000	2,000,000	....	....	2,700,000.00	90	3,000,000.00
59	‡80,000	....	....	1,100,000	165,000.00	70	235,714.29
60	277,500	212,268	....	....	30,000.00	95	31,589.47
Total	9,412,500	7,486,951	42,146,185	2,286,532	$7,052,869.91	84	$8,379,542.51

‡ Cotton yarns purchased.

COTTON CLOTHS, WARPS, WEBS, THREADS AND YARNS—Closed Mills.

TABLE No. 3.—Capacity for Production.

Number of Establishment.	Looms formerly in operation.	Spindles formerly in operation.
61	......	5,000
62	18	1,792
63	12	2,640
64	21	3,616
65	......	1,200
66	280	12,000
67	104	6,000
68	179	8,000
69	180	9,000
70	......	600
71	......	5,000
72	......	1,200
Total	794	56,048

COTTON CLOTHS, WARPS, WEBS, THREADS AND YARNS.

TABLE No. 4. — Assessments and Amounts Paid in Taxes — Division by Towns.

Town.	Assessment on Grand List, 1897.	Amount paid in taxes, 1897.
Ansonia	$38,000	$836.00
Bridgeport	78,000	936.00
Brooklyn	542,142	5,692.50
Bozrah	23,350	233.50
Canterbury	2,050	24.60
Colebrook	14,740	221.10
Columbia	18,460	276.90
Eastford	800	12.80
East Haddam	175,473	2,281.66
East Lyme	6,200	74.40
Farmington	11,587	139.04
Glastonbury	95,255	1,428.82
Griswold	788,850	7,888.50
Haddam	39,000	663.00
Hamden	64,950	974.25
Huntington	140,000	2,100.00
Killingly	578,557	8,677.35
Mansfield	53,220	698.29
Middlefield	40,600	730.80
Middletown	352,910	5,791.10
Montville	269,023	4,304.37
New Hartford	326,040	3,912.48
Norwalk	21,360	427.20

COTTON CLOTHS, WARPS, WEBS, THREADS AND YARNS — *Concluded.*

TABLE No. 4. — Assessments and Amounts Paid in Taxes — Division by Towns — *Concluded.*

Town.	Assessment on Grand List, 1897.	Amount paid in taxes, 1897.
Norwich	$2,117,734	$19,534.57
Plainfield	837,770	10,053.24
Putnam	742,700	14,111.29
Sprague	290,000	4,350.00
Stonington	180,350	3,707.88
Thompson	745,696	8,948.35
Vernon	106,650	713.25
Voluntown	115,000	2,070.00
Waterbury	75,000	2,475.00
Westport	17,500	175.00
Windham	1,394,745	32,069.13
Windsor Locks	112,150	1,121.50
Woodstock	4,657	55.88
Total	$10,370,519	$147,209.75

COTTON — Closed Mills.

Assessments and Taxes Paid, Divided by Towns.

Town.	Assessment on Grand List, 1897.	Amount paid in taxes, 1897.
Glastonbury...	$95,255	$1,428.82
East Haddam..	68,321	942.76
Colebrook	14,740	221.10
Voluntown..	40,000	720.00
Killingly........	19,560	293.40
Bozrah...	23,350	233.50
Eastford..	800	12.80
Montville...	2,482	39.71
Woodstock..	4,657	55.88
Total...	*$269,165	*$3,947.97

*Included in Table No. 4.

SYNOPSIS.

A synopsis of the foregoing shows that in the seventy-two establishments which appear in the tabulation, and which in-cludes the mills which were closed during the period covered by the investigation, there were in 1897, 1,094,068 spindles, active and idle. The number of looms idle and in operation being 21,874. The total assessments against all the establish-ments represented, closed mills included, was $10,370,519, and the amount paid by them in taxes to the several towns $147,209.75, an average rate of $14\frac{2}{10}$ mills. The average rate of assessment in the entire State, computed on the basis of number of spindles, was $9.48 per spindle.

WAGE RATES AND RENT.

The table which follows shows the average wage rates which obtain in the sixty establishments which were in opera-tion in 1897. A division in number of weavers and spinners, and information as to number of hours worked in the entire year by each individual not being obtainable, the actual average rate of wages cannot be shown. The accompanying table, however, contains an accurate statement as to the rates of wages for weavers and spinners which were paid in 1897 by each establishment.

The table also shows the number of tenements owned or controlled by the manufacturers represented, together with an approximate statement as to the number of rooms contained in each and the rate of monthly rental for each class. The total number of tenements reported as being occupied by employes in the cotton mills of the State was 3,084; the num-ber of rooms contained in each ranging from 2 to 10, and the rate paid for rent from 90 cents to $11.00 per month.

COTTON CLOTHS, WARPS, WEBS, THREADS AND YARNS.

TABLE No. 5.—Wage Rates and Rates Paid for Rent.

Number of Es and shmen	WEAVERS. Weekly wage rates.			SPINNERS. Weekly wage rates.			Tenements owned.	Rooms in each.	Rent per month.
	Highest.	Lowest.	Average.	Highest.	Lowest.	Average.			
1	$12.00	$5.00	$7.00	$10.00	$8.50	$8.75	50	3 to	$2.00 to $4.17
2	13.22	3.00	6.27	11.92	7.00	9.15	248	3 to	1.86 to 3.73
3	8.50	5.00	7.00	9.00	6.00	8.00	52	4 to	2.25 to 4.00
4	7.50	3.50	5.75	9.80	6.00	7.90	52	3 to 7	2.24 to 4.56
5	10.50	6.25	7.50	14.00	10.25	12.00	450	3 to 7	2.50 to 5.00
6	7.00	5.90	6.50	8.00	8.00	8.00	32	3 to 6	3.36 to 4.17
7	10.50	6.00	7.00	10.00	6.00	8.50	......	....	....
8	9.10	4.56	6.82	9.00	8.60	8.72	39	3 to 7	3.50 to 7.00
9	12.00	6.60	7.00	10.50	9.00	9.50	110	4 to 8	2.43 to 5.42
10	8.88	4.39	6.17	8.48	7.25	8.23	57	4 to 6	3.25 to 6.50
11	11.80	5.40	7.80	6.24	2.55	4.65	......	....	....
12	7.50	5.00	6.00	10.50	5.50	7.00	25	3 to 6	2.00 to 4.00
13	8.82	4.00	6.25	6.18	3.00	4.75	73	3 to 7	3.00 to 5.42
14	12.00	5.00	7.00	10.00	8.50	8.75	48	5 to 7	4.00 to 5.00
15	8.50	6.00	7.78	9.00	7.50	8.34	56	4 to 7	3.43 to 5.25
16	8.00	5.00	6.00	9.00	7.00	7.50	160	4 to 7	2.80 to 3.20
17	9.49	4.06	6.66	7.09	3.50	5.00	123	3 to 7	3.60 to 7.00
18	10.97	3.10	6.56	11.33	8.92	9.70	175	3 to 9	1.82 to 5.20
19	12.00	5.00	7.00	10.00	8.50	8.75	59	3 to 7	2.00 to 4.17
20	9.00	4.80	6.00	5.50	2.56	4.00	50	3 to 8	2.00 to 4.00
21	7.50	4.00	5.00	5.10	3.00	4.60	40	5 to 10	1.50 to 6.25
22	8.00	4.50	5.50	5.50	3.50	5.00	150	2 to 10	.90 to 9.00
23	11.52	5.01	8.10	10.59	3.00	4.94	55	6	6.00

COTTON CLOTHS, WARPS, WEBS, THREADS AND YARNS—*Continued.*

TABLE No. 5.—Wage Rates and Rates Paid for Rent —*Continued.*

Number of Estab'shmen	WEAVERS. Weekly wage rates.			SPINNERS. Weekly wage rates.			Tenements owned.	Rooms in each.	Rent per month.
	Highest.	Lowest.	Average.	Highest.	Lowest.	Average.			
24	$7.50	$6.00	$7.00	$6.00	$5.00	$5.75	7	6 to 8	$3.50 to $4.00
25	9.00	6.50	7.25	7.00	6.00	6.75	12	5	5.00
26	10.25	4.00	6.00	6.30	1.80	4.16	150	3 to 8	3.25 to 8.66
27	7.00	5.00	6.00	8.00	6.00	7.25	31	5 to 7	2.50 to 3.75
28	12.00	4.00	7.00	5.64	1.92	4.00	80	3 to 8	2.70 to 8.00
29	......	......	......	......	......	......	......	....	....
30	10.50	7.50	9.50	6.00	4.50	5.00	54	3 to 7	3.00 to 5.12
31	10.50	4.50	8.00	14.00	9.00	11.00	68	3 to 5	2.00 to 6.00
32	15.00	6.00	9.00	8.40	5.50	6.00	72	7	6.00
33	......	......	......	8.25	6.00	7.00	12	4 to 7	3.00 to 6.00
34	......	......	......	9.00	6.00	7.25	4	5	3.50
35	......	......	......	6.30	4.50	5.40	62	3 to 7	2.20 to 5.00
36	......	......	......	10.00	7.00	8.50	13	3 to 6	3.00 to 6.25
37	......	......	......	5.00	4.50	4.87	13	6 to 10	4.00 to 7.00
38	......	......	......	6.50	4.00	5.00	16	5 to 7	4.00 to 6.00
39	......	......	......	10.00	8.00	9.00	......	....	....
40	......	......	......	5.00	4.00	4.25	6	6 to 10	2.50 to 4.50
41	......	......	......	6.00	4.80	5.40	......	....	....
42	......	......	......	7.00	4.00	5.00	18	4 to 10	2.00 to 6.25
43	30.00	8.00	18.00	......	......	......	......	....	....
44	14.00	5.00	7.00	......	......	......	......	....	....
45	21.00	9.00	15.00	......	......	......	......	....	....
46	6.00	2.00	5.40	6.00	2.00	5.40	14	2 to 6	1.25 to 4.00

COTTON CLOTHS, WARPS, WEBS. THREADS AND YARNS — *Concluded.*

TABLE No. 5.—Wage Rates and Rates Paid for Rent — *Concluded.*

Number of Es and shmen .	WEAVERS. Weekly wage rates.			SPINNERS. Weekly wage rates.			Tenements owned.	Rooms in each.	Rent per month.
	Highest.	Lowest.	Average.	Highest.	Lowest.	Average.			
47	$21.00	$5.00	$14.00	......	......	....	......	....	....
48	12.00	6.00	8.00	......	......	....	......	....	....
49	12.00	8.00	9.00	......	......	....	22	6 to 9	$8.00 to $10.00
50	......	......	......	$14.50	$6.00	$9.00	30	6 to 8	7.00 to 11.00
51	......	......	......	6.00	4.80	5.60	......	....	....
52	......	......	......	8.00	4.00	5.00	......	....	....
53	......	......	......	8.00	4.00	4.50	32	5 to 6	3.00 to 5.00
54	......	......	......	8.00	1.80	4.50	23	4 to 7	1.60 to 4.00
55	......	......	......	14.00	6.00	9.00	6	4 to 9	4.00 to 10.00
56	......	......	......	9.00	5.00	6.50	12	4	4.17
57	......	......	......	8.00	6.00	6.75	20	4 to 6	2.50 to 4.00
58	......	......	......	13.00	5.50	6.97	178	3 to 8	2.50 to 10.00
59	......	......	......	12.00	5.75	7.25	7	6 to 8	5.00 to 7.00
60	......	......	......	8.00	6.50	7.00	18	4 to 6	2.75 to 4.00

ILLUSTRATIONS.

The following exhibits are taken from the completed
schedules of different manufacturers of all grades of cotton
goods, the purpose being to show the number of spindles per
employe, the number of yards produced per loom, and the per
cent. of product value paid in wages by establishments.

As has been before stated, much of the information secured
by the Bureau for publication in this chapter of the report was
obtained with the understanding that the identity of the establishment furnishing the data was not to be disclosed. The
twelve schedules presented herewith, however, while giving
the amount paid in wages, together with the value of product,
separately, do not in any degree violate the agreement made
as to concealment of the identity of the establishments with
which such agreement had been entered into.

EXHIBIT 1.

Year 1897.
307 looms,   14,640 spindles,
Produced 2,663,505 yards sheetings, shirtings and twills.
Average number employed, 126.
Number spindles per employe, 116.19.
Average yards produced per loom, 8,676.
Value of product, $99,000.00.
Amount paid in wages, $43,000.00.
Per cent. of product value paid in wages, 43.4.

EXHIBIT 2.

Year 1897.
282 looms,   15,296 spindles,
Produced 1,500,000 yards cotton cloth.
Average number employed, 157.
Number spindles per employe, 97.43.
Average yards produced per loom, 5,319.
Value of product, $115,000.00.
Amount paid in wages, $38,475.97.
Per cent. of product value paid in wages, 33.5.

EXHIBIT 3.

Year 1897.
451 looms, 21,080 spindles,
Produced 3,871,165 yards sheetings.
Average number employed, 190.
Number spindles per employe, 110.95.
Average yards produced per loom, 8,584.
Value of product, $120,870.27.
Amount paid in wages, $47,527.36.
Per cent. of product value paid in wages, 39.3.

EXHIBIT 4.

Year 1897.
2,775 looms, 118,938 spindles,
Produced 24,000,000 yards cotton cloth.
Average number employed, 1,500.
Number spindles per employe, 79.29.
Average yards produced per loom, 8,649.
Value of product, $1,200,000.00.
Amount paid in wages, $500,000.00.
Per cent. of product value paid in wages, 41.7.

EXHIBIT 5.

Year 1897.
172 looms, 10,704 spindles,
Produced 1,650,000 yards sheetings and twills.
Average number employed, 99.
Number spindles per employe, 108.12.
Average yards produced per loom, 9,218.
Value of product, $75,865.86.
Amount paid in wages, $26,317.04.
Per cent. of product value paid in wages, 34.7.

EXHIBIT 6.

Year 1897.
300 looms, 13,280 spindles,
Produced 2,556,580 yards sheetings.
Average number employed, 142·
Number spindles per employe, 93.52.
Average yards produced per loom, 8,522.
Value of product, $128,791.61.
Amount paid in wages, $41,909.17.
Per cent. of product value paid in wages, 32 5.

EXHIBIT 7.

Year 1897.
648 looms,   23,640 spindles,
Produced 3,723,535 yards sheetings.
Average number employed, 274.
Number spindles per employe, 84.73.
Average yards produced per loom, 5,746.
Value of product, $222,315.30.
Amount paid in wages, $77,671.53.
Per cent. of product value paid in wages, 34.9.

EXHIBIT 8.

Year 1897.
451 looms,   19,348 spindles,
Produced 3,833.814 yards sheetings, shirtings and twills.
Average number employed, 173.
Number spindles per employe, 111.84.
Average yards produced per loom, 8,501.
Value of product, $142,000.00.
Amount paid in wages, $55,000.00.
Per cent. of product value paid in wages, 38.7.

EXHIBIT 9.

Year 1897.
308 looms,   13,520 spindles,
Produced 2,556,946 yards sheetings, shirtings and twills.
Average number employed, 120.
Number spindles per employe, 112.67.
Average yards produced per loom, 8,302.
Value of product, $97,000.00.
Amount paid in wages, $42,000.00.
Per cent. of product value paid in wages, 43.3.

EXHIBIT 10.

Year 1897.
690 looms,   25,000 spindles,
Produced 2,827,080 yards cambrics, satines and twills.
Average number employed, 266.
Number spindles per employe, 93.98.
Average yards produced per loom, 4,097.
Value of product, $189,960.79.
Amount paid in wages, $82,641.87.
Per cent. of product value paid in wages, 43.5.

EXHIBIT 11.

Year 1897.

508 looms,   20,656 spindles,

Produced 3,537,496 yards sheetings and twills.

Average number employed, 202.

Number spindles per employe, 102.26.

Average yards produced per loom, 6,967.

Value of product, $126,934.08.

Amount paid in wages, $50,000.00.

Per cent. of product value paid in wages, 39.4.

EXHIBIT 12.

Year 1897.

700 looms,   30,000 spindles,

Produced 6,054,779 yards fine yarn goods.

Average number employed, 350.

Number spindles per employe, 85.71.

Average yards produced per loom, 8,650.

Value of product, $278,055.26.

Amount paid in wages, $104,325.79.

Per cent. of product value paid in wages, 37.5.

COMPARATIVE CONDITIONS.

Manufacturers and employes engaged in the cotton industry in Connecticut have been mutually interested in the extension of cotton manufacturing in the South, and its effect upon the industry in Connecticut. In New England nearly uniform laws respecting hours of labor and employment of children make the conditions more equal in the competition of these States. In the large cotton centers of Massachusetts and Maine a reduction has been made in wages, the manufacturers claiming that it was necessary to enable them to make goods in competition with the low wages and long hours in the South. The cotton industry, occupying as it does such a prominent place in Connecticut, comparisons with former conditions are of interest.

In the United States Census of 1890, Connecticut ranks fourth in the number of cotton spindles, having 934,155, or 5.6 per cent. of the entire number, being exceeded, respectively, by Massachusetts, Rhode Island and New Hampshire, in the order named.

From the same source the figures show that there were employed in the cotton industry 13,411 persons with a yearly pay-roll aggregating $4,524,483. The value of the product is given as $15,409,476. It has been said that, while the prestige long held by New England as the cotton manufacturing stronghold was fast departing on account of the gigantic advance and competition in the South, Connecticut was not holding its own in the strife. A study of the following table, compiled from Dockham's Textile Directory for a period of ten years, 1887–1896, the accuracy of which is to be assumed, shows the assertion to be true.

NUMBER OF COTTON SPINDLES.

	1887.	1889.	1891.	1892.	1894.	1896.	Percentages of increase + or decrease − in 1896 as compared with 1887.
NEW ENGLAND STATES.							
CONNECTICUT....	1,092,524	1,023,928	1,046,399	1,020,070	1,033,935	1,045,937	−4.26.
Maine...............	824,432	884,722	917,169	923,541	931,116	916,304	+11.14
New Hampshire....	1,180,648	1,207,312	1,245,021	1,288,351	1,296,606	1,308,802	+10.85.
Vermont...........	63,868	62,775	72,848	80,271	102,303	106,583	+66.88
Massachusetts.......	5,330,120	5,905,875	6,308,925	6,847,744	7,160,480	7,790,642	+46.16.
Rhode Island.......	1,856,982	1,948,958	2,036,519	2,086,087	2,076,665	2,104,060	+13.31
SOUTHERN STATES.							
Alabama...........	104,791	96,647	102,519	138,471	170,159	231,011	+120.45.
Georgia............	406,330	442,148	484,983	501,512	550,510	731,238	+79.96.
Kentucky..........	27,500	42,500	47,287	49,143	50,043	58,779	+113.74
Mississippi.........	47,050	54,800	57,420	57,968	54,484	72,258	+53.58
North Carolina.....	227,348	321,070	423,192	510,190	656,480	910,474	+300.48.
South Carolina......	232,692	351,040	463,424	508,404	626,883	997,185	+328.54
Tennessee..........	100,277	116,783	124,911	117,841	121,984	145,428	+45.03
Virginia............	68,912	79,612	91,760	111,756	139,356	134,696	+95.46

THE INDUSTRY IN CONNECTICUT AND IN THE SOUTH — 1890.

The data available for comparison respecting the conditions in Connecticut and in those Southern States in which the manufacture of cotton goods has had its greatest increase are to be found in the United States Census, and being brought up to 1890 only, can only form the basis of broad, general inferences as to product, wages, employes, etc.

The following table summarizes this information, and presents certain percentages so as to show the facts clearly from the latest returns, namely, those for the year 1890.

COTTON INDUSTRY IN CONNECTICUT AND THE SOUTH — 1890.

States.	Value of goods made.	Value of stock used.	Value of industry product.	Amount of wages paid.	Profit and minor expense fund.	Percentages of industry product paid in wages.	Percentages of industry product devoted to profit and minor expenses.
CONNECTICUT	$15,409,476	$8,208,111	$7,201,365	$4,239,546	$2,961,819	58.95	41.05
Alabama........	2,190,771	1,459,048	731,723	402,908	328,815	55.06	44.94
Georgia.........	12,035,629	7,778,026	4,257,603	2,167,036	2,090,567	50.90	49.10
Kentucky.......	1,000,668	643,949	356,719	170,573	186,146	47.82	52.18
Mississippi.......	1,333,398	871,970	461,428	263,997	196,431	57.21	42.79
North Carolina.	9,563,443	6,238,352	3,325,091	1,475,932	1,849,159	44.39	55.61
South Carolina..	9,800,798	6,816,820	2,983,978	1,510,494	1,473,484	50.62	49.38
Tennessee.......	2,507,719	1,765,062	742,657	444,573	298,084	59.86	40.14
Virginia.........	1,732,648	1,197,234	535,414	373,993	161,421	69.85	30.15

It will be seen from the foregoing figures that the value of cotton goods made in Connecticut in 1890 amounted to $15,409,476, exceeding the product of any of the Southern group, Georgia leading with $12,035,629, South Carolina standing next with a product of $9,800,798, and North Carolina next with a product of $9,563,443.

The value of the stock used in Connecticut, including under that term not only all that may be called raw material, but also all the incidental items of stock or material which enter into the product or which are consumed in the process of manufacture, was $8,208,111. In Georgia the value of stock used was $7,778,026; in South Carolina $6,816,820, and in North Carolina $6,238,352. By deducting the value of stock used and material consumed, as shown by these figures, from the value of goods made, there remains what may be termed the "industry product," or the value product actually created in the cotton industry. By this method it is found that the value of the industry product in Connecticut was $7,201,365; in Georgia $4,257,603; in South Carolina $2,983,978, and in North Carolina $3,325,091.

This industry product may be divided into two parts, one being the aggregate sum paid in wages, and the other constituting a fund from which all the minor expenses of manufacture, such as taxes, insurance, interest, etc., must be paid, and from which, after these minor expenses have been provided for, profits are derived. It follows that as the portion of industry product devoted to wages is increased or diminished, the balance devoted to profit and minor expenses will be diminished or increased.

In order to note the relative proportions in each of the States it is only needed to refer to the percentages of industry product paid in wages, and of industry product devoted to profit and minor expenses, as shown in the last two columns of the table. It is there shown that in the year under consideration 58.95 per cent. of the industry product in Connecticut was divided among the operatives in the form of wages, leaving a balance of 41.05 per cent. to be devoted to profits and the minor expenses of manufacture, expenses, which it should be borne in mind, are only termed "minor" in comparison with the greater expense of wages and stock used, inasmuch as in themselves they may constitute a considerable percentage of expense.

It will be noted that there are two States in the Southern group in which the percentage paid in wages is higher than in Connecticut. These are Tennessee and Virginia, but the product is comparatively small.

The Commissioner of the Massachusetts Bureau of Labor Statistics, in a report on this same subject, says, "It is probable that the establishments were not so effectively organized as the others."

As against the 41.05 per cent. devoted to profits and minor
expenses in Connecticut, there remained in Georgia 49.10, in
South Carolina 49.38 per cent., and in North Carolina 55.61 per
cent. Of course these percentages show nothing conclusively
as to profits, since the element of minor expense is not deter-
minable from the figures and may be greater or less than in
Connecticut. If less, then on the basis of these figures, a larger
share of the industry product could be devoted to profits in
these States than in Connecticut. If greater, it might still be
possible to secure the same profits as in Connecticut, unless
they were so great as to overcome the larger proportion which,
in the aggregate, appears as a profit and minor expense fund.

COMPARATIVE FIGURES FOR 1880.

For the purpose of showing historically the growth of the
cotton industry in Connecticut and the Southern States, during
the ten years preceding 1890, the following table is introduced,
derived from the Census of 1880.

States.	Value of goods made.	Value of stock used.	Value of industry product.	Amount of wages paid.	Profit and minor expense fund.	Percentages of industry product paid in wages.	Percentages of industry product devoted to profit and minor expenses.
CONNECTICUT	$16,069,771	$8,029,127	$8,040,644	$3,632,639	$4,408,005	45.18	54.82
Alabama........	1,228,019	783,711	444,308	239,998	204,310	54.02	45.98
Georgia.........	6,481,894	4,019,673	2,462,221	1,135,184	1,327,037	46.10	53.90
Kentucky.......	418,286	253,818	164,468	63,850	100,618	38.82	61.18
Mississippi......	679,093	337,149	341,944	133,214	208,730	38.96	61.04
North Carolina.	2,554,482	1,463,645	1,090,837	439,659	651,178	40.30	59.70
South Carolina..	2,895,769	1,808,300	1,087,469	380,844	706,625	35.02	64.98
Tennessee.......	874,717	553,761	320,956	161,071	159,885	50.18	49.82
Virginia........	1,040,962	640,391	400,571	169,789	230,782	42.39	57.61

In this year it will be seen that the total value of goods
made in Connecticut was $16,069,771, or 4.11 per cent. less than
in 1890. This may properly be accounted for by the cheaper
cost of material, thus lessening the selling price of the product.

During this period Georgia practically doubled her product, and North and South Carolina both show a gain of more than 235 per cent.

Without considering the other figures in the table, it is interesting to note the percentages of industry product paid in wages and devoted to profit and minor expenses in the leading States in 1880, as compared with those before cited for 1890. As to the percentage of industry product paid in wages, Connecticut, in 1890, shows 45.18, as against 58.95 in 1890, a considerable increase in the latter year. Georgia shows a slight increase, namely, from 46.10 per cent. to 50.90 per cent. South Carolina rose from 35.02 to 50.62, and North Carolina from 40.30 to 44.39. It is seen that in each of these States wages consumed a larger portion of the industry product in 1890 than in 1880, but the gain was greater in Connecticut than in any of the other States, except Mississippi, South Carolina and Virginia.

The table further shows that while in 1880 54.82 per cent. of the industry product was devoted to profit and minor expenses, this percentage fell to 41.05 per cent. in 1890, while on the other hand, the percentage in Georgia fell only from 53.90 to 49.10, and in North Carolina from 59.70 to 55.61. In South Carolina the decline was from 64.98 per cent. to 49.38 per cent.

PERCENTAGES OF STOCK AND WAGES OF PRODUCT, 1880–1890.

The table that follows shows the percentages of the value of stock used and wages paid of the value of goods made—that is, of the selling price of the product in 1880.

PERCENTAGES OF STOCK AND WAGES OF PRODUCT.

States.	Stock used of product.	Wages paid of product.
CONNECTICUT..........................	48.68	22.61
Alabama...............................	63.82	19.54
Georgia...............................	62.01	17.51
Kentucky..............................	60.68	15.26
Mississippi...........................	49.65	.19.62
North Carolina.......................	57.30	17.21
South Carolina.......................	62.45	13.15
Tennessee.............................	63.31	18.41
Virginia..............................	61.52	16.31

In Connecticut the value of stock consumed represented 48.68 per cent. of the selling price of the product, while wages represented 22.61 per cent.   In Georgia stock represented 62.01 per cent. and wages 17.51 per cent.   In North Carolina stock 57.30 per cent. and wages 17.21 per cent.   In South Carolina stock 62.45 per cent. and wages 13.15 per cent.

To put it another way, out of every $100 received for the product, $48.68 was expended for stock and $22.61 for wages in Connecticut, and $57.30 for stock and $19.62 for wages in North Carolina.

It will be noticed that in Connecticut the percentage paid in wages was larger than any of the other States. For purpose of comparison the same figures for 1890 are arranged in the table that follows:

States.	Stock used of product.	Wages paid of product.
CONNECTICUT.	53.27	27.51
Alabama	66.60	18.39
Georgia	64.63	18.01
Kentucky	64.35	17.05
Mississippi	65.39	19.80
North Carolina	65.23	15.43
South Carolina	69.55	15.41
Tennessee	70.39	17.73
Virginia	69.10	21.59

From this table it appears that in 1890 the value of the stock consumed in Connecticut was 53.27 per cent. of the selling price of the product, and wages 27.51 per cent. The percentage of wages paid of selling price is, as in 1880, larger in Connecticut than in any of the Southern States, and very much larger than in North and South Carolina, which show percentages of 15.41 and 15.43, respectively. Georgia shows a percentage of 18.01.

The difference between the amount of wages paid, considered as a percentage of the selling price of the product in Connecticut as compared with North and South Carolina and Georgia, is still wider in 1890 than in 1880, and greatly so in North Carolina.

In 1890 the difference between North and South Carolina is small as compared with 1880.

COMPARISON OF AVERAGE WEEKLY EARNINGS.
1890.

States.	Operatives and skilled employes.			Unskilled employes.
	Males above 16 years.	Females above 15 years,	Children.	Males above 16 years.
CONNECTICUT..........................	$7.68	$5.69	$3.35	$7.92
Alabama.................................	5.31	4.19	1.78	4.77
Georgia.................................	5.75	4.55	1.96	6.09
Kentucky...............................	5.89	4.02	1.89	5.40
Mississippi.........................	7.09	4.66	1.67	7.09
North Carolina........................	5.25	3.21	1.84	4.71
South Carolina........................	5.17	3.90	1.93	5.00
Tennessee..............................	6.31	3.24	2.30	6.10
Virginia...............................	6.29	3.54	2.11	6.30

In this table the operatives and skilled employes are classified separately from the unskilled employes, and each class is subdivided into groups of males above 16 years of age, females above 15 years of age, and children.

It will be seen that the wages of the skilled employes in Connecticut, $7.68, $5.69 and $3.35 for the respective grades, is greater than in any of the Southern group. The lowest being males above 16 years, in Georgia, $5.75. For females above 15 years, in North Carolina, $3.21, and for children, in Mississippi, $1.67. No quotation is given for Connecticut for females and children in the unskilled class. That given for males above 16 years is $7.92. The lowest is in North Carolina, $4.71. It will be noted, however, that notwithstanding these apparent differences in nominal wages, the labor cost appears to be more nearly equalized when put upon the basis of cost per spindle, as shown in the following table.

It is not pretended that the conditions that existed in 1890 exist to-day. In but two States are the figures collected annually under statute law (Massachusetts and North Carolina). The last report of the North Carolina Bureau of Labor Statistics, covering the year 1897, has interesting data which may be compared with similar data collected by this Bureau, covering the same period.

COMPARISONS RELATING TO COST OF MANUFACTURE SHOWN BY THE CENSUS OF 1890.

The tables that follow are for the purpose of showing a comparison of different elements entering into the cost of manufacture in each of the States considered.

The first shows the average cost per pound of cotton, percentages of children of total wage-earners, number of spindles per employe, labor cost per spindle and cost of fuel, on basis of spindles, derived from the Census of 1890.

COMPARISONS RELATING TO COST OF MANUFACTURE SHOWN BY 1890 CENSUS.

States.	Average cost per pound of cotton.	Per cent. of children of total wage-earners.	Number of spindles per employe.	Labor cost per spindle.	Cost of fuel on basis of spindles.
CONNECTICUT...............	$.1076	7.90	70.66	$4.54	$ .22
Alabama......................	.0932	23.99	37.95	5.09	0.30
Georgia...	.0064	23.85	43.19	4.86	0.32
Kentucky....................	.0964	21.76	52.50	3.97	0.20
Mississippi.....................	.0939	26.52	49.40	4.63	0.49
North Carolina...............	.1008	24.32	39.67	4.37	0.30
South Carolina................	.0975	26.52	41.23	4.54	0.33
Tennessee....................	.0985	20.20	45.92	4.56	0.49
Virginia......................	.1018	23.92	47.38	3.97	0.18

It appears from the table that the average cost per pound of the cotton used in Connecticut was .1076. This is higher than in any of the other States, but only slightly higher than in Virginia.

When the percentages of children of total wage-earners is considered, a very different condition appears in Connecticut than in the other States. The percentage in Connecticut is 7.90 ; in South Carolina it is 26.52; in North Carolina 24.32, and in Georgia 23.85.

In number of spindles per employe, Connecticut shows 70.66, while North Carolina returned but 39.67, South Carolina 41.23, and Georgia 43.19.

In a comparison of the labor cost per spindle per employe, in Connecticut, the figures are $4,54, while it is $4.37 in North Carolina, $4.54 in South Carolina, and $4.86 in Georgia. How much conditions have changed since these figures were collected it is impossible to say. Correspondence was had with officials of the Southern States to ascertain, if possible, what the present conditions are, but without success.

* "A general decline in the net price of cotton, unaccompanied by a relative change in freight and other charges which finally determine its price at the mill, would probably bear equally upon all the States, and would simply change the amounts of the figures without changing their returns."

It is probable, however, that the proportion of children of total wage-earners has been changed, as the age at which children may be employed has been raised from thirteen years, as it was at the time these figures were collected, to fourteen years at the present time.

The cost of fuel, on the basis of spindles, was but 22 cents in Connecticut, while it was 33 cents in South Carolina, 32 cents in Georgia, and 30 cents in North Carolina.

In connection with the cost of fuel, the table that follows shows this cost computed as a percentage of the value of the product (this being the fairest basis of comparison), and includes other data relating to fuel and motive power.

---

* Mass. Report.

COMPARISONS RELATING TO COST OF MANUFACTURE, CENSUS 1890.

States.	Relative proportions of cost of fuel.			Percentages of motive power.		Percentages of cost of fuel of value of product.
	Coal.	Wood.	Other fuel.	Steam.	Water.	
CONNECTICUT.	87.12	0.50	12.38	35.13	64.87	1.31
Alabama	82.69	17.31	....	58.20	41.80	1.09
Georgia	89.17	10.19	0.64	35.43	64.57	1.17
Kentucky........	86.21	13.79	....	95.29	4.71	0.87
Mississippi.......	58.05	41.95	....	98.18	1.82	2.11
North Carolina..	44.57	51.38	4.05	47.57	52.43	1.05
South Carolina..	83.45	13.60	2.95	42.38	57.62	1.13
Tennessee........	88.84	11.16	....	81.08	18.92	1.90
Virginia..........	97.67	2.33	....	17.87	82.13	0.99

This table presents the relative proportions of coal and wood used in the different States considered, the relative proportions of steam and water power of the entire motive power in the industry, and the percentages which the cost of fuel constitutes of value of product.

In Connecticut coal represented 87.12 per cent. of the entire fuel consumed, other fuel 12.38 per cent., and wood only .50.

In Georgia coal represented 89.17 per cent. and wood 10.19 per cent. In South Carolina coal represented 83.45 per cent. and wood 13.60 per cent., but in North Carolina coal represented only 44.57 per cent., and the percentage of wood rose to 51.38.

In Connecticut 64.87 per cent. of the motive power was derived from water, and only 35.13 from steam.

In Georgia steam represented 35.43 per cent. and water 64.57 per cent. In North Carolina steam represented 47.57 per cent. and water 52.43 per cent., and in South Carolina the percentage of steam was 42.38 per cent. and water 57.62 per cent.

In Connecticut the expense of fuel amounted to 1.31 per cent. of the value of the product.

In Georgia 1.17 per cent.; in North Carolina 1.05 per cent., and in South Carolina 1.13 per cent.

Notwithstanding the differences in certain elements of manufacture, by combining the value of stock and materials consumed and the amount of wages paid, and computing them as a percentage of the total value of product, it is found that there is a very slight difference between the States.

In some instances this percentage is higher in the Southern States than in Connecticut. The figures are brought together in the table that follows.

PERCENTAGES OF STOCK AND WAGES OF VALUE OF PRODUCT.

CONNECTICUT	80.78
Alabama	84.99
Georgia	82.64
Kentucky	81.40
Mississippi	85.19
North Carolina	80.66
South Carolina	84.96
Tennessee	88.12
Virginia	90.69

In Connecticut the combined value of stock and wages represented 80.78 per cent. of the selling price of the product. In Georgia it was 82.64 per cent., South Carolina 84.96 per cent., and in North Carolina 80.66 per cent., the smallest of any of the Southern States.

WOOLEN.

The following tables refer to those establishments in the State which were engaged in the manufacture of goods composed wholly or in part of wool. The computation as to quantity of material used is based on the amount of "scoured wool" used, to which, it must be stated, the amount of "other material used" should be added. This "other material" consists of "woolen rags," "shoddy," "mixed stock" and "cotton."

It is found, therefore, that the quantity of wool used in the fifty-four establishments represented in the tabulation amounted to 17,626,388 pounds during the year 1897, to which amount should be added 4,041,171 pounds of "other material."

As to amount of capital invested, it should be borne in mind that the total amount as shown in the tables, refers to "capital originally invested," or "capital stock of corporation," which, obviously, is not intended to include accumulations or surplus. The amount thus given as being invested in the woolen industries of Connecticut in 1897 was $6,906,000.00. There were 417 sets of cards in use, 3,213 looms, and 91,928 spindles in operation during the year. The total average number employed in all establishments was 7,738, of which 4,761 were men, 2,507 women, and 470 boys and girls under 16 years of age. The proportion of boys and girls of total number employed was 6.1 per cent.

WOOLEN.

TABLE No. 1.— Capacity for Production.

Number of Establishment.	Capital invested.	Horse power.	Sets of cards.	Looms in operation.	Spindles in operation.	Pounds of wool used in 1897.	Average number employed during 1897.				
							Men.	Women.	Boys.	Girls.	Total.
1	$10,000	150	2	36	1,244	[1] 27,531	33	19	4	2	58
2	35,000	50	2	21	792	[2] 40,000	36	10	4	2	52
3	18,000	75	2	14	792	125,000	40	4	2	....	46
4	300,000	300	19	88	......	405,000	129	63	5	....	197
5	50,000	200	5	22	1,480	275,000	53	19	5	2	79
6	24,000	125	7	38	2,140	200,000	60	30	....	....	90
7	240 000	270	9	109	......	[3] 308,556	200	88	15	8	311
8	200,000	350	......	50	3,732	300,000	25	25	20	20	90
9	25,000	80	4	20	1,680	[4] 90,000	35	9	....	....	44
10	100,000	125	12	58	3,784	378,662	90	53	....	3	146
11	100,000	250	15	76	......	123,400	192	60	....	....	252
12	200,000	150	......	63	......	[3] 840,000	35	100	....	25	160
13	25,000	80	3	28	816	[5] 17,000	31	17	....	....	48
14	32,000	100	4	25	936	240,000	37	20	3	....	60
15	200,000	300	20	125	......	273,228	209	78	7	5	299
16	300,000	300	9	160	3,500	288,500	264	95	8	8	375
17	160,000	200	10	54	3,690	312,000	71	41	2	....	114
18	250,000	500	5	114	......	275,000	216	64	8	15	303
19	75,000	120	4	19	1,800	[6] 100,000	70	15	2	....	87
20	10,000	160	1	24	288	[7] 55,000	20	6	....	....	26
21	250,000	400	20	67	6,000	627,451	100	70	2	3	175
22	75,000	150	5	70	1,584	[8] 300,000	60	35	....	....	95
23	100,000	200	7	46	......	325,000	84	23	3	4	114

[1] 22,100 pounds other material used.
[2] 45,000 " " " "
[3] Including worsted yarns purchased.
[4] 15,000 pounds other material used.
[5] 27,500 " " " "
[6] 125,000 " " " "
[7] 100,000 " " " "
[8] 500,000 " " " "

WOOLEN — *Continued.*

TABLE No. 1. — Capacity for Production — *Continued.*

Number of Establishment.	Capital invested.	Horse power.	Sets of cards.	Looms in operation.	Spindles in operation.	Pounds of wool used in 1897.	Average number employed during 1897.				
							Men.	Women.	Boys.	Girls.	Total.
24	$10,000	160	6	43	......	[9] 150,000	50	25	5	....	80
25	25,000	40	4	27	600	[10] 180,448	32	21	....	....	53
26	200,000	180	14	......	......	[11] 491,946	60	10	....	....	70
27	75,000	150	8	36	2,800	500,000	70	50	....	....	120
28	100,000	225	7	40	2,150	[12] 221,053	78	25	3	1	107
29	45,000	116	5	35	1,680	371,200	65	35	....	....	100
30	50,000	180	7	35	2,688	[13] 558,568	75	28	....	....	103
31	100,000	350	16	118	3,080	1,200,000	215	75	....	7	297
32	20,000	75	3	16	1,040	132,000	26	6	2	....	34
33	150,000	300	3	17	864	[14] 475,000	60	20	4	....	84
34	15,000	60	4	42	960	[15] 25,000	24	14	3	....	41
35	40,000	65	4	28	2,080	80,000	23	13	4	3	43
36	15,000	75	4	17	1,320	40,000	40	10	3	2	55
37	15,000	85	5	27	1,968	[16] 65,000	61	9	4	4	78
38	1,500,000	1,200	25	424	13,444	2,700,000	412	423	32	36	903
39	75,000	150	10	88	......	430,000	100	50	....	....	150
40	50,000	125	6	35	2,800	300,000	80	20	....	....	100
41	200,000	125	6	60	1,520	120,000	64	30	3	3	100
42	25,000	75	3	14	800	60,000	28	8	....	....	36
43	400,000	300	17	100	5,600	595,845	175	80	20	25	300
44	150,000	200	14	70	......	328,000	80	60	3	2	145
45	7,000	60	......	......	1,200	21,000	12	......	....	....	12
46	65,000	70	3	32	......	[17] 7,000	34	16	4	....	54

[9] 300,000 pounds other material used.
[10] 14,381 " " " "
[11] 47,474 " " " "
[12] 25,500 " " " "
[13] 13,500 " " " "
[14] 35,000 " " " "
[15] 100,000 " " "
[16] 128,216 " "
[17] 295,000 " "

WOOLEN — *Concluded.*

TABLE No. 1. — Capacity for Production — *Concluded.*

Number of Establishment.	Capital invested.	Horse power.	Sets of cards.	Looms in operation.	Spindles in operation.	Pounds of wool used in 1897.	Average number employed during 1897.				
							Men.	Women.	Boys.	Girls.	Total.
47	$60,000	150	8	65	......	285,000	100	60	10	10	180
48	35,000	120	9	112	......	[18] 4,000	80	60	8	9	157
49	150,000	200	12	77	......	378,000	95	70	6	8	179
50	25,000	100	7	70	......	[19] 1,000	55	60	10	7	132
51	150,000	200	17	86	5,792	600,000	215	85	....	....	300
52	100,000	150	......	......	5,280	450,000	52	60	....	....	112
53	150,000	250	13	87	......	[20] 150,000	110	70	8	10	198
54	125,000	200	12	85	......	580,000	100	70	10	14	194
Total	$6,906,000	10,371	417	3,213	91,928	17,626,388	4,761	2,507	232	238	7,738

[18] 717,500 pounds other material used.
[19] 910,000   "   "   "   "
[20] 620,000   "   "   "   "

WOOLEN PRODUCTION.

This table has reference to the number of yards of goods produced during the year 1897 in the fifty-four establishments represented in the tabulation as manufacturers of cloths composed wholly or in part of wool, and also exhibits the value of product per yard and in total, together with the amount paid in wages. The latter amount, for reasons which have been hereinbefore explained, appears in the aggregate only.

It will be noticed that in two instances there are no figures given stating the number of yards of goods produced. This is explained by the footnote accompanying the table. It is proper, however, to state here that the material produced by the two establishments above mentioned, while composed of wool, was not used by themselves in the manufacture of woolen goods, but entered into the finished product of other establishments. In order, then, that the average value of production per yard be accurate, the amount of the production above referred to should be deducted from the total value of manufactured product, which has been done as shown in the table.

The number of yards of goods produced by all establishments was 17,235,929. The stated value of this production was $12,176,827.67. Deducting from this amount the value of product "reported elsewhere," and the net product value of the quantity of goods reported as having been manufactured during the year 1897 was $11,887,227.67, or 69 cents per yard.

The total amount paid in wages, exclusive of salaries, during the year was $2,667,953.07. The proportion of product value paid in wages was, therefore, 22 per cent.

WOOLEN.

TABLE No. 2. — Capacity for Production.

Number of Establishment.	Yards of goods produced during 1897.	Value of product manufactured.	Value per yard.	Per cent. production of full capacity.	Value of product, full capacity.
	274,608	$68,652.00	$0.25	80	$85,815.00
2	100,000	100,000.00	1.00	100	100,000.00
3	75,000	49,920.00	.67	100	49,920.00
4	154,067	120,000.00	.78	32	375,000.00
5	115,768	175,000.00	1.51	100	175,000.00
6	150,000	162,000.00	1.08	65	249,230.77
7	321,428	450,000.09	1.40	83	542,168.92
8	80,000	140,000.00	1.75	25	560,000.00
9	101,516	65,000.00	.64	100	65,000.00
10	84,836	151,766.00	1.79	60	252,943.33
11	204,853	284,264.62	1.39	83	342,487.49
12	540,000	330,000.00	.61	95	347,368.42
13	270,000	60,000.00	.22	90	66,666.66
14	120,000	240,000.00	2.00	67	358,208.96
15	221,230	339,700.00	1.54	60	566,166.67
16	360,000	664,000.00	1.84	83	800,000.00
17	520,000	200,000.00	.38	95	210,526.32
18	450,000	750,000.00	1.67	80	937,500.00
19	175,000	200,000.00	1.14	100	200,000.00
20	180,000	12,600.00	.07	50	25,200.00
21	279,122	248,637.65	.89	60	414,396.08
22	900,000	198,000.00	.22	100	198,000.0
23	160,000	200,000.00	1.25	60	333,333.33

WOOLEN — *Continued.*

TABLE No. 2. — Capacity for Production — *Continued.*

Number of Establishment.	Yards of goods produced during 1897.	Value of product manufactured.	Value per yard.	Per cent. production of full capacity.	Value of product, full capacity.
24	216,000	$125,812.00	$0.58	100	$125,812.00
25	48,707	40,000.00	.82	60	66,666.67
26	136,508	114,666.72	.84	90	127,407.47
27	450,000	250,000.00	.56	90	277,777.78
28	181,148	110,558.40	.61	66	167,512.73
29	104,000	208,000.00	2.00	95	218,947.37
30	242,396	162,106.54	.67	100	162,106.54
31	400,000	500,000.00	1.25	100	500,000.00
32	105,000	57,750.00	.55	80	72,187.50
33	90,000	65,000.00	.72	45	144,444.44
34	550,000	86,000.00	1.56	90	95,555.56
35	150,000	60,000.00	.40	83	72,289.16
36	25,000	25,000.00	1.00	33	75,757.58
37	102,500	192,187.00	1.87	100	192,187.00
38	1,296,187	1,109,306.74	.86	60	1,848,844.57
39	2,250,000	200,000.00	.09	90	222,222.22
40	240,000	140,000.00	.58	100	140,000.00
41	600,000	225,000.00	.38	100	225,000.00
42	118,300	26,400.00	.22	90	29,333.33
43	323,569	487,000.00	1.50	100	487,000.00
44	260,000	275,000.00	1.06	90	305,555.56
45	*........	25,000.00	......	100	25,000.00
46	190,169	97,500.00	.51	100	97,500.00

*Appears elsewhere.

WOOLEN — *Concluded.*

TABLE No. 2. — Capacity for Production — *Concluded.*

Number of Establishment.	Yards of goods produced during 1897.	Value of product manufactured.	Value per yard.	Per cent. production of full capacity.	Value of product, full capacity.
47	275,000	$300,000.00	$1.09	95	$315,789.47
48	799,017	218,400.00	.27	100	218,400.00
49	275,000	268,000.00	.97	85	315,294.12
50	700,000	144,000.00	.21	100	144,000.00
51	500,000	520,000.00	1.04	90	577,777.78
52	*........	264,600.00	......	100	264,600.00
53	450,000	325,000.00	.72	100	325,000.00
54	320,000	345,000.00	1.08	100	345,000.00
Total	17,235,929	†$12,176,827.67	‡$0.69	‡78	$15,439,900.80

* Appears elsewhere.
† Value of product, less goods produced, reported elsewhere, $11,887,227.67.
‡ Average.

WAGES AND RENT.

The scale of wages as shown in the tables are given by establishments only, an accurate average wage rate not being possible to obtain. As will be seen $18.20 per week was the highest wages reported as having been paid weavers, while in one instance $3.00 per week was reported as being the lowest wages paid. The highest average rate of wages reported by any establishment was $12.04 per week, the lowest average weekly wages paid weavers being $5.50.

The highest wages paid spinners was reported to have been $14.20 per week, $3.70 per week being the lowest. The highest average weekly wages paid spinners, as reported, was $12.00, and the lowest average rate $4.75 per week.

There were 1,117 tenements owned by the several manufacturers of woolen goods. The number of rooms in each ranging from three to twelve, and the rate for rent from $2.08 to $13.00 per month.

WOOLEN.

TABLE No. 3.—Wage Rates and Rates Paid for Rent.

Number of Establishment.	WEAVERS. Weekly wage rates.			SPINNERS. Weekly wage rates.			Tenements owned.	Rooms in each.	Rent per month.
	Highest.	Lowest.	Average.	Highest.	Lowest.	Average.			
1	$10.00	$6.00	$8.00	$9.00	$9.00	$9.00	9	5 to 8	$2.50 to $7.00
2	12.00	9.00	10.50	7.50	7.50	7.50	2	6 and 11	5.00 and 7.00
3	12.00	......	9.00	......	......	7.92	10	4 to 6	2.17 to 4.34
4	10.50	6.00	8.25	10.00	8.00	9.00	57	6	4.17
5	15.60	......	10.18	12.80	......	9.40	16	6 to 11	6.00 to 13.00
6	......	......	8.50	......	......	7.75	......	....	....
7	18.00	4.50	8.50	......	......	......	1	8	7.00
8	......	......	12.00	......	......	......	10	5 to 7	7.00 to 10.00
9	9.00	6.00	8.00	7.50	7.50	7.50	8	5	4.50
10	9.90	7.56	8.73	10.44	10.38	10.41	21	5	3.50
11	15.00	5.00	8.60	......	......	8.10	......	....	....
12	......	......	8.00	.....	......	......	......	....	....
13	10.00	......	8.00	......	......	......	7	6	5.00
14	......	......	9.00	......	10.50	......	17	4 to 8	3.50 to 8.00
15	14.07	9.69	12.04	8.21	5.79	7.39	......	....	....
16	......	......	8.45	......	......	6.60	12	4 to 8	5.00 to 12.00
17	9.93	7.50	8.12	12.14	10.83	11.20	27	6 to 8	4.00 to 7.00
18	18.00	5.50	10.00	8.17	4.84	7.00	6	6 to 8	6.00 to 8.00
19	13.00	7.50	9.00	8.10	8.10	8.10	22	4 to 9	2.08 to 8.00
20	10.50	5.00	7.50	10.50	10.50	10.50	10	5 to 6	3.00
21	12.00	6.00	9.00	9.00	5.00	7.00	30	5	5.00
22	10.00	6.00	8.75	10.00	9.00	9.75	20	4 to 8	4.00 to 8.00
23	12.00	5.00	8.50	9.00	9.00	9.00	12	4 to 10	5.50

WOOLEN — *Continued.*

TABLE No. 3.—Wage Rates and Rates Paid for Rent — *Continued.*

Number of Establishmen t	WEAVERS. Weekly wage rates.			SPINNERS. Weekly wage rates.			Tenements owned.	Rooms in each.	Rent per month.
	Highest.	Lowest.	Average.	Highest.	Lowest.	Average.			
24	$11.10	$7.65	$8.88	$11.00	$7.50	$8.46	6	4 to 5	$3.50 to $5.00
25	10.00	6.00	7.50	8.70	8.70	8.70	3	6 to 7	5.00 to 8.00
26	......	......	......	......	......	......	12	8	6.30
27	13.00	10.00	11.00	9.00	9.00	9.00	35	8	4.00
28	11.00	7.50	9.00	10.00	6.00	7.35	14	4 to 7	4.00 to 7.00
29	......	......	9.50	......	......	10.50	23	4 to 8	4.00 to 8.00
30	•12.00	7.30	10.54	14.20	8.60	10.58	12	5 to 8	4.00 to 7.00
31	12.00	7.50	9.00	11.00	8.00	9.00	54	4 to 8	3.00 to 8.00
32	9.00	6.00	7.00	12.00	7.50	9.48	10	3 to 6	3.00 to 6.00
33	12.50	3.00	7.50	9.60	9.60	9.60	......	......	......
34	......	......	8.00	......	......	12.00	6	5 to 6	3.00 to 4.00
35	10.00	5.00	8.00	9.00	6.00	8.00	10	4 to 7	3.00 to 6.25
36	12.00	9.00	10.00	9.00	-7.50	8.00	8	4	4.00
37	12.00	9.00	10.00	9.50	8.00	8.50	......	......	......
38	18.20	4.50	9.00	8.40	3.70	4.75	240	3 to 8	3.45 to 11.25
39	9.50	7.50	8.25	12.00	10.50	11.00	28	4 to 9	4.00 to 7.00
40	10.00	7.00	8.50	11.00	6.00	8.50	12	3 to 4	2.50 to 6.00
41	13.00	7.00	8.10	12.00	9.00	10.20	42	4 to 12	3.50 to 7.50
42	12.00	8.00	8.75	7.20	7.20	7.20	14	6	5.00
43	12.00	7.50	9.00	9.00	6.50	7.50	77	4 to 10	3.50 to 8.00
44	13.00	8.50	10.00	10.00	7.00	7.75	28	4 to 8	4.00 to 8.00
45	......	......	......	9.00	6.25	7.80	......	......	......
46	12.00	6.00	8.00	12.00	10.00	10.50	10	3 to 5	3.50 to 4.50

WOOLEN — *Concluded.*

TABLE No. 3.—Wage Rates and Rates Paid for Rent — *Concluded.*

| Number of Establishment | WEAVERS. Weekly wage rates. | | | SPINNERS. Weekly wage rates. | | | Tenements owned. | Rooms in each. | Rent per month. |
	Highest.	Lowest.	Average.	Highest.	Lowest.	Average.			
47	$13.00	$9.00	$10.50	$12.00	$9.50	$11.00	......	....	....
48	13.00	5.00	6.50	13.00	9.00	10.00	9	3 to 4	$3.00 to $4.25
49	12.00	7.00	8.75	10.00	6.00	7.50	30	3 to 5	3.00 to 5.00
50	8.00	5.00	5.50	10.00	7.00	8.50	6	4 to 5	3.00 to 4.00
51	12.00	6.50	10.00	10.00	7.00	9.00	71	4 to 6	4.00 to 6.00
52	......	......	......	12.00	8.00	9.00	30	4 to 6	4.00 to 7.00
53	12.00	6.00	7.50	12.00	7.00	8.00	20	3 to 5	3.00 to 4.00
54	13.00	6.00	10.00	......	......	......	10	3 to 6	4.00 to 7.00

ASSESSMENTS AND TAXES.

The fifty-four establishments represented in the foregoing were located in twenty-eight different towns. The assessment laid against them for purposes of taxation, in 1897, was $4,549,798.00, and the amount paid by them for taxes to the several towns was $58,686.30. The average rate of taxation was 13 mills. The following table shows the amount of assessment and the amount paid in taxes, divided by towns.

WOOLEN GOODS.

Assessments and Taxes Paid, Divided by Towns.

Town.	Assessment on Grand List, 1897.	Amount paid in taxes, 1897.
Bridgeport	$110,000	$1,320.00
Coventry	12,575	188.62
East Lyme	31,450	377.40
East Windsor	205,350	3,080.25
Enfield	652,250	11,109.88
Glastonbury	81,235	1,218.52
Greenwich	69,900	908.70
Killingly	124,250	1,863.75
Ledyard	7,300	109.50
Manchester	77,799	1,166.98
Meriden	112,700	2,366.70
Middletown.	15,780	157.80
Montville.	20,375	326.00
Norwalk	158,500	3,170.00
Norwich	258,835	1,682.43
Plainfield	154,100	1,849.20
Preston	69,975	1,119.60
Putnam	164,151	3,118.87
Seymour	74,000	1,480.00
Somers	113,205	1,358.46
Sprague	6,300	94.50
Stafford	275,559	5,511.18
Stonington	14,000	175.00

WOOLEN GOODS — *Concluded.*

Assessments and Taxes Paid, Divided by Towns — *Concluded.*

Town.	Assessment on Grand List, 1897.	Amount paid in taxes, 1897.
Thompson	$37,075	$444.90
Torrington	98,000	1,372.00
Winchester	5,000	65.00
Woodbury	35,712	535.68
Vernon	1,564,422	12,515.38
Total	$4,549,798	$58,686.30

CLOSED MILLS.

There were found to be in the State fifteen establishments which had been engaged in the manufacture of woolen goods previous to the period covered by this investigation. These establishments, when in operation, had 79 sets of cards in use and 543 looms in operation, and were assessed in the grand list of 1897 at $183,826.00, and paid $3,113.25 in taxes to the different towns in which they were located. Three of the establishments reported as being "closed mills" were not assessed for purposes of taxation, and although they appear in the tabulation referring to sets of cards and number of looms, no reference is made to the locality of the mills in the exhibit of assessment and taxes paid to towns.

WOOLENS — Closed Mills.

TABLE No. 3. — Capacity for Production.

Number of Establishment.	Sets of cards.	Number of looms.
55..	8	54
56..	17	101
57..	4	20
58..		4
59..	1	8
60..	5	37
61..	2	16
62..	5	38
63..	......	2
64..	4	56
65..	5	28
66..	11	56
67..	8	40
68..		3
69..	7	80
Total..	79	543

WOOLEN GOODS — Closed Mills.

Assessments and Taxes Paid, Divided by Towns.

Town.	Assessment on Grand List, 1897.	Amount paid in taxes, 1897.
Bethlehem..	$6,111	$48.89
Coventry...	23,800	357.00
Eastford...	1,000	16.00
Montville...	2,900	46.40
New London...	20,000	640.00
Newtown..	15,180	166.98
Norwalk..	38,000	760.00
Norwich...	32,800	328.00
Southbury..	500	7.50
Sprague..	25,643	384.64
Stafford...	10,000	200.00
Willington...	7,892	157.84
Total..	$183,826	$3,113.25

ILLUSTRATIONS.

The following exhibits are made up from the returns made by ten manufacturing establishments, the product of which consisted of broadcloths, cassimeres, cloakings, woolens and worsteds, and have been prepared for the purpose of showing the proportion of product value which was paid for wages, and also to show the average number of yards produced per loom and per employe, by establishments.

The same explanation should apply to these illustrations as has been made in the preceding chapter concerning the cotton industry.

A most interesting comparison can here be made with the figures contained in the report of the Commissioner of Industrial and Labor Statistics for the State of Maine which has just been issued, and covers the same period as does this report. The publication referred to gives the statistics from twenty-five establishments engaged in the manufacture of woolen goods. The total value of product of these establishments in 1897 was $3,630,312, and the total amount paid in wages $911,037. The proportion of product value paid in wages was 25 per cent.

Making comparisons with the ten establishments in Connecticut shown in the following exhibits, it is found that the total value of product of these was $2,406,616.62, and the amount paid by them in wages $571,962.73, this being 24 per cent. of product value.

It must be remembered, however, in making comparisons that the proportion of product value paid in wages by the fifty-four establishments covered by this investigation was 22 per cent.

EXHIBIT 1.

Year 1897.
36 looms,   2 sets of cards,
Produced 274,608 yards cassimeres.
Average number employed, 58.
Average yards produced per loom, 7,628.
Average yards produced per employe, 4,735.
Value of product, $68,652.00.
Amount paid in wages, $18,792.09.
Per cent. of product value paid in wages, 27.4.

EXHIBIT 2.

Year 1897.
21 looms,   2 sets of cards,
Produced 100,000 yards fancy worsteds.
Average number employed, 52.
Average yards produced per loom, 4,762.
Average yards produced per employe, 1,923.
Value of product, $100,000.
Amount paid in wages, $18,000.00.
Per cent. of product value paid in wages, 18.

EXHIBIT 3.

Year 1897.
22 looms,   5 sets of cards,
Produced 115,768 yards wool uniform cloths.
Average number employed, 79.
Average yards produced per loom, 5,262.
Average yards produced per employe, 1,465.
Value of product, $175,000.00.
Amount paid in wages, $32,525.90.
Per cent. of product value paid in wages, 18.6.

EXHIBIT 4.

Year 1897.
109 looms,   9 sets of cards,
Produced 321,428 yards cassimeres and worsteds
Average number employed, 311.
Average yards produced per loom, 2,949.
Average yards produced per employe, 1,034.
Value of product, $450,000.00.
Amount paid in wages, $122,142.83.
Per cent. of product value paid in wages, 27.1.

EXHIBIT 5.

Year 1897.
20 looms,   4 sets of cards,
Produced 101,516 yards cassimeres and cloakings.
Average number employed, 44.
Average yards produced per loom, 5,076.
Average yards produced per employe, 2,307.
Value of product, $65,000.00.
Amount paid in wages, $15,525.00.
Per cent. of product value paid in wages, 23.9.

EXHIBIT 6.

Year 1897.
76 looms,   15 sets of cards,
Produced 204,853 yards woolens, worsteds and cassimeres.
Average number employed, 252.
Average yards produced per loom, 2,695.
Average yards produced per employe, 813.
Value of product, $284,264.62.
Amount paid in wages, $71,935.12.
Per cent. of product value paid in wages, 25.3.

EXHIBIT 7.

Year 1897.
28 looms,   3 sets of cards,
Produced 270,000 yards union cassimeres.
Average number employed, 48.
Average yards produced per loom, 9,643.
Average yards produced per employe, 5,625.
Value of product, $60,000.00.
Amount paid in wages, $17,000.00.
Per cent. of product value paid in wages, 28.3.

EXHIBIT 8.

Year 1897.
125 looms,   20 sets of cards,
Produced 221,230 yards fine worsteds and woolens.
Average number employed, 299.
Average yards produced per loom, 1,770,
Average yards produced per employe, 740.
Value of product, $339,700.00.
Amount paid in wages, $96,489.79.
Per cent. of product value paid in wages, 28.4.

EXHIBIT 9.

Year 1897.
160 looms,   9 sets of cards,
Produced 360,000 yards woolens and worsteds.
Average number employed, 375.
Average yards produced per loom, 2,250.
Average yards produced per employe, 960.
Value of product, $664,000.00.
Amount paid in wages, $136,500.00.
Per cent. of product value paid in wages, 20.6.

EXHIBIT 10.

Year 1897.

54 looms,   10 sets of cards,

Produced 520,000 yards carriage and broad cloth.

Average number employed, 114.

Average yards produced per loom, 9,630.

Average yards produced per employe, 4,561.

Value of product, $200,000.00.

Amount paid in wages, $43,052.00.

Per cent. of product value paid in wages, 21.5.

KNIT GOODS.

Classified as manufacturers of knit goods are those establishments the product of which consists of hosiery, men's, women's and infants' underwear, the material used being made up of both cotton and wool. Accurate division of this material being impossible, the quantity used is given in the aggregate and includes all material used in the process of manufacture except the amount of cotton yarn purchased of other manufacturers, the amount of the material for the manufacture of which appears in the table referring to cotton warps, webs, threads and yarns.

There were twenty-three establishments in operation in the State during the year 1897. The amount of capital invested (exclusive of surplus) being $1,863,000.00. The number of cards reported as being in use was 126 sets. There was also in operation in all the establishments shown in the tabulation 38 looms, 53,514 spindles and 1,204 knitting and other machines. It should be stated that one establishment was reported as being closed, the capacity of which was 11 sets of cards and 45 machines, thus making the total number of cards 137, and 1,249 machines, total capacity for production being considered.

The total amount of material used (exclusive of cotton yarns purchased) was 5,451,392 pounds. The average number of persons employed during the year was 3,006, of which 913 were men, 1,921 women, 68 boys and 104 girls, the two last named classes being under 16 years of age. The proportion of children of total number employed, therefore, was 5.7 per cent.

The production of all the establishments for the year covered by the investigation amounted to 706,964 dozen of the various kinds of hosiery and knit goods, in addition to which there was manufactured 100,000 square yards and 348,000 pounds of other goods, the nature of which was such as to render it impossible to classify as to number of pieces.

The total value of product manufactured by these establishments during the year 1897 was $3,630,550.52, and the

amount paid in wages (exclusive of salaries) for the same
period $967,752.47, this being 26.7 per cent. of product value.

WAGES AND RENT.

As previously stated, the actual average wage rate was not
obtainable, the highest and lowest average only can be given,
which were, for knitters $11.00 and $4.50 per week, respectively, and to spinners the highest average rate paid was $14.40
and the lowest $7.15 per week.

There were 137 tenements reported as being owned by the
several establishments, the number of rooms in each ranging
from 4 to 10, and the rate paid for rent from $3.00 to $12.00
per month.

ASSESSMENTS AND TAXES.

The total assessment laid against all establishments for
purposes of taxation, by the towns in which these industries
were located, was $1,505,528; and the amount paid in taxes
$21,134.47, the average rate of tax being 14 mills.

KNIT GOODS.

TABLE NO. 1. — Capacity for Production.

Number of Establishment.	Capital invested.	Horse power.	Sets of cards.	Number of looms.	Number of machines.	Number of spindles.	Pounds of material used.	Average number employed during 1897.				
								Men.	Women.	Boys.	Girls.	Total.
1	$30,000	280	......	......	80	6,000	55,000	25	60	3	......	88
2	13,000	6	......	......	40	....	*........	2	34	......	......	36
3	40,000	20	......	......	18	....	*13,000	10	26	......	......	36
4	15,000	3	......	....	24	....	*.......	2	20	......	......	22
5	2,000	6	......	......	12	....	*.......	5	......	......	......	5
6	150,000	120	11	....	50	2,640	212,000	50	100	......	5	155
7	50,000	70	3	....	25	768	32,000	17	33	......	......	50
8	300,000	300	20	....	....	9,500	261,572	124	328	6	17	475
9	150,000	150	13	....	72	2,600	150,000	40	100	25	30	195
10	125,000	150	9	......	60	3,264	287,500	50	125	3	3	181
11	100,000	125	5	....	125	566	360,000	40	120	5	10	175
12	75,000	125	8	....	32	2,040	240,000	40	100	1	6	147
13	40,000	125	10	10	37	2,736	475,127	93	71	2	2	168
14	60,000	300	6	12	68	2,496	176,000	30	40	6	6	82
15	50,000	150	8	16	....	2,100	300,000	40	70	......	......	110
16	350,000	200	13	......	185	4,500	1,500,000	150	250	......	......	400
17	8,000	25	1	......	6	....	53,000	2	5	......	......	7
18	60,000	100	7	....	67	2,304	123,300	50	116	6	10	182
19	50,000	75	7	......	60	1,800	189,893	45	75	......	......	120
20	80,000	200	......	......	115	3,000	360,000	35	120	5	7	167
21	60,000	150	5	....	24	2,200	278,000	28	80	3	5	116
22	5,000	3	......	......	18	....	*........	1	10	......	......	11
23	50,000	150	......	......	86	5,000	385,000	34	38	3	3	78
Total	$1,863,000	2,833	126	38	1,204	53,514	5,451,392	913	1,921	68	104	3,006

Closed Establishments.

1	....	....	11	......	45	....	....	......	......	......	......	......

* Yarns purchased.

KNIT GOODS.

TABLE No. 2. — Capacity for Production.

Number of Establishment.	Dozens of goods produced during 1887.	Value of product manufactured.	Per cent. production of full capacity.	Value of product, full capacity.
1	5,000	$66,000.00	25	$264,000.00
2	15,000	30,000.00	75	40,000.00
3	20,000	64,000.00	75	85,333.33
4	25,000	24,000.00	100	24,000.00
5	12,000	4,750.00	75	6,333.33
6	34,254	70,000.00	60	116,666.67
7	25,000	26,000.00	60	43,333.33
8	47,000	460,000.00	50	920,000.00
9	67,000	100,000.00	60	166,666.67
10	14,000	250,000.00	85	294,117.65
11	65,000	275,000.00	96	286,458.33
12	28,000	140,000.00	80	175,000.00
13	36,857	300,642.56	95	316,465.95
14	8,500	63,000.00	68	92,647.06
15	40,000	280,000.00	100	280,000.00
16	75,000	425,000.00	100	425,000.00
17	*........	10,000,00	60	16,666.67
18	56,000	220,000.00	100	220,000.00
19	13,753	286,657.96	61	469,931.08
20	60,000	240,000.00	95	252,631.58
21	58,000	135,000.00	100	135,000.00
22	1,600	6,500.00	33	19,696.97
23	†........	154,000.00	60	256,666.67
Total	706,964	$3,630,550.52	74	$4,906,615.29

* 100,000 square yards.
† 348,000 pounds

KNIT GOODS.

TABLE No. 3. — Wage Rates and Rates Paid for Rent.

Number of Es ald shmen	KNITTERS. Weekly wage rates.			SPINNERS. Weekly wage rates.			Tenements owned.	Rooms in each.	Rent per month.
	Highest.	Lowest.	Average.	Highest.	Lowest.	Average.			
1	$12.00	$4.20	$7.20	$12.00	$6.60	$7.40	13	5	$5.00
2	10.00	6.00	7.00	......	......	......	......	....	....
3	10.50	10.50	10.50	......	......	......	......	....	....
4	10.00	6.00	7.50	......	......	......	......	....	....
5	8.00	5.00	6.00	......	......	......	......	....	....
6	12.00	5.40	7.50	12.00	9.00	10.00	......	....	....
7	8.10	6.90	7.50	12.00	9.00	10.50	6	7	3.00 to 6.00
8	......	......	......	12.00	7.00	10.00	......	....	....
9	......	......	......	10.00	6.60	8.10	2	....	8.00
10	10.00	5.00	8.00	8.00	6.00	7.50	25	5 to 10	5.00 to 12.00
11	9.00	6.90	8.10	10.80	6.60	8.70	1	7	6.00
12	12.00	9.00	9.50	12.00	10.00	10.50	7	7	9.00
13	11.00	9.00	10.00	11.00	9.00	10.00	37	4 to 8	4.00 to 9.00
14	8.00	7.00	7.50	7.50	6.75	7.15	12	6	4.50
15	10.50	6.00	8.00	12.00	6.00	7.50	......	....	....
16	12.00	7.50	11.00	12.00	7.50	11.00	34	4 to 5	Average 10.00
17	6.00	6.00	6.00	......	......	......	......	....	....
18	12.00	9.00	10.50	16.50	12.00	14.40	......	....	....
19	12.00	9.00	9.50	12.00	9.00	9.50	......	....	....
20	12.00	7.00	10.50	12.00	7.00	10.50	......	....	....
21	12.00	8.10	11.00	12.00	8.10	11.00	......	....	....
22	6.00	3.00	4.50	......	......	......	......	....	....
23	......	......	......	12.00	8.50	11.25	......	....	....

KNIT GOODS.

Assessments and Taxes Paid, Divided by Towns.

Town.	Assessment on Grand List, 1897.	Amount paid in taxes, 1897.
Bridgeport..	$11,000	$132.00
Bristol...........	100,610	1,226.61
Derby...	296,533	2,668.79
Glastonbury...	50,125	721.87
Hartford......	6,500	130.00
Huntington...	60,000	660.00
Madison..	400	4.00
Manchester...	34,400	516.00
Naugatuck..	8,225	119.26
New Britain...........................	417,000	8,340.00
New Haven..	10,000	240.00
Norfolk..	22,000	264.00
Plainville..	80,476	724.28
Stamford..	4,125	86.62
Sterling..	39,900	518.70
Trumbull...	1,900	22.80
Vernon...	60,000	480.00
Waterbury..	50,000	1,400.00
Windsor..	14,000	182.00
Windsor Locks..	133,600	1,336.00
Winchester...	104,734	1,361.54
Total..	$1,505,528	$21,134.47

SILK GOODS.

The silk manufacturing industry in Connecticut is a very important one, and the nature of the product is such that to undertake to describe in detail the different kinds or varieties of goods produced, or to endeavor to show the number of yards, pieces or pounds manufactured would, in a greater or less degree, violate the agreements made with the establishments that have furnished the Bureau with detailed information, and for this reason the table referring to silk goods contains only the data secured which shows the capital invested (not including accumulation or surplus) by firm, individual or corporation engaged in the business in 1897. The table also shows the number of horse power used by the several establishments, the number of pounds of silk consumed in the process of manufacture, the value of manufactured product, the amount paid in wages (aggregate only), and the average number employed by all establishments, together with the average weekly wage rate paid weavers and spinners.

Information was secured from twenty-five establishments engaged in the silk industry, which were in operation in 1897. The aggregate amount of capital invested in these (exclusive of surplus) was $4,008,000.00. 1,607,150 pounds of silk were consumed in the process of manufacture, the value of manufactured product being $7,488,485.05, and the amount paid in wages (exclusive of salaries) $1,734,739, this amount being 23 per cent. of product value. The total average number employed in all establishments was 5,154, of which 2,093 were men, 2,590 women and 471 boys and girls under 16 years of age. 9.1 per cent. of the total number employed, therefore, being children.

The highest average wages paid weavers was found to be $15.00 per week; the lowest average being $7.50 per week. $10.00 per week was the highest average wage rate paid spinners, and the lowest $4.50 per week.

SILK.

TABLE No. 1. — Capacity for Production.

Number of Establishment.	Capital invested.	Horse power.	Pounds of silk used in 1897.	Value of product manufactured.	Average number employed during 1897.					Average weekly wage rate.	
					Men.	Women.	Boys.	Girls.	Total.	Weavers.	Spinners.
1	$12,000	30	10,000	$24,000.00	3	16	1	......	20	......	$6.75
2	50,000	70	3,000	40,000.00	......	50	2	3	55	$7.50	......
3	100,000	80	41,523	91,496.25	23	72	......	......	95	......	7.50
4	1,000,000	140	88,650	926,000.00	35	200	30	20	285	......	7.75
5	20,000	40	15,000	100,000.00	15	30	10	10	65	......	7.00
6	145,000	100	25,000	150,000.00	25	100	......	......	125	7.50	7.00
7	6,000	15	6,533	21,492.00	3	7	......	2	12	......	9.25
8	150,000	30	28,000	250,000.00	50	52	7	......	109	......	10.00
9	25,000	40	13,553	106,000.00	18	42	......	......	60	......	8.75
10	15,000	20	7,500	30,000.00	5	15	......	......	20	......	7.25
11	60,000	150	60,892	200,000.00	12	90	......	......	102	......	7.50
12	640,000	150	22,948	231,226.48	80	125	7	......	212	15.00	......
13	15,000	15	17,539	70,156.00	10	43	5	4	62	......	7.50
14	60,000	25	*150	65,000.00	10	20	......	......	30	13.00	......
15	25,000	25	12,000	50,000.00	48	13	2	2	65	13.25	......
16	75,000	150	65,000	200,000.00	100	50	......	......	150	11.50	......
17	100,000	250	100,000	600,000.00	240	160	30	40	470	11.00	......
18	50,000	30	30,000	150,000.00	5	50	......	......	55	......	6.25
19	1,000,000	1,850	*750,362	3,139,211.32	1,096	855	75	139	2,165	8.70	7.50
20	60,000	75	11,500	150,000.00	27	130	4	8	169	9.00	4.50
21	60,000	100	3,000	33,903.00	35	35	......	......	70	10.00	4.60
22	100,000	125	95,000	375,000.00	150	150	10	10	320	11.50	......
23	100,000	100	65,000	170,000.00	50	120	4	4	178	......	7.00
24	15,000	50	35,000	65,000.00	8	40	6	6	60	......	7.25
25	125,000	200	100,000	250,000.00	45	125	15	15	200	......	8.50
Total	$4,008,000	3,860	1,607,150	$7,488,485.05	2,093	2,590	208	263	5,154	......	......

* Other material purchased.

Total amount paid in wages, all establishments, $1,734,739.
Proportion wages paid of product value, 23 per cent.

	Value of product manufactured.	Per cent. production of full capacity.	Value of product, full capacity.
All establishments.............	$7,488,485.05	†77	$9,725,777.28

† Average.

ASSESSMENTS AND TAXES.

As will be seen by referring to the preceding table, there
were twenty-five establishments in the State actively engaged
in the manufacture of silk goods in 1897. It should be noted,
however, that there were two establishments reported as being
closed during that period.

The total number of establishments against which assessments for purposes of taxation were laid was, therefore, twenty-seven. These were located in twenty-two different towns,
as will be seen by the following table. The total amount of
assessment laid (including assessments against closed mills),
was $2,292,381, and the amount paid in taxes to the several
towns by all establishments was $35,166.36. The average rate
of taxation was 15 mills.

SILK GOODS.

Assessments and Taxes Paid, Divided by Towns.

Town.	Assessment on Grand List, 1897.	Amount paid in taxes, 1897.
Bridgeport	$150,100	$1,801.20
Coventry	4,025	60.37
Danbury	15,550	311.00
Hamden	3,050	45.75
Hartford	70,000	1,400.00
Hebron	31,900	446.60
Manchester	1,421,561	21,323.41
Mansfield	3,252	48.78
New Haven	6,500	156.00
New London	110,400	3,532.80
Norfolk	15,000	180.00
Norwalk	2,500	50.00
Norwich	28,500	470.20
Preston	13,000	208.00
Putnam	31,000	589.00
Stonington	14,720	331.20
Vernon	151,000	1,208.00
Watertown	119,823	1,318.05
Winchester	45,000	585.00
Windham	37,000	851.00
Windsor Locks	5,500	55.00
Total	$2,279,381	$34,971.36

Closed Mills.

Mansfield	$1,000	$15.00
Marlborough	12,000	180.00
Total	$13,000	$195.00

SUMMARY.

A summary of the foregoing is presented herewith and shows, in a condensed form, the results of the work of the Bureau in the investigation of the subject of the condition of the textile industries in the State.

It will be noted that in the case of the silk industry the mechanical appliances used in manufacture and the quantity of goods produced, has been omitted from the tabulation. The reason for this omission has been explained elsewhere. The value of product and the total amount paid in wages is given, however, thus indicating the per cent. of product value paid in wages.

Goods Manufactured.	Number of establishments considered.	Number of horse power.	Capital invested, 1897.	Value of product manufactured, 1897.	Amount paid in wages, 1897.	Per cent, wages paid of product value.	Average per cent. of full capacity production.	Value of product, full capacity.	Average number employed. Males.	Average number employed. Females.
Cotton	60	30,499	$15,671,700	$15,540,584.42	$4,830,023.37	31.1	89	$17,426,369.45	7,767	7,870
Woolen	54	10,371	6,906,000	11,887,227.67	2,667,953.07	22.	78	15,439,900.80	4,993	2,745
Knit	24	2,833	1,863,000	3,630,550.52	967,752.47	26.7	74	4,906,615.29	981	2,025
Silk	25	3,860	4,008,000	7,488,485.05	1,734,739.00	23.	77	9,725,777.28	2,301	2,853
Total	163	47,563	$28,448,700	$38,546,797.66	$10,200,467.91	26.5	81	$47,499,162.82	16,042	15,493

Goods Manufactured.	Sets of cards in use, 1897.	Looms in operation, 1897.	Machines in use, 1897.	Spindles in operation, 1897.	Cards idle, 1897.	Looms idle, 1897.	Machines idle, 1897.	Spindles idle, 1897.	Total number. Cards.	Total number. Looms.	Total number. Machines.	Total number. Spindles.
Cotton	....	21,080	....	1,088,020	....	794	....	56,048	....	21,874	....	1,094,068
Woolen	417	3,213	....	91,928	79	543	....	....	496	3,756	....	91,928
Knit	126	38	1,204	53,514	11	....	45	....	187	38	1,249	53,514
Total	543	24,331	1,204	1,183,462	90	1,337	45	56,048	683	25,668	1,249	1,239,510

Goods Manufactured.	Pounds of cott used in 1897.	Pounds of woo used in 1897.	Pounds of sil used in 1897.	Pounds of oth material used in 1897.	Yards of goo produced in 18	Dozens of goo produced in 18	Pounds of go produced in 18
Cotton	53,104,000	......	......	5,000	204,214,178	2,286,532	7,486,951
Woolen	......	17,626,388	......	4,041,171	17,235,929	......	......
Knit	......	......	......	*5,451,392	100,000	706,964	348,000
Silk	......	......	1,607,150	......	......	......	......
Total	53,104,000	17,626,388	1,607,150	9,497,563	221,550,107	2,993,496	7,834,951

* Exclusive of yarns purchased.

Goods Manufactured.	Total assessment on Grand List, 1897.	Total amount paid in taxes, 1897.	Number of tenements owned.	Rooms in each.	Rate of rent per month.	Average weekly wages.					
						Weavers.		Spinners.		Knitters.	
						Highest.	Lowest.	Highest.	Lowest.	Highest.	Lowest.
Cotton	$10,370,519	$147,209.75	3,084	2 to 10	$ 90 to $11.00	$18.00	$5.00	$12.00	$4.00	......	......
Woolen	4,733,024	61,799.55	1,117	3 to 12	2.08 to 3 00	12.04	5.50	12.00	4.75	......	......
Knit	1,505,528	21,134.47	137	4 to 10	3.00 to 2 00	......	......	14.40	7.15	$11.00	$4.50
Silk	2,292,981	35,166.36	......	......	......	15.00	7.50	10.00	4.50	......	......
Total	$18,902,052	$265,310.13	4,338	......	......	......	......	......	......	......	......

In closing the portion of this report devoted to the subject of the manufactures of textiles in Connecticut, an interesting comparison can be made with existing conditions in North Carolina, the material for which is taken from the report of the Bureau of Labor Statistics of that State for the year 1897.

It appears in the publication referred to that in the year named there were 208 establishments in the State engaged in the manufacture of cotton and hosiery goods, with 24,517 looms, 1,044,385 spindles and 1,410 machines in operation, requiring the use of 43,000 horse power in running the plants.

The largest number of looms in operation in any one establishment was 1,366, and of spindles 28,350. The largest amount of capital invested in any one establishment is reported as being $500,000.

The total number employed in these mills was 25,887, of which 5,363 or 20.7 per cent. were children.

Comparisons made with the conditions which obtain in the establishments manufacturing similar goods in Connecticut make it apparent that conditions are more favorable in this State than in the South, for the investigation made by this Bureau into the prevailing conditions here develops the information that in the same year as was covered by the report of the Bureau of Labor Statistics of North Carolina there was found to be 84 establishments actively engaged in the manufacture of cotton and hosiery goods in this State, having 21,118 looms, 1,091,534 spindles and 1,204 machines in operation during the year. The horse power required for the running of these establishments was 33,332. The largest number of looms in use in any one establishment was 2,947 and of spindles 118,938. In amount of capital $2,000,000 was the largest invested in any establishment.

In the matter of employes there was a total number of 18,643 engaged in all the establishments which were in operation, 1,724 or 9.2 per cent. being children. Obviously, the laws governing the employment of children in the factories of Connecticut are beneficent ones, and in comparison to the conditions as they exist in North Carolina (where there is no age limit for the employment of children) are operating in the interests of the working classes, and in no way detrimental to the interests of manufacturers.

In this connection it is interesting and appropriate to make the following extract from the report of the North Carolina Bureau of Labor Statistics, comment being unnecessary and superfluous :

"The wages of our cotton operatives are much lower than the wages paid in the mills of the North, and while the Northern States have passed laws regulating the hours of labor in the factory, our State has let the matter rest on the same basis as on the farm, in the mine and in the forest."

Further information gleaned from the same report develops the rather interesting fact that the average hours of labor in the mills of this one of the Southern group of textile manufacturing States are 69 per week, while in Connecticut the average is but 60 hours per week, and as affecting the employment of women and children it is unlawful in this State "that the hours of labor exceed sixty in a week."

Another most interesting comparison can be made as to the number of spindles operated by the employes in the two States considered, for it appears that in North Carolina there were employed 25,887 persons for the operation of 1,044,385 spindles, this being 40.34 spindles per person employed, while in Connecticut, where the hours of labor are nine hours per week less than in North Carolina, the average number of spindles operated per employe was 58.55. It should be borne in mind that this comparison has been made with establishments in both States which were engaged in the manufacture of cotton goods and hosiery. It must also be borne in mind that the percentage of children of total number employed is much less in Connecticut than in North Carolina, which may account in a measure for this wide discrepancy in number of spindles operated per employe.

The hours of labor which prevail in the States in which the manufacturing industries consist largely of textiles is an important factor, and the following synopsis of the laws which have been enacted is herewith presented.

SYNOPSIS OF THE LAWS RELATING TO THE
HOURS OF LABOR AND THE EMPLOYMENT
OF WOMEN AND CHILDREN.

NEW ENGLAND STATES—SOUTHERN STATES.

EMPLOYMENT OF CHILDREN.

NEW ENGLAND STATES.

CONNECTICUT.—

No child under fourteen years of age shall be employed in
any mechanical, mercantile or manufacturing establishment.
None shall be employed between fourteen and sixteen years
of age who cannot read and write unless they produce a certificate from a teacher of an evening school that they have
attended eighteen consecutive sessions of the current month.
Inspection of establishments is made by agents of the State
Board of Education. ' Penalty for violation not more than
sixty dollars. Each week of employment to be considered a
separate offence.*

MAINE.—

If under twelve years of age children may be employed if
at school taught by a qualified teacher for four months of each
year preceding time of employment. Under fifteen years of
age, three months under same conditions. Penalty for violation is $100. School committee investigates and reports to
County attorney who shall prosecute.

NEW HAMPSHIRE.—

None to be employed under ten years of age. None under
sixteen years of age to be employed that cannot read and

---

*Eleven prosecutions for violations were brought during the current year, nine
of which were for illegal employment in Textile manufactories.

write, during the time the public schools are in session in the district in which they reside. If under sixteen years of age and over fourteen years, they must furnish certificate of twelve weeks' attendance at school. If under fourteen and over twelve years of age, six months or such portion of time as schools may be open. If under twelve and over ten years of age they must attend all the time the schools are open.

Penalty not to exceed $50 for each offence. Duty of school board to prosecute. Failure on their part to do so subjects them to penalty of $20 for each neglect.

VERMONT.—

None under ten years of age. Over ten and under fourteen years of age may be employed when in possession of certificate showing attendance at public school of twenty weeks during year preceding employment. Penalty not less than $5 and not more than $25. Inspection and prosecution by truant officer.

MASSACHUSETTS.—

None to be employed under thirteen years of age. Between thirteen and fourteen years of age may be employed during vacation of public schools, if in possession of certificate showing thirty weeks' attendance at school during year preceding employment. Penalty not less than $20 and not more than $50. None can be employed under fourteen years of age who cannot read and write the English language. Inspection by truant officer, who may prosecute.

RHODE ISLAND.—

None to be employed under twelve years of age. None over twelve and under fifteen while the public schools are in session who cannot write his or her name, age and place of residence legibly. Between twelve and fifteen years of age children may be employed if in possession of certificate showing eighty days' attendance at school or certificate showing that they have acquired the elementary branches taught in the public schools. May also be excused by school committee.

SOUTHERN STATES.

ALABAMA.—

No limit in manufacturing.   In mines none allowed under ten years of age.

GEORGIA.—

No limit.

NORTH CAROLINA.—

No limit.

SOUTH CAROLINA.—

No limit.

TENNESSEE.—

In factories and mines none under twelve years of age. Penalty not less than $50 and not more than $500.

VIRGINIA.—

No limit.

KENTUCKY.—

No limit.

MISSISSIPPI.—

No limit.

HOURS OF LABOR.

NEW ENGLAND STATES.

CONNECTICUT.—

No minor under sixteen years of age, and no woman shall be employed more than sixty hours per week.

NEW HAMPSHIRE.—

No minor under eighteen years of age, and no woman shall be employed more than sixty hours per week.

VERMONT.—

No one under fifteen years of age shall be employed more than sixty hours per week.

MASSACHUSETTS.—

No woman or minor under eighteen years of age shall be employed between hours of 10 P. M. and 6 A. M., nor more than fifty-eight hours per week.

MAINE.—

No woman or minor under sixteen years of age shall be employed more than sixty hours per week.

RHODE ISLAND.—

No woman or minor under eighteen years of age shall be employed more than sixty hours per week. Penalty not exceeding $20 for each offence.

SOUTHERN STATES.

ALABAMA.—

No limit.

GEORGIA.—

Minors (under twenty-one years of age), sunrise to sunset. In cotton or woolen mills sixty-six hours per week. Penalty not less than $20 and not more than $500 for each offence.

NORTH CAROLINA.—

No limit.

SOUTH CAROLINA.—

Sixty-six hours per week; may be seventy hours to make up for lost time. Penalty not less than $50 and not more than $100 for each offence.

TENNESSEE.—

No limit.

VIRGINIA.—

No minor under fourteen years of age, and no woman shall be employed more than sixty hours per week. Penalty not less than $5 and not more than $20.

KENTUCKY.—

No limit.

MISSISSIPPI.—

No limit.

PART II.

ORGANIZED LABOR IN CONNECTICUT.

1. WAGES.

2. HOURS OF LABOR.

3. BENEFITS.

ORGANIZED LABOR IN CONNECTICUT.

No question of social economy occupies a more deservedly prominent place in the thoughts of the people than does the labor movement of the day. In all the cities of the State there are found, bonded together, fellow craftsmen in many of the various trades. In order that the purposes of these associations may be known and understood, a careful investigation of their condition and needs has been undertaken, and its results are set forth in the following pages. The "workingmen" of Connecticut appear at every session of our General Assembly, advocating the passage of laws which they assert are for the betterment of their condition. The laws which have already been passed, such as those providing for factory inspection, clean bake-shops, limitation of the hours of labor, and weekly payment of wages, are the result of concerted movement by the organized labor of the State. Concerning the labor movement as it now exists, Hon. Carroll D. Wright, United States Commissioner of Labor, in an address before the National Association of Labor Commissioners, said :

"The labor question occupies a different position each succeeding decade or generation. What it may have been once does not indicate what it is now. Formerly the labor question was a very narrow one, and consisted simply in the proposition, How can wages be raised or the working hours per day reduced? And the demand of the wage-worker in former times was for an increase of wages, or a decrease in the hours of labor, or both, with a view to elevating his standard of life. You should remember that when this demand was first made wages were paid in accordance with David Ricardo's old and well known 'iron law of wages,' under which the rate of wages was fixed at a point which simply covered the absolute physical necessities of a man, his clothing, his food and his shelter. This much was to be granted for day labor, simply that the physical machine, the working anatomy, should not depreciate in value ;

(103)

but in the last generation or two there has come something beyond this which means more than the mere physical wants
of man, and this something else relates to the workingman's
interest in society, how he can receive wages enough to enable
him to become what he has been made everywhere, a political,
a social, and a moral factor in the community. He now receives in wages from 10 to 15 per cent. margin above the rate
which the 'iron law of wages' would fix as his compensation
for so much labor rendered. This extra demand for some of
the elevating and spiritualizing influences of life lies at the
bottom of the labor question to-day ; and so it means sociology
as a whole, the science of society—how can society grow, and
grow in the very best way, so that all men shall receive something of the things in this life which mean culture, education—art, even.

  " This demand wherever you meet it is evidenced by what we
call 'social unrest,' and it is the function of these offices which
we represent to contribute facts, and facts only, which shall
help us to understand the meaning of this social unrest and
enable us to determine, if possible, whether there shall be any
danger in it, or whether the social unrest means something that
shall carry civilization still farther up in the advance of the
times. Then what is the labor question concretely stated ? The
underlying factors of the labor question had their origin so
long ago, that history gives no account of them, as far back as
when a certain tribe lived on the table lands of Central Asia,
away back of the historic period, and so far back that all we
know of it comes from the Sanscrit. This tribe grew refined ;
it became intelligent; it built boats, and steered them in the
streams with a rudder, and propelled them with oars as we do to-
day; it wove cloth; it did many things that indicate a higher
sense of true civilization ; and then, gentlemen, commenced that
great fever of unrest, which has followed the Aryan race to
this moment, and will follow it until the end, whenever that
may be, thousands or millions of years hence, and it is to this
unrest that our Western Hemisphere owes its existence as a
populated land. As soon as this tribe, that grew somewhat refined, found itself in that position, the ambition seized its members and a portion of the old tribe came down from the table
lands of Central Asia and found itself wandering westward.
Other sections came down behind them and pushed on those
that were in advance, and they crossed the eastern waters
and settled the Hellenic States. They made Central Europe
what it is, and finally, crossed the English Channel and settled
Great Britain, and soon they found themselves fretting on the
outmost western rock of the Irish coast, with just as much unrest in their souls as they ever had during the centuries back of
them, and they peered into the western ocean and finally one of
their number, one day in October, in 1492, found himself still
peering from the deck of his battered little caravel into the

west, and this great continent was discovered. More of his tribe kept sweeping on and sweeping on, settling a fringe all along the Atlantic coast, crossing the rivers, and finding themselves at last beyond the Mississippi, until now the sons of this old, ambitious Aryan race are fretting on the outmost western coast of this country. Whether or not they will in time sweep over the Pacific and reach again the table lands of Central Asia, is a great question in sociology, but my reason for referring to this fact is to show you that the unrest which made this country what it is, is of the remotest origin; and we Americans find in our veins to-day the very life blood which made those characters thousands of years ago distinctive, and this unrest has followed us, and is following us, and we are feeling it in accessions as the generations pile up in the passage of time.

"This, gentlemen, concretely, is the labor question of to-day. What shall be done with this unrest; how shall it be shaped; not whether it can be killed, but whether the struggle under it can be softened, can be guided, can be moulded into some force which shall mean the very best for human conditions. * * * * * There is a great deal of pathetic talk about unrest, about discontent, and there are several kinds of discontent which prevail; but the discontent that is legitimate is that which impels men, always and ever, to seek better conditions. That is what has brought millions across the stormy western ocean to settle in this land; that is what has made the United States what it is; that is what is building the South into a great industrial empire. Now as facts are collected, classified, and systemized, we find that out of them all, which means the knowledge of conditions as they are, there is growing a new political economy. * * * * * Dr. William T. Harris, the Commissioner of Education, has defined a crank. He says a crank is a man who sees something very clearly, but not in its relations, and it is so in the attempts to solve phases of the labor problem. One man sees a thing very clearly; he sees that the temperance question involves the happiness and economic conditions of men, and he thinks that if temperance principles could only prevail the world would be happy. Another man ignores that and says, 'If you can only establish industrial arbitration you will settle all your difficulties.' Another man thinks that the eight-hour day would solve the problem and remove all difficulties attending industrial conditions. All these things are good, but they must be considered together in their relations one to the other, or else you are simply setting up bricks to be knocked down. Our duty, then, whether as Commissioners of Labor, or in whatever capacity we may serve, is to help contribute to the sum of knowledge which shall ultimately soften this struggle without attempting to remove that divine discontent which makes the world what it is, and which gives us whatever civilization now exists."

The work of securing the desired statistical information has been somewhat difficult, principally due to a fear on the part of many of the unions that the facts elicited would be used to their detriment. Accompanying the information blank and the letter requesting that it be filled out, was the following circular letter, which was sent to all the unions in the State the addresses of which could be ascertained, and which greatly aided the Bureau in securing information that otherwise would have been withheld :

"HARTFORD, Conn., April 1, 1898.

To Organized Labor of Connecticut:

"FELLOW WORKERS :—Your attention is respectfully called to the accompanying blank form, issued by the Commissioner of Labor Statistics, and his letter requesting your organization to have the same filled and returned to him. Grouped in totals, by trades and localities, these facts will be disseminated by the Bureau, and will prove of inestimable value to our cause. It is plain to all of us that hitherto the lack of statistical information of this character placed Organized Labor at a great disadvantage when it had under consideration matters pertaining to wages and hours. Members of a trade in one part of the State should always know the exact economic status of their fellow craftsmen in other sections so that they may act intelligently on subjects affecting their welfare. The diffusion of knowledge concerning the income of the workers, the number unemployed and the causes of idleness at stated periods would unquestionably lead to a universal discussion of the subject, and bring about a reformation of the social system that would eventually provide permanent employment for the toilers at living wages and reduced daily working time. Moreover, the public generally, and business men particularly, will be more apt to heed the reasonable demands of the Unions if they have at their command official statistics proving the justness of their claims.

"Much more could be written in favor of the Commissioner's plan, but we believe that sufficient has been said to show that labor's interests will be advanced materially if the organizations will promptly send him the required statistics.

"We, therefore, strongly urge every member of your organization to take a personal interest in this matter and co-operate with the Commissioner of Labor Statistics in his efforts in labor's behalf. We heartily commend his work in this direction, and trust it will be a complete success.

"Fraternally yours,

"ELI BRUNELL,

"Prest. Conn. State Branch A. F. of L.

"J. D. COWPER,

"State Organizer."

THE QUESTIONS ASKED TO WHICH ANSWERS WERE DESIRED WERE:

(1) Name of organization.

(2) Date of organization.

(3) Number of men,   Women,   when organized.

(4) Number of men,   Women,   at present time.

(5) Trade wages (per day): Highest, $ Lowest, $ Average, $

(6) What benefits are provided?

(7) Hours of labor (weekly),   On Saturday.

(8) How many weeks in the year can members usually obtain employment?

(9) Have wages been increased or decreased as a result of organization?

(10) If increased, was it voluntary, by demand or by strike?

(11) Have hours of labor been increased or decreased as a result of organization?

(12) Do you favor shorter hours with a proportionate reduction of pay?

(13) Has your Union engaged in any strikes? If so, for what object? Was it successful or unsuccessful?

(14) How many of the members of your Union are employed?

(15) How many of the members of your Union are unemployed?

(16) What is your estimate as to the number of your trade that is unorganized in your locality?

(17) How do the wages paid organized and unorganized labor in your trade compare?

(18) Has organization been of benefit to your trade?

(19) Suggest anything that will improve the condition of the craft.

The answers given to Question No. 3 were so unsatisfactory, owing to loss of their records by several of the unions, that no attempt has been made to collate them.

Question No. 12 was answered in the negative by all save seven unions. A barber's union states that the same amount of work could be done in a shorter time, and would not call for a reduction of pay. Only six unions gave an affirmative answer. The others want shorter hours and the same pay.

The answers given to Question No. 10 were so largely "guesswork" that the tabulation has been omitted.

In answer to Question No. 17 it was stated by nearly all that wages had been increased from 15 to 35 per cent. as a result of organization, and by the others that organization had prevented the reduction of wages. As to the general benefits that have been secured by organization, the information is best given under the heading "Notes from the Unions." Answers were received, in all, from 105 unions.

In addition to the unions, from which replies were received, there are 34 from which it has been impossible to get any return whatever. Requests were made two, three and in some cases, four times, but the request was repeatedly ignored, notwithstanding the fact that stamped envelopes were enclosed for reply.

The location and names of the unions, failing to make reply, follow:

ANSONIA.—
    Buffers and Polishers.

BRIDGEPORT.—
    Bricklayers and Plasterers.
    Engineers.
    Elastic Goring Weavers.
    Granite Cutters.
    Suspender Weavers.

BRISTOL.—
    Buffers and Polishers.

DANBURY.—
    Engineers.

DERBY.—
    Plumbers and Gas Fitters.

HARTFORD.—
    Core Makers.
    Cornice Makers.
    Horseshoers.
    Locomotive Firemen.

HARTFORD.—*Continued.*
    Machine Woodworkers.
    Painters.
    Rubber Goods Workers.
    Screwmakers.
    Stone Cutters.
    Stone Masons.
    Stone Tenders.
    Tailors.

MERIDEN.—
    Iron Moulders.
    Granite Workers.

NAUGATUCK.—
    Iron Moulders.

NEW HAVEN.—
    Brewers.
    Buffers and Polishers.
    Stereotypers.

NORWICH.—
    Bricklayers and Plasterers.

SHELTON.—
    Knife Grinders.

WALLINGFORD.—
    Buffers and Polishers.

WATERBURY.—
    Brewers.
    Carpenters.
    Iron Moulders.

In nearly every instance the blanks were returned correctly and intelligently filled out. An invitation was extended to the unions to state what, in their opinion, would benefit the condition of the several organized crafts, and the great majority of them made use of the opportunity thus afforded. With but few and slight alterations, the answers are given as received, under the heading "Notes from the Unions." Two replies which were redolent with anarchy have not been used, as it is not the work of this Bureau to disseminate economic theories, foreign in their origin, unsuited to our labor conditions, and opposed by the vast majority of the intelligent workmen of the State. That these workmen are intelligent, no one will question after reading the matter given under the caption above referred to.

An analysis of the figures shows that of the one hundred and five unions reporting, forty-nine have been organized during or since 1890. Further analysis shows that organization has been of immense benefit to the men directly interested, and also to the general public by the avoidance of strikes and the general disorder which follow them.

In this State it cannot be claimed by any one that the uniting together of men of the various crafts is for the purpose of antagonizing the manufacturers of the State. On the contrary, it is asserted that never has there been a better understanding between the men employed in the shops and mills in Connecticut and the employers than exists at the present time. Union men recognize, as never before, the fact that one manufacturer cannot pay high wages and run his mill a reasonable number of hours in competition with his fellow-manufacturer in the same line of goods who pay low wages and keeps his power going for an unlimited time.

In view of this fact, organized labor, not only in Connecticut but all over the country, is concentrating its efforts to secure uniform laws concerning hours of labor, and by thorough co-operation a uniform rate of wages. During the year past a number of unions have been formed among the textile workers. To them this question of hours and wages is of vital importance. In the South, as is shown in another chapter of this report, low wages and long hours are the prevailing rule. A cotton mill owner, interested in four mills in this State, stated to an officer of this Bureau that they had no desire to reduce wages or increase the hours of labor to meet this competition and that they were in complete harmony with the efforts of organized labor to secure national legislation tending to equalize conditions.

Thus far, organized labor in Connecticut has shown itself to be a conservative and self-respecting body. The rules and regulations governing most of the unions make it impossible for one or two men to precipitate a strike. Before one is ordered every possible means must be used to effect a settlement of any question which may be in dispute between employer and employe. That these unions are acting up to this principle is evidenced by the fact that in the whole history of the one hundred and five unions represented in this report but twelve strikes have occurred. The record covers a period extending from 1850 to the present time. It is to be understood that these figures do not refer to unorganized trades. The investigation further shows that, since one of a similar character made in 1891 (see Seventh Annual Report), the number of unions and their membership has been largely increased.

The deductions that may fairly be drawn as a direct result of this investigation clearly indicate that trades unionism in the State is, in general, in a healthy and prosperous condition, that it aims primarily to ameliorate the condition of the employe and not to antagonize the employer, that its needs and shortcomings are known and understood, and that intelligent and continual effort is being put forth to improve the standing and efficiency of all organized craftsmen. The letter from the locomotive engineers demonstrates what may be accomplished by a thorough understanding between employer and employe, and the general plea for an efficient apprentice law indicates a praiseworthy regard for the future well-being of the Connecticut laborer.

NATIONAL ORGANIZATIONS REPRESENTED IN CONNECTICUT.

Amalgamated Woodworkers Association.
American Federation of Labor.
Brewery Workers.
Bricklayers and Plasterers International Union.
Brotherhood of Bookbinders.
Brotherhood of Locomotive Engineers.
Brotherhood of Locomotive Firemen.
Brotherhood of Painters and Decorators.
Brotherhood of Railway Trainmen.
Elastic Goring Weavers Amalgamated Association.
International Association of Machinists.
International Brotherhood of Brass Workers.
International Cigarmakers Union.
International Typographical Union.
Iron Moulders Union of North America.
Journeymen Bakers and Confectioners International Union.
Journeymen Barbers International Union.
Journeymen Horseshoers National Union.
Journeymen Tailors Union of America.
Knights of Labor and Industry.
Metal Polishers and Buffers International Union.
Musicians Protective Association.
National Association of Fur Hat Makers.
National Association of Hat Finishers.
National Association of Stationary Engineers.
National Beamer Tenders Association.
National Brotherhood of Electrical Workers.
National Cotton Weavers Union.
National Loom Fixers Association.
National Mule Spinners Association.
National Silk Workers Association.
National Union of Stone Masons.
Printing Pressmen Union.
United Association of Journeymen Plumbers.
United Brotherhood of Carpenters and Joiners.
United Hatters of North America.

AMERICAN FEDERATION OF LABOR.

The Connecticut Branch of the American Federation of Labor was formed in Hartford in 1887, mainly through the efforts of the Central Labor Union of Hartford. Representatives were present from thirty-five local and central bodies. The trades represented were :

Bakers,	Hatters,
Barbers,	Hodcarriers,
Boxmakers,	Iron Moulders,
Bricklayers,	Masons' Tenders,
Carpenters and Joiners,	Printers,
Cigarmakers,	Tailors,
Clerks,	Woodcarvers.
Horseshoers,	

At its first meeting it declared its objects to be :

" I. To assist in establishing National and International Trades Unions, based upon a strict recognition of the autonomy of each trade, and the promotion and advancement of such bodies.

" II. The encouragement and formation of local Trade and Labor Unions in every city and town in this State, and the combination of these bodies into a State Federation of Trade and Labor Unions, to assist and aid each other.

" III. To secure State legislation in the interests of the working people, and to influence public opinion by peaceful and legal methods in favor of organized labor.

" IV. To aid and encourage the labor press of our State, and to establish an organ of the State Federation as soon as deemed advisable."

This organization holds a convention each year in some place designated by the preceding convention. It has had an active growth, having at the present time affiliated with it eighty unions and central bodies. The number of members represented by the affiliated unions is stated to be 5,000.

The basis of representation is that—

" Each Union having one hundred members or less shall be entitled to one delegate, and one additional delegate for each additional hundred members or majority fraction thereof. Each central body shall be entitled to but one delegate."

Since 1896 a State organizer has been kept in the field organizing new unions and visiting the weaker ones. He re-

ports that during this present year twenty-four (24) new
unions have been formed, with a membership of fourteen
hundred and forty-four (1,444).

CENTRAL LABOR UNIONS.

These organizations, of which there are eight in the State,
are composed of representatives from the local unions situated in their immediate vicinity. Their object is the same as
that of the State Branch. These organizations are located in—

Bridgeport,	New Britain,
Danbury,	New Haven,
Hartford,	Norwich,
Meriden,	South Norwalk.

JOURNEYMEN BAKERS AND CONFECTIONERS IN-TERNATIONAL UNION OF AMERICA.

The Journeymen Bakers and Confectioners International
Union of America was organized January 13, 1886, at Pitts-
burg, Pa.

"OBJECT OF THE ORGANIZATION.

" The Union aims at the promotion of the material and intellectual welfare of all workmen in the baking trade: (1) By
organization; (2) by education; (3) by the reduction of the
hours of labor; (4) by gradually abolishing such evils as may
prevail in the baking trade; (5) by establishing labor bureaus
wherever possible; (6) by assisting members in legal causes in
matters concerning the Union; (7) by agitating the abolition
of nightwork, and by using its influence with the lawmakers of
each State to secure the passage of Sanitary Bake-shop Laws.

"MEMBERSHIP—DUTIES AND RIGHTS.

" No person shall become a member of this organization
until he has worked at least three years at some branch of the
trade. After that period he may become a member on the
recommendation of a member of this organization. No distinction shall be made on account of race, sex, creed or
nationality.

"STRIKES.

"Section 1. In case of difficulties between employes and
employers, it becomes the duty of the Local Union to prevent
strikes as much as possible by attempting to settle such difficulties in a peaceful way. Only in the event that all attempts

at a peaceful settlement shall prove of no avail, or if the demands of the employers should be beneath the dignity of the employes and contrary to the principles of a Unionist, a strike shall be resorted to.

"Section 2. Should a strike in one locality seem unavoidable, then it shall be attempted to limit such strikes to as few shops as possible, so as to enable those remaining at work to support their fellow-members on strike.

"Section 4. Strikes can only be declared when three-fourths of the members in good standing vote in favor thereof. The same vote is required to declare a strike ended.

"Section 5. No member shall receive a strike benefit in the first week of a strike.

"Section 6. If a Local Union proposes to go on a strike subject to being aided by the International Union, such Union must make an application to the Executive Board before going on strike, wherein all the reasons must be stated that lead to that strike, together with a statement of the attempts that were made to accomplish a peaceful settlement of the difficulties; also a statement as to how many members may eventually become involved in such a strike.

"Section 8. No strikes shall be decided upon unless every member has been invited in writing, or personally, by an officer of the Union to attend the meeting where it is to be acted upon."

A sick benefit of five dollars per week and a death benefit of one hundred dollars is paid to members in good standing.

BROTHERHOOD OF CARPENTERS AND JOINERS.

The National Brotherhood of Carpenters and Joiners was organized in Chicago, Ill., April, 1881. Several attempts had been made previous to that time, but the unions formed were not of long duration, owing largely to lack of concerted action. Its jurisdiction extends over all the States of the Union. The society is governed by an executive board of five members, elected by the local unions within ten miles of the city selected as headquarters. The qualifications for membership are that the applicant must be a carpenter and joiner, engaged at woodwork, and competent to command average wages, not more than sixty years of age, of good moral character and sound health, and not afflicted with any disease or subject to any complaint likely to endanger life. Any stairbuilder, millwright, planing mill hand or any cabinet-maker, engaged at carpenter work, or any carpenter running woodworking machinery, is eligible to membership, if possessed of the above qualifications.

Any member who engages in the sale of intoxicating liquors must withdraw from the organization.

At the beginning, the object was purely protective in its character, upholding wages, struggling to advance them, and to shorten the hours of labor. At the National Convention, held in Philadelphia in 1882, it laid down the settled policy of advocating the adoption of nine hours as a day's work. That is the rule now prevailing in Connecticut. The policy of the order is to avoid strikes and to render them almost impossible. To order a strike requires a two-thirds vote by secret ballot of the members, and all members must have two weeks' notice to attend the meeting. Then the consent of the General Executive Board must be obtained, and, if granted, the "Protective Fund" of the entire Brotherhood is at the command of the local union in trouble. But before the union takes a ballot on the subject, an arbitration committee from the union must wait on the employers and endeavor to adjust the difficulty. Members in good standing are entitled to the following benefits : Member's death, $200.00 ; funeral of wife, $50.00 ; for total disability by accident while at work, $200.00 ; sickness, $3.00 per week.

The order has a membership of over fifty thousand.

CIGARMAKERS INTERNATIONAL UNION OF AMERICA.

The Cigarmakers International Union was organized in New York City on June 21, 1864, by twenty-three persons as delegates from several local unions. Previous to this time efforts to organize had been of a local or State character, and had met with varying success.

The more active and wisest among the craft foresaw that no lasting results could be obtained unless the fragmentary elements composing the scattered local bodies could be bound together in one compact organization. Step by step, and by dint of perseverance and self-sacrifice, it has now reached a membership of thirty-two thousand, and has a very large reserve fund to draw upon in aiding its members.

The principal objects of the order are declared to be—

" The sustenance of the unfortunate and distressed among our members ; the promotion and protection of our social, economic and political interests, and the advancement of education upon those subjects, a broad and intelligent conception of which is most necessary to a true solution of the labor problem and the final emancipation of the wage-worker."

The Bureau is indebted to Mr. G. W. Perkins, President of the International Union, for the following facts :

The initiation fee is $3, and the weekly dues are 30 cents.

It pays the following benefits : $5 per week in case of strike; $3 per week out-of-work benefit; $5 per week sick benefit; traveling loan benefit; death benefit from $50 to $550, and a wife and widowed mother funeral benefit of $40.

In the past eighteen years it has expended, all told, in benefits, the munificent sum of $3,718,686.38.

The following table presents the total benefits paid for the last eighteen years and two months:

BENEFITS PAID IN EIGHTEEN YEARS AND TWO MONTHS.

Year.	Strike benefit.	Sick benefit.	Death benefit.	Traveling benefit.	Out-of-work benefit.
1879	$3,668.23	....	....	....	....
1880	4,950.86	....	....	$2,808.15	....
1881	21,797.68	$3,987.73	$75.00	12,747.09	....
1882	44,850.41	17,145.29	1,674.25	20,386.64	....
1883	27,812.13	22,250.56	2,690.00	37,135.20	....
1884	143,547.86	31,551.50	3,920.00	39,632.08	....
1885	61,087.28	29,379.89	4,214.00	26,683.54	....
1886	54,402.61	42,225.59	4,820.00	31,835.71	....
1887	13,871.62	63,900.88	8,850.00	49,281.04	....
1888	45,303.62	58,824.19	21,319.75	42,894.75	....
1889	5,202.52	59,519.94	19,175.50	43,540.44	....
1890	18,414.27	64,660.47	26,043.00	37,914.72	$22,760.50
1891	33,531.78	87,472.97	38,068.35	53,535.73	21,223.50
1892	37,477.60	89,906.30	44,701.97	47,732.47	17,460.75
1893	18,228.15	104,391.83	49,458.33	60,475.11	89,402.75
1894	44,966.76	106,758.37	62,158.77	42,154.17	174,517.25
1895	44,039.06	112,567.06	66,725.98	41,657.16	166,377.25
1896	27,446.46	109,208.62	78,768.09	33,070.22	175,707.25
1897	12,175.09	112,774.63	69,186.67	20,067.04	117,471.40
Total	$662,772.99	$1,116,525.82	$501,849.66	$652,557.26	$784,980.65

Total benefits paid in 1896... $424,266.64
Total benefits paid in 1897... 340,674.83
Grand total of benefits paid........................... .... 3,718,686.38

In addition to these benefits it has succeeded in raising the wages of its members from 20 to 50 per cent., and in shortening the hours of labor to eight per day. The eight-hour day has been in operation since May 1, 1886, being inaugurated and gained independent of any other craft at the time.

The successful achievements of the International Union are so many and varied, that space will not permit me to give even a synopsis of them. However, chief among them was the adoption of an admirable financial system and the payment of high dues; the shortening of the hours of labor; the adoption of a splendid chain of benefits and the adoption of the "Blue Label."

The payment of high dues is considered one of the most potent factors that has led up to our present success, as it has allowed the accumulation of a large reserve fund, which is largely responsible for our success, and thereby enabled us to not only keep our membership intact, but to increase its numerical strength.

It is a fact that since this fund assumed fair proportions, we have succeeded in raising wages in a large number of instances without strike or any expense to the International Union. Employers hesitate in the face of such formidable weapons to bring on a contest, and in recent years, as a rule, when our demands have been tempered with justice, they have been readily acceded to.

We gained more advances with our present fund and expended less money for strike benefit with our 36,000 members, than we did in former years with 12,000 members. In other words, more strike benefit was paid when we had only 12,000 members and a small defense fund than we expend now with about 36,000 members and a large defense fund, and still the percentage of increases in wages is greater now than at the former period.

During the unprecedented industrial and commercial depression now drawing to a close, we have expended thousands of dollars to our unfortunate members out of employment, which to say the least, enabled them to retain their standing and claim on benefits.

The order has a membership of 757 in Connecticut, among whom are three women, distributed among eleven local unions.

THE BROTHERHOOD OF LOCOMOTIVE ENGINEERS.

In April, 1863, a few engineers in the employ of the Michigan Central Railroad Company conceived the idea of forming an association to promote the welfare and interest of their profession and elevate their standing and character as men. With these objects in view, they assembled at the house of one of their number, in the city of Marshall, Mich. The result of their deliberation was the issuing of an invitation to the engineers employed on the adjacent roads to meet in the city of Detroit on the fifth day of May. In response to the invitation, at the appointed time, ten delegates assembled, who, with but little formality in their organization, entered upon their duties, and, with the assistance of a few engineers residing in Detroit, a constitution and by-laws were presented and adopted, embodying the fundamental principles of the present organization.

The necessity of something further on the part of engineers than the common consent to become and remain members of the association so long as suited their own convenience became apparent to the minds of the delegates, and an obligation, as a bond of union, was formulated and unanimously adopted, and on the 8th day of May, 1863, twelve engineers joined hands and hearts, pledging themselves to support the constitution and by-laws, assist the needy and maintain the right.

Officers were elected, and Detroit Division No. 1, Brotherhood of the Footboard, stood forth as the pioneer in the great work of reformation and elevation of the locomotive engineers of this continent.

During the first year of its existence, forty-four sub-divisions were organized. On the 17th of August, 1864, the first convention was held in the city of Indianapolis, Ind., with forty-four division representatives, at which time the name and title of the organization was changed to its present one, making it international in character, so that all locomotive engineers, regardless of nationality, would be eligible.

The organization has been in existence, as a society, thirty-five years, and during that time has gradually increased in numbers and importance ; emerging almost silently from its original obscurity. At the present time the Brotherhood has a membership of 32,000, distributed among 538 divisions, three divisions are located in Connecticut with a membership of 378. Their membership contains nine-tenths of the best locomotive engineers on this continent; and they have gained an enviable position by a strict adherence to their mottoes: "Sobriety, Truth, Justice and Morality," "Vigilance, not Violence," and "Do unto others as ye would that they should do unto you, and so fulfil the law." They stand aloof from all political bodies and sects and ignore all questions of creed and race, and look only to the improvement and protection of the locomotive engineers and their families.

At the convention held in the city of Boston in November, 1866, the publication of a monthly journal, to be devoted exclusively to the interests of the profession, was authorized and the first number was issued in January, 1867, composed of 16 pages; it now has 112 pages and has at the present time a circulation of nearly 37,000, including among its subscribers residents of Europe and India. It contains a list of all subdivisions, together with the names of the officers and where they are located.

On the 3rd of December, 1867, there was established an insurance association, which pays to the heirs of deceased members, or to a member who is unfortunate enough to lose a hand, arm, limb, or eyesight, the full amount of the policy or policies held. Policies are for $1,500, and a member may carry one, two or three, making $1,500, $3,000 or $4,500. The cost of carrying one policy of $1,500 is from 23 to 25 dollars a year. In the aggregate, the sum of $5,771,214.61 has been paid to injured brothers and heirs of deceased members, besides disbursing, out of their hard earnings, thirty-five to forty thousand dollars among the widows, orphans and needy of the order at every convention.

A large number of the divisions have a weekly indemnity insurance, each having their own law, which vary in the amount of dues and indemnity. The weekly indemnity is usually about twelve dollars.

The organization has contracts with 107 railroad companies, which include nearly all the great trunk lines. These contracts embody rates of pay and rules and regulations governing overtime, treatment of the employes and for the prevention of unjust discharge or suspension.

Through the instrumentality of this organized effort, the remuneration for services has been greatly increased, overtime allowance properly adjusted, and the character of those who comprise it elevated and educated, and peace and harmony maintained between the employer and employe.

(EXTRACTS FROM CONSTITUTION.)

"SECTION 1. This organization shall be known under the name and title of the 'GRAND INTERNATIONAL BROTHERHOOD OF LOCOMOTIVE ENGINEERS,' and its purpose shall be to more effectually combine the interests of locomotive engineers, to elevate their standing as such, and their character as men. * * * * * No person shall become a member of the Brotherhood unless he is a white man 21 years of age, and can read and write, and is a man of good moral character, temperate habits, and a locomotive engineer in good standing, and in actual service as a locomotive engineer when proposed, and has had experience as such at least one year, each Division to be the judge of what constitutes one year's experience. * * * * * No member of this organization shall be allowed to join any other labor organization, under penalty of expulsion by his Division. * * * * * The influence or sympathy of the Brotherhood, as a body, shall never be enlisted or used in favor of any political or religous organization whatever ; no member of this brotherhood shall be permitted to discuss in any manner in Division, or while discussing Division matters, any religious matter, or criticise the religious belief of any member, and any Division permitting the same to be done shall have their charter suspended, and all members participating in such discussion shall be expelled."

IRON MOULDERS UNION OF NORTH AMERICA.

The iron moulders had local organizations early in the century. In Cincinnati they were sufficiently organized in 1849 to maintain a strike that lasted for nine months, and in which they were eventually successful. On July 5, 1859, the various local unions came together and formed the Iron Moulders Union of North America. The constitution of the union provides the following stringent regulations for the government of strikes:

"Any subordinate union requiring the assistance of this union to vindicate its rights and privileges under this constitution, shall be required to conform to the following sections, and shall await an official answer.

" When a difficulty occurs under the jurisdiction of any local

union through a reduction of wages or through the principles
of our organization being jeopardized in any manner, the
union under whose jurisdiction the trouble exists shall hold a
meeting at once to consider the same. If, in its judgment, the
matter is worthy the attention of the executive officer, it shall
lay the case before him. The president shall then, either by
deputy or in person, proceed to the place at once and make a
thorough examination as to the facts in the case. He shall do
his utmost to settle the trouble amicably between employers
and employed. Failing to adjust the difficulty, he shall lay the
matter before the executive board immediately, which board,
in conjunction with the president, shall have absolute control of
all strikes and lockouts. They shall see that no more strikes
are on hand at any one time than the organization is able to
handle. They shall concentrate the whole prestige and force
of the National Union, financially and otherwise, in the direction most needed. It shall be considered sufficient cause for
expulsion from the National Union should any local union
attempt to assume responsibility of striking without their
grievance being considered by the president and having the
sanction of the executive board before going out."

Since 1880 it has paid a death benefit of $100 to the families
of all members in good standing at death. Over fifteen per
cent. of its income has been thus expended.

MUSICIANS PROTECTIVE UNION.

The Musicians Protective Union, while not strictly a labor
organization, can properly be classed as such, as the object of
the union is declared to be "To unite the instrumental portion
of the musical profession for the better protection of its interests in general, the establishment of a minimum rate of prices
to be charged by the members of said union for their professional services, and the enforcement of good faith and fair
dealing between its members."

Any musician of good moral standing, who takes an engagement for money, is eligible to membership.

No member of the union is allowed to play with a resident
non-union member, but may play with any musician living out
of the town where the union is located, provided, always, that
the scale of prices adopted by the union is adhered to.

"Until all indebtedness for musical services rendered by any
member of the union, to any society, organization, or individual,
shall have been satisfactorily settled for, all members shall be

restricted from taking or filling any engagement with the society, organization or individual." A scale of prices is fixed by each local union covering nearly every form of service likely to be called for.

INTERNATIONAL TYPOGRAPHICAL UNION.

The organized printers have existed as an " International " body since 1869. In 1852 they were known as the National Union, but the title was changed in 1869 in order to admit the members of the craft residing in Canada. A National convention of printers met in New York in 1850 and in Baltimore in 1851, but little progress was made toward a permanent organization. At the convention held in 1852 the National Typographical Union was formed. From that time the organization has grown in strength and power.

The International Union regards strikes as inexpedient and to be deprecated, except where principles and rules of the order have been violated. Recognizing strikes as detrimental to the best interests of the craft, it directs subordinate unions not to order a strike until every possible effort has been made to settle the difficulty by arbitration.

In case it shall be considered by a subordinate union that a strike is necessary, the consent of the " National Executive Council " of the order must first be obtained.

The constitution provides as follows :

"An Executive Council, consisting of the president of the International Typographical Union, the chief organizer and a vice-president or state deputy, shall be convened, when necessary, by the president of the International Typographical Union. It shall be the duty of the Executive Council to consider all appeals for aid for strikes or lockouts from subordinate unions, to investigate such matters, and it shall decide in all cases. When a strike has been approved by the Executive Council it shall notify the subordinate union, and, in its discretion, order an assessment of from two to twenty-five cents per capita to be paid to the subordinate union making the appeal. Any union inaugurating a strike, without the approval of the Executive Council, shall receive no benefit on account of the strike from the strike fund ; *provided*, that where a union strikes in case of emergency, without consent as above, they shall be entitled to all benefits if the strike be subsequently approved by the Executive Council."

A funeral benefit of $60 is paid by the International Union. Sick benefits are paid by the local unions.

"OBJECTS OF THE ORGANIZATION.

" Section 2. The objects of this Union shall be the maintenance of a fair rate of wages, the encouragement of good
workmen and the exposition and prevention of all subterfuge
whatever by persons employed in the printing business, as journeymen, in working under any arrangement whereby less than
the established rates are paid ; to endeavor to replace strikes by
arbitration and conciliation in the settlement of all disputes
concerning wages and conditions of employment, and also to
relieve the deserving needy and provide for the burial of deceased members."

At the quadrennial meeting of the National Body, held in
Denver, Colorado, in 1894, it was decided that the time had now
come when a demand should be made for a nine-hour workday,
and a committee, styled " Shorter Workday Committee," was appointed to make preparations for such a demand.   The question
had been discussed and approved in every subordinate branch
of the order since that time, and it was decided that the time
had come when the demand should be made.   The committees
of the allied printing trades met with the committee of the
United Typothetæ, an association of employing printers, at
Syracuse, New York, October 10th, and asked that an agreement might be made to establish nine hours as a day's work.
The subject was discussed for several days, and a compromise
was effected whereby a nine-and-one-half-hour day should be
given after November 21st, 1898, and a nine-hour day after
November, 1899.   These conditions were agreed to by the
Connecticut Branch of the Typothetæ at a meeting held in
New Haven in October.

The arrangement is now in effect in all the leading printing
establishments in this State, beginning November 21, 1898.

SICK AND DEATH BENEFITS PAID.

Bakers.—
    For sickness, $5.00 per week, not exceeding 26 weeks.
    For death, $50.00 to $100.

Barbers.—
    For sickness, $5.00 per week, not exceeding 13 weeks.
    Death, $50.

Bricklayers and Plasterers.—
    $5.00 per week for sickness or disability.

Buffers and Polishers.—
    $5.00 per week during a strike.

Carpenters and Joiners.—
    Wife's funeral, $50.
    Disability of member, $100 to $400.
    Member's death, $300.

Cigarmakers.—
    In case of strike, $5.00 per week.
    Out of work, $3.00 per week.
    Sickness, $5.00 per week.
    Death of member, $50 to $500.
    Wife or widowed mother's funeral, $40.

Cotton Weavers.—
    $5.00 per week while on strike

Drivers Protective Association.—
    Sickness, $5.00.
    Death, $50.

Elastic Goring Weavers.—
    Death benefit, $100.

Hatmakers.—
    Burial benefit, $100.

Hat Trimmers.—
    Burial benefit, $300.

Horse Nail Workers.—
    Sickness, $5.00 per week.
    Death, $50.

Horseshoers.—
    $5.00 per week for sickness, not exceeding 10 weeks.

Loom Fixers.—
    Weekly benefit during strike or shut down.

Machinists.—
    Sickness, $5.00 per week.
    Death, $50.

Mule Spinners.—
    $5.00 while on strike.

Printing Pressmen.—
    Death benefit, $250.

Railway Trainmen.—
    Insurance, death or loss of limb, $1,200.

Tailors.—
    Sickness, $5.00 per week.
    During strike, $6.00.
    Death, $100.

RATES OF WAGES AND HOURS OF LABOR OF ORGANIZED LABOR.

BAKERS AND CONFECTIONERS.

Town.	Name of organization.	Organized.	Wages per day.			Hours of labor		Average number weeks employed.
			Highest.	Lowest.	Average.	Weekly.	Saturday.	
New Haven...	Bakers Union No. 11.............	1886	$3.00	$2.00	$2.50	72	14	52
Hartford......	Bakers Union No. 8.............	1886	2.50	1.70	2.25	72	13	52
Bridgeport....	Bakers Union No. 38...'.........	1886	3.25	1.25	2.25	90	19	52
Meriden.......	Bakers Union No.	1891	2.66	2.00	2.25	73	13	52
New Britain...	Bakers Union No. 107..........	1892	2.65	1.65	2.15	68	13	52
Danbury......	Bakers Union No. 193..........	1897	3.00	1.75	2.25	60	12	52

JOURNEYMEN BARBERS.

Town.	Name of organization.	Organized.	Highest.	Lowest.	Average.	Weekly.	Saturday.	Average number weeks employed.
Danbury......	Barbers Union No. 175.........	1895	2.25	2.00	2.00	74	14	52
Meriden.......	Barbers Union No. 88..........	1896	2.33	1.67	2.00	61	17	52
Norwich.......	Barbers Union No.	1897	2.50	1.65	2.00	74	14	52
New London..	Barbers Union No. 136.........	1898	....	.....	....	73	15½	52

BOOKBINDERS.

Town.	Name of organization.	Organized.	Highest.	Lowest.	Average.	Weekly.	Saturday.	Average number weeks employed.
Hartford......	Bookbinders....................	1892	3.25	2.25	2.75	59	9	50

BRASS MOULDERS.

Town.	Name of organization.	Organized.	Highest.	Lowest.	Average.	Weekly.	Saturday.	Average number weeks employed.
Meriden.......	Brass Moulders..................	1886	3.00	2.25	2.50	54	9	40

RATES OF WAGES AND HOURS OF LABOR OF ORGANIZED LABOR — *Continued.*

BREWERY WORKERS.

Town.	Name of organization.	Organized.	Wages per day.			Hours of labor		Average number weeks employed.
			Highest.	Lowest.	Average.	Weekly.	Saturday.	
Hartford......	Brewers Union No.	1887	$2.60	$2.50	$2.50	60	10	52
Meriden.......	Brewers Union No.	1895	3.33	2.00	2.50	60	10	52
Waterbury....	Brewers Union No.	1897	2.60	2.50	2.50	60	10	52

BRICKLAYERS AND PLASTERERS.

Town.	Name of organization.	Organized.	Highest.	Lowest.	Average.	Weekly.	Saturday.	Average number weeks employed.
Hartford......	Bricklayers and Plasterers No. 1	1885	4.00	3.50	3.75	54	9	40

BUFFERS AND POLISHERS.

Town.	Name of organization.	Organized.	Highest.	Lowest.	Average.	Weekly.	Saturday.	Average number weeks employed.
Meriden.......	Buffers and Polishers No. 48....	1886	3.00	2.00	2.50	54	9	40
Waterbury....	Buffers and Polishers No.	1895	2.50	1.75	2.25	60	10	40
Bridgeport....	Buffers and Polishers No.	1896	3.50	1.25	2.00	59	9	40
Middletown...	Buffers and Polishers No.	1897	2.50	1.75	2.50	59	9	36

CARPENTERS AND JOINERS.

Town.	Name of organization.	Organized.	Highest.	Lowest.	Average.	Weekly.	Saturday.	Average number weeks employed.
Hartford......	Carpenters and Joiners No. 43..	1882	3.00	2.00	2.50	54	9	45
New Britain ..	Carpenters and Joiners No. 97..	1885	2.75	1.75	2.25	54	9	40
Bridgeport....	Carpenters and Joiners No. 115.	1885	2.50	1.50	2.00	54	9	40
Norwich......	Carpenters and Joiners No. 137.	1886	2.50	1.75	2.00	54	9	40
Norwalk	Carpenters and Joiners No. 746.	1891	2.50	2.00	2.25	54	9	50
New Haven...	Carpenters and Joiners No. 79..	1892	3.00	1.50	2.00	54	9	40
Stamford......	Carpenters and Joiners No. 210.	1897	2.88	1.75	2.50	53	8	45
Shelton........	Carpenters and Joiners No 127.	1898	2.75	1.75	2.50	60	10	40
Meriden.......	Carpenters and Joiners No.	1885	3.00	1.25	2.50	54	9	42

RATES OF WAGES AND HOURS OF LABOR OF ORGANIZED LABOR — *Continued.*

CIGARMAKERS INTERNATIONAL UNION.

Town.	Name of organization.	Organized.	Wages per day.			Hours of labor		Average number weeks employed.
			Highest.	Lowest.	Average.	Weekly.	Saturday.	
New Haven...	Cigarmakers Union No. 39......	1871	$3.75	$1.50	$2.00	48	8	44
Hartford......	Cigarmakers Union No. 42......	1880	3.60	1.50	2.25	48	8	48
Long Hill......	Cigarmakers Union No. 139.....	1881	3.00	2.00	2.50	44	4	45
So. Norwalk..	Cigarmakers Union No.	1880	3.00	1.50	1.75	48	8	50
Danbury......	Cigarmakers Union No. 180....	1882	2.50	1.50	1.75	46	6	36
Suffield........	Cigarmakers Union No. 156.....	1883	3.50	1.50	2.50	48	8	48
Bridgeport....	Cigarmakers Union No. 282.....	1886	2.50	1.50	2.00	48	8	40
Ansonia.......	Cigarmakers Union No. 103.....	1884	2.50	......	......	48	8	50
New London..	Cigarmakers Union No. 189.....	1893	2.00	1.50	1.75	48	8	50
Waterbury....	Cigarmakers Union No. 395.....	1897	2.50	1.50	1.70	46	6	46
Norwich.......	Cigarmakers Union No. 407.....	1898	3.00	1.50	2.00	48	8	52

DRIVERS PROTECTIVE UNION.

Town.	Name of organization.	Organized.	Highest.	Lowest.	Average.	Weekly.	Saturday.	Average number weeks employed.
Hartford......	Drivers Protective Union.......	1895	2.50	1.50	1.75	60	10	52

ELECTRICAL WORKERS UNION.

Town.	Name of organization.	Organized.	Highest.	Lowest.	Average.	Weekly.	Saturday.	Average number weeks employed.
Hartford......	Electrical Workers..............	1897	2.50	2.50	2.50	60	10	40

ENGINEERS, LOCOMOTIVE.

Town.	Name of organization.	Organized.	Highest.	Lowest.	Average.	Weekly.	Saturday.	Average number weeks employed.
New Haven...	Brotherhood Locomotive Eng'rs	1866	4.50	2.00	3.50	8	8	52
Hartford......	Brotherhood Locomotive Eng'rs	1883	4.00	3.00	3.50	8	8	52
New London..	Brotherhood Locomotive Eng'rs	1888	3.50	2.50	2.75	8	8	52

RATES OF WAGES AND HOURS OF LABOR OF ORGANIZED LABOR — *Continued.*

ENGINEERS, STATIONARY.

Town.	Name of organization.	Organized.	Wages per day.			Hours of labor		Average number weeks employed.
			Highest.	Lowest.	Average.	Weekly.	Saturday.	
Meriden.......	Stationary Engineers...........	1883	$4.50	$2.50	$3.00	....	....	52

HATTERS UNIONS.

Danbury......	Hatters Assembly, K. of L., No. 4236......................	1885	.....	.....	.....	60	8	30
"	Hatters Assembly, K. of L., No. 7923......................	1886	.....	.....	.....	60	8	30
"	Beaver Assembly, K. of L., No. 2824......................	1884	.....	.....	.....	60	8	40
"	Hatmakers Union...............	1850	*.....	*.....	*.....	60	8	30
"	Hat Finishers Union.............	1855	5.00	1.50	2.00	60	8	30
"	Hat Coverers and Slippers Union	1885	3.00	.....	3.00	60	8	30
Norwalk	Hatmakers Union...............	1860	4.00	1.50	1.60	55	5	35
"	Hat Finishers Union..	1860	4.50	1.50	2.50	60	10	35

HORSESHOE NAIL WORKERS.

Hartford......	Horse Nail Workers No. 1.......	1892	3.50	1.50	1.80	59	9	50

HORSESHOERS UNION.

New Haven...	Horseshoers Union No. 26.......	1893	3.50	2.50	2.75	59	9	45
Ansonia.......	Horseshoers Union No.	1898	3.00	2.00	2.50	60	10	52

*See notes from the unions.

RATES OF WAGES AND HOURS OF LABOR OF ORGANIZED LABOR — *Continued.*

HOUSE PAINTERS.

Town.	Name of organization.	Organized.	Wages per day.			Hours of labor		Average number weeks employed.
			Highest.	Lowest.	Average.	Weekly.	Saturday.	
New Britain ..	House Painters Union	1890	$3.00	$2.25	$2.50	54	9	35

IRON MOULDERS.

Norwalk.... .	Iron Moulders Union No. 209....	1869	4.00	2.00	2.50	60	10	45
Norwich.......	Iron Moulders Union No. 126....	......	3.00	2.00	2.50	59	9	45
Bridgeport....	Iron Moulders Union No. 110....	1879	3.00	1.80	2.25	59	9	45
Branford.....	Iron Moulders Union No. 82.....	1880	2.50	2.00	2.25	60	10	50
Hartford......	Iron Moulders Union No. 72.....	1888	3.50	2.25	2.50	60	10	50
Ansonia.......	Iron Moulders Union No. 52.....	1889	3.25	2.00	2.50	60	10	45
Rocky Hill....	Iron Moulders Union No. 302....	1892	3.00	2.00	2.25	60	10	36
New Haven...	Iron Moulders Union No.	1878	2.75	1.50	2.50	54	9	50
Stamford	Iron Moulders Union No.	......	4.00	2.50	3.00	60	10	48
New Britain..	Iron Moulders Union No.	......	2.50	1.50	2.00	60	10	48

MACHINISTS AND TOOL MAKERS.

Bridgeport....	Machinists and Tool Makers Benefit Association..........	1891	3.50	2.50	2.75	59	9	48
"	International Association of Machinists....................	......	3.25	2.00	2.75	59	9	48
Hartford......	International Association of Machinists................	1893	3.50	2.00	2.50	59	9	52
New Britain'..	International Association of Machinists....................	1894	4.00	2.00	2.75	60	10	52

RATES OF WAGES AND HOURS OF LABOR OF ORGANIZED LABOR — *Continued.*

MUSICIANS UNIONS.

Town.	Name of organization.	Organized.	Wages per day.			Hours of labor		Average number weeks employed.
			Highest.	Lowest.	Average.	Weekly.	Saturday.	
			$	$	$			
Meriden.......	Musical Protective	1889	*.....	......	......	.....	....	......
Hartford......	Musical Protective	1890	*.....	......	......	.....	....	......
Bridgeport....	Musical Protective	1896	*.....	......	......	.....	....	......
Danbury......	Musical Protective	1897	*....	......	......	.....	....	......
Norwalk	Musical Protective	1897	*.....	......	......	.....	....	......

JOURNEYMEN PLUMBERS.

Hartford......	United Association of Journey-men Plumbers.................	1892	3.50	2.00	2.50	54	9	50
Meriden.......	Plumbers, Steam and Gas Fitters	1893	3.50	2.50	2.75	54	9	40
Norwich	Plumbers, Steam and Gas Fitters	1897	2.75	2.00	2.50	54	9	40
New Britain..	Plumbers, Steam and Gas Fitters	1894	3.00	2.50	2.75	54	9	52
New Haven...	Plumbers, Steam and Gas Fitters	1887	3.50	2.50	3.00	54	9	50

PRINTING PRESSMEN.

New Haven...	Printing Pressmens Union No. 74	1896	4.25	2.50	3.50	†59	9	52
Hartford......	Printing Pressmens Union No. ...	1897	5.50	2.25	2.75	†59	9	52

*See notes from the unions.

†These hours apply to the job printers only. Newspaper pressmen work from six to seven hours daily.

RATES OF WAGES AND HOURS OF LABOR OF ORGANIZED LABOR — *Continued.*

RAILWAY TRAINMEN.

Town.	Name of organization.	Organized.	Wages per day.			Hours of labor		Average number weeks employed.
			Highest.	Lowest.	Average.	Weekly.	Saturday.	
			$	$	$			
New Haven...	Brotherhood of Railroad Trainmen.............................	1883	3.00	1.50	2.00	60	10	52
Hartford......	Brotherhood of Railroad Trainmen.............................	1885	2.25	1.95	2.00	60	10	52
Bridgeport....	Brotherhood of Railroad Trainmen.............................	1887	3.00	1.95	2.00	60	10	52
Danbury......	Brotherhood of Railroad Trainmen.............................	1889	2.75	1.90	1.95	60	10	52

SHOEMAKERS.

Town.	Name of organization.	Organized.	Wages per day.			Hours of labor		Average number weeks employed.
			Highest.	Lowest.	Average.	Weekly.	Saturday.	
Danbury......	Shoemakers Union..............	1895	*.....	......	......	....	....	......

STONE MASONS.

Town.	Name of organization.	Organized.	Wages per day.			Hours of labor		Average number weeks employed.
			Highest.	Lowest.	Average.	Weekly.	Saturday.	
New Haven...	Stone Masons Union............	1883	†.43	3.60	†.40	54	9	35

TAILORS.

Town.	Name of organization.	Organized.	Wages per day.			Hours of labor		Average number weeks employed.
			Highest.	Lowest.	Average.	Weekly.	Saturday.	
Danbury......	Journeymen Tailors Union.....	1885	2.50	1.50	2.00	‡...	‡...	26

*See notes from unions.
†Per hour.
‡No limit.

RATES OF WAGES AND HOURS OF LABOR OF ORGANIZED LABOR— *Concluded.*

TEXTILE WORKERS.

Town.	Name of organization.	Organized.	Wages per day.			Hours of labor		Average number weeks employed.
			Highest.	Lowest.	Average.	Weekly.	Saturday.	
Bridgeport....	Silk Weavers Association.......	1898	$1.75	$.50	$1.00	65	10	40
Norwalk.......	Elastic Goring Weavers.........	1885	3.50	1.50	1.75	55	5	......
Norwich	Loom Fixers Union	1889	1.88	1.70	1.80	60	6¼	49
"	Mule Spinners Union...........	1889	2.00	1.58	1.70	60	6¼	49
"	Weavers Union..................	1898	1.58	.37	1.00	60	6¼	49
"	Beamer Tenders Union.........	1898	1.75	1.50	1.60	60	6¼	49

TYPOGRAPHICAL UNION.

New Haven...	Typographical Union No. 47....	1860	4.16	2.50	3.00	59	9	52
Norwich	Typographical Union No. 100...	1867	3.50	2.50	3.00	59	9	52
Hartford......	Typographical Union No. 127...	1883	3.50	2.50	3.00	59	9	52
Bridgeport....	Typographical Union No. 252...	1889	3.00	2.00	2.50	59	9	52
Danbury......	Typographical Union No. 143...	1897	3.00	2.00	2.50	59	9	52
Meriden.......	Typographical Union No.	1892	3.00	2.40	2.50	60	10	52

WOODWORKERS.

Hartford......	Amalgamated Woodworkers...	1896	3.50	2.00	2.25	54	9	50

The preceding tables give the names of organizations, where located, highest, lowest and average of standard of wages, weekly hours of labor, hours employed on Saturday, and the average number of weeks employed per annum.

It is found that of the "outdoor" workers, the painters and stone masons lose the most time, their average being only 35 weeks in the year. Of the "indoor" workers, the tailors average but 26 weeks and the hatters 30 weeks in the year. This is explained by the fact that their work is governed by what is called "season work."

The highest, lowest and standard wage by trades is found to be as follows :

	Highest.	Lowest.	Standard.
Bakers	$3 50	$1 25	$2 25
Barbers	2 50	1 65	2 00
Beamer Tenders	1 75	1 50	1 60
Bookbinders	3 25	2 25	2 75
Brass Moulders	3 00	2 25	2 50
Brewers	3 33	2 00	2 50
Bricklayers	4 00	3 50	3 75
Buffers	3 00	2 00	2 50
Carpenters	3 00	1 50	2 50
Cigarmakers	3 75	1 50	2 25
Cotton Spinners	2 00	1 58	1 70
Cotton Weavers	1 75	50	1 10
Drivers	2 50	1 50	1 75
Electrical Workers	3 00	2 50	2 50
Elastic Goring Weavers	3 50	1 50	1 75
Hat Finishers	5 00	1 50	2 00
Horse Nail Workers	3 50	1 50	1 50
Horseshoers	3 50	2 00	2 50
House Painters	3 00	2 00	2 50
Iron Moulders	4 00	1 50	2 25
Locomotive Engineers	4 50	2 00	3 50
Loom Fixers	1 88	1 70	1 80
Machinists	4 00	2 00	2 75
Plumbers	3 50	2 00	2 75
Printers	4 16	2 00	2 50
Printing Pressmen	5 50	2 25	2 75
Railway Trainmen	3 00	1 50	2 00
Silk Weavers	1 75	50	1 00
Stationary Engineers	4 50	2 00	3 00
Stone Masons	3 87	3 00	3 00
Tailors	2 50	1 50	2 00
Woodworkers (machine)	3 50	2 00	2 25

TOTAL NUMBER ORGANIZED AND NUMBER UNEMPLOYED—INCREASE OF WAGES—DECREASE OF HOURS.

Trade or calling.	Number of organizations.	Number organized.			Number unemployed.			Benefits derived.	
		Men.	Women.	Total.	Men.	Women.	Total.	Increased wages.	Shorter hours.
Bakers......................	6	163	.....	163	15	....	15	4	4
Barbers....................	4	87	.....	87	1	....	1	1	2
Brewers...................	3	79	.....	79	2	....	2	4	3
Buffers....................	4	795	.....	795	45	....	45	3	1
Carpenters...............	9	1,224	.....	1,224	146	....	146	6	7
Cigarmakers...............	11	754	3	757	44	....	44	10	10
Hatters...................	9	2,627	1,123	3,750	570	224	794	7	2
Horseshoers..............	2	30	.....	30	.....	....	.....	1	2
Iron Moulders............	10	552	.....	552	24	....	24	8	1
Locomotive Engineers...	3	378	.....	378	20	....	20	3	3
Machinists................	4	237	.....	237	.....	....	.....	3	....
Miscellaneous......	12	902	109	1,011	33	....	33	7	5
Musicians.................	5	345	4	349	.....	....	.....	5	....
Plumbers..................	5	163	.....	163	48	....	48	3	3
Printers...................	6	305	13	318	43	1	44	6	4
Printing Pressmen.......	2	45	.....	45	.....	....	.....	....	1
Railway Trainmen.......	4	276	.....	276	.....	....	....	4	3
Textiles..................	6	336	187	523	15	3	18	3	3
Total..............	105	9,298	1,439	10,737	1,004	228	1,232	78	54

This table summarizes the membership by sex, the number unemployed, the number of unions which have had wages increased, and the number of unions which have had the hours of labor decreased as a result of organization. The table represents the 105 unions which made reports. The first column gives the name of the organization and the second the number of unions of that craft. The number of male members is 9,298 and females 1,439. The total membership is. 10,737. Of the males 1,004, or 10.9 per cent., and females 228, or 15.8 per cent., were out of employment at the time the report was made. The total number out of employment was. 1,232, or 11.5 per cent. The number of unions which have had wages increased since, and as a result of, organization is 78, and the number which have had the hours of labor shortened is 54. A study of the returns shows that the increase in wages was secured by 12 strikes, 33 demands and 33 by action of the employers on petition of the employes. The decrease in hours. of labor has been secured largely by the action of the National bodies of the several crafts forbidding their members to work beyond a specified time.

NOTES FROM THE UNIONS.

BAKE-SHOPS.

HARTFORD.—BAKERS AND CONFECTIONERS INTER-
NATIONAL UNION NO. 8.

The only suggestion we have to make is that there be a well conducted labor agitation. Anything else in our trade is of no benefit, because the "bosses" sign a contract and after a few weeks are over discharge the union men for some cause or other. Therefore, as above mentioned, agitation in favor of the union label is the only means to uphold the union and strengthen our craft. The union label certifies that the product bearing it is made in a clean, sanitary shop, under union rules.

BRIDGEPORT.—BAKERS AND CONFECTIONERS INTER-
NATIONAL UNION NO. 38.

What will improve our craft? I answer, a strict enforcement of the "Bake-shop law," passed by our last legislature, for clean and healthy shops.

In this city there are two bakers' unions, besides the one to which I belong. Both are independent, have no national head, and have no affiliation with organized labor. They are joined together to cut wages. They will not listen to labor talkers, or even go to a meeting called for their benefit.

BARBERS.

DANBURY.—JOURNEYMEN BARBERS INTERNATIONAL UNION
OF AMERICA, LODGE NO. 175.

Sunday closing would greatly benefit our craft. The hours of labor, if reduced from twelve to ten hours for a day's work, would also greatly improve our condition. There would be no need to reduce our pay of $2.00 per day, which is little enough.

MERIDEN.—JOURNEYMEN BARBERS INTERNATIONAL UNION
OF AMERICA, LODGE NO. 88.

Organized barbers' unions should consist of all barbers who
have served a three years' apprenticeship. Barber schools
should be abolished.

NORWICH.—NATIONAL BARBERS ASSOCIATION NO. 26.

Our craft can best be helped by the barbers who are not
members of a union becoming such.

NEW LONDON.—JOURNEYMEN BARBERS INTERNATIONAL
UNION NO. 136.

We desire a barbers' license law, as in some other States, requiring persons having practiced the trade in this or in another
State for at least three years, and is possessed of the requisite
skill in said trade to properly perform all the duties thereof; to
register within ninety days from date of passage, punishing
any one without a certificate, by a fine or imprisonment, or both.
Study the trade as an apprentice under a qualified and practical
barber, whether in a shop or a student in barber schools; all to
be examined by a board of examiners. Under such laws and
regulations, you would have skilled workmen, which would be
a benefit and protection to the patrons, as well as those who
have to compete with unskilled and cheap labor.

BRASS MOULDERS.

MERIDEN.

We should like steady employment, except during the vacation period in January and July. Eight hours' pay for eight
hours' work is the general desire of the Brass Moulders' Union.

BREWERS.

MERIDEN.

We want shorter hours per day and more thorough organization.

HARTFORD.

If people would purchase only the stock that bears the union
label it would help our organization. The label is a guarantee
that the product has been made by union men.

BRICKLAYERS AND PLASTERERS.

HARTFORD.—UNION NO. 1 OF CONNECTICUT.

Organization has been of great benefit to us, as before we formed the union we were working ten hours a day for whatever wages we could get. Now we work but nine hours and receive not less than $3.50 for a day's work. Some receive $4.00, but the majority receive $3.75.

BUFFERS AND POLISHERS.

BRIDGEPORT.

To have every buffer and polisher a member of our union will help us more than anything else.

CARPENTERS AND JOINERS.

HARTFORD.—UNITED BROTHERHOOD OF CARPENTERS AND JOINERS NO. 43.

Organization has been a benefit to the carpenters and joiners in this city, as it has reduced the hours of labor per week. Union men are also receiving fifty cents a day more than non-union men. The apprenticeship system would also be of benefit to us. As an organized body we have had no strike for any cause.

NEW BRITAIN.—NO. 27.

Organization here has not been of as much benefit as it ought to be. The reason, no doubt is, is because we are, as a trade, not fully organized. To be fully benefited our craft should have in its union membership all the carpenters in the town, or nearly all. If we had three-quarters of them we would be in a position to demand better wages and get them.

One of the worst features of our trade is the lack of thoroughly efficient workmen. To correct and avoid this condition it would be helpful if the apprenticeship system was established by enactment of the legislature of a law compelling a person to learn the trade before offering himself as a tradesman. The law should compel every workman to show, when asked, a certificate of his ability, and the certificate should bear the seal of the county.

BRIDGEPORT.—NO. 115.

If all the journeymen carpenters were in our organization, our wages would.be $3.00 per day of nine hours.

The contractors are in favor of organization. It is the men's fault that cheap labor reigns supreme here. Our city directory shows 560 men classed as carpenters.

NORWALK.—NO. 746.

It would greatly benefit our craft if the laws regarding liens on buildings could be amended so that a journeyman could get his wages where an irresponsible contractor fails to pay his men, for the reason that he has taken a contract for a less price than a responsible one could have taken it and pay for his labor and material.

This would make people more careful about who they let contracts to. It would benefit responsible contractors as well as the journeymen, if the journeymen could contract his wages from the owner of the building.

Our experience here is that if one can possibly collect his wages from one of this class of contractors, it usually costs more than the wages amount to.

The journeymen carpenters are alone to blame that they do not get their share of the good things of this world, by not coming into the union and being thoroughly organized for their own benefit. Our craft certainly furnishes more tools, more brains and runs more risk of loss of life than any other branch of the building trade, or any other trade, and we receive about the least wages for our labor.

DERBY.—NO. 127.

Organization is the keynote to our success in trying to better our condition. This union is only in its infancy. We are trying to get a complete organization so that when we attempt to get higher wages and shorter hours we shall be reasonably sure of success. We aim not only to get our hours of labor reduced, but to maintain the present rate of wages.

I believe that reducing the hours of labor is a matter of prime importance, because it gives employment to a greater number of men, hence more money in circulation and more business. Where there is a demand for labor, wages will adjust themselves.

MERIDEN.—NO. 2.

At the present time our union is in poor condition owing to two reasons. Trade is at a standstill here and many of our members have sought work elsewhere. Our laws provide that if a member takes jobs, or contracts for three months, he shall lose his standing in the union. Most of our members have had to do this—become contractors—in order to live. Consequently we have lost in membership so many that we hold no regular meetings. The Central Labor Union, however, attends to matters for us and gives attention to all grievances and by so doing holds for us the ground we gained by organization.

I know of no union man wholly out of employment, as the public have come to understand that the most devoted union man is the most likely to be the best mechanic and do his work well.

Jealousy among workingmen is the worst thing we have to contend with, for if one is active in all the branches of organized labor, he is said to be "after something" for himself. There is nothing that will help us so much as education will along these lines, and I sincerely believe that there is no better educator in this country, save the church, than the labor union. The man who becomes a member of one of these unions with the sole view in his mind of helping to improve the condition of his fellowman, will find his own improving and his own happiness increasing.

CIGARMAKERS.

NEW HAVEN.—CIGARMAKERS INTERNATIONAL UNION OF AMERICA NO. 39.

Organization has increased wages and shortened the hours of labor.

A strike was made for the increase of wages. It is believed that nearly all members of the craft in this city are members of the union. The members will be benefited by the enforcement of the "Trade Label Law" and the enactment of a strict sanitary law.

HARTFORD.—NO. 42.

By organization wages have been increased and hours of labor decreased, both being secured by a strike after a request had been made and refused. Before the formation of the union wages were from 25 per cent. to 30 per cent. less than now. As far as known all members of the craft in this section are organized. As to what would improve the condition of the craft, I am of the opinion that the abolition of the tenement house cigar factory would be of vast benefit to our craft, and also to the smoking public, who are liable to contract disease from the product of such factories. Hon. Theodore Roosevelt, Assistant Secretary of War, when he was a member of the New York State Assembly, spoke as follows on the bill to prohibit the making of cigars in tenement houses: "I have visited these pestholes personally, and I can assure you if smokers could only see how these cigars are made we would not need any legislation against this system at all." The New York *Sun* had this to say under the caption of "The Cigars of Death:" "The tenement house inspectors, now making their rounds, have found nothing in any quarter of New York more dangerous to public health, family virtue and common decency than the huge tenement house cigar factories which have frequently, during the past few years, been forced upon the notice of the Board of Health, but which, for some reason—through some means—are still allowed to exist"

We have persistently sought to get legislative action against this system wherever it existed, but without much success. However, we have been more successful in fighting this system since the adoption of our blue label, more especially in the past ten years, when our label has become better known. This label, when placed upon a box of cigars, is a guarantee that the cigars contained therein have been made under clean and healthy conditions.

SOUTH NORWALK.

Wages were increased and hours decreased by the manufacturers when request for the same was made to them after we organized a union in this city. There are about forty unorganized men at work here. They receive from $1.00 to $3.00 per week less than the others. Continuous agitation in favor of the use of goods bearing the "Union Label," which is a guarantee of their being made in a clean shop, will greatly assist the craft. Sale of prison-made cigars should be prohibited.

LONG HILL.—NO. 139.

Organization has been of decided benefit to us, as a craft, as our wages have been increased and the hours shortened as a result of such action. Both were granted by the employers when asked for. All cigarmakers in town are members of the union. Prison labor should be abolished and not be allowed to compete in the market with fair and honest labor.

The craft would be strengthened and greatly helped if all would purchase only goods bearing the " Blue Label," which is evidence that they have been made in a clean and sanitary shop.

DANBURY.—NO. 180.

Since the cigarmakers' union was formed here our wages have been increased, and we do not have to put in so many hours per day. We have had no strike or difficulty with our employers. There are but two cigarmakers in the place who do not belong to the union. There should be laws preventing the employment of child and prison labor. The Bureau of Labor Statistics should be continued and have the same support as does the Board of Agriculture and other State departments.

SUFFIELD.—NO. 156.

Wages were raised and hours decreased after a strike. We consider organization a great benefit. All cigarmakers here are members of the union.

ANSONIA.—NO. 103.

In 1886 a demand was made for an increase of wages, which was granted. We have had no occasion to strike. Our working time has also been decreased. All members of the craft here are members of the union.

Thorough organization of workingmen in every branch of trade and calling will naturally improve the condition of our craft, inasmuch as organized labor recognizes only union-made goods.

We believe unions are equally good for manufacturers and employes. Manufacturers in a locality, who run strictly union shops, have no advantage over one another in the matter of wages, as they are governed alike by the scale of prices they pay, as far as wages are concerned. They cannot cut prices to any great extent on finished products, as the cost of manufacture, etc., is nearly the same, thus proving that it is equally good for both employer and employe.

Now, on the other hand, how is it with non-union manufacturers? They are not governed by any union scale of prices. They pay their employes what they will take, which generally is a great deal less than union wages. In this way such a manufacturer will, because of less cost of manufacture, to secure trade, sell his goods for less the difference of wages than his union competitor; so where is the advantage or benefit he has derived? His goods cost him less, but he also sells them for less. We fail to see where it is any benefit to run a non-union shop. The only thing they can say is that they can hire employes at any wages they see fit to pay them, and perhaps they consider it to their advantage to run factories under conditions which would not be tolerated by union people, as the same has cost the unions many thousands of dollars in various ways to abolish.

BRIDGEPORT.—NO. 282.

We have had our wages increased and secured a shorter workingday by organization. We have had two strikes, the first being for an increase of wages, and was successful. The second was for the enforcement of union regulations, and was only partially successful. Our weekly wages average $8.08 per week on an actual working time of 32 hours per week.

NEW LONDON.—NO. 189.

While our hours have been decreased as a result of organization, wages have not improved. Unorganized men are working as low as $8.00 per week. What we lack is a thorough organization. More are out of the union than in. The city is full of scab goods. If union men would stop buying them and purchase only those goods bearing the union label it would be of great benefit to the cigarmakers' union, which stands for clean goods made in clean places.

WATERBURY.—NO. 395.

Previous to organization the members of the craft residing in Waterbury were members of Union No. 103, at Ansonia. All work here is regulated by the union scale. We work on the piece system.   There are but four cigarmakers here who are not union men.   They receive from $2.00 to $5.00 per week less than union men do.   We consider organization as a benefit to us.

NORWICH.—NO. 407.

Our wages have been increased and daily working hours decreased as a result of organization.   Both were granted us by the manufacturers without trouble.   There are about twelve men who are not yet in the union here.   A better patronage of the "Blue Label" goods will help us more than anything else.

ELECTRICAL WORKERS.

HARTFORD.—BROTHERHOOD OF ELECTRICAL WORKERS OF AMERICA, LOCAL NO. 37.

For the improvement of the condition of our craft I would suggest the establishment of a State law governing an apprentice system.   I would also favor the licensing of all men professing to be first-class electrical workers, after putting each and every one through an examination, this examination not to be on purely technical subjects, but on matters pertaining to trade, and issue a license accordingly.   Some time ago the local to which I belong, brought before the ordinance committee of this city a bill in which the above conditions were stated, together with numerous remarks from prominent insurance men of this city, and a meeting was called of the above-mentioned committee at which meeting our bill was ordered tabled and we were told that we would be notified when it came up.   After waiting about two months without hearing from the committee we started a committee out to send a tracer after the bill, with the result that up to the present time we have not been able to find out what happened to it.   In bringing this matter before my organization I was instructed to request you, as far as it were possible for you to do, to help us get this bill passed.   If at any time you should desire other information about this or any other matter, I assure you that by writing me I will do all in my power to aid you.

LOCOMOTIVE ENGINEERS.

NEW HAVEN.

As the rate of wages varies according to the service performed, the scale paid the New Haven division is here given
as an illustration of the method of apportionment.

"The engineers on the New Haven system of the N. Y.,
N. H. & H. R. R. work under a written contract, which we
denote a schedule, signed by the company on their part and a
committee of engineers on our part, which is termed the mileage system. It originated with our organization, and we
consider it the fairest and most equitable system that has yet
been introduced, equally as just for the company as for the
engineers, viz.: 100 miles or less constitutes a day's work on
passenger or freight trains, 3½ cents per mile for passenger
and 4 cents per mile for freight trains; work trains $100 per
month of 26 working days. Hours are not considered in passenger trains as they run on schedule time. On most of the
divisions freights are paid overtime if out over 12 hours, time
to begin at 10 hours at the rate of 35 cents per hour; also work
trains are paid overtime under the same ruling as regards
hours for freights. A day's pay is $3.50 for passenger and
$4.00 for freight. Firemen promoted to engineers are paid on
switch engines $2.50 first year, $3.00 second year and $3.50
third year, 8 hours to constitute a day's work; all over time
pro rata. If assigned to road work, to be paid the rate as per
schedule in the class in which they are employed. This rate
applies to the New York, Hartford, Shore Line, Air Line,
Shepang, and New Haven divisions; the Berkshire, Danbury
& Norwalk and Naugatuck divisions work under what is called
the trip system, which also includes overtime after being out a
given number of hours. The rate runs from $3.00 to $7.00
per day. The $7.00 rate is a long day's work for an engineer
and is divided between two men running alternate days. All
things being considered, the Brotherhood of Locomotive Engineers favor the mileage system and the privileges that it
confers on them in preference to any other system of pay. In
the aggregate they are the gainers both in hours of labor and
a higher rate of pay."

STATIONARY ENGINEERS.

The National Association of Stationary Engineers is in no
sense a labor organization in the usual acceptance of the term,
therefore this fact precludes the possibility of definitely an-
swering all of the questions required in the schedule.

Education is the first consideration—in fact, the foundation
stone of our order and the principle for which we are united.
We realize that the interests of the manufacturer (employer)
and the engineer are identical. The more economically and
efficiently that an engineer can operate a steam plant the more
useful he is both to himself and his employer, and we have
found that sooner or later true merit meets with just recognition and reward.

Our weekly meetings are devoted largely to the consideration of practical questions relating to the generation and
transmission of power and kindred subjects.

There is one desideratum, namely, an honest engineer's
license law. That such laws, requiring that every operating or
superintending engineer in the State of Connecticut shall demonstrate his ability to safely control the enormous natural forces
with which he has to deal, also to prove himself able to successfully meet any emergency arising in the plant under his charge,
would be greatly beneficial to employer and engineer alike
there cannot be the slightest doubt, as the results of such laws,
enacted by Massachusetts, New York City and other communities throughout the United States bear witness. For years the
subordinate associations of this State have been striving for
such laws and sooner or later these laws must come.

Regarding wages, would state that we have no "scale,"
rather believing that merit will be met with just and sufficient
compensation. Some of the members of this subordinate association are qualified to take full charge of any steam plant in
the State, and some have never had charge of anything larger
than a twenty horse-power plant. The question of wages is not
given the first consideration by our organization. In many
instances wages have been voluntarily increased, or at least
increased for the mere asking, after certain members have been

with us for a year or so, due to the greater knowledge of the profession which they have attained through the educational feature which is given the first consideration in our order.

Engineers, as a rule, have a great deal of work to attend to that cannot be done in running hours, also more or less time to devote to their plants on Sundays, such as cleaning boilers, making extensive repairs or adjustments to engines and steam appliances, which is part and parcel of the duties of an engineer and for which, usually, there is no extra compensation. On the other hand whenever a holiday of any kind turns up the time of the engineer is his to use as his judgment dictates, provided, first of all, that his plant does not need his attention in any of its details.

HATMAKERS.

DANBURY.—HATMAKERS OF DANBURY.

Our craft is much different from any other, as we have what we call Fall and Spring trade, which lately has lasted about ten weeks each. The remainder of the year we have parts of the day perhaps, which would be from 60 cents to $1.20 for the time worked. Take for instance the shop which I am employed in. There has been no work in it since the 15th of April, 1898, and no prospects of any until after the 15th of July, when the Fall trade usually starts. Before the depression $3 was considered the day's wages for the average man (though there were men who could make $4), and when it went under that there was a grievance, which was investigated, and if it was found the manufacturer was at fault he would be compelled to either pay more per dozen or change his mixtures so that men could do enough to bring their wages up to that standard, the men remaining at work pending the settlement. There are some branches of the trade at the present time, where men have full work, at which $5.00 or $6.00 per day can be made, but they are very few. The majority make from $2.00 to $2.50 in good times. You can see from the amount of work they have in a year that it is impossible to live on that. The only way I can see that our craft can be benefited is for the manufacturers to stop cutting each other in the market, or the people of the country to patronize hats that bear the union label of the United Hatters of North America, as that insures the purchaser that the men making them receive the best wages, and that they receive more than in the shops of firms who pay what they please to their help, and if they say anything against it are discharged. Others take their places, and for what the manufacturers choose to pay them. If such firms as these did not receive the patronage of the people they would be compelled to make their factories fair, pay fair wages, and could not go into the market with the advantage they now have over manufacturers who are disposed to deal fairly with their employes. There is much that could be said on what would be a benefit to the hatting trade, but I must content myself with what I have said.

DANBURY.—HAT FINISHERS ASSOCIATION.

Encourage organized labor by purchasing only such goods as bear the union label when they are to be had.

NORWALK.—HATMAKERS ASSOCIATION.

The Hatmakers Association allows members to work only by the piece, except the foreman and one assistant. Ten hours constitute a day's labor, to be done between the hours of 7 A. M. and 6 P. M. The association says all work must cease at 12 o'clock, noon, on Saturday.

The United Hatters of North America is composed of about 5,000 members, and is supported by the different local hatters' associations. It has had for a number of years a label, to be placed in all union-made hats, and we believe it has been a great success. The association advocates the purchase of all union-made goods. We favor an eight-hour law.

NORWALK.—HAT FINISHERS.

An increased demand on the part of the consumers for goods bearing our union label. Our wages and conditions are not such as skilled mechanics should enjoy. But we realize that there are many whose necessities compel them to exchange their labor for even less than we receive. We have not even a fighting chance to improve our wages. We might succeed in forcing manufacturers to raise our wages, thereby making it harder for them to meet the competition of the employers of cheap and unorganized labor. But we feel that this policy would eventually work their ruin and ours too.

HORSESHOERS.

NEW HAVEN.—JOURNEYMEN HORSESHOERS UNION NO. 26.

Horseshoeing is hard work, and I would like to see ten hours form a day's work for five days and five hours on Saturdays.

ANSONIA.—JOURNEYMEN HORSESHOERS UNION NO. 87.

In answer to your last question I will state, for myself, that education will improve the condition of any craft, for the more we read and study the better we can find a way to improve the condition of our craft and ourselves. It also opens a way for expressing our opinions on any subject that may come before us for discussion. The labor question is something that needs lots of study, and we must not jump at conclusions too soon, for we are all liable to be mistaken sometimes. We must go at this labor question in a cool manner so that we may all understand it when it is brought before us for discussion. Educate your men on this question and they will soon find a way to improve their condition.

Now, in regard to wages by the day, there are two branches of workmen in the horseshoeing trade who are known as the firemen and the floormen. The former receive more pay than the latter, so you will see by my figures that a fireman receives $3 a day and a floorman $2 a day. In regard to working hours we always worked ten hours on Saturday until our union was organized, and when we asked for nine hours on Saturday we got it right away.

In regard to benefits of organized labor there are a good many. In the first place it brings men together for the purpose of bettering their condition in life, not only socially, but financially. It creates a good feeling, and that is always necessary to make a success of anything you undertake to do. We had a case right here in our own union. Two men who had not spoken a word to each other for two years became members of the union, and to-day they are working hand in hand for the benefit of the union.

IRON MOULDERS.

It has long been a mooted question as to how to secure justice to the day wage-worker.   In many of the trades where good
organization prevails a reasonable amount of justice has been
secured, but the trades of lesser organization the men are at the
mercy of the employers.   Often even a hearing is denied them.
Many times men make mistakes by not giving attention to surrounding or distant economic conditions, but in the cases I now
have in mind, even if they were thus fortified, it would avail
them little personally.

In disputes between employer and employe I believe there
should be a board possessing judicial power and making attendance compulsory on part of employer and employe.   This
board, having power to determine, should also have power to
enforce their decisions.   This may not be a solution of the
labor problem, but it would at least cause the employer to
recognize the reasonable claims of his employes, and not needlessly destroy the peaceful serenity of our different localities.

That which will be of the most benefit to our craft is a
thorough organization.   This accomplished, we shall secure a
workingday of eight hours, and thereby give an opportunity
for some of the idle ones — not from choice — to secure work.
Another help would be the restriction of immigration.

The curse of our business is the piece system, which prevails
in most shops.   Our trade is filling up with Hungarians and
Poles who are willing to work cheaper than the English-
speaking people can.   They live very cheap; in fact, in a
manner that is a disgrace to civilization.   It is humiliating, to
say the least, to American manhood and womanhood to be
obliged to compete with them, let alone having to endure their
presence which is often revolting in the extreme, and I must
add that it is such people that get the preference with some of
our manufacturers.

· The majority of them do not intend to remain here.   They
accumulate until they have sufficient to buy land where they

came from and then they return.   Others then come and take
their places.   If any of them die the town generally has to bury
them.

You may think this is not so, but I assure you that it is..
Shame to us that our American-born young men are walking
the streets for lack of employment on account of these people
being given the preference.   Many of them have enlisted and
are now fighting for our country and its flag.   These people
will not do that; they did not come here for that purpose.   I
might say much more but will refrain from doing so as I think
I have given the Labor Commissioner some idea of our
grievance.

HARTFORD.—NO. 72.

More thorough organization is the most important of the
thousand and one suggestions that may be offered for the betterment of our condition.

ROCKY HILL.—NO. 302.

If our organization was more thoroughly organized it would
be more beneficial to the members of our craft.   We would
have less strikes, and the money spent in strikes if spent in per-
fecting organization, would secure better wages and shorter
hours.   Our firm tells us that they cannot compete with firms
making the same class of goods because they have to pay
higher wages to union men.

Every iron moulder should be a union man.   There should
be a paid organizer to visit about for the purpose of adding to
the unions.   Our organization has been visited but once since
its formation.

MACHINISTS.

BRIDGEPORT.—INTERNATIONAL ASSOCIATION OF MACHINISTS.

To my mind organization outclasses all reforms offered for
the betterment of the laboring classes, save some form of so-
cialism.   Free trade, with the single tax, high tariff or low
tariff have proved fruitless to stem the tide of falling wages.
The single tax is being tried in New Zealand, I believe, and

from reports the results obtained are not to be compared with
what could be obtained by organized labor thoroughly organized. The reasons Bridgeport is so poorly organized are
various. Some cannot bear the thought of the financial investment required, while othere are fearful that if their employers
knew of their joining the union their jobs would be jeopardized,
while the bulk, I must say, are not awake to the real necessity
of the times. Few of the laboring class know anything of
political economy, in fact hardly know the application of the
same. We of Bridgeport believe in shortening the number of
hours for a day's work, thereby employing the surplus and
opening chances for better pay made by the increased demand
for labor.

NEW BRITAIN.—INTERNATIONAL ASSOCIATION OF MACHINISTS.

An eight-hour day with eight hours' pay would be a great
benefit to our trade. We also desire to see the apprenticeship
system introduced, which would be a surety that all machinists
were capable, trained men. The system would also be of inestimable benefit to the public as well as the trade.

BRIDGEPORT.—MACHINISTS AND TOOLMAKERS ASSOCIATION.

Thorough organization of the machinists and toolmakers
under one head, working for the benefit of each other, with no
heavy values to pay, and the dues heavy enough to have a substantial weekly benefit in case of sickness or disability. A competent committee to arbitrate all grievances so as to avoid a
strike if possible. A more friendly feeling to a new hand coming into a shop—in fact a living down of the petty jealousies
that exist, I am sorry to say, to a greater extent than one not in
the trade is aware of.

I would like to say just a few words on the subject of unionism in the machinists and toolmakers' trades. We have been in
existence now nearly seven years, first as a local union for two
years, then we were affiliated with the International Machinists'
Union three years, and for the last two years we have been just
a local benefit association, doing our best to organize the men,
and, I tell you, it is an uphill, thankless job in this city. But
there are a few of us that think we know what a thorough organization would mean for us all, and we dislike to give it up.

MUSICAL PROTECTIVE UNION.

BRIDGEPORT.—AMERICAN FEDERATION OF MUSICIANS NO. 63.

Musicians, though not strictly a trade union, should certainly organize to assist the other class of wage-workers. We have splendid success, because we do not have corporations and monopolies to fight, but deal more with individuals. In this city, for instance, we have given the unions the biggest boom they have had for years, and will continue to do so. We are the only body of musicians in this State with a national head. The other locals would improve greatly should they join the American Federation of Musicians, 20,000 strong.

DANBURY.

I think it would be well, if practical, to establish a bill of prices in all musical unions in the State, the same price to be paid in each city for all engagements of the same character.

The musicians of this city are obliged to compete with union musicians of other cities, and have to play at lower prices than we play the same business at home or lose the business. I refer, of course, to business outside of our own city.

SOUTH NORWALK.

Our union, although a young organization, is at present in a thriving condition, and I can think of no suggestion whereby the members could be benefited. We are striving to get the applications of the few non-union musicians in town, and hope soon to have every player of ability in the organization.

PLUMBERS.

HARTFORD.—UNITED ASSOCIATION OF JOURNEYMEN PLUMBERS.

It would be a great help to plumbers if the city ordinances in regard to registering plumbers were put into effect by the Board of Health. As it now stands apprentices do a great deal of the work that journeymen ought to be doing, thereby throwing skilled men out of work. This is the sentiment of every journeyman plumber, union or non-union, in Hartford.

MERIDEN.—PLUMBERS, GAS AND STEAM FITTERS UNION.

We need the passage of a law by the State that would require a strict inspection of all plumbing by inspectors who are masters of this trade in all its branches.

NORWICH.—PLUMBERS, GAS AND STEAM FITTERS UNION.

Trade is very dull in this vicinity. Owing to this fact and that we have been organized but a short time we have made no effort to have wages increased. The master plumbers cut prices in competition with each other, and this has a tendency to keep wages down. There are a great many journeymen here who have not yet united with the union. Some say they can get along without union membership. We still hope to induce them to unite with us.

NEW BRITAIN.—UNITED ASSOCIATION OF JOURNEYMEN PLUMBERS.

We want a State law that will compel plumbers to pass an examination and take out a license. This will improve our craft and be a still greater benefit to the public health.

NEW HAVEN.—PLUMBERS, GAS AND STEAM FITTERS UNION.

We need more thorough organization of all journeymen plumbers. As it is now, men have to take what wages are offered.

PRINTING PRESSMEN.

HARTFORD.—NO. 75.

A shorter workday without reduction of wages. Other trades have it, and I think we should also, as I believe as much work would be done under ordinary circumstances in a nine-hour day as is done in ten hours. I do not think the employers would lose anything in the long run, and the shorter workday would help them as well as the pressmen, as they would be able to make up for it in better prices for work without any perceptible difference in the amount of work finished, as the whole thing amounts to a raise in wages and would spur the pressmen on, and they would work the harder, and the result would be satisfactory to the employers as well as the employes.

SHOEMAKERS.

DANBURY.—SHOEMAKERS PROTECTIVE UNION.

The largest number of members of our organization are self-employing. But notwithstanding that, when the trade was not organized, there was a strong tendency to lower the price charged for the work done by the several shoemakers, and therefore partially reducing the profit—that is, their wages. Since we organized we have a standard price for the different kinds of work we do, based on a fair day's wages.

The difference between the cost of material employed and expense (rent, light, heat. etc.), and the price charged for work is our wages, being the share due for the work we perform.

STONE MASONS.

HARTFORD.—UNION NO. 7, OF CONNECTICUT.

About seven years ago the stone masons were receiving forty cents per hour. Our work is very hard, and on account of the weather we lose a large amount of time. We struck for forty-five cents per hour. The "bosses" offered forty-three cents. We held out for one year, and did not consider the strike a success. Our organization has been of benefit to us, but we are troubled by outsiders coming in to work for less than union rates. I mean unorganized labor ; and if they will work for less than the standard rate there is always some contractor ready to hire cheap labor. Some are working as low as twenty-five cents per hour. As high as forty-three is paid by some of the "bosses," but the standard rate is forty cents. Those receiving the lower rate are inferior workmen.

I am opposed to strikes except when there is no other way. Every means possible should be tried before a strike is ordered.

TEXTILE WORKERS.

NORWICH.—NATIONAL LOOM FIXERS.

We favor a national eight-hour day law.

NORWICH.—NATIONAL MULE SPINNERS ASSOCIATION.

We had quite a lot of trouble lately. We had a two-weeks' strike against a reduction of ten per cent. The strike brought it to an average of eight, and was the cause of organizing the weavers and part of the carding room, and I am under the impression that they mean to keep it up, for they have seen how it would have benefited them if they had been organized about one year ago. They would have been able to resist the reduction much better.

Looking at the depression of the cotton trade at the present time, in my humble opinion it would be a good thing to lessen the hours of labor in factories. It would help our trade and benefit the men, women and children employed, as well as have a tendency to prolong our lives. I would like to know why they want us to work ten hours a day in factories, in a congested atmosphere, when the masons, carpenters and others, out doors, only work nine hours. There is nothing to remedy this but organization and the ballot.

NORWICH.—WEAVERS.

Having been organized only a short time, organization has not yet shown the benefit of such action. The employers have taken advantage of our not being organized to cut and cut our wages, not a general plan, but in changing weaving from time to time to different patterns. Shorter hours would help us. Our reason for desiring this is that the manufacturers tell us "the market is overstocked." Shorter hours will lessen the production and create a larger demand for woven goods and give more regular employment. Better wages can also be paid.

BRIDGEPORT.—SILK WORKERS ASSOCIATION.

Pass a law that will punish employers who discharge their employes who join labor organizations.

Also a law that shall make nine hours a legal day's work, except Saturday, when it shall be eight.

This will reduce production and give a chance for the surplus labor to be used, and then with a better demand we shall receive better wages. This will not only benefit the employes, but the general public as well.

The only way for the industrial classes of this country to

better their condition is to organize for the purpose of protection and education. They should seek such legislation as will
work for their betterment, which, in many cases, is most
desirable.

NORWALK.—ELASTIC GORING WEAVERS AMALGAMATED ASSOCIATION.

Our branch has had no local strike. We have had, however,
three strikes in the trade against a reduction of wages and were
successful each time.

Our trade has been in a very depressed condition for the last
five years on account of the change of style of shoes. I do not
think we have averaged more than two days a week during that
time.

TYPOGRAPHICAL UNION.

NEW HAVEN.—NO. 47.

The enrollment of all non-union men in this city of our
trade would be of great benefit to us and also to the non-
unionists.

I think a shorter workday would be of great benefit to the
workingmen of this country. It would certainly, if it became
adopted by workingmen generally throughout the country,
give employment to some of that "vast army of unemployed"
we hear so much about.

NORWICH.—NO. 100.

A shorter workingday would furnish employment for the
surplus printers of this country! The use of the union label
would benefit us.

HARTFORD.—NO. 127.

To have all printed matter bear our label. If this is done
the public will know that whenever work is done and bears this
label the help employed on said work are receiving fair and
living wages. We will never be satisfied until the above is
accomplished.

Being reorganized since December 3, 1883, makes us in
existence, next December, fifteen years. During this time we

have had one strike, and we tried all possible means to avoid
that. We do not believe in strikes. Our members in said strike
were discharged one by one and girls put in their places, receiving from $6.00 to $9.00 per week.

Naturally most people will think since the introduction of
machinery that we are losing ground. No. We are much
stronger at the present time than six years ago, or thereabouts,
when the Mergenthaler was introduced in our trade.

The only thing that will improve our condition is the label.

BRIDGEPORT.—NO. 252.

Members holding situations in newspaper offices have steady
work all the year round, while those in job printing offices are
generally on short time during the late summer and early fall.
Eight hours constitute a day's labor on morning newspapers
and nine and nine and one-half on evening. Our membership
is continually fluctuating, through arrivals and withdrawals,
but generally we have about half a dozen members not holding steady situations. Machinery, during the last two or three
years, has considerably lessened our membership. A thorough
organization of the printing trades, all branches, in this city,
and working in harmony with proprietors, would improve
conditions.

DANBURY.—NO. 143.

There is nothing that I can suggest under this head except
that thorough organization, under present conditions, is the
only thing that will improve the condition of the craft. Get all
other trade unions to call for the typographical union label on
their printing, and patronize only goods bearing the labels of
fraternal organizations. If possible seek to better the wage-
earners' condition by political ends, and gain points by legislation in the same manner that the firemen did when they got
the State Firemen's Association incorporated.

In other words, get the workmen as well protected as are
the gigantic corporations, holding valuable charters granted by
the State.

MERIDEN.

At the present time all the printers in this city are employed,
and are in complete harmony with the employers.

FROM A MERIDEN GLASS CUTTER.

That organization among the workingmen has been the means of elevating their condition is a fact which cannot be disputed.

It was through the influence of organized labor that the various States established the Bureaus of Labor Statistics to investigate and report the actual condition of the working classes with a view to improving the same. For that reason there can be found in our State to-day, as well as in others, men who have no sympathy for, or interest in, the elevation of the masses of the people (men whom the workingmen themselves elect to the legislatures to make laws for them), who would, if they had their way, abolish the offices of the Commissioner of Labor Statistics and Inspector of Factories entirely, knowing that the investigation and exposure of the unsanitary conditions of factories and mills, sweat-shops, dangerous and unguarded machinery, elevators, etc., would create an agitation and comment which would result in some action being taken to remedy the same.

It was through the influence and at the request of organized labor that laws were passed by the several States in the interest of education by restricting the employment of children of tender age in the factories and mills. It is a fact worthy of consideration that in States where there are no labor organizations to speak of (particularly in the South) neither are there any such laws on their statute books restricting child labor as in States where labor is well organized. This has been referred to by several of the leading newspapers recently in commenting on the great cotton mills strike throughout New England against a reduction of wages, and which led to an attempt by the owners of the mills in Massachusetts to have the laws restricting child labor in that State repealed by the last legislature in order that they might be better able to compete with the South. This could be properly classed as a movement in the interest of illiteracy.

I will quote from a paper read at the ninth annual convention of the International Association of Factory Inspectors, held at Providence, R. I., September 3, 1895, by Deputy Inspector Jordan, of New York, and who also presented a table

originally prepared by Assistant Factory Inspector John Fra-
ney, of New York, entitled, "Table showing percentage of illiteracy, population, child labor, etc., in the United States." Mr.
Jordan stated, among other things: "It is discouraging to find
the illiteracy of North Carolina in 1890 as high as 37.7 per cent.,
while in 1850 the illiteracy of free negroes was only 21.32 per
cent. and the whites only 13.30 per cent. It is surely no mere
coincidence, but more likely cause and effect, that a State which
has (proportionately) more than ten times the child labor of
New York should have trebled its illiteracy during the last
forty-five years, while the 'little red school-house,' in Fourth
of July oratory at least, has been marching on in triumph everywhere else except, of course, in South Carolina. This State
had 10.25 per cent. child labor and 45 per cent. illiteracy in 1890,
but less than 10 per cent. free negroes illiterate and less than 6
per cent. among the whites before the war. Alabama also
stands out with 40 per cent. illiteracy in 1890 and 4.50 per cent.
child labor, but less than 11 per cent. of negroes and 8 per cent.
of whites in 1850. Even Rhode Island, with over 8 per cent.
child labor, had over 9 per cent. illiteracy in 1890, but only 7.27
per cent. for negroes and 2.32 per cent. of whites in 1850. This
looks like the worst kind of reaction—certainly not like progress. * * * Is it not humiliating that California and Vermont should be worse than Belgium, Holland and Russia, allowing children to work at 10 years, and that Maine and Rhode
Island should not rise higher than the low limit of 12 years of
those continental countries? That New Jersey and Louisiana
should not rise to the level of France and Germany, that of 13
years? * * *"

The above is certainly a gloomy picture of the condition
of the working classes in those and other States from an educational standpoint, and should receive earnest attention and
action to remedy the same, not only from organized labor, but
from our legislators and others who have any regard for the
future welfare and greatness of our Nation.

It is written, "A Nation's greatness depends, not on acres,
but upon the education of its people." In order to remedy the
above and make other improvements in the condition of the
working class of a permanent nature, and put them into effect,
organized labor must discard its old policy and motto of "No
politics," and adopt the reverse, "All politics," as it is only

through legislation that the above and other permanent improvements can be accomplished. Workingmen themselves must be the legislators and the desired laws passed by their votes instead of begging of and trusting to others to do it for them. As evidence that organized labor has already taken this view, I will state that in 1897 seventeen unions affiliated with the State Branch American Federation of Labor, voted in favor of calling a convention for political action while only four voted against it.

PART III.

CONDITION OF MANUFACTURES.

1. DIVISION BY INDUSTRIES AND ESTABLISHMENTS.

2. PERSONS EMPLOYED.

3. WAGES.

4. BUSINESS DONE.

5. DIVISION BY LOCALITIES.

CONDITION OF MANUFACTURES.

Part III. of this report is devoted to the condition of the manufacturing industries of the State, the investigation having been made along the same lines as last year, with the view that an intelligent comparison can be made with previous years, the same industries being considered.

It will be noticed that the number of establishments represented in the tabulation which follows is considerably less than the number which appeared in the chapter of the report for 1897 devoted to the same subject. This is explained in part by the fact that the means at the command of the Bureau were insufficient for the employment of the necessary assistance required to make a canvass of the entire State, and, furthermore, in the chapter of the report relating to the Textile Industries of Connecticut will be found a statistical abstract of the manufactures of cotton, hosiery, knit, silk and woolen goods, covering in a measure the same matters as are shown in Part III.

There are many reasons why meagre returns are given by some manufacturers and especially so when the period of unusual financial stringency and depression, which has prevailed in the State for some years past, is taken into consideration.

There is considerable pride among manufacturers regarding their business, and naturally there is some reluctance in making a return when the conditions of any year have been to their disadvantage. Some of those having capital invested in manufactories or mills feel that they could not make a good showing, and, perhaps, thoroughly disheartened, do not wish to make a report. It is pleasing to note, however, that as the aims and objects of the department become better understood there is less objection to answer the questions propounded. It should be stated here that as much consideration is given in

(167)

the collection of the returns from an establishment employing
five or six individuals as that from one with as many hundred
employes. Those taken from small concerns are just as valuable for purposes of statistics as those gotten from the larger
ones.

An improvement in industrial conditions is made manifest
by the result of the investigation shown in the following
tables, and while the figures show that the manufacturing
interests of the State have not, as yet, reached the former
highly prosperous condition, yet, assuming that the amount of
money paid out to the wage-earner is a true barometer from
which to draw inferences as to the exact industrial situation,
conditions are slowly but surely approaching the normal stage
of success and prosperity which prevailed throughout the State
during the years preceding the period of depression from which
the people of Connecticut have so long been suffering.

Concerning the table which shows the increase or decrease
in number of persons employed and the ratio of amount disbursed as wages for the three periods of 1896-7-8, in the
several localities considered in the tabulation, it should be
understood that the number of establishments, the number
employed or the amount paid in wages does not include all
manufactories or establishments in the specified localities, but
only those, the data from which was at hand in the office of
the Bureau, with which to make comparisons. Therefore, in
the event that the amount shown as having been paid in wages
in 1898 should appear as being less than in a previous year, it
by no means follows that a less amount has been disbursed in
the entire community, but in those establishments only to
which the table has reference.

It should be added further, as regards the number employed, that, as is shown by the tables, the number of persons
on the pay-rolls of the several establishments on the specified
date of July 1st is taken as the basis for the computation, and
it must not be inferred that the number so specified is the
actual or average number for the year, for by the method
above described it is rendered possible to show the number of
employes to have been less in 1898 than in a previous year,
while the amount disbursed as wages is shown to have been
materially in excess of the amount paid out by the same
establishments during the preceding year.

INDUSTRY : BRASS AND BRASS GOODS.

Number of Establishment.	Persons employed July 1.		Per cent. number employed.		Amount paid in wages during year ending July 1.		Per cent. amount paid in wages.		Estimated per cent. business done of full capacity.
	1897.	1898.	Increase.	Decrease.	1897.	1898.	Increase.	Decrease.	
1	427	497	16.4	....	$180,500	$221,332	22.6	....	100
2	650	800	23.1	....	316,557	385,000	21.6	....	100
3	60	50	....	16.7	21,000	26,899	28.1	....	75
4	157	164	4.5	....	86,735	95,755	10.4	....	70
5	70	60	....	14.3	32,494	31,200	....	4.	70
6	234	207	....	11.5	100,909	104,080	3.1	....	75
7	716	834	16.5	....	388,523	468,217	20.5	....	100
8	201	187	....	7.	85,504	82,504	....	3.3	70
9	109	112	2.7	....	34,252	36,452	6.4	....	80
10	761	1,005	32.1	....	376,142	521,287	38.1	....	100
11	8	6	....	25.	3,488	2,973	....	14.8	50
12	9	13	44.4	....	4,068	4,856	19.3	....	85
13	220	226	2.7	....	111,971	117,639	5.1	....	80
14	26	25	....	3.8	11,368	10,844	....	4.6	85
15	13	13	....	....	5,067	5,280	4.2	....	70
16	12	13	8.3	....	10,000	10,343	3.4	....	75
17	86	76	....	11.9	46,269	44,188	....	4.5	98
18	8	8	....	....	3,100	3,100	....	....	70
19	6	5	....	16.6	2,000	2,600	30.	....	90
20	533	559	4.9	....	249,195	129,329	....	48.1	60
21	268	250	....	6.7	129,254	143,787	11.2	....	95
22	73	82	12.3	....	37,727	42,218	11.8	....	75
23	118	124	5.1	....	57,691	64,157	11.2	....	85
24	188	200	6.4	....	76,672	81,692	3.8	....	85
25	3	3	....	....	2,260	2,310	2.2	....	75
26	233	240	3.	....	115,575	135,474	17.2	....	100
27	11	7	....	36.3	6,000	3,000	....	50.	30
28	299	226	....	24.4	184,509	141,522	....	23.3	60
29	545	674	23.7	....	244,673	261,714	6.9	....	100
30	10	9	....	10.	3,847	3,809	....	9.	50
31	460	385	....	16.3	219,956	238,307	8.3	....	80

INDUSTRY: BRASS AND BRASS GOODS — *Concluded.*

Number of Establishment.	Persons employed July 1.		Per cent. number employed.		Amount paid in wages during year ending July 1.		Per cent. amount paid in wages.		Estimated per cent. business done of full capacity.
	1897.	1898.	Increase.	Decrease.	1897.	1898.	Increase.	Decrease.	
32	1,461	1,870	28.	....	$742,925	$905,165	21.8	....	100
33	50	56	12.	....	24,000	24,900	3.7	....	80
34	15	13	....	13.3	9,000	5,674	....	36.9	50
35	4	4	....		1,680	1,680			50
36	211	220	4.3	....	105,700	114,705	8.5	....	95
37	169	190	12.4	....	69,965	88,492	26.5	....	67
38	600	653	8.8	....	300,500	351,011	16.8	......	75
39	5	20	300.	....	2,600	5,709	119.6	....	100
40	98	101	3.1	....	57,157	50,384	....	11.8	95
41	321	450	40.2	....	172,615	210,352	21.8	....	100
42	35	40	14.3	....	5,000	18,200	264.	....	100
43	93	85	....	8.6	51,189	48,636	....	5.	50
44	442	496	12.2	....	230,066	282,698	22.9	....	100
45	954	1,272	33.3	....	248,463	576,763	132.1	....	100
46	38	36	....	5.2	20,377	20,351	....	1.	100
47	39	25	....	35.9	16,534	16,185	....	2.1	70
48	83	84	1.2	....	60,986	62,129	1.9	....	100
49	348	450	26.2	....	138,894	236,296	70.1	....	90
50	10	10	....	....	5,825	5,960	2.3	....	75
51	8	14	75.	....	2,184	6,630	203.6	....	100
52	30	34	13.3	....	15,000	16,779	11.9	....	97
53	44	27	....	38.6	17,000	15,373	....	9.6	70
54	150	125	....	16.6	50,000	22,000	....	56.	90
55	612	800	30.7	....	377,044	429,290	13.9	....	100
56	100	135	35.	......	33,556	40,912	21.9	....	85
57	17	21	23.5	....	10,000	12,540	25.4	....	60
58	30	40	33.3	....	14,200	15,000	4.9	....	65
59	21	27	28.5	....	13,000	13,800	6.2	....	25
60	123	130	5.7	....	49,919	59,864	19.9	....	95
61	1,052	1,134	7.8	....	480,184	569,537	18.6	....	90
Total	13,677	15,622	14.2		$6,472,869	$7,648,823	18.2		*89.6

* On basis of wages paid.

INDUSTRY : BUTTONS, BUCKLES AND PINS.

Number of Establishment.	Persons employed July 1.		Per cent. number employed.		Amount paid in wages during year ending July 1.		Per cent. amount paid in wages.		Estimated per cent. done of full capacity.
	1897.	1898.	Increase.	Decrease.	1897.	1898.	Increase.	Decrease.	
62	70	79	12.9	....	$25,000	$33,000	32.	....	70
63	62	68	9.7	....	24,500	26,000	8.6	....	100
64	22	20	....	9.1	6,755	9,207	36.3	....	80
65	23	24	4.3	....	8,750	9,961	13.8	....	100
66	7	14	100.	....	4,525	1,471	....	67.4	20
67	65	84	27.7	....	17,714	28,262	59.5	....	100
68	84	106	26.1	....	43,710	57,720	32.1	....	80
69	45	52	15.5	....	10,000	14,700	47.	....	80
70	50	65	23.	....	12,500	17,300	38.4	....	100
71	17	17	....	....	7,277	10,742	47.6	....	85
72	12	15	25.	....	3,700	4,805	29.9	....	70
73	300	381	27.	....	140,000	173,300	23.7	....	100
74	263	375	42.6	....	87,643	137,936	57.4	....	100
75	250	250	....	....	75,000	121,019	61.4	....	100
76	99	126	27.1	....	30,815	39,161	27.1	....	85
77	76	84	10.5	....	33,190	32,788	....	1.2	80
Total	1,445	1,760	21.8		$531,079	$717,372	35.1		*92.3

*On basis of wages paid.

INDUSTRY: CARRIAGES AND CARRIAGE PARTS.

Number of Establishment.	Persons employed July 1.		Per cent. number employed.		Amount paid in wages during year ending July 1.		Per cent. amount paid in wages.		Estimated per cent. business de of full capacity.
	1897.	1898.	Increase.	Decrease.	1897.	1898.	Increase.	Decrease.	
78	25	22	....	12.	$15,000	$9,639	....	35.7	60
79	25	25	....	....	11,000	15,000	36.4	....	50
80	32	26	....	18.7	14,397	11,267	....	21.7	20
81	15	15	....	....	14,000	14,200	1.4	....	100
82	13	16	23.1	....	17,996	15,951	....	11.4	70
83	185	200	8.1	....	125,000	128,000	2.4	....	80
84	52	66	26.9	....	35,000	42,000	20.	....	65
85	21	26	23.8	....	15,300	23,677	54.7	....	80
86	100	100	....	....	69,317	69,400	.1	....	75
87	35	40	14.2	....	20,000	17,350	....	13.3	60
88	12	12	....	....	5,600	5,600	....	....	25
89	12	11	....	8.3	8,325	7,449	....	10.5	75
90	3	4	33.3	....	1,800	1,800	....	....	80
91	13	17	30.8	....	5,850	6,665	....	13.9	75
92	27	21	....	22.2	14,200	13,000	....	8.4	50
93	17	15	....	11.8	9,100	8,000	... ...	12.1	83
94	10	10	....	....	6,200	7,000	12.9	....	80
95	2	2	....	....	1,144	1,144	....	....	50
96	42	40	....	4.8	27,040	26,507	....	1.9	70
97	38	34	....	10.2	15,578	16,418	5.3	....	40
98	22	22	....	....	15,470	15,610	.9	....	100
99	19	20	5.2	....	12,500	13,600	8.8	....	55
Total	720	744	3.3		$459,817	$469,277	2.1		*64.8

* On basis of wages paid.

INDUSTRY : CORSETS.

Number of Establishment.	Persons employed July 1.		Per cent. number employed.		Amount paid in wages during year ending July 1.		Per cent. amount paid in wages.		Estimated per cent. business done of full capacity.
	1897.	1898.	Increase.	Decrease.	1897.	1898.	Increase.	Decrease.	
100	59	60	1.7	....	$14,340	$19,000	32.5	....	85
101	250	250	....	....	85,000	85,000	....	....	85
102	275	300	9.1	....	60,000	66,000	10.	....	90
103	896	934	4.2	....	296,145	332,194	12.2	....	85
104	732	772	5.3	....	215,056	241,597	12.3	....	90
105	205	208	1.4	....	66,269	81,856	23.5	....	95
106	75	91	21.3	....	20,885	26,234	25.6	....	100
107	1,400	1,400	....	....	456,000	510,180	11.9	....	100
108	70	38	....	45.7	15,000	7,703	....	48.6	35
109	380	363	....	4.4	110,000	112,289	2.	....	100
Total	4,342	4,416	1.7		$1,338,695	$1,482,053	10.7		*91.9

* On basis of wages paid.

INDUSTRY: CUTLERY AND TOOLS.

Number of Establishment.	Persons employed July 1.		Per cent. number employed.		Amount paid in wages during year ending July 1.		Per cent. amount paid in wages.		Estimated per cent. business done of full capacity.
	1897.	1898.	Increase.	Decrease.	1897.	1898.	Increase.	Decrease.	
110	46	47	2.1	....	$15,246	$18,395	20.6	....	75
111	5	4	....	20.	3,000	2,500	....	16.6	45
112	22	25	13.6	....	8,300	10,800	30.1	....	85
113	60	50	....	16.6	19,600	25,516	30.2	....	50
114	45	60	33.3	....	17,000	23,409	37.7	....	50
115	70	80	14.3	....	32,000	36,000	12.5	....	30
116	31	34	9.7	....	12,047	15,422	27.1	....	85
117	148	148	....	....	60,629	72,326	19.3	....	33
118	7	13	85.7	....	6,276	5,402	....	13.9	70
119	50	57	14.	....	23,466	23,689	.9	....	95
120	4	4	....	....	1,520	2,037	34.	....	40
121	55	42	....	25.5	31,476	35,506	12.8	....	50
122	75	75	....	....	36,058	39,936	10.9	....	100
123	48	45	....	6.2	14,219	18,888	32.8	....	40
124	120	125	4.2	....	45,000	50,000	11.1	....	100
125	8	9	12.5	....	2,915	3,241	11.2	....	50
126	90	121	34.4	....	46,033	62,580	35.9	....	100
127	99	108	9.1	....	29,324	37,702	21.7	....	90
128	267	320	19.8	....	125,454	130,559	4.1	....	100
129	60	90	50.	....	30,000	40,000	33.3	....	40
130	2	2	....	....	1,350	1,050	....	22.2	40
131	20	20	....	....	10,044	11,681	16.3	....	100
132	5	4	....	20.	2,100	2,000	....	4.7	50
133	14	16	14.3	....	7,540	9,976	32.3	....	65
134	132	201	52.2	....	63,049	84,818	34.5	....	100
135	27	37	37.	....	15,300	11,250	....	26.4	75
136	53	56	5.7	....	25,499	33,263	30.4	....	100
137	106	156	47.2	....	48,255	61,151	50.6	....	95
138	30	34	13.3	....	5,880	11,985	103.8	....	100
139	58	58	....	....	30,852	39,351	27.5	....	100

INDUSTRY : CUTLERY AND TOOLS — *Concluded.*

Number of Establishment.	Persons employed July 1.		Per cent. number employed.		Amount paid in wages during year ending July 1.		Per cent. amount paid in wages.		Estimated per cent. business done of full capacity.
	1897.	1898.	Increase.	Decrease.	1897.	1898.	Increase.	Decrease.	
140	18	17	....	5.5	$16,283	$5,911	....	63.7	50
141	9	8	....	11.1	2,311	2,879	24.6	....	75
142	69	76	10.1	....	34,000	47,500	39.7	....	80
143	4	4	....	....	3,500	4,500	28.5	....	60
144	10	5	....	50.	3,680	1,200	....	67.4	30
145	20	27	35.	....	10,138	13,500	33.2	....	75
Total	1,887	2,178	15.4		$839,344	$995,923	18.7		*67.6

* On basis of wages paid.

INDUSTRY: FIRE ARMS.

Number of Establishment.	Persons employed July 1.		Per cent. number employed.		Amount paid in wages during year ending July 1.		Per cent. amount paid in wages.		Estimated per cent. business done of full capacity.
	1897.	1898.	Increase.	Decrease.	1897.	1898.	Increase.	Decrease.	
146	40	55	37.5	....	$19,661	$24,675	25.5	....	100
147	65	68	4.6	....	24,000	35,611	48.4	....	100
148	260	164	....	33.1	130,000	82,637	....	36.4	50
149	7	9	28.6	....	5,600	3,777	....	32.6	20
150	406	611	50.5	....	237,176	301,826	27.2	....	80
151	16	15	....	5.5	7,200	8,500	18.1	....	70
152	12	12	....	....	7,850	8,000	1.9	....	75
Total	806	934	15.9		$431,487	$465,026	7.8		*72.1

* On basis of wages paid.

INDUSTRY: GENERAL HARDWARE.

Number of Establishment.	Persons employed July 1.		Per cent. number employed.		Amount paid in wages during year ending July 1.		Per cent. amount paid in wages.		Estimated per cent less done of full capacity.
	1897.	1898.	Increase.	Decrease.	1897.	1898.	Increase.	Decrease.	
153	12	8	....	33.3	$7,200	$4,000	....	44.4	40
154	49	60	22.4	....	23,281	22,710	....	2.4	75
155	656	765	16.7	....	336,000	372,027	11.	....	85
156	238	233	....	2.1	68,512	68,600	.1	....	70
157	65	60	....	7.6	28,434	36,944	29.9	....	80
158	372	379	1.9	....	150,422	164,190	9.1	....	75
159	7	7	....	....	2,589	2,800	8.1	....	70
160	81	86	6.2	....	33,927	42,940	26.6	....	75
161	50	58	16.	....	20,526	23,210	13.1	....	63
162	41	44	7.3	....	13,122	13,705	4.4	....	70
163	70	79	12.9	....	32,289	29,592	....	8.3	65
164	41	53	29.2	....	13,056	19,012	45.6	....	50
165	14	25	78.5	....	6,969	10,979	57.5	....	75
166	50	50	....	....	18,078	22,430	24.1	....	75
167	60	75	25.	....	24,700	32,000	29.6	....	90
168	413	446	7.9	....	207,343	224,911	8.5	....	58
169	100	100	....	....	50,000	52,800	5.6	....	75
170	35	42	20.	....	20,000	25,000	25.	....	100
171	38	45	18.4	....	20,000	20,000	....	....	80
172	192	187	....	2.6	68,636	86,927	26.6	....	100
173	10	10	....	....	6,257	7,914	26.4	....	75
174	30	30	....	....	14,827	16,679	12.4	....	50
175	13	15	15.4	....	6,458	6,902	6.9	....	65
176	12	22	83.3	....	2,000	2,592	29.6	....	75
177	123	57	....	53.6	49,279	35,567	....	27.8	60
178	83	40	....	51.8	43,393	18,674	....	56.9	30
179	44	44	....	....	19,527	19,387	....	.7	75
180	13	10	....	23.1	3,974	9,215	132.5	....	50
181	135	122	....	9.6	60,000	74,512	24.2	....	90
182	54	66	22.2	....	19,595	23,245	18.6	....	69

INDUSTRY: GENERAL HARDWARE — *Concluded.*

Number of Establishment.	Persons employed July 1.		Per cent. number employed.		Amount paid in wages during year ending July 1.		Per cent. amount paid in wages.		Estimated per cent. class due of full capacity.
	1897.	1898.	Increase.	Decrease.	1897.	1898.	Increase.	Decrease.	
183	276	325	17.7	....	$112,380	$156,015	38.8	....	100
184	36	37	2.8	....	18,704	19,429	3.9	....	45
185	210	206	....	1.9	73,324	82,300	12.2	....	100
186	9	11	22.2	....	4,316	5,000	15.8	....	40
187	21	21	....	....	9,000	10,000	11.1	....	65
188	54	55	1.8	....	19,862	27,073	36.3	....	75
189	36	18	....	50.	8,493	10,254	23.8	....	100
190	205	215	4.7	....	84,048	89,000	5.8	....	100
191	15	18	20.	....	24,354	21,678	....	10.9	90
192	169	183	8.3	....	80,000	89,242	11.6	....	100
193	1,300	1,200	....	7.7	613,836	581,595	....	5.2	80
194	150	175	16.6	....	81,042	72,616	....	10.3	90
195	23	6	....	73.9	10,288	12,000	16.6	....	85
196	15	14	....	6.6	7,500	2,500	....	66.7	25
197	1,093	1,123	2.7	....	413,488	416,000	.6	....	75
198	41	43	4.8	....	22,520	26,538	17.8	....	50
199	168	191	13.7	....	69,000	87,533	26.8	....	95
200	46	45	....	2.2	23,047	23,546	2.2	....	50
201	672	774	15.2	....	250,000	300,000	20.	....	90
202	12	12	....	....	2,700	2,900	7.4	....	50
203	280	279	....	.4	100,000	98,000	....	2.	65
204	70	76	8.6	....	25,000	28,180	12.7	....	75
205	7	34	385.7	....	3,553	8,300	133.3	....	65
206	8	7	....	12.5	3,592	4,193	16.7	....	65
Total	8,017	8,286	3.4		$3,430,431	$3,664,356	6.8		*74.2

* On basis of wages paid.

INDUSTRY: HATS AND CAPS.

Number of Establishment.	Persons employed July 1.		Per cent. number employed.		Amount paid in wages during year ending July 1.		Per cent. amount paid in wages.		Estimated per ct. business done of full duty.
	1897.	1898.	Increase.	Decrease.	1897.	1898.	Increase.	Decrease.	
207	187	184	....	1.6	$91,500	$102,500	12.1	....	95
208	125	125	....	....	54,757	57,743	5.4	....	55
209	165	205	24.2	....	50,000	56,000	12.	....	100
210	70	75	7.1	....	30,000	30,000	....	....	50
211	125	150	20.	....	48,178	66,998	39.1	....	75
212	69	78	13.	....	43,161	46,151	6.9	....	80
213	40	55	37.5	....	9,000	25,000	188.9	....	100
214	140	144	2.9	....	36,688	44,300	20.7	....	95
215	175	180	2.8	....	50,000	52,000	4.	....	75
216	13	14	7.7	....	12,000	5,000	....	58.3	25
217	201	201	....	....	103,478	64,690	....	37.4	75
218	46	72	56.5	....	28,129	45,664	61.9	....	90
219	304	275	....	9.5	138,443	126,570	....	8.5	70
220	28	32	14.3	....	9,111	12,975	42.4	....	75
221	28	28	....	....	8,763	8,759	....	....	90
222	168	207	23.2	....	79,886	90,124	12.8	....	95
223	254	198	....	22.1	102,600	103,363	.7	....	67
224	60	58	....	3.3	22,000	23,000	4.5	....	68
225	120	115	....	4.2	71,235	71,285	....	....	69
226	42	42	....	....	14,727	7,269	....	50.6	50
227	225	220	....	2.2	103,300	101,027	....	2.2	60
Total	2,585	2,658	2.8		$1,106,956	$1,140,418	3.		*73.5

* On basis of wages paid.

INDUSTRY: IRON AND IRON FOUNDRIES.

Number of Establishment.	Persons employed July 1.		Per cent. number employed.		Amount paid in wages during year ending July 1.		Per cent. amount paid in wages.		Estimated per cent. business done of full capacity.
	1897.	1898.	Increase.	Decrease.	1897.	1898.	Increase.	Decrease.	
228	25	27	8.	....	$14,217	$16,000	12.5	....	65
229	50	80	60.	....	26,000	35,000	34.6	....	100
230	365	432	18.2	....	131,820	169,299	28.5	....	45
231	68	80	17.6	....	36,436	45,500	24.8	....	35
232	100	110	10.	....	48,000	51,323	6.9	....	50
233	71	70	....	1.4	29,818	40,196	34.8	....	75
234	66	94	42.4	....	32,600	43,300	32.8	....	56
235	135	176	30.4	....	68,422	101,830	48.8	....	100
236	517	505	....	2.3	320,000	350,000	9.3	....	85
237	130	106	....	18.4	58,300	54,607	....	6.3	85
238	218	316	44.9	......	125,263	145,846	16.4	....	80
239	6	4	....	33.3	5,000	1,000	....	80.	20
240	300	325	8.3	....	175,000	177,000	1.1	....	85
241	19	21	10.5	....	10,400	12,100	16.3	....	40
242	225	313	39.1	....	170,000	175,000	2.9	....	75
243	25	153	512.	....	70,000	62,000	....	11.4	20
244	41	45	9.7	....	16,800	19,300	14.5	....	40
245	57	51	....	10.5	28,000	22,000	....	21.4	85
246	12	12	....	....	8,639	9,637	11.6	....	60
247	71	80	12.7	....	39,000	42,000	7.7	....	75
248	427	358	....	16.1	208,312	212,061	1.8	....	75
249	40	30	....	25.	23,000	20,000	....	13.1	60
250	30	23	....	29.9	20,598	14,205	....	31.	80
251	10	39	290.	....	6,000	20,195	236.5	....	100
252	13	10	....	23.1	7,538	7,473	....	.9	75
253	40	35	....	12.5	16,000	16,675	4.2	....	100
254	8	8	....	....	3,507	3,492	....	.4	90
255	185	192	3.8	....	124,500	114,700	....	7.8	80

INDUSTRY : IRON AND IRON FOUNDRIES — *Concluded.*

Number of Establishment.	Persons employed July 1.		Per cent. number employed.		Amount paid in wages during year ending July 1.		Per cent. amount paid in wages.		Estimated per cent. business done of full capacity.
	1897.	1898.	Increase.	Decrease.	1897.	1898.	Increase.	Decrease.	
256	175	140	....	20.	$80,000	$70,200	....	12.2	40
257	20	17	... .	15.	11,000	8,317	....	24.4	40
258	35	44	25.7	....	19,567	25,294	29.3	....	50
259	10	6	....	40.	3,600	3,636	1.	....	25
260	28	28	....	....	11,000	11,000	....	....	100
Total	3,522	3,930	11.6		$1,948,332	$2,100,186	7.8		*63.9

* On basis of wages paid.

INDUSTRY: LEATHER GOODS.

Number of Establishment.	Persons employed July 1.		Per cent. number employed.		Amount paid in wages during year ending July 1.		Per cent. amount paid in wages.		Estimated per business done of full capacity.
	1897.	1898.	Increase.	Decrease.	1897.	1898.	Increase.	Decrease.	
261	28	26	....	7.1	$7,385	$10,201	38.1	....	100
262	15	15	....	....	9,979	8,650	....	3.3	25
263	5	5	....	....	3,146	3,146	....	....	70
264	100	97	....	3.	96,320	77,000	....	20.	40
265	30	35	16.6	....	4,000	6,000	50.	....	80
266	17	17	....	....	11,553	11,484	....	.6	70
267	84	80	....	4.7	39,102	41,580	6.3	....	70
268	10	10	....	....	4,580	5,200	13.5	....	60
269	30	29	....	3.3	13,500	16,438	21.8	....	60
270	7	12	71.4	....	5,000	7,800	56.	....	80
271	25	26	4.	....	5,000	12,708	154.2	....	100
272	12	8	....	33.3	3,000	3,047	1.6	....	60
273	55	41	....	25.5	25,000	17,000	....	32.	40
274	150	180	20.	....	69,708	73,714	5.7	....	80
275	15	16	6.6	....	7,200	7,650	6.2	....	75
Total	583	597	2.4		$304,473	$301,618		.9	*56.5

* On basis of wages paid.

INDUSTRY : MACHINE SHOPS.

Number of Establishment.	Persons employed July 1.		Per cent. number employed.		Amount paid in wages during year ending July 1.		Per cent. amount paid in wages.		Estimated per cent. business done of full capacity.
	1897.	1898.	Increase.	Decrease.	1897.	1898.	Increase.	Decrease.	
276	33	36	9.1	....	$25,130	$20,426	....	18.7	50
277	192	281	46.3	... .	84,887	110,845	30.6	....	85
278	7	7	....	....	4,200	3,840	....	8.6	90
279	141	223	58.1	....	62,744	91,118	45.2	....	93
280	7	5	....	18.5	4,500	3,665	....	18.5	30
281	48	46	....	4.2	25,150	29,206	16.1	....	55
282	9	8	....	11.1	5,344	5,335	....	.2	60
283	5	4	....	20.	2,470	2,300	....	6.8	60
284	40	32	....	20.	25,448	22,072	....	13.2	70
285	10	8	....	20.	6,500	8,190	26.	....	100
286	26	27	3.8	....	12,956	11,289	....	12.1	80
287	30	38	26.6	.:......	14,495	15,603	7.6	....	50
288	308	286	....	7.1	164,805	181,700	10.2	....	68
289	6	6	....	....	4,160	5,634	35.4	....	75
290	1,012	1,022	.9	....	638,879	655,103	2.5	....	75
291	25	36	44.	....	19,563	19,000	....	2.9	50
292	106	135	27.3	....	60,000	57,600	....	4.	95
293	12	8	....	33.3	2,924	3,644	24.6	....	65
294	23	20	....	13.	12,676	11,947	....	5.7	70
295	6	5	....	16.6	3,640	2,000	....	45.1	25
296	57	80	40.3	....	35,000	50,000	14.3	....	100
297	19	19	....	....	7,852	14,116	79.8	....	50
298	9	9	....	....	5,000	5,000	....	....	50
299	13	14	7.7	....	8,400	9,000	7.1	....	100
300	12	13	8.3	....	6,375	7,280	14.2	....	60
301	125	145	24.	....	90,187	95,099	5.4	....	100
302	20	47	135.	....	14,866	20,600	38.5	....	65
303	90	80	....	11.1	57,715	51,340	....	11.	70
304	55	50	....	9.1	20,824	22,000	5.6	....	75
305	3	3	....	....	4,334	2,930	....	32.4	50

INDUSTRY : MACHINE SHOPS — *Continued.*

Number of Establishment.	Persons employed July 1.		Per cent. number employed.		Amount paid in wages during year ending July 1.		Per cent. amount paid in wages.		Estimated per cent. business done of full capacity.
	1897.	1898.	Increase.	Decrease.	1897.	1898.	Increase.	Decrease.	
306	2	2			$1,549	$1.500		3.1	25
307	361	398	10.2		229,834	232,025	.9		90
308	8	12	50.		5,500	6,700	21.8		65.
309	8	10	25.		2,650	2,540		4.1	50
310	10	10			10,000	10,000			50
311	26	25		3.8	15,687	16,770	6.9		75.
312	12	10		16.6	8,750	7,500		14.2	70
313	20	25	25.		8,100	12,000	48.1		75.
314	97	109	12.4		46,000	51,214	11.3		75
315	15	17	13.3		5,000	7,000	40.		85.
316	88	90	2.2		57,167	66.037	15.5		100
317	19	30	57.9		27,037	38.000	40.5		65.
318	60	79	31.7		29,610	30,868	4.2		100
319	106	115	8.5		60,433	62,730	3.8		70
320	4	3		25.	2,100	1,950		7.1	50
321	34	54	58.8		14,898	27,158	82.3		90
322	333	191		42.6	267,319	255,181		4.5	100
323	1,007	681		32.4	578,000	867,427	50.		100
324	213	156		26.7	106,730	108,690	1.8		100
325	855	853		.2	509,606	513,795	.8		80
326	18	26	44.4		11,992	19,212	60.2		100
327	50	60	20.		25,711	30,395	18.2		100
328	47	50	6.4		25,000	29,000	16.		75
329	7	6		14.3	4,147	3,718		10.3	65
330	50	37		26.	15,000	22,000	46.6		40
331	48	50	4.2		19,789	17,198		13.1	70
332	61	70	14.7		32,091	18,426		42.5	78
333	16	19	18.7		4,411	7,000	58.6		75.
334	54	36		33.3	31,200	19,424		37.7	25.
335	1,269	1,158		8.7	603,582	725,403	20.2		100

INDUSTRY : MACHINE SHOPS—*Concluded.*

Number of Establishment.	Persons employed July 1.		Per cent. number employed.		Amount paid in wages during year ending July 1.		Per cent. amount paid in wages.		Estimated per cent. business done of full capacity.
	1897.	1898.	Increase.	Decrease.	1897.	1898.	Increase.	Decrease.	
336	87	75	....	13.8	$56,594	$44,578	....	21.2	40
337	106	100	....	5.6	43,398	48,037	10.7	....	70
338	6	5	....	16.6	2,083	1,968	....	5.5	50
339	15	12	....	20.	13,000	10,000	....	23.1	25
340	54	57	5.6	....	36,611	38,100	4.1	....	85
341	100	100	....	....	50,000	62,000	24.	....	100
Total	7,715	7,424		3.8	$4,391,603	$5,253,426	19.6		*91.6

*On basis of wages paid.

INDUSTRY: MUSICAL INSTRUMENTS AND PARTS.

Number of Establishment.	Persons employed July 1.		Per cent. number employed.		Amount paid in wages during year ending July 1.		Per cent. amount paid in wages.		Estimated per cent. business done of full capacity.
	1897.	1898.	Increase.	Decrease.	1897.	1898.	Increase.	Decrease.	
342	225	230	2.2	....	$95,409	$96,300	.9	....	50
343	45	40	....	11.1	25,200	18,780	....	25.5	25
344	7	8	14.3	....	3,600	3,700	2.8	....	60
345	163	205	25.7	....	77,857	100,989	29.7	....	100
346	8	8	....	....	3,500	3,600	2.8	....	100
347	302	352	16.5	....	121,634	158,438	30.2	....	100
348	50	50	....	....	25,712	30,622	19.1	....	95
Total	800	893	11.6		$352,912	$412,429	16.9		*72.5

* On basis of wages paid.

INDUSTRY: PAPER AND PAPER GOODS.

Number of Establishment.	Persons employed July 1.		Per cent. number employed.		Amount paid in wages during year ending July 1.		Per cent. amount paid in wages.		Estimated per cent. business done of full capacity.
	1897.	1898.	Increase.	Decrease.	1897.	1898.	Increase.	Decrease.	
349	18	21	16.6	....	$8,079	$11,098	37.3	....	75
350	52	49	....	5.7	10,741	11,698	8.9	....	80
351	45	43	....	4.4	16,386	15,836	....	3.3	67
352	7	7	....	....	2,593	2,593	....	....	30
353	160	145	....	9.4	56,974	58,172	2.1	....	50
354	22	20	....	9.1	8,249	8,688	5.2	....	99
355	44	42	....	4.5	13,600	13,700	.7	....	67
356	70	70	....	....	30,000	24,400	....	18.7	85
357	144	144	....	....	59,535	70,000	17.6	....	75
358	32	32	....	....	15,284	15,691	2.6	....	75
359	48	52	8.3	....	25,660	26,439	3.	....	100
360	16	16	....	....	7,376	6,725	....	8.8	92
361	23	25	8.7	....	7,500	10,000	33.3	....	100
362	187	187	....	....	70,183	70,183	....	....	50
363	35	35	....	....	19,520	16,872	....	13.5	75
364	25	20	....	20.	7,500	6,500	....	13.3	60
365	9	7	....	22.2	5,500	5,000	....	9.1	85
366	480	480	....	....	200,676	195,000	....	2.8	75
367	45	43	....	4.4	13,500	25,000	85.2	....	100
368	30	39	30.	....	9,215	12,349	34.	....	75
369	14	14	....	....	2,500	2,500	....	....	75
370	76	76	....	....	25,000	25,000	....	....	75
371	47	50	6.6	....	18,000	19,736	9.6	....	80
372	9	14	55.5	....	3,500	5,035	43.8	....	75
373	10	12	20.	....	4,200	3,464	....	17.5	50
374	68	56	....	17.6	21,992	21,595	....	1.8	65
375	41	53	29.3	....	16,144	12,641	....	21.7	75
376	7	7	....	....	2,374	3,036	29.9	....	100
377	22	13	....	40.9	4,370	4,346	....	.5	35
378	7	8	14.3	....	2,990	3,003	.4	....	90

INDUSTRY: PAPER AND PAPER GOODS—*Concluded.*

Number of Establishment.	Persons employed July 1.		Per cent. number employed.		Amount paid in wages during year ending July 1.		Per cent. amount paid in wages.		Estimated per cent. business done of full capacity.
	1897.	1898.	Increase.	Decrease.	1897.	1898.	Increase.	Decrease.	
379	13	12	....	7.7	$3,577	$4,867	36.1	....	50
380	7	5	....	28.5	1,722	1,696	....	1.5	85
381	90	90	....	....	39,000	40,000	2.6	....	90
382	10	10	....	....	4,479	4,348	....	2.9	100
383	17	19	11.8	....	6,800	7,500	10.2	....	67
384	62	62	....	....	36,000	30,000	....	16.7	75·
385	3	2	....	33.3	475	750	57.9	....	33
386	30	30	....	....	7,500	8,200	9.3	....	50
387	19	26	36.8	....	10,900	14,000	28.8	....	100·
388	24	24	....	....	10,000	10,000	....	....	70
389	12	18	50.	....	6,730	7,274	8.1	....	89·
390	40	40	....	....	10,000	13,206	32.	....	90
391	30	33	10.	....	10,700	11,290	5.5	....	85·
392	7	12	71.4	....	2,593	5,000	92.8	....	50
393	63	75	19.	... ...	20,039	24,258	21.1	....	75
394	22	15	....	31.8	15,363	14,139	....	7.9	70
395	17	17	....	....	5,100	5,700	11.8	....	50
396	90	86	....	4.4	30,000	31,898	6.3	....	100
397	68	64	....	5.9	22,283	22,563	1.2	....	100
Total	2,417	2,420	.1		$932,402	$962,989	3.3		*71.8·

* On basis of wages paid.

INDUSTRY: RUBBER GOODS.

Number of Establishment.	Persons employed July 1.		Per cent. number employed.		Amount paid in wages during year ending July 1.		Per cent. amount paid in wages.		Estimated per cent. business done of full capacity.
	1897.	1898.	Increase.	Decrease.	1897.	1898.	Increase.	Decrease.	
398	64	60	....	6.2	$27,700	$26,000	....	6.1	70
399	292	298	2.1	....	226,462	237,068	4.7	....	100
400	33	162	390.9	....	21,492	70,000	225.7	....	100
401	205	225	9.8	....	77,551	88,000	13.5	....	80
402	30	39	30.	....	11,957	15,682	31.2	....	95
403	115	135	17.4	....	57,500	65,000	13.	....	60
404	1,233	1,298	5.2	....	450,045	642,050	42.7	....	100
405	1,500	1,400	....	6.6	511,218	736,666	44.1	....	100
406	18	11	....	38.8	4,500	6,000	33.3	....	100
407	15	14	....	6.7	7,500	5,013	....	33.2	25
408	250	263	5.2	....	50,000	54,320	8.6	....	100
409	32	39	21.9	....	19,275	21,893	13.6	....	35
410	236	236	....	....	105,466	109,831	4.1	....	65
411	45	75	66.6	....	20,667	34,647	67.6	....	100
Total	4,068	4,255	4.6		$1,591,333	$2,112,170	32.7		*91.7

* On basis of wages paid.

INDUSTRY : SHOES.

Number of Establishment.	Persons employed July 1.		Per cent. number employed.		Amount paid in wages during year ending July 1.		Per cent. amount paid in wages.		Estimated per cent. business done of full capacity.
	1897.	1898.	Increase.	Decrease.	1897.	1898.	Increase.	Decrease.	
412	137	194	41.6	....	$40,000	$49,218	23.	....	100
413	61	60	....	1.6	26,600	22,948	....	13.7	50
414	100	50	....	50.	49,187	10,200	....	79.3	25
415	7	9	28.5	....	4,000	5,000	25.	....	60
416	34	34	....	....	14,339	13,743	....	4.1	85
417	35	44	25.7	....	5,822	22,786	291.4	....	100
418	10	10	....	....	3,500	3,500	....	....	75
419	75	60	....	20.	30,000	30,000	....	....	100
420	75	71	....	5.3	30,000	27,000	....	10.	70
Total	534	532		.4	$203,448	$184,395		9.4	*71.9

* On basis of wages paid.

INDUSTRY: SILVER AND PLATED WARE.

Number of Establishment.	Persons employed July 1.		Per cent. number employed.		Amount paid in wages during year ending July 1.		Per cent. amount paid in wages.		Estimated per cent. business done of full capacity.
	1897.	1898.	Increase.	Decrease.	1897.	1898.	Increase.	Decrease.	
421	217	229	5.5	....	$118,544	$129,282	9.1	....	65
422	20	20	....	....	7,659	10,999	43.6	....	100
423	23	25	8.7	....	11,082	17,500	57.9	....	75
424	66	70	6.1	....	31,625	40,364	27.6	....	90
425	8	4	....	50.	3,900	2,726	....	30.1	75
426	113	103	....	8.8	57,494	55,795	....	3.	75.
427	29	44	51.7	....	14,099	18,230	29.3	....	55
428	220	251	14.1	....	77,988	88,230	13.2	....	70
429	80	80	....	....	44,579	38,516	....	13.6	67
430	180	180	....	....	80,376	90,349	12.4	....	90
431	882	915	3.7	....	425,607	492,344	15.6	....	65.
432	540	553	2.4	....	267,279	315,328	17.9	....	80.
433	95	100	5.2	....	51,599	52,781	2.3	....	65.
434	74	80	8.1	....	31,030	34,100	9.9	....	55
435	200	250	25.	....	94,154	111,000	17.9	....	85.
436	72	50	....	30.6	25,251	18,514	....	26.6	75
437	125	100	....	20.	52,000	50,000	....	3.8	65.
438	128	129	.8	....	62,557	62,449	....	.2	75.
439	114	121	6.1	....	58,000	60,000	3.4	....	80.
440	90	100	11.1	....	35,000	40,200	....	14.9	65.
441	75	81	8.	....	44,994	47,076	4.6	....	50.
442	100	107	7.	....	52,589	53,583	1.9	....	50.
443	12	9	....	25.	7,200	3,900	....	45.8	33
444	15	30	100.	....	7,570	11,870	58.6	....	100
445	95	50	....	47.4	54,500	50,000	....	8.3	70
446	120	190	58.3	....	64,204	98,100	52.8	....	100
447	215	212	....	1.4	89,235	100,750	12.9	....	65
Total	3,908	4,083	4.5		$1,870,065	$2,093,986	12.		*70.5

* On basis of wages paid.

INDUSTRY: STONE CUTTING AND QUARRYING.

Number of Establishment.	Persons employed July 1.		Per cent. number employed.		Amount paid in wages during year ending July 1.		Per cent. amount paid in wages.		Estimated per cent. business done of full capacity.
	1897.	1898.	Increase.	Decrease.	1897.	1898.	Increase.	Decrease.	
448	2	2	....	....	$800	$800	....	....	25
449	25	25	....	....	9,262	10,742	15.9	....	100
450	302	440	45.7	....	87,937	243,359	176.8	....	75
451	5	3	....	40.	2,576	1,680	....	34.7	80
452	12	10	....	16.6	9,500	4,750	....	50.	80
453	151	130	....	13.9	45,612	40,997	....	10.1	33
454	207	43	....	79.2	63,032	50,791	....	19.2	86
455	21	20	....	4.8	9,133	9,283	1.6	....	90
456	5	9	80.	....	4,300	7,020	63.3	....	85
457	12	9	....	25.	7,200	5,000	....	30.6	65
Total	742	691		6.9	$239,352	$374,422	56.4		*67.3

* On basis of wages paid.

INDUSTRY: WIRE AND WIRE GOODS.

Number of Establishment.	Persons employed July 1.		Per cent. number employed.		Amount paid in wages during year ending July 1.		Per cent. amount paid in wages.		Estimated per cent. business done of full capacity.
	1897.	1898.	Increase.	Decrease.	1897.	1898.	Increase.	Decrease.	
458	3	3	....	....	$1,609	$2,000	24.3	....	67
459	4	4	....	....	1,500	3,500	133.3	....	100
460	60	60	....	....	16,797	17,000	1.2	....	95
461	15	15	....	....	7,042	6,000	....	14.8	45
462	146	161	10.3	....	74,052	71,071	....	4.	90
463	3	3	....	....	1,400	1,400	....	....	75
464	206	256	24.3	....	87,736	115,714	31.9	....	75
465	100	100	....	....	30,000	34,215	10.7	....	55
466	125	125	....	....	53,000	52,000	....	1.8	100
467	18	13	....	27.7	7,200	7,662	6.4	....	60
468	30	34	13.3	....	15,175	20,170	32.9	....	100
Total	710	774	9.		$295,511	$330,732	11.9		*78.7

* On basis of wages paid.

INDUSTRY: WOOD-WORKING.

Number of Establishment.	Persons employed July 1.		Per cent. number employed.		Amount paid in wages during year ending July 1.		Per cent. amount paid in wages.		Estimated per cent. business done of full capacity.
	1897.	1898.	Increase.	Decrease.	1897.	1898.	Increase.	Decrease.	
469	34	41	20.6	....	$25,789	$22,052	....	14.4	75
470	67	50	....	25.4	36,500	35,000	... .	4.1	60
471	30	22	....	26.6	12,500	12,000	....	4.	90
472	30	30	....	....	7,453	8,490	13.9	....	40
473	20	21	5.	....	9,000	15,000	66.7	....	100
474	98	100	2.	....	32,100	33,000	2.8	....	75
475	50	20	....	60.	26,000	13,500	....	48.1	60
476	35	45	28.6	....	18,200	25,000	31.9	....	100
477	12	12	....	....	7,020	7,696	9.6	....	100
478	5	5	....	....	2,248	2,223	....	1.1	25.
479	15	20	33.3	....	7,500	10,000	33.3	....	66.
480	30	33	10.	....	15,722	18,124	15.3	....	90
481	145	170	17.2	....	80,239	77,649	....	3.2	70
482	6	6	....	....	3,952	4,000	1.2	....	75
483	10	10	....	....	4,500	8,000	77.8	....	50
484	20	15	... .	25.	19,000	14,000	....	26.3	33
485	18	14	....	27.7	9,163	8,100	....	11.6	50
486	25	36	44.	....	6,623	11,871	79.2	....	80
487	10	51	410.	....	1,837	23,000	1152.	....	100
488	52	32	....	38.5	20,000	13,500	....	32.5	50
489	8	8	....	....	4,500	4,457	....	1.	65
490	6	3	....	50.	2,109	1,000	....	52.5	25
491	49	20	....	59.1	16,255	14,911	....	8.3	85
492	2	2	....	....	950	1,760	85.3	....	20
493	28	29	3.5	....	13,823	17,941	29.8	....	80
494	112	89	....	20.5	50,741	65,890	29.9	....	100
495	52	54	3.8	....	34,628	33,494	....	3.3	75
496	14	14	....	....	4,200	4,300	2.4	....	75
497	6	3	....	50.	3,000	3,500	16.6	....	85
498	9	8	....	11.1	8,000	10,000	25.	....	100

INDUSTRY: WOOD-WORKING — *Concluded.*

Number of Establishment.	Persons employed July 1.		Per cent. number employed.		Amount paid in wages during year ending July 1.		Per cent. amount paid in wages.		Estimated per cent. business done of full capacity.
	1897.	1898.	Increase.	Decrease.	1897.	1898.	Increase.	Decrease.	
499	23	25	8.7	....	$12,175	$18,885	55.1	....	50
500	18	24	33.3	....	11,000	16,928	53.9	....	100
501	56	58	3.6	....	31,000	31,000	....	....	100
502	35	26	....	25.7	15,600	12,596	....	19.2	50
503	433	430	....	.7	159,338	188,440	18.2	....	100
504	4	5	25.	....	1,400	2,038	45.6	....	75
505	245	320	30.6	....	99,117	153,422	54.8	....	60
506	55	20	....	63.6	16,507	12,289	....	25.5	70
507	23	23	....	....	7,020	9,332	32.9	....	75
508	28	32	14.3	....	27,954	11,060	....	60.4	50
509	30	25	....	16.6	20,000	15,000	....	25.	55
510	20	45	125.	....	6,647	11,428	71.9	....	50
Total	1,968	1,996	1.4		$891,310	$1,001,876	12.4		*72.3

* On basis of wages paid.

INDUSTRY: MISCELLANEOUS.

Number of Establishment.	Persons employed July 1.		Per cent. number employed.		Amount paid in wages during year ending July 1.		Per cent. amount paid in wages.		Es imated per cen business done of ull capacity.
	1897.	1898.	Increase.	Decrease.	1897.	1898.	Increase.	Decrease.	
511	17	12	....	29.4	$3,914	$7,150	82.7	....	100
512	35	36	2.8	....	14,097	18,707	32.7	....	100
513	24	22	....	8.3	8,700	8,919	2.5	....	25
514	48	35	....	27.1	14,000	12,000	....	14.3	75
515	4	4	....	....	1,184	1,663	40.4	....	75
516	30	26	....	13.3	25,000	15,642	....	37.4	50
517	30	23	....	23.3	13,864	15,283	10.2	....	75
518	10	9	....	10.	3,666	5,658	54.3	....	75
519	13	13	....	....	6,000	8,000	33.3	....	100
520	14	14	....	....	12,456	11,602	....	6.8	80
521	21	29	38.1	....	8,750	11,600	32.6	....	20
522	9	9	....	....	6,086	6,136	.8	....	75
523	40	36	....	10.	29,328	29,640	1.1	....	100
524	64	65	1.6	....	34,000	33,000	....	2.9	85
525	15	16	6.6	....	3,900	4,500	15.4	....	50
526	5	6	20.	....	2,500	2,500	....	....	50
527	23	25	8.7	....	13,447	14,184	5.5	....	66
528	16	14	....	12.5	6,342	6,815	7.4	....	80
529	39	37	....	5.1	31,000	27,568	....	11.1	75
530	22	20	....	9.1	15,390	16,700	8.5	....	80
531	186	173	....	6.9	100,270	120,000	19.6	....	100
532	22	18	....	18.2	6,920	6,866	....	.8	66
533	20	21	....	5.	12,711	11,113	....	12.6	90
534	20	15	....	25.	9,000	8,000	....	11.1	90
535	17	17	....	....	7,067	7,662	8.4	....	25
536	14	20	14.5	....	6,057	7,550	24.6	....	100
537	29	30	3.4	....	9,768	17,000	74.	....	75
538	57	56	....	1.7	26,000	31,200	20.	....	95
539	13	13	....	....	5,800	6,000	3.4	....	100
540	6	6	....	....	2,335	2,437	4.2	....	70

INDUSTRY: MISCELLANEOUS—*Concluded.*

Number of Establishment.	Persons employed July 1.		Per cent. number employed.		Amount paid in wages during year ending July 1.		Per cent. amount paid in wages.		Estimated per cent. business done of full capacity.
	1897.	1898.	Increase.	Decrease.	1897.	1898.	Increase.	Decrease.	
541	9	10	11.1	....	$5,123	$5,252	2.5	....	80
542	31	36	16.3	....	19,500	22,665	16.2	....	75
543	18	18	....	....	7,643	2,262	....	70.4	90
544	8	11	....	....	6,300	8,000	27.	....	50
545	11	7	....	36.3	3,475	1,769	....	49.1	20
546	14	14	....	....	5,000	5,000	....	....	100
547	25	20	....	20.	8,000	8,000	....	....	60
548	68	67	....	1.4	28,336	32,408	14.3	....	100
549	3	3	....	....	1,825	1,825	....	....	25
550	25	36	44.	....	11,000	16,000	45.5	....	100
551	87	87	....	....	29,918	30,878	3.2	....	75
552	27	28	3.7	....	11,494	12,780	11.2	....	85
553	95	101	6.3	....	62,500	67,600	8.2	....	90
554	6	6	....	....	2,925	2,972	1.6	....	50
555	16	16	....	....	9,000	9,000	....	....	90
556	10	10	....	....	4,000	4,000	....	....	80
557	15	12	....	20.	6,700	3,250	....	51.5	50
558	72	68	....	5.5	25,572	29,573	15.6	....	50
559	10	10	....	....	5,200	1,500	....	71.2	33
560	19	19	....	....	5,285	6,241	18.1	....	90
561	12	13	8.3	....	4,705	6,217	32.1	....	65
562	20	20	....	....	11,812	11,800	....	.1	90
563	17	16	....	5.8	9,000	9,000	....	....	40
564	30	28	....	6.7	15,000	14,100	....	6.	75
Total	1,511	1,476		2.3	$738,865	$787,182	6.5		*72.5

* On basis of wages paid.

RECAPITULATION.

Industry.	Number of Establishments reporting.	Persons employed July 1.		Per cent. number employed.		Amount paid in wages during year ending July 1.		Per cent. amount paid in wages.		Estimated per cent. business done of full capacity on basis of wages paid.
		1897.	1898.	Increase.	Decrease.	1897.	1898.	Increase.	Decrease.	
Brass and Brass Goods.	61	13,667	15,622	14.2	....	$6,472,869	$7,648,823	18.2	....	89.6
Buttons, Buckles and Pins...................	16	1,445	1,760	21.8	....	531,079	717,372	35.1	....	92.3
Carriages and Carriage Parts................	22	720	744	3.3	....	459,817	469,277	2.1	....	64.8
Corsets.................	10	4,342	4,416	1.7	....	1,338,695	1,482,053	10.7	....	91.9
Cutlery and Tools.......	36	1,887	2,178	15.4	....	839,344	995,923	18.7	....	67.6
Fire Arms..............	7	806	934	15.9	....	431,487	465,026	7.8	....	72.1
General Hardware......	54	8,017	8,286	3.4	....	3,430,431	3,664,356	6.8	....	74.2
Hats and Caps..........	21	2,585	2,658	2.8	....	1,106,956	1,140,418	3.	....	73.5
Iron and Iron Foundries.................	33	3,522	3,930	11.6	....	1,948,332	2,100,186	7.8	....	63.9
Leather Goods..........	15	588	597	2.4	....	304,473	301,618	....	.9	56.5
Machine Shops..........	66	7,715	7,424	....	3.8	4,391,603	5,253,426	19.6	....	91.6
Musical Instruments and Parts.............	7	800	893	11.6	....	352,912	412,429	16.9	....	72.5
Paper and Paper Goods	49	2,417	2,420	.1	....	932,402	962,989	3.3	....	71.8
Rubber Goods..........	14	4,068	4,255	4.6	....	1,591,333	2,112,170	32.7	....	91.7
Shoes....................	9	534	532	....	.4	203,448	184,395	....	9.4	71.9
Silver and Plated Ware	27	3,908	4,083	4.5	....	1,870,065	2,093,986	12.	....	70.5
Stone-cutting and Quarrying.............	10	742	691	....	6.9	239,352	374,422	56.4	....	67.3
Wire and Wire Goods...	11	710	774	9.	....	295,511	330,732	11.9	....	78.7
Wood-working..........	42	1,968	1,996	1.4	....	891,310	1,001,876	12.4	....	72.3
Miscellaneous..........	54	1,511	1,476	....	2.3	738,865	787,182	6.5	....	72.5
Total................	564	61,957	65,669	6.		$28,370,284	$32,498,659	14.6		79.9

STATISTICS OF MANUFACTURES.

The statistical presentations contained in this chapter of the report are based upon the returns made by 564 identical establishments for each of the years 1897 and 1898, and presents a clear statement of the condition of manufactures in the State.

The total number of persons on the pay-rolls of all establishments considered on July 1, 1898, was reported as being 65,669, an increase of six per cent. over the number reported on the payrolls of the same establishments on the same date in 1897. The estimated proportion of business done of full capacity by these establishments, based on the amount paid in wages, during the year 1898 was 79.9 per cent., while in 1897 the proportion was 74 per cent., reached by the same method, and in 1896 the proportion of normal business done by all establishments included in the computation in that year was 79.7 per cent. It should be remembered, however, in making comparisons with previous years that the results above shown bear relation to identical establishments only for the years 1897 and 1898. Comparisons made, therefore, with the figures for 1896 should be predicated upon the results obtained from all establishments, and in the aggregate only.

The total amount disbursed for wages by all establishments during the year ending July 1, 1898, was $32,498,659, an increase of 14.6 per cent. over the amount paid in wages by the same establishments in 1897. Thus it appears that while the number employed increased but 6 per cent., the per cent. of increase in amount paid in wages was in excess of this, which can be explained by stating that the number reported as being employed refers to the specified date of July 1, 1898, and by no means can be considered as the average for the year. Hence it can readily be seen that it is thus rendered possible to show a decrease in number employed and an increase in amount paid in wages, and the reverse can also be equally possible.

BY INDUSTRIES.

BRASS AND BRASS GOODS.

Sixty-one manufacturers of lamps, bells, plumbers' fittings, electrical goods, brass foundries and mills reported as having 15,622 persons on their several pay-rolls on July 1, 1898. On the corresponding date in 1897 there were 13,677 individuals employed by the same establishments, 14.2 per cent. being the increase in number employed in 1898 over 1897. The amount paid in wages during the year ending July 1, 1898, by these establishments, was $7,648,823, an increase of 18.2 per cent. over the previous year. The estimated per cent. business done of full capacity, based on wages paid, was 89.6. Comparisons made with the report of this industry in 1897 show that the 67 establishments which reported to the Bureau in that year did a business of 76 per cent. of full capacity, and in 1896 the reports from the same number of establishments, not identical however, showed a business of 83.5 per cent. of normal capacity.

BUTTONS, BUCKLES AND PINS.

Following the same method, and it is found that in the industry classified as buttons, buckles and pins, that on July 1, 1898, there were 1,760 persons employed in the 16 establishments reporting to the Bureau, this being an increase in number employed by the same establishments on the same date in 1897 of 21.8 per cent. The increase in the amount paid in wages by the identical firms during the year ending July 1, 1898, over the same period in 1897, being 35.1 per cent.; and the proportion of business done in 1898 was 92.3 per cent.; in 1897, 76 per cent.; and in 1896, 77.5 per cent. of full capacity.

CARRIAGES AND CARRIAGE PARTS.

Twenty-two establishments engaged in this industry reported to the Bureau, having on July 1, 1898, 744 persons on their several pay-rolls, an increase over 1897 of 3.3 per cent. The increase in amount paid in wages in 1898 over 1897 was 2.1 per cent.; the proportion of business done in 1898 being 64.8 per cent.; in 1897, 63 per cent.; and in 1896, 72 per cent. of full capacity.

CORSETS.

From the manufacturers of corsets there were ten establishments which made reports to the Bureau, 4,416 being the number on all pay-rolls on July 1, 1898, an increase of 1.7 per cent. in number employed, while the wages paid in 1898 shows an increase of 10.7 per cent. over 1897. The business done of full capacity in 1898 was 91.9 per cent.; in 1897, 63 per cent., and in 1896, 87.6 per cent.

CUTLERY AND TOOLS.

Thirty-six establishments engaged in the manufacture of table and pocket cutlery, machinists' tools, files, etc., reported to the Bureau as having 2,178 persons on their various pay-rolls on July 1, 1898. The same establishments reported in 1897 that on the same date of that year there were 1,887 persons employed, hence the increase in 1898 over 1897 was 15.4 per cent. The increase in the amount paid in wages for the same period was 18.7 per cent.; and 67.6 per cent. of full capacity was the estimated proportion of business done.

FIRE ARMS.

The seven establishments in this industry included in the tabulation, report 934 employes on July 1, 1898, an increase of 15.9 per cent. over the number employed in the same establishments for the corresponding period in 1897. The amount paid in wages increased 7.8 per cent., 72.1 per cent. being the proportion of business done of full capacity on the basis of wages paid. The reports from this industry in 1897 showed 60 per cent. as being the proportion of business done of full capacity, and in 1896 it was 57.3 per cent.

GENERAL HARDWARE.

Classified in the tabulation as general hardware are manufacturers of builders' and furniture hardware, toys, saddlery and harness trimmings. The 54 establishments which reported to the

Bureau had 8,286 persons on all pay-rolls on July 1, 1898. The increase over the corresponding period in 1897 was 3.4 per cent., while the amount paid in wages during the same period increased 6.8 per cent., the per cent. of normal business being 74.2.

HATS AND CAPS.

Twenty-one establishments engaged in the hatting industry reported having 2,658 persons on their several pay-rolls on July 1, 1898, an increase in number employed over the previous year of 2.8 per cent. The increase in amount paid in wages by the same establishments during the same period was 3 per cent.; the proportion of business done of full capacity in 1898 was 73.5 per cent.; in 1897 it was 70 per cent., and in 1896, 75.8 per cent.

IRON AND IRON FOUNDRIES.

The thirty-three concerns classified as manufacturers of iron goods, including iron founders, report 3,930 persons as being employed on July 1, 1898. The percentage of increase was 11.6 over the corresponding date in 1897. The increase in amount paid in wages, however, was but 7.8 per cent.; the proportion of business done was reported as 63.9 per cent. of full capacity. In 1897 this industry showed a business of 69 per cent., and in 1896, 83.6 per cent. of normal capacity.

LEATHER GOODS.

Fifteen manufacturers of leather goods made reports to the Bureau, having 597 persons employed on July 1, 1898, an increase in the number on the pay-rolls of the same establishments on the same date in 1897 of 2.4 per cent. In amount paid in wages a decrease of .9 per cent. was shown; 56.5 per cent. of full capacity was the proportion of business done in 1898. The percentage in 1897 was 65 per cent., and in 1896, 80 per cent.

MACHINE SHOPS.

The number of establishments classified as machine shops which made reports to the Bureau was 66, having 7,424 persons on all pay-rolls on July 1, 1898, as against 7,715 employed by the same concerns on the same date in 1897, a decrease of 3.8 per cent. The amount disbursed as wages by these establishments during the year ending July 1, 1898, however, was $5,253,426, an increase of 19.6 per cent. over the amount paid in wages by the same establishments for the same period in 1897. The proportion of business done in 1898 was reported as being 91.6 per cent. of full capacity; in 1897 this proportion was given as 79, and in 1896, 87 per cent.

MUSICAL INSTRUMENTS AND PARTS.

The seven establishments manufacturing this class of goods reported having 893 employes on July 1, 1898, an increase of 11.6 per cent. over 1897. The increase in amount paid in wages was 16.9 per cent., and the proportion of business done in 1898, 72.5 per cent.; in 1897 this industry reported 70 per cent. as the proportion of business done for that year, and in 1896, 69.4 per cent.

PAPER AND PAPER GOODS.

Forty-nine manufacturers of paper and paper goods reported to the Bureau. The number of employes on the pay-rolls of these establishments on July 1, 1898, was 2,420, an increase of .1 per cent. over the number employed by the same establishments at the corresponding date in 1897, while the amount paid in wages during the year ending July 1, 1898, increased 3.3 per cent. over the amount for the same period in the previous year; 71.8 per cent. of full capacity was the proportion of business done in 1898; in 1897, this was reported as 70, and in 1896, 69.3 per cent.

RUBBER GOODS.

In the rubber industry there were 4,255 persons reported as being on the pay-rolls on July 1, 1898, of the 14 establishments which made reports, this being an increase of 4.6 per cent. over the number reported as being employed by the same establishments at the same date in 1897. The amount paid in wages during the same period increased 32.7 per cent.; and the proportion of business done of full capacity was reported as being 91.7 per cent. in 1898, 72 per cent. in 1897, and 63.7 per cent. in 1896.

SHOES.

Nine manufacturers of shoes made reports, the number of employes on July 1, 1898, being 5.32, a decrease from the number employed by them at the same date in 1897 of .4 per cent. The wages paid by the same establishments, as shown by the returns made, decreased 9.4 per cent. The proportion of business done of full capacity in 1898 was reported as 71.9 per cent.; in 1897, 88 per cent., and in 1896, 83.9 per cent.

SILVER AND PLATED WARE.

Manufacturers of silver and plated ware to the number of 27 reported having 4,083 employes on their several pay-rolls on July 1, 1898, showing an increase over the number employed by the same establishments in 1897 of 4.5 per cent. In amount paid in wages by the identical establishments the increase for the year ending July 1, 1898, over the same period in 1897, was 12 per cent.; 70.5 per cent. of full capacity was the proportion of business reported for 1898; in 1897 it was estimated as being 63 per cent., and in 1896, 73.6 per cent.

STONE-CUTTING AND QUARRYING.

The number of persons reported as being on the pay-rolls of the 10 establishments engaged in this industry on July 1, 1898, was 691, a decrease from the number employed by the same establishments on the same date in 1897 of 6.9 per cent. An increase of 56.4 per cent. was shown in the amount paid in wages by these establishments in the two periods. The proportion of business done of full capacity in 1898 was estimated as being 67.3 per cent.; in 1897, it was 58 per cent., and in 1896, 72.2 per cent.

WIRE AND WIRE GOODS.

The 11 establishments reporting as being engaged in the manufacture of wire and wire goods had 774 persons on their various pay-rolls on July 1, 1898. Nine per cent. was the increase in number employed over the corresponding period in 1897. The increase in amount paid in wages during the same period was 11.9 per cent., and the proportion of business done of full capacity 78.7 per cent. This was reported as being 65 per cent. in 1897, and 78.4 per cent. in 1896.

WOOD-WORKING.

Engaged in this industry there were 42 establishments which made reports, the number employed on July 1, 1898, was stated as being 1,996, an increase in number employed by the same establishments at the same date in 1897 of 1.4 per cent. There was a reported increase of 12.4 per cent. in amount paid in wages in 1898 over the amount paid by tne same establishments during the same period in 1897; 72.3 per cent. of full capacity was the estimated proportion of business done in 1898 by all establishments reporting. In 1897 it was reported as being 74 per cent., and in 1896, 76.8 per cent.

MISCELLANEOUS.

By the 54 establishments classified as miscellaneous there were 1,476 persons employed on July 1, 1898, showing a decrease of 2.3 per cent. from the number on the pay-rolls of the same establishments at the same date in 1897. There was, however, an increase of 6.5 per cent. in amount paid in wages by the identical concerns during that period. The proportion of business done of full capacity in 1898 was reported to have been 72.5 per cent.; in 1897 it was 79 per cent., and in 1896, 82.2 per cent.

DIVISION BY LOCALITIES.

Locality.	Number of Establishments reporting.	Persons employed July 1.		Per cent. Increase + Decrease − 1898 compared with		Amount paid in wages during year ending July 1.		Per cent. Increase + Decrease − 1898 compared with	
		1897.	1898.	1896.	1897.	1897.	1898.	1896.	1897.
nsonia	9	2,250	2,490	+48.2	+10.6	$1,083,583	$1,275,797	+37.5	+17.7
ridgeport.......	76	8,693	9,845	+14.	+13.3	3,762,873	4,320,378	−15.2	+14.8
ristol...........	17	1,289	1,311	−.1	+1.7	622,237	612,035	+7.	−1.6
anbury	24	2,076	2,088	+.9	+.6	910,153	893,921	−1.1	−1.8
artford.........	69	6,996	6,916	−6.7	−1.1	4,053,394	4,446,730	+.2	+9.7
illingly....	10	1,002	1,077	+10.9	+7.4	273,697	887,074	+54.4	+41.4
eriden	28	3,446	3,765	+2.5	+9.3	1,694,368	1,627,421	−1.5	−4.
iddletown......	14	1,646	1,764	−8.9	+7.2	563,269	601,077	−7.4	+6.7
ew Britain......	20	3,859	3,910	−11.6	+1.3	1,534,301	1,667,665	−13.4	+8.7
ew Haven......	70	5,358	5,408	−4.	+.9	2,279,740	2,646,204	−7.8	+16.1
ew London.....	9	1,441	1,684	+14.2	+16.9	501,114	607,349	+22.8	+21.2
orwalk...	11	1,567	1,626	+8.5	+3.8	561,355	614,137	+11.3	+9.4
orwich..........	26	4,155	4,095	−9.2	−1.4	1,441,684	1,527,683	−15.6	+6.
utnam..........	12	864	918	+28.3	+6.3	280,727	297,234	+4.1	+5.9
ockville.........	11	1,429	1,557	+7.9	+9.	402,662	507,652	+9.1	+26.1
tafford.........	12	824	997	+21.	+21.	282,933	367,030	+17.2	+29.7
tamford.........	7	1,105	1,358	+18.	+22.9	507,698	583,189	−.3	+14.9
orrington.......	6	1,369	1,598	+27.	+16.7	657,088	815,247	+26.4	+24.1
allingford......	10	1,505	1,667	+16.1	+10.8	722,825	895,900	+22.7	+23.9
aterbury.......	44	8,531	9,001	+5.1	+5.5	3,892,248	4,874,117	+11.	+25.2
illimantic......	5	1,817	1,907	+1.4	+5.	573,316	632,569	−11.6	+10.3
insted..........	19	1,211	1,237	+11.4	+2.1	500,620	501,207	+14.2	+.1

DIVISION BY LOCALITIES.

This table is designed to show the increase or decrease of the number of persons employed on July 1, 1897, and July ·1, 1898, also the gross amount distributed as wages by the establishments represented, during the two years ending on the dates above given in twenty-two selected cities and towns.

This comparison has reference to the same establishments in all cases. As has been said elsewhere it does not represent all of the establishments of any given locality, only those which have reported being considered.

An analysis shows a gratifying increase in the number of persons employed and the amount of wages distributed. Of the twenty-two localities considered, sixteen show an increase over 1896, and twenty an increase over 1897 in the number of persons employed, Stafford showing the largest, an increase of 21 per cent.

In the distribution of wages thirteen localities show an increase over 1896, and nineteen an increase over 1897. The greatest increase is shown in Killingly, where it is 41 per cent., Stafford following with 29 per cent., and Wallingford 23.9 per cent. But six of the localities considered in 1897 showed an increase over 1896.

PART IV.

LABOR LEGISLATION,
1897-8.

LABOR LEGISLATION.

THREE bills were before the Fifty-fifth Congress which are of interest to organized labor. Two of them, one creating a National Arbitration Board to mediate in disputes between common carriers and their employes, and the other authorizing the "Appointment of a nonpartisan commission" to collate information and to consider and recommend legislation to meet the problems presented by labor, agriculture and capital, were passed. The full text of each is here given:

An Act Concerning Carriers Engaged in Interstate Commerce and Their Employees.

Be it enacted by the Senate and House of Representatives of the United States of America in Congress assembled, That the provisions of this Act shall apply to any common carrier or carriers and their officers, agents, and employees, except masters of vessels and seamen, as defined in section forty-six hundred and twelve, Revised Statutes of the United States, engaged in the transportation of passengers or property wholly by railroad, or partly by railroad and partly by water, for a continuous carriage or shipment, from one State or Territory of the United States, or the District of Columbia, to any other State or Territory of the United States, or the District of Columbia, or from any place in the United States to an adjacent foreign country, or from any place in the United States through a foreign country to any other place in the United States.

The term "railroad" as used in this Act shall include all bridges and ferries used or operated in connection with any railroad, and also all the road in use by any corporation operating a railroad, whether owned or operated under a contract, agreement, or lease; and the term "transportation" shall include all instrumentalities of shipment or carriage.

The term "employees" as used in this Act shall include all persons actually engaged in any capacity in train operation or train service of any description, and notwithstanding that the cars upon or in which they are employed may be held and oper-

(211)

ated by the carrier under a lease or other contract; Provided, however, That this Act shall not be held to apply to employees of street railroads and shall apply only to employees engaged in railroad train service. In every such case the carrier shall be responsible for the acts and defaults of such employees in the same manner and to the same extent as if said cars were owned by it and said employees directly employed by it, and any provisions to the contrary of any such lease or other contract shall be binding only as between the parties thereto and shall not affect the obligations of said carrier either to the public or to the private parties concerned.

Sec. 2. That whenever a controversy concerning wages, hours of labor, or conditions of employment shall arise between a carrier subject to this Act and the employees of such carrier, seriously interrupting or threatening to interrupt the business of said carrier, the chairman of the Interstate Commerce Commission and the Commissioner of Labor shall, upon the request of either party to the controversy, with all practicable expedition, put themselves in communication with the parties to such controversy, and shall use their best efforts, by mediation and conciliation, to amicably settle the same; and if such efforts shall be unsuccessful, shall at once endeavor to bring about an arbitration of said controversy in accordance with the provisions of this Act.

Sec. 3. That whenever a controversy shall arise between a carrier subject to this Act and the employees of such carrier which can not be settled by mediation and conciliation in the manner provided in the preceding section, said controversy may be submitted to the arbitration of a board of three persons, who shall be chosen in the manner following: One shall be named by the carrier or employer directly interested; the other shall be named by the labor organization to which the employees directly interested belong, or, if they belong to more than one, by that one of them which specially represents employees of the same grade and class engaged in services of the same nature as said employees so directly interested: Provided, however, That when a controversy involves and affects the interests of two or more classes and grades of employees belonging to different labor organizations, such arbitrator shall be agreed upon and designated by the concurrent action of all such labor organizations; and in cases where the majority of such employees are not members of any labor organization, said employees may by a majority vote select a committee of their own number, which committee shall have the right to select the arbitrator on behalf of said employees. The two thus chosen shall select the third commissioner of arbitration; but, in the event of their failure to name such arbitrator within five days after their first meeting, the third arbitrator shall be named by the commissioners named in the preceding section. A majority of said arbitrators shall be competent to make a valid and binding award under the provisions hereof. The submission shall be in writing, shall be signed by the employer and by the labor organization representing the employees, shall specify the time and place of meeting of said board of arbitration, shall state the questions to be decided, and shall contain appropriate provisions by which the respective parties shall stipulate, as follows:

First. That the board of arbitration shall commence their hearings within ten days from the date of the appointment of the third arbitrator, and shall find and file their award, as provided in this section, within thirty days from the date of the appointment of the third arbitrator; and that pending the arbitration the status existing immediately prior to the dispute shall not be changed: Provided, That no employee shall be compelled to render personal service without his consent.

Second. That the award and the papers and proceedings, including the testimony relating thereto certified under the hands of the arbitrators and which shall have the force and effect of a bill of exceptions, shall be filed in the clerk's office of the circuit court of the United States for the district wherein the controversy arises or the arbitration is entered into, and shall be final and conclusive upon both parties, unless set aside for error of law apparent on the record.

Third. That the respective parties to the award will each faithfully execute the same, and that the same may be specifically enforced in equity so far as the powers of a court of equity permit: Provided, That no injunction or other legal process shall be issued which shall compel the performance by any laborer against his will of a contract for personal labor or service.

Fourth. That employees dissatisfied with the award shall not by reason of such dissatisfaction quit the service of the employer before the expiration of three months from and after the making of such award without giving thirty days' notice in writing of their intention so to quit. Nor shall the employer dissatisfied with such award dismiss any employee or employees on account of such dissatisfaction before the expiration of three months from and after the making of such award without giving thirty days' notice in writing of his intention so to discharge.

Fifth. That said award shall continue in force as between the parties thereto for the period of one year after the same shall go into practical operation, and no new arbitration upon the same subject between the same employer and the same class of employees shall be had until the expiration of said one year if the award is not set aside as provided in section four. That as to individual employees not belonging to the labor organization or organizations which shall enter into the arbitration, the said arbitration and the award made therein shall not be binding, unless the said individual employees shall give assent in writing to become parties to said arbitration.

Sec. 4. That the award being filed in the clerk's office of a circuit court of the United States, as hereinbefore provided, shall go into practical operation, and judgment shall be entered thereon accordingly at the expiration of ten days from such filing, unless within such ten days either party shall file exceptions thereto for matter of law apparent upon the record, in which case said award shall go into practical operation and judgment be entered accordingly when such exceptions shall have been finally disposed of either by said circuit court or on appeal therefrom.

At the expiration of ten days from the decision of the circuit court upon exceptions taken to said award, as aforesaid, judgment shall be entered in accordance with said decision unless during said ten days either party shall appeal therefrom to the circuit court of appeals. In such case only such portion of the record shall be transmitted to the appellate court as is necessary to the proper understanding and consideration of the questions of law presented by said exceptions and to be decided.

The determination of said circuit court of appeals upon said questions shall be final, and being certified by the clerk thereof to said circuit court, judgment pursuant thereto shall thereupon be entered by said circuit court.

If exceptions to an award are finally sustained, judgment shall be entered setting aside the award. But in such case the parties may agree upon a judgment to be entered disposing of the subject-matter of the controversy, which judgment when entered shall have the same force and effect as judgment entered upon an award.

Sec. 5. That for the purposes of this Act the arbitrators herein provided for, or either of them, shall have power to administer oaths and affirmations, sign subpoenas, require the attendance and testimony of witnesses, and the production of such books, papers, contracts, agreements, and documents material to a just determination of the matters under investigation as may be ordered by the court; and may invoke the aid of the United States courts to compel witnesses to attend and testify and to produce such books, papers, contracts, agreements and documents to the same extent and under the same conditions and penalties as is provided for in the Act to regulate commerce, approved February fourth, eighteen hundred and eighty-seven, and the amendments thereto.

Sec. 6. That every agreement of arbitration under this Act shall be acknowledged by the parties before a notary public or clerk of a district or circuit court of the United States, and when so acknowledged a copy of the same shall be transmitted to the chairman of the Interstate Commerce Commission, who shall file the same in the office of said commission.

Any agreement of arbitration which shall be entered into conforming to this Act, except that it shall be executed by employees individually instead of by a labor organization as their representative, shall, when duly acknowledged as herein provided, be transmitted to the chairman of the Interstate Commerce Commission, who shall cause a notice in writing to be served upon the arbitrators, fixing a time and place for a meeting of said board, which shall be within fifteen days from the execution of said agreement of arbitration: Provided, however, That the said chairman of the Interstate Commerce Commission shall decline to call a meeting of arbitrators under such agreement unless it be shown to his satisfaction that the employees signing the submission represent or include a majority of all employees in the service of the same employer and of the same grade and class, and that an award pursuant to said submission can justly be regarded as binding upon all such employees.

Sec. 7. That during the pendency of arbitration under this Act it shall not be lawful for the employer, party to such arbitration, to discharge the employees, parties thereto, except for inefficiency, violation of law, or neglect of duty; nor for the organization representing such employees to order, nor for the employees to unite in, aid or abet, strikes against said employer; nor, during a period of three months after an award under such an arbitration, for such employer to discharge any such employees, except for the causes aforesaid, without giving thirty days' written notice of an intent so to discharge; nor for any of such employees, during a like period, to quit the service of said employer without just cause, without giving to said employer thirty days' written notice of an intent so to do; nor for such organization representing such employees to order, counsel, or advise otherwise. Any violation of this section shall subject the offending party to liability for damages: Provided, That nothing herein contained shall be construed to prevent any employer, party to such arbitration, from reducing the number of its or his employees whenever in its or his judgment business necessities require such reduction.

Sec. 8. That in every incorporation under the provisions of chapter five hundred and sixty-seven of the United States Statutes of eighteen hundred and eighty-five and eighteen hundred and eighty-six it must be provided in the articles of incorporation and in the constitution, rules, and by-laws that a member shall cease to be such by participating in or by instigating force or violence against persons or property during strikes, lockouts, or boycotts, or by seeking to prevent others from working through violence, threats, or intimidations. Members of such incorporations shall not be personally liable for the acts, debts, or obligations of the corporations, nor shall such corporations be liable for the acts of members or others in violation of law; and such corporations may appear by designated representatives before the board created by this Act, or in any suits or proceedings for or against such corporations or their members in any of the Federal courts.

Sec. 9. That whenever receivers appointed by Federal courts are in the possession and control of railroads, the employees upon such railroads shall have the right to be heard in such courts upon all questions affecting the terms and conditions of their employment, through the officers and representatives of their associations, whether incorporated or unincorporated, and no reduction of wages shall be made by such receivers without the authority of the court therefor upon notice to such employees, said notice to be not less than twenty days before the hearing upon the receivers' petition or application, and to be posted upon all customary bulletin boards along or upon the railway operated by such receiver or receivers.

Sec. 10. That any employer subject to the provisions of this Act and any officer, agent, or receiver of such employer who shall require any employee, or any persons seeking employment, as a condition of such employment, to enter into an agreement, either written or verbal, not to become or remain a member of any labor corporation, association, or organization; or shall threaten any employee with loss of employment, or shall unjustly discriminate against any employee because of his membership in such a labor corporation, association, or organization; or who shall require any employee or any person seeking employment, as a condition of such employment, to enter into a contract whereby such employee or applicant for employment shall agree to contribute to any fund for charitable, social, or beneficial purposes; to release such employer from legal liability for any personal injury by reason of any benefit received from such fund beyond the proportion of the benefit arising from the employer's contribution to such fund; or who shall, after having discharged an employee, attempt or conspire to prevent such employee from obtaining employment, or who shall, after the quitting of an employee, attempt or conspire to prevent such employee from obtaining employment, is hereby declared to be guilty of a misdemeanor, and, upon conviction thereof in any court of the United States of competent jurisdiction in the district in which such offense was committed, shall be punished for each offense by a fine of not less than one hnudred dollars and not more than one thousand dollars.

Sec. 11. That each member of said board of arbitration shall receive a compensation of ten dollars per day for the time he is actually employed, and his traveling and other necessary expenses; and a sum of money sufficient to pay the same, together with the traveling and other necessary and proper expenses of any conciliation or arbitration had hereunder, not to exceed ten thousand dollars in any one year, to be approved by the chairman of the Interstate Commerce Commission and audited by the proper accounting officers of the Treasury, is hereby appropriated for the fiscal years ending June thirtieth, eighteen hundred and ninety-eight, and June thirtieth, eighteen hundred and ninety-nine, out of any money in the Treasury not otherwise appropriated.

. Sec. 12. That the Act to create boards of arbitration or commission for settling controversies and differences between railroad corporations and other common carriers engaged in interstate or territorial transportation of property or persons and their employees, approved October first, eighteen hundred and eighty-eight, is hereby repealed.

Approved, June 1, 1898.

An Act Authorizing the Appointment of a Nonpartisan Commission to Collate Information and to Consider and Recommend Legislation to Meet the Problems Presented by Labor, Agriculture, and Capital.

Be it enacted by the Senate and House of Representatives of the United States of America in Congress assembled, That a commission is hereby created, to be called the "Industrial Commission," to be composed as follows: Five members of the Senate, to be appointed by the presiding officer thereof; five members of the House of Representatives, to be appointed by the Speaker, and nine other persons, who shall fairly represent the different industries and employments, to be appointed by the President, by and with the advice and consent of the Senate.

Sec. 2. That it shall be the duty of this commission to investigate questions pertaining to immigration, to labor, to agriculture, to manufacturing, and to business, and to report to Congress and to suggest such legislation as it may deem best upon these subjects.

Sec. 3. That it shall furnish such information and suggest such laws as may be made a basis for uniform legislation by the various States of the Union, in order to harmonize conflicting interests and to be equitable to the laborer, the employer, the producer, and the consumer.

Sec. 4. That the commission shall give reasonable time for hearings, if deemed necessary, and if necessary it may appoint a subcommission or subcommissions of its own members to make investigation in any part of the United States, and it shall be allowed actual necessary expenses for the same. It shall have the authority to send for persons and papers and to administer oaths and affirmations. All necessary expenses, including clerks, stenographers, messengers, rent for place of meeting, and printing and stationery, shall be paid from any money in the Treasury not otherwise appropriated; however, not to exceed fifty thousand dollars per annum for expenditures under this section.

Sec. 5. That it may report from time to time to the Congress of the United States, and shall at the conclusion of its labors submit a final report.

Sec. 6. That the term of the commission shall be two years. The salary of each member of this commission appointed by the President shall be three thousand six hundred dollars per annum. Each member of the commission shall be allowed actual traveling expenses.

Sec. 7. That any vacancies occurring in the commission by reason of death, disability, or from any other cause shall be filled by appointment by the officer and in the same manner as was the member whose retirement from the commission creates the vacancy. That in case the term of a Senator or Representative expires while a member of this commission, said Senator or Representative shall not thereby cease to be a member of said commission, but shall serve until the expiration of the term for which he was appointed, drawing pay from the time his term as Senator or Representative expires, at the same salary as those members of the commission appointed by the President of the United States.

Sec. 8. That a sum sufficient to carry out the provisions of this Act is hereby appropriated out of any money in the Treasury of the United States not otherwise appropriated.

Approved, June 18, 1898.

A bill to regulate the hours of labor, known as the "Eight
Hour Bill," passed in the House, is now before the Senate, with
the amendments added by the Senate Committee on Education
and Labor, and reported without recommendation. The text of
the bill, as it is now written, follows:

55th Congress, Second Session.
H. R. 7389.

Passed the House of Representatives May 17th, 1898,

IN THE SENATE OF THE UNITED STATES.
May 18, 1898.

Read twice and referred to the Committee on Education and
Labor.
June 29, 1898.

Reported by Mr. Kyle, with amendments, but without recommendation.

Amended in the Senate Committee by the insertion of the part
printed in italics.

AN ACT

Limiting the hours of daily services of laborers, workmen, and
mechanics employed upon the public works of, or work done
for the United States, or any Territory, or the District of
Columbia.

Be it enacted by the Senate and House of Representatives of
the United States of America in Congress assembled, That the
time of service of all laborers, workmen, and mechanics employed upon any public works of, or work done for the United
States, or any Territory, or the District of Columbia, whether
said work is done by contract or otherwise, is hereby limited and
restricted to eight hours in any one calendar day; and it shall be
unlawful for any officer of the United States, or of any Territory,
or the District of Columbia, or any person acting for or on behalf of the United States, or any Territory, or said District, or
any contractor or subcontractor for any part of any public works
of, or work done for the United States, or any Territory, or said

District, or any person whose duty it shall be to employ or to direct and control the services of such laborers, workmen, or mechanics, or who has in fact the direction or control of the services of such laborers, workmen, or mechanics, to require or permit them, or any of them, to labor more than eight hours in any one calendar day, except in cases of extraordinary emergency caused by fire, flood, or danger to life or property, *or except to* work upon public military or naval works or defences in time of war.

Sec. 2. That each and every contract to which the United States, any Territory, or the District of Columbia is a party, and every contract made for or on behalf of the United States, or any Territory, or said District, which contract may involve the employment of laborers, workmen, or mechanics, shall contain a stipulation that no laborer, workmen, or mechanic in the employ of the contractor or any subcontractor doing or contracting to do any part of the work contemplated by the contract, shall be required or permitted to work more than eight hours in any one calendar day, *except in cases of extraordinary emergency caused by fire, flood, or danger to life or property, or except to work upon public, military, or naval works or defenses in time of war,* and each and every such contract shall stipulate a penalty for each violation of the stipulation directed by this Act of ten dollars for each laborer, workman, or mechanic, for each and every calendar day in which he shall labor more than eight hours; and the inspector or other officer or person whose duty it shall be to see that the provisions of any such contract are complied with, shall report to the proper officer of the United States, or any Territory, or the District of Columbia, all violations of the stipulation in this Act, provided for in each and every such contract, and the amount of the penalties stipulated in any such contract shall be withheld by the officer or person whose duty it shall be to pay the moneys due under such contract, whether the violations for which said penalties were imposed were by the contractor, his agents, or employees, or any subcontractor, his agents, or employees. No person on behalf of the United States, or any Territory, or the District of Columbia, shall rebate or remit any penalty imposed under any stipulation herein provided for unless upon a finding which he shall make up and certify that such penalty was imposed by reason of an error of fact.

Sec. 3. That any officer of the United States, or any Territory, or the District of Columbia, or any person acting for or on behalf of the United States, or any Territory, or the District of Columbia, who shall violate the provisions of this Act, shall be deemed guilty of a misdeameanor and be subject to a fine or im--

prisonment, or both, at the discretion of the court, the fine not to exceed five hundred dollars, nor the imprisonment one year.

Sec. 4. That all acts and parts of acts inconsistent with this Act, in so far as they are inconsistent, be, and the same are hereby, repealed. But nothing in this Act shall apply to any existing contract, or to soldiers and sailors enlisted, respectively, in the Army or Navy of the United States, or to seamen on seagoing vessels, *or to the transportation of mails, merchandise, or passengers, or to common carriers in any way.*

Laws have been enacted during this period in a number of the States relating to labor. The subject of legislation and the State enacting the law is here given.

UNITED STATES.—

Forbidding importation of convict-made goods. Appointing a nonpartisan commission to collate information and recommend legislation to meet labor problems. Appointing a Board of Mediation and Arbitration in disputes between common carriers and their employes.

COLORADO.—

Creating a State Board of Mediation and Arbitration. Forbidding blacklisting and boycotting. Requiring horseshoers to pass an examination and be licensed before practicing their trade.

DISTRICT OF COLUMBIA.—

Requiring plumbers and gas-fitters to pass examination and be licensed before practicing their trade.

ILLINOIS.—

Requiring horseshoers to pass an examination and be licensed before practicing their trade.

KENTUCKY.—

Requiring the payment of wages in cash and making the "truck system" unlawful.

MARYLAND.—

Requiring steam engineers, plumbers and horseshoers to pass an examination and be licensed before practicing their trade.

MASSACHUSETTS.—

Requiring gas-fitters to pass examination and be licensed before practicing their trade. Requiring street railway companies to use vestibule cars.

MINNESOTA.—

Requiring barbers, horseshoers and plumbers to pass examination and be licensed before practicing their trade.

NEBRASKA.—

Requiring street railway companies to use vestibule cars.

NEW JERSEY.—

Requiring street railway companies to use vestibule cars.

NEW YORK.—

A general labor law providing for vestibuled cars on street railways. Eight-hour workday for State employes. Ten-hour workday for service and electric railway and brickyard employes. Weekly payment of wages. Wages of employes to be a preferred claim. Wages to be paid in cash. Providing for examination of scaffoldings used in the erection of buildings. Forbidding the employment of alien laborers on public works.

PENNSYLVANIA.—

Forbidding the employment of women and minors more than sixty hours in any one week. Providing for the inspection of bake-shops. Eight-hour workday for State or municipal employes. Forbidding discharge of an employe for belonging to a labor organization.

VIRGINIA.—

Creating a Bureau of Labor Statistics. Protection of "Trade Marks" of trade unions. Requiring street railway companies to use vestibuled cars.

WASHINGTON.—

Creating a Bureau of Labor Statistics. Requiring contractors for State, county, municipal or other public works to file a bond that wages of all employes shall be paid. Requiring plumbers to pass an examination and be licensed before practicing their trade.

WISCONSIN.—

Requiring convict-made goods to be branded. Requiring plumbers to pass an examination and be licensed before practicing their trade. Requiring bake-shops to be examined for sanitary conditions.

INDEX.

INDEX.

PART I.

PART II.

Organized Labor in Connecticut.

PART III.

Condition of Manufactures.

PART IV.

Labor Legislation.

16th and 17th

ANNUAL REPORTS

OF THE

State Board of Charities

OF

CONNECTICUT,

FOR THE

Years Ending Sept. 30, 1897, and Sept. 30, 1898.

PRESENTED TO THE GOVERNOR IN DECEMBER, 1897 and 1898.

HARTFORD, CONN.:
Press of The Case, Lockwood & Brainard Company.
1898.

TABLE OF CONTENTS.

RECAPITULATION

OF

RECOMMENDATIONS FOR LEGISLATIVE ACTION.

———

It is recommended by the State Board of Charities:

1. That the principle of the Indeterminate Sentence be incorporated in some form in the statute laws concerning the commitment of criminals, (pages 49 and 55).

2. That Industrial Training be provided for all inmates of the Connecticut School for Boys at Meriden, (page 50).

3. That the Commitment of Boys under Ten Years of Age to the Connecticut School for Boys, except upon conviction for a felony, be by law prohibited, (page 51).

4. That a Special Agent be appointed to have oversight of all boys released on parole from the Connecticut School for Boys, (page 51).

5. That a State Reformatory for Women be established, (pages 53 and 57).

6. That Sections 3385, 3386, and 3387 of the General Statutes, relating to the Commitment of Insane Prisoners by County Commissioners, be repealed, (page 59).

7. That a State Commission in Lunacy be appointed to act in connection with the State Board of Charities, (page 62).

8. That a separate Department for Epileptics be established in connection with some one of the State or State-aided institutions, (page 62).

9. That a separate Department for Incurable Children be established in connection with one of the County Temporary Homes, (page 72).

FORMER MEMBERS OF THE STATE BOARD OF CHARITIES.

NAMES.	RESIDENCE.	DATE OF APPOINTMENT.	TERMINATION OF SERVICE.
Benjamin Stark,	New London.	Sept. 18, 1873.	Resigned March 27, 1879.
Levi Ives,	New Haven.	Sept. 18, 1873.	Resignation accepted May 1, 1875.
Samuel F. Jones,	Hartford.	Sept. 18, 1873.	Resigned March 27, 1879.
Miss Lucy Alsop,	Middletown.	Sept. 18, 1873	Resigned 1878.
Mrs. Marie Pettee,	Meriden.	Sept. 18, 1873.	Resignation accepted August 7, 1874.
H. W. Buell,	Litchfield.	May 1, 1875.	Resigned March 27, 1879.
Mrs. G. A. Hoyt,	Stamford.		Resigned 1878.
Willis R. Austin,	Norwich.	March 18, 1881.	Resigned 1883.
S. Rutledge McNary,	Hartford.	March 18, 1881.	Resigned 1883.
Wm. H. Hotchkiss,	New Haven.	March 18, 1881.	Resigned 1883.
Mrs. Augusta C. Pease,	Hartford.	March 18, 1881.	Resigned 1882.
Miss Hannah L. Ripley,	Norwich.	March 18, 1881.	Resigned 1882.
Mrs. Virginia T. Smith,	Hartford.	July 17, 1882.	Resigned 1882.
Harlow P. Harris,	Salisbury.	April 18, 1883.	Died in office.
James Gallagher,	New Haven.	April 18, 1883.	Reappointed 1887. Term expired July 1, 1891.
Henry E. Burton,	Middletown.	April 18, 1883.	Reappointed 1887. Term expired July 1, 1889.
Mrs. Virginia T. Smith,	Hartford.	April 18, 1883.	Reappointed 1887–9. Term expired July 1, 1893.
Mrs. Francis Bacon,	New Haven.	April 18, 1883.	Reappointed 1887–9. Term expired July 1, 1893.
Leverette W. Wessels,	Litchfield.	Nov. 3, 1885.	Reappointed 1887. Term expired July 1, 1891.
George H. Wood,	Hartford.	July 1, 1889.	Term expired July 1, 1893.

PRESENT MEMBERS

OF

THE STATE BOARD OF CHARITIES.

		DATE OF APPOINTMENT.	TERM EXPIRES.
HEMAN C. WHITTLESEY,	Middletown.	July 1, 1893.†	July 1, 1899.
GEORGE F. SPENCER,	Deep River.	July 1, 1893.†	July 1, 1899.
MISS REBEKAH G. BACON,	New Haven.	July 1, 1893.*	July 1, 1901.
MISS MARY HALL,	Hartford.	July 1, 1893.*	July 1, 1901.
EDWIN A. DOWN, M.D.,	Hartford.	July 1, 1897.	July 1, 1901.

Organization of the Board.

HEMAN C. WHITTLESEY, Middletown, *President.*
MISS R. G. BACON, New Haven, *Special Agent for County Homes.*
MISS MARY HALL, Hartford, *Special Agent for County Homes.*

CHARLES P. KELLOGG, Waterbury, *Secretary and General Agent.*

---

* Appointed by the Governor, with the consent of the Senate, for four years (General Statutes, Section 1884). Reappointed 1897.

† For the unexpired portion of the term of four years from July 1, 1891. Reappointed 1895.

THE STATE BOARD OF CHARITIES,

MEMBERS AND AGENTS.

As provided in the General Statutes of Connecticut, the State Board of Charities consists of five members, three men and two women, who are appointed by the Governor with the advice and consent of the Senate to serve for a period of four years each, three members being appointed during the Legislative session of 1889 and quadrennially thereafter, and two during the session of 1891 and quadrennially thereafter, the term of office to date from the first day of July succeeding the appointment.

The Board has an office in the Capitol at Hartford where its records, papers, and books are preserved. A meeting is held on the first Wednesday of each month—and special meetings, also, as occasion requires. The members and officers of the Board, excepting the secretary and agents, receive no compensation for their services, but the traveling and other necessary expenses incurred in the performance of their official duties are paid by the State.

In accordance with an Act of the General Assembly of 1895, a secretary is now chosen from outside the membership of the Board, who serves during the pleasure of the Board, and gives his whole time to the duties of the office. The secretary has all the powers of a member of the Board, except that of voting at meetings, acts as general agent of the Board in making any visitations required by statute or custom, is a member of the Board of Management of one of the County Temporary Homes, and performs such other duties as are connected with the position, including the preparation of the Board's annual reports.

Under another Act of the same year, two special agents have been appointed by the Board to assist in the placing out and supervision of children from the County Homes. A fuller statement of their work may be found in the General Report in the paragraphs on County Temporary Homes.

POWERS AND DUTIES.

An examination of the General Statutes and the Public Acts relating to the State Board of Charities shows that its powers and duties are largely advisory, constituting it a board of visitation and inspection for all institutions in the State designed for the restraint and care of its dependent, defective, and delinquent classes. The Board is empowered to correct any abuses found to exist in these institutions in such manner as not to conflict with any personal, corporate, or statutory rights, acting, so far as practicable, through the persons in charge of the institutions and with a view to sustain and strengthen their rightful authority.

The chief executive functions of the Board are to be found in connection with the County Temporary Homes, each of which is under the direction of a board of management consisting of the three County Commissioners and one representative each from the State Board of Charities and the State Board of Health. The Board of Charities and its agents are further authorized to recommend to the boards of management suitable family homes for the children in charge of the Temporary Homes, to visit families in which the children may be placed for the purpose of ascertaining whether they are properly treated and whether the homes are suitable ones for their welfare, and to exercise a general supervision over dependent and neglected children who are under the care of the County Temporary Homes.

In accordance with statutory requirements visits are made by members of the Board, at least one of each sex, as often as once in three months, to the State Prison, the Industrial School for Girls, the Connecticut School for Boys, and the State Hospital for the Insane, without previous notice to the persons in charge. The inmates of these institutions have the right of private communication with members of the Board either by personal conversation or by sealed correspondence, and shall be informed of their rights in this respect by the persons in charge to the satisfaction of the Board.

All asylums for the restraint and care of the insane and persons suffering from mental or nervous diseases are visited and inspected as often as once in six months, and quarterly statistical returns are made by their managers to the Board, stating the name, age, and sex of each patient confined therein, the time when committed, and by whom, and such other information as the Board may prescribe.

The county jails are examined from time to time and in-spection is made of institutions for the care of the deaf, the blind, and the feeble-minded. Visits are made to hospitals, both those that receive State aid and others, and to Fitch's Home for Soldiers at Noroton. Private institutions for the care of the indigent, aged, and young are visited, and all houses or premises used for the boarding of infants are open to inspec-tion by the Board.

Examination is made of the almshouses or other provision for the poor in all towns of the State as well as of the alms-house for State paupers at Tariffville. It is also the duty of the Board to collect information and statistics relating to pau-perism and the administration and operation of the poor laws and State charities, and to embody the same, with such sug-gestions as they may deem best, in an annual report.

As may be seen from the foregoing paragraphs, the Board of Charities, beyond its strict limitations as such, embodies also the functions of a prison commission and of a lunacy commis-sion, so far as these obtain in this State. Up to the present time, however, there is nothing in the name of the Board to suggest its combined nature.

GENERAL STATUTES OF CONNECTICUT, 1888,

with subsequent Acts and Amendments.

STATE BOARD OF CHARITIES.

Title XXVII, Chapter CXVI, Page 410.

Appointment.

Section 1884. There shall continue to be a State Board of Charities, composed of five members, of whom three shall be men and two shall be women. During the regular session of the General Assembly in 1889, and quadrennially thereafter, three members shall be appointed by the Governor, with the advice and consent of the Senate, and in like manner two mem-bers shall be appointed during the regular session of the General Assembly in 1891, and quadrennially thereafter, who shall hold their respective offices for four years from the first day of July next succeeding their respective appointments. Any vacancy not occurring from the expiration of a term of office shall be filled by the Governor during the unexpired portion of the term.

SEC. 3. The Governor shall have power to remove any of the members of the State Board of Charities for cause. P. A. 1 Ch. 31

Inspection of Almshouses, Homes for Dependent Children, Asylums, Hospitals, etc.

Sec. 1885. The Board may inspect all almshouses, homes for neglected or dependent children, asylums, hospitals, and all provisions or institutions for the care or support of the dependent or criminal classes; and they shall inspect all institutions in which persons are detained by compulsion, to ascertain whether their inmates are properly treated, and, except in cases of detention upon legal process, to ascertain whether any have been unjustly placed or are improperly held therein, and may examine witnesses, and send for persons and papers, and correct any abuses found to exist, in such manner as not to conflict with any personal, corporate, or statutory rights, acting so far as practicable, through the persons in charge of such institutions, and with a view to sustain and strengthen their rightful authority; and no measure shall be adopted without the assent of the persons so in charge, except at a meeting of the Board, at which at least four members shall be present, or by a written order, signed by a majority of the Board. An appeal may be taken to the Governor from any action of the Board by the persons in charge of such institutions.

Certain Institutions to be Visited Monthly — Their Inmates to have Opportunity of Private Communication with Members of the Board.

s amended
. A. 1893,
Ch. 92. **Sec. 1886.** The State Prison, the Connecticut School for Boys, the Industrial School and State Insane Asylum, shall be visited as often as once a month, and by at least one member of each sex. No previous notice of such visits shall be given to the persons in charge of the institution visited, and at every such visit an opportunity shall be offered to each inmate for private conversation with some member of the Board. Any communication directed to said Board, or to any member thereof, by any inmate of said institutions, shall be immediately forwarded, post-paid, to the post-office, by the persons in charge, without inspection ; and any inmate of said institutions may personally deliver to any member of said Board, and any member of said Board may receive any communication, without interference or inspection of the person or persons in charge. The inmates of said institutions shall be informed of their rights under this section by the persons in charge, to the satisfaction of said Board, or any visiting member thereof.

. A. 1895,
Ch. 311. **SEC. I.** Section 1886 of the general statutes is hereby amended by substituting the words "once in three months" for "once a month" in the third line thereof.

Homes for Dependent and Neglected Children.

Sec. 3656. In each county the County Commissioners thereof, with one member of the State Board of Charities and one member of the State Board of Health, shall constitute a Board for   .   .   .   the general supervision of such temporary home or homes in the county, etc.

Sec. 3658. Any Court of Probate, the Judge of any City or Police Court   .   .   .   or any Justice of the Peace may   .   .   .   . upon petition of   .   .   .   the State Board of Charities commit any child belonging to the class enumerated in Sec. 3655, to any Temporary Home that may have been established under this chapter, etc.

. A. 1895;
Ch. 298. **SEC. I.** The State Board of Charities may recommend to the boards for the management and supervision of the temporary homes in the several counties suitable family homes for the dependent and neglected children in charge of said temporary homes, and may visit any family home in which any such child has been placed by the county board in any county; or any place in which any such child has been placed at employment by any county board, to ascertain whether such child is properly treated, and whether such home is a suitable one, having in view the welfare of the child.

SEC. 2. Whenever it shall be found that any such child is not properly treated in any family home, or that any such home is not a suitable one, and is of such character as to jeopardize the welfare of any child so placed therein, the State Board of Charities shall report the facts in the case to the county board which placed the child in such family home, and said county board, upon being satisfied of the ill treatment of the child, or the unsuitableness of the home, shall remove the child from such home and take such further action as shall be necessary to secure the welfare of the child.

Overseers of the Poor to Keep Records and Make Returns.

Sec. 3312. Overseers of the poor shall keep full and accurate records of the paupers fully supported, the persons relieved and partially supported, and the travelers and vagrants lodged at the expense of their respective towns, together with the amount paid by them for such support and relief, and shall annually, in October, make return of the number of such persons supported and relieved, with the cost, to the State Board of Charities.

Boarding of Infants.

Sec. 2612. Such house or premises shall, at all hours during the day, and before nine o'clock in the evening, be open to visits of inspection by any officer or agent of the   .   .   . State Board of Charities, provided that such visit be made in company with a selectman of the town in which such house is located, or with some other proper person appointed by the selectmen of such town, etc. Such authorized visitors may direct and enforce such suitable measures respecting such children and premises as they may deem proper.

Sec. 2613. Any person violating any provision of the preceding section, or refusing admission to any of the persons specified in Section 2612, shall be fined not less than fifty nor more than five hundred dollars, or imprisoned not more than one year, or both.

Asylums for the Insane.

SEC. 22. Every keeper of an asylum in this state shall, quarterly, make written return to the State Board of Charities, containing the name, age, and sex of each patient confined therein, and the time when committed, and by whom, and such other information and in such form of return as said Board of Charities may prescribe. P. A. 18 Ch. 256

SEC. 23. All asylums in this state shall be subject to the inspection and visitation of the State Board of Charities, and shall be so visited and inspected at least once in six months in each year.

Officers, Records, etc.

Sec. 1888. The Board shall have an office in Hartford, where its records, papers, and books shall be preserved ; and shall meet at least once in two months, and as much oftener as it shall deem best, and three members shall constitute a quorum. It shall make such by-laws as it shall deem necessary or desirable for the conduct of its business; and shall appoint a secretary or superintendent, describe his duties, and fix his compensation, which shall be paid like other salaries. The members and officers of the Board, excepting the secretary or superintendent, shall receive no compensation for their services, but their traveling and other necessary expenses shall be paid by the state as audited by the Comptroller.

. A. 1895,
Ch. 311.
SEC. 2. The secretary or superintendent of the State Board of Charities shall hold office during the pleasure of the board ; his compensation shall not exceed fifteen hundred dollars per annum, and he shall give his whole time to the duties of his office. He shall have all the powers of a member of the Board except that of voting at meetings, and may make any visitations required by statute of a member of the Board, and be a member of boards of management of temporary homes. The Board may commit to him any powers or duties which may be exercised by it, but, in the exercise and performance thereof, he shall always be subject to the direction and control of the Board. If any member of the Board of Charities appointed by the Governor shall be appointed secretary or superintendent, his office, as a member appointed by the Governor, shall become vacant, and the vacancy shall be filled as by law provided.

. A. 1895,
Ch. 298.
SEC. 3. The State Board of Charities may authorize its secretary or superintendent, or any agent appointed by it, to visit family homes in which dependent and neglected children in charge of temporary homes in the several counties may be placed, to recommend suitable family homes to the county boards, and perform such further duties in connection with the dependent and neglected children in charge of such temporary homes as said State Board of Charities may prescribe ; but it shall not pay any agent appointed by it more than three dollars per day for time actually employed, and the total compensation of its secretary and any such agents shall not exceed two thousand dollars in any one year.

Estimates of State Expenses to be Made Biennially.

Sec. 379. It shall be the duty of the persons mentioned in the next section, on or before the first day of December, in the year eighteen hundred and eighty-eight, and biennially thereafter, to make and transmit to the Treasurer estimates of the amount of money required in their respective departments and offices of the State government for the two fiscal years commencing on the first day of the following July. Such estimates shall be itemized to such an extent and in such manner as may be required by law, and by any rules, instructions, or regulations adopted by the Treasurer and Secretary.

By Whom to be Made.

Sec. 380. The estimates for the different classes of expenditure shall be made as follows, to wit: .   .   .   For the State Board of Charities, by the Comptroller.

Annual Report.

Sec. 1887.   It shall be the duty of said Board to collect information and statistics relating to pauperism, and the administration and operation of the poor laws and State charities, and to embody the same, with such suggestions as they may deem best, in an Annual Report.

SEC. 1.   All reports heretofore or hereafter required to be made by State departments, institutions, commissions, boards, or any recipients of State money shall, from and after the passage of this act, be made to the Governor, and by him transmitted to the General Assembly. P. A. 18(Ch. 294

SEC. 2.   All reports above referred to shall be made to and including the thirtieth of September, 1895, and annually thereafter, and shall be published on or before the thirty-first day of December following.   .   .   .

Number of Annual Reports to be Printed.

Sec. 331.   The Comptroller shall annually cause to be printed, at the expense of the State, such number of copies of each of the following annual reports as is hereinafter stated :   .   .   .   of the State Board of Charities, two thousand   .   .   .

LIST OF INSTITUTIONS VISITED

BY

The State Board of Charities

In 1897 and 1898.

The Connecticut State Prison, ...	*Wethersfield*
The Connecticut Industrial School for Girls, . . .	*Middletown*
The Connecticut School for Boys, ...	*Meriden*
The Connecticut Hospital for the Insane, ...	*Middletown*
The Connecticut School for Imbeciles, ...	*Lakeville*
The Retreat for the Insane, ...	*Hartford*
Fitch's Home for the Soldiers, ...	*Noroton*

— 7

COUNTY JAILS.

Hartford County, ...	*Hartford*
New Haven County, ...	*New Haven*
New London County, ...	*Norwich*
New London County, ...	*New London*
Fairfield County, ...	*Bridgeport*
Fairfield County, ...	*Danbury*
Windham County, ...	*Brooklyn*
Litchfield County, ...	*Litchfield*
Middlesex County, ...	*Haddam*
Tolland County, ...	*Tolland*

— 10

PRIVATE SANITARIUMS FOR NERVOUS AND MENTAL DISEASES.

Spring Hill Home, ...	*Litchfield*
Kensett, ...	*Norwalk*
Elmcroft, ...	*Enfield*
The Westport Sanitarium, ...	*Westport*
Stamford Hall, ...	*Stamford*
Grey Towers, ...	*Stamford*
Hall-Brooke, ...	*Stamford*

— 7

INSTITUTIONS FOR THE DEAF.

The American School at Hartford for the Deaf, . .	*Hartford*
The Mystic Oral School, ...	*Mystic*

—

INSTITUTIONS FOR THE BLIND.

The Connecticut Institute and Industrial Home, . .	*Hartford*

—

HOSPITALS.

The New Haven Hospital, ...	*New Haven*
The Hartford Hospital, ...	*Hartford*
The Bridgeport Hospital, ...	*Bridgeport*
The Waterbury Hospital, ...	*Waterbury*
The Danbury Hospital, ...	*Danbury*
Grace Hospital, ...	*New Haven*

The Meriden Hospital, ... *Meriden*
The Norwalk Hospital, ... *Norwalk*
The Memorial Hospital, ... *New London*
The William W. Backus Hospital, ... *Norwich*
The Stamford Hospital, ... *Stamford*
The Day-Kimball Hospital, ... *Putnam*
St. Francis' Hospital, ... *Hartford*
The Emergency Hospital, ... *Bridgeport*
The Emergency Hospital, ... *Danbury*
The Sheltering Arms, ... *Norwich*
Cromwell Hall, ... *Cromwell*
Dr. Bowman's, ... *Greenwich*
Crestview Sanitarium, ... *Greenwich*
Dr. Hills' Private Hospital, ... *Willimantic*

— 20

COUNTY TEMPORARY HOMES.

Hartford County, ... *Warehouse Point*
New Haven County, ... *New Haven*
New London County, ... *Preston*
Fairfield County, ... *Norwalk*
Windham County, ... *Putnam*
Litchfield County, ... *Winsted*
Middlesex County, ... *Haddam*
Tolland County, ... *Vernon Center*

— 8

HOMES FOR THE AGED.

The Old People's Home, ... *Hartford*
The Church Home, ... *Hartford*
The Lawson C. Ives Widows' Home, ... *Hartford*
The Widows' Home, ... *Hartford*
St. Mary's Home, ... *West Hartford*
The Erwin Woman's Home, ... *New Britain*
The Old Ladies' Home, ... *New Haven*
The Trinity Church Home, ... *New Haven*
The Ellen M. Gifford Home for Incurables, . . . *New Haven*
The Home for the Friendless, ... *Fair Haven*
The Curtis Home, ... *Meriden*
The Southmayd Home, ... *Waterbury*
The Smith Memorial Home, ... *New London*
The Eliza Huntington Home, ... *Norwich*
St. John's Home, ... *Stamford*
The Harriet M. Makinster Home, ... *Middletown*

— 16

HOMES FOR THE YOUNG.

The Hartford Orphan Asylum, ... *Hartford*
St. James's Asylum, ... *Hartford*
The Watkinson Juvenile Asylum and Farm School, . . *Hartford*
Home for Incurable Children, ... *Newington*
The New Haven Orphan Asylum, ... *New Haven*
St. Francis' Asylum, ... *New Haven*
Children's Branch of Home for the Friendless, . . . *Fair Haven*
Children's Branch of Curtis Home, ... *Meriden*
Mt. Carmel Children's Home, ... *Hamden*
The Rock Nook Home, ... *Norwich*
The Bridgeport Orphan Asylum, ... *Bridgeport*
The Danbury Children's Home, ... *Danbury*
The Children's Home, ... *Norwalk*
The Children's Home, ... *Stamford*
The Gilbert Home, ... *Winsted*
The Middlesex County Orphans' Home, ... *Middletown*
The Maplewood Farm, ... *East Canaan*

— 17

Total, . . 88

LIST OF TOWNS VISITED

BY

The Board to Inspect Almshouses

And Other Provision for Town Poor

In 1897 and 1898.

HARTFORD COUNTY.

Hartford,	Enfield,	Plainville,
Avon,	Farmington,	Rocky Hill,
Berlin,	Glastonbury,	Simsbury,
Bloomfield,	Granby,	Southington,
Bristol,	Hartland,	South Windsor,
Burlington,	Manchester,	West Hartford,
Canton,	Marlborough,	Wethersfield,
East Granby,	New Britain,	Windsor,
East Hartford,	Newington,	Windsor Locks.
East Windsor,		

NEW HAVEN COUNTY.

New Haven,	East Haven,	North Haven,
Waterbury,	Guilford,	Orange,
Ansonia,	Hamden,	Prospect,
Bethany,	Madison,	Seymour,
Branford,	Meriden,	Wallingford,
Cheshire,	Middlebury,	Wolcott,
Derby,	Naugatuck,	Woodbridge.

NEW LONDON COUNTY.

New London,	Griswold,	Old Lyme,
Norwich,	Groton,	Preston,
Bozrah,	Ledyard,	Sprague,
Colchester,	Lisbon,	Stonington,
East Lyme,	Lyme,	Waterford,
Franklin,	North Stonington,	Voluntown.

FAIRFIELD COUNTY.

Bridgeport,
Danbury,
Bethel,
Brookfield,
Darien,
Greenwich,
Huntington,

Monroe,
New Canaan,
New Fairfield,
Newtown,
Norwalk,
Redding,

Ridgefield,
Sherman,
Stamford,
Weston,
Westport,
Wilton.

WINDHAM COUNTY.

Windham,
Putnam,
Ashford,

Brooklyn,
Canterbury,
Plainfield,

Pomfret,
Thompson,
Woodstock.

LITCHFIELD COUNTY.

Litchfield,
Winchester,
New Milford,
Bridgewater,
Canaan,
Cornwall,
Goshen,

Harwinton,
Kent,
Norfolk,
North Canaan,
Plymouth,
Roxbury,
Salisbury,

Sharon,
Thomaston,
Torrington,
Washington,
Watertown,
Woodbury.

MIDDLESEX COUNTY.

Middletown,
Chatham,
Chester,
Cromwell,

Durham,
East Haddam,
Essex,
Middlefield,

Old Saybrook,
Portland,
Saybrook,
Westbrook.

TOLLAND COUNTY.

Tolland,
Andover,
Coventry,
Ellington,

Hebron,
Mansfield,
Somers,

Stafford,
Vernon,
Willington.

ALMSHOUSE FOR STATE PAUPERS, - Tariffville.

Total, - - 138.

SIXTEENTH ANNUAL REPORT

OF

THE STATE BOARD OF CHARITIES.

For the year ending September 30, 1897.

OFFICE OF THE STATE BOARD OF CHARITIES, }
Room 80, Capitol, Hartford, Conn. }

To His Excellency, Lorrin A. Cooke, Governor of the State of Connecticut :

SIR :—We have the honor to submit herewith the Sixteenth Annual Report of the Board for the year ending September 30, 1897 :

THE WORK OF THE BOARD.

During the year under review regular meetings of the Board have been held monthly at its office in the Capitol, and special meetings, also, as occasion has required. The business then transacted has been duly recorded in the minutes of the meetings, and the reports and documents in connection therewith have been filed for reference in the Board's office.

In conducting the work of the Board in accordance with the statutory requirements, regular visits of inspection have been made to the State Prison, the Connecticut School for Boys, the Industrial School for Girls, and the State Hospital for the Insane, as often as once in three months, as provided in Section 1886 of the General Statutes and its amendment, Chapter 311 of the Public Acts of 1895. Additional visits have been made to these institutions from time to time, whenever occasion has required, and an effort has been made by the Board to keep in touch with their methods and work throughout the year. Inspections have been made of the Hartford Retreat for the Insane, and of the other private asylums, eight in number, the

School for Imbeciles at Lakeville, the American School at Hartford for the Deaf, the Mystic Oral School, the Perkins Institute for the Blind at Boston, where are twenty Connecticut beneficiaries, the Connecticut Institute and Industrial Home for the Blind, Fitch's Home for Soldiers at Noroton, Hospitals, both those that are State-aided and others, the County Jails, the County Temporary Homes for Dependent and Neglected Children, and a number of private charitable institutions for the care of the indigent aged and young; the almshouse for State paupers at Tariffville has been inspected, and fifty-five towns, also, have been visited to examine the almshouses or other provision made for the care of the town poor. In accordance with statutory provision, it is the custom of the Board to make the visits referred to without previous notice to the persons in charge. Except in a very few instances, the visitors have been well received, and the managers of the institutions have shown a commendable willingness to exhibit all departments of the same and to give any desired information in regard to their condition and methods of work.

The chief functions of the Board are of an advisory nature, and its efforts in this direction have resulted in the accomplishment of certain improvements that have been recommended and in the consideration of plans for others not already carried out. Much still remains to be done, however, in certain directions, but it is nevertheless the belief of the Board that the majority of the institutions in Connecticut present conditions of humane and careful management. Over the others, which are now deficient in these respects, constant supervision will be maintained in the hope of accomplishing finally their permanent improvement.

Since the date of the last report, September, 1896, a number of changes have been made in matters which concern the charities of the State. Additional buildings and increased facilities have been provided in some of the institutions, but the total of these operations does not equal that of the preceding year, which was a period of unusual activity in these directions.

Certain statutes were enacted by the General Assembly of 1897 in relation to the dependent, defective, and criminal classes of the State, and it is hoped that the carrying out of their provisions will prove beneficial to those for whom they were intended.

THE STATE PRISON.

Doubtless the most important change undertaken at the State Prison during the year has been the erection of the ward for insane criminals, the need of which has been greatly felt for several years. It is a substantial structure, directly adjoining the west wing of the Prison, and in its interior arrangement is designed in accordance with modern ideas as to the treatment of the insane. Accommodations are furnished for sixty inmates in single bedrooms, besides separate dormitories for excited cases and those of a suicidal tendency. Sitting-rooms for use in the daytime, dining and work-rooms, and other needful conveniences are also provided.

When the building is ready for occupancy, which it is expected will be about January 1, 1898, the insane convicts at present confined at the State Hospital at Middletown will be removed to this new department of the Prison, and hereafter the frequent transfer of convicts to and fro between Wethersfield and Middletown, with all the dangers incident thereto, will be abolished.

Under the law establishing the insane ward at the Prison, a consulting physician, learned in the treatment of the insane, has been appointed by the Governor, who shall visit the insane ward every month, or whenever requested by the Prison officials, or by the Governor, and shall examine the condition and treatment of the persons confined there.

In connection with the establishment of this new department, it is recommended that a careful study be made of the probable causes of insanity in the Prison, with a view toward adopting such measures as shall tend to reduce the number of cases of this terrible affliction.

Another change of considerable importance has been the construction of two additional tiers of cells in the west end block which is reserved for prisoners of the first grade. This makes a total of sixty-four cells in this department, all of which are occupied with the exception of about seven, which are kept open as an incentive to men in the second grade to strive for promotion.

Other improvements completed during the year, some of which were in contemplation at the time of the last Report, consist in the enlargement of the chapel by the addition of the old schoolroom, the fitting up of a new schoolroom just beyond the old one, and the equipment of a separate hospital room for patients who are afflicted with pulmonary diseases. An inclosed balcony near the hospital door has been added for the exercise of convalescent patients who are unable to descend the long stairs to the yard below. Five temporary cells or booths have been added in the women's department to accommodate the increased number of inmates there, and the system of heating and ventilating in that wing of the building, as well as in the hospital, has been thoroughly renovated in accordance with modern theories. The whole Prison has been wired for electric lights, the work being done almost entirely by prisoners at a comparatively small expense, and it is hoped to adopt that improved system of illumination at an early date.

The passage of the law providing for the release on parole of certain classes of prisoners by the State Board of Pardons is in accord with the progressive spirit of prison reform now shown in several of the states, and the effect of its operation in Connecticut will be watched with interest. Up to the close of the fiscal year no paroles had been granted.

The number of inmates in the Prison during the past year has exceeded all previous records in the history of the institution, having reached a total of four hundred and fifty-one, and showing a steady increase toward the close of the year. Practically all of the cells are occupied, and a considerable number of prisoners who have already received sentence are still detained in the County Jails awaiting admission to the Prison. Inquiry made has revealed the fact that there are a number of cells vacant in several of the jails, and it has been suggested that some of the Prison inmates whose terms are nearly expired be transferred to these places in accordance with the law permitting such action, and that room thus be made for the more serious offenders now awaiting removal to Wethersfield.

The marked increase in the number of inmates in the penal institutions of the State is in itself a strong argument for the establishment of a State Reformatory in the near future, but until that time arrives, it is desirable that every successful expedient known to modern prison reform be employed in our own State Prison. The changes and improvements accomplished there during the last few years show an effort made in this direction, and in general it may be said that the institution presents, in addition to a commendable condition of cleanliness and decent comfort, evidences of a progressive tendency on the part of its directors.

THE CONNECTICUT SCHOOL FOR BOYS.

The School for Boys at Meriden has passed through another year with little, if any, change in the general features of its management. Whenever visited, the School has presented an admirable appearance of neatness and good order, but it is regretted that no greater advances have been made in methods and resources for the definite improvement of the inmates. No provision has yet been made for the introduction of systematic physical exercise, and the lack of any such means of development, as well as of a suitable gymnasium, is still one of the marked defects in the equipment of the School. The recommendation made in the last Report is here repeated, viz.:— that some systematic method of physical exercise, such as the Ling or Swedish system of gymnastics, be adopted for all inmates of the School at an early date.

The classes in working trades have been carried on as before, with only a few boys in each, and the work accomplished, with the exception of that done in printing and telegraphy, has been almost wholly in the line of the School's daily routine or in the nature of repairs to the School's property.

The whole number of boys so employed is small in comparison with the total population of the School, and the large majority of them are still engaged in the monotonous and uninspiring occupation of caning chairs. The arguments made in the Board's last Report for the introduction of a more varied system of trades instruction for the whole School, together with Sloyd work for the younger and less experienced boys, still hold good, and are too obvious to require repetition. The School is not a jail and can never fulfill its true purpose with jail industries. In these matters of trades instruction and physical development, the Connecticut School is sadly inferior to those of our neighbor states, New York and Massachusetts, and other enlightened commonwealths, and the suggestion is here offered that the best features of these more progressive schools be adopted, with such modifications as are necessary, in our own institution. The expense of so doing would doubtless be considerable, but there is reason to believe that it would prove a profitable investment in the increased usefulness to the State hereafter of the graduates of the School as self-sustaining, law-abiding citizens.

One matter that merits criticism at the School is the employment of the boys from both the south and the north divisions of the main building, the older and more vicious with the younger and less hardened, in the same workshop. As another workroom stands vacant near by, the boys can easily be separated; the change will require merely the employment of one more supervisor at a small additional expense, comparatively, and will prove a great benefit to the boys. It is hoped that this separation may be made at an early date.

The chief improvement accomplished at the School during the year has been a complete renovation of the plumbing of the several buildings, with the introduction of modern sanitary fixtures; preparations have also been made for replacing the old wooden fences around the playgrounds of the congregate departments with a more secure iron structure of neat and substantial design.   This, it is hoped, will be completed at an early date and will prove effective in lessening the number of escapes from the institution, which has been considerable during the past year, although most of the runaways have been afterward recovered. As a part of good discipline, too much stress cannot be laid upon the necessity of employing every safeguard to prevent such escapes, and of using every means to recover any boys who may possibly elude the School's vigilance.

In regard to the disposition that is made of the boys who are released from the School because they have attained the Honor Grade, or for other cause, it is noticed that the same large proportion as usual are returned to parents or friends; during the last year two hundred and twenty-four out of a total of two hundred and sixty-five released having been so placed. In many cases the homes and companions to which the boys return are of the most degraded nature, and they soon lapse into evil habits with no one to warn or encourage them. As the State, through the School, is the legal guardian of these boys during their minority, it will always seem remiss in the performance of its duty until it makes provision for a State Agent whose duty it shall be to find suitable homes and employment for boys who are released, to return them to the School when they fail to conduct themselves properly outside, and in general to maintain a careful supervision over all wards of the School who are released on probation.

THE CONNECTICUT INDUSTRIAL SCHOOL FOR GIRLS.

At the Industrial School for Girls at Middletown, an important addition to the equipment has been made in the erection of the so-called Honor Home.   This is situated in the southern part of the grounds and is an attractive three-storied structure of brick, with broad piazzas on all sides.   The cost, which is about $17,000, has been met by the reserve funds of the institution, and no call has been made upon the State treasury for the purpose.   When occupied, which will probably be about December 1st, it will make complete the system of classification adopted in the School, by furnishing an intermediate residence between the other seven Homes and positions in families outside the School.   Accommodations are provided for twenty-six girls, who will here be tested by the enjoyment of a period of comparative freedom to prove their fitness for life in the world outside.

Girls who have reached the honor grade and have been placed out in family homes are systematically visited by the School's Agent, and the records continue to show that a large proportion of them do well in their new surroundings.

The School always presents an admirable condition of neatness, comfort, and kindly discipline when visited, and it is a pleasure to commend this institution as one of which the State may well be proud.

Every year, however, bears stronger witness to the need for some suitable institution other than the County Jails, where young women over sixteen years of age (which is the limit set for admission to the Industrial School) who have committed minor offenses may receive proper restraint and instruction and be reclaimed before it is too late.   Connecticut must have a Women's Reformatory before many years.

COUNTY JAILS.

The changes and alterations in the buildings and equipment of several of the County Jails which were noted in the Board's last Report as being then undertaken, were completed in due season and have been fully justified by the improved conditions they have effected.

In the case of the Hartford County Jail the increased cell room and workshop accommodations have been greatly appreciated.   The new hospital department was opened for use in January and has proved a valuable addition to the Jail's equipment. The whole is furnished with modern sanitary apparatus and is under the charge of a hospital steward.

Since January 1st all of the prisoners in the Jail have been supplied with neat uniforms, and the clothes that they wore at the time of entrance are preserved, after a thorough cleaning and fumigating, in separate racks, and are returned to the owners when they leave the institution. This system insures a neat appearance of the men while in the Jail and prevents them from replenishing their wardrobes at the public expense. It is a feature that might be adopted to advantage in the other large Jails of the State. All departments of this Jail show signs of careful and efficient management, and the institution as a whole may be favorably compared with any of the same class in the country.

At the New Haven County Jail the addition of the new cells in both the male and female departments, which was noted in the last Report, has relieved in a measure, only, the severity of the overcrowding formerly felt there. With a total of two hundred and fifty cells available for men, the jail has been compelled to shelter at times from three hundred and twenty-five to three hundred and fifty male prisoners, and recourse is thus necessarily had to the pernicious system of " doubling up " two men in the same cell. Unless the pressure upon its accommodations is relieved in the near future by the establishment of a State Reformatory, the New Haven County Jail will soon require another extensive addition to its plant. The jail in general exhibits a commendable degree of neatness and good management in spite of its overcrowded condition.

The Windham County Jail is now settled in its new building, which was described in the last Report and which appears to be in every respect well adapted to the purpose and sufficient to meet the needs of the county for some time to come.

No changes of importance have occurred during the year in the jails of other counties, and each presents substantially the same condition as a year ago.

In spite of the extensive improvements made in recent years in the material equipment of several of these institutions, the county jail system as maintained in Connecticut continues to be unsatisfactory as ever as a means of reducing crime or of permanently improving the moral and social condition of the persons committed to their custody. Supt. Brockway of the Elmira Reformatory has stated in a recent letter that more

than a true share of attention has been paid to the felon criminals and the prisons used for their confinement and treatment, to the neglect of the more important matter of the repression of crime with the misdemeanants, the class of offenders
out of which are recruited the felon criminals who commit the
more serious offenses.   He states that the application of a reformatory regime to misdemeanants can be as readily accomplished as its application to felons in the modern reformatories,
and expresses the belief that the probability of successful treatment of misdemeanants is greater than of felons.   "There is
not," he declares, "a more promising field of usefulness to
society by diminishing criminal offenses than the field of those
convicted of misdemeanors."   The reformatory system could
be applied, however, to the county prisons only by bringing
them under a uniform administration and the centralized control of the State.

A possible solution of the reformatory problem in Connecticut might be the State control of all the county prisons
and the conversion of two of the larger ones into reformatories
for men and women, respectively, leaving the others for the
restraint of the less serious offenders and the detention of
prisoners bound-over for trial in the higher courts.

STATE REFORMATORY.

The history of the movement to establish a State Reformatory in Connecticut is still fresh in the minds of those who followed the discussion of the subject in the last General Assembly,
and does not need to be reviewed here.   An extended series of
hearings on the matter was held before the Committee on Humane Institutions, during which the arguments for and against
the location and plans chosen for the Reformatory were presented and the whole question of the desirability of such an institution in this State was thoroughly discussed.   At the conclusion of the hearings, the Committee made a report which
coincided with the last Report of this Board in objecting to the
site chosen on account of its distance from railway communication and the lack of sufficient land to carry on suitable farming
operations.   The final paragraph deserves repetition here.

"In concluding their report, your Committee would urge
that the idea of a reformatory be not abandoned.   In the last
eight years the people of this State have spent in the improvement and extension of jails more than three hundred thousand

dollars. In a short time additional expense in this direction must be incurred. It costs no more to build a reformatory than it costs to build a jail, and a reformatory established on the lines suggested in this report will maintain its inmates at a less expense. There is in the jails a class of prisoners whose chances of reformation would be much greater in a reformatory. This would mean to the State a gain in manhood and womanhood which it is hard to estimate in dollars and cents. In her charities Connecticut stands in the front rank of her sister states. In the reformation of her criminals she may have attempted too much at first and so faltered. But she should take no backward step. She should at least stand with her face to the light."

In connection with the report the Committee submitted a resolution and a bill, both of which were passed by the General Assembly. The bill repealed the Act of 1895 which established the Reformatory, and in presenting it the Committee said: " We feel that in this matter it is best to begin again from the lowest foundation. The many admirable provisions of the present act can all be retained in the bill which may be submitted to the next General Assembly for its consideration and approval." The resolution authorized the Governor to appoint a commission of three persons, who, serving without compensation, shall have power to sell the present reformatory site, and whose duty it shall be to investigate the whole subject of a reformatory in this State and to recommend to the next General Assembly such legislation on the subject as may seem wise and proper.

The commission was appointed as provided, but no definite action has yet been taken toward selling the reformatory property, and the report, of course, will not be forthcoming until a year hence.

It is superfluous to emphasize the need of a reformatory in Connecticut if one studies at all the present condition of our penal system. The new features introduced of late at the State Prison are good so far as they go, but it would require a complete upheaval of existing customs and traditions there to make of it a true reformatory, and even then a new State Prison would have to be erected elsewhere to accommodate such criminals as are not amenable to reformatory influences.

It is especially hoped that the commission appointed will recommend the establishment at the earliest possible date of the women's department of the reformatory. Many cases are known of young women who have passed the age of sixteen (the limit for admission to the Girls' Industrial School), who need just the instructive and improving influences of such an institution, and for whom a short term in jail may mean only the beginning of a life of evil.

THE STATE HOSPITAL FOR THE INSANE.

At the State Hospital for the Insane at Middletown, the year under review has been marked by a steady increase in the number of patients, the total having risen as high as eighteen hundred and over. The new cottage, adjoining the south end of the North Hospital, the construction of which was mentioned in the last Report, was occupied soon after and has furnished additional accommodations for fifty female patients. To meet the constantly increasing demand for admission, another cottage of corresponding style is being erected to connect with the north end of the same Hospital, and, when finished, will provide room for fifty more male patients. Upon the completion of the insane ward at the Prison, the removal there of the insane convicts now at the Hospital will relieve in a measure the crowded condition of the latter institution, but for a brief period only, it is feared, as there are already many pauper and indigent insane in the State waiting for a chance to be admitted.

The Board of Charities has been instrumental during the year in effecting the transfer of a number of deserving cases of the insane from town almshouses to the State Hospital and has still under supervision several others whose entrance is anticipated as soon as there are vacancies.

The crowded condition of the institution became a matter for discussion in the last General Assembly, and a resolution was passed appointing a commission of seven persons, " who shall serve without compensation and whose duty it shall be to investigate the necessity for additional accommodations for the insane in this State, to consider the expediency of erecting new buildings for this purpose, to inquire into the desirability of the site which the people of Norwich have offered to give to the State for an asylum for the insane, or the desirability of any other site which any other town may propose to donate, and to report the result of their investigations to the next legislature at the beginning of its session."

The appointment of this commission revives the question

whether the already extensive establishment at Middletown should be still further enlarged or another institution be erected in a different locality, and whether the insane wards of the State may not best be cared for in separate institutions, one a hospital for the scientific treatment of acute cases, and the other an asylum for the restraint and humane care of the so-called chronic or incurable cases. It is earnestly hoped that the work of this commission may be effective in bringing about a more adequate provision for this unfortunate class of persons than exists at present in the State.

In spite of its crowded condition, the Hospital, whenever visited, has presented its customary appearance of neatness and necessary comfort and bears evidence to its prudent and intelligent management.

PRIVATE ASYLUMS.

An important measure in regard to the status of private asylums for the insane in Connecticut was the bill passed by the General Assembly of 1897 requiring a license from the Governor for the maintenance of any such institution. The action was instituted in the first place by the State Board of Charities, and is in accord with the practice of many other states. The bill provides that every such institution shall be in charge of a physician, registered under the laws of this State, who has had at least three years' experience as medical attendant in some institution for the treatment of insane persons, and that he shall reside upon the premises.

In accordance with the provisions of this act all of the private asylums in the State, it is believed, have procured licenses, with the exception of the Louden Sanitarium at Greenwich, whose superintendent wrote to the Board that they would not need one, as they were going out of the business. A later visit to the place, however, revealed the fact that it was still being conducted under the guise of a boarding-house, and that four of the six boarders then present were persons who had formerly been committed to Mr. Louden's care as insane. In defense of this action it was claimed that these persons had been examined by physicians and declared not insane, but in view of their advanced age and the unscientific nature of their treatment it is difficult to see how such sudden recoveries could have been effected. It is evidently a case of "a distinction without a difference," and deserves a careful investigation by the proper authorities.

The other seven asylums present practically the same conditions as a year ago. Cromwell Hall at Cromwell, under the charge of the Drs. Hallock, as noted in the last Report now receives only nervous patients and declines to admit the strictly insane.

Stamford Hall, Dr. A. J. Givens' sanitarium at Stamford, has been enlarged by the erection of new buildings until it now has accommodations for one hundred patients. The other institution at Stamford, formerly known as The Stamford Home, has passed from under the charge of Dr. Kindred to that of the Drs. Barnes and MacFarland, and is now known as Grey Towers.

Perhaps the first step toward the development of a joint State commission of lunacy and charity in Connecticut has been taken in the appointment to the State Board of a physician who is experienced in the treatment of the insane, and it is hoped that the future may bring a still further advance along these lines.

THE LAKEVILLE SCHOOL FOR IMBECILES.

No important change has taken place during the year at the School for Imbeciles at Lakeville, the only material addition being in the nature of increased facilities for the kitchen and sewing-room departments. The present year, however, brings the promise of enlargement in the general work of the School under an appropriation of eight thousand dollars, which was made by the last General Assembly in consideration of the release by the School of all its claims under the long-contested Marett bequest. This, it is hoped, will make possible the construction of the additional schoolrooms and other buildings that have been so long needed. With increased accommodations, the School will be enabled to enlarge the scope of the valuable remedial and educational work that it is accomplishing for unfortunates of this class.

THE AMERICAN SCHOOL AT HARTFORD FOR THE DEAF.

The School for the Deaf at Hartford has experienced another year of continued effort and substantial progress. As has been the custom for many years, instruction in articulation and lip-reading has been continued in connection with the manual method and sign language, and gratifying progress has been shown by the pupils in all branches. With the opening of the present term a class has been formed whose instruction is being conducted under the exclusive oral method, and which, it is possible, may prove to be the beginning of a pure oral department in the School. In the report of the Committee on Humane Institutions to the last General Assembly on the subject of schools for the deaf, it was said: " It will be a consummation devoutly to be wished if we had in the State one school for the education of the deaf, with separate departments for the use of the combined and oral methods, so that pupils could be placed in one or the other, and transferred from one to the other, according to their needs, and from no consideration of selfishness or of competition."

The contemplated removal of the School, mentioned in the last Report, from its present property on Asylum avenue to quieter and more extensive grounds in the suburbs, has not yet been effected, but a committee of trustees has been appointed for the purpose and plans are being considered in that direction. With new, modern buildings and improved facilities in all departments, the School will be better fitted than ever to care for the deaf wards of the State.

THE MYSTIC ORAL SCHOOL.

No changes of importance have taken place at the Mystic Oral School during the year, and practically the same conditions are existent as described in the last Report. The peculiar status of the institution still continues, being a private school in receipt of State-aid, but having no representative of the State connected with its management.

The arguments formerly made against the maintenance of two schools by the State for the instruction of its deaf wards are equally valid to-day.

THE CONNECTICUT INSTITUTE AND INDUSTRIAL HOME FOR THE BLIND.

This dual institution, with its kindergarten department on Asylum avenue and its Industrial Home on Wethersfield avenue in the city of Hartford, has had another busy year of effort in behalf of its unfortunate wards. A class of five children have been graduated from the kindergarten and have gone to the

Perkins Institute for the Blind in Boston, to continue there a more advanced course of instruction.

In the industrial department, an important change has been the removal of the broom-shop, which employs some thirteen persons, to quarters in the town of Colchester. The rooms vacated in the Wethersfield avenue building are being re-modeled as a dormitory for the young women of the institution, who, upon the completion of the alterations, will be transferred thither from their present quarters in the kindergarten on Asylum avenue. This will place them in more convenient proximity to the Institute store and to the printing-office, in which some of them are employed.

The practice is still continued of maintaining a concert company, which spends a large part of the time in traveling through this and neighboring States, giving entertainments for the benefit of the Institute. Several of the performers are supposed to be acquiring a knowledge of useful trades at the same time in the Institute, but the intervals of continued work in Hartford are so brief and so constantly interrupted that their progress toward self-support must be necessarily slow.

Under the existing system of management in the Institute, it seems necessary to revise the natural idea one would have of the place as an industrial school, where, after a few years' training, its pupils shall be fitted to take their places as self-sustaining citizens in the world at large, and to consider it rather as an industrial home whose unfortunate inmates shall be supported there by the State for an indefinite period, giving in return such labor as they may while in the institution.

HOSPITALS.

The number of these important institutions in the State has not been increased during the year, but those already in service have made the usual repairs and minor improvements and, whenever visited, have given evidence of good management and conscientious treatment of patients.

The movements to establish public hospitals in New Britain, Middletown, and Winsted, which were noted in the last Report, have progressed slowly during the year, but will doubtless result in the opening of the desired institutions at no very distant date.

COUNTY TEMPORARY HOMES.

Among the acts passed by the General Assembly of 1897 which concern the County Temporary Homes was one raising from two to four years the age limit until which children may be retained in almshouses. The natural effect of this will probably be to decrease the number of very young children who are committed to the County Homes and thus to lessen somewhat their total population. In accordance with Chapter 210 of the Public Acts of 1897, the word sixteen is changed to eighteen in all acts relating to the County Temporary Homes (except in the second line of Section 3658 of the General Statutes), so that all these acts may be construed in complete accordance with the law of 1895 which gives to the Boards of Management of the several Homes control of their wards until they reach the age of eighteen years. Chapter 28 specifies which are the proper courts of probate to approve agreements for the adoption of children who have been committed to the Homes. A bill was introduced in the General Assembly to transfer the cost of support of children in the County Homes from the State, where it now rests almost wholly, to the towns from which the children are committed, but the measure was finally defeated.

Certain material changes in the buildings and equipment of the several Homes have taken place during the past year and may be noted as follows:

In the Home at New Haven a new wing has been added to the building which provides increased dining-room and kitchen facilities and an enlarged dormitory for the boys; the plumbing of the whole house has been completely renovated and new sanitary fixtures introduced throughout.

At the Fairfield County Home the grounds have been neatly graded and a new steam heater has been provided in the building. A line of electric cars has been extended from Norwalk to Westport and now passes the door of the Home.

The Middlesex County Home at Haddam has been enlarged by a substantial addition which provides a new schoolroom and increased facilities for carrying on the work of the Home which have been long needed.

At the Gilbert Home in Winsted, which provides quarters, also, for the Litchfield County Home, a neat gymnasium has been completed, and plans are under consideration for the enlargement and improvement of the hospital cottage.

In the case of both the New London and the Fairfield County Homes, new matrons have succeeded to the positions of those who were formerly in charge.

The system of boarding out a large number of the children for hire, which has been practiced in New Haven County during the last year, is considered to be satisfactory by those who have the work in charge. The adoption of some such plan was made necessary by the inadequacy of the Home to accommodate the numbers committed to its charge. As a rule it is the younger children who are boarded out, and the older boys and girls, who are more likely to be placed in families, receive temporary shelter in the County Home. It is not believed by the management that this system decreases the number of family homes that would otherwise receive the children without pay, and every effort is made to place the children in the usual way whenever possible.

The records of the County Homes for the past year show the usual large number of dependent and neglected children cared for, and a statistical summary of the operations of the Homes is appended herewith. The number of family homes secured for the children is about the same as that for the preceding year and exceeds by more than one-half the record for 1895. In this connection mention should be made of the special agents appointed by the State Board whose purpose it is to work in friendly co-operation with the Boards of Management and the Town Committees in the several counties; to stimulate thus the placing out of children throughout the State and to aid thereafter in maintaining a careful supervision over them so long as they are wards of the Homes. Material assistance may be given in many cases where local conditions or other circumstances make it difficult for the Town Committees to act. Due credit should be given, however, to the efforts of the latter who serve voluntarily and who often devote valuable time and strength to the furtherance of this important work. It was never designed that the duties of the special agents should supplant those of the Town Committees. Such a result would not be possible under existing circumstances, even if it were desirable. To cover the whole field would require at least twice the present number of agents who should give their whole time to the work.

As an aid to the systematic oversight of County Home wards, an effort is being made by the State Board to prepare a directory of all those up to eighteen years of age who are

living in family homes.   This will be arranged like a library
card catalogue, indexed by towns, and will be revised monthly
from the reports which are made by the County Homes to the
special agents.

The successful placing of the children in desirable family
homes and the supervision of them thereafter will doubtless
continue to be the most difficult as well as the most important
features in the operation of the Homes.   It goes without
saying that no child should ever be transferred from one family
to another without the sanction of the County Home of which
it is a ward, and it would be well if all persons taking children
were required to sign agreements to notify the Homes of any
future changes of address that might be made.

The steady increase year by year in the number of children
committed to their care has necessarily resulted in making the
management of the Homes more complex and difficult than
it was in the earlier years of their existence.   Hasty critics of
occasional defects in the present operations should bear in
mind the fact that difficulties now exist which were unknown
before, when the work was comparatively small and simple.

SUMMARY OF STATISTICS FOR THE EIGHT COUNTY TEMPORARY HOMES.

For the year ending September 30, 1897.

Number in Homes October 1, 1896,	598
Received during year ending September 30, 1897 (new cases),	337
Returned to Homes during year ending September 30, 1897,	204
Total,	1,139

Placed in family homes (new cases),	154
Replaced in family homes,	128
Returned to friends,	164
Sent to Protestant Asylums,	1
Sent to Catholic Asylums,	10
Given to priests,	3
Sent to School for Boys,	9
Sent to Industrial School,	8
Sent to Lakevile School,	2
Sent to School for Deaf,	3
Sent to Institute for Blind,	2
Discharged by Board of Management,	12
Recalled by Selectmen,	5
Died,	3
Remaining in Homes, October 1, 1897,	635
Total,	1,139

TOWN ALMSHOUSES AND ALMSHOUSE FOR STATE PAUPERS.

Of the one hundred and sixty-eight towns in Connecticut, seventy have almshouses which are owned by the respective towns and nineteen others maintain almshouses which are owned by private individuals. A large part of these have been inspected by the Board during the year and visits have been made, also, to a number of other towns which make different provision for poor-relief.

The general condition of the almshouses throughout the State may be said to be about the same as in recent years, although the changes that have been made are along the lines of improvement rather than in the nature of a retrograde movement. The majority of these places present an appearance of cleanliness, good order, and decent comfort, and give evidence of humane treatment of the inmates; some which now show signs of indifference and neglect might be readily improved by a little effort on the part of the proper authorities, and a few only are positively unfit for use and ought to be abolished.

Suggestions for improvements in various directions which have been made by the Board have been received with favor, in some instances, by the keepers and town officials, and have been put into effect with reasonable promptness. In other cases, the authorities have been slow to comply with the recommendations made, and repeated efforts have been required to accomplish the desired ends.

A special effort has been made of late by the Board in the investigation of cases of insanity and phthisis in the almshouses. Of the former, several have already been transferred to the State Hospital at Middletown, in compliance with recommendations made, and others are only awaiting vacancies in that crowded institution. In the better class of almshouses it has been found that sufferers from phthisis are given separate sleeping-rooms, being secluded to that extent, at least, from the other inmates. In other places, however, instances have been discovered of persons in various stages of the disease who were occupying the same bedrooms with apparently well persons, and in all such cases an effort has been made by the Board to have them provided with separate apartments.

But few cases of children over the prohibitory age have been discovered in almshouses, and in almost every instance the Board has been successful in securing their prompt removal to most suitable places. Since the limit of age until which they may be retained in these institutions has been raised by the Act of 1897 from two to four years, it is expected that the number of such cases hereafter will be even less than in the past.

In the absence of a State almshouse or State farm in Connecticut, the contract for the support of State paupers which existed between the Comptroller's office and the late Mr. Marvin Sanford of Tariffville, and which expired on August 1, 1897, was renewed for another period of years with Mr. Morton Sanford, brother of the former manager.

The house at Tariffville which is used for the purpose has been somewhat improved during the year in the matters of lighted halls, improved beds, and added protection against fire, but it is, nevertheless, very old and unsuitable both in size and arrangement for the accommodation of any considerable number of persons. Several of the inmates are of the lowest, most depraved natures, but the cells in the basement in which some of these wretched creatures are confined at night are not fit for any human beings.

When last visited, there were thirty-five inmates present, of whom only ten were State paupers. If only the State paupers were cared for here, the accommodations would be ample and satisfactory, but the other twenty-five are boarded at the place by the several towns upon which they are lawfully dependent. This practice is continued in direct violation of Section 3310 of the General Statutes, which provides that " all paupers shall be supported at some place or places within the town to which they belong, and it shall not be lawful for any town, or the selectman thereof, to remove any pauper out of the town to which such pauper belongs to be supported in any other town." It is extremely desirable that some means should be devised for enforcing the provisions of this statute, at least to the extent that the unfortunate poor of a town should not be subject to such associations as now prevail in the case of some of the inmates of the so-called State almshouse at Tariffville.

NATIONAL CONFERENCE OF CHARITIES AND COR-
RECTION.

For the first time in its history, the National Conference of Charities and Correction met this year outside the borders of the United States, the twenty-fourth annual session having been held in July, 1897, in the city of Toronto, Canada. Perhaps owing to this fact, and also to the extreme heat which prevailed at the time, the number of persons in attendance was slightly smaller than that of the preceding year. There were representatives present, however,. from thirty different states and territories, besides Canada, Mexico, and England. The Connecticut State Board was represented by four delegates, who bore also credentials from the Governor as representatives of the State.

The meetings proved interesting and profitable as ever, and a most hospitable reception was accorded to the conference by the citizens of the place.

A considerable number of interesting institutions in Toronto for the care of the delinquent, defective, and dependent classes were inspected by the delegates, and on the journey thither visits were made to the state hospitals for the insane at Utica and Rochester, N. Y., to the state prison at Auburn, to the penitentiary at Albany, and to the State Industrial School for Boys and Girls at Rochester. At several of these places valuable suggestions were received which might, with modifications, be advantageously applied to similar institutions in Connecticut.

The Conference of 1898 will be held in New York city, and the Connecticut Board is recognized in its make-up by the appointment of its delegates to membership in committees and to other official positions. As the quarter-centennial of the Conference, its sessions will doubtless be of unusual interest, and, being held in a city so near to us, should attract many persons from this State. Workers and students in all lines of philanthropic and reformatory effort will find attendance at these annual conferences an experience of much practical value.

RECENT LEGISLATION REGARDING STATE INSTITUTIONS AND CHARITIES.

Several statutes were enacted by the General Assembly of 1897 which directly concern the institutions and charities of the State. The most important of them may be mentioned as follows:

Chapter 111 of the Public Acts repealed the Act of 1895, which provided for the establishment of a State Reformatory, and under a special act, No. 286, a commission of three persons was appointed to sell the present site for the reformatory, to investigate the whole subject of a reformatory in this State, and to recommend to the next General Assembly such legislation on the subject as may seem wise and proper.

Chapter 177 provided for the erection of a ward for insane criminals at the State Prison, and in connection therewith for the appointment by the Governor of a consulting physician, learned in the treatment of the insane, who shall advise as to the condition and treatment of the persons confined there.

Under the provisions of Chapter 231, power is given to the State Board of Pardons to release on parole, by a majority vote of the Board, any inmate of the State Prison who has served at least one-half of the full term of his sentence, who is not known to have suffered a previous conviction for felony, and who is not serving a life sentence; provided that his prison record has been such as to afford reasonable probability that he would, if released, lead a law-abiding life, and provided, also, that suitable employment be obtained for him before the release is granted. Any prisoner so released shall remain while at large in the legal custody of the Board, and subject at any time during his term of sentence to be re-imprisoned for sufficient cause.

Chapter 103 amended Section 3343 of the General Statutes, which permitted the warden of the State Prison to employ not more than ten prisoners at a time outside the walls of the prison, so that now there may be employed such number of prisoners as may be approved by the board of directors outside the prison walls, but within two miles thereof.

Chapter 215 provides that no institution for the treatment or detention of insane persons shall be conducted or maintained within the State except under a license granted by the Governor. Every such institution shall be in charge of a physician, registered under the laws of this State, who has had at least three years' experience as medical attendant in some institution for the treatment of insane persons, and who shall reside upon the premises.

Under the Special Law, No. 455, a commission of seven persons was appointed whose duty it shall be to investigate the necessity of additional accommodations for the insane of the State, to consider the expediency of erecting new buildings for the purpose, to inquire into the desirability of the site which the people of Norwich have offered to give to the State for an asylum, to inquire into the desirability of any other site which any other town may propose to donate, and to report the result of their investigations to the next Legislature.

In accordance with Chapter 210 of the Public Acts, the word sixteen is changed to eighteen in all acts relating to the County Temporary Homes (except in the second line of Section 3658 of the General Statutes), so that all these acts may be construed in complete accordance with the law of 1895, which gives to the Boards of Management of the several Homes control of their wards until they reach the age of eighteen years.

Chapter 28 specifies which are the proper courts of probate to approve agreements for the adoption of children who have been committed to the County Homes.

The limits of age between which children may not be retained in almshouses have been raised by Chapter 206 from two to four years, and from sixteen to eighteen years; so that Section 3657 of the General Statutes now reads: "It shall be unlawful for overseers of the poor to place or retain children between the ages of four and eighteen years in almshouses after, etc."

EXPENSE TO STATE AND TOWNS.

In this State, with a population in 1890 of 750,000, it is known that the following institutions are maintained for the restraint and care of its delinquent, defective, and dependent classes. For —

Criminals and Offenders,	. 11	(State Prison and County Jails).
Juvenile Offenders, .	. 2	(School for Boys and Girls' Industrial School).
The Insane, . . .	. 9	(State Hospital, Hartford Retreat, 7 Private Asylums).
The Feeble-Minded,	. 1	(Lakeville School for Imbeciles).
The Deaf, . . .	. 2	(American School and Mystic Oral School).
The Blind, . . .	. 1	(Institute and Industrial Home).
The Sick and Injured, .	. 17	(Hospitals, Public and Private).
Old Soldiers, . . .	. 1	(Fitch's Home for Soldiers).
Dependent Children,	. 8	(County Temporary Homes).
Paupers, ...	. 89	(Town Almshouses, Almshouse for State Paupers).
The Aged, Private Provision,	15	(Old People's Homes).
The Young, Private Provision,	14	(Orphan Asylums and Homes).
Total, . . .	. 170	

The amount of State aid which has been applied to the support of a part of the institutions in the above list was, as shown by the appended table, for the year 1897, $732,858. This, as compared with the sum of $662,329 expended for similar purposes in 1896, and $588,721 expended in 1895, shows a steady increase in the cost to the State of the criminal and dependent classes year by year. A certain amount of increase is to be expected with the constantly growing population of the State, and, as shown in the preceding review, some of the institutions mentioned are still in need of more liberal appropriations for the successful accomplishment of their legitimate purposes. There is reason to believe, however, that in other directions a more prudent economy could be practiced without detriment to the work of the institutions concerned.

The amount paid by the towns for the relief and support of their poor population in the year 1896 was $724,594, as compared with $780,104 for the year 1895, showing a gratifying decrease in this department of public expense.

Notice has been sent by the Board during the year to the selectmen of the various towns calling their attention to Section 3312 of the General Statutes, and hereafter request will be made each October for the annual return of statistics of poor relief therein provided for. In this way it is hoped that the cost of town poor relief for the current year may be noted in each annual report of the Board.

Respectfully submitted,

HEMAN C. WHITTLESEY, Middletown,
REBEKAH G. BACON, New Haven,
MARY HALL, Hartford,
GEORGE F. SPENCER, Deep River,
EDWIN A. DOWN, M.D., Hartford,
Members of the State Board of Charities.

CHARLES P. KELLOGG, Waterbury,
Secretary.

SEVENTEENTH ANNUAL REPORT

OF

THE STATE BOARD OF CHARITIES.

For the year ending September 30, 1898.

OFFICE OF THE STATE BOARD OF CHARITIES, }
Room 80, Capitol, Hartford, Conn. }

To His Excellency, the Governor of the State of Connecticut:

SIR: — We have the honor to submit herewith the Seventeenth Annual Report of the Board for the year ending September 30, 1898:

THE WORK OF THE BOARD.

Since the adoption of Chapter 294 of the Public Acts of 1895, the Report of the Board has been prepared annually, instead of biennially as was customary from 1886 to 1895. The Report for the year ending September 30, 1897, was presented in typewritten form, and is now printed with this year's Report for presentation to the Governor and to the General Assembly of 1899.

During the past year regular meetings of the Board have been held monthly at its office in the Capitol, and special meetings, also, as occasion has required. The business then conducted has been duly recorded in the minutes of the meetings, and the reports and documents in connection therewith have been filed for reference in the Board's office.

In the exercise and performance of the Board's statutory powers and duties, regular visits of inspection have been made to the State Prison, the Connecticut School for Boys, the Industrial School for Girls, and the State Hospital for the Insane, as often as once in three months, as provided in Section 1886 of the General Statutes and its amendment, Chapter 311 of the Public Acts of 1895. Additional visits have been made at intervals as occasion has demanded, and it has been the purpose of the Board to keep thoroughly informed in regard to the work of these institutions. Inspections have been made of the American School at Hartford for the Deaf, the Mystic Oral School, the Connecticut Institute and Industrial Home for the Blind, the Hartford Retreat for the Insane, and the other private asylums, nine in number, the School for Imbeciles at Lakeville, eighteen hospitals, both those that are State-aided and others, Fitch's Home for Soldiers at Noroton, the ten County Jails, the eight County Temporary Homes for Dependent and Neglected Children, and twenty-nine private charitable institutions for the care of the indigent aged and young; the almshouse for State paupers at Tariffville has been inspected, and ninety-eight towns have been visited to examine the almshouses or other provision made for the care of the town poor, sixteen of which were visited also in 1897.

As directed by statute, the visits referred to have been made, as a rule, without previous notice to the persons in charge and, with few exceptions, a general willingness has been shown by the managers to exhibit all departments of the institutions and to give any desired information in regard to their work and methods.

In general it may be said that in the departments of charity and correction, Connecticut maintains a position of cautious conservatism as compared with many of her sister states. The members of the Board have been forcibly impressed with the limitations of the work along these lines in their own State when they have visited the public institutions of neighboring commonwealths or have met their representatives in the sessions of the National Conference of Charities and Correction.

A number of Connecticut's institutions may bear favorable comparison with any others of their respective classes in the country, but there is reason to believe that the introduction of new ideas and new life in some cases, and the application of increased or more wisely directed appropriations in others, would effect a considerable advance in their work of practical beneficence. It is true that the cry of the State for the past two years has been for decreased expenditures along all lines, but there is a point at which economy may cease to be a virtue and may become mere parsimony. It is quite as desirable, often, to increase the revenues as it is to decrease the disbursements. The State can make no more profitable investment than the employment of all necessary funds to secure the best men and the best methods for the conduct of all preventive and curative work (such, for example, as the care and education of neglected children, the reformation of offenders, both juvenile and adult, etc.), and to insure to society an adequate protection by the custodial care of all members of the hopelessly defective classes.

In spite of the conservative influences surrounding the charities of the State, it is found, on reviewing the field for a period of years, that there has been a considerable increase in the number of institutions established; and a marked development in the work of those already in existence. The departments of child-saving and of the care of the sick and insane are especially noticeable in these respects. The supervision of all charitable and correctional institutions by a duly organized State board is generally believed to be productive of much good in bringing to the public attention many things in their administration that ought to be known, and in preventing the growth of certain well-recognized evils that are not uncommon when the institutions are left wholly to themselves and their own directors. As the work of charities and correction increases year by year, the work of the State Board of Charities must increase in a corresponding degree, if Connecticut is to keep pace with the advance of other enlightened commonwealths along these lines.

THE STATE PRISON.

The history of the past year at the State Prison has been marked by a steady increase in the number of convicts committed to its charge. All of the cells in the institution have been filled, and at times a considerable number of persons sentenced to the prison have been detained in the County Jails waiting for an opportunity to be admitted. This pressure upon the accommodations of the prison will have to be relieved at an early date, and it has been suggested that the old east end, now occupied by the women's department, be remodeled to contain a block of one hundred and fifty cells, which would be connected with the present guardroom and thus be controlled by the officers stationed there. Perhaps this is the best solution of the problem for the present, for, until Connecticut shall possess a reformatory for the younger class of criminals, her State Prison stands in great need of increased accommodations.

A number of improvements in equipment have been effected during the year, among the most important being the introduction of electric lights in all departments and the completion of the ward for insane criminals. This has proved already to be a valuable addition to the institution in that it does away with the frequent transfers of prisoners to and from the hospital at Middletown, and also provides a place where convicts suffering from a temporary derangement of the nervous system may receive proper treatment amid favorable surroundings.

It is possible that at present some of the prisoners who are reported and punished on the ground of being vicious and unruly may be in reality the victims of mental hallucinations, and in all such cases it is recommended that a personal examination be made by experts in mental diseases in order that suitable treatment may be applied without delay.

It is still the belief of the Board that occasional opportunities for conversation among the majority of the prisoners — always under proper supervision and restraint — together with greater liberality in the matter of secular literature, would be beneficial in stimulating the mental condition of the men and in preventing many a case of mental depression and disease.

The considerable number of cases of insanity occurring at the prison, and the large proportion of the deaths there due to pulmonary phthisis, have caused the State Board of Charities to collect data in regard to these diseases from a number of penal institutions throughout the country, the result of which may be found in another part of this Report.

On the occasion of the quarterly visits to the prison made by members of the Board, it is their practice to hold private interviews with those prisoners who, by means of the customary cards, have signified their desire to obtain a hearing. Special visits also have been made for this purpose when it has seemed advisable from the nature or circumstances of the complaints. In some cases the grievances are found upon investigation to be of a trivial nature; in others, the requests made are not within the province of the Board to grant; but in many cases it is known that the simple rehearsal of his troubles is a relief to the prisoner otherwise subjected to continual silence, and the mere knowledge that there is a friendly power at hand to which appeal can be made in case of need is in itself an aid to courage and patience under discipline.

The system of classifying the inmates in distinctive grades, which was established at the prison in 1896, is in accord with the practice of some other states during recent years, and was adopted with the intention of keeping in touch with modern methods of prison management. The provisions of the parole law of 1897, which supplements in a degree the grading system, have been exercised in only four instances at the date of writing, and it may be doubted whether such a restricted use of the measure as exists under the present arrangement can ever develop a fair test of its merits.

Another feature of modern prison methods which is recommended for careful consideration at the Wethersfield institution is the application in some form of the principle of the indeterminate sentence. Leading experts in penology declare this measure to be one of the most effective yet devised for the permanent reformation of criminals and the consequent protection of society.

After all schemes and methods for the inspiration and regeneration of criminals have been introduced in an institution, the fact still remains that it is not in any system that the best results in prison reform are to be obtained, but in the personal character and conception of duty of those in whose custody prisoners are placed for punishment and reformation. Too much stress, therefore, cannot be laid upon the importance of having in all official positions at the Connecticut State Prison men of right principle and honorable habits.

THE CONNECTICUT SCHOOL FOR BOYS.

Once more it becomes necessary to report the year's record at the School for Boys as an unsettled one, and to note another change in the superintendency, Mr. Charles M. Williams, formerly superintendent of the public schools in Meriden, and a man of comparatively little experience in reformatory work, having been appointed to the position by the trustees in July last.

The School has made little progress in methods or resources for the development of its inmates since the Board's last published Report, and the same defects still call for the same criticisms. The lack of systematic physical exercise for all the boys and the want of a gymnasium and physical instructor, are serious shortcomings that should be made good in the near future. "A sound mind in a sound body," is a motto that might well be adopted by the School, and the recommendation

4

made in previous reports is here repeated — that some regular method of physical exercise, such as the Ling or Swedish system of gymnastics, be provided for all of the boys at an early date.

The so-called " industrial classes " at the School have been continued in a small way, but with the exception of those in printing and telegraphy their members have been engaged almost entirely in the daily routine work of the School, or upon repairs to the School's property. By far the largest part of the boys are still employed for six hours each day in the " jail-bird " industry of caning chairs. The arguments in previous reports against this as an occupation for young boys presumably receiving reformatory influences, are almost too obvious to be repeated and yet a continual dropping may wear away stones. The work has absolutely no element of reformatory or educational influence, and often proves a positive detriment rather than a benefit to a boy after he leaves the School. The few thousands of dollars yearly realized from this industry toward the School's support are a poor compensation for the failure to arouse the latent abilities of the boys by a more varied and interesting system of work, and will be more than counterbalanced by the future cost to the State of those graduates of the School who drift into careers of crime on account of lack of early instruction in useful occupations.

It is contended that the best boys, who would be the ones to receive the greatest benefit from trades instruction, are those who remain in the School for the shortest periods of time, but the records show that the average residence of the boys is twenty-two months, and no boy can earn his way out in less than eleven months. Surely, in either of these periods, the ground work of instruction in a useful trade could be laid, which in many cases would prove the salvation of the boys when released.

For all of the younger and duller boys there should be introduced a system of Sloyd work, comprising elementary instruction in the use of hands and tools, which has proved successful to a marked degree in similar institutions in stimulating and developing hands, eyes, and brains. It is desirable, also, that a greater number of boys should be employed in farm work than is the case at present. Constant employment in a variety of healthful and interesting occupations is one of the most effective forces in the reformation of offenders — juvenile or adult.

During the last two years twenty-one small boys under ten years of age — mere children, in fact — have been committed to the School, some of them for no more serious offense than the lack of a suitable home, and since the opening of the School three hundred and forty-nine such children have been received. With a suitable Home for Children in operation in each county of the State, there can be no excuse for this practice, and its continuance cannot be too strongly condemned. It is, therefore, recommended that hereafter no boy under ten years of age be committed to the School except upon conviction for a felony.

As noted in the last Report, the same large proportion of boys released upon probation have been returned to relatives or friends, two hundred and twelve of the two hundred and seventy-six boys discharged during the past year having been so located. Many instances are known where the homes and companions to which the boys have been returned are of the lowest order. The rule requiring boys to report their condition to the School every six months is not generally obeyed, and there is no one to help them with friendly warning or advice.

As the State, through the School, is the legal guardian of these boys during their minority, it is recommended that provision be made for the appointment of an agent whose duty it shall be to find suitable homes and employment for boys at the time of their release, to return them to the School when they fail to conduct themselves properly outside, and in general to maintain a careful supervision over all wards of the School during their time of probation. Furthermore, it should be the business of this agent to investigate the cases of all boys on trial for commitment to the School upon any other charge than that of a felony, with a view to improving the home discipline and thus reducing the number of those who are sentenced for " incorrigibility " and similar offenses, which, in too many cases, are but ill-defined.

It is greatly to be regretted that a work of such far-reaching importance as the reformation of boy offenders should be allowed to drag on in Connecticut along the lines of narrow vision and of a " what-has-been-is-good-enough " policy, which has marked its course so long. A personal comparison of the Connecticut School with the boys' industrial schools of neighboring commonwealths makes one grieve for our own State's neglect of duty toward its delinquent youths.

The developments which were brought to light in the recent examination of the School's affairs by the legislative committee of investigation reflected serious discredit upon the managing board of the institution, and showed that the weakness of the School was not alone in the superintendent's office. It is doubtful if the School will ever achieve success until there is a thorough reorganization of the higher as well as of the lower powers, and a consequent freedom from any possible influence of local politics in the management of the institution. The Connecticut School for Boys needs not only a superintendent of experience, ability, and tact, but also a board of trustees composed of broad-minded, philanthropic citizens at large of this commonwealth.

THE CONNECTICUT INDUSTRIAL SCHOOL FOR GIRLS.

Satisfactory progress in all departments is the record of the year under review for the Industrial School for Girls at Middletown. Whenever visited, evident conditions of commendable neatness, good discipline, and homelike comfort have been noted, and it may be safely said that the School stands in the front rank of similar institutions throughout the country.

The completion and opening of the Henry D. Smith Home, or Honor Home, is an advanced step in the development of the School's facilities for the cultivation of true womanly character among the girls committed to its charge. During the months that it has been in use, it has amply fulfilled the expectations entertained for its success, and already it has proved not only a great benefit to its own inmates, but also a valuable influence for good throughout the School.

The dressmaking and cooking schools maintained in the institution have been continued with gratifying results and have proved of much greater value than the box-making industry which they supplanted, although the latter was a source of some revenue to the School. It would be a decided improvement if the cane-seating work at the Boys' School were as wisely displaced in favor of some instructive form of employment.

In regard to girls who have been placed out in family homes, it may be said that they are kept under careful supervision by the visiting agent of the school, and the records continue to show that fully 90 per cent. of them follow honorable lives in the communities in which they reside.

The limit of age until which girls may be committed to the School is fixed at sixteen years, and once more it becomes a duty to emphasize the necessity of establishing at an early date a Women's Reformatory, where young women, who have passed that age limit and have committed minor offenses, may be placed under suitable restraining and improving influences and may thus be led into careers of honest respectability before it is too late.

COUNTY JAILS.

No material changes in the equipment or management of the County Jails have been made during the past year. The additions and improvements noted in the Board's reports for the two years previous, particularly in the jails of Hartford, New Haven, Windham, and Litchfield counties, have proved the value of their adoption in the enlarged accommodations and increased facilities for work thus provided. The old condition of overcrowding has not been wholly relieved, however, and in the New Haven Jail, especially, the cell capacity is still inadequate to accommodate properly the average number of inmates.

The general condition of the larger jails may be said to reveal an effort on the part of the officers in charge to conduct them along the lines of good order, decent comfort, and humane discipline. In some of the smaller institutions, however, a want of neatness and cleanliness and an evident looseness of discipline warrant the inference that no adequate appreciation is felt of the importance of the work in hand, or else that there exists a willingness to let it drag along in the old ruts of indifference and neglect.

The serious defects of the County Jails as maintained in Connecticut have been pointed out frequently in the Board's reports, and it is probable that these institutions will never accomplish much toward the repression of crime or the permanent improvement of their inmates until there is a radical change in the system now in vogue.

A plan for bringing all county prisons under the centralized control of the State, which was referred to in the Board's last report, has been widely discussed in Massachusetts, and in this connection General Brinkerhoff of Ohio, president of the National Prison Association, may be quoted as saying: " My experience in dealing with county prisons has long since led me to believe that the only way to make any large progress in their improvement is to place them under state control. The experience of England in the matter is conclusive evidence of the advantages of such control. Prior to 1877 the county jails of England were duplicates of our American jails, and were unspeakably bad, but with state control, which began in 1877, all has been changed, and the county prisons of all the British Islands are now models for the world, and crime from that date has steadily decreased. Not only are prisoners better cared for, but expenses have vastly decreased."

Superintendent Brockway of the Elmira Reformatory, in an address before the recent meeting of the National Prison Association, said: " More than 90 per cent. of recorded crimes are misdemeanors, not felonies; that is to say, are crimes punishable by imprisonment for periods less than a year in jails, workhouses, county penitentiaries, etc. More attention in the future should be given to offenses and offenders of this class. There can be no effective repression of the great body of crimes by the laws and prisons, without very important changes of public sentiment, of penal statutes and of imprisonment for misdemeanors and misdemeanants."

Some months ago there appeared in the *Hartford Daily Times* an article which stated so clearly the inherent weakness of the county jail system that it is desired to reproduce here the following paragraphs:

" Many arguments have been made to show that a reformatory is needed in Connecticut on grounds of humanity because the jails and the State Prison merely make men worse. No doubt this statement of the effect of jails and prisons is substantially true. It expresses the opinion usually held by sheriffs and wardens and by all who have studied the subject.

" When every one knows that the system followed in jails and prisons makes men worse, why is it not reformed? Why do we attempt to put up a separate institution which shall do for those committed to it what the jails and prisons neglect to do for their inmates?

" The only solid reason is that no legislature in any state has dared to destroy this vast patronage. A reformatory succeeds because it is managed by experts with no regard to politics; the jails and prisons fail because in the former the chief office is always a political prize, and in the latter politics has its influence. No sheriff is elected because he understands the problem of treating criminals or cares a row of pins about it. He is chosen as a politician, and with a perfect understanding that he is to pay political debts by appointments and favors. It is the purest accident when a man who has any conception of the problem of a jail is put in charge of one.   With the State Prisons it is often a little better.   The warden is sometimes appointed with plain reference to his understanding of the work he has to do, but very often the appointing power is so grossly ignorant of the questions involved that it does not dream of more than finding a man of fair character who is a disciplinarian, as the phrase goes, and it is usually expected that politics shall be considered in the appointment of minor offices, and very often in the purchase of supplies.

" Not many years ago, everybody concerned — legislators included — could plead ignorance of any better way than the old one known to their fathers.   Now the case is changed. The utility and ultimate economy of reformatory methods are demonstrated.   No one has a right to legislate on the subject without knowing something about it.   No one has a right to help maintain the villainous, wasteful, corrupting jail system. But nothing is done towards reforming it.   Those who study the whole subject are hopeless of accomplishing anything in jails at present.   They seek to improve the State Prisons; they try to establish reformatories, but they practically admit that the abuses of the jails are too strongly entrenched to be attacked until a different popular feeling has been created."

If such words as these could be sounded again and again in the ears of legislators and intelligent citizens at large, there is reason to believe that a popular sentiment would be aroused which would demand the inauguration of a new and better order of things without delay.

The suggestion made in the Board's last report in regard to the State control of county prisons is therefore repeated, and it is further recommended that all of the penal institutions in the State be placed under the direction of a State commission, and that, so far as possible, all such reformatory measures as the indeterminate sentence, release on parole, and the grading of prisoners be introduced into both county and state prisons.

STATE REFORMATORY.

Among the many matters to be considered at the coming session of the General Assembly will doubtless be a revival of the project to establish a State Reformatory, which was so gracefully buried by the legislative committee on humane institutions in 1897.

The special commission of three persons which was appointed at that time to sell the Reformatory property and to recommend to the next General Assembly desirable measures of legislation on the subject has thus far maintained a condition of masterly inactivity. An effort was made by the trustees of the American School for the Deaf to secure the Reformatory site for the uses of the School, but there was a failure between the parties concerned ·to agree upon terms that were mutually satisfactory. It is sincerely hoped that the commission is not retaining the property with the idea that a Reformatory will ultimately be erected there, for the same objections to the location for the purpose of such an institution, which were noted in the Board's last printed report, are equally valid to-day. At the date of writing it is known that the members of the commission have not visited any of the reformatories in other states for the purpose of studying the conditions and problems of their management with relation to the establishment of a similar institution in Connecticut.

The overcrowded condition of the State Prison and the County Jails, and the presence in the Boys' School at Meriden of offenders who are too old to be amenable to its influences, are only familiar illustrations of well-known arguments for the necessity of establishing without delay a State Reformatory worthy of the name. If the suggestion made in another part of this report for the State control of county prisons could be carried into effect, it would then be possible to reorganize two of them as reformatories for men and women, respectively, and thus to make a practical test of the reformatory idea in Connecticut at a minimum cost to the State.

While there is no doubt of the value of farm labor as an adjunct to a reformatory institution, and of the principle that more men *ought* to adopt it for an occupation than is now the case, there is no gainsaying the fact that the majority of men committed to penal institutions in Connecticut will *not* engage in farming except under compulsion. For a large proportion of reformatory inmates, therefore, in this State, there should be provided a variety of industrial occupations, and for those persons who enter the institution totally unskilled, practical instruction in useful trades.

When an institution controls the industries carried on within its limits, and credits the men engaged therein with the average market rate of wages befitting their labor and ability, it is difficult to see how any degrading competition is brought upon the free labor of the State.   If a man is working for average wages, what does it matter whether he is within walls or without?   " Degradation " is incurred when the labor of an institution's inmates is let out to contractors at cut-throat prices which cannot be met by other workmen in open competition. It would be well if the contract system were abolished from all of our public institutions, and the labor of the inmates were directly controlled by the authorities in charge.

Connecticut will ever be remiss in the performance of duty toward its delinquent classes and toward the people of the State in general until it shall possess for men and women two reformatories, with grounds and buildings separate so far as practicable.   The women's reformatory, especially, should be established at the earliest possible opportunity, for it is the young women past the age limit of admission to the Industrial School for whom the conditions of our County Jails are most harmful, and for whom the preventive and regenerative influences of a suitable institution might often work their permanent reform.

THE STATE HOSPITAL FOR THE INSANE.

The past year has brought a change in the superintendency of the Hospital for the Insane, owing to the death of the former incumbent of that office, Dr. Olmstead, who, by his unceasing devotion to the work in all its details, caused those who knew him well to believe that he sacrificed his life in the service of the State.   To fill the position the trustees selected Dr. Charles W. Page, formerly superintendent of the Hospital for the Insane at Danvers, Mass., who assumed charge of the institution at Middletown in the month of July last.   Dr. Page's successful record at Danvers, and his reputation for intelligent progressiveness promise well for the conduct of the Connecticut Hospital.

The constant increase year by year in the number of patients committed to the Hospital has continued during the last biennial period, and, with nominal accommodations for eighteen hundred patients, the institution has been compelled to shelter at times as many as nineteen hundred and over.   It is clear that the original plans for the care of the State's insane wards have been outgrown long since, and that materially enlarged provision for this purpose must be made very soon either at Middletown or elsewhere.   The report of the commission appointed by the General Assembly of 1897 to investigate this subject is awaited with interest.

In the meantime, however, a scheme of re-organization has been adopted at Middletown which provides in reality for a combined or three-fold institution, in that two of the buildings are to be reserved as hospital and infirmary for the scientific treatment of acute cases, while the remaining buildings are to be utilized as asylums for the custodial care of the chronic insane.   There is practically no limit of size to which such a combined institution can be developed and the present location possesses many natural advantages for the operation of a great establishment.

A plan has been submitted, also, for the construction of a large congregate dining-room for the use of the chronic insane patients, but this cannot be carried into effect without obtaining a suitable appropriation for the purpose from the General Assembly.   By the adoption of this plan, twenty or more small ward dining-rooms now in use, would be refitted as dormitories and the capacity of the institution would be increased by about three hundred beds at a comparatively small expense, and without the erection of additional buildings for dormitory purposes.

The financial management of the Middletown Hospital has been conducted in such a careful manner that the actual cost to the State per patient, in the way of direct appropriations, has been remarkably small.   The initial cost of establishing a second hospital in another part of the State would be very large, and it is possible that local rivalry and jealousy, with disagreeable complications, might be engendered between two institutions.

On the other hand, however, it is necessary to look beyond the needs of the State in this department for the immediate future and to consider what provision is best for the State's insane wards for several decades to come.   Bearing in mind the steady increase in the number of insane persons committed each year, the possible size of one great institution after the lapse of several years looms up in significant proportions.   It is the practice in some other states to limit the number of patients in a public hospital to about one thousand, and it is stated that there are not more than a dozen institutions for the insane in the country which contain greater numbers.   With all due regard for the State's financial interests, the question of what is the best system for the cure or improvement of individual patients must not be ignored.   In the present case in Connecticut, an attractive site for a new hospital has been offered to the State, and it is claimed that, once the original plant is established, the expense of additions for two institutions will be no greater than for one.   It is believed, also, that another large hospital might offer a place where persons of moderate means, who can well afford to pay more than the low rate charged at Middletown, but not the higher prices of the private sanitariums, could board insane relatives or friends on reasonable terms.

Several cases still occur each year at the Middletown hospital where insane prisoners from the County Jails are committed by order of the County Commissioners under the provisions of Sections 3385 and 3386 of the General Statutes.   This law contains a grave defect in that it makes no provision for the convict's care if his insanity continues longer than the term of his sentence to jail.   Chapter 46 of the Public Acts of 1893, which puts the committing power in the hands of the Governor, contains a remedy for this defect and was intended to supersede the old law, but no definite repealing clause was inserted. As the later law covers all the points of the earlier statutes and is altogether more desirable, it is recommended that repeal be made of Sections 3385, 3386, and 3387 of the General Statutes.

The transfer of thirty insane convicts to the State Prison upon the completion of the insane ward there has removed an exceedingly troublesome group of inmates from the Hospital, but has not relieved, materially, the pressure upon its accommodations.

Upon the occasion of a recent visit to the Hospital, the ventilation in some of the wards was found to be decidedly poor, and it is therefore suggested that more effective apparatus be obtained for this purpose and that some form of power be supplied, if necessary, to keep in circulation artificial currents of air.   In general, it may be said that the institution, when visited, has always given evidence of careful management and of good order and reasonable comfort in the treatment of the inmates.

PRIVATE SANITARIUMS FOR MENTAL AND NERVOUS DISEASES.

The act of the General Assembly of 1897 which requires all private sanitariums for the care of mental diseases to procure a license from the Governor of the State has been generally complied with, and is believed to be a valuable measure in the recognition which it gives to all legally conducted institutions and in the protection which it affords from the possible establishment or maintenance of improperly conducted places. In the absence of a State commission in lunacy in Connecticut, the work of the Board of Charities in this department during the past year has led it to bring two institutions, which were dilatory in this respect, into compliance with the law.

The number of these institutions within the Board's knowledge has been increased by one during the year, Dr. D. W. McFarland, formerly connected with Grey Towers at Stamford, having opened an independent establishment called Hall-Brooke, in the vicinity of the same city. Another sanitarium of this class was in operation during the summer months in the town of Old Saybrook under the charge of a woman physician from New Jersey, who utilized it as a summer outing-place for some of her patients from that state, and who procured a license for the purpose in accordance with the Connecticut statute.

As noted in the last report, Dr. Hallock at Cromwell now makes it a rule to admit only cases of nervous diseases, and his sanitarium is therefore enrolled under the head of private hospitals. Stamford Hall has been enlarged by the erection of new buildings, and Dr. Bowman's establishment, formerly known as Fairlea at Noroton, has been removed to Greenwich, where it occupies a large and handsomely appointed house.

The nine institutions of this class at present in the State exhibit various degrees of material comfort and different methods of management, and range from the small sanitariums which are designed to receive a few wealthy patients, to the larger establishments which are equipped for the care of greater numbers and are provided with some wards for persons of small means where luxuries are not expected. A majority of the patients come from other states than Connecticut, and in many cases the forms of commitment which are legal where the patients reside are accepted as sufficient. An occasional superintendent, however, is more exact in his methods, and has his patients committed by the court of probate for the district in which the sanitarium is situated. A considerable number of patients are designated as voluntary cases, but in some other instances patients are received by order of commitment from physicians,—a practice which is in violation of the Connecticut law governing the care of the insane.

CENSUS OF INSANE AND COMMISSION IN LUNACY.

That the number of insane persons under restraint in the State of Connecticut has increased considerably in recent years may readily be seen by a little study of the institutions provided for their care. Their present distribution is very nearly as follows:

In State Hospital for the Insane, ...	1,895
In Hartford Retreat for the Insane, ...	150
In Private Asylums, ...	250
Among Town Poor, ...	430
	2,725

Under the last heading are many chronic cases who have been under treatment at the State Hospital, but who have been returned to the almshouses when, on account of the overcrowded condition of the institution, their removal became necessary in order to provide accommodations for acute cases in need of immediate treatment. Others have gradually become insane, but have never been examined and adjudged so by any competent authority. Many of both classes would doubtless be benefited by the remedial treatment of a hospital had our State institution sufficient room for them.

The total number of insane persons under restraint is a large one, but does not necessarily prove that this unfortunate class is growing in disproportion to the growing population of the State. Its increase may be accounted for in a considerable degree by the enlarged accommodations provided for the reception of patients at the State Hospital and the reduced cost of maintenance there, by which many who formerly would have been kept at home are now placed in the institution; and, also, by the increased number of private asylums, most of whose inmates are not residents of this State.

In addition to the numbers of insane persons mentioned above, new cases frequently develop in establishments such as the State Prison, County Jails, Hospitals, etc., in which large numbers of persons are confined. With the exception of the insane ward at the State Prison, the present provision for the diagnosis and restraint of such cases is temporary and insufficient.

In recognition, therefore, of the importance of securing for all members of this defective class scientific and humane treatment, the recommendation made in previous reports is herewith repeated, viz: that a commission in lunacy be appointed to act in connection with the State Board of Charities, and be authorized to ascertain that the commitment and detention of patients is in accordance with the provisions of the statutes, to examine and prescribe for new cases in the County Jails, Hospitals, and other institutions, and to exercise a general supervision in the interest of insane persons throughout the State. The appointment in 1897 to the State Board of a physician who is experienced in the treatment of the insane may be regarded as the first step toward the establishment of a joint commission of lunacy and charity in Connecticut, and it is hoped that further developments may be made along these lines.

THE LAKEVILLE SCHOOL FOR IMBECILES.

The School for Imbeciles at Lakeville has had another year of satisfactory effort in behalf of its unfortunate wards. The plan noted in the last report for the erection of a new building, under an appropriation which was made to the School by the State in lieu of the Marett bequest, has not yet been carried into effect but arrangements are now being made to do so at an early date.

The completion of this new building will provide increased facilities for the School's work that have long been needed, but it is desirable that other buildings also should be added, in order to furnish sufficient accommodations for all suitable applicants for admission and to render possible a more exact classification of the inmates. It would be especially fitting if a separate cottage department could be established here for the care of all epileptics in the State who may need the restraining and corrective influences of a specialized form of treatment. The so-called colony plan, by which separate departments are provided for teachable imbeciles, epileptics, and custodial cases, is believed to be most effective in giving each class the treatment best fitted for its needs and in accomplishing the greatest measure of preventive and positive service.

The excellent results already effected at the Lakeville School, and the enlargement of its remedial and educational work that would be possible with increased facilities, warrant the recommendation that a broader and more liberal policy be adopted in the interests of this institution.

THE AMERICAN SCHOOL, AT HARTFORD, FOR THE DEAF.

The contemplated plan for the erection of new buildings for the American School for the Deaf has not as yet been carried into effect, owing to the inability of the trustees to secure at a satisfactory price the desired property which was originally designed for the State reformatory. As the School for many years has expended thousands of dollars from its own endowment funds upon the education of the State's deaf wards, in addition to the public moneys received for that purpose, it would seem to be only fitting that the State, through its agents, should requite the School in this matter with a fair degree of liberality.

The managers of the School will not cease, however, their efforts to provide a suitable domicile and equipment for this successful and respected institution, and if the desired location cannot be obtained, it is possible that new buildings will be erected in the near future upon the present site.

In its present buildings, nevertheless, the School has enjoyed another year of satisfactory progress in all departments. The favor with which it is regarded by the authorities in Massachusetts, a state justly recognized as leading in educational matters and possessing within its own borders two well-known oral schools, is shown by the fact that the number of pupils sent to the School from that state almost equals the number of pupils from Connecticut.   In addition, it may be noted that the number of Connecticut pupils received during the last school year was the largest in the history of the institution.

The class under instruction by the exclusive oral method, which was organized a year ago, has been continued this year with gratifying success, and, in the contemplated alterations at the School, may form the basis of a pure oral department.

The American School strives to follow the golden mean in the education of the deaf, placing first in importance mental development and a knowledge of written language, and adding thereto in the case of every child speech and lip-reading to the degree that his capacity and adaptability allow him to acquire them.

THE MYSTIC ORAL SCHOOL.

Within the past year, the Mystic Oral School has been incorporated under the general laws of the State governing the formation of joint-stock companies. While this action gives the School a nominal standing as an established corporation, it is, nevertheless, more a change of name than of nature, for in reality almost all of the stock is held by the actual manager, Mrs. McGuigan, and by her husband, and a few shares only stand in the names of residents of Mystic and vicinity. No provision has yet been made to represent the State in the management of the institution.

The School has been visited a number of times by representatives of the Board since the publication of the last Report, and on every occasion the actual classroom work of the several divisions has been carefully exhibited by the teachers in charge. Creditable results were shown in some instances, but in many cases it was noticed that the proficiency of a pupil in the use of intelligible speech depended largely upon the amount of hearing possessed or upon a former ability to speak before the hearing was lost.

The acquired speech of almost all deaf persons is, as a rule, very imperfect, sometimes muffled, sometimes harsh, and since their own articulation is so incomplete, it is doubtful if satisfactory intercourse can ever be had among themselves through the channels of lip-reading and speech. Moreover, the great difficulty that is usually experienced by the average hearing person—not a teacher of the deaf—in attempting to converse with orally instructed deaf pupils, makes it probable that the value in after life of their laboriously acquired speech has been considerably overestimated. While it may be true that instruction by the exclusive oral method is desirable for a certain class of deaf pupils, there is, nevertheless, reason to believe that the intellectual development of the majority of deaf persons is greatly stimulated by a judicious use of the sign language as employed in the combined method.

If the pure oral class, already established at the school in Hartford, could be developed sufficiently to satisfy any demand there might be in the State for instruction by this method, there would then be no apparent reason for Connecticut to support longer two institutions for the education of its deaf wards.

THE CONNECTICUT INSTITUTE AND INDUSTRIAL HOME FOR THE BLIND.

As may be seen by reference to the more detailed paragraphs upon the subject in the body of this Report, the provision made by the State for the care of its blind wards is directed by the State Board of Education of the Blind largely toward the institution bearing the title mentioned above.

It is difficult to understand upon just what ground a special State board is maintained in the interests of this private corporation, involving, as it does, a considerable expense to the State in the matter of salaries, office expenses, etc. There appears to be no more valid reason for having a separate Board of Education of the Blind than there would be for having a Board of Education of the Deaf, or any other class of beneficiaries requiring special instruction. So far as known after inquiry made, Connecticut is the only state which indulges in the luxury of an independent Board of Education of the Blind.

An effort was made by the active head of the Connecticut institution during the last session of the General Assembly to have that establishment included in the category of the purely educational institutions of the State, and thus relieved from supervision by the State Board of Charities. The attempt failed deservedly, and in this connection it is desired to call attention to a recent decision of the Court of Appeals in the state of New York in the case of the right of a State Board of Charities to maintain supervision over schools for the blind and the deaf. The verdict is one that might, with equal fitness, be made applicable to conditions in Connecticut.

The case was a most interesting and important one and was commenced at the instance of the New York Institution for the Blind, which denied that it was a charitable institution or was subject to the supervision of the Board. Among the important points settled by this decision of the court of last resort were the following: (1) The mere fact that an institution is partly educational does not exclude it from the provisions of the statutes placing charitable institutions under the supervision of the State Board of Charities. If an institution is both educational and charitable, it falls within those provisions. (2) An institution is to be regarded as charitable in so far as it clothes, educates, and maintains indigent pupils at public expense or by donations from individuals; and as to such pupils, it is subject to the supervision of the State Board of Charities.

The work, of the Connecticut Institute has been continued during the year with more or less of activity in the several departments. In regard to the kindergarten on Asylum avenue, there is little to criticise in the matters of reasonable comfort and satisfactory instruction. While it does not as yet possess some of the advantages of the generously endowed kindergarten department connected with the Perkins Institution at South Boston, where it was formerly the custom to send Connecticut children, it may, nevertheless, have compensating features in the way of accessibility from the children's homes and of the local interest which is aroused by the presence of such an institution in our midst.

The matter of instructing blind persons of more mature years in useful trades, with the idea that they will ultimately become self-supporting, is one that involves more serious difficulties. The experience of the New York Institution with its workshops for the blind, which were maintained for a long period of years, proved so disastrously expensive that it was finally compelled to abolish them.

The Connecticut Institute in its industrial department has been experimenting since its organization with a variety of occupations for the blind. Occasionally, an individual is found who, by inherent ability and faithful application to the work in hand, is finally encouraged to attempt the unequal competition with his seeing brethren, but in the majority of cases it is probable that the blind person will always be dependent in a greater or less degree upon some form of assistance. In fact, the president of the Institute himself has declared in public that blind women must not be expected to become wholly self-supporting, but that a home must be furnished them where, in suitable employment, they may assist somewhat in providing for their own maintenance. The statement of the same official formerly made, that a period of two years of industrial training should be sufficient for the average blind person to become self-supporting at his chosen occupation, must therefore be received with material limitations, at any rate in so far as it relates to the training provided at the Connecticut Institute under its present system of management.

The practice of maintaining a concert company, whose members spend much time traveling through this State and others for the ostensible purpose of interesting people in the work of the institution, and incidentally of raising additional funds for its uses, has been continued with great regularity. During the last school year several blind persons, for each of whom the State was paying three hundred dollars and upward annually in order that they might receive "instruction in the simple branches of education," as provided by law, were included among the number who were thus conducted about the country for the purpose of advertising the institution. Their industrial training at the Institute, for which, presumably, the State funds were being drawn, must have been seriously interrupted, and it is therefore recommended that hereafter no beneficiaries of the State be permitted to have a part in these traveling companies.

When last visited, the industrial department was found to be without a resident superintendent, and it was stated that an effort had been made for some time to dispense with the services of such an official. In the hope, however, of securing systematic direction and effective discipline, the managers of the Institute have since found it necessary to engage a superintendent who will reside upon the premises.

In the last published report of the institution, for the year ending September 30, 1897, a very commendable profit was shown in the cash transactions of the upholstery and printing departments. In addition, there was an apparent balance to the good of almost four thousand dollars from the proceeds of the concert company, besides some twenty-five hundred dollars of receipts from other entertainments and from private contributions. The allowance made by the State of three hundred to three hundred and thirty dollars a year for each blind beneficiary is liberal when compared with the amount paid for the support and instruction of other classes, namely, two hundred dollars for the deaf and one hundred and four dollars for children in the County Homes. In spite of these very considerable receipts from various sources, the financial condition of the institution was frequently reported to be unsatisfactory. When one considers the extremely simple style in which the inmates of the Institute live and the nature of the instruction which is afforded them, it would appear that this imputed financial embarrassment must be due to a lack of skill or exactness in conducting the business affairs of the institution. Attention, therefore, is called to these noticeable defects, and it is urged that measures be adopted in its management which shall have special reference to an economical and accurate administration. A published statement in detail of receipts and expenditures and an explanation of its financial difficulties would be of great value to persons who are interested in the work of the Institute, and would make possible a more intelligent estimate of its needs than can be formed at present.

The State Board of Charities appreciate most fully the difficulties which are necessarily involved in the conduct of any young and struggling institution, and they realize the importance of providing for the unfortunate victims of blindness all practicable forms of employment, as much for the purpose of relieving their otherwise enforced idleness as for the purpose of assisting them to become self-supporting, wholly or in part. It may be that the time has come when Connecticut should support an industrial home, in the real meaning of that term, where the blind beneficiaries of the State may receive shelter and care for an indefinite period of time, and where they may give in return such labor as they are capable of so long as they remain in the institution. The State Board of Charities would be the last body of persons to intentionally discourage a worthy effort for the encouragement and improvement of any class of unfortunate persons, but they nevertheless know that it is their duty to render criticism where criticism is due.

HOSPITALS.

St. Francis' Hospital, at Hartford, is the latest institution of this class to come within the notice of the Board, having been opened on September 1, 1897. It is under the charge of the Roman Catholic order of the Sisters of St. Joseph, but no distinctions of creed or residence are made in the reception of patients.

At Grace Hospital, in New Haven, a large new building of modern design and equipment has been completed at a cost of forty thousand dollars, of which amount twenty-five thousand dollars were appropriated by the State some years ago and the balance has since been raised by private contributions.

At Norwalk, a new hospital building is now in process of erection and will be ready for occupancy, it is expected, in the spring of 1899. In the case of the other hospitals already in service, the usual repairs and improvements have been made and, whenever visited, the institutions in general have given evidence of good management and careful treatment of patients.

At New Britain, the building purchased for the purpose of a public hospital was opened temporarily for the reception of volunteer soldiers in the recent war who were suffering from fevers or other diseases, and an effort is being made to provide for the continuance of the hospital's work on a more permanent basis.   The movements to establish public hospitals in Middletown and Winsted, which were noted in a previous Report, have progressed slowly.

In regard to the employment of State funds in furthering the work of these beneficent institutions, it is desired to draw the attention of the managers and of the general public anew to the fact that the provision of the statute is that the annual appropriation in each case is to be " expended for the support of charity patients and so used as to benefit the different towns as they may from time to time make application."

COUNTY TEMPORARY HOMES.

The work of the eight County Temporary Homes in caring for dependent children has been marked by a large increase in the number of children committed to their charge during the past year.   Reference to the statistical tables, which are included in the chapter on this subject in the body of the Report, will show that three hundred and ninety-three new commitments were made to the Homes, an increase of fifty-six over the number committed during the year previous.   This fact bears evidence to the growing willingness of town officials to have large numbers of children committed to the Homes through the medium of the courts, for under this procedure the cost of their maintenance in the institutions is paid from the State treasury and the towns are thus relieved from the burden of their support.

There would appear to be no more valid reason that a town should avoid the responsibility of supporting its dependent children than that it should do so with regard to the adult poor who have a claim upon it.   If the cost of support in the County Homes were transferred from the State to the towns, where it more properly belongs, there is reason to believe that the number of children committed to their care would be considerably decreased, for the town authorities would then feel it incumbent upon them to make every effort to discover relatives or friends who would provide for the children in their time of need.   It has been suggested that, in some instances, this method might involve suffering in the possible neglect of deserving cases, but it is believed that public opinion is too well educated in these matters at the present day to knowingly permit any such abuses.

The number of family homes that have been secured during the year for children from the County Homes through the efforts of the boards of management, the official visitors in the several towns, and the special agents of the State Board, is three hundred and twenty-two, exceeding by forty the number so secured in the preceding year. This result reveals a commendable activity on the part of the persons concerned, but, in spite of their efforts, the number of children still remaining in the county institutions shows a marked increase, being due largely to the fact that a greater proportion of very young children are now committed to their care for whom it is difficult to secure family homes.

Unless it is desired to make of the County Temporary Homes large institutions in which the tendency will be toward the more permanent residence of their inmates, it will be necessary to check these steadily increasing numbers by the adoption of radical measures. The change from State to town support, it is believed, would prove to be one of the most effective in this respect.

The act of the General Assembly of 1897, which permits the retention of children in almshouses until the age of four years, has not had the desired effect of reducing the total number of children in the county institutions. In regard to the provisions of this act, there has been a question whether children less than four years old should be received, but it is believed to be the general consensus of opinion that the matter rests within the discretion of the board of management, as was formerly the case in respect to children under two years of age.

Probably the most difficult feature connected with the County Home system is the work of securing for the children family homes which shall approach at all closely to the standards of the county institutions in matters of comfort, kindly discipline, and secular and religious instruction. It remains, therefore, for the boards of management and the town committees to put forth every effort for the successful accomplishment of this object, in order that the children may enjoy the advantages of life in family homes, which, other things being equal, is generally conceded to be more conducive to their normal development than that in the best of institutions.

The system of boarding out children in selected family homes, which was adopted in New Haven County two years ago in order to avoid the necessity of erecting extensive buildings, has been continued with results that are considered satisfactory by those who have charge of the work.   It has not decreased the number of family homes that receive children without pay, as was feared by some persons, and every effort is still made to place out the children in the usual way whenever possible.

In the past autumn the buildings of the Windham County Home at Putnam were completely destroyed by fire, but fortunately no loss of life was incurred.   A part of the children are now boarded in family homes in the neighborhood, and plans are under consideration for the erection of new buildings upon the same location.   Fire also destroyed the large barn belonging to the Tolland County Home at Vernon Center earlier in the summer, but a new one has since been completed to replace the loss.

At the Fairfield County Home a substantial brick building especially designed and equipped for hospital purposes has been added to the plant of the institution at a cost of about five thousand dollars.   It has accommodations for about fifty beds, and when not otherwise occupied, may be utilized as a detention cottage for children during the first few weeks of their life in the Home.

The increased pressure upon the accommodations at the New London County Home has made necessary the consideration of plans for an enlargement of its building in all departments, which will probably be carried into effect in the near future.   In the case of the other County Homes, the usual repairs and improvements have been made during the year and all present an appearance of good order and reasonable comfort.

An annual meeting at which the town committees and other interested persons have been present with the board of management, has been held in each of the counties, with the exception of New Haven and Windham, the meeting at the latter having been prevented by the destruction of the Home buildings.   The value of these meetings in providing an opportunity for mutual conference and discussion of the problems involved in the work, makes it important that the board of management in every county should comply with the provisions of the statute law on the subject.

The death rate of children under the charge of the County Homes is remarkably low, especially when one considers the vitiated inheritances which many of them possess and the conditions of poverty and neglect from which they are taken.   In a total of more than a thousand children cared for during the year, only four deaths were reported, a proportion much less than that for the general population of the State.   This fact certainly speaks well for the careful treatment that the children receive in the Homes, and may be accounted for in part by their simple but wholesome style of living, their regular habits, and freedom from exposure in attending school, most of the Homes having schoolrooms directly connected with the main buildings.

Several attempts have been made during the year by selectmen or other officials to place defective children or those suffering from incurable diseases in the County Homes, but in all cases it has been necessary to refuse them admission in accordance with the provisions of the statute, as well as for the general good of the County Home inmates.   Other cases are known where unfortunate children of these classes have, of necessity, been allowed to remain in town almshouses under all their pauperizing influences because no other adequate provision is made for their care.

It is therefore recommended that a separate cottage department be established in connection with one of the County Homes, where all such children who become dependent upon public support, may receive suitable medical care and nursing and may be kept under the supervision of responsible State and county officials.

POOR RELIEF.

Almost all of the one hundred and sixty-eight towns in Connecticut have been visited by representatives of the State Board since the publication of the last printed report, for the purpose of inspecting the provision made for the relief and support of the dependent poor.

In regard to the general condition of the almshouses which are maintained in eighty-eight of the towns, it must be said that they represent widely varying standards of management. The degree of excellence or unfitness, moreover, does not always correspond to the size and wealth of the town in which the house is situated.   In some instances the country farmhouse, which is utilized for the purpose, presents an appearance of greater comfort and neatness than the larger but occasionally ill-kept institution of a more populous town. The majority of almshouses, it is believed, are marked by conditions of reasonable comfort and humane management; a few, only, are positively bad and ought to be replaced.

In several places changes and improvements have been made in equipment and methods during the year, notably at the Hartford almshouse which is rapidly becoming one of the best of its class. Recommendations along these lines, which have been made by the Board, have been well received in a number of instances and have been carried into effect with reasonable promptness.

The chief defects in almshouse arrangements, which have been pointed out in previous reports also, are the want in some cases of a sufficient separation of the sexes, inadequate water supply and facilities for bathing, insufficient provision for heating halls and bedrooms, and the absence of any organized effort to keep the able-bodied " old timers " systematically employed. The lack of regular religious services, of suitable reading matter, and of any social intercourse with people in the world outside, are also noticeable in a number of instances, and it is therefore suggested to the kindly-disposed members of a community that they include the town almshouse in their round of friendly visits.

The Board have been successful during the year in securing the removal of a number of insane persons from almshouses to the State Hospital at Middletown, and the majority of those remaining, it is believed, are cases of a chronic and harmless nature. Many of them, however, would be benefited by removal to surroundings better adapted to their unfortunate condition, if the State institution had accommodations sufficient to receive them.

The few children above the prohibitory age who have been found in almshouses are, for the most part, defective, or sufferers from incurable diseases, and consequently not eligible for admission to the County Homes.

The so-called " State almshouse " at Tariffville, where the small number of regular State paupers are boarded under contract with the Comptroller's office, has been visited several times during the year by members of the Board, and on almost every occasion has given evidence of some unsatisfactory condition. Certain alterations have been effected at the instigation of the Board, chiefly in the matters of separating the sexes and of removing a number of sleeping cells from the basement, but the house in its general arrangement and equipment is still unsuited for the use of any large number of persons.

The immediate care of the establishment has been in the hands of a resident matron, concerning whom so many complaints of ill-treatment of inmates were received that it became necessary for the Board to secure her removal. In view of the low character and offensive habits of some of the inmates, it would appear extremely desirable that a man and his wife should be employed as resident superintendents who, in respect to character and habits, should be above reproach.

If the State paupers only were cared for here, the accommodations would be ample, but a majority of the inmates are boarded at the place by the several towns to which they belong, in direct violation of Section 3310 of the General Statutes. This law provides that " it shall not be lawful for any town or the selectmen thereof, to remove any pauper out of the town to which such pauper belongs to be supported in any other town." An effort should be made, therefore, to devise some measure by which the unfortunate poor of a town may not be forced into such associations as prevail under the present system of management at the Tariffville institution.

In the case of the town of Danbury, which possesses a new almshouse the equal of any in the State, it was found that the old building, which had previously been condemned as unfit for use, was still being employed by the selectmen as lodgings for a large number of dependent families. It was, in fact, an almshouse full of children and disorderly adults, all living in an atmosphere of pauperism and disease. After repeated visits to the place by members of the Board, assisted also by members of the State Board of Health, the removal of the inmates to more suitable quarters was secured. A more detailed account of the investigation may be found in the body of the Report.

In regard to towns which maintain no almshouses, but which board the dependent poor in such families as the town officials see fit to select, it is found that the visits of the State Board of Charities often result in materially improving the condition of the poor. The boarding places chosen are frequently with families who live on back roads in retired rural districts where they are seldom disturbed by inquiring visitors, or even by the town officials themselves. Without serious intention, perhaps, the care of the boarder is in some cases gradually neglected, until instances have been discovered where the rooms and clothing supplied have been poor beyond description. In a number of cases a radical improvement of existing conditions, or removal to a more desirable boarding place, has been effected through the efforts of the Board.

In previous years it has been the custom of the Board to prepare tables of statistics of the cost of public poor relief by gathering the facts from the printed reports which the selectmen of the towns annually prepare and present to their several communities. On account of the fact that the town reports are published at widely varying dates and that the work of collecting them was often delayed, it was never possible for the Board to publish more recent statistics than those for the preceding year.

With the intention of securing the statistics for the current year under review, an effort has been made by the Board to effect a compliance on the part of town selectmen with the provisions of Section 3312 of the General Statutes, which states that "Overseers of the poor shall annually, in October, make return of the number of persons supported and relieved, with the cost, to the State Board of Charities."

For this purpose a circular letter was sent to all town selectmen in October, 1897, notifying them that the returns of statistics, as provided for in the statute, would be called for in the fall of 1898. In October of this year, therefore, a blank form for statistical returns, accompanied by an explanatory letter, was sent to the selectmen in every town. Second and third copies had to be sent to many of them before replies could be secured, and even by the middle of November, eight towns had failed to answer the repeated requests, among the delinquent officials being the selectmen of Waterbury, whose office is in close proximity to that of the Board's secretary.

The answers made to the simple questions asked were in some cases so imperfect that it is feared that the statistical tables for the present report will not be so complete as is desirable, but it is hoped that by another year measures may be adopted which will insure a more prompt and accurate return of the desired information.

The disbursement of the so-called "outdoor relief" is a matter that involves the expenditure of thousands of dollars annually by the selectmen or other officials entrusted with the direction of public charity, and that affords frequent opportunities for the possible exercise of favoritism and political patronage. It would be well if a more frequent statement than the annual town report were required of all such officials, at least every three months, for instance, which should show in detail the manner of disbursing such relief and the recipients thereof, and should be open to the inspection of any authorized and responsible person.   In the larger cities, especially, where charity organization societies are already in existence, it is desirable that active co-operation should be maintained between them and the official overseers of the poor, in accordance with the recognized principles of such societies, with a view to preventing, so far as possible, a re-duplication of relief, and of securing the greatest measure of benefit for all concerned with the least practicable expenditure.

PRIVATE PROVISION FOR AGED AND YOUNG.

Although not in receipt of public moneys and therefore not included in the category of public charities, the number of Private Homes throughout the State for the care of the dependent aged and young supplement in a measure the work of the public institutions provided for these classes. On this account and in order to make a more complete record of charitable effort in the State, it has been customary during recent years to visit these establishments occasionally and to include a brief description of them in the Board's Report.   In certain instances, circumstances warrant the belief that these private institutions might with advantage be placed under the closer supervision of responsible officials.

The number of these institutions to come under the notice of the Board has been increased by three within the last year, and new and enlarged buildings have been added to several of those already established.

With reference to the conditions of the organization of these institutions, it is to be regretted that the scope of their work is so closely confined, being generally governed by denominational differences, local sentiment, and limitations in deeds of trust in the case of those founded by bequests.

NATIONAL CONFERENCE OF CHARITIES AND CORRECTION.

The quarter-centennial meeting of the National Conference of Charities and Correction was held in New York city in May, 1898, and was marked by an enthusiasm and brilliancy in matters of attendance, speakers, addresses, and discussions that well befitted the unusual character of the event.

The leading thought of the Conference this year was the relation of the State to its delinquent, defective, and dependent classes, and the various sessions proved to be of unusual interest and profit. Opportunity also was enjoyed for the inspection of a number of important charitable and reformatory institutions of the city under personal direction, and a most cordial hospitality was extended to the delegates by many leaders in philanthropic effort.

Connecticut was represented by the managers of the Industrial School for Girls and of the Lakeville School, by members of the State Board of Charities, who bore also credentials from the Governor as representatives of the State, and by a number of scattering delegates. It is a cause for regret that the managers of other institutions in Connecticut do not attend these annual gatherings, where the personal meeting with expert workers in similar lines of effort and the consequent interchange of thought and discussion of methods might often result in improved conditions in our own State.

The Conference of 1899 will be held in Cincinnati, Ohio, and will undoubtedly be of much practical benefit for all who attend its meetings. The Connecticut State Board is represented in the make-up of its committees and officers, and it is urged that many of the institutions, also, in the State send delegates there.

. During the summer vacation, visits were made by two representatives of the Board to a number of institutions in New Hampshire, among them being the State Prison and the State Hospital for the Insane at Concord and the State Industrial School for Boys and Girls at Manchester, besides the county jail, poorhouse, workhouse, and insane asylum near the latter city. Considerable information of value was gained in regard to their working methods, particularly in the case of the county institutions.

EXPENSE TO STATE.

In this State, with an estimated population in 1897 of 850,000, it is known that the following institutions are maintained for the restraint and care of its delinquent, defective, and dependent classes. For —

Criminals and Offenders,	. 11	(State Prison and County Jails).
Juvenile Offenders,	. 2	(School for Boys and Industrial School).
The Insane, . . .	. 11	(State Hospital, Retreat, 9 Private Asylums).
The Feeble-Minded,	. 1	(School for Imbeciles).
The Deaf, ...	. 2	(American School and Mystic Oral School).
The Blind, . . .	. 1	(Institute and Industrial Home).
The Sick and Injured,	. 18	(Hospitals, Public and Private).
Old Soldiers, . . .	. 1	(Fitch's Home for Soldiers).
Dependent Children,	. 8	(County Temporary Homes).
Paupers, ...	. 89	(Town Almshouses, Almshouse for State Paupers).
The Aged, Private Provision,	16	(Old People's Home).
The Young, Private Provision,	16	(Orphan Asylums and Homes).

Total, ... 176

The total amount of State aid which has been applied to the support, in whole or in part, of these institutions during the year was $658,190.20. As compared with the total amount so expended for the fiscal year 1897, a considerable reduction is noticed, which may be partly accounted for by the fact that some $58,000 less was devoted to building operations than in the former year. The most noticeable increase of expenditure is seen in the case of the County Temporary Homes and the Home for Disabled Soldiers, in both of which departments, there has been a considerable increase in the number of inmates supported.

The work of the special committee that was appointed by the General Assembly of 1897 to investigate the condition of the State's receipts and expenditures has brought to light during the year an inexactness in the methods of handling the public funds at more than one of the State-aided institutions. This carelessness, if no severer word be used, was shown in one instance at least to be an accompaniment to a long-continued practice that was originated, it may be, with no intention of irregularity. Too much attention, however, cannot be given at every institution which is in receipt of appropriations from the public treasury to the matters of expending all such funds with the greatest advantage to the State's beneficiaries, and of rendering a just and accurate account of the stewardship entrusted to it.

The amounts paid by towns for the support and relief of their poor population may be found by reference to the statistical tables contained in the chapter on poor relief in the body of the Report.

The total sum expended for the care of the criminal and dependent classes is a large one for a State of the size and population of Connecticut, but, as may be seen in the foregoing review of the several departments, certain institutions are still in need of more generous appropriations for the development of legitimate and desirable purposes. The conclusion is therefore reached that greater liberality should be shown in some instances and a more intelligent economy be exercised in others.

Respectfully submitted,

HEMAN C. WHITTLESEY, Middletown,
REBEKAH G. BACON, New Haven,
MARY HALL, Hartford,
GEORGE F. SPENCER, Deep River,
EDWIN A. DOWN, M.D., Hartford, ·
Members of the State Board of Charities.

CHARLES P. KELLOGG, Waterbury,
Secretary.

EXPENSE TO THE STATE

FOR THE

Delinquent, Defective, and Dependent Classes,

For the Two Years ending September 30, 1897 and 1898.

	Year ending Sept. 30, 1897.	Year ending Sept. 30, 1898.
Connecticut State Prison, . . .	$48,583.92	$40,342.61
" State Prison, Building, . .	30,000.00	21,000.00
" Prison Association, .	3,020.00	2,995.00
" State Board of Pardons, . .	355.25	299.55
" State Reformatory, Building, .	17,783.30	1,099.84
" Industrial School for Girls, .	42,301.05	42,004.81
" School for Boys, . .	71,353.69	67,713.81
" School for Boys, Building, .	5,000.00	5,000.00
Prisoners in Jails, eight counties, .	123,077.88	114,493.76
Connecticut Hospital for Insane, .	*105,793.22	86,467.21
Hartford Retreat for Insane, .	3,157.13	3,162.58
Connecticut School for Imbeciles, .	17,872.13	19,279.00
Connecticut School for Imbeciles, Building,	8,000.00	. . . .
American School for Deaf, . .	13,211.85	13,942.17
Mystic Oral School, . .	4,657.95	5,307,62
Perkins Institution for the Blind, .	5,572.93	5,325.23
Connecticut Institute for the Blind, .	14,389.95	15,155.64
State Board of Education of the Blind, .	3,248.57	3,523.54
New Haven Hospital, . .	5,000.00	5,000.00
Grace Hospital, . . .	5,000.00	5,000.00
Grace Hospital, Building, .	25,000.00	. . . .
Hartford Hospital, . , .	5,000.00	5,000.00
Bridgeport Hospital, . .	5,000.00	5,000.00
Danbury Hospital, . .	5,000.00	5,000.00
Memorial Hospital, New London, .	5,000.00	5,000.00
Backus Hospital, Norwich, .	5,000.00	5,000.00
Meriden Hospital, . .	3,000.00	3,000.00
Waterbury Hospital, . .	2,500.00	3,000.00
Norwalk Hospital, . .	. . . .	3,125.00
Day-Kimball Hospital, Putnam, .	875.00	1,750.00
Fitch's Home for Soldiers, . .	70,000.00	80,000.00
Burial of Soldiers, . .	10,617.50	10,052.50
Soldiers' Orphans, . .	3,574.40	3,215.72
Temporary Homes, eight counties, .	59,914.29	66,348.33
State Paupers, . . .	4,998.37	5,586.28
	$732,858.38	$658,190.20

Total for year ending Sept. 30, 1896, . $662,329.76
Total for year ending Sept. 30, 1895, . $588,721.61

* Fourteen months.

THE CONNECTICUT STATE PRISON,
. WETHERSFIELD.

Under the control of a Board of seven Directors appointed by the Governor with the advice and consent of the Senate.

MR. JABEZ L. WOODBRIDGE, *Warden.*

Visited quarterly by two members of the Board.

The Connecticut State Prison is located at Wethersfield, four miles south from Hartford, and is easily reached by electric cars which pass the Prison grounds. The buildings are of brownstone and brick, placed well back from the street, and are surrounded by twenty-six acres of land extending from the street in front to the Connecticut River in the rear.

The central portion contains the guardroom and on the upper floors the Prison offices and quarters for the officers. The part to the left of the entrance, which is now called the west end, was built in 1827 and formed the whole of the original Prison. The east end, in the rear of the warden's residence, was added in 1835 and is now used as the women's department. In 1886 there was built the main block of cells, which extends directly back from the guardroom.

MAIN CELL BLOCK.

The main block is built of brick and contains three hundred and ninety-six cells arranged in five tiers. It is completely surrounded by a wide hallway and is divided longitudinally by a passway on each tier which contains the water and ventilating pipes and permits each cell to be inspected from the rear by the guard officer. The halls and cells are well lighted and ventilated by long windows in the outer walls and by a system of pipes which connect with the outer air by ventilators in the roof.

As a measure of safety, it is desirable that the guardroom should be enlarged by an addition of several feet upon the west side so that officers stationed there might then be able to survey both sides of the main block without leaving their post of duty.

All the cells are identical in size and measure on the inside, 7 feet $4\frac{1}{2}$ inches in height, 8 feet in length, and 4 feet $11\frac{1}{2}$ inches in width. Each is furnished with a single bed, sheets and

6

blankets, pillow and pillow-case, and a chair. A small shelf in each cell, to be attached to the door for use at meal times, is a convenient addition to the furnishings. At the back of the cell are a water-closet and wash-stand supplied with running water and soap and towel. The cells are lighted by electric lights, as are all departments of the institution, the work having been completed about a year ago. Each prisoner is held responsible for the condition of his cell, and is expected to keep his quarters so neat and clean that they will pass a daily inspection. Every man is required to bathe weekly and is furnished with a clean set of underclothing. Shower baths, sixteen in number, of modern sanitary design, are situated in a room adjoining the main block.

KITCHEN, STOREHOUSE, AND PRINTING-OFFICE.

The kitchen and bakery are situated at the northeast corner of the main block, and are equipped with all needful apparatus for the preparation of food in large quantities. A window connects the kitchen with the hall surrounding the main block, and through it the rations are served to the men as they pass to their cells. The food is plain but wholesome, and for the main body of prisoners is selected from a reasonable variety of staple articles.

The storehouse, situated near the northwest corner of the main block, furnishes room for the systematic arrangement of large quantities of supplies. The storekeeper has an office in the building, and a system is maintained of drawing requisitions thereon for all supplies needed in the various departments. On the first floor, also, is a small printing-office, where the job-printing required in the institution is done, and where, under the direction of the chaplain, a monthly paper is published to which the prisoners contribute a considerable portion of the contents.

CHAPEL, NIGHT SCHOOL, AND LIBRARY.

The chapel is situated on the first floor at the left of the guardroom, and, as enlarged a year ago by the addition of the old schoolroom, contains about five hundred and fifty sittings. Religious services are held every Sunday morning as follows: from nine to ten o'clock a service is conducted by a Roman Catholic priest; between ten and eleven o'clock, Sunday-school classes, both Protestant and Roman Catholic, at which the attendance is optional, are held in the same room.

The former are taught by teachers from the Hartford Young Men's Christian Association, and the latter by young men sent down from the Roman Catholic churches of the city. From eleven to twelve o'clock a Protestant church service is conducted by the chaplain, which is attended by the prisoners in a body. The women prisoners are placed in the gallery and are so screened as not to be seen by the men below. On Monday evenings are held the meetings of the Christian Endeavor Society, composed of about twenty-five prisoners who have records of the better class and are interested in religious matters.

In the schoolroom on Tuesday, Wednesday, and Friday evenings instruction is given, under the direction of the chaplain, assisted by teachers from among the prisoners, to a limited class of men whose records are good and who wish to obtain the elements of education, such as reading and writing. About one-third of the convicts, many of whom are foreigners, are unable to read or write, and it has not been thought best to attempt any of the higher branches of education.

The library contains about four thousand volumes, which have been purchased from time to time by means of an annual appropriation of three hundred dollars made for that purpose by the State. It is under the direction of the chaplain, and on Mondays and Fridays the men are allowed to make selections from the catalogue, a copy of which is placed in each cell.

During the winter a number of entertainments are given for the improvement and amusement of the prisoners. They consist of musicales, readings, lectures, stereopticon exhibitions, etc., and are given voluntarily by clubs, societies, and individuals.

HOSPITAL.

The hospital is situated over the chapel and schoolroom and is a large airy room, well lighted and ventilated by long windows on the south side and by a cupola overhead. On one side is a row of beds for convalescent patients and on the other a series of six rooms for those who are seriously ill. An inclosed balcony near the hospital door gives opportunity to enjoy sunshine and fresh air to convalescent patients who are unable to descend the long stairs to the yard below.

Between the main hospital and the ward for contagious diseases beyond, is a room where patients are isolated who are suffering from pulmonary phthisis in an aggravated form. Prisoners who are afflicted with the disease in an incipient stage, but who are yet able to work in the shops, occupy a row of contiguous cells in the main block, with which special sanitary precautions are taken.

During the past year the plan was adopted of having a resident physician stationed at the Prison, who has charge of the hospital and looks after the physical condition of the prisoners in general.

WEST END.

The west end now contains a block of sixty-four steel cells of modern design, arranged in four tiers, the upper two tiers having been completed under an appropriation from the General Assembly of 1897, and first used about a year ago.   They are completely furnished and are occupied by prisoners of the first grade, as noted later.   At the end of this block is a special kitchen from which meals are served for this department and also for the new insane ward which adjoins it beyond.

INSANE WARD.

The insane ward, for which an appropriation of $38,000 was made by the General Assembly of 1897, was completed and first occupied in January, 1898, the thirty insane criminals at that time confined in the Hospital for the Insane at Middletown being then transferred to this new department of the Prison.

The building is a substantial one of brick and brownstone, two stories and basement in height, and is built in the manner known as mill or slow-burning construction.   It stands at right angles to the west end of the Prison, with which it is connected by a dining-room, with a workshop above.   The main building contains rooms for sixty inmates, besides sitting-rooms for use in the daytime, wards for disturbed or suicidal cases, officers' rooms, bath and toilet rooms, etc.   The plumbing, heating, and ventilating systems are all of the most approved modern design.   An inclosed yard furnishes opportunity for out-of-door exercise, and employment is provided for all who can avail themselves of it in the workroom.

In connection with the insane ward, a consulting physician in lunacy has been appointed whose duty it is to visit this department at least once a month, or whenever requested by the Prison officers, or by the Governor, and to examine the condition and treatment of the persons there confined.

CLASSIFICATION OF PRISONERS AND PAROLE SYSTEM.

In accordance with the system of classifying the inmates of the Prison which was adopted in 1896, three grades are established, of which the second includes the general body of prisoners and is the one in which all newcomers are enrolled on arrival.   From this grade, promotions to the first grade may be made by the Board of Directors upon the written recommendation of the warden, in recognition of a prisoner's general cheerfulness and obedience to rules, steady effort in labor, and exemption from punishment for a period of at least six months prior to the recommendation.   A serious violation of the rules and a violation of the qualifications for promotion subjects a prisoner to forfeiture of membership in the first grade.   Reduction from this grade is made by the warden, and no prisoner so reduced is eligible for re-entrance within a year thereafter. Members of the second grade wear suits of a dull gray color.

Any prisoner who seriously or persistently violates the rules is reduced to the third grade by the warden for a period of thirty days.   At the expiration of that time, if the prisoner has been obedient, he is restored to the second grade, but a continued violation of the rules subjects him to detention in the third grade for another period of thirty days.   Any further extension of time in this grade may be made at the discretion of the Board of Directors.   Members of the third grade are clad in suits of bright red and are deprived of all privileges.

The members of the first grade wear neat uniforms of cadet blue, occupy the new cells in the west end, and enjoy a number of extra privileges in matters of food and tobacco, letter-writing, and the reading of certain secular weekly newspapers.   In addition, one hour a fortnight is granted for debate or literary exercises under the direction of the chaplain, for which purpose a club organization has been adopted, officered by the prisoners. . These meetings are suspended during the summer months, as are also those of the Christian Endeavor Society.

All convicts on entering the Prison receive a thorough physical and mental examination, and a variety of physical measurements is taken of every man according to the Bertillon system, which are of such a nature as to insure his future identification.   The data thus obtained are entered, together with photographs of the subject considered, upon cards which are then filed for reference.   When a central bureau of the system is established, as expected, at Washington, D. C., its usefulness as a means of correspondence between penal institutions will be greatly increased.

The parole law, which was enacted by the General Assembly of 1897, authorizes the State Board of Pardons, under such regulations as it may establish, to release upon parole first-term convicts who have served at least half their full sentence, whose record in the Prison suggests probable reformation, and for whom suitable employment has been obtained.

WORKSHOPS.

In the Prison yard, west of the main block, are the workshops, where five of the rooms are occupied with the industry of shoe-making. The work is carried on under contracts made for a period of five years, and employs the services of two hundred and forty-five men at the rate of fifty cents per day for each. The amount thus earned during the year ending September 30, 1897, was $35,963.75, and during that ending September 30, 1898, $35,805.38.

About the first of September, 1895, the industry of shirt-making was begun in shop No. 4. This work, also, is under a five-year contract which calls for the services of from sixty to one hundred men. At a recent visit there were ninety employed. The price paid for this work is on the piece-work plan, by which the State receives fifty cents per dozen shirts, and it was expected that each man would turn out about that number a day. The amount received on the contract during the year ending September 30, 1897, was $6,966.61, and during that ending September 30, 1898, $8,254.50.

The working hours for all the shops are, in summer, from 7 A. M. until noon, and from 1 till 6 P. M. In winter the hours are necessarily shorter, as the shops are purposely not supplied with artificial lights, so that the prisoners are kept at work only so long as daylight lasts.

REPAIR SHOP AND LAUNDRY.

The State shop, so-called, is a detached two-story brick building situated in the yard east of the main block and is used as a repair shop and laundry. Here is also the tailoring department, where two men are employed in cutting and making all the prison uniforms. All such work as the re-binding of library books, repairing and making tin mess pans and cups, shoe and harness mending, painting and varnishing, blacksmithing, tire setting, or any incidental work, is carried on in this building.

The laundry has an average weekly washing of about three thousand pieces and is well-equipped with steam wringer, drying-frame, and a large steam sterilizer through which all the bedding and clothing are passed, thus destroying any disease germs.

OUT-OF-DOOR WORK AND EXERCISE.

A part of the land attached to the Prison and an adjoining tract leased from outside parties are cultivated by the prisoners, who raise considerable quantities of vegetables and general farm produce. All prisoners who are employed outside the walls are clad in conspicuous suits of black and white stripes.

It is now the stated intention of the authorities to give each prisoner, who is employed in the workshops, one hour's exercise in the open air per week, when the weather is pleasant. The men are taken to the east yard at 7:30 o'clock in the morning, one shop squad at a time, and are put through the setting-up exercises of the United States Army and the covering at quickstep of a distance from two to three miles. This exercise is omitted during the months of June, July, and August, on the ground that the weather then is too hot for its enjoyment; but in view of the early morning hour for which it is scheduled, the reason given for its discontinuance appears to be of little value. It is urged, therefore, that this slight opportunity for healthful exercise be provided at all seasons of the year.

WOMEN'S DEPARTMENT.

This department is situated in the east wing, under the charge of a matron, and consists of a large room with two tiers of five cells each, ranged on the north side, and on the south side a row of five temporary wooden cells constructed to accommodate an increased number of women prisoners. The cells are larger than those used for the male convicts and are more comfortably furnished. The heating and ventilating apparatus in this department, as well as that in the hospital, was thoroughly renovated about a year ago in accord with the modern system in use in other parts of the Prison. The women inmates are all regularly employed; they have the use of sewing-machines and make and mend all the sheets, pillow-cases, and shirts used in the Prison, and mend all of the underwear. They also do the laundry work for the officers of the institution in an adjoining room. A small court, enclosed by a high stone wall, serves as a drying yard and also as an exercise ground for the women in fair weather.

EXECUTION HOUSE.

The present execution house, a one-story brick structure situated in the east yard, contains two steel cells, comfortably furnished, where the condemned man (or two if circumstances so require), spends his last hours under the close supervision of the death watch. In an adjoining room is the machine by which the hanging is performed; it has been used for several executions and is considered by the authorities to be satisfactory.

REGULATIONS, PUNISHMENTS, AND REPORTS.

On entering the institution, each inmate is provided with a set of the Prison rules and regulations. Men who are reported for petty violation of rules, are warned in the first instance, but on successive repetitions are, according to circumstances, placed in solitary confinement, kept upon short rations, or, what they feel most keenly of all, are docked a portion of their good time allowance, which would otherwise accumulate at the rate of five days per month for good behavior and would be deducted from the period for which they were sentenced. No officer is allowed to strike a prisoner except in self-defense. Reduction from a higher to a lower grade, under the present system of classifying the prisoners, is also employed as a measure of discipline.

Six light punishment cells for the confinement of less serious offenders are situated in a room adjoining the main cell block and are well ventilated and entirely above ground. Here unruly prisoners are restrained for varying periods of time, and in some cases are required to stand with an arm chained to the wall at about the height of one's head.

In the cellar under this room are six cells for solitary confinement, which are built of brick, each independent of the others, and have double steel doors in front, with apertures and gratings through which food may be passed to the more violent persons confined. The cells are dry and well ventilated, but are sufficiently dark and lonely to make confinement in them undesirable. Prisoners confined here are given bread and water twice a day and are visited daily by the Prison physician. In another part of this cellar is a secluded cell for the punishment of especially vicious prisoners, which, by its peculiar wedge-shaped construction, precludes the possibility of unforeseen attack upon an officer by the person confined therein.

An elaborate system of daily reports is kept, which gives

to the warden a complete record of the condition and occupation of all the prisoners.

NUMBER OF INMATES AND COST OF SUPPORT.

Since the completion of the new cells in the west end, the Prison contains a total of four hundred and seventy-five cells, besides the twelve devoted to the uses of light punishment and solitary confinement.   For the years ending September 30, 1897 and 1898, the statistics of the Prison were as follows:

	1897.	1898.
Number of inmates October 1, 1896 and 1897, .	386	446
Number admitted during year, . . .	221	294
Total present, ...	607	740

	1897	1898
Discharged by expiration of sentence, . .	141	204
Discharged by Board of Pardons, . . .	3	4
Released on parole, ...	0	4
Died in hospital from phthisis, . . .	5	5
Died in hospital from other causes, . .	0	4
Died by suicide, ...	1	0
Died in insane ward, other causes, . .	0	1
Executed by hanging, ...	2	3
Pardoned by President of U. S., . . .	0	1
Sent to Insane Hospital, Middletown, . .	8	0
Sent to Insane Hospital, Washington, D. C., .	1	1
Remaining in prison September 30, '97 and '98,	446	513
	607	740

	1897	1898
Highest number present, 1897 and 1898, . .	451	517
Lowest number present, 1897 and 1898, . .	382	443
Average number present, 1897 and 1898, . .	432.5	505.6
Number of insane convicts, Sept. 30, '97 and '98,	32	31
Number of prisoners in First Grade, Sept. 30, .	42	64
Number in Second and Third Grades, . .	404	449
Number of female prisoners present Sept. 30, .	15	9

The annual increase in the number of prisoners during the last few years is very marked and, unless checked by influences now unforeseen, will demand a material enlargement of the Prison's accommodations at an early date.

The amounts paid by the State for the maintenance of the Prison have been:

For the year ending September 30, 1897,   .   . $48,583.92
For the year ending September 30, 1898,   .   . 40,342.61

These sums include the expenses of the directors, the services of examiners in lunacy, etc., in addition to the amounts necessary to make good the deficiency in the earnings of the Prison to support its inmates.

VISITORS.

Under the present regulations visitors from the general public are admitted to the Prison on Wednesdays at the discretion of the warden, but on other days only on a written permit from the warden or one of the directors. Each prisoner in the first and second grades is allowed to receive one visit a month on Fridays from relatives or friends in the presence and hearing of an officer.

CONNECTICUT PRISON ASSOCIATION,
HARTFORD.

MR. JOHN C. TAYLOR, *Secretary and Agent.*

Since the date of its incorporation in 1879, this Association has carried on a systematic and continuous work in assisting prisoners at the time of their discharge to reach their families or friends and to secure honest employment. The Society is supported by private contributions and donations and receives also an annual appropriation from the State of three thousand dollars, almost all of which is spent in actual assistance to the prisoners.

A committee from the Society visits the Prison every month and there interviews each prisoner who is to be discharged during the month succeeding, giving him an opportunity to discuss his plans for the future and to avail himself of the Association's help. At the time of his release, he is met by the agent, who accompanies him to the Society's office in the Capitol and assists him in determining upon the first steps of his new life.

It is the stated design of the Association to stand by each man with material assistance until he can have honest, self-supporting employment, and in the event of his getting out of employment to assist him again to get other work. Also as an incentive to good behavior, it is agreed with each man that if he lives an upright, industrious life, steps will be taken to secure a passage of a resolution by the Legislature restoring to him his forfeited rights as a citizen (after having given evidence of his reform by continuing in the right path for a year or more).

The work of such an organization, when rightly conducted, ought to prove of considerable value, but there is reason to believe that more effective agencies than the Society now provides, would be required to complete the reformation of any great number of criminals.

A brief statistical statement of the Society's work for the last two years is as follows:

	Year Ending Sept. 30, '97.	Year Ending Sept. 30, '98.
Discharged by expiration of sentence, .	. 141	203
Discharged by Board of Pardons, . .	. 3	4
Paroled by Board of Pardons, . .	. 0	4
Pardoned by President of United States, .	. 0	1
Total, ...	. 144	212
Assisted by the Association, . .	. 144	212
Assisted those discharged previously, .	. 17	9
Assisted prisoners discharged from jails, .	. 3	7
Total, ...	. 164	228

The amounts expended by the Association for the aid of discharged prisoners were:

For the year ending September 30, 1897, . . $2,363.27
For the year ending September 30, 1898, . . 3,132.59

REFORMATORIES.

THE CONNECTICUT SCHOOL FOR BOYS,
MERIDEN.

Under the management of a Board of twelve Trustees, appointed by the Senate, one from each County, and four from the vicinity of the Institution.

MR. CHARLES M. WILLIAMS, *Superintendent,*
(Formerly Superintendent of Public Schools in Meriden).
Visited quarterly by two members of the Board.

The Connecticut School. for Boys, as the State Reform School has been known since its change of title by the Legislature of 1893, is pleasantly situated on a high elevation of land fronting on Colony street, about half a mile north of the center of Meriden.   The buildings are built of brick and consist of a large main building, five detached cottages, a chapel, shop for repair work and outbuildings; a large brick barn of modern design and equipment has been completed recently to replace the former one destroyed by fire.

The main building is used for the congregate department, so called, which is arranged in two divisions and usually comprises about two hundred boys, although the building has total accommodations for more than three hundred and fifty.   Each division has its separate schoolroom, playroom, dormitory, and dining room, all of which are neatly furnished.   The south division contains the older and more vicious fellows, while the north division is composed of younger boys who are not adapted for admission to the cottages.   The fourth story of the central portion has been fitted up for hospital purposes and has been thoroughly renovated during the past year.   In many respects it is ill-adapted to such use, and by reason of its height from the ground, suggests dangerous possibilities in case of fire.   A separate cottage hospital with provision for isolating cases of contagious diseases is greatly needed.

A wing in the rear of the main building contains the kitchen, bakery, and laundry, each of which employs a squad of half a dozen boys. On the upper floors are the tailorshop, shoe-shop, printing-office, classroom for telegraphy, and a large shop for cane-seating chairs, which is used by the two divisions in common. About a dozen boys are employed in the tailor-shop, where the trousers, vests, and shirts used in the School are manufactured, and about eight others in the printing-office, where they conduct a general printing business and publish the monthly paper of the School. On both sides of this wing are yards for exercise and recreation, which are inclosed with high fences and, for reasons of cleanliness and safety, are paved throughout with asphalt. New iron fences of substantial frame work, covered with corrugated sheet iron, were completed about a year ago under an appropriation from the General Assembly of 1897, which provided, also, for the complete renovation of the plumbing in the main building.

Each of the five detached cottages has accommodations for fifty boys, and contains a dormitory, dining room, schoolroom, playroom, and workshop for cane-seating chairs. Each cottage is under the supervision of a man and his wife, who make an effort to conduct them on the family plan, kindly discipline and restraint taking the place of bolts and bars and high fences. The more tractable boys are lodged in the cottages, being assigned among the several households as their natures and dispositions prove most suitable, while the unruly and vicious characters are confined in the main building. A pleasant playground is set apart for each cottage, and the boys from the different houses occasionally come together for ball games or other athletic contests.

The usual daily routine consists of six hours for work in the various departments, three hours in the schoolrooms, and ten hours allotted for sleep, while the remaining five hours are devoted to meals, incidental duties, and recreation. The eight schools in the institution are graded and provide instruction in all the ordinary branches of a common-school education. It has not been customary for the boys in the printing-office to attend school, the work there being considered equivalent to instruction in the ordinary English branches, but plans are now under consideration to arrange certain classes for their benefit. Devotional exercises are held morning and evening during the week, and on Sundays preaching and Sunday-school services are conducted in the chapel. It is expected that a chaplain will be employed hereafter to take charge of the Sunday services and to act as moral preceptor for the boys. Roman

Catholic priests are in attendance for mass once in two weeks. Entertainments of various sorts are given at intervals through the winter months.

At the rear of the buildings lies the School farm of one hundred and ninety-five acres, upon which a group of about a dozen boys is employed under the direction of the farmer. About the same number are engaged in caring for the School grounds, while the boys of the several cottages exercise considerable rivalry in the cultivation of vegetable gardens. A building is provided for classes in working trades, but little is done in this direction beyond the accomplishment of minor repairs upon the School property. By far the largest part of the boys are engaged in the occupation of cane-seating chairs. The School band furnishes opportunity for instruction in music to a class of about thirty.

Boys under sixteen years of age may be committed to the guardianship of the School during their minority by any court of record in the State. Through uniform good conduct, a boy may earn successive promotions and reach the honor grade in a year from the time of entrance, when he is eligible for dismissal on probation. The average time of residence is twenty-two months. When released on probation, it is expected that each boy will report to the School once in six months, but the rule is not uniformly followed and little supervision is exercised over the boys on parole.

For petty offenses the punishment is transfer to a lower grade, which involves a lengthened stay in the School. Other means of discipline are deprivation of privileges, and solitary confinement in small rooms for reflection, with no occupation and with a diet of bread and water. For serious or repeated offenses, corporal punishment may be inflicted, but in severe cases usually in the presence of the superintendent.

In connection with the maintenance of effective discipline, and in consideration of the record for the past year, stress is laid upon the necessity for unceasing care upon the part of the management to prevent the escape of boys from the School, and in the event of such escapes, to employ every possible means for the prompt recovery of the runaways.

The general statistics of the School are as follows:

	Year Ending Sept. 30, 1897.	Year Ending Sept. 30, 1898.
Number in School October 1, 1896 and 1897, .	469	443
Received during the year, ...	164	159
Received on old commitments, . . .	56	93
Returned themselves, ...	17	15
Boarders, ...	2	2
	708	712

Returned to parents or friends, . . .	224	212
Placed with farmers, ...	27	37
Placed at trades, ...	6	4
Discharged in other ways, . . .	7	21
Died, ...	1	2
Remaining in the School Oct. 1, '97 and '98,	443	436
	708	712

FOR WHAT OFFENSE COMMITTED.

Incorrigibility, ...	52	50
Theft, ...	43	49
Truancy, ...	20	27
Vagrancy, ...	19	7
Burglary, ...	17	14
Other offenses, ...	13	12
	164	159

Whole number of boys since opening, March 1, 1854,   6,141

The State allowance per capita is $3 per week.

The cost to the State has been :—

For the year ending September 30, 1897, .   .   . $71,353.69
For the year ending September 30, 1898, .   .   . 67,713.81

THE CONNECTICUT
INDUSTRIAL SCHOOL FOR GIRLS,
MIDDLETOWN.

Under the control of a self-perpetuating Board of twelve Directors ·and the Governor, Lieut.-Governor, and Secretary of State, as State Directors, *ex officio.*

Mr. W. G. Fairbank, ... · . *Superintendent.*
Mrs. W. G. Fairbank, *Visiting Agent and Assistant Superintendent.*

Visited quarterly by two members of the Board.

This School is not a State institution, but a private charity which was established by individual contributions. It was incorporated in 1868, received its first inmates in January, 1870, and has granted to the State the use of its facilities for the guardianship and instruction of girls between the ages of eight and sixteen years who are leading idle, vagrant, or vicious lives, or are in manifest danger of falling into evil habits. All such cases may be committed by judges of probate, of city courts, or justices of the peace, upon satisfactory written complaint, to the guardianship of the School during their minority, unless sooner lawfully discharged; when so committed they become wards of the State, for whose support the State pays a fixed sum. Its purpose is not one of punishment, but of prevention and reformation by giving to its inmates that special physical, mental, moral, social, and industrial training necessary to fit them for useful lives, which they were not likely to receive in the surroundings from which they were taken.

The School is finely situated about two miles west from the center of the city, upon high ground commanding extensive views of the surrounding country. The buildings are of brick, neat and attractive in style, and comprise eight family homes, designed for about two hundred and eighty inmates, a chapel - and school building, Superintendent's house, dressmaking shop, farmhouse, and barn. Fessenden Hall contains on the first floor a large cooking school, a dining-room for Directors' meetings, etc., and a primary schoolroom for the youngest girls. On the floor above are a pleasant assembly room for meetings, entertainments, etc., and a library room. In the basement are two large rooms, of which one is used as a gymnasium and is equipped with all needful apparatus.

These eight homes provide facilities for a careful classification of the inmates. . The Browning Home is reserved for the youngest girls, and the Russell Nos. 1 and 2 for those of vicious and unruly natures. These latter attend school in their own building, and in their schedule of work, study, and recreation live as a separate family. The other homes are graded according to the age and character of their inmates. The girls from the different homes are never brought together except in the schoolrooms and in the religious and other meetings, and then always under the watchful eyes of teachers, so that the danger of corruption from evil associates is not great.

The last-established of the eight homes is the Henry D. Smith Home, or Honor Home, as it is sometimes called, which was opened for use in February, 1898. The house is an attractive one, three stories in height, and has pleasant piazzas on all sides. This home makes complete the system of classification adopted for the School by supplying an intermediate residence between the other seven homes and positions in families outside. Here girls are brought from the other homes who, by their general deportment, have proved themselves worthy of promotion, and here they are tested through a period of comparative freedom to prove their fitness for positions in the outside world. Girls who fail in the test are returned to the homes from which they came, while the placing-out of girls in families is done largely from this home. The life of the Smith Home is that of a family and not of an institution. There are accommodations for twenty-eight girls, and each one has for her own use a good-sized room, tastefully furnished. The occupants of the home are placed upon their honor as far as possible, and act as monitors and assistants in certain positions for the rest of the School. The periods of residence in the Honor Home range from three to six months in duration.

The daily routine of the School consists of four hours of work in the various departments, four hours in the schoolrooms, and the remainder of the time for meals, reading, and recreation. The discipline of the establishment is kind but firm. Reproof is the most common form, but for willful disobedience and other offenses the punishment is confinement in a room for reflection for a period not exceeding three days, except by special order of the Superintendent. Corporal punishment has been employed in rare instances only.

The cooking school and the dressmaking school are important features of the institution's industrial work along lines that are of great value to the girls after they leave the School. Each is under the charge of an expert teacher, and furnishes instruction to classes comprising forty-eight of the older girls who have satisfactory records.

The schools in the institution are arranged in nine grades, which are intended to conform as closely as possible to the standards of public grammar schools. Besides these are the two ungraded schools in the Russell Home. On two evenings a week singing classes are held in Fessenden Hall, where oral instruction in music is given to the whole School. Instruction in moral and religious principles, also, is made an influential part of the School life.

Marks are awarded according to a standard of good behavior and good work, and are made up once a month, thus determining the grades to which the girls belong. By uniformly good conduct a girl may reach the honor grade and be eligible for dismissal or placing out in a family within ten months from the date of commitment.

When placed in outside families the girls are accompanied to their new homes and are visited twice a year or oftener and kept under observation until they reach the age of twenty-one. With few exceptions, homes are chosen within the limits of the State, and every effort is made in their selection that the families and the girls may be mutually satisfactory.

The statistics of the School for the last two years are as follows:

	1897.	1898.
Number in School October 1, 1896 and 1897,	241	258
Received during the year (new cases),	63	49
Returned on old commitments,	48	36
Totals,	352	343
Placed in families (new cases),	22	21
Replaced in families,	11	13
Placed with relatives,	46	31
Died,	0	1
Dismissed by expiration of minority,	2	4
Dismissed in other ways,	13	16
Remaining in School October 1, 1897 and 1898,	258	257
	352	343

CAUSES OF COMMITMENT.

	1897.	1898.
Manifest danger of falling into vice, . .	31	26
Truancy or vagrancy, . . .	9	3
Incorrigibility and disobedience, . .	10	7
Theft, ...	6	4
Offenses against chastity, . . .	4	6
Other causes, ...	3	3
	63	49

Whole number received since opening of School,   1,369
Whole number placed out (including those returned and replaced),   .   .   .   2,288

The cost to the State, on the basis of $3 per week for each inmate, has been:

For the year ending September 30, 1897, .   . $42,301.05
For the year ending September 30, 1898, .   .   42,004.81

PROVISION FOR THE INSANE.

CONNECTICUT HOSPITAL FOR THE INSANE,

MIDDLETOWN.

Under the management of a Board consisting of the Governor and twelve Trustees appointed by the Senate; one from each county and four from the vicinity of the Institution.

CHARLES M. PAGE, M.D., *Superintendent and Physician,*
Formerly Superintendent of the Hospital for the Insane at Danvers, Mass.

Visited quarterly by two members of the Board.

The State Hospital for the Insane was organized by an act of the Legislature in 1866, and the main building was opened for the reception of patients on April 30, 1868. It was soon filled, and since that time applications for admission have steadily increased. To meet this demand additional buildings have been erected from time to time, until now the institution comprises four main hospitals, an annex and five cottages, besides several farm and other outbuildings. They furnish a nominal capacity for about eighteen hundred patients, which is somewhat increased by skillful arrangement. Although its advisability has been variously discussed, it has been the policy of the State to increase the capacity of the institution at Middletown as occasion has demanded, rather than to establish additional hospitals in other parts of the State. The location has many natural advantages in the way of an abundant water supply and a simple method of sewage disposal by surface irrigation over the farm, and is easily accessible both for patients and the reception of supplies by freight. More than four hundred and fifty acres of land are included in the Hospital property, and the buildings are finely situated on a high ridge which commands extensive views of the surrounding country.

At a recent meeting of the Board of Trustees, plans were adopted, upon the recommendation of the new superintendent, for a complete re-arrangement of the patients in the several buildings, and the sum of $5,000 was appropriated to make the necessary alterations and improvements. Upon their completion the North Hospital will be reserved for the reception of new patients and the treatment of acute cases under scientific hospital conditions. The first floor of the south annex of this building will contain laboratories for clinical and pathological research, and an expert pathologist has been engaged who will have charge of this work, and will study also the actual condition of patients in the wards. Other rooms on this floor will be equipped with various forms of baths and apparatus for hydropathic and therapeutic treatment. A lecture room, also, will be provided, where classes of attendants will receive instruction from the physicians in charge, and in this way a practical training school may be developed.

Other features of the re-arrangement are that the South Hospital is to constitute an infirmary for those who are in a feeble or invalid condition, and for noisy and disorderly cases; the Main Building is to be devoted to female chronic patients, and the Middle Hospital and main cottage are to be occupied by male chronic patients. It is expected that these changes will be completed and the new system be fully established early in the coming year, 1899.

Each of the four main hospitals is now under the charge of a resident physician, assisted by a staff of supervisors who have the immediate direction of the ward attendants and instruct them in their duties. All the patients are classified according to their bodily and mental condition. Those who are quiet and easily controlled are associated together in common wards or dormitories, while those afflicted with acute mania are confined in separate rooms. The latter are watched at night by attendants who patrol the corridors once an hour, while in the wards night attendants are always on duty. Patients who are suspected of suicidal tendencies and epileptic patients are under the constant supervision of a staff of nurses.

By far the largest proportion of the inmates of the Hospital is of the pauper and indigent classes, both of which are now paid for by the towns or persons committing them at the same rate of two dollars per week, the balance of the cost of support being paid by the State. Only when there are vacancies not desired by applicants of these classes are private patients admitted.

Many of the able-bodied inmates are regularly employed

·on the farm, about the premises, in the sewing-room and work-shop, and in various departments of housework, while evening entertainments in the winter months, outdoor exercise and various amusements are regular features of the Hospital life.

The general statistics of the Hospital are as follows:

For the year ending September 30, 1897:

	Males.	Females.	Total.
Number of inmates October 1, 1896,	846	936	1,782
Number admitted during the year,	198	152	350
Total present,	1,044	1,088	2,132
Number discharged—Recovered,	42	30	72
Improved,	39	19	58
Stationary,	39	27	66
Died,	59	49	108
Remaining September 30, 1897,	865	963	1,828
Totals,	1,044	1,088	2,132

For the year ending September 30, 1898:

	Males.	Females.	Total.
Number of inmates October 1, 1897,	865	963	1,828
Number admitted during the year,	216	195	411
Total present,	1,081	1,158	2,239
Number discharged—Recovered,	30	31	61
Improved,	40	28	68
Stationary,	60	36	96
Died,	69	50	119
Remaining September 30, 1898,	882	1,013	1,895
Totals,	1,081	1,158	2,239

	1897.	1898.
Causes of death—Phthisis,	14	21
Heart diseases,	15	13
General paresis,	4	15
Epilepsy,	5	7
Apoplexy,	13	16
Suicide,	0	0
Other causes,	57	47
	108	119
Number of insane epileptics present September 30,	91	95

Number remaining September 30, 1897 and 1898, were supported as follows:

	1897.	1898.
By State and towns (paupers),	1,104	1,214
By State and friends (indigent),	564	542
By State alone,	112	93
By self or friends (paying),	22	19
Insane soldiers,	26	27
Totals,	1,828	1,895

Number of insane convicts September 30—From State Prison, 42 — 0
From County Jails, 10 — 12

52 — 12

For the maintenance of the institution the State paid:

For the year ending September 30, 1897, . . $195,793.22
For the year ending September 30, 1898, . . 86,276.94

RETREAT FÓR THE INSANE,

HARTFORD.

HENRY P. STEARNS, M.D.,   *Physician and Superintendent.*
JAMES R. BOLTON, M.D.,   *Assistant Physician.*

Visited September 14, 1898.

The Hartford Retreat for the Insane is the third in point of age among institutions in this country designed for the exclusive treatment of mental diseases, having received its charter from the State in 1821. The institution was formally opened for the reception of patients on April 1, 1824. The location is a pleasant one in the southern part of the city and the grounds comprise some thirty acres, bounded by Washington street, Retreat avenue, and Maple avenue, with the principal entrance on Washington street. It is distant from the City Hall about a mile and a half and may be reached in a few moments by electric cars on the Vernon street or Cedar Hill lines. Broad stretches of lawn, diversified with walks, driveways, and shade trees, furnish attractive surroundings for out-of-door recreation and gentle exercise.

The main building consists of a central administration section with several wings on either side, which have been added from time to time as occasion has required. In later years three cottages, also, have been erected at a short distance from the main building in order to provide a greater degree of luxury and home-like seclusion for patients whose means enable them to enjoy these privileges. Meals for the cottage patients are conveyed by an underground tramway, which connects with the kitchen of the main building. The whole establishment has comfortable accommodations for one hundred and fifty-five patients.

All departments are comfortably furnished and particular care has been taken to insure wholesome sanitary conditions. During the past two years the steam-heating system of the whole institution has been completely renovated in accordance with the most approved modern principles, and electric lights have been introduced throughout all departments.

The Retreat is, perhaps, the only institution of its class in the country that maintains a chaplain and daily religious services. An attractive and commodious chapel on the west side of the grounds was erected in 1875 through the generosity of the president of the board of directors and was appropriately furnished. The services are well attended and, aside from their religious influence, are believed to effect a beneficial result in varying the routine of the daily life. During the winter season a course of evening entertainments is given in the music hall in the main building. The course consists of concerts, dances, drills, readings, musical and dramatic entertainments, etc., in the production of which local clubs and societies and private individuals generously assist. Much attention is devoted to out-of-door exercise and amusements when the weather permits, and numerous excursions for the quieter class of patients are made to towns and localities in the vicinity.

The institution is under the charge of a Board of Directors and a Board of Managers. Six medical visitors, including physicians from different sections of the State, make monthly inspections of the Retreat in turn and at such visits give full opportunity to the patients to confer with them privately in regard to any personal grievances they may have. Visits have been made at intervals by representatives from the State Board of Charities, and quarterly statistical returns are rendered to the Board in accordance with the practice of the smaller private sanitariums.

The number of attendants provided to care for the patients is liberal and in their daily employment and instruction they constitute a practical training-school. Two valuable farms which are connected with the institution furnish the necessary supplies of fruits, vegetables, milk, etc.

The Retreat occupies a somewhat unique position among institutions for the insane in Connecticut from the fact that, although a private corporation in form, it was for many years the only place of treatment for the insane in the State and, as such, received consequently a large number of State patients. Since the establishment of the State Hospital, the Retreat has been patronized chiefly by patients who desire the advantages of greater comfort and more individual treatment, but, at the same time, a number of State patients have been committed to its care each year.

On September 30, 1898, there were in the Retreat one hundred and fifty-two patients, of whom one hundred and nineteen were residents of Connecticut. Thirty-one of the whole number were State patients and six others were being supported without charge. A large proportion of the patients present pay less than the average cost of maintenance per week and the drain upon the resources of the institution is consequently great.

The amount paid for the support of State beneficiaries was:

For the year ending September 30, 1897, . . . $3,157.13
For the year ending September 30, 1898, . . . 3,162.58

The statistics of the Retreat, as shown in its annual reports for the last two years, are as follows:

	YEAR ENDING MARCH 31, '97.	YEAR ENDING MARCH 31, '98.
Number of patients March 31, 1896 and 1897,	143	154
Admitted in the year, . . .	116	104
Re-admitted in the year, . . .	13	10
Total present in the year, . .	272	268
Daily average for the year, . . .	148	147
Discharged — Recovered, . .	29	39
Much improved, . .	14	12
Improved, . . .	30	27
Stationary, . . .	28	25
Died, ...	15	17
Not insane, . . .	2	2
Total discharged in the year, . . .	118	122
Remaining at the end of the year, . .	154	146
	272	268

PRIVATE SANITARIUMS
FOR MENTAL AND NERVOUS DISEASES.

Of the eight institutions of this class in Connecticut noted in the last Report, one, the Louden Sanitarium at Greenwich, has been closed through the efforts of the State Board on account of its failure to comply with the provisions of the Act of 1897 governing the establishment and maintenance of such institutions.

Two new sanitariums have been opened since the date of the last Report, but of these the one in the town of Old Saybrook was in operation during the summer months, only, as a resort for the patients of a New Jersey physician. Of the nine institutions that are now licensed for the purpose by the Governor of the State, two are enrolled under the title of Private Hospitals on account of the fact that they do not make a general practice of receiving the insane, but treat almost entirely patients who are suffering from nervous diseases.

The nine institutions are visited at intervals by representatives of the State Board, and the resident physicians in charge render quarterly statistical returns to the Board in accordance with the provisions of Chapter 256 of the Public Acts of 1895. The average number of patients cared for during the year was two hundred and thirty and the prices charged range, according to the nature of the accommodations and treatment required, from $7.00 to $50.00 a week, or even higher in certain cases.

A brief description of the sanitariums in the order of their establishment, together with the statistics of patients treated during the year, and statutes relating to the care of the insane and to this class of institutions follow hereupon. As may be seen by reference to the statistical tables, by far the largest proportion of the patients admitted are the so-called " voluntary " cases, many of whom are not insane, but are victims of alcoholic and narcotic excesses. A comparatively small number are formally committed by courts of probate as provided in the statutes.

SPRING HILL HOME
FOR NERVOUS INVALIDS,

LITCHFIELD.

UNDER THE CHARGE OF DR. J. L. BUEL.

Visited April 1, 1898.

This sanitarium was established in 1847, and is the oldest private institution for nervous and mental diseases in the State. Its buildings are attractively situated on high ground at the head of North street, about half a mile from the center of the town, and command pleasant views of the surrounding country.

There are in all five houses for the use of patients, besides the residence of the doctor in charge, of which three are designed for women, furnishing accommodations for thirteen patients, and two, one of which is small and is called "the chalet," are reserved for men and accommodate nine patients. All the inmates are under the charge of individual attendants and have opportunities for driving and for exercise and recreation on the grounds surrounding the houses. Some of them have their meals in common in the south cottage, while others are served in their rooms. The buildings are heated by steam and hot air, and the rooms, many of which are in suites, are pleasant and comfortably furnished. A well-kept farm of two hundred acres adjoins the Home.

Voluntary applicants are received, but all other cases are required to observe the legal formalities of commitment. A fair number of recoveries are reported each year.

KENSETT,

NORWALK.

UNDER THE CHARGE OF DR. EDWIN EVERETT SMITH,

Formerly connected with the Hospital for Insane at Morris Plains, N. Y.

Visited April 27 and September 19, 1898.

The institution was opened in June, 1886, for the treatment of nervous diseases, especially those affecting the brain, and for persons suffering from alcoholic and narcotic excesses.

The place occupied for the purpose was formerly a private residence and is finely situated on high ground four miles north of Norwalk, and not far from the South Wilton station on the Danbury division of the New York, New Haven and Hartford Railroad. Besides the main house, there are several cottages on the grounds, the whole furnishing accommodations for about twenty patients. It is the aim of the place to provide the inmates with all material comforts and the extensive grounds furnish abundant opportunities for out-of-door exercise and recreation. A farm of five hundred acres, a part of which is under cultivation, is connected with the sanitarium. During the past three years it has been the practice of Dr. Smith to remove all such patients as were able to Bethlehem, N. H., for the summer months, where they have enjoyed the beneficial mountain air in a comfortable cottage amid quiet surroundings.

The majority of the patients at Kensett are from New York, and all of them, other than voluntary cases, are committed according to the forms prescribed by the laws of the State in which they reside.

ELMCROFT,
ENFIELD.

UNDER THE CHARGE OF DR. EDWIN S. VAIL.

Visited November 3, 1898.

Dr. Vail's institution has been mentioned in previous Reports of the Board under the title of private hospitals, but it should more fittingly be included among sanitariums for the insane, for the patients treated are, as a rule, of that class, and a license for the purpose has been obtained from the State.

The sanitarium was opened in 1888 and two years later was removed to the present location on Enfield street, about one mile south from the railway station at Thompsonville on the Hartford division of the New York, New Haven & Hartford Railroad. Electric cars on the line between Warehouse Point and Longmeadow pass the grounds.

The building used for the sanitarium is a brick house, three stories in height, formerly a private residence, and contains a number of large rooms which are handsomely appointed.   The house is equipped throughout with steam heat and electric lights and has an excellent water supply and system of drainage.   Not more than five patients are accommodated as a rule, for each one has a large room and one or more attendants, as the nature of the case may demand.   The service is liberal and the prices charged vary somewhat, according to the accommodations and the treatment required.

Fifty acres of shady lawns, fruit orchards, meadow, and woodland surround the house and furnish abundant opportunity for out-of-door exercise in pleasant weather.   Extensive views in all directions make the place an attractive one for nervous invalids.

THE WESTPORT SANITARIUM,

WESTPORT.

Dr. F. D. Ruland, *Superintendent and Physician,*
Formerly connected with the Brunswick Home at Amityville, L. I.
Dr. L. H. Wheeler, *Assistant Physician.*

Visited April 27, and September 19, 1898.

The Westport Sanitarium differs from other private asylums in the State in the fact that it is owned by a joint stock company, incorporated under the laws of the State of Connecticut, and is controlled by a board of directors to whom the resident superintendent is directly responsible.   It was opened for the reception of insane patients and sufferers from nervous diseases in January, 1891.

The Sanitarium is situated near the center of the town and may be reached easily by electric cars which run from the Westport station on the New York, New Haven and Hartford Railroad directly by the main entrance to the grounds.   The buildings consist of a comfortable mansion and the Sanitarium proper, a large three-storied wooden structure especially designed for the purpose. The patients are classified in wards according to the nature of their cases, each ward consisting of a pleasant hall or sitting-room with bedrooms opening from it.   There are separate dining-rooms for the several wards, all communicating by dumb-waiters with a common kitchen.   The whole building is heated by steam and lighted by electric lights and gasoline, and provision is made for fire-escapes and lines of fire hose. During the past year a new steam-heating boiler has been placed in the main building and the plumbing in the mansion has been entirely renovated.

The grounds about the institution comprise some fifty acres, laid out in an ornamental manner, and give the patients daily opportunity for exercise and recreation when the weather permits.   Indoor games and occasional entertainments are provided and religious services are held at times.

The whole institution furnishes accommodations for about seventy patients; at the date of the last visit there were fifty-two under treatment, thirty men and twenty-two women, for whom a sufficient number of attendants was provided.   A majority of the patients are from New York, and in many cases are committed by the judge of probate in Westport in order to satisfy the exact letter of the Connecticut statute.   Voluntary cases, also, are received on condition that each one signs an agreement to remain and follow a prescribed course of treatment for a definite period.

STAMFORD HALL,

STAMFORD.

UNDER THE CHARGE OF DR. AMOS J. GIVENS,

Formerly connected with the Hospitals for the Insane at Westboro, Mass., and Middletown, N. Y.

Visited October 1, 1897, and April 15, 1898.

Stamford Hall, for the care and treatment of mental and nervous diseases, was opened in January, 1892.   As one of the few sanitariums in the country belonging to the homeopathic school of medicine, it receives patients from many different states.

The buildings are pleasantly located on high ground on

Summer street, about a mile and a half north from the center of Stamford, and consist of a main house and several cottages, having total accommodations for more than one hundred patients. All the buildings are heated by steam, lighted by electricity, and are comfortably furnished. The patients are classified in the different houses according to the nature and severity · of their cases. Voluntary patients sign a statement that they are inmates of the Hall of their own free will, and on the part of the Hall it is agreed that they shall be at liberty to leave on giving three days' notice in advance. All other patients are committed according to the usual legal requirements.

GREY TOWERS,

STAMFORD.

UNDER THE CHARGE OF DR. F. H. BARNES.

Visited December 4, 1896, October 1, 1897, and April 15, 1898.

Grey Towers is the institution which was noted in the Board's last Report as the Stamford Home, and was originally established in the town of Darien in January, 1894. The Stamford branch was opened in September, 1895, and in May, 1896, the two departments were consolidated. . After the removal to New York of Dr. Kihdred, the former physician in charge, the sanitarium was conducted for a time by Drs. Barnes and McFarland, until the latter withdrew in April, 1898, to open an independent institution.

Grey Towers is situated on Summer street, about two miles north from the center of the city, on a tract of land some twenty-five acres in extent. A grey stone house, formerly a private residence, is reserved for the treatment of alcoholic and narcotic habitués, and for such mild cases of mental disease as desire the higher-priced accommodations. Near by is a cottage for female patients of more limited means.

The main building of the institution is a wooden structure three stories in height, of which the second is reserved for women and the third for men. The rooms are small but comfortably furnished, and the whole building is heated by hot-air furnaces and lighted by electricity. An annex for male patients of small means and for the more violent forms of mental

8

disease furnishes accommodations which are in keeping with the prices required.

The sanitarium has a total capacity of sixty patients, and the considerable variety of prices here established makes it possible to receive persons of widely varying means and position.

HALL–BROOKE,

STAMFORD.

UNDER THE CHARGE OF DR. D. W. McFARLAND,

Formerly assistant physician at the Manhattan State Hospital, N. Y., and at the New Jersey State Asylum.

Visited July 18, 1898.

This is the latest of the institutions of this class established in the State for the treatment of mental and nervous diseases, having been opened for the reception of patients on the first of May, 1898.

The place leased for the use of the sanitarium was formerly a country residence, and is situated near the Springdale station and about two and three-quarters miles northeast from the Stamford city hall. The house is a wooden structure, three stories in height, and is equipped with modern plumbing and heating apparatus. The water supply is abundant and the drainage and other sanitary conditions are considered satisfactory. About twenty acres of land are included in the place, which provide opportunity for a variety of out-of-door exercise. A stable, garden, and orchard furnish the usual attractions of a pleasant rural life.

The sanitarium is designed to receive persons suffering from mental and nervous diseases, as well as those addicted to alcoholic and drug habits. There are accommodations for about twenty patients, and a number of attendants are provided to care for their wants. The prices are reasonable and vary according to the accommodations and the treatment desired.

GENERAL STATISTICS FOR NINE SANITARIUMS,

For the year ending September 30, 1898.

Number of patients September 30, 1897, .	235
Admitted during the year, . . .	280
Total present during the year, . .	515
Patients discharged during the year, . .	268
Number remaining September 30, 1898, .	247

Ages of Persons Admitted.

Under 20, ...	11
20 to 30, ...	80
30 to 40, ...	59
40 to 50, ...	53
50 to 60, ...	43
60 to 70, ...	23
70 to 80, ...	4
80 and over, ...	1
Unknown, ...	6
	280

Civil Condition.

	MALES.	FEMALES.	TOTAL.
Single, ...	74	57	131
Married, ...	71	63	134
Widowed, ...	4	11	15
Total, ...	149	131	280

How Committed.

	MALES.	FEMALES.	TOTAL.
Judges of Probate, ...	15	8	23
Judges of Superior Court, . . .	0	1	1
New York Physicians, . . .	5	3	8
Connecticut Physicians, . . .	7	8	15
Voluntarily, ...	122	111	233
Total, ...	149	131	280

PUBLIC ACTS OF 1895,

CHAPTER 256.

An Act concerning Insane Persons.

SECTION I.   In this act the words and expressions following shall have the several meanings hereby assigned to them, unless there is something in the subject or context repugnant to such construction, that is to say: Asylum means any public or private hospital, retreat, institution, house, or place in which any insane person is received or detained as a patient for compensation; but shall not include any state prison, county jail, or poorhouse, nor any public reformatory or penal institution of this state; insane person means and shall include every idiot, *non compos*, lunatic, insane, and distracted person; patient means any person detained and taken care of as an insane person; the words "keeper of an asylum" mean any person, body of persons, or corporation, who have the immediate superintendence, management, and control of an asylum and of the patients therein.   Words importing the masculine gender may be applied to females.

SEC. 2.   The jurisdiction of the commitment of an insane person to an asylum shall be vested in the court of probate for the district in which such person resides, or, when his place of residence is unknown, in which he may be at the time of filing the complaint, except in cases where it is otherwise expressly provided by law.   Courts of probate shall exercise such jurisdiction only upon written complaint alleging in substance that such person is insane and is a fit subject to be confined in an asylum.   Such complaint may be made by any person, and if any insane person shall be at large and shall be dangerous to the community, it shall be the duty of the selectmen of the town in which he resides, or in which he shall be at large, to make such application.

SEC. 3.   Except when otherwise specially provided by law, no person shall be committed or admitted to or detained in an asylum without an order of a court of probate, as hereinafter provided; *provided*, that when a person who has suddenly become clearly and violently insane is brought to an asylum chartered by the laws of this state, such person may be received and detained there for not more than forty-eight hours without special order of a court of probate; but in such case the keeper of the asylum shall see that the proper proceedings are forthwith commenced in the probate court.

SEC. 4.   Upon such complaint being filed in the probate court, such court shall thereupon assign a time, not later than ten days thereafter, and a place for hearing such complaint, and shall cause reasonable notice thereof to be given to the person alleged to be insane, and to such relative or relatives and friends as it may deem proper; such court may also issue a warrant for the apprehension and bringing before it of the person complained of, and shall see and examine such person, if in its judgment his condition or conduct renders it necessary and proper so to do; or state in its final order why it was not necessary or advisable so to do.

SEC. 5. If the court of probate shall be satisfied that the person alleged to be insane is a dangerous person to be at large, it may make such order for his restraint and custody while the proceedings are pending as it may deem proper, but no such person shall be prevented from having all reasonable opportunities to consult counsel and friends, and to prepare and make his defense to such application.

SEC. 6. In addition to such oral testimony as may be offered at such hearing, the court shall require the sworn certificates of at least two reputable physicians, whom it shall find to be graduates of legally organized medical institutions and to have been practitioners of medicine at least three years within this state, and not connected with any asylum nor related by blood or marriage to the complainant nor to the person alleged to be insane, and one of whom shall be selected by the court, to the effect that they have personally examined such person within ten days of such hearing, and that in their opinion such person is insane and a fit subject for confinement in an asylum.

SEC. 7. If on such hearing the court shall find that the person complained of is insane and a fit subject for treatment in an asylum, or that he ought to be confined, it shall make an order for his commitment to an asylum to be named in such order, there to be confined while such insanity continues or until he shall be discharged in due course of law, and commanding some suitable person to convey him to such asylum, and deliver him, with a copy of such order and of said certificates, to the keeper thereof. In appointing a person to execute such order, courts shall give preference to a near relative or friend of the insane, so far as they shall deem it practicable and judicious.

SEC. 13. When any person shall be held in confinement as an insane person under the order of a court of probate, such court, upon proper application and satisfactory proof that such person has been restored to reason, may order his discharge. Such court may, for reasonable cause shown, order any person confined in an asylum to be removed to any other asylum in this state.

SEC. 15. When any person shall be found to be insane, upon proceedings had under this act, all fees and expenses incurred upon such proceedings shall be paid out of the estate of such insane person, if he has sufficient estate, and if not, by his relatives liable to support him, if of sufficient ability, and if there be none such, then by the town to which he belongs.

SEC. 17. All insane persons confined in an asylum in this state shall be entitled to the benefits of the writ of habeas corpus, and the question of insanity shall be determined by the court or judge issuing such writ, and if the court or judge before whom such case is brought shall decide that the person is insane, such decision shall be no bar to the issuing of said writ a second time, if it shall be claimed that such person has been restored to reason. Said writ may be applied for by said insane person or on his behalf by any relative or friend or person interested in his welfare.

Sec. 19.   The keeper of any asylum in this state may receive and detain therein as a patient any person who is desirous of submitting himself to treatment and makes written application therefor, but whose mental condition is not such as to render it legal to grant an order of commitment as an insane person in his case, under the provisions of this act.   No such patient shall be detained for more than three days after having given notice in writing of his intention or desire to leave said asylum.

Sec. 20.   An attorney at law retained by or on behalf of any patient in any asylum, or any medical practitioner designated by such patient, or by any member of his family, or by a relative or friend of such patient, shall be admitted to visit such patient at all reasonable hours, if in the opinion of the keeper of said asylum such visit would not be injurious to such patient, or if a judge of the superior court first orders in writing that such visit be allowed.

Sec. 21.   All persons detained as insane shall at all times be furnished with materials for communicating under seal with any proper person without the asylum, and such communications shall be stamped and mailed daily.   Should the patient desire it, all rational communications shall be written at his dictation and duly mailed to any relative or person named by the patient.

Sec. 22.   Every keeper of an asylum in this state shall, quarterly, make written return to the state board of charities, containing the name, age, and sex of each patient confined therein, and the time when committed, and by whom, and such other information and in such form of return as said board of charities may prescribe.

Sec. 23.   All asylums in this state shall be subject to the inspection and visitation of the state board of charities, and shall be so visited and inspected at least once in six months in each year.

Sec. 24.   Every person who wilfully causes or attempts to cause, or who conspires with any other person to cause to be committed to an asylum any person who is not insane, and any person who shall wilfully certify falsely to the insanity of any person in any certificate provided for in this act, and any person who, under the provisions of sections 487 and 3683 and 3692 of the general statutes, shall wilfully report falsely to any court or judge that any person is insane, shall be punished by a fine not exceeding one thousand dollars, or by imprisonment in the state prison not exceeding five years, or both.

Sec. 25.   Every keeper of an asylum who shall wilfully violate any of the provisions of sections three, eighteen, nineteen, and twenty of this act shall be guilty of a misdemeanor, and may be punished by a fine not exceeding two hundred dollars, or by imprisonment in a common jail not exceeding one year, or both, at the discretion of the court.

PUBLIC ACTS OF 1897,
CHAPTER 215.
An Act concerning Asylums for the Insane.

SECTION 1.   No institution for the treatment or detention of insane persons shall be conducted or maintained within this state after the first day of July, 1897, except under a license granted by the governor in conformity to the provisions of this act.

SEC. 2.   Any person desiring a license to conduct such an institution shall file with the governor a written application for such license, verified by the applicant's oath, stating the proposed location of such institution, the number of persons for whom accommodations will be provided, the name of the person to be placed in charge, and the previous experience which such person has had in the care and treatment of insane persons.

SEC. 3.   Within twenty days after the filing of an application, as provided in section two of this act, the governor, if satisfied that the location is a suitable one and that the applicant is a proper person to receive the same, shall issue a license to said applicant to conduct an institution for the treatment and detention of insane persons under the provisions of this act, which license shall specify the location of such institution and the name of the person to have charge of the same.

SEC. 4.   Every such institution shall be in charge of a physician, registered under the laws of this state, who has had at least three years' experience as medical attendant in some institution for the treatment of insane persons, and he shall reside upon the premises.

SEC. 5.   Whenever the licensee of any such institution shall desire to place in charge of the same a person other than the one specified in the license, application shall be made to the governor in the manner provided in section two of this act for permission to make said change, which application shall be determined within ten days from the date of the filing of the same with the governor.

SEC. 6.   Any license issued under the provisions of this act may be revoked by the governor upon proof that the institution for which such license was issued is being improperly conducted, or for the violation of any of the provisions of this act; *provided, however,* that the licensee shall first be given a reasonable opportunity to be heard in reference to such revocation.

SEC. 7.   Every person to whom a license is issued under the provisions of this act shall pay to the state treasurer the sum of fifty dollars, and shall annually thereafter, on the first day of July, pay to said treasurer the sum of twenty-five dollars.

SEC. 8.   Every person who shall conduct any institution for the treatment or detention of insane persons contrary to the provisions of this act shall be fined not more than one thousand dollars, or imprisoned not more than six months, or both.

SEC. 9.   The provisions of this act shall not apply to any state hospital for the insane.

SEC. 10.   This act shall take effect from its passage.

Approved, June 9, 1897.

PROVISION FOR THE FEEBLE-MINDED.

CONNECTICUT SCHOOL FOR IMBECILES,
LAKEVILLE.

DR. GEORGE H. KNIGHT, *Superintendent.*

Visited September 17, 1897, and October 6, 1898.

The School was established in 1859 by the late Dr. H. M. Knight, is regularly incorporated, and is under the management of a Board of Trustees.   In its form and organization it is a private institution, but, as the only provision in the State for the care of the feeble-minded, it is the custodian of the State's wards of that class and is the recipient of State appropriations for maintenance and necessary additions.   The State authorizes the payment of $2.50 a week for the support of each pauper or indigent imbecile who may be committed to its care under the approval of the Governor.   An annual report containing a detailed account, by the Superintendent, of the School's work and results is submitted to the General Assembly by the Board of Trustees.

, The School is favorably situated on high ground on the north shore of Wononscopomoc Pond, about a quarter of a mile from the railway station.   The property comprises about nineteen acres sloping toward the south and includes pleasant playgrounds for the children in fine weather besides a well-kept farm.   The direct sunlight, good drainage, and fine air of this location are conducive to health in the School as is shown by the records.   The buildings consist of a main house containing dormitories, dining and school rooms, gymnasium, etc., a custodial building for incurables, and a hospital cottage, which is a valuable adjunct to the School, not only as a place for the care of the sick away from the noise of the main house but also as a quarantine station for newly-admitted children. The buildings are protected against fire by stand-pipes running through the halls and a plentiful supply of hose on each landing.

The capacity of the School is limited, furnishing comfortable accommodations for only one hundred and fifty inmates, which are somewhat increased, however, by careful arrangement, and applicants for admission are often turned away for lack of sufficient room. It has been found necessary, also, to utilize certain rooms on the third floor as dormitories, which were never intended for the purpose and are unsatisfactory, both in location and arrangement.

Plans are under consideration for the erection at an early date of another building which will contain new schoolrooms, gymnasium, and teachers' quarters, and will thus permit the use in other ways of the rooms at present employed for those purposes. Nevertheless, increased dormitory accommodations and other features considered desirable in modern schools will still be urgently needed.

For all pupils who are at all teachable a systematic course of training and studies is pursued throughout the year with the exception of a vacation during July and August. In the kindergarten department the pupils are employed with charts and exercises that require the application of only the feeblest intellect and that gradually lead up to an intelligent study of the common English branches. The results are very gratifying, the handwriting, spelling, and other exercises in many cases comparing favorably with those of children in the common schools. During the winter months a series of entertainments, in which the brighter pupils often take part, is held weekly in the gymnasium.

For occupations the older girls sew and assist in the lighter forms of housework, while the boys are employed a part of the time in useful work upon the farm and around the premises. No opportunities for manual training have yet been provided, and it is desirable that these features should be introduced as soon as practicable for the benefit of those pupils who are fitted to acquire the knowledge of some productive occupation.

In a recent report the Superintendent states that " the most hopeful future for the care of the feeble-minded may be looked for in the adoption of the colony plan, in which the teachable imbeciles of both sexes are cared for in the main buildings, from which there is easy access to the schoolrooms. Not too far off should be other buildings which are devoted to the epileptics of both sexes. And still farther off may be buildings which shall be for the custodial cases of both sexes.

Under this system not only do we teach the imbecile class in all its various grades, and give to the epileptic class the care and treatment necessary to them, but we can make use of the adult imbeciles who have been trained in the school in caring for the custodial cases. This is the most economical way and with it we get the best results.

Most important of all, the outcome of the colony plan is the fact that when we have found a method which shall care for the custodial case, whom no one wants, and the epileptic, who becomes a custodial by degrees unless his disease is arrested, and the bright imbecile who can be taught to help his weaker brother, and the moral imbecile who can have the outlet of occupation and safeguard of restraint and constant oversight, and, most necessary of all and most difficult to procure for him and his depraved tendencies, that ' charity which suffereth long and is kind ' — when we have brought this about we shall have made a tremendous gain of preventing among imbeciles that disgrace to our civilization, the reproduction of their own kind."

With its present facilities, even, this School renders a valuable form of preventive service for the common good of society and provides a positive agency for the improvement of a sadly defective class of human beings.

A brief summary of the statistics of the School for the last two years is as follows:

	Year End'g Sept. 30, '97.	Year End'g Sept. 30, '98.
Number in School October 1, '96 and '97,	161	166
Number received during the year,	26	23
Totals,	187	189
Number discharged, improved,	10	3
Number discharged, stationary,	6	2
Died,	5	5
Remaining in School October 1, '97 and '98;	166	179
Totals,	187	189
Number of epileptics in School,	?	33
Whole number of State beneficiaries,	159	163

The amount received from the State for the support of its beneficiaries was:

For the year ending September 30, 1897, . . $17,872.13
For the year ending September 30, 1898, . . 19,279.00

The cost for the support of a pauper or indigent imbecile child averages about $100 per annum more than the amount authorized by the statutes, and in such case this difference is paid by the town from which the child was committed.

GENERAL STATUTES, 1888.

COMMITMENTS TO THE SCHOOL FOR IMBECILES.

SECTION 489. Whenever there shall be found in any town in this State any pauper or indigent imbecile child who would be benefited by being sent to the School for Imbeciles at Lakeville, the selectmen of such town shall make application to the court of probate for the district in which such town is situated, for the admission of such child to said school, and if upon inquiry said court shall find that said child is a proper subject to be received into said school, it shall order said selectmen to take such child to said school to be kept and supported for such length of time as said court may deem proper. But said selectmen shall not take or commit any such child to said school, until the order of said court has been approved by the governor, and no child shall be received at said school to be supported in any manner by the State, without the approval of the governor. There shall be taxed by the comptroller $2.50 a week for each week such child shall remain at said school, and the principal of said school shall make his bill therefor quarterly and present it to the governor, upon whose approval it shall be paid by the State treasurer, and the balance shall be paid by the parents or friends of said child; or, if the child is a pauper, by the town in which said child belongs.

PUBLIC ACTS OF 1895,

CHAPTER 325.

SECTION 1. No man or woman, either of whom is epileptic, imbecile, or feeble-minded, shall intermarry, or live together as husband and wife, when the woman is under forty-five years of age; any person violating or attempting to violate any of the provisions of this section shall be imprisoned in the state prison not less than three years.

SEC. 2. Any selectman or any other person who shall advise, aid, abet, cause, or assist in procuring, or countenance any violation of section one of this act, or the marriage of any pauper when the woman in such marriage is under forty-five years of age, shall be fined not less than one thousand dollars, or imprisoned not less than one year, or both.

SEC. 3. Every man who shall carnally know any female under the age of forty-five years who is epileptic, imbecile, feeble-minded, or a pauper, shall be imprisoned in the state prison not less than three years. Every man who is epileptic who shall carnally know any female under the age of forty-five years, and every female under the age of forty-five years who shall consent to be carnally known by any man who is epileptic, imbecile, or feeble-minded, shall be imprisoned in the state prison not less than three years.

CHAPTER 350.

Nothing contained in Chapter 325 of the public acts of the present session shall be construed as affecting the mutual relations of any man and woman lawfully married.

PROVISION FOR THE DEAF.

THE AMERICAN SCHOOL, AT HARTFORD, FOR THE DEAF.

Under the control of a self-perpetuating Board of Directors, with the Governors and Secretaries of State of the New England States as Members of the Board *ex officio.*

MR. JOB WILLIAMS, ... *Principal*
Visited March 17 and November 23, 1897, and May 27 and October 11, 1898.

This is the oldest School for the instruction of the deaf in the United States, having been incorporated in 1816 and opened for the reception of pupils in April, 1817. The buildings are located on Asylum avenue, a short distance west from the center of the city, and may be reached by electric cars which pass the grounds. Erected in 1821, they have given good service for a long term of years, but the feeling has been entertained for some time that the welfare of the School would be promoted by the erection of more modern and conveniently arranged buildings. A committee of the trustees has had the matter in hand for a year or more, and plans have been adopted recently, which provide for the erection on the present grounds of a new house for the use of the primary and pure oral departments, and for a thorough renovation of the main building.

All of the New England states make provision through their legislatures for the education and support of deaf mutes and send many of them for instruction to the American School. The numbers of pupils so sent for the last two school years ending in June, 1897 and 1898, are as follows:

	1897.	1898.
Maine, ...	7	5
New Hampshire, ...	12	11
Vermont, ...	8	10
Massachusetts, ...	66	68
Connecticut, ...	63	74
	156	168

Rhode Island now provides for the education of its deaf wards at the school in Providence, and it is not expected that any new state pupils will be received from Maine hereafter, since the school in Portland is now conducted as a state-aided institution.

The number of Connecticut pupils admitted last year is the largest in the history of the School. The per capita appropriation is $200 a year, and the cost to the State for the last two years is as follows:

For the year ending September 30, 1897, .   . $13,211.85
For the year ending September 30, 1898, .   . 13,942.17

The system of instruction in the School is eclectic. Speech, writing, pictures, the manual alphabet, signs and natural action are all made use of to secure mental development and an easy use of the English language, oral and written. Each pupil receives much individual attention, and, so far as possible, the method is adopted in each case under which it appears probable that the pupil will make satisfactory progress and receive the most practical benefit.

As an efficient means for the rapid exchange of thought, for imparting and receiving information, and for developing the intellectual faculties, the free use of the sign language is considered invaluable. For the ordinary vocations of life, however, the necessity for and worth of such facility in intelligible speech as deaf mutes are capable of acquiring is clearly recognized, and particular attention is, therefore, paid to articulation. A teacher was first employed to give instruction by this method in 1857, and since that date, with the exception of a period of five years, special instructors in articulation have been regularly employed. A searching and prolonged trial is made by expert teachers of all newcomers to determine their proficiency in acquiring speech and speech-reading, and each pupil who shows promise of reasonable success receives one hour's instruction in this branch daily throughout the course.

At the beginning of the last school year, a class of about a dozen members was formed whose instruction was conducted entirely by pure oral methods. The results were so satisfactory that the class has been continued this year and it may form the basis for a pure oral department when the School acquires its new buildings.

In speaking of the increased attention paid to the oral instruction of the deaf, a recent report stated: " The danger is that teachers in their new-found zeal will conclude that oral teaching is sufficient and best for all. A large percentage of the deaf under proper methods can obtain a very useful amount of speech and lip-reading, but there is also a large percentage of them that would be greatly restricted in their mental development, if allowed no other means of instruction."

The pupils, under a staff of eighteen instructors, four of whom are teachers of articulation, are in school from 9 A. M. until noon, and from 2 to 4 P. M. Visits were made to various schoolrooms while the classes were in session, and the methods of instruction by reading, speech, lip-reading, manual spelling, pictures, pantomime, and the sign language were seen in actual operation. The pupils acquitted themselves most creditably, and proved that they had been under thorough and painstaking instruction.

It has been found by experience that eight years is the earliest age at which it is expedient to receive children into the School. The usual length of time required for the education of a pupil in passing from the position of a beginner in the kindergarten department up to and through the highest grade is ten years.

In addition to the cultivation of mental discipline, all the boys who are old enough to work receive instruction in departments of manual training. Two shops connected with the School, and under the charge of shop masters, are used for shoe and cabinet-making, respectively. In the shoe shop, twenty boys are employed in repairing the shoes worn by the inmates and in making various grades of footwear for sale.

In the cabinet shop, where about the same number are employed, the chief occupation is making tables, washstands, chests of drawers, and repairing broken or worn-out pieces of furniture; book-cases, chiffoniers, and other articles are made to order when required. The time spent in shop work is from 7 to 8.45 A. M., and from 4.30 to 5.45 P. M., daily. For the younger boys a class in Sloyd work has been formed, which, it is expected, will prove of considerable value.

Other departments in the School course are systematic drill in Swedish gymnastics and instruction in drawing for the technical education of those who show a taste and capacity in that direction. Religious services are held in the chapel on week day mornings and twice on Sundays.

The girls' duties before and after school hours consist of sewing and mending, and light housework in the dining-room and dormitories; two hours per day are usually thus occupied.

A class in practical dressmaking, also, is conducted for a group of the older girls.

Separate playgrounds are provided for boys and girls, and there is also a detached building for use for amusement purposes in bad weather, and during the winter season. In midsummer there is a vacation of eleven weeks, which it is expected that the pupils will spend at home. The change of scene and chance for holiday recreation are an advantage to them, and their absence from the School gives an opportunity for the necessary repairs and house-cleaning.

THE MYSTIC ORAL SCHOOL,

MYSTIC.

Mrs. J. I. McGuigan, *Superintendent.*

Visited June 7 and November 2, 1897, and June 8 and October 24, 1898.

The Mystic Oral School is the institution which, for some twenty years, was conducted as the Whipple Home School for the Deaf by various persons of that name and family. After the sudden disappearance of the former principal, Mrs. Margaret Whipple Hammond, in the session of 1894-5, the School was reorganized under its present title by Mrs. J. I. McGuigan, who is Mrs. Hammond's only surviving daughter. Mrs. McGuigan resides in Philadelphia and visits the School occasionally when its affairs require her presence.

Within the past year, the School was incorporated under the general laws of the State governing the formation of joint-stock corporations, being capitalized at $8,500, of which 20 per cent. only was paid in at the time. A few shares of the capital stock are held by residents of Mystic and vicinity, but by far the largest part stands in the names of Mrs. McGuigan and her husband. The State is not represented in the management of the institution.

The School is situated on high ground about two miles north of the village of Mystic, and occupies a large wooden house which was formerly used as a private residence. The building is heated by stoves and lighted by lamps, but is provided with a fire-escape and has a sufficient water supply. Owing to an increased number of pupils this year, the sleeping apartments are very crowded, and it has been necessary to rent a small house in the neighborhood to accommodate some of the teachers. The schoolrooms are located in a detached wooden building, a story and a half high, and are equipped with needful apparatus.

The pure. oral system of instruction, which has been followed from the founding of the School, is still continued under the direction of a principal teacher and several assistants. Conventional signs are not taught in the classes and the pupils are instructed in the common English branches by articulation and lip-reading. Classes are conducted in language, geography, arithmetic, United States history, current events, and drawing, and individual training is given in addition to class instruction. Kindergarten work is provided when there are younger pupils who require it, and gymnastic exercises are arranged for the whole School. Five hours a day are spent in the schoolrooms, and the school year extends from the middle of September to the middle of June, with a short vacation for the Christmas holidays.

The School has been visited twice a year by representatives of the Board, and upon these occasions the work of the classes in the several branches has been examined. A fair degree of proficiency was shown in some instances, but it was noticed that the aptitude of a pupil to acquire intelligible speech depends largely upon the amount of hearing possessed, or upon a previous ability to speak before the hearing was lost.

At the date of the last visit, there were thirty-four pupils enrolled, of whom four had not yet returned on account of illness. One or two feeble-minded children were noted who should, more fittingly, be placed in the Lakeville School. Besides the teachers and matron, there are two attendants in charge of the boys and girls, and three persons who assist in the teaching in return for the training received in articulation and lip-reading.

When not in school, the boys assist in out-of-door work and the girls are instructed in sewing and the lighter forms of housework. The only manual training provided is knife work and wood carving, and no opportunity is offered for learning useful trades. On Sundays a part of the children attend church in the village when the weather is fair, and in the afternoon all have Bible lessons at the School.

During the last two years the State has expended the following sums for the maintenance of this private school on the basis of two hundred dollars a year for each pupil:

For the year ending September 30, 1897, . 　 . 　$4,657.95
For the year ending September 30, 1898, . 　 . 　5,307.62

9 .

PROVISION FOR THE BLIND.

THE CONNECTICUT INSTITUTE AND INDUSTRIAL HOME FOR THE BLIND,

HARTFORD.

Visited March 3 and November 3, 1897, and February 3, and October 11, 1898.

The Connecticut Institute and Industrial Home for the Blind is a private corporation under the direction of a board of six trustees, assisted by an advisory board, and was established in 1893. Its stated objects are to furnish opportunity for instruction in useful trades to those blind persons who, having passed the limit of age (eighteen years), are ineligible for admission to the Perkins Institution at South Boston, or to any blind persons of suitable age and capacity, who may, or may not, have enjoyed the advantages of any school for the blind in their earlier years, and also to provide care and primary education for young blind children until they shall be fitted for the more advanced department of the Massachusetts school. Prior to the opening of the Connecticut Institute, the only provision for the education of blind persons in the State was an arrangement under which they were cared for at the Perkins Institution.

The State Board of Education of the Blind, which was organized under an Act of the General Assembly of 1893, has a controlling influence in the management of the Connecticut institution, its two active members serving also as president and secretary of the corporation, and contracts with its officers for the care of many of the blind wards of the State.

The organization and equipment of the institution in the first instance were secured through private contributions, the aid of friendly societies, and the amounts received from concerts and entertainments given by the blind. To assist in the payments for buildings, machinery, furniture, etc., the State has made appropriations, through the Board of Education of the Blind, for the use of the Institute, of $15,000 in 1895, and of $1,200 in 1897. These sums were in addition to the regular allowance of three hundred or three hundred and thirty dollars per year for each pupil provided by legislative acts.

It is provided in the statute establishing the Board of Education of the Blind, that all resident blind persons of suitable age and capacity shall receive such instruction in the simple branches of education as the Board may deem expedient. In its published rules the Board deems it expedient that all persons admitted to the privileges of State pupils shall receive a continuous course of instruction calculated to encourage self-reliance, and to qualify pupils to enter upon some self-sustaining occupation. For the accomplishment of these ends, therefore, the Institute and Industrial Home was organized with two distinct departments.

KINDERGARTEN.

The kindergarten department is located at Nos. 1205 and 1207 Asylum avenue, and may be reached by a five-minutes walk from the terminus of the electric car line at Woodland street. Children who have attained school age are received as State pupils and are given instruction in the simple exercises of kindergarten work and primary studies, while enjoying at the same time the care of a comfortable home. As soon as they become sufficiently advanced, it is the intention to send them from the kindergarten to be educated in the ordinary English branches at the Perkins Institution. While there the progress of their studies will be carefully watched, and it will be noted in which directions they individually show the greatest lack or proficiency. At the end of a few years it will be possible to determine whether it would be better to allow a child to remain and have the advantages of the higher grades of instruction of a full course, or to remove and place him in surroundings better suited to his taste and capacity. During the last two years, seven children have graduated from the kindergarten department and have been transferred to the Institution at South Boston.

The buildings consist of a double brick house which has accommodations for thirty children, and at the rear a commodious brick structure, three stories in height, which is now used for the purposes of a schoolhouse, and provides, also, rooms for the teachers and the domestics employed in the household. The first floor forms a large hall for entertainments and for exercise which consists of systematic training in easy gymnastics. Both of the buildings have been equipped throughout with electric lights during the past year, and in their general furnishings present an appearance of comfort and good order.

When last visited there were twenty-three children in attendance in this department, ranging in age from five to fourteen years, who were under the charge of two matrons and a staff of four resident teachers, besides the instructor in music and a teacher of Sloyd, who visits the school once a week and gives instruction in wood-working and clay-modeling.

The young women inmates of the Institute, who were formerly cared for in this department, were removed in February last to the Industrial Home on Wethersfield avenue, but they still visit the kindergarten department for the purpose of receiving instruction in music.

INDUSTRIAL HOME.

This department was opened in November, 1893, and is located at No. 334 Wethersfield avenue in a building erected especially for the uses of the Home. It contains on the ground floor a general store called " The Pioneers," which is conducted partly by blind persons, and the printing-office of the Institute, where several young women are employed in the branches of the work which do not require skilled labor, such as feeding the presses, folding and stitching pamphlets, etc. The type-setting, proof-reading, etc., are all done by seeing persons who are employed for the purpose.

The upper floors of the building contain the living rooms and dormitories, which are occupied largely by the young women inmates who, at the last visit, numbered eleven. The few young men who are regular inmates of the Industrial Home are provided with rooms in the house at No. 335 on the opposite side of the street. An occasional pupil is given instruction in cane-seating chairs or in broom-making. The manufacture of mattresses is continued in a small building at the rear, but is now leased to private parties, as the Institute did not find it profitable. The general work of broom-making, conducted by the Institute, was transferred somewhat over a year ago to quarters in the town of Colchester, where it has since engaged the services of about ten blind men under the direction of a superintendent, who, also, is without eyesight.

At the date of the last visit to the Industrial Home, plans were under consideration for the introduction soon of basket-making as an industry for some of the young women, and of piano-tuning as a means of employment for any pupil whose talent might be cultivated in that direction.

A prominent feature of the Institute is its concert company, whose members spend much of their time traveling through Connecticut and other states and giving entertainments to acquaint people with the work of the institution and to raise additional funds to meet its demands.

The whole number of State pupils under the charge of the Board of Education of the Blind during the last year was sixty-six, of whom sixteen were supported at the Perkins Institution at South Boston, and fifty at the Connecticut Institute, twenty-six being in the kindergarten department and twenty-four in the Industrial Home.

The cost to the State for the care and education of its blind wards on the basis of from three hundred to three hundred and thirty dollars a year in each case, has been:

For the year ending September 30, 1897, .   . $23,211.45
For the year ending September 30, 1898, .   _   24,004.41

PUBLIC ACTS OF 1893,

CHAPTER 156.

AN ACT FOR THE EDUCATION OF THE BLIND.

All Blind Persons Entitled to Receive Instruction.

SECTION 1.   All blind persons, or persons so nearly blind that they cannot have instruction in the public schools, who are of suitable age and capacity for instruction in the simple branches of education, and who are legal residents of this State, shall be entitled to receive such instruction and for such a length of time as may be deemed expedient by the Board of Education of the Blind hereinafter provided for; the expense of such education to be paid by the State, to an amount not exceeding three hundred dollars for each of said persons in any one year, except that where the parents of such blind persons are not able to provide for his or her clothing and transportation, an additional sum of thirty dollars per year may be allowed for those expenses.

Organization of the Board of Education.

SEC. 2.   The Board of Education of the Blind is hereby established. The Board shall consist of four members, of whom the governor of the State and the chief justice of the supreme court, for the time being, shall be permanent members. The other two members shall be appointed by the governor and shall be a man and a woman, one of whom shall be a blind person, both residents of this State. Their term of office shall commence on the first day of July, in the year when they are appointed, and shall continue for four years, except that one of the members appointed the first year shall hold his or her office for only two years, the governor designating at the time of the appointment which of the two shall thus hold for only two years. The governor may for a reasonable cause remove any one of these two members and appoint another person to fill·the vacancy, the appointment thus made to be only for the unexpired part of the term of the member removed.

Secretary and Treasurer, Expenses.

SEC. 4. Said Board shall appoint a secretary, who shall also act as treasurer, and prescribe his or her duties and compensation, which office shall be held subject to the pleasure of the Board. No member of the Board shall receive compensation for services rendered unless such services shall be special and specially requested by the Board, in which case a moderate allowance may be made for the time actually spent. The actual and necessary expenses of the members and of the secretary shall be paid, and a certified statement of such expenses . . . . shall be filed with the.comptroller. . . .

Board may Contract with Institutions.

SEC. 5. The Board is authorized to contract with any institution or institutions within this State, or in any other state, having facilities for the instruction of the blind, for the education of the blind persons from this State found by the Board to be fitted for such instruction, but within the expenditure therefor provided in the first section of this act.

Board may Compel Attendance.

SEC. 6. Said Board shall be empowered to compel attendance of any minor blind child at any such institution. . . .

PUBLIC ACTS OF 1895,

CHAPTER 303.

AN ACT RELATING TO INSTRUCTION OF THE BLIND.

Provision for Education of the Blind.

SECTION 1. The State Board of Education of the Blind may, by a unanimous vote of all the members, provide such suitable buildings, furniture, machinery, tools, implements, and apparatus for the use of the Connecticut Institute and Industrial Home for the Blind as it shall deem necessary to enable said institution successfully to carry out the rules adopted by said Board, providing for the instruction of the Blind; but shall not expend more than fifteen thousand dollars for such purposes during the next two years.

State Lien on Buildings.

SEC. 3. The payment of any sum hereunder shall create a lien on the land and buildings of said Connecticut Institute and Industrial Home for the Blind, which lien shall be foreclosed on behalf of the State of Connecticut, if said land or buildings are ever diverted from their present use.

CHAPTER 319.

Approval of Expenditures.

SEC. 3. Hereafter the Board of Education of the Blind shall not receive or undertake the education of any additional pupils or incur any expense, without the affirmative vote or order of at least three members of said Board.

PROVISION FOR THE SICK.

HOSPITALS.

There is now either public or private hospital provision in each of the seventeen cities in the State, with the exception of Ansonia, Derby, Rockville, and Middletown. The building in New Britain, which was purchased for the purpose of a hospital, as noted in the last Report, was opened temporarily for the care of sick soldiers of the recent Spanish-American war, and plans are now being made for its continued operation on a more permanent basis.

Charters were granted by the General Assembly of 1895 to certain citizens of Middletown and Winsted, incorporating them under the names of the Middlesex Hospital and the Litchfield County Hospital, respectively, but the movements to establish the institutions in active operation have progressed slowly.

There are at present in the State:

Thirteen General Hospitals (including New Britain).
Two Emergency Hospitals.
One Cottage Hospital (available for local patients).
Four Private Hospitals (three of which are for nervous cases chiefly).

For the General Hospitals annual appropriations from the State, showing the total amount, have been granted as follows:

For the year ending Sept. 30, 1897, to 11 hospitals, .   . $41,375.00
For the year ending Sept. 30, 1898, to 11 hospitals, .   . 45,875.00

In addition to these amounts there was paid as a special appropriation for building purposes in 1897 the sum of $25,000 to Grace Hospital in New Haven.

A detailed account of the Hospitals classified as (1) Hospitals aided by the State, and (2) Hospitals not aided by the State, is given in the following pages:

I. HÓSPITALS AIDED BY THE STATE.

THE GENERAL HOSPITAL SOCIETY OR THE NEW HAVEN HOSPITAL,

CEDAR STREET, NEW HAVEN.

MR. J. H. STARKWEATHER, *Superintendent.*

Visited March 29, 1898.

The New Haven Hospital is the oldest in the State, having been established in 1827.   It is situated in the southwestern part of the city and occupies a block of about seven and a half acres.   Electric cars on Congress and Sylvan avenues pass near the entrance.   The central building is an ancient structure of stuccoed brick erected in 1833, and contains the administration offices, rooms for private patients, and a maternity ward.   The nurses' dining-room and the general kitchen are also situated here, and the latter has proved to be badly located as well as inconvenient and unhealthful for those who work in it. An entirely new administration building is urgently needed, but, as there is no immediate prospect of securing the necessary funds, plans have been prepared for the erection first of a new kitchen and nurses' dining-room to adjoin the old building, on which it is hoped to begin work during the coming year.

Adjoining the administration building on the south side is a large three-storied structure of brick, erected in 1873, which contains the five principal wards classified as medical, surgical, and mixed, besides one for children.   Each ward has its own dining-room and pantry connected by dumb-waiter with the general kitchen.   An improved system of ventilation has been

introduced throughout the building and fire-escape towers at
the corners furnish ready means of egress from all the wards.

Beyond this building and connected with it is the Farnam
operating theater, which was given to the Hospital in memory
of Dr. George B. Farnam of New Haven, and was occupied
first in January, 1889. The operating room proper is well
lighted by means of a glass roof and is surrounded by abruptly
rising tiers of seats for the use of students from the Yale
Medical School. It contains all the improved apparatus required in modern surgery and is equipped with a complete set
of antiseptic furnishings. There are additional rooms for
etherizing, recovery, etc., and an accident room for the treatment of emergency cases.

To the north of the administration building, and also connected with it, are the Chapel and the Gifford Home for Incurables, a charitable foundation under the management of the
Hospital directors, of which a more detailed statement may be
found under the head of Private Provision for the Aged and
Infirm.

Two detached cottages on the grounds are used for purposes of isolation in an emergency, but the rules of the Hospital
forbid the admission of patients insane or suffering from contagious diseases.

Among the improvements contemplated by the Hospital
management is the erection of a separate building or wing for
a new maternity ward to take the place of the present temporary and contracted quarters. A piece of property valued at
$50,000 has also been bequeathed to the Hospital Society to
build and equip a separate ward for children, and, pending its
sale, the rental thereof will be applied to the building fund.

During the year 1897 the total number of patients under
treatment was one thousand, one hundred and fifty-four. Of
these only ninety-eight paid the full cost of their support; eight
hundred and thirty were partially, and two hundred and twenty-
six wholly supported by the funds of the Society. There were
three hundred and sixteen town patients who received the
benefit of the State appropriation (five thousand dollars)
at the rate of $2.63 per week. The average cost of
supporting each patient in the Hospital was eight dollars
and ninety-five cents per week. As but seven dollars a week
is charged in the wards for so-called " self-paying " patients,
and but five dollars a week for town patients, a large deficit
annually has to be made good from the funds of the Society.

The patients admitted during the year came from seventy-two different towns and villages in this State, and from fifteen other states and countries. The largest number of patients in one day was one hundred and thirty-seven; the smallest number one hundred and one, and 'the daily average one hundred and eighteen. The number of ambulance calls was two hundred and seventy-seven. United States marine and State soldier patients are admitted under a contract with the government and in accordance with the provisions of the general statutes.

During the summer and fall months of 1898, a total of one hundred and sixty-five soldiers of the recent Spanish-American war received treatment at the Hospital. Tents were erected on the grounds, and the Chapel was filled with beds to meet the requirements of the emergency. Graduate nurses and citizens volunteered their services to care for the sick men, and the people of New Haven were generous in their efforts for the soldiers' comfort.

The Connecticut Training School for Nurses was established in connection with the Hospital twenty-five years ago. Pupils are received from any state and remain in the School for a period of two years, pursuing their studies and daily routine of work under the charge of the superintendent of nursing. Each nurse is assigned to the several departments in turn, and in the course of a year has studied medical, surgical, and obstetrical nursing, and also the preparation of special dishes for invalids and convalescents. The number of pupils, together with the head nurse and assistant, averaged forty-one during the past year.

THE HARTFORD HOSPITAL,

HARTFORD.

Mr. Benjamin S. Gilbert, *Superintendent.*

Visited September 14, 1898.

The Hartford Hospital was incorporated by act of the General Assembly in 1854, and is the second oldest institution in
Connecticut for the care of the sick and injured.   It occupies
a triangular piece of property of about seven acres in extent,
situated in the southern part of the city and bounded by Retreat
avenue, Jefferson and Hudson streets, and may be reached by
electric cars from the City Hall.   The large main building,
substantially built of brownstone, was erected in 1857 and has
been enlarged by several additions, so that at present the Hospital furnishes accommodations for something over two hundred patients.   All parts of the institution are well lighted and
ventilated and are supplied with systems of hot-water heating
and gas lighting.   Electric lights would be a desirable improvement which it is hoped to introduce in the near future.   Connection is had with the city's departments of water and sewers.

There are six organized sections for the treatment of cases,
as follows: Medical, surgical, orthopoedic, eye and ear,
gynecological, and obstetrical.   In addition to the general
wards, there is maintained a separate ward for children with
accommodations for twenty-one patients.   A spacious veranda
on the south end of the children's ward serves as a convenient
playroom and airing-place for convalescents.

A detached building for the special care of contagious diseases has accommodations for thirty patients besides the attending staff of doctors and nurses.   The disinfecting apparatus
and the system of heating and ventilating are of the best
modern type, and all details of construction and appointments
are planned with reference to the latest developments in medical
science.

The medical staff of the Hospital is composed of a resident
physician and a resident surgeon with an assistant for each,
and seventeen visiting physicians and surgeons of the city who
serve according to a fixed schedule.   The price for patients in

the general wards is six dollars a week, which includes medical and surgical attendance, food, nursing, and washing.   Patients in private rooms pay according to the accommodations and service received.

The operating room is located on the second floor, and has been entirely renovated within the past year by the addition of a tiled floor and wainscoting and the introduction of new plumbing of the most approved design.   These improvements, together with the tables, sterilizers, and apparatus, which are of modern aseptic pattern, make the room one which may be compared favorably with the operating rooms in many more recently erected hospitals.   An elevator for the transportation of patients from the floor below is still one of the urgent needs of the Hospital.

The desirability of providing an isolated building for the treatment of pulmonary phthisis has been under consideration for some time, and a suitable pavilion for the purpose may be erected on the Hospital farm at Cedar Hill.   The farm, consisting of one hundred and eight acres, is situated not far from the city, and provides the Hospital with valuable supplies of milk, cream, fruit, and vegetables.

The Training School for Nurses in connection with the Hospital was established in 1877, and offers the usual two-years' course of instruction in professional nursing by means of lectures, recitations, and practical work in the wards.   During the past year the house formerly used as a superintendent's residence has been occupied by a number of nurses, but it furnishes only a part of the accommodations required for the purpose.   An effort is being made at present to devise means for the establishment of a suitable house for the use of the Training School and the resident nurses.

During the year ending September 30, 1898, the total number of patients under treatment was one thousand, seven hundred and eighty-three, and the average cost per week for each patient was $8.55.   The annual appropriation from the State of $5,000 was applied to the relief of one thousand and ninety patients at the rate of $1.01 each per week.   Sixty-three soldiers of the Spanish-American war were received prior to the first of October, and forty-one were admitted after that date, making a total of one hundred and four who received treatment.

Visitors are welcome to the Hospital every week day between the hours of 2 and 5 P. M., and on Sundays for the purpose of attending the religious services.

THE BRIDGEPORT HOSPITAL,

BRIDGEPORT.

MR. JOHN H. BEACH, *Superintendent.*

Visited July 19, 1898.

The Hospital is situated in East Bridgeport about two miles from the center of the city and one block from the Barnum avenue line of electric cars. The location is a fine one, on high ground, and commands extensive views of the city and of Long Island Sound. The Hospital was chartered in 1878 and in 1881 the State granted $50,000 on condition that a site should be furnished and an equal amount raised from other sources. This was accompished in 1882, and the Hospital was completed and occupied in 1884.

The building is a large one of brick and consists of a main portion containing the administration offices, quarters for the superintendent and resident physicians, and private rooms for patients, and of two wings containing the medical wards for men and women, each one story high and well lighted and ventilated. Another wing, which was added in 1895, the generous gift of Mrs. Mary Wood of Bridgeport, contains on the first floor the men's surgical ward, additional rooms for patients, closets, etc., and on the second floor an etherizing room, surgeons' consultation room, and a large operating room equipped with all the most improved appliances required by modern surgery, which are models of cleanliness and freedom from infection. The room has tiled walls and floor, and a glass roof sloping toward the north. An elevator also is situated in this part large enough to accommodate a cot or stretcher at full length. There are total accommodations in the Hospital for eighty patients.

The women's surgical ward is situated in the main building, and the corresponding ward, formerly used for men, is now occupied as a children's ward. This was completely equipped by an association of ladies in the city, who provide also clothing, etc., for the children. It is daintily and comfortably furnished in light colors, the walls are hung with pretty pictures, and the room has a cheerful appearance unusual in a hospital ward.

The whole Hospital is lighted by gas and is furnished with a complete system of steam heating and ventilation. During the past year, the water supply has been increased by the completion of an additional driven well, together with a windmill which forces the water to all parts of the buildings.

The whole number of patients treated during the year ending September 30, 1898, was eight hundred and nineteen, who represented forty-three different towns in Connecticut, besides thirty-seven other states and countries. The average cost per patient was $8.68 a week. The ordinary price for treatment in the general wards is $7 per week, but for town patients only $4 a week is charged.

The Hospital is in receipt of an annual appropriation of $5,000 from the State, and during the year free treatment was given to one hundred and seventeen patients. Eighteen free beds are supported from the income from endowment funds given for this purpose. Soldiers of the Spanish-American war were cared for to the number of twenty-five.

A Training School for Nurses is carried on in connection with the Hospital, and a class of nine members graduated in April last. A home for the nurses, entirely separate from the Hospital building, is greatly desired.

THE WATERBURY HOSPITAL,

WATERBURY.

Miss M. A. Andrews, *Matron.*

Visited December 10, 1898.

The matter of establishing a hospital in Waterbury was first brought to public notice through the medium of the local press in 1882, and a charter for the purpose was secured from the General Assembly of 1883. An appropriation of $25,000 to assist the project was made by the Legislature in 1887 on condition that $50,000 be collected from private contributions, and by March, 1889, the whole of the required amount had been raised.

Among the early contributions received was the generous bequest from Mr. E. L. DeForest of Watertown of $25,000, which enabled the corporation to purchase in 1886 the property now in use. This consists of six acres of land artistically laid out with walks, driveways, trees, and flowering shrubs, and a brick house finely located on a commanding eminence. It is distant about three-quarters of a mile from the center of the city and may be reached by a short walk from the end of the West Main street railway.

The Hospital was opened in January, 1890, and at present consists of the main house and a two-storied addition containing male and female wards, with provision for forty-four beds. The main house contains six rooms for private patients and an operating room equipped with modern antiseptic furnishings.

An attractive cottage, comprising ten bedrooms besides reception and other rooms, was erected on the grounds in 1893 for the use of the nurses, and was presented completely furnished to the Hospital by one of its directors. Through the generosity of the same person, two dining-rooms for the use of convalescent patients have been added to the wards since the last Report, and a neat cottage dormitory for the domestic servants is now being completed. Other buildings included in the Hospital property are an isolated cottage for the treatment of contagious diseases, and a detached structure in which the entire laundry work for the institution is laboriously done by hand. Modern laundry apparatus, operated by power, is urgently needed in this department.

During the year ending December 10, 1898, the total number of patients treated was four hundred and six, who represented nineteen different towns in Connecticut and towns in three other states. The highest number of patients at any one time was fifty-one. The wards, especially, are almost always well filled, and additional wards, in which the surgical cases may be separated from the medical, are greatly needed.

The Hospital is in receipt of an annual appropriation of $3,000 from the State, and a large number of town and charity patients are assisted thereby every year. Several other hospitals in the State, which treat a smaller number of patients, receive appropriations of $5,000 each annually, and it would appear to be eminently fitting that the allowance for this worthy institution should be increased to the same amount. The average cost per week for each patient in the Hospital is about ten dollars.

The attending medical staff consists of eight local physicians and surgeons, who serve in turn, two at a time, for periods of three months each. A consulting staff of four physicians and surgeons, who reside in neighboring towns, is also connected with the Hospital. The usual number of nurses in attendance is twelve.

THE DANBURY HOSPITAL,

DANBURY.

Mrs. S. W. Cutler, *Superintendent.*

Visited January 26 and June 28, 1898.

The movement to establish a hospital in Danbury first took definite shape in March, 1882, when a public meeting was held for the purpose and a Board of Managers was appointed. Until more permanent quarters could be secured, two cottages, which a Danbury physician had built for a private hospital, were purchased by the Association in 1885, and were used for the purpose until the opening of the present building on February 1, 1890. The institution was incorporated by the General Assembly in 1886, and the collection of a building fund was then actively begun. In this way $14,000 were raised and an equal sum was secured from appropriations made by the State at various times.

The Hospital is a wooden structure pleasantly situated on high ground about a mile northwest from the center of the city, and is surrounded by four acres of land. A noticeable improvement during the past year has been the grading of the grounds and the erection of a neat stone wall at the personal expense of one of the managers of the Hospital. The drainage is excellent and the water supply received from a lake at a distance is abundant. A large water tank in the upper part of the building affords a uniform pressure and an ample protection against fire. The building has accommodations for twenty-four patients with separate wards for men and women, and is heated by steam and lighted by gas throughout. On the second floor are a well-equipped operating room and a number of private rooms for patients. The demand for the latter has exceeded the supply to such an extent that it is hoped to erect a new wing, containing an additional number of private rooms, at an early date. A detached pavilion for contagious diseases and more adequate accommodations for the nurses in training are also urgently needed.

The services of the ambulance, which is maintained in connection with the emergency room in the City Hall, can be secured at any time by telephone.

During the year ending April 1, 1898, one hundred and ninety-seven patients received treatment, of whom sixty were wholly and seventy-one were in part supported by the State appropriation and by other funds of the Association. They came from seventeen Connecticut towns, besides towns in three other states. The regular charge for treatment to patients in the general wards is $5 a week. Each patient choses his or her own physician, as there is no medical staff officially connected with the institution. The Hospital is open to all schools of practice as selected by the patients, and the physicians are paid for their services by the patients and not by the Association.

A training school for nurses was opened in connection with the Hospital in April, 1894. A class of four members graduated in July, 1898, and at the last date of visit nine nurses were receiving instruction through recitations, lectures by physicians of various schools, and practical work in the Hospital departments.

GRACE HOSPITAL,

NEW HAVEN.

MRS. J. B. HAM, *Matron.*

Visited April 21, 1898

Grace Hospital is located on West Chapel street in the heart of one of the residence portions of the city, and may be reached by electric cars which pass the door. It was chartered by the General Assembly of 1889, and was opened for the reception of patients in November, 1892.

A large private residence, standing in a spacious yard of four acres, was remodeled and equipped for its new uses and provided comfortable accommodations for about twenty-five patients. The demand upon its capacity increased, however, to such an extent that arrangements were made for the erection of a new building, which was completed and first occupied during the past summer. The cost of construction was about $40,000, which was met by an appropriation of $25,000 from the State and by private contributions sufficient to realize the balance of the amount.

The new hospital adjoins the original building, and is a substantial structure of brick, three stories in height, providing accommodations for about ninety patients. The first and second floors are for men and women, respectively, and each contains a well-arranged ward, a sun-room with southern exposure for the use of convalescents, and a number of rooms for private patients. Locker rooms for the clothing of patients in the wards, diet kitchens and ample toilet and bath rooms, equipped with model plumbing, are provided on each floor.

The operating room is situated on the third floor and is a large, well-lighted apartment, furnished with modern apparatus of the most approved fashion. In convenient proximity are the sterilizing, etherizing, and recovery rooms, while a commodious elevator, large enough to receive a rolling bed at full length, renders them all easy of access from the lower floors and from the ambulance entrance to the Hospital. A special room, also, for the treatment of emergency cases is provided on the first floor.

All departments of the building are equipped with gas and electric lights and with scientific systems of heating and ventilation. A small, separate ward is arranged in both the male and female departments for the treatment of patients who desire a somewhat greater degree of seclusion than the general wards afford, but who cannot pay the higher prices required in the private rooms. The customary rates in the wards are $7 and $10, respectively, but $5, only, a week is charged for town patients.

Since the completion of the new building, the original house is used for the administrative department, and contains still a few rooms for private patients which were furnished as memorials by friends of the Hospital.

The method of treatment is homeopathic, exclusively. Patients are attended by a staff of twelve physicians and surgeons of that school of medicine, who serve for periods of two months in rotation. Other homeopathic physicians are admitted when desired by private patients, and a resident physician also is connected with the Hospital. At present Grace Hospital is the only one of the homeopathic school in the State.

A training school for nurses was opened in connection with the Hospital in September, 1895, and at the date of visit had eleven pupils in attendance. A two years' course of instruction is conducted by means of recitations, lectures by the attending physicians, and practical work in the Hospital departments.

THE MERIDEN HOSPITAL,

MERIDEN.

Miss Bessie Livingston Webb, *Matron.*

Visited June 17, 1898.

The Hospital in its present form dates from December 21, 1892, at which time it was publicly opened for the reception of patients. It is situated on Cook avenue in the southwestern part of the city, and occupies a large wooden house of three stories, which was formerly a private residence and stands well back from the street.

The State appropriated $25,000 in aid of the institution, and this amount, together with the contributions from private sources, enabled the trustees to buy the property, consisting of the house and three acres of land, to remodel the house for its present purpose, and to furnish it with the necessary hospital appliances. It has accommodations for twenty-one patients in wards and private rooms, is heated by hot water and lighted by gas. It is fitted also with an elevator running from basement to attic. A convenient operating room is equipped throughout with antiseptic furnishings of modern design.

The medical staff consists of five physicians and five surgeons, two of whom serve alternately for a period of two months. The general charge for patients is $6 per week, which includes medical and surgical attendance, food, nursing, and washing.

A corps of four nurses is in training, and after a two-years' course of practical and theoretical instruction diplomas are awarded to those who pass satisfactory examinations.

During the year ending November 1, 1898, the whole number of patients under treatment was one hundred and thirty-four, who represented five different towns in Connecticut and thirteen other states and countries. The Hospital is in receipt of an annual appropriation of $3,000 from the State, and a considerable number of town patients were received during the year at the rate of five dollars per week for each. The regular charges per week for treatment are $6 in the wards and $10 in the private rooms. Eleven soldiers of the recent war were cared for at State expense during the summer.

A visiting committee composed of fifty-two ladies, two of whom serve in turn for two weeks in succession, generously assist in the support of the institution, and in the performance of kind offices for the comfort of the inmates.

THE NORWALK HOSPITAL,

NORWALK.

Miss Helen Brown, *Head Nurse.*

Visited September 19, 1898.

The Norwalk Hospital Association was organized in December, 1892, under the general laws of the State, and in July, 1893, the house at No. 24 Leonard street was opened for hospital purposes with accommodations for about ten patients. The Hospital maintains an efficient ambulance service, and has been especially useful in accident and emergency cases.

The medical staff consists of eight physicians and surgeons, who are members of the Norwalk Medical Association, and who serve in turn, two at a time, for periods of two months each.   The head nurse has two assistants besides the matron of the house.   The ordinary charge for treatment is seven dollars a week, which includes medical and surgical attendance, together with medicines, nursing, and washing.   Members of a board of lady visitors call at the Hospital every week and do quiet but effective work in supplying additional comforts for the inmates.

The Hospital is supported largely by the contributions of churches, societies, and friends, and by the fees from members of the Association; since 1895, however, it has been in receipt of an annual appropriation of $2,500 from the State.   The total number of patients treated during the year ending December 1, 1898, was seventy-two, and the average cost for each patient was $19.07 per week.

Some four years ago the directors purchased a portion of an estate situated about half way between Norwalk and South Norwalk, on the summit of a hill back of the Armory and not far from the main avenue connecting the two places.   At the date of visit, foundations were completed for the construction of a new hospital building on the site, and it is expected that it

will be completed and ready for use early in 1899. The building will cost about $20,000, and almost the whole amount has
been secured through voluntary subscriptions and the dues
from life directors of the Association.

The plans adopted call for a wooden structure in the colonial
style, with a central administration department, containing also
a number of private rooms, and adjoining wings comprising
wards for male and female patients, respectively. An elevator will be provided in the main building, and a convenient
operating room will be furnished with antiseptic apparatus of
modern design. The building will be equipped throughout
with gas and electric lights and with scientific systems of heat-·
ing and ventilation.

The new Hospital will have accommodations for about
thirty patients and will furnish greatly increased facilities for
the work of this beneficent institution.

THE MEMORIAL HOSPITAL,

NEW LONDON.

Miss M. J. Wallace, *Superintendent.*

Visited June 7, 1897, and February 11, 1898.

The Memorial Hospital of New London is situated on Garfield avenue about three-quarters of a mile west from the
center of the city. A fine site comprising about five acres of
land on a high ridge was contributed by the city for the use of
the Hospital Association. A charter was granted to the incorporators by the General Assembly of 1893, and on August 1st of
that year the building was opened for the reception of patients.

The main building and the ward now used for men were the
generous gift of the Hon. J. N. Harris of New London. An
additional wing, which contains separate wards for women and
children, besides several rooms for private patients, was erected
in 1895 through the liberality of the Hon. George F. Tinker,
and gives the Hospital a total capacity for about thirty patients.

The ordinary charge to patients in the wards is $10 a week,
which includes medical and surgical attendance, nursing, medi-

cines, food, and washing.   Since 1895, the Hospital has been
in receipt of an annual appropriation of $5,000 from the State,
and it is assisted further by the voluntary contributions of
friends.   One free room was handsomely furnished and endowed by Mrs. Nellie Osgood Tyler, who also presented the
Hospital with an ambulance of modern construction and complete equipment.

The Hospital is connected with the city's systems of water
and sewers, and, since the last Report, has been equipped
throughout with electric lights.   In July, 1897, the care of
marine patients, which had been discontinued for a time, was
resumed under contract with the United States government,
but the work is now restricted principally to the care of emergency cases.

The medical board consists of fifteen physicians and surgeons of the city representing both schools of practice; three
members of the board compose the visiting staff, who are assigned to duty in regular rotation, and serve for periods of two
months each.

A training school for nurses is maintained in connection
with the Hospital, in which the pupils receive a two-years'
course of training and instruction by the attending physicians
and surgeons and by the superintendent of nurses.   Stated examinations are held and those whose conduct and work are
satisfactory for the whole period receive the diplomas of the
School.

The Memorial Aid Association, representing the various
churches and societies of New London and vicinity, was organized in March, 1893, and assists the Hospital in providing
necessary articles of clothing and bedding, books, delicacies,
etc.

During the year ending March 1, 1898, the whole number
of patients treated was one hundred and sixty-four, who represented fifteen Connecticut towns and twenty-four other states
and countries.   The average cost for each patient was $12.88
per week, and 130 patients were assisted wholly or in part by
the State appropriation.

THE WILLIAM W. BACKUS HOSPITAL,

NORWICH.

MR. FREDERICK SYMINGTON, *Superintendent.*

Visited August 9, 1898.

This institution is a conspicuous instance of the expenditure from private sources of a large amount for hospital purposes without the solicitation of any aid whatever from the State, and forms a splendid tribute to the generosity and public spirit of certain citizens of Norwich, who together contributed the necessary funds.

The Hospital was formally opened with befitting ceremonies on October 4, 1893. It is conveniently situated on the Norwich Town road about one mile and a half north from the center of the city, and may be reached by electric cars which pass the grounds. The property includes eighteen acres and extends from the street on the east to the high bank of the Yantic River on the west.

All the buildings are of pressed brick with light stone trimmings. The main or administration building contains the offices, operating and accident rooms, and rooms for private patients. Two long enclosed corridors, one above the other, extend towards the west, and connect on the south side with two wings of two stories each, which contain the general wards for men and women, respectively. An elevator large enough to contain an invalid's bed is used for the service of the Hospital. The wards and private rooms together furnish accommodations for sixty-three patients.

Other buildings in the group are the nurses' home, a detached pavilion specially designed for patients suffering from infectious and contagious diseases, and a service building convenient to all departments and containing the laundry, kitchen, boiler equipment, and servants' quarters. All of these may be reached by covered passageways without exposure to the open air.

No pains have been spared in furnishing the institution throughout with the most improved styles of heating, ventilating, and sanitary appliances. The operating room in particular is distinguished for the superior excellence of its appointments.

The floors and walls are of polished white marble, and the table, stands, and other fittings are either of glass or iron work finished in white.   Every detail in its construction has been scientifically planned with a view to making its antiseptic conditions as nearly perfect as possible.

The medical department consists of two resident physicians and a visiting staff composed of twelve city physicians and surgeons, two of whom serve in turn for a period of two months. The force is further strengthened by the addition of a consulting physician and surgeon, and of an ophthalmic and aural specialist.

Since the last Report, a convenient ambulance of modern design has' been presented to the Hospital by a number of ladies in Norwich.   It is kept at a stable in the city, subject to call by telephone, and is a valuable acquisition to the Hospital's equipment.

The number of patients under treatment in the Hospital during the year ending September 30, 1898, was four hundred and forty-one.   The new admissions represented forty-six different towns in Connecticut and towns in eighteen other states. The average cost per week for each patient was $12.03, being less than the corresponding figure for recent years, but still high owing to the large fixed expenses necessary in conducting such an extensive establishment for a comparatively small number of patients.   As the ordinary charge for paying patients in the wards is only $7 per week, a large deficit annually has to be made good from the funds of the corporation. The daily average number of patients was thirty-two, and the attendants and other residents averaged twenty-four.   Support and treatment amounting to $8,293.83 were given in charity during the year, divided among two hundred and sixty-five patients.   The rate for town patients has been reduced since the last Report from $5 to $3 per week.

Since 1895 the Hospital has been in receipt of an annual appropriation of $5,000 from the State.   An out-patient department, or free dispensary, is maintained in connection with the Hospital, and during the year furnished free treatment to eight hundred and sixty-four poor persons, representing twenty-six hundred and fifty-one visits.

A training school for nurses is under the direction of the matron and provides for the usual two-years' course of instruction with periodical examinations and final awarding of diplomas.   During the year ten pupils were in attendance, of whom three graduated in June, 1898.

THE DAY--KIMBALL HOSPITAL,

PUTNAM.

Miss Caroline F. Brigham, *Superintendent.*

Visited June 30, 1898.

This Hospital was opened on February 22, 1893, in a house on Bolles street, and was named the Day-Kimball Hospital in memory of a son of Mrs. Susan Kimball of Boston, a generous donor to the fund for a more permanent building.

An attractive site for the new building was selected on the Pomfret Street road about one mile northwest from the center of Putnam. A substantial three-story structure of wood was erected and appropriately dedicated in November, 1895. It contains a reception room, operating and etherizing rooms, a ward for women, and private rooms for male and female patients. The whole building is heated by steam and lighted by electricity. It affords accommodations for about twenty patients, and cost about eight thousand dollars. An appropriation of $5,000, made by the General Assembly of 1895, assisted materially in obtaining the new grounds and building.

The need is already felt of a special ward for male patients, and plans are under consideration for an addition to the building for this purpose. The introduction of an elevator, also, would be a desirable acquisition to the Hospital's equipment.

As the only public hospital in Windham County, the Day-Kimball Hospital receives patients from all parts of that county, and its board of twelve visiting physicians represents seven different towns. In addition there is a board of four consulting physicians, who are residents of Putnam.

The General Assembly of 1897 granted an appropriation of $3,500 to the Hospital for the following biennial period, and assistance is otherwise received from the contributions of friends, churches, and societies. During the year ending May 31, 1898, the total number of patients admitted was one hundred and one, of whom ninety-six were from Connecticut.

An association of ladies in Putnam and vicinity has rendered the Hospital valuable aid with gifts of funds and useful articles, and has supported one of the four free beds that it contains.

II. HOSPITALS NOT AIDED BY THE STATE.

THE STAMFORD HOSPITAL,

STAMFORD.

MRS. J. E. NOTTINGHAM, *Matron.*

Visited October 2, 1897, and July 18, 1898.

The Stamford Hospital was opened for the reception of patients on April 7, 1896. A charter was granted to the incorporators by the General Assembly of 1893 which voted, also, an appropriation of $25,000 to aid in establishing the Hospital on the condition that $75,000 should be obtained from other sources. This amount was readily subscribed by a number of wealthy and generous citizens, and a desirable piece of property, consisting of a large private residence surrounded by twenty-two acres of land, was purchased for the purpose. It is located on East Main street, about one mile from the center of the city, and may be reached by the Myrtle avenue line of electric cars which pass the grounds.

The building was thoroughly renovated and equipped with all features suitable for its new uses, and provides total accommodations for thirty patients. There are pleasant wards for men and women and a well-lighted operating room completely furnished with modern apparatus of antiseptic properties. A number of attractive rooms are provided for private patients, several of which are arranged in suites with bathrooms attached. The building is heated throughout with hot water and lighted by gas, and is connected with the city's system of water and sewers.

During the hospital business year ending May 1, 1898, two hundred and ten patients received treatment, more than half of whom were charity patients. A large proportion of the cases treated were of a surgical nature. Seven free beds are maintained in the Hospital from endowments made by private individuals. Up to the present time, the Hospital has not been in receipt of annual appropriations for support from the State.

A staff of five visiting physicians and surgeons of the established school of medicine is connected with the Hospital, whose members serve for periods of two months each in rotation.   Patients in private rooms may engage homeopathic physicians, if desired, at their own expense.

ST. FRANCIS' HOSPITAL,

HARTFORD.

UNDER THE CHARGE OF THE SISTERS OF ST. JOSEPH.

Visited November 3, 1898.

St. Francis' Hospital was established through the contributions of a number of benevolent members of the Roman Catholic Church, headed by the Right Reverend Bishop of the Diocese, and was opened for the reception of patients on September 1, 1897.   A spacious residence at the corner of Woodland and Collins streets was purchased for the purpose and was thoroughly refitted and equipped to meet its new uses.   It is believed to be the only Roman Catholic institution of the kind in the State.

The Hospital has accommodations for thirty-two patients, and contains wards for men and women, a small number of private rooms, and operating and etherizing rooms furnished with modern apparatus.   The building is heated by hot water and lighted by gas, and the general sanitary conditions appear to be satisfactory.

There is a board of directors connected with the institution, and the actual management is in the hands of Sisters of the Order of St. Joseph, of whom there were five in attendance at the date of visit, assisted by two lay nurses.   No restrictions are observed in regard to the creed or residence of patients admitted.

During the year ending September 1, 1898, three hundred and fourteen persons received treatment, representing forty-one different towns in Connecticut, besides towns in Massachusetts and Maine.   The usual prices charged are $6.00 a week in the wards and $15.00 a week in the private rooms, but a considerable number of cases were charity patients.   The éxpenditures of the Hospital were just met, however, by the receipts from patients, which may be accounted for by the fact that the Sisters in charge give their services voluntarily. The city of Hartford makes an allowance to the Hospital of one-half the regular rates for five patients, to provide for any needy cases it may send there, but, aside from this, the institution is not in receipt of public appropriations.

A staff of sixteen physicians and surgeons of Hartford is provided, two of whom, together with a specialist in gynecology, visit the Hospital every day. Patients have the privilege of engaging any other reputable physician, not on the Hospital staff, at their own expense.

THE EMERGENCY HOSPITAL,

BRIDGEPORT.

MR. J. N. BRENNAN, *Superintendent.*

Visited June 7, 1898.

The Hospital is located in the central part of the city on Middle street, in the large brick building of the Board of Public Charities of Bridgeport, and is under the direction of a sub-committee of that Board. The location is a good one and is especially convenient for sufferers from accidents or injuries on the railroad.

A well-equipped ambulance service is maintained ready for use at a moment's notice, and here victims of accidents from any cause whatsoever may be brought directly and treated. Serious cases are afterward transferred to the Bridgeport Hospital or to their homes, as the case may be. The Hospital contains an operating room equipped with all appliances for ordinary cases, and a comfortable ward which can be enlarged to meet any reasonable demands. A staff of four city physicians is retained in the Hospital service and makes visits at stated hours.

A free dispensary, also, is maintained from which medicines are supplied to the sick and worthy poor. The ambulance surgeon is on duty all day and may be reached for calls of necessity at night.

The records of the Hospital for the fiscal year ending April 1, 1898, show that the ambulance was called out two hundred and fifty-one times; that one thousand, three hundred and thirty cases were treated, and that three thousand, two hundred and twenty-three prescriptions were filled out.

The whole cost of maintaining the Hospital is borne by the city, and plans are under consideration for its removal after another year to quarters in the City Hall, which will probably be enlarged and remodeled in the near future. Sleeping accommodations for vagrants are provided in the cellar of the present building, which is comfortably heated by steam.

THE EMERGENCY HOSPITAL,

DANBURY.

DR. N. M. SILLECK, *Physician in charge.*

Visited October 7, 1898.

The Emergency Hospital of Danbury was opened in April, 1894, to serve as an adjunct to the Police Department of the city. A room in the City Hall on Main street was set aside for the purpose and was furnished with the necessary appliances for the treatment of injuries from accidents and cases of sudden illness until they can be removed to the general Hospital. The city ambulance is kept at a neighboring stable and can be had at a moment's notice.

The Emergency room is under the direction of the Superintending police surgeon, and during the year ending February 28, 1898, provided treatment in ninety-five cases. From March 1st to December 1, 1898, fifty-one cases were treated.

PRIVATE HOSPITALS.

THE SHELTERING ARMS,

NORWICH.

Miss H. E. De Launcey, *Matron.*

Visited August 9, 1898.

The Sheltering Arms is a private, non-sectarian charity, which is supported by individual contributions and is managed by members of the United Workers' Society in the interest of poor people of Norwich who require hospital care and treatment.   Incurable cases are not received, and it is purposed to make the character of the place more that of a home than of a formal institution.

The charity was established in 1878 and occupies a comfortable house near the Norwich Town road and not far from the Backus Hospital.   Within the past year a two-storied addition has been built over the kitchen wing, which contains rooms for eight persons, and gives the house total accommodations for twenty-four inmates.

Patients who can do so pay something toward their expenses, usually about one-half of the cost of their support. Their own physicians are called in attendance, and the professional services are given free of charge.   At the date of visit there were seventeen patients present and five helpers in the household.   Religious services are held every Sunday in the upper hall of the house, except during the months of July and August.

DR. HILLS' PRIVATE HOSPITAL,

WILLIMANTIC.

Visited September 26, 1898.

This is a small hospital connected with the practice and under the direction of Dr. T. Morton Hills and Dr. Laura Heath Hills, and is the only institution for hospital purposes maintained in Willimantic. It is located in a part of Dr. Hills' house, near the main street and the railroad, and is useful in cases of accidents. The majority of the cases received for treatment are surgical. Rooms for private patients are available, and it is expected in the near future to employ the whole house for hospital purposes.

CROMWELL HALL,

CROMWELL.

UNDER THE CHARGE OF DR. FRANK K. HALLOCK.

Visited July 30, 1897, and July 22, 1898.

Since the publication of the Board's last printed report, the class of patients received and the system of treatment followed at Cromwell Hall have undergone a gradual but complete change. As the second oldest sanitarium in the State, having been opened in December, 1877, it offered treatment during a number of years to patients suffering from various forms of mental disease.

Some three years ago, however, in view of the steadily increasing proportion of simply nervous cases among the inmates, it was decided to limit the admission exclusively to that class of patients and to refuse thereafter all cases of insanity. Persons suffering from nervous prostration in all its forms now represent the chief class of patients admitted. A license from the State, however, was obtained by the managers on account of the presence in a distant cottage belonging to the sanitarium, of four or five insane persons for whose lifelong support in the institution arrangements had previously been made.

The distinctive feature of the treatment is what is known as the "Program Method," under which a varied schedule of treatment and hygienic living is carefully arranged for each patient. Out-of-door life and exercise, with sun, air, and water baths are made much of in the daily routine. For this purpose the hillside back of the main house is laid out in attractive fashion with groups of trees and winding walks, and is provided with the necessary fenced enclosures within which patients receive the various baths.

The sanitarium is finely situated on high ground, about one mile north from the railway station at Cromwell, and commands extensive views of the Connecticut River and valley. The buildings consist of a large octagonal house of stone, three stories in height, and two pleasant cottages near by, which are reserved for men and women respectively. There are total accommodations for about twenty-five patients, and the number of nurses and attendants provided is liberal.

Since the recent death of Dr. W. B. Hallock, the institution is conducted under the charge of his son, Dr. Frank K. Hallock, and is maintained at its customary high standard.

DR. BOWMAN'S SANITARIUM,

GREENWICH.

UNDER THE CHARGE OF DR. J. E. BOWMAN,

Formerly connected with the Long Island Home, Amityville, and the New York Home for Epileptics.

Visited October 1, 1897, and September 20, 1898.

Dr. Bowman's Sanitarium, which was established at Noroton in August, 1895, was removed within the past year to Greenwich, where it is pleasantly situated about three miles northeast from the center of the town on what is known as the North Cos Cob road.

The house occupied was formerly a private residence, but

II

was extensively remodeled to suit the new requirements.   The building is equipped throughout with steam heat and modern plumbing, and all of the rooms are handsomely furnished after the fashion of an attractive home.

A limited number of patients are received and, as almost all of them are sufferers from nervous diseases, the institution is classed under the title of private hospitals rather than under that of sanitariums for mental diseases.   A license, however, has been obtained from the State, so that the institution is duly authorized to receive cases of mental disorder whenever it is desired to do so.

CREST VIEW SANITARIUM,

GREENWICH.

Under the charge of Dr. H. M. Hitchcock.

Visited September 20, 1898.

Crest View Sanitarium is pleasantly situated about one and a half miles north from the Greenwich station on the New York, New Haven & Hartford Railroad, and is designed for the care and treatment of nervous invalids.

The buildings comprise three cottages which are attractively furnished and are provided with all modern conveniences.   The grounds of the Sanitarium and the surrounding country furnish opportunity for driving, walking, and out-of-door exercise.   The rest treatment and various forms of baths, massage, and electricity are employed as desired.

While it is not the practice of this institution to receive cases of mental disease, the distinction between the nervous and the mental disorders is often such a close one, that it is recommended by the Board that every establishment of this class should be provided with a license from the State as a guarantee against any possible irregularities.

PROVISION FOR DISABLED VOLUNTEER SOLDIERS.

FITCH'S HOME FOR SOLDIERS,

AND

SOLDIERS' HOSPITAL OF CONNECTICUT,

NOROTON HEIGHTS.

CAPT. JAMES N. COE, *Superintendent.*

Under the management of the Soldiers' Hospital Board of Connecticut.

Visited October 1, 1897, and July 1, 1898.

The Home is favorably located on an elevated site a few rods west of the Noroton station, and commands an extensive view of the surrounding country and Long Island Sound. The institution had its origin in the generous gift by its founder, Mr. Fitch, of a plot of land and a building which he had set apart for the use of soldiers' orphans. The property was taken over by the State in 1887, and since that time has been conducted under State and National auspices as Fitch's Connecticut Home for Disabled Volunteer Soldiers and Sailors. The grounds now include a total of about twenty acres, and present an inviting appearance of good order and tasteful arrangement.

The general disposition of the buildings is in the form of a hollow square. The main group of buildings on the left contains the offices, dormitories, messrooms and commissary departments. Over against the main building and separated from it by a broad stretch of lawn, stand the chapel and hospital, which form the second side of the square. A small cottage dormitory, the laundry, and carpenter's shop make up the third side, while the fourth is bounded by the public high-

way. In the center of the square a tall flagstaff from which
daily float the national colors, and mounted cannon standing
on either side, give an appropriate military aspect to the
grounds. Within the past year a commodious house has
been erected near the main building, which provides quarters
for all of the staff officers of the institution, except the superintendent and the assistant surgeon.

DORMITORIES AND COMMISSARY DEPARTMENT..

The dormitories are arranged on the congregate plan and,
although well-filled, are kept in a clean and orderly condition.
With the exception of the top story, each floor is supplied with
a stand-pipe and fire hose, in addition to a fire-escape and easy
exits. Verandas are attached to each floor of the main building on the south side and add greatly to the comfort of the
inmates during the summer months.

The second building of the main group was completed and
first occupied on February 1, 1896. It is connected with the
older building by a covered passageway and contains on the
first floor a large dining-room with a comfortable seating capacity of 340, commodious kitchen and bakeshop equipped with
modern fittings, and well-arranged storerooms and cold-stor-
age for the preservation of supplies. The upper floor comprises a large dormitory with bathrooms and lavatory attached, barber-shop, shoe-shop, and clothes-rooms. The
erection of this building increased the total capacity of the
Home to accommodate four hundred and fifty-eight inmates.

All the buildings of the Home are heated by steam and
lighted by gas, and are provided with an excellent water supply and system of drainage. A thorough inspection of every
department is made on Saturday of each week, and any error
or omission in order or management is marked for correction.
With the exception of hospital patients, each inmate is required
to bathe weekly. Forty-six men are regularly employed in the
carpenter's shop, kitchen, baking house, and other departments
where civilian labor would otherwise be required, and are paid
in proportion to the quantity and worth of their labor. In connection with the daily routine, men are detailed in rotation for
duty in the laundry, dining-rooms, etc.; for which no compensation is given.

The building containing the amusement room and library
is located at the east end of the main building, and provides
a comfortable place for the inmates to spend much of their time

in reading, smoking, and games. Magazines, daily and weekly
newspapers (generously contributed), games of various kinds,
and a library of twelve hundred volumes are at hand for recreation and instruction. The building is still too small to serve
the purpose adequately, and plans are under consideration for
its enlargement at an early date.

THE HOSPITAL.

One of the most important departments of the institution is
the hospital. The accommodation so far provided consists of
two independent wards, of one story each, offices for medical
staff and dispensary practice, and a sitting-room for convalescent patients, etc. The wards are fitted with modern appliances throughout, and are well lighted and ventilated.

In the natural course of events, as the years pass on, an increasing number of old soldiers become subjects for hospital
treatment. The effect of this natural movement has already
been felt at Noroton, where the hospital wards, with twenty-
five beds in each, have proved to be unequal to the necessities
of the case. Rooms which were not intended for service as
wards are used for the overflow. A two-storied addition to the
hospital, also, was erected in 1893, which contains on the first
floor a well-equipped diet kitchen, and on the upper story
rooms of suitable size and furnishings which are reserved for
such cases as require to be isolated.

MANAGEMENT.

The working of the Home is constantly in evidence. At
the end of every ten days the superintendent is required to hand
in a report to the United States Government. Bi-weekly visits
are also made by the Executive Committee of the Soldiers'
Hospital Board of Connecticut, who inspect the premises and
audit the accounts. The institution is regularly inspected by a
representative of the Government who is a member of
the Board of Managers of the National Home for Disabled
Volunteer Soldiers, and it receives formal visits of the same
kind from members of the Grand Army. The Woman's Auxiliary Corps appoint a succession of monthly visitors, who by
charitable gifts and kindly acts, not strictly within the scope
of government aid, have contributed in many ways to the comfort and cheer of the inmates. Religious services are held in
the chapel on Sunday afternoons by local pastors.

An act of Congress authorizes the payment to any State of $100 per annum for each disabled volunteer soldier maintained in a Soldiers' Home on the condition that such homes shall be inspected and a report made by the Board of Managers for the information of Congress. The expense for support in excess of the Government allowance for the Connecticut Home is met by the State. The State appropriated:

For the year ending September 30, 1897, . . $70,000.00
For the year ending September 30, 1898, . . 80,000.00

The average cost of maintenance per capita in 1897 was $159.33.

The following statistics are for the years ending June 30, 1897 and 1898:

Total number admitted, ... 253 199
Total number cared for, ... 641 651
Average number cared for, ... 437 470
Number present and absent June 30th, . . 457 481

A large proportion of the inmates are in receipt of pensions. The money is sent by check, enclosed in envelopes, which may be opened only by the persons to whom they are addressed.

Pensioners are required to file their certificates with the superintendent on admission, and to make over to the Soldiers' Hospital Board the amount of each pension respectively, with the understanding that it is to be used for their own wants or for dependent relatives or friends.

	1897.	1898.
Number of pensioners present June 30th, .	240	380
Number of pensioners present June 30th, under act of June 27, 1890, ...	160	296
Total amount of pensions received, .	$44,912.60	$43,518.22
Total amount sent to dependents, .	19,052.87	18,362.94

Each inmate receives a copy of the rules and regulations for the government of the Home on admission. The superintendent records violations of the rules and other offenses, and for repetition of the same has authority to warn and finally discharge the offender. The State furnishes a uniform which is worn so long as the person receiving it remains in the Home, and on his discharge is returned to the superintendent.

All permits for admission to the Hospital or Home are issued by the Chairman of the Executive Committee, Soldiers' Hospital Board, Bridgeport, Connecticut, to whom all applications and communications should be addressed.

SOLDIERS' ORPHANS.

Under Chapter CCXXVII, Section 3648, of the General Statutes, it is ordered that there shall be paid from the State Treasury $1.50 per week for the benefit of each child of this State under the age of fourteen years who has no other adequate means of support, and is not in any poorhouse, whose father served as a Connecticut soldier or enlisted from this State in the United States Navy in the war for the suppression of the rebellion, and died by reason of wounds received or disease contracted while in such service.

The selectmen of each town and the treasurers of the New Haven and Hartford Orphan Asylums are required to return to the Comptroller, quarterly, a written list of the names and ages of all such children, and certify that they are entitled to the State bounty. Within ten days after the commencement of the quarter the Comptroller draws his order on the Treasurer for the amount payable for such children.

The amount paid by the State under the above statute was :

For the year ending September 30, 1897,   .   . $3,574.40
For the year ending September 30, 1898,   .   .   3,215.72

PROVISION FOR MISDEMEANANTS.

THE COUNTY JAILS.

In connection with the County Jails the following statistics relating to their population are taken from the annual returns of the County Commissioners for the two years ending June 30, 1897 and 1898. The table of receipts and expenses is taken from the same source, and shows the relative amounts received from the State and from the earnings of the prisoners to meet the cost of their support. It is provided in Section 3359 of the General Statutes, and in Chapter 4 of the Public Acts of 1893; that the County Commissioners, in their respective counties, shall fix the sum to be received for boarding prisoners, not exceeding two dollars and twenty-five cents a week each.

The cost to the State for the board of prisoners in the County Jails was:

For the year ending September 30, 1897,   .   . $123,077.88
For the year ending September 30, 1898,   .   .   114,493.76

STATISTICS OF JAILS FOR YEAR ENDING JUNE 30, 1897.

Committed.	Hartford County.	New Haven County.	New London County.	Fairfield County.	Windham County.	Litchfield County.	Middlesex County.	Tollard County.	Totals.
Number of commitments,	2,470	2,875	870	2,077	343	363	262	72	9,332
Males,	2,193	2,619	808	1,877	339	355	253	71	8,515
Females,	277	256	62	200	4	8	9	1	817
Males under twenty-one years,	144	153	78	156	11	23	8	3	576
Females under twenty-one years,	13	13	1	20	0	1	2	0	50
In prison before,	1,350	2,060	442	1,276	161	151	141	0	5,581
Discharged during year,	2,482	2,823	838	2,122	354	345	284	66	9,314
By expiration of sentence,	1,391	1,750	531	1,431	267	218	234	41	5,863
By Co. Commrs. and State's Attorney,	93	169	11	200	25	11	2	4	515

STATISTICS OF JAILS FOR YEAR ENDING JUNE 30, 1898.

Committed.	Hartford County.	New Haven County.	New London County.	Fairfield County.	Windham County.	Litchfield County.	Middlesex County.	Tolland County.	Totals.
Number of commitments,	2,085	2,841	914	1,981	401	343	243	97	8,905
Males,	1,855	2,414	875	1,789	399	335	231	94	7,992
Females,	230	427	39	192	2	8	12	3	913
Males under twenty-one years,	135	151	64	142	13	18	7	4	534
Females under twenty-one years,	8	17	0	20	0	1	0	0	46
In prison before,	1,231	1,722	455	1,236	216	161	162	12	5,195
Discharged during year,	2,101	2,883	915	1,980	399	354	230	69	8,931
By expiration of sentence,	1,084	1,819	577	1,306	318	249	175	65	5,593
By Co. Commrs. and State's Attorney,	88	169	21	142	26	18	2	4	470

CLASSIFICATION OF OFFENSES FOR WHICH COMMITTED, 1897.

Classification.	Hartford County.	New Haven County.	New London County.	Fairfield County.	Windham County.	Litchfield County.	Middlesex County.	Tolland County.	Totals.
Offenses against order,	1,568	2,115	661	1,122	255	243	198	54	6,216
Offenses against property,	550	388	142	506	42	68	32	7	1,735
Offenses against the person,	206	144	30	284	24	34	26	8	756
Offenses against morals,	105	135	20	95	5	12	1	1	374
Other offenses,	41	93	17	70	17	6	5	2	251
Totals,	2,470	2,875	870	2,077	343	363	262	72	9,332

CLASSIFICATION OF OFFENSES FOR WHICH COMMITTED, 1898.

Classification.	Hartford County.	New Haven County.	New London County.	Fairfield County.	Windham County.	Litchfield County.	Middlesex County.	Tolland County.	Totals.
Offenses against order,	1,243	2,144	673	1,108	317	253	178	77	5,993
Offenses against property,	488	413	179	415	50	59	35	3	1,642
Offenses against the person,	220	74	26	275	22	20	23	13	673
Offenses against morals,	105	151	13	131	3	5	5	4	417
Other offenses,	29	59	23	52	9	6	2	0	180
Totals,	2,085	2,841	914	1,981	401	343	243	97	8,905

RECEIPTS AND EXPENSES OF COUNTY JAILS.

1897. Counties.	Received from the State.	Earnings of Prisoners and Sales.	Due from State and Earnings.	Expenses.
Hartford,	$35,336.10	$1,803.14	$3,823.53	*$32,057.71
New Haven,	36,561.64	4,208.84	......	*28,828.18
New London,	8,791.82	2,039.56	......	9,116.67
Fairfield,	24,627.12	1,234.36	1,672.44	24,148.73
Windham,	5,157.94	2,460.42	1,881.46	9,652.26
Litchfield,	6,062.46	475 88	1,613.76	7,463.18
Middlesex,	4,426.05	458.53	822.20	7,375.96
Tolland,	1,074.12	......	......	2,861.15
Totals,	$122,037.25	$12,680.73	$9,813.39	$121,503.84

* In addition to these amounts there was expended for buildings, in Hartford Co., $44,000.00; in New Haven Co., $16,682.02.

1898. Counties.	Received from the State.	Earnings of Prisoners and Sales.	Due from State and Earnings.	Expenses.
Hartford,	$32,013.29	$2,144.65	$2,545.67	*$34,300.91
New Haven,	43,140.42	4,608.28	......	*27,596.23
New London,	11,147.37	1,404.64	1,368.91	9,650.02
Fairfield,	16,697.76	945.61	9,134.41	25,596.79
Windham,	7,136.81	730.06	1,877.68	9,642.90
Litchfield,	6,119.99	42.65	2,120.36	7,800.27
Middlesex,	3,721.16	1,146.75	699 95	6,930.68
Tolland,	1,573.10	......	.....	3,392 43
Totals,	$121,549.90	$11,022.64	$17,746.98	$124,910.23

* In addition to these amounts there was expended for buildings, in Hartford Co., $9,500.00; in New Haven Co., $6,393.14.

THE HARTFORD COUNTY JAIL,

HARTFORD.

Mr. E. J. Smith, *Sheriff;* Mr. M. D. Connors, *Deputy Jailer.*

Visited September 24, 1897, February 3 and May 27, 1898.

The Jail buildings are situated in a good-sized lot occupying all but one corner of a block, on Seyms Street in the northern part of the city, and may be reached by a short walk from the Main Street or Albany Avenue lines of street cars. A pleasant house for the Jailer stands at the center of the south front, while entrance to the Jail proper is had at one side through the office.

The original part, which still remains unchanged, contains the main block of one hundred and thirty-six cells arranged in four tiers and substantially built of brick. A smaller block extending to the right contains twenty-four cells of somewhat larger size, arranged in three tiers, which are used exclusively for "bound-over" men. Straw mattresses, blankets, sheets, pillows, and pillow-cases are provided for the beds, and ventilation is secured for each cell independently by a system of pipes which discharge into openings above the block. The corridors surrounding the block are well lighted and ventilated by series of long windows and openings in the outer walls.

The Jail was built in 1873-4, and for over twenty years served the steadily increasing demands of the County upon its accommodations without alteration. Its overcrowded condition at last became so serious, however, that in 1896 extensive additions and improvements were undertaken, for the completion of which total appropriations of ninety-five thousand dollars were made by the County legislators.

The most important feature in the alterations was the addition of a substantial brick wing, extending one hundred and eight feet beyond the bound-over block in an easterly direction. Within this is a block of one hundred and twenty steel cells arranged in four tiers about the sides of a central court,

twenty-five feet in width, from which they are screened by walls
and doors of solid steel, pierced only by peep-holes for the purpose of inspection. This court is well lighted and ventilated
by a large skylight in the roof, and furnishes a convenient place
for the daily exercise of those prisoners who are not employed
in the workshop, while the solid steel walls prevent communication from one side to the other of the block. Galleries surround the court on all sides, providing easy access to the several
tiers, and are heavily grated from top to bottom. The block
is further surrounded by an outer corridor on each tier from
which the cells receive abundant light and air, and from which
they are separated by heavy steel gratings. Each cell is provided with proper bedding and a bunk which hangs by chains
from the wall and can be turned up when not in use. No
plumbing whatever is introduced into the cells. This block
is connected by doors with the corridor of the main building,
and together they provide a total capacity for the Jail of two
hundred and eighty cells for the use of male prisoners.

- Parallel with the new block and connected with the north
end of the main hall, is another new wing containing the hospital, which was opened for use in January, 1897. This department is under the charge of a special hospital steward,
and contains a pleasant ward with twelve beds, sitting and
dining-room, bathroom, and dispensary, all comfortably
equipped with modern furnishings. The rooms which were
formerly used for hospital purposes are now employed as shops
for the tailoring and shoe-making required in the institution.

Since January 1, 1897, uniform clothing has been provided
for all inmates of the Jail, and the garments that the prisoners
possess at the time of entrance are taken from them, systematically preserved, and returned to their owners when they leave
the institution. This method insures the neat appearance of
the men while in the Jail, and prevents them from replenishing
their wardrobes unduly at the public expense. The officers
of the Jail wear appropriate uniforms. Twelve shower baths
of modern design are provided for the use of male prisoners,
and a change of clean clothing is furnished weekly for each
man.

The workshop is situated at the rear of the main block,
and, as enlarged in the course of the general improvements,
now provides accommodations for two hundred and twenty-five
men. The industry carried on is cane-seating and manufacturing chairs under contract, and all the prisoners, with the

exception of "bound-over" men and those who are ill or assigned to duty in other departments, are regularly employed. The working hours are from 7 A. M. till noon and from 1 to 5 P. M.

The chapel of the Jail is situated over the workshop and is a room of good size and cheerful appearance. A partition separates the men in the body of the chapel from the women, who, together with visitors, are seated in the rear. Religious services are held every Sunday by the chaplain.

The department for women is located in a wing on the west side of the main block and contains thirty-six cells available for their use. The hall about the cells receives an abundance of air and sunlight from windows in the southern wall. The women are under the charge of a matron and do the laundry work and mending and make the sheets and shirts that are used in the Jail. The basement under the women's department contains the laundry which is provided with stationary tubs, steam-driers, and other facilities, and a well-arranged bathroom, furnished with convenient showers, tubs, etc.

The kitchen, bakery, and storehouse are situated in a one-story brick wing, which stands in the angle between the main building and the women's wing, and opens into both by means of windows through which the rations are served. All departments are equipped with modern fittings and are well adapted for the purpose. The cooking is done entirely by men, and rations are served as follows: breakfast, beef or fish hash, bread and coffee; dinner, either bean soup, meat stew, corned beef, or fish hash, with bread; supper, mush and milk or mush and molasses.

All parts of the Jail have presented evidences of neatness, good order, and effective discipline, when visited, and the institution may fairly be said to compare well with any of the same class in the country.

NEW HAVEN COUNTY JAIL,

NEW HAVEN.

Mr. A. B. Dunham, *Sheriff ;* Mr. J. J. Hart, *Deputy Jailer.*

Visited November 11, 1897, and September 17, 1898.

The Jail is situated in a large lot on Whalley Avenue in the northwestern part of the city and may be reached by a line of street cars which pass the premises. Near the center of the south front of the buildings is a comfortable house for the Jailer's use, while the entrance to the Jail itself is at one side through the office. The main building was originally erected in 1857, and was subsequently changed and enlarged to meet increasing demands. It contains the main block of cells, one hundred and fifty in number, which are arranged in three tiers, and are substantially built of brick. Light and air are received through long windows in the outer walls of the building, and in addition each cell is ventilated independently by a system of pipes which communicate with openings above the block. The cells are alike in size and are furnished uniformly, each with a bed which is supplied with a tick filled with straw, a pillow, pillow-case, blankets, and one sheet.

This Jail, also, suffered severely from overcrowding for a number of years, until, in 1896, an extensive enlargement of all departments was effected at a cost of about eighty thousand dollars.

The interior of the old workshop, a two-storied brick structure situated just to the east of the main building, was torn out, and within its walls was built a new block of one hundred and two steel cells, arranged in three tiers. The cells are constructed on the usual plan, back to back, and are separated by a narrow passway which extends through the length of the block on each tier and permits inspection of the cells from the rear. A wide corridor surrounds the block and is sufficiently lighted and ventilated by windows in the outer walls.

The north end of this building is still divided into two stories as before, the upper one of which forms a large room for use as a chapel.   Here services are conducted every Sunday by local religious organizations, and on alternate Sundays mass is said by a Roman Catholic priest.   The space under the chapel may be occupied by another section of cells, one tier in height, when a further addition seems advisable.   At present, there are situated here two detached steel cells which are carefully padded throughout for the use of prisoners who are violent with delirium tremens.

Shower baths of modern design are provided in both the new and the old departments, and the plumbing of the Jail is equipped throughout with sanitary fixtures.   All the prisoners are required to bathe once a week and a change of clean clothing is provided weekly.   The bedding and shirts belonging to the Jail are washed by the female prisoners, while men who possess undergarments of their own are expected to wash them every week in one of the bath-tubs.   Clothing is furnished to a number of the prisoners who are in actual need, while others continue to wear the garments which they had at the time of arrival.   As a measure of ultimate economy, however, it would seem desirable to equip all of the men with uniform clothing, and upon their discharge to return to them the apparel with which they entered the institution.

The new workshop of the Jail adjoins the rear of the main block, and is a commodious, three-storied structure of brick, whose several floors provide convenient quarters for the manufacture of bent-wood chairs in its various departments.   The industry is carried on under contract with a local company, and there are ample accommodations for the employment of more than two hundred men at the same time.   The working hours are from 7 A. M. to 12, and from 1 to 6 P. M., and all of the men, with the exception of those who are ill, assigned to other duty, or bound over for trial, are regularly employed in this department.

The women's department is located in a wing at the west side of the main building, and is under the charge of a matron. It contains forty cells, arranged in three tiers, and is provided with an abundant supply of bath-tubs, shower baths, and toilet fixtures, accessible from each tier.   The women work in the kitchen and laundry, make the men's shirts and all other clothing and bedding used in the Jail, and do the mending.   These duties, together with certain branches of housework, keep them employed for a part of each day.

12

The kitchen of the Jail is situated between the main block and the women's department, and is equipped with all needful apparatus.   Rations are served to the general body of prisoners as follows: for breakfast, hash and bread; for dinner, bread with bean soup, beef soup, or corned beef and vegetables; for supper, rice, oatmeal, or mush,. with milk.   The bread is obtained fresh every day from a local baker.

Over the kitchen is a large room which is comfortably furnished and is used for hospital purposes when occasion requires.   The general health of the prisoners is good, and only one death has occurred within the last two years.

The alterations and improvements in the Jail accomplished in 1896 have relieved in a measure, only, its former overcrowded condition, for at present there are but two hundred and fifty cells available for men, and the Jail often has to accommodate from three hundred to three hundred and fifty male prisoners. The unfortunate practice of " doubling-up " two men in the same cell is still continued of necessity, and unless a State Reformatory is established in the near future, the New Haven Jail will soon require another extensive enlargement.

THE NEW LONDON COUNTY JAILS.

Two jails are maintained in New London County; one in Norwich and one in New London.   The expense and inconvenience are proportionately greater under this arrangement, and it is admitted that it would be a benefit to the county and to all concerned if the differences arising from local interest and prejudice could be satisfactorily settled and the two Jails united into one institution.

NEW LONDON.

MR. GEORGE O. JACKSON, *Sheriff;* MR. J. B. ROGERS, *Deputy Jailer.*

Visited February 11, 1898.

The New London Jail is situated at the corner of Franklin and High streets, a short distance west from the center of the city.   It consists of an old part, solidly built of stone in 1846, which contains fourteen cells and a dungeon, and a new part built of brick in 1876, which contains the main block of forty-two cells arranged in three tiers.   The wide corridor surrounding the block is well ventilated and lighted by long windows in the outer wall, and each cell is also ventilated separately by a system of pipes leading to the roof.   The walls and ceilings of the cells are whitewashed, and the beds are provided with straw ticks, blankets, sheets and pillow-cases.   It had not been customary, formerly, to furnish pillow-cases in the men's department, and their adoption merits approval, not only as a matter of cleanliness and comfort, but also as a means of economy in preserving the pillows.

The building is heated by steam from a boiler in the old part of the Jail.   There is no water closet, but buckets are used in the cells both during the day and at night.   A bath-tub stands in the corridor at one end of the block, which partially screens it from view, and the prisoners are required to bathe once a week.

There is no steady work for the men, but employment is given as opportunity offers in re-seating cane chairs, beating

carpets, and doing such other odd jobs as can be accomplished
in the hall and in the Jail yard.   No land is connected with the
Jail, except the yard immediately surrounding the building, a
portion of which is cultivated as a kitchen garden.   Four or
five men on an average are employed inside the building, and
from six to eight outside.   On three Sundays in the month
services are held in the Jail chapel under the direction of various religious organizations of the city.   The chapel room is
also used for hospital purposes when necessity requires it.

The department for women is located on the north side of
the building between the main block and the Jailer's house.
It contains eight cells arranged in two tiers, and presented an
appearance of commendable neatness and good order.   The
women prisoners are employed in the kitchen, and rations
are served to the prisoners as follows: for breakfast, bread
and coffee; for dinner, corned beef, fish chowder, soup, or baked
beans; for supper, oatmeal, rice, or mush, with molasses.   At
the date of visit, there were forty-two inmates present, all of
whom were men.

THE NORWICH JAIL,

NORWICH.

Mr. D. J. Champlin, *Deputy Jailer.*

Visited August 9, 1898.

The Norwich Jail is located on Jail Hill, so called, an abrupt
elevation not far from the center of the city.   It was solidly
built of stone in 1838, and retains in general its original form
to the present day.   The Jailer's house is attached to the front
of the building, and commands an attractive view.

The main part of the Jail is used for male prisoners and
contains a block of thirty-six cells which are arranged in two
tiers, and are surrounded by a corridor twelve feet wide.   Long
windows in the outer walls and openings in the ceiling provide
sufficient light and ventilation.   The building is heated throughout by steam and is connected with the water and sewer systems of the city.   A bath-tub is situated at the end of the corridor and is screened from view by the main block.   Here also,
as at New London, there is no water-closet, and buckets are

used in the cells by day as well as by night.   Each cell contains a single bed, furnished with a tick filled with straw, sheets, blankets, pillow and pillow-case, the last-named article having been introduced about three years ago.

At the date of visit there were forty inmates present, thirty-six of them being men.   When the male prisoners outnumber the cells provided for them, additional accommodation is provided by using settees and cots as temporary beds in one side of the general corridor, and the practice of doubling-up the men in the cells is thus avoided.   Under such circumstances, however, it is difficult to maintain effective discipline.

There is no workshop connected with the Jail, and no means have yet been devised for keeping the men regularly employed at some useful industry.   The corridor on one side of the block, however, has been furnished in a somewhat primitive fashion with a carpenter's bench, tailor's table, racks, etc., and here the men are occupied with such odd jobs as can be obtained from the townspeople.   The ordinary occupations are mattress-making, re-seating cane chairs, and upholstering furniture.   Carpet-beating is also carried on in the small yard which comprises all of the land connected with the Jail.   The supply of work is not uniform and is not sufficient to keep more than a part of the men employed.

The combined kitchen and laundry adjoins the building on the west side, and overhead are situated the women's quarters, which contain ten cells.   The latter were clean and comfortable in appearance and supplied with proper sanitary conveniences. The women prisoners, whenever present, do the sewing and mending for the Jail inmates, and make such garments as are needed.   There is no hospital room in the Jail, and prisoners who are seriously ill are removed to the city hospital.

The usual bill of fare is as follows: breakfast, bread and coffee; dinner, either corned beef, beef stew, soup, beans, or fish, with bread and potatoes; supper, mush with milk or molasses.   The various articles of food appeared wholesome and sufficient.   Male prisoners perform the cooking, baking, and washing required for the Jail, and the men and women inmates are consequently not associated in any department of work.

The city missionary, who, on three Sundays in the month, conducts religious services, visits the Jail often and makes a practice of helping discharged prisoners by securing employment for them when possible.   His work in this direction has met with encouraging results.

THE FAIRFIELD COUNTY JAILS.

Fairfield County supports two Jails; the principal one being at Bridgeport and the other at Danbury.   The latter stands in the relation of a dependency to the larger institution at Bridgeport, and is used, as a rule, for the detention of short-term men only.

THE BRIDGEPORT JAIL,

BRIDGEPORT.

Mr. S. E. Hawley, *Sheriff ;* Mr. Wm. Scofield, *Deputy Jailer.*

Visited June 7, 1898.

The Bridgeport Jail is situated in a large lot at the corner of North and Fairmount avenues in the northern part of the city, and may be easily reached from the North avenue line of electric cars.   It stands on high ground and receives an abundance of light and air from all sides.

The building is a substantial one of brick, and consists of an old part built some twenty years ago and a new part erected in 1890 of modern design and construction.   The latter contains a massive steel cage, which is built within and practically distinct from the brick walls surrounding it, and has a main floor and roof of steel and heavy gratings of steel bars that extend from top to bottom.   The cage is divided into three tiers, each of which comprises two rows of thirteen cells facing outward.   The flooring of each tier is extended to a width of five feet beyond the cells and is carried the whole length of the block, thus forming a secure promenade enclosure for each section of cells.   The doors to the respective enclosures are always kept locked, but the doors of the cells are not locked during the day, and the " bound-over " prisoners who are not required to work, and those who from sickness or other good reasons are confined to their cells, are allowed the freedom of the promenade on their tier. In this part each cell is provided with a closet, wash basin and running water, and is fitted with an independent system of ventilation. One room on each tier also is furnished as a bathroom, which in winter months is warmed and supplied with an abundance of hot water. Access to the several tiers is gained from a series of narrow galleries that surround the cage on all sides.

The women's department, which is also situated at this side of the Jail, contains a total of twenty-four cells available for female prisoners. The women are under the charge of a matron, and assist in the kitchen and laundry work, and do the mending for the institution.

The old part of the Jail extends directly back from the office and contains a substantial brick block of one hundred and twenty cells arranged in three tiers. The floor of the lowest tier is a trifle below the level of the ground outside, and, having no cellar underneath, is consequently quite damp at certain seasons. It would be well if a cellar could be made of this bottom tier itself, and another tier be constructed above the block to replace the cells thus abandoned.

Each cell at present is connected with a system of ventilating pipes extending to the roof, but it was found that their utility is much impaired by the inmates in their practice of stuffing them with old rags, papers, etc. In some other respects, also, the condition of the cells revealed a lack of that perfect neatness which is desirable in an institution of this kind. Every cell is furnished with an iron bed provided with a tick filled with straw, blankets, one sheet, pillow, and pillow-case. The use of pillow-cases was introduced about a year ago, after an urgent recommendation by the Board to that effect. Shower baths are situated at the end of the block, and the men are required to bathe every week. The clothing of the prisoners is taken from them at the time of their arrival and is thoroughly fumigated. During the period of confinement, each prisoner wears plain but decent clothing belonging to the Jail, and when discharged, goes out possessed of the same garments with which he entered the institution.

The workshop is a commodious brick building of two stories forty by one hundred feet, and adjoins the end of the old part with which it is connected by a simple doorway. The first floor is used as a storeroom for materials, finished products, etc., while the upper floor forms the workshop proper. This room receives an abundance of light and air from all sides and furnishes ample quarters for the employment of all of the prisoners, except the " bound-over " men and those who are detailed for other duty in and around the Jail.   The industry carried on is cane-seating chairs under contract, which is governed by the results accomplished in a given time without regard to the number of men employed.   The working hours are from 7 A. M. to 12, and from 12.30 to 5.30 P. M.

In feeding the prisoners the ordinary bill of fare is: breakfast, meat or fish hash, bread and coffee; dinner, bread and potatoes with corned beef, beef stew, soup, or beans; supper, mush with syrup, or bread and tea.

Two rooms situated over the Jailer's office may be utilized for hospital purposes when required, but are seldom so employed.   All ordinary cases of illness are treated in the cells. Religious services are held in the chapel every Sunday from October 1st to June 1st, and are conducted by delegations from various churches and organizations in the city.

The Jail, in general, gives evidence of good management and, if the prisoners were compelled to keep their cells in' neater condition, would satisfy all reasonable requirements.

THE DANBURY JAIL,

DANBURY.

MR. W. M. SCOTT, *Deputy Jailer.*

Visited January 26, 1898.

The Jail is conveniently located on the main street near the center of the city. It is a medium-sized building, the front part of which is used by the Jailer as his private quarters.   The Jail apartments are attached to the rear, and are screened from the street by a board fence which extends above the windows. It has a total capacity of twenty-eight cells, twenty-two of which are for men, and six for women.   The beds are provided with sheets and blankets, and each man has his own towel.

Stoves are used for heating purposes and for drying the men's clothing, which, when washed, is hung on lines in the corridor.   The bath-tub and closet at the end of the block were not partitioned off in any way, and the use of a movable screen was recommended as a means of securing privacy at a little expense.   Sanitary fixtures are provided and all departments are connected with the city's system of sewers.

As this Jail is used, as a rule, for the detention of short-term men only, it has not been thought advisable to introduce a system of employment; it would also appear from the plan of the building that none was contemplated at the time of its erection.   Men who are committed by the Danbury Court are, in many cases, not detained long in the local Jail.   The understanding is that when prisoners are sentenced for a period of thirty days or longer, the Jailer shall notify the Sheriff, who will then direct the transfer of the men to the Bridgeport Jail, where they will thenceforth be regularly employed; the cost of transportation in such cases is willingly met by the party who has the work under contract.

The short-term men who serve out their sentences in Danbury spend their days in idleness, and either occupy their cells or sit in the halls and read.   The bill of fare is wholesome, but is purposely not so hearty as it would be if the men were regularly employed.   The daily menu is: breakfast, hash, bread, and coffee; dinner, bread and milk; supper, mush and milk.

The Jail is clean and has the appearance of being well conducted.   Religious services are held on alternate Sundays by members of the Women's Christian Temperance Union.

THE WINDHAM COUNTY JAIL,

BROOKLYN.

MR. P. B. SIBLEY, *Sheriff ;* MR. C. H. OSGOOD, *Deputy Jailer.*

Visited October 15, 1897, and September 27, 1898.

The Jail is located at Brooklyn, six miles south from the Pomfret station on the Midland division of the N. Y., N. H. & H. R. R., and four miles west from Danielson on the Norwich division of the same railway.   Brooklyn is the old county seat of Windham County, but for some years past the sessions of the courts have been held for the most part in the larger towns of Putnam and Windham.

The building which was formerly used for the purpose of a Jail at last became so utterly unfit to meet the necessary requirements, that an entirely new structure was erected in 1896, at a total cost of about $45,000, upon the same site. The new Jail is substantially built of brick in a simple but pleasing style of architecture, and consists of a long main building extending north and south, and a smaller part extending east and west which connects the main building with the Jailer's house. The latter is the only part of the old Jail which is still preserved, and it has been thoroughly renovated to be in keeping with the new structures.

The main building consists of three divisions, of which the southernmost and largest contains the main block of sixty cells disposed in three tiers. The cells are solidly constructed of steel and are placed back to back, each tier being divided by a narrow passage which runs through the length of the block and permits the inspection of the cells from the rear by the officer in charge. Light and air are received from long windows in the outer walls, and each cell is further ventilated independently by a system of pipes which extend to the roof. Every cell contains a good bed and bedding, and is provided with a sanitary bucket, inclosed in a ventilated compartment. In the northern division is another block of thirty-six cells, similar in design and equipment to those in the larger block. Shower baths and lavatories are accessible from each tier in both divisions, and every prisoner is required to bathe once a week. Steam heat is supplied in all departments of the Jail.

The central part of the main building contains a convenient hospital room, with bathroom attached, and on the upper floor a pleasant chapel, where religious services are conducted every Sunday. In the basement is a well-equipped laundry which contains also a steam sterilizer, where the clothing of the men, which is taken from them at the time of entrance, is thoroughly fumigated; clothing and shoes are provided for the inmates by the Jail during their time of residence.

The smaller part of the Jail contains a well-arranged kitchen and bakery, from which rations are served conveniently to the inmates of both the north and south divisions. The usual bill of fare is: for breakfast, bread and coffee, and hash for those who are actively employed; for dinner, corned beef and vegetables, soup, or beans, with bread; for supper, bread and tea, with meat for the workers.   Pleasant offices for the Jailer are situated in this part of the building, and on the upper floor are several large rooms designed for workshops, where the bedding and much of the clothing used in the Jail are manufactured by the inmates.   One of these rooms is occupied by the women prisoners, who are usually few in number, as the cells designed for them in the north block did not prove, suitable for the purpose.

Twenty-four acres of land are directly connected with the Jail, a considerable part of which is cultivated by the prisoners. A model stable, barn, and creamery, situated on the premises, furnish healthful employment for a number of men.   During the past year, new sheds and outbuildings have been erected by means of the Jail labor, and on all sides are evidences of careful and efficient direction.   An adjacent farm of two hundred acres, also, is owned by the County, and here a majority of the prisoners are employed in clearing up the land and in raising large quantities of farm-produce.   In addition, groups of men are let out to assist the farmers in the neighborhood, as occasion requires.

By the erection of the new buildings the County is committed no doubt to the policy of maintaining the Jail in Brooklyn for a number of years to come.   Since their completion, it possesses a penal institution in every respect adequate and suitable to meet its requirements.

THE LITCHFIELD COUNTY JAIL,

LITCHFIELD.

Mr. E. A. Nellis, *Sheriff* ; Mr. J. M. Benton, *Deputy Jailer.*

Visited April 1, 1898.

The Jail has an attractive situation in the center of the town at the corner of North and West streets, and is surrounded by a small but well-kept yard.   It consists of a large dwelling-house, erected in 1811, in which the Jailer has his office and private quarters, and adjoining it in the rear the Jail buildings proper.

The first of these buildings is a small structure, solidly built of brick and containing at present sixteen cells arranged in two tiers. For many years these constituted the total cell capacity of the Jail, until at last its utter inadequacy for the purpose became so marked that in 1895 a suitable addition and other improvements upon the property were undertaken at a cost of about $22,000. The new building, a substantial brick structure of two stories, is directly connected with the older one, and contains the main block of twenty-eight cells, arranged in two tiers. The block is built of brick with a solid iron floor dividing the tiers. All of the cells are furnished with the regulation prison cots with proper coverings, and are provided with convenient receptacles for sanitary buckets, having thorough ventilation to the roof. The hall surrounding the block is well lighted and ventilated by means of windows in the outer walls. In addition to the main block, there are in each of two corners of the building two steel cells for the restraint of more desperate criminals, and at the other end a single dark cell for the purpose of solitary confinement. Two guard rooms command a view of both sides of the block, and at the southeast corner of the corridor opens a well-appointed bathroom.

The workshop occupies the whole of the upper floor of the main part, and receives good light and air from windows on the north and south sides. The industry carried on is cane-seating chairs under contract with a Bridgeport agent. An ell on the north side contains in the basement the boilers which supply both the new and the old buildings with steam heat, and on the first floor a well-arranged kitchen and pantries. On the second floor is a store-room in connection with the workshop for the storage of materials, finished product, etc., and also a good-sized room for use as a hospital for men.

The improvements made in the front part of the Jail included a thorough renovation of the upper rooms which are now occupied by women prisoners, except when the crowded condition of the Jail necessitates their use for men. In such case the women, if any are present, are transferred to a new room on the third floor of an ell which was added to the north side of the house. This ell contains also a new kitchen, pantries, etc., for the Jailer's household, besides several convenient storerooms. Women prisoners are employed in the kitchen and laundry, and do the sewing and mending required in the institution.

A library of over three hundred volumes is available for the use of the inmates, and religious services are held in the Jail every Sunday. Neat uniforms are worn by the Jailer and his assistant, and all departments give evidence of careful and efficient management.

THE MIDDLESEX COUNTY JAIL,

· HADDAM.

MR. T. S. BROWN, *Sheriff;* MR. W. E. ODBER, *Deputy Jailer.*

Visited July 23, 1898.

The Jail is located at Haddam, on the Valley Division of the N. Y., N. H. & H. R. R., and stands facing the main street of the town on a hill back of the station. It is solidly built of granite, and is provided with quarters on the north side for the use of the Jailer's family. A door in the Jailer's office leads directly into the Jail proper, which consists of a good-sized hall, with the majority of the cells ranged in two tiers on the north side. The main portion of the hall constitutes the old part and contains twenty single cells, whose interior dimensions are eight feet long, four and one-half feet wide, and six and one-half feet high. An addition built on to the eastern end several years ago forms the new part, and contains ten cells, which are somewhat larger and are fitted in each case with accommodations for two inmates. The room is chiefly lighted and ventilated by a row of windows on the south side.

All of the cells are cared for by their respective inmates, and are furnished with single beds provided with ticks filled with straw, pillows, and blankets. At the date of the last visit there were no sheets and pillow-cases in evidence, and the suggestion made by the Board of Charities some time ago that their use be adopted had evidently never been put into effect. As a measure of cleanliness and common decency, their prompt introduction is strongly urged.

The building is supplied with a steam-heating apparatus, the pipes of which extend along the south wall of the corridor, at a considerable elevation from the floor. It has not operated successfully, and a coal-burning stove in the northwest corner is depended upon as the mainstay for heating purposes. Dur-

ing the days in the winter months when there is no work offering, the men who are at large in the corridors draw wooden
benches near the stove and sit huddled together around it.   On
the opposite side of the room is the bathtub.   A movable ·
screen stands near by and can be readily adjusted so as to conceal the tub from public view.

The plumbing and general sanitary fixtures of the Jail are
inadequate and ill-arranged; when last visited, it was found that
a new iron bath-tub had replaced the old one, but no other improvements were noticed.   The bath-tub still discharges into
an open drain and thence by a pipe through the wall to a tank
outside.   The drain is so shallow that it overflows, and keeps
the floor wet and nasty in the neighborhood of the tub.   As
noted in the Board's last Report, all the laundering for the inmates is done in the main corridor.   No tubs are provided and
there are no facilities for heating the water except the stove
above mentioned.   A kettle placed on the top of the stove is
used for the purpose and the washing is done in the bath-tub;
the garments are then hung on lines in the corridor to dry.

The women's department is situated over the kitchen, with
which it has been connected by a new staircase since the last
Report.   It consists of four cells, besides one dark cell for
solitary confinement, and is furnished with pitchers and basins
for toilet purposes.   The women are employed in the kitchen
as circumstances require.   The food supplied to the prisoners
is sufficient and of good quality.   The ordinary bill of fare is:
for breakfast, bread and coffee, with beans, hash, or cold meat;
for dinner, bread, with corned beef and vegetables, fish, soup,,
or beans; for supper, some variety of cereal food with tea. ·

There is no workshop connected with the institution, and
the men are not regularly employed.   They are engaged in
cultivating the Jail farm of forty acres during the season, and
in the spring and autumn do a part of the work upon the roads
and bridges in the town, and are occasionally hired out by the
day to the neighboring farmers.   The net results are very
small.   Religious services are held in the Jail every Sunday
afternoon by the minister of the local church.

In matters of equipment, neatness, and good order, it must
be said that the Middlesex County Jail is not up to the standard
of other institutions of the kind in the State, and it is, therefore,
urgently recommended that steps be taken at an early date to
effect a thorough renovation of the Jail, and an improvement in
its general furnishings and sanitary conditions.

THE TOLLAND COUNTY JAIL,

TOLLAND.

Mr. A. P. Dickinson, *Sheriff ;* Mr. J. A. Brown, *Deputy Jailer.*

Visited March 18, 1898.

The County Jail is inconveniently situated in Tolland and is reached from the nearest three railway stations by a drive of five miles from Rockville, of six miles from Vernon on the Highland division of the N. Y., N. H. & H. R. R., or of three miles from the Tolland station on the Central Vermont Railroad.

As it now stands the Jail is a small stone building, and consists of an old part built in 1865, and a new part which was added four years ago; the former contains two tiers of eight cells each, constructed of brick, and the latter the same number, constructed of iron, making thirty-two cells in all. The tiers are ranged along the north wall of the building and open on to a wide corridor, which is lighted by a series of windows facing the south and is ventilated by them and by openings in the ceiling. The floor of the corridor is about five feet below the level of the ground.

The cells contain single beds, which are furnished with excelsior mattresses, sheets, blankets, pillows, and pillow-cases. The bath-tub at one end of the corridor, and the closet at the other are decently enclosed by wooden partitions. The men do their own washing, and have the use for this purpose of a row of stationary wash-tubs conveniently placed and supplied with hot and cold water. The clothes are hung on lines in the corridor to dry. At the time of visit certain evidences were noted of a lack of care in preserving conditions of neatness and cleanliness in the Jail quarters.

There is no workshop attached to the Jail; the men are not employed in any way, except in doing occasional odd jobs about the premises, and there are, therefore, in this instance no receipts from the earnings of prisoners. The ordinary bill of fare is: breakfast, crackers and coffee, with sugar and milk;

dinner, meat and potatoes, meat stew, hash, or beans, with bread; supper, crackers and tea, with sugar and milk.

The Jailer's residence is connected with the Jail, and is provided with telephone communication from Rockville. In the back part over the kitchen are located the women's quarters, consisting of two good-sized rooms with accommodations for four inmates. A general condition of improvement was evident in this department at the date of visit. The rooms are heated by steam and are provided with a closet. Adjoining the women's department is a large room which is designed for use as a hospital and seems well adapted for the purpose.

Although Tolland County Jail is the smallest one in the State, it is the only Jail whose accommodations usually exceed the requirements.

PROVISION FOR DEPENDENT AND NEGLECTED CHILDREN.

THE COUNTY TEMPORARY HOMES.

Under the provisions of the General Statutes a Temporary Home for dependent and neglected children is maintained in each of the eight counties of the State.   The law authorizing their establishment grew out of a movement whose object was to prevent the placing of children over two years of age in town almshouses, a concerted inquiry having previously demonstrated the fact that it was a common practice on the part of overseers of the poor to place dependent children in almshouses, and that large numbers of them, many of whom were between the ages of two and sixteen, were still under the influence of such objectionable surroundings.

The law was passed in January, 1883, and preparations were made to put its provisions into effect with as little delay as possible.   One Home was opened on September 10, 1883; others followed suit at somewhat later dates, and by January 1, 1884, all had been established and were in active operation.

The original locations that were selected for the Homes have not been retained in a single instance.   At the time of their organization the Homes were in the experimental stage of a new departure, and provisions in regard to amount of land, kind of buildings, and points of location, etc., have since been determined by various causes.

A brief account of their present situation and condition, in the order of their foundation, together with a compendium of the laws governing their establishment and management, tables of statistics concerning their population, etc., is given in the following pages.

THE MIDDLESEX COUNTY HOME.

The Home was opened in Middletown on September 10, 1883; was moved to Higganum in April, 1884, and in November, 1886, to Haddam, its present location.   The situation is a

13

good one, being on a considerable elevation above the Connecticut River and on the main road of the town, about half a mile south from the Haddam station and only a few rods distant from the flag-station at Arnold's.

The building occupied is a large wooden structure, three stories in height, constructed especially for the purpose and enlarged about a year ago by a commodious addition on the north side.   The new wing contains a well-lighted schoolroom, with additional dormitories, bathrooms, etc., on the upper floors, and increases the capacity of the Home to accommodations for eighty children.   New iron beds, painted white, have been introduced in the dormitories, and all departments present an attractive appearance of comfort and good order.   The building is provided with iron fire-escapes from the upper stories.

An abundant supply of good water is piped into the house from a neighboring hill, and the system of drainage into the river is effective.   It is desirable, however, that the water main to the house should be replaced by one of larger size, which would permit the introduction of fire plugs and hose · in the hallways, as a means of protection in case of need.

Between four and five acres of land surround the Home, of which a portion is cultivated as a kitchen garden, but the larger part is used solely as a recreation ground.   On Sundays the children attend church and Sunday-school in the town.

THE HARTFORD COUNTY HOME.

The Hartford County Temporary Home was opened in Bloomfield on October 1, 1883; was afterwards moved to East Hartford, and again in 1889 to its present location at Warehouse Point.   It is finely situated on a hill one mile east from the railway station at Windsor Locks, and one mile and a half south from the Warehouse Point station.   A large brick house, formerly used as a private residence, was remodeled to suit the Home's purposes.   The grounds in front of the house are laid out in an ornamental manner, and those on the north and east are cultivated as a kitchen garden and orchard, about eleven acres of land in all being connected with the institution.

To remedy its overcrowded condition a few years ago, a large brick addition, two stories in height, was erected in connection with the main house, and by a careful arrangement can be made to accommodate about one hundred children. The dormitories, etc., are neat and attractive, but no provision is made for a playroom for the girls in the building, and the desirability of furnishing some place for the purpose is heartily recommended. The boys' playroom in the basement, although well-lighted and aired, is a barren and cheerless apartment, and should be made more attractive by the introduction of simple games.

The main house is now reserved for the use of the Superintendent's family, teachers, assistants, etc., with the exception of a large dining-room for the children and a room on the third floor which is used for hospital purposes when needed. The total number of children belonging to the Home is, as a rule, considerably in excess of the accommodations provided in the institution, and it has, therefore, been the practice for some time to board a certain class of them with a housekeeper in the town.

A new and commodious schoolhouse was erected in 1896, for the use of the Home. It is a one-story brick structure, situated at a short distance from the main building, and contains two schoolrooms having accommodations for fifty pupils each. The rooms are well-lighted and equipped with improved systems of heating and ventilation, and are further provided with convenient coat and toilet-rooms adjoining.

THE LITCHFIELD COUNTY HOME.

The Home was opened in New Milford on October 1, 1883. In April, 1884, it was removed to East Canaan, and on April 1, 1889, it was removed, on the invitation of the founder, to the Gilbert Home in Winsted.

Under this arrangement the county does not support an institution of its own as a Temporary Home. The county and Gilbert Home children occupy the same building, the county paying $1.50 per week to the Home trustees for the support of each child of the former class. A description of the Gilbert Home is given elsewhere in this Report under the heading of Private Provision for Children, and a reference to it will show that the county is fortunate in having the privileges of so well equipped an institution available for its dependent children under such favorable conditions. The same regulations in regard to committing and placing out of county children apply here as in the other Temporary Homes. The inmates attend school on the premises.

THE WINDHAM COUNTY HOME.

The Home was opened at Putnam Heights on November 1, 1883, and was moved on November 1, 1886, to a location on the public highway between Putnam and Thompson, and about two miles east from the Putnam station.

The buildings, which consisted of a large house, a succession of outbuildings, and a large barn, the whole appearing more like a comfortable farming establishment than a county institution, were destroyed by fire in the fall of the present year. Fortunately, no lives were lost, and the children have been boarded since, for the most part, at neighboring farmhouses. A few have been accommodated with the superintendent's family in a detached cottage on the Home grounds, which was erected in 1895 for the purpose of a hospital, and which, alone, of all the Home buildings, escaped destruction.

The property consists of a productive farm of about sixty-five acres, and, as the location was a desirable one for the Home, it is planned to erect new buildings on the same site at the earliest practicable opportunity.

It is still the practice of the Home children to attend the district school near by, and on Sundays to attend service and Sunday-school at a neighboring church.

THE TOLLAND COUNTY HOME.

The Home was opened in Andover on November 1, 1883, and was later moved to Vernon Center, where it has remained since. It has an unusually pleasant location on high ground facing the main road of the town, about a mile and a quarter northeast from the Vernon station and half a mile east from the Vernon Center depot, which, however, is merely a flag station.

The house now occupied was formerly a tavern and, when bought by the county, was remodeled to suit its new purpose. A two-storied addition was erected in 1895, and increased materially the capacity of the Home. Its first floor forms a large playroom for the use of all the children, and the second floor a comfortable dormitory for boys. Convenient bathrooms and toilet facilities also are provided. All of the dormitories are furnished with white enamelled bedsteads and present a neat and attractive appearance. A large room on the third floor is used for hospital purposes when required. The building is heated by steam, and an abundant supply of pure spring water is piped into the house.

About twelve acres of land are attached to the Home, a part of which is cultivated as a garden.   The large barn belonging to the Home was destroyed by fire during the past year, but a new and commodious structure has since been erected to replace it.   Several head of stock are kept, and the boys and girls enjoy practically all the best features of country life under healthful conditions.

The children attend the district school near by, and are present at Sunday services in the village church.   The life of the Home is that of a large family, and is characterized by features of homelike care and comfort.

THE NEW HAVEN COUNTY HOME.

The Home was opened in Tyler City on January 1, 1884, and on July 1, 1885, was moved to its present location in New Haven, at the corner of Shelton avenue and Bassett street. A line of electric cars runs past the place and makes this the most accessible of all the Homes.

The Home stands in a large lot which furnishes a good playground, but, on account of its location within the city limits, the place lacks many of the features of country life that children in the other Homes enjoy.   In this instance, also, the Home was formerly a private residence, and was remodeled and enlarged to suit its purposes.   The last alterations were made in 1897, and provide improved dining-room and dormitory accommodations, together with a thorough renovation of all the plumbing in the building in modern sanitary fashion.

In the year 1895-6 a plan was adopted by the Board of Management of boarding out all the younger children belonging to the Home in selected family homes, not more than four being placed in any one family.   This was done in order to relieve the overcrowded condition of the Home, which had been growing steadily worse for a number of years, and to avoid the necessity of erecting new and extensive buildings with their usual tendency toward a more permanent form of institution.

The Home at present shelters chiefly the older children, for whom places in family homes are more readily secured, and thus preserves, so far as possible, the temporary character intended in its organization.   The children receive instruction in two schoolrooms connected with the Home, and on Sundays attend service and Sunday-school at neighboring churches.

It is not found that the boarding-out system affects the number of family homes that receive children without remuneration, and an effort is made to place them in the usual manner whenever possible.

THE NEW LONDON COUNTY HOME.

The Home was opened in Norwich on January 1' 1884, but shortly afterwards was moved into the town of Preston. It may be reached from Norwich by a Taftville electric car to Eighth street, and a short walk thence across the river.

The house now occupied was formerly a private residence, and was remodeled and enlarged at the time of purchase. In 1894 a wing was added, providing a schoolroom on the first floor and a dormitory for boys above. The dormitory is low between joints and is warmed by the heated air that rises through registers from the schoolroom below. The girls' dormitory is situated over the playrooms. The Home can accommodate forty-five children comfortably, or fifty when crowded. Of late the pressure upon its accommodations has become so serious that plans are now under consideration for the enlargement of all departments at an early date by the construction of another addition to the building.

The house is heated by steam and lighted by oil lamps. A fair supply of water is obtained from a well and a cistern, and the drainage is conducted by pipes to the river. A few acres of land surround the house and are used chiefly as playgrounds for the children. A simple wooden building on the premises is used as a playhouse in stormy weather or in summer heat (since there are no trees on the place to furnish protection), and is greatly enjoyed by the inmates of the Home. On Sundays the children attend church and Sunday-school in the suburb of Norwich directly across the river from the Home.

THE FAIRFIELD COUNTY HOME.

The Home was opened in Stratford on January 1, 1884, and was later removed to Norwalk, where it has a fine location on high ground, about three-quarters of a mile northeast from the

· center of the city. Electric cars between Norwalk and Westport pass the premises.

For the use of the Home the county erected a commodious
brick building at a cost of seventeen thousand dollars, and in
1892 it was opened for the reception of children. It is a well-
built structure, unusually well lighted and ventilated, and has
accommodations for about eighty children. As the average
number of children belonging to the Home is one hundred or
more, it has been customary for several years to board from
ten to twenty of them at Greenfield Hill, about five miles north
of Norwalk, in the families of an ex-matron of the Home and
one of her neighbors. For some time, also, a number of
children have been boarded with a former assistant in the
Home at Southwick, Mass., and with her sister in Springfield.
Although the circumstances in this case were exceptional, the
general principle of boarding County Home children outside
the limits of the State cannot be regarded with favor.

In 1895 a two-storied brick building for school purposes was
erected at the Home, and is connected with the main building
by a covered passage. Two well-arranged schoolrooms are
under the charge of efficient teachers. On Sundays the children attend service and Sunday-school at churches in Norwalk.

Within the past year a hospital building, also of brick and
one story high, has been completed at a cost of about five
thousand dollars. It is situated at a sufficient distance from
the main building and contains two large, airy wards for boys
and girls, respectively, with possible accommodations for fifty
beds. In connection with each ward is a bathroom equipped
with modern sanitary fixtures. The central portion of the
building contains two bedrooms for nurses and a well-furnished
kitchen. The building is heated by steam and lighted by gas,
and every precaution has been taken to insure admirable sanitary conditions.

THE WORKING ORGANIZATION
OF THE
COUNTY HOMES.

BOARDS OF MANAGEMENT AND TOWN COMMITTEES.

Each Home is under the charge of a Board of Management, which, under the present law, consists of the County Commissioners, a member of the State Board of Health, and a member of the State Board of Charities. This Board appoints the Superintendent and Matron, and also appoints committees of men or women in each town in the county, who serve without compensation, who have the right to visit and inspect the Home, make suggestions of changes and improvements to the Board, and whose duty it is to assist in the careful selection of family homes, and in the visitation of children when placed out. The town committees appoint a Secretary, who correponds with the other members in regard to the interests of children placed in families, etc., etc.

Under the provisions of an Act of 1895, the Board of Management has full guardianship and control of each child committed to the Temporary Home in that county until the child reaches the age of eighteen years, or until such guardianship is legally transferred; and the Board is further empowered in certain cases to give any child under its care in adoption in the same manner as any other legal guardian might do. It is provided, however, by an Act of 1893, that any child who has been committed to a Temporary Home may, upon the petition of its parents or guardians to the Board of Management, or to the court that made the commitment, be released and discharged from the Home when it is shown that the causes for which the commitment was made no longer exist. In many instances there is reason to believe that children are so released without sufficient examination into the circumstances of the persons making the petition, and that the conditions to which the children are returned are often as bad as those from which they were originally removed. Great care, therefore, should be exercised to investigate all cases of this sort before granting such petitions.

.In placing children in family homes, the rule is that when strangers apply at the Home, they shall present a written recommendation from one or more of the town committees. If the application is granted the children are placed in the applicants' care, under the condition that until eighteen years old (unless sooner discharged by law) they will be at all times subject to the care and control of the Board of Management. The committee for the town to which the children go is then notified, and is expected by visits and observation to keep a careful watch and to report to the Board any failure on the part of the family to care for the children in a satisfactory manner. Two special agents, appointed by the State Board of Charities under the provisions of an Act of 1895, also assist in the work of securing family homes and in maintaining supervision over the children thus placed out.

In the fall months an annual meeting is held at the Home of the members of the Board of Management, town committees and all others who are interested. A financial statement is presented, reports are given by the town committees of their visits and observations, and the details of the working of the Home for the past year are fully discussed. .

TOWN AND STATE GUARDIANSHIP.

According to Section 3657 of the General Statutes, neglected and dependent children may at any time be placed by the Selectmen of the town under the protecting care of the Home in that county, without the previous observance of formalities of any sort. The Home has a fixed charge of not less than $1.50 nor more than $2.00 per week for the support of each inmate. The Selectmen know the rate, and if they place a child in the institution it is fully understood that the town, through them, will be expected to pay for the child's board at the rate in question.

Children so placed are retained as wards of the town. Their temporary support is paid for by the town, and when the conditions which had called for their immediate care are replaced by those which admit of their return to home or friends, they may be removed by the town Selectmen with the same informality.

Under another statute, Section 3658, Justices of the Peace.

Judges of Probate, or Judges of any city or police court may, by due process of law, formally commit children deserted, neglected, or cruelly treated to any one of the Temporary Homes. The children then become wards of the State. Their temporary support is paid for by the State, and until they reach the age of eighteen years, the State expects that the Board of Management will satisfactorily perform its duties in behalf of State wards by temporarily protecting them for only so long a time as shall be absolutely necessary for the placing of the children in well-selected family homes. Under this system the towns are relieved from the burden of supporting the children removed from the several localities, and in consequence the practice of committing children to the Homes through the medium of the courts has become wellnigh universal.

ERRORS IN COMMITMENT.

There is no question that in most cases the committals to the Homes have been made properly, and in the right understanding of the conditions in question, but at the same time mistakes have occurred, and with a view to reducing the percentage of such errors to the smallest limit, it is well to point out the desirability of holding a thorough investigation previous to taking the decisive step.

In certain cases children have been committed where less hasty action and an inquiry into the circumstances would have discovered near relatives or friends who would have been willing to take the children under their care.

It happens, too, as a matter of course, that now and again the propriety of certain commitments will be called into question, and it will be alleged with much force that the courts' authority has been wrongfully and arbitrarily exercised. It is well understood that if children are really destitute and exposed to vicious influences, it is a duty to remove and protect them from such conditions, but in all cases too much stress cannot be laid upon the foundation principle that children should not be lightly removed and families broken up and parents permitted to shirk their responsibility if, consistently with the best interests of the children, it can be prevented.

HOMES

FOR

DEPENDENT AND NEGLECTED CHILDREN.

GENERAL STATUTES, 1888,

CHAPTER CCXXVIII.

WITH SUBSEQUENT ACTS AND AMENDMENTS.

(Amended words and clauses are in italics.)

To Be Provided in Each County.

Section 3655. For the better protection of children between the ages of two and *eighteen* years, of the classes hereinafter described, to wit: waifs, strays, children in charge of overseers of the poor, children of prisoners, drunkards, or paupers, and others who are or may hereafter be committed to hospitals, almshouses, or workhouses, and all children within said ages, deserted, neglected, cruelly treated, or dependent, there shall be provided in each county one or more places of refuge, to be known as Temporary Homes. Said homes shall be distant not less than one-half mile from any penal or pauper institution; and no pauper or convict shall be permitted to live or labor therein; and they shall not be used as a permanent provision or residence for any child, but for its temporary protection, for so long a time only as shall be absolutely necessary for the placing of the child in a well-selected family home. Children demented, idiotic, or suffering from incurable or contagious diseases, are not included in the provisions of this chapter.
As amended by P. A. 1897, Ch. 210.

How Managed — Town Committees.

Sec. 3656. In each county the County Commissioners thereof, with one member of the State Board of Charities and one member of the State Board of Health, shall constitute a board for the location, organization, management, and general supervision of such temporary home or homes in the county. Said board may use, with their consent, orphan asylums now in operation in any county. as temporary homes for that county; and the County Commissioners may lease, purchase, hold, sell, and convey real and personal estate
As amended by P. A. 1893, Ch. 28.

for the purposes of such temporary home or homes; and the board may, when desirable for economical reasons, and when consistent with the welfare of the children to be provided for, establish such temporary homes in desirable private families; *provided*, that in no instance shall such home be under the same care or management as an almshouse, workhouse, or penal institution. Said board may appoint such superintendents or agents, and may make such rules, regulations, and by-laws as may be necessary or convenient for the order and government of the temporary home and its officers; and they shall appoint a committee of one man or woman in each town of the county, *or more than one in accordance with the population and area of the town*, who shall serve without compensation, and who shall have at all times the right to visit and inspect the home or homes of their county, and to suggest to said board such provisions, changes, or additions as they may think desirable; and shall assist said board in the careful selection of family homes for the children in the temporary home or homes, and in the visitation of children when placed in selected families; which visitation shall be made by said board, or by its agents, or through said committees, at least once in every three months; and said board shall remove any child from the family in which it may be placed to a temporary home or to another family, at their discretion, subject to the intents and purposes of this chapter.

Board of Management to Meet Once in Three Months.

895,   SEC. 1. In each county the board for the management of temporary homes for dependent children shall meet at least once in each three months for the purpose of attending to the duties imposed upon it by law, and notice of such meetings shall be sent to each member by mail at least three days prior thereto by the chairman of said board.

Town Committees to Meet with Board of Management.

SEC. 2. At the meeting of said board held in each county in the fall months of each year, the town committees of the several towns in the county shall meet with said board for the purpose of suggesting such provisions, changes, and additions as they may think desirable in the temporary home, and assisting said board in the selection of family homes for the children in the temporary home, and advising said board of the results of their visitations of children when placed in family homes; and like notice of said meeting shall be given the town committees at least five days prior thereto by the chairman of said board.

Board to have Guardianship of Children until Eighteen Years.

SEC. 3. Said board in each county shall have full guardianship and control over each child committed to the temporary home for such county until such child shall have reached the age of eighteen

years, or such guardianship and control shall have been legally transferred, or another guardian appointed by the probate court with the
consent of said board; and said board in each county shall have full
power to place any child committed to the temporary home of the
county at such employment, and cause the child to be instructed in
such branches of useful knowledge as may be suited to the years and
capacity of the child for such term of years not extending beyond
the child's becoming eighteen years of age, as may be, in the judgment of said board, necessary to secure the welfare and future benefit
of the child; and said board may give any such child, being an orphan
or having been in charge of the county home for more than one year,
in adoption in the same manner as any other legal guardian might
do, and may at its discretion apply to the proper probate court for
the appointment of a guardian of any such child. Said board may
authorize the chairman or secretary to execute on behalf of the board
any papers or instruments, or do any acts necessary or proper to the
exercising of the powers herein given.

Parents Not Entitled to Earnings.

SEC. 4. Parents whose children have been supported by a temporary home for three years shall not be entitled to their earnings or services after they have become eighteen years of age.

Probate Courts to have Jurisdiction in Adoption.

SEC. I. The court of probate, in the district where there is a tem- P. A. 189
porary home for dependent or neglected children, shall have exclusive Ch. 28.
jurisdiction for the approval of every agreement by such home giving
in adoption any child, and in cases where the natural parent or guardian
of a child enters into an agreement giving a child in adoption; either
the court of probate in the district where such natural parent or
guardian resides or the court of probate in the district where the
adopting parent resides shall have jurisdiction for the approval of such
agreement, and such agreement may be exhibited to the court of probate in either of such districts.

SEC. 2. All acts or parts of acts inconsistent herewith are hereby
repealed.

SEC. 3. This act shall take effect from its passage.   Approved,
March 15, 1897.

State Board of Charities May Recommend Homes.

SEC. I. The State Board of Charities may recommend to the boards P. A. 189
for the management and supervision of the temporary homes in the Ch. 298.
several counties suitable family homes for the dependent and neglected
children in charge of said temporary homes, and may visit any family
home in which any such child has been placed by the county board
in any county, or any place in which any such child has been placed

at employment by any county board, to ascertain whether such child
is properly treated and whether such home is a suitable one, having
in view the welfare of the child.

To Report Ill Treatment.

SEC. 2.   Whenever it shall be found that any such child is not properly treated in any family home or that any such home is not a suitable
one and is of such character as to jeopardize the welfare of any child
so placed therein, the State Board of Charities shall report the facts in
the case to the county board which placed the child in such family
home, and said county board, upon being satisfied of the ill treatment
of the child, or the unsuitableness of the home, shall remove the child
from such home and take such further action as shall be necessary to
secure the welfare of the child.

May Delegate Duties to Secretary or Agent.

SEC. 3.   The State Board of Charities may authorize its secretary or
superintendent, or any agent appointed by it, to visit family homes in
which dependent and neglected children in charge of temporary homes
in the several counties may be placed, to recommend suitable family
homes to the county boards, and perform such further duties in connection with the dependent and neglected children in charge of such
temporary homes as said State Board of Charities may prescribe.

Children Not to be Placed or Retained in Almshouses—Expenses of Sup-port, How Paid, etc.

nded by
897,
.

SEC. 3657.   It shall be unlawful for overseers of the poor to place
or retain children between the ages of *four and eighteen* years in almshouses after they shall have been notified by said board that a temporary home in their county is open for the reception of such children;
and upon such notice they shall cause all such children in almshouses
to be removed to such home: *provided*, that, if one of the parents of
such children who is a person of good moral character shall be committed to the almshouse with and may there care for them, such children may remain with such parent in the almshouse for a period of not
more than thirty days in any one year. The necessary expenses of supporting children in temporary homes, or in family homes until they
shall reach the age of twelve years for girls and fourteen for boys,
shall be paid by the town committing them to the temporary home,
said town so paying having a right of action upon this statute for re-
imbursement from the towns to which said children, if paupers, would
be legally chargeable, at not less than one dollar and fifty cents nor
more than two dollars weekly per child: but nothing herein shall be
construed as requiring payment for the support of children in private
families when in the opinion of said board they may be placed by it in
such families to its satisfaction, consistently with the best interests of

the child and with the provisions and purposes of this chapter, without such payment. Overseers of the poor may place children in the temporary home for their county upon such terms, as to the time of their stay therein, as may be agreed upon by them with said board. Said board may, in its discretion, permit children to be cared for in the temporary home at the expense of private persons. The placing of children with the lowest auction bidder is hereby prohibited.

Forfeiture for Neglect to Place Child in Temporary Home.

Any selectman, overseer of the poor, or town, placing or retaining any child between the ages of two and *eighteen* years in an almshouse, in violation of the provisions of section 3657 of the general statutes, shall forfeit fifty dollars for each month of such violation, to be recovered by information in the superior court by the state's attorney.

P. A. 189 Ch. 313.
As amen P. A. 189 Ch. 210.

Children under Two Years May be Placed in County Home.

Children less than two years of age may be placed by overseers of the poor in any county temporary home if its board of management shall consent to receive them, and the expense of their support shall be paid in accordance with Section 3657 of the General Statutes.

P. A. 189 Ch. 323.

Vicious Children Not to be Committed to Jail, Almshouse, or Workhouse.

Sec. 3658. No court or justice of the peace shall commit any child under sixteen years of age as vicious, truant, or incorrigible, to any jail, almshouse, or workhouse. Any court of probate, the judge of any city or police court sitting in chambers, or any justice of the peace may, upon proceedings instituted in the manner provided for the commitment of children to the Industrial School or Connecticut School for Boys, or upon petition of the Connecticut Humane Society or the State Board of Charities, commit any child belonging to the class enumerated in Sec. 3655 to any temporary home that may have been established under this chapter until such child shall be *eighteen* years of age, unless sooner discharged by said board of management of temporary homes, and the costs of such commitment, and the expense of the support of such children after such commitment, shall be paid in the same manner as in other cases referred to in *this* section.

As amen P. A. 188 Ch. 28, ar 1897, Ch.

Certain Children Not to be Sent to Connecticut School for Boys or Industrial School Unless—

Sec. 3659. No child belonging to either of the classes specified in Sec. 3655 shall be sentenced or committed by any court or justice of the peace to the Connecticut School for Boys or the Connecticut Industrial School for Girls, unless such child is found to have committed an offense punishable by law, or is leading an idle, vagrant, or vicious life, or the court or magistrate is of opinion that the child's previous circumstances and life have been such as to make it desirable that such child should be placed under the restraint, care, and guardianship of one of said schools.

Transfer of Children from School for Boys or Industrial School to County Homes.

Sec. 3660.   The directors of either of said schools may at their discretion transfer any child belonging to either of the classes specified in Sec. 3655, sentenced or committed to such school, to the county home of the county from which such child was sentenced or committed, after reasonable notice to the board of managers thereof.   The superintendent of such school shall immediately notify the comptroller of such transfer, and the expense of supporting the child in such home shall be paid by the State as provided in case of children committed to temporary homes by process of law.

Guardianship of Such Child Not Affected.

Sec. 3661.   Such transfer shall not divest the school from which the child is transferred of its guardianship and control over such child, unless the same be relinquished by the board of directors of such school.

Appeals from Commitment of Children to Public Institutions. — To what Courts Appeals May be Taken.

893,

SEC. 1.   Chapter CLXXI of the Public Acts of 1889 is hereby amended to read as follows: An appeal shall lie from any judgment, order, or decree of a court of probate, judge of a city or police court, or justice of the peace committing any child to the Connecticut School for Boys, to the Connecticut Industrial School for Girls, or to any County Home for Dependent or Neglected Children, to the next criminal term of the Court of Common Pleas to be held within and for the county where such judgment is rendered, but in towns of which the District Court of Waterbury has appellate jurisdiction in criminal cases, such appeal shall be taken to the next criminal term of said district court, and in cases not in the jurisdiction of such Court of Common Pleas or District Court to the next criminal term of the Superior Court.

Who May Take Appeal.

SEC. 2.   Such appeal may be taken by any parent or guardian of the child so committed, or by the selectmen of the town in which such judgment is rendered, within twenty days hereafter; and the appellant shall enter into a recognizance, with surety to the State; conditioned to answer to the complaint and abide the order and judgment of the court thereon.

Criminal Complaint Against to be Tried by Jury on Appeal.

SEC. 3.   Complaints under sections 3628, 3641, and 3658 of the General Statutes shall, on appeal, be tried by a jury, and such child shall be produced in court during trial and to receive final judgment, by the appellant or by the person or persons having such child in their possession or control; and the jury shall render a verdict of guilty, or not guilty, or of proven or not proven, as the facts proved may warrant; and on a verdict of guilty or proven, sentence of commitment may follow as provided in said sections of the General Statutes.

Children May be Discharged or Transferred from Temporary Homes.

SEC. 1. Any child committed to a temporary home by virtue of the provisions of Chapter CCXXVIII of the General Statutes, or transferred or committed to any suitable person or institution, by the provisions hereof, may, upon petition of the parents or guardian of such child to the board of managers, or the court of authority that made the commitment or transfer, be released and discharged from said temporary home, and from the authority of said board of managers, said persons, or institutions, to such parents or guardians, when it is shown upon inquiry had that the causes for which the commitment was made no longer exist, and said board, court, or authority may transfer any child from such home to the keeping of any suitable person or institution upon the petition of the parents or guardian therefor, upon said board, court, or authority being satisfied and assured, after due inquiry had that such transfer will be for the welfare and best interest of said child; *provided, however,* that the town which committed any child to the temporary home, or the town to which said child, if a pauper, would be legally chargeable, shall not be liable for the expense of supporting such child after such transfer; *and provided that any child who has been or shall be transferred to a private institution shall cease to be a charge to the State or county; and provided, further, that said application or petition be made within a year from the date of the commitment of the child to the county home;* and further provided, that the words " court or authority " shall not be so construed as to include justices of the peace.

P. A. 189
Ch. 255.
As amen
by P. A.
Ch. 228.

To whom Children May be Committed.

SEC. 2. Commitments of children by virtue of the provisions of said chapter may be made by authority designated in said chapter, to any suitable person or institutions consenting thereto, designated by the parents or guardians of such children, upon being satisfied, after due inquiry made, that such a commitment will be for the welfare and best interest of such children; *provided, however,* that the town from which any child is committed under the provisions of this section, or the town to which said child, if a pauper, would be legally chargeable, *or the State or the county* shall not be liable for the expense of supporting such child by the person or institution, *other than the county home,* to which such child is committed.

Religious Instruction.

SEC. 3. Ministers of the gospel shall have free access to the several places of commitment and residence of children of their respective communions for the purpose of administering moral and religious instruction at such reasonable time as shall be designated by the board of managers of said temporary homes.

Children to be Subject to Authority of Board of Management.

SEC. 4. All children committed or transferred in accordance with the provisions hereof shall be subject to the authority and supervision of the board of managers of the temporary home of the county in which the commitment or transfer takes place, and said board of managers, or their agents, may visit said children in the several places of commitment provided therein, in the same manner and with the same authority as is provided in Section 3656 of the General Statutes, in reference to the visitation of selected families, and said managers may for good and sufficient cause remove temporarily to the temporary home of said county any child so committed or transferred until such cause is terminated; *provided*, that if said cause be not terminated within thirty days, then said managers may find private family homes for said children in accordance with the provisions of Chapter CCXXVIII of the General Statutes.

Religious Instruction.

893, 3.

SEC. 1. Equal privileges shall be granted to clergymen and parents of all religious denominations to impart religious instruction to the inmates of the temporary homes for dependent and neglected children, and every reasonable opportunity shall be allowed such clergymen and the parents of said inmates to give to such inmates as belong to their respective denominations such religious and moral instruction as they may desire, and the boards of management of said temporary homes shall prescribe reasonable times and places when and where such instruction may be given.

County Tax for Support of Home — When to be Laid.

SEC. 3662. To provide for the expenses of temporary homes in excess of the sum received under Section 3657, said board shall present annually to the county representatives and resident senators of such county an estimate of the expense of such homes for the succeeding year; and said representatives and senators may, and in case sufficient funds are not already in the treasury for such maintenance shall, at their biennial meeting, or, in years in which no biennial meeting is held, at any special meeting duly called in such year, lay a county tax for the maintenance of such home or homes in their county.

Extra School Expense Incurred by Town or School District — How Paid.

SEC. 3663. The necessary extra expense incurred by any town or school district in providing school accommodations and instruction for the inmates of any temporary homes located therein shall be paid by the county as provided in the preceding section.

Audit and Approval of Such Expenses.

Sec. 3664. The board of managers of temporary homes in any county shall be the judge of what are necessary extra expenses, under the preceding section, for school accommodations and instruction for inmates of temporary homes located therein, and no such expense shall be allowed or collected of such county unless it shall have been incurred with the approval of such board of managers, nor until the account of the same shall have been audited and approved by such board.

Schools in County Homes — Enumeration of Children.

. SEC. 1. The children legally committed to county homes shall be enumerated in the districts in which said county homes are located, as provided in Section 2224 of the General Statutes, as amended by Chapter XXVI of the public acts of 1889, but the enumerator shall make a separate list of the children in the county home, and certify said list to the school visitors of the town as provided in Section 2225 of the General Statutes, as amended by Chapter XXVI of the public acts of 1889.

P. A. 189
Ch. 222.

County Commissioners May Establish Schools at County Homes.

SEC. 2. The county commissioners may establish schools at the county homes if in their opinion it is for the interest of the children. In case the county commissioners establish and maintain such a school in any county, the treasurer of the town in which the school is located shall pay to the county commissioners from the amount paid to the town by the comptroller that proportionate part which was derived from the enumeration of the children in the county home. Said commissioners shall apply the sum so named to the payment of the teacher, and to no other purpose. Said schools shall be open during the same days and hours and terms as the schools in the district in which the school is located, and the branches taught shall be those prescribed by the proper school officers for the schools of the town.

Concerning Teachers and School Visitors.

SEC. 3. The county commissioners may employ and pay as teachers of the schools at the county homes persons found qualified as provided in this section, and shall provide books for the children and apparatus for teaching. It shall be the duty of the state board of education to examine the persons employed by the county commissioners, and if the candidates are found qualified in respect of character, education, and teaching ability, to give them certificates authorizing them to teach in said schools, and said board may revoke such certificate, and the county commissioners shall not employ any person who does not hold such certificate.   The said board shall appoint an acting visitor or acting visitors who shall inspect and examine said schools at least twice in each term, and the county commissioners shall not pay any teacher nor maintain said school unless said acting visitor shall certify in writing that said school has been for each month kept in conformity to the laws relating to public schools.

Penalty for Removing Child from Temporary or Private Home.

Sec. 3665.   Every person who shall remove or cause to be removed any child from a temporary home, or from a private home provided by the board of management of temporary homes, which child has been committed to a temporary home by a town or by any court, shall be fined not less than ten or more than thirty dollars, or imprisoned not more than twenty days, or both; *provided,* that children so committed may be withdrawn upon the authority of said board or of the selectmen so committing them.

Statistics of County Homes for Years ending September 30, 1897 and 1898.

	Hartford County.	New Haven County.	New London County.	Fairfield County.	Windham County.	Litchfield County.	Middlesex County.	Tolland County.	Totals.
Number in Homes, Oct. 1, 1896,	103	157	39	96	43	71	52	37	598
Received (new cases),	44	98	48	66	20	28	19	14	337
Returned to Homes,	36	61	18	12	8	46	20	3	204
Totals,	183	316	105	174	71	145	91	54	1,139
Placed in family homes (new cases),	22	42	14	23	10	27	9	7	154
Replaced in family homes,	15	28	11	16	5	38	10	5	128
Returned to friends,	23	60	33	17	7	6	15	3	164
Sent to Protestant Asylums,	0	1	0	0	0	0	0	0	1
Sent to Catholic Asylums,	5	5	0	0	0	0	0	0	10
Given to priests,	0	0	0	3	0	0	0	0	3
Sent to School for Boys,	2	5	1	0	0	1	0	0	9
Sent to Industrial School,	4	1	2	0	0	1	0	0	8
Sent to Lakeville School,	0	2	0	0	0	0	0	0	2
Sent to School for Deaf,	0	3	0	0	0	0	0	0	3
Sent to Institute for Blind,	0	2	0	0	0	0	0	0	2
Discharged by Board of Management,	0	0	0	12	0	0	0	0	12
Recalled by Selectmen,	0	1	0	0	0	4	0	0	5
Died,	1	2	0	0	0	0	0	0	3
Remaining in Homes, Oct. 1, 1897,	111	164	44	103	49	68	57	39	635
Totals,	183	316	105	174	71	145	91	54	1,139
Number in Homes, Oct. 1, 1897,	111	164	44	103	49	68	57	39	635
Received (new cases),	46	79	60	98	36	45	22	17	393
Returned to Homes,	35	65	19	14	13	52	8	12	218
Totals,	192	308	113	215	98	165	87	68	1,246
Placed in family homes (new cases),	27	37	15	34	20	26	6	11	176
Replaced in family homes,	20	44	15	6	9	41	7	4	146
Returned to friends,	16	43	22	41	8	4	13	2	149
Sent to Protestant Asylums,	0	0	0	0	0	0	0	0	0
Sent to Catholic Asylums,	0	1	0	0	0	0	0	0	1
Given to priests,	3	0	0	0	0	0	0	0	3
Sent to School for Boys,	0	3	1	0	0	1	1	1	7
Sent to Industrial School,	2	3	0	2	0	0	0	1	8
Sent to Lakeville School,	0	0	0	2	0	0	0	0	2
Sent to School for Deaf,	0	2	0	0	0	0	0	0	2
Sent to Institute for Blind,	0	2	0	0	0	0	0	0	2
Discharged by Board of Management,	0	1	0	11	0	0	0	2	14
Recalled by Selectmen,	0	3	1	0	0	0	0	0	4
Died,	0	1	0	1	1	1	0	0	4
Remaining in Homes, Oct. 1, 1898,	124	168	59	118	60	92	60	47	728
Totals,	192	308	113	215	98	165	87	68	1,246

Statistics from the Date of Opening, January 1, 1884, to September 30, 1898.

COUNTIES.	Received.	Placed in Family Homes.	Returned to Friends.	Given to Priests.	Sent to Protestant Asylums.	Sent to Catholic Asylums.	Sent to School for Boys.	Sent to Industrial School.	Sent to Lakeville School.	Sent to Blind Institute.	Sent to Schools for Deaf.	Recalled by Selectmen.	Died.	Remaining in County Homes.
Hartford,	903	451	327	89	...	5	8	11	1	...	2	5	10	124
New Haven,	1,241	549	446	13	9	136	36	18	5	6	8	25	20	168
New London,	535	236	235	10	5	...	7	2	5	...	1	18	4	59
Fairfield,	824	314	322	28	7	...	22	5	4	...	...	10	16	118
Windham,	304	167	81	1	...	...	...	...	1	...	...	14	4	60
Litchfield,	414	363	57	7	...	...	2	3	...	...	...	10	13	92
Middlesex,	299	146	119	...	...	...	3	1	...	...	1	4	5	60
Tolland,	226	133	29	11	...	...	4	3	...	2	...	5	8	47
Totals,	4,746	2,359	1,616	159	21	141	82	43	16	8	12	91	80	728

RECEIPTS AND EXPENSES OF COUNTY HOMES.

The following brief statements of the receipts and expenses of the eight County Homes are taken from the returns of County Commissioners for the two years ending June 30, 1897 and 1898, and show the relative amounts paid by the State and by the towns for the support of their respective wards :

1897. COUNTIES.	Received from the State.	Received from Towns.	Total.	Expenses.
Hartford,.............	$11,039.63	$13.14	$11,052.77	$12,403.24
New Haven,........	16,160.94	136.01	16,296.95	23,061.59
New London, ...	4,547.22	———	4,547.22	3,812.68
Fairfield, ...	8,928.43	398.29	9,326.72	11,080.30
Windham,..........	4,714.40	....	*5,068.80	5,097.36
Litchfield, ...	4,505.87	1,048.43	5,554.30	5,558.71
Middlesex,..........	5,274.27	———	5,274.27	5,861.86
Tolland,...........	5,112.86	156.00	5,268.86	3,720.36
Total,....	$60,283.62	$1,751.87	$62,389.89	$70,596.10

* Included in this amount : sales at the Home, $354.40.

1898.				
Hartford,............	$11,042.10	———	$11,042.10	$11,857.50
New Haven,........	16,639.56	$112.30	16,751.86	22,547.36
New London,.......	4,548.44	———	*4,558.44	3,478.87
Fairfield, ...	10,286.82	315.70	*10,791.52	12,733.28
Windham,..........	5,402.75	———	*5,844.95	5,964.80
Litchfield, ...	4,644.68	753.18	5,397.86	5,470.42
Middlesex,..........	6,397.38	———	6,397.38	†7,437.26
Tolland,............	3,036.26	———	*3,187.77	4,727.58
Total,..........	$61,997.99	$1,181.18	$63,971.88	$74,217.07

* Included in these amounts: from School fund, Fairfield County, $189.00 ; sales at the Home, New London County, $10.00; Windham County, $442.20; Tolland County, $151.51.

† In addition to this amount, Middlesex County expended on buildings, $3,689.38.

EXPENSE TO THE STATE.

The State has paid for the support of its wards in the eight County Homes :

For the year ending September 30, 1897, ... $59,914.29

For the year ending September 30, 1898, ...   66,348.33

HARTFORD COUNTY TEMPORARY HOME.

BOARD OF MANAGEMENT.

Chairman, Mr. ROBERT A. POTTER, Bristol,
Secretary, Mr. WILLIAM C. CHENEY, So. Manchester, } *County*
    Mr. EDWARD W. DEWEY, Granby, } *Commissioners.*
Dr. C. A. Lindsley, New Haven, of the State Board of Health ;
Miss Mary Hall, Hartford, of the State Board of Charities.

SECRETARY OF TOWN COMMITTEES.

Mrs. Charles E. Stowe, ...   Simsbury.

TOWNS.	COMMITTEES.	POST OFFICE ADDRESSES.
Hartford,	Mrs. John A. Crilly,	Hartford.
Avon,	Mrs. C. K. Frankhauser,	Avon.
Berlin,	Mrs. R. E. Ensign,	Berlin.
"	Mrs. A. A. Hart,	Kensington.
Bloomfield,	Mrs. Nathan Miller,	Bloomfield.
Bristol,	Mrs. E. F. Judson,	Bristol.
"	Mrs. R. A. Potter,	"
Burlington,	Mrs. Isaac Barnes,	Burlington.
Canton,	Mrs. M. P. Dowd,	Collinsville.
East Granby,	Mrs. I. E. Clark,	East Granby.
East Hartford,	Mrs. C. M. Hill,	East Hartford.
East Windsor,	Mrs. H. O. Allen,	Broad Brook.
"	Mrs. John Middleton,	Melrose.
"	Mrs. James Price,	Warehouse Point.
"	Mrs. Charles Heath,	"
Enfield,	Mrs. George T. Mathewson,	Enfield.
"	Mrs. J. P. Davis,	Thompsonville.
"	Mrs. J. C. Simpson,	"
	Mrs. E. F. Parsons,	"
"	Mrs. John Twiss,	Shaker Station.
Farmington,	Miss J. S. Porter,	Farmington.
"	Mrs. D. D. Marsh,	Unionville.
Glastonbury,	Mrs. F. W. Dean,	Glastonbury.
"	Mrs. W. S. Goslee,	"
"	Mrs. D. H. Keene,	"
"	Mrs. James S. Williams,	"
Granby,	Mrs. F. M. Colton,	Granby.
Hartland,	Mrs. Hattie H. Gaylord,	West Hartland.
Manchester,	Miss Adeline Cheney,	South Manchester.
"	Mrs. C. G. Walkins,	"
Marlborough,	Miss Ida Veasey,	Marlborough.

TOWNS.	COMMITTEES.	POST OFFICE ADDRESSES.
New Britain,	Mr. A. S. Finch,	New Britain.
Newington,	Mrs. E. A. Deming,	Newington.
"	Miss E. A. Root,	"
Plainville,	Mrs. J. B. Minor,	Plainville.
"	Mrs. D. W. Fox,	"
"	Dr. T. G. Wright,	"
Rocky Hill,	Mrs. L. A. Griswold,	Rocky Hill.
"	Mrs. F. A. Warner,	"
Simsbury,	Mrs. Charles E. Stowe,	Simsbury.
"	Mrs. William Whitehead,	"
Southington,	Mrs. Estelle Barnes,	Southington,
"	Mrs. T. H. McKenzie,	"
South Windsor,	Mrs. Roswell Grant,	South Windsor.
Suffield,	Mrs. M. G. Dibble,	Suffield.
"	Mrs. Harvey Lindsley,	"
West Hartford,	Mrs. W. E. Goodwin,	Elmwood.
Wethersfield,	Miss Mary Harris,	Wethersfield.
Windsor,	Mrs. W. W. Loomis,	Windsor.
"	Mrs. R. O. Holcomb,	Poquonock.
Windsor Locks,	Mrs. J. H. Adams,	Windsor Locks.
"	Mrs. J. A. Whipple,	"

SUPERINTENDENT AND MATRON,

Mr. and Mrs. H. M. Adams, ... Warehouse Point.

NEW HAVEN COUNTY TEMPORARY HOME.

BOARD OF MANAGEMENT.

Chairman, Mr. Hart D. Munson, New Haven,   ⎫   *County*
Secretary, Mr. Jacob D. Walter, Cheshire,   ⎬ *Commissioners.*
    Mr. Albert B. Dunham, Seymour,   ⎭

Prof. W. H. Brewer, New Haven, of the State Board of Health ;
Miss Rebekah G. Bacon, New Haven, of the State Board of Charities.

SECRETARY OF TOWN COMMITTEES.

Mrs. G. F. Newcomb, ... 90 York Square, New Haven.

TOWNS.	COMMITTEES.	POST OFFICE ADDRESSES.
New Haven,	Mrs. B. J. Lum,	19 Compton Street.
"	Mrs. G. W. Bacon,	32 High Street.
"	Miss M. D. Skinner,	144 College Street.
Waterbury,	Mrs. F. E. Castle,	Waterbury.
Ansonia,	——	——
Beacon Falls,	Mrs. Julius A. Hart,	Beacon Falls.
Bethany,	Mrs. Jerome A. Downs,	Bethany.
Branford,	——	
Cheshire,	Mrs. Norman Platt,	New Haven.
"	Mrs. Gillette,	Cheshire.
"	Mrs. George Bell,	West Cheshire.
Derby,	Mrs. A. B. Shaw,	Derby.
East Haven,	——	——
Guilford,	Mrs. E. O. Blatchley,	Guilford.
Hamden,	Miss Carolyn Dickerman,	Hamden.
Madison,	Mrs. Josephine Scranton,	Madison.
Meriden,	Mrs. Eli I. Merriman,	Meriden.
Middlebury,	Miss M. L. Townsend,	Middlebury.
Milford,	Mrs. D. Clark,	Milford.
"	Miss J. Beach,	"
Naugatuck,	Mrs. B. B. Tuttle,	Naugatuck.
"	Mrs. Geo. D. Buck,	"
North Branford,	Mrs. Nathan Harrison,	North Branford.
North Haven,	Mrs. P. B. Orcutt,	North Haven.
Orange,	Mrs. Stiles Woodruff,	Orange.
Oxford,	Mrs. S. P. Sanford,	Oxford.
Prospect,	Mrs. W. H. Phipps,	Prospect.
Seymour,	Mrs. A. T. Dunham,	Seymour.

Towns.	Committees.	Post Office Addresses.
Southbury,	Mrs. Merwin Mitchell,	South Britain.
Wallingford,	——	——
Wolcott,	Mrs. M. R. Carter,	Wolcott.
"	Mrs. J. R. S. Todd,	"
Woodbridge,	Mrs. LeRoy C. Beecher,	Woodbridge.

Superintendent and Matron,

Mr. and Mrs. Willard Matthews, ... New Haven, Conn.

NEW LONDON COUNTY TEMPORARY HOME.

BOARD OF MANAGEMENT.

Chairman, Mr. JOHN T. BATTY, Groton,
Secretary, Mr. GILBERT L. HEWITT, Norwich,
Mr. R. W. CHADWICK, Lyme,
} *County Commissioners.*

Dr. G. W. Wilson, Meriden, of the State Board of Health ;
Mr. Charles P. Kellogg, Waterbury, of the State Board of Charities.

SECRETARY OF TOWN COMMITTEES.

Mrs. F. S. Camp, ... Norwich.

TOWNS.	COMMITTEES.	POST OFFICE ADDRESSES.
New London,	Mrs. Frank Hawkins,	New London.
"	Mr. G. F. Tinker,	"
Norwich,	Mrs. F. S. Camp,	Norwich.
"	Mrs. F. A. Mitchell,	Thamesville,Norwich.
Bozrah,	Mrs. S. W. Haughton,	Bozrah.
Colchester,	Mrs. George O. Jackson,	Colchester.
East Lyme,	Mrs. S. K. Luce,	Niantic.
Franklin,	Miss Ella I. Smith,	Franklin.
Griswold,	Mrs. George A. Haskell,	Jewett City.
Groton,	Miss Abbie M. Clark,	Groton.
Lebanon,	——	
Ledyard,	Mr. George Fanning,	Ledyard.
Lisbon,	Mrs. H. L. Reade,	Jewett City.
Lyme,	Mr. Frederick Fosdick,	North Lyme.
Montville,	Mrs. Charles Johnson,	Norwich.
North Stonington,	Mrs. John D. Avery,	North Stonington.
Old Lyme,	Mrs. William W. Wallace,	Old Lyme.
Preston,	Mrs. Austin Chapman,	Preston.
Salem,	——	——
Sprague,	Mrs. Ethan Allen,	Hanover.
Stonington,	Mrs. N. P. Trumbull,	Stonington.
Voluntown,	Mrs. E. Dewhurst,	Voluntown.
Waterford,	Mrs. J. L. Payne,	Waterford.

MATRON,

Miss Jessie Gibson, . . , ... Preston.

FAIRFIELD COUNTY TEMPORARY HOME.

BOARD OF MANAGEMENT.

Chairman, Mr. WHITMAN S. MEAD, Greenwich,   } *County*
Secretary, Mr. JAMES E. MILLER, Redding,   } *Commissioners.*
Mr. HENRY LEE, Bridgeport,   }

Dr. N. E. Wordin, Bridgeport, of the State Board of Health ;
Miss Rebekah G. Bacon, New Haven, of the State Board of Charities.

SECRETARY OF TOWN COMMITTEES.

Miss Ellen Merrill, ... 26 France Street, Norwalk.

TOWNS.	COMMITTEES.	POST OFFICE ADDRESSES.
Bridgeport,	Mr. D. C. Phelps,	Bridgeport.
"	Mrs. H. H. Scribner,	38 Prospect Street.
"	Mr. W. H. Bunnell,	132 Seaview Avenue.
Danbury,	Mrs. Mary L. Ward,	356 Main Street.
Bethel,	Mrs. Frank W. Smith,	Bethel.
Brookfield,	Miss Amelia J. Northrup,	Brookfield Center.
Darien,	Mr. Charles A. Lounsbury,	Darien.
Easton,	Miss A. F. Seeley,	Easton.
Fairfield,	Mrs. Samuel Glover,	Fairfield.
Greenwich,	Dr. L. P. Jones,	Greenwich.
Huntington,	Miss Jennie Curtis,	Shelton.
Monroe,	Mrs. John G. Stevens,	Monroe.
New Canaan,	Miss Leonora I. Clark,	New Canaan.
New Fairfield,	Mrs. John J. Treadwell,	New Fairfield.
Newtown,	Mrs. E. L. Johnson,	Newtown.
Norwalk,	Mr. Charles Burr,	24 Center Avenue.
"	Miss G. H. Benedict,	South Norwalk.
Redding,	Mrs. A. A. Weed,	Danbury.
Ridgefield,	Mrs. L. W. Abbott,	Ridgefield.
Sherman,	Mrs. Maltby G. Gelston,	Sherman.
Stamford,	Mrs. Arthur C. Bruce,	Stamford.
Stratford,	Mrs. Rufus W. Bunnell,	Stratford.
Trumbull,	Miss Cora E. Beach,	Trumbull.
Weston,	Dr. Frank Gorham,	Lyons Plains.
Westport,	Mrs. William T. Wood,	Westport.
Wilton,	Miss Katharine A. Sturges,	Wilton.

MATRON,

Miss Martha A. Boughton, ... Norwalk.

WINDHAM COUNTY TEMPORARY HOME.

BOARD OF MANAGEMENT.

Chairman, Mr. E. H. Hall, Windham,   ⎫ *County*
Secretary, Mr. E. L. Palmer, Danielson,   ⎬ *Commissioners.*
        Mr. E. H. Corttiss, Thompson,   ⎭

Mr. George P. Ingersoll, New Haven, of the State Board of Health;
Dr. Edwin A. Down, Hartford, of the State Board of Charities.

SECRETARY OF TOWN COMMITTEES.

Mrs. E. A. Whitmore, ... ¯ Putnam.

TOWNS.	COMMITTEES.	POST OFFICE ADDRESSES.
Ashford,	Mrs. Davis A. Baker,	Ashford.
Brooklyn,	Mrs. C. A. Potter,	Brooklyn.
Canterbury,	Miss Olive D. Sanger,	Canterbury.
Chaplin,	Mrs. Merrick Barton,	Chaplin.
Eastford,	Mrs. Timothy J. Walker,	Eastford.
Hampton,	Mrs. Nellie C. Cleveland,	Hampton.
Killingly,	Miss Mary Dexter,	Danielson.
Plainfield,	Mrs. George Loring,	Central Village.
Pomfret,	Mrs. T. W. Williams,	Pomfret.
Putnam,	Mrs. E. A. Whitmore,	Putnam.
Scotland,	Mrs. Charles A. Brown,	Scotland.
Sterling,	Mrs. George C. Spooner,	Sterling.
Thompson,	Mrs. M. D. Elliot,	Thompson.
Windham,	Miss Annie H. Tingley,	Willimantic.
Woodstock,	Mrs. F. L. Corbin,	Woodstock.

SUPERINTENDENT AND MATRON,

Mr. and Mrs. J. D. Converse, ...   Putnam.

LITCHFIELD COUNTY TEMPORARY HOME.

BOARD OF MANAGEMENT.

Chairman, Mr. N. L. WEBSTER, Thomaston, ⎫
Mr. S. N. PETTIBONE, BakerVille, ⎬ *County Commissioners.*
Mr. G. W. HALL, Canaan, ⎭

Dr. R. S. Goodwin, Thomaston, of the State Board of Health ;
Miss Mary Hall, Hartford, of the State Board of Charities.

SECRETARY OF TOWN COMMITTEES.

Miss Mary P. Hinsdale, ... West Winsted.

TOWNS.	COMMITTEES.	POST OFFICE ADDRESSES.
Litchfield,	Mrs. M. B. McLaughlin,	Litchfield.
"	Mrs. Geo. M. Woodruff,	"
"	Mrs. Dwight Kilborn,	East Litchfield.
"	Mrs. Amos Kilborn,	Milton.
Barkhamsted,	Mrs. E. J. Youngs,	Pleasant Valley.
"	Mrs. Wallace Case,	Barkhamsted.
Bethlehem,	Mrs. William Harrison,	Bethlehem.
Bridgewater,	Mrs. C. H. Jessup,	Bridgewater.
"	Mrs. E. R. Wooster,	"
Canaan,	Mrs. W. L. Millard,	Falls Village.
"	Mrs. James Hakes,	Huntsville.
Colebrook,	Mrs. Ralph Turner,	Colebrook.
"	Miss Sarah Carrington,	"
"	Miss Bass,	Robertsville.
Cornwall,	Mrs. Katharine M. Sedgwick,	Cornwall Hollow.
"	Mrs. T. S. Gold,	West Cornwall.
"	Miss Susie E. Harrison,	Cornwall Hollow.
"	Mrs. Victory Beers,	Cornwall Bridge.
Goshen,	Mrs. Delton Ostrem,	Goshen.
"	Mrs. H. E. Small,	"
Harwinton,	Mrs. Abijah Catlin,	Harwinton.
"	Mrs. Martin Goodwin,	"
Kent,	———	———
Morris,	Mrs. H. R. Stockbridge,	Morris.
"	Miss Louise Mason,	"
New Hartford,	Mrs. Geo. W. Bancroft,	New Hartford.
"	Mrs. Walter Woodruff,	"
"	Mrs. S. N. Pettibone,	Bakerville.
New Milford,	Mrs. Dr. Bacon,	New Milford.
"	Mrs. T. P. Marsh,	"

Towns.	Committees.	Post Office Addresses.
Norfolk,	Mrs. Alice E. Bridgeman,	Norfolk.
"	Mrs. Ralph J. Crissy,	"
North Canaan,	Mrs. A. G. Stevens,	Canaan.
"	Mrs. George Adam,	"
Plymouth,	Mrs. George Langdon,	Plymouth.
"	Mrs. Andrew Gaylord,	Terryville.
Roxbury,	Mrs. Leverett Castle,	Roxbury.
"	Mrs. L. I. Pons,	"
Salisbury,	Mrs. H. P. Harris,	Salisbury.
"	Miss Almira Cleveland,	"
Sharon,	Mrs. Dr. Knight,	Sharon.
"	Mrs. M. F. Whitney,	"
Thomaston,	Mrs. Wm. Simpkins,	Thomaston.
"	Mrs. Chauncey Benedict,	"
Torrington,	Mrs. E. C. Hotchkiss,	Torrington.
"	Mrs. John Burr,	Burrville.
"	Miss Mary Brooker,	Torrington.
Warren,	Mrs. Gardiner,	Warren.
Washington,	Mrs. Wm. G. Brinsmade,	Washington.
"	Mrs. Mary E. Kinney,	Washington Depot.
Watertown,	Mrs. W. S. Munger,	Watertown.
"	Mrs. Merritt Heminway,	"
Winchester,	Miss Mary P. Hinsdale,	West Winsted.
"	Mrs. Caleb Camp,	"
Woodbury,	Mrs. James Huntington,	Woodbury.
"	Mrs. C. P. Crane,	"

SUPERINTENDENT AND MATRON,

Mr. and Mrs. Dwight S. Case,   .   .   .   ·   Winsted, Conn.

MIDDLESEX COUNTY TEMPORARY HOME.

BOARD OF MANAGEMENT.

Chairman, Mr. John J. Hubbard, Middletown, ⎫
Secretary, Mr. George A. Olcott, Clinton, ⎬ *County Commissioners.*
Mr. William H. Scoville, East Haddam, ⎭

Dr. G. W. Wilson, Meriden, of the State Board of Health;
Mr. George F. Spencer, Deep River, of the State Board of Charities.

SECRETARY OF TOWN COMMITTEES.

Mrs. J. H. Bunce, ... Middletown.

TOWNS.	COMMITTEES.	POST OFFICE ADDRESSES.
Middletown,	Mrs. Henry Ward,	Middletown.
"	Mrs. J. H. Bunce,	"
"	Mrs. Thomas Walsh,	"
"	Mrs. M. D. Murphy,	"
Haddam,	Mrs. G. A. Dickinson.	Haddam.
"	Miss Hannah M. Walkley,	Higganum.
Chatham,	Mrs. Wm. H. Bevins,	East Hampton.
"	Mrs. A..H. Conchlin,	"
Chester,	Mrs. Joseph E. Silliman,	Chester.
"	Mrs. Merritt S. Brooks,	"
Clinton,	Mrs. George E. Elliot,	Clinton.
"	Miss Marietta Hull,	"
Cromwell,	Mrs. Harriet W. Wheelock,	Cromwell.
"	Mrs. A. N. Pierson,	"
Durham,	Mrs. Earl Mathewson,	Durham Center.
"	Mrs. Wm. C. Hubbard,	"
East Haddam,	Mrs. E. W. Chaffee,	Moodus.
"	Mrs. W. H. Scoville,	East Haddam.
"	Mrs. F. W Swan,	Millington.
Essex,	Mrs. Alfred M. Wright,	Centerbrook.
"	Mrs. J. B. Northrop,	Ivoryton.
"	Mrs. C. H. Hubbard,	Essex.
Killingworth,	Mrs. Nathan H. Evarts,	Killingworth.
"	Mrs. Julius Buell,	"
Middlefield,	Miss Mary E. Lyman,	Middlefield.
"	Mrs. Henry S. Steele,	"
Old Saybrook,	Mrs. J. H. Grannis,	Saybrook.
"	Mrs. W. E. Clark,	"
"	Miss Mabel C. Holman,	"

15

Towns.	Committees.	Post Office Addresses.
Portland,	Mrs. E. L. Sears,	Portland.
"	Mrs. Henry Kilby,	"
"	Mrs. John H. Sage,	"
Saybrook,	Mrs. Milon Pratt,	Deep River.
"	Mrs. Lozelle L. Platt,	"
"	Mrs. Henry M. Snell,	"
Westbrook,	Mrs. C. C. Champlin,	Westbrook.
"	Mrs. Charles L. Clark,	"

Superintendent and Matron,

Mr. and Mrs. J. H. Odber, ... Haddam.

TOLLAND COUNTY TEMPORARY HOME.

BOARD OF MANAGEMENT.

Chairman, Mr. JOHN H. BUELL, Gilead,
Secretary, Mr. M. P. J. WALKER, Stafford Springs, } *County Commissioners.*
Mr. JOHN THOMPSON, Ellington,

Mr. T. H. McKenzie, C. E., Southington, of the State Board of Health;
Mr. H. C. Whittlesey, Middletown, of the State Board of Charities.

SECRETARY OF TOWN COMMITTEES.

Mrs. E. C. Pinney, ... Stafford.

TOWNS.	COMMITTEES.	POST OFFICE ADDRESSES.
Andover,	Mrs. Myron P. Yeomans,	Andover.
"	Mrs. Charles B. Stearns,	"
Bolton,	Mrs. C. M. Loomis,	Bolton.
"	Mrs. Orlando Sperry,	"
Columbia,	Mrs. Wm. H. Yeomans,	Columbia.
"	Mrs. Abbott Little,	"
Coventry,	Mrs. H. W. Mason,	South Coventry.
"	Mrs. H. R. Hoisington,	Coventry.
Ellington,	Mrs. James M. Talcott,	Ellington.
"	Mrs. Albert Pinney,	Vernon.
Hebron,	Mrs. J. H. Buell,	Gilead.
"	Mrs. N. E. Lord,	Hebron.
Mansfield,	Mrs. E. G. Sumner,	Mansfield Center.
"	Mrs. W. H. Gardner,	Spring Hill.
Somers,	Mrs. H. M. Gager,	Somers.
"	Mrs. A. D. Noble,	Somersville.
Stafford,	Mrs. G. H. Baker,	Stafford Springs.
"	Mrs. M. P. J. Walker,	"
"	Mrs. E. C. Pinney,	Stafford.
Tolland,	Mrs. E. S Agard,	Tolland.
"	Mrs. Wm. D. Holman,	"
"	Mrs. Oscar Leonard,	"
Union,	Mrs. E. W. Upham,	Union.
Vernon,	Mrs. William Butler,	Rockville.
"	Mrs. Robert McChristie,	"
"	Mrs J. S. Thrall,	"
"	Mrs. G. G. Tillinghast,	Vernon.
Willington,	Mrs. Annie A. Preston,	Willington.

SUPERINTENDENT AND MATRON,

Mr. and Mrs. E. S. Talbot, ... Vernon Center.

PROVISION FOR THE POOR.

ALMSHOUSE FOR STATE PAUPERS,

TARIFFVILLE.

Visited September 29, 1897, February 18, May 10, and November 19, 1898.

Connecticut owns neither a State Almshouse nor a State Farm. It has had a comparatively small number of State paupers to support, and it has been, therefore, the custom for the Comptroller's office to contract with some individual for their support. Since the death in 1896 of Mr. Marvin Sanford of Tariffville, with whom the contract had been placed for a number of years, the paupers have been under the charge of his brother, Mr. Morton Sanford, and the contract with the latter has been renewed for a period of three years, dating from August 1, 1897.

The house reserved for the use of the paupers is situated on a hillside at a short distance from the railway station, and is under the direct management of a matron, the superintendent-contractor occupying a private dwelling near by. The almshouse is an old-fashioned wooden building, two stories high, with basement and garret, and, aside from incidental repairs, maintains in general its original arrangement and condition. The ceilings are low, the halls contracted, and the stairways steep, and there are none of the conveniences and sanitary appliances of modern houses. No special provision is made for the care of the sick and the insane.

Men and women occupy separate portions of the house, but meet in a common dining-room in the basement for meals. The rooms in the basement and first story are heated by stoves, while those above receive whatever warm air rises from the rooms below. The water supply is received from a single pipe in the basement kitchen, but, owing to the lack of pressure, is not carried to the upper stories. The only provision for protection against fire is a supply of water pails and hand-grenades hung in different parts of the house.

A number of improvements in equipment have been made

within the past year, comprising the introduction of neat iron bedsteads in a part of the rooms, the remodeling of the wretched cells in the basement, and the removal of most of their former occupants to a small house on the premises, the separation of the yards for men and women, and the addition in a detached wash-house of a separate bath-tub for the use of the female inmates. All of the inmates are required to bathe once a week, and the bath-tub for men is located in a small out-building in their yard. One end of this out-building is partitioned off for the use during the daytime of a number of men who are unfit by their natures and habits to associate with the other inmates.

With the exception of a few cases of the unfortunate poor, the majority of the inmates represent low types, and may be classified in general as tramps, victims of drink, or persons affected with loathsome diseases. Some, too, are ugly in disposition and will not yield to ordinary discipline, while others are idiotic or insane and are unable to care for their persons decently. About one-half of the men can be made to work, and they are employed upon the farm or the large woodpile that stands at one end of the yard. The number of inmates when last visited was forty-six, of whom fourteen, only, were beneficiaries of the State. In view of the low nature and troublesome habits of many of the inmates, it would seem to be very desirable that a reliable man and his wife should reside in the building as keepers in order to prevent any possible disturbances, especially at night.

In addition to the State paupers at the date of last visit, the town poor of Avon (four), Barkhamsted (three), and Bloomfield (two), were cared for under contract, and paupers were boarded from other towns as follows: Bridgeport (two), Brookfield (two), Cromwell (four), East Granby (one), Meriden (two), North Canaan (four), North Haven (three), Orange (one), West Hartford (two), Windsor Locks (two). The authorities of all these towns maintain this practice in direct violation of Section 3310 of the General Statutes, which provides that, "it shall not be lawful for any town, or the selectmen thereof, to remove any pauper out of the town to which such pauper belongs to be supported in any other town."

By the terms of the contract with the Comptroller's office, $2.75 per week is paid for the board of each State pauper. The cost to the State was:

For the year ending September 30, 1897, . . $4,998.37
For the year ending September 30, 1898, . .   5,586.28

GENERAL STATUTES, 1888.

Support by the State.

Section 3311. All persons needing relief, who have no settlement in any town in this State, shall, when needing relief, be provided for by the Comptroller, for the period of six months next after they come into this State, and no longer, etc.

Sec. 3316. The Comptroller may, from time to time, contract with any person for not more than five years, for the relief and support of State paupers, and may remove any State pauper from any town, and place him with such contractor, adjust any demands arising under such contract, and draw orders on the State Treasurer for the payment thereof.

TOWN ALMSHOUSES.

There are 168 towns in Connecticut, of which 68 maintain almshouses owned by the town, and 20 others have almshouses which are owned and managed by private persons.

The total number of persons receiving almshouse support in the year, as shown in the selectmen's returns to the State Board of Charities, is as follows:

Hartford County,	711
New Haven County,	955
New London County,	251
Fairfield County,	388
Windham County,	155
Litchfield County,	75
Middlesex County,	71
Tolland County,	88
	2,694

GENERAL STATUTES, 1888.

Support by Towns.

Section 3295. All persons who have not estate sufficient for their support and have no relations of sufficient ability who are obliged by law to support them, shall be provided for and supported at the expense of the town where they belong; and every town shall maintain and support all the poor inhabitants belonging to it, whether residing in it or in any other town in the State.

Sec. 3296. It shall be unlawful for any town, or the selectmen or agent thereof, to make any contract for the support of any person liable to be supported by such town. All persons supported by any town shall be supported in an almshouse or other place or places provided by such town, etc.

Sec. 3303. Paupers shall be liable to be removed to such places as the selectmen may lawfully designate, to be supported as the town or selectmen may direct, etc.

Sec. 3310. All paupers shall be supported at some place or places within the town to which they belong, and it shall not be lawful for any town, or the selectmen thereof, to remove any pauper out of the town to which such pauper belongs to be supported in any other town.

HARTFORD COUNTY.

There are twenty-nine towns in Hartford County, of which fifteen maintain almshouses owned by the town, and three have almshouses owned and managed by private individuals. Visits have been made to the towns mentioned in the appended list, and reports on the condition of the poor are presented as follows:

HARTFORD.

Visited by Miss Hall, April 15, 1898, and by Miss Hall and Mr. Kellogg, September 24, 1897, and November 3, 1898.

Almshouse is owned by town. About 100 acres of land are attached.

Keeper, Mr. W. W. Stillman, who is also superintendent of public charities for the city.

Terms, $2,000 a year as superintendent.

Prisoners are not received.

Number of inmates at date of last visit, 271; 171 men, 100 women, and 6 infants under four years.

Number of insane, 27; 11 men, 16 women; of whom 4 men and 4 women have previously been in the State Hospital.

Number of inmates able to work, 75; 40 men, 35 women.

The men are employed upon the farm, and in carpenter work and painting about the place. The women are engaged in housework, sewing, mending, etc.

The house is a large brick structure two stories high, and was built in 1886. A large number of improvements have been made within the last two years. The old bedrooms have been torn out, and large airy dormitories for men and women, respectively, containing forty-three beds each, have been arranged in their place.

The former quarters used for insane inmates have been remodeled as a well-equipped laundry, and a new insane ward has been provided. The hospital ward for women who are too feeble to go to the dining-room has accommodations for forty beds. The children's nursery has been thoroughly renovated and pleasantly furnished.

It is also planned to enlarge a wing in the rear of the building, providing on the upper floor a ward for consumptives, and on the lower floor quarters for those who are untidy in their habits. New bath-rooms and toilet facilities have been provided in several departments.

Religious services are held in the chapel every Sunday, under the alternate direction of Protestant and Roman Catholic leaders. All departments 'show signs of careful management, and the almshouse is rapidly becoming one of the best in the State.

AVON.

Visited by Miss Hall, September 22, 1898.

Avon has no almshouse, but at the date of visit was boarding six paupers in the Almshouse for State Paupers at Tariffville. One other woman was being assisted at the same date.

BERLIN.

Visited by Miss Hall, June 16, 1898.

Almshouse is owned by town. About 75 acres of land are attached.

Keeper, Mr. Alonzo Sweet, whose contract expires April 1st, annually.

Terms, $40 per month, not including out-door relief.

Prisoners are received occasionally, and are kept separate from the rest of the paupers.

Number of inmates at date of visit, 3; 2 men, 1 woman.

The house was found in good condition, the beds being especially clean, and the general appearance one of comfort.

BLOOMFIELD.

Visited by Miss Hall, April 22, 1898.

Bloomfield has no almshouse, but at the date of visit was boarding four men at Tariffville, and one at the State Hospital for the Insane.

Three other persons were being assisted with partial relief. The town has a contract for fifteen years, under which it boards the majority of its dependent poor at the Almshouse for State Paupers, for $500 a year.

BRISTOL.

Visited by Mr. Kellogg, September 14, 1897, and by Miss Hall, October 3, 1898.

Almshouse is not owned by town; is managed by private parties, and is situated two and one-half miles northwest from the railway station.

Keepers, Mr. and Mrs. Chauncey N. Atwood, whose contract expired in October.

Terms, $2.50 per week for each inmate.

Prisoners are not received.

Number of inmates at date of last visit, 4; 3 men and 1 woman.

Number of insane, 1 woman, who had previously been in the State Hospital.

Number able to work, 2 men, who are employed in general farming.

The house appeared dirty and disorderly, and there was a general appearance of indifference to the comfort of the inmates.

Recommendations for improvements were made, and the Board have been informed since the last visit that the town poor were removed in November to the care of Mr. Bailey on Fall Mountain.

BURLINGTON.

Visited by Mr. Kellogg, September 29, 1897, and by Miss Hall, March 25, 1898.

Almshouse is not owned by town, but is managed by private parties.

Keeper, Mr. John Green, whose contract expires January 1, 1899.

Terms, $350 a year.

Prisoners are not received.

Number of inmates at date of visit, 8; 3 men, 5 women.

Number of insane, 1 woman, who had previously been in the State Hospital.

Number of feeble-minded, 2; 1 man and 1 woman.

Number able to work, 4; 2 men, 2 women.

Occupations, farm work and housework.

The house is old, but the beds and rooms were clean, and the inmates appeared well fed and cared for.

Six hundred dollars is the limit that may be expended for

clothing, provisions, medical attendance, etc., and this must include the out-door relief also, for which the keeper has to make account to the selectmen.

CANTON.

Visited by Mr. Kellogg, September 29, 1897.

Almshouse is not owned by town; is managed by private parties and is situated one and a half miles north from Collinsville.

Keepers, Mr. and Mrs. L. D. Dowd, whose contract expires January 1st, annually.

Terms, $1,500 a year, which includes also out-door relief.

Prisoners are not received.

The only inmate at the date of visit was one woman, who was mildly insane, and had previously been in the State Hospital. She does some small work about the house, and appeared to be well cared for.

A two-story ell to the house contains a pleasant sitting-room and eight bedrooms, all comfortably furnished, which may be used for the town poor whenever their numbers require it.

EAST GRÁNBY.

Visited by Miss Hall, October, 1897.

There is no almshouse in East Granby, but at the date of visit three persons were being boarded by the town in private families.

EAST HARTFORD.

Visited by Miss Hall, February 16 and September 23, 1897, and August 19, 1898.

Almshouse is owned by town. About nineteen acres of land are attached.

Keepers, Mr. and Mrs. John Rouff, whose contract expires April 1st.

Terms, $400 a year, not including out-door relief.

Prisoners are not received.

Number of inmates at date of last visit, 5; 4 men, 1 woman.

Number of insane, 1 man, who had previously been in the State Hospital.

Two men are able to do some work about the place.

A new bath-tub has been added during the last year, and the house appeared comfortable and well kept. A large number of tramps are given shelter during the winter.

EAST WINDSOR.

Visited by Miss Hall, September 21, 1897, and July 8, 1898..

Almshouse is owned by town, and about seventy-five acres of land are attached.

Keeper, Mr. Thomas J. Coleman, whose contract expires April 1st.

Terms, $425 a year, not including out-door relief.

Prisoners are not received.

Number of inmates at date of last visit, 7; 3 men, 4 women.

Number of insane, 1 woman.

The house was in fair condition, and the inmates were made passably comfortable. Several of them assist in the housework and about the place.

ENFIELD.

Visited by Miss Hall, May 6, 1897.

Almshouse is owned by town, and about 100 acres of land are attached.

Keeper, Mr. Merrick Lamphere, whose contract expires in October.

Terms, $450 a year, not including out-door relief.

Prisoners are not received.

Number of inmates at date of visit, 12; 8 men, 4 women.

Number of insane, 3 men, all of whom have previously been in the State Hospital.

All of the inmates were able to do some work, and assisted in the house and about the place. They appeared to be humanely treated. The house is always in good order, and visitors are welcome.

FARMINGTON.

*Visited by Miss Hall, September 3, 1897, and by
Miss Bacon, April 19, 1898.*

Almshouse is owned by town, and about 300 acres of land are
  attached.
Keeper, Mr. Patrick C. Gilbert.
Terms, $600 a year, not including out-door relief.
Prisoners are not received.
Number of inmates at date of last visit, 14; 5 men, 3 women,
  and 6 children between the ages of two and sixteen years.
Number of insane, 1 woman, who had previously been in the
  State Hospital.

The house is old and in poor repair. It was, however, clean
and the inmates were comfortable. When last visited a family
of eight persons were there; father, mother, and six children.
The children were to be removed soon after. Farmington
needs a new almshouse with modern provision for heating,
bathing, etc.

GLASTONBURY.

*Visited by Miss Hall, February 16, and September 22, 1897, and
August 19, 1898.*

Almshouse is owned by town, and about one acre of land is
  attached.
Keepers, Mr. and Mrs. Charles W. Matson.
Terms, $250 a year, not including out-door relief.
Prisoners are not received.
Number of inmates at date of last visit, 10; 5 men, 5 women.
Number of insane, 1 man.
Number of feeble-minded, 1 man.
All of the inmates are able to work a little about the place.

This is one of the best-kept almshouses in the State. The
house has been equipped with steam heat during the past year,
and the sleeping-rooms were clean and attractive.

GRANBY.

Visited by Miss Hall, October 10, 1898.

There is no almshouse in Granby, but four persons are
boarded by the town in private families, and one is supported
at the Retreat for the Insane in Hartford.

HARTLAND.

Visited by Miss Hall, June 24, 1898.

Hartland has no almshouse, but at the date of visit was boarding one man and one woman in the town; also one woman at the State Hospital for the Insane. Out-door relief is given to individuals as occasion requires.

MANCHESTER.

Visited by Miss Hall, January 12, and October 10, 1897.

Almshouse is owned by town, and about 100 acres of land are attached.

Keeper, Mr. Charles E. Taylor, whose contract expires April 1st.

Terms, $600 a year, not including out-door relief.

Prisoners are not received.

Number of inmates at date of last visit, 29.

Number of insane, 15; 5 men, 10 women; all of whom had previously been in the State Hospital.

A number of the inmates assist in housework and about the place. The house has been enlarged since the last report, and presented an appearance of good order. The inmates have comfortable beds and plenty of well-cooked food. A bath-room, however, is greatly needed.

MARLBOROUGH.

Visited by Miss Hall, August, 1897, and September 20, 1898.

Marlborough has no almshouse, but at the date of last visit was supporting two families entirely, one of them consisting of ten persons, of whom the father was very ill with consumption. Two other women are assisted partially, with weekly payments.

NEW BRITAIN.

Visited by Miss Hall, September 15, 1897, and June 28, 1898, by Mr. Kellogg, September 28, 1897, and by Mr. Whittlesey and Mr. Kellogg, April 2, 1898.

Almshouse is owned by town, and is situated two miles southeast of center. About 80 acres of land are attached.

Keepers, Mr. and Mrs. L. B. Boughton, whose contract expires April 1st.

Terms, $700 a year, not including out-door relief.

Prisoners are not received.

Number of inmates at date of last visit, 48; 26 men, 22 women, and one infant under two years.

Number of insane, 12; 7 men, 5 women, of whom 7 in all have been in the State Hospital.

Number of feeble-minded, 7 men.

A number of the inmates assist in the housework, and eight men are employed upon the farm.   Much dissatisfaction was found with the condition of the house at the time of the earlier visits, many rooms being very dirty and ill-kept. After urgent recommendations by the Board, the town authorities made a change of keepers on April 1, 1898. Under the present managers the condition of the house and of the inmates has been much improved.   The present selectman assisted greatly in effecting the improvements. The part of the house reserved for men is very old, however, and difficult to keep in good order. It should be replaced by a new building better befitting a city of the size and standing of New Britain.   Other improvements in the sanitary arrangements of the present building are urgently needed.

NEWINGTON.

Visited by Miss Hall, September 15, 1897.

There is no almshouse in Newington, and the few town poor are either boarded in private families or assisted in their own homes.

PLAINVILLE:

Visited by Miss Hall, June 28, 1898.

There is no almshouse in Plainville, but at the date of visit four persons were being boarded in private families. Partial relief at the same time was being given to ten families. The Strong fund assists materially in the care of the town poor. Three insane persons are reported at the State Hospital.

ROCKY HILL.

Visited by Miss Hall, September 20, 1897.

Rocky Hill has no almshouse, but at the date of visit was boarding seven persons in private families at the rate of $2 a week for each. Of these persons, two were insane and had formerly been in the State Hospital, and two others were feeble-minded.

SIMSBURY.

Visited by Miss Hall and Mr. Kellogg, September 29, 1897, and by Miss Hall, February 25, 1898.

Almshouse is owned by town, and is situated three miles north of Simsbury center. About 150 acres of land are attached.
Keepers, Mr. and Mrs. Wesley Case, whose contract expires April 1st.
Terms, $450 a year, not including out-door relief.
Prisoners are not received.
Number of inmates at date of last visit, 6; 4 men, 2 women.
Number of feeble-minded, 1 woman.
Three of the inmates assist in housework and about the place.

The women room in the keeper's house, and the men occupy a detached building at a short distance. All take their meals in the main house. The men care for their own rooms, and conditions of greater neatness were advised. The house is fairly well-kept and the food sufficient.

SOUTHINGTON.

Visited by Miss Bacon, October 25, 1897, and by Miss Hall, October 3, 1898.

Almshouse is owned by town.
Keeper, Mr. Thomas S. Case, whose contract expires April 1st.
Terms, $500 a year.
Prisoners are not received.
Number of inmates at date of last visit, 12; 5 men, 7 women.
Number of insane, 1 man, who had previously been in the State Hospital.

Six of the inmates assist in work about the place. The general condition of the house was not so clean or neat as could be desired.   Four old women were present, who were very untidy in their habits, and the keepers were advised to supply them with special conveniences.

SOUTH WINDSOR.

Visited by Miss Hall, June 30, 1897, and July 7, 1898.

Almshouse is owned by town, and about 30 acres of land are attached.

Keepers, Mr. and Mrs. C. C. Kibbe, whose contract expires April 1st.

Terms, $500 a year, not including out-door relief.

Prisoners are received occasionally, and are kept separate from the paupers.

Number of inmates at date of last visit, 3; 2 men, 1 woman.

The house was clean and in good order, and the inmates appeared to be well-cared for.   A large number of tramps are sheltered in a separate building during the winter.   East Windsor Hill is the nearest railway station.

SUFFIELD.

Visited by Miss Hall, November 16, 1898.

Almshouse is owned by town; about 80 acres of land are attached.

Keeper, Mr. James W. Pomeroy, whose contract expires April 1st.

Terms, $425 a year, not including out-door relief.

Prisoners are not received.

Number of inmates at date of visit, 5; 3 men, 2 women.

Number of insane, 1 man.

Number of feeble-minded, 1 woman.

Number able to work, 3 men, who were engaged in work upon the farm.

The house is well-kept, and is one of the cleanest in the county.   The food supplied is excellent, also.

16

WEST HARTFORD.

Visited by Miss Hall, April 18, 1898.

West Hartford has no almshouse, but boards its dependent poor in the Almshouse for State Paupers at Tariffville. At the date of visit, two men were being boarded there at the rate of $2.50 for each. Two other feeble-minded persons were being supported at the time, and five persons were boarded in the State Hospital for the Insane.

WETHERSFIELD.

Visited by Miss Hall, June 23, 1897.

Almshouse is owned by town.

Keeper, Mr. George Treadwell, whose contract expires in November.

Terms, $375 a year, not including out-door relief.

Prisoners are not received.

Number of inmates at date of visit, 2 men; 1 of whom had previously been in the State Hospital for the Insane.

The house appeared to be in fair condition, and the inmates expressed themselves as contented with their treatment. 2,400 tramps were given shelter during the previous year.

WINDSOR.

Visited by Miss Hall, January 11, 1897, and September 12, 1898.

Almshouse is owned by town, and about 10 acres of land are attached.

Keeper, Mr. William McDonald, whose contract expires in April.

Terms, $400 a year, not including out-door relief.

Prisoners are not received.

Number of inmates at date of last visit, 3; 1 man, 1 woman, and 1 boy under sixteen years.

A bath-tub is greatly needed in the house, and more attention should be paid to the condition of the bedrooms. The boy, Joseph Grotto, about nine years of age, was soon after removed to the County Home, upon the recommendation of the visitor.

WINDSOR LOCKS.

Visited by Miss Hall, October 9, 1897, and in July, 1898.

There is no almshouse in Windsor Locks, but at the date of last visit, the town was supporting ten persons entirely, and assisting five families in their homes. Three insane persons were boarded at the State Hospital.

NEW HAVEN COUNTY.

There are twenty-six towns in New Haven County, of which eleven have almshouses owned by the town. Visits have been made to the towns mentioned in the appended list, and reports on the condition of the poor are presented as follows:

NEW HAVEN.

Visited by Miss Bacon, October 26, 1897, and by Miss Bacon and Dr. Down, March 23, 1898.

Almshouse is owned by town, and is situated four miles west from the city hall, and one and one-half miles from the Westville post-office. About 400 acres of land are attached, of which 50 acres are cultivated.

Keeper, Mr. Sucher.

Prisoners are not received.

Number of inmates at date of last visit, 370, including 17 infants under four years of age.

Number of insane, 80.

The house is beautifully situated on what is known as Springside Farm, and consists of a large brick building three stories and attic in height, which was erected at a cost of $225,000. It is heated by steam, lighted by gasoline, and is connected with the city's systems of water and sewers. All departments are complete in their appointments, and are kept in a clean condition, great care being taken to keep the beds free from vermin. Since the consolidation of town and city governments, the almshouse is under the control of the Bureau of Public Charities.

WATERBURY.

Visited by Miss Bacon, May 31, 1897 ; by Miss Hall, June 8, 1898 and by Mr. Kellogg, September 6, 1898.

Almshouse is owned by town, and is situated about two miles northwest from the city hall, near the Watertown road. About 120 acres of land are attached.

Keepers, Mr. and Mrs. Thomas Moran, whose contract expires April 1st.

Terms, $800 a year, not including out-door relief.

Prisoners are received occasionally, chiefly cases of delirium
tremens, and are kept in a separate department provided
with convenient cells.

Number of inmates at date of last visit, 97; 49 men, 37 women,
3 children between four and eighteen years of age, and 8
infants under four years.

Number of insane, 12; 4 men, 8 women; of whom 1 man and 5
women have previously been in the State Hospital.

Number of feeble-minded, 9; 3 men, 6 women.

Number able to work, 50; 35 men, 15 women.

Occupations, housework and farmwork.

The house, which is a large brick structure of three stories,
stands on high ground, and was first occupied in February,
1894. It is heated by steam, lighted by electricity, and provided with an abundant supply of water. The several floors
contain pleasant rooms for elderly people and comfortable
dormitories for the general body of inmates, men and women
occupying separate wings of the building. Sitting and read-
ing-rooms are provided, as well as hospital wards and a chapel
where occasional religious services are held. All necessary
comforts and conveniences are furnished, and the whole establishment appeared clean and in good order.

Two of the three children, who were in the house when
visited, were removed soon after at the instigation of the visitors. The third is a cripple, who is ineligible for admission to
the County Home.

Two or three of the insane inmates should, more properly,
be in the State Hospital.

ANSONIA.

Visited by Mr. Kellogg, July 21, 1898.

Almshouse is owned by town, and is situated one and one-half
miles north from the center, on the Seymour road on the
west side of the river. About 50 acres of land are attached.

Keepers, Mr. and Mrs. Peter Foy, whose contract expires
January 1st.

Terms, $700 a year, not including out-door relief.

Prisoners are not received.

Number of inmates at date of visit, 12; 5 men, 7 women.

Number of insane, 2; 1 man, 1 woman, both of whom have been in the State Hospital.

Number of feeble-minded, one man.*

Two of the women assist in the housework.

The almshouse is a wooden building, old, but neat and comfortable. It is heated by steam, and lighted by lamps. Separate sitting and dining-rooms for men and women are provided, and the food appeared sufficient and of good quality. Separate yards surrounded by high board fences are provided for men and women, but of these, the women's yard is much too small for the purpose.

BETHANY.

Visited by Miss Bacon, July 18, 1898.

Bethany has no almshouse, and during the past year had only two families receiving poor relief. Three persons are supported at the Hospital for the Insane.

BRANFORD.

Visited by Miss Bacon, November, 1898.

Almshouse is owned by town.

Keeper, Mr. Jerry Miller.

Number of inmates at date of visit, 8; 5 men, 3 women.

The condition of the house was found to be much improved since the previous visit. The place was clean and warm, and the inmates appeared to be comfortable. All of the inmates are too old to do any work.

There is still room for improvement in some departments of the house.

CHESHIRE.

Visited by Miss Bacon, October 26, 1897, by Mr. Kellogg, July 26, 1898, and by Miss Hall, October 4, 1898.

Almshouse is owned by town, and is situated one and one-half miles northeast from the center. About 75 acres of land are attached.

Keepers, Mr. and Mrs. C. H. Hodge, who assumed charge
   April 1, 1898.
Terms, $500 a year, not including out-door relief.
Prisoners are not received.
Number of inmates at date of last visit, 4 ; 2 men, 2 women.
Number able to work, 3 ; 1 man, 2 women.
Occupation, housework.

The house is well-arranged and comfortable, but the management in some respects is not so careful as is desirable. The
food appeared sufficient and of good quality. Tramps are
cared for in a separate building.

DERBY.

Visited by Mr. Kellogg, July 21, 1898.

Derby has no almshouse, but at the date of visit was boarding three men at William Nolan's place near the New Haven
road. The place was visited, and the inmates found to be comfortably cared for. The town pays $2.75 a week for each
boarder, and furnishes clothing in addition. A few other dependent persons are boarded at Joseph Martin's, in the town
of Huntington, and in other families in the town of Derby.

EAST HAVEN.

Visited by Miss Bacon, July 25, 1898.

There is no almshouse in East Haven, and at the date of
visit two families were partially supported by the town. Two
insane persons are boarded in the State Hospital, and one child
in the School for Imbeciles at Lakeville.

GUILFORD.

Visited by Miss Bacon, January 20, 1897.

Almshouse is owned by town. A few acres only are attached.
Keeper, Mr. William Bowen.
Terms, $125 a year, not including out-door relief.
Number of inmates at date of visit, 2 ; 1 man, 1 woman, neither
   of whom is able to work.

The house is very old, but as there are so few occupants, they are made reasonably comfortable. A building for tramps has been erected on the premises, and a large number of them were sheltered during the winter.

HAMDEN.

Visited by Miss Bacon, December 28, 1896.

Almshouse is owned by town, and about 120 acres of land are
 attached.
Keeper, Mr. George B. Zorn.
Terms, $450 a year, not including out-door relief.
Prisoners are not received.
Number of inmates at date of visit, 8; 2 men, 6 women.
Number of feeble-minded, 3 women.
Number able to work, 2 women.

Everything about the place appeared neat and comfortable. The inmates had no complaints to make, and all spoke well of the keeper.

MADISON.

Visited by Miss Bacon, July 22, 1898.

Madison has no almshouse, and at the date of visit only one pauper was wholly supported by the town. Four families were assisted with partial relief. The town supports five persons in the Hospital for the Insane, and one child in the County Home. About fifty tramps were given shelter and meals during the winter.

MERIDEN.

*Visited by Miss Hall and Mr. Whittlesey, September 4, 1897, and
by Miss Bacon and Mr. Kellogg, June 17, 1898.*

Almshouse is owned by town, and is situated on Capitol avenue
 two miles northwest of the center; about 12 acres of land
 are attached, and a small farm at some distance, also belongs to the town.
Keepers, Mr. and Mrs. M. H. O'Brien, whose contract expires
 January 1st, annually.

Terms, $800 a year, not including out-door relief.

Prisoners are received, chiefly cases of drunkenness, and are not separated from the paupers.

Number of inmates at date of visit, 46; 25 men, 19 women, 2 infants under four years.

Number of insane, 21 : 14 men, 7 women; of the women, 5 had previously been in the State Hospital.

Number able to work, 13 : 8 men, 5 women.

Occupations, housework and farmwork.

The main house is a two and a half story wooden building, old and ill arranged. It is, however, kept in a neat and clean condition, and the beds are good. The building is heated by stoves and lighted by lamps, and should be provided with fire-escapes.

In the women's dormitory are eight cells, in which the inmates are locked at night. The men occupy a detached wooden house which is provided with outside staircases for use in times of necessity.

After the visit, recommendation was made to the selectmen that a number of the worst cases of insanity be removed to the State Hospital, and this was done soon afterward. It was also recommended that a new building be erected, or extensive improvements made upon the present structure.

MIDDLEBURY.

Visited by Mr. Kellogg, July 11, 1898.

Middlebury has no almshouse, and at the date of visit no poor persons wholly supported by the town. Three families were being assisted with partial support.

NAUGATUCK.

Visited by Miss Bacon, June 1, 1897, and by Mr. Kellogg, May 6, 1898.

Almshouse is owned by town, and is situated about one mile west of the center, on the Millville road. About 200 acres of land are attached.

Keepers, Mr. and Mrs. C. F. Blumenauer, who took charge May 1, 1896.

Terms, $1,000 a year, not including out-door relief.

Prisoners are not received.

Number of inmates at date of visit, 20: 10 men, 8 women, 2 infants under four years.

Number of feeble-minded, 6: 3 men, 3 women.

Number able to work, 9: 6 men, 3 women.

The building was formerly an old farmhouse, and in many ways is unfit for its present use. It is heated by stoves only, and there is no means of heating the bath-room, which might be better equipped with toilet facilities. Considerable improvement was noticed, however, in the condition of the house under its new keepers, and all departments appeared clean and tidy. The town should have a new building better adapted for the purpose.

NORTH HAVEN.

Visited by Miss Bacon, December, 1898.

There is no almshouse in North Haven, but at the date of visit the town was supporting two men and one woman in the Almshouse for State Paupers at Tariffville. One woman is boarded in a private family, and other persons are assisted from time to time in their own homes, as occasion requires. Three insane persons are supported in the State Hospital.

ORANGE.

Visited by Miss Bacon, July 30, 1898.

Orange has no almshouse, but at date of visit about thirty persons were being assisted with partial support.

The town boards eight insane persons at the State Hospital.

PROSPECT.

Visited by Mr. Kellogg, July 15, 1898.

There is no almshouse in Prospect, but at the date of visit the town was supporting two persons in private families, one at the Hospital for the Insane, and one in the New Haven Hospital.

SEYMOUR.

Visited by Miss Bacon, December 2, 1898.

Seymour has no almshouse, though at the date of visit 19 persons were being wholly supported.   Twenty-one others were receiving partial support.

With so many persons dependent upon the town, it would seem advisable that they should be brought together and cared for on a town farm.

Three insane persons are boarded at the State Hospital.

WALLINGFORD.

Visited by Miss Bacon, January 23, 1897, and February 17, 1898.

Almshouse is owned by town, and about 20 acres of land are attached.

Keeper, Mr. A. H. Leonard.

Terms, $700 a year.

Prisoners are not received.

Number of inmates at date of last visit, 15 ; 8 men, 7 women.

The almshouse has been greatly improved since the last report by the erection of a large addition, and the introduction of new heating and bathing arrangements.   The inmates appear well cared for, and everything is in a neat and orderly condition.   The house is one of the best in the State.

WOLCOTT.

Visited by Mr. Kellogg, August 6, 1898.

Wolcott has no almshouse, and at the date of visit, no one wholly supported by the town.   A number of persons are helped with partial support when necessary.

WOODBRIDGE.

Visited by Miss Bacon, July 18, 1898.

There is no almshouse in Woodbridge, but during the year eight persons were assisted by the town with partial support.

Three insane persons are boarded in the State Hospital.

NEW LONDON COUNTY.

There are twenty-one towns in the county, of which ten maintain almshouses owned by the town, and two have alms-houses owned and managed by private individuals. The towns mentioned in the appended list have been visited, and reports on the condition of the poor are presented as follows:

NEW LONDON.

Visited by Mr. Spencer and Mr. Kellogg, June 7, 1897, and by

Mr. Whittlesey and Mr. Kellogg, February 11, 1898.

Almshouse is owned by town, and is situated at the corner of Garfield and Jefferson avenues, three-fourths of a mile west from the city hall. About 18 acres of land are attached. ·

Keepers, Mr. and Mrs. Charles H. Walden, who have had charge since 1880.

Terms, $850 a year, not including out-door relief.

Prisoners are not received.

Number of inmates at date of last visit, 51 : 25 men, 24 women, and 2 infants under four years.

Number of insane, 16 : 10 men, 6 women, of whom 4 men and 3 women have previously been in the State Hospital.

Number of feeble-minded, 8 : 4 men, 4 women.

Number able to work, 13 : 5 men, 8 women.

Occupations, housework and farmwork.

The house is a three-story structure of brick with basement, and is connected with the city systems of water and sewers. All departments are heated by hot-water pipes, and electric lights have recently been introduced throughout. Neatness and good order prevail in all parts of the house, and its general condition reflects great credit upon the keepers.

Since the recommendation two years ago of the State Board, three meals a day are now furnished to the inmates in winter as well as in summer. The food is abundant and of excellent quality.

NORWICH.

Visited by Mr. Kellogg, August 9, 1898.

Almshouse is owned by town, and is situated on the west side of the Yantic river, one and a half miles west from the city hall.   West-side electric cars pass within a third of a mile from the house.   About 30 acres of land are attached.

Keepers, Mr. and Mrs. Marvin L. Bailey, whose contract is renewed April 1st, annually.

Terms, $800 a year, not including out-door relief.

Prisoners are not received.

Number of inmates at date of visit, 68 : 33 men, 35 women.

Number of insane, 8 : 2 men, 6 women ; of whom 1 man and 1 woman have been in the State Hospital.

Number of feeble-minded, 1 man.

Number able to work, 7 : 4 men, 3 women.

Occupations, farmwork and housework.

The house is a brick structure three stories high, and is heated by steam and lighted by gas.   All departments presented an appearance of neatness and comfort.   As in the case of New London, three meals a day are now served here in the winter, since the Board's recommendation to that effect.   The food is varied and sufficient.

Three violently insane persons were awaiting transportation to Middletown.   The house is visited every month by a committee of ladies from the United Workers Association of the city, and religious services are conducted on Sundays by delegations from the churches and other organizations.

BOZRAH.

Visited by Mr. Kellogg, June 9, 1898.

Bozrah has no almshouse, and at date of visit was boarding one aged woman in the village of Leffingwell at the rate of $2 a week.

Other persons are helped in their homes as needed, and two insane persons are supported at the State Hospital.

COLCHESTER.

Visited by Miss Hall, August 17, 1897, and by Miss Hall and Mr. Kellogg, February 16, 1898.

Almshouse is owned by town, and is situated one-half mile south from the railway station. About 90 acres of land are attached, besides 150 acres of woodland.

Keepers, Mr. and Mrs. Frederick I. Phillips, whose contract is renewed April 1st, annually.

Terms, $400 a year, not including out-door relief.

Prisoners are received occasionally, and are kept in two cells that open out from the living-room of the house.

Number of inmates at date of last visit, 10 : 4 men, 6 women.

Number of insane, 1 man, who had previously been in the State Hospital.

Number of feeble-minded, 3 women.

Number able to work, 4 : 1 man, 3 women.

Occupations, farmwork and housework.

The house was provided with a hot-air furnace in 1897, that heats most parts of the house very well. It is ingeniously arranged, and wood from the town land is used for fuel. All portions of the house appeared neat and comfortable, and the inmates seemed to be well cared for.

A bath-tub is still needed in the house. Tramps are given lodging in a detached building.

EAST LYME.

Visited by Mr. Kellogg, May 11, 1898.

There is no almshouse in East Lyme, but at the date of visit, three persons were being partially supported at rates varying from $2 to $5 a week.

FRANKLIN.

Visited by Mr. Kellogg, June 9, 1898.

The town has no almshouse, but at the date of visit was boarding two persons at Daniel McCarthy's, between Smith's Corners and Baltic, at the rate of $2 a week for each. The inmates were treated as members of the family, and had no complaints to make. Greater attention to neatness in some respects was recommended.

GRISWOLD.

Visited by Mr. Kellogg, June 10, 1898.

Almshouse is owned by town, and is situated four and a half
miles northeast of Jewett City.   About 125 acres of land
are attached.

Keepers, Mr. and Mrs. Frank Ray, since April, 1896.

Terms, $450 a year, not including out-door relief.

Prisoners are not received.

Number of inmates at date of visit, 6: 3 men, 3 women.

Number of insane, 1 man, 3 women, of whom the man and
two of the women had previously been in the State
Hospital.

Number of feeble-minded, 1 man.

Number able to work, 2 men, 1 woman.

Occupations, farmwork and housework.

Quarters for the poor are situated in an ell of the building,
and are clean and comfortable.   There is a common sitting
and dining-room, and the food is cooked in the keeper's house.
Tramps are given shelter in a small building near by.

GROTON.

Visited by Mr. Kellogg, May 12, 1898.

Almshouse is owned by town and is situated two and a half
miles west from Mystic village, or four miles east from
Groton village.   About 75 acres of land are attached.

Keepers, Mr. and Mrs. Owen H. Williams, whose contract is
renewed March 1st, annually.

Terms, $360 a year, not including out-door relief.

Number of inmates at date of visit, 10: 6 men, 4 women.

Number of insane, 1 man, who had previously been in the State
Hospital.

Number of feeble-minded, 3 women.

Number able to work, 5: 3 men, 2 women.

Occupations, farmwork and housework.

The town farm was presented to Groton by Capt. Elihu
Spicer, who left in his will $5,000 to be devoted to the mainten-
ance and repair of the buildings at the farm.   About $4,000
of this sum were expended in the erection of a large addition
to the keeper's house, which was first occupied in October,
1894.   It contains seventeen bedrooms, with accommodations

for twenty-two inmates, also sitting-room, bath-room, etc., and is heated throughout by steam. The quarters are exceptionally neat and attractive. · All departments gave evidence of good management, and the inmates appeared to be kindly treated.

LEDYARD.

Visited by Mr. Kellogg, May 12, 1898.

Almshouse is owned by town, and is situated six miles north
    of Mystic village, and three miles east of Ledyard center. .
    About 200 acres of land are attached.
Keepers, Mr. and Mrs. Henry Gallup. The town pays $2 a
    week for the board and clothing of each inmate, and
    furnishes medical attendance in addition when required.
Number of inmates at date of visit, 4: 1 man, 3 women.
Number of insane, 2 women, one of whom had previously
    been in the Hartford Retreat.
Number of feeble-minded, 1 man.
The man assists somewhat in work about the place.

The place was formerly known as the Charles Park farm, and was purchased by the town in March, 1895. The house is very old, but fairly comfortable. The bathing and sanitary arrangements are primitive, as in most old farmhouses. The inmates are given two regular meals a day in winter, and a light lunch on retiring.

LISBON

Visited by Mr. Kellogg, June 9, 1898.

Lisbon has no almshouse, but at the date of visit was boarding two persons in private families. One aged woman at the home of Frank Ames, six miles north from Norwich, and near the village of Versailles, was visited, and was found to be comfortably situated.

LYME.

Visited by Mr. Kellogg, May 11, 1898.

Lyme has no almshouse, and at the date of visit was wholly supporting only one person. Others were helped with partial support as necessary.

NORTH STONINGTON.

Visited by Mr. Kellogg, May 12, 1898.

There is no almshouse in North Stonington, but at the date of visit the town was supporting four persons in private families, and was assisting a number of others with partial relief.

OLD LYME

Visited by Mr. Kellogg, May 11, 1898.

Almshouse is owned by town, and is situated two miles north from the railway station. About 10 acres of land are attached.

Keeper, Mrs. A. H. Maynard, whose contract is renewed April 1st, annually.

Terms, $3 a week for each inmate, the town furnishing clothing and medical attendance in addition.

Prisoners are not received.

Number of inmates at date of visit, 3 men.

Number of feeble-minded, 1 man.

Number able to work, 2 men.

Occupation, small work about the place.

The place is a fairly comfortable farmhouse, but greater attention to neatness should be observed in some respects. One aged cripple, who is confined to his room, should have had a more comfortable chair, and recommendation to that effect was made to the town authorities.

PRESTON.

Visited by Mr. Kellogg, June 10, 1898.

Preston has no almshouse, and at date of visit was wholly supporting only one person. Other persons are assisted with partial relief, and eight inmates are boarded at the State Hospital for the Insane.

SPRAGUE.

Visited by Mr. Kellogg, June 9, 1898.

Almshouse is not owned by town, but is managed by private parties. It is situated two miles north of Baltic, or ten

17

miles north of Norwich, on a cross road between the Scotland and Hanover roads.

Keeper, Mr. James Valette.

Terms, $2 a week for each inmate.

Prisoners are not received.

Number of inmates at date of visit, 5 : 1 man, 4 women.

Number of insane, 4 women, of whom 2 had previously been in the State Hospital.

Number of feeble-minded, 1 man.

The inmates all room in a separate building, but the cooking is done in the keeper's house. The building is old, but fairly comfortable, and the inmates appeared to be well cared for.

STONINGTON.

Visited by Mr. Kellogg, May 12, 1898.

Almshouse is owned by town, and is situated three and a half miles north from the railway station. About 150 acres of land are attached.

Keepers, Mr. and Mrs. F. C. Dixon, who took charge March 25, 1898.

Terms, $600 a year, which includes clothing and all other provisions for the inmates.

Prisoners are not received.

Number of inmates at date of visit, 21 : 14 men, 6 women, 1 infant under four years.

Number of insane, 2 men, 1 woman.

Number of feeble-minded, 2 men, 2 women.

Number able to work, 11 : 7 men, 4 women.

Occupations, farmwork and housework.

The house is old, but fairly comfortable. The women occupy rooms on the upper floor of the main part, while the men's quarters are situated in an ell. Steam heat is provided in the halls, and the bedrooms are fairly neat. Separate sitting-rooms are provided for men and women, who meet in a common dining-room for meals.

One insane man, 50 years old, had a very dirty room and bed, and while out-of-doors was fastened with a ball and chain. Recommendation was made to the town authorities that he be removed to the Hospital for the Insane at once. Some improvements were noticed since the installation of the new keepers, new iron beds being supplied, and the halls being freshly painted.

WATERFORD.

Visited by Mr. Kellogg, February 12, 1898.

Almshouse is owned by town, and is situated five miles northwest from the city of New London. About 115 acres of
land are attached.

Keepers, Mr. and Mrs. N. D. Getchel, who have held the position since 1882, with an interval of three years.

Terms, $300 a year, not including out-door relief.

Prisoners are not received.

Number of inmates at date of visit, 7 : 6 men, 1 woman.

Number of insane, 2 : 1 man, 1 woman.

Number of feeble-minded, 1 man.

The house is very old, and most of the inmates occupy small
rooms in the ell directly under the roof, which must be ex-
cessively hot in summer, and bitterly cold in winter. The
house was found unchanged since previous visits, but was in
fairly good order.

The insane woman was in the same miserable room as
before, which has a cement floor and no furnishings, but a tick
filled with straw. She was unable to care for herself decently,
and it was impossible to keep her properly clothed. The
visitor called upon the second selectman and urged her early
removal to the State Hospital for the Insane.

The insane man was found tied in a chair, and his removal
to Middletown, also, was advised. A thorough remodeling of
the old house, or the construction of an entirely new one, is
greatly needed.

VOLUNTOWN.

Visited by Mr. Kellogg, June 10, 1898.

Voluntown has no almshouse, but at the date of visit was
supporting three persons in private families. Two insane persons were boarded at the State Hospital.

FAIRFIELD COUNTY.

There are twenty-three towns in Fairfield County, of which seven maintain almshouses owned by the town, and five have almshouses owned and managed by private individuals. Visits have been made to the towns mentioned in the appended list, and reports on the condition of the poor are presented as follows:

BRIDGEPORT.

Visited by Mr. Kellogg, March 18, 1898.

Almshouse is owned by town, and is situated on Asylum street, one and a half miles north from the railway station. The East Main street line of electric cars runs near the place. About 113 acres of land are attached.

Keepers, Mr. and Mrs. Michael Logan, who have been in charge since 1866.

Terms, $2,080 a year for the keepers and two assistants. This does not include out-door relief.

Prisoners are received occasionally, and are not separated from the paupers.

Number of inmates at date of visit, 165: 117 men, 40 women, 8 infants under four years.

Number of insane, 46: 30 men, 16 women, of whom 16 men and 8 women had previously been in the State Hospital.

Number of feeble-minded, 13: 5 men, 15 women.

Number able to work, 51: 36 men, 15 women.

The men work upon the farm, in the blacksmith and carpenter shops, and care for their part of the house. The women are employed in housework, sewing, mending, etc. The almshouse is a brick building, but some parts are old and ill arranged for the purpose. It is also overcrowded at times, and the ventilation in the men's department is poor. A new building for men would be a great improvement. A new two-story extension of brick contains quarters for insane women on the ground floor, and a chapel above. Services are held twice a month, Roman Catholic and Protestant alternately. The whole place is neat and clean, and appears to be well-managed. The food is abundant and of good quality.

DANBURY.

*Visited by Miss Hall and Mr. Kellogg, September 18, 1897,
and by Mr. Whittlesey, November 15, 1898.*

Almshouse is owned, by town, and is situated on Osborn street, one mile northwest from the center.   About 78 acres of land are attached.

Keepers, Mr. and Mrs. George P. Foote, who took charge in June, 1896.

Terms, $900 a year, not including out-door relief.

Number of inmates at date of visit, 56: 41 men, 15 women.

Number of insane, 9: 4 men, 5 women, of whom the men and 2 of the women had previously been in the State Hospital.

Number of feeble-minded, 1 man, 1 woman.

Number able to work, 20: 16 men, 4 women.

Occupations, farmwork and housework.

The almshouse is a handsome, three-story structure of brick, situated on high ground, and was first opened in November, 1894.   It is heated throughout by steam and is lighted by gas. Bath and toilet-rooms are located on every floor.   The second floor is arranged as dormitories and the third floor in single rooms.   Large hospital rooms are also provided for men and women. · The house is a model one in its way and appears to be exceptionally well managed by the new superintendents. Interest in the inmates and an ambition to keep all departments in good order were evident.   Religious services are held every Sunday under the auspices of the Women's Temperance Union.

BETHEL.

Visited by Mr. Kellogg, September 18, 1897.

Bethel has no almshouse, but boards its dependent poor in private families.   A visit was made to the home of Eugene Burcham, where were boarded two old men at the rate of $3 a week each, and two colored boys aged three and four years, respectively.   The house was comfortable, but not so neat as is desirable.   The children had previously been in the County Home, but had been dismissed on account of a hereditary disease.

BROOKFIELD.

Visited by Mr. Kellogg, September 18, 1897.

Brookfield has no almshouse, but assists the town poor with relief in their own homes. Visit was made to the second selectman and facts learned in regard to the amount of relief distributed. During the year, the town supported five adult dependents, besides a family of small children in their home.

DARIEN.

Visited by Miss Hall and Mr. Kellogg, October 1, 1897.

Almshouse is not owned by town, but is rented for the purpose, and is situated one-half mile south from the railway station.

Keeper, Mrs. Sarah E. Hall.

Terms, $3 a week for each inmate besides clothing and medical attendance.

Number of inmates at date of visit, one man, who does some small work about the place. The old man inmate had been provided with a better bed since the last visit, as recommended, but the house still lacked in matter of cleanliness and neatness, and greater care in these respects was urged. Visit was made to the first selectman and certain improvements were recommended.

GREENWICH.

Visited by Miss Bacon and Mr. Kellogg, November 16, 1897.

Almshouse is owned by town, and is situated four miles north of the center on the Round Hill road. About 125 acres of land are attached.

Keepers, Mr. and Mrs. Maurice Nolan, whose contract is renewed January 1st, annually.

Terms, $500 a year not including out-door relief.

Prisoners are not received.

Number of inmates at date of visit, 23 : 12 men, 8 women, 1 boy ten years old, and 2 infants under four years.

Number of insane, 1 man, who had previously been in the State Hospital.

Number of feeble-minded, 1 man.

Number able to work, 6 : 4 men, 2 women.

Occupations, farmwork and housework.

The house is a large wooden structure and appeared very

comfortable and well-kept. All parts were clean and neat. A new steam-heating apparatus was being introduced at the time of visit. The ten-year-old boy had formerly been in the County Home, but was returned on account of a serious impediment in his speech. An attempt was made to place him in the school for the deaf, but he did not appear to be a suitable pupil for the school.

HUNTINGTON.

Visited by Mr. Kellogg, January 27, 1898.

The town has no almshouse, but boards its dependent poor in private families. The visitor called at one place two miles east from Monroe center, where he found an aged woman who had miserable quarters in a cold garret. The house was very dilapidated and all the surroundings indicated neglect. Upon the recommendation of the Board, the woman was soon after removed to a more comfortable boarding place near Huntington center.

The visitor called also at the house of Joseph L. Martin at Huntington center, four miles west of Derby, where there was an old colored woman belonging to the town of Huntington, and a colored boy seven years old, belonging to the town of Derby. Both boarders appeared to be contented and well cared for. The boy was formerly in the Fairfield County Home, but was discharged on account of a constitutional disease.

MONROE.

Visited by Mr. Kellogg, January 27, 1898.

Monroe has no almshouse, but boards its dependent poor in private families. The visitor called at David Laborie's, two miles east of the center, where one man was cared for in miserable quarters. The man is very dirty in his habits, and sleeps on a miserable bed in the hay-loft of the barn. It was said to be his own choice, but the keepers were advised to put him in better condition.

NEW CANAAN.

Visited by Mr. Kellogg, October 2, 1897.

Almshouse is owned by town, and is situated three miles north-
east from the center.   About 80 acres of land are attached.
Keepers, Mr. and Mrs. Charles B. Rider, whose contract is
renewed April 1st, annually.
Terms, $575 a year, not including out-door relief.
Prisoners are not received.
Number of inmates at date of visit, 4 : 3 men, 1 woman.
Number of insane, 1 woman, who had previously been in the
State Hospital.
Number of feeble-minded, 1 man.
Number able to work, 1 man, 1 woman.
Occupations, farmwork and housework.

The house is old, but thoroughly comfortable and neat.
The rooms are pleasantly furnished, and the food is sufficient.
Inmates appeared to be well cared for.

NEW FAIRFIELD.

Visited by Miss Hall and Mr. Kellogg, October 7, 1898.

There was no almshouse in operation in New Fairfield at
the time of visit, but the few persons dependent upon the town
were boarded in private families.   One woman was visited
who had a comfortable home.   A man who was said to be very
troublesome to care for, was found in miserable condition,
occupying a very dirty loft in a barn.   The visitors recommended that he be removed to better surroundings, and he was
soon after transferred to the State Hospital for the Insane.

The town has purchased a building near the center, formerly
used as a wagon-shop, and may utilize it as an almshouse, if
the number of dependent poor warrants such action.

NEWTOWN.

Visited by Mr. Kellogg, January 27, 1898.

Almshouse is not owned by town, but is managed by private
parties, and is situated three miles southeast from the
Newtown railway station.
Keeper, Mrs. Martin Lynch.

Terms, $3 a week for each person, in addition to clothing and
medical attendance.

Number of inmates at date of visit, 8 : 5 men, 3 women.

Number of feeble-minded, 2 : 1 man, 1 woman.

Number able to work, 5 : 3 men, 2 women.

The house is old, but is fairly comfortable. The women
occupy rooms down stairs, while the men are accommodated
in a large loft over the rear of the house. One young man,
an epileptic, is difficult to care for properly. The town boards
several other persons in other families, and might do better if
they were all cared for in one place.

NORWALK.

Visited by Mr. Kellogg, April 26, 1898.

Almshouse is owned by town, and is situated one and a fourth
miles east from the center, on the Strawberry Hill road.
About 40 acres of land are attached.

Keepers, Mr. and Mrs. Charles E. Hoyt, whose contract is
renewed November 1st, annually.

Terms, $450 a year, not including out-door relief.

Prisoners are received occasionally, but are not separated from
the paupers.

Number of inmates at date of visit, 36 : 20 men, 15 women, 1
boy, two and one-half years old.

Number of insane, 1 woman, who had previously been in the
State Hospital.

Number of feeble-minded, 12 : 6 men, 6 women.

Number able to work, 30 : 17 men, 13 women.

Occupations, farmwork and housework.

The building is a three-story wooden structure with basement, and is heated throughout by steam. As at the date of
the previous visit, there were no fire-escapes, and the only
water supply was a pump in the basement kitchen. Better
facilities in these respects were recommended, also the addition of a bath-room to the house.

There were no lights in the halls or dining-room, and only
oil lamps in the kitchen. The introduction of electric lights
would be a great improvement. It has been the practice to
furnish only two meals a day during the winter. The house appeared to be in good order, and the inmates seemed to be well
cared for.

REDDING.

Visited by Mr. Kellogg, September 18, 1897.

Almshouse is not owned by town, but is managed by private
    parties.   It is situated in West Redding, about three miles
    northeast from the railway station at Branchville.
Keepers, Mr. and Mrs. Frank C. Lee, since February, 1897.
Terms, $3 a week for each inmate.
Prisoners are not received.
Number of inmates at date of visit, 4 : 3 men, 1 woman.
Number of feeble-minded, 1 woman.
Number able to work, 1 man, 1 woman.

The man does light work about the place and the woman
assists in the housework.   The inmates live in a little structure built at a short distance from the house.   It contains also
a blacksmith-shop and must be cold in winter.   Meals are
carried out from the main house.   The three men, of whom
one was a consumptive, all slept in a small room, and it was
recommended that the consumptive be given a room by himself.

There is opportunity for improvement in the general conditions of comfort.

RIDGEFIELD.

Visited by Mr. Kellogg, September 18, 1897.

Almshouse is owned by town, and is situated three miles north
    from the center.   About 50 acres of land are attached.
Keepers, Mr. and Mrs. Smith Remington, since April, 1897.
Terms, $300 a year, not including out-door relief.
Prisoners are not received.
Number of inmates at date of visit, 11 : 6 men, 5 women.
Number of feeble-minded, 1 man, 1 woman.
Number able to work, 5½ men, 3 women.

The women assist about the house and the men in light
work upon the farm.   The rooms for the inmates are all up-
stairs, but are clean and comfortable.   The beds are old, but
clean.   One man, a consumptive, has a bedroom alone.

SHERMAN.

Reported September 17, 1897.

Sherman was not visited, but at the date of visit to an adjoining town, report was made that there were no paupers wholly supported in the town of Sherman. Families and individuals are assisted from time to time as occasion requires.

STAMFORD.

Visited by Mr. Kellogg, October 2, 1897.

Almshouse is owned by town, and is situated seven miles north from the center. About 100 acres of land are attached.

Keepers, Mr. and Mrs. J. H. Parker.

Terms, $600 a year, not including out-door relief.

Prisoners are received occasionally, and are not separated from the paupers.

Number of inmates at date of visit, 38 : 13 men, 25 women.

Number of insane, 10 : 2 men, 8 women, of whom both of the men and four of the women had previously been in the State Hospital.

Number of feeble-minded; 7 : 2 men, 5 women.

Number able to work, 11 : 4 men, 7 women.

The men work on the roads and the farm, and the women are employed in various kinds of housework. The almshouse is a large wooden building, with a recent addition three stories in height. The halls, sitting-rooms, and hospital-rooms are heated by steam. The water supply is obtained from a driven well and is pumped into a large tank. Separate bath-rooms, equipped with modern plumbing, are provided for men and women.

All departments of the main house appeared clean and comfortable, and the inmates seemed contented. In a small wooden building at the rear were confined three women whose mental condition and bodily habits made them difficult to care for. Soon after the visit, one of these women attacked the keeper, who died during the encounter from heart-failure, as was reported afterwards. It had previously been recommended by the Board that the woman should be removed to the Hospital at Middletown, and after this unfortunate occurrence she was transferred there.

WESTON.

Visited by Mr. Kellogg, April 27, 1898.

Weston has no almshouse, and at the date of visit was wholly supporting only one person, a married woman, at that time living in the town of Easton. Other needy persons in the town are helped as occasion demands.

Two insane persons are boarded at the State Hospital.

WESTPORT.

Visited by Mr. Kellogg, April 27, 1898.

Almshouse is not owned by town, but is the property of the second selectman, and is situated two and a half miles north from the village.

Keeper, Mrs. Dignam, who receives $5 a month and her living, the town furnishing in addition all clothing, supplies, etc.

Number of inmates at date of visit, 5 : 4 men, 1 woman.

Number of feeble-minded, 1 man.

Number able to work, 1 man.

The house was very old, but fairly comfortable. More attention to neatness and cleanliness in some respects was recommended. One man, who was seriously ill, should have received greater care, but the inmates, as a whole, had no complaints to make.

WILTON.

Visited by Mr. Kellogg, April 27, 1898.

Almshouse is not owned by town, but is managed by private parties. It is situated on the main road two miles north from Wilton center, and five miles south from Ridgefield.

Keeper, Mr. R. W. Keeler.

Terms, $2 a week for each inmate, in addition to clothing and medical attendance.

Prisoners are not received.

Number of inmates at date of visit, 3 : 2 men, 1 woman.

Number of insane, 1 man, who had previously been in the State Hospital.

Number of feeble-minded, 1 woman.

All of the inmates are able to do some little work about the place. The house for the paupers is a small wooden structure, containing four small bedrooms and a living-room. Rooms and beds were comfortable, and were fairly neat. Meals are cooked in the keeper's house near by, and are carried out. A few tramps are received at 50 cents each per night.

WINDHAM COUNTY.

There are fifteen towns in the county, of which seven have almshouses owned by the town, and one maintains an almshouse owned by a private individual. The towns mentioned in the appended list have been visited and reports on the condition of the poor are presented as follows:

WINDHAM.

(*Willimantic.*)

Visited by Mr. Kellogg, April 29, 1898.

Almshouse is owned by town, and is situated on West Main street, one mile west from the railway station. About 70 acres of land are attached.

Keepers, Mr. and Mrs. John M. Palmer, whose contract is renewed April 1st, annually.

Terms, $720 a year, not including out-door relief.

Prisoners are received occasionally, and have quarters in the basement of the building entirely separate from the other inmates.

Number of inmates at date of visit, 47 : 27 men, 20 women.

Number of insane, 1 woman.

Number of feeble-minded, 1 man, 2 women.

Number able to work, 6 men, 6 women.

The women are engaged in housework, and the men cut wood and do other small work about the place. The house is a large three-story wooden building, heated throughout by steam and lighted by gasoline.

There is one fire-escape from the top floor and fire-hose is provided in all the halls. A store is situated in the basement, from which provisions, etc., are delivered on orders to the outside poor under the direction of the keeper. All departments were in good order, and the inmates appeared to be kindly treated.

PUTNAM.

Visited by Mr. Kellogg, June 30, 1898.

Almshouse is owned by town, and is situated two miles southwest from the center, on the Pomfret road. About 180
acres of land are attached.

Keepers, Mr. and Mrs. Herbert Maples, since May 1, 1898.

Terms, $400 a year, which includes also the work of distribut-
ing supplies to the outside poor.

Prisoners are not received.

Number of inmates at date of visit, 14 : 3 men, 8 women, 1 boy
five years old, and 2 infants under four years.

Number of insane, 2 women, of whom one had previously
been in the State Hospital.

Number of feeble-minded, 1 man.

Number able to work, 2 men, 3 women.

Occupations, farmwork and housework.

The women have rooms in the main house, while the men
are accommodated in an older building near by which is heated
by stoves.

The main house is provided with a hot-water heating apparatus and a good bath-room. All departments appeared
neat and comfortable, and the inmates seemed contented. The
five-year-old boy and one of the infants were afterward taken
away by their mother, upon recommendation of the Board to
that effect.

BROOKLYN.

Visited by Mr. Kellogg, September 27, 1898.

The town owns no almshouse, but boards its dependent
poor with Mrs. C. M. Spaulding, who lives three miles north
from the center, and the same distance south from the railway
station at Pomfret.

The terms are $3 a week for each inmate.

No prisoners are received. At the date of visit one old man
was being boarded; also a woman and three children who
were said to belong to the town of Sprague. Eight other
persons, chiefly old people, were being assisted in their homes.
Three insane persons were supported at the State Hospital.
The boarders at Mrs. Spaulding's appeared reasonably comfortable, but the old man's room was dirty and should be kept
in better condition.

ASHFORD.

Visited by Mr. Kellogg, April 30, 1898.

Ashford has no almshouse, but boards its dependent poor with Mr. and Mrs. Arnold Upton, who live about four miles east from Willington center.   The town pays $1.50 a week for each person, and furnishes in addition clothing and medical attendance.

At the date of visit there were two persons supported there. Mr. and Mrs. Upton care also for the town poor of Willington, and had others present belonging to the towns of Tolland and Ellington.

Separate sitting-rooms are provided for men and women, and the inmates appeared to be contented.

CANTERBURY.

Visited by Mr. Kellogg, August 10, 1898.

Almshouse is owned by town, and is situated at Canterbury Plains, six miles west from the railway station at Plainfield.   About 100 acres of land are attached.

Keepers, Mr. and Mrs. John Kinne, since April, 1898.

Terms, $1.75 a week for each inmate, in addition to which the town furnishes clothes, bedding, and medical attendance.

Prisoners are not received.

Number of inmates at date of visit, 3 : 1 man, 2 women.

Number of insane, 1 woman.

The almshouse is a wooden building two stories high.   The quarters reserved for the poor are somewhat limited, but appeared cleaner and more comfortable than at the previous visit.

The inmates have the same fare as the family, and made no complaints.   One woman is bedridden and is difficult to care for.

PLAINFIELD.

Visited by Mr. Kellogg, August 10, 1898.

Almshouse is owned by town, and is situated three miles northeast from the railway station at Plainfield, or one mile east from the station at Central Village.   About 70 acres of land are attached.

Keepers, Mr. and Mrs. George L. Stetson, whose contract is
   renewed March 23d, annually.
Terms, $400 a year, not including out-door relief.
Prisoners are not received.
Number of inmates at date of visit, 11 : 4 men, 7 women.
Number of insane, 4 women, all of whom had previously been
   in the State Hospital.
Number of feeble-minded, 1 man, 1 woman.
Number able to work, 2 men, 2 women.

   The house is old, but is kept neat and in good order. The
beds are clean and the food appeared varied and sufficient.

   A bath-room and improved toilet facilities are greatly
needed. A large number of tramps were given lodging in a
detached building during the winter.

POMFRET.

Visited by Mr. Kellogg, July 1, 1898.

   Pomfret has no almshouse, but at the date of visit was
boarding three dependent persons; two in the town of Pomfret
and one in the town of Brooklyn, besides two insane persons
in the State Hospital and one inmate at the School for Imbeciles.

   One of the persons boarded in the town of Pomfret was
visited and found to be comfortably cared for.

THOMPSON.

Visited by Mr. Kellogg, June 30, 1898.

Almshouse is owned by town, and is situated six miles north-
   east from the railway station at Putnam.   About 100 acres
   of land are attached.
Keepers, Mr. and Mrs. George W. Cutler, since October, 1896.
Terms, $300 a year, not including out-door relief.
Prisoners are not received.
Number of inmates at date of visit, 7 : 4 men, 3 women.
Number of insane, 1 man.
Number of feeble-minded, 1 man, 2 women.
Number able to work, 1 man, 1 woman.
Occupations, housework and farmwork.

   The house is old, but comfortable, and the inmates appeared
to be well treated.   The bedsteads at the time of visit were

old wooden affairs, but were afterwards replaced by newer ones of iron, after recommendation by the Board.   A furnace and a bath-room are both greatly needed in the house.   In winter it is customary to serve but two regular meals a day, but a light lunch is given before bedtime if desired.

WOODSTOCK.

Visited by Mr. Kellogg, July 1, 1898.

Almshouse is owned by town, and is situated nine miles north-
    west from the railway station at Putnam.   About 140
    acres of land are attached.

Keepers, Mr. and Mrs. B. W. Bates, whose contract is renewed
    April 1, annually.

Terms, $400 a year, not including out-door relief.

Prisoners are not received.

Number of inmates at date of visit, 13 : 6 men, 6 women, and
    1 feeble-minded boy, 16 years old.

Number able to work, 3 men, 6 women.

Occupations, housework and farmwork.

The house is situated on a high hill which commands fine views of the surrounding country.   On account of its exposed situation and for reasons of safety and economy, a furnace should take the place of the numerous stoves which are now in use.   Recommendation to that effect, and also for the intro-duction of a bath-room, was made to the town selectmen.

The feeble-minded boy has been in the house for nine years, but it has never been deemed advisable to send him to the Lakeville School.

The house is well kept in all respects, and the inmates ap-peared comfortable and contented.

18

LITCHFIELD COUNTY.

There are twenty-six towns in the county, of which nine maintain almshouses owned by the town, and three have alms-houses owned and managed by private individuals. Visits have been made to the towns mentioned in the appended list, and reports on the condition of the poor are presented as follows:

LITCHFIELD.

Visited by Miss Bacon, May 29, 1897, and by Mr. Kellogg, April 1, 1898.

Almshouse is owned by town, and is situated two and a half miles northeast from the center, near the Torrington road. About 200 acres of land are attached.

Keepers, Mr. and Mrs. Moses Doyle, since April, 1896.

Terms, $600 a year, not including out-door relief.

Prisoners are not received.

Number of inmates at date of visit, 13 : 9 men, 4 women.

Number of insane, 2 men, 1 woman, of whom both of the men had previously been in the State Hospital.

Number of feeble-minded, 2 men, 1 woman.

Number able to work, 3 men, 2 women.

Occupations, farmwork and housework.

The house is a large wooden structure and has an exposed situation on a high hill. A hot-air furnace was added in 1896, which heats the inmates' part of the building fairly well. The house appeared clean and in good order, and the inmates expressed themselves as contented.

It was recommended that some means be adopted for lighting the halls and stairways.

WINCHESTER.

(*Winsted.*)

Visited by Mr. Kellogg, October 12, 1898.

Almshouse is owned by town, and is situated one and three-fourths miles east from the railway station. About 100 acres of land are attached.

Keepers, Mr. and Mrs. Joseph Poole Jr., whose contract is renewed April 1st,' annually.

Terms, $3,200 a year, which includes also the care of the outside poor.

Prisoners are not received.

Number of inmates at date of visit, 9: 5 men, 2 women, 1 boy four years old, and 1 boy two years old.

Number of insane, 1 man, who had previously been in the State Hospital.

Number of feeble-minded, 1 woman.

Number able to work, 1 man, 2 women.

Occupations, farmwork and housework.

The house is a neat-looking brick building, and presented an appearance of comfort and good order. The only water supply is obtained from a well which at times becomes dry. Increased facilities in this respect should be provided. The cellar, on the other hand, is often very wet, and should be drained. Recommendations to this effect were made to the town selectmen.

NEW MILFORD.

Visited by Miss Hall and Mr. Kellogg, September 17, 1897.

Almshouse is owned by town, and is situated two and a half miles south from the center. About 100 acres of land are attached.

Keepers, Mr. and Mrs. James H. Osborn, whose contract expires April 1st.

Terms, $350 a year, not including out-door relief.

Prisoners are not received.

Number of inmates at date of visit, 6: 3 men, 2 women, 1 feeble-minded girl, ten years old. One man had previously been in the State Hospital for the Insane, and two of the women were feeble-minded.

The house is very old, and should be replaced by a more modern structure. New beds had been added since the last visit, and the house appeared as well kept as such an old place could be. Recommendation was made that the feeble-minded girl, who was also a cripple, be removed to the Lakeville School, and this was soon after complied with.

BRIDGEWATER.

Visited by Miss Hall, September 18, 1897.

Bridgewater has no almshouse, but at the date of visit three dependent persons were being wholly supported by the town. One of these was in the State Hospital for the Insane.

CANAAN.

Visited by Mr. Kellogg, September 17, 1897.

Canaan has no almshouse, and at the date of visit no town poor wholly supported in the town. One man was boarded in Housatonic, Massachusetts, and two insane persons in the State Hospital. Other individuals and families are assisted in their homes as necessary.

CORNWALL.

Visited by Mr. Kellogg, September 17, 1897.

Cornwall has no almshouse, but at the date of visit four persons were being boarded in private families. One of these was visited at the house of Mr. S. J. Adams, two and a half miles north from West Cornwall, and was found to be comfortably situated. An interview was had with the first selectman, and it was learned that two insane persons were being supported in the State Hospital.

GOSHEN.

Visited by Mr. Kellogg, June 15, 1898.

Goshen has no almshouse, but at the date of visit was boarding one man in the town at the rate of $2.50 a week. Other persons are assisted with partial relief as necessary, and one insane person was supported at the State Hospital.

HARWINTON.

Visited by Mr. Kellogg, June 15, 1898.

Harwinton has no almshouse, but at the date of visit was supporting two persons in the town. Other persons were assisted with partial relief as needed. Three insane persons were supported in the State Hospital.

KENT.

Visited by Miss Hall, September 17, 1897, and October 5, 1898, and by Miss Hall and Mr. Kellogg, January 27, 1898.

Almshouse is owned by town, and is situated five miles northwest from the railway station. About 130 acres of land are attached.

Keepers, Mr. and Mrs. Lewis Ives.

Terms, $500 a year, which includes also out-door relief.

Number of inmates at date of last visit, 1 man.

On the occasion of the first visit reported, three old women were found alone in the house, with their rooms and beds in a very dirty condition, and recommendations for improvements were made. At the last visit, however, it was found that all of the old women had died. The quarters reserved for the town poor consist of a small extension to the keeper's house, which contains a common sitting and dining-room for men and women, and three very small bedrooms opening from it. If any considerable number of persons are to be cared for here, the accommodations should be enlarged and improved at an early date.

NORFOLK.

Visited by Miss Hall and Mr. Kellogg, September 16, 1897.

Almshouse is owned by town, and is situated three miles east from the center. About 275 acres of land are attached.

Keepers, Mr. and Mrs. Thomas Carroll, who receive the use of the farm and $1 a week for each inmate.

Prisoners are not received.

At the date of visit, there was only one inmate present, a woman who assists in work about the house. The place is a comfortable farmhouse, and the room of the single inmate was neat and clean.

Rooms on the upper floor reserved for tramps are superior to the usual accommodations for this purpose, in points of comfort and cleanliness.

NORTH CANAAN.

Visited by Mr. Kellogg, October 6, 1898.

Almshouse is not owned by town, but is owned by private
 parties.

Keepers, Mr. and Mrs. Miles Rockwell.

Terms, $2.50 a week for each inmate, besides clothing and
 medical attendance.

Number of inmates at date of visit, 1 man, who does some light
 work about the place.

The house is situated at Canaan Valley, five miles northeast from the railway station at Canaan, and three miles northeast from the one at East Canaan. It is an old weather-beaten structure, but the only inmate appeared to receive fairly good care.

The town also supports three other persons in private families, and boards four dependents in the Almshouse for State Paupers at Tariffville.

PLYMOUTH.

*Visited by Mr. Kellogg, September 14, 1897, and February 19, 1898;
 and by Miss Hall, June 8, 1898.*

Almshouse is not owned by town, but is managed by private
 parties. It is situated in the East Church district, about
 two miles north from the railway station at Terryville.

Keeper, Mr. Franklin B. Scott, since 1865.

Terms, $800 a year, which includes also out-door relief.

Prisoners are not received.

Number of inmates at date of last visit, 3 : 1 man, 2 women.

At the date of first visit, the rooms were found very dirty and the beds full of vermin. The inmates are old and feeble, and are difficult to care for. At the last visit the house was found to be somewhat improved after recommendations made. There is still need, however, of efficient help in the house to keep it clean and orderly, and to care for the inmates. A material improvement in the general conditions will be looked for at the next visit.

ROXBURY.

Visited by Miss Hall, September 18, 1897.

There is no almshouse in Roxbury, and at the date of visit only two persons were being wholly supported by the town; one man boarded with his son at $2 a week, and one child boarded at the rate of $1.50 a week.

SALISBURY.

Visited by Miss Bacon, July 15, 1897

Almshouse is owned by town, and is situated one and a half miles south from the center and an equal distance from the railway station at Lakeville. About 150 acres of land are attached.

Keepers, Mr. and Mrs. H. J. Melius, whose contract is renewed April 1st, annually.

Terms, $360 a year, not including out-door relief.

Number of inmates at date of visit, 10: 6 men, 2 women, 2 children over four years of age.

The house was formerly an old tavern, but has been kept in good repair, and presented an appearance of comfort. The inmates are well cared for and generally contented. The two children present were suffering from a skin disease which rendered them unfit to be placed with other children in the County Home.

SHARON.

Visited by Miss Hall, September 17, 1897, and October 5, 1898.

Almshouse is owned by town, and is situated three and a half miles east from Sharon Village, and four miles northwest from the railway station at Cornwall Bridge. About 200 acres of land are attached.

Keeper, Mr. Henry Ingraham.

At the date of the first visit it was learned that the almshouse was rented temporarily to private parties, and that four dependent persons were being boarded elsewhere in the town. At the second visit, however, it was found that the house had been recently reopened, and that two inmates were present. Some ten other persons, who were being supported in different parts of the town, were soon to be removed to the almshouse.

THOMASTON.

Visited by Mr. Kellogg, March 26, 1898.

Thomaston has no almshouse, and at the date of visit was supporting only two dependent persons; one, an old man, in the Waterbury almshouse, and another younger man in the town of Bethlehem. Other individuals and families are assisted as occasion requires.

The town supports seven inmates in the State Hospital for the Insane.

TORRINGTON.

Visited by Mr. Kellogg, June 15, 1898.

Almshouse is owned by town, and is situated four miles north-
    west from the center. About 200 acres of land are
    attached.
Keepers, Mr. and Mrs. Andrew Palmer, since April 1, 1898.
Terms, $540 a year, with clothing and medical attendance fur-
    nished in addition. This does not include out-door relief.
Prisoners are not received.
Number of inmates at date of visit, 6: 4 men, 2 women.
Number of feeble-minded, 2 men.
Number able to work, 3 men, who assist in work upon the farm.

The poor have comfortable quarters in an annex to the keepers' house, which contains thirteen bedrooms, separate sitting-rooms for men and women, and a bath-room supplied with hot and cold water.

Rooms on the first floor and the upper halls are warmed by a hot-air furnace. All parts of the house appeared clean and comfortable and seemed to be well managed.

WASHINGTON.

Visited by Miss Hall, September 18, 1897.

There is no almshouse in Washington, but at the date of visit thirteen poor persons were being supported in the town, besides two at the State Hospital for the Insane, and one in the Hartford Retreat.

Other persons are assisted with partial relief as necessary. Plans were under consideration at the time of visit for the establishment of an almshouse in the town.

WATERTOWN.

Visited by Mr. Kellogg, July 11, 1898.

Watertown has no almshouse, but at the date of visit was supporting four persons in the town at rates varying from $2 to $3 a week.   Families and individuals in need are assisted as occasion requires.   One young woman is supported in the State Hospital for the Insane.

WOODBURY.

Visited by Miss Bacon, August 30, 1898.

Almshouse is owned by town; about 65 acres of land are
    attached.
Keepers, Mr. and Mrs. George W. Rowe.
Prisoners are not received.
Number of inmates at date of visit, 7: 3 men, 4 women.

The town bought the place about a year ago. It is a comfortable farmhouse, delightfully situated on high ground, and all the surroundings indicate excellent management by the keepers.

The testimony of the inmates and their tidy appearance made it plain that they were in excellent hands.

The house was neat and presented a home-like appearance.

MIDDLESEX COUNTY.

There are fifteen towns in Middlesex County, of which seven have almshouses owned by the town. Visits have been made to the towns mentioned in the appended list, and reports on the condition of the poor are presented as follows:

MIDDLETOWN.

Visited by Mr. Whittlesey, October 17, 1896.

Almshouse is owned by town, and about 50 acres of land are
  attached.
Keepers, Mr. and Mrs. A. C. Ware, whose contract expires
  April 1st.
Terms, $700 a year, not including out-door relief.
Prisoners are not received.
Number of inmates at date of visit, 29 : 15 men, 14 women.
Number of insane, 8 men, of whom 4 had previously been in
  the State Hospital.
Number of feeble-minded, 6 women, of whom 3 had been in the
  State Hospital for the Insane.
Number able to work, 6 : 4 men, 2 women.
Occupations, farmwork and housework.

The house is old and ill-arranged. It lacks, also, a sufficient water supply, especially when one considers its nearness to the railroad and the consequent danger of fire from the sparks of passing locomotives.

The ventilation is imperfect, and the sexes are not separated as carefully as is desirable.

The place is kept in good order, however, and appears to be well managed. Religious services are held on Sunday afternoons.

CHATHAM.

Visited by Miss Hall, August 30, 1897, and August 16, 1898.

Almshouse is owned by town. About 75 acres of land are
  attached.
Keeper, Mr. H. C. Ackley.

Terms, $300 a year, not including out-door relief.

Number of inmates at date of visit, 7 : 5 men, 2 women.

The general condition of the house was not satisfactory. The sleeping-rooms, especially, showed little care and the beds were dirty.

The visitor called on the selectmen and recommended improvements, which will be looked for at the next visit.

CHESTER.

Visited by Mr. Spencer, September 21, 1898.

Chester has no almshouse, but at the date of visit was boarding two persons in private families. Other persons are assisted with partial relief, as needed, and two insane persons were supported at the State Hospital.

CROMWELL.

Visited by Mr. Whittlesey, October 17, 1896.

Almshouse is owned by town. About 65 acres of land are attached. .

Keepers, Mr. and Mrs. Charles Hodge, whose contract expires April 1st.

Terms, $360 a year, not including out-door relief.

There were no inmates at date of visit. The keeper cares for the farm and works the town roads. Two men who support themselves during the summer are assisted at the almshouse through the winter.

DURHAM.

Visited by Mr. Whittlesey, September 17, 1898.

The town has no almshouse, and at the date of visit was supporting only three persons. One of them lives in Durham and the other two are boarded in private families in New Haven. Other persons are assisted temporarily from time to time as they need town aid.

EAST HADDAM.

Visited by Mr. Spencer, October 31, 1896.

Almshouse is owned by town.   About 120 acres of land are
    attached.
Keepers, Mr. and Mrs. W. W. Gates, whose contract expires
    April 1st.
Terms, $350 a year, not including out-door relief.
Prisoners are not received.
Number of inmates at date of visit, 15: 5 men, 8 women, 2
    infants, one four years, the other six months, old.
Number of insane, 2 women, who had previously been in the
    State Hospital.
Number of feeble-minded, 3 women.
Number able to work, 4 men, 4 women.
Occupations, farmwork and housework.

The building is a comfortable one and is heated by stoves.
The four-year-old boy had previously been in the County
Home, but was dismissed as being feeble-minded.

ESSEX.

Visited by Mr. Spencer, October 30, 1896.

Almshouse is owned by town, and about one acre of land is
    attached.
Keeper, Mr. Charles Waterhouse.
There were no inmates at date of visit.

MIDDLEFIELD.

Visited by Mr. Whittlesey, June 25, 1898.

The town has no almshouse, but boards its dependent poor
with relatives or in private families, at rates varying from $1.25
to $1.50 a week.   One inmate is supported in the State Hos-
pital for the Insane.

The whole number of dependents at the date of visit was
six adults and a family of children.

OLD SAYBROOK.

Visited by Mr. Whittlesey, August 3, 1898.

The town formerly maintained an almshouse, but several years ago it ceased keeping it for that purpose, and rented it to outside parties.   During their occupancy the house was destroyed by fire.

The town now boards a few dependent persons at private houses within the town limits, and a few others with relatives in neighboring towns.

PORTLAND.

Visited by Miss Hall, August 21, 1897, and September 16, 1898.

Almshouse is owned by town, and is situated three miles east of the center, on the road to Cobalt.   About 80 acres of land are attached.

Keepers, Mr. and Mrs. Thomas B. Pitkin, whose contract expires April 1st.

Terms, $400 a year, not including out-door relief.

Prisoners are not received.

Number of inmates at date of last visit, 23 : 5 men, 16 women, 1 girl over four years of age, and one female infant under four years.

Number of insane, 2 men, both of whom had previously been in the State Hospital.

Number of feeble-minded, 1 man, 1 woman.

Number able to work, 8 : 5 men, 3 women.

Occupations, housework and farmwork.

The buildings are in good repair, but are not kept as well as is desirable.   The beds and bedding were very dirty.   The visitor called upon the selectmen and recommended new beds and bedding, also the introduction of a bath-room in the house and more attention to conditions of neatness and cleanliness. The child is said to be boarded in the keeper's family, but the distinction between that condition and the almshouse is a vague one, and the child should be removed to more suitable surroundings.

SAYBROOK.

Visited by Mr. Spencer, November 30, 1897.

The town owns an almshouse, but rents it to private parties, as there is not a sufficient number of paupers to pay for maintaining it as an almshouse. Various persons are assisted with partial relief, as needed, and one insane person is supported in the State Hospital.

WESTBROOK.

Reported to Mr. Whittlesey, September 30, 1898.

The town has no almshouse, but at the date of report was supporting seven dependents, two of whom were in the State Hospital for the Insane.

Several persons were assisted by the town with partial relief. Three of them were bad cases, who cost the town from $4 to $7 a week each.

TOLLAND COUNTY.

There are thirteen towns in the County, of which two maintain almshouses owned by the town, and five have almshouses which are owned and managed by private individuals. Visits have been made to the towns mentioned in the appended list and reports on the condition of the poor are presented as follows:

TOLLAND.

Visited by Miss Hall and Dr. Down, March 18, 1898.

The town has no almshouse, but at the date of visit was supporting six persons in private families, also three inmates in the State Hospital for the Insane. Among the six dependents in the town was an insane woman, in regard to whom it was recommended that she be removed to more suitable surroundings at an early date.

ANDOVER.

Visited by Miss Hall, April 7, 1898.

Andover has no almshouse, and at the date of visit was wholly supporting only one person. Other persons are assisted with partial relief as needed.

COVENTRY.

Visited by Mr. Kellogg, August 4, 1897.

Almshouse is not owned by town, but is managed by private parties. It is situated in North Coventry, about twelve miles northwest from Willimantic, or three miles west from Mansfield depot on the Central Vermont railway.

Keepers, Mr. and Mrs. Henry C. Walker, since October, 1894.

Terms, $3 a week for each inmate, including clothing, medical attendance, etc.

Prisoners are not received.

Number of inmates at date of visit, 6 : 2 men, 4 women.
Number of feeble-minded, 2 men, 1 woman.
Number able to work, 1 woman, who assists in the housework.

The house for the paupers is a detached building which is very plain, but fairly comfortable. Only two meals a day are served during the winter. The inmates made no complaints.

ELLINGTON.

Visited by Miss Hall and Miss Bacon, October 18, 1897.

Ellington has no almshouse, but at the date of visit was supporting three aged persons in private families.

HEBRON.

Visited by Miss Hall, August 24, 1897.

The town owns no almshouse, but boards its dependent poor with Mr. Charles C. Buell at the rate of $2 a week for each.

The place is a comfortable farmhouse, one and a half miles west from the center and four and a half miles northwest from the railway station at Turnerville. The inmates eat at the same table with the family and appeared to be well cared for.

MANSFIELD.

Visited by Mr. Kellogg, August 4, 1897.

Almshouse is not owned by town, but is managed by private parties. It is situated six miles north from Willimantic, and near the Spring Hill post-office.
Keepers, Mr. and Mrs. William H. Gardiner since 1861.
Terms, $1,200 a year, which includes out-door relief.
Prisoners are not received.
Number of inmates at date of visit, 15 : 7 men, 8 women.
Number of insane, 1 man, 1 woman.
Number of feeble-minded, 3 men, 1 woman.
Number able to work, 3 men, 2 women.
Occupations, housework and light farmwork.

The house for the inmates stands at a short distance from

the keepers' house, and, although old, is comfortable and home-like. The house is heated by coal-burning stoves in winter, and meals are carried out from the keepers' house. It is customary to serve but two regular meals a day during the winter, with a light lunch before retiring for those who desire it. The three feeble-minded men, one of whom was perfectly helpless, occupied a room over a detached workshop, which is only reasonably comfortable.

SOMERS.

Visited by Mr. Kellogg, April 30, 1898.

Almshouse is not owned by town, but is managed by private
    parties. It is situated two and a half miles northwest
    from Somers, and three miles east from the railway station
    at Hazardville.
Keepers, Mr. and Mrs. Thomas Dwyer.
Terms, $2.50 a week for each inmate, including also clothing
    and medical attendance.
Prisoners are not received.
Number of inmates at date of visit, 5 men, one of whom was
    feeble-minded.

    Two of the men do some light work about the place. The inmates have a comfortable living room, and a number of well-kept bedrooms. They have the freedom of all parts of the house, and expressed themselves as well satisfied with their treatment.

    Tramps are given supper, lodging, and breakfast at fifty cents a head.

STAFFORD.

Visited by Mr. Kellogg, April 30, 1898.

Almshouse is owned by town, and is situated on the main road
    in West Stafford, three miles west of Stafford Springs.
    About 3 acres of land are attached.
Keepers, Mr. and Mrs. W. S. Shepard, whose contract expires
    May 20th.
Terms, $400 a year, the town furnishing, in addition, pro-
    visions, clothing, and medical attendance.
Prisoners are not received.
Number of inmates at date of visit, 10: 3 men, 7 women.

    19

Number of insane, 2 women, of whom one had previously been
 in the State Hospital.

Number of feeble-minded, 3 men, 2 women.

Number able to work, 2 men and 2 women, who assist in various forms of housework, and in work about the place.

The almshouse is a large double house, one side of which
is used for the town poor. They have a large comfortable
sitting-room, and the sleeping-rooms are provided with good
beds. Three meals a day are provided in winter as well as in
summer. One woman suffering from consumption has a room
by herself. Religious services are held occasionally.

VERNON.

*Visited by Miss Hall and Miss Bacon, October 20, 1897, and by
Miss Hall and Dr. Down, March 18, 1898.*

Almshouse is owned by town, and is situated one mile south
 from Rockville, or four miles northeast from Vernon
 Station. About 85 acres of land are attached.

Keeper, Mr. E. R. Holman, whose contract expires April 1st.

Terms, $600 a year, not including out-door relief.

Prisoners are not received.

Number of inmates at date of visit, 22 : 13 men, 9 women.

Number of insane, 9 women.

Number able to work, 13 men, 3 women.

Occupations, farmwork and housework.

The house is a two-story brick structure, with a large
addition three stories in height. The building is heated by
steam, and is comfortably furnished. Bath-rooms and toilet-
rooms are provided.

The house presented its usual appearance of cleanliness
and neatness, all departments being in excellent condition and
well warmed and ventilated. Recommendation was made that
one of the insane women be removed to the State Hospital.

WILLINGTON.

Visited by Mr. Kellogg, April 30, 1898.

Willington owns no almshouse, but boards its dependent
poor with Mr. and Mrs. Arnold Upton, who live four miles east
of Willington Center, and nine miles from Stafford Springs.

At the date of visit, two women and one man were being boarded at the place at the rate of $1.50 a week, in addition to which the town furnishes clothing, medical attendance, etc.

The town poor of Ashford are also boarded at the same place, and they have in addition a few paupers from the towns of Tolland and Ellington.

Separate sitting-rooms are provided for men and women, and the inmates eat at the same table with the family.

The place was reasonably comfortable, and the inmates appeared satisfied with their treatment.

STATISTICS BY COUNTIES RELATING TO THE SUPPORT OF THE POOR.

The selectmen and treasurer of each of the one hundred and sixty-eight towns in Connecticut render to the taxpayers an annual report of the receipts and expenses, etc., and, except in the case of a few of the smaller towns, these reports are printed. It is noticeable in an examination of the reports that there is a marked dissimilarity in the manner of presenting the accounts. The ground covered is substantially the same in each, but local usage prevails rather than a uniform system. In a few reports the numbers and names of almshouse inmates are given, but as a rule those features are omitted; while as regards those who receive outside support, it is not possible from the data given to gather anything but approximate information. It is to be regretted that in a matter of so much interest and importance a more careful and detailed classification is not adopted, by means of which the exact numbers in receipt of public aid both in and out of almshouses, and the amount so spent, may be plainly shown.

In order to ascertain what provision is made for the relief of the poor population, it has been customary in previous years to request the selectmen to forward copies of their reports to the Board's office, and to incorporate in the Board's Report statistics taken therefrom relating to the annual expenditure for the support of in and out-door poor.

Owing to the varying dates at which the reports are published, and to the difficulties encountered in the attempt to collect them promptly, it has never been possible hitherto to publish statistics more recent than those for the year preceding the Board's Report.

With the present Report, however, an effort has been made to collect statistics for the current year, and in more complete form, by requesting from the selectmen of the several towns an active compliance with Section 3312 of the General Statutes, which provides that " Overseers of the poor shall keep full and accurate records of the paupers fully supported, the persons relieved and partially supported, and the travelers and vagrants lodged at the expense of their respective towns, together with the amount paid by them for such support and relief, and shall annually in October make return of the number of such persons supported and relieved, with the cost, to the State Board of Charities."

For this purpose blank forms for statistical returns, accompanied by an explanatory letter, were sent to the selectmen of every town, and from the answers received in reply thereto the following tables of statistics have been compiled.

From the returns thus presented, the total expense to the towns for poor relief has been collated as nearly as possible under two headings, as follows:

1. Cost of almshouse support.
2. Cost of all poor outside almshouse.

Under these headings are included the cost for the support of the sick and insane poor, and of dependent children. In addition are given the number of almshouse inmates during the year, the number of persons supported and relieved outside of the almshouses, the number of insane poor not in asylums, and the number of these that have been at any previous time inmates of an asylum.

TOWNS.	Population, Census 1890.	Cost of Almshouse Support, 1898.	Cost of all Poor Outside Almshouse, 1898.	Total Cost of Poor, 1898.	Tax per Capita of Population for Support of Poor, 1898.	Number of Almshouse inmates during Year.	Number of Poor Outside Almshouse.	Insane Poor not in Asylums.	Number of these formerly in Asylums.
Hartford,	53,230	$38,885	*$47,633	$86,518	$1.63	514	887	25	8
Avon,	1,182	.....	800	800	.68	0	5	4	1
Berlin,	2,600	500	450	950	.37	4	24	2	2
Bloomfield,	1,308	.....	480	480	.37	0	25	0	0
Bristol,	7,382	696	*8,479	9,175	1.24	7	113	2	0
Burlington,	1,302	950	109	1,059	.81	9	7	6	1
Canton,	2,500	450	1,050	1,500	.60	5	34	1	1
East Granby,	661	.....	639	639	.97	11	15	0	0
East Hartford,	4,455	1,180	1,275	2,455	.55	9	112	0	0
East Windsor,	2,890	2,532	1,628	4,160	1.44	18	15	4	4
Enfield,	7,199	1,459	*4,763	6,222	.86	18	76	6	1
Farmington,	3,179	862	3,269	4,131	1.30	10	45	1	0
Glastonbury,	3,457	1,186	1,884	3,070	.89	0	20	10	0
Granby,	1,251	.....	765	765	.61	0	14	0	0
Hartland,	565	.....	352	352	.62	0	4	0	0
Manchester,	8,222	1,834	6,216	8,050	.98	21	167	6	1
Marlborough,	582	.....	329	329	.57	0	15	0	0
New Britain,	19,007	4,925	*18,139	23,064	1.21	48	130	6	0
Newington,	953	.....	145	145	.15	0	4	3	2
Plainville,	1,993	.....	1,548	1,548	.78	0	26	0	0
Rocky Hill,	1,069	.....	852	852	.80	0	6	2	1
Simsbury,	1,874	1,017	315	1,332	.71	5	2	0	0
Southington,	5,501	2,023	1,705	3,728	.68	15	28	6	2
South Windsor,	1,736	978	1,487	2,465	1.42	3	22	0	0
Suffield,	3,169	1,833	1,219	3,052	.96	6	17	3	0
West Hartford,	1,930	.....	1,360	1,360	.70	0	17	0	0
Wethersfield,	2,271	2,564	691	3,255	1.43	5	11	0	0
Windsor,	2,954	607	507	1,114	.38	3	22	0	0
Windsor Locks,	2,758	.....	2,588	2,588	.94	0	27	3	3
	147,180	$64,481	$110,677	$175,158	$1.19	711	1,890	90	27

* Included in this amount for Sick and Insane: Hartford, $30,953; Bristol, $1,212; Enfield, $2,286; New Britain, $4,427.

NEW HAVEN COUNTY.

TOWNS.	Population, Census 1890.	Cost of Alms-house Support, 1898.	Cost of all Poor Outside Almshouse, 1898.	Total Cost of Poor, 1898.	Tax per Capita of Population for Support of Poor, 1898.	Number of Alms-house inmates during Year.	Number of Poor Outside Alms-house.	Insane Poor not in Asylums.	Number of these formerly in Asylums.
New Haven,	86,045	$36,035	*29,128	$65,163	$0.76	517	1,680	101	59
Waterbury,	33,202	15,178	*21,120	36,298	1.09	220	1,400	12	4
Ansonia,	10,342	2,394	*5,277	7,671	.74	23	190	3	1
Beacon Falls,	505	.....	552	552	1.09	0	7	0	0
Bethany,	550	.....	118	118	.21	0	4	0	0
Branford,	4,460	1,800	4,204	6,004	1.35	14	120	1	1
Cheshire,	1,929	2,800	458	3,258	1.69	7	8	1	
Derby,	5,969	700	3,650	4,350	.73	3	50	0	0
East Haven,	955	.....	432	432	.45	0	4	2	0
Guilford,	2,780	694	806	1,500	.54	3	60	1	0
Hamden,	3,882	1,170	1,926	3,096	.80	9	5	3	0
Madison,	1,429	.....	800	800	.56	0	18	2	2
Meriden,	25,423	8,585	*22,975	31,560	1.24	89	415	18	6
Middlebury,	566	.....	71	71	.13	0	0	0	0
Milford,	3,811	.....	2,442	2,442	.64	0	55	0	0
Naugatuck,	6,218	4,100	*8,640	12,740	2.05	52	144	2	0
North Branford,	825	.....	119	119	.14	0	2	0	0
North Haven,	1,852	.....	1,181	1,181	.63	0	16	2	0
Orange,	4,537	.....	4,730	4,730	1.04	0	72	0	1
Oxford,	902	300	537	837	.93	3	18	0	0
Prospect,	445	.....	303	303	.70	0	5	0	0
Seymour,	3,300	.....	3,757	3,757	1.14	0	40	0	0
Southbury,	1,689	.....	572	572	.52	0	13	0	0
Wallingford,	6,584	2,700	2,200	4,900	.74	15	99	4	4
Wolcott,	522	.....	24	24	.05	0	6	0	0
Woodbridge,	926	.....	878	878	.95	0	10	1	0
	209,058	$76,456	$116,900	$193,356	$0.92.5	955	4,445	150	78

* Included in this amount for Sick and Insane: New Haven, $8,000; Waterbury, $7,895; Ansonia, $1,745; Meriden, $4,437; Naugatuck, $2,800.

NEW LONDON COUNTY.

TOWNS.	Population, Census 1890.	Cost of Alms-house Support, 1898.	Cost of all Poor Outside Almshouse, 1898.	Total Cost of Poor, 1898.	Tax per Capita of Population for Support of Poor, 1898.	Number of Alms-house Inmates during Year.	Number of Poor Out-side Alms-house.	Insane Poor not in Asylums.	Number of these formerly in Asylums.
New London,	13,757	$5,947	*$11,178	$17,125	$1.24	82	529	14	5
Norwich,	23,048	6,000	19,272	25,272	1.10	77	489	6	2
Bozrah,	1,005	......	424	424	.42	0	18	1	1
Colchester,	2,988	1,540	1,584	3,124	1.05	13	56	0	0
East Lyme,	2,048	......	544	544	.26	0	3	0	0
Franklin,	585	......	299	299	.51	0	3	0	0
Griswold,	3,113	450	1,292	1,742	.56	8	55	.5	3
Groton,	5,539	1,300	2,230	3,530	.64	12	41	3	3
Lebanon,	1,670	......	2,100	2,100	1.26	0	24	0	0
Ledyard,	1,183	416	1,056	1,472	1.24	4	13	0	2
Lisbon,	548	......	376	376	.69	0	4	2	1
Lyme,	977	......	408	408	.42	0	7	1	0
Montville,	2,344	1,055	1,177	2,232	.95	10	27	0	0
North Stonington,	1,463	......	1,318	1,318	.90	0	18	3	1
Old Lyme,	1,319	551	1,450	2,001	1.52	3	16	1	0
Preston,	2,555	......	1,157	1,157	.45	0	20	2	1
Salem,	481	......	229	229	.48	0	5	0	1
Sprague,	1,106	572	1,688	2,260	2.04	5	23	2	0
Stonington,	7,184	2,372	2,640	5,012	.70	31	141	4	2
Voluntown,	1,060	......	†787	787	.74	0	20	0	0
Waterford,	2,661	1,785	732	2,517	.95	6	48	1	0
	76,634	$21,988	$51,941	$73,929	$0.96	251	1,560	45	21

* Included in this amount for Sick and Insane : New London, $4,100 ; Norwich, $4,800.
† No answer to repeated inquiries was received from Voluntown, so figures of 1897 are used.

FAIRFIELD COUNTY.

TOWNS.	Population, Census 1890.	Cost of Almshouse Support, 1898.	Cost of all Poor Outside Almshouse, 1898.	Total Cost of Poor, 1898.	Tax per Capita of Population for Support of Poor, 1898.	Number of Almshouse Inmates during Year.	Number of Poor Outside Almshouse.	Insane Poor not in Asylums.	Number of these formerly in Asylums.
Bridgeport,	48,866	$14,560	*$27,800	$42,360	$0.87	175	3,062	47	20
Danbury,	19,473	8,519	*22,064	30,583	1.57	72	406	12	6
Bethel,	3,401	.....	3,003	3,003	.90	0	75	0	0
Brookfield,	989	.....	406	406	.41	1	6	0	0
Darien,	2,276	422	2,004	2,426	1.07	0	20	4	0
Easton,	1,001	.....	523	523	.52	0	16	0	0
Fairfield,	3,868	.....	*4,220	4,220	1.09	0	46	1	1
Greenwich,	10,131	2,331	*9,878	12,209	1.20	30	86	1	0
Huntington,	4,006	.....	2,192	2,192	.55	0	65	0	0
Monroe,	934	.....	653	653	.66	0	5	1	1
New Canaan,	2,701	1,177	1,230	2,407	.89	4	69	1	1
New Fairfield,	670	.....	984	984	1.47	8	10	0	0
Newtown,	3,539	878	2,800	3,678	1.04	40	25	1	0
Norwalk,	17,747	2,725	*16,672	19,397	1.09	0	336	4	0
Redding,	1,546	.....	1,343	1,343	.87	0	17	1	0
Ridgefield,	2,235	1,189	1,067	2,256	1.01	11	21	1	0
Sherman,	668	.....	456	456	.68	0	9	0	0
Stamford,	15,700	4,126	*8,411	12,537	.80	38	150	4	1
Stratford,	2,608	.....	1,106	1,106	.42	0	30	4	4
Trumbull,	1,453	.....	300	300	.21	0	16	0	0
Weston,	772	.....	225	225	.29	0	4	0	0
Westport,	3,715	625	2,500	3,125	.84	6	60	2	1
Wilton,	1,722	506	621	1,127	.65	3	5	1	1
	150,081	$37,058	$110,458	$147,516	$0.98	388	4,539	80	36

* Included in this amount for Sick and Insane: Bridgeport, $14,000; Danbury, $4,700; Fairfield, $1,000; Greenwich, $3,000; Norwalk, $3,400; Stamford, $2,800.

WINDHAM COUNTY.

TOWNS.	Population, Census 1890.	Cost of Alms-house Support, 1898.	Cost of all Poor Outside Almshouse, 1898.	Total Cost of Poor, 1898.	Tax per Capita of Population for Support of Poor, 1898.	Number of Alms-house inmates during Year.	Number of Poor Out-side Alms-house.	Insane Poor not in Asylums.	Number of these formerly in Asylums.
Windham,	10,032	$3,251	*$9,758	$13,009	$1.30	69	225	3	1
Putnam,	6,512	1,378	5,758	7,136	1.10	17	195	1	0
Ashford,	778	200	570	770	.99	2	2	0	0
Brooklyn,	2,628	421	1,269	1,690	.64	4	12	0	0
Canterbury,	947	450	130	580	.61	3	4	0	0
Chaplin,	542	......	150	150	.28	0	4	0	0
Eastford,	561	......	233	233	.42	0	4	0	0
Hampton,	632	......	425	425	.67	0	7	1	0
Killingly,	7,027	†1,724	*3,227	4,951	.70	20	120	0	0
Plainfield,	4,582	†1,883	1,650	3,533	.77	18	70	1	0
Pomfret,	1,471	......	762	762	.52	0	12	0	0
Scotland,	506	......	524	524	1.04	0	9	5	0
Sterling,	1,051	......	534	534	.51	0	5	0	0
Thompson,	5,580	1,080	2,800	3,380	.70	8	64	0	0
Woodstock,	2,309	873	583	1,456	.63	14	18	3	1
	45,158	$11,260	$28,373	$39,633	$0.88	155	751	13	2

* Included in this amount for Sick and Insane: Windham, $1,658; Putnam, $1,706; Killingly, $1,012.
† No answers to repeated inquiries were received from Killingly and Plainfield, so figures of 1897 are used.

LITCHFIELD COUNTY.

TOWNS.	Population, Census 1890.	Cost of Alms-house Support, 1898.	Cost of all Poor Outside Almshouse, 1898.	Total Cost of Poor, 1898.	Tax per Capita of Population for Support of Poor, 1898.	Number of Alms-house inmates during Year.	Number of Poor Outside Alms-house.	Insane Poor not in Asylums.	Number of these formerly in Asylums.
Litchfield,	3,304	$1,781	$2,147	$3,928	$1.19	14	44	2	1
Winchester,	6,183	1,053	2,237	3,290	.53	9	51	0	0
New Milford,	3,917	1,351	*2,665	4,016	1.03	10	51	0	0
Barkhamsted,	1,130	......	875	875	.77	0	12	3	0
Bethlehem,	543	......	245	245	.45	0	4	3	1
Bridgewater,	617	......	553	553	.90	0	14	0	0
Canaan,	970	......	1,058	1,058	1.09	0	17	0	0
Colebrook,	1,098	......	362	362	.33	0	14	0	0
Cornwall,	1,283	......	857	857	.67	0	15	0	0
Goshen,	972	......	929	929	.96	0	34	0	0
Harwinton,	943	......	1,496	1,496	1.59	0	31	0	0
Kent,	1,383	450	156	606	.44	3	1	0	0
Morris,	584	......	700	700	1.20	0	6	0	0
New Hartford,	3,160	600	1,738	2,338	.74	6	40	0	0
Norfolk,	1,546	356	1,300	1,656	1.07	1	20	1	1
North Canaan,	1,683	......	2,800	2,800	1.66	1	10	7	0
Plymouth,	2,147	555	961	1,516	.71	3	14	0	0
Roxbury,	936	......	387	387	.41	0	11	0	0
Salisbury,	3,420	†1,060	*1,300	2,360	.69	15	40	1	1
Sharon,	2,149	......	1,898	1,898	.88	0	20	0	0
Thomaston,	3,278	......	1,966	1,966	.60	0	24	0	0
Torrington,	6,048	804	*3,408	4,212	.70	5	86	0	0
Warren,	477	......	529	529	1.11	0	7	1	1
Washington,	1,633	......	1,786	1,786	1.09	0	21	1	0
Watertown,	2,323	......	762	762	.33	0	15	1	1
Woodbury,	1,815	1,022	2,384	3,406	1.88	8	26	2	1
	53,542	$9,032	$35,499	$44,531	$0.83	75	628	22	6

* Included in this amount for Sick and Insane: New Milford, $935; Salisbury, $650; Torrington, $1,900.
† No answer to repeated requests was received from Salisbury, so figures of 1897 are used.

MIDDLESEX COUNTY.

TOWNS.	Population, Census 1890.	Cost of Alms-house Support, 1898.	Cost of all Poor Outside Almshouse, 1898.	Total Cost of Poor, 1898.	Tax per Capita of Population for Support of Poor, 1898.	Number of Alms-house Inmates during Year.	Number of Poor Outside Alms-house.	Insane Poor not in Asylums.	Number of these formerly in Asylums.
Middletown,	15,205	$4,110	*$11,222	$15,332	$1.01	38	140	5	3
Haddam,	2,095	......	800	800	.38	0	28	2	0
Chatham,	1,949	644	493	1,137	.58	5	12	0	0
Chester,	1,301	......	557	557	.43	0	9	0	0
Clinton,	1,384	......	815	815	.59	0	7	2	0
Cromwell,	1,987	......	*1,184	1,184	.60	0	23	0	0
Durham,	856	......	442	442	.52	8	8	0	0
East Haddam,	2,599	1,128	740	1,868	.72	0	24	4	1
Essex,	2,035	......	1,437	1,437	.71	0	22	1	0
Killingworth,	582	......	329	329	.57	0	5	1	0
Middlefield,	1,002	......	431	431	.43	0	8	1	1
Old Saybrook,	1,484	......	1,158	1,158	.78	0	22	0	0
Portland,	4,687	2,354	*3,808	6,162	1.31	20	161	2	2
Saybrook,	1,484	......	†1,062	1,062	.72	0	15	0	0
Westbrook,	874	......	909	909	1.04	0	7	0	0
	39,524	$8,236	$25,387	$33,623	$0.85	71	491	18	7

* Included in this amount for Sick and Insane: Middletown, $4,429; Cromwell, $500; Portland, $1,300.
† No answer to repeated requests was received from Saybrook, so figures of 1897 are used.

TOLLAND COUNTY.

TOWNS.	Population, Census, 1890.	Cost of Alms-house Support, 1898.	Cost of all Poor Outside Almshouse, 1898.	Total Cost of Poor, 1898.	Tax per Capita of Population for Support of Poor, 1898.	Number of Alms-house inmates during Year.	Number of Poor Outside Alms-house.	Insane Poor not in Asylums.	Number of these formerly in Asylums.
Tolland,	1,037	......	$979	$979	$0.94	0	14	2	1
Andover,	401	......	178	178	.44	0	3	1	1
Bolton,	452	......	899	899	1.99	0	14	1	0
Columbia,	740	......	539	539	.73	0	9	0	0
Coventry,	1,875	$660	1,716	1,716	.92	4	17	1	0
Ellington,	1,539	......	679	679	.44	0	11	0	0
Hebron,	1,039	......	125	370	.36	3	18	0	0
Mansfield,	1,911	245	363	1,563	.82	15	2	4	0
Somers,	1,407	1,200	692	1,432	1.02	5	16	1	0
Stafford,	4,535	740	*1,972	2,856	.63	16	37	3	0
Union,	231	884	376	376	.87	0	6	2	2
Vernon,	8,808	......	6,778	9,167	1.04	41	114	3	0
Willington,	906	2,389	485	797	.88	4	16	0	0
	25,081	$6,430	$15,121	$21,551	$0.86	88	277	17	4

* Included in this amount for Sick and Insane: Stafford, $900; Vernon, $2,463.

SUMMARY FOR THE STATE.

COUNTIES.	Population, Census, 1890.	Cost of Alms-house Support, 1898.	Cost of all Poor Outside Almshouse, 1898.	Total Cost of Poor, 1898.	Tax per Capita of Population for Support of Poor, 1898.	Number of Alms-house Inmates during Year.	Number of Poor Outside Alms-house.	Insane Poor not in Asylums.	Number of these formerly in Asylums.
Hartford,	147,180	$64,481	$110,677	$175,158	$1.19	711	1,890	90	27
New Haven,	209,058	76,456	116,900	193,356	.92.5	955	4,445	150	78
New London,	76,634	21,988	51,941	73,929	.96	251	1,560	45	21
Fairfield,	150,081	37,058	110,458	147,516	.98	388	4,539	80	36
Windham,	45,158	11,260	28,373	39,633	.88	155	751	13	2
Litchfield,	53,542	9,032	35,499	44,531	.83	75	628	22	6
Middlesex,	39,524	8,236	25,387	33,623	.58	71	491	18	7
Tolland,	25,081	6,430	15,121	21,551	.86	88	277	17	4
Total for State,	746,258	$234,941	$494,356	$729,297	$0.97.7	2,694	14,581	435	181
Total for year 1896,	746,258	227,818	496,776	724,594	.97.1	....	....	....	....
Population, 1898, [ESTIMATED]	850,000	......	......	......	.85.8	....	....	....	....

PRIVATE PROVISION

FOR THE

AGED, INDIGENT, AND INFIRM.

An account is given below of Homes in the State which, in addition to the public institutions provided, furnish accommodations for the care of aged and infirm men and women.

The Homes have, as a rule, been duly incorporated and are supported in some cases by private charity alone, and in others by the receipts from entrance fees and payments for board.

THE OLD PEOPLE'S HOME,

HARTFORD.

Mr. B. S. Gilbert, *Superintendent;* Mrs. E. J. Fox, *Matron.*

Visited September 14, 1898.

The Old People's Home is under the same management as the Hartford Hospital, and was organized by an act of the General Assembly in 1873, amending the Hospital's charter for that purpose.   An attractive three-storied building of brick and stone was erected for the use of the Home on Jefferson street opposite the Hospital grounds, and has accommodations for eighty-five inmates.   On the first floor are the offices, reception-room, and rooms for men; the upper floors are reserved for women.

Applicants for admission to the Home must be citizens of Hartford County, persons of good character, not under sixty years of age, and in reduced circumstances.   For several years applications for admission have exceeded so greatly the means of the Home to support them that it has been necessary to raise the entrance fee to $1,000 for permanent inmates.   A few boarders are received at fixed sums per week.

Although managed with due care and economy, it is impossible for the Home to be self-supporting, and the admission fee will of necessity be kept high until such time as the Home shall be sufficiently endowed to provide an adequate income.

The rooms are large and well furnished, and everything is provided which will insure to the occupants the conveniences and comforts of a well-appointed home.   Religious services are held on Sunday afternoons and are conducted in turn by clergymen of different denominations.

The friends of inmates and the public generally may visit the Home on Thursdays between the hours of 10 and 12 o'clock A. M., and from 2 to 4 P. M.   At other times visitors will be admitted only by permission of the superintendent or matron.

THE CHURCH HOME,

HARTFORD.

Visited November 2, 1898.

The Church Home of Hartford was incorporated in 1876, and is under the management of an association which includes the rectors and certain lay members of all the parishes of the Protestant Episcopal Church in the diocese of Hartford.

The property formerly occupied by the Home on Bellevue street has been sold since the last Report, and a new house has been erected at No. 115 Retreat avenue, between Hudson and Seymour streets, especially designed for the uses of the Home. The new building is substantially constructed of brick in the Colonial style of architecture, and has accommodations for seventeen inmates.   Every convenience required in a comfortable home has been provided, and the heating, lighting, and plumbing systems are of the best.

All of the inmates who are able to do so are required to care for their own rooms and to assist in the lighter domestic duties. Religious services are conducted daily by the chaplain or the matron, and an appropriate chancel is provided in the parlor of the new building, which may be shut off from the room when not in use.

The object of the Home, as stated in the constitution, is to provide maintenance for such aged and infirm persons as it may receive and have under its care, and to establish and carry on such other branches of charitable and reformatory work as may be deemed expedient. Such aged persons or others may be admitted to the privileges of the institution as the Board of Managers may deem fit, and on such terms and conditions as the board may establish. The usual entrance fee is $400 for permanent inmates. All persons who are admitted as permanent beneficiaries are required to sign an agreement conveying to the Home, under certain conditions, such property as they may then possess or may acquire afterward. Applications for admission must be made to the chairman of the house committee.

An annual report of the Home is published, giving the names of officers, house rules, etc., and a detailed statement of the entire receipts and disbursements from the time of its organization to the date of report.

THE WIDOWS' HOMES,

HARTFORD.

Visited November 2, 1898.

The Widows' Home on Market street was established in 1854 as the gift of Mr. George Beach, a resident of Hartford, and still occupies the original building at No. 133, about one block east from Main street. The Home contains twelve suites of apartments of three rooms each. The inmates do their own work, live independently, and pay a rental of about $2 per month.

The Home is under the management of a Board of Trustees, which was incorporated by the General Assembly in 1860, and consists of the rectors and wardens of the Protestant Episcopal churches in the city of Hartford.

After the establishment of the Market street Home, other bequests were made from time to time to the Board, until, in 1895, they were enabled to open a second Home of similar character on South Hudson street. The building is a substantial and well-appointed structure, and contains, like the pioneer Home on Market street, twelve suites of rooms. The apartments in both Homes are all filled and applications for vacancies are on file.

20

THE LAWSON C. IVES WIDOWS' HOMES,

HARTFORD.

Visited November 2, 1898.

The Widows' Homes at Nos. 848 and 850 North Main street, now renamed Windsor avenue, were established in 1867 by the will of Mr. Lawson C. Ives, an honored citizen of Hartford, who died in that year.   The two Homes are under the management, respectively, of the pastors and prudential committees of the Park Congregational Church and of the Pearl Street Congregational Church, who were incorporated for that purpose by the General Assembly of 1867.

Each Home contains twelve apartments of three rooms each, and all occupants who are able to do so, pay a monthly rental of $2 for front and $1.50 for back rooms.   The buildings provide a welcome home for a number of self-respecting women who, in the vicissitudes of life, have become unable to provide permanent homes for themselves.

ST. MARY'S HOME FOR THE AGED,

WEST HARTFORD.

Visited September 29, 1898.

St. Mary's Home is located on Albany avenue, about three miles from Hartford, and commands an unusually fine view of diversified country.   It is under the sole charge of the Sisters of Mercy, fifteen of whom have entire care of the Home and its inmates.

The Home was opened in October, 1880, and a new and commodious building was erected and first occupied in April, 1896.   It is a handsome structure of brick and brownstone, three stories in height, with a high basement entirely above ground, and consists of two parts, of which the central or administration building contains the reception-rooms, quarters for the Sisters, a beautifully appointed chapel, dining-rooms for men and women, kitchen, laundry, etc.   The domestic departments are equipped with the most approved labor-saving apparatus, and, like all other parts of the Home, are models of cleanliness and good order.   The north wing contains sixty-five single rooms for aged women, all of which were occupied at the date of visit.   A pleasant sitting-room is provided on each floor, as well as convenient bath and toilet rooms, and a comfortable infirmary is reserved for those who are feeble or ill.   The whole building is heated by steam and lighted by gas, and is provided with easily accessible fire-escapes.

As soon as the necessary funds can be obtained, another wing to adjoin the administration building on the south will be added for the use of old men.   The men are now quartered in the original building, which has accommodations for thirty inmates; there were twenty present at the date of visit.

There are no restrictions in regard to the residence or age of applicants for admission.   An entrance fee of $1,000 is required of all permanent inmates who have sufficient means, and others who are able to pay are boarded at rates of $3.50 to $5 a week; a considerable number, however, of the inmates are supported free of charge.

A valuable farm of one hundred and sixteen acres is connected with the Home, and the men whose health will permit assist in its cultivation.   Large supplies of vegetables and general farm produce are raised annually.

The Home is not endowed, and has not yet been in receipt of annual subscriptions of fixed amounts, nor of a yearly donation day offering.   It depends for its support upon what the inmates are able to pay, upon the sale of its farm supplies, and upon funds raised by the Sisters of Mercy.   It is the only Roman Catholic institution of its kind in the State.

THE ERWIN WOMAN'S HOME,

NEW BRITAIN.

Visited September 28, 1897.

The Erwin Home was established in accordance with a provision of the will of the late Mr. Cornelius B. Erwin, who designed it as a home for worthy but indigent women of the town of New Britain.   It was opened on May 1, 1892.

The Home is located on the corner of Bassett and Ellis streets in a quiet part of the city, and consists of a series of

suites of apartments having separate entrances; they are all
under one continuous roof and are connected by broad corridors to which the suites have direct access.   The original
building had twenty-four suites of two rooms each, but owing
to the demand for admission, an addition of six suites was
erected in 1894.   Each occupant keeps house independently;
she furnishes her room herself, has her own stove and sink,
cooks her meals and does her own housework.   Lighting and
steam heat are provided by the trustees for the halls and public parts of the building, and can be supplied to the private
suites if required.

Applicants for admission must be endorsed by some responsible person or society, and persons so admitted are required
to serve one month on probation.   Tenements are let for one
year, or for a term less than one year, and are practically free,
with the exception of a nominal charge for rental of less than
$2 per month.   By the terms of the founder's will, the man-
agement is in the hands of the pastor and standing committee
of the South Congregational Church of New Britain, who were
incorporated by an act of the General Assembly of 1893 for the
purpose of controlling the affairs of the Home.

THE ELLEN M. GIFFORD HOME FOR
INCURABLES,

NEW HAVEN.

Mr. J. H. Starkweather, *Superintendent.*

Visited March 29, 1898.

The Home was opened on July 14, 1892, and is under the
management of the directors of the General Hospital Society.
It occupies a building which is practically independent, having
a free exposure to light and air on three sides, but on the
eastern end is connected by a wide corridor with the main
building of the New Haven Hospital on the right, and with the
Gifford Chapel on the left.   A bronze tablet bearing the following inscription has been placed on the wall in the main corridor of the Home:

ELLEN M. GIFFORD HOME FOR INCURABLES
was founded in 1889 under the will of
ELLEN MARTHA GIFFORD,
the only child of Philip Marett of New Haven,
and is supported by funds bequeathed
in part by each.

The building is divided into two wards for men and women, respectively, and accommodates forty-four patients in all. One end of each ward is conveniently fitted up with surgical cabinets, pantry, linen closets, nurses' dining-room, etc., and the other forms an attractive semi-circular sitting-room, which is enclosed with glass and serves as a sun parlor.

The Gifford fund is a charity fund, and the income may be used for the support of poor patients only. It is designed in particular for patients who are suffering from incurable diseases which require and may be alleviated by skillful nursing and medical treatment.

In 1896, free support and treatment were furnished to fifty-nine patients, amounting to one thousand and forty weeks, and in 1897 to thirty-six patients, for a total of one thousand and fifty-three weeks.

THE HOME FOR THE FRIENDLESS,

FAIR HAVEN.

Miss M. J. SLATER, *Matron.*

Visited September 17, 1898.

The object of this institution is to provide a temporary home for friendless and homeless women and girls who, through necessity or crime, have no other refuge, and to give them employment and instruction with the ultimate design of providing for them a more permanent situation, or of fitting them to maintain themselves; also to provide a home for small children and for infants with their mothers. More particular mention of this branch of the work is made in a following portion of this Report. It is the only free, non-sectarian home for aged women in the State.

The Home was incorporated in June, 1867, and is governed by an advisory board and a board of managers, consisting of representatives from each church in the city. It is located at the corner of Clinton avenue and Pine street, and may be reached by a short walk from the Fair Haven line of electric cars. Since the last Report, the original wooden building has been replaced by a substantial three-storied structure of brick, which was erected through the generosity of Mrs. Lucy H. Boardman, and was opened for use in November, 1897. It is adjoined by a large brick wing, previously constructed, which contains apartments for the old ladies, and has been enlarged by the addition of a third story. · The whole building is heated by steam and lighted by gas, and is supplied with all the conveniences of a comfortable home.

There is no positive restriction in regard to place of residence, but the preference for admission is given to applicants who are residents of New Haven. There were twenty-six adults present at the date of visit. All the inmates who are able to do so are under obligations to pay a small sum weekly for board. The Home is supported by the income from a small endowment fund, by annual subscriptions, and by a yearly " donation day " contribution. It is the aim of the management to make the domestic life of the place homelike and elevating. Religious services are held in the Home every Sunday afternoon.

THE OLD LADIES' HOME,

NEW HAVEN.

Mrs. Harriet A. Scranton, *Matron.*

Visited September 17, 1898.

The Home, which is located at 124 Wall street, has accommodations for twelve inmates, and was opened in 1871. It is under the management of a committee of the Center Church, and is intended for aged and destitute women who are resident members of that church in New Haven.

Women without resources are supported free of expense, but it is required that those inmates who are able to do so shall pay $4 per week for board. As opportunities are offered, through vacancies in the Home, women from other churches may be received on payment of the same weekly rate. It is a bright, pleasant Home, suitable in size and appointments, and is well maintained under the attentive care of the matron, who has been in charge since it was opened. The number of inmates at date of visit was nine, for whose care five nurses and domestics were provided.

THE TRINITY CHURCH HOME,

Miss Elizabeth T. Smythe, *Matron.*

Visited September 17, 1898.

The Home is located at No. 303 George street, and was built in 1868 and conveyed in trust to the corporation of Trinity Church under a provision of the will of the late Mr. Joseph E. Sheffield. It was created for the purpose of establishing and maintaining in the city of New Haven a refuge for the poor and friendless members of Trinity parish, and such others as the Board of Managers may think entitled to its benefits.

The Home contains rooms for twenty inmates, and is comfortably furnished and provided with modern conveniences. Members of other religious denominations may also be admitted, but in such cases it is required that a fixed sum per week shall be paid for their support. The number of inmates at date of visit was thirteen, of whom only seven were members of Trinity parish. Religious services are held in the Home every week by the chaplain.

THE CURTIS HOME,

MERIDEN.

Miss Hannah K. Peck, *Matron.*

Visited June 17, 1898.

The Curtis Home was founded in accordance with a provision of the will of the late Mr. Lemuel J. Curtis, its object being to found a home for aged and indigent women. The Home is under the control of St. Andrew's Episcopal Church of Meriden, whose rector, wardens, and vestrymen were incorporated for the purpose in 1885. The corporation annually appoint a Board of Managers, composed of representatives from all of the Protestant churches of the city, who have general charge of the internal affairs of the Home through a number of committees.

The conditions for the admission of applicants are that they shall be over sixty years of age, and shall have lived in the town of Meriden for at least one year prior to the date of application; it is also required that they shall be in good mental and bodily condition, and shall serve a probationary term of three months. No charge is made for support, but when admitted to permanent residence inmates must convey such property as they possess to the institution.

The Home is finely situated on a hill at the end of Crown street, about a mile south from the center of the city, and commands a widely extended view to the south and west. The building is a handsome structure of yellow brick in the Colonial style, and is three stories in height, with a central portion of four stories. It was designed especially for the purpose and was first occupied in April, 1896. Attractive reception-rooms, dining-room, and chapel occupy the first floor, while the upper floors are devoted to private apartments for the inmates, the fourth floor being reserved for use as a hospital. All departments are finished in the most complete manner and are equipped with every appliance for the comfort and convenience of the inmates. A passenger elevator furnishes easy access to the upper floors, and the heating, ventilating, and plumbing systems are of the most approved design. The kitchen and other domestic departments are situated in a semi-detached wing, and the main building is provided with a fireproof hall and stairway.

The Home has accommodations for thirty inmates, and is amply endowed. At the date of visit there were sixteen aged women enjoying its advantages.

THE SOUTHMAYD HOME,

WATERBURY.

Mrs. Thomas Donaldson, *Superintendent.*

The Southmayd Home is the latest of the institutions established for the care of aged and indigent women, and was opened for the reception of inmates in September, 1898. It was established through the contributions of a considerable number of charitably disposed residents of the city, and is under the direction of a board of trustees and a board of women managers.

The property purchased for the purpose is located on North Main street, opposite Division street, and consists of a large yard and two houses, one of which is rented to assist in the support of the Home. The house reserved for the use of the Home is a pleasant, wooden structure, and has accommoda-

`tions for seven inmates. ·It is heated by a hot-water system and lighted by gas, and is supplied with all needed conveniences. The various rooms in the house have been attractively furnished by several of the churches and charitable societies in the city and by private individuals.

The price of board at the Home ranges from $3 to $4 per week, according to the location of the room, and includes lodging, board, and washing. All old ladies who are without homes, and whose friends and relatives can pay the small weekly rate required, and who come suitably recommended, are eligible as inmates.

THE SMITH MEMORIAL HOME,

NEW LONDON:

Mrs. John Sizer, *Matron.*

Visited October 25, 1898.

The Home occupies a large house pleasantly situated at the corner of Union and Masonic streets, directly opposite the City Hall. It was the gift of Dr. Seth Smith, and is designed as a Home for the needy and respectable poor women of New London. It was opened for use in December, 1885, and has accommodations for thirty inmates. The control of the Home is vested in a self-perpetuating Board of Trustees composed of six gentlemen of the city, and is entirely non-sectarian in its character.

Applicants for admission must have resided in New London for at least five years, and must be not less than sixty-five years of age, except in special cases to be determined by the trustees. Persons accepted as inmates are required to pay an entrance fee of $100 and to convey to the Home all property owned by them.

The institution is liberally endowed and the annual income is more than sufficient to meet the current expenses. Part of it is derived from an adjoining apartment house and a cottage which may be used to increase the capacity of the Home when needed. The rooms are pleasant and comfortably furnished, and everything is done by the management to make the Home attractive. There were twenty-one inmates at the date of visit.

THE ELIZA HUNTINGTON MEMORIAL HOME,

NORWICH.

Miss Adelaide Gorton, *Matron.*

Visited August 9, 1898.

The Home is located at No. 99 Washington street and oc-cupies a pleasant old-fashioned house surrounded by attractive grounds.   It was formerly the residence of Mr. Jedediah Hunt-ington, whose generosity established the Home as a memorial to his wife.   The original endowment has been increased until it now amounts to about fifty thousand dollars, and the income from this largely supports the Home.

The inmates are limited to eight old ladies, each of whom must be not less than sixty years of age and must pay an en-trance fee of $500.   Applicants for admission must be resi-dents of Norwich at the time of entrance, or must have lived in the city previously.   The Home is non-sectarian in character.

ST. JOHN'S HOME,

STAMFORD.

Miss Elizabeth Walker, *Matron.*

Visited October 2, 1897.

The Home is maintained in connection with St. John's Protestant Episcopal Church for the care of the aged and infirm and of orphaned and destitute children connected with the Episcopal Church in Stamford.   Admission is granted by vote of the trustees.

The house occupied for the purpose is the end one of a large wooden block on Pacific street, about one-third of a mile south from the railway station, and may be reached by the Summer street line of electric cars, which pass the door.   There are accommodations for about ten inmates, and at the date of visit there were seven present.

The trustees of the Home have purchased a building lot on the opposite side of the same street, adjoining a small chapel which also belongs to St. John's Church, and have begun the collection of a fund which, it is hoped, will enable them to erect in the near future a building especially designed for the use of the Home.

THE HARRIET MAKINSTER HOME,

MISS BERTHA BOWMAN, *Matron.*

Visited September 21, 1897, and September 22, 1898.

The Home was established in 1860 under the name of St. Luke's Home, and in 1892 was moved into a new and commodious building on the corner of Pearl and Liberty streets, the fund for which was given by Mrs. Harriet M. Makinster. Since that time the house has borne her name.

It is an attractive, three-storied structure of brick and has accommodations for fourteen inmates. The rooms are comfortably furnished, and no pains have been spared to make it a bright, cheerful, and well-conducted home. At the date of visit all the rooms were occupied, and it is hoped to enlarge the house in the near future.

The liberality of its management is shown in the provision that aged and destitute women may be admitted without regard to their place of residence or creed. As a rule, no inmates are received under sixty-five years of age. No entrance fee is charged, but each inmate is expected to pay something towards her board. Full board is placed at the sum of $3.50 per week, but the management have authority to receive persons at lower rates in special cases. In such event, however, it is agreed that the inmate shall give to the Home all funds which she may have or acquire.

The Home is supported by annual subscriptions and private contributions, and is under the management of trustees and a board of seventeen lady managers. The latter serve as visitors to the Home, two every month in turn, and each member calls twice a week during her month of service.

PRIVATE PROVISION FOR THE YOUNG.

ASYLUMS AND HOMES,

Holding, with but few Exceptions, Charters from the State.

THE HARTFORD ORPHAN ASYLUM,
(PROTESTANT)

HARTFORD.

REV. AND MRS. GEORGE DUSTAN, *Superintendent and Matron.*

Visited February 3, 1898.

The Asylum has a commanding location in a large lot in the southwestern part of the city, on Putnam street, and may be easily reached from the Parkville or Zion street lines of electric cars. It is a commodious brick building of attractive design, and stands on an eminence well back from the highway. A charter was first granted to the incorporators in 1833. The original charter, however, was revised in 1865, when the Hartford Orphan Asylum and the Hartford Female Beneficent Society were united into one institution, called the Hartford Orphan Asylum.

The institution is designed for the protection and education of orphans, half-orphans, and neglected and destitute children of the city of Hartford, and has the power and authority to make such provision for the temporary support and maintenance of poor and indigent children as may be found necessary and expedient. Children from out of town may be received as the accommodations permit, on the payment of the full amount of a fixed weekly rate.

During the fiscal year ending in June, 1898, the average number of inmates was one hundred and thirty, of whom fourteen were supported entirely by the Asylum and sixteen by the city of Hartford. Forty-two new children were received during the year, and twenty-two were removed by parents, friends, ' or selectmen. A majority of the inmates of the Asylum are partially supported by relatives or friends. Children are placed out in family homes by indenture, or given in adoption as opportunities are found, great care being exercised to prevent placing in any but well-recommended families.

An average number of ninety boys and girls attend the public school on Lawrence street. They begin in the kindergarten department, and are from five to six years in completing the school's course. A few who are sufficiently advanced pursue their studies in either the upper grades of the South District School or the Hartford Public High School.

The girls assist in the performance of minor household duties in the dormitories and dining hall, and during vacation time receive two hours' instruction in sewing daily, Saturdays excepted. The boys also help in various departments of housework, and, under the guidance of the Superintendent, work in the home garden during the summer vacation and raise a large variety of vegetables.

The pressure upon the Asylum for enlargement was partially met by the opening in February last of a second nursery, or intermediate department, where a dozen children between four and six years of age receive elementary kindergarten training.

Among the building improvements of the year may be noted a complete renovation of the plumbing system and the introduction of an electric elevator, which runs from the basement to the third floor. A room in the upper part of the building (connected with the dining-room by a dumb-waiter) is used as a hospital and answers the purpose fairly well, although experience has shown that a detached hospital cottage would be preferable.

Devotional exercises are held on week-day mornings and evenings, and religious services and Sunday-school on Sunday afternoons.

Two members of a committee of the Board of Lady Managers visit the institution officially once a month. The Asylum is chiefly supported by the income from invested funds and by annual contributions. The various departments present an appearance of good order and cleanliness, and the institution in general gives evidence of excellent management.

THE WATKINSON JUVENILE ASYLUM AND FARM SCHOOL,

HARTFORD.

Mr. E. B. SMEAD, *Principal.*

Visited September 29, 1898.

The School was established under a provision of the will of the late Mr. David Watkinson, and was first opened in an experimental way in 1884 on the property at the corner of Putnam and Park streets, adjoining that of the Hartford Orphan Asylum. The object of the School is to care for and instruct worthy homeless boys and boys in danger of acquiring habits of vice and crime. They are not formally committed according to the usual process, but show their desire to enter by applying to the managers for admission, and on approval of their applications are enrolled as inmates. The ages at which they are received are, as a rule, between twelve and fourteen. Boys from any part of the State may be admitted, but the preference is usually given to residents of Hartford.

Through the liberality of a Hartford gentleman, a valuable farm of one hundred and twenty-five acres, located at the corner of Albany and Bloomfield avenues, about two and a half miles northwest from the center of the city, was afterward purchased and put into a favorable condition for tillage. The farm bears the name of the Handicraft Farm, and is under the management of a board of trustees, whose object is to establish schools in connection therewith, which will afford the inmates an opportunity to combine life and work upon a farm with instruction in English branches, and in departments of manual training in the common handicrafts of life. It is believed that this plan will further the work of the Watkinson Farm School, and that it will be of lasting benefit to such boys as may choose to come as day pupils.

For a nominal consideration a sufficient portion of the farm was leased in perpetuity to the trustees of the Watkinson Farm School for its use, and an attractive brick building was erected thereon from the School's funds, thus making the institution the first of the Handicraft Schools. The building was first occupied in July, 1895, and has accommodations for sixty boys; at the date of visit there were twenty-two present. All departments are exceptionally well-arranged and are provided with improved systems of heating, lighting, and ventilation.

A distinguishing feature of the institution is its home-like character; the boys are made to feel that they are members of a common family, and that they are expected to share in the varied duties and responsibilities of domestic life. They begin by taking care of their own rooms and clothes, and from that they pass on to the care of the halls, dormitories, dining-room, schoolroom, heating apparatus, etc. When their training in the latter course is finished they are given charge of the different classes of live stock. There is daily instruction in the common English branches in a schoolroom on the premises, and a portion of the time is also spent according to a fixed schedule in doing general work upon the School farm and garden. Model barns, piggery, and poultry houses are part of the School's equipment, and, in connection with the Handicraft School, instruction is provided in working in wood and iron, painting and bricklaying.

Opportunity is offered the boys to earn money for themselves during their spare hours by extra work upon the farm, and in some cases sufficient sums have been accumulated to assist the owners in pursuing further courses at the Storrs Agricultural College or at the Mt. Hermon School. While the boys are in the Watkinson School, parents or friends, when able to do so, are expected to pay a nominal sum, from $1 to $2 per week, toward their support. The average period of residence in the School is from three to three and a half years, and an effort is made to secure suitable employment for the boys when they leave the institution. On Sundays the boys attend the Center Church and Sunday-school, and in the afternoon religious services are held at the School.

The management do not lose sight of the pupils after they have left the School, but keep in touch with them by interchange of visits and correspondence and continually exercise a paternal care in regard to their welfare. It is pleasant to note that the boys who have graduated from the School have formed a plan for maintaining their interest in the institution, and for preserving early recollections and friendship, by organizing an alumni association, with a list of officers, regulations, etc., and by holding annual reunions at the School Home.

One matter of regret to be noted in connection with the School is the fact that, with ample and admirable accommodations for more than twice the present number of inmates, the advantages of its life and training are not extended to a greater number of beneficiaries. An enlargement of its work in this direction would doubtless yield gratifying results.

ST. JAMES'S ASYLUM,

(ROMAN CATHOLIC)

HARTFORD.

Under the direction of the Sisters of Mercy ; Rev. John Mulcahy, V.G.,

Superintendent.

Visited October 26, 1898.

This institution is located on Church street in a central part of the city, and occupies the westernmost of three buildings which formerly comprised the dual establishment of St. Catherine's Girls' Orphanage and St. James's Asylum for Boys.

Under the present arrangement it is the intention to limit St. James's Asylum, so far as possible, to the reception of children from the church parish with which it is connected. The easternmost building is now occupied entirely by the Sisters of Mercy and is called St. Catherine's Convent, while the central building, which was designed originally as a hospital, is devoted to various uses of the parish.

The inmates include orphans, half-orphans, and children of dissipated and neglectful parents, and numbered twenty at the date of visit, four girls and sixteen boys. The earliest age at which children are received is two years, and the usual system is followed of placing them in family homes as opportunity offers. The inmates attend the parochial school on Allyn street. The average rate of board in the Asylum is about $6 a month, and an annual appropriation of $500 has been received from the town of Hartford.

HOME FOR INCURABLE CHILDREN,

NEWINGTON.

Under the Management of the Connecticut Children's Aid Society.
MRS. M. E. SARLE, *Matron.*

Visited September 14, 1898.

The Home for Incurable Children is an institution which the Connecticut Children's Aid Society has been endeavoring for some years to establish. A location for the purpose was finally purchased in the town of Newington, and the Home was opened for the reception of children on June 15, 1898.

The property is situated about a quarter of a mile east from the trolley station at the center of the town. It consists of about fifty acres of farm land, a barn, and a small, two-storied wooden house which was refitted to meet the new requirements. The rooms on the lower floor are heated by stoves, while those on the upper floor receive whatever warm air rises from the rooms below. Water from a mountain spring is conducted into a storage tank at the top of the house.

There are accommodations for ten children and at the date of visit the full number was present. Since that time four more children have been received, taxing the capacity of the house to the utmost. The ages of those present when visited ranged from five to thirty years, and the mental condition of several of them indicated that they should, more suitably, be inmates of the School for the Feeble-minded at Lakeville.

The names of eight physicians are enrolled as medical advisers for the Home, of whom five reside in Hartford, two in New Britain, and one in New Haven. They make no charge for their services, and visit the Home about once in two weeks, or whenever their attendance is required. The whole care of the children is in the hands of the matron and an assistant, but in view of the diseased and enfeebled condition of many of them, it seems to be most desirable that an experienced nurse should be employed also.

No provision has yet been made for systematic instruction in educational branches, but three friends of the Home volunteer their services twice a week each for the purpose of conducting classes. Two of the children attend the public school in the village.

21

It is the desire of the society to erect a new building for the use of the Home, as soon as the necessary funds can be collected. A charge of about $2 a week each is now made for the board of children in the Home.

In this connection, mention may be made of a later visit of a representative of the State Board to the office of the Children's Aid Society in Hartford, where an interview was had with the general agent of the society in regard to its work. The stated object of the society is to search out and care for dependent and neglected children who are not otherwise provided for, and, in addition, considerable activity is maintained in behalf of unfortunate girls and women with young children, who desire places in families where they may support themselves and their children.

The society was incorporated in November, 1896, under the general laws of the State regulating the formation and organization of associations without capital stock.

NEW HAVEN ORPHAN ASYLUM,
(PROTESTANT)

NEW HAVEN.

MRS. JOHN HUNT, *Matron.*

Visited September 17, 1898.

This Asylum was chartered by the State in 1833 and was established for the protection and education of orphans, half-orphans, and homeless and destitute children. The charter provides that the children must be residents of the town of New Haven, and that none shall be received who are over ten years of age. It is under the control of a board of nine trustees, citizens of New Haven, and of a board of sixty lady managers, who visit the Home at regular intervals and have a general oversight of its internal management.

The regular expenses are met by the income from endowment funds, by annual subscriptions, and by a " donation day " contribution, which is received every year in the autumn. In 1897 this amounted to $5,300, and included also a large variety of useful articles, such as books, toys, clothing, household supplies, utensils, etc. The town of New Haven appropriates $2,000 annually towards the Asylum's expenses, and may in turn exercise the right to send to the institution such children as are legally chargeable to the town. The total receipts, as given in the treasurer's report for the year ending May 15, 1898, were $15,849.60.

The Asylum, which is a commodious brick building and was first occupied in 1855, is situated in a spacious enclosure of six acres comprising the block bounded by Elm, Beers, and Platt streets and Edgewood avenue; electric cars pass the grounds. A part of the property is used as a playground for the children. The Asylum has accommodations for about one hundred and forty inmates, and the average number during the year 1897-98 was one hundred and thirty-nine. Sixty-one new children were admitted in the year, forty-one were returned to friends, and six were placed at service.

The children in the Asylum attend school in a detached building on the grounds. The teachers are engaged by, and the school is under the supervision of, the State Board of Education. The same terms and holidays are observed as in the public schools. In addition, the girls are given two hours' exercise in sewing each week under competent instructors, and a number of the older boys are taught the use of tools in a carpenter's shop. In another part of the Asylum yard stands a hospital building which is intended for children suffering from contagious diseases. Within the last two years, it has been found necessary to use it on two occasions only.

The Nina-Lynette Nursery for infants, which was given as a memorial by friends of the institution, is an attractive cottage located in one corner of the grounds and has accommodations for twelve inmates. Here infants are retained until they reach the age of two or two and a half years, when they are transferred to the main building.

When the children reach the age of twelve years, an effort is made to place them in selected family homes, and after they have been so placed the intention is to visit them once a year, or to have them visit the Asylum, until they reach the age of eighteen.

All the departments of the Asylum are admirably clean and in good order, and bear evidence of being under careful and experienced management.

ST. FRANCIS' ORPHAN ASYLUM,

(ROMAN CATHOLIC)

NEW HAVEN.

REV. J. F. CORCORAN, *Treasurer.*

Visited in May, 1898.

The Asylum is favorably located on Whitney avenue, about a mile and a half from the City Hall. It stands on high ground and commands an extensive view of the eastern portion of the city. It first existed as a private parochial institution, which was founded in 1852 by the Rev. E. J. O'Brien. In 1864 the present property was purchased, and in June, 1865, the institution was regularly incorporated under the laws of the State. It is designed for the reception and care of orphans, half-orphans, and homeless and destitute children, whose parents are of the Roman Catholic faith. Children are received from all parts of the State, but those living outside Connecticut are not eligible, unless in exceptional cases.

At the time of a child's admittance it is required that there shall be a written communication with reference thereto from either a parish priest or one of his subordinates, or from the town authorities, to the end that responsibility for the payment of the child's board may be definitely secured; one hundred dollars a year is the usual charge for each inmate. As a rule, children are between the ages of three and seven when sent to the Asylum; none under two years of age are received. The inmates attend school on the premises, and enjoy the advantages of six large and well-appointed schoolrooms. The girls are also taught sewing, and assist in the kitchen, laundry, and bakery work, according to their age and capacity. The boys sweep and dust and perform other minor duties.

An annual appropriation of $2,000 is received from the town, and in return the Asylum gives support to a large number of children who are committed to it by the town authorities. It has the use also of an income from invested funds, which it has received from time to time in the form of bequests, and is materially helped by annual subscriptions, and a " donation day " contribution of cash and generous gifts of toys, books, clothing, etc.

The Asylum was enlarged in 1896 by the addition of a large wing, which is substantially built of brick, is three stories in height, and contains additional accommodations for two hundred inmates.

It is the practice of the management to place children in Roman Catholic families according to opportunity. In the case of those who have been committed by the town, written permission is first received from the town agent.

The various departments of the Asylum are kept in perfect order and cleanliness and bear marks of excellent management. It has not been the custom to publish an annual report.

(See Supplementary Report in Appendix.)

THE CHILDREN'S BRANCH OF THE HOME FOR THE FRIENDLESS,

FAIR HAVEN.

Visited September 17, 1898.

The Children's Branch is a department of the Home for the Friendless, and occupies the same building and is under the same management. Its purpose is to provide a temporary home for young children, and for infants with their mothers. The advantages of the new building and equipment, described in the paragraphs on the Home's department for aged women, are shared by the Children's Branch in common with the rest of the institution.

At the date of visit there were seventeen children present, between the ages of two and eight years, besides three infants with their mothers. It is the intention of the management to limit the number of children accommodated to fifteen, as a rule.

The older children attend the public school near by, while the little ones are cared for and given kindergarten instruction in the Home.

Only such children are taken as are ineligible for admission to the Orphan Asylums, and can find, for the time, no other home, and they are returned to their parents or guardians as soon as these persons are able to again properly care for them. In cases where parents or guardians are unable or unfit to longer have the custody of children, good homes are found for them by the managers of the Home.

The children's board is paid for either by friends or relatives, or by members of the Board of Management representing one of the city churches.

MOUNT CARMEL CHILDREN'S HOME,

HAMDEN.

Mrs. A. M. D. Chamberlin, *Matron.*

Visited in October, 1898.

The Mount Carmel Children's Home was formally opened in September, 1896, and the promoters of the enterprise obtained a charter from the General Assembly of 1897.

A published report of the Home states that its object is to form a basis of co-operation for the various Protestant churches of the State whereby a home may be provided for children of Protestant Christian parentage, who, for various causes, may be left homeless. Its declared purpose is to fill a distinct field, and in no way to seek to do the work of existing state, county, or city orphan asylums.

The property secured for the use of the Home comprises sixteen acres of land and a large wooden house, formerly a private residence. As only a part of the purchase price could be paid at the time, much of the effort of the organizers is still necessarily devoted to the work of reducing the debt incurred.

At the date of visit there were twelve children present, and the number previously had been as high as eighteen under crowded conditions. Until the Home attains a more satisfactory financial condition, it is the rule that the board of each child present shall be paid as far as possible by its friends or by some interested organization.

The matron and one assistant have the whole care of the children and of the house, and an effort is made to have all the children who are old enough assist in some useful employment in the household. The need of more caretakers was evident to the visitor.

Permanent homes have been found for a number of children who were admitted to the Home without either father or mother living, and in other cases the circumstances of the parents have become so improved as to make it possible for the children to be returned to their care.

THE CHILDREN'S BRANCH OF THE CURTIS HOME,

MERIDEN.

Miss Hannah K. Peck, *Matron.*

Visited June 17, 1898.

The Children's Branch of the Curtis Home occupies an attractive, two and a half story, brick house, which was formerly devoted to the care of the aged women in the Home, until the new building was completed for that purpose in 1896, as hitherto described. The two departments are situated on adjoining grounds.

The general object of the Home is to provide care and instruction for orphans and destitute children, with the ultimate purpose in view of fitting them to provide for self-support, and of opening a way to permanent employment. The conditions of admission are that the children to be received shall have lived in the town of Meriden for at least one year before the date of application, and that they shall not be less than two nor more than ten years of age. It is essential also that they should be in good mental and physical condition. Children may be received as boarders, but not to the exclusion of those who are orphaned or destitute.

During the last two years, five children were placed in family homes, of whom one was afterward adopted. While in the Home, the girls receive instruction in sewing and the lighter forms of housework, and the boys have simple duties about the place.

The older children attend the public school in the neighborhood, and primary instruction for the little ones is provided in the Home. All are expected to be present at the regular

services at the Episcopal Church. The Home has accommodations for fifty inmates; thirty-two were under care at the
time of visit. Everything that can contribute to their comfort and well-being is provided without charge.

THE ROCK NOOK HOME,

NORWICH.

Miss A. D. Holmes, *Matron.*

Visited August 9, 1898.

This worthy charity was established in 1882, and is conducted under the auspices of the United Workers' Society.
The house and seven acres of land were the gift of a gentleman of Norwich, and are situated on the Norwich Town line
of electric cars about two miles north from the center of the
city. A two-storied addition to the house contains pleasant
nurseries for day and night use and other convenient rooms.

The Home has accommodations for thirty children, and
although there is no positive restriction, the intention is to
limit admission to children between the ages of four and
twelve.

Preference is given to children of the town and city of Norwich. The inmates attend the public school, and at the date
of visit numbered twenty-six, ten boys and sixteen girls. A
majority of the children in the Home are boarded there by
relatives, friends, or charitably disposed persons.

It is the intention of the management to place the children
in family homes so far as possible, and, when so placed, they
are kept under supervision until they reach the age of twenty-
one years. In certain cases they are given in adoption. The
Home is conducted on a non-sectarian basis and is doing excellent work.

BRIDGEPORT PROTESTANT ORPHAN ASYLUM,

BRIDGEPORT.

Mrs. Walter Wells, *Matron.*

Visited March 22, 1898.

The Asylum was established in 1868, and up to the present time has occupied the house originally built for the purpose at No. 119 Lafayette street. The house was designed to accommodate thirty-five children, and during the past year it has been more than full.

Orphaned children are received at the age of three years or over and are kept at the Asylum until they are twelve years old, when the usual plan is followed of placing them out in family homes. Supervision is maintained over them thereafter for a number of years by an annual interchange of visits between the children and the Asylum.

The officers of the Asylum consist of a board of trustees and a board of management of about forty ladies. The children attend school in the building and are also taught sewing and other useful branches. The Asylum is entirely supported by private charity, and for twenty-one years has been under the devoted care of the present matron, Mrs. Wells.

In May, 1894, a piece of land comprising about two acres at the corner of Fairfield avenue and Church street, in the Black Rock district, was purchased for the purpose of erecting a new building for the use of the Asylum. At the date of visit actual work was begun, and it was expected that the building would be ready for occupancy in the spring of 1899. The new home will be a well-arranged structure of brick, with accommodations for at least seventy-five inmates, and will be equipped with all modern conveniences. The Fairfield avenue line of electric cars pass the grounds.

THE DANBURY HOME FOR DESTITUTE AND HOMELESS CHILDREN,

DANBURY.

Miss E. A. Westerfield, *Matron*.

Visited January 26, 1898.

This is a non-sectarian institution whose object, as stated in its constitution, is " to provide a suitable temporary home for orphans, homeless, and destitute children, and to relieve and help to support, and to temporarily provide for and succor, those children whose parents, guardians, and relatives are unable to wholly support, maintain, and educate them." It is under the direction of a board of management composed of eighteen men and women of the city, and has no endowment fund, but depends for its support largely upon the gifts and subscriptions of its friends.

A few of the children are beneficiaries of the Home; the board of others is paid by their friends or by the town at the rate of two dollars a week. Admission is not restricted to Danbury children, although in most cases they are given the preference. It is customary to return the children to their parents, guardians, or friends as soon as their circumstances make it advisable to do so, or to place them out in family homes, where watch is kept of their future development by the managers of the Home. Children under two years of age are not received.

The Home occupies a comfortable two-storied house situated on high ground not far from the center of the city, and is surrounded by a pleasant yard. There are accommodations for from fifteen to twenty inmates, and at the date of visit eleven children were being cared for. All who are of suitable age attend the public school in the neighborhood.

THE CHILDREN'S HOME,

NORWALK.

Mrs. Joanna Lewis, *Matron.*

Visited April 26, 1898.

The Home was opened in 1879 and occupies the building formerly used as the town almshouse. It is situated about one-half mile west from the present almshouse, and is supported by the town of Norwalk for the benefit of such children as are destitute, neglected, or badly treated.

The children attend the public school in East Norwalk and as opportunity offers are placed in suitable family homes. At the date of visit there were sixteen inmates present. The accommodations are plain but comfortable, and the children receive excellent care from the resident matron. Her faithful work deserves more competent assistance than the town at present provides.

THE CHILDREN'S HOME,

STAMFORD.

Mrs. Williams, *Matron.*

Visited July 18, 1898.

This is one of the most recently established of the private homes for children in the State, having been opened in December, 1895. It is under the direction of a committee from the Charity Organization Society of the city, and is designed to care for any destitute or neglected children who may come under its charge. Parents do not relinquish control of the children when placed in the Home, but may withdraw them when circumstances render such action advisable.

In April, 1898, the Home was removed from its original location on Oak street to a house on Lockwood avenue in the eastern part of the city. The building, which was formerly a private residence, is well-adapted for the purpose, and it is hoped to purchase the property as soon as the necessary funds can be obtained. The land about the house comprises an acre and a half in extent and provides pleasant playgrounds for the children.

Children under three years of age are not received, and all who are sufficiently advanced attend the public school. At the date of visit there were thirteen inmates, four girls and nine boys.

A charge of $2 a week for board is made in all cases where the relatives or friends are able to assist in the support of the children, but special rates are granted at the discretion of the managers. The Home depends largely for its support upon the gifts of its friends and the charitably disposed people of the city.

THE GILBERT HOME,

WINSTED.

MR. AND MRS. DWIGHT S. CASE, *Superintendent and Matron.*

Visited October 12, 1897.

The Home is so named after the donor, the late Mr. W. S. Gilbert of Winsted, who, shortly before his decease, planned a home for children on a liberal scale, and endowed it so generously that the management are in the happy position of having no cause to apprehend any embarrassment from lack of available funds.

The object of the institution is to provide a home where, for a nominal sum per week, parents or friends may board children for such length of time as circumstances may require. In cases where families are broken up and it is not possible to provide home comforts and training, and in cases where daily employment or condition of health prevents mothers from properly caring for their children, relief may be had by temporarily placing them in charge of the Gilbert Home. As inmates they are well trained and kindly cared for, and taught the common English branches. For this service a charge is made of $1 a week. A significant feature is that the children thus received are not placed out in families, but are kept at the Home under the assurance that they will be given back to parents or friends whenever it is convenient or possible for the latter to care for them suitably.

The spot selected for the site was a piece of high ground in the western part of Winsted. A wooded tract of nineteen acres, with running streams, fruit orchards and shade trees, was purchased for a home lot. A large main building, especially designed for the purpose, was erected on the hillside, and by April 1, 1889, it was completed and ready for inmates. It is built of brick and is designed to accommodate two hundred. The rooms are large and are well lighted and ventilated. Verandas extend from each floor, and the view from them covers a wide tract of pleasant country. A neat wooden building was also erected by the managers of the Home for hospital purposes, and stands at a short distance from the main building. It contains rooms for isolating cases of contagious diseases, a nurse's room, sun-parlor, and other conveniences. In some respects it has proved inadequate to satisfy all requirements, and it is therefore hoped to provide improved facilities in this department in the near future.

To meet the demand for school accommodations for the steadily increasing number of inmates a separate school building was afterward erected. It is a handsome brick structure, and is connected with the main building by a covered corridor. In addition to four well-arranged and completely equipped schoolrooms, it contains also on the upper floor an attractive hall with a seating capacity for two hundred and fifty, and in the basement separate playrooms for boys and girls. A special gymnasium, forty by fifty feet in size, was later added to the Home's equipment, and is also connected with the covered corridor mentioned.

The Home is conducted on a non-sectarian basis, and there is no restriction in regard to applicants for admission; children may be received from any part of the State. The number present on September 30, 1898, was one hundred and thirty-five, in addition to ninety-two County Home children who are here cared for as described in the chapter on County Temporary Homes. The management is in the hands of a self-perpetuating board of sixteen trustees, and the provisions of the will under which the Home was founded require that, having defrayed the necessary expenses out of the Home's funds, they shall annually, for a period of one hundred years, lay by a fixed sum as an addition to the original endowment fund. The superintendent and matron report to the trustees once a month on the working of the Home.

The institution presents an attractive appearance of cleanliness and good order whenever visited, and gives evidence of faithful and efficient management. It is a noble charity, and the scope of its usefulness increases year by year.

MIDDLESEX COUNTY ORPHANS' HOME,

MIDDLETOWN.

Miss Mary Fennell, *Matron.*

Visited September 28, 1897, and September 21, 1898.

The Home is a private charity under the management of a board of Middletown ladies, and in 1881 received a charter from the State. It occupies a pleasant house at No. 66 Wyllys avenue, which has possible accommodations for twenty inmates, although ten is the largest number that has yet been cared for.

Dependent and neglected children and those in particular who are too young to be eligible for admission to the County Temporary Homes are received and cared for at the usual rate of $2.00 per week. The management is liberal, and children are received from all parts of the State. At the date of last visit there were seven present, four of whom were being boarded by the towns, and three by relatives or friends. Some confusion has arisen from the similarity of its name to that of the Middlesex County Temporary Home at Haddam; the two institutions, however, are entirely distinct, and it is hoped that the Middletown Home will alter its title in the near future.

MAPLEWOOD FARM,

EAST CANAAN.

Visited October 6, 1898.

Maplewood farm is a place where it was formerly the custom to receive a considerable number of young children to board.

At the date of visit it was found that only one child under the age of ten years, prescribed in the statutes governing the boarding of infants, was then being cared for. In addition there were present a twelve-year-old boy, who is a ward of the Litchfield County Home, and one or two other children who were connected with the family.

RIGHTS OF SELECTMEN WITH REGARD
TO DEPENDENT CHILDREN.

With reference to the authority of selectmen in the case of dependent children, it is provided by the General Statutes in Section 1740 that:

" If any person who has had relief from any town shall suffer his children to misspend their time, and shall neglect to employ them in some honest calling, or if any person does not provide competently for his children, whereby they are exposed to want, or if any poor children in any town live idly or exposed to want, and there are none to take care of them, the selectmen of such town, with the assent of a justice of the peace, shall indenture such children to be apprentices to some proper trade for said term; and may indenture them in like manner to any society incorporated for the purpose of educating and relieving orphans or destitute children whose place of business is in this State, and may contract with such society to defray wholly or in part the expenses of such child while in the institution, to an amount not exceeding $1.50 per week; and such society shall have the same authority with regard to such children as over those surrendered to them by their parents."

The Hartford and New Haven Orphan Asylums have power and authority to accept a surrender in writing by the father, or, when there is no father, by the mother or guardian, or from the selectmen, under the written approval of the judge of probate for the district, of any indigent child, as described in the act aforesaid.

These Asylums have also the right to indenture for adoption or apprenticeship any such child or children thus surrendered to their care and control.

BOARDING OF INFANTS.

GENERAL STATUTES, 1888.

Section 2610. Any person who shall make a business of taking children under ten years of age, other than members of such person's family, to entertain or board, in any number exceeding two in the same house at the same time, shall within three days after the reception, removal, or death of any such child, give written notice thereof to the selectmen of the town within which such house is situated, specifying the name and age of such child, the place of residence of the parties so undertaking its care, and the birthplace and parentage of said child, if known.

Sec. 2611. Said selectmen, or some proper person appointed by them, shall visit and inspect such premises as often as once in each month, and within one week after such visit make a written report containing a statement of the number of such children in said house, the number received and removed since the last visit, the number of deaths and the causes thereof, the condition of the premises and of the children, which report, when accepted by said selectmen, shall be kept on file in the office of the town clerk of said town.

Sec. 2612. Such house or premises shall at all hours during the day and before nine o'clock in the evening be open to visits of inspection by any officer or agent of the   ·   .   .   State Board of Charities, provided that such visit be made in company with a selectman of the town in which such house is located, or with some other proper person appointed by the selectmen of such town, etc.   .

Sec. 2613. Any person violating any provision of the three preceding sections, or refusing admission to any of the persons specified in Section 2612, shall be fined not less than fifty nor more than five hundred dollars, or imprisoned not more than one year, or both.

PUBLIC ACTS OF 1895,

CHAPTER 102.

AN ACT CONCERNING MATERNITY HOSPITALS, AND THE BOARDING OF INFANTS.

SECTION 1. No person shall keep a maternity hospital, or lying-in place, unless such person has previously obtained a license therefor, duly issued by the mayor, or board of health of the city, or health officer of the town wherein such maternity hospital or lying-in place is situated.

22

SEC. 2. Within six hours after the departure, removal, or withdrawal of any child born at such maternity hospital, or lying-in place, the keeper thereof shall make a record of such departure, removal, or withdrawal of such child, and the names and residences of the persons who took such child, and whatever disposition of such child, or its body, is made, and the place where it is taken and left, which record shall be produced by the keeper or licensee of said hospital, or lying-in place, for inspection by and upon the demand of any person authorized so to do by the mayor or board of health or health officer of the city or town in which such hospital, or lying-in place, is located.

SEC. 3. No keeper of any such hospital, or lying-in place, or any of his servants or agents, shall refuse permission to any person, so authorized to make such inspection, to enter such hospital, or lying-in place, for the purpose of such inspection, and shall permit such person so authorized, as aforesaid, to inspect such hospital and all its appurtenances for the purpose of detecting any improper treatment of such child.

SEC. 4. Every person so authorized may take and remove any article, which he thinks presents evidence of any crime being committed therein, and deliver the same to the coroner of the county, to be disposed of according to law.

SEC. 5. Any person violating any provision of this act shall be fined not less than fifty, nor more than five hundred dollars, or imprisoned not more than one year, or both.

CHAPTER 324.

AN ACT CONCERNING THE ESTABLISHMENT OF PRIVATE ASYLUMS.

No asylum, home, or institution for defective, deformed, or incurable persons shall be established or maintained within the limits of any town without the consent of said town, unless under express legislative authority.

APPENDIX.

SPECIAL REPORT

ON THE

CAUSES OF INSANITY AND TUBERCULOSIS,

AT THE

CONNECTICUT STATE PRISON.

BY

EDWIN A. DOWN, M.D., HARTFORD,

Member of the State Board of Charities.

The inquiry into the causes of insanity and tuberculosis which had been noticeably prevalent in the Connecticut Prison during several years past, began with a comparison of methods and statistical findings between our own institution and those of a similar character throughout the country. The results are based upon periods extending over three years, embracing the time comprised in the reports of the directors for the years 1894, 1895, 1896.

The statistics furnished by other institutions for the same periods represent a prison population of eighty thousand persons distributed throughout the United States. A series of questions bearing upon this subject sent to prison officials in various parts of the country, resulted in bringing to our knowledge a large number of facts of a practical nature, and useful also for purposes of comparison.

The inquiry did not stop here. Personal visits to penal and reformatory institutions in other states by members of our Board, interviews with leaders in the science of penology and criminology, and a closer scrutiny of jails and other places of detention which act as feeders to our prison population, were important accessories in the line of this investigation. Supplementing these was the inspection of a number of prisons and reformatories in the Canadian provinces during the session of the National Conference of Charities and Correction held at Toronto during July of last year.

In the report of the warden of the Connecticut Prison, for the year 1894, we are told that nine cases of insanity occurred in the Prison. The following year twenty-five prisoners were adjudged insane, and during 1895 eighteen persons succumbed to this malady. These figures indicate a percentage of four and four-tenths to the total prison population for the year ending September 30, 1895. When compared with the number of cases occurring in the general population of the State, it was discovered that insanity was exhibiting itself twelve times as frequently in the State Prison as in the community at large. The succeeding year has a record of eighteen cases. This was an improvement over the preceding year, but the fact that one out of every thirty-two persons confined in the Prison was becoming insane, was not looked upon as an encouraging feature of prison reform, nor in keeping with advances made in other directions.

The following table shows the percentage of insane and tuberculous subjects in the prison population throughout the country and in our own Prison at Wethersfield.

PRISON POPULATION, COUNTRY AT LARGE.

Insanity: six-tenths of 1 per cent.

Tuberculosis: eight-tenths of 1 per cent.

CONNECTICUT STATE PRISON.

Insanity: more than 3 per cent.

Tuberculosis, two and six-tenths per cent.

Having ascertained that the percentage of these maladies in the Connecticut Prison was largely in excess of the average of the country at large, the next step was to discover the institution which presented the minimum of these two forms of disease, as well as the conditions under which they existed. A comparison of these associated conditions with those pertaining to our own prison should prove helpful where prison construction and organization are contemplated.

The prison at Santa Fe, New Mexico, is the one selected for this purpose; and the following table of comparisons is self-explanatory:

SANTA FE PRISON.

Situation high; more than 1,000 feet above tide water.
Sanitary conditions excellent.
Occupations: chiefly out of doors.
Fresh air and sunshine unlimited.
No history of malaria.
Conversation permitted between cell-mates.
Bucket system; no water-closets in cells.
Ratio of insane: 1 to 567.
Ratio of tuberculous: 1 to 567.

CONNECTICUT STATE PRISON.

Situation low; soil marshy.
Sanitary conditions, until recently, not first-class.
Occupations: chiefly confined to shops.
Out-of-door recreation almost *nil*.
Out-of-door air and sunshine mainly procured in walking from the main building to the shops, and returning:
Malaria abounds.
Conversation prohibited; silent system.
Water-closet in each cell, connected with sewer.
Ratio of insane: 1 to 32.
Ratio of tuberculous: 1 to 40.

These tables represent the two extremes in the line of comparison, but it seems to be conclusively shown that moral and physical hygiene are important factors in determining for or against the class of disorders under review, and that these are not necessarily the direct product of a vitiated ancestry. There are also other points of difference between these two institutions, worthy of notice and careful reflection. Let us compare the attitude of the law in Connecticut toward her convict class, with that of her western sister.

" The Connecticut State Prison," the report for 1895 tells us, " was built for a penal institution and not for a reformatory — the construction of the Prison is such that any extended reformatory measures cannot be carried out." In New Mexico the prevailing sentiment prompts the warden of the prison to state that "while the object of this institution — to be a terror to all evil-doers — has been paramount to all other considerations, the reformatory features of this prison have received the next and very close attention. Many convicts have been taught trades, and many others have received primary knowledge of the same."

From sociological and psychological points of view, these reformatory measures are of prime importance. In one case the offender, after the expiration of his sentence, finds himself in possession of mechanical skill, which will enable him to provide himself with the necessaries of life in an honorable manner; and he places himself in the ranks of the constructive members of society. Having in mind the postulate that the integrity and normal action of the cerebral centers are dependent upon their healthful exercise, the conclusion that variety in movements, which are the external representatives of these centers, is a wholesome feature of most forms of labor, leads to the ready acceptance of this favorite dictum of modern psychiatry.

On the other hand, where reformatory features are disregarded, the last state of the culprit is worse than the first. Worse, from the fact that he is kept in ignorance of the progress of events outside his own prison-house during a long term, it may be, and he finds it difficult upon his discharge to adjust himself readily to the new order of things; and there appears to be no other resource than to resort to his former practice of procuring dishonestly what he is unqualified to obtain by honorable methods.

It is encouraging to note that the initial steps in the direction of the reformatory idea have been taken by our prison officials, and efforts to make men and law-abiding citizens out of prison material are rapidly superseding practices resulting from the too close application of the primitive and barbaric dogma of "an eye for an eye, and a tooth for a tooth," which is out of harmony with an intelligent conception of social evolution. Setting generalities aside for the time being, let us examine some of the different classes of cases as they are presented for examination.

As an example, let us take the case of a young man who does not apply himself closely to any one pursuit, but prefers to encounter the risks involved in changing from one position to another, thus securing a certain amount of excitement attendant upon frequent change of environment, which accords very well with a disposition in which are compounded a spirit of adventure and careless independence. When from any cause this man is found guilty of an offense requiring a given length of time in the State Prison, an opposite polarity in currents of thought and action is established. Before his incarceration his acts were aggressive, and currents of thought and emotion were in an outward direction, being chiefly centrifugal.

Under prison discipline this order of things is reversed. Aggressive movements have now become inhibited functions; thought processes take an inward or centripetal direction and introspection becomes an enforced habit.

With those whose intellectual training has been meager, there appears to be lacking the requisite mental resiliency and adaptive qualities which in others renders it comparatively easy to exercise the inevitable philosophy of making the "best" of the situation; and the proper corrective for this condition of introspection not appearing, the transition to a depressive form of mental impairment is an occasional result.

This brief outline of a case is not a mere hypothesis invoked in aid of some abstract theory, but has as its basis, features not uncommon in the histories of a class of prisoners whose records are kept on file at the Prison.

Right here we may be confronted with the inquiry, Would not this man have become insane had he remained at large? And was it not his lack of mental equilibrium which caused his incarceration? An affirmative answer would furnish an easy solution of a disturbing question in prison economics; but in the judgment of the writer such a conclusion is erroneous. In his opinion, the case cited might have remained in a rational and normal state under the influence of his customary environment and have died without a question of his mental responsibility having been raised.

To assert that mental impotence was the cause of his committing crime would be equivalent to affirming that most criminals were insane prior to commitment. This proposition is as incautious as it is unsafe and inaccurate. Cases similar to the one just described are included in the class known as accidental criminals in contradistinction to the habitual criminal or recidivist. In the former class are found those who are not intentionally bad, but who in an unguarded moment may be over-persuaded by those older in crime to commit an offense for which they may be apprehended, while the promoters of the transaction escape. Such acts may also be involuntary; for I have in mind a young man who came into my office during the past summer and related the story of his having been met by two men on one of the roads leading to Hartford, and was invited by them to assist in robbing a farmhouse. Upon his refusing, they attempted to use force in compelling him to accede to their proposal, but, their noise attracting attention, he was released, the others seeking safety in some woods. This story is not unique.

With the habitual criminal matters are very different. He understands the nature and result of his act, and at the expiration of his sentence expects to pass through the same cycle of events, at the same time hoping that he may not be apprehended. A few months or years in prison are not terrifying to such an individual, but with the " accidental " the remorse is sometimes intense, and mental derangement not infrequently results.

Of course, we meet with the degenerative cases quite frequently, But the doctrine of Lombroso, that all criminals belong to a degenerative type, should not be allowed to overshadow obvious facts, even though this 'dogma appears to furnish an easy and comfortable method of dealing with this part of our subject.

Among those who may be considered mentally defective before conviction are included individuals who, at the suggestion of counsel, have entered the plea of " guilty " in the hope of securing the clemency of the court. After such plea sentence soon follows, and any latent or semi-apparent defects in the prisoner's mental equipment are overlooked or disregarded, the true mental state not being fully recognized until after varying periods subsequent to his commitment.

One of the effects of seclusion is the resort to the habit of self-abuse, and this practice as a factor in the production of insanity has attained considerable prominence. After careful deliberation I am convinced that this is not the fruitful source of mental derangement which it has become popular to affirm. Masturbation may be assumed to be the cause or the effect of the disturbed mental state with which it is associated; and when other depressing and debilitating causes are in operation, it may be merely the accidental precipitant amongst a congeries of causes. Excess in other directions might be capable of exerting similar influence, and become the chief objective symptom, while other antecedent but less apparent indications could be easily overlooked. The prevalence of this habit outside prison walls is too common to warrant the assertion that masturbation *per se* is responsible for the large number of cases of insanity associated with it. A full discussion of this feature of our subject cannot be accomplished within the limits of this report, but must be reserved for publication in some of our medical journals.

Other cases becoming insane during imprisonment belong to the class in which are included the recurrent forms of mental disorder, so called from the fact that after a varying interval, during which the person has a marked remission or a true intermission of the morbid symptoms, there is a recurrence of the phenomena which characterized the preceding attack. During such remission or intermission he may be convicted of crime, his insanity not manifesting itself for months or perhaps a year or more after his incarceration. These are the cases which often find their way to this country from foreign shores, it being an easy matter to bring or send them here during the quiet interval between the attacks.

Doubtless, at the time of their admission into the prison many convicts are physically below the average; but this is true of most prisons, and the superintendent of the New Mexico institution takes the pains to state that " It should be remembered that nearly three-fourths of the convicts come to this institution suffering from chronic blood affections and diseases of long standing and almost incurable."

In the Connecticut Prison the estimate is 70 per cent. Such chronic and specific disorders are, doubtless, predisponents to certain forms of mental disability, and many of the ataxic and paralytic forms should be placed to their credit.

It would be obviously impossible in a report of this character to discuss at length the various agencies at work in the production of the disorders under review, but attention should be drawn to a few remaining facts which assume a position of prime importance, in the writer's estimation. These include the germ-laden soil beneath and surrounding the Prison, and the geographical position of the institution itself. Referring to the warden's report for the fiscal year ending September 30, 1894, we learn that from an unknown period prior to that year ordinary rules of sanitation had been overlooked. For example, he tells us that " every roof on the premises except the warden's house and contractor's shop was leaking like a riddle

— steam pipes through the institution were twisted and warped so that it was impossible to get heat." "Sewer pipes were twisted and leaking, and permitting the escape of sewer gas into every department." Added to this the warden states that sewage had been permeating the soil for an indefinite period. and that doubtless the ground beneath the Prison had been saturated with this material for a number of years.

Under the present regime these defects have been remedied, and an inspection of the Prison should convince the most skeptical that the system of heating, ventilating, and cleanliness, the care in the selection and preparation of food, besides the facilities for hospital care and treatment, leave little to be desired in these directions.   But the same soil is there, and the surrounding atmosphere contains the miasmatic poison; and while the cellar beneath the "block" is orderly and well kept, the soil contains microbic agencies which have not been devitalized by a layer of a few inches of sand.

Regarding the location of the Prison, it is a safe assumption that with our present knowledge of disease, its causation and treatment. no intelligent committee would consider a proposal which involved the purchase of a site conspicuous for its miasmatic and other unwholesome conditions.   Among these conditions may be mentioned the proximity of the outlet of the Franklin avenue sewer, materials from which may be seen on the river bank at the rear of the Prison, during low tide.   In the second place the marshy character of the soil and concomitant barometric and hygrometric conditions, all of which lend material aid in the production of the malarial cachexia. Supplementing these. the testimony of Warden Woodbridge and Dr. Edward G. Fox, who for many years and until recently occupied the office of prison physician, and Dr. Thayer, who succeeded him, fortifies the position assumed, and leaves scarcely the remnant of a doubt that malarial poisoning is endemic in and about the Prison, and its effects, immediate and remote, are responsible for a large percentage of the maladies appearing within the prison walls.   The concurrent testimony of these officers shows that the use of quinine and other antimalarial remedies constitutes a very important part of the medical treatment, and their employment by the officers and employes is a matter of routine.

This matter of the locality of the Prison and the effects upon the inmates is not new to many, and has been clearly recognized by several boards of directors during the last thirty years.

In the directors' report for 1882, we read that " In view of the fact that the hygienic condition of our Prison, at least so far as malarial sickness is concerned, rapidly deteriorating for years, has at last reached a point which must awaken the gravest apprehensions, an investigation into the causes is plainly demanded by every dictate of justice and humanity. While the inmates of the Prison who are suffering the penalty of violated law have forfeited their right to freedom, they are surely entitled to pass their confinement under circumstances not unfavorable to health."

On the board of directors at that time were the Hon. Francis Wayland of New Haven and Judge McManus of this city. These gentlemen consulted with Colonel Waring of New York, who visited the Prison, and, after a careful examination of the premises, recommended the construction of a blind drain to carry off the surplus water from the soil about the building. The General Assembly of 1883 appropriated twenty-five hundred dollars for the purpose of improving the drainage and other needed repairs. After this the health of the prisoners seemed to improve, but there was still a large surplus of moisture, which required the use of fires during the months of July and August of the same year to render the atmosphere comfortably respirable.

As far back as 1871 the General Assembly appointed a commission to investigate and report upon the sanitary and hygienic conditions of the State Prison. Their report refers to the old prison, which is now used as a chapel and assembly room, but the new part is on the same level, and is practically an " L " to the old building. In describing some of the conditions found, the report further states that " The bottom of the cellar, in which we have sometimes found water standing, is only a little, if at all, above the level of the highest water in the Wethersfield Cove." Regarding the location, the committee was moved to say " it would seem too obvious for argument that the Prison should be on ground high enough to secure good air and natural drainage, and to be free from miasmatic exhalations. It needs no expert to tell us that the present site combines with almost ideal completeness every unfavorable feature which can be well conceived of for such an institution." The committee also recommended " the erection as speedily as may be, of another State Prison in a different and better place."

The gift of prophetic inspiration is not essential to either professional or layman to enable him to foretell that, given

such conditions as have been briefly outlined, a lowering of
mental and physical functions will be a logical result; and in
the opinion of the writer, this acquired defective vital resistance
is the touchstone which brings into the foreground any latent
tendencies to disease which, under the influence of more salu-
tary environs, would not have been suspected.

Owing to a lack of proper data, the opinion has been occasionally expressed that such diseases existed before the person
was apprehended; and in some instances a too ready acceptance and loose application of one of the theories of modern
science that nothing " happens," account for a flavor of dog-
matism with which sporadic and off-hand conclusions are
tinctured. ' The fact is that there are many offenders outside
of prison walls; the only difference between such and the man
on the inside is that the former have not been convicted; but
no one would care to assume the responsibility of declaring all
of them insane.

The subject of inherited mental stigmata merits attention,
and presents some seeming contradictions, or at least peculiarities. If we accept the sweeping proposition that most crimes
are the result of an inherited intellectual flabbiness, how shall
we account for the small percentage of females in the convict
class? In the classification of insanity, the description of the
various types applies to male and female alike. Mania is
mania, and melancholia is melancholia, whether in the male or
female; and homicidal impulses are of the common gender.

Without attempting a full discussion of this interesting
question, the writer presents the proposition that many traits
and tendencies are acquired rather than inherited, and are as
often responsible for the resulting criminal act. If we institute
a comparison between a few of the prominent traits in the
female with those of the opposite sex, we discover that in the
former there is a cultivated habit to appear as favorably as possible before others, and secure the good opinion and admiration
of the general public; and she endeavors to regulate her conduct accordingly. Such habits carefully nurtured through a
series of years become an element of the personality of the
woman and furnish safeguard against the forces of impulse
which beset male and female alike. Greater timidity, less independence in action, and more lenient treatment at the hands
of men have also been presented as reasons for the small number of females in our state prisons.

With men the case appears almost the reverse. Independent, possessed of a courage verging on temerity, and rendering themselves callous to public opinion, the response to an impulse, be it morbid or the reverse, is different from that observed in the female under the conditions previously outlined, and frequently results in crime. A large excess in point of numbers, among those who are the subjects of alcoholic addiction occuring in males, explains very satisfactorily the more frequent association of some forms of crime with the sterner sex.

When the individual's insanity does not appear until a variable period after his incarceration, it is a fair deduction that prison life is an important factor in the production of the morbid condition found to exist; and this is notably true in cases of a first attack. The sanitary conditions by which the prisoner is surrounded have already been alluded to. The effect of physical conditions upon mental states are well exhibited in a prison atmosphere; and demonstrate the close relationship and interaction of the cerebro-spinal and sympathetic nervous systems, rendering the proposition, " if one member suffers, all the other members suffer with it," not only morally sound but scientifically accurate.

It is instructive to note in connection with the study of the insane cases, that these present symptoms belonging to the depressive forms of insanity to a great extent. This is perfectly consistent with the conditions of repression under which the prisoners exist, and is another point in evidence going to show the fallacy of considering so many persons mentally out of adjustment before committal. In comparing the forms of mental disorder existing in the general population with those occurring in prisons, we find that the forms characterized by excitement and an exaltation of the functions preponderate in the former, while depression and inhibition are the prominent features of the latter. Some difficulty is experienced in obtaining reliable statistics regarding the forms of mental disorder from which the patients suffer, and some of the answers to the questions touching upon the character of the insanity — whether excitement or depression prevailed — were as follows: " No record," " Mixed," " Excitement and Depression," " Various," etc. In some instances, where the person was the subject of delusions which were depressive in their nature, a transitory condition of violence and excitement manifested itself when force was employed to compel the subject of these delusive concepts to perform some task or duty which was inimical to his interests, or even safety, according to the dictates of his morbid ideas.

Under these accidental circumstances, such cases have been considered maniacal; whereas the prevailing emotion has been one having an opposite direction, and some confusion in classification has resulted. In some of the prisons carefully kept records show the mental state of those becoming insane; while in the majority of the reports received, it is very evident that the importance of this feature of a convict's or criminal record has not impressed itself upon the minds of those having the preparation of the prison reports and records under their immediate supervision.

TUBERCULOSIS.

The brief outline of causes of the insane condition is analogous to that pertaining to the disorder known as tuberculosis or consumption. The subject of consumption in state prisons has been very carefully handled by the physician to the New Jersey State Prison in his report for 1895, and an abstract of his conclusions is well worth the time devoted to its perusal. He begins by stating that " So general, indeed, is the existence of this disease in prison life, that so reliable an authority as Baer has stated that in the autopsies of prisoners dying from all causes it is the exception to find the lungs free from tubercle. While the mortality from it in the human family is generally reckoned at one-seventh, or 14 or 15 per cent., in prisons it almost invariably reaches 40, 50, or 60 per cent., the last figures being probably the nearest approximation to the accurate, as applied to the cellular system of prisons."

In the last report of this prison, which corresponds very closely with the Connecticut Prison, we find that 75 per cent. of the total deaths of the Prison were chargeable to tuberculosis. But this is only part of the story. It must be borne in mind that numbers of prisoners who are discharged at the expiration of their sentences bear away with them the marks of an incipient, and not infrequently an advanced, tuberculosis. The rational treatment of tuberculosis consists mainly in placing the patient in an atmosphere containing a minimum of moisture, and permeated with sunlight. If the climates of Egypt and Colorado are ideal ones for the consumptive, then our prison atmosphere must be the reverse, for the conditions are reversed.

Just how and when the infection of the prisoners occurs is not apparent. This was partly explicable when such cases were treated in their cells in the block, prior to the establishment of the hospital.

In forming an estimate of the conditions, favorable or otherwise, in which our convicts exist, it should be remembered that there are four hundred water-closets in the room where the prisoners live and sleep, each closet connected with the sewer. During " high water " in the river, the mouth of the sewer is closed, and it is more than probable that any gases which may be present are forced by hydraulic pressure through the traps in the closets.

This has not been practically demonstrated, but it is a question whether or not the closet plan can replace the bucket system which is in use in most of the prisons of the country. The great advantage with the bucket system is the impossibility of sewage contamination, and as the buckets are exposed to out-of-door air and sunlight during the day, their presence is less objectionable than the stationary closet. This opinion is concurred in by many of the wardens of the prisons visited, as well as those who supplied the information through the circular of inquiry.

While the foregoing is intended for a report only, some portions appear to have been discussed at length; but this has been necessary in order to insure an approach to lucidity in dealing with this interesting but abstruse subject.

In summarizing, the following propositions appear reasonable in view of the facts presented:

1. That the location of the State Prison is not desirable from a sanitary point of view, owing to the presence of miasmatic elements dependent upon conditions of soil, proximity to city sewer, and other features previously recorded.

2. That malaria is endemic in and about the Prison.

3. That chronic malarial poisoning, devitalizing in its effects, is directly responsible for the appearance of many of the cases of insanity and tuberculosis within the Prison.

4. That the conclusion that a large majority of the convicts are insane prior to incarceration has no basis in fact.

5. That reformatory methods are helpful in averting mental and physical disorders.

6. That industrial features are not substitutes for fresh air and sunlight in promoting the health of prisoners.

7. That it is problematical if the stationary water-closet in

the cell where the prisoner lives, eats, and sleeps is a wholesome substitute for the portable bucket which is in use in most of the prisons in the United States and Canada.

It was designed to have prepared a statement regarding the atmospheric conditions of the Prison for the purpose of showing to what extent the bacillus or germ of tuberculosis was present, but this could not be accomplished in time for our report.

In conclusion, our Board desires to express acknowledgments for the courteous manner in which the inquiries have been answered by the officers of the institutions visited and corresponded with, as well as those connected with our own Prison; and it does not appear to be an unreasonable expectation that, with the data regarding the causation of the diseases referred to at hand, a marked decrease in the number of cases will be recorded in each succeeding report, and thus afford a basis for the hope of their ultimate extermination.

ST. FRANCIS' ORPHAN ASYLUM,

NEW HAVEN.

SUPPLEMENTARY REPORT.

In addition to the report of this Asylum in the preceding chapter on Private Provision for the Young, it is desired to present the following statements, which were received too late for insertion with the former report.

The Asylum is under the management of a self-perpetuating board of trustees, composed of the parish priests' of the St. Francis' Orphan Asylum district and of lay members from the Catholic parishes of the city of New Haven. There is also a board of managers selected by the trustees, who have charge of the financial and secular affairs of the orphanage. The internal management of the institution is intrusted to the Sisters of Mercy, who serve without remuneration, and devote their lives faithfully to the highest welfare of the children under their charge.

In addition to the household duties mentioned in the former report, in which the children are employed, it is the expectation of the management, as soon as their means will permit, to establish manual and industrial training schools for boys and girls, respectively, where such children as cannot be provided with suitable homes may be taught useful trades by which they may earn an honest livelihood after leaving the institution.

The number of children cared for during the year 1898, representing twelve different nationalities, was 517, of whom 141 were newly admitted in the year. The total number of children discharged during the year was 205, of whom 73 were placed out in Catholic homes, 86 were returned to parents, and 21 were returned to other relatives or friends. The number of children remaining in the Asylum, December 31, 1898, was 312, of whom 197 were boys and 115 girls. The current expenses for all purposes of running the Asylum in 1898 were $23,085.

The main building of the Asylum is a large, three-storied structure of brick, and was first occupied in November, 1876.

23

It contains dormitories, schoolrooms, recreation halls, refectories, and chapel, and is well heated, lighted, and ventilated. In addition, there are detached buildings used for laundry, bakery, and stable purposes. About thirteen acres of land are included in the property, furnishing opportunity for the cultivation of considerable farm produce.

Children who are placed in family homes are subject to the supervision of the parish priests, and are kept within the jurisdiction of the Asylum to the effect that they may be recalled if, at any time, the conditions of the new homes prove undesirable. Children suffering from incurable or contagious diseases, or those who are feeble-minded, crippled, vicious, or incorrigible, are not received in the Asylum.

REPORT

ON THE

Special Investigation of the Hillside Almshouse at Danbury.

During the fall and early winter of 1897-8, a special investigation was made by the State Board of Charities into the condition of the so-called Hillside Farm (formerly the town almshouse) at Danbury, in which the representatives of the Board were assisted by two members of the State Board of Health.

A copy of the following letter was sent to the selectmen of Danbury on the date given, together with a copy of the report of the State Board of Health to the State Board of Charities, which is subjoined herewith.

On the occasion of later visits to the place, it was found that the recommendations of the Board had been complied with, the inmates of the house had been removed to other quarters, and the building was empty and closed. At the special request of several influential citizens of Danbury, copies of these reports were afterward published in the *Danbury Evening News*.

WATERBURY, CONN., March 16, 1898.

To the Selectmen of Danbury:

GENTLEMEN: — On Sept. 18, 1897, Miss Mary Hall of the State Board of Charities and I visited the place in Danbury which was formerly used as the town almshouse, but which, since its abandonment for that purpose, has been occupied by families aided by the town. We found the building and the premises in very bad condition and swarming with children who were growing up in an atmosphere of pauperism and disease. We so reported the case at the next monthly meeting of the State Board of Charities held on October 6th, and were authorized by them to confer with your board of selectmen in regard to a more suitable disposition of the place and its inmates. Accordingly, on October 14th, I met your board in Danbury and discussed the matter (Miss Hall being detained by accident), and then presented the recommendation of the State Board that the dependent families be removed to more suitable quarters and that some fitting disposition be made of the building and premises.

A report of this conference was given to the next meeting of the State Board on Nov. 3d, and as some time elapsed without any move being made on your part to improve the condition of the place, another conference was had with your board by Miss Hall and me on January 26, 1898. At this time the recommendation of the State Board made at the former meeting was repeated and emphasized, but no agreement was made by your board as to the action you would take in the matter. Miss Hall and I called the same day upon your town health officer, who expressed the earnest wish that the place might be destroyed at an early date, as the best means of improving its sanitary condition. We should have visited the building again at that time, but for the fact that an epidemic of diphtheria, which had been raging there, had but recently subsided.

Before taking final steps in the matter, it was the desire of some members of the State Board to obtain detailed information in regard to the inmates of the place, and for that purpose I again visited it on February 28th last, and interviewed at considerable length and with great care every family living there.

On March 8th, Dr. Lindsley of New Haven and Dr. Wordin of Bridgeport, members of the State Board of Health, accompanied me in another visit to the place in order that they might examine it in its sanitary aspects chiefly. A copy of their report is enclosed herewith, and speaks for itself. It is based, as before stated, on the result of a careful inspection in person, and is, we submit, entitled to your thorough consideration.

There were then in the main building six families, which consisted of twelve adult persons and twenty-five children, ranging in age from five months to fourteen years. Besides these, in a small building close by, was a young woman with an infant. The woman was not very bright, and was represented to us as suffering from a contagious and loathsome disease. Although her rooms were separate from those of the other families, she frequented their apartments and used the same conveniences. Her influence upon the children with whom she mingled freely could not fail to be of the very worst.

Of the six families, four have been residents of, the place for a period of three years or more, another for two years and eight months, while only one family has been there less than a year. Therefore the argument made that the rent given them here is a temporary expedient does not appear to be a valid one.

All of the families were receiving weekly orders from the town varying in amount from $1.50 to $3.00, besides supplies of coal and wood, with the exception of one, of whom the head of the family was working in a hat factory. This fact clearly marks the inmates as dependent upon the town for support, and, in this case, as dependent poor who are supported upon a portion of your town farm property. Competent legal authorities have advised us that this makes the place practically an almshouse, although you have another institution for that purpose, and that your Board by retaining children in the place are rendering yourselves liable to a fine of fifty dollars a month as provided in Chapter 313 of the Public Acts of 1895 and amended by Chapter 210, Section 2, of the Public Acts of 1897.

At least three of the men appeared to be able to earn a part, if not the whole, of their means of subsistence, did they not find it easier to receive support from the town. For them and for several of the women also, there would be a better chance to obtain employment if they occupied tenements nearer the center of the city. The chief trouble with the men appeared to be the intemperate use of alcoholic liquors, supplies of which, I was informed, they introduced into the building with the result of noisy carousals. A lively fight between two families was in progress at the time of my arrival and similar disturbances, I learned, were of frequent occurrence.

The fact of twenty-five young children all growing up in an atmosphere of pauperism, disease, and immorality under the patronage of the town authorities is alone enough to condemn the present use to which the building is put, to say nothing of its wretched sanitary condition. Five children have been born in the families during their residence in the place, of whom two were fortunately relieved from lives of suffering and evil by early death. One girl of fourteen years, it became necessary to place in the House of the Good Shepherd at Albany, after she had been evilly treated by one of the men who is still allowed to continue his residence in the place.

It is plain that the town authorities of Danbury are here encouraging the propagation and development of a new generation of paupers, and that it would prove ultimately a measure of economy if the families now occupying the place were given rents elsewhere in the city and the present buildings were completely demolished. The place as conducted at present is a disgrace to the town, and it is unfortunate that Danbury is not satisfied with possessing the best almshouse in the State, but must at the same time wish to maintain the worst.

In conclusion, we wish to convey to your board of selectmen the recommendation of these two State Boards that the present use of the place be discontinued at as early a date as possible, that more suitable provision be made for the dependent families now occupying it, and that the building be disposed of as may best suit your convenience.

Awaiting the favor of an early reply, I remain,

Yours very truly,

CHARLES P. KELLOGG, *Secretary*.
For the State Board of Charities.

NEW HAVEN, CONN., March 9, 1898.

To the Connecticut State Board of Charities:

The undersigned respectfully beg leave to report to your Honorable Board, that, in response to a request from your Secretary, that the State Board of Health join him in an inspection of a certain locality in Danbury, we were appointed by the President of the said Board of Health to that duty.

On the 8th of March we went to Danbury and, in company of your Secretary, Mr. Kellogg, inspected a building and surroundings situated in the suburbs of the city, which building might be designated as an annex to the poorhouse. We were informed that some years ago it was the poorhouse, but that a new poorhouse had been erected and this one abandoned because it had become unfit for the habitation of paupers; that subsequently it had been partially repaired, and for the last four years or more it had been appropriated for the use of impoverished families who were allowed to occupy the rooms rent free, and were supplied with fuel and, to some extent, with furniture and other needs.

The building showed no evidence of recent repairs. On the contrary, it is so nearly in the last stages of usefulness that any attempt at satisfactory repairs to adapt it to the purposes of family housekeeping will be, probably, equivalent in cost to entire reconstruction.

It is doubtful if a more striking example of an utterly worn-out tenement for human habitation, still occupied by so many people, can be found elsewhere in Connecticut.

Fortunately, there is but little plumbing in the building. It would be better if there were none. Every family, however, is provided with a sink in one of the rooms; some of them are trapped and some are not; but they are all alike — malodorous from neglect of cleanliness.

The pipes from them lead to drains which are obstructed, and the sewage sets back in the cellar. It will improve the sanitary condition to entirely remove every sink from the building.

The whole house reeks with fetid odors, the result of years of nasty housekeeping.

At the time of our visit there were thirty-six residents in the place, of the human species, and several cats. We saw no dogs.

Of the thirty-six persons dwelling here, twenty-five were children ranging in age from five months to fourteen years.

One family, of a father and four children, slept together in two beds in one little room. Among them was a boy fourteen years old and a girl of twelve. The house is large and many rooms are unoccupied simply because they are positively uninhabitable. There is a cellar under only a small part of the building; what is under the rest of it we were satisfied to guess at by the sense of smell.

The external surroundings were quite in keeping with the interior. Nastiness and filth were the most prominent features.

It will be tedious to describe in detail the many sanitary objections to its present use; they are tersely and correctly described in the statement given for the original abandonment of the house, to wit: — " unfit for the habitation of paupers."

We were told that the town authorities claimed that it is not in a legal sense an almshouse, and therefore the law relating to the maintenance of children there is not violated.   But it is town property, filled, as we understood, by the permission of the town authorities with a company of improvident and impoverished townspeople, who are, in part, supported by the town.   If the institution is wanting in anything to complete the requirements of a poorhouse, it is a resident superintendent, with authority to control the inmates and insist upon some degree of decent living.

And by that want it is by so much worse than any other poorhouse in the State.

It is doubtful if in our largest cities there are so-called slums, where children are born and reared under more unpromising conditions for their future, than prevail in this unique institution of Danbury.

It is the conviction of the undersigned that giving aid to the town poor in this way encourages pauperism in the adults, and becomes a school of immorality and vice for the children.

But the latter remarks are gratuitous, as our opinion is only asked upon the sanitary condition of the place.

We therefore unhesitatingly declare that in our judgment the building itself is no longer fit for human habitation; that its unfitness and its objectionable surroundings are greatly aggravated by the character of its present occupants, without the supervision of a resident superintendent in authority.   And we further believe that its continuance in its present condition is a menace to the health of the vicinity.

C. A. LINDSLEY, M.D., New Haven,
N. E. WORDIN, M.D., Bridgeport,
Committee for the State Board of Health.

BY-LAWS

OF THE

STATE BOARD OF CHARITIES.

What Officers — Their Election.

SECTION 1. The Board shall have a President and a Secretary who shall be elected by the Board in June or July of each year, at a regular meeting, or at a special meeting called for the purpose.

Terms of Office.

They shall hold their offices until the first day of July in the year next succeeding the year of their elections, and until their successors shall be elected, unless they shall sooner die, resign, or be removed by the Board for cause, upon charges and specifications filed by a member of the Board, after reasonable notice thereof, and full hearing thereon before the Board.

Duty of President.

SEC. 2. It shall be the duty of the President to preside at all meetings of the Board.

May Issue Notices of Meetings.

He may issue notices of meetings of the Board, both regular and special, in the manner hereinafter provided.

To Perform His Duties as a Member, Unless —

He shall, unless excused by vote of the Board, do his part of its work as a member thereof, in addition to his duties as its President.

President Pro T.em.

In his absence from any meeting a President *pro tem.* shall be elected.

Duties of the Secretary.

SEC. 3. It shall be the duty of the Secretary to keep a record of the proceedings of the Board; to conduct its correspondence; to prepare its annual reports; to give notice of its regular meetings; to make, at each regular meeting, and at special meetings when called for, a report of his work since the last preceding regular meeting; to inspect, yearly, the

State Almshouse, and all institutions in which the State has beneficiaries; to procure, so far as possible, the reports of Boards of Charities of other States and of National Conferences of Charities and Corrections, and deposit the same in the office of the Board; and, in general, to perform such duties as the Board shall by vote assign to him as its Secretary.

If a Member, to do Duties as Such in Addition —

If he be a member of the Board, he shall do his part of its work as such member, in addition to his work as its Secretary.

Secretary Pro Tem. — His Duties.

In his absence from any meeting a Secretary *pro tem.* shall be elected, who shall make the record of the proceedings at such meeting, and shall transmit the same to the Secretary within three days thereafter.

The President and Secretary to Bring the Petitions of the Board in Certain Cases.

SEC. 4. The authority of the Board, under the fourth section of the Act entitled *An Act to Provide Homes and Care for Dependent and Neglected Children*, to petition for the commitment of children to the Temporary Homes provided for in said act, shall be exercised by its President and Secretary, as its committee, with the full powers of the Board; petitions brought by them shall be signed in the name of the Board by its Secretary, and shall be countersigned by its President.

Duties of Agents for County Homes.

SEC. 5. It shall be the duty of the special agents appointed by the Board in connection with the work of the County Temporary Homes, to visit family homes in which dependent and neglected children under the charge of the Temporary Homes in the several Counties may be placed, to recommend suitable family homes to the County Boards, and to perform such further duties in connection with the dependent and neglected children under the charge of such Temporary Homes as the Board may prescribe.

Regular Meetings, When and Where Held.

SEC. 6. The regular meetings of the Board shall be held at its office, in Hartford, on the first Wednesday of each month.

Notices of Regular Meetings, When and How to be Given — What to Contain.

Notices of regular meetings shall be given to all members of the Board by mail, postpaid, not less than seven days in advance, exclusive of the first and inclusive of the last day; and shall name the day, date, and hour of meeting; and shall mention any matters of special importance to be acted upon thereat, so far as they may be known to the officer giving the notice at the time of issuing the same; and any member intending to bring forward any matter of special importance at any regular meeting shall file with the Secretary written notice of such intention, with a written statement of the particular matter to be so brought up, sufficient to clearly indicate its character and scope, not less than twelve days before such meeting; but nothing contained in this sixth section shall limit the power of the Board to act upon any matter brought before it at a regular meeting.

Special Meetings, by Whom and Where Called — Not to be at Private Residence, Except —

SEC. 7. Special meetings may be called by the President, the Secretary, or any three members of the Board, at the office of the Board, in Hartford, or at any State institution; but they shall not be called at any private residence, except with the written consent of all the members of the Board previously obtained.

Notices of Special Meetings, When and How Given — What to Contain.

. Notices of special meetings shall be given to all members of the Board by mail, postpaid, or by telegram, not less than three days in advance, exclusive of the first and inclusive of the last day; and shall name the day, date, hour, and place of meeting; and shall mention the purpose of calling the same.

Limitation of Action At.

No matter not included in the purpose of the meeting, as stated in the notice, shall be acted upon thereat, except by the unanimous consent of all members of the Board, both present and absent.

Quorum.

SEC. 8. Three members of the Board shall constitute a quorum for business at its meetings.

Order of Business.

The order of business shall be as follows:

1. Reading the minutes of the last meeting.

2. Secretary's report of his work since the last regular meeting — at regular meetings only, unless called for.

3. Reports by members of their work since the last regular meeting — at regular meetings only, unless called for — to be made in the order of their appointments; and to be reduced to writing, and filed with the Secretary, when required by the vote of the Board.

4. Unfinished business.

5. New business, including, at regular meetings, assignments of members, or officers, to visitations, required by the statutes, or by the Board, during the month.

REPORT

—OF THE—

BOARD OF EDUCATION

OF THE BLIND,

—FOR THE—

STATE OF CONNECTICUT.

FISCAL YEARS ENDING SEPTEMBER 30th, 1897 & 1898.

PRESS OF
INDUSTRIAL HOME FOR THE BLIND,
HARTFORD, CONN.

FIFTH ANNUAL REPORT

—OF THE—

SECRETARY OF THE BOARD OF EDUCATION

OF THE BLIND.

To, His Excellency, George E. Lounsbury, Governor, State of Connecticut

SIR:—

I have the honor to submit herewith the Fifth Annual Report of the State Board of Education of the Blind.

During the fiscal year ending September 30th, 1898, the number of State pupils coming under the care and supervision of the State Board of Education of the Blind was sixty-nine (69). Of this number, eighteen (18) attended the Perkins Institution for the Blind, at South Boston, Mass.

Twenty-five (25) were at the Kindergarten, one (1) being a day pupil, twenty-five (25) at the Industrial Home for the Blind and one whose attendance was divided, between the Perkins Institution and the Industrial Home. Of this number three were absent a portion of the time.

Assuring your Excellency, that the education of the young children in the Kindergarten, and the older children at the Perkins Institution, is progressing under the most favorable conditions attainable, we must refer those who would learn more concerning the methods employed for their instruction and the results obtained, to previous reports, the last of which will be found bound with the present report. These children have crossed the danger line and for the present are in a safe harbor protected by barriers raised by the humanity of a past generation, and the enlightened sympathy of the present. Our duty of the hour is to take our place by the side of those who were the children of yesterday, but who to-day are battling with the waves outside the breakwater. Waves made angry by the same spirit of selfishness that combated the establishment of free schools for the seeing, and has disputed every advancing step made by the vanguard of enlighten-ment, humanity and civilization. Waves that are made more angry in the impending struggle, by error born of prejudice and piqued by successive failures, into a persistent opposition. Six years ago the genius of Connecticut awakened to her duty, decided that she would no longer leave her blind children to a fate determined by chance, but that henceforth they should receive every advantage that had been gained and secured to her children whose days were brightened by the sunlight. Experience had taught her that it was not enough to establish free schools in which the children of the poor, might stand side by side with the children of the rich without being classified as paupers, but there must be a Board of Education established, charged with a duty of securing the attendance in such schools, of the children of slothful, careless or selfish parents.

What measure then in the light of experience would be more likely to secure the best results in the case of her less fortunate children, than to. establish a Board of Education of the Blind? A Board, one member of which should be a woman, who with a mother's heart, stirred by tender and loving solicitude, would take in her arms each little neglected, sightless child, and with a knowledge prompted by love, fan the God-given spark of intelligence until it should illuminate the mind and thus strengthen and equip her little charge to begin its journey along the dark and sunless path, it must soon learn to walk alone. And when her charge, a young man grown, should reach the shore of the unknown and sunless sea, and be compelled to launch his frail barque upon its waves, he shall not, at this, the most criti-cal time of his life, be deserted and abandoned to founder upon unknown shoals, for there shall be at hand a pilot, who, as master of his own ship, has sailed this sea for twenty years. A pilot, who, with chart in hand, shall point out the dangerous reefs, encourage and sustain her charge until, with confidence born of knowledge, he can be safely trusted with the helm. Nor should this work be undertaken until there shall be wise and just provisions made to safeguard the interest of the people.

Hence as members of this Board, the chosen chief magistrates of the State shall be entrusted to exercise a just and wise discretion and stand as guardians of the interest of the people, to prevent all unnecessary or unwarranted expenditures of public funds. Thus fortified, the genius of Connecticut stands forth the champion of this new and sacred trust.

Two years ago the Connecticut Legislature appointed a commission charged with the duty of examining into state expenses and making a report to the General Assembly of 1899, pointing out how these expenses could be reduced. This commission in order to save a little money for the State, proposes, among other saving measures, to withdraw the support which the state has hitherto granted to our Industrial Home.

Before considering what has been accomplished since the organization of the State Board of Education of the Blind, it will be well to understand how the blind people of Connecticut fared when everything was left to chance, and it was the business of no one to look after their interests, or to see that the money expended by the State accomplished the intended purpose.

A glance at the record shows that the number of State beneficiaries, up to the time the State Board of Education of the Blind was created, was fifty-seven, covering a period of twenty-eight years.

All of these were young children when they entered the Perkins Institution at Boston, and for every pupil the State paid three hundred dollars a year or any fractional part of a year. Of these, nine remained one year or less.

It is safe to say that over $11,000 expended by the State for the children who staid two years or less was practically thrown away.

The twelve who did not stay out their full time undoubtedly fell far short of the benefit they would have received had they completed their course. Of the whole number, not one-third as many became self-sustaining as the records of the Industrial Home will show as the results of its labors during the past five years.

This commission, however, proposes to dig a grave and bury therein the new born hopes and aspirations of the Blind. They have on their side this advantage, most people do not understand nor realize what it is possible for blind people to accomplish; therefore, when they say that what we claim can be done is not practical, and that we are attempting more than we can accomplish at the State's expense, they quite readily obtain converts to their ideas.

For example, this commission says in its report that our printing department is not and cannot be a success. It will not be pretended that more than two members of this commission have ever visited our Institution and then only for a flying visit, nor will it be pretended that either of these two gentlemen personally know anything about the printing business.

When this claim was made by one of these gentlemen two years ago in the Senate we answered it by inviting representatives from leading printing and publishing offices in Hartford to visit our printing department and judge for themselves. The Case, Lockwood & Brainard Co., Fowler, Miller & Co., and the printing establishment of C. M. Gaines complied with our request and as a result of their visit we were able to publish in the Hartford papers the following:

"This is to certify that the undersigned, by the request of the officials of the Industrial Home for the Blind at Nos. 334 and 336 Wethersfield Ave., Hartford, Conn., have this day visited and inspected the job printing department of said Institution, and we there saw a number of blind persons engaged in various kinds of work in job printing. Two were feeding power presses, two were printing on hand presses, another was binding pamphlets and showed his ability to take the work from the hands of the pressman and do all that was necessary to complete the work, making use of the wire staple binding machine in so doing, others were folding and making packages ready for the mail.

"The work was well done and in our opinion it is possible and practicable for one seeing person to keep from six to eight blind persons profitably employed in the job printing business. We also inspected the plant and outfit and upon being told that the cost did not exceed twenty-four hundred dollars, we are of the opinion that it was purchased exceedingly cheap and that the results attained fully justify the outlay."

MARCUS A. CASE,
Vice President C. L. & B. Co.
J. E. FLANIGAN,
Foreman, Fowler & Miller Co.
CHAS. M. GAINES,
Printer.

Hartford, May 28, 1897.

The volume of business done by the printing department, can be roughly estimated, from the fact, that in addition to over $800 charged on the books during the last year and four months, the cash receipts reported by Ella B. Kendrick, amounted to $6,439.17

NOTE.—Ella B. Kendrick, who makes the following statement and has charge of the work done by the Blind in the printing office and is also editor of the magazine, published by the Industrial Home for the Blind, had eight years experience in the printing business, before entering the employment of the Institution and no one can be better qualified to judge than she now is of the practicability of employing Blind people in the printing and publishing business.

"Before assuming the management of the Printing Department of the Industrial Home for the Blind, I had never been associated with blind people and had no knowledge of their capabilities. In fact, I rather shared the opinion prevalent among seeing people, that the Blind must of necessity be partially helpless. Consequently, when Mr. Cleaveland, in his enthusiasm, talked of his plans, I was sceptical, although willing to do all in my power to assist him to realize his hopes.

After nearly a year and a half in the work, coming into contact with many young blind people, who display all the different characteristics which belong to seeing people, I am satisfied in my own mind that under the right conditions a very large percentage of the Blind can be taught occupations to which they are adapted and that they can become self-supporting.

We have in our department young women who feed power presses, running at the same speed that our seeing people use; they do the same work that our seeing people do, which is the work of an average printing office. We publish a magazine, TALKS AND TALES, and the work rendered necessary by this keeps many of the blind pupils busy. One of the pupils gathers the forms, another we depend upon to stitch the books (she using a power wire stitcher) and we have also pupils who assist in covering the magazines.

All our pupils have learned to fold sheets and their work is well and rapidly done. Two of our young women operate a type-writer, using the same keyboard that seeing people use and doing good work.

The envelopes in which we send out our magazines, are all addressed by these pupils on a type-writer that is used by seeing persons and with no special arrangements for the use of the Blind.

It has been proven that our Blind girls can use type-writers exactly as seeing people do, learning the keyboard as we all learn the keyboard of the piano. They operate their machines with neatness and speed, taking care of them without assistance. After they become familiar with one machine they can readily use a different make. Feeding a cylinder press is also another work that our pupils have demonstrated can be done by the Blind.

There are some parts of the work in a printing office that blind people cannot do, but I speak with conviction when I state that, given the same adaptability to the work that we require in a seeing person, blind people *can* earn a living in a printing office. The only difficulty in their way is the lack of faith on the part of seeing people.

Frequently, the question is asked me, "Would anyone employ a blind person in a printing office?"

I have but one reply to that question: "With my personal knowledge of the ability of the Blind, *I* would."

I repeat, the only obstacle in the way of the blind person is the prejudice of the seeing person."

ELLA B. KENDRICK,
Business Manager Printing Department,
Editor TALKS AND TALES.

Hartford, Feb. 23, 1899.

"I have had about seventeen years experience in the printing business, have been foreman in several printing offices and was foreman in the office of the "New England Home," when in existence, for four years.

Before I became foreman of the printing department of the Industrial Home for the Blind at Hartford, Conn., I should never have thought it possible for blind people to do anything in a printing office, that would be of any practical value; but, with the opportunity I have had as foreman of this department for the last year and a half to judge, I now fully endorse all that has been said in the foregoing statement of Ella B. Kendrick, which I have carefully read, and should not hesitate if I was conducting a printing office to employ Blind people.

It may be thought by some that there is more danger of blind people being injured by machinery run by power in a printing office, than there would be, to seeing people, but what danger there would otherwise be, has been eliminated. The belting that runs the power printing presses and stitcher all come up through the floor, instead of the over-head system, and the gearings of all the machinery are covered so as to secure them from injury."   D. L. HONDLOW.

Hartford, Conn.. Feb. 24, 1899.

"I am requested by Mr. Cleaveland, to give the opinion I have formed as the result of my observations of the practicability of employing the blind in the printing business. I have been the owner and publisher of several newspapers, and have had seven years experience in the business in every department from devil, to editor. For the last two years and a half I have been editor and part owner of the "Farmington Valley Herald, and Journal. '

I have been in this printing office and seen the blind people at work scores of times; no one could have been more sceptical than I was of the possibility of a blind person working successfully in a printing office.

The foregoing statement by Ella B. Kendrick, has been read by me and I fully endorse all that she has said, concerning the work in this department by the blind. '   JOHN A. NORTH.

Just at this point we think will be a good place to reproduce the following:

"AS ITHERS SEE US."

A COMMUNICATION FROM THE PEN OF THE REV. F. F. THAYER, PASTOR OF THE BAPTIST CHURCH OF AYER, MASS., TAKEN FROM THE FITCHBURG "EVENING STAR," OF JAN. 24, 1899.

To the citizens of Ayer :—

"Believing that our townspeople who have of late shown their regard in a most substantial manner for one of our number, Edwin E. Warren, would like to know something of the Institution to which he has gone as the result of their kindly aid, I have taken the liberty to write the following as my impressions of that Institution: We arrived there at 1 o'clock, Saturday, January 14, and were invited into the music room by the superintendent. This we found a very delightful apartment, several pianos and other musical instruments being there, and used by the students, to many of whom we were introduced. Later in the dining room we found every thing in perfect order, and it is safe to say that after four hours riding, Mr. Warren and myself did justice to the very bountiful dinner provided. The kitchen was an equally attractive room and with the dining room constituted an excellent place to live. At 2.30 we had the pleasure of once more meeting F. E. Cleaveland, President of the Institution, whom we met a few weeks before in Ayer at the concert so beautifully rendered by students of the Institution. They were at this time preparing for a similar trip to New Jersey. * * * I was greatly impressed by the kind-hearted and loving care shown by Mr. Cleaveland and his assistants. In one room young ladies were making baskets, in another running printing presses under the direction of Mrs. E. B. Kendrick, editor of their monthly magazine. Across the hallway was the store and a very bright, though blind young woman, dealing out goods to her customers in a manner so quick and ready as to put to shame some of our clerks who are blessed with sight. Next, in the rear, we found men making brooms and mattresses, and caning chairs. This was the department where Mr. Warren is to receive instruction from a blind man. In a few months Mr. Warren will be able to make from eighteen to twenty brooms a day, and so let the housekeepers of Ayer be ready to buy their brooms from our fellow citizen, when Edwin comes marching home again.''

What follows above the signature of Mr. Thayer is a statement showing contributions received amounting to $186.85 to assist Mr. Warren who was a young blind man living in Ayer, Mass., and struggling to exist by occasionally getting a job of sawing wood.

The action of the reverend gentleman and other friends of the young man was the result of the visit to the town of Ayer, of the concert company from our Industrial Home for the Blind at Hartford, Conn., and the opportunity thus offered to explain the work of our Institution and the needs of the Blind. This is only a notable instance of what is happening right along, the only occasion for regret being our inability to keep pace with the demands upon our Institution.

This commission in its report gives as one reason why the Industrial Home for the Blind should not be continued in Connecticut, that there is no such institution in Vermont, New Hampshire, Maine nor Rhode Island, and that Connecticut can send its pupils, as these other states do, to the Perkins Institute at Boston.

They fail to inform the General Assembly however, that no person over 18 years of age will be received as a pupil at that Institution and that our Industrial Home simply undertakes to cover the ground that the Institution at Philadelphia, which they commend, covers, and does not trench upon the ground covered by the Perkins Institution at Boston, but on the contrary, we send our own state pupils, after they finish their course in the Kindergarten and primary department, to the Perkins Institution.

Again, it is no argument to advance to the citizens of Connecticut, that they should wait for other New England states to perform their duty. Connecticut is proud of the part its citizens have taken in the progress of civilization and works of philanthropy. It was the citizens of Connecticut who formulated the first written constitution; it was in Connecticut that the first Institution in America, for the education of the deaf and dumb was established. It was a citizen of Connecticut, Mrs. Harriet Beecher Stowe, author of Uncle Tom's Cabin, who made converts by the thousands to the doctrine of anti-slavery and thus made the abolition of slavery possible; it was a citizen of Connecticut, John Brown of Torrington, who drew his sword and cut the Gordion knot that fastened the system of slavery to the backs of a people who had declared for freedom; it was also citizens of Connecticut who stoned the seminary where a brave Connecticut lady admitted a colored girl to equal privileges with white children, and it was a General Assembly of the State of Connecticut, that years after that act purged the State of this disgrace.

Now, when we are considering the advance work that is being done in this state for the Blind, is it any discredit to Connecticut that, at the recent bi-ennial meeting of the American Association of the Instructors of the Blind, where representatives from the old established Institutions for the Blind in Boston, New York and Philadelphia, as well as from all parts of the United States and Canada, were present, that a representative of this State was chosen chairman of a committee appointed to wait upon the Congress of the United States to secure legislation which by resolution of that assembly was deemed desirable. *

Let us now introduce some statements from those who know and realize, better far than any seeing person can possibly do, the good the Industrial Home for the Blind at Hartford, Conn., is accomplishing along the line of the special work it has undertaken. We refer to those, the barren monotony of whose lives spent in an unending night, has been broken by the appearance of a ray of light which, through this Institution, has been shed upon their pathway.

For obvious reasons, in some instances, we refrain from giving more than the initials of some of the persons to whom these statements refer.

I am acquainted with John Sullivan of Willimantic, who became totally blind about nine years ago, while employed by the N. Y., N. H. & H. R. R.

2

Co., through the carelessness of a fellow workman by the premature explosion of dynamite.

I applied for his admission to the Industrial Home for the Blind at Hartford, Connecticut, where he learned the trade of broom making. For the past four years, he has been carrying on business in Willimantic and has earned for himself a comfortable livelihood. This young man was without means and friendless, and but, for the opportunity thus afforded him by the Industrial Home for the Blind, would have been compelled to spend the remainder of his days in the poor house, to which he had already made application."

A. C. ANDREWS,
Dealer in Music and Musical Instruments.

Willimantic, Conn., Feb. 15, 1899.

"My daughter, S—— C——, who has been blind since her childhood, was educated at the Perkins Institution for the Blind at Boston. After losing my husband her support and care fell upon me.

My health for years has been very poor, but for a long time I labored faithfully to provide a home for us both, and whenever employed, I was compelled to leave her at home alone, as I had no other children to stay with her. No mother, until she has been in my place, can imagine the anxiety I felt for the safety of my child on these occasions. At the alarm of fire, it seemed as though my heart would cease to beat until I had counted the strokes of the fire alarm bell. The thought of dying and leaving my daughter alone in the world was simply unbearable, but now all is changed and this change has come to us on account of the opportunity which the Industrial Home for the Blind at Hartford has afforded my daughter to earn her own living. She is in every way a different person. Then she was the reverse of the animated, happy, and self reliant girl she now is. She now earns her own living and for nearly ten months in the year, is paid a salary of six dollars a week, and many times when her mother has been ill and unable to work, she has furnished the money to meet home expenses, and how anyone can wish to deprive the Blind, of the benefits which this Institution confers, by withholding from it, the support and patronage it deserves, I am unable to comprehend."

MRS. EMMA CLARK

Hartford, February 16, 1899.

I am acquainted with C———— O————, formerly of Georgetown, Conn. He became totally blind some eight or nine years ago.

He learned the trade of broom and mattress making at the Industrial Home for the Blind at Hartford, Conn., and has been carrying on business for himself in Georgetown, and later in New Canaan, Conn., for the last four years, maintaining himself and family, consisting of himself, his wife and his mother.

I received a letter from his wife, who is my sister, less than four weeks ago, and she wrote that C————— was getting on finely with his business."

W. E. OFFICER,

Wethersfield, Conn., Feb. 16, 1899.

NOTE.—When this young man became blind he was the only son of a widow who depended upon him for support. He applied to the Perkins Institute at Boston for admission only to be told that he was just too old to be admitted, owing to the rule which had fixed an 18 year limit.

In despair at what seemed to him to be the failure of his last chance to escape from being dependent upon his mother or spending his days in the poor house, he attempted to take his own life, but was discovered in time to prevent the consummation of his purpose. It was shortly after. that our Industrial Home was started and he became its first pupil.

"I was formerly a pupil at the Industrial Home for the Blind in Hartford, Conn. I there learned the lesson that a blind person by the cultivation of self-reliance and business habits could readily become self-sustaining. Since I ceased to be a pupil at the Institution, though totally blind, I have during the past three years, in addition to supporting myself, saved from my salary an average of three dollars per week."

CHARLOTTE M. HINMAN,

W. C. A. Building, Church St.

Hartford, Conn., Feb. 15, 1899.

"G———— P————, a former pupil of the Industrial Home for the Blind, after leaving the Institution commenced the manufacture of brooms, with the assistance of the Institution, in Danbury Conn., where he remained in business about six months, and then removed to Bridgeport.

When he entered the Institution his wife wrote him, that on account of his blindness she had been advised that it would not be judicious nor wise for her to live with him again. He was greatly depressed with this double affliction, and for several months was unable to apply himself in a satisfactory manner to the acquirement of a trade.

Since leaving the Institution, his wife has consented to live with him again, and they are now located in Bridgeport, Conn., where he expects, as soon as a suitable place can be procured, to begin again the manufacture of brooms.

In a conversation with me to-day, he stated that when working at his trade, he could make eighteen first-class brooms in a day. These brooms when disposed of to consumers at the usual prices, would yield a profit of $1.50 per dozen.

JOHN A. NORTH.

Collinsville, Conn., Feb. 15, 1899.

"I lost my sight when a mere child. After I left the Perkins Institution until I became a pupil at the Industrial Home for the Blind in Hartford, Conn., my home was first with one kind friend and then with another who provided for my needs. But while I was always kindly treated and well provided for, I longed to be able to take care of myself and to enjoy the satisfaction of knowing that I was neither dependent upon others nor expected at all times to conceal my preferences, fearing they might come in conflict with the plans which others had made for me. No one can imagine, what a source of happiness it has been to be able to feel that I could at last realize this dream and hope of my life.

I received voice culture, while at the Industrial Home for the Blind, which has enabled me during the past three years to support myself. I have been able not only to support myself, but have saved from my earnings a little over four hundred dollars."

EMMA L. PATTERSON.

Feb. 18, 1899, 3024 14th Street, N. W., Washington. D. C.

NOTE.—The advantages received by this young lady at the Industrial Home, were not limited to the development and cultivation of a naturally sweet and musical contralto voice; but, she acquired a good practical knowledge of printing which should her voice ever fail, would enable her to still maintain herself.

D. L. HONDLOW,
Foreman, Printing Dept.

"William D. Smith, was a pupil of the Industrial Home for the Blind at Hartford, Conn., and I was his instructor. He was a married man, having a wife and several children and was totally blind.

He was a very apt pupil and learned the trade of broom making thoroughly in less than four months.

We have kept up a correspondence since he returned to his home. He informs me that he has established for himself a good business and is taking care of himself and family.

I have also been in correspondence with Harry E. Whitten, a former pupil of the Institution, who was also a married man with a family. He also was totally blind.

When he left the Institution, he could make from eight to ten brooms a day and with the help of his children to sort his corn, would be able to make from twelve to fourteen brooms a day, which when sold to the consumer, would yield a profit of from a dollar and a half to a dollar and seventy-five cents per dozen.

From his letters I learn that he has not been quite as successful as Mr. Smith, for want of capital to procure stock, but under favorable circumstances would undoubtedly be self-sustaining,"

ARTHUR SKINNER, 16 Preston St.

Hartford, Conn., Feb. 15, 1899.

NOTE.—The case of Mr. Whitten was one that would appeal to every person capable of any feeling for his fellow man, for in the statement which he made when he appealed for admission he says, "I lost my house by fire, my wife was removed to the hospital in a critical condition, and I became blind all within three months.

The following correspondence between Mr. Smith, Mr. Cleaveland, President of the Institution and Mr. Hondlow, foreman of the Printing Department, tell the whole story better than we can tell it in volumes.

It contains the whole argument for the existence and support of the Industrial Department of our Institution.

"F. E. Cleaveland, President of the Pioneers Institution for the Blind, Hartford, Conn.

DEAR SIR—I am a young man, have been blind for the last ten years. Not until two years ago did I learn of the Institution for the Blind at South Boston, Mass., at which time I made application, only to learn that I was too late. * * * I am strong and active, handy with tools, having done things that have puzzled seeing people. I am not afraid of work, having gone about sawing and splitting cord wood, but I am denied even that, the dealers doing it cheaper by means of their horses. I now submit the above for your careful consideration and humbly ask, if there is any possibility of my being instructed in some art in your Institution that I may be enabled in the future to support myself. Can furnish references from either clergy or business men. Hoping that the only ray of hope that remains may not be crushed by your reply, I am your obedient servant,"

W. D. SMITH, P. O. Box 120.

Sept. 6, 1897.

To the foregoing the writer sent the following reply:

"MY DEAR MR. SMITH:

Replying to your favor of the sixth inst., just received, I would say that we will most gladly welcome you in our Institution just as soon as it will be possible for us to receive you without placing a greater strain upon its resources than they are able to bear.

If our young people meet with the usual success this fall in their concert work, or if the magazine, the publication of which we have just commenced, is favorably received by the public, we can undoubtedly make a place for you this winter.''   Most cordially yours,

                                        F. E. CLEAVELAND.

MY DEAR MR. HONDLOW:

"Five·months have passed since I left Wethersfield Avenue and not one week has passed that I did not at some time think of the promise so faithfully made that I should write and let you know how I was getting along, and cannot blame you if you have long since come to the conclusion, that the little Scotchman never intended to write at all. But after all I am convinced if you knew my circumstances you would be charitable enough to excuse the delay. I was without a dollar, requiring a workshop, machinery and broom supplies, and the worst of the jig was, the people did not think I had been long enough away to decently look over the Institution, instead of learning a business that was intended to support my family, but nevertheless I got what I required and started to make brooms last month. I have got small orders from most of the merchants and they have promised me all their trade when they sell the stock on hand. They all like my brooms and I have just received an order for twenty-five dozen from the paper company here, and if they suit I will get the trade. It is the second largest paper company in the country and use a pile of brooms and they pay a good price for them.

  *   *   *   *   *   ~   *   *

Hoping this may reach you in good season, I am yours very truly,''

                                        W. D. SMITH,
                                        P. O. Box, 120.

Aug. 23, 1898.

"At the request of the President of the Institute for the Blind at Hartford, Conn., I visited the following named blind persons, who have received instruction at the Industrial Home. My first call was on James Girken at 1578 State St., New Haven, Conn. I found that he was out on business, but Mrs. Girken showed me his shop and in answer to my queries as to how he was getting on with his broom manufacturing business, replied: 'Very nicely indeed.' He is supporting his family, consisting of a wife and two children. He has a horse and wagon which he uses for delivering his goods and at the same time he takes orders for chairs to be caned by Burdett Knapman, who was also formerly a pupil of the Industrial Home at Hartford. Mrs. Girken was enthusiastic in her praise of the Institution and what it had done for her husband. Mr. Girken occupies as a work shop a store immediately under the tenement in which he lives. It is fitted up with all the appliances and machinery used for broom making, all of which

I am told, was furnished him by money raised by the Industrial Home, to give him a business start after he had finished learning his trade at the Institution.''

"I then called upon William Arion of 21 Avon St., New Haven, Conn. I had seen him at the Institution nearly two years ago and he recognized my voice at once. He also has a shop for broom making and chair caning nicely fitted up, and he has no trouble in getting all the work that he can do. He is self-sustaining and he spoke of the Institution and what it had done for him in the highest of terms, and when told that it was having a struggle to continue its work, he exclaimed, 'If I could do anything to help it along, I would go on my knees from New Haven to Hartford.' He regarded the Institution as one of the greatest possible blessings that had ever come to the assistance of the blind.''

"My next call was on Thomas Donahue, corner of State and Newhall streets, New Haven. Mrs. Donahue met me and when I asked her how Thomas was getting along in his business, she said, 'Very well, indeed, he is out in the shop at work, now.' She added that he was very contented. I was then shown his shop which was built for his use in the rear of his dwelling. There was no light in the shop but he was busily working. He has a large family of children one of whom accompanied me with a lantern His shop was well fitted up with machinery and tools for broom making and in answer to my question asking how he was getting on, he said that he had all that he could do and was supporting his family by his own labor. He said, 'It was a God-send to me when I met Mr. Cleaveland at a fair the blind people gave in New Haven' adding 'If I had not met him I should have been crazy or dead before this time, for then I was sitting around brooding over my condition; without exercise my weight had increased until it was a burden, but since I have been at work at my trade learned at the Industrial Home in Hartford, I have got back to my old weight where I was when I worked at the Winchester Fire Arms shop before I became blind. The Winchesters buy all the brooms they use of me, and I supply the leading hotels of the city and the clock shops.' He also mentioned other customers. Mr. Donahue also spoke in the warmest terms of the Institution and said he would do anything in his power to help it on in the work it was doing for the Blind.''

ALEXANDER ANGUS, 31 Warner St.,

Hartford, Conn., Feb. 17, 1899.

NOTE.—William Arion, referred to by Mr. Angus, was not a state pupil, as he was too old to be admitted, but while at the Institution he earned, besides his support, a sufficient amount to purchase his broom machinery and tools, with which he started in business. The Institution also furnished

Thomas, Donahue instruction, board, washing and mending for a year without receiving any compensation from the state therefor, he too, being considered at the time, too old to come within the provisions of the state law.

"In January of '98, the Connecticut Industrial Home for the Blind, opened its doors to Miss Grace Copeland, of Brooklyn, Conn.

Sickness had deprived her of hearing, and she was fast becoming blind. Owing to her last misfortune she had failed to gain entrance to the American Institute for the Deaf.

Under the instructions of the undersigned she was enabled to thoroughly learn the art of chair caning. On leaving us in June she had mastered the trade, and was equiped by the Institution with tools and cane for a proper start in business. Since that time she has written several letters to her teacher, speaking with much feeling of the great happiness which has come to her since she has been able to do something toward her own support.

In a recent letter she speaks of having finished seven chairs and was expecting more. All her letters breathe the gratitude she feels towards the Institution for placing within her grasp this means of self-support."

C. M. HINMAN.

"I became blind when a mere lad. I graduated at the Perkins Institution for the Blind, but was not fitted by my instruction there to enter upon any industry or employment by which I could earn my living, and I did nothing towards my support for seven years. I was living at the home of my father, when my brother-in-law, after visiting the Industrial Home for the Blind at Hartford, Conn., made arragements for my admission. Four months after I was admitted, I began by my services to pay my own way, and have since earned on an average of $2.50 per week and my living expenses.

For the past nineteen months I have been using my spare time to study law. During this time I have transcribed into Braille, which is a point system used by the blind in reading, and I have mastered the contents of the following law books: Harriman on Contracts, Bigelow on Torts, May on Criminal Law, Benjamin on Sales, Mecham on Agency, Schonler on Domestic Relations, The Practice Art of Connecticut, Andrews and Fowler's Digest of Connecticut Reports of 1896.

I have also transcribed into Braille, about one hundred and fifty legal forms, with which I have become more or less familiar. I expect to apply for admission to the Bar, and I feel confident that I will succeed in my chosen profession.

I am sincerely grateful to the Institution and its management for the opportunity that has been afforded me to carry forward my life plans."

A. J. HOSKING.

"I was in the employ of the New York & New Haven Railroad Co., as Baggage Master at East Hampton, Conn., when I lost my sight. I was then about nineteen years of age. I applied to be admitted to the Perkins Institution for the Blind, but was refused admission on the ground that I was over eighteen years of age. I afterwards heard of and was admitted to the Industrial Home for the Blind at Hartford, Conn.

At this Institution I received instruction in music, and it is my expectation to earn my living by teaching music. While at the Industrial Home for the Blind I learned to print and bind pamphlets, that is, I could feed a power press, bind pamphlets on the power stitcher and do many other things about a printing office, so that if my preference ran that way I could undoubtedly earn my living at the printing business.

I am at present earning from four to five dollars a week, in addition to my living expenses."   · HARRY L. BILL.

"Prior to my admission to the Industrial Home for the Blind at Hartford, I was living with my uncle in Wethersfield, Conn, this place being my old home. My uncle was giving me my living as I was able to do nothing for my support.

At the Industrial Home besides working in the mattress shop, I was instructed in vocal and instrumental music and since leaving the Institution, I have been self-sustaining. I am at present receiving a salary of five dollars per week and my expenses, with a chance of receiving more, contingent upon the profits of the business in which I am engaged.

The one thing which I consider was of the greatest value to me was the determination which I formed at the Institution to make a success of life and I am satisfied that every blind man, who has half a chance, with the right amount of push, can do this."

HARRY C. GREEN,

—|—

MARGARET BILL, Witness.

"My home is in New Haven, Conn. I became blind when about six years of age. Prior to my being admitted to that Industrial Home for the Blind at Hartford, Conn., I was supported by my parents. For nearly three years since I ceased being a State pupil at the Institution, I have earned my own living and an average of $4.50 per week. I am not very robust, and at present in quite poor health.

I am satisfied that nothing but ill health, will prevent my continuing to be self-sustaining, and I give the Industrial Home for the Blind full credit for giving me the chance to accomplish what I have."

THOMAS V. McCOY,

—|—

MARGARET BILL, Witness.

"I wish to state that I was a pupil at the Industrial Home for the Blind at Hartford, Conn. That while there I received instruction in music and that since ceasing to be a State pupil, I have had employment that has enabled me to support myself. With the exception of about two months in the summer, I am able to earn, and have earned from four to five dollars a week, over and above my expenses.

I know that the Industrial Home, at Hartford, has been a great help to other blind people. When I was in New Haven, about New Year's I saw Burdette Knapman, who is a friend of mine, who was also a pupil at the Industrial Home for the Blind. He told me he was doing a good business and I know he is earning his own living.

EDWARD NORTHROP.

—|—

MARGARET BILL, Witness.

"I learned the trade of broom making at the Industrial Home for the Blind at Hartford, Conn., and now consider myself competent to earn my own living. As soon as I can get a start in the way of broom machinery tools and broom material.

I am working for the Institution now and have been for the past few months, earning from two to three dollars a week. The Institution has been of great assistance to me and I am very grateful for the help I have received, as I have not been able myself to make any return to it for what it has done for me except by my labor. I am not totally blind, but so nearly so, that I am compelled to work as blind people do, and what sight I now have is gradually failing."

M. J. GILMORE.

—|—

MARGARET BILL, Witness.

NOTE:—The following letter was received from Miss Grace Copeland after the statement concerning her, by her teacher, Miss Hinman, was in print, but believing our readers would like to hear direct from our only pupil who was deaf, dumb and almost entirely blind, we have concluded to print the letter just received.

BROOKLYN, CONN., FEB. 18, 1899.

Mr. Cleaveland,

"Dear Sir:—The Institution has done a great deal for me. At the Kindergarten I learned to knit and crochet, and make hammocks. I also learned a little about sewing, and received the first lessons in chair caning there. Then I finished learning chair caning at the Institution, and when I came home last June, the Institution gave me a good start in business, by providing me with a complete outfit of tools and material, and I have earned quite a little since I came home, by caning chairs and crocheting slippers. And I cannot begin to tell you how happy it makes me to know that I am really earning something towards my own support. I am *very very, grateful* to those who have done so much for me. May God bless and prosper the Institution which is doing so much for the Blind."

Yours very gratefully,
GRACE M. COPELAND.

"The Connecticut Industrial Home has recently taken up the new industry of basket making, which seems to be a departure of great promise for future helpfulness for the Blind girls.

An Indian woman was employed for two months, who taught them to make many different kinds of fancy baskets. Now they are going on with the work with very little help from one who can see, and after sufficient practice they will undoubtedly be able to do without help.

One great advantage of this work is that it can be carried on in their homes or boarding places. As one of the young ladies said recently, 'There is no place like this. The Perkins Institute educates them, but then they go home and sit down and do nothing, now we will have something to do to help at least toward our own support.'

Another advantage in their work is that it is light and pleasant and the girls enjoy it and consider it a recreation after the harder work of the printing office. Those who have the taste for it are studying music, both piano and violin, which will be of incalculable benefit in their after lives."

MISS M. E. GORHAM, Girls' Preceptress.

Among the pupils who finished their course of instruction in the Industrial Department of the Institution last June, were two young men totally blind, one named Watson Higgins, the other Samuel Brooks, both from Greenwich, Conn.

Mr. Higgins was strong and became an expert broom maker, but Mr. Brooks was of a delicate constitution. Both, before they entered the Institution, were wholly dependent upon friends for support. With money raised by the Institution, a fine shop was fitted up with machinery and appliances for broom making and chair caning, for these two young men, and they started in with a flourishing business.

The writer has learned through Mr. Higgins and the friends of Mr. Brooks, that while Mr. Higgins is going on with business at the shop as usual, Mr. Brooks has removed his chair caning business to the house of his sister, where he makes his home. There is no question about Mr. Higgins being self-sustaining, and while Mr. Brooks lives with his sister, his time will be occupied and he will contribute very largely to his support, as I am informed he has plenty of work to do. But if this home should fail him and our Industrial Home was not in existence to receive him, this delicate young man, whose gentle, Christian spirit has won all hearts, would be doomed to end his days in the poor house, as he has not the physical ability to carry on any business by himself.

Thomas Connolley of Southington, Conn., another pupil of the Industrial Department, who finished his course of instruction last June, is in business for himself in Southington, and in course of conversation with the Town Clerk of Southington to-day, (Feb. 24,) the writer was assured that Connolley was self-supporting. Connolley for many years was an inmate of the poor house in Southington. He is a man of middle age, and his support might have cost the town of Southington during the remainder of his life, more than the instruction necessary to make ten blind men self-sustaining, would cost at the Industrial Home.

Two of the former pupils of the Industrial Department, namely, P. K. Root and Rose Nichols, gained their sight to such an extent that they have been able to secure employment as seeing people, the former as a traveling agent of the Singer Sewing Machine Co.; the latter as a domestic.

Two others, whom we will not mention by name, have not up to the present time, succeeded in becoming self-sustaining, the cause in neither case being lack of sight. One is afflicted by the same disease or condition of mind, which operates to make the career of seeing people unsuccessful, that is, using plain language, the only reason which the writer can assign, is a want of disposition to put forth an effort to succeed, and an indisposition to follow anything that requires any amount of labor or application. The other one has ambition enough for two people, but is lacking in good judgment, a character frequently met with in the seeing world, and possessed by persons usually spoken of as a "Jack of all trades and master of none."

THE DARK SIDE.

The reader of the foregoing statements, would undoubtedly, if he had an opportunity, ask these questions: Have all the Blind people who have become pupils of this Industrial Home, been successful? Are there no failures to record?

We should be compelled to answer, that there have been a few cases in which self-support thus far has not been attained, but the history of these cases furnishes the best argument for the continuance of the Industrial Home, as will be readily agreed to by the reader.

Two of the cases the writer has in mind, like Mr. Connolley, spent years in town poor houses. Both are able-bodied men, both after learning broom making have been started in business for themselves, one by the Institution, and the other by the selectmen of the town. Either of these men could have succeeded as easily as any of those above mentioned. Had the Industrial Home been open to them, when they first lost their sight, before they lost their ambition and self-respect, both of these men would have scorned to have received assistance from the town. Having once been supported by the town however, and knowing that they have only to ask for assistance to receive it, I am told that they are only partially self-supporting, as they frequently call upon the selectmen in the towns where they live, for assistance.

There are three other most unfortunate cases to mention. Two of these people, one a man of middle age, the other a young woman, had become so addicted to the use of opium, that the Institution could do nothing for them. The saddest case of all is that of a young woman who became blind at fifteen years of age, up to which time she had been proficient in her studies in the common school. It was the fate of this young girl to have this misfortune overtake her, at a time when it was no one's business in this State to look after the education of the Blind.

Being helpless and friendless she was sent to the poor house where she remained till she was twenty-four years of age, when she was brought to our Home by the overseer of the poor. Her condition was simply indescribable. To all appearances she was both a physical and mental wreck.

Our success with one other case of this kind, prompted us to see what could be accomplished in this case, but after three years of patience and perseverance on the part of caretakers and instructors, we are unable to report any more than partial success. The Industrial Institution, however, is the best place for her. She is no longer a charge upon the State, and whenever she seems to be sinking into the old condition of apathy, her instructors have only to mention that our Industrial Institution is not for idle people and that she will have to return to her old home, to obtain from her the very best service of which she is capable.

Among other things alluded to by this commission in its report (page 122, item 6,) as expended by the State for the State Board of Education of the Blind, is a statement of the aggregate sum without specifying that it contained the salary of the Secretary, the salary of the Assistant Secretary, the traveling expenses of both for a year, the cost of stationery, printing the annual report, the cost of clothing and the traveling expenses authorized by the State in cases of the pupils whose parents were unable to provide these necessities.

The first time this mistake was made, was when a former Secretary of the State Board of Charities, referred to this aggregate sum as the salary received by the Secretary of this Board. When his attention was called to this mistake and it was pointed out to him, that it would greatly prejudice many friends against the cause, to whom we were appealing for support and co-operation, he admitted it was an oversight, said he was sorry for it, but refused to make a public acknowledgement of the error, on the ground that he did not wish to stultify himself in that way.

The Commission on State Receipts and Expenditures above referred to, has come so near repeating this blunder, that several members of the present Legislature, have asked, if that was the amount of salary paid to the writer.

The itemized statement following this article, showing the amount of money received and how it was disbursed, will show just what salary the writer received as well as the amount which the Industrial Home receives as its share of the appropriation made by the State. It will be found as a matter of fact, that the writer receives a trifle over one-third as much as the Secretary of the State Board of Education for the seeing.

Let it not be understood, however, that the writer here undertakes to express an opinion that the salary of the State official referred to is too large. On the contrary, the writer believes that the office of the head of no department of the State should have a salary attached to it, which bids for finer or greater qualities of mind than should be possessed by the head of the MIND TRAINING department of the State.

To come back to the point however, to which the writer has referred as being of so much importance, it can be plainly read between the lines of the report of this commission, that its members are of the opinion, that to pay even such a small salary to a blind man, is a foolish and unnecessary expenditure. This again resolves itself into the proposition that the State has no need of the knowledge and experience acquired by the Blind, in solving the problem of what kind of training is needed by, and will prove most beneficial to, the sightless.

One step further and we have reached the real reason that has plainly influenced the members of this commission to make the recommendations they have made and that is, they share with most seeing people the belief that blind persons are necessarily and irrevocably chained to a condition of hopeless dependence.

Upon this issue then, cleared of all obstructions, let the decision be reached by the present General Assembly. Before we proceed to discuss this question further, let us crave the sympathy of all fair-minded and considerate people. Not because we are blind, but because, despite the constitutional provision that no man's life should be twice placed in jeopardy for the the same offence, our cause is for the fourth time placed in jeopardy by the persistency of our opponents, after three times making good our defence before the chosen representatives of the people.

Does it count for nothing with this commission that the Board of Education of the Blind was created and its powers defined upon the advice and unanimous approval of the joint standing committee on Judiciary of the General Assembly of 1893, composed of such men as Senator Fox of New Haven, Messrs. Wood of Manchester, Hale of Glastonbury, Judd and Stoddard of Litchfield, Beardsley of Bridgeport, Corttis of Thompson, Palmer of Norwich, and Wilcox of Berlin.

Is the General Assembly aware that the whole subject of the advisability of the State lending its aid and encouragement to the work that is being done by this same Industrial Home for the Blind was thoroughly gone over and inquired into by the General Assembly of 1895, and that the Committee on Humane Institutions consisting of Senator Bernd, Messrs. Newton, of New Haven; Whiton, of Manchester; Fuller, of Suffield; Saunders, of Waterford; Lounsbury, of Darien; Barber, of Putnam; Battey, of Columbia; and Booth, of New Milford, after the most thorough canvass and consideration of the whole subject, made a unanimous report in favor of continuing the methods employed by the Board and favored an appropriation to the Industrial Home for the Blind for the full amount it then asked for?

Do the gentlemen of this commission know that their idea of abolishing the State Board of Education of the Blind and passing over its work to the Board of Education for the seeing did not originate with them, but that Judge Newton of New Haven, House Chairman of the Committee on Humane Institutions of the General Assembly of 1895, advanced this proposition, but, becoming thoroughly convinced that any such change would be unwise, he subsequently agreed with the committee, thus making their approval of the measure submitted to them unanimous.

Does it count for nothing with the members of this commission, that their opinions are opposed to those entertained by the late Governor Morris, Ex-Governor O. Vincent Coffin, Ex-Governor Lorrin A. Cooke and Chief Justice Charles B. Andrews without whose co-operation, sanction and approval the work they seek to undo could never have been carried forward ?

Does it count for nothing with them that their opinion and judgment is opposed to the opinion and judgment of such men as Mr. Rodney Dennis, President Connecticut Humane Society; Rev. Joseph H. Twichell, Dr. Henry P. Stearns, Superintendent and Director of Hartford Retreat; Dr. G. Pierrepont Davis, General Arthur L. Goodrich, Ex-Lieutenant-Governor Ernest Cady, Colonel George Pope, Treasurer Pope Manufacturing Co.; Prof. A. R. Merriam, of the Hartford Theological Seminary and the Rev. Dr. George M. Stone, all of whom as members of the Advisory Board of the Institution, have become familiar with the affairs of the Industrial Home, and have had opportunities for judging the merits of its work during the past six years, a hundredfold greater than any information that the commission could have acquired through its sub-committee ?

NOTE.—One member of this sub-committee had previous to the creation of this committee paid a flying visit to the Industrial Home, which visit was afterwards repeated in the company of another member of the commission.

In order that the State at large should be more fully represented on the advisory board of our Institution, the following named gentlemen with their consent and approval, have been added:

Hon. George E. Lounsbury, Ridgefield,
Major Richard O. Cheney, South Manchester,
Hon. Allan W. Paige, Bridgeport,
Hon. H. Lynde Harrison, Guilford,
Lieut-Gov. Lyman A. Mills, Middlefield,
Hon. Charles E. Searles, Thompson,
Hon. Charles Phelps, Atty.-Gen., Rockville,
Gen. Louis N. Van Keuren, Bridgeport,
Hon. Daniel N. Morgan, Bridgeport,
Col. Norris G. Osborn, New Haven.
Dr. S. B. St. John, Hartford,
Richard G. Beebe, Stafford,
Hon. J. Henry Roraback, Canaan,
Erastus Gay, Farmington,
P. H. Woodward, Hartford,
Dr. Jos. E. Root, Hartford,

Herbert H. White, Hartford,
Morris W. Seymour, Bridgeport,
Charles M. Jarvis, Berlin,
Ex-Gov. Thomas M. Waller, New London,
Gen. Wm. B. Rudd, Lakeville.

Knowing this fact will the General Assembly not think that it will be as well to wait before undoing the work of the past six years until this board informs a future General Assembly that such action is desirable?

Is the commission not aware that all the reasons advanced in its report on which it bases its recommendations, were urged by the opponents of the work for the Blind before the General Assembly of 1897?

That, in addition to these reasons, all the evidence was in, including the advice of the State Board of Charities, which insists upon classifying the Blind with imbeciles, convicts, insane and paupers. That all this evidence was fully weighed and considered by Gov. Cooke before the writer, whose term of office expired in the following July, was reappointed to continue his labors in behalf of the Blind.

For a more thorough presentation of what it is possible for blind persons to accomplish, citing many cases which will be found most interesting, see Article, pages 12 to 20 inclusive, in the report of this Board for the fiscal year ending September 30th, 1897, a copy of which is bound with this report.

Before drawing this reply to a close, it would be well to summarize all the points upon which the Committee on State Receipts and Expenditures, base their advice to the General Assembly, to abolish the State Board of Education of the Blind and to withdraw the support the State has hitherto given to the Industrial Home for the Blind.

FIRST. On page 27, lines 36, 37 and 38 of the printed report of this committee, they say, "The work that is done here is not as practical as we could wish; nor do we believe that satisfactory results can ever be attained under existing conditions."

We submit that this is merely the expression of opinion and not a statement of evidence obtained by them, upon which if found to be true, the lawmakers of the State could exercise their own judgment.

The gentlemen have evidently expected the members of the General Assembly to take their opinions ready made, without being furnished the evidence upon which they are based.

In our reply to this mere statement of opinion we furnish the foregoing written statements, which as evidence, show what the result really has been.

SECOND. In the first four lines of page 28, the language of the report is as follows: "Surely, the art of printing will not appeal to an unprejudiced person, as at all adapted to blind people. They cannot set type, and they cannot operate the press, except when running at a reduced speed."

In reply to these conclusions, which again is a mere expression of opinion, without furnishing the General Assembly a particle of evidence, we offset the statements of former pupils, and the foregoing written statements of six expert printers, three of whom are at the head of some of the largest printing and publishing houses in the State, while it will not be pretended that either of the gentlemen who visited our printing department in the interest of the Commission have any knowledge of the printing business whatever.

The most notable thing about the statement just quoted, however, is to be found in the words, "Surely the art of printing will not appeal to an unprejudiced person as at all adapted to blind people." Here we have the key, which admits us to a position where we can easily see the exact mental process, which resulted in the conclusions reached. We submit again that this committee here furnishes no light whatever. The state did not need the services of a special commission to inform it that nine seeing people out of ten would say without hesitation, that the printing business could not be successfully followed by blind people. Every one of the expert witnesses we introduce, entertained the same opinion before they were compelled by the most satisfactory evidence to reach a different conclusion.

THIRD. The language employed by the gentlemen in lines 5, 6 and 7, on the same page is as follows: "A number of persons in the Home are members of a musical company, travelling about the country giving concerts, which necessarily interrupts their work in the several departments." Our reply to this is, that the concert company referred to, during the past four years has consisted mainly of former pupils, who are musicians, and by this very employment are not only furnished a means of earning their own living, but as will be seen in the letter from the Rev. Mr. Thayer, given on page 8 of this (our own) report, was the means of accomplishing one of the very objects for which the Institution was founded.

Whenever during the past four years we have taken out pupils with the concert company, it has always been those pupils who intended to employ their musical talent as a means of gaining their living. Therefore, the incentive to greater application to prepare for these concerts, as well as the actual training which the concert work affords, furnished the very best reasons for doing just what the members of this commission criticise as being unwise. I may here add, that the question raised by this objection was raised by the State Board of Charities several years ago, and that it then received full and careful consideration by the Governor and chief justice and that the concert work was continued with their approval. At present there is only one state pupil who is a member of the concert company.

FOURTH. We quote again from the same page, the language of which is as follows, (line 8,): "The financial management of the Home has not been a success."

Here is an assertion, without evidence. Our reply that the financial management has not been a success, is, that it is untrue. Not a year has passed that our income from the workshops of the Institution, from money raised by concerts and in other ways, has not nearly equalled the sum received from the state for the board and tuition of state pupils, in the Industrial Department. Our statement of assets and liabilities, pages 6 and 7, of our report for the fiscal year ending September 30, 1897, a copy of which is bound with this report, shows that starting with nothing, in 1893 up to July 1, 1897, the assets of the Institution exceeded the liabilities by $32,409.78. Of this sum, as the committee show in their own report, aside from the same allowance made for the board and tuition of state pupils which this state was making and has always made Perkins Institution for the Blind, our Institution had only received from the state the sum of $14,970.44, see committee's report, page 122, item 6, under head of "Appropriations for Buildings." Thus, up to the time mentioned, the Institution had saved and invested in the purchase and improvement of the real and personal property of the Institution, the sum of $17,439.34.

In the statement of assets and liabilities above referred to, nothing was allowed for the appreciation of the value of the real estate, and to show that no unwise investments have been made by the management we publish the following:

HARTFORD, CONN., July 29th, 1897.

"We hereby certify that we are fully acquainted with the real estate owned by the Conn. Institute and Industrial Home for the Blind, in Hartford Conn., and know its value and that in our judgment, placing the same at a low and conservative valuation, the Trustees would be fully warranted by the appreciation in its value, during the past four years, to appraise the same in their statement of assets at $10,000 more than the original purchase price of the same, exclusive of improvements.

Signed.

EDWARD SHELTON,
Broker and Real Estate Dealer.
ROBERT D. BONE,
Chairman Board of Assessors.

"In a letter dated July 29th, 1897, addressed to the President of the Institution, A. W. Scoville, architect, making use of substantially the same language as above, places the appreciation in value of the real estate of the Institution, for the past four years, at $11,980, instead of $10,000."

We now come to the financial struggle of the Industrial Home for the Blind for the past two years, intelligence of which coming to the ears of the commission undoubtedly gave rise to the assertion to which we are now replying.

This struggle was precipitated by the success of our opponents, who, taking advantage of the general demand for the reduction of the State expenses, succeeded in preventing the State from carrying out the obligations it was under to said Institution, for money expended, and obligations incurred, by authority af an act passed by the General Assembly of 1895.

Believing, as the members of ihe Board of Education of the Blind certainly did, that said Board was authorized by law to "Provide such suitable buildings, furniture, machinery, tools, instruments and apparatus for the Connecticut Institute and Industrial Home for the Blind, as it shall deem necessary," the Board decided to proceed to erect buildings, furnish and equip them, at a cost of $29,000, this being the amount which the original plans called for.

These original plans were submitted to, and carefully examined by, the Governor and Chief Justice, and the work as it proceeded was personally inspected by them. The Governor in behalf of the State submitted the plans to an expert of his own choosing, which expert subsequently acted as inspector in the interest of the State.

Fifteen thousand dollars of the appropriation of the General Assembly of 1895 was available as the work proceeded, and the balance was to be available at the expiration of two years under the general law, the only condition imposed being the unanimous approval of the Board. The General Assembly of 1897, however, by its law providing for specific appropriations, and its failure to make a specific appropriation to carry out the provisions of the law above referred to, left our Institution in a situation that presented a problem not easily solved.

On the first day of July, 1897, the floating indebtedness of the Institution was $14,843.69. There was due it from the State for the board and tuition of State pupils, the sum of $4,663.31, and on account of money expended and obligations incurred for the erection, furnishing and equipment of buildings, the sum of $13,583.13 which if paid, would have enabled us to discharge our entire floating indebtedness, and would have left a balance of $3,402.77, besides a small amount in outstanding accounts due the Institution, with which to begin the new year. As it was however, we only received from the State the sum of $4,663.31, which when expended, left us to start the new year with a floating indebtedness of $10,180.38. In addition to carrying this burden, the management must provide for the support of sixty-four blind persons, pay for the running expenses of the Institution, including salaries of Superintendent, teachers, matrons, caretakers and servants, until the 10th day of January following, before it could call upon the State for more money, at which time the Institution would receive, one-third of the amount allowed for the board and tuition of State pupils. The burden must then be carried for three months, longer, until the second payment from the State became due, and again three months until the third and last payment for the year.

Then another stretch of six months and so on through the second year. Although we receive the same amount per capita, which the State pays the Perkins Institution, that Institution has no pupils to care for from July 1st to September 20th; while there are many pupils attending our Institution whom we have been compelled to care for during the summer months, as they had no other homes to go to, and this was also true in the case of three homeless children, for which the Perkins Institution received the annual allowance.

To solve the problem thus presented at a time during which the Free Silver agitation made it difficult to obtain credit, even upon good security at the banks, and at the same time to carry through successfully a project to establish and place on a paying basis, a monthly magazine that should furnish employment for our homeless girls, was a task which only those who have been placed in a similar situation can understand or appreciate, and yet this Committee say in their report that, "The financial management has not been a success," and this, too, when in addition to bringing this Institution safely through this crisis, we have raised and expended nearly six hundred and fifty dollars, for tools, machinery and stock, to start in business the pupils who had finished their course of instruction.

But let us pass on to the next point raised by this commission in lines 9 and 10, page 28, they say, "and we seriously doubt if its inmates can ever become sufficiently proficient in the trades as taught at this Institution, to become self-supporting."

Our only reply to this, which is merely an expression of their opinion, is to refer the reader back to the statements in this report made by the blind people themselves, who have finished their course of instruction at the Institution, and to ask the gentlemen to point out any other Institution, even with resources much greater than ours, that shows any better results.

We have already replied to everything in the report until we reach line 35 of page 28, which we quote, "Apparently no provision is made for blind persons over eighteen years of age."

This follows a statement that the commission had investigated and learned what is being done for the blind, in New England, New York, New Jersey and Pennsylvania.

They then say, "Pennsylvania owns no institution where adult blind persons may be educated. However, it contributes to the support of the working home for men and women in the city of Philadelphia, which is a shop for the blind with a boarding house or home attached. The institution is conducted on business principles, and the results attained have been eminently satisfactory. The provisions for adult blind seem to be very meagre in every state we have mentioned with the exception of Pennsylvania. Connecticut is the only one of the states mentioned in which there is a separate Board of Education for the Blind."

This finishes the statement of the commission upon which it bases its recommendation. The language of the last quotation, appears to the writer to offer the very best reasons why the work in Connecticut, should be allowed to go on, and ample provision made for its support.

The commission neglected to state that the Institution for the adult blind in Philadelphia, is the result of the labors of the present efficient head and manager, who is a blind man, and therefore was in a position to know what was most needed by the Blind.

STATEMENT OF DISBURSEMENTS

——FOR THE——

FISCAL YEAR ENDING SEPTEMBER 30TH, 1898.

The total amount disbursed under the direction of the State Board of Education of the Blind was $22,569.96 as follows:

1.	Amount paid Perkins Institution for the Blind	$5,325.23
2.	Kindergarten for the Blind	7,406.64
3.	Industrial Home	6,489.00
4.	Salary of Secretary	1,200.00
5.	Salary of Assistant Secretary	600.00
6.	Traveling and Office expenses of Secretary	70.69
7.	Expenses reported by Assistant Secretary	137.97
8.	Traveling Expenses, Chief Justice Andrews	5.50
9.	Cash paid for clothing and transportation of Pupils at Industrial Home (Pioneers)	255.99
10.	Stationery	10.30
11.	Cash expended for transportation and clothing of other State Pupils	750.34
12.	Printing Report and Expense	318.30
	TOTAL	$22,569.96

It will be observed that items 3, 4 and 9, representing $7,944.99, is the amount chargeable to the Industrial Home and the salary of the Secretary of this Board. As soon as the work for the young adult blind, neglected in the past, has been carried forward long enough to clear the State of these cases, and we begin to settle down to a normal condition, attending only to such cases as arise from year to year, the amount required for this purpose will yearly be less and less, until not more than $3000, per year will be required to continue this branch of our work. It is quite possible, with the help of the State to pay off the indebtedness of the Institution incurred for the buildings, furniture and equipments, that our Industrial department will in the near future become self sustaining.

Our Industrial Home is only a little over five years old. It is only half through its struggling to reach a firm foundation. Philanthropy will unquestionably come to our aid, but thus far the only bequest received by our Institution has been the work bench, tools and books, of one of our young blind people. In case the death blow, threatened by the proposed legislation of this commission, is successful, more blind people, now taking care of themselves through the employment which our Institution furnishes, will be thrown upon the towns to support, then they (the towns) will be able to take care of with the money withheld from the Institution by the State. Our blind people, who have never yet been paupers, are of the same quality of feeling, and would suffer as great distress, as the sons and daughters of any of our citizens.

In closing let me say to the people of the State of Connecticut that they could do no greater wrong than to close the door of hope that has been opened to the Blind and we most earnestly trust that no such grave mistake will be made.

Most Respectfully Submitted,
F. E. CLEAVELAND.

STATEMENT OF ASSETS AND LIABILITIES

OF THE CONNECTICUT INSTITUTE AND INDUSTRIAL HOME FOR THE BLIND.

ASSETS.

Value of Plant Sept. 30, 1895, Value at Cost, . .	$27,072.46
Cash paid out for purchase of property and improvement of plant by Treasurer for year ending Sept. 30, 1896, .	4,771.38
Cash paid out for purchase of property and improvement of plant by Ass't Treasurer for year ending Sept. 30, 1896,	1,079.59
Cash paid out by State for erection and equipment of buildings, ...	14,970.44
Cash paid out for purchase of property and improvement of plant for nine months ending June 30, 1897, by Treas.	5,372,76
Cash paid out for purchase of property and improvement of plant for nine months ending June 30, 1897, by Ass't Treasurer, ...	2,359.42
Cash paid out by State for furnishing broom shop, . .	1,200.00
Cash paid out for purchase of property and improvement of plant for fifteen months ending Sept. 30, 1898, by Treasurer, ...	3,049.35
Cash paid out for purchase of property and improvement of plant for fifteen months ending Sept. 30, 1898, by Ass't Treasurer, ...	1,661.28
Appreciation in value of Land (see appraisal page 28,) .	10,000.00
Inventory Sept. 30, 1898.	
Merchandise Department, ...	475.66
Mattress Department, ...	450.00
Broom Department, ...	463.54
Printing Department, ...	130.82
Hay, Feed and other supplies, ...	50.00
Musical Instruments, ...	600.00
Other property acquired by Institute, . . .	125.00
Bills and accounts receivable, ...	2,362.89
Improvement of plant represented by outstanding obligations,	1,047.74
Industrial Home Kindergarten, ...	1,940.86
	———— $79,183.19

LIABILITIES.

Mortgage Indebtedness, Kindergarten, . . .	$14,597.44
Mortgage Indebtedness, Ind. Home, · . . .	4,774.76
Bills and accounts payable, ...	6,702.12
*Temporary loans, ...	7,900.00
Allowance for shrinkage in value personality . .	500.00
	———— $34,474.32

NOTE: Had the personal property of the Institution not been purchased at greatly reduced rates, granted by dealers to Institution, a larger allowance would have been made for shrinkage in its value. It is believed the excess of the Assets over the Liabilities, namely, $44,708.87, fairly represents the property interest of the Institution.

* Long standing accounts bearing interest have been included above under the classification of temporary loans.

34

STATEMENT BY E. ECHOLS, ACCOUNTANT,

SHOWING RECEIPTS AND DISBURSEMENTS OF THE INSTITUTION
FOR THE FISCAL YEAR ENDING SEPT. 30, 1898.

Dr.

To Balance on hand Oct. 1, 1897,	$ 84.46
" Cash from Treasurer, (State Receipts,)	13,895.64
" " " " (Other Sources,)	3,189.60
" " " Ass't Treas., (Kindergarten Dept.,)	3,856.82
" " " Donations and sources unclassified,	803.32
" " " Temporary Loans,	3,367.46
" " " Broom Department,	3,595.33
" " " Upholstery Department,	2,660.24
" " " Printing Department,	557.49
" " " Property Department,	35.00
" " " Merchandise sold in Inst. Store,	1,833.61
" " " Concert Company,	4,681.31
" error in balance by former clerk, July 1, 1898,	1.58
	$38,561.86

Cr.

By Paid Ass't Treas. amount due Sept. 30, 1897,	$ 103.67
" " " " (Kindergarten Department,	10,481.43
" " Temporary Loans,	3,537.91
" " On account Broom Department.	4,687.40
" " " " Upholstery Department,	1,894.65
" " " " Printing Department,	919.17
" " " " Property Department,	2,215.25
" " " " Merchandise Department,	1,718.77
" " " " Concert Company,	1,902.25
" " " " Current Expenses,	5,096.16
" " " " Salaries and Wages,	5,916.10
" Balance on hand Sept. 30, 1898,	89.10
	$38,561.86

HARTFORD, CONN., March 8, 1899.

This certifies that we have examined the accounts of the Connecticut Institute and Industrial Home for the Blind, for the fiscal year ending Sept. 30th, 1898, compared the same with the vouchers and found the same correct. The balance of cash in the hands of the clerk on said date was eighty-nine dollars and ten cents ($89.10.)

Signed, FRANKLIN B. NOYES,) Auditors of
D. WARD NORTHROP,) Public Accounts.

KINDERGARTEN ACCOUNT,

MRS. H. L. OLMSTED, ASSISTANT TREASURER.

	Dr.
To Cash From Contributions and Entertainments, . .	$3,528.40
" " " Rhode Island, Board of James Waterhouse,	300.00
" " " Sale of Cow, ...	21.00
" " " Sundries, ...	6.41
" " Due Ass't Treasurer, (error in contributions), .	1.01
" " From Treasurer During Year, . . .	6,728.28
	$10,585.10

	Cr.
By Paid Balance Due Ass't Treasurer, Sept. 30, 1897, . .	$ 103.67
" " for Salaries and Services, ...	4,285.58
" " " Provisions, etc., ...	2,466.83
" " " Fuel, ...	684.26
" " " Water, ...	73.50
" " " Insurance, ...	71.00
" " " House Furnishings and Repairs, . . .	506.49
" " " Current Expenses, ...	534 56
" " " Property Account, ...	1,259.89
" Balance on hand, Sept. 30, 1898, ...	599.39
	$10,585.10

HARTFORD, CONN., March 8, 1899.

This certifies that we have examined the accounts of the Connecticut Institute and Industrial Home for the Blind, Kindergarten Department, for the fiscal year ending Sept. 30th, 1898, compared the same with the vouchers and found the same correct. The balance of cash on hand on said date was five hundred and ninety-nine dollars and thirty-nine cents ($599.39)

Signed,   FRANKLIN B. NOYES, } Auditors of
       D. WARD NORTHROP, } Public Accounts.

ABSTRACT.

Showing signatures of prominent citizens of many of the principal cities and towns in the State, in aid of Senate Bill 'No. 88; pending before the General Assembly, entitled An Act Concerning the Instruction and Employment of the Blind.

To the members of the joint standing committee on appropriations, and through them to the members of the General Assembly.

GENTLEMEN:—This abstract has been prepared to afford a ready reference to a list of names which we believe will impress you as being worthy of your consideration as evidence that the people of this State are in hearty accord with what has been done and what it is proposed to do for the elevation, enlightenment and general welfare of the Blind.

HARTFORD.

Joseph H Twichell
Rodney Dennis
Ernest Cady
G Pierrepont Davis
Francis Goodwin
Henry C Robinson
Arthur L Goodrich
Frank L Burr
George M Stone
Jonathan B Bunce
H P Stearns
Charles M Lamson
George Pope
Jacob L Greene
Meigs H Whaples
Ralph W Cutler
George F Hills
Atwood Collins
James Nichols
Thomas W Russell
Chester D Hartranft
W B Clark
J G Batterson
Charles E Gross
John R Buck
Henry L Bunce
Samuel G Dunham
John Addison Porter
Charles E Chase

Herbert H White
Miles B Preston
Waldo S Pratt
Edwin Knox Mitchell
S. B. St John
Job Williams
Henry Ferguson

NEW HAVEN.

Pierce N Welch
Oliver S White
Charles R Ingersoll
Charles E Grases
Newman Smythe
T T Munger
Wilbur F Gay
A W DeForest
Morris F Tyler
Henry F English
Henry G Newton
E Hayes Trowbridge
Ezekiel G Stoddard
Francis Wayland
George P Fisher
S E Merwin
E B Bowditch
Henry T Blake
H B Harrison
John K Beach
A D Osborne
Eli Whitney

Gardner Morse
Leonard M Daggett
George D Watrous
L. W. Cleaveland
Henry C White
Timothy Dwight
Theodore S Woolsey
Simeon E Baldwin
Henry W Farnham

BRIDGEPORT.

Frank E Clark
A Stewart
Fred Seeley
William A Barnes
James Staples
Benjamin Fisk
J B Prindle
John T Sterling
Russell I Whiting
H M Knapp
John Neal
Richard B Coggswell
F W Marsh
Henry H Pyle
George Comstock
J H McMahon
C Y Beach
W B. Beach
P W Wren
W W Starr

R C Giddings
Bernard Keating
F C Mullens
A W Wallace
W S Wilson
F Garrett
Joseph Smith
H G Scofield
L N Middlebrook
T B Ford
C F Washburn
Lyman W Wilson
Frederick E Stevens
James Richardson
Frank D Bell
Edward T Bartram
J E Foster
C K Macomber
C R Brothwell
Walter B Bostwick
R S Neithercut
M Moody Downer
Phillip L Holzer
Frank W Beers
D M Rowland
Orland Smith
Wm H May
F W Storrs
Walter Nichols
Louis Van Deusen

WATERBURY.

F J Kingsbury
F W Kellogg
H L Wade
Leroy Upson
E L Frisbie Jr
A M Dickinson
J Richard Smith
Earl Smith
E C Lewis
G W Beach
John D Elton
Gilmore C Hill
B G Bryan
A I Chatfield
Thomas D Barlow
Nathaniel Bronson
J M Burral
R N Blakesley

MIDDLETOWN.

O Vincent Coffin
Richard L de Zeng
Simon Spear
James Donovan
Isaac Spear
Geo A Coles
Henry Woodward
Conrad G Bacon
W U Pearne
Eldow B Birdseye
Geo T Meech
E E Ellsworth
C H Lewis
Lucien R Hazen
Chas Reynolds
C Barrows
G Burr
W D Thayer
Jas J McNulty
J A Broach
A Jameson
R C Kelsey
Wm E Hale
Henry Burnhart
A W Bidwell
J W Stenck
J S Fairchild
Wilbur A Snow
Ernest King & Son
Richard Murphy
Christian Bischel
Richard Cody
James Young
John Conway
Henry S Beers
J Williams
Samuel Russeil
Joseph J Noxon
Wm S Whitney
M B Copeland
Seth H Butler
Arthur B Califf
Daniel J Donahoe
John T Walsh
Orrin D Stoddard
John D Ryan
Geo A Craig
Edward G Camp

Earl C Butler
F G Chaffee
Samuel T Camp
Geo Bull
O H Cone
T F Nolan
P M Camp
John J Murphy
Michael Wall
James Lawton
M Lawton
J H Seiferman
W B Griswold

WESTFIELD,

Rev D B Hubbard
Albert Bacon
Marcus Wilcox
James H Ross
Julius C Atkins
Wm H Wilcox
T M Carckin
Edgar H Burns
Geo Goodrich
A L Congdon
Henry Wilcox

NORWICH.

Anros T Otis
C H Preston Rich
A L Story
Charles F Thayer
Gilbert S Raymond
J H Welles
F T Sayleo
Nathan Small
Ira L Peck
C L Hopkins
D L Underwood
Stephen H Hall
Charles B Chapman
Henry D Johnson
Hams Rasmusson
William S Hemstead
Adam Reid
Hull Brothers
D T Ruby
W H Cardwell.
Porteous & Mitchell

Joseph S Cunningham
A W Pearson,
　　Editor Bulletin
Lewellyn Pratt
Jonathan Trumbull
H H Gallup
A H Brewer
Archibald S Spalding
Luther S Eaton
D H Hough
C J King
Charles C Caulkins
O H Reynolds
E R Thompson
Charles Bard
Henry W Bard
Lewis A Hyde
Henry L Bennett
W F Crandall
Nathaniel A Gibbs
Warren K Dowe
George W Swan
S B Meech
C C Johnson
Charles D Foster
Frank Hempstead
George D Coit
Edward Harland
John M Brewer
George E Bachelder
Charles W Comstock
Henry H Burnham
Paul B Greene
Stephen D Moore
A A Browing
Franklin H Brown
Andrew Miller
James Duggan
H I Palmer
C W Hill
James A Brown
Samuel H Freeman
George E Parsons
F L Osgood
Irving N Gifford
Justin Holden
Sidney L Geer
L W Carroll
F L Klein

Nathan D Bates
N Douglas Sevin
Patrick Cassidy
George W Kies
H O Rallion
Edson S Bishop
Charles W Gale
W A Briscoe
John T Wait
F T Brown

MERIDEN.

W N Catlin
R S Norton
A Chamberlin
C S Perkins
J J Anderson
C L Upham
Phillip C Rand
George A Fay
S J Hall
John L Billard
John Ives
F J Wheeler
Walter Hubbard
George M Curtis
Frank A Camp
George Rockwell
E B Everett
C E Stockder Jr
S T Thomas
A J Fletcher
Asher Anderson
Samuel Dodd.
Levi E Coe
Wilbur F Davis
Edwin W Husted
G W Miller
Wm W Wheeler
Herman Hess
E B Moss
Charles H S Davis
F H Cushing
W R Mackay
John McWherry
C W Cahill

NEW LONDON.

James P. Johnson,
　　Mayor of City

P Hall Shurts
F H Parmlee
H A Hull
T W Potter
C A Benjamin
Isaac Knowles
W H Rowe
F E Barker
Arnold Rudd
George M Coles
Alfred Poole Grint
Benjamin Stark
F D Crandall
John E Darrow
William F M Rogers
A T Hale
W G Wilbur
Geo T Strong
C A Williams
Edmund S Neilan
A T Hatch
E D Stone
Walter Davis
Daniel Latham
Charles H Goss
W H Bentley
C J Vick
D T Morsh
E N Caulkins
R S Smith
Clark E Smith
Charles W Strickland
Henry H Stoddard
Herbert L Crandall
Lee S Denison
Franklin G McKeever
John C Nichols
H H Daboll
H J Civiker
H E Harris
C S Broddock
B F Mahon
D J Lucy
W H Chapman
E D Barker
William T May
Charles B Ware
Henry D Stanton
S Leroy Blake

KILLINGLY.

Anthony Ames
W H Chollar
C C Young
A D Putnam
Joseph W Stone
George C Foote
Edward Dexter
Samuel D Danielson
J Q A Stone
F W Chapman
James E Keech
R R James
H H Green
C P Backus
E L Palmer
J A Gilbert
E J Mathewson
R F Lyon
C H Burroughs
C E Carpenter
Frank T Preston
E O Wood
W F Bidwell
W E LaBelle
E M Randall
W C Darrow
A B Potter
M P Dowe
H M Clemons
Clarence E Young
H F Clark
O W Bowen
C H Bacon
G P Hall
Rev H S Brown
S S Waldo
E S Carpenter
James H Potter
John W Law
H C Atwood
L S James
S R Gilbert
W F Day
W P Kelley
Frank W Bennett
Rev. John Deans
H L Hammond M D
William Y Harrington
H J Miller

BRISTOL.

J F Chidsey
W W Russell
John S Lyon
W Hart
Williard E Goodwin
George W Mitchell
W T Shepard
Samuel M Steele
Charles H Buck
Thomas M Miles
H B Cook
L M Bennett
A B Judd
C B Abell
S K Montgomery
George W Baker
Miller Card
Arthur G Muzzy
William B Adams
W T Smith
C S Cook
M E Wilden
William Madden
James D Rowe
E W Whitman
Perry M Holley
Lee Roberts
W B Hinkley
W S Jones
H O Palmer
William H Adams
H S Bartholomew
Stephen N Wells Jr
George P Allen
R B Codling
L G Mesick
M D Edgerton
Francis O Lewis
Edson M Peck
T H Patterson
Epapheoditus Peck

WINSTED.

Rufus E Holmes
Henry Gay
Lucius V Pinney
Ralph W Holmes
Darwin S Moore
M H Marines

Wm P Gladwin
J J Whiting
A W Healy
H Skinner
C Halstead
C A Bristol
Rev G W Remington
H C Price
Edward Ferris
George S Rowe
D C Roraback
Geo H Spencer
Edward Jones
Fred H York
John W Moore
G L Fancher
Charles J Ryan
C S Foster
K L Preston
H S Rising
E W King
J R Griswold
Sam S Newton
James C Kelley
S N Lincoln
J O Houlihan
W H Gillette
Charles Pulver
David E Jordan
John F Coffee
W M Johnson
H O Atkins
Wallace Persons
S H Alford
E Larkin
W J Sparks
F G Gates
W C Plant
John P Cook
L C Colt
J T Morgan
H B Stevens
W H Miles
A W Clark
J C Burwell
S C Wheeler
J H Alvord

MANCHESTER.

Thos J Gardiner
Wm S Hutchinson

A L Geer
W B Porter
W H Coates
J G Trotter
John P Cheney
Charles Cheney
Edward Cadman
S T Bidwell
Rich O Cheney
K D Cheney
James W Cheney
Saml Richmond
William C Cheney
Geo Davidson
Alex Miller
B J Bartlett
Loren Davis
James Britton
H. G. Brown
John Wright Jr
Wm Dongan
Charles McKee
Edward McKee
Frank Hobley
James Fallow
Geo W Ferris
J B Grimes
L B Bade
John Hickey
Harry Nelson
Arthur Sault
Geo H Acheson
Wm H Wright
Henry W Leidholdt
John M Shewey
B A Cadman
John Wright
W W Cheney
H F Brown
Wm Ferguson
Frederick Waldo
Theo H Bidwell
D C Y Moore M D
Thos S Cadman
Jos Watkin
John Cadman
L N Hebner
Wm N Keating
M L Chapman
B F T Jenny

Chas F House
Fred W Mills
C L Leacey
James Hutchinson
James H Miniken
Arthur W Cone
C Tiffany
A H Skinner
D Wadsworth
J H Bilser
Isaac M Quinn
F H Ladd
O B Taylor
Wm Arnoth
Alexander Arnoth
Thomas P Aitkin
Thomas Simms
W H Grant
C G Watkins
Julian S Wadsworth
Wm E Keith
A E Peterson
F A Verplanck

SOUTHINGTON.

Stephen Walkley
E E Stowe
John Heminway
Enoch Nichols
Edwin G Lewis
Hial S Grannis
Rev T C Hanna
L E Southwith
W S Gould
Geo S Allen
Geo W Blakeslee
Theo Buckley
Wm H Cowles
R W Cowles
A W Lewis
T B Atwater
Chas W Bushnell
W H Cummings
W A Finch
H D Smith
Wm Cook
W G Steadman
E W Twitchell
E P Hotchkiss
L C Clark

Jno C Breaker
Ralph T Ives
J H Martin
A N Cheney
J H Pratt
O D Woodruff
L K Curtis
N A Barnes
Chas D Barnes
William Hutton
T H McKenzie
O N Lamson
T E Barnes
J Bond
J H Baldwin
Wallace A Johnson
C F Hamlin

PLYMOUTH.

George Langdon
W M Bull
Arthur Beardsley
A S Beardsley
Frank Blakesley
Rev C H Smith
M W Beach

BERLIN.

A A Barnes
Benj K Field
Charles W Janes
E W Stearns
Geo H Sage
J B Barnes
Arthur W Upson

SOUTHBURY

Wm H Barrows
Sherman Tuttle
A W Guthrie
D M Wheeler
H H Brown
J P Welch
H R Stone
Herman Perry
B M Tuttle
Theodore Mallory
George A Smith
William E Beecher
J S Bennett
H A Mathews

S L Tuttle
Henry B Russell
Timothy Reynolds
Charles E Smith
James E Baldwin
Benjamin S Hicock
C S Brown
H W Beecher
H V Peck
Samuel O Barton
Stephen Collins
Joel U Strong
Oscar W Ambler
C W Wheeler
Charles K Osborne
Walter Hicock
William Morris
C O Hine
E P Hine
A L Hine

STRATFORD.

Joel S Ives
William B Cogswell
W H Smith
M Fryer
F W Judson
Paul A Carey
John R Lattin
William Chichester
Lewis Curtis
Charles Sanford
James A Sanford
Perry Beardsley
William H Feyer
George T Jewell
E M Wells

NOANK.

Robert Palmer
John E McDonald
R P Wilbur
Amos R Chapman
J E Stark
C I Fitch
William E Spencer
Gurdon L Daboil
W A Fraser

UNION.

Benjamin B Hopkinson

J W Winch
W G Howard
E W Upson
R B Horton
E M Horton
George Wallace
Rev O Sherwood Terry
George W Crawford
A T Allen
Fayette Crawford
G W Thayer
Chelsea Young
Williard Richards
F B Johnson
F S Upham
N B Booth
C R Webster
L M Reed
H F Corbin
D C Mathews

NEW HARTFORD.

Edwin R Carter
Edgar H Lane
J P Hawley
W C Woodruff
C E Moorehouse
Frederick R Jewell
Frank P Marble
Calvin Aldrich
R G Foster
Frederick M Tarrill
George W Barrempt
Walter M Smith
Orrin Fitch
Fred O Clark
P N Chamberlin

POMFRET

Francis H Bird
Ezra B Pike
Edward L Williams
Joseph E Stoddard

CROMWELL.

A N Pierson
R Ludwig
P Anderson
W B Hallock & Son
E S Coe
R S Griswold

C R Frisbie
William E Hurlburt
George S Wilcox
Russell Frisbie
W R McDonald
M W Austin
George P Savage
C E Bush
H G Marshall
George W Stevens
William G Keighley
W A Bugbee
C E Penniman
Arthur Boardman
Thomas Beaumont
Maguire Pierson

ELMWOOD.

George T Goodwin
P A Sears
R N Francis
N E Sears
Charles E Lord
H B Goodwin
Cyrus Brown
Fred A Handall
Charles W Perry
J H Raymond
J W Hayer
H L Lamb
J M Shaw
H Hurlburt

NEWINGTON.

Joshua Belden
F H Belden
Mary E Belden
Julia M Belden
Agnes W Belden
John S Kirkham
Mary K A Kirkham
Minnie L Petsner
Edwin Stanley Wells
Daniel W Fish
J N Merrill
G N Downs
C M Kilbourne
Gaylord Morgan
Erastus Kilbourne
R S Kilbourne
Horace Kilbourne

42

S H Kilbourne
C L Bayington
Fred H Bayington
SIMSBURY.
C D Shaw
George O Butler
A S Chapman
F N Hoskins
Edwin Chase
George H Noble
Burton J Noble
William C Mather
A Eberg M D
Nelson St Thomas
E D Jones
W S Holcomb
S H Alger
J T Monks
Geo W Carr
TARIFFVILLE.
J E Heald
C A Ensign
Morton Ensign
Wm H Pease
H Higinbotham
Harvey Tucker
J L Dewey
S M Griffin
A Buncus
Frank Wilkinson Mfg Co
Fred Jones
C M Wooster
NEW FAIRFIELD.
I S Knapp
J K Hatch
J J Ticadwell
R J Scudder
Henry Barker
H O Leach
David S Barnum
John A Waldron
H H Wildman
S E Knapp
E Jennings
A M Couch
H W Jennings
W B Yale
S B Gilbert
A B Brush

G W Trusdale
J F Myer
Emory Kirk
D J Gross
A A Brush
ASHFORD.
Henry C Barlow
Anson G Barlow
Cicero D Chapman
Geo H Whitaker
SAYBROOK.
Amos S Chesebrough
John T Bushnell
J H Mannip
W C Booth
D A Kellogg
O H Kirtland
Edward E Bacon
Robert T Chuther
J H Chase
Thos C Aston Jr
John Sangle
G A Bushnell
W R Bushnell
J D S Pardee
D W Clark
Isaac N Devoe
F F Bradley
F A Curtis
D C Spencer
N D Spencer
John Allen
Sam H Pratt
G Walker
N L Kelsey
Robert Chapman
Joseph M Pratt
Joseph L Hayden Rept.
E. WINDSOR HILL.
George O Clapp
Wm B Parmelee
Frank Bancroft
J D Weyart
J W Clark
C Z Parmelee
W R Wood
J R Noble
D Busbee
R M Burnham

Henry Chapman
Geo S Bissell
ESSEX.
James Phelps
Thomas D Coulter
Chas D Hubbard
Percy I Fenn
J T Mather & Co
Chas Harrison
Mack & Burrows
G W Hayden
W H Parmlee
S M Morley
N H Williams
P Murdock
M W Johnson
J E Knowles
Charles Neitzel
L L Wooster
E E Dickinson & Co
Louis P Parker
Julius L Wilder
L H Parker
H T Phelps
Geo A Dowd
F Halliday
Wm Halliday
S W Ingersoll
Wm Bowen
Edwin T Pratt
James L Pratt
Selden Spencer
Edwin Pratt
N F Stevens
B E Case
Chas E Pratt
Henry R Stevens
Alfred A Pratt
Henry L C Stephenson
Wm P Chapman
Wm E Williams
E C Williams
A C Fenn
J T Lancaster
J Minke
W E Peabody
N E Gladding
M J Beebe
Geo D Dickinson

E C Strong
W E Stephens
Chas Munger
A Shaffer

NORTH HAVEN.

M D Marks
Wm S Stiles
Jas H Halligan
W P Leetes
Wm Lush
H P Smith
C G Malmgieth
Amos A Tuttle
Ezra L Stiles
E D L Goodyear
E A Heminway
H F Potter
L P Tuttle
G W Doolittle
F Hayden Toddy
P A Alson
A F Austin
Theopilus Eaton
D L Clinton
G F Cooper
C O Saxton
Henry C Terrill
D W Tucker
E L Ball
R Harrison

ROCKY HILL.

H R Merriam
F C Warneu
E F Belden
R W Griswold
John North
Geo H Bugbey
A P Shipman
Timothy Gilbert
W A Hammond
Elizabeth Gilbert
Jane Blinn
Geo E Belden
Henry D Trinkons
Fred E Fowler
Chas A Fowler
Elmer E Brown
Wm G Robbins
Geo Risley

Geo B Stillman
Frank G Sherwood
Fred Morton
M J Merriam

NORTH BRANFORD.

F Countryman
Geo C Linsley
Andrew J Russell

EAST HARTFORD.

Edw F King
A G Olmsted
Joel H Brown
E O Goodwin
C P Risley
J E Cawall
Chas Merriway
F W Richardson
G W Darlin
John L Jinks
Wm Duff
Wm G Stoughton
Henry L Goodwin
D C Burnham
W E Bartlett
J W Elmer
M J Hickey
L P Gale
E C Walker
F E Hyde
F H Hammer
P S Bryant
Edward P Carroll
Jos O Goodwin
James S Forbes
C R Forbes
Wm N Lowey
E W Pratt
H W Vinton
Sam O Goodwin
S A Barrett
John Houghton
William A Foley
Charles W Roberts
William S Jasman
L H Forbes
W E Truesdell
W H Chapman
Julius Levy
William J Foley

J W Forbes
Charles Olmstead
John McVay
E Ackerly
F C Gould
Abner Track
L V Lister
D E Lane
William B Noble
William P Stanley
Norman S Brewer
Alme Von W Wickham

NEWTOWN.

Rev Otis W Barker
Allison P Smith
   Editor Newtown Bee
George T Linsley
   Rector Trinity Church
Chas Northrop Treas
   Newtown Saving Bank
M J Houlihan
M J Bradley
      Judge of Probate
H S Clark
N S Clark
W A Leonard
A G Baker
R H Beers (merchant)
Edgar F Hawley
Charles H Peck
Aaron Sanford M of H
M F Houlihan M of H

SALEM

A Morgan
Rev Jarius Ordway
N E Miner
Donald Macrus
Rev E W Merritt
J A Rix
F S Dewolf
G F Allyn

CHESTER.

E W Smith
Ira C Tucker
C H Watrous
E K Cone
J H Wilcox
C A Wright
I L Abbey

E W Clark
J Egerter
F Y Sallum
J A Parker
S E Ackley
E G Smith
W L Bates
C N Smith
R B Jones.
Henry C Scoville
E W Tyler
H C Lewis
G W Warner
A Cooper
E C Hungerford
Julius Smith
George W Smith
A L Osborne
Fred Summer Smith
Fredrick W Silliman
John B Hardy
Rudolf Davis
J K Dennison
H D Selden
W A Warner
C E Smith
H H Clark
A J Smith
H K White
H C Parker
E F Alexander
C Holmes
S G Arnold
W A Foster
D F Hood
H B Crok
James S Deuse

PUTNAM.

Chauncey Morse
F D Sargent
George E Shaw
F W Perry
W C Sharpe
J R Champlin
C A Smith
F W Sewall
E G Wright
E F Whitmore
E C Bohamm

A W Bowen
Edgar M Warner

TERRYVILLE.

William Alfred Gay
Henry E Hinman
M P Robinson
Frederick T Cook
George A Scott
O D Hunter
A D Gaylord
Jason C Fenn
T F Higgins
H A Barton
F E Williams·
H Plumb
J A Russell
C H Baldwin
M A Shurts
Otis B Hough
Frank L Mather
E E Baldwin
P Salmon
C K Palmer·
A B Beach
Geo M Bayington
W D Duffy
J N Keefe
W Atwater
C W Plumb
H D Allen
W A Tilden
J M Gilbert
E I Barnes
Wm C Bates
Albert Griffen
John E Knox
W T Goodwin
Wm L Norton
Charles W Judson
George F Carr
C E Chapman
William W Carr
H O Sullivan
W S Webb
A P Clark
A C Holcomb
Arthur P Clow
F H Pond
E Clayton Goodwin

E Goddard
F R Alford
J M Clemens
A A Place
William Robinson

GRISWOLD.

Clayton T Williard
W Moulding Baker
C F Griswold
J D Welles
George Harris
C H Dilling
S N Woodside
Stephen Churchill
Levi B Churchill
Fredrick G Churchill
H D Shepard
W E Griswold
R S Griswold

WOODSTOCK.

C H Hiscox
H R Lowe M D
G N Lyon
Prescott P Hammond
R F Williams
Rev George L Putnam
F L Corbin
J T Hall
Frank R Jackson
G Clinton Williams
C E Tomburd
N D Skinner

FARMINGTON.

S Porter
M M Porter
E G Porter
Mr & Mrs F L Scott
E F McKien
Mr & Mrs D R Hawley
F H Root
J S Porter
Richard H Gay
M A Howe
M H Smith
M C Gay
Edward H Deming
Alfred Hardy
J Backus

FOURTH ANNUAL REPORT

Conn. Institute and Industrial Home

FOR THE BLIND,

AT HARTFORD, CONN.

TO SEPTEMBER 30, 1897

PRESS OF
THE CONN. INSTITUTE AND INDUSTRIAL HOME
FOR THE BLIND.

FOURTH ANNUAL REPORT,

To His Excellency, Lorrin A. Cooke, Governor, State of Connecticut,

SIR :—

I have the honor to submit herewith the Fourth Annual Report of the State Board of Education of the Blind, and an accompanying statement showing the work of the "Connecticut Institute and Industrial Home for the Blind" organized at the instance of said Board.

The number of State pupils receiving instruction during the year was sixty-seven (67), being less by five than the number receiving instruction at the expense of the State during the previous year. Of these sixty-seven, nineteen (19) were in attendance at the Perkins Institution for the Blind at South Boston, forty-eight (48) at the Connecticut Institution, twenty-one (21) of whom were adults and twenty-seven (27) were children in the Kindergarten Department. In addition to the foregoing number of State pupils, the Institution has been able to furnish profitable employment for sixteen (16) adult blind people, seven (7) of whom are employed as instructors in the several departments.

The special work accomplished in gathering in young children and their progress made in the Kindergarten Department, has been most satisfactory. A detailed account of which will be given further on in this report in the form of a statement by the Assistant Secretary under whose immediate charge this branch of the work has been carried on.

Little more can be said of the pupils at the Perkins Institution than that with one exception the Director of that Institution has reported satisfactory progress. In the case of this exception, the pupil, by vote of this Board at its last meeting, was dismissed.

In our last Annual Report we endeavored to emphasize the importance of the part taken by the Industrial Home in preparing the pupils of the State to enter successfully some useful and self-sustaining occupation. The failure of the Legislature to provide an adequate appropriation for the need of this Department, and the consequent struggle it has undergone to maintain an existence, is well set forth in a circular issued by authority of the Trustees and Advisory Board of said Institution, which circular is here submitted in full.

CIRCULAR.

"To all public spirited and benevolent people of Connecticut, who believe that our State should not fail to keep abreast with other states and countries, in the discharge of its duty to its citizens; and all who may feel a kindly interest in the efforts of the undersigned to establish and maintain in Connecticut, an Institution for the instruction and employment of the Blind.—

GREETING:—

"Four years ago the General Assembly of the State of Connecticut created a State Board of Education of the Blind, of which the Governor and Chief Justice were *ex-officio* members.

"This Board was charged by law with the duty of inquiring into the condition of the Blind children and youth of this State, and was empowered to adopt any and all measures necessary to secure for them a continuous course of instruction calculated to obtain the best results in the way of enabling them to become self-reliant and self-sustaining citizens.

"This Board deemed it necessary to provide for the establishment of an Institution in this State, with two departments, one to be known as the Kindergarten and Primary Department, and the other to be a Manual Training School and Industrial Home.

"Up to this time no appropriation had been made to provide the necessary buildings, furniture and equipment for such an Institution, but the whole matter, with the recommendations of the Board, was referred to the next General Assembly which in turn referred the recommendations and report to the Committee on Humane Institutions.

"This Committee made a thorough and exhaustive investigation and were unanimous in recommending the carrying into effect all the recommendations of the Board, and granting the full amount of the appropriation asked for.

"In pursuance of this recommendation, the Legislature passed the following:— Section 1, of Chapter 303 Public Acts of 1895. 'The State Board of Education of the Blind, may by a unanimous vote of all the members, provide such suitable buildings, furniture, machinery, tools, implements and apparatus, for the use of the Connecticut Institute and Industrial Home for the Blind, as it shall deem necessary to enable said Institution successfully to carry out the rules adopted by said board, providing for the instruction of the blind.' The committee on appropriations, feeling constrained so to do, by the condition of the State Treasury, limited the appropriation for the following two years, to fifteen (15) thousand dollars, saying to the friends and promoters of the work for the Blind, that they must look to the next General Assembly, for an additional appropriation.

"The Board of Education and the Trustees of the Institution, which, with the help of friends, had already made a beginning, were agreed that this fifteen (15) thousand dollars could not be economically expended to meet the needs of the Institution, by erecting any smaller buildings than were called for by the original plans.

These called for the expenditure of $26,000 for additions to the buildings which the Trustees had already secured, and relying upon the probable action of the General Assembly, of 1897, for an appropriation to carry into effect the provisions of the law passed in 1895, they took necessary steps to erect, furnish and equip the buildings needed; obtaining temporary loans and credits for that purpose.

"The General Assembly of 1897, finding that the expenses of the State had for some time exceeded its income, felt it necessary to postpone the relief and assistance needed by this Institution, and consequently appropriated only twelve (12) hundred dollars, and limited the expenditure of this sum to providing additional accommodations made necessary by the growth of the Institution, thus admitting that the accommodations already afforded were insufficient; as the result of this action, the Trustees of the Institution find themselves called upon to meet obligations which they will be unable to meet, unless a loan can be guaranteed by the persons to whom this circular letter is addressed, as the buildings erected from the money advanced by the State are subject to a lien in behalf of the State, for the amount advanced, and also subject to a mortgage in favor of the State Savings Bank, given at the time the original purchase was made.

"They are confident, however, that by securing a loan which the guarantee asked for will enable them to do, they will be able within the next five years, to raise a sum sufficient to pay the same and thus discharge the guarantors from all further liability, even if the next General Assembly should also refuse to comply with the law of 1895, above referred to.

"A statement of the assets and liabilities of the Institution will be found hereunto annexed. The undersigned officers and members of the Advisory Board most earnestly appeal for the sympathy and support of the citizens of Connecticut, in this work, and if the person to whom this circular letter is forwarded feels inclined to respond to this appeal, he or she will kindly fill out the enclosed certificate of guaranty and return the same to the REV. JOSEPH H. TWICHELL, No. 125 Woodland Street, Hartford, Conn., President of the Advisory Board of said Institution.

Most respectfully submitted,

Statement of Assets and Liabilities of

The Conn. Institute and Industrial Home for the Blind.

July 1st, 1897.

ASSETS.

1.	Value of plant September 30, 1895, valued at cost	$27,072.46
2.	Cash paid out for purchase of property and improvement of plant, by Treasurer, for year ending Sept. 30th, 1896	4.771.38
3.	Cash paid out for purchase of property and improvement of plant by Asst. Treasurer, for year ending Sept. 30th, 1896	1,079.59
4.	Amount appropriated by State for new buildings	15,000.00
5.	Cost of property purchased and improvement of plant for nine months ending June 30, 1897, Treasurer's account.	5,372.76
6.	Cost of property purchased and improvement of plant for nine months ending June 30th, 1897, Asst. Treasurer's account.	2,359.42
7.	Amount due from State for board and tuition of pupils	4,663.31
8.	Amount due from State for printing, etc.	132.23

INVENTORY JUNE 30TH, 1897.

9.	Mattress Department	346.88
10.	Broom "	898.15
11.	Merchandise "	734.33
12.	Printing "	69.82
13.	Hay, feed and other supplies	20.90
14.	Musical instruments acquired by Institution, by means of concerts and donations	600.00
15.	Other property acquired by Institution	125.00
16.	Bills and accounts receivable	1,770.81
17.	Cash on hand	186.43

Total $65,203.47

LIABILITIES.

18.	Balance of principal due on Kindergarten mortgage	$13,600.00
19.	Interest from January 1, to July 1, 1897	340.00

	Brought over..	13,94
20.	Principal due on School fund mortgage................................	4,35
21.	Interest from July 1, 1896. to July 1, 1897.................	26
22.	Bills and accounts payable for the purchase of property and improvement of plant..	4,61
23.	Bills and accounts payable for stock and material for mattress, broom, printing and merchandise departments, and current expenses...........	5,83
24.	Temporary loans and interest to date...	3,79

Total $32,79

Assets	$65,203.47
Liabilities	32.793.69
	$32,409.78

LETTERS SENT WITH CIRCULAR.

Rev. Joseph H. Twichell, Chairman Advisory Board:

MY DEAR SIR :—

"In submitting the foregoing statement of Assets and Liabilities, permit m call your attention to the fact that had the general Assembly of 1897 appropri the amount needed to carry into effect Section 1, Chapter 303, Public Acts of 1 the State would have paid over to our Treasurer the sums represented by items 5 and 6, amounting to $13,583,15; this added to items 7, 8 and 17 would have nished the sum of $18,565.12, which would have been available to disch liabilities represented by items 19, 21, 22, 23 and 24, amounting to $14.843.69 leave a balance in treasury of $3,721.43, which added to bills and accounts rece ble, and stock and materials on hand, as represented by items 9, 10, 11, 12, 13 16, would have furnished a capital of $7,562.32 with which to enter upon the of the succeeding year.

"Your attention is also called to the fact that in less than four years, (the en time being within the period of business depression) the management, aide devoted friends, have been able to acquire the difference between assets and lia ties, less the $15,000 received from the State, which amounts to $17,409.78 to wh by the appraisal made by A. W. Scoville, Architect, Edward Shelton, broker real estate dealer, and Robert D. Bone, Chairman of the Board of Assessors; 1 would be entitled to add the sum of at least $10,000 covered by the appreciatio value of the real estate purchased for the Institution.

Most respectfully submitted,

F. E. CLEAVELAND.

HARTFORD, CONN., July 29th, 18ç

"We hereby certify that we are fully acquainted with the real estate owned the Conn. Institute and Industrial Home for the Blind, in Hartford, Conn., know its value and that in our judgment, placing the same at a low and conservative valuation, the Trustees would be fully warranted by the appreciations in its value during the past four years, to appraise the same in their statement of assets at $10,000 more than the original purchase price of the same, exclusive of improvements.

Signed,

EDWARD SHELTON,

Broker and Real Estate Dealer.

ROBERT D. BONE,

Chairman Board of Assessors.

"In a letter dated July 29th, 1897, addressed to the President of the Institution, A. W. Scoville, architect, making use of substantially the same language as above, places the appreciation in value of the real estate of the Institution, for the past four years, at $11,980, instead of $10,000."

The necessity for issuing the foregoing appeal would never have occurred had not the General Assembly failed to appropriate an amount sufficient to provide for carrying into effect the provisions of Sec. 1, Chapter 303 of the Public Acts of 1895, above cited; and the surface reason for such failure was not the real reason, namely a depleted treasury, but one that lay much deeper and one which will continually operate to embarrass and hamper the work of the Board of Education of the Blind in the discharge of its duty under the law, unless the people of the State can be made to understand and appreciate its significance, and relation to the future success of the efforts of this department.

Within the easy recollection of the citizens of the Capital of this State, the people of Hartford were shocked and thrown into a great state of excitement by the sudden collapse in the night of one of the principal hotels. Had this hostelry at the time been known to be unoccupied, its collapse would have occasioned but a passing interest; but all knew that buried beneath the debris of timbers and brick there were many persons who undoubtedly were yet alive. Following quickly upon the intelligence of the wreck of the hotel, came an alarm of fire, and it was known that those buried beneath the ruins, who were yet alive, were in imminent danger of perishing amid the flames.

The city was stirred to its center. The people with but a single impulse thronged the streets. The militia was summoned and the Fire and Police Departments, with unparalled energy began the work of rescue, nor did their activity abate until every brick and timber that might hold down and imperil the life of a human being had been cleared away. And as one after another of the buried victims of the disaster were lifted out of their perilous position, there went up from the assembled thousands a glad and triumphant shout.

Let us suppose that at this time some would-be guardian of the City Treasury had undertaken to hinder the work of rescue by raising the question of expense, by pointing out that there was a depleted treasury, and that the city could not afford to expend money for this purpose. How would such a proposition have been received by its citizens?

Again let us suppose, and we but relate the facts of cases within our knowledge, as follows:

Case number one.—A young man, the only son of a widowed mother, who has stepped manfully forward and assumed the burden of her support, and who, when he is in a fair way to succeed,. is suddenly and without his fault, stricken with blindness. He looks into the future and believes he is compelled to choose between being a burden upon his parent, or spending a lifetime as a pauper in the town poor-house. He chooses rather to take his own life, and is only prevented from so doing by the timely appearance of a friend. While in this extremity, he is taken by the hand and led up and out of a condition of despondency, bordering on despair, and given the opportunity of learning a useful trade, by means of which he will be able not only to provide for his own support, but to again successfully undertake the support of his mother.

When this has been accomplished, has not the life of this young man been as truly saved, as any who were rescued from the burning ruin of the building men-tioned in the preceding illustration?

Case number two.—An orphaned child, at fifteen years of age, becomes blind, and being friendless, she becomes the inmate of a poor-house. When she became blind she was bright and as far advanced in her studies in the common school as any girl of her age. At twenty-four years of age, through the inactivity of mind and body, she has become a mental and physical wreck.

Case number three.—A child blind from birth and supported at the expense of the town, is allowed to grow up in ignorance and become a life-long pauper.

Multiply these cases with varying conditions of hardship, until we have an average of one in every thousand inhabitants, and let it be understood that by pro-viding a suitable Institution to receive, instruct, and by paternal oversight furnish employment for, the blind, where by the cultivation of self-reliance and habits of industry they can maintain themselves in a comfortable home amid pleasant sur-roundings, with agreeable companionship.

Press this upon the attention of the Legislature of a state until it sees its duty plainly, and creates a commission consisting of the Governor and the Chief Justice, as the responsible and trusted representatives of the interests of the State, who call to their assistance other men, well known for their business ability, wisdom, and probity. Entrust with this commission the establishment of an Institution that shall be conducted so as to accomplish for the blind what we have pointed out as both possible and practicable.

Let this Commission report to the next General Assembly of the State; have its action approved, its recommendations adopted, and provision made to carry them into effect.

Let the work be carefully and conscientiously carried forward, relying upon the State to fulfill its obligations by coming to the support of its trusted servants. Let buildings be erected, furnished and equipped with necessary machinery and apparatus pursuant to an Act which provides that these buildings and their furnish-ings shall be paid for by the State. Let indebtedness and obligations be incurred and then let the next General Assembly refuse to make an appropriation to meet these obligations, and you will have a brief history of the work begun and carried forward in the State of Connecticut, to provide for the instruction and employment of the blind up to the time when it became necessary for officers and trustees of the Connecticut Institute and Industrial Home for the Blind to issue the appeal before cited.

It now becomes incumbent upon us to point out the real reason underlying or explaining the action of the last General Assembly. It is just as impossible to believe that there could be found a single representative of the people, who, as a member of this honorable body, would take the ground that the State obligations to the blind should be thus ignored, on account of the condition of its Treasury, as to believe there could be found a citizen of Hartford who would have raised a similar question to arrest the work of rescuing the victims of the Park Central disaster.

The real reason, then, was the same that influenced the young man in Case No. 1, above cited, to attempt to take his own life, and it is the same reason that every blind person who has attempted to rise above a condition of dependence. and who has succeeded in the attempt, will agree is an obstacle an hundred times more difficult to surmount, than to accomplish without sight every other condition or requirement precedent to success. The reason then, is the belief on the part of those who see that blindness is such a condition of hopeless disability that it is folly for them to attempt to become proficient in any walk of life, or to do effective work that will enable them to throw off the burden of dependence and become self-reliant, self-sustaining and useful members of society. Hence that it is folly for the State to spend money in furtherance of this object.

To make this still plainer, let us suppose that the great inventors, Morse or Bell, had not been able to demonstrate the possibilities of the telegraph and telephone, but relying on theory, had either of them appeared before the General Assembly, asking for an appropriation to lay a cable across the Atlantic Ocean or construct a telephone plant similar to thousands now in operation throughout the United States. It would be easy to foresee that many generations would have come and gone before the practical utility of these great inventions could have been established, but, like Morse and Bell, the blind people of this generation are able to demonstrate that it is possible and practicable for every blind person who is not otherwise handicapped, if afforded a reasonable opportunity, to become proficient and succeed in many different occupations and professions.

The most discouraging and difficult feature of the problem. however, is to discover or foresee how many times we shall be obliged to make out a case, and before how many different General Assemblies of the State we shall be summoned to appear and be required to meet and overcome the same prejudices, or, more correctly, prejudgment of persons wholly unacquainted with the achievements of the blind.

This is certainly a problem, to attempt the solution of which is most difficult and disheartening, especially when the testimony of the most advanced thinkers on the subject, and the most experienced educators of the blind, is to be lightly thrown aside by servants of the State whose knowledge on the subject comes only from a mere surface opinion.

The men entrusted by the last General Assembly to consider, approve or disapprove the measures which this Board deemed were necessary to enable it to proceed successfully with its work, were outspoken in their opinion that any attempt to make the blind self-supporting was a mere waste of time, and to expend the money of the State for this purpose was the height of folly. We were compelled to listen without an opportunity to reply to a man who, in addressing one branch of this General Assembly, (House of Representatives) and who, from his position, held the fate of the measure in his hand, held that it was impossible for blind people to accomplish that which, for the past twenty-five years has been and is being successfully accomplished by them in nearly every Working Home for the blind in the United States.

We quote now from a leading authority on the subject who for many years has been connected with institutions for the blind, Dr. E. Park Lewis, of the New York Institute. He says:

"There are two things to be done: First, to impress upon the blind themselves the fact that they have within themselves possibilities worth developing, though they may lie in quite different lines from any they have heretofore followed; second, to make the individual members of this great Commonwealth understand that there are obligations in relation to the blind which far transcend the mere giving of alms.

"Assistance, to be effective, must be ready in two ways: It is imperative that the State should establish and maintain industrial training schools for adults, as well as schools for children, and the various trades should be taught thoroughly. Of the few whom the State has already educated, a large number have been successful in their work. But, that a larger proportion may become so, the assistance must not cease at the critical time, when the blind man starts out to face an uninformed and practically unsympathetic public, equipped to earn his own living. *This public, while it would contribute collectively, this support, were he in a poor-house or asylum, would not individually, know how to receive him.*"

It is at this point that French philanthropy has been more far seeing than our own, and that chiefly through the eyes of a blind man. Maurice de la Sizeranne, appreciating the difficulties that his blind co-workers were obliged to meet, established by indefatigable effort an organization well-nigh perfect in its details, one chief function of which is to bring the educated blind in touch with those by whom their services might be required.

A church in need of an organist may secure one through this association; firms wanting chair-caners, mattress or broom-makers, may be supplied; and good piano-tuners are furnished upon application.

Professor C. F. Fraser, the blind principal of the Canadian Institution for the Blind, at Halifax, N. S., which is one of the most, if not *the* most, successful institution in America, in securing to its pupils the greatest and most permanent benefit through its methods of instruction and subsequent paternal oversight, and Dr. F. J. Campbell, (also blind,) principal of the Royal Normal College for the Blind, of Great Britain, justly celebrated as the greatest and most advanced educator of the blind in Europe or America, are both most emphatic in their estimation of the value of work along the lines indicated by Dr. Lewis, in the language just quoted, and any endeavor that fails in this most important, not to say indispensible feature of our labors in behalf of the sightless, would be like planting and nourishing the growth of a tree only to leave the fruit unplucked to wither and decay.

Notwithstanding that this testimony, in a previous report, has been pressed by us upon the attention of all who were called upon to pass judgment upon this question, we have a youthful servant of the State, whose duty it is to visit one hundred and sixty-eight different institutions in the State, and to know more about what is required for the proper management and successful administration of the affairs of each than those in charge of the work, coming forward with his private judgment and opinion that the work undertaken in this State for the blind cannot be successfully accomplished. He makes, as he must in all cases, a flying visit to our Institution, and he is able to say that the Printing Industry of the Institution which we consider an unqualified success, is of little use. If our information is correct, our critic is not especially qualified by experience or knowledge of the printing business to pass such a summary judgment, and in order that the public might have the benefit of the judgment of experts in the business, the men at the head of the leading printing and publishing houses in the State were requested by us to inspect this department, see our blind people at work, and pass their judgment on the practicability of employing the blind in this industry.

The following statement which we were able to publish for the information of the public, was the result: .

"This is to certify that the undersigned, by the request of the officials of the Industrial Home for the Blind at Nos. 334 and 336 Wethersfield Avenue, Hartford, Conn., have this day visited and inspected the job printing department of said Institution, that we there saw a number of blind persons engaged in various kinds of work in job printing. Two were feeding power presses, two were printing on hand presses, another was binding pamphlets and showed his ability to take the work from the hands of the pressman and do all that was necessary to complete the work, making use of the wire staple binding machine in so doing, others were folding and making packages ready for the mail.

"The work was well done and in our opinion it is possible and practicable for one seeing person to keep from six to eight blind persons profitably employed in the job printing business. We also inspected the plant and outfit and upon being told that the cost did not exceed twenty-four hundred dollars, we are of the opinion that it was purchased exceedingly cheap and that the results attained fully justify the outlay."

MARCUS A. CASE,
Vice-President C. L. & B. Co.
J. E. FLANIGAN,
Foreman, Fowler & Miller Co.
CHAS. M. GAINES,
Printer.

Hartford, May 28, 1897.

———

It would appear that although the State created and especially commissioned this Board to superintend and provide for the instruction of the blind in this State, and that notwithstanding under the rules which it has been authorized to make, it has proceeded with the approval of all its members, and the sanction of all the members of the Advisory Board of the Institution, it must nevertheless, convince this gentleman and the Board which he represents that it is not attempting an impossibility, or it will be compelled to meet and answer his objections before each succeeding General Assembly.

Realizing as we do, that his ideas are held in common by the majority of seeing people, we therefore undertake, from the standpoint of the blind to prove that a more careful and thorough knowledge of the subject will enable the people of this State to form a different opinion. We believe he thinks he is conscientiously discharging his duty to the State, and we therefore appeal to him and the Board that he represents to listen impartially to the presentation of the proof that it is possible for the blind, WITH PROPER OPPORTUNITIES, to cease to be dependent, and by their own labor win the right to demand that they shall no longer be classified with insane persons, convicts, imbeciles, paupers and other incapables.

We therefore appear as an advocate before a Tribune of the people who, we shall imagine, has all the prejudices and disbelief in the ability of the blind, shown by our critics.

My first witness shall be your own REASON, from a different standpoint than the one you now occupy. When the hopes, aspirations and all that is worth living for in the lives of the blind are to be placed on one side of the scale, the Judge who is to hold the balance, should be an ideal judge. , Let me therefore place over your eyes a bandage; for the wisdom of the ages has created as its ideal a Goddess of Justice with bandaged eyes. Now that you cannot see, a Venus or Hebe might appear to testify and your judgment remain as undisturbed and dispassionate as though you were listening to a story of a poor but honest washer-woman.

Again, while you are thus deprived of sight, let me for the sake of argument, ask you to imagine the limitation *permanent.* Have you any objection now to be classed with imbeciles, insane persons, paupers and convicts? If I should ask you if the loss of sight did not place you in as hopeless a situation as the imbecile or insane, would you not reply: "No, a thousand times no! The eye is but the servant of the brain, I am far better off than the insane because my reason is not dethroned."

Yes, you are right. Your REASON is like a king who in his palace sits enthroned. Your sense of sight is but one of five grand avenues of approach along which swift-footed messengers bring tidings of what transpires throughout your kingdom. You lose this sense of sight and you have but closed the palace gates of *one* of these grand avenues. But the messengers who are thus debarred, are only HINDERED, not dismayed. For quickly they approach the throne along the other four. Before you lost your sight you thought that little more could be accomplished for the blind than to provide them food, raiment and shelter, but now, with plenty of time to think it over and revise your former opinion, shall you feel compelled to resign the office you now hold and live in idle dependence on your fortune or friends, or perchance, if your fortune and friends should be swept away, will you be content to take a place in some neglected corner of a town poor-house? Or will you say in your mind, what blind men have accomplished may be again accomplished by the blind? Remembering Mr. Faucett, who was chosen by Gladstone as a Cabinet Minister, would you not say if it was possible for him to make an eminently successful Postmaster General of a great empire, will it not be possible for me to retain the office I now hold, and still find a way in which I can faithfully discharge my duty as a public servant?

Would you think it possible for a blind man to use the eyes of others as men use spectacles, and become one of the most celebrated naturalists of his day? Turn to your encyclopedia and read the life of Huber who is still the leading authority on the particular lines he followed out. Let us have his testimony in his own words on this point. We quote his language to a friend who could see.

"I am much more certain of what I declare to the world than you are, for you publish what your own eyes only have seen, while I take the mien among many witnesses."

It is related of Michael Angelo that on an occasion when out walking with a friend, he pointed out a rough, unhewn rock, and inquired of his friend what he saw. The reply was, "I see nothing, but a huge, rough rock." "But I," said Michael Angelo, "see lying concealed in that rock the form of an angel." And later, this celebrated sculptor released from its imprisonment the angel he had seen.

But you reply, "Michael Angelo was not blind. You do not mean to affirm that the blind can enter the domain of art successfully? Yet note what is said of John Conelli, in a book entitled "Achievements of the Blind," published at Rochester, N. Y., by Artman & Hall in 1872.

"Perhaps the most complete triumph of tactual perfection over want of sight that history records, is to be found in the artistic skill of John Conelli, sometimes called Gambasio, from the place of his birth in Tuscany. This remarkable person lost his sight at the age of twenty, and after having been in this condition about ten years, he first manifested a taste for sculpture. His first work in this art was to imitate a marble figure representing Cosmo de Medici, which he formed of clay, and rendered a strikingly perfect likeness of the original. His talent for statuary soon developed itself to such a degree that the Grand Duke Ferdinand, of Tuscany, sent him to Rome to model a statue of Pope Urban VIII, which he completed to the entire satisfaction of his patron. It is supposed that this is the same famous blind sculptor whom Roger de Piles met with in the Justinian Palace where he found him modeling in clay a figure af Minerva.

"It is related that the Duke of Bracciano, who had seen him at work, doubted much that he was completely blind, and in order to set the matter at rest he caused the artist to model his head in a dark cellar. It proved a striking likeness. Some, however objecting that the Duke's beard which was of patriarchal amplitude, had made the operation of producing a seeming likeness too easy, the artist offered to model one of the Duke's daughters which he accordingly did, and this also proved an admirable likeness. Among his numerous other works is a marble statue of Charles I of England, said to be finely finished."

Let us now ask you to turn once more to your Britanica, and read that James Holman, an officer in the English army, after losing his sight, became one of the most famous travelers of his time; that in 1835 he published a four volume edition of his travels entitled "A Voyage Around the World," of which the author of the article in the Britanica writes:

"The works of Holman, besides the interest attaching to them from his incidental references to the peculiarities of his circumstances arising from his physical defect, and his methods of triumphing over his difficulties, occupy a unique place in literature as products of very extraordinary energy and perseverance, while on account of variety of their information and their frequently graphic descriptions, they are of considerable value as books of travel."

Entering the domain of poetry and history, it is hardly necessary to ask you to recall that Homer completed the Illiad and composed the Odyssey after he became blind. That it was not until after Milton was turned from his political career by his becoming blind that he wrote "Paradise Lost," and that our own Prescott, author of "Ferdinand and Isabella," "Conquest of Mexico" and "Conquest of Peru," gathered his material and produced these valuable contributions to history after losing his sight.

We are living in an age of wonderful achievements of the mind, and the triumph of inventions. If any noted scientist should announce that he had opened up communication with the inhabitants of another planet, *who* among us would stake our lives or fortunes that he could not demonstrate the truth of his declaration? And yet, let me summon the most noted scientists and inventors of this generation before you and ask them if they have not seen more that was of service to them in their labors when their heads were lying on their pillows and their eyes were closed, than at any other time.

Did you ever consider that the messenger whom we are now able to send around the world in thirty minutes was never seen by Mr. Morse or any of his successors in electrical experiments, and that it was to his sense of hearing and not his sense of sight that the world is indebted for the invention of the telegraph?

Blind men as clergymen have attained to the greatest eminence. Thomas Blacklock, D. D., who was born in Scotland, lost his sight while an infant, but became an eminent divine and author. (Achievements of the Blind, page 70.)

The Rev. Richard Lucas, D. D., was a noted divine and author. (Achievements of the Blind, page 52.)

There is to-day a physician in active practice in the city of Hartford, holding an important office under the law, who is so nearly blind that there could be found many pupils in any institution for the blind whose percentage of sight is very much greater.

William E. Cramer, of Milwaukee, as a journalist and at one time editor of t Albany Argus, and later editor and proprietor of the Evening Wisconsin, at M waukee, ranks among the distinguished men of that vocation in this country.

Mr. Herreshoff, of Bristol, R. I., has held the palm against all seeing co petitors. The yachts made after his designs and under his supervision have proud borne the stars and stripes, leading in every contest with the swiftest sailing yach constructed by the most skillful of our British cousins.

The "Mentor," a work published in Boston, and devoted to the interests of t blind, records the following instances:

"Printing and book-binding successfully attempted." (Vol. I, page 121.)

"Successful Telegraph Operators." (Vol. I, page 356, also Vol. 3, page 313.)

"Farming and Mining." (Vol. I, page 251.)

"Typewriting." (Vol. I, page 17.)

"Piano Tuning." (Vol. 2, page 263.)

"Stenography and Editorial Work." (Vol. 2, page 56.)

"Crystal Cutter." (Vol. 3, page 221.)

"David Wood, of Philadelphia, an organist at the head of his profession." (Vc 3, page 41.)

"John Metcalf, Yorkshire, England, remarkably successful as a contractor a builder." (Vol. 3, page 25.)

"Watch and Clockmaking, by William Huntly and William Kennedy (Achievements of the Blind, page 250.)

To these the more ordinary pursuits of brushmaking, basket making, cha caning, mattress making and broom making may be added.

In England there has existed for a number of years an association of phila thropists, known as the British and Foreign Association, who have charged the selves with the work of creating opportunities and facilities for furnishing emplo ment for the adult blind.

In Connecticut, we have had many associations for the advancement of ma worthy objects, including a State Association for the prevention of cruelty animals, and a State Board of Charities, but until the friends of the present wo which has resulted in the establishment of a "State Board of Education of the Blind began their labor, no one, not even the State Board of Charities, had made it b business to look after the elevation and advancement of this class of our citizens.

An interesting account of the founding of an institution in Brazil will be foul in Vol. I, page 130, of "The Mentor," from which we select the following:

"In 1872 was laid the foundation of a building sufficiently large, when complete to receive six hundred pupils,—four hundred boys and two hundred girls. T annual receipts of five lotteries were appropriated to this institution, this sum, wi the accumulating interest and various donations which would be given, to constitu a fund for the maintainance of the establishment.

"The accommodations thus provided for six hundred pupils are far from me ing the needs of the country. Recent statistics show the number of blind childre between the ages of six and fourteen years, in the Empire of Brazil to be abo 12,000. Accordingly, six other schools for the blind are to be established in t chief towns of the provinces of Para, Pernambuco, Bahia, Minas-Geraes, Sao Paul and Rio Grande de Sul. In connection with each of these schools a workshop w be provided to give employment to those who cannot earn a livelihood by music the liberal professions. The Institution at Rio will then become a training school furnish teachers for the provincial establishment.

"The pupils of this institution are supported and educated at the expense of tl government. The first teachers were seeing persons, and their appointments we for life. In 1886 three vacancies occurred, and these were filled by former pupils of the school who had been assistants. The religious teaching is given by an ecclesiastic, and in three other branches—namely, natural sciences, playing of wind instruments, and the needlework for girls—the training is given by teachers who have sight; but in all other departments of the school—in the elementary classes in Portugese, arithmetic, algebra, geometry, geography, history, French, the piano, harmony, piano-tuning, printing and book-binding,—the instruction is given by blind teachers.

"Among the successful graduates of this school are cited two wealthy farmers; one man who has earned a competency by raising stock; another, a poet, novelist and musician, who is organist in the richest church in Rio; a fifth who is a teacher of the French language; and a sixth who, as a piano-tuner, music-teacher, and conductor of an orchestra, has reared a family in comfortable circumstances and will probably become rich. Among the girls who have graduated, are mentioned one who became a distinguished pianist, and another who is a charming vocalist."

Now, then, if it please the Court, let us stop a moment, and see where we are.

Are we assuming too much if we claim that we have succeeded in maintaining the following propositions: First, that *blindness itself* is not an impassable barrier preventing a person with this limitation from becoming a self-reliant, self-sustaining and useful member of society? Second, that the only reason why all blind people who are otherwise mentally and physically sound, do not become self-sustaining, is not because they are *blind*, but because the general belief entertained by all their seeing friends, (including their parents,) has in the case of children, robbed them of that training and discipline essential to a successful career even on the part of those who can see, and in the case of the adult blind operating to confirm *them* in the belief that they are rendered helpless by the loss of sight. Third, that Connecticut, in its labors for the blind, (to say nothing of what our sister states have done,) is twenty years behind even our neighbors in South America.

It is possible that we may not have sufficiently emphasized the importance of educating the seeing public on these points. So important, however, is this phase of the work, that all else sinks to insignificance compared with it. You may teach the blind as much as you please, they may become even more skillful and proficient in what they undertake than any of their seeing competitors, as Mr. Herreshoff undoubtedly is. But, when you send them forth into the world and they run up against the solid wall of public disbelief in their ability to accomplish anything without sight, they in ninety-nine cases out of a hundred will give up the struggle and settle back into a condition of idle dependence. Now this same public will receive them without question, where, in their apparent helplessness, they but serve to confirm the public in its erroneous belief.

Some years before the locomotive had found its way into Utah, a small army of Mormon proselytes started to march from Denver to Salt Lake City, drawing their luggage and supplies with them in handcarts. This march, known in history as the "Handcart Expedition," was begun later in the fall than was expected and before they had covered half the distance winter had set in. The extreme cold, driven by the bleak winds, chilled the very marrow in their bones and their trail was easy to follow for years after by the skeletons of those who perished. Only a mere handful out of that large company ever reached their goal.

The blind persons who have attained success, in spite of the disbelief of the world in their ability to do so, may be compared with the survivors of this ill-fated expedition.

Just what a train of cars drawn by a locomotive over the iron rails that now bind Denver to Salt Lake City would have done for these poor, perishing Mormon, the education of the seeing public on the point in issue will do for the blind; and if I could summon before the Tribune the two thousand successful blind people out of the sixty-two thousand in the United States in 1890, every one would tell you the same story that the brave girl writes me in a letter which I here introduce:

"I graduated in the Ohio School for the Blind in the class of 1889 and entered the Cleveland College of the Western Reserve University, in the following September.

"It was my ambition on leaving college, to obtain a position in some seeing school, to teach those branches which I had found by careful investigation, that a properly trained blind teacher could teach seeing pupils quite as well as a seeing teacher. I felt sure that if I could succeed in this, I might open a field for those of the blind who could fit themselves for such work, and break down a little of the aversion to our doing anything practicable. It is hardly necessary however, for me to say that, though I did my utmost, and though I had the best of commendations, I failed to find anyone who would give me a trial. There were plenty of seeing teachers seeking employment, and those who had positions to give either did not believe that I could do their work, or they were unwilling to try the experiment. Perhaps if I had had influential friends in some of the schools, it might have been otherwise.

"In the meantime, I maintained myself by private teaching, tutoring and writing, until my failing health made it necessary for me to have country air and outdoor exercise. I believe that the blind, properly trained, and conveniently located, can do nicely in each of the above named fields, and it is easier to overcome prejudice where only the individual is concerned.

"At present I am not doing much of anything but trying to regain my strength. Yet I hope to be able to go to work soon. Like yourself, I am deeply interested in our class, and I hope we may become better acquainted. It is hardly necessary for me to add that if I can be of any assistance to you in your work I am entirely at your service."

Yours truly,

ROBERTO ANNA GRIFFITH.

We have several times cited a book entitled "Achievements of the Blind." I now ask you to receive in evidence the testimony of its authors on the point we are now considering. We take the following from the introduction:

"We will not weary the reader's patience with an elaborate preliminary, nor with apologies for offering the present work to the public. We have been induced to enter the arena of book-makers by a desire to disseminate a more correct and extended knowledge of blindness and its effects upon mental and physical development than the reading public has hitherto possessed. In this way we hope to remove some of the most formidable obstacles that hedge up the way to usefulness and independence for all who are placed in this condition; a condition to which, by the vicissitudes of life, every person is exposed, and in whose dark and inauspicious night more than five hundred thousand of our race are at present enshrouded, in almost every state of our Union, as well as in those of Europe. Charity, with her angelic hand, has raised within the present century institutions dedicated to the sacred purpose of giving the light of science and a knowledge of some of the useful arts to those who behold not the beautiful earth and serene sky. But sad experience has taught us that until society in general better understands and appreciates the abilities of the blind, all the knowledge and skill we can acquire at these establishments are not available as means of self-support but tend only to awaken a keener sense of our privation and dependence. To illustrate: A young man graduates at one of our institutions for the blind, after receiving a thorough course of instruction in the theoretical and practical sciences. Elated with the hope of henceforth being able to earn for himself a respectable livelihood as a teacher of music, or of some other science, he hears of a vacant situation and makes the necessary application, but is informed that as he cannot see, he cannot, of course, discharge the requisite duties. The next time an opportunity offers he determines to go in person, say a hundred miles and in winter, too, to show that he is qualified. If a knowledge of music is required, he performs with proficiency; if of literature, philosophy or mathematics, he is ready and clear and proves himself competent to the discharge of all the duties of the employment that he seeks. But the idea that one who can see is more serviceable than one who cannot, still erects an impenetrable wall between him and success. And thus the prejudice which his condition creates opposes him on every side.

"Without hesitation we say, that all the most painful disadvantages with which we have been obliged to contend under the absence of sight, have arisen entirely from ignorance on the part of communities of our capability and resources.

"Sympathy, like the atmosphere, surrounds us on every side, but like the atmosphere, is too light to sustain life. To acknowledge that our present work may have faults and imperfections, is only to admit that it has been produced by human agency. But we certainly cannot ask to have them excused or loved in consequence of our peculiar condition. No; attribute them to our ignorance, carelessness, or stupidity, but we pray thee, reader or critic, attribute them not to blindness, for this we must deem rather an advantage than an inconvenience in the art of composition."

After a quarter of a century's experience, during which time we have taken an active part in the affairs of life, and attained a certain measure of success, we here solemnly affirm that nine-tenths of the difficulties experienced have been due to the unwillingness of the public to believe in our ability to accomplish what we undertook. And now, Your Excellency, turning from our imaginary Tribune, we propose to take the public somewhat into our confidence. We confess that we foresaw that as soon as the work for the blind in Connecticut assumed the proportions that it was bound to assume if we discharged our duty faithfully, we should meet with serious opposition from those who did not understand the importance of the work, and from those who have always stood in the way of human progress, just as the public school system (which is the proudest monument Connecticut has ever erected to bear testimony to the enlightenment and civilization of her people,) was persistently opposed.

It was in order that we should be prepared to meet the storm when it came, that we have labored in season and out of season, and that our young blind people have given exhibitions in nearly every town in the State, so as to raise up friends for the work, who would understand and appreciate its importance and who would stand by us when the battle was on.

We felt that we had accomplished what we had undertaken, when we were able to support our recommendations by a memorial to the General Assembly containing such names as, Ex-Gov. Charles R. Ingersoll, Pres. Dwight, of Yale College, Theodore S. Woolsey, Rev. Newman Smythe, Rev. T. T. Munger, Ex-Gov. H. B. Harrison, Judge Simeon E. Baldwin, of New Haven, and Bishop Williams and Ex-Gov. O. Vincent Coffin, of Middletown, Henry C. Robinson, James G. Batterson, Rev. Francis Goodwin, Dr. Chester D. Hartranft, John R. Buck, and Chas. E. Gross, of Hartford, with twelve hundred and fifty prominent and representative names from all the principal cities and towns in the State, standing not only for a large majority of its voting population, but representing three-fourths of the grand list of the State. These memorials referred to the Committee on Appropriations, formed but a part of the hearing a report of which appeared in the Hartford Courant on the morning following the day assigned, and which report we here quote:

After referring to the presentation of the needs of the Institution for the Blind, by the Secretary of the State Board of Education of the Blind, the report proceeds as follows:

"Rodney Dennis spoke in favor of the appropriation and viewed it from the standpoint of duty the State owed to the blind.

"The Rev. J. H. Twichell said: 'By making this appropriation, the State will only be following where others have led. Many individuals have put aside comfort in order to help the blind. Of course it is a matter of pity that we are obliged to come before the Committee in the present state of affairs and ask for money. A good father once admonished his son not to be a spendthrift but to keep within his salary if he had to borrow money to do so. If necessary, we should do that way, rather than neglect the crying wants of humanity.

"Ex-Lieut-Gov. Cady said that one thing that should lead the State to aid the blind was that they were doing all they could to help themselves. Other unfortunates had been provided for, but none could be more worthy than these poor people. They had got into debt and asked for aid. It seemed to him there was an obligation the State ought to assume. In closing, he said: 'I hope the appropriation may be met as far as you gentlemen see fit.'

"The Rev. Dr. G. M. Stone called attention to the fact that the blind movement started in the slums. This fact should be especially considered in its favor. The object was such a worthy one that he felt it would be rightly met.

"Prof. A. R. Merriam, of the Theological Seminary, had for a long time been interested in watching the blind work go on. The reports of their work were most favorable and the State should help them obtain the pecuniary aid they needed.

"Prof. J. J. McCook favored the bill and urged that the requirements be met. 'The most we can do,' he said, 'for these poor people is to bring the light of enlightenment to them.'

"T. M. Crowley, speaking for organized labor, said he was heartily in favor of the appropriation and was willing to do all he could as an individual to aid its being brought about.

"A blind man spoke of how he had been benefited by learning the trade of broom-making at an Industrial School for the Blind.

"Mrs. Foster, Ass't. Secretary of the Board of Education of the Blind,, related instances where the blind had been helped and stated that in certain cases blind eyes might be opened by giving them proper care. Others who spoke in favor of the appropriation were Mr. Job Williams (head of the School for Deaf-mutes,) Mrs. Whitmore, and Mrs. Olmsted.

"Mr. Cleaveland exhibited articles showing the work the Blind are capable of doing; he also showed a printed abstract of the names of prominent people of forty-five cities and towns who supported the bill. The list represented two-thirds of the grand list of the State and half the voters, he said."

From this it will be seen that to all appearances we were prepared to show good reasons why the State should go steadily forward with the work for the blind and make amends as soon as possible for past neglect.

We had made out a case before the Committee which we believed was unanswerable. And as no one appeared to controvert what had been said, or oppose the passage of the bill under consideration, we believed that all had been done that could be done to insure a favorable report. But you may imagine our surprise when a report was made which did not even provide for the payment of the obligation that had been incurred for the buildings and their equipment, which the law (hereinbefore cited) had fully empowered our Board to erect and furnish.

It would appear that the memorial to which we have referred, an abstract of which will be annexed to this report, was considered to be of no more account than so much waste paper, although every person who signed this memorial had a printed copy of the measure submitted to him, and those who know the men whose names appear therein, must believe that they are men who would not attach their names to any document of that character without due consideration.

Is the voice of the people, thus expressed to an assembly of the people's representatives, to be thus lightly put aside and ignored by a committee of that body, and a hearing to count for naught wherein a large number of esteemed and prominent citizens give expressions to their views favoring the measure under consideration, when not a voice is heard in opposition?

We can only hope that the Joint Standing Committee on Appropriations appointed by the next General Assembly will more carefully consider such measures of relief and assistance as this Board may deem it advisable to recommend, bearing in mind that those who have been appointed and commissioned under the law to ascertain the needs of these people and study into the methods best calculated to promote the objects for which it was created, should be given due weight.

We submit herewith a statement from the Superintendent of the Industrial Home for the Blind, and if the results for the past year do not come fully up to the expectation of our critics, let them try to appreciate what it means to be unexpectedly called upon to bear up and continue a work under a load of indebtedness contracted by authority of law, and which they had every reason to believe would be promptly met by the last General Assembly.

Most respectfully submitted,

F. E. CLEAVELAND, Sec'y.

REPORT OF

FRED D. CHILD, General Superintendent.

Dr.		Cr.	
To Balance from acct. of George Marshall, Treas., Oct. 1, '96	543 84	By Cash Paid out on acct. of Broom Dept.	1459
"Balance from acct. of H. L. Olmsted, Asst. Treas. Oct. 1, '96	343 12	"Cash paid out on acct. of Upholstery Dept.	2563
" Broom Dept. for year ending Sept. 30, '97	1619 57	" Cash paid out on acct. of Current Expenses	5931
" Upholstery Dept.	3980 71	" Cash paid out as above by Asst. Treas.	2840
" Cash from other than State pupils and sources not classified	1040 25	" Cash paid out on acct. of Salaries and Wages	8569
" Cash from Assistant Treas. and sources not classified	24 52	"Cash paid out as above by Asst. Treas.	3756
" Merchandise sold in Institution store	2726 54	"Cash paid out on account of Temporary Loans	2658
" Cash from Concert Co.	6195 50	" Cash paid out on acct. of Merchandise Dept.	2673
" Contributions entered and reported by Asst. Treas.	2529 94	" Cash paid out on acct. of Concert Co.	2631
" Printing Dept.	509 16	"Cash paid out on acct. of Printing Dept.	79
" Cash from George Marshall, Treas.	9726 64	" Check made over to Treas. from Concert Co.	181
" Cash from Ernest Cady, Treas.	4663 31	"Cash paid out for property and permanent improvement	4093
" " " " from Contributions from Concert Co., and other sources	669 04	" Cash paid out as above by Asst. Treas.	1279
" Cash from Ernest Cady, Treas. —Contributions from Asst. Treas.	659 54	"Balance	84
" Temporary Loans	3467 68		$38,803.
" Cash from Mrs. Olmsted, money contributions	103 67		
	$38,803.03		

HARTFORD, CONN., April 28th, 1898.

This certifies that we have examined the accounts of the Connecticut Institu and Industrial Home for the Blind for the fiscal year ending Sept. 30, 1897. Co pared the same with the Vouchers and found the same correct. The balance cash in the hands of the Superintendent on said date was Eighty-four Dollars a Forty-six Cents. ($84.46.)

FRANKLIN B. NOYES, ⎫ Auditors
D. WARD NORTHROP, ⎬ of
⎭ Public Accounts.

REPORT OF

SECRETARY

BOARD OF EDUCATION OF THE BLIND

YEAR ENDING SEPTEMBER 30, 1897.

KINDERGARTEN DEPARTMENT.

Of the twenty-seven blind children cared for during the year past, Hartford is represented by six, New Haven by four, and seventeen other towns of the State by one pupil each. This number includes only the children in the Hartford school and not those in Boston. Of this number, one child's sight was so much improved by medical and nurse's care, wholesome food, good air, and regular habits, that she was scarcely a subject for our Institution longer. Two of the older ones were discontinued, their progress being insufficient to warrant our keeping them longer at the State's expense, and five of our pupils were prepared to enter the Perkins Institute of Boston. From that Institution we have received most gratifying reports of their standing, which we feel is an assurance of the qualification and work of our teachers. We parted with these children with genuine heart-ache, they having been so long with us, and, shall we acknowledge, some reluctance, as they were our "Stars" in our school exhibitions; but their advancement demanded the transfer.

This transfer to Boston for the more advanced education, we deem a valuable advantage. First, it breaks the monotony of their school years; again, the promotion to a distant and larger school proves a great incentive to our older children, as well as to our instructors.

Our schedule of work is as follows:

A complete course of Kindergarten training. (It seems almost as if Froebel had received his inspiration in this direction to meet the peculiar needs of blind children, it being so wonderfully adapted to them.) Two years of primary school work. Included in this primary work is reading by "line type," reading and writing by the "Braille," method, writing in "square" hand, (this being done with a grooved board and pencil.) Number work by means of a type slate, language, history, and zoology. This last study is one of the most interesting, it being so satisfactorily comprehended by means of stuffed or clay models. Anything that comes within the *touch* of a blind child it feels it "can see."

PHYSICAL TRAINING is of the utmost importance also; it strengthens and straightens forms, and encourages active and free movement. Few of our children have ever had any free exercise before coming to us, and strong bodies will strengthen minds, we know.

> "Our feet are free to come and go,
> While theirs are *chained* with doubt and fear."

The loss of sight hampers them in walking. Running is almost an unknown power unless urged upon them. Physical inactivity can but result in impaired health; so, generally speaking, our work is begun here. Gymnastic drills, timed by chime-bells, are of great benefit, too. Musical dumb-bells enable us to do much work in classes which, without the aid of sound, would have to be taught individually. "*Sloyd*" *knitting* is also a factor in both mental and manual training.

We have been greatly favored by a kind friend to our School, Miss Louise Lee, of Hartford, (herself blind) who has furnished a special teacher, (a graduate of Pratt Institute,) and material for a class in "*Sloyd*" *carpentry work*. Interest and ambition has been awakened in some of the boys of this class, when efforts in all other directions had failed to arouse them. The knowledge and use of carpenter's tools as a foundation for trades, in the years to come, is of inestimable value.

Here I must refer to the Industrial Department of our Institution, and say that I should have but little heart to work with many of our children if it were not for its existence; and I trust by the time these who to-day are youth or children, need such a Home, it will be firmly established, "tried and true." Not by any means do I feel that all, or even a majority of our pupils will necessarily have to resort to it; we believe that many of these will go out into the world and make their way; but however high our hopes or standards may be for them, there will always be those to whom this Industrial Home will be a need and a boon.

MUSIC is a prime factor in the education of the blind. We do not teach it merely as an accomplishment; it means far more than that; it trains, it develops, it refines, and as a source of livelihood for many of those deprived of sight, it has been the most available of all pursuits. Many of this class have stood among the first musicians the world over.

While we do not claim that all blind people are musical, yet naturally, living in a world of sound, as our people do, the sense of hearing is highly cultivated and becomes acute. This cultivated hearing, together with their power for stronger mental concentration, we must accept as being greatly to their advantage in the sphere of music.

Our instructor in this department has attained more than satisfactory results during the past year; he has had about twenty children under his care, instructing individually, in chorus, duet (instrumental and vocal,) rhythm, and writing "Musical Braille." It is safe to say few professionals can distinguish and name chords, as struck upon the piano, major or minor, ("glad or sad," as the children say,) tell the key, and name the notes which compose the chords as readily and accurately as some of these little children.

A most pleasant and interesting feature of our musical department is the "Children's Orchestra." The instruments used are termed "toy" instruments, consisting of autoharps, harmonicas, fife, flageolet, drum, and, for the tiny children tambourines, triangles, cymbals, etc. They are accurately trained in their solo, trio and "full band" parts. While this is in the nature of diversion, and is more interesting to them than the monotony of their other work, it is, nevertheless, a valuable training in time and tune.

Some better idea of the work done may be given by including here the program of our exhibition at the close of the school year in June, 1897. I will also submit an original paper composed and read by one of our little girls—in the Zoology Class. The paper read is as follows:—

"There are two kinds of camels, the Bactrian and Arabian. The Arabian camel is found mostly in Arabia, Syria and Northern Africa, and the Bactrian in Central Asia.

"The Bactrian camel has two humps on its back, while the Arabian has only one. The camel has a small head and small ears, prominent eyes, a long neck, long legs, and cleft hoofs.

"As our good Creator has fitted us all for our different kinds of work, so he has fitted the camel to cross the desert.

"The camel can go without eating for several days because he stores a great deal of his food away in the humps on his back where it changes into fat, which nourishes him while crossing the desert. He can also go without drinking for several days, because he stores a good supply of water in his stomach, which he can draw from at any time he wishes. The camel's teeth are made so that he can chew the wiry grass and thistles which he may find in the desert. His stomach is also

fitted to digest them. He can close his nostrils at any time he wishes, to prevent the sharp, cutting sand from blowing into his nose. He has long heavy eyelashes, which protect his eyes from the rays of the sun. The camel has callous places on his chest and on the joints of his legs, which protect him from the hot sand when he kneels to take his burden. He has wide, clumsy feet which do not sink into the sand. He has pads on the bottom of them so that the hot sand does not burn them.

"The camel has very woolly hair which in summer may be pulled from the skin very easily. It is very useful to the Arab; he weaves it into different kinds of cloth; the coarser cloth is used as a covering for his tent, the finer is made into clothes. The skin of the camel can be made into very good leather.

"The camel belongs to the animal kingdom, to the branch vertebrata, because it has a back-bone; to the class mammalia, because it gives milk to its little ones; to the order ruminantia, because it is a cud-chewing animal, and it is a quadruped, or four-footed animal."

"JESSIE."

PROGRAM.

1. March and Gymnastic Drill.
2. Piano Duet, - - - - - Jessie and Anna.
3. Class in Zoology, - - - - - Paper and Classifying.
4. Violin Solo, - - - - - - Arthur Washington.
5. Sloyd Knitting, - - - - - Class.
6. Square Hand Writing, - - - - Class.
7. Piano Solo, - - - - - Jessie.
8. Kindergartners' - . - - March and Games.
9. Polka, - - - - - - Children's Orchestra.
10. Duet, - - - - - - Alice and Sadie.
11. Reading and Recitation, - -
12. Mocking Bird, - - - - - Children's Orchestra.
13. Waltz, . - - - - - - " "
14. Chorus, - - - - - - { (a) Old, Old Story. (b) Good-night Song.

We would not give the impression that with us it is "all work and no play." Our children live in an atmosphere of love—Heart-Sunshine abides with them. In *surroundings adapted* to them, the blind child can be made most happy. "There is no substitute for a child's way of being a child," and to the child-lover nothing can be more fascinating (however pathetic) than to watch these little ones at their play. Being so imaginative, and such mimics of sound, voices, etc., often while listening to them we "see ourselves as others see us," or rather *hear* ourselves as others *hear* us, so clever is their impersonation of matron, teacher, doctor or whoever it may be.

Our "Children's Matron" has one noble work, and her peculiar gift appears to be in character building.

Our teachers and care-takers have been faithful and zealous in their work, and satisfactory results have been fully realized from their efforts. Aside from their regular duties, (and they are onerous in this service,) they have given many extra hours of thought and labor for the comfort, happiness and welfare of the children.

With thankful hearts—we state that we have been spared the existence, and even serious alarm of illness during the entire year.

We are under the deepest obligations to Mr. St. John and his associate, Dr. Waite, Oculists, who have performed five operations for cataract and have taken devoted care of their little patients, in our home hospital rooms. This, and much more, they have done gratuitously.

Our work assumes to be only a Kindergarten course, and the first and second years of a primary course of instruction,—but as a matter of fact, at the present age and stage of our school it would be impossible to put into writing where our work begins or ends. In regard to this *special* work, there are several reasons why such a statement is necessarily so indefinite. One great reason is because of the recent beginning of this home-work for the blind children of Connecticut, in consequence of which we have not been able to get our children young enough for a normal beginning. We have to go back, undo, correct the waste and injury which the loss of these early and most important of years has meant to them. I am speaking here of children who are even possible candidates for our Kindergarten course.

There is another class whom we have found at ten, twelve, even fourteen years of age, whose training and development has been utterly neglected. I am glad to state that this condition of affairs is already beginning to yield. The best intentioned and most intelligent parents we have had to deal with are the ones who, after their children have been with us for a few weeks or months, have expressed themselves as appreciating most keenly that the observation, study, and experience with blind children, which are essential for their most intelligent development, are impossible to attain in the private home.

Up to two years ago, of thirty children gathered, but two applications had been made by parents. That at least four such applications have been made during the past year, is a gratifying evidence that the work is becoming known and more appreciated. Another most natural reason why we may hope to get the children younger is that parents are more reconciled to allowing them to attend school within the State's border. Again, we are learning of these children even while they are infants, and we can keep trace of them and look after them in *proper* time. This leads me to refer once more to the undue number of children whom we have termed "backward"—a result in almost every case of not being taken in time. Undeveloped mentally and physically, untrained and helpless, muscles feeble, vitality low for want of exercise, the brain and entire nervous system either in a condition of over-excitement, or the other extreme, benumbed and dormant. The result of our work in many of these cases has gladdened our hearts and this part of our labor might well be termed "rescue work," while in several instances (although we can claim to have *helped* all) we have been forced to relinquish hope after hope as to satisfactory progress, or at least results sufficient to warrant us in keeping them at the State's expense—and so have given them up.

Above, I said "undue number" of these "backward" children. I mean by this, that after the State is once thoroughly canvassed and "cleared up" by *systematic oversight*, such as it is the design of the "State Board of Education of the Blind," to exercise together with the help of the law to "prevent blindness," passed in 1893, by the State Board of Health, we trust this class of cases will be greatly reduced in the future.

Getting these children while young does not mean that our State is going to be financially overburdened in this direction—there being a fair estimate of one case of blindness to a thousand inhabitants (only a small proportion of these are children,) we believe the average number in attendance in our Hartford School during the ten years to come will not exceed thirty. But what the fact of getting these children *early* does mean, is in favor of *both the child and the State.*

"Good the beginning, good the end shall be." Give the normal, trusting mind —before it has been wrought upon by isolation, deception, and repeated shocks; the little body,— before it has outgrown the unused muscles; give the sensitive and the impressionable years to the teacher and Kindergarten environment, and we may hope uniform development will result. This will mean stronger and abler men and women, while the same effort removed along the life of a child five or eight years, can only yield at most, a partial result for good.

It is an established fact the world over, that it pays to educate the blind—that it is not only a duty, but an *economy*—looking to a depth and height beyond the question of dollars and cents, what a *privilege!* Is there a Gospel more vital than that of educating, "giving light to," the blind?

Respectfully submitted,

EMILY WELLS FOSTER, Asst. Sec'y.

CONTRIBUTIONS.

Contributions to Connecticut Nursery and Kindergarten for the Blind, fo years ending September 30, 1897—as per audited accounts of Mrs. H. L. Ol Asst. Treasurer.

Allen, Mrs. B. R.,	$45 00	Chapin, Mr. F. H.,
Allen, Mrs. S. H.,	10 00	Clark, Miss Mary,
Andrews, Miss Kate,	1 00	Cole, Mrs. Charles J.,
Avery, Mrs. Geo. W.,	6 00	Coffin, Mrs. H. R., Windsor Locks,
Avery, Miss Helen & little friends,	3 00	Collins, Mrs. Atwood,
Anonymous,	100 00	Collins, Miss E.,
Barbour, Mrs. Lucius A.,	30 00	Collins, Miss Mary F.,
Barbour, Mrs. S. L.,	5 00	Cooley, Mr. F. B.,
Barney, Mrs. D. Newton,		Cooley, Mrs. F. B.,
Farmington,	210 00	Cone, Mrs. Jas. B.,
Barney, Mrs. S. E.,	50 00	Cook, Mrs. Albert S.,
Beach, Mrs. Geo.,	15 00	Cooke, Mrs. John W.,
Batterson, Mrs. James G.,	5 00	Corning, Mr. John W.,
Blythe, Misses Margaret and		Crosby, Mrs. A. A.,
Elizabeth,	5 00	Clapp, Mrs. S. M.,
Brainerd, Miss L. A.,	30 00	Cowles, Mrs. John, Farmington,
Bridges, Miss Fidelia, Canaan,	15 00	Curtis, Mrs. Edward,
Brace, Miss Emily,	2 00	Church, Mrs. S. J.,
Bradley, Mrs. H. E.,	1 00	Daniels, Mrs. L. C.,
Belden, Mrs. Harriet, Litchfield,	4 00	Davenport, Mr. James,
Brewster, Mrs. Jas. H.,	4 00	Davenport, Miss Julia,
Bronson, Mrs. A. H.,	1 00	Davenport, Miss Martha,
Boston Branch, "Great cake sale,"	4 00	Davis, Dr. and Mrs. G. Pierrepont,
Brown, Miss Annie,		Davison, Mrs. C. J..
Brooklyn, N. Y.,	10 00	Day, Miss Caroline,
Buck, Mrs. T. R., Wethersfield,	5 00	Dennis, Mr. Rodney,
Buck, Mrs. T. R.'s Sons,		Dobson, Mrs. John, Vernon,
Wethersfield,	5 00	Day, Mrs. Thos. M.,
Bullard, Mr. Herbert,	1 00	Dunham, Miss Mary E.,
Bulkley, Mrs. Geo. L.,	12 00	Dunham, Miss S. R.,
Bushnell, Mrs. Horace,	35 00	Dunham, Mrs. S. G.,
Bunce, Mrs. Jonathan B.,	40 00	Dunham, Mrs. Sylvester,
Bunce, Miss Alice,	1 00	Dix, Mrs. E. F., Lancaster, Mass.,
Burton, Mrs. Richard E.,	4 00	Ellsworth, Mrs. P. W.,
Burr, Mrs. F. L.,	1 00	Enders, Mrs. Thomas A.,
Camp, Misses Cornelia and Kate,	10 00	Enos, Mrs. D, C.,
Camp, Mrs. John S.,	15 00	Erwin, Mrs. Robert R.,
Chamberlin, Mrs. F.,	10 00	Field, Mrs. Chas. H. & Sons,
Chase, Mr. Geo. L,.	75 00	Forbes, Fred and George,
Chase, Mrs. Chas. E.,	1 00	Foster, Mr. A. L.,
Cheney, Mrs. L. R.,	25 00	
Child, Mrs. Nath'l R., Litchfield,	2 00	Total.....................$1,3

Brought forward,	$1,306 50	Jewell, Mrs. Lyman B.,
Franklin, Mrs. W. B.,	2 00	Jewell, Mrs. Pliny,
Frisbie, Mrs. Charles G.,	5 00	Johnson, Little Ned,
Forrest, Mr. Chas. R.,	25 00	Jones, Mrs. F. C.,
"A Friend," Niles St.,	10 00	Jones, Mrs. George A.,
Friends in Rockville, by Mrs.		Judd, Mrs. J. F.,
W. H. Prescott and Miss		Kennedy, Mrs. Henry,
J. A. Maxwell,	98 85	Lee, Mrs. W. H.,
Friend, an unknown,	100 00	Lee, Miss Louise,
Friend, A,	2 00	Langdon, Mrs. George,
Friend, A,	2 00	Lincoln, Mrs. Charles G.,
Gay, Mrs. Julius, Farmington,	5 00	Lyman, Mrs. Theodore,
Goodman, Mrs. A. G.,	5 00	Lord, Miss,
Goodwin, Mrs. Chas. S. and		Manning, Miss Augusta,
daughters,	6 00	May, Mr. W. J.,
Goodwin, Mrs. James J.,	400 00	Mather, Mr. Roland,
Goodwin, Jamie,	2 00	Merriam, Miss M. C., Springfield,
Gordy, Mrs. W. F.,	2 00	Miles, Margaret (3 months old),
Greene, Col. Jacob L.,	50 00	Mills, Mr. Hiram,
Gross, Mr. Chas. E.,	10 00	Mills, Miss Isabel,
Gross, Mrs. Chas. E.,	20 00	Mitchell, Mrs. Edwin Knox,
Hall, Mr. John H.,	15 00	Moore, Mrs. Geo. W.,
Hansel, Miss Caroline,	2 00	Morgan, Mrs. H. K.,
Hapgood, Mrs. M. H.,	1 00	Morris, Mr. J. F.,
Havemeyer, Mrs, Chas. H.,	75 00	Munyan, Mrs. C. G.,
Henry, Miss Esther,	2 00	Mite-box, from a,
Hamersley, Miss E.,	1 00	Mite-box at Kindergarten,
Hills, Miss Anna,	20 00	Newton & Burnet,
Hills, Mrs. Geo. F.,	5 00	Newton. Mrs. R. W.,
Heublein, Mr. G. F.,	25 00	Ney, Mr. J. M.,
Hitchcock, Mrs. Henry R.,	1 00	Page, Mrs. Charles W.,
Hammond, Mrs. E. P.,	3 00	Palmer, Mrs. S. A., Albany,
Harrison, Mrs. M. E.,	5 00	Palmer, Mrs. W. H.,
Hillyer, Miss Clara E.,	26 00	Palmer, Miss Emelyn,
Hillyer, Mrs. Appleton R.,	10 00	Pardee, Miss Sarah A.,
Hillyer, The Misses,	6 00	Parker, Mr. R. B.,
Holt, Mr. Chas. W.,	1 00	Peck, Mrs. N. F.,
Hull, Mr. A. E.,	1 00	Peck, Miss Cornelia,
Holbrook, Mrs. C. M.,	5 00	Perkins, Mrs. Edward,
Hooker, Mrs. B. E.,	5 00	Perkins, Mrs. George C.,
Howard, Mrs. Chas. F. and		Perkins, Miss Mabel H.,
Miss Howard,	10 00	Plimpton, Wm. F.,
Howard, Mrs. James L.,	10 00	Porter, Mrs. Clara Pond,
Howe, Mrs. D. R.,	10 00	Porter, Mrs. Josephine E. S.,
Howe, Rita,	2 00	Porter, Mrs. Wm. Jr.,
Howard, Miss E. M.,	1 00	Pratt, Mrs. Waldo S.,
Huntington, Miss Maria,	3 00	Plimpton, Mrs. Lucinda F.,
Huntington, Miss Sarah B.	3 00	Risley, Mrs. Elisha,
Hyde, Mrs. A. P.,	4 00	Roberts, Mrs. George,
In memory of M. C. H.	400 00	Roberts, Mrs. Henry,
Hunt, Mrs. A. L.,	2 00	
Ingalls, Miss H.,	50	Total.....................$3,

Brought forward.	$3,833 15	Strong, Mrs. M. E. C.,
Root, Mrs. M. C.,	10 00	Taintor, Mrs. Henry E.,
Russ, Ers. Chas. T.,	20 00	Taintor, Mrs. James U.,
Rowell, Miss Harriet,	2 00	Talcott, Miss M. K.,
Russell, Mrs. Gordon W.,	10 00	Talcott, Mrs. Seth,
Sawyer, Mrs. George O.,	4 00	Tallman, Mrs. J. H.,
Schutz, Mrs. Augustus,	15 00	Talcott, Mr. Charles H.,
Schrepfer, Mr. M.,	5 00	Towne, Miss E. A.,
Seymour, Miss Emily,	5 00	Taintor, Miss Alice,
Sexton, Mrs. George,	5 00	Terry, Mrs. Stephen,
Shepherd, Mrs. George R.,	2 00	Tucker, Mrs. James Erastus,
Shipman, Mrs. Nath'l.,	10 00	Uhlhorn, Mrs.,
Skinner, Mrs. W. C.,	50 00	Van Ingen, Mrs. E. H.,
Skilton, Mrs. D. W.,	20 00	Walker, Mrs. George Leon,
Slosson, Mrs. Annie T:,	10 00	Warner, Mrs. Charles Dudley,
Sisson, Mr. Thomas,	10 00	Welch, Mrs. A. A.,
Smith, Mrs. Charles B.,	55 00	Welch, Mrs. H. K. W.,
Smith, Mrs. Charles H.,	10 00	Wells, Mr. Edward,
Smith, Mrs. E. A. and Sons,	120 00	Whaples, Mr. M. H.,
Smith, Mrs. Geo. Williamson,	15 00	White, Mr. J. H.,
Smith, Miss Clara G.,		Williams, Mr. George G.,
Poquonock,	2 00	Williams, Miss Sarah, Danielson,
Sperry, Mrs. H. T.,	1 00	Williams, Mrs. George C. F.,
Spring, Miss Helen, Springfield,	10 00	Woodford, Miss Ada, .
Stillman, Mrs. H, A.,	1 00	Well-wisher, A
Stillman, Miss.	1 00	Woodruff, Mrs. H. A.,
Stoughton, Mrs. John A.,		
East Hartford,	2 00	Total, General Subscribers, $4,

NEW HAVEN SUBSCRIBERS.

Champion, Mrs. Henry,	2 00	Seymour, Mrs. T. D.,
Daggett, Miss M. J.,	5 00	Smith, Mrs. C. F.,
Dana, Mrs. J. D.,	5 00	Shipman, Miss C.,
Deites, Mrs. F. B.,	5 00	Shipman, Miss M. B.,
Everitt, Mrs. Richard M.,	2 00	Tyler, Mrs. Morris F.,
Ehni, Mr. Robert,	10 00	Terry, Mrs. J. R.,
Farnam, Mrs. Henry,	75 00	Terry, Miss Frances,
Hadley, Mrs. A. J.,	5 00	Woolsey, Mrs. T. D.,
Hermance, Mrs. E. L.,	1 00	Woolsey, Miss Edith,
Hollister, Mrs. John C.,	1 00	Wallace, Mrs. Edward,
Kitchel, Mrs. Cornelius,	2 00	White, Mr. Oliver S.,
Munger, Mrs. T. T.,	1 00	Winchester, Miss Charlotte,
Moran, Mrs.,	2 00	Friends at 44 Wall St.,
Porter, Mrs. F. C.,	1 00	Hillhouse, Miss Josephine,
Prichard, Miss E. M.,	5 00	Welch, Mrs. Pierce N.,
Peck, Mrs. John M.,	2 00	Peets, Mrs. C. Berry,
Reed, Mrs. Edward M.,	10 00	
Smyth, Mrs. Newman,	1 00	Total, New Haven Subscribers, $

NEW LONDON SUBSCRIBERS.

Barnes, Miss,	2 50
Harris, Mrs. J. N.,	5 00
Palmer, Mrs. E. L.,	5 00
Palmer, Mrs. F. L.,	5 00
Stoddard, Mrs. and Miss,	5 00
Mead, Miss Stella H.,	5 00
Turner Mrs. P. C. & family,	5 00

Mrs. Charlotte Crandall, Mrs. J.P. Johnston, Miss Woodruff, Mrs. H. C. Weaver, Mrs. Wilbur and others,

Total, New London Subscribers, $

CONTRIBUTIONS FROM SUNDAY SCHOOLS.

Asylum Hill Cong'l Church, Hartford,	43 06
Asylum Hill Cong'l Church, Hartford, Primary Dept.,	20 38
Center Church S. S., Hartford,	10 00
Park Church, Hartf'd, Primary Department,	5 00
Prospect Ave. S. S., Hartford,	15 00
Mrs. Havens' class, N. Methodist Church, Hartford,	5 00
Rockville S. S. birthday box,	5 00

Congregational Church S. S. Washington, Conn.,
Primary Department S. School, Colchester,
Pilgrim Church S. S. Home Department, Canaan,
Woodford Congregational Ch., Derring. Me.,
S. School, Hallowell, Me.,

Total from Sunday Schools, $1

CONTRIBUTIONS FROM CHURCHES.

Asylum Hill Cong'l Hartford,	325 89
First Baptist, Hartford,	26 00
Wethersfield Congregational, (Thanksgiving),	20 00

Suffield Baptist and Congregational, (Thanksgiving),

Total from Churches, $3

CONTRIBUTIONS FROM KING'S DAUGHTERS' CIRCLES.

Hearty Workers, Farmington,	10 00
Union Circle, Rockville,	9 00
Helpful Circle, Ch Redeemer, Hartford,	10 00
Comforting Circle, Hartford,	5 00

Olive Branch Circle, Hartford,
Louise Circle, Hartford,

Total from King's Daughters, $

CONTRIBUTIONS FROM CHRISTIAN ENDEAVOR AND MISSION CIRCLES.

Mission Circle, Park Ch., Htf'd,	25 00
Mission Circle, Windsor Ave. Church, Hartford,	12 00
Junior Endeavor N. Congregational Ch., New Hartford,	5 00

Young People's Society Pilgrim Church, Canaan,

Total from Mission Circles, etc., $

CONTRIBUTIONS FROM OTHER CLUBS, CIRCLES, ETC.

Clover Leaf Club, W. Hartford, 10 00
Farmington Ave. Literary and
   Benevolent Circle, Htf'd, 26 50
Klavier Club, 1 25
L. L. T. Society, 6 00

Teacher and pupils, room G.,
   West Middle School, Htf'd,
   by Miss Skilton,

Total from "Other Clubs," etc., $

FROM ENTERTAINMENTS.

Scenes, Mother Goose, at house
   of Mrs. James J. Goodwin, $350 50
"A Living Calendar," at Dr.
   Reid's School, 114 61
Benefit Concert in New Haven, 162 40
Concert at Kindergarten by
   Mr. Marshall, 175 00

Recital by friends in Stonington,
"Tea" in Lakeville by Mrs. F. E.
   Randall,

Total from Entertainments, $

ACKNOWLEDGEMENTS,

Besides the foregoing contributions in money, the managers of the Nu and Kindergarten have to acknowledge many useful donations of food, clot house furnishings and various acceptable articles, as well as valuable aid and en agement of other kinds.

It may be impossible to enumerate all the friends to whom we are inde Among the donors are the following:

Professional Services—Dr. S. B. St. John and his associate, Dr. Waite G. S. Segur. Dr. Joseph E. Root, Dr. N. J. Goodwin.

Miss Louise Lee, outfit of carpenter's tools, benches and working mat and teacher of sloyd carpentering since the spring of 1896.

The Junior Branch of the Good Samaritan Chapter of King's Daught violin, and violin lessons for six months for Arthur Washington.

The Good Samaritans, fifty-five new books.

Rev. Mr. Miel and Trinity Church, a prayer-book.

Mr. Edward Dillingham, Book of Psalms in raised print.

The Hartford Courant Co., their indispensable daily paper.

Mr. Franklin Smith, eight dozen tablets for Kindergarten.

FOR GIFTS OF FOOD.

Lee, Mrs. W. H.
Robertson, Mrs. W. P.
Strong, Mrs. M. E. C.
Collins, Miss M. F.
Palmer, Mrs. W. H.
Collins, Miss E.
Goodwin, Mrs. James J.
Mitchell, Prof. E. K.
Watkinson Farm School,
Phillips, Mr. E. F., Farmington
Stillman, Mrs. Benjamin
Root, Miss M. C

Quiggle, Mrs. Elmer C.
Porter, Agnes
Warner, Mrs. George H.
Hart, Mrs., Farmington,
Miel, Rev. Mr.
Olmsted, Mrs. H. L.
Tallman Mrs. James H.,
Smith, the Misses, and pupils of
   side Seminary,
Hapgood, Ruth and Alice,
May, Mr. W. J.
Schrepfer, Mr. M,

For House Furnishings and Fuel.

Howe, Mrs. D. R.
Palmer, Mrs. W. H.
Collins, Miss E.
Dunham, Mrs. S. G.
Lee, Mrs. W. H.
Pratt, Mr. W. S.
Cheney, Mrs. L. R.
Robinson, Miss E. T.

Smith, Misses, Woodside Seminary
Dixon, Miss
Welling, Mrs. James
Perkins, Mrs. George C.
Smith, Mrs. T. M.
Olmsted, Mrs. H. L.
Knox, Mr. and Mrs. Frank

For Clothing.

Hartford Branch Needlework Guild (100 garments),
Wethersfield Branch Needlework Guild,
Dunham, Mrs. S. G.
Roberts Mrs. George
Loomis, Miss and friends,
Beach, Mrs. C. C.
Ferguson, Mrs. H. A.
Jewell, Mrs. Pliny
Olive Branch Circle, King's Daughters, Hartford,
Mission Circle, Park Church, by Mrs. John S. Camp,
Hyacinth Circle, King's Daughters,
Louise Circle, King's Daughters,
Cheerful Workers Circle, King's Daughters, West Hartford,
Skinner, Mrs. W. C.
Collins, Mrs. Atwood,
Palmer, Mrs. W. H.
Havens, Mrs. D. W.
Friends in New Haven,

Barbour, Mrs. S. L.
Hart, Mrs. G. W.
Bartlett, Miss
Frazier, Mrs. C. U.
Foster, Mrs. Emily Wells
Avery, Mrs. G. W.
Ensworth, Mrs. L. L.
Davis, Mrs. G. P.
Penrose, Mrs. Morris
Goodwin, Mrs. James J.
Hovey, Mrs.
Larned & Hatch, Messrs.
Perkins, Mrs.
Taintor, Mrs. H. E.
Kline, Mrs.
Brewster. Mrs. J. H.
Burbank, Miss J.
Smith, Mrs. Charles L.
Shepherd, Mrs. Geo. R.
Bowman's Mrs. Circle, East Hart
White, Mrs. H. H.

For Playthings and Rocking-horses.

Children of West Middle School,
Barbour, Mrs. S. L.
Woolley, Mrs. George
Fisher, Walter

Gross, Mrs. Charles E.
Mitchell, Spencer
Shaker Station, Conn., by Mr. Twiss.

Entertainments to the Children.

Captain Norton, Graphophone Exhibition at Kindergarten.
The Misses Smith, Woodside Seminary, Christmas Treat and presents.
Miss Katharine Andrews, Piano and Violin Music at her house.
Mrs. Dr. J. F. Wright, Piano and Violin Music at her house.
Drives—by Mrs. Elmer C. Quiggle.

From Individuals.... .... $4,924.95
   "   Sunday Schools................,................................... 141.14
   "   Churches 375.60
   "   King's Daughters... 42.00
   "   Mission Circles, etc........................ .... 46.80
   "   Clubs, etc 54.25
   "   Entertainments.. 934.01

                                    Total $6,518.75

NOTE. The above detailed account covers two years—one year of which was submitted
to the Governor by the General Superintendent at the close of 1896. This explains the
apparent difference between the sums reported as received from contributions, by the General Superintendent and the Assistant Treasurer.

DONATIONS.

INDUSTRIAL HOME DEPARTMENT, 1897.

AUDITED.

First Congregational Church, Gardiner, Mass., through D. H. Rand, Treas.,	15 72
Second Congregational Church, Manchester, Conn., Levi Drake, Treas.....	2 60
Park Congregational Church, through Willis E. Smith................	34 83
L. D. Carpenter, Providence, R. I............	1 00
C. W. Fitch. South Norwalk, Conn..........................	1 00
Mrs. E. M. Hatch, Collinsville, Conn............................	7 00
Ever Ready Circle, King's Daughters...............................	2 00
Jerush W. Kilbourne............................	5 00
Mrs. H. E. Beach..	3 35
Union Circle, King's Daughters, So. Norwalk, by C. E. Marion, Sec'y........	5 00
Central Band, King's Daughters..	5 00
Donation	5 00
Donation...	1 00
Whatsoever Circle, King's Daughters, Newington, Conn., by Miss H. H. Merrill, Sec'y.................................	5 00
Donation...................................	5 00
John C. Goddard...	1 25
A Well Wisher..	75 00
Second Congregational Church Sunday School of Manchester, by John P. Fitch..	23 37
Ladies' Aid Society, Wethersfield Congregational Church, by A. M. Smith.	15 60

Radford B, Smith..

F. S. Bartram, No. 126 Williams' Street, N. Y..

Thos. R. Taylor, Bridgeport, Conn...

Mr. John Little, Pawtucket, R. I...

Total $22

Donations other than money we gratefully acknowledge as follows:—

From The Good Samaritan Circle of King's Daughters' and Sons, Hartf

1 Patent Rocker, 1 Large Lamp.

From Mrs. Hunt, Hartford, 1 Center Table.

From Circle of King's Daughters, East Hartford, 1 Art Square.

From merchants who have in many instances allowed liberal discount on t

From kind friends for entertainments, clothing, fruit, flowers etc., which have so thoughtfully sent in.

FORMS OF BEQUEST.

I give, devise and bequeath to the Connecticut Institute and Industrial H for the Blind at Hartford, Conn., (here describe property devised or bequeat

....

....

to be used by the trustees of that corporation to promote its interests at their cretion.

I give, devise and bequeath to the Connecticut Institute and Industrial H for the Blind at Hartford, Conn., for the sole use of the Kindergarten for the F the sum of................................. Dollars.

I give, devise and bequeath to the Connecticut Institute and Industrial for the Blind at Hartford, Conn., for the sole use of the Industrial Home the of................................. Dollars.

OFFICERS OF CORPORATION.

ANNUAL REPORT

.. OF ..

CONNECTICUT

SCHOOL FOR IMBECILES,

LAKEVILLE, CONN.

1898.

BRIDGEPORT, CONN.
PRESS OF THE MARIGOLD PRINTING COMPANY.
1899.

OFFICERS OF THE INSTITUTION.

REPORT OF DIRECTORS.

To His Excellency,

GOVERNOR GEORGE E. LOUNSBURY:

SIR:—The Directors of the Connecticut School for Imbeciles respectfully transmit to you their report for two years ending Oct. 1, 1898.

The number of children connected with the Institution during the year ending Sept. 30, 1897, was 188. For the year ending Sept. 30, 1898, the number was 189.

The number of State beneficiaries connected with the Institution for the year ending Sept. 30, 1897, was 158. The number for the year ending Sept. 30, 1898, was 163. The number present Oct. 1, 1897, was 145. The number present Oct. 1, 1898, was 158.

The amount received from the State for their support, including $104.00 for the care of a harmless lunatic, was $17,872.13, as follows:—

For quarter ending Sept. 30, 1896,	.	. $ 4,255.21
For quarter ending Dec. 31, 1896,	.	. 4,431.86
For quarter ending Mar. 31, 1897,	.	. 4,534.79
For quarter ending June 30, 1897,	.	. 4,650.27
Total income for the year,	.	. $38,339.94

For the year ending Sept. 30, 1898, the amounts were as follows:—

For quarter ending Sept. 30, 1897,	.	. $ 4,657.57
For quarter ending Dec. 31, 1897,	.	. 4,776.28
For quarter ending Mar. 31, 1898,	.	. 4,830.59
For quarter ending June 30, 1898,	.	. 4,954.56
		$19,219.00
Total income for the year,	.	. $39,853.94

Your attention is respectfully called to that part of the Superintendent's report which refers to the need of a separate school building. The sum of money already in the hands of the Directors is not sufficient to build and heat the school building necessary for the proper prosecution of the Institution work. There is urgent need of such a building, therefore we ask that the sum of five thousand dollars be appropriated by the present legislature to enable this Board to authorize the erection of suitable school accommodations at once.

For the Board,

GEORGE B. BURRALL, *President.*

TREASURER'S REPORT.

T. L. NORTON, *Treasurer.*

In account with THE CONNECTICUT SCHOOL FOR IM-
BECILES.

Dr.

Amount on hand, ... $ 8,128.60

The table of expenditures is as follows:—

For year ending Sept. 30, 1897.

Salaries and Wages, ...	$ 15,466.55
Provisions and Supplies, ...	17,221.09
Periodicals, Postage, etc., and Misc., .	3,730.74
Interest and Insurance, ...	261.40
Improvements and Repairs, . . .	1,660.16
	$38,339.94

For the year ending Sept. 30, 1898.

Provisions and Supplies, ...	$ 19,081.93
Salaries and Wages, ...	15,855.96
Miscellaneous, etc., ...	3,262.17
Insurance, ...	975.00
Improvements and Repairs, . . .	678.88
	$39,853.94

SUPERINTENDENT'S REPORT.

To the Directors:

I hereby submit the report of the Institution under my charge for the two years ending Oct. 1, 1898.

For the year ending Oct. 1, 1897, there were connected with the Institution 188 children. For the year ending Oct. 1, 1898, there were connected with the Institution 189 children.

The number present Oct. 1, 1897, was 171. The number present Oct. 1, 1898, is 179. During the two years we have had ten deaths.

For the year ending Oct. 1, 1897, four from epilepsy and one from paresis. For the year ending Oct. 1, 1898, three from epilepsy, one from nephritis and valvular disease of the heart and one from organic heart trouble.

The report of the school work is as follows:

Pupils in School,	74
Reading,	46
Chart,	19
Primer,	3
Second Reader,	12
Fourth Reader,	12
Arithmetic,	48
Addition,	6
Subtraction,	7
Multiplication,	13
Division,	12

Fractions,	7
Compound Numbers,	4
Interest and Percentage,	1
Geography,	10
Singing,	60
Writing,	23
Gymnastics,	74
History,	10
Language,	12

Kindergarten.

Coming in daily for kindergarten work,	64
Coming in for fancy work,	10
Daily entering kindergarten games,	60
Sewing cards,	49
Folding,	47
Weaving,	47
Coloring,	47
Gifts Nos. 1, 2, 3,	32
Gift No. 5,	13
Stick Laying,	48
Pegs and Tiles,	57
Bead Stringing,	57
Drawing,	48
Cutting and Pasting,	37
Plain Sewing,	11
Painting, (mixing colors),	10

Our applications are becoming more and more numerous and we have reached nearly the limit of our capacity. In fact, at present we can only receive children who are eligible to a group in which we have a vacancy.

Your attention has been called before to the pressing need of a school building separate but easy of access from the main house.

The present sum in the treasury is not quite sufficient to build and properly equip such a building, involving as it does enlarging the boiler house. I would therefore suggest that the present legislature be asked to appropriate a sum in addition to that we already have, sufficient to erect this building since our present need of it is imperative.

It is gratifying to be able to report that as in former years the health of our institution has been excellent.

Our death rate for the past year of but five in so large a number enables us to maintain the standing of the institution among the first for healthfulness.

I wish especially to call your attention to the high character of the work done by our teachers to whom too warm commendation cannot be given.

We have also been exceedingly fortunate in the excellence of the service in all the departments of our Institution home.

In accordance with your request I have presented in this report the paper read by me at the last National Conference of Charities and Corrections held in New York last May. It is given for the purpose of showing that the aim of the sociologist of to-day is largely prevention. It is gratifying to call attention again to the fact that in effective legislation in this direction Connecticut still leads.

Respectfully submitted,

GEO. H. KNIGHT, Supt.

ADMISSION OF PUPILS.

Feeble-minded children, who are so peculiar or deficient in intellect as to be incapable of being educated at an ordinary school, may be admitted by the Superintendent.

The parents or next friends of those in whose behalf applications are made for admission as pupils, are expected to make answer, in writing, to such questions as the Superintendent may prescribe.

All pupils will be expected to come provided with a good supply of neat and substantial clothing, of dark color, and plainly marked with the child's full name.

There will be a vacation during the months of July and August, at which period all pupils must be removed by the parents or guardians, unless otherwise directed by the Superintendent.

In case of indigence, applications may be addressed to His Excellency the Governor, for aid from the State appropriation.

Where aid from the towns should also be afforded, application is made to the judge of probate of the district where the child resides. Blanks will be furnished on application.

Application for the admission of pupils, and all general correspondence, should be directed to Geo. H. Knight, M. D., Lakeville, Conn.

PREVENTION FROM A LEGAL AND MORAL STANDPOINT.

I recently saw in print the following statement that "of the entire population of the United States an average of one person in every five is at the present time in a public almshouse or other charitable institutions, or is being assisted by some relief-giving organization." This statement is not only startling, but it brings forcibly to the minds of thinking people the question whether we are not at the present time giving too much attention to the care and relief of the dependent classes, and too little to the study of prevention.

The consideration and discussion of the best way of providing for the feeble-minded, including the epileptic as well, have been so generally taken up at the various sessions of this conference, that the subject long ago escaped from the narrow point of view of the specialist. At the present time it is fortunate enough to claim the intelligent thought of the average citizen interested in charity in its general sense. I use the word fortunate advisedly in this connection.

It is as true in matters of reform as it is in business, that if you want to accomplish anything satisfactorily, you must bring it into the every-day thought and experience of as many people as possible. The State Boards of Charity have helped the Superintendents of institutions to familiarize the public with those facts which the pioneers in this work felt compelled to harp upon constantly in the early days. The National Conference of Charities and Corrections has spread broadcast, through its members, the knowledge of what has been done by teaching, by custodial care, by manual training, and by medical oversight for those grades of the defective class which comes under the head of the feeble minded. That which is now being so success-fully worked out in the colony for the epileptic we hope in the near future to accomplish for every one of this class. There is no longer need of argument to persuade an intelligent community that "it pays" to provide state care for the mentally and morally deficient.

That the imbecile cannot work in competition with the normal man is self evident. An intelligent state policy demands that he shall be housed, fed, nursed, clothed, and taught as far as may be, and when we shall have put him in the way of following the common laws of order and decency, we have started him on the up grade. Even the simplest custodial care is a great step in advance of the neglect of former years. We have reached our sober second thought for the imbecile. The plain facts in the case do not warrant us in claiming for him the high degree of attainment our early enthusiasm led us to hope for. My own conviction is that as time goes on we shall do less in the school room, and more in the workshop and field. Institutions we must have and in them we must be able to combine minimum of cost with maximum care, since all placing out systems are valueless in this work,

All who have had experience in finding homes for children know that the slightest physical defect is a great detriment even when there is perfect mental bal-ance. Nothing is truer than that we all judge and are influenced by appearances. Consider then the difficul-ties when to the physical defect almost universal in the imbecile, there is added the mental peculiarities which set him apart from his fellows. There is no remedy for this; no logic, no appeal to sentiment, charity or humanity will avail with the mass of people. It is a state of affairs we must accept and provide for. Nobody wants the imbecile, not even those who are bound most closely to him by ties of blood. He is an innocent element of disorder everywhere outside of associations with his own kind.

Defenseless, easy victims to injustice and neglect, their very weakness appeals to the best that lies in humanity. That is why it is possible to secure for him the high order of individual teaching necessary for each case, no matter how large the institution is. Every institution for the feeble minded stands as an object lesson in advanced civilization.. The pauper can sometimes be made self-supporting, the incorrigible, so-called, may sometimes be given a new start, the insane have a chance of recovery, every class of dependent and delinquent has one or more chances of altering his condition. The feeble minded alone is the exception. He, unfortunately, is handicapped from the cradle to the grave. When you have done your very best for him, his highest attainment is to become what some one has called "two-thirds of a man."

The question that we must face in view of the terrible yearly increase of this class, is not what shall we do with this fraction of humanity, but, how shall we get rid of it? How shall we cut off the supply? That insanity, pauperism and crime imbecility we know— that imbecility produces these in turn we are beginning to find out. That heredity is a direct cause of imbecility no one denies who has given the problem intelligent study. How shall we wipe out heredity?

For the so-called wards of the State, those who are already in institutions, the answer is comparatively easy. State care for a life time is the simplest, most civilized and economical solution of the problem. In the case of these we can consider that the remedy lies in our own hands. But in face of the fact that there are at least one hundred thousand feeble minded persons of various ages and conditions who are outside of the direct restraining influences of an institution, it is clear no half-way measures will prevent the increase of this number. What is considered the sacred law of individual right places it within the power of a large percent of these to marry, and inevitably to reproduce their own kind.

If we are to strike a telling blow in the interests of prevention we must influence public sentiment and legislation for the sake of morality and permanent good.

In effect according to the statute, we are all wards of the state under a certain age. However bright mentally or strong physically, we can neither make a will, convey property, nor marry except through the agency and written consent of a parent or guardian. Without the said consent the registrar who issues a certificate of marriage to a minor is subjected to a heavy penalty. Now if the state can enact such laws for the protection of its normal citizens, what shall hinder its placing the age limit of the feeble minded at that unattainable period for them, which is commonly called years of discretion? I use the term feeble minded in its broadest sense. Under that head will come the epileptic, incorrigible or moral imbecile, and the insane, as well as the idiot and imbecile of the ordinary type.

I am well aware that this suggestion carried out would strike a blow directly at the root of what is called the law of individual right, but I claim that the mentally unfit have no individual right to reproduce themselves. Being mentally unfit we cannot expect the moral side of the case to appeal to any one of them. We

cannot instill into the feeble minded any sense of responsibility for bringing either a legitimate or an illegitimate child into the world. They are and must remain
illegitimate parents of illegitimate children from first to
last. That which they will not, cannot do for themselves, the law of the land must do for them. The
sane, normal, every day people of this country must
have a chance.

As Professor Brewer of Yale, said, at the New
Haven Conference a few years ago: "Thanks to modern
science, charity and humanity, we are saving everything that is unfit and it is the greatest test that can be
brought to bear upon our civilization. Once here, save
them we must for humanity's sake. As far as we can,
let us cut off the supply at the fountain head."

In the words of Dr. Maudsley, "it is certain that
lunatics and criminals are as much manufactured articles as are steam engines and calico-printing machines,
only the processes of the organic manufactory are so
complex that we are not able to follow them. They
are neither accidents nor anomalies in the universe, but
come by law and testify to casuality; and it is the business of science to find out what the causes are and by
what laws they work."

That which I advocate could never become what is
called a federal law. Perhaps never is a strong word,
but at the least calculation, it would take years to bring
it about, and we cannot afford to wait. With an annual
increase of over two thousand of the feeble minded
alone, we absolutely cannot afford to wait. But let each
state enact its own law.

We move slowly in conservative Connecticut, but
we have had upon the statute books the past three
years the following prohibitory law:

An Act Concerning Crimes and Punishments.

SECTION 1. No man and woman either of whom is epileptic, imbecile or feeble minded, shall intermarry, or live together as husband and wife, when the woman is under forty-five years of age. Any person violating or attempting to violate any of the provisions of this section shall be imprisoned in the state prison not less than three years.

SEC. 2. Any selectman or any other person who shall advise, aid, abet, cause, or assist in procuring, or countenance any violation of section one of this act, or the marriage of any pauper when the woman in such marriage is under forty-five years of age, shall be fined not less than one thousand dollars, or imprisoned not less than one year, or both.

SEC. 3. Every man who shall carnally know any female under the age of forty-five years who is epileptic, imbecile, feeble-minded, or a pauper, shall be imprisoned in the state prison not less than three years. Every man who is epileptic who shall carnally know any female under the age of forty-five years, and every female under the age of forty-five years who shall consent to be carnally known by any man who is epileptic, imbecile, or feeble-minded, shall be imprisoned in the state prison not less than three years.

Approved July 4, 1895.

Every man here, every member of this Conference, every State Board of Charity, can influence legislation in this matter.

Science is slow. To become science, detail must above everything else be accurate. To prove every step takes time. Nothing is harder to get at than truth in the history of cases, as every medical superintendent of an institution for the idiot and imbecile can testify. This will exist so long as imbecility is looked upon as a disgrace instead of a misfortune. A physical or mental imperfection is in the popular mind, a greater affliction than a moral one. The statement that we are all sinners, we accept pretty passably. The statement that we are all feeble in mind, because of that, or feeble in will, even in the least degree, we should resent to a man. This universal feeling acts against making rapid progress in getting at the hidden causes which result in the production of defective human beings. The mystery of life is too great. There is too much theory to overcome, but when we do feel firm ground under our feet we must advance. When we can prove as we have that a certain definite per cent. of the histories of children received into the institutions for the feeble minded show epilepsy as a cause or as a complication, and that hitherto we have placed no legal obstacle in the way of repeating these conditions, our way is clear in this direction at least.

Morally every citizen is responsible for the legal increase of imbecility in his own community. Morally he is responsible for the increase of illegitimate imbecility in his own community. Every man *is* his brother's keeper to this extent. In the face of the terrible increase of this class by what we may call known methods, every one of us must strike a blow for prevention. At least let us wipe out the stain of legalizing the production of idiocy, imbecility, insanity and crime.

HARTFORD HOSPITAL.—SOUTH WINGS.

43^D ANNUAL REPORT

OF THE

Executive Committee

OF THE

HARTFORD HOSPITAL

INCLUDING THE

FOURTEENTH ANNUAL REPORT

OF

OLD PEOPLE'S HOME

AND THE

TWENTY-FIRST ANNUAL REPORT

OF THE

HARTFORD HOSPITAL
TRAINING SCHOOL FOR NURSES

HARTFORD, CONN.
Press of The Case, Lockwood & Brainard Company
1898

OFFICERS OF THE HARTFORD HOSPITAL.

*Elected at the Annual Meeting of the Corporation December 8, 1897,
and at the Annual Meeting of the Directors December 15, 1897.*

GURDON W. RUSSELL, M.D., *President.*
JONATHAN B. BUNCE, *Vice-President.*
WARD W. JACOBS, *Secretary and Treasurer.*

Executive Committee.

HENRY K. MORGAN, 108 Farmington Ave.
HARMON G. HOWE, M.D., 137 High St.
THOMAS SISSON, 729 Main St.

Committee on Finance.

JONATHAN B. BUNCE.
HENRY A. REDFIELD,
HENRY C. DWIGHT.

Auditors.

JONATHAN B. BUNCE,
HENRY A. REDFIELD.

Librarian.

WILLIAM W. KNIGHT, M.D.

Directors.

GURDON W. RUSSELL, M.D.,
JONATHAN B. BUNCE,
HENRY C. ROBINSON,
HENRY K. MORGAN,
THOMAS SISSON,
HARMON G. HOWE, M.D.,
HENRY A. REDFIELD,
MELANCTHON STORRS, M.D.,
HENRY C. DWIGHT,
JAMES J. GOODWIN,
G. PIERREPONT DAVIS, M.D.,
ATWOOD COLLINS,
MILES B. PRESTON, Mayor, *ex-officio.*

4

RUSSELL, WILLIAM C.
SHIPMAN, NATHANIEL
SISSON, THOMAS
WELLES, MRS. JOHN S.

Members for Life. — $50.

ALLEN, JEREMIAH M.
BACON, DR. WILLIAM T.
BARNARD, HENRY
BEACH, CHARLES M.
BIDWELL, PITKIN & CO.
BLANCHARD, HOMER
BOARDMAN, WILLIAM F. J.
BRABAZON & McGOWEN
BRINLEY, EDWARD H.
BRAINARD, LEVERETT
BUCK, REV. GEORGE
BUDDE, AUGUSTUS W.
BURR, ALFRED E.
CAMPBELL, JAMES, M.D.
CARPENTER & BARTLETT
CLARK, FRANKLIN
COLLINS, ATWOOD
COOK, HAPGOOD & CO.
DAVISON, MRS. SUVIA T.
DAY, GEORGE H.
DENNIS, RODNEY
DIMOCK, IRA.
DUNHAM, EDWARD
DUNHAM, MARY
FISHER, HUBERT
FORREST, CHARLES R.
FRANCIS, WILLIAM
GEER, ELIHU'S SONS
GLAZIER, A. JUDSON
GLEASON & WILLARD
GOODRICH, STEPHEN & CO.
GOODWIN, MRS. LESTER H.
GREENE, JACOB L.
GRIFFING, ROBERT A.
GROSS, CHARLES E.
GOLDSCHMIDT, HERMAN
HALL, JAMES P.
HANSEL, HARRIET DAY

HARBISON, HUGH
HEUBLEIN, G. F. & BRO.
HILLIARD, ELISHA C.
HILLS, GEORGE F.
HOLLANDER, ABRAHAM
HOOKER, EDWARD B., M.D.
HOWARD, MRS. CHARLES F.
HOWE, MRS. DANIEL R.
HOWE, HARMON G., M.D.
HUBBARD, CHARLOTTE H.
HYDE, WILLIAM WALDO
INGALLS, PHINEAS H., M.D.
JACOBS, WARD W.
JEWELL, CHARLES A.
JEWELL, P. & SONS,
JOHNSON, HORACE
JUDD, EDWIN D.
LEE & DEANE
MANDLEBAUM, JACOB
McNARY, JAMES M. B.
MORRIS, JONATHAN F.
MUNSILL, GAIL B.
NICHOLS, JAMES
NORTHAM, CHARLES H.
PATTERSON, CALDWELL
PERKINS, MRS. EDWARD H.
PERKINS, MRS. GEORGE C.
POWELL, JAMES B.
PULSIFER, NATHAN T.
ROBERTS, MRS. GEORGE, SR.
ROBERTS, MRS, HENRY
ROCKWELL, FRED C.
ROGERS, WILLIAM, MANUF'G CO.
ROOD, DAVID A.
RUSSELL, MRS. GURDON W.
SMITH, CHARLES B.
STEBBINS, LUCIUS
SUGDEN, WILLIAM E.

TAINTOR, ALICE
TALCOTT, CALEB M.
TAYLOR, SAMUEL
TERRY, MRS. STEPHEN

THOMSON, JAMES M.
WELLES, JAMES G.
WHITING, CHARLES B.
WOOLLEY, G. W. & W. P.

Members for Five Years.— $25.

HAAS, LOUIS B.

WEBSTER, JOHN C.

Elected Members.

SWIFT, ROWLAND
MATSON, WILLIAM L.
REDFIELD, HENRY A.
ELMORE, SAMUEL E.
CLARK, WILLIAM B.
STORRS, MELANCTHON, M.D.
CLEMENS, SAMUEL L.
BURR, FRANKLIN L.
ROOT, JOHN G.

DWIGHT, HENRY C.
CLARK, CHARLES HOPKINS
SKINNER, WILLIAM C.
WOODWARD, P. HENRY
BULKELEY, MORGAN G.
* BUNCE, EDWARD M.
WARNER, CHARLES DUDLEY
SMITH, HERBERT KNOX

* Deceased.

ɩ

BIRD'S EYE VIEW.—NORTH WINGS.

HARTFORD HOSPITAL.

EXECUTIVE OFFICERS OF THE HARTFORD HOSPITAL.

At the beginning of the fiscal year, September 30, 1898.

Executive Committee.

HENRY K. MORGAN, 108 Farmington Ave.
HARMON G. HOWE, M.D., 137 High St.
THOMAS SISSON, 729 Main St.

Superintendent.

BENJAMIN S. GILBERT.

Resident Physician.

WILLIAM S. REOCH, M.D.

Resident Surgeon.

ALBERT M. ROWLEY, M.D.

Assistant Surgeon.

IRVING D. BLANCHARD, M.D.

Assistant Physician.

HEMAN A. TYLER, JR., M.D.

Matron and Lady Superintendent of Training School.

Miss ELIZABETH M. FRIEND.

Night Matron.

Miss SARAH L. HARRISON.

HEAD NURSES.

Miss CONSTANCE A. HOLDEN,
Miss FRANCES AULD,
Miss CAROLINE TOBEY,
Miss CARLOTTA MUNOZ.

Teacher of Cooking School.

Mrs. ELIZABETH SLUYTER AYERS.

Apothecary.

HENRY W. FULLER.

Clerk.

JAMES W. S. TOBEY.

Housekeeper.

Miss EMMA E. BEEBE.

CORRIDOR.—MALE SIDE.

THE FORTY-THIRD ANNUAL REPORT

OF THE

Executive Committee of the Hartford Hospital.

To the Directors of the Hartford Hospital:

The Executive Committee take pleasure in presenting to you the following as the Forty-third Annual Report of the Hartford Hospital for the year ending September 30, 1898. Included in its pages are the Treasurer's Report to you in full, the Superintendent's Report to us, the Matron's Report to us of the Training School for Nurses, and the Reports of the House Medical and Surgical Staff to us of the medical and surgical work of the Hospital during the past year, as well as other data of interest to you and the public pertaining to the institutions under our care.

Although the work of the past year has been unusually heavy, taxing the endurance of all to an unusual degree, it has been accomplished with little friction, and in a manner creditable to the heads of departments, and demonstrating the satisfactory working of the various changes in the internal management of the Hospital which were instituted last year. The sole purpose of the founding of this institution was the care of the patient and divining ways and means to promote his recovery. This principle we aim to impress upon all persons connected with the actual care of the sick, and that by the conscientious discharge of the small duties of each individual nurse, orderly, or physician is built up the success of the institution as a whole.

The greatest number of patients any one day was 205, the average number for the year being 158; the total number of admissions 1,622; the total number under care, 1,783; the total number of weeks' board and care, 8,152; the average residence being 4.57 weeks. The cost of maintenance per week was $8.55 per patient. Comparing this with last year, there were 64 more admissions, and 101 more under care, and an increase of 622 weeks of residence in the Hospital; an increase of the average time of residence from 4.48 to 4.57 weeks; an increase of the average cost of maintenance per week from $8.26 to $8.55. The receipts from paying patients increased from $17,-359.65 to $18,478.39. This class of patients includes all private-room cases, who pay more than the actual cost of board, and, therefore, help to balance the loss on all patients sent in by the towns who pay less than the cost, as well as those who are admitted free. To the actual cost of board of the private-room patients must be added, however, light, heat, and extra personal attention in estimating the expense of their care. The demand for these private rooms has increased considerably, and, at times, application has had to be made in advance.

Owing to a change in the method of closing the books of the Hospital promptly on the thirtieth of September, the last quarter of the state appropriation of $1,250 was not drawn until after this date. Other bills due from towns at the close of the quarter were not collected until after the close of the financial year, and do not appear in the receipts.

Early in August we were apprised of the suffering of the United States troops for want of hospital accommodations, and, therefore, offered to care for 75 patients, which offer was accepted. We, therefore, made preparations for this number at considerable expense to us. No patients were sent until September, although we were in daily expectation of them. At the close of the year we have 63 soldiers in the wards of the Hospital, nearly all being cases of typhoid fever, and members of the First Regiment Connecticut Volunteers, or of the Batteries enlisted from the state. Owing to the necessity of hiring additional nurses from outside of the regular force, the increase of the Training School to 39, and the additional maids required in the wards and kitchens, the item of salaries has increased from $19,430.30 to $21,822.04.

Repairs have cost $4,514.99, as compared with $3,401.40 last year. The total expenditure increased from $62,261.41 to $69,737.95, while the total receipts decreased from $38,242.53 to $36,467.66, owing to the change of method of bookkeeping referred to before, actually, however, increasing about $2,000.

The treasurer's report this year shows an actual expenditure for all purposes of $71,925.98, and an actual income from all sources of $56,259.40, making an actual loss of $15,666.58. After deducting the amount paid for insurance and other expenses of the Treasurer's office, we have a loss of $13,478.55, or $5,617.68 more than last year.

The percentage of improvements and recoveries of total number under care was 76.8 per cent., and of admissions during the year was 84.4, or 4 per cent. more than last year. The death rate of total under care was 9.5 per cent, or 2 per cent. less than last year, the total being 170. Of this number 17 were due to accident and lived but a few hours, 25 were hopeless cases and lived but a short time, and 19 died of consumption. Excluding this class of deaths, 61 in number, 3.7 per cent. of the total admissions, or 35.8 per cent. of the total deaths, we have 1,561 admissions of persons having some chance of being benefited by hospital care, with a death list of 109, or rate of 6.3 per cent. Considering that all classes of disease and accident are received, including contagious diseases, this rate is perfectly satisfactory, being 1.3 per cent. less than last year.

The surgical wards have been well filled, and the class of work accomplished fully up to our past records. There have been 588 operations performed, 80 more than last year. Of these there were 38 cases of appendicitis, 35 of whom were operated upon, with 2 deaths; 20 cases of hernia, 18 of which were operated upon, with 2 deaths; 5 hysterectomies, with 2 deaths; 3 intestinal adhesions, with one death; 9 ovariotomies, with one death: 79 laparotomies from all causes, with 9 deaths.

In the Eye and Ear Department there have been 62 cases

cared for in the wards of the Hospital, and 170 in the out department. Forty-five cases have been cared for in the Orthopedic Department. One hundred and twenty-one mothers and children have been accommodated in the lying-in wards, and 155 in the Gynecological Department. In the Medical Department 137 cases of typhoid fever have been cared for, with a record of six deaths. A part of this number were United States Volunteers. Typhoid fever has not been as prevalent in this locality as during some years past.

MEDICAL AND SURGICAL STAFF.

The members of the Medical and Surgical Staff of the Hospital have been regular in attendance and painstaking in their work, which is a voluntary contribution on their part, no pay for services rendered being allowed. There have been few changes in the ranks. Dr. James Campbell resigned as visiting physician, and Dr. Charles C. Beach was appointed to the vacancy. Dr. Ansel G. Cook and Dr. James Campbell were appointed assistant surgeons, and Dr. Everett J. McKnight was appointed orthopedic surgeon in place of Dr. Ansel G. Cook. No appointment to the position of Pathologist was made, Dr. Philip D. Bunce, Bacteriologist, performing the duties of both positions.

HOUSE STAFF.

Dr. Howard Franklyn Smith and Dr. Thomas W. Chester have completed their term of two years' service on the House Staff, and have both opened offices in the city. Dr. Irving D. Blanchard and Dr. Heman A. Tyler, Jr., have been appointed as interns during the year. At the close of the fiscal year the House Staff is as follows:

· Dr. William S. Reoch, Chief of Staff and House Physician.
Dr. Albert M. Rowley, House Surgeon.
Dr. Irving D. Blanchard, Assistant House Surgeon.
Dr. Heman A. Tyler, Jr., Assistant House Physician.

Much depends upon the ability and judgment of the House Staff, and the absence of any considerable friction is due to their conscientious endeavors to carry out the house rules and to perform their duties in a manner creditable to the Hospital, for which the thanks of the officers of the Hospital are due.

THE EXECUTIVE DEPARTMENT.

The position of Superintendent has been ably filled by Benjamin S. Gilbert, who was appointed September, 1897, to fill the vacancy caused by the death of Leander Hall, who had efficiently served in this position for twenty-four years.

Miss Katherine Emory, the Matron and Lady Superintendent of the Training School at the opening of the year, resigned from the position, to take effect February 1st. The vacancy was filled by the promotion of Miss Elizabeth M. Friend from the position of Night Matron. Miss Friend has been connected with the Hospital in various capacities for some time, and we feel that she is eminently qualified to govern the school and Hospital. She is ably supported by Miss Sarah L. Harrison as Night Matron, and an excellent corps of head nurses, the Misses Auld, Holden, Munoz, and Toby.

THE KENEY FUND.

The income from the Keney Fund, $2,295.83, has been applied to the support of 127 patients, supported entirely by the charity of the Hospital, occupying 358.4 weeks at $6.40 per week.

IMPROVEMENTS.

Three wards have been renovated and painted, the Obstetric, Gynecological, and Ward 2. The entire cornice, window casings and frames, and gutters have also been painted. The operating room has been thoroughly renovated and tiled, fitted with modern plumbing and utensils, and is now modern in every way. Window screens have also been supplied to some of the wards. Now all the ground floor is screened. . New mattresses have gradually been bought, until now each Hospital bed is provided with a good hair mattress. Some atten-

2

tion has been paid to the lawns and courts about the Hospital, and flowers and shrubs added where they were thought to be needed to make them seem as attractive as possible for the patients. It is proposed to lay out walks and to plant shrubbery about the grounds and to make more use of them in future during the warm weather and give a place of recreation for the convalescents, who heretofore have used the balconies and the sidewalks. Most of the private rooms have been renovated and painted during the year, as have also many of the rooms occupied by nurses in the basement story. A small building was fitted up to be temporarily used for contagious cases during September and October, allowing us to use the thoroughly renovated pavilion as a convalescent ward for the soldiers. Electric bells connected with enunciators have been placed in every private room.

BEQUESTS AND DONATIONS.

It gives us pleasure to announce the following bequests received:

Estate of John C. Parsons	$ 1,000.00
Estate of Amanda M. Whitney	10,528.24
Estate of Martha W. Brown	38,877.67
Estate of Susan S. Clark	4,850.00
	$55,255.91

Also a donation from Louis B. Haas of $25.

Many friends of the Hospital have brightened the wards with flowers and brought donations of fruit, clothing, books, toys, *et cetera*, a full list of which may be found in the Superintendent's Report, for which we wish to express our thanks. There is never a time when these offerings are not gratefully received by our inmates. A little attention to the Hospital patients from visitors helps to while away the time of sickness wonderfully.

Religious services have been held as usual by friends of the institution, and your committee wish to express their thanks to the participants, especially also to those who have carried Christian consolation to the bedside.

NECESSITIES.

During the past year we have cared for more people in a better manner, with less friction, and with a lighter death rate, everything considered, than ever before. With a daily average of 158 patients, a great proportion of whom were acute cases, the capacity of the wards, as well as the capability of the officers, physicians, and nurses, and the discipline of the institution, have been at times severely taxed.

We have now 39 members of the Training School for Nurses, 4 head nurses, and 1 night matron, on our regular force. They are housed at the Old People's Home, the former Superintendent's house, and in the basement of the annex, and the Children's Ward. We cannot increase the school for lack of room for them to sleep. We find that the extra strain of hard work required of them during the past summer has affected those who occupied rooms under the Children's Ward, and we attribute it to overcrowding and to dampness. Your Executive Committee have been convinced that an effort should be made this fall to raise money for the proposed building of the Training School, with a full belief that the many friends of humanity in this city and community will liberally respond to the call for financial aid.

The growing tendency to bequeath to public charities moneys in trust is to be encouraged, as in no other way can a permanent fund of an institution be established. But for this reason when a time for building comes before us we have no other resource but to make a special call upon the public for the specific purpose.

The income from the permanent fund last year was only 26 per cent. of the expenses. We should have a fund double its present size to keep up with the natural growth of the Hospital, and to allow of our keeping pace with the modern idea of what a hospital should be.

The care of patients suffering from phthisis is still before us unsolved. We are convinced that this dread disease will always be with us, and that some method of isolation in the near future must be installed. We assure you that we are in no condition to bring to our aid the best methods for the treatment of this class of patients without special accommodations for them. We sincerely hope that some friend of humanity will give us a special fund for the erection and maintenance of such a building.

The growth of the Lying-in and Gynecological Departments will necessitate the erection of another story over the children's ward before many years. The work of this department carries with it our warmest appreciations, it brings invalid mothers back into homes, with renewed life and strength, to take up their daily toil, who would without this help languish and die.

Electric lighting has been again postponed for lack of funds to accomplish it. The wants are so numerous and pressing in other directions that we do not wish to urge its immediate acceptance beyond reason. We are satisfied that the most economical method will be to buy the electricity from outside. The expense of the plant for the manufacture would be so large that we find it would not be wise to endorse it. The expense of wiring the institution would be about $1,000.

WILDWOOD FARM.

The milk supply from the farm has been materially increased during the year by its efficient manager, Clarence A. Hawks, and we are gratified in being able to report that it is now on a paying basis. This fall we propose to erect an ice house, also to build a short dam for the forming of a pond for ice, proposing to cut our own ice in future.

Respectfully submitted.

HENRY K. MORGAN,
HARMON G. HOWE,
THOMAS SISSON.

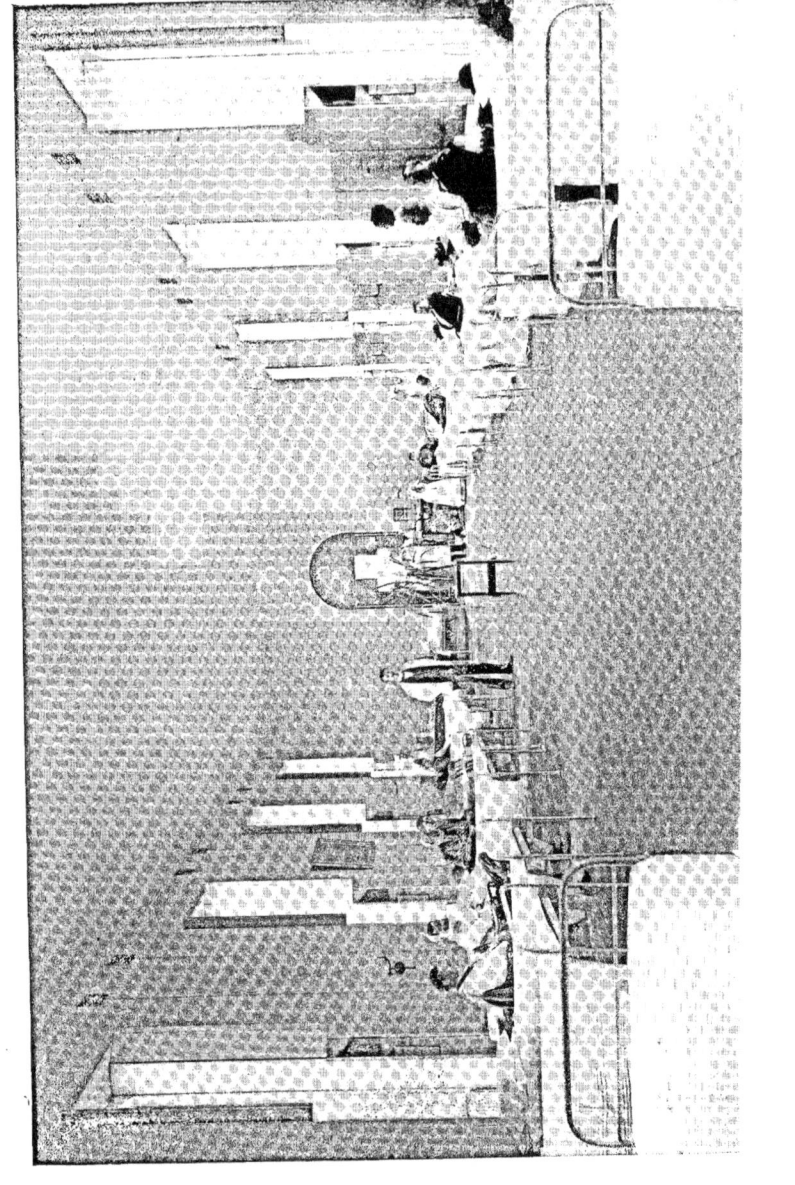

TREASURER'S REPORT.

TREASURER'S REPORT,

CLOSE OF FISCAL YEAR, SEPTEMBER 30, 1898.

RECEIPTS.

Balance cash from 1897 report, ...			$2,964.21
Bequest of John C. Parsons, . . .	$1,000.00		
' " Amanda M. Whitney, . .	10,528.24		
' '" Martha W. Brown, . . .	38,877.67		
' ·'' Susan S. Clark, . . .	4,850.00—		55,255.91
Donation of Louis B. Haas, ...			25.00
Hartford Street Railway Company, one-half amount paid for land and right of way. Newington Avenue, "Wildwood Farm,"			750.00
Interest, net, ...			16,899.30
Keney Fund income, net, ...			2,295.83
Rents, Wooster Street property, net, . .	$217.98		
" Congress " " gross, .	693.11—		911.09
Received from Superintendent for board of patients at Hospital, ...			36,467.66
Bills receivable, real, No. 1, H., ...			19.00
" " · ' E. M. Watkinson Trust Fund, . .			450.00
" " " Keney Fund, part payment of note, .			15,000.00
Bonds, Gurdon Fox Fund, 5,000 Chicago, Rock Island & Pacific Railway, 5s of 1934, redeemed, . . .			5,000.00
Bank Stocks, Mercantile National Bank, Hartford, in liquidation, 30 per cent. repayment of 100 shares capital stock,			3,000.00
Bank Stocks, Merchants National Bank, New Haven, 30 per cent. repayment of 50 shares capital stock, . .			750.00
Gas Stocks, New Britain Gas Light Company, one-third share sold, ...			9.00
Cemetery Stocks, Cedar Hill Cemetery, 4 shares retired, balance, ...			200.00
Old People's Home, loans paid, ...			10,800.00
E. M. Watkinson Trust Fund Income, ...			169.50
Bills payable, ...			2,500.00

$153,466.50

HARTFORD HOSPITAL.

CLOSE OF FISCAL YEAR, SEPTEMBER 30, 1898.

DISBURSEMENTS.

Paid Executive Committee's orders for		
General Expenses at Hospital,	$69,737.95	
Portraits,	276.25	
Tablet,	19.95—	$70,034.15
Bonds, Gurdon Fox Fund, bought 5,000 Lehigh Valley Railway of New York, 4½s of July 1, 1940,	5,000.00	
" E. M. Watkinson Trust Fund, bought 1,000 Lehigh Valley Railway of New York, 4½s of July 1, 1940,	1,000.00	
" F. A. and Martha W. Brown Fund, bought 9,000 Lehigh Valley Railway of New York, 4½s of July 1, 1940,	9,000.00	
" Susan S. Clark Fund, bought 5,000 Lehigh Valley Railway of New York, 4½s of July 1, 1940,	5,000.00—	20,000.00
Premium Account and Sinking Fund, permanent funds,		635.62
Bills receivable, real, No. 1, H.,		1,000.00
" " " Keney Fund,		15,000.00
Bills payable,		13,500.00
E. M. Watkinson Trust Fund Income, paid Miss C. M. Ely for Miss Susan Buck,		90.00
Congress Street property, repairs, etc.,		314.48
Insurance on Hospital buildings and contents, one year,		1,125.00
Expense, telephone, one year,	30.00	
" Legal services,	25.00	
" Cedar Hill Cemetery, for care of lot and monument of Junius S. Morgan,	61.50	
" Stationery and printing,	16.50	
" Salary of Treasurer, one year to September 30, 1898,	600.00	
" Incidentals,	33.83—	766.83
Permanent Funds, uninvested,		30,711.42
Trust Funds, uninvested,		250.00
Balance cash,		39.00
		$153,466.50

TREASURER'S REPORT — Continued.

Close of Fiscal Year, September 30, 1898.

ASSETS.
Bank Stocks.

Shares.					Book Value.	Market Value.
50	Ætna	National, Hartford,	.	.	$5,000.00	$7,250.00
200	American	"	"	. .	10,000.00	14,000.00
18	Charter Oak	"	"	. .	1,800.00	1,620.00
24	Hartford	"	"	. .	2,400.00	3,312.00
100	Mercantile	"	" in liquidation,		2,000.00	1,000.00
200	National Exchange,	"		. .	10,000.00	12,000.00
22	Phœnix National,	"		. .	2,200.00	2,706.00
50	Merchants	"	New Haven,	. .	1,750.00	1,820.00
25	Second	"	"	. .	2,500.00	4,300.00
80	First	"	Norwich,	. .	8,000.00	8,000.00
50	Thames	"	"	. .	5,000.00	7,500.00

Insurance Stocks.

37	Ætna,	Hartford,	.	.	3,700.00	10,101.00
46	Connecticut Fire,	"	.	.	4,600.00	8,464 00
11	Hartford	" "	.	.	1,100.00	5,610.00
25	Orient,		.	.	1,250.00	2,175.00
12	Travelers,		.	.	1,200.00	3,180.00

Railroad Stocks.

40	New London Northern, . .	.	4,000.00	7,000.00
37	New York, New Haven & Hartford,	.	3,700.00	7,030.00
108	Chicago, Burlington & Quincy, .	.	10,800.00	12,366.00
83	Detroit, Grand Rapids & Western (55.02 scrip), . . .	.	1,253.25	3,342.00
100	Erie & Pittsburgh, . .	.	5,000.00	6,800.00
100	Ft. Wayne & Jackson, preferred, .	.	10,000.00	13,000.00
100	Kansas City, St. Louis & Chicago, pref., .		10,000.00	14,000.00
40	Pittsburgh, Ft. Wayne & Chicago,	.	4,000.00	6,840.00

Miscellaneous Stocks.

177	Broad Brook Company, . . .	4,425.00	708.00
5	Collins Company, ...	500.00	565.00
100	Farnham Type-Setter Mfg. Co. (par $2,500),	1.00	1.00
28	Hartford Carpet Company, . .	2,800.00	1,736.00
46	Hartford City Gas Light Company, .	1,150.00	1,932.00
13	New Britain " " "	325.00	455.00
9	Adams Express Company, . .	900.00	990.00
32	Spring Grove Cemetery Association (par $800), ...	1.00	1.00

Bonds.

	Book Value.	Market Value.
State of North Carolina, 4s, July 1, 1910,	$1,650.00	$1,699.50
City of Omaha, 5s, Sept. 1, 1907,	10,000.00	10,900.00
Chic., Burl. & Quincy R. R., 5s, Sept. 1, 1903,	2,000.00	2,280.00
" " " " 7s, July 1, 1903,	1,000.00	1,150.00
Chicago, Mil. & St. Paul Ry.		
South-Western Div., 6s, July 1, 1909, .	15,000.00	17,550.00
South Minnesota Division, 6s, July 1, 1910,	5,000.00	5,850.00
Canada Southern Ry., 5s, Jan. 1, 1908,	1,000.00	1,090.00
Det., Gd. Rapids & Western R. R. 4s, April 1, 1946 (par $8,297.20),	5,808.04	7,218.56
Det., Monroe & Toledo R. R., 7s, Aug. 1, 1906,	10,000.00	12,200.00
Joliet & Northern Ind. R. R., 7s, July 10, 1907,	3,000.00	3,480.00
Kansas City, St. Jo. & C. B. R. R., 7s, Jan. 1, 1907,	15,000.00	18,000.00
Milwaukee & Madison R. R., 6s, Sept. 1, 1905,	10,000.00	11,700.00
New York & New England R. R., 7s, Jan. 1, 1905,	16,000.00	19,200.00
N. Y., N. H. & Hartford R. R., 4s, April 1, 1908,	1,500.00	2,415.00
N. Y. Cent. & Hudson River R. R., 4s, May 1, 1905,	5,000.00	5,200.00
Bills receivable, real, No. 1, H.,	13,000.00	13,000.00
" " " No. 2, W.,	5,100.00	5,100.00

Real Estate.

Hospital buildings and grounds,	1.00	1.00
Old People's Home, original lot,	1.00	1.00
Superintendent's residence,	1.00	1.00
One-half interest in "Wildwood Farm,"	1.00	1.00
Double house, 21 and 23 Congress Street,	6,600.00	6,600.00
One-half interest in 51 and 51½ Wooster Street,	2,500.00	2,500.00
West Virginia lands,	1.00	1.00
Loans to Old People's Home,	20,000.00	20,000.00
Balance cash,	39.00	39.00

PERMANENT FUNDS.

F. A. and Martha W. Brown Fund.

BONDS.

Lehigh Valley Ry, of N. Y., 4½s, July 1, 1940,	9,000.00	9,225.00
Balance cash, uninvested,	29,877.67	29,877.67

Cheney Brothers Fund.

BONDS.

Chicago & West. Indiana R. R., 6s, Dec. 1, 1932,	5,000.00	6,000.00

Susan S. Clark Fund.

BONDS.

	Book Value.	Market Value.
Lehigh Valley Ry. of N. Y., 4½s, July 1, 1940,	$5,000.00	$5,125.00

Gurdon Fox Fund.

BONDS.

Cleveland, Cincinnati, Chicago & St. Louis Ry., 4s, Nov. 1, 1990 (par $4,000),	3,685.00	3,920.00
Lehigh Valley Ry. of N. Y., 4½s, July 1, 1940,	5,000.00	5,125.00
Balance cash, uninvested,	465.00	465.00

Moses Fox Fund.

BONDS.

Cleveland, Cincinnati, Chicago & St. Louis Ry., 4s, Nov. 1, 1990 (par $5,000),	4,631.25	4,900.00
Balance cash, uninvested,	368.75	368.75

Keney Fund.

BONDS.

Port Reading R. R., 5s, Jan. 1, 1941,	15,000.00	15,600.00
West Chicago Street Railroad Tunnel Co., 5s, Feb. 1, 1909,	10,000.00	10,000.00
Bills receivable, real,	25,000.00	25,000.00

Mary J. Keney Fund.

BONDS.

Chicago & Western Ind. R. R., 6s, Dec. 1, 1932,	10,000.00	12,000.00

E. M. Watkinson Trust Fund.

BONDS.

Lehigh Valley Ry. of N. Y., 4½s, July 1, 1940,	1,000.00	1,025.00
Bills receivable, real,	4,750.00	4,750.00
Balance cash, uninvested,	250.00	250.00
Premium Account and Sinking Fund, permanent funds,	635.62	635.62
	$400,220.58	$471,248.10

LIABILITIES.

Fund, . . .		. .	.	$171,335.05
George Hall	Fund, .	.	.	31,020.00
Harriet Hall	" .	.	.	18,800.00
Daniel P. Crosby	" .	.	.	5,000.00
Charles H. Northam	.	.	.	5,000.00
Henry I. Wright	" .	.	.	10,000.00
Mary J. Keney	.	.	.	10,000.00
Junius S. Morgan	" .	.	.	20,000.00
Keney	.	.	.	50,000.00
Gurdon Fox	" .	.	.	9,150.00
F. A. and Martha W. Brown	" .	.	.	38,877.67
Susan S. Clark	" .	.	.	4,850.00
Miles A. Tuttle	" Free Bed,	.	.	1,000.00
Daniel Goodwin	" "	.	.	2,000.00
Charles F. Pond	" "	.	.	3,900.00
Nathan M. Waterman		.	.	3,000.00
Cheney Brothers		.	.	5,000.00
Moses Fox	" "	.	.	5,000.00
Ellen M. Watkinson Trust Fund,	.	.	.	6,000.00
" " " " " income,	.	.	.	82.62
Orthopedic Fund, .	.	.	.	187.24
Subscription for Training School Building, .	.	.	.	18.00
				$400,220.58

AUDITORS' CERTIFICATE.

HARTFORD, CONN., November 8, 1898.

We hereby certify that we have this day examined the books of Ward W. Jacobs, Treasurer of the Hartford Hospital, including the department of Old People's Home, compared vouchers for all cash-book disbursements made during the year ended September 30, 1898, and have checked the balance sheets.

We have also examined the lists of Assets, and find all of the several items as stated.

J. B. BUNCE,
H. A. REDFIELD, } *Auditors.*

SUPERINTENDENT'S REPORT.

To the Executive Committee:

GENTLEMEN — I herewith submit for your consideration the following as the forty-third annual report of the management of the Hartford Hospital, consisting of a detail of the receipts and disbursements, number of patients under care, results of treatment, and such other items as may be of interest.

The number of patients in the Hospital September 30, 1897, was 161 — 103 males and 58 females.

During the year 1,622 have been admitted, making an aggregate of 1,783 under treatment — 1,097 males and 686 females.

Of this number, 1,157 have recovered, 212 have improved, 46 not improved, 170 have died, and 198 remain under treatment — 137 males and 61 females. Of the deaths, 17 were the result of accidents, and lived but a few hours after admission, 25 were hopeless cases, and lived but a short time; 19 were due to consumption.

There were 52 births — 28 males and 24 females.

The whole number of weeks occupied was 8,152, of which citizens occupied 7,971.04, state beneficiaries 57.68, and United States marine patients 23.28.

There have been 127 patients occupying 358.4 weeks supported entirely by charity.

The appropriation from the State of $3,750 has partially supported 1,090 patients at the rate of 76 cents per week for each patient.

The number of state beneficiaries was 6.

The number of marine patients was 6.

The daily average of patients was 158.

CHILDREN'S WARD.

The greatest number any one day was 205.

The least number was 119.

The average duration of patients was 4.57 weeks.

The average cost per week for each patient was $8.55.

There have been 887 Americans, 695 foreigners, and 40 of unknown nativity.

Patients have been received from 73 different towns in the State.

The HARTFORD HOSPITAL in account with B. S. GILBERT, Supt.

Dr.		Cr.	
1897–8. To amount paid for—		· 1898. By amount received from—	
Anesthetics,	$143.23	W. W. Jacobs, Treasurer,	$69,737.95
Barn expenses,	211.58	Board of patients from	
Breadstuffs,	1,992.92	various towns in the	
Butter and eggs,	2,411.39	State,	13,255 85
Fruits and vegetables,	2,486.22	Paying patients,	18,478.39
Freights, etc.,	87.19	State appropriation,	3,750.00
Fuel,	5,197.29	State beneficiaries,	225.21
Furniture,	4,469.27	Marine patients,	149.00
Gas,	1,530.56	Services of nurses,	122.57
Groceries,	2,357 74	Sales,	417.89
Ice,	401.85	Registrar of births and	
Instruments,	986.99	deaths,	68.65
Meat, fish, and fowl,	9,935.57		
Medicine,	881.39		
Milk,	4,170.14		
Miscellaneous,	1,782.94		
Printing and stationery,	791.38		
Repairs,	4,514.99		
Salaries,	21,822.04		
Surgical dressings,	2,214.20		
Soap and washing soda,	333.82		
Water,	379.50		
Whiskey, etc.,	635.75		
Total current expenses,	$69,737.95		
Amount paid Treasurer,	36,467.66		
	$106,205.61		$106,205.61

Detailed Statement of the Receipts of the HARTFORD HOSPITAL
from September 30, 1897, to September 30, 1898.

Received from the State Appropriation:

December 31, 1897, ...	. $1,250.00
March 31, 1898, ...	. 1,250.00
June 30, 1898, . . , . .	. 1,250.00

3,750.00

Received from various towns in the State:

December 31, 1897, ...	. $3,920.12
March 31, 1898, ...	. 1,667.55
June 30, 1898, ...	. 7,120.30
September 30, 1898, ...	. 547.88

13,255.85

Received from paying patients:

December 31, 1897, ...	. $4,863.29
March 31, 1898, ...	. 4,192.15
June 30, 1898, ...	. 5,272.72
September 30, 1898, ...	. 4,150.23

	18,478.39
Received from State for care of beneficiaries, . .	225.21
Received from U. S. Collector for marine patients, .	149.00
Received for services of nurses, ...	122.57
Received from sales, ...	417.89
Received from Registrar of Births and Deaths, .	68.75
Total receipts, ...	. $36,467.66

Number of Patients who have received the Benefits of the HART-
FORD HOSPITAL *during the Year ending September 30, 1898.*

	Male.	Female.	Total.
Number of patients in the Hospital, October 1, 1897, ...	103	58	101
Admitted during the year, . . .	994	628	1,622
Total, ...	1,097	686	1,783
Of this number have been discharged:			
Recovered, ...	697	460	1,157
Improved, ...	127	85	212
Not Improved, ...	28	18	46
Died, ...	108	62	170
Total, ...	960	625	1,585
Remaining October 1, 1898; . . .	137	61	198

Monthlyt Admissions from September 30, 1897, to September 30, 1898.

	Male.	Female.	Total.		Male.	Female.	Total.
October,	81	66	147	May,	85	54	139
November,	83	46	129	June,	85	63	148
December,	96	49	145	July,	82	39	121
January,	85	55	140	August,	61	48	109
February,	58	46	104	September,	148	60	208
March,	66	50	116				
April,	64	52	116	Total,	994	628	1,622

Occupation of Patients.

Actors,	2	Fact'yOp'ratives,	68	Printers,	4
Agents,	3	Firemen,		Plumber,	1
Burnishers,	2	Foremen,		Porter,	1
Bakers,	15	Gardeners,		Peddlers,	15
Barbers,	3	Grinders,	5	Painters,	30
Bartenders,	11	Gunsmiths,	3	Polishers,	11
Butchers,	9	Hostlers,	15	Photographers,	2
Blacksmiths,	8	Harnessmakers,	15	Quarrymen,	2
Brakemen,	21	Housekeepers,	310	Secretary,	1
Bookkeepers,	6	Journalist,	1	Stenographers,	2
Bookbinders,	2	Lathers,	10	Shoemakers,	3
Bottlers,	3	Laundresses,	22	Seamstress,	1
Cutters,	3	Lawyers,	6	Seamen,	4
Clergyman,	1	Linemen,	7	Stonecutters,	3
Cabinetmakers,	2	Laborers,	233	School girls,	9
Civil Engineers,	3	Music Teacher,	1	School boys,	11
Clerks,	39	Machinists,	35	Salesmen,	15
Cooks,	29	Moulders,	12	Salesladies,	3
Cigarmakers,	10	Merchants,	6	Students,	13
Carpenters,	30	Masons,	30	Soldiers,	3
Domestics,	135	Mechanics,	42	Tailors,	13
Draughtsmen,	3	Manufacturers,	2	Tailoresses,	3
Dressmakers,	15	Messenger,	1	Teachers,	8
Dentist,	1	Nurses,	33	Teamsters,	13
Engineers,	6	None,	188	Waiters,	12
Electricians,	6	Office boy,	1	Waitresses,	8
Farmers,	75	Physician,	1	Weavers,	9

Residence of Patients.

Ashford,	Bloomfield,	Danbury,
Avon,	Canton,	Essex,
Ansonia,	Chatham,	East Hartford,
Branford,	Colchester,	East Windsor,
Baltic,	Cromwell,	Enfield,
Burlington,	Cheshire,	East Hampton,
Bristol,	Chaplin,	East Haddam,
Bridgeport,	Cornwall,	Ellington,
Berlin,	Chester,	East Granby,

Residence of Patients — Continued.

Farmington,	Newington,	Simsbury,
Groton,	New Haven,	Tolland,
Glastonbury,	New Hartford,	Torrington,
Hebron,	Portland,	Vernon,
Harwinton,	Plainville,	Woodbury,
Hartford,	Plymouth,	Wallingford,
Haddam,	Rocky Hill,	Waterbury,
Lyme,	Stamford,	Wethersfield,
Manchester,	Stafford,	West Hartford,
Meriden,	Southington,	Windham,
Middletown,	Suffield,	Windsor Locks,
Mansfield,	Saybrook,	Willington,
Norfolk,	Salisbury,	Winchester,
Naugatuck,	Somers,	Windsor.
New London,	Stonington,	
New Britain	South Windsor,	

DONATIONS.

Through the kindness of the editors, we have received the *Hartford Daily Times*, the *Hartford Daily Courant*, the *Hartford Daily Post*, the *Hartford Daily Telegram*, and the *New York Medical Journal*.

BOOKS, PAPERS AND MAGAZINES.

Mrs. L. D. Fisk, Mrs. J. J. Goodwin, Mrs. Sanborn, Mrs. Edward Hickmott, Mrs. C. H. Barbour, Mrs. A. J. Hyde, Mrs. Atwood Collins, Mrs. C. C. Beach, Mrs. Jacob Knous, Mrs. E. H. Crosby, Miss Alice O'Brien, Mrs. J. A. Smith, Mrs. George F. Spencer, Mrs. E. Parsons, H. J. Gillette, Grant D. Brower, George L. Chase, J. D. Armes, George Avery, J. M. Parker, Jr., New York Club, St. John's Church, S. S. W. W. S. S., Miss Martha Schwab, Mrs. J. D. Tucker, C. H. Adams.

CLOTHING, OLD LINEN AND COTTON.

Miss Alice Hills, Mrs. W. A. Dudley, Mrs. George Taintor, Mrs. M. A. Hart, Mrs. Jacob Knous, Mrs. Mills Munsill, Mrs. J. B. Powell, Mrs. Newton, Mrs. Harriett Bosanco, Mrs. H. G. Howe, Mrs. Alex. Allen, Mrs. G. M. Johnson, Mrs. A. C. Hills, Mrs. M. S. Peck, Mrs. L. D. Fisk, Mrs. Burdick, Mrs. W. B. Clark, Mrs. Francis Goodwin, Mrs. Baker, Mrs. Carey, First M. E. Church Epworth League, Hartford Branch of the N. G. Association, Young Ladies' Benevolent Society of the Church of the Redeemer, Union for Home Work Park Church Mission Circle, Mission Circle Canton Church, Mrs. Henry Hart, Mrs. George A. Hunn, Mrs. William H. Hendson, W. Stone Wilson, Mrs. G. P. Davis, Mrs. John Allen.

FRUITS AND FLOWERS.

Mrs. Henry S. Redfield, Misses Pardee, Mrs. Judson Rockwell, Miss Parker, Mrs. D. H. Wright, Mrs. John Coombs, Mrs. B. S. Gilbert, D. W. Brooks, L. B. Haas, J. F. Morris, Wethersfield Flower Mission.

MISCELLANEOUS.

Mrs. J. Gilman, one swing; Mrs. Harriet Bosanko, toys; Mrs. Newton, toys; King's Daughters, one dozen cushions.

CHRISTMAS AND THANKSGIVING.

InAsMuch Ten King's Daughters, Bristol, Conn., scrap books and dolls; Raymond Tracey, toys; Misses Dunham, toys; Mrs. H. A. Redfield, box of oranges; the North West School, one box oranges; Misses Pardee, $10.00.

Many others have kindly left different gifts without leaving any name. Some names may have been unintentionally omitted. To all, however, we extend our thanks.

B. S. GILBERT,
Superintendent.

GENERAL STATISTICS

YEARS.	Admitted during the year.	NUMBER EACH YEAR.						Remaining at the end of the year.	Daily average for the year.	NO. EACH DAY.	
		Under care.	Discharged.	Recovered.	Improved.	Not improved.	Dead.			Greatest.	Least.
1860–1861,	45	45	32	21	7	1	3	13	12	14	1
1861–1862,	258	271	214	159	20	12	23	57	27	85	14
1862–1863,	107	164	141	103	15	5	18	23	18	57	11
1863–1864,	157	180	149	103	14	8	24	31	27	45	21
1864–1865,	132	163	142	102	2	9	29	21	27	31	21
1865–1866,	196	277	172	133	5	8	26	45	35	49	21
1866–1867,	221	266	211	176	8	5	24	55	44	59	29
1867–1868,	251	306	250	183	16	15	36	56	50	63	38
1868–1869,	259	315	260	192	18	16	34	55	55	67	42
1869–1870,	248	339	298	220	21	20	37	41	50	62	36
1870–1871,	329	370	303	210	28	18	50	64	63	67	39
1871–1872,	347	411	345	215	42	46	41	66	62	71	59
1872–1873,	370	436	368	206	70	31	55	68	69	76	56
1873–1874,	452	520	422	299	36	29	58	98	79	98	63
1874–1875,	492	590	486	323	53	29	53	104	95	119	71
1875–1876,	603	707	573	376	64	35	57	134	113	136	90
1876–1877,	599	733	613	378	85	49	72	120	130	149	112
1877–1878,	914	1,034	944	591	117	66	100	90	101	122	80
1878–1879,	538	628	533	307	93	37	68	95	97	113	87
1879–1880,	597	692	589	362	93	38	66	103	94	109	78
1880–1881,	649	752	360	392	99	33	102	92	96	107	83
1881–1882,	736	828	734	404	154	62	89	94	97	115	90
1882–1883,	723	817	720	391	161	63	95	97	94	117	83
1883–1884,	701	798	697	362	158	69	93	101	98	118	86
1884–1885,	747	848	746	392	177	81	85	102	114	139	92
1885–1886,	741	843	743	404	178	60	90	100	107	130	63
1886–1887,	770	870	760	402	162	66	117	110	108	139	83
1887–1888,	745	855	764	436	146	56	108	91	108	137	87
1888–1889,	845	936	831	496	148	61	117	105	111	143	83
1889–1890,	998	1,103	983	566	183	71	144	120	127	156	105
1890–1891,	928	1,048	946	522	195	82	145	102	110	132	83
1891–1892,	1,074	1,176	1,079	581	271	75	152	97	120	137	89
1892–1893,	1,169	1,266	1,155	645	254	97	159	111	122	145	88
1893–1894,	1,151	1,292	1,126	657	216	90	163	136	130	153	101
1894–1895,	1,295	1,431	1,133	854	233	74	141	129	138	160	102
1895–1896,	1,563	1,692	1,568	1,128	189	71	180	124	144	160	91
1896–1897,	1,558	1,682	1,521	991	265	78	187	161	144	166	113
1897–1898,	1,622	1,783	1,585	1,157	212	46	170	198	158	205	119

Table of Diseases, Injuries, Etc.,

TREATED IN

THE HARTFORD HOSPITAL

During the Year Ending September 30, 1898.

MEDICAL CASES.

	Under treatment Sept. 30, 1897.	New cases admitted.		Recovered.	Improved.	Unimproved.	Died.	Remaining Sept. 30, 1898.
		Male.	Female.					
Constitutional Diseases.								
Alcoholism, Acute,	1	..	..	1	..	..	..	..
" Chronic,	1	3	..	1	..	..	3	..
Debility,	..	..	3	1	1	1	..	..
Glycosuria,	..	1	..	...	1	..	..	..
Insolation,	..	1	..	1	..	..	..	..
Marasmus,	..	1	1	1	..	..	1	..
Lumbago,	1	4	..	4	1	..	..	..
Rheumatism, Acute Art.,	..	13	3	8	5	..	..	3
" Chronic,	3	15	3	4	11	3	2	1
" Muscular,	1	4	..	2	1	..	1	1
" Sub-acute,	1	3	3	5	2	..	..	..
Rheumatoid, Arthritis,	3	..	..	..	1	2	..	..
Senility,	..	2	1	..	1	1	1	..
Uraemia,	..	1	1	..	..	..	2	..
Diseases of Circulation.								
Anaemia,	..	2	3	..	3	..	2	..
" Cardiac,	..	1	..	..	1	..	..	..
Aneurysm,	..	1	..	..	..	..	1	..
Apoplexy,	3	5	1	..	1	2	5	1
Arterio-Sclerosis,	1	5	1	..	3	1	1	2
Endarteritis,	..	1	..	..	..	..	1	..
Cerebral Embolism,	..	..	1	1	..	..	..	..
Heart, Fatty Degen. of,	..	1	..	..	..	1	..	..
" Mitral Regurg. of,	1	3	2	..	2	1	2	1
Hemiplegia,	..	1	1	..	..	1	..	1
Leukaemia,	..	1	..	..	..	1	..	..

MEDICAL CASES.— Continued.

	Under treatment Sept. 30, 1897.	New cases admitted. Male.	New cases admitted. Female.	Recovered.	Improved.	Unimproved.	Died.	Remaining Sept. 30, 1898.
Diseases of Cutaneous System.								
Dermatitis Simplex,	..	..	1	1	..	..	..	..
Eczema of Arms,	..	..	1	1	..	..	..	..
" " Hands,	..	1	..	1	..	..	..	..
" " Head,	..	..	1	1	..	..	..	..
" Papulosum,	..	1	..	1	..	..	..	..
" Squamosum,	..	..	1	..	..	1	..	..
Impetigo Contagiosum,	1	1	..	..	..	..	..	1
Pemphigus Vulgaris,	..	2	1	3	..	..	..	..
Psoriasis,	..	..	1	..	1	..	..	..
Scabies,	..	..	1	1	..	..	..	..
Urticaria,	..	..	2	..	2	..	..	..
Diseases of Digestive System.								
Dentition,	..	..	1	1	..	..	..	..
Dysentery,	1	4	8	8	..	..	3	2
Dyspepsia,	..	1	..	1	..	..	..	..
Fecal Impaction,	..	..	1	1	..	..	..	..
Entero-Colitis,	1	1	..	2	..	..	..	..
Gastritis, Acute,	1	5	4	6	3	1	..	..
" Alcoholic,	..	2	3	3	..	..	..	2
" Chronic,	1	13	3	8	8	1	..	..
Gastric Ulcer,	1	..	..	1	..	..	..	..
Gastralgia,	1	..	1	2	..	..	..	..
Glossitis,	..	1	1	2	..	..	..	..
Hepatic Colic,	..	..	1	1	..	..	..	..
Intestinal Paralysis,	..	..	1	1	..	..	..	..
Jaundice, Catarrhal,	..	1	2	1	..	..	..	2
" Obstuctive,	..	..	1	1	..	..	..	..
Liver, Carcinoma of,	..	1	..	..	..	..	1	..
" Cirrhosis of,	1	4	..	1	1	..	2	1
" Hypertrophy of,	..	1	..	..	1	..	..	..
Mesentery, Carcinoma of,	1	..	..	..	..	..	1	..
Peritonitis,	..	1	4	4	1	..	..	..
Perityphlitis,	..	1	..	1	..	..	..	..
Stomach, Dilitation of,	..	2	..	..	2	..	..	..
Diseases of Nervous System.								
Acute Melancholia,	..	2	..	..	..	2	..	..
Cephalaegia,	..	3	..	2	1	..	..	..
Cerebral Tumor,	1	..	..	..	..	1	..	..
Chorea,	..	..	1	..	1	..	..	..
Dementia,	..	1	1	..	1	1	..	..
Epilepsy,	..	2	3	2	3	..	..	..
Gumma of Brain,	..	1	..	..	..	..	..	1
Hysteria,	..	2	3	2	2	1	..	..
" and Epilepsy,	..	2	..	..	1	1	..	..
" " Neurasthenia,	..	..	1	..	1	..	..	..

MEDICAL CASES.— Continued.

	Under treatment, Sept. 30, 1897.	New cases admitted.		Recovered.	Improved.	Unimproved.	Died.	Remaining Sept. 30, 1898.
		Male.	Female.					
Diseases of Nervous System.— *Continued.*								
Hysteria and Puerperal Convulsions,	..	..	1	..	1	..	..	..
Locomotor Ataxia,	..	1	..	..	1	..	..	..
Mania á Potu,	..	1	..	1	..	..	..	..
" Bell's.	..	..	1	..	..	1	..	..
Meningitis, Basilar,	1	..	..	..	..	..	1	..
" Cerebral,	..	1	..	..	..	..	1	..
" Cerebro-Spinal,	..	..	1	..	..	..	1	..
Myelitis, Chronic,	..	1	..	..	1	..	..	..
Neurasthenia,	..	3	5	3	4	1	..	..
Neuralgia, Facial,	..	1	2	2	1	..	..	..
" Intercostal,	..	1	..	1	..	..	..	..
Neuritis, Alcoholic,	..	4	2	3	2	..	1	..
" Multiple,	..	1	2	..	1	..	..	2
Paralysis, Agitans,	..	1	..	..	..	..	..	1
Paresis,	..	1	..	..	..	..	..	1
Polyomyelitis, Acute Ant.,	..	..	1	..	1	..	..	..
Sciatica, Acute,	..	2	1	3	..	..	..	..
" Chronic,	..	..	3	..	..	..	2	1
Diseases of Respiratory System.								
Bronchitis, Acute,	2	2	3	6	..	..	.	1
" Capillary,	..	..	1	1	..	..	..	..
" Chronic,	..	9	5	6	4	..	3	1
" and Asthma,	1	..	..	1	..	..	..	..
Emphysema,	1	4	3	4	4	..	..	..
Empyema,	1	..	..	1	..	..	..	..
Gangrene of Lungs,	..	1	..	..	1	..	..	..
Laryngitis,	..	2	..	2	..	..	..	..
Oedema of Lungs,	..	1	..	..	..	..	1	..
Phthisis Pulmonalis,	5	33	12	..	18	2	24	6
" " Acute,	..	2	..	..	..	1	1	..
" Fibrinous	2	2	..	..	2	1	1	..
" and Influenza,	..	1	..	..	1	..	..	..
Pleurisy, Acute,	..	1	..	1	..	..	..	..
" Fibrinous,	..	1	2	2	1	..	..	..
" Serous,	..	3	2	3	..	..	2	..
" Sero-Fibrinous,	..	2	..	1	1	..	..	..
Pleuridynia,	..	1	..	1	..	..	..	..
Pneumonia, Broncho,	..	5	2	7	..	..	..	..
" Catarrhal,	..	1	..	1	..	..	..	..
" Lobar,	5	30	7	35	2	..	5	..
" Double,	..	2	1	..	..	..	3	..
" and Nephritis,	..	1	1	1	..	..	..	..
" " Syphilis,	..	1	..	..	1	..	..	..
Tonsilitis, Follicular,	..	3	7	10	..	..	..	..
Tonsils, Hypertrophy of,	..	2	..	1	1	..	..	..

MEDICAL CASES.— Continued.

	Under treatment Sept. 30, 1897.	New cases admitted.		Recovered.	Improved.	Unimproved.	Died.	Remaining Sept. 30, 1898.
		Male.	Female.					
Diseases of Urinary System.								
Bladder, Atony of, ...	..	I	..	I	..	..	..	..
Nephritis, Chronic Diffuse, . . .	..	I	..	..	I	..	..	..
" and Anæmia, . .	I	..	..	..	..	..	I	..
" " Tachycardia, . .	I	..	..	..	..	..	I	..
" Interstitial, ...	..	I	..	..	I	..	..	..
Pyonephrosis, ...	..	2	..	I	I	..	..	..
Infectious Diseases.								
Diphtheria, ...	..	2	3	4	..	..	I	..
Erysipelas, ...	..	5	5	10	..	..	..	..
Intermittant Fever, ...	2	30	7	35	I	..	..	3
Measles, ...	..	I	I	2	..	..	..	..
La Grippe, ...	3	10	4	15	2	..	..	..
Remittant Fever, ...	..	3	I	4	..	..	..	..
Scarlet Fever, ...	2	21	15	37	..	..	I	..
Typhoid Fever, ...	21	98	18	56	..	..	6	75
Typho-Malaria, ...	I	..	..	I	..	..	..	..
Varicella, ...	..	I	..	I	..	..	..	..
Multiple Diseases.								
Acute Gastritis and Endometritis, .	..	..	I	I	..	..	..	..
Alcoholism and Pneumonia, . .	..	..	I	..	..	..	I	..
Chronic Bronchitis and Myocarditis, .	..	I	..	I	..	..	..	..
Diabetes and Sciatica, . .	..	I	..	..	..	I	..	..
Myocarditis and Internal Injuries, .	..	..	I	..	..	..	I	..
Phthisis and Endocarditis, . .- .	..	..	I	..	..	I	..	..
Pleurisy and Asthma, . . .	..	I	..	..	I	..	..	..
Pneumonia and Empyema, . .	..	..	I	..	..	..	I	..
Pulmonary Congestion and Pneumonitis, .	..	I	..	..	..	..	I	..
Poisons.								
Carbolic Acid, ...	..	I	I	2	..	..	..	..
Chloroform, ...	..	I	..	I	..	..	..	..
Illuminating Gas, ...	..	2	..	I	..	..	..	I
Lead, Chronic, ...	..	I	..	..	I	..	..	..
Opium, ...	..	..	I	I	..	..	..	..
Ptomaine, ...	..	I	I	2	..	..	..	..
Rhus Toxicodendron, ...	..	2	..	2	..	..	..	..
Unclassified Diseases.								
Alcoholism, ...	..	I	..	I	..	..	..	..
Malingerer, ...	..	2	I	3	..	..	..	..
No Disease, ...	..	4	5	6	..	..	..	3
Spasmodic Torticollis, ...	..	I	..	..	..	I	..	..
Total, includ'g Obstetrics and Gynecology,	85	480	442	588	135	34	110	140
Total, not including Obstetrics and Gynecology.	75	452	202	377	117	31	89	115

OBSTETRICS AND GYNECOLOGICAL DISEASES.

	Under treatment Sept. 30, 1897.	New cases admitted.		Recovered.	Improved.	Unimproved.	Died.	Remaining Sept. 30, 1898.
		Male.	Female.					
Gynecology.								
Amenorrhœa,	..	..	3	3	..	..	..	..
Cervix Uteri Carcinoma of,	..	..	4	..	2	1	1	..
" " Laceration of,	..	..	7	6	1	..	..	..
" " " and hemorrhoids,	..	..	3	3	..	..	..	..
" Uteri, Papilloma of,	..	..	1	1	..	..	..	..
Cystocele,	..	..	2	2	..	..	..	..
Dysmenorrhœa,	..	..	8	8	..	..	..	..
Endometritis, Acute,	2	..	12	12	2	..	..	..
" Chronic,	2	..	16	10	1	..	..	7
" and Lacerated cervix,	..	..	5	5	..	..	..	..
" " perineum,	..	..	3	3	..	..	..	..
" Retroversion,	..	..	1	..	1	..	..	..
" Sciatica,	..	..	1	..	1	..	..	..
" Vaginitis,	..	..	1	1	..	..	..	..
Fistula, Vesico-Vaginal,	..	..	1	1	..	..	..	..
Menorrhagia,	..	..	2	2	..	..	..	..
Oöphoralgia,	..	..	2	2	..	..	..	..
Ovarian cyst,	..	..	6	5	..	..	..	1
" " double,	..	..	2	2	..	..	..	..
" " and carcinoma,	..	..	1	1	..	..	..	..
" " " neuralgia,	..	..	1	1	..	..	..	..
Perinéum, Laceration of,	..	..	8	7	..	..	..	1
" and cervix, Laceration of,	..	..	14	14	..	..	..	..
" " " " and Endometritis,	..	..	1	1	..	..	..	..
" " " Laceration of, and Rectocele,	..	..	1	1	..	..	..	..
" Laceration of, and hemorrhoids,	..	..	1	1	..	..	..	..
" " " Anæmia,	..	..	1	1	..	..	..	..
" " " thro' Sphincter,	..	..	1	..	..	..	..	1
Pelvic Cellulitis,	..	..	12	8	..	..	2	2
" " and Abscess,	..	..	2	1	1	..	..	..
" " " Oöphoralgia,	1	..	..	..	1	..	..	..
" " " Peritonitis,	..	..	1	..	1	..	..	..
Prolapsus Uteri,	..	..	4	2	2	..	..	..
Pyosalpinx,	..	..	2	2	..	..	..	..
Salpingitis,	..	..	1	..	1	..	..	..
Uterus, Carcinoma of,	..	..	5	..	..	..	2	3
" Displacements of,	..	..	..	..	..	..	..	..
" Anteversion,	..	..	1	1	..	..	..	..
" Retroflexion,	..	..	1	1	..	..	..	..
" Retroversion,	..	..	1	..	..	..	..	1
" and Adhesions,	2	..	..	..	2	..	..	..
" Fibromata of,	..	..	8	7	..	1	..	..
" Subinvolution of,	..	..	1	1	..	..	..	..
Vulva, Oedema of,	..	..	1	1	..	..	..	..
" Papilloma of	..	..	1	1	..	..	..	..

OBSTETRICS AND GYNECOLOGICAL DISEASES.— Continued.

	Under treatment Sept. 30, 1897.	New cases admitted.		Recovered.	Improved.	Unimproved.	Died.	Remaining Sept. 30, 1898.
		Male.	Female.					
Obstetrics.								
Abortion, ...	..	..	3	3	..	..	..	..
" Threatened, ...	..	..	1	1	..	..	..	..
Miscarriage, ...	..	..	1	1	..	..	..	..
Mastitis, ...	..	..	1	1	..	..	..	..
Pregnancy, ...	3	..	54	45	2	..	1	9
" and Albuminuria, . . .	..	..	1	1	..	..	..	..
" " Contracted Pelvis, .	..	..	1	..	..	1	..	..
" " Chorea, . . .	..	..	1	..	..	..	1	..
" " Hyperemisis, . .	..	..	1	1	..	..	..	..
" " Secondary Hemorrhage, .	..	..	1	..	..	..	1	..
Puerperium, ...	..	..	1	1	..	..	..	..
Infants, Full term, ...	..	23	21	39	..	..	5	..
" Still born, ...	..	5	3	..	..	..	8	..

WM. S. REOCH,
House Physician.

SURGICAL CASES.

	Under treatment Sept. 30, 1897.	New cases admitted.		Recovered.	Improved.	Uninproved.	Died.	Remaining Sept. 30, 1898.
		Male.	Female.					
Injuries of Head, Face, and Neck.								
Abrasion of Face,	..	1	1	2	..	..	..	..
Adenitis of Neck,	..	..	3	2	1	..	..	..
Burn of Face and Neck,	..	1	..	1	..	..	..	..
Cervical Abscess (Potts),	..	1	..	..	..	1	..	..
Compression of Brain,	..	1	..	..	..	..	1	..
Concussion " "	..	4	1	4	..	..	1	..
Contusion of Face,	..	5	..	5	..	..	..	..
" " Head and Arm,	..	1	..	1	..	..	..	..
Fracture of Base of Skull,	..	4	..	1	..	..	3	..
" " Inferior Maxilla,	..	1	..	1	..	..	..	..
" " Skull (Compound),	..	1	..	..	..	..	1	..
" " " Base of and Dislocation of Clavicle,	1	..	..	1	..	..	..	..
Hare Lip,	..	1	..	..	..	..	1	..
Lipoma of Neck,	..	1	..	1	..	..	..	..
Necrosis of Face,	..	..	1	1	..	..	..	..
" " Inferior Maxilla,	..	1	..	1	..	..	..	..
" " Parietal Bone,	..	1	..	1	..	..	..	..
Periostitis of Inferior Maxilla,	..	3	2	4	1	..	..	..
Tubercular Glands of Neck,	1	4	1	6	..	..	..	..
Wounds, Gunshot of Jaw,	..	1	..	1	..	..	..	..
" " " Neck,	..	1	..	1	..	..	..	..
" Incised of Chin,	..	1	..	1	..	..	..	..
" " " Face,	..	4	1	4	1	..	..	..
" " " Forehead,	..	2	..	2	..	..	..	..
" " " Scalp,	..	3	..	2	1	..	..	..
" Infected of Nose,	..	1	..	1	..	..	..	..
" Lacerated of Scalp,	..	2	..	2	..	..	..	..
Injuries of Upper Extremities, Axilla and Spine.								
Amputation of Fingers (Traumatic),	..	1	..	1	..	..	..	..
" " Thumb,	..	1	..	1	..	..	..	..
Burn of Arm (Carbolic),	..	1	..	..	..	..	1	..
" " " and Thorax,	1	..	..	..	1	..	..	..
" " Hand,	..	1	..	1	..	..	..	..
" " " (Double),	..	1	..	1	..	..	..	..
Caries of Carpi (Tubercular),	..	1	..	1	..	..	..	..
" " Phalanx of Finger,	..	..	1	1	..	..	..	..
" " Metacarpi,	..	1	1	1	..	..	..	1
Cellulitis of Arm,	..	3	..	2	..	..	1	..
" " " and Hand,	..	2	..	2	..	..	..	..
" " Hand,	..	1	1	1	..	..	..	1
Contusion of Arm,	..	1	1	2	..	..	..	..
" " Hand,	..	1	..	1	..	..	..	..
" " Shoulder,	..	1	..	1	..	..	..	..

SURGICAL CASES.— Continued.

	Under treatment Sept. 30, 1897.	New cases admitted.		Recovered.	Improved.	Unimproved.	Died.	Remaining Sept. 30, 1898.
		Male.	Female.					
Injuries of Upper Extremities, Axilla, and Spine — *Continued.*								
Crush of Finger,	..	1	..	1	..	..	..	..
" " Hands,	..	1	..	1	..	..	..	..
Dislocation of Elbow,	..	1	..	1	..	..	..	..
" " Shoulder,	..	3	1	4	..	..	..	..
" " Thumb,	..	1	..	1	..	..	..	..
Foreign Body in Hand,	..	..	1	1	..	..	..	..
Fracture of Colles,	..	..	2	2	..	..	..	..
" " " (double),	..	1	..	..	..	..	..	1
" " Finger,	..	2	..	2	..	..	..	..
" " Humerus (neck),	2	3	1	5	..	..	..	1
" " " (shaft),	..	6	2	7	..	..	..	1
" " " (compound and comminuted)	..	1	..	..	1	..	..	..
" " Radius,	..	2	..	2	..	..	..	..
" " " and Ulna,	1	1	1	3	..	..	..	..
" " " " compound),	..	..	1	1	..	..	..	..
" " Spine,	..	2	..	..	..	..	I.	1
Gangrene of Finger,	..	2	..	2	..	..	..	..
Necrosis of Meta Carpi,	..	1	..	1	..	..	..	..
" " Phalanges,	..	..	1	1	..	..	..	..
Periostitis of Finger,	..	1	..	1	..	..	..	..
Rupture of Phalangeal Tendon,	..	1	..	1	..	..	..	..
Sprain of Elbow,	..	1	..	1	..	..	..	..
" " Shoulder,	..	2	..	1	..	..	..	1
" " Wrist,	..	2	..	2	..	..	..	..
" " " and Alcoholism,	..	1	..	..	..	..	1	..
Wound, Gunshot of Hand,	1	..	..	1	..	..	..	..
" " " Arm,	..	..	1	1	..	..	..	..
" Incised of Hand,	..	2	..	2	..	..	..	..
" Infected of Finger,	..	1	..	1	..	..	..	..
" " " Hand,	..	1	..	1	..	..	..	..
" Lacerated of Arm,	..	1	..	1	..	..	..	..
" " " Finger,	1	1	..	2	..	..	..	..
" " " Hand,	2	3	..	5	..	..	..	..
" " " " and Finger,	..	1	..	1	..	..	..	..
" " " Wrist,	..	1	..	1	..	..	..	..
Injuries of Lower Extremities and Groin.								
Amputation of Thigh, Traumatic,	..	1	..	..	..	..	1	..
Aneurism of Popliteal Artery,	..	1	..	..	1	..	..	..
Burn of Foot,	..	..	1	1	..	..	..	..
Bursitis of Patella,	1	1	1	2	1	..	..	..
Callosity of Toe,	..	..	1	1	..	..	..	..
Caries of Femur (Tubercular),	..	1	..	1	..	..	..	..

	Under treatment Sept. 30, 1897.	New cases admitted.		Recovered.	Improved.	Unimproved.	Died.	Remaining Sept. 30, 1898.
		Male.	Female.					
Injuries of Lower Extremities and Groin. *Continued.*								
Cellulitis of Foot,	..	2	..	2	..	..	..	..
" Leg,	..	2	..	2	..	..	..	..
" " and Alcoholism,	..	1	..	..	..	..	1	..
Contusion of Foot,	..	2	..	1	..	..	..	1
" Hip,	..	1	..	1	..	..	..	..
" Thigh,	..	1	..	1	..	..	..	..
Crush of Foot,	..	2	..	1	..	..	..	1
" Leg,	..	3	..	3	..	..	..	..
" Thigh,	..	1	..	..	..	..	1	..
Dislocation of Ankle,	..	2	..	2	..	..	..	..
" Knee,	..	1	..	1	..	..	..	..
Fracture of Femur (neck),	2	1	3	5	..	..	1	..
" " (shaft),	3	11	3	12	..	..	..	5
" " (compound),	..	1	..	1	..	..	..	..
" (" comminuted),	..	1	..	..	..	..	1	..
" Fibula,	..	..	1	1	..	..	..	..
" (double),	..	1	..	1	..	..	..	..
" (compound),	..	..	1	1	..	..	..	..
" Potts'),	1	8	4	13	..	..	..	..
" Patella,	1	..	..	1	..	..	..	..
" (compound comminuted),	1	..	..	1	..	..	..	..
.. Tibia,	1	1	..	2	..	..	..	..
" " (compound),	..	1	..	1	..	..	..	..
" " and Fibula,	2	8	..	9	..	..	1	..
" " " (double),	..	1	..	1	..	..	..	..
" " " (compound),	1	2	..	1	..	..	1	1
" Leg (multiple),	..	1	..	..	..	..	..	1
Foreign Body in Foot,	..	..	1	1	..	..	..	..
Frost-bite of Foot,	..	2	..	2	..	..	..	..
" Toes,	..	1	..	1	..	..	..	..
Gangrene of Foot (diabetic).	1	..	..	1	..	..	..	..
" " (senile),	1	1	..	..	..	..	1	1
Necrosis of Femur,	1	1	..	2	..	..	..	..
" Fibula,	1	1	..	1	1	..	..	..
" Os Calcis,	..	1	..	..	..	..	..	1
" Tibia,	2	2	..	3	1	..	..	..
Painful Stump of Leg,	1	..	..	1	..	..	..	..
Periostitis of Fibula,	..	..	1	1	..	..	..	..
Raynaud's Disease,	..	2	..	2	..	..	..	..
Sinus of Buttock,	..	2	..	1	1	..	..	..
Sprain of Ankle,	..	2	4	6	..	..	..	..
" " and Knee,	..	..	1	1	..	..	..	..
" Hip,	..	2	1	3	..	..	..	..

SURGICAL CASES.— Continued.

	Under treatment Sept. 30, 1897.	New cases admitted. Male.	Female.	Recovered.	Improved.	Unimproved.	Died.	Remaining Sept. 30, 1898.
Injuries of Lower Extremities and Groin. *Continued.*								
Sprain of Knee, ...	..	3	..	1	2	..	..	..
Synovitis of Ankle (acute), ...	..	2	..	2	..	..	..	..
" " (chronic) . . .	..	2	..	..	2	..	..	..
" Knee (acute), ...	..	1	..	1	..	..	..	..
" " (sub-acute), . . .	1	2	1	1	2	1	..	..
" " (chronic), . . .	..	..	1	1	..	..	..	..
Ulcer of Foot (Varicose), ...	2	..	..	2	..	..	..	..
" " (traumatic), ...	..	2	..	2	..	..	..	..
" Leg (indolent), ...	1	..	..	1	..	..	..	..
" " (rodent), ...	..	..	1	..	1	..	..	..
" " (traumatic), ...	1	2	..	2	1	..	..	..
" " (tubercular), ...	..	..	2	1	..	..	..	1
" " (varicose), ...	1	4	9	10	2	..	..	2
Varicose Veins of Leg and Thigh, . . .	..	3	..	1	2	..	..	..
Wounds, Gunshot, of Foot, ...	..	1	..	1	..	..	..	..
" " Knee, ...	..	1	..	..	..	1	..	..
" " Thigh, ...	1	..	..	1	..	..	..	..
" Incised, of Foot, ...	..	1	..	1	..	..	..	..
" " Leg, ...	..	1	..	1	..	..	..	..
" " Thigh, ...	..	1	..	1	..	..	..	..
" Infected, of Foot, ...	..	1	..	..	..	..	..	1
" Lacerated, of Leg, ...	..	1	..	1	..	..	..	..
" Puncture of Scrotum and Thigh,	1	..	..	1	..	..	..	..
" Stab of Thigh, ...	..	1	..	..	..	..	1	..
General Surgical Diseases and Injuries.								
Abdominal Adhesions, ...	..	1	1	1	..	..	1	..
Abscess of Abdomen, ...	2	1	..	2	1	..	..	..
" Axilla, ...	..	2	1	3	..	..	..	..
" Back, ...	1	..	..	1	..	..	..	..
" Buttock, ...	..	1	2	2	..	..	..	1
" Elbow, ...	..	..	1	1	..	..	..	..
" Face, ...	..	1	..	1	..	..	..	..
" Finger, ...	..	..	1	1	..	..	..	..
" Groin, ...	1	..	..	1	..	..	..	..
" Hand, ...	..	1	..	1	..	..	..	..
" Ischio-Rectal, ...	..	4	1	3	2	..	..	..
" Jaw, ...	..	1	..	1	..	..	..	..
" Knee, ...	1	..	..	1	..	..	..	..
" Leg, ...	1	3	..	4	..	..	..	..
" " (diabetic), ...	1	..	..	..	1	..	..	..
" " with Procedentia Uteri, .	1	..	..	1	..	..	..	..

SURGICAL CASES.— Continued.

	Under treatment Sept. 30, 1897.	New cases admitted.		Recovered.	Improved.	Unimproved.	Died.	Remaining Sept. 30, 1898.
		Male.	Female.					
General Surgical Diseases and Injuries. *Continued.*								
bscess of Mammary Gland,	..	..	1	1	..	..	..	..
" Neck,	..	1	2	3	..	..	..	..
" Perineum,	..	1	..	1	..	..	..	..
" Side,	..	1	..	1	..	..	..	..
" Scalp,	..	1	..	..	..	..	..	1
" Thigh,	..	..	1	1	..	..	..	..
" Thorax,	1	1	..	1	1	..	..	..
Appendicitis,	6	19	15	34	..	..	4	2
" and Cystic Ovary,	..	..	1	1	..	..	..	..
" and Fecal Fistula,	1	2	1	1	1	..	2	..
" and Peritonitis,	1	..	..	1	..	..	..	..
Burn of Face and Hand,	..	3	..	3	:	..	..	..
" Hand, Side, and Apoplexy,	..	1	..	..	..	..	..	1
" Trunk,	..	2	..	2	..	..	..	..
" " and Lower Extremity,	..	..	2	..	..	..	2	..
" Multiple,	..	..	1	1	..	..	..	..
Contusion of Back,	..	3	..	3	..	..	..	..
" Body,	..	3	..	3	..	..	..	..
" Shoulder,	..	1	..	1	..	..	..	..
" Side,	..	2	1	3	..	..	..	..
" Thorax,	..	3	..	3	..	..	..	..
" " and Hip,	..	1	..	1	..	..	..	..
Dislocation of Elbow and Fractured Elbow,	..	1	..	1	..	..	..	..
Erysipelas of Face,	..	1	..	1	..	..	..	..
Fecal Fistula,	..	1	..	..	1	..	..	..
Fissure in Ano,	..	..	2	2	..	..	..	..
" " and Hemorrhoids,	..	..	1	1	..	..	..	..
Fistula in Ano,	..	4	1	3	1	..	..	1
" Vesico-Rectal,	1	1	..	..	1	..	..	1
Foreign body in Stomach,	..	1	..	1	..	..	..	..
Fracture of Clavicle,	1	5	1	7	..	..	..	..
" " and Mania à Potu,	1	..	..	1	..	..	..	..
" Femur and Mania à Potu,	..	1	..	..	..	..	1	..
" Multiple,	..	2	..	1	..	..	1	..
" of Pelvis and Internal Injuries,	..	1	..	..	..	..	1	..
" Ribs,	..	2	..	2	..	..	..	..
" " and Internal Injuries,	..	1	..	..	1	..	..	..
" " Radius and Ulna,	..	1	..	..	..	..	1	..
" " and Tibia,	..	..	1	1	..	..	..	..
" Scapula,	..	3	..	3	..	..	..	..
" Skull and Femur,	..	1	..	..	..	..	1	..
" Jaw and Femur,	..	1	..	..	..	..	1	..
Hemorrhoids,	..	9	5	13	..	1	..	..

SURGICAL CASES.— Continued.

	Under treatment Sept. 30, 1897.	New cases admitted. Male.	Female.	Recovered.	Improved.	Unimproved.	Died.	Remaining Sept. 30, 1898.
General Surgical Diseases and Injuries. *Continued.*								
Hernia, Infantile,	..	2	..	2	..	..	..	..
" Inguinal,	1	8	2	9	..	..	..	2
" " (strangulated),	..	2	..	1	..	..	1	..
" " and Alcoholism,	1	.	..	..	..	..	1	..
.. Scrotal,	..	1	..	1	..	..	..	..
" Umbilical,	..	..	1	1	..	..	..	..
" " (strangulated),	..	..	..	1	..	..	1	..
:: Ventral,	1	2	..	1	..	..	1	1
" and Hydrocele,	..	1	..	1	..	..	..	..
Intestinal Obstruction,	..	2	1	..	..	..	3	..
Imperforate Anus,	..	..	2	1	..	..	1	..
Peritonitis, Traumatic,	..	..	1	..	..	..	1	..
" Tubercular,	..	..	1	..	..	1	..	..
Sinus of Abdomen,	1	1	..	2	..	..	..	..
" Breast,	..	..	1	1	..	..	..	..
Sprain of Back,	..	8	2	10	..	..	..	..
Stricture of Anus,	..	2	..	2	..	..	..	..
Tubercular Glands of Neck and Peritonitis,	..	..	1	1	..	..	..	..
" " and Spondylitis,	..	..	1	..	..	..	1	..
Tumor, Carcinoma of Breast,	..	..	8	5	..	2	..	1
" " Intestine,	..	..	2	..	1	1	..	..
" " Rectum,	..	..	1	..	..	..	1	..
" " Tongue,	..	..	1	..	..	1	..	..
" Adenoma of Breast,	..	..	1	1	..	..	..	..
" " Chest,	..	..	1	1	..	..	..	..
" Epithelioma of Axilla,	..	..	1	1	..	..	..	..
" " Face (recurrent),	1	..	..	..	..	..	..	1
" " Lip,	..	..	2	2	..	..	..	..
" " Tongue,	..	1	..	..	..	..	1	..
Lipoma of Abdomen (diffuse),	..	..	1	1	..	..	..	..
" of Buttock,	..	1	..	1	..	..	..	..
" of Shoulder,	..	..	1	1	..	..	..	..
Multiple Cancer,	..	..	1	..	..	..	1	..
Osteo-Sarcoma of Femur,	..	1	..	1	..	..	..	..
" " Rib,	..	..	1	..	..	1	..	..
Sarcoma of Foot,	..	1	..	..	..	..	1	..
" Leg,	..	1	1	1	..	1	..	..
" Neck,	1	..	..	..	..	..	1	..
" Palate,	..	1	..	..	..	..	1	..
" Testicle,	..	2	..	1	..	..	1	..
Wounds, Gunshot, of Back,	..	1	..	1	..	..	..	..
" " Pelvis,	..	1	..	..	..	..	..	1
" Incised, of Back and Scalp,	..	1	..	1	..	..	..	..

SURGICAL CASES.—CONTINUED.

	Under treatment Sept. 30, 1897.	New cases admitted. Male.	New cases admitted. Female.	Recovered.	Improved.	Unimproved.	Died.	Remaining Sept. 30, 1898.
General Surgical Diseases and Injuries. *Continued.*								
Wounds, Lacerated, of Lung,	..	2	..	..	..	..	2	..
" " Rectum,	..	1	..	..	..	..	1	..
" " Scalp and Buttock,	..	1	..	1	..	..	..	..
" Penetrating, of Abdomen,	..	1	..	1	..	..	..	..
" Punctate, of Tongue,	..	1	..	1	..	..	..	..
" Stab, of Abdomen,	..	2	..	2	..	..	..	..
Genito-Urinary Diseases and Injuries.								
Atony of Bladder,	..	3	..	2	1	..	..	..
Cystitis and Hypertrophied Prostate,	..	2	..	..	1	..	1	..
Cystitis,	..	1	..	1	..	..	..	..
Hydrocele,	..	3	..	3	..	..	..	..
" and Hypertrophied Prostate,	..	1	..	..	..	..	1	..
Hydro-Nephrosis,	..	..	1	..	1	..	..	..
Hypertrophied Prostate and Cystitis and Hydrocele,	..	2	..	..	1	..	1	..
Lacerated Penis,	..	1	..	1	..	..	..	..
Nephro-lithiasis,	..	..	1	..	..	..	..	1
Paraphymosis,	..	1	..	1	..	..	..	..
Post Parotitic Orchitis,	..	1	..	1	..	..	..	..
Pyonephrosis,	..	1	1	1	1	..	..	..
Varicocele,	..	4	..	4	..	..	..	..
Vesical Calculus,	..	1	..	1	..	..	..	..
" Fistula,	..	2	..	2	..	..	..	..
Venereal Diseases.								
Chanchroids,	..	1	..	1	..	..	..	..
" and Venereal Warts,	..	1	..	1	..	..	..	..
Condyloma of Anus,	1	..	..	..	1	..	..	..
Epididymitis,	..	1	..	1	..	..	..	..
Epididymo-Orchitis,	..	1	..	1	..	..	..	..
Gonorrhœa, (acute),	..	12	2	14	..	..	..	..
" (chronic),	..	2	..	1	1	..	..	..
" and Bubo,	..	2	..	2	..	..	..	..
" " Balanitis and Phymosis,	..	1	..	1	..	..	..	..
" " Paraphymosis,	..	1	..	1	..	..	..	..
" " Phymosis,	..	3	..	3	..	..	..	..
" " Prostatitis,	..	4	..	4	..	..	..	..
Gonorrhœal Orchitis,	..	11	..	11	..	..	..	..
" Rheumatism,	..	3	..	2	..	..	..	1
Syphilis, Primary,	1	..	..	..	1	..	..	..
" Secondary,	..	1	2	..	2	..	..	1
" Tertiary,	..	9	7	..	12	1	..	3

SURGICAL CASES.— Continued.

	Under treatment Sept. 30, 1897.	New cases admitted.		Recovered.	Improved.	Unimproved.	Died.	Remaining Sept. 30, 1898.
		Male.	Female.					
Venereal Diseases.— *Continued.*								
Syphilitic Gumma,		1	..	..	1	..	..	..
" Nodule of Scalp, .	1	..	..	1	..	..	..	..
" Ulcer of Leg,	..	1	2	2	..	..	..	1
Stricture of Urethra, .	..	5	..	3	..	..	1	1
" " " and Cystitis,	..	2	..	2	..	..	..	..
" " " " Gleet, .	..	1	..	1	..	..	..	..
" " " " Gonorrhœa,	..	1	..	1	..	..	..	..
Total, ...	67	444	158	498	57	12	59	43

ORTHOPEDIC DISEASES.

	Under treatment Sept. 30, 1897.	New cases admitted.		Recovered.	Improved.	Unimproved.	Died.	Remaining Sept. 30, 1898.
		Male.	Female.					
Orthopedic Diseases.								
Ankylosis of Knee,	2	1	1	2	2	..	..	..
" " Hip,	..	..	1	1	..	..	..	..
Contraction of Knee, .	..	..	1	..	1	..	..	..
Exostosis of Fibula,	..	..	1	1	..	..	..	..
Genu Valgum, .	..	1	..	1	..	..	..	..
" " and Varum, .	..	..	1	..	1	..	..	..
Hammer Toe, .	..	..	1	1	..	..	..	..
Hypertrophied Tendon of Foot,	..	..	1	1	..	..	..	..
Morbus Coxarius,	1	6	3	1	3	..	..	6
Pes Planus, .	..	1	..	1	..	..	..	..
Potts' Disease of Spine,	..	9	1	..	5	..	..	5
Richitis, .	..	3	..	2	1	..	..	..
Talipes Equinus, .	1	..	..	1	..	..	..	..
" Equino-Varus,	..	1	2	3	..	..	..	..
Torticollis, .	..	..	2	2	..	..	..	..
Tubercular Elbow,	..	1	..	1	..	..	..	..
" Knee Joint Disease, .	..	2	1	..	1	..	1	1
Total, ...	4	25	16	18	14	..	1	12

DISEASES OF EAR, EYE, NOSE, AND THROAT (INDOOR).

	Under treatment Sept. 30, 1897.	New cases admitted. Male.	New cases admitted. Female.	Recovered.	Improved.	Unimproved.	Died.	Remaining Sept. 30, 1898.
Abscess of Cornea,	..	2	..	2	..	..	..	..
Blepharitis Marginatis,	1	2	..	3	..	..	..	..
Caruncle Lachrymalis,	..	..	1	1	..	..	..	..
Cataract,	..	1	3	4	..	..	..	..
" (Congenital),	..	..	1	1	..	..	..	..
" (Traumatic),	..	1	..	1	..	..	..	..
Choroiditis,	1	..	..	1	..	..	..	..
Conjunctivitis (Croupous),	..	1	..	1	..	..	..	..
" (Traumatic),	..	1	..	1	..	..	..	..
" and Iritis,	..	1	..	1	..	..	..	..
Epithelioma of Orbit,	..	..	1	1	..	..	..	..
Foreign Body in Eye,	..	1	..	1	..	..	..	..
Frontal Sinusitis,	..	1	..	1	..	..	..	..
Hemorrhage of Retina,	1	..	..	1	..	..	..	..
Hypertrophied Tonsil,	..	1	..	..	..	..	..	1
Iritis,	..	1	..	1	..	..	..	..
Kerato Iritis, (Syphilitic),	..	1	..	..	1	..	..	..
Lachrymal Stricture, (Double),	..	..	1	..	..	..	..	1
Mastoiditis, (Chronic),	..	1	..	..	1	..	..	..
" (Sub-acute),	..	1	..	..	1	..	..	..
Opacity of Cornea,	..	3	2	5	..	..	..	..
Opthalmia, (Gonorrhœal),	1	2	.	3	..	..	..	..
" (Neonatorum),	..	..	1	1	..	..	..	..
Otitis Media (Acute),	..	1	..	1	..	..	..	..
" " Chronic,	..	1	..	..	1	..	..	..
" Externa,	..	1	..	1	..	..	..	..
Panophthalmitis,	..	3	..	3	..	..	..	..
Ptosis,	..	2	1	2	1	..	..	..
Strabismus,	..	..	1	1	..	..	..	..
Trachoma and Keratitis,	..	1	..	1	..	..	..	..
Ulcer of Cornea,	..	8	..	6	1	..	..	1
" " " and Dermatitis of Face,	1	..	..	1	..	..	..	..
Wounds, Contused of Eyeball,	..	2	..	2	..	..	..	..
" Gunshot of Eyeball,	..	1	..	1	..	..	..	..
" Lacerated of Cornea,	..	1	..	1	..	..	..	..
" Incised of Cornea,	..	1	..	1	..	..	..	..
" " " Eyeball,	..	1	..	1	..	..	..	..
" Shot of Eyeball,	..	1	..	1	..	..	..	..
Total,	5	45	12	53	6	..	..	3

DISEASES OF EAR, EYE, NOSE, AND THROAT (OUTDOOR).

	Male.	Female.
Adenoids of Pharynx, ...	1	1
Albumeno Retinitis, ...		1
Astigmatism, ...		2
Atrophy of Optic Nerve, ...	3	
Blephero Adenitis, ...		2
Blepharitis Marginalis, ...	3	7
Cataract, ...	4	1
Catarrh, Nasal, ...	1	1
Chalazion, ...	1	4
Conjunctivitis, Catarrhal, ...	4	5
" Chronic, ...	1	1
" Granular, ...		1
Phlyctenular, ...	1	4
Deflected Septum, ...		1
Error of Refraction, ...	6	10
Foreign Body in Eye, ...	1	1
Glaucoma, ...		1
Hypertrophied Terbinated Bone, ...	1	1
Impacted Cerumen, ...	1	
Iritis, ...	1	2
Keratitis Interstitial, ...	2	
" Phlyctenular, ...		2
Glaucoma, ...	3	
Opacity of Cornea, ...	1	
Ophthalmia Purulent, ...		1
Optic Neuritis, ...	1	1
Otitis Media, Acute, ...	1	
" " Chronic, ...	4	6
" " Sub-acute, ...	1	1
" " Suppurative, ...	4	3
" " Et External, ...	1	
Panophthalmitis, ...	2	
Pterigium, ...		1
Ptosis, ...		1
Strabismus, ...	2	1
Stricture of Lachrymal Duct, ...	2	7
Enlarged Tonsils, ...		3
Trachoma, ...	3	5
Ulcer of Cornea, ...	4	
Wound of Cornea, ...		-
" " " with Prolapse of Iris, ...	1	
Total, ...	49	79

SUMMARY OF SURGICAL PATIENTS.

	Under treatment Sept. 30, 1897.	New cases admitted.		Recovered.	Improved.	Unimproved.	Died.	Remaining Sept. 30, 1898.
		Male.	Female.					
Injuries of Head, Face, and Neck,	2	45	11	46	4	1	7	..
" Genito-Urinary System,	..	23	3	17	5	..	3	1
" Upper Extremity, Axilla, and Spine,	8	63	15	73	2	..	4	7
" Lower Extremity and Groin,	28	105	37	127	17	2	9	15
" and Diseases. General,	26	144	79	182	11	8	35	13
" Venereal,	3	64	13	53	18	1	1	7
" Orthopedic,	4	25	16	18	14	..	1	12
" Eye and Ear (Indoor),	5	45	12	53	6	..	..	3
Total (Indoor),	76	514	186	569	77	12	60	58
Eye and Ear (Outdoor),	..	61	79	..	..	..	..	..
Total of all Patients Treated,	..	575	265	..	..	..	..	..

A. M. ROWLEY, M.D.,
House Surgeon.

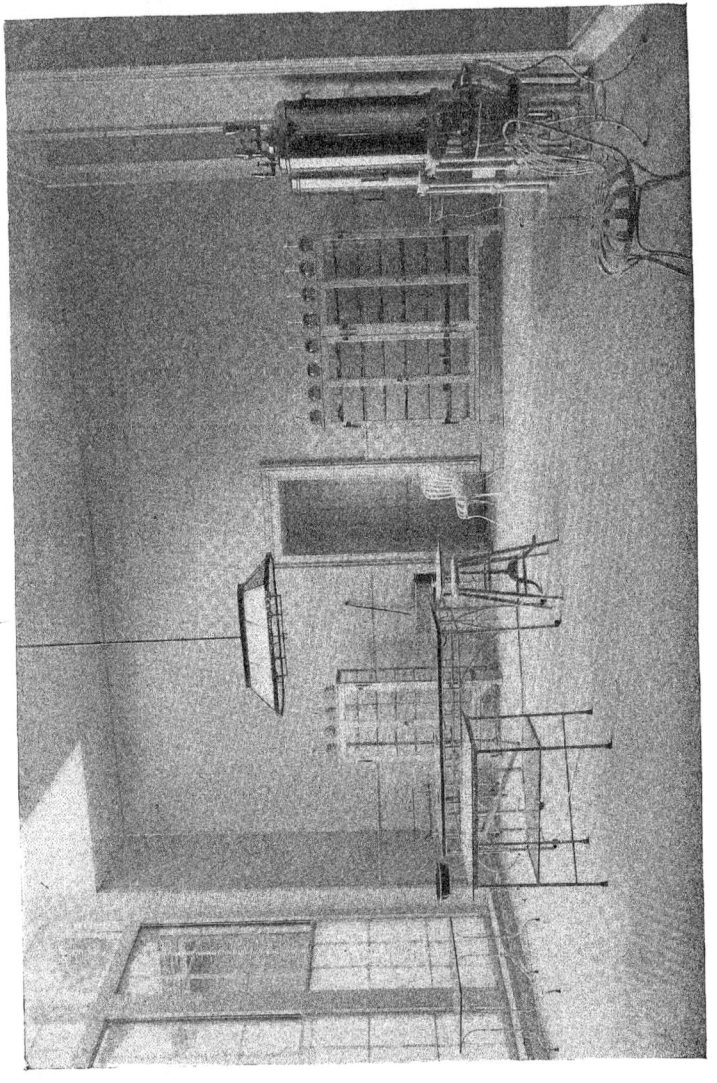

OPERATING ROOM.

TABLE OF OPERATIONS.

	Male.	Female.		Male.	Female.
Accouchement Forcé, .	..	1	Curetting Uterus, . . .	..	28
Amputation of Arm, . .	1	..	Uterus and Perineorrhaphy,	..	7
of Breast, ...	..	5	and Amputation of Cervix,	..	1
of Finger, ...	2	1	and Perineorrhaphy and } Trachelorrhaphy,	..	16
of Fingers, . . .	2	2	and Trachelorrhaphy, .	..	10
of Foot, ...	1	..	for Secundines, . .	..	4
of Hand, . . .	2	2	Dilatation of Cervix Uteri, .	..	1
of Leg, ...	3	..	of Lachrymal Stricture, .	1	6
of Shoulder Joint, .	1	..	of Urethral Stricture with } Ext. Urethrotomy,	1	..
of Thigh, ...	6	1	Ectropion, ...	1	..
of Thumb, ...	1	..	Elevation of Depressed } Fracture of Skull,	2	..
of Toes, ...	5	..	Enucleation of Eye, . .	2	..
Application of forceps in } labor,	..	2	Examination of Abdomen, .	..	2
of plaster cast to arm, .	1	..	of Bladder for Calculus, .	2	..
of plaster cast to leg, .	2	1	of Eye, ...	1	1
Aspiration of Abdomen, .	1	1	of Fecal Fistula, .	1	..
of Bladder, . . .	2	..	of Fractured Tibia, . .	1	..
of Knee Joint, . . .	4	1	of Rectum, . . .	..	1
of Thorax, . . .	2	..	of Sprain of Shoulder, .	1	..
Arthrectomy of elbow joint } (Tubercular),	1	..	of Tumor of Palate, . .	1	..
Atresia of Arms, . .	..	1	of Urethra, . . .	2	..
Bowman's operation for } Cystitis,	1	..	of Uterus and Kidney, .	..	1
Breaking up Adhe'ns of Hip,	1	1	Excision of Adenoma of Neck,	1	..
of knee, . .	..	1	of Carcinoma of Breast, .	..	1
of knee and ankle, .	2	..	of Carcinoma of Side, .	..	1
Cantholomy, ...	1	2	of Chalazion, . . .	2	1
Castration, ...	2	..	of Cystoma of Nares, .	..	1
Castration (double), .	1	..	of Cystoma of Neck, .	1	..
Cauterization of Condyloma } of Arms,	2	..	of Cystoma (Tubercular) } of Arm,	..	1
of Cornea, . . .	5	2	of Epithelioma Cervix Uteri,	..	1
of Thigh, ...	1	..	of Epithelioma of Lip, .	1	1
Circumcision, . . .	8	..	of Epithelioma of Orbit, .	..	1
and opening Bubo, .	1	..	of Epithelioma of Scalp, .	1	..
Colparrhaphy, . . .	..	1	of Exostosis of Fibula, .	..	1
Costotomy, . . .	3	..	of Glands of Axilla (Tuberc.)	..	1
Curetting Abscess of Axilla,	2	..	of Glands of Neck (Tuberc.),	3	4
Abscess of Breast, .	..	1	of Submaxillary, . .	1	..
Abscess of Thigh, .	..	2	of Lipoma of Abdomen, .	..	1
Abscess of Scalp, .	2	..	of Lipoma (Diffuse) of } Abdomen,	..	1
Eyelids for Trachoma, .	3	2	of Lipoma of Back, . .	1	1
Sinus of Abdomen, .	2	1	of Lipoma of Neck, . .	2	..
Sinus of Hand, . .	2	1	of Lipoma of Shoulder, .	1	..
Sinus of Heel, . .	2	..	of Needle from Hand, .	..	1
Sinus of Ischio-Rectal, .	1	..	of Nerves of Face, . .	..	1
Sinus of Leg, . . .	1	..	of Osteoma of Skull, .	1	..
Tubercular Ulcer of Leg, .	..	2	of Osteo-Sarcoma of Tibia, .	..	1
Ulcer of Cornea, . .	1	..	of Papilloma of Hand, .	..	1
Ulcer of Foot (Raynaud's)	1	..			

TABLE OF OPERATIONS. — Continued.

	Male.	Female.		Male.	Female.
Excision of Papilloma of Vulva,	..	1	Incision and Curetting Abscess of Face,	1	..
Exsection of Hip Joint,	1	..	and Curetting Abscess of Foot,	1	..
of Knee Joint,	..	3	and Curetting Abscess of Groin,	1	..
of Prolapsed Rectum,	1	..	and Curetting Abscess of Knee,	..	1
Extraction of Cataract,	..	5	and Curetting Abscess of Leg,	2	..
of Foreign body in Eye,	2	..	and Curetting Abscess of Neck,	4	2
of Foreign body of Leg,	1	..	and Curetting Abscess of Perineum,	2	..1
of Foreign body in Nose,	1	..	and Curetting Abscess of Psoas,	..	2
of Teeth,	2	..	and Curetting Abscess of Scalp,	1	..
Hare Lip,	1	1	and Curetting Abscess of Side,	1	..
Herniotomy, Femoral,	..	1	and Curetting Abscess of Thigh,	1	2
Inguinal,	4	..	and Curetting of Ankle Joint,	..	1
Hysterectomy,	..	5	and Curetting of Buboe,	2	..
Incision for Abscess of Abdomen,	..	1	and Curetting of Hand,	..	2
of Axilla,	1	..	Sinus of Breast	..	1
of Breast,	..	5	Incision & removal of Breast,	4	2
of Leg,	1	..	Imperforate Anus,	1	..
of Pelvis,	2	4	Iridectomy,	1	1
of Prepaletta Bursea,	..	2	Laparotomy for Appendicitis,	19	15
of Thorax,	1	..	Appendicitis & Ovariotomy,	..	1
of Vagina,	..	1	Abdominal Sinus,	1	..
of Caruncle,	..	1	Exploratory (Cancer of Omentum),	1	.
Incisions for Cellulitis of Arm,	3	1	Exploratory,	1	..
for Cellulitis of Foot,	1	..	Fecal Fistula,	1	..
for Cellulitis of Hand,	2	1	Hernia (Ing. Strangulated),	6	1
for Cellulitis of Leg,	1	..	Umbilical,	..	1
Fistula in Ano,	7	1	Ventral,	3	2
Hæmotoma of Leg,	1	..	Intestinal Adhesions,	1	2
Lachrymal Stricture,	1	4	" Obstruction,	1	..
Lymphangitis of Arm,	..	1	Ovariotomy,	..	2
Periostitis of Inf. Max.,	2	2	" (double),	..	6
Periostitis of Finger,	..	..	Peritonitis,	..	3
Periostitis of Fibulae,	..	1	Salpingotomy,	..	1
Prepuce for Paraphymosis,	2	..	Ligation of Artery (Femoral),	1	..
Prepuce for Phymosis,	2	..	Post Circumflex,	..	1
of Sarcoma of Leg,	1	..	of Hæmorrhoids,	8	5
of Tonsil,	1	..	and Cauterization,	..	2
Incision and Curetting of Abscess of Abdomen,	2	..	of Hæmorrh'ds and op'n'g Ischio-Rectal Abscess,	1	..
and Curetting Abscess of Axilla,	1	..			
and Curetting Abscess of Multiple,	1	..			
and Curetting Abscess of Back,	1	2			
and Curetting Abscess of Breast,	..	1			
and Curetting Abscess of Buttock,	2	..			

TABLE OF OPERATIONS. — Continued.

	Male.	Female.		Male.	Female.
Ligation of Hæmorrhoids and incision for Fecal Fistulæ,	1	..	Resection of Radia and Ulna,	1	..
			Sequestrotomy of Carpi, .	1	..
of Hæmorrhoids and Prolapsed Rectum,	1	..	of Femur, . . .	3	..
			of Inf. Maxilla, . .	2	..
Meotomy, . . .	1	..	of Metacarpi, . .	2	..
Nephrotomy, . . .	2	..	of Oscalcis, . ,	1	..
Nephro-lithotomy, . .	..	2	of Radeus and Ulna, .	1	..
Neurectomy of Inf. Maxilla,	1	..	of Tibia, . . .	5	..
Osteotomy for Genu. Valgum,	1	..	of Tarsi, . . .	..	1
Parecentesis of Membrana Tympani,	2	2	Skin grafting of Arm, . .	..	1
			of Leg, . . .	1	..
Ptosis, acquired, . . .	..	1	of Thigh, . . .	1	..
Congenital, . . .	1	..	Strabotomy, . . .	2	..
Passive Motion of Knee Joint,	1	3	Stretching Sphincter Ani for Fissure,	2	3
of Knee Joint and Wrist, .	..	1	for Stricture, . .	1	..
Perineorrhaphy, . . .	..	1	Suturing Incised Wound of Chin,	1	..
with Trachelorrhophy, .	..	6			
with Colporrhaphy, . .	..	2	of Face, . . .	3	..
with Ligation of Hæmorrhoids,	..	2	of Thigh, . . .	2	..
			Lacerated Wound of Eye, .	2	..
with Amputation of Cervix,	..	2	Lacerated Wound of Foot and Hand,	2	..
Phelps' Operation for Talipes,	1	2			
Phlebotomy for Popliteal Cervix,	1	..	Lacerated Wound of Head,	2	..
for Varicocele, . .	4	..	Lacerated Wound of Thorax and Shoulder,	2	..
Probing for Bullet, . .	2	..	Ununited Fract. of Femur,	2	..
Reduction of Fracture of Femur,	1	1	Compound Fract'e of Tibia,	2	..
Fracture of Inf. Maxilla, .	1	..	Tapping Hydrocele, . .	3	..
Fracture of Leg (compound),	2	..	Tonsilotomy, . . .	..	2
Fracture of Nasi, . .	1	..	Trephining for Fracture of Skull,	2	..
Fracture of Scapula, .	1	..			
of Hernia, . .	4	..	Urethrotomy, Ext and Int.,	5	..
of Luxation of Ankle, .	1	..	Internal, . . .	1	..
of Luxation of Elbow, .	1	..	Internal and Meaotomy, .	1	..
of Luxation of Knee Joint,	1	..	Internal and Circumcision,	1	..
of Luxation of Shoulder, .	1	..	Ventral Fixation, . .	..	1
of Luxation of Thumb, .	2	..	Version and Ext't'n of Fœtus,	..	1
Recto-Vaginal Fistula, .	..	1			
Recto Vesical Fistula, .	2	..	Total, ...	319	269

Ether has been administered, ... 334 times.

Chloroform " " 98

Cocaine, " " . . . . . , . . 70

No anæsthesia; " 86

A. M. ROWLEY, M.D.,

House Surgeon.

RULES

ADMISSION OF PATIENTS TO THE HARTFORD HOS-PITAL.

1. All patients are admitted by permits from one of the Executive Committee, or from the Superintendent, who shall arrange the price per week, according to the circumstances of the case and accommodations required.

2. All permits are subject to the approval of the Executive Committee, at their regular Hospital meeting.

3. Those who are able to contribute toward their support are received at an agreed rate.

4. The ordinary charge per week is $6.00, which includes medical and surgical care, together with medicine and nursing.

5. Persons who are desirous of extra accommodations are charged according to circumstances.

6. Persons who are destitute of friends and means are provided for in various ways.

7. Those persons only who are carried directly from the place of accident are admitted without a certificate from the Executive Committee or Superintendent.

8. No persons having venereal or contagious diseases are admitted into this institution (except by special permit).

Copy of Bond.

HARTFORD, CONN., 18 .

Upon the admission of of into the "HARTFORD HOSPITAL," at Hartford, I engage to provide or pay for a sufficiency of clothing for use, and pay the Treasurer of said institution dollars per week for board, medicine, and medical attendance; cause said patient to be removed when discharged, and, in the event of death, to pay the expenses of burial.

Principal.

For value received, I hereby engage to become responsible for the fulfillment of the above stipulations.

Surety.

RULES FOR THE ADMISSION OF VISITORS.

1. Visitors are welcome to the Hospital every week-day, between the hours of 2 and 5 P. M., and on Sunday, for the purpose of attending Divine worship, but on that day they must leave the wards when the services are ended.

2. Visitors shall not enter the wards without the consent of the Superintendent or Matron.

3. Visitors must deposit with the Superintendent or Matron any articles of food or delicacies intended for patients, which articles will be distributed as requested, if not inconsistent with the condition of said patient.

ACTS OF LEGISLATION.

ACT INCORPORATING HARTFORD HOSPITAL.

Resolved by the Senate and House of Representatives in General Assembly convened:

SECTION 1. That David Watkinson, Ebenezer Flower, A. S. Beckwith, S. S. Ward, A. W. Butler, A. M. Collins, Wm. T. Lee, Job Allyn, Samuel Colt, James B. Crosby, Albert Day, Chester Adams, James G. Bolles, George Beach, Thomas Smith, Jonathan Goodwin, A. W. Birge, Lucius Barbour, and Charles T. Hillyer, and all such persons as are from time to time associated with them, for the purpose of establishing and maintaining a hospital in the city of Hartford, and their successors, be, and they hereby are, incorporated for said purpose, and made a body corporate and politic, by the name of the Hartford Hospital, and by that name shall be capable of suing and being sued, pleading and being impleaded, and may make purchases, take, receive, hold, sell, and convey estate, real and personal, to such an amount as may be necessary for the purposes of said corporation; may have a common seal, and the same may alter and change at pleasure, and may make and execute such by-laws and regulations, not contrary to the laws of this State or of the United States, as shall be deemed necessary for the well-ordering and conducting the concerns of said corporation.

SEC. 2. That said corporation shall be governed by the following articles:

ARTICLE 1. This corporation shall be called the Hartford Hospital. Persons contributing for the use of the corporation at any one time the sum of fifty dollars shall be members for life. Persons contributing the sum of five hundred dollars shall be vice-presidents for life, and also directors for life; those contributing two hundred dollars shall be directors for life; those twenty-five dollars shall be members for five years; and those ten dollars shall be members for one year.

ART. 2. In order to the better carry into effect the object of said corporation, the members thereof shall, at an annual meeting, to be held at such time and place as the by-laws of the said corporation shall direct and appoint, elect from their own number by ballot, and by a majority of the votes given at such election, twelve persons as directors of the said corporation; and the persons so elected, together with the mayor of the city of Hartford for the time being, shall constitute a board of directors. The directors so elected shall hold their offices for one year, and until others are elected in their places. In case of any vacancy in the board the remainder of the directors shall have power to fill such vacancy until the next election.

ART. 3. The board of directors shall, annually, as soon as may be convenient after the said annual election, elect by ballot from among their own number a president, a vice-president, and shall also elect a secretary and treasurer, who shall hold their offices for one year, and until others are elected in their stead. But as many directors may be chosen as there may be directors by subscription.

ART. 4. The said board of directors shall have power to manage and conduct all the business and concerns of the corporation, and to make such laws as may be necessary for the management and disposition of the estate and concerns of the corporation, and to appoint such officers and servants as they may deem necessary. The medical officers, including all attending and consulting physicians and surgeons, shall be appointed annually. Vacancies occurring before the expiration of the year from the time of any appointment shall be filled by the directors as soon as the same can be conveniently done.

ART. 5. A majority of the corporators shall call the first meeting for the election of officers at such time and place in the city of Hartford as they shall appoint, giving three days' notice thereof by publishing the same in the daily papers of the city; and the annual meeting of said corporation shall be held at such time and place and on such notice as shall be fixed by the by-laws of said corporation.

ART. 6. This act may be altered, amended, or repealed by the General Assembly.

Approved, May Session, 1854.

RESOLUTION AMENDING THE CHARTER OF THE HARTFORD HOSPITAL.

Resolved, That additional members of said corporation may hereafter be elected at any annual meeting by a two-thirds vote of those present without the payment of any sum of money on the part of members so elected.

Approved, January Session, 1881.

AMENDMENT OF THE CHARTER OF THE HARTFORD HOSPITAL.

Resolved by the Senate and House of Representatives in General Assembly convened:

SECTION 1. That, in addition to the powers already conferred upon the Hartford Hospital, said corporation are hereby authorized to establish, in connection with the present hospital buildings, and upon the hospital grounds, or elsewhere, an Old People's Home, or a department or home for the accommodation, support, and maintenance of such aged and infirm persons as shall, from time to time, be admitted to the comforts and privileges of such department or home, and erect the necessary buildings therefor, and sustain the said Home with such funds and means as shall be given for that purpose, or paid by or for the benefit of the persons admitted to said Home. The board of directors of said Hartford Hospital shall have the power to make and execute any and all such by-laws, rules, and regulations in relation to such department or home, and the management of the same, and the funds pertaining thereto, and generally all the concerns of said department, not contrary to the laws of this State or of the United States, as shall be deemed necessary or proper for the well-ordering and conducting the concerns of said department, and the same to repeal or change at pleasure, and may appoint, if deemed expedient, a board of managers for said department, with such powers as they shall deem proper, and also such officers and servants as they may deem necessary.

All the rights and privileges conferred by the charter of the Hartford Hospital upon persons contributing for the use of said corporation shall be had and enjoyed by persons and parties limiting their contributions to the use of the department for the aged and the infirm as fully and to the same extent as if no such limitation was connected with such contribution.

All the money and funds already, or which shall be, given or contributed for the uses and purposes of the Hartford Hospital shall be confined to and used for the benefit of the hospital department, and all moneys and funds in any way given or contributed for the aged and infirm department shall be held and used exclusively for that department, under such rules and regulations as may be adopted in relation to a division of the common expenses pertaining to the two departments, which cannot be kept separately and accurately divided.

This department of the Hartford Hospital shall be known as the Old People's Home, and any and all moneys, gifts, legacies, devises, bequests, or other contributions given to the

Old People's Home, or for its uses, or to the Hartford Hospital, or to any other trustee or trustees, for or in trust for the use of the Old People's Home, shall be good and effectual, and shall be for the use of this department for the aged and infirm created under this act.

SEC. 2. This resolution may be altered, amended, or repealed at the pleasure of the General Assembly.

Approved, June 19, 1873.

FORM OF BEQUEST.

I give to the Hartford Hospital of the city of Hartford ....dollars, for the uses and purposes of said Hospital.

FORM OF BEQUEST FOR FREE BED.

I give to the Hartford Hospital of the city of Hartford, the sum of five thousand dollars, to be used in the maintenance of a free bed in said Hospital.

PAVILION FOR CONTAGIOUS DISEASES.

TRAINING SCHOOL FOR NURSES.

HARTFORD HOSPITAL
TRAINING SCHOOL FOR NURSES.

OFFICERS.

Executive Committee.

HENRY K. MORGAN, 108 Farmington Ave.
HARMON G. HOWE, M.D., 137 High St.
THOMAS SISSON, 729 Main St.

Superintendent of the Hospital.

BENJAMIN S. GILBERT.

Matron and Lady Superintendent of the Training School.

Miss ELIZABETH M. FRIEND.

Night Matron.

Miss SARAH L. HARRISON.

Teacher of Cooking School.

Mrs. ELIZABETH SLUYTER AYERS.

Head Nurses.

Miss FRANCIS AULD,
Miss CONSTANCE A. HOLDEN,
Miss CAROLINE TOBEY,
Miss CARLOTTA MUNOZ.

THE TWENTY-FIRST ANNUAL REPORT

OF THE

HARTFORD HOSPITAL TRAINING SCHOOL FOR NURSES.

To the Directors of the Hartford Hospital:

The Executive Committee take pleasure in presenting to you the following report as the twenty-first annual report of the Hartford Hospital Training School for Nurses for the fiscal year ending September 30, 1898, including the Lady Superintendent's report to us and other items of interest connected with the school.

We take pleasure in commending the work of the school for the past year and consider that it ranks well up among the best schools in the country. The graduates, seventeen in number, start out from the institution as well-equipped for their work as it is possible to make them in the short space of two years.

The large number of applications for admission (120) show somewhat the popularity of the school. The probation period of one month has been changed to two months, and it has been a question of discussion between us whether it was not best to make the term of residence in the Hospital three years, instead of two, but action was postponed until such time as we can have a separate building for the school.

We consider that we are allowing daily conditions of inconvenience, hygiene, and discomfort in connection with the Training School which is strongly calling for a proper building for the training of the young ladies, every one of whom is working hard to fit herself to enter our own families as a friend in

5

adversity as well as to perform the work of the Hospital itself in a creditable manner. We expect this fall to open a subscription list for the purpose of raising the necessary funds for the erection of such a building as we need. We hope that every graduate nurse will remember the sore want and will contribute her mite, as well as every friend of the Hospital.

Miss Katherine Emory, the Lady Superintendent at the opening of the year, resigned her position, taking effect February 1st of the present year. Miss Elizabeth Friend, our former night matron, was promoted to fill the vacancy. We consider Miss Friend an able teacher and a good disciplinarian, and are satisfied that the school is well conducted.

The matron is ably assisted by Miss Sarah L. Harrison as night matron, and the Misses Auld, Holden, Tobey, and Munoz as head nurses. During the whole year the work has been laborious, but especially so during the latter part, after the Hospital began to receive the typhoid fever cases from the army, but the esprit de corps in the school is excellent, and we have had a ready response to orders by all.

Graduating exercises will be held as usual in the Portrait Gallery of the Hospital on the first Wednesday in October, where we are glad to welcome all the friends of the school who can be accommodated. Mr. Charles Dudley Warner will present the annual address to the school.

Respectfully,

HENRY K. MORGAN,

HARMON G. HOWE, M.D.,

THOMAS SISSON.

REPORT OF THE SUPERINTENDENT OF THE TRAINING
SCHOOL FOR NURSES TO THE EXECUTIVE COMMIT-
TEE OF THE HARTFORD HOSPITAL, FOR THE YEAR
ENDING SEPTEMBER 30, 1898.

———————

The Training School began its twenty-first year with thirty-
six members, which number was increased to thirty-eight during the year. By this increase we are able to keep two nurses
at the Old People's Home all of the time, without interfering
with the work in the Hospital.

The health of the nurses at the Home on Jefferson street
has been uniformly good; but of those who have occupied
rooms under the children's ward in the basement, three have
resigned temporarily and one permanently on account of sickness.

Out of 120 applicants for admission to the Training
School, 55 have been accepted. Thirty probationers have been
admitted, three of whom have been obliged to leave on account of ill-health, two were dropped at the end of their probation month, and one was discharged for cause.

Seventeen nurses have been graduated, four of whom are
taking post-graduate courses, two are at home, one is married, one has taken a Hospital position, and the other nine are
doing private nursing.

All nurses have spent two hours weekly in class; the members of the senior class have each had ten lessons in massage.
The members of the visiting staff have very kindly given their
time for weekly lectures from September 22 to June 23, 1898.
The lectures have been very helpful and were much appreciated

by the nurses.   Daily clinical instruction has been given by the members of the house staff and the head nurses.

In reviewing the past year I think we can safely say that the work done by the nurses has kept pace with the many improvements in the Hospital.

Respectfully submitted,

ELIZABETH M. FRIEND,

Superintendent of Training School.

LIST OF MEMBERS

OF

THE TRAINING SCHOOL.

SEPTEMBER 30, 1898.

Miss Mabel McNaughton,
Miss Isabel F. Pasco,
Miss Edith A. Roth,
Miss Sarah E. Blenkhorne,
Miss Katherine Jordan,
Miss Alice Goodrich,
Miss Martha S. Ball, ·
Miss Elizabeth Connor,
Miss Alice Lee,
Miss Mary Wolcott,
Miss Mary B. Smart, *
Miss Bertha Davis,
Miss Clara B. Case,
Miss Isabel Shannon,
Miss Eva J. Edwards,
Miss Josett Linn,
Miss Annie L. Garvie;
Miss Sarah Garrity,
Miss Harriet Cunningham,

Miss Janet Campbell,
Miss Alice Bosanko,
Miss Helen A. Gilbert,
Miss Vesta McLaulin,
Miss Bessie L. Colter,
Miss Alice M. Godwin,
Miss Ellen Jenny,
Miss Nellie F. Hackett,
Miss Amelia Armstrong,
Miss Ruth A. Morton,
Miss Mary J. Daley,
Miss Flora B. Martin,
Miss Mary Stiles,
Miss Daisey Carlton,
Miss Sarah A. Carroll,
Miss Clara Bachand,
Miss Cora M. Cooke,
Miss Grace Widdison,
Miss Edna F. Titus.

LIST OF GRADUATES.

HARTFORD HOSPITAL TRAINING SCHOOL FOR NURSES.

1879.

Mrs. Caroline A. House,
Miss Hannah M. Callahan,
[1] Miss Amelia Cooke,

Mrs. Annie Morrell,
Miss Lydia S. Woodward.

1880.

[2] Miss Lizzie T. Oliver,
Miss Mary E. Crane.

Miss Ida F. Barnes.

1881.

Miss Kate E. Kinne,
[2] Miss Alice M. Noble,
[2] Miss Alice M. Delano,
[2] Miss Georgette T. Rogers,

Miss Annie C. Abbe,
Miss Marion E. Kingsley,
Miss Annie M. Wakefield.

1882.

[2] Miss Mattie Kingsley,
[2] Miss Mary I. Denison,
[2] Miss Elizabeth L. Goodale,

Miss Lydia B. Roberts,
Miss Jennie McLaughlin.

1883.

[2] Miss Alice Ewen,
[2] Miss Harriet M. Hosking,
Miss Lucy A. Kirk,
[1] Mrs. Zoe M. Tucker,

Miss Sarah M. Sheldon,
[2] Miss Eliza C. Smith,
Mrs. Charlotte F. Schultz,
Miss Hannah L. Russell.

1884.

[2] Miss Emma Strickland,
[2] Miss Harriet E. Fuller,
[2] Miss Maria A. Clark,
[12] Miss Josie L. Hubbard,

Miss Emma J. Osborn,
Miss Jennie M. Beardsley,
Miss Alice M. Gardiner.

1885.

Miss Lucy Way,
[2] Miss Minnie L. McLese,
[2] Miss Emile M. Pugsley,
Miss Mary E. Brown,

Miss Mary A. Murphy,
Miss Lillian C. Catlin,
Miss Mary H. Patch.

[1] Died.   [2] Married.

Miss Martha B. Parker,
Miss Hattie E. Crocker,
. Miss Ella J. Holcomb,
² Miss Gertrude E. Morley,
Miss Emma L. Terrell,

¹ Miss Carrie Swettenham,
Miss Annie C. McNeil,
Miss Annie Figgis,
Miss Emma Carver,

Miss Maria A. Wakefield,
² Miss Hattie B. Smith,
Miss Jennie McCollister,
² Miss Jessie T. Jeffrey,

Mrs. Ida D. Lewis,
² Miss Annie E. North,
Miss Allie Cornelius,
² Miss Henrietta E. Willet,

Miss Alice M. Smith,
Miss Jennie R. Field,
Mrs. Addie R. Young,
² Miss Alma A. Robinson,
Miss Nancy R. Cornelius,

Miss Mary M. Brown,
¹ Miss Emma J. Lyman,
Miss Lillie Wind,

Miss Annie E. Palmer,
Miss Mary A. Rogers,
Miss Minnie I. Bacon,
² Miss Mary L. Marsh,
Miss Mary A. Farnsworth,

Miss Lillian M. Alexander,
Miss Janie McNeil,
Miss Lois Pomeroy,
Miss Annie E. Brazos,
ᴵ Miss Ellen S. Richardson,
² Miss Minnie A. Havens,
² Miss Lillian A. Dermont,

1886.
Miss Minnie Hicks,
¹ Miss Elma A. Bennett,
Miss Rebecca LaMonte,
Miss S. Alice Griswold.

1887.
Miss Jennie B. Methven,
² Miss Nellie T. Manning,
Miss Jennie McKean,
Miss Juliette A. Parsons.

1888.
Miss Helen McCloy,
Miss Delia L. Bridgeman,
Miss Annie Black.

1889.
Mrs. Addie L. Lloyd,
Miss Ella E. Gibbs,
Miss Bessie C. Taber,
Miss Rilla J. Perry.

1890.
Miss Delia M. Smith,
Miss Harriet A. Lorber,
Miss Martha J. Wilkinson,
Miss Isabella M. Snelling,
² Miss Mary J. Barr.

1891.
Miss Emma B. Richards,
Miss Etta A. Straw,
¹ Mrs. Eva C. Swift.

1892.
Miss Jessie M. Randall,
² Miss Mary J. Harrison,
Miss Hattie E. Allen,
Miss Lois S. Peck,
² Miss Ella J. French.

1893.
Miss Eleanor Campbell,
Miss Carmel Cretcher,
Miss Mildred E. Sherwood,
Miss Emily A. Dalton,
Miss Harriet Hendrick,
Miss Eva Trenholm.

¹·Died.   ²·Married.

1894.

Miss Margaret Cunningham,
Miss Eliza MacKean,
Miss Julia E. Ferguson,
[2] Mrs. Lilly W. Stevens,
Miss Mary E. Jennison,
Miss Sarah L. Harrison,
Miss Adelaide M. Throop,

[1] Miss Christine J. Rae,
Miss Mary A. Rood,
[1] Miss Fanny Nichols,
Miss Frances O. Mather,
[1] Miss Geneva Dunning,
Mrs. Inez L. Fowler,
Miss Arrette E. Jenkins.

1895.

[2] Miss Josie M. Brown,
Miss Minnie P. Cheeny,
Miss Lottie Beck,
[2] Miss Bertha S. Holt,
Miss Winnefred B. Hardiman,

Miss Annie L. Lynde,
Miss Hattie I. Waterman,
Miss Daisy Lewis,
Miss Anna A. Keller,
Miss Florence E. Carman.

1896.

[2] Miss Lillie D. Philips,
Miss C. E. Shermerhorn,
Miss Margaret Spitzli,
Miss Katherine D. Arthur,
Miss Ruby E. Gates,
Mrs. E. K. Morehouse,

[1] Miss Grace W. Cushman,
Miss Jessie K. Denison,
Miss Eliza Barker,
Miss Mary F. Jons,
Miss Jane A. Bryson,
Mrs. Minnie A. Stafford.

1897.

Miss Marie Miellez,
Miss Mary C. MacGarry,
Miss Emma L. Ward,
Miss Theresa M. Townsend,
Miss Caroline Tobey,
Miss Clara H. Hearle,
Miss Jessie E. Knapp,

Miss Mary J. Wright,
Miss Mary C. Johnson,
Miss Carlotta Munoz,
Miss Grace C. Ballou,
Miss Margaret M. Bramly,
Miss Helen M. Jones.

1898.

Miss Margaret D. Hunter,
Miss Elizabeth M. Abbie,
Miss Lena I. Pratt,
Miss Mary H. Nutting,
Miss Francis A. Bingham,
Miss Annie E. Shepard,
Miss Mary E. Snow,
Miss Jane A. Dunn,
[2] Miss Ida A. Kauffman,

Miss Edith Childs,
Miss Margaret A. Doyle,
Miss Sarah A. Wheeler,
Miss Sarah H. Ripley,
Miss Idella M. Pardee,
Miss Lucy A. Bates,
Miss Katherine E. Boies,
Miss Maude M. Carter.

---

[1] Died. [2] Married.

A—MALE SURGICAL WARD.—WARD 5.

LIST OF LECTURES AND SUBJECTS TO BE DELIVERED
TO THE TRAINING SCHOOL FOR NURSES
DURING THE ENSUING YEAR.

THURSDAYS, 4 P. M.

DATE.	LECTURER.	SUBJECT.
Sept. 22, 1898,	Dr. Knight,	Skeleton.
" 29, "	" "	Muscles.
Oct. 6, "	" "	Nerves.
" 13, "	" "	Topographical anatomy.
" 20, "	Dr. Fuller,	Respiration, circulation, blood.
" 27, "	" "	Nursing of heart cases.
Nov. 3, "	" "	Nursing of lung cases.
" 10, "	" "	Physiology of digestion.
" 17, "	Dr. Campbell,	The sick room ventilation.
Dec. 1, "	" "	Fever nursing.
" 8, "	" "	Management of diet.
" 15, "	Dr. Root,	Infection and contagion.
" 22, "	" "	Sterilization of apparatus, excreta, and food.
Jan. 5, 1899,	" "	Special nursing in contagious cases.
" 12, "	Dr. Howe,	Emergencies.
" 19, "	" "	Emergencies.
" 26, "	Dr. Hall,	Anesthetics and their administration.
Feb. 2, "	" "	Nursing surgical cases. Shock.
" 9, "	Dr. Downs,	The brain and its functions.
" 16, "	" "	The abnormal mind.
" 23, "	" "	Common forms of insanity.
Mar. 2, "	" "	Neurasthenia and hysteria.
" 9, "	Dr. Beach,	Anatomy of the skin.
" 16, "	" "	Care of the skin.
" 23, "	" "	Nursing sick children.
" 30, "	Dr. Ingalls,	Obstetrics.
April 6, "	" "	Obstetrics.
" 13, "	" "	Gynæcology.
" 20, "	" "	Laparotomy. Preparation and nursing.
" 27, "	Dr. Bacon,	Nursing of ear and throat.
May 4, "	Dr. St. John,	The eye.
" 11, "	" "	Nursing of eye.
" 18, "	Dr. McKnight,	Fractures and splints.
" 25, "	" "	Orthopædic surgery.
June 1, "	Dr. Cook,	Materia medica.
" 8, "	" "	Toxicology.
" 15, "	Dr. Bunce,	Bacteriology.
" 22, "	" "	Urinalysis.

LIST OF LECTURES AND SUBJECTS DELIVERED TO THE
TRAINING SCHOOL FOR NURSES DURING
THE PAST YEAR.

THURSDAYS, 4 P. M.

DATE.	LECTURER.	SUBJECT.
Sept. 23, 1897,	Dr. Knight,	The skeleton.
" 30, "	" "	The muscles:
Oct. 7, "	" "	The nerves.
" 14, "	" "	Topographical anatomy.
" 21, "	Dr. Fuller,	Respiration and circulation of blood.
" 28, "	" "	Auscultation, percussion, and nursing of heart and lung cases.
Nov. 4, "	" "	Auscultation, percussion, and nursing of heart and lung cases.
" 11, "	" "	Physiology of digestion.
" 18, "	Dr. Davis,	Air and ventilation.
" 25, "	" "	The sick room.
Dec. 2, "	Dr. Root,	Infection and contagion.
" 9, "	" "	Sterilization of apparatus, clothing, excreta, and food.
" 16, "	" "	Management of diet.
" 23, "	Dr. Howe,	Emergencies.
" 30, "	" "	Emergencies.
Jan. 6, 1898,	Dr. Hall,	Anæsthetics, their administration.
" 13, "	" "	Nursing surgical cases. Shock.
" 20, "	Dr. Downs,	The brain and its functions.
" 27, "	" "	The abnormal mind.
Feb. 3, "	" "	Common forms of insanity.
" 15, "	" "	Special nursing of the insane.
" 17, "	Dr. Beach,	Anatomy of the skin.
" 24, "	" "	Care of the skin.
Mar. 3, "	" "	Nursing sick children.
" 10, "	Dr. Ingalls,	Obstetrics.
" 17, "	" "	Obstetrics.
" 24, "	" "	Gynecology.
" 31, "	" "	Laparotomy. Preparation. Nursing.
April 7, "	Dr. Cook,	Fractures and splints.
" 14, "	" "	The foot. Orthopedic surgery.
" 21, "	" "	Administration of medicines.
" 28, "	Dr. Bacon,	Nursing of eye, ear, nose, and throat.
May 5, "	Dr. Campbell,	Fever nursing.
" 12, "	" "	Special nursing in contagious diseases.
" 19, "	Dr. Bunce,	Surgery of the brain.
" 26, "	" "	Surgery of the nerves.
June 2, "	" "	Not announced.
" 9, "	Not supplied.	" "
" 16, "	" "	" "
" 23, "	" "	" "

TRAINING SCHOOL FOR NURSES.

ADMISSION OF PUPILS TO THE TRAINING SCHOOL.

1. The Directors of the Hartford Hospital have made arrangements for giving at the Hospital a two-years training to women desirous of becoming professional nurses. The demand for hospital-trained nurses is great, and a well-trained nurse is practically sure of sufficient work after graduation.

2. Persons wishing to receive the course must apply to the Lady Superintendent of the Training School, when, upon approval of the Executive Committee, they will be received as pupil nurses in the school.

3. Candidates must be unmarried or widowed, over twenty-one and under thirty-five years of age; they must present a certificate of sound health from their physician; also a certificate from some responsible person of their good character.

4. Applicants will be received for two months on probation, during which time they will be boarded and lodged at the expense of the Hospital, but will receive no compensation if they leave before the expiration of the second month or are found incompetent.

5. The Lady Superintendent of the school will have full power to decide as to the fitness of the nurses for the work, and will report to the Executive Committee the propriety of dismissing or retaining them at the end of the month for trial.

6. The same authority can discharge them in case of misconduct or inefficiency, subject to the approval of the Executive Committee.

7. They will reside in the Hospital, and serve as assistants in the wards of the Hospital; the second year they will be assigned by the Lady Superintendent, either to act as nurses in the Hospital, or to be sent to private cases among the rich or poor. When in service they are expected to wear the Hospital uniform.

TRAINING.

Those persons complying with the foregoing conditions will be accepted as pupils by signing a written agreement to remain at the school for two years, and to conform to the rules of the Hospital.

The instruction includes:

1. The dressing of blisters, burns, sores, and wounds; the preparation and application of fomentations, poultices, and minor dressing.

2. Application of leeches and subsequent treatment.

3. Administration of enemas, the use of the female catheter, and giving of baths.

4. The care of the patient's room, the principles of ventilation, and their practical application.

5. The best method of friction to the body and extremities.

6. Management of helpless patients, moving, changing, managing positions, and preventing bed sores.

7. Emergencies and their treatment, bandaging, making bandages and rollers, and lining splints.

8. Making beds and changing sheets while the patient is in bed.

9. That no part of the Hospital is clean if it can be made cleaner.

The pupils are taught to prepare food, drinks, and stimulants for the sick; all that pertains to night in distinction from day nursing; to report to the physician accurate observations of the state of the secretions, excretions, pulse, skin, appetite, temperature of the body, intelligence (as to delirium or stupor), breathing, sleeping, conditions of wounds, eruptions, formation of matter, effect of diet, stimulants, and medicine, and to learn the management of convalescents.

Instruction will be given by attending and resident physicians and surgeons at the bedside, and in various other ways by the Matron and her assistants, and under their direction by the head nurses.

The pupils will pass through the various wards, serving and being taught. They will be supplied with board and lodging, and will be paid for their clothing and personal expenses ten dollars a month for the first and fourteen dollars a month for the second year. This sum, with their education, is considered a full equivalent for their services. When the full term of two years is completed, the nurses thus trained, after passing a final examination, will receive diplomas, certifying to their knowledge of nursing, their ability and good character. The medal and diploma, or either, of any graduate of the Training School may be revoked for cause by the Executive Committee.

Copy of the paper to be filled out in the candidate's own handwriting and sent to the Lady Superintendent of the Hartford Hospital Training School for Nurses, Hartford, Conn.

Questions to be answered by the candidate:

1. Name in full, and present address of candidate?
2. Are you a single woman or a widow?
3. Your present occupation or employment?
4. Age last birthday, and date and place of birth?
5. Height? Weight?
6. Where educated?
7. Are you strong and healthy, and have you always been so?
8. Are your sight and hearing perfect?
9. Have you any physical defects?
10. If a widow, have you children? How many? Their ages? How are they provided for?

11. Where (if any) was your last situation? How long were you in it?

12. The names in full, with addresses, of two persons to whom you refer. State how long each has known you. If previously employed, one of these must be the last employer.

13. Have you ever been a pupil of any other training school?

14. Have you read, and do you clearly understand, the regulations?

I declare the above statement to be correct.

    (Signed)   ....

Date...

For information regarding the reception of pupils in the Training School, or copies of the above application, apply in writing or personally to the Lady Superintendent of the Hartford Hospital Training School for Nurses, Hartford, Conn.

OLD PEOPLE'S HOME.

OFFICERS OF THE OLD PEOPLE'S HOME.

Executive Committee.

HENRY K. MORGAN, 108 Farmington Ave.
HARMON G. HOWE, M.D., 137 High St.
THOMAS SISSON, 729 Main St.

Superintendent.

BENJAMIN S. GILBERT.

Physician.

JOSEPH B. HALL, M.D.

Matron.

Mrs. ELIZABETH J. FOX.

Assistant.

Miss CARRIE M. FOX.

THE FOURTEENTH ANNUAL REPORT

OF THE

OLD PEOPLE'S HOME.

To the Directors of the Hartford Hospital:

Your Executive Committee respectfully submit the following as the fourteenth annual report of the Old People's Home for the year ending September 30, 1898.

At the beginning of the year there were 63 inmates — 51 females and 12 males, 57 permanent and 6 boarders, resident in the Home. The ages were as follows:

Between the age of 60 and 70 . . .	11
Between the age of 70 and 80 . . .	33
Between the age of 80 and 90 . . .	17
Over the age of 90	2

Twelve permits have been issued during the year.

Five permanent inmates have died during the year, as follows:

Addison Wheeler, aged 69; residence, 7 years 11 months.

Florinda A. Hills, aged 89; residence, 9 years and 13 days.

Althea M. Lord, aged 64; residence, 6 months.

Spencer Read, aged 81; residence, 8 years and 6 months.

Emma J. Cornwell, aged 71; residence, 2 years and 7 months.

At the close of the year the total number of inmates was 73 — 57 females and 16 males, 64 permanent and 9 boarders, their ages being as follows:

Between the ages of 60 and 70 . .	13
Between the ages of 70 and 80 . .	22
Between the ages of 80 and 90 . .	25
Over the age of 90	4

6

The total expense account for the past year is as follows:

House expenses	.	.	.	$11,424.20
Insurance on buildings and contents				292.50
Officer's expenses (treasurer's)		.		43.00
Total	.	.	.	$11,759.70

The receipts were as follows:

Board of inmates	.	.	.	$1,851.33
Board of nurses	.	.	.	12.36
Rent of rooms to nurses	.	.		380.00
Sales	.	.	.	.	6.00
Income from permanent fund		.		3,634.13
Total		.		$5,883.82

There has been a net loss of $5,875.83 for the year, being $573.08 more than last year. There has been received $10,000 in permanent inmates' fees, which gives an actual gain of $4,124.12 for the year, and has allowed us to pay a portion of our indebtedness to the Hospital.

There have been received the following bequests:

Estate of Amanda M. Whitney	.		$10,528.25
Estate of Sarah Tuttle	.	.	5,000.00
Estate of Martha W. Brown	.		6,803.59
Estate of Susan S. Clark	.	.	4,850.00
Total	.		$27,181.84

These bequests, we sincerely hope, may be followed by many more, that we may before many years announce that this noble charity stands upon a firm financial basis, allowing your Executive Committee to accept some of the worthy applicants who are destitute of the necessary means to permit of their admission.

As a whole the family has been a happy and contented one, the table plain but wholesome and in good quantity. We have kept two nurses from the Hospital on duty during the past year, one for day and one for night service. We feel that the emergencies attending upon advanced age are foreseen and cared for as well as can be done. Dr. Hall has attended upon the old people during the past year, and has discharged his duties in a faithful manner, serving without pay. Religious services have been held in the building by kind friends of the Home.

CONTRIBUTIONS.

Miss Mary Clark — October 8th, ice-cream and cake; Thanksgiving, ice-cream, cake, and charlotte russe; Christmas, ice-cream and cake; Easter, cards, ice-cream, cake, and flowers; April 11th, charlotte russe; June 7th, carriage hire for all the inmates; June 13th, ice-cream and cake.

Mrs. Mary J. Munsill — November 3d, one and one-half barrels of apples; January 3d, two boxes oranges; February 19th, two boxes of oranges; September 3d, two baskets of peaches; and September 6th, two baskets of peaches and melons.

A Friend — Thanksgiving, $5 and flowers; Christmas, $20; March 19th, box of oranges; Easter, two boxes of oranges.

The Williams & Carleton Co. — November 25th, six pounds of coffee.

Mrs. B. S. Gilbert — Thanksgiving flowers.

Mrs. H. R. Redfield — Box of oranges Christmas.

Mrs. E. A. Smith — Box of oranges.

Fowler & Hunting — Figs and pop-corn.

C. S. Brewer & Co. — Figs.

J. C. Parsons — March 14, flowers.

Mrs. Caroline Knous — Clothing.

Books from the Public Library.

Mrs. Mary E. Sessions, Bristol, Conn. — April 28, two boxes of sandwiches.

Flowers every Thursday from the Wethersfield Mission.

St. Andrew's Brotherhood — Leaflets every Monday.

ENTERTAINMENTS.

October 18th. — Musicale by the young people of the Advent Church.

January 4th. — Music by the young people of the Universalist Church; also ice-cream and cake.

Through the kindness of the editors, we have received the *Hartford Daily Times*, the *Hartford Daily Courant*, the *Hartford Daily Post*, and the *Ladies' Home Journal*.

Mrs. Fox continues to fill the position of matron, and, assisted by her daughter, Miss Carrie Fox, has administered the affairs of the Home in a satisfactory manner.

Appended to this report is that of the Treasurer to you and of the Superintendent to us, as well as other items of interest.

Respectfully,

SUPERINTENDENT'S REPORT.

The OLD PEOPLE'S HOME *in account with* BENJ. S. GILBERT, *Sup't.*

1897–8. To amount paid for		1898. By amount received from	
Breadstuffs,	$391.45	W. W. Jacobs, Treas.,	$11,424.20
Butter and Eggs,	607.94	Board of Inmates,	1,851.33
Burials,	40.50	Board of Nurses,	12.36
Fruits and Vegetables,	767.21	Rent of Rooms to Nurses,	380.00
Fuel,	1,370.10	Sales,	6.00
Furniture,	388.58		
Gas,	656.63		
Groceries,	656.39		
Ice,	60.00		
Meats and Fish,	2,331.44		
Milk,	784.65		
Miscellaneous,	103.55		
Repairs and Improvements,	580.49		
Salaries,	2,497.52		
Washing Soda and Soap,	19.59		
Stationery,	3.16		
Water,	165.00		
Total current Expenses,	$11,424.20		
Amount paid Treasurer,	2,249.69		
	$13,673.89		$13,673.89

TREASURER'S REPORT.

Close of Fiscal Year,

RECEIPTS.

Balance Cash from 1897 report, ...		$6,596.80
Bequest, Amanda M. Whitney, . . .	$10,528.25	
" Sarah Tuttle, ...	5,000 00	
" Martha W. Brown, . . .	6,803.59	
" Susan S. Clark, . . .	4,850.00—	27,181.84
Hartford Street Railway Company, one-half amount paid for land and right of way, Newington Avenue, "Wildwood Farm, ...		750.00
Bonds, Charles E. Fox Fund, 5,000 Chicago, Rock Island & Pacific Railway 5s of 1934, redeemed, . .		5,000.00
Fund No. 2, from Deceased Inmates, . . .		774.46
Interest, Net, ...		1,134.13
Keney Fund, Income.		2,500.00
Received from Superintendent for board of Inmates at Old People's Home, ...		2,249.69
Permanent Inmate Fees, ...		10,000.00
Savings Banks, drawn and paid to Inmates, . .		370.47
Inmates' Accounts to new year, . . .		9,908.87
		$66,466.26

DISBURSEMENTS.

Balance of Inmates' Accounts from 1897 Report, . .		$9,744.44
Paid Executive Committee's Orders for General Expenses at Old People's Home, . . .	$11,424.20	
Tablet, ...	22.80—	11,447.00
Bonds, Elizabeth C. Bacon Fund, bought 6,000 Lehigh Valley Railway of N. Y. 4½s of July 1, 1940, .	6,000.00	
" Charles E. Fox Fund, bought 5,000 Lehigh Valley Railway of N. Y. 4½s of July 1, 1940, ...	5,000.00	
" William F. Tuttle Fund, bought 5,000 Lehigh Valley Railway of N. Y. 4½s of July 1, 1940, ...	5,000.00	
" F. A. Brown Fund, bought 5,000 Lehigh Valley Railway of N. Y. 4½s of July 1, 1940, ...	5,000.00	
" Martha W. Brown Fund, bought 2,000 Lehigh Valley Railway of N. Y. 4½s of July 1, 1940, ...	2,000.00	
" Susan S. Clark Fund, bought 5,000 Lehigh Valley Railway of N. Y. 4½s of July 1, 1940, ...	5,000.00—	28,000.00
Premium Account and Sinking Fund, Permanent Funds,		813.76
Express Stocks, 8 shares Adams Express Company, received on account of Permanent Inmate Fees, . .		1,200.00
Savings Banks, deposited on account of various Inmates, .		165.92
Insurance on building and contents one year, . ,		292.50
Bills Payable, ...		10,800.00
Incidental Expenses, . . , . .		20.20
Permanent Funds, uninvested, ...		485.00
Balance Cash, ...		3,497.44
		$66,466.26

OLD PEOPLE'S HOME.

SEPTEMBER 30, 1898.

ASSETS.

Railroad Stock.

Shares.		Book Value.	Market Value.
10	St. Johnsb'y & Lake Champ'n (par $500).	$1.00	$1.00

Manufacturing Stock.

	Book Value.	Market Value.
100 Farnham Type-Setter Manufacturing Co. (par $2,500), ...	1.00	1.00

Express Stocks.

	Book Value.	Market Value.
8 Adams Express Company, . .	1,200.00	880.00

Real Estate.

	Book Value.	Market Value.
Buildings and Grounds, . . .	1.00	1.00
Half interest in Wildwood Farm, . . .	1.00	1.00

Inmates' Trust Accounts.

	Book Value.	Market Value.
Savings Bank Deposits, . . .	4,065.15	4,065.15
Miscellaneous Investments, . . .	2,500.00	2,500.00

Elizabeth C. Bacon Fund.

Bonds.

	Book Value.	Market Value.
Lehigh Valley Railway of N. Y. 4½s, July 1, 1940, ...	6,000.00	6,150.00

F. A. Brown Fund.

Bonds.

	Book Value.	Market Value.
Lehigh Valley Railway of N. Y. 4½s, July 1, 1940, ...	5,000.00	5,125.00

Martha W. Brown Fund.

Bonds.

	Book Value.	Market Value.
Lehigh Valley Railway of N. Y. 4½s, July 1, 1940, ...	2,000.00	2,050.00

Susan S. Clark Fund.

Bonds.

	Book Value.	Market Value.
Lehigh Valley Railway of N. Y. 4½s, July 1, 1940, ...	5,000 00	5,125.00

88

Charles E. Fox Fund.

Bonds.

Cleveland, Cincinnati, Chicago & St. Louis Railway 4s, Nov. 1, 1990 (par $4,000),	3,665.00	3,920.00
Lehigh Valley Railway of N. Y. 4½s, July 1, 1940, ...	5,000.00	5,125.00
Balance Cash, uninvested, . . .	485.00	485.00

Keney Fund.

Bonds.

Hartford Street Railway 5s, May 1, 1916, .	25,000.00	25,500.00
Brooklyn Wharf & Warehouse Co. 5s, Feb. 1, 1945, ...	25,000.00	22,000.00

Catherine Tuttle Fund.

Bonds.

Lehigh Valley Terminal Railway 5s, Oct. 1, 1941, ...	2,000.00	2,240.00

William F. Tuttle Fund.

Bonds.

Lehigh Valley Railway of N. Y. 4¼s, July 1, 1940, ...	5,000.00	5,125.00

Miscellaneous.

Premium Account and Sinking Fund, Permanent Funds, . . .	813.76	813.76
Estate of John H. Most, . . .	69 88	69.88
Profit and Loss Account, . . .	30,581.21	30,581.21
Balance Cash, ...	3,497.44	3,497.44
	$126,881.44	$125,256.44

LIABILITIES.

Fund Account No. 2, Deceased Inmates, . . .	$12,168.98
Bills Payable, ...	20,000.00
Elizabeth C. Bacon Fund, ...	6,000.00
F. A. Brown Fund, ...	4,859.71
Martha W. Brown Fund, ...	1,943.88
Susan S. Clark Fund, ...	4,850.00
Charles E. Fox Fund, ...	9,150.00
Anna L. Franklin Fund, ...	1,000.00
Keney Fund, ...	50,000.00
Catherine Tuttle Fund, ...	2,000.00
William F. Tuttle Fund, ...	5,000.00
Inmates' Trust Accounts, ...	9,908.87
	$126,881.44

TERMS OF ADMISSION.

ARTICLE I. Applicants for admission to the Old People's Home must be citizens of the County of Hartford, persons of good character, not under sixty years of age, and in reduced circumstances.

ARTICLE II. The preliminary conditions of admission for permanent inmates will be as follows, viz.:

Applicants over the age of sixty years will be required to pay $1,000 on admission.

This admission fee must be paid to the Treasurer of the Hospital upon the entrance of applicant.*

Applicants for temporary accommodations in the Home will be charged such a sum as the Executive Committee may find necessary to cover the expenses of board, washing, etc.

Such occupancy will be limited at the discretion of said committee.

ARTICLE III. A probationary period of four months will be required before the applicant can be confirmed as a permanent inmate of the Home.

ARTICLE IV. Applications for admission must be made to the Executive Committee, and a full statement of the circumstances of the applicant must be given.

ARTICLE V. Every person admitted as a permanent inmate shall sign and execute, in a book kept by the Superintendent, the agreement and conveyance hereto annexed.

ARTICLE VI. No article of furniture shall be brought into the institution without the consent of the Executive Committee; such articles as shall be admitted shall be and become the absolute property of the Hospital.

---

*If from any cause an individual is not confirmed, the amount paid will be refunded, after deducting the price of the board, etc., while a resident of the Home.

ARTICLE VII. Form of agreement: The undersigned having been received as a permanent inmate and beneficiary of the Old People's Home, a department of the Hartford Hospital, in the city of Hartford, now, in consideration of the benefits assured to me as such beneficiary and of my admission thereto, I do hereby assent to and promise compliance with the rules and regulations of such Home as they exist at the date hereof, and as the same shall be made, amended, or modified thereafter, and I do hereby sell, assign, set over, and convey unto the Directors of the Hartford Hospital, and their successors and assigns forever, all the goods, chattels, effects, and personal property of every kind, and all real estate, wheresoever the same may be situated, which I now possess, or to which I shall hereafter become entitled during my residence at the Home; and I hereby make and appoint the Treasurer of the Hartford Hospital, and his successor and successors in office, my attorney and trustee irrevocable, with full power and authority to demand, receive, collect, and recover said property, effects, and claims for the purposes hereinbefore and hereinafter stated, to pay and deliver the same to said Home. It is also understood that I may at any time terminate my connection with the Home, and that the Executive Committee of the Hospital may in their discretion, at any time, require me to do the same. It is, however, understood that, upon payment to said Hospital of such sum or sums of money as fixed by the Executive Committee as a fair compensation for my support, and charges against me to the full extent, and for all the term in which I shall have been an inmate of said Home, then I am to receive from said Hospital such property as I have transferred to it, or the proceeds of such property as the Executive Committee may have disposed of.

HOUSE RULES.

Article I. — Duties of Matron.

The Matron shall have the general care of the domestic affairs of the Home and of the inmates, subject to the direction of the Superintendent and Executive Committee. No person will be permitted to interfere or find fault with the Matron; but if any inmate has cause for complaint, application must be made to the Executive Committee, who will receive any statement and take action thereon as they think proper. She shall see that all inmates, who are able to do so, shall take their meals at the family table, and that proper order is preserved; also, that suitable food shall be provided for the sick.

Article II. — Duties of Inmates.

Any inmate wishing to leave the house to visit friends or otherwise must apply to the Matron for her assent, stating where he or she intends going, and when he or she expects to return. Every inmate who is able to do so will be required to keep his or her room neat and clean, and the furniture in order, and make themselves generally useful. Any inmate who shall be guilty of circulating reports injurious to the reputation of the Home, criticising or finding fault with the management, creating dissatisfaction or disturbance among its inmates, shall be admonished, and on repetition of such offense shall hereby forfeit his or her privileges, and be dismissed from the institution. It shall not be allowable for the male or female inmates to visit each other's rooms, but they may meet in the corridors, which will always be open to them.

Article III. — Visitors.

The friends of inmates, and the public generally, may visit the Home on Thursday, between the hours of 10 and 12 o'clock A. M., and from 2 to 4 o'clock P. M. At other times visitors will be admitted only by permission of the Superintendent or Matron.

ARTICLE IV. — PHYSICIANS.

No physician except those connected with the Hospital will be allowed to attend the inmates, except by permission of the Chairman or some member of the Executive Committee.

ARTICLE V.

No spirituous liquors shall be brought into the Home, nor shall any be used by any inmate, unless the same be prescribed by the attending physician, and placed in charge of and administered by the Matron.

ARTICLE VI.

The lights shall be extinguished in the rooms of the inmates at nine in the evening, and in the halls and corridors at 10 P. M., unless the Matron, for good reasons, directs otherwise.

ARTICLE VII.

Upon the death of an inmate, the Matron shall immediately notify the Executive Committee, and also the friends, as far as their address may be ascertained. Should the funeral take place from the Home, the arrangements shall be uniform in all cases, and shall be made under the direction of the Executive Committee. The friends of the deceased may defray the expenses, or remove the remains elsewhere for interment by permission of the Superintendent.

ARTICLE VIII.

Willful violation of any of these rules or regulations by any of the inmates shall render such person liable to dismissal, in which case he or she shall not be entitled to a return of any moneys paid by such individual; such clothing or other personal effects belonging to the person dismissed may be taken. The Executive Committee may make such dismissal. Persons expelled will not be permitted to visit the Home under any circumstances. In all matters of difference between the inmates the decision of the Superintendent shall be conclusive, until modified or reversed by the Executive Committee. The orders of the Superintendent and Matron, in all matters relating to the domestic government of the family, must be observed by all inmates; such orders must be reported to the Executive Committee.

FORM OF BEQUEST.

I give to the Hartford Hospital of the city of Hartford, dollars, for the uses of the Old People's Home, a department of said Hospital.

FORM OF BEQUEST FOR FREE BED.

I give to the Hartford Hospital of the city of Hartford the sum of five thousand dollars, to be used in the maintenance of a free bed in the Old People's Home, a department of said Hospital.

TWENTY-SEVENTH REPORT

OF THE

BOARD OF TRUSTEES

OF THE

CONNECTICUT HOSPITAL FOR THE INSANE

OF THE

STATE OF CONNECTICUT,

WITH THE

SUPERINTENDENT'S AND TREASURER'S REPORTS,

FOR THE

Biennial Period Ending September 30, 1898.

Presented to the General Assembly at its Session in January, 1899.

BY ORDER OF THE GENERAL ASSEMBLY.

MIDDLETOWN, CONN.:
PELTON & KING, PRINTERS AND BOOKBINDERS.
1898.

Officers of the Hospital.

BOARD OF TRUSTEES.

THE GOVERNOR OF CONNECTICUT.

COSTELLO LIPPITT,	New London County,	Norwich.
TIMOTHY E. HOPKINS,	Windham County,	Killingly.
WILBUR B. FOSTER,	Tolland County,	Rockville.
WM. D. MORGAN, M. D.,	Hartford County,	Hartford.
HENRY WOODWARD,	Middlesex County,	Middletown.
WM. BISSELL, M. D.,	Litchfield County,	Lakeville.
JAMES G. GREGORY, M. D.,	Fairfield County,	Norwalk.
HART D. MUNSON,	New Haven County,	New Haven.
ELIJAH K. HUBBARD,		Middletown.
FRANK B. WEEKS,		Middletown.
SAMUEL RUSSELL,		Middletown.
E. IRVING BELL,		Portland.

M. B. Copeland, - - - - - - - - *Treasurer.*

RESIDENT OFFICERS.

CHARLES W. PAGE, M. D.,	*Superintendent and Physician.*
HENRY S. NOBLE, M. D.,	*Assistant Superintendent.*
WILLIAM E. FISHER, M. D.,	
CHARLES E. STANLEY, M. D.,	
JAMES M. KENISTON, M. D.,	
ARTHUR B. COLEBURN, M. D.,	*Assistant Physicians.*
JOHN W. DUKE, M. D.,	
ROSS E. SAVAGE, M. D.,	
THOMAS M. DURFEE,	*Clerk.*
P. W. SANDERSON,	*Farmer.*
MRS. MARGARET DUTTON,	*Matron.*

All communications relative to the admission, etc., of patients, should be addressed to the Superintendent. Blanks will be furnished on application.

TRUSTEE'S REPORT.

————•••————

To His Excellency the Governor of Connecticut:

The Trustees of the Connecticut Hospital for the Insane take pleasure in presenting this twenty-seventh report for the information of the General Assembly.

The work accomplished by the hospital during the two years just ended will compare favorably with the past record of the institution.

The last report mentioned the addition of a new wing to the south end of the North Hospital, and since that time the Trustees have built an additional wing to the north end of the same hospital, thereby making accommodations for fifty additional patients.

These additions have provided room for all patients who have applied, but the hospital is over full, and we are obliged to care for the insane in places that are not entirely suitable for such purposes, including several wood cottages, which we are obliged by the exigencies of the situation to retain in use.

This north wing was erected at an expense of $17,623.

There has also been erected a Mortuary building of stone and brick, with a tiled roof, at an expense of $6,524.54.

There has been placed in position a substantial iron fence on both the north and south sides of Silver Street, in front of the main grounds.

At the South Hospital there have been added two large verandas, three stories high, enclosed with wire guards, which provide valuable space where patients can sit in pleasant weather as a relief from confinement indoors.

More room being required for farm stock, a large barn, constructed on modern principles, has been erected to provide stabling for 100 cows. This barn is constructed with brick walls, iron frame, and cement floors, making it practically fire-proof. The cost of this barn was $16,902.10.

At an expense of $610.96, a fire-proof waiting room has been erected at the foot of the grounds, opposite the terminal of the electric car line. The necessity for such a shelter for hospital employés and visitors to the hospital, as well as the importance of its control by the hospital, fully justified the investment in the opinion of the Trustees.

The removal of the insane convicts to Wethersfield has afforded a much desired relief, and has vacated quarters, not altogether desirable, it is true, which are occupied by a class of our patients who have broken laws, but have been adjudged "not guilty" by reason of insanity, or who have been convicted of some crime and served out their sentence, but cannot be restored to liberty because of mental disorder.

The hospital requires many additions and improvements, which will absorb all the funds now available for immediate use. The Trustees have at times, in former reports, questioned the expediency of enlarging this hospital, but heretofore the Legislature has not coincided in such views. If the State should again conclude that it is in the line of economy and good policy to continue to add to the number of patients here, we shall adopt a plan which has been presented, and which, we are convinced, will do away with the objections that have heretofore operated to influence the Trustees in their opinion.

The plan contemplates a system of classification, as discussed at length in the Superintendent's report, and the erection of a large congregate dining room to accommodate all the quiet and more orderly patients in the hospital. This plan, by doing away with the present ward dining rooms, will furnish dormitory space for 250 beds.

The estimated cost of the proposed building and connections will not exceed $100,000.

If the Legislature desires the Trustees to provide further accommodations for the insane, and upon the line suggested, an appropriation from the State treasury will be necessary.

Since our last report one of our Trustees, Mr. Horace F. Boardman, has died, and the vacancy has been filled by the appointment of Mr. E. I. Bell, of Portland.

It becomes our painful duty to report the death of our late Superintendent, Dr. James Olmstead, who for nearly twelve years had so ably administered the affairs of the hospital. Having previously served nine years as assistant physician, he entered upon the duties of Superintendent upon the death of Dr. Shew, and brought to the position untiring energy and a love for the work that has contributed largely to the financial success and usefulness of the hospital. His tender care for the unfortunate inmates of the hospital will long be remembered by all who were associated with him. His life was one of singular devotion to duty, and his best energies were always at the command of the State.

After the death of Dr. Olmstead, Dr. H. S. Noble, the Assistant Superintendent, was placed in charge, and filled the position for nine months to the entire satisfaction of the Board. But as he declined to permanently bear the responsibility of the position, the Trustees elected as Superintendent, Dr. Charles W. Page, who assumed the duties of the office on the first day of September, 1898. Dr. Page brings to the position a long experience, having formerly been connected with the Hartford Retreat, and for the last ten years having had charge of the State Hospital, at Danvers, Mass.

The terms of the following-named Trustees will expire July 1st, 1899, viz.: Hart D. Munson, James G. Gregory, M. D., William Bissell, M. D., Henry Woodward, E. Irving Bell, and Samuel Russell.

Respectfully submitted,

LORRIN A. COOKE,
HENRY WOODWARD,
ELIJAH K. HUBBARD,
E. IRVING BELL,
FRANK B. WEEKS,
COSTELLO LIPPITT,
WILBUR B. FOSTER,
WM. D. MORGAN, M. D.,
JAMES G. GREGORY, M. D.,
WILLIAM BISSELL, M. D.,
HART D. MUNSON,
TIMOTHY E. HOPKINS.

SUPERINTENDENT'S REPORT.

To the Board of Trustees of the Connecticut Hospital for the Insane:

GENTLEMEN:—Complying with the by-laws of the institution, I herewith submit a report of its operations during the biennial period closing with September 30, 1898, to which is appended the usual statistical tables.

The number of patients present at the beginning of the fiscal year 1896–97 was 1,782, of whom 846 were men and 936 were women. At the end of the same fiscal year, September 30, 1897, there were present 865 men and 963 women, a total of 1,828. At the close of the hospital year 1897–98, the whole number present had increased to 1895, of whom 882 were men and 1,013 were women.

Reference to Table 1 shows that during the biennial period 643 patients have been discharged from the hospital. Of this number 227 have died, 162 were discharged stationary, 126 had improved sufficiently to dispense with hospital care and resume their places in home and society, and 133 were regarded as fully restored to mental health. Many of those discharged improved were, at the time of release, in a fair way to recover, and have since undoubtedly completed their convalescence. While the percentage of recoveries does not seem large if reckoned on the average number present, this is accounted for largely by the fact that nearly all the chronic insane of the State are cared for at this institution and enter into the statistics year after year. If the recovery rate be reckoned on the number of admissions, as is done by the Commissioners on Lunacy for the State of New York, a much fairer showing of the institution's work will be obtained.

The subject of recoveries is one of absorbing interest to all hospital men inasmuch as it is, primarily, the end and object toward which all their efforts are directed, although the desired goal may not always be attained.

The Commissioners on Lunacy for the State of New York, in their last report, comment upon the excellent work done by the hospitals of that State since the adoption of improved methods of treatment, and give statistics showing the percentage of recoveries which have occurred during the period beginning with October 1, 1888, and ending with September 30, 1897, covering a space of nine years. The recovery rate is ascertained to be 27.5 per cent. for the whole period, which is an excellent showing when we take into account the advanced stage of the disease at which patients are usually committed to hospitals for treatment, and the discouraging character of many of the cases, such as paretics, dotards, and imbecile, among whom a recovery is manifestly impossible. This percentage is, however, reckoned on what are termed "original admissions," or cases admitted from homes, and excludes from the computation all those transferred from other institutions. This would seem to be a fair deduction to make, even though almshouses were included, where patients are often kept five, ten, and twenty years, to be finally committed to some hospital on account of the development of dangerous or troublesome symptoms in the advanced stages of the disease. We observe also that the criminal and convict classes are likewise omitted, inasmuch as the statistics of the Matteawan State Hospital for Insane Criminals do not appear in the computation. The existence of this institution in the State of New York presumably relieves the other State hospitals of the care and treatment of insane criminals, so that this element, so notoriously discouraging as far as recoveries are concerned, is likewise eliminated. Statistics like these are interesting as well as encouraging, affording as they do an opportunity for comparing the results of old methods of treatment with those of the new in the same, and in different hospitals. The interest excited by these facts presented in the New York Commissioners' report has prompted us to prepare similar statistics from the tables of the Connecticut Hospital for the Insane, covering the same period, and making practically the same deductions from the whole number of admissions. It is undoubtedly the custom in most hospitals to reckon among the recoveries those cases of insanity of toxic origin which, after a longer or shorter period of treatment, regain their normal mental condition, and are enabled to resume their positions in society as useful, law-abiding citizens. In the annual statistics of the Connecticut Hospital for the

Insane these cases have always been reckoned among the
"Stationary" on account of their known liability to relapse,
although it is perhaps questionable whether such liability is
greater in this than in some other forms of mental disease.
In order, however, to satisfy the most exacting, the percentage
of recoveries has been computed both with and without these
cases. Until January 1, 1898, all the convict and criminal
insane of Connecticut were treated at this hospital, whereas in
the State of New York they are cared for at Matteawan, and
thus the other State hospitals are relieved of their presence.
In order, therefore, to institute anything like a fair comparison
between the recovery rates in the two States, it is necessary to
eliminate from the admissions to this hospital all who belonged
to the convict and criminal classes, and who are committed as
such after having been convicted and confined for a longer or
shorter period in some penal institution. All those acquitted
of crime on the ground of insanity and committed to this hospital direct from the courts, are reckoned in these statistics the
same as ordinary admissions from homes. With these necessary explanations we herewith submit the percentage of recoveries reckoned on the admissions for the period of nine years
ending September 30, 1897:

Whole number admitted from September 30, 1888, to Octo-
ber 1, 1897, - - - - - - - - - 3,500
Whole number recovered during the same period exclusive
of those from toxic insanity, - - - - - 696
Whole number recovered in the period including those from
toxic insanity, - - - - - - - 798
Number of admissions in the period less those received from
other hospitals, - - - - - - - - 3,184
Percentage of recoveries reckoned on this number, - - 21.8
Percentage of recoveries reckoned on this number including
those from toxic insanity, - - - - - - 24.7
Number of admissions in the period less criminals and those
received from other hospitals, - - - - - 2,950
Percentage of recoveries reckoned on this number, - - 23.5
Percentage of recoveries reckoned on this number including
those from toxic insanity, - - - - - - 26.7
Number of admissions in the period, less old almshouse
cases, criminals, and those from other hospitals, - - 2,610
Percentage of recoveries reckoned on this number, - - 26.6
Percentage of recoveries reckoned on this number including
those from toxic insanity, - - - - - - 30.2

The movement of population during the biennial period is shown in Table 1. During the latter part of 1896 and beginning of 1897 we were unable to receive either male or female patients without delay, owing to lack of room for their accommodation. During the past year, however, no inconvenience has been experienced from that cause, as patients of both sexes have been promptly received.

That the hospital has been, and is, overcrowded is a fact patent to any observer. Attics, stair landings, sitting rooms, alcoves in the corridors, and removable cots on the halls, have all been utilized to meet and relieve the ever-increasing pressure. The opening of the Annex building for females, at the North Hospital, which was in process of erection when the last biennial report was issued, afforded only a temporary relief, as it contains accommodations for only fifty patients. As was anticipated in the last report, "delay in the admission of male patients continued to increase until a corresponding addition at the other extremity of the North Hospital for the care of men" became an imperative necessity. This was accordingly built and furnished, and was opened for the reception of patients, April 26, 1898. This building is located at the northeastern extremity of the North Hospital, and, like its counterpart for females at the opposite end of the building, is separated from it, but in close proximity.

It was designed by the same architects, Messrs. Curtis & Johnson of Hartford, contains fifty beds, and is heated from the North Hospital boilers. Architecturally it is in harmony with the remainder of the block, while its internal arrangements and construction, as well as its location, are such as to adapt it for the care of the disturbed class of patients for whom it was designed. The wards are connected with the dining room by a covered passage the same as at the other extremity of the building, through which the patients go to and from their meals without the risk of escape or exposure.

On January 1 of the current year, in conformity with the provisions of an act passed by the General Assembly at its last session and approved May 25, 1897, all the convicts remaining at this institution whose sentences had not expired, were transferred to the new quarters provided for them in connection with the prison at Wethersfield. This left the Annex building, where they had formerly been cared for, nearly vacant, and rendered thirty-three beds available for male patients. These, with your permission, were utilized in caring for the criminal insane, and the convicts whose sentences had expired but who were still insane. The building is quite well adapted for this class on account of its greater security, its yard for exercise, and the workshop in connection with it.

During the month of August, 1898, the city authorities of New Haven removed from the hospital to their almshouse twenty-eight patients (fifteen men and thirteen women) of the quiet, chronic class, who required little other than custodial care.

On March 14, 1898, a room on the third floor of the center building of the Main Hospital, formerly a part of the old chapel, was fitted up as a dormitory for the accommodation of nineteen female patients of a quiet class, selected from the wards of the Main building.

By means of the increased accommodation above mentioned, supplemented by the ordinary and extraordinary discharges, we have been able, during the past year, to wipe out entirely the list of waiting applicants and receive all patients, male and female, without delay. It will be necessary, however, during the coming year, to adopt some adequate means to relieve the overcrowded condition of the hospital and provide for the ordinary annual increase in the number to be cared for. By reference to Table 1 it will be seen that the increase during the fiscal year 1896–97 was 46, and for the year 1897–98 it was 67. The average annual increase for the past ten years has been 60.3.

The health of this vast household has been, in the main, satisfactory during the biennial period just closed, although the average number sick in bed has been a trifle larger than in former years. This, however, should occasion no surprise if we take into account the number of patients received in the last stages of their disease, many of whom were so far reduced as to be unable to walk and required to be carried to the ward and bed from which they were destined never to rise again. It is also noted that during the past few years the number of patients of advanced age who have been admitted has markedly increased. During the biennial period fifty-one persons over seventy years of age have been received. There is a growing tendency to consign to the care of this hospital the aged, helpless, paralyzed, and bed-ridden, if only they present the symptoms of mental impairment required to admit of their being classed as insane. It is likewise a sad fact that the early period of life is not without its representatives in the wards of the institution, thirty-six persons under twenty years of age having been admitted during the past two years.

No epidemic of contagious disease is to be recorded, and the fact that two years have passed without the occurrence of a suicide is one for which we may well feel profoundly grateful.

The table on page 12 indicates the mode of commitment and source of support of the patients present at the close of the biennial period.

COMMITMENT BY COUNTY COMMISSIONERS.

Although the matter was referred to in the last biennial report of the late Dr. Olmstead, it seems desirable to again call attention to the commitment of insane patients by the County Commissioners. It is to be observed that although Chapter XLVI., Acts of 1893, was intended to supersede the law governing commitments by County Commissioners, the latter not having been specifically repealed, the Commissioners in some Counties continue to commit under the old law, and will undoubtedly do so until this is accomplished. The law empowering the Commissioners to send patients to the hospital has been found to be somewhat defective in its operation, as it makes no provision for the care and treatment of the patient after the expiration of the period for which he was sentenced to jail, no matter how insane or dangerous to the community he may be. The provisions of the law are quite sufficient in the event of recovery, for he is then to be returned to jail to complete his sentence. But should he still be insane at the expiration of his sentence, there is no legal authority for his further detention except through a new order of commitment obtained from some other source.

COMMITMENTS AND SUPPORT OF PATIENTS.

PATIENTS.	Committed By					Supported By					
	Probate Courts.	Police Court.	Superior Court.	County Commissioners.	Governor's Orders.	State and Towns.	State and Friends.	Private Funds.	Soldiers' Board.	State Alone.	
Pauper Patients, -	1,186				1	1,186					} Pub. Acts 1895, Chap. 180 (see Appendix).
Indigent Patients,	542						542				} Pub. Acts 1895, Chap. 256.
Private Patients, -	15							15			} Pub. Acts 1895, Chap. 256.
Veteran Soldiers,	27								27		Gen. Stat., Sec. 3762.
Criminals, acquitted, insane,		22	54			27		4		45	Gen. Stat., Sec. 1601.
Criminals awaiting trial, -			2		1					3	Gen. Stat., Sec. 1600.
Convicts sentenced to County Jails, -				5						5	Gen. Stat., Sec. 3385–86.
Convicts sentenced to County Jails, -					6					6	Pub. Acts 1893, Chap. 46.
Convicts, sentence expired, -			2		8	1				8	} Pub. Acts 1893, Chap. 46. Gen. Stat., Sec. 3683.
Non-residents, -					24					26	Pub. Acts 1893, Chap. 241.
Total, - -	1,770	22	58	5	40	1,214	542	19	27	93	

IDIOTS AND IMBECILES.

Although the institution is designated by the title of "Hospital," we are expected to receive as "patients" idiots and imbeciles, as long as the forms of law are complied with in the matter of their commitment. It would seem desirable that some legal restrictions should be placed upon the commitment of these classes of persons to the hospital, or some discretionary power be given to the Board of Trustees relative to their admission, especially at times when the institution is crowded beyond its normal capacity.

CONSTRUCTION AND REPAIRS.

To obviate the risk of fire in the drying room of the laundry it was thoroughly lined with tin, and the steam pipes protected from any possible contact with wood or clothing by wire netting. The laundry extension and the above-mentioned repairs involved an expense of $800. In order to remove still another of the fire risks common to nearly every ward in the institution, certain changes have been made in the dry closets. Heretofore these have been provided with wood racks placed over the steam coils on which clothing might be placed to dry. In some instances the wood was in contact with the pipes, and twice in our experience had become ignited. The wood has been removed from all these closets, and racks of galvanized wire cloth substituted. The doors and casings have also been lined with tin, so that it does not now seem that any risk of fire in these localities need be apprehended.

Metal ceilings have been put up in five dormitories at the Middle Hospital, in one corridor and five dormitories at the South, and in the Assistant Superintendent's sleeping room at the Main Hospital. One hundred white enamel bedsteads, with woven wire mattresses, have been purchased to enable us to dispense with wood bedsteads in the Main Hospital, which is the beginning of a change contemplated and authorized throughout the hospital, and to be accomplished as rapidly as circumstances will permit.

At several points where the fire risk was regarded as particularly hazardous, viz., in kitchen and bakery; over stage in Assembly Room; in carpenter shop, laundry, and dry room; carpenter and paint shops, and laundry dry room, a system of automatic sprinklers was installed by the Walworth Manufacturing Company at a cost of $720.24. The water pressure in the sprinklers placed at the highest elevation is thirty-one pounds, while in those at lower points it varies from sixty to seventy pounds. Twenty-five pounds pressure is considered amply sufficient to render them effective, and any increase beyond this renders protection more complete in consequence of the greater volume of water discharged.

The North Annex for male patients at North Hospital, already mentioned, was erected at a cost of $17,623.

WAITING STATION.

As a considerable part of the patronage on the Silver Street portion of the trolley-line is from visitors to the hospital, an iron waiting station has been provided, which contributes materially to the comfort of arriving and departing guests. The contract for the station was awarded to the Berlin Iron Bridge Company for the sum of $500. Some additional work was found necessary after the completion of the contract, such as laying a coping and stone walk, grading, etc., at an additional outlay of $110.96.

COW BARN.

As the institution has increased in numbers the consumption of milk has necessarily become greater. In order to meet this demand we have for several years past been obliged to purchase about half as much milk as we produced, as there were no facilities for keeping more cows. The new cow barn, which will afford stabling for one hundred cows, was built in accordance with modern ideas from plans prepared by architect J. D. Sibley, of Middletown. The committee having the matter in charge visited and inspected similar structures in adjoining States, where the most recent sanitary appliances had been carried into effect. The total cost of the new barn, including heating apparatus, was $16,720.62.

SAFETY VAULT.

At no time since the hospital has been in operation has it been provided with any receptacle where its medical and financial records could be stored, where they would be reasonably safe from destruction in case of fire. A commodious fire-proof vault has finally been constructed, contiguous to the ˙dispensary and convenient to the offices, where all commitments, vouchers, and records can be stored and no apprehension be felt for their safety.

WARMING CLOSETS.

One of the recent movements inaugurated for the purpose of improving the dietary is the installation of warming closets in all congregate dining rooms, where food may be kept hot until ready to be served. This plan will undoubtedly secure as satisfactory results as are possible under the present system of organization. In an institution as large as our own the disadvantages of a multiplicity of dining rooms become more and more apparent to anyone familiar with their operation. The fewer dining rooms we have, the less the number of divisions to be made of the food, and consequently the greater economy. Moreover, as less time is consumed in getting the food before the patients, it reaches them in a warmer and more palatable condition. The fewer the dining rooms, the more readily can proper inspection of the food and service be made.

Other improvements which might be mentioned are the following: Stone coping and five-foot iron fence on both sides of Silver Street; 2½-inch galvanized iron stand-pipe, with fire hose attached, in each ward of the North, Middle, and South Hospitals; fire-escape stairs and balconies attached outside to rear wall of each wing of Middle and South Hospitals, from uppermost story to the ground; fire-escape stairs from third story of North, Middle, and South centers to roof over first story; storm windows on most exposed portions of North Hospital.

TRAINING SCHOOL.

In this hospital, as well as in most others of a similar character, the training school for attendants has become a permanent feature, although it seems to be more properly an adjunct to the treatment of acute cases of insanity than to the simpler and less arduous care of the chronic insane. The sessions of the school closed for the year with the month of May, and were followed by oral and written examinations of the classes. The instruction is given almost entirely by means of text-books and recitations, supplemented by lectures, demonstrations, and clinical teaching. Seven members of the senior class passed their oral and written examinations with credit, and received certificates showing that they had completed the course. All are required to attain a percentage of 70 on the scale of 100, on recitations through the year, on the oral, and on the written examinations. The highest percentage attained was 291.37 out of a possible 300, and the lowest was 255.38.

FINANCIAL STATEMENT.

The financial statement for each of the two years past, notwithstanding the heavy drafts made upon our funds by the construction expenses mentioned in another place, still shows a moderate balance in our favor. Contemplated changes, however, which will enable the hospital to care for the patients already here, as well as a considerable number in addition, better and more economically than is now done, will undoubtedly absorb the greater part of the funds accumulated for that purpose. No serious catastrophe having occurred which would involve a loss of these funds belonging to the State, it seems eminently fit and proper that they should be devoted to the improvement of the hospital which created them, so as to enable it to carry on the better its philanthropic work.

ACKNOWLEDGMENTS.

I desire to express my personal obligations to the clergymen of the various denominations who, often at the sacrifice of personal convenience and comfort, have conducted the Sunday afternoon religious services.

The Assembly Room still maintains its place as one of the potent remedial agents at our command. The evening entertainments are looked .forward to, enjoyed, remembered, and discussed pleasantly, for days after their occurrence by a vast majority of our patients. The privilege of attending these gatherings induces efforts at self-control in the excited, weak, and impulsive, and diverts the thoughts of the depressed into happier and more healthful channels. The choir and orchestra, under the leadership of Dr. Keniston, have contributed in no small degree to the entertainment of our people, and are deserving of hearty commendation. Special thanks are also due to those benevolent friends of the hospital who have cheerfully contributed time and talents to afford pleasure to those less fortunate than themselves.

The following is a list of the entertainments provided for the household:

Concerts by Hospital Company, Dr. Keniston, leader, six evenings.
Readings by Miss Edith M. Norton, two evenings.
Stereopticon Lectures, "France and the French," by Prof. H. E. Northrop.
Readings by Mrs. Helen Stuart-Richings, two evenings.
Musical and Literary Entertainments, by Hospital Company, Drs. Keniston and Noble, managers.
Stereopticon Lecture, "Norway, Sweden, and Russia," by Prof. H. E. Northrop.
Phonographic Exhibition, by Mr. Charles D. Mowry.
Dramatic Entertainment, two plays by Middletown Dramatic Club.
Stereopticon Lecture, "Greenland," by Hugh J. Lee.
Reading, by Miss Alice A. Belding.
Reading, by Miss Marie G. Stubbs.
Stereopticon Lecture, by Dr. Coleburn.
Reading, by Prof. R. G. Hibbard.
Stereopticon Lecture, "German Army and Students," by Prof. H. E. Northrop.
Stereopticon Lecture, "Children of Europe," by Prof. H. E. Northrop.
Stereopticon Lecture, "Overland to California," by Mr. T. M. Durfee.
Lecture, "Sunshine," by Prof. Cosgrove.
"Living Pictures of War Time," by G. A. R., H. R. Young, manager.
Concert, by Mr. William B. Davis, assisted by Hospital Orchestra.
Ventriloquism, by Prof. Harry Bryant.
Drama, "The Donation Party," by members of the Y. P. C. U. of the Universalist Church.
Concert by Choir of North Congregational Church, assisted by Prof. and Mrs. Cone.
Stereopticon Lecture, "Atlantic and Pacific Coasts," by Dr. Stanley.
"Magic, Mimicry, and Mirth," by Prof. Aitchjaydee.
Stereopticon Lecture, "Italy and Italian Lakes," by Prof. H. E. Northrop.
Musical and Dramatic Entertainment, by Misses Hollinger and Ives, Prof. S. J. MacWatters and Mr. Charles Myers, assisted by Hospital Orchestra.
Dancing parties, twenty-four evenings.
Fourth of July exercises.

Our list of entertainments would be incomplete if we failed to mention the exercises in commemoration of the Nation's birthday, and which likewise served to celebrate the American victory over the Spanish forces at Santiago. The programme opened at 9:30 A. M., with a concert on the lawn of vocal and instrumental music, the former of which consisted of patriotic songs, and the latter of national and popular airs rendered by an orchestra of eleven pieces. This was followed by athletic contests, in which prizes were offered to the successful contestants in order to increase the enthusiasm and interest. Following the award of prizes by the Master of Ceremonies, Dr. Duke, the usual refreshments were served to the entire household. A considerable part of the afternoon was pleasantly passed by patients and attendants in witnessing a game of base ball. At 7 o'clock in the evening there was a bicycle parade, in which sixty-five riders took part, all of whom were in fancy costume and with their wheels tastefully decorated. A display of fireworks closed the festivities of the day, which was keenly enjoyed by everyone whose condition permitted them to be present. It is a matter for congratulation that, although enthusiasm ran high, everything passed off quietly and without accidents and escapes. It is no small matter to control a crowd of such dimensions, composed of both sexes, when out upon the grounds in the enjoyment of unusual freedom and excitement, and keep them good-natured, orderly, and happy. During the display of the fireworks nearly nine hundred patients were out upon the lawn and not a single escape occurred or was attempted. The day was certainly one which will be long and pleasantly remembered by the patients of the Connecticut Hospital for the Insane.

Reading matter, especially illustrated periodicals, are always acceptable, a fact which has apparently been realized by the numerous friends of the hospital who contribute them, some of whom still regard it of greater importance that good deeds should be done than that the author should be known. We can, however, express our sense of obligation for the following contributions:

DONATIONS.

Illustrated papers and magazines, by Mrs. Andrew D. Clark, Mrs. F. E. B. Nichols, Mrs. Andrew Brown, Mr. L. R. Hazen, Mr. and Mrs. Durfee, Mrs. O. V. Coffin, Mrs. E. E. Smith, Rev. H. A. Starks.

Religious papers, by Prof. Wm. North Rice, Mrs. Nellie Christenson, Mrs. Lydia J. Persons.

Agricultural reports, by Mr. T. S. Gold.

Melodeon, by Dr. H. S. Noble.

Number of palms and other valuable plants, by Jos. S. Smith, of Norwich.

DONATIONS FOR FOURTH OF JULY.

One box of cigars, by Mr. R. M. Seyms.
Two drinking cups, by Mr. Henry Woodward.
One pair sleeve buttons, by Horseford & Rothschild.
One bicycle suit, Willis & Wilson.
Cash, $5, Stoddard & Kimberly.

Copies of the following papers have been mailed to the hospital regularly, for which we tender to the publishers our grateful acknowledgments:

The Courant, daily, Hartford.
The Times, weekly, Hartford.
The Religious Herald, weekly, Hartford.
The Connecticut Catholic, weekly, Hartford.
The Morning News, daily; New Haven.
The Tolland County Journal, weekly, Rockville.
The Standard, weekly, Bridgeport.

It has been customary in previous reports of the hospital to mention changes in the *personnel* of the Medical Staff. Through the favor of a kind Providence it has heretofore been necessary on only one occasion to record the solemn fact that the last great change, the birthright of all mankind, had come to one of our fraternity of co-workers. The death of a public servant to whose hands great and varied interests have been confided is an occasion of profound anxiety for those on whom his duties may chance to fall. In the death of Dr. Olmstead the hospital was deprived of an honest, faithful, conscientious head. Dr. Jessie M. Weston resigned her position on the medical staff, June 1st, 1897, and the vacancy thus created remains unfilled. Shortly after the death of Dr. Olmstead your Finance Committee empowered the Acting Superintendent to employ such temporary medical assistance as the emergency required, and Dr. Ross E. Savage, of Bristol, N. H., was called to assume the duties of Junior Assistant, and still remains. The other members of the medical staff continue at their several posts of duty, and their long experience and familiarity with the routine of the institution have enabled them to render invaluable service in carrying on the work of the hospital, for which I desire to express my thankfulness and appreciation. Your faithful and competent Matron, Supervisors, and heads of the various departments continue at their respective posts of duty, and contribute in no small measure to the successful administration of this great charity.

The preceding statements, and comments upon the operations of the hospital for the past two years, were written by Dr. Henry S. Noble, Assistant Superintendent, who is personally familiar with the facts from his long-time connection with the hospital, and who most successfully managed its affairs from the date of Dr. Olmstead's retirement in November, 1897, until September 1, 1898, one month ago, at which time I assumed the duties of Superintendent.

At the commencement of my administration it seems important to consider the present condition of the hospital, anticipate its future, reaffirm the policy that is to guide its management, and to adopt a comprehensive scheme of organization, and possible expansion, before taking any decisive steps in the way of changes or additions. This survey of the hospital conditions is presented with a clear conception of the time and expense involved in the changes proposed, and without expectation that they must, or can, be readily accomplished. But when a definite plan, sufficiently broad to embrace the whole institution, has been decided upon, single lines of progress can be undertaken, and operations can commence at various points, and yet when ultimately completed the several parts will present the desired relation to each other, and the whole will constitute a unified establishment.

It is plain to see that this hospital has outgrown the lines of organization upon which it was founded. At the time it was established leading authorities upon lunatic hospital construction advocated small hospitals for the insane. They insisted upon restricting the number of patients, so the medical superintendent could personally direct the treatment and management of each case.

But such ideal hospitals have seldom existed long in any State, because the increase of insanity at large has forced overcrowding and additions until the large institution is now the rule.

The supposed advantages of the small hospital have never been lost sight of by the past management of this institution, and the enlargements, that from time to time have been made here, have been made under protest, and were calculated to provide little beyond immediate requirements. Naturally, under such conditions, a complex system of organization and management has resulted.

Considering this state of affairs and the probable demand for still further enlargement, radical changes in the classification of patients, and the introduction of some new features of treatment, and management, seem desirable. The various annexes and secondary hospitals, which from time to time have been erected upon the hospital grounds, are in the main very well located and adapted for the desired reorganization.

The acute and curable cases should be so assembled that special care, study, and treatment can be given them. They should have the benefit of special medical oversight, be placed in wards equipped and managed in accordance with hospital ideas. Trained female nurses should be employed not only in the women's department, but to a considerable extent in the male wards.

Apparatus for hydrotherapy should be provided, and a convenient laboratory for both clinical and pathological work should be added. In fact, no legitimate expense should be spared in efforts to restore to health and reason all cases having a prospect of recovery.

The number of patients requiring such special treatment is comparatively small, but it is difficult to give them the requisite attention in the wards of the large central hospital, associated as they necessarily are with a much larger number of chronic cases.

For various reasons it seems best to make use of the North Hospital for the reception and treatment of acute, curable and interesting cases. It is much smaller than the Main building, and yet amply large to accommodate all the acute cases. It occupies the most prominent and sightly position on the hospital grounds. Besides, it is nearest the city, and most easily accessible from the car station and the street. Some interior alterations and improvements will be required to best fit the buildings for the purposes suggested, and eventually some additions may be considered necessary.

An assistant physician with special training in pathology should be employed to combine clinical observation with pathological investigation. Such an officer can accomplish little without a full laboratory equipment, and I would recommend that the ground floor of the south addition to the North Hospital be re-arranged as a laboratory, and that the necessary fixtures, library, instruments, chemicals, etc., be purchased.

The dormitory at the east end, with additional windows and interior changes, would make a good room for microscopical work. Other small rooms in that end of the ward would accommodate bacteriological work, electric, photographic, and other apparatus. One small dark room would be required for ophthalmic examinations and developing photographs, and the bath room could be easily converted into a chemical laboratory.

At the west end of the ward the sleeping rooms could be fitted with hydriatric apparatus, douche room, needle bath, hot air cabinets, etc., etc., all of which are quite requisite for the successful treatment of nervous invalids. The day room is remarkably well adapted to the purposes of a lecture room, where the medical staff meeting could be daily held for the discussion of cases, and where lectures to training school pupils and medical students could be given.

If the acute and curable cases are provided for, and treated, in the North Hospital, there will remain a considerable number of chronic patients that require careful medical supervision. The turbulent, the noisy, the destructive, the habitually untidy and the physically infirm should also be placed in quarters specially adapted to their condition, and such accommodations should be apart from other wards of the hospital.

The South Hospital, by reason of its outlying position, should be utilized for the care of such cases. Minor alterations and improvements in the wards will be required to adapt them to the new classification. Some wards will need to be made a little more secure—double doors and double windows should be provided for a number of rooms, and possibly additional dormitory space will be required, since the patients we propose to treat there should be watched at night as well as by day, and large dormitories facilitate careful supervision at night.

Utilizing the North Hospital and the South Hospital as suggested, the Main Hospital, the Middle Hospital, and the Main Cottage will be left to provide for the larger number of the more quiet and able-bodied members of our permanent population.

As the capacity of the Main Hospital nearly equals the combined capacity of the other two buildings, it seems advisable to still further classify, by placing women only in the Main Hospital, and men only in the Middle Hospital and Main Cottage.

The patients thus centralized would require for the most part simply custodial care. They could be properly treated at less expense than other classes of patients; and yet the State, having seen fit to isolate them and circumscribe their liberties, is in duty bound to make their lives here as free from irritation and as full of cheer and natural interest as is consistent with their welfare, and is possible by a judicious expenditure of the funds received for their support. With the limited means at our command more could be accomplished in this direction by concentrating our efforts to favorably affect this class in a mass, rather than by treating them in small companies or as isolated individuals.

To further this very desirable object, a convenient and commodious daily meeting place should be provided. The Main Hospital, the Middle Hospital, and the Main Cottage are so grouped around an open space in the rear of the Main Hospital that the inmates of these buildings could conveniently meet for their meals in a large congregate dining room located on that square. Such a dining room should be located upon the second floor of the building, and be connected with the whole central group of hospital buildings by elevated passageways or bridges.

Much can be said in favor of large congregate dining rooms. The economy possible by concentrating labor and simplifying the distribution of food, both cooked and uncooked, is favored by large dining rooms; and the above proposition contemplates closing two large kitchens and twenty-three various sized dining rooms.

But the other phase of advantage in this plan, the humane purposes which it would subserve, ought to insure its adoption. The dining room should constitute the heart of any institution as large as this has become. It should be managed as the most vital spot in the organization—the point where the personal influence of the Superintendent could be most effectively applied, and the centre from which helpful influence would naturally radiate into the wards, cheering, stimulating, and toning up the whole institution. With such ends in view, the dining room should be light and airy, and should be made attractive by a profusion of growing plants, palms, ferns, and flowers, against the walls and about the tables. The tables should be spread with white cloths and ordinary table ware.

No food should be placed upon the tables until all the patients are seated, when it should be served in a systematic, orderly manner.

The size of the proposed room would present no obstacle to the rapid serving of food, but haste is to be avoided. While in a large dining room a single course could be served to all within five minutes, there should be waits between the courses, and a full hour should be allowed for the serving of dinner, and nearly as much time both for breakfast and supper.

Meantime there should be music from a well-drilled orchestra, such as nearly all large institutions maintain by selecting musical attendants. Piece after piece should be given at short intervals throughout the hour, and music of a high grade should be selected, as the best effect will follow the rendering of the finer varieties of music. One can readily understand that good music would be helpful in making an hour in an institution dining room pass quickly and agreeably with the nervous and the insane. But it would accomplish much more than that when used in connection with an attractive, well-appointed dining room.

The combined influence of such a dining room, with flowers and music, would promote self-control and self-respect. The ordinary monotony of institution life would be well-nigh abolished; the privilege of going regularly to meals in the dining room, depending, as it must, upon proper behavior there, would be so appreciated it would have a powerful influence with each individual for good, and thus there would be planted in the mind of each patient a healthful and constantly acting motive to right conduct, which is a great advance upon rules and coercive measures looking to the same end.

With the present number of patients under treatment and custody here, a large central congregate dining room should be erected to perfect the plan of reorganization, to centralize and simplify the distribution of food, to facilitate thorough supervision of both employés and patients, to promote the comfort of the patients and revive in them natural sentiments leading to self-respect and self-control.

And if the hospital is to provide accommodations for an increased number of patients, the large dining room becomes the first consideration. By no other plan could so many additional patients be provided for with a given sum of money. The twenty-three dining rooms now used in the central group of buildings, which could be converted into dormitories, would easily accommodate 250 additional beds. Then the large dining room would not only simplify the design and management of the hospital, but it would admit of extensive enlargement of the hospital without complicating or marring the unity of design which the proposed reorganization would establish.

South and east of the square upon which the dining room should be located there is ample room for several large buildings, which could be readily connected with the dining room by overhead passageways. The necessary day room and associate dormitories to accommodate a large number of patients could be provided in such buildings at a low cost rate per capita.

The location of a large congregate dining room on the second floor of a building is desirable for several reasons. When connected with the second story of the other buildings by covered bridges, it permits the passage of patients to and from their meals without interfering with the approaches to, or the ordinary business of, the hospital. It also minimizes the total amount of stair climbing required of the patients who assemble there from the various floors of the hospital. Besides, it insures a dry passage in stormy weather, and a safe passage at all times.

Then the basement story would be available for the more convenient location of various departments that should be close to the dining room. The kitchen, store rooms, vegetable cellar, milk and butter, meat and cold storage rooms should be established there. It being the most central and easily accessible place, it should also afford room for a large rain bath and swimming pool, which can displace, economically, the majority of ward bath rooms, thus increasing the rapidity, safety, and satisfaction with which the patients can be bathed.

The present kitchen for the Main Hospital is far from satisfactory as regards space, fixture, and their arrangement. The room it now occupies is greatly needed by the bakery, which should have more convenient and more suitable storage room than it now has for flour, meal, bread, etc. If, after providing for a new kitchen and store room on the ground floor, under the proposed dining room, sufficient space remains to accommodate the laundry, that could be advantageously relocated there, and the present laundry building could be utilized for a large central sewing room, where dry goods and clothing could be stored and where wearing apparel, bedding, etc., could be made for the whole institution, by a large force of patients under competent supervision.

If the present store room be vacated, the ground floor of that building can be used as a meeting place, or sort of club room, for employés. There is a large force of employés connected with the hospital. The rules regarding their service and conduct are quite strict. The management has always recognized the importance of giving the employés some respite from the exacting duties required of them, some hours of freedom as often as convenient, but it has not provided a suitable recreation room for them. "Off duty," under present circumstances, does not mean recreation, or change of scene, etc., unless the excused person goes into the city among strangers, and where the readiest welcome can be found in saloons.

If there were provided a reading room, a smoking room, and a larger room where general conversation, music, etc., could be enjoyed, the employés would not only spend their leisure time upon the premises, where they could be quickly found if unexpectedly required, and where they would escape the temptations of the city, but their self-respect would be fostered, and their services would be correspondingly more valuable to the institution.

By increasing the night service of the hospital, which will be my policy, all the day nurses and attendants can be excused from ward duty at least one hour each day. But relaxation from nervous strain, incident to their occupation, is in some degree dependent upon a convenient, well-appointed meeting place, and I submit, the hospital is in duty bound to provide something for its employés in the line suggested.

The second story of the old store-room building would make a good sleeping place for the outside men, while the upper story of the laundry would afford similar accommodations for the outside female help, as it does at present.

The future development and economical success of the institution depends so much upon the large dining room and the re-location of the several domestic departments, a plan of such a building with the estimated cost has been prepared.

In order to be sure of ample space for the present needs and permit of a prospective increase in the number of patients for several years to come, a dining room 100 by 250 feet has been designed; and in order to provide the necessary room on the ground floor for the different departments as suggested, the first story has been extended on both sides of the building. In building a room where 1,500 patients are to be assembled three hours each day, every possible precaution against fire should be taken; especially is provision to avoid fire necessary where that room is located above a large kitchen and laundry.

The cost of brick walls, steel frame and granolithic floors, is now sufficiently reasonable to warrant such construction, and the estimated cost of the proposed building ($75,000) is based upon figures made by the Berlin Iron Bridge Co., the Eastern Expanded Metal Co., and Messrs. Curtis & Johnson, the architects, who have made a sketch and calculated the cost of foundations, brick work, roofs, etc.

The figures given do not cover cost of the elevated passage-ways, cold storage, and the necessary heating apparatus; to furnish which will probably bring the whole cost up to $100,000. Then there will be considerable expense for extras which have not been carefully considered in the hasty sketch submitted.

The importance of a more or less complete electric plant will be pressing if we attempt to re-locate machinery. Not only should the power required in the various departments, laundry, kitchen, carpenter shop, etc., be distributed by electricity from a central power station, but exhaust fans for ventilation purposes are needed to a considerable extent in each group of buildings, and electric power is absolutely necessary in driving such fans. If electricity were adopted for motive power by day, the same machinery would generate electricity for lights at night. Expert mechanics agree that where steam is required for heating purposes, power for generating electricity can be gotten from that steam before it goes into the heating system, with little, if any, extra cost for the work it can be made to do in an engine. In this institution some 5,000 tons of coal are consumed annually for heating purposes, and it would certainly be a decided economy to get some power as well as heat out of that coal.   An electric plant such as is required here would cost from $15,000 to $20,000.

Summing up the cost of these several propositions, it appears that at least $125,000 should be expended for the new building, electric plant, etc., as soon as the work could be performed.   It is impossible for the hospital to accomplish the needed changes without a special appropriation from the State.

I would therefore recommend that the State Legislature be petitioned for $100,000, to be expended upon the new buildings as herein suggested.   The additional $25,000 can probably be taken from the hospital treasury within twelve months with safety, but I think that sum the maximum amount that can be prudently expended from the hospital treasury for construction the coming year.

The cost of the proposed laboratory, with fixtures, equipments, etc., at the North Hospital, will be about $5,000.

The Hubbard Cottage should be renovated and altered over to provide a home for the North Hospital nurses, and the Roberts Cottage should be treated in the same way to accommodate the South Hospital nurses.

Other repairs and alterations, incident to the plan of reorganization, will draw heavily upon the hospital resources the next two years, and, in my opinion, it would be decidedly unsafe to reduce the Treasurer's balance below $50,000.   If after having depleted the hospital treasury, some accident or unforeseen emergency should require the immediate use of funds, the hospital would be in a crippled condition—especially so, since the Trustees have no authority to borrow money for the State, and the Legislature meets but once in two years. An extra session of the Legislature called to provide funds for an exhausted hospital treasury, would unfortunately add greatly to the financial burdens of the State.

In conclusion, I wish to thank your Board for the honor it has conferred upon me by trusting to my hands such extensive and vital interests as the management of this hospital involves.

Respectfully submitted,

CHARLES W. PAGE, M. D.,
Superintendent.

SEPTEMBER 30, 1898.

TABLE I.

GENERAL STATISTICS.

	1896–97.			1897–98.		
	Males.	Females.	Total.	Males.	Females.	Total.
Number at the beginning of the year,	846	936	1,782	865	963	1,828
Persons admitted in the year,	198	152	350	216	195	411
Total present in the year,	1,044	1,088	2,132	1,081	1,158	2,239
Discharged—Recovered,	42	30	72	30	31	61
Improved,	39	19	58	40	28	68
Stationary,	39	27	66	60	36	96
Died, - - - -	59	49	108	69	50	119
Remaining at the end of the year,	865	963	1,828	882	1,013	1,895
Average present during the year,	856.89	944.64	1,801.53	873.61	996.83	1,870.44

Received on First and Subsequent Admissions.

NUMBER OF THE ADMISSIONS.	1896–97.			1897–98.		
	Males.	Females.	Total.	Males.	Females.	Total.
First, - - -	168	122	290	174	156	330
Second, - - -	20	15	35	29	26	55
Third, - - -	7	9	16	5	4	9
Fourth, - - -	2	—	2	5	4	9
Fifth, - - -	1	3	4	2	5	7
Sixth, - - -	—	3	3	1	—	1
Seventh, - - -	—	—	—	—	—	—
Eighth, - - -	—	—	—	—	—	—
Ninth, - - -	—	—	—	—	—	—
Tenth, - - -	—	—	—	—	—	—
Total, - - -	198	152	350	216	195	411

TABLE II.

ADMISSIONS AND DISCHARGES SINCE THE OPENING OF THE
HOSPITAL, APRIL 30TH, 1868.

	MALES.	FEMALES.	TOTAL.
Cases admitted, - - - - -	4,492	3,954	8,446
Cases discharged—Recovered, - -	895	813	1,708
Improved, - -	704	546	1,250
Stationary, - -	874	674	1,548
Died, - - - - - - -	1,137	908	2,045

Average Number Present Each Year Since the Opening of the Hospital.

YEARS.	MALES.	FEMALES.	TOTAL.
1868–69, - - - - - -	79.35	6.12	85.47
1869–70, - - - - - -	110.63	114.54	225.17
1870–71, - - - - - -	115.97	117.72	233.69
1871–72, - - - - - -	124.21	118.44	242.65
1872–73, - - - - - -	132.11	132.43	264.54
1873–74, - - - - - -	146.43	193.29	339.72
1874–75, - - - - - -	198.54	227.19	425.73
1875–76, - - - - - -	225.60	227.02	452.62
1876—April 1st to November 30th, -	228.39	228.57	456.97
1876–77, - - - - - -	231.45	232.43	463.88
1877–78, - - - - - -	236.11	238.06	474.17
1878–79, - - - - - -	244.57	253.76	498.34
1879–80, - - - - - -	250.08	263.95	514.63
1880–81, - - - - - -	293.17	315.39	608.51
1881–82, - - - - - -	357.26	432.01	789.27
1882–83, - - - - - -	385.61	468.89	854.50
1883–84, - - - - - -	402.58	480.64	883.22
1884—December 1st to June 30th, 1885,	427.55	518.76	946.31
1885–86, - - - - - -	487.86	589.98	1,077.84
1886–87, - - - - - -	541.00	652.87	1,193.87
1887–88, - - - - - -	560.40	709.84	1,270.24
1888–89, - - - - - -	598.38	740.76	1,339.14
1889–90, - - - - - -	607.38	746.40	1,353.78
1890–91, - - - - - -	640.15	783.93	1,424.08
1891–92, - - - - - -	687.53	811.35	1,498.88
1892–93, - - - - - -	698.08	810.01	1,508.09
1893–94, - - - - - -	730.09	824.77	1,554.87
1894–95, - - - - - -	758.02	835.05	1,593.07
1895—July 1st to September 30th, 1896,	815.64	907.90	1,723.54
1896–97, - - - - - -	856.89	944.04	1,801.53
1897–98, - - - - - -	873.61	996.83	1,870.44

TABLE III.

AGES OF PATIENTS ADMITTED.

AGE.	1896–97.						1897–98.					
	When Admitted.			When Attacked.			When Admitted.			When Attacked.		
	M.	F.	T.	M.	F.	T.	M.	F.	T.	M.	F.	T.
Under 15, -	1	—	1	14	5	19	3	2	5	12	8	20
15 to 20, -	10	7	17	16	12	28	5	8	13	8	15	23
20 to 25, -	26	14	40	19	16	35	19	17	36	24	25	49
25 to 30, -	28	18	46	26	18	44	31	21	52	28	18	46
30 to 35, -	23	17	40	21	25	46	25	20	45	21	27	48
35 to 40, -	26	25	51	19	19	38	18	23	41	18	22	40
40 to 45, -	23	11	34	19	10	29	39	22	61	31	20	51
45 to 50, -	14	12	26	14	7	21	19	12	31	13	10	23
50 to 60, -	20	24	44	14	18	32	25	29	54	19	17	36
60 to 70, -	12	14	26	10	6	16	17	20	37	14	17	31
70 to 80, -	9	8	17	5	7	12	7	11	18	6	7	13
80 and over, -	3	2	5	—	1	1	3	8	11	3	2	5
Unknown, -	1	—	1	19	8	27	4	—	4	18	5	23
Not insane, -	2	—	2	2	—	2	1	2	3	1	2	3
Total, -	198	152	350	198	152	350	216	195	411	216	195	411

TABLE IV.

NUMBER AT EACH AGE SINCE THE OPENING OF THE HOSPITAL.

AGE.	WHEN ADMITTED.			WHEN ATTACKED.		
	Males.	Females.	Total.	Males.	Females.	Total.
Under 15, -	15	14	29	182	89	271
15 to 20, -	185	129	314	301	260	561
20 to 25, -	470	361	831	547	506	1,053
25 to 30, -	618	457	1,075	591	560	1,151
30 to 35, -	573	481	1,054	518	493	1,011
35 to 40, -	533	495	1,028	426	464	890
40 to 45, -	476	436	912	370	351	721
45 to 50, -	408	404	812	306	312	618
50 to 60, ' -	557	576	1,133	416	375	791
60 to 70, -	351	316	667	282	199	481
70 to 80, -	188	159	347	110	113	223
80 and over, -	52	82	134	24	35	59
Unknown, -	17	21	38	370	174	544
Not insane, -	49	23	72	49	23	72
Total, -	4,492	3,954	8,446	4,492	3,954	8,446

TABLE V.

NATIVITY OF PATIENTS ADMITTED.

NATIVITY.	1896–97.			1897–98.			Since the Opening.		
	Males.	Females.	Total.	Males.	Females.	Total.	Males.	Females.	Total.
Alabama, - - -	—	—	—	—	—	—	3	1	4
California, - - -	1	1	2	—	—	—	2	3	5
Connecticut, - -	107	58	165	98	89	187	2,347	1,698	4,045
Florida, - - -	—	—	—	—	—	—	2	—	2
Georgia, - - -	—	—	—	—	—	—	1	3	4
Illinois, - - -	—	—	—	—	—	—	1	3	4
Indiana, - - -	—	—	—	—	—	—	2	—	2
Iowa, - - -	—	—	—	—	—	—	2	—	2
Kansas, - - -	—	—	—	1	—	1	1	1	2
Kentucky, - - -	—	—	—	—	—	—	2	1	3
Louisiana, - - -	—	—	—	—	—	—	4	2	6
Maine, - - -	1	—	1	—	—	—	18	13	31
Maryland, - - -	—	—	—	1	—	1	7	6	13
Massachusetts, - -	5	2	7	8	6	14	131	88	219
Michigan, - - -	—	—	—	1	—	1	4	2	6
New Hampshire, -	—	—	—	—	1	1	9	6	15
New Jersey, - -	2	2	4	—	1	1	24	14	38
New York, - -	6	7	13	10	17	27	237	225	462
North Carolina, - -	1	—	1	2	—	2	14	3	17
Ohio, - - -	—	—	—	1	1	2	4	7	11
Pennsylvania, - -	1	1	2	3	—	3	26	17	43
Rhode Island, - -	—	—	—	2	2	4	48	26	74
South Carolina, - -	—	—	—	—	—	—	2	1	3
Tennessee, - -	—	—	—	—	—	—	3	—	3
Texas, - - -	—	1	1	—	—	—	—	2	2
Vermont, - - -	1	1	2	1	1	2	21	17	38
Virginia, - - -	—	1	1	—	1	1	20	21	41
Wisconsin, - - -	—	—	—	—	1	1	1	1	2
Austria, - - -	3	2	5	6	2	8	19	9	28
Bermuda, - - -	—	—	—	—	—	—	1	—	1
Canada, Dominion of,	1	3	4	9	3	12	87	49	136
China, - - -	—	—	—	1	—	1	1	—	1
Cuba, - - -	—	—	—	—	—	—	1	5	6
Denmark, - - -	2	—	2	1	—	1	12	6	18
England, - - -	7	8	15	7	3	10	148	141	289
France, - - -	1	—	1	—	—	—	10	11	21
Germany, - - -	8	11	19	14	16	30	222	240	462
Ireland, - - -	29	36	65	28	40	68	823	1,145	1,968
Italy, - - -	3	1	4	4	1	5	31	10	41
Japan, - - -	1	—	1	—	—	—	1	—	1
Norway, - - -	—	—	—	—	—	—	3	2	5
Russia, - - -	3	4	7	8	1	9	33	25	58
Scotland, - - -	—	1	1	1	3	4	23	30	53
Spain, - - -	—	—	—	—	—	—	6	—	6
Sweden, - - -	11	4	15	6	6	12	67	72	139
Switzerland, - -	1	2	3	—	—	—	12	6	18

TABLE V.—(Continued.)
NATIVITY OF PATIENTS ADMITTED.

NATIVITY.	1896–97.			1897–98.			SINCE THE OPENING.		
	Males.	Females.	Total.	Males.	Females.	Total.	Males.	Females.	Total.
Turkey, - - -	—	—	—	—	—	—	—	·1	1
Wales, - - -	—	2	2	1	—	1	6	3	· 9
West Indies, - -	—	—	—	—	—	—	—	1	1
Unknown, - - -	3	4	7	2	—	2	50	37	87
Total, - - -	198	152	350	216	195	411	4,492	3,954	8,446

TABLE VI.
RESIDENCE OF PATIENTS ADMITTED.

RESIDENCE.	1896–97.			1897–98.			SINCE THE OPENING.		
	Males.	Females.	Total.	Males.	Females.	Total.	Males.	Females.	Total.
State at Large, - -	29	4	33	26	2	28	478	39	517
Hartford County, -	47	42	89	50	41	91	918	892	1,810
New Haven County, -	56	44	100	50	62	112	1,157	1,153	2,310
New London County,	7	9	16	17	19	36	397	391	788
Windham County, -	3	10	13	11	4	15	143	156	299
Litchfield County, -	10	7	17	12	12	24	226	239	465
Middlesex County, -	12	11	23	7	16	23	363	356	719
Tolland County, -	8	3	11	2	6	8	113	128	241
Fairfield County, -	26	22	48	41	33	74	687	598	1,285
Elsewhere, - - -	—	—	—	—	—	—	10	2	12
Total, - -	198	152	350	216	195	411	4,492	3,954	8,446

TABLE VII.
OCCUPATION OF THOSE ADMITTED.

OCCUPATION.	1896–97.			1897–98.			SINCE THE OPENING.		
	Males.	Females.	Total.	Males.	Females.	Total.	Males.	Females.	Total.
Accountants,	2	—	2	3	—	3	44	—	44
Actors,	—	—	—	—	—	—	3	3	6
Agents,	1	—	1	1	1	2	49	1	50
Artists,	—	—	—	2	—	2	10	1	11
Brokers,	—	—	—	—	—	—	3	—	3
Clerks,	2	—	2	5	1	6	99	4	103
Clergymen,	1	—	1	—	—	—	16	—	16
Dentists,	—	—	—	—	—	—	6	—	6
Domestics,	—	28	28	—	27	27	—	707	707
Druggists, -	—	—	—	1	—	1	19	—	19
Factory employés,	11	10	21	3	10	13	405	285	690
Farmers,	29	—	29	26	—	26	717	—	717
Fishermen,	—	—	—	—	—	—	11	—	11
Housekeepers,	—	5	5	—	8	8	—	237	237
Housewives,	—	58	58	—	85	85	—	1,620	1,620
Journalists,	—	—	—	—	—	—	4	—	4
Laborers, -	52	—	52	51	—	51	1,047	—	1,047
Landlords,	—	—	—	—	—	—	6	—	6
Lawyers, -	—	—	—	2	—	2	10	—	10
Machinists,	11	—	11	11	—	11	140	—	140
Manufacturers,	—	—	—	2	—	2	31	—	31
Mechanics,	6	—	6	3	—	3	450	—	450
Merchants,	—	—	—	3	—	3	92	1	93
Newsboys,	—	—	—	—	—	—	8	—	8
No employment,	23	35	58	31	44	75	335	736	1,071
Nurses,	—	3	3	—	1	1	—	18	18
Peddlers, -	2	—	2	1	—	1	19	1	20
Physicians,	—	—	—	—	—	—	16	—	16
Railroad employés,	3	—	3	3	—	3	62	—	62
Sailors,	1	—	1	2	—	2	59	—	59
Saloon keepers, -	1	—	1	3	—	3	30	1	31
Speculators,	—	—	—	—	—	—	2	—	2
Soldiers,	—	—	—	—	—	—	2	—	2
Students, -	1	1	2	—	2	2	27	32	59
The trades,	45	4	49	55	12	67	616	146	762
Teachers, -	—	5	5	1	3	4	20	98	118
Teamsters,	3	—	3	4	—	4	78	—	78
Telegraph operators, -	1	—	1	—	1	1	5	1	6
Unknown, -	—	2	2	2	—	2	36	61	97
Undertakers,	—	—	—	—	—	—	1	—	1
Waiters,	3	1	4	1	—	1	14	1	15
Total,	198	152	350	216	195	411	4,492	3,954	8,446

TABLE VIII.
CIVIL CONDITION OF THOSE ADMITTED.

	1896–97.			1897–98.			Since the Opening.		
	Males.	Females.	Total.	Males.	Females.	Total.	Males.	Females.	Total.
Single, - - - -	108	65	173	120	66	186	2,281	1,544	3,825
Married, - - - -	72	63	135	84	95	179	1,813	1,758	3,571
Widowed, - - -	16	24	40	12	34	46	327	606	933
Unknown, - - -	2	—	2	—	—	—	71	46	117
Total, - - -	198	152	350	216	195	411	4,492	3,954	8,446

TABLE IX.
HOW COMMITTED.

	1896–97.			1897–98.			Since the Opening.		
	Males.	Females.	Total.	Males.	Females.	Total.	Males.	Females.	Total.
By Friends, - - -	—	—	—	—	—	—	138	107	245
Probate Judges, - -	158	148	306	183	192	375	3,704	3,788	7,492
Judges of Superior Court,	5	—	5	3	1	4	190	15	205
Governor's Orders, - -	16	2	18	15	1	16	164	14	178
Soldiers' Hospital Board,	5	—	5	1	—	1	126	—	126
Justice or Police Courts, -	10	1	11	12	1	13	125	27	152
Order of General Assembly,	—	—	—	—	—	—	1	1	2
County Commissioners, -	4	1	5	2	—	2	44	2	46
Total, - - -	198	152	350	216	195	411	4,492	3,954	8,446

TABLE X.
HOW SUPPORTED.

	1896–97.			1897–98.			Since the Opening.		
	Males.	Females.	Total.	Males.	Females.	Total.	Males.	Females.	Total.
By Self or Friends (paying),	1	—	1	2	—	2	164	123	287
State and Friends (indigent),	55	67	122	63	73	136	1,531	1,793	3,324
State and Town (pauper),	113	82	195	125	122	247	2,296	2,001	4,297
State alone, - - -	29	3	32	26	—	26	501	37	538
Total, - - -	198	152	350	216	195	411	4,492	3,954	8,446

TABLE XI.

FORM OF DISEASE OF THOSE ADMITTED.

FORMS OF DISEASE.	1896-97.			1897-98.			SINCE THE OPENING.		
	Males.	Females.	Total.	Males.	Females.	Total.	Males.	Females.	Total.
Mania—Acute, - -	31	22	53	16	16	32	924	748	1,672
Sub-acute, -	—	—	—	—	—	—	20	7	27
Chronic, -	31	31	62	17	47	64	1,019	1,110	2,129
Melancholia—Acute, -	50	30	80	55	32	87	706	674	1,380
Chronic,	23	12	35	41	24	65	375	333	708
Attonita,	—	—	—	—	—	—	7	7	14
Dementia—Acute, -	1	—	1	—	—	—	30	20	50
Chronic, -	7	10	17	2	19	21	194	257	451
Organic, -	3	2	5	8	4	12	59	37	96
Epileptic Insanity, -	10	3	13	13	6	19	243	125	368
Hysterical " -	—	—	—	—	—	—	—	16	16
Neurasthenic " . -	—	1	1	—	—	—	2	5	7
Puerperal " -	—	3	3	—	4	4	—	97	97
Recurrent " -	3	9	12	6	11	17	93	128	221
Senile " -	11	13	24	17	18	35	183	221	404
Toxic " -	9	5	14	9	4	13	205	42	247
Paranoia, - - -	3	6	9	4	1	5	76	17	93
General Paresis, - -	8	—	8	20	—	20	174	23	197
Imbecility, - - -	6	5	11	7	7	14	133	64	197
Not Insane, - -	2	—	2	1	2	3	49	23	72
Total, - -	198	152	350	216	195	411	4,492	3,954	8,446

TABLE XII.

COMPLICATIONS (OF NERVOUS SYSTEM) IN THOSE ADMITTED.

COMPLICATIONS.	1896–97.			1897–98.			SINCE THE OPENING.		
	Males.	Females.	Total.	Males.	Females.	Total.	Males.	Females.	Total.
Aphasia, - - -	—	—	—	—	—	—	7	—	7
Apoplexy, - - -	1	2	3	7	3	10	44	24	68
Chorea, - - -	—	—	—	—	1	1	17	15	32
Epilepsy, - - -	10	3	13	13	6	19	245	125	370
Hemiplegia, - -	1	2	3	—	3	3	19	29	48
Hysteria, - - -	—	3	3	—	3	3	—	42	42
Hereditary tendency, -	45	56	101	29	65	94	992	986	1,978
Neuritis, alcoholic, -	—	—	—	1	—	1	5	2	7
Paraplegia, - -	—	—	—	—	1	1	10	6	16
Paralysis agitans, -	—	—	—	—	—	—	1	1	2
Pseudo - hypertrophic } paralysis, - - }	—	—	—	—	—	—	—	1	1
Progressive muscular } atrophy, - - - }	—	—	—	—	—	—	1	1	2
Spinal paralysis, -	—	—	—	—	—	—	3	—	3
Syphilis, - - -	—	2	2	2	1	3	21	27	48
Without complications,	141	84	225	164	112	276	3,127	2,695	5,822
Total, - - -	198	152	350	216	195	411	4,492	3,954	8,446

TABLE XIII.

NUMBER OF ATTACKS IN THOSE ADMITTED.

ATTACK.	1896–97.			1897–98.			SINCE THE OPENING.		
	Males.	Females.	Total.	Males.	Females.	Total.	Males.	Females.	Total.
First, - - -	163	125	288	182	173	355	3,383	3,121	6,504
Second, - - -	14	13	27	12	9	21	402	406	808
Third, - - -	2	3	5	4	4	8	105	124	229
Fourth, - - -	1	2	3	3	2	5	50	49	99
Fifth, - - -	1	3	4	2	1	3	22	34	56
Sixth, - - -	1	—	1	2	—	2	15	15	30
Seventh, - - -	—	—	—	—	—	—	7	6	13
Eighth, - - -	—	—	—	—	1	1	2	9	11
Several, - - -	1	—	1	—	—	—	78	22	100
Unknown, - - -	13	6	19	10	3	13	379	145	524
Not insane, - -	2	—	2	1	2	3	49	23	72
Total, - - -	198	152	350	216	195	411	4,492	3,954	8,446

TABLE XIV.

DURATION OF INSANITY BEFORE ENTRANCE OF THOSE
ADMITTED.

DURATION.	1896–97.			1897–98.			SINCE THE OPENING.		
	Males.	Females.	Total.	Males.	Females.	Total.	Males.	Females.	Total.
Less than 1 month, -	15	7	22	19	18	37	527	503	1,030
1 to 3 months, - -	34	21	55	38	16	54	630	459	1,089
3 to 6 " - -	25	17	42	20	8	28	439	371	810
6 to 9 " - -	15	7	22	13	12	25	288	237	525
9 to 12 " - -	6	4	10	8	2	10	149	106	255
12 to 18 " - -	19	12	31	15	17	32	359	320	679
18 to 24 " - -	4	3	7	15	4	19	139	112	351
2 to 3 years, - -	19	15	34	16	15	31	374	341	715
3 to 5 " - -	11	14	25	19	21	40	344	390	734
5 to 10 " - -	10	22	32	9	44	53	347	427	774
10 to 15 " - -	8	5	13	9	11	20	192	187	379
15 to 20 " - -	5	5	10	6	7	13	100	104	204
20 to 25 " - -	3	9	12	7	2	9	63	67	130
25 to 30 " - -	2	2	4	—	2	2	43	32	75
30 and over, - -	3	—	3	2	7	9	48	80	128
Unknown, - - -	17	9	26	19	7	26	401	195	596
Not insane, - - -	2	—	2	1	2	3	49	23	72
Total, - - -	198	152	350	216	195	411	4,492	3,954	8,446

TABLE XV.

CAUSES OF INSANITY IN THOSE ADMITTED.

CAUSES ALLEGED.	1896–97. Males.	1896–97. Females.	1896–97. Total.	1897–98. Males.	1897–98. Females.	1897–98. Total.	Since the Opening. Males.	Since the Opening. Females.	Since the Opening. Total.
Anxiety of mind, - -	3	2	5	3	6	9	161	82	243
Arsenic habit, - - -	—	—	—	—	—	—	—	1	1
Abortion, - - -	—	1	1	—	—	—	—	10	10
Apoplexy, - - -	1	2	3	5	3	8	58	28	86
Cerebral tumor, - -	—	—	—	—	—	—	1	—	1
Cerebro-spinal meningitis,	—	—	—	—	—	—	—	8	8
Confinement, - - -	1	—	1	—	—	—	20	—	20
Chloral habit, - - -	—	—	—	—	—	—	—	1	1
Congenital defect, - -	6	4	10	6	4	10	71	33	104
Connected with the affections	4	5	9	5	10	15	108	216	324
Domestic difficulties, -	1	4	5	1	3	4	36	111	147
Diabetes mellitus, - -	—	—	—	—	—	—	—	1	1
Dissipation, - - -	—	—	—	—	—	—	12	11	23
Epilepsy, - - -	10	3	13	11	6	17	218	124	342
Excessive venery, - -	1	—	1	1	—	1	24	1	25
Fluctuations of fortune, -	1	1	2	4	3	7	70	31	101
Fevers, - - ·- -	3	—	3	—	2	2	22	25	47
Hysteria, - - -	—	—	—	—	1	1	—	20	20
Ill health, - - -	3	9	12	1	5	6	217	360	577
Influenza, - - -	1	—	1	3	1	4	10	7	17
Injuries to head and spine,	6	2	8	10	5	15	124	21	145
Intemperance, - -	28	6	34	44	9	53	712	158	870
Masturbation, - - -	2	1	3	5	1	6	193	37	230
Menopausis, - - -	—	5	5	—	3	3	—	94	94
Menstruation, disorders of,	—	—	—	—	—	—	—	24	24
Meningitis, - - -	—	—	—	—	—	—	—	4	4
Nervous shock, - -	—	1	1	—	1	1	11	16	27
Nostalgia, · · ·	—	—	—	—	—	—	4	7	11
Not insane, - - -	2	—	2	1	2	3	49	23	72
Old age, - - - -	9	13	22	7	15	22	121	169	290
Over-study, - · - -	—	—	—	—	—	—	16	21	37
Opium habit, - - -	—	2	2	—	2	2	10	21	31
Over-work, - - -	2	6	8	3	4	7	103	136	239
Partial insolation, - -	2	—	2	4	1	5	60	6	66
Phthisis pulmonalis, -	—	—	—	—	—	—	2	5	7
Puerperal state, pregnancy, etc., - - -	—	4	4	—	11	11	—	174	174
Religion, ⸱ - -	2	1	3	—	2	2	50	68	118
Syphilis, - - -	—	2	2	4	—	4	30	25	55
Tobacco, - - -	1	—	1	—	—	—	13	—	13
Tuberculosis, - - -	—	—	—	—	—	—	1	—	1
Uterine disease, - -	—	2	2	—	1	1	—	43	43
Starvation and privation,	1	1	2	—	2	2	2	15	17
Unknown, - - -	108	75	183	98	92	190	1,963	1,817	3,780
Total, - - -	198	152	350	216	195	411	4,492	3,954	8,446

TABLE XVI.

RECOVERED OF THOSE ATTACKED AT THE SEVERAL AGES
SINCE THE OPENING OF THE HOSPITAL.

AGE WHEN ATTACKED.	NUMBER RECOVERED.			PER CENT. RECOVERED.		
	Males.	Females.	Total.	Males.	Females.	Total.
Under 15, - - -	—	4	4	—	4.49	1.48
15 to 20, - - -	55	55	110	18.23	21.15	19.60
20 to 25, - - -	126	125	251	23.03	24.60	23.82
25 to 30, - - -	124	117	241	20.98	20.89	20.76
30 to 35, - - -	138	112	250	26.64	24.74	24.72
35 to 40, - - -	120	106	226	28.16	22.83	25.39
40 to 45, - - -	95	86	181	22.97	21.65	25.10
45 to 50, - - -	83	64	147	27.12	20.51	23.78
50 to 60, - - -	87	103	190	20.91	27.46	24.62
60 to 70, - - -	55	34	89	19.14	17.08	18.10
70 to 80, - - -	10	6	16	9.09	5.30	7.17
Over 80, - - -	2	1	3	8.33	2.08	5.08
Total, - - -	895	813	1,708	—	—	—

TABLE XVII.

RECOVERED AFTER VARIOUS DURATIONS OF DISEASE
BEFORE TREATMENT SINCE THE OPENING.

DURATION.	NUMBER RECOVERED.			PER CENT. RECOVERED.		
	Males.	Females.	Total.	Males.	Females.	Total.
Under 1 month, - -	281	253	534	53.32	50.94	51.74
1 to 3 months, - -	240	215	455	38.09	46.60	41.80
3 to 6 " - -	138	149	287	31.43	40.16	35.43
6 to 9 " - -	68	62	130	20.13	26.16	24.76
9 to 12 " - -	50	24	74	32.21	22.64	29.01
1 to 2 years, - -	59	56	115	11.92	12.98	11.16
2 to 3 " - -	37	21	58	9.89	6.15	8.11
3 to 5 " - -	13	17	30	3.75	4.35	4.08
5 to 10 " - -	5	10	15	1.44	2.34	1.93
Over 10 " - -	4	6	10	.61	.89	.66
Total, - - -	895	813	1,708	—	—	—

TABLE XVIII.

DURATION OF TREATMENT OF THOSE RECOVERED SINCE
THE OPENING.

DURATION.	NUMBER RECOVERED.		
	Males.	Females.	Total.
Under 1 month, - - - -	91	34	125
1 to 2 months, - - - -	162	89	251
2 to 3 " - - - -	134	140	274
3 to 6 " - - - -	217	247	464
6 to 9 " - - - -	104	105	209
9 to 12 " - - - -	66	62	128
12 to 18 " - - - -	54	55	109
18 to 24 " - - - -	16	25	41
2 to 3 years, - - - -	28	24	52
3 to 5 " - - - -	17	20	37
Over 5 " - - - -	6	12	18
Total, - - - - - -	895	813	1,708
Average duration of all, - -	6.65 + mos.	8.09 + mos.	7.53 + mos.

TABLE XIX.

DURATION OF DISEASE OF THOSE RECOVERED SINCE THE
OPENING.

DURATION.	NUMBER RECOVERED.		
	Males.	Females.	Total.
Under 1 month, - - - -	40	13	53
1 to 2 months, - - - -	93	34	127
2 to 3 " - - - -	83	51	134
3 to 6 " - - - -	164	214	378
6 to 9 " - - - -	136	154	290
9 to 12 " - - - -	99	103	202
12 to 18 " - - - -	108	81	189
18 to 24 " - - - -	47	41	88
2 to 3 years, - - - -	66	49	115
3 to 5 " - - - -	40	39	79
Over 5 " - - - -	19	34	53
Total, - - - - -	895	813	1,708
Average duration of all, - -	11.84 + mos.	13.63 + mos.	12.72 + mos.

TABLE XX.

FORM OF DISEASE OF THOSE RECOVERED SINCE THE OPENING.

DISEASE.	NUMBER RECOVERED.			PER CENT. RECOVERED OF EACH FORM ADMITTED.		
	Males.	Females.	Total.	Males.	Females.	Total.
Mania—Acute, - - -	426	311	737	46.10	40.24	44.07
Sub-acute, - -	20	2	22	100.00	28.56	81.48
Chronic, - -	60	90	150	5.00	8.10	7.04
Melancholia—Acute, -	252	222	474	35.83	32.93	34.34
Chronic, -	57	71	128	15.20	21.02	18.07
Attonita, -	—	1	1	—	14.28	7.14
Dementia—Acute, - -	6	5	11	20.00	25.00	22.00
Epileptic Insanity, - -	4	1	5	1.64	.80	1.35
Hysterical " - -	—	9	9	—	56.25	56.25
Neurasthenic " - -	1	3	4	50.00	60.00	57.14
Puerperal " - -	—	59	59	—	60.82	60.82
Recurrent " - -	38	31	69	40.86	24.37	31.17
Toxic " - -	31	8	39	14.63	19.04	15.79
Total, - - -	895	813	1,708	—	—	—

TABLE XXI.

CAUSES (EXCITING) OF DISEASE OF THOSE RECOVERED SINCE THE OPENING.

CAUSES.	NUMBER RECOVERED.			PER CENT. RECOVERED OF EACH FORM ADMITTED.		
	Males.	Females.	Total.	Males.	Females.	Total.
Abortion, - - - -	—	2	2	—	20.00	20.00
Anxiety of mind, - -	45	30	75	37.95	36.59	37.24
Connected with the affections,	40	57	97	37.03	26.38	31.21
Connected with fluctuations } of fortune, - - - }	19	6	25	27.42	19.35	24.75
Connected with religion, -	21	21	42	42.00	30.88	35.59
Domestic difficulties, -	11	29	40	30.55	27.27	27.21
Epilepsy, - - - -	4	1	5	1.83	.80	1.43
Excessive venery, - -	6	—	6	25.00	—	20.00
Fevers, - - - -	7	2	9	31.81	8.00	17.02
Ill health, - - - -	54	94	148	24.88	26.11	25.66
Intemperance, - -	207	46	253	29.21	12.77	29.08
Injuries to nervous system,	23	7	30	18.54	33.33	20.68
Masturbation, - - -	27	7	34	14.98	18.91	14.65
Menopausis, - - -	—	14	14	—	14.89	14.89
Nostalgia, - - -	—	1	1	—	•14.28	9.09
Over-study, - - -	4	4	8	25.00	19.04	21.62
Partial insolation, - -	7	—	7	11.66	—	10.60
Puerperal state,pregnancy,etc.	—	75	75	—	43.10	43.10
Tobacco, - - - -	4	—	4	30.76	—	30.76
Confinement, - - -	10	—	10	50.00	—	50.00
Over-work, - - -	25	36	61	24.27	26.17	25.52
Syphilis, - - - -	1	5	6	3,33	20.00	10.90
Opium, - - - -	1	5	6	10.00	23.80	19.35
Starvation and privation, -	—	4	4	—	26.66	23.52
Unknown, - - -	379	367	746	19.30	20.18	19.37
Total, - - -	895	813	1,708	—	—	—

TABLE XXII.
AGES AT DEATH.

AGE.	1896–97.			1897–98.			SINCE THE OPENING.		
	Males.	Females.	Total.	Males.	Females.	Total.	Males.	Females.	Total.
Under 15, - - - -	—	—	—	—	—	—	—	1	1
15 to 20, - - - -	—	—	—	—	—	—	11	10	21
20 to 25, - - - -	1	—	1	1	2	3	31	26	57
25 to 30, - - - -	3	2	5	2	2	4	56	46	102
30 to 35, - - - -	1	2	3	10	2	12	79	49	128
35 to 40, - - - -	4	2	6	5	3	8	115	87	202
40 to 45, - - - -	6	2	8	9	3	12	124	64	188
45 to 50, - - - -	3	5	8	10	5	15	114	91	205
50 to 60, - - - -	11	9	20	9	7	16	200	169	369
60 to 70, - - - -	9	16	25	12	8	20	203	145	348
70 to 80, - - - -	14	7	21	7	16	23	142	148	290
80 to 90, - - - -	7	2	9	3	2	5	60	61	121
Over 90, - - - -	—	2	2	1	—	1	2	11	13
Total, - - -	59	49	108	69	50	119	1,137	908	2,045

TABLE XXIII.
DEATHS AND THE CAUSES.

CAUSES.	1896–97.			1897–98.			SINCE THE OPENING.		
	Males.	Females.	Total.	Males.	Females.	Total.	Males.	Females.	Total.
Abscess, lumbar, - -	—	—	—	—	—	—	—	1	1
Abscess, lungs, -	1	—	1	—	—	—	2	—	2
Abscess, tonsils, - -	—	—	—	—	—	—	1	—	1
Aneurism, aorta, - -	—	—	—	—	=	—	1	—	1
Aneurism, carotid, - -	—	—	—	—	—	—	—	1	1
Arteritis, chronic (atheromatous), - - - -	3	1	4	—	3	3	17	11	28
Arteritis, chronic (osseous),	—	—	—	—	—	—	1	—	1
Arteritis, chronic (aneurismal),	—	—	—	—	—	—	1	1	2
Apoplexy, - - -	6	7	13	10	6	16	109	79	188
Asphyxia, - - -	—	—	—	—	—	—	—	1	1
Bright's disease, acute, -	—	—	—	1	—	1	4	2	6
Bright's disease, chronic, -	1	2	3	2	1	3	29	22	51
Bronchitis, capillary, - -	—	2	2	2	1	3	6	7	13
Carcinoma, - - -	1	2	3	—	2	2	12	23	35
Carbuncle, - - -	—	—	—	—	—	—	2	—	2
Cerebral atrophy, - -	1	—	1	—	1	1	2	4	6
Cerebral embolism, - -	—	—	—	—	—	—	4	—	4
Cerebral softening, - -	3	1	4	4	—	4	18	7	25
Chorea, - - - -	—	—	—	—	—	—	1	3	4

TABLE XXIII.—(Continued.)

DEATHS AND THE CAUSES.

CAUSES.	1896–97. Males.	1896–97. Females.	1896–97. Total.	1897–98. Males.	1897–98. Females.	1897–98. Total.	SINCE THE OPENING. Males.	SINCE THE OPENING. Females.	SINCE THE OPENING. Total.
Cyst, ovarian, - - -	—	—	—	—	—	—	—	1	1
Cystitis, chronic, - -	—	—	—	—	—	—	6	—	6
Diphtheria, - -	—	—	—	—	—	—	—	1	1
Drowning, accidental, -	—	—	—	—	—	—	2	—	2
Diabetes mellitus, - -	—	—	—	—	—	—	1	1	2
Dysentery, - - -	—	—	—	1	—	1	8	11	19
Epilepsy, - - - -	2	3	5	4	3	7	75	35	110
Empyema, - - -	—	—	—	1	—	1	3	3	6
Endocarditis, - -	—	1	1	—	—	—	—	1	1
Enteritis, - - - -	—	—	—	5	6	11	19	31	50
Erysipelas, - - -	2	1	3	—	—	—	29	14	43
Fracture of femur, -	—	1	1	—	—	—	—	2	2
Gangrene, lungs, - -	—	—	—	1	—	1	6	4	10
Gangrene, senile, - -	1	2	3	—	—	—	1	2	3
General paresis, - -	3	1	4	13	2	15	171	28	199
Hemorrhage, secondary, -	1	—	1	—	—	—	1	—	1
Hemorrhage, uterine, -	—	—	—	—	—	—	—	2	2
Heart, hypertrophy of, -	—	—	—	—	—	—	1	—	1
Heart, paralysis of, - -	—	—	—	—	—	—	6	5	11
Heart, rupture of, - -	1	—	1	—	—	—	3	—	3
Heart, fatty degeneration of,	—	1	1	—	—	—	5	6	11
Heart, valvular disease of,	5	6	11	4	9	13	72	60	132
Hernia, strangulated, -	—	—	—	—	—	—	1	2	3
Intestinal obstruction, -	—	—	—	—	—	—	1	1	2
Injuries from fall, - -	—	—	—	—	—	—	4	—	4
Leucocythaemia, - -	—	—	—	1	—	1	1	1	2
Liver, cirrhosis of, - -	—	—	—	—	—	—	4	3	7
Liver, fatty degeneration of,	—	—	—	—	—	—	1	1	2
Lung, oedema of, - -	1	—	1	1	1	2	3	3	6
Lymphadenoma, - -	—	—	—	—	—	—	—	1	1
Mania, acute, exhaustion from,	1	—	1	—	—	—	43	34	77
Mania, chronic, " "	1	1	2	—	—	—	47	48	95
Melancholia, " "	3	3	6	1	—	1	26	34	60
Marasmus, - - -	—	2	2	—	—	—	17	28	45
Meningitis, - - -	3	2	5	1	2	3	19	9	28
Osteoarthritis, - - -	—	—	—	—	—	—	1	—	1
Paralysis, exhaustion from,	3	1	4	2	1	3	23	5	28
Pericarditis, suppurative, -	—	1	1	—	—	—	—	1	1
Phthisis, catarrhal, - -	6	3	9	8	11	19	131	176	307
Phthisis, tubercular, - -	2	4	6	1	1	2	14	16	30
Phlebitis, - - - -	—	—	—	—	—	—	—	1	1
Pleuritis, - - - -	—	—	—	—	—	—	6	1	7
Pneumonia, - - -	7	—	7	3	—	3	60	35	95
Peritonitis, acute, - -	1	1	2	1	—	1	10	7	17
Peritonitis, chronic, - -	—	—	—	—	—	—	3	1	4
Pyaemia, - - - -	—	—	—	—	—	—	3	1	4
Pyonephrosis, - - -	—	—	—	—	—	—	—	1	1
Senility, - - - -	—	—	—	—	—	—	54	104	158
Septicaemia, - - -	—	—	—	1	—	1	2	1	3
Shock from injuries, - -	—	—	—	—	—	—	—	1	1
Strangulation from food, -	—	—	—	—	—	—	4	—	4

TABLE XXIII.—(Continued.)
DEATHS AND THE CAUSES.

CAUSES.	1896–97.			1897–98.			Since the Opening.		
	Males.	Females.	Total.	Males.	Females.	Total.	Males.	Females.	Total.
Suicide, - - - -	—	—	—	—	—	—	20	12	32
Syphilis, - - - -	—	—	—	—	—	—	5	2	7
Sclerosis, spinal, - -	—	—	—	—	—	—	1	—	1
Sclerosis, diffused cerebral,	—	—	—	—	—	—	—	1	1
Tetanus, - - - -	—	—	—	—	—	—	1	—	1
Tonsillitis, - - -	—	—	—	—	—	—	—	1	1
Tumor, cerebral, - -	—	—	—	1	—	1	3	—	3
Tumor, ovarian, - -	—	—	—	—	—	—	—	1	1
Tumor, uterine, - -	—	—	—	—	—	—	—	1	1
Undetermined, - - -	—	—	—	—	—	—	6	4	10
Ulceration of gall bladder,	—	—	—	—	—	—	1	—	1
Violence, - - - -	—	—	—	—	—	—	3	1	4
Total, - - -	59	49	108	69	50	119	1,137	908	2,045

TABLE XXIV.
DURATION OF INSANITY OF THOSE WHO DIED SINCE THE OPENING OF THE HOSPITAL.

DURATION.	From Admission into the Hospital.			From the Attack.		
	Males.	Females.	Total.	Males.	Females.	Total,
Under 1 month, -	141	86	227	16	18	34
1 to 2 months, -	89	46	135	30	22	52
2 to 3 " -	89	34	123	21	7	28
3 to 6 " -	116	75	191	43	31	74
6 to 9 " -	77	56	133	47	23	70
9 to 12 " -	65	35	100	37	17	54
12 to 18 " -	103	74	177	101	29	130
18 to 24 " -	34	51	85	64	48	112
2 to 3 years, -	91	81	172	114	104	218
3 to 5 " -	92	116	208	150	119	269
5 to 10 " -	126	131	257	156	169	325
10 to 15 " -	67	74	141	109	95	204
15 to 20 " -	30	33	63	58	64	122
20 to 25 " -	14	13	27	42	47	69
25 to 30 " -	3	3	6	25	24	49
30 to 40 " -	—	—	—	23	34	57
40 to 50 " -	—	—	—	15	17	32
Unknown, - -	—	—	—	86	40	146
Total. - -	1,137	908	2,045	1,137	908	2,045
Average of all, -	37.28 months.	47.87 months.	42.67 months.	6.75 years.	8.69 years.	7.72 years.

TABLE XXV.
REMAINING AT THE END OF THE YEAR.

AGE.	MALES.	FEMALES.	TOTAL.
Under 15, - - - - -	1	2	3
15 to 20, - - - - -	5	10	15
20 to 25, - - - - -	32	36	68
25 to 30, - - - - -	80	58	138
30 to 35, - - - - -	113	81	194
35 to 40, - - - - -	127	136	263
40 to 45, - - - - -	141	128	269
45 to 50, - - - - -	105	110	215
50 to 60, - - - - -	161	229	390
60 to 70, - - - - -	84	140	224
70 to 80, - - - - -	29	63	92
80 to 90, - - - - -	3	18	21
Over 90, - - - - -	1	2	3
Total, - - - - -	882	1,013	1,895

TABLE XXVI.
REMAINING AT THE END OF THE YEAR.—DURATION OF THE DISEASE.

DURATION.	SINCE ADMISSION.			SINCE THE ATTACK.		
	Males.	Females.	Total.	Males.	Females.	Total.
Under 1 month, -	12	15	27	1	—	1
1 to 2 months, -	15	16	31	2	2	4
2 to 3 " -	23	17	40	3	6	9
3 to 6 " -	43	30	73	18	10	28
6 to 9 " -	38	40	78	11	7	18
9 to 12 " -	18	37	55	12	5	17
12 to 18 " -	44	48	92	29	27	56
18 to 24 " -	38	39	77	25	20	45
2 to 3 years, -	82	80	162	57	59	116
3 to 5 " -	117	136	253	94	93	187
5 to 10 " -	205	229	434	170	206	376
10 to 15 " -	135	166	301	123	178	301
15 to 20 " -	65	96	161	102	133	235
20 to 25 " -	30	29	59	59	83	142
25 to 30 " -	10	31	41	37	48	85
30 to 40 " -	7	4	11	27	46	73
Over 40 " -	—	—	—	20	36	56
Unknown, - -	—	—	—	92	54	146
Total, - -	882	1,013	1,895	882	.1,013	1,895

TABLE XXVII.—Census Each Year Since the Opening of the Hospital.

PATIENTS.	Yr End. Mar 31, 1869	Mar 31, 1870	Mar 31, 1871	Mar 31, 1872	Mar 31, 1873	Mar 31, 1874	Mar 31, 1875	Mar 31, 1876	Per. End. Nov 30, 1876	Nov 30, 1877	Nov 30, 1878	Nov 30, 1879	Nov 30, 1880	Nov 30, 1881	Nov 30, 1882	Nov 30, 1883	Nov 30, 1884	Per. End. June 30, 1885	June 30, 1886	June 30, 1887	June 30, 1888	June 30, 1889	June 30, 1890	June 30, 1891	June 30, 1892	June 30, 1893	June 30, 1894	June 30, 1895	Per. End. Sept 30, 1896	Sept 30, 1897	Sept 30, 1898	Total.
Admitted—Males,	165	78	49	56	43	93	122	108	59	92	101	75	73	193	177	135	121	103	175	182	193	193	197	234	190	169	212	208	281	198	216	4492
Females,	103	56	26	36	31	160	88	58	29	61	60	88	71	159	171	136	122	106	186	193	202	193	171	188	176	169	145	172	251	152	195	3954
Total,	268	134	75	92	74	253	210	166	88	153	161	163	144	352	348	271	243	209	361	375	395	386	368	422	366	338	357	380	532	350	411	8446
Recovered—Males,	35	27	14	11	8	16	24	33	12	26	20	20	16	33	39	46	26	13	25	35	49	39	36	44	28	42	39	42	62	42	30	895
Females,	—	16	6	6	3	21	17	12	6	15	12	13	14	20	42	26	26	15	48	52	51	46	39	41	34	32	26	28	48	30	31	813
Total,	35	43	20	17	11	37	41	45	18	41	32	33	30	53	81	72	52	28	73	87	100	85	75	85	62	74	65	70	110	72	61	1708
Improved—Males,	11	8	8	11	8	9	19	23	11	20	14	13	15	16	17	17	6	6	14	31	39	29	44	31	29	34	21	25	42	39	40	704
Females,	—	10	5	6	5	20	25	23	11	20	14	17	14	4	17	25	7	8	15	24	39	27	26	28	31	42	27	15	28	19	28	546
Total,	11	18	13	17	13	29	44	46	22	40	28	30	29	20	34	42	14	14	29	55	54	56	70	59	60	76	48	40	70	58	68	1250
Stationary—Males,	6	8	6	10	9	13	14	18	12	20	21	23	26	25	31	35	28	16	38	35	43	45	57	40	29	34	32	32	42	39	40	874
Females,	—	9	8	10	9	15	20	14	5	14	15	14	8	8	12	24	20	16	17	19	34	31	21	24	58	42	49	38	39	27	36	674
Total,	6	17	14	20	18	28	34	32	17	34	36	37	33	33	43	59	48	32	55	54	77	76	78	64	87	76	81	70	77	66	96	1548
Died—Males,	14	18	11	12	8	16	24	21	21	26	27	16	32	47	44	44	34	19	37	41	57	45	48	49	87	57	59	59	77	59	69	1137
Females,	1	3	6	9	3	21	17	18	11	19	13	14	12	32	32	27	34	20	40	40	48	53	57	48	58	61	43	59	67	49	50	908
Total,	15	21	21	26	12	37	41	39	32	45	40	30	44	79	71	59	48	39	77	81	105	98	105	97	145	118	101	118	144	108	119	2045
Whole number in the year,	268	343	307	329	336	524	605	548	619	629	644	654	880	1079	1113	1113	1103	1132	1380	1521	1639	1678	1705	1799	1860	1844	1893	1960	2194	2132	2239	—
Number at end of the year,	209	232	237	262	271	395	450	460	466	468	481	510	528	731	842	860	929	1019	1146	1244	1292	1337	1377	1494	1506	1535	1589	1662	1782	1828	1895	—

TABLE XXVIII.

ADMISSIONS AND DISCHARGES.—RATIO PER CENT.

	1896–97.	1897–98.	SINCE , THE OPENING.
Admission from causes:			
Anxiety of mind and over-study, - -	1.42	2.14	3.30
Apoplexy, - - - - - -	.85	1.94	.94
Connected with the affections, - -	2.57	3.60	3.83
Connected with fluctuations of fortune,	.57	.73	1.19
Connected with religion, - - -	.85	.48	1.39
Epilepsy, - - - - - -	3.71	4.13	4.04
Ill health, - - - - - -	3.40	1.43	6.83
Intemperance, - - - - -	9.71	12.89	10.30
Masturbation, - - - - -	.85	1.43	2.71
Old age, - - - - - -	6.26	5.35	3.43
Puerperal, - - - - - -	1.14	2.67	2.06
Unknown, - - - - - -	52.29	46.22	44.73
Recovered of all cases admitted:			
Under one year, - - - - -	29.13	33.76	39.90
One year and over, - - - -	8.06	6.22	4.81
Deaths of all under care, - - -	5.06	5.31	24.21
Deaths of average number in hospital,	5.99	6.36	7.20

TREASURER'S REPORT.

Annual Statement of the Treasurer of the Connecticut Hospital for the Insane, for the Year ending September 30, 1897.

RECEIPTS.

Balance of cash on hand, October 1, 1896, -	$43,145 65
Amount of revenue from Hospital in October,	55,160 08
" " " " November,	18,922 33
" " " December,	14,503 68
Amount of interest to date on balance in bank,	466 36
Amount of revenue from Hospital in January, 1897,	37,617 74
Six months' interest on Sargent Fund of $1,000,	20 00
Amount of revenue from Hospital in February,	7,651 06
" " " " March,	24,205 76
" " " " April,	30,536 75
" " " " May,	17,801 17
" " " " June,	18,033 99
Amount of interest to date on balance in bank,	1,073 05
Six months' interest on Sargent Fund of $1,000,	20 00
Amount of revenue from Hospital in July,	34,794 41
" " " " August,	20,538 60
" " " " September,	13,107 39
	$337,598 02

DISBURSEMENTS.

Amount of Superintendent's orders paid in October, 1896,	$18,914 61
" " " " November,	20,414 83
" " " " December,	21,121 47
" " " " January, 1897,	22,815 98
" " " " February,	20,094 09
" " " " March,	17,911 90
" " " " April,	20,967 89
" " " " May,	20,106 18
" " " " June,	21,667 43
" " " " July,	23,820 53
" " " " August,	24,619 58
" " " " September,	60,820 35
Balance on deposit in Middletown National Bank, September 30,	44,323 18
	$337,598 02

M. B. COPELAND, *Treasurer.*

MIDDLETOWN, Conn., October 1, 1897.

This certifies that we have examined the accounts of M. B. Copeland, Treasurer of the Connecticut Hospital for the Insane, for the fiscal year ending September 30, 1897, compared them with the vouchers, and found them correct. The balance in the hands of the Treasurer on September 30, 1897, was forty-four thousand three hundred twenty-three dollars and eighteen cents ($44,323.18).

FRANKLIN B. NOYES, } *Auditors*
D. WARD NORTHROP, } *of Public Accounts.*

MIDDLETOWN, Conn., December 21, 1897.

TREASURER'S REPORT.

Annual Statement of the Treasurer of the Connecticut Hospital for the Insane, for the Year ending September 30, 1898.

RECEIPTS.

Balance of cash on hand, October 1, 1897, - - - - -	$44,323 18
Amount of revenue from Hospital in October, - - - -	36,337 13
" " " " November, - - - -	20,237 52
" " " " December, - - - -	14,071 72
" " " " January, 1898, - - -	32,345 30
" " " " February, - - - -	24,599 92
" " " " March, - - - -	12,948 85
" " " " April, - - - -	31,096 49
" " " " May, - - - -	23,701 77
" " " " June, - - - -	12,249 50
" " " " July, - - - -	35,021 53
" " " " August, - - - -	20,254 93
" " " " September, - - - -	14,716 83
Amount of interest received from Middletown National Bank, -	1,128 26
One year's interest on Sargent Fund of $1,000, - - - -	40 00
	$323,072 93

DISBURSEMENTS.

Amount of Superintendent's orders paid in October, - -	$19,354 16
" " " " November, - -	23,652 23
" " " " December, - -	24,150 94
" " " " January, 1898, - -	17,776 98
" " " " February, - -	19,164 96
" " " " March, - -	18,904 83
" " " " April, - -	21,624 06
" " " " May, - -	18,551 39
" " " " June, - -	24,110 30
" " " " July, - -	25,428 27
" " " " August, - -	26,888 30
" " " " September, - -	18,524 89
Balance of cash on hand, September 30, 1898, - - - -	64,941 62
	$323,072 93.

M. B. COPELAND, *Treasurer.*

MIDDLETOWN, Conn., October 1, 1898.

This certifies that we have examined the accounts of M. B. Copeland, Treasurer of the Connecticut Hospital for the Insane, for the fiscal year ending September 30, 1898, compared them with the vouchers, and found them correct. The balance in the hands of the Treasurer on September 30, 1898, was sixty-four thousand nine hundred forty-one dollars and sixty-two cents ($64,941.62).

FRANKLIN B. NOYES, } *Auditors*
D. WARD NORTHROP, } *of Public Accounts.*

MIDDLETOWN, Conn., December 21, 1898.

SUPERINTENDENT'S FINANCIAL STATEMENT.

Year ending September 30, 1897.

DEBTOR.

Oct.	1,	1896.	Cash,	-	-	-	-	-	-	$257 52
"	1,	"	Treasurer's balance,		-	-	-	43,109 33
"	31,	"	Revenue,	-	-	-	-	-	55,160 08
Nov.	30,	"	"	-	-	-	-	18,922 33
Dec.	31,	"	"	-	-	-	-	14,503 68
Jan.	31,	1897.	"	-	-	-	-	38,102 10
Feb.	28,	"	"	-	-	-	-	7,651 06
Mch.	31,	"	"	-	-	-	-	24,205 76
Apr.	30,			-	-	-	-	30,536 75
May	31,	"	"	-	-	-	-	17,801 17
June	30,	"	"	-	-	-	-	19,107 04
July	31,			-	-	-	-	34,814 41
Aug.	31,	"	"	-	-	-	-	20,538 60
Sept.	30,	"	"	-	-	-	-	13,107 39
									$337,817 22

CREDITOR.

Oct.	31,	1896.	Vouchers,	-	-	-	-	$18,948 59
Nov.	30,	"	"	-	-	-	-	20,755 11
Dec.	31,	"	"	-	-	-	-	22,290 50
Jan.	31,	1897.	"	-	-	-	-	21,783 83
Feb.	28,	"	"	-	-	-	-	19,944 18
Mch.	31,	"	"	-	-	-	-	17,858 09
Apr.	30,	"	"	-	-	-	-	20,836 60
May	31,	"	"	-	-	-	-	20,287 97
June	30,	"		-	-	-	-	21,493 58
July	31,	"		-	-	-	-	23,825 19
Aug.	31,	"		-	-	-	-	24,619 54
Sept.	30,	"	"	-	-	-	-	61,996 50
"	30,	"	Treasurer's balance,	-	-	42,777 49
"	30,	"	Cash balance,	-	-	-	400 05
								$337,817 22

OUTSTANDING ORDERS.

No. 24874,	-	-	-	-	$2 03	No. 28291,	-	-	-	$198 05
No. 25291,	-	-	-	-	14 60	No. 28325,	-	-	-	67 38
No. 25383,	-	-	-	-	2 40	No. 28327,	-	-	-	115 76
No. 27394,	-	-	-	-	13 71	No. 28328,	-	-	-	1,131 76
	Total,	-	-	-	-	-	-	$1,545 69

Sept. 30, 1897. Balance,	-	-	-	-	-	-	-	$42,777 49
Outstanding orders,	-	-	-	-	-	-	-	1,545 69
Treasurer's balance,	-	-	-	-	-	-	-	$44,323 18

This certifies that we have examined the accounts of the Superintendent of the Connecticut Hospital for the Insane for the fiscal year ending September 30, 1897, compared them with the vouchers, and found them correct. The balance in the hands of the Superintendent on September 30, 1897, was four hundred dollars and five cents ($400.05).

FRANKLIN B. NOYES, } *Auditors*
D. WARD NORTHROP, } *of Public Accounts.*

MIDDLETOWN, Conn., December 21, 1897.

SUPERINTENDENT'S FINANCIAL STATEMENT.

Year ending September 30, 1898.

DEBTOR.

Oct. 1, 1897.	Cash, - - - - -	$400 05	
" 1, "	Treasurer's balance, - - - -	42,777 49	
" 31, "	Revenue, - - - - -	36,337 13	
Nov. 30, '	" - - - - -	20,237 52	
Dec. 31, "	" - - - - -	14,395 59	
Jan. 31, 1898.	" - - - - -	32,345 30	
Feb. 28, "	" - - - - -	24,619 92	
Mch. 31, "	" - - - - -	12,948 85	
Apr. 30, '	" - - - - -	31,096 49	
May 31, '	" - - - - -	23,701 77	
June 30, '	" - - - - -	13,073 89	
July 31, '	" - - - - -	35,021 53	
Aug. 31, '	" - - - - -	20,254 93	
Sept. 30, '	" - - - - -	14,716 83	
			$321,927 29

CREDITOR.

Oct. 31, 1897.	Vouchers, - - - -	$18,608 41	
Nov. 30, "	" - - - -	23,245 08	
Dec. 31, "	" - - - -	24,205 06	
Jan. 31, 1898.	" - - - -	17,483 39	
Feb. 28, "	" - - - -	19,347 97	
Mch. 31, "	" - - - -	18,849 41	
Apr. 30, '	" - - - -	21,903 87	
May 31, "	" - - - -	18,229 70	
June 30, '	" - - - -	24,413 73	
July 31, '	" - - - -	25 137 59	
Aug. 31, '	" - - - -	27,037 16	
Sept. 30, '	" - - - -	18,278 80	
" 30, "	Treasurer's balance, - - - -	64,892 34	
" 30, "	Cash balance, - - - -	294 78	
			$321,927 29

OUTSTANDING ORDERS.

No. 24874, - - - -	$2 03	No. 27394, - - -	$13 71
No. 25291, - - - -	14 60	No. 29253, - - -	14 29
No. 25383, - - - -	2 40	No. 29346, - - -	2 54
Total, - - - - - -	$49 57		

Sept. 30, 1898. Balance, - - - - - -	$64,892 34	
Less error in orders 28975, 29066, 28726, - - - - -	29	
	$64,892 05	
Outstanding orders, - - - - - - - -	49 57	
	$64,941 62	

This certifies that we have examined the accounts of the Superintendent of the Connecticut Hospital for the Insane for the fiscal year ending September 30, 1898, compared them with the vouchers, and found them correct. The balance in the hands of the Superintendent on September 30, 1898, was two hundred ninety-four dollars and seventy-eight cents ($294.78).

FRANKLIN B. NOYES, }   *Auditors*
D. WARD NORTHROP, } *of Public Accounts.*

MIDDLETOWN, Conn., December 21, 1898.

ABSTRACT OF VOUCHERS FOR YEAR ENDING SEPTEMBER 30, 1897.

1896–'97.	Salaries of Officers.	Pay of Employés.	Furniture and Fixtures.	Fuel and Lights.	Dry Goods and Clothing.	Stationery, Books, and Postage.	Provisions.	Fish.	Flour.	Meat.	Groceries.	Farm and Garden.	Construction.	Drugs.	Burial.	Refunded.	Repairing.	Insurance.	Miscellaneous.	Supplies.	Total.
Oct., -	$1137.14	$5892.43	$133.74	$1111.00	$679.73	$210.03	$1535.74	$412.16	$36.72	$2128.93	$690.05	$1001.67	$1730.67	$303.35	$12.25	$217.50	$1015.59	—	$221.77	$480.12	$1848.5
Nov., -	1192.14	5924.42	949.81	58.30	1435.22	110.59	1960.91	903.40	—	2321.70	1682.09	816.69	2277.01	52.59	10.50	123.04	691.46	—	177.55	67.69	20755.1
Dec., -	1194.14	5702.39	895.11	1059.30	718.97	146.81	2170.38	258.58	1517.02	2596.69	1566.89	764.55	1896.14	498.63	—	94.77	844.70	—	225.77	148.66	22290.5
Jan., -	1190.14	5797.30	234.27	79.86	2308.71	126.20	2275.26	531.27	11.75	2036.07	1749.53	1459.72	2686.91	245.20	10.25	44.08	787.83	—	245.96	463.52	21783.8
Feb., -	1192.14	5635.04	499.07	—	1208.32	542.34	2149.83	615.22	1623.75	2384.29	934.41	543.38	1840.15	94.01	—	75.86	291.64	—	223.48	91.25	19944.1
Mar., -	1142.14	5549.38	582.90	1428.35	454.49	79.10	2080.22	463.68	155.48	3224.87	774.53	602.02	164.88	62.84	10.50	146.93	691.39	—	29.78	214.61	17858.0
April,-	1189.25	5563.28	973.93	123.64	1375.17	233.19	1794.11	425.21	2536.50	1503.75	1490.07	1048.06	1119.50	249.35	26.00	101.94	629.84	—	255.04	208.36	20836.0
May, -	1200.47	5699.39	809.61	—	979.40	78.29	3105.08	725.46	77.40	2626.76	1488.90	729.48	1393.75	106.81	10.50	117.01	470.36	—	207.78	472.02	20287.9
June, -	1210.80	5647.13	288.53	798.51	1572.73	55.41	2171.66	358.22	769.85	3000.31	1348.88	657.10	1890.03	275.92	—	56.27	558.55	—	439.54	394.14	21493.
July, -	1206.80	5613.69	1464.12	4317.00	908.59	97.05	1871.42	375.35	1182.50	2915.67	1566.54	800.74	374.60	248.94	23.00	41.43	623.05	$1874.00	175.55	19.15	23825.1
Aug., -	1153.80	5625.01	100.15	4117.30	307.22	99.30	1802.97	345.54	167.50	2824.74	912.51	460.17	383.64	101.63	15.50	53.58	344.40	—	146.95	313.63	24619.
Sept., -	1145.46	5670.66	60.44	8984.70	2036.72	182.80	1827.67	280.28	1355.00	4770.60	2332.87	851.12	30866.30	217.83	11.70	9.36	1005.72	149.92	97.35	140.00	61996.
Total, -	14154.42	68420.12	6991.68	22068.96	13985.27	1961.11	24745.25	5694.37	9433.47	37334.38	16037.27	9734.70	50093.58	2457.10	117.70	1081.77	7954.53	2023.92	2446.52	2993.56	2946.39.

ABSTRACT OF VOUCHERS FOR YEAR ENDING SEPTEMBER 30, 1898.

1897-98.	Salaries of Officers.	Pay of Employés.	Furniture and Fixtures.	Fuel and Lights.	Dry Goods and Clothing.	Stationery, Books, and Postage.	Provisions.	Fish.	Flour.	Meat.	Groceries.	Farm and Garden.	Construction.	Drugs.	Burial.	Refunded.	Repairing.	Insurance.	Miscellaneous.	Supplies.	Total.
Oct.,	$1153.80	$5585.61	$78.55	$99.57	$1468.33	$184.58	$2979.72	$434.74	$690.00	$1110.73	$2574.61	$622.05	$512.35	$156.28	$15.25	$3.57	$533.84	—	$326.33	$78.50	$18608.41
Nov.,	1146.64	5640.90	305.90	2867.18	1132.79	84.20	3514.37	518.89	12.75	2803.56	1407.10	369.65	1837.22	58.47	10.50	70.86	892.83	—	170.11	401.16	23245.08
Dec.,	1192.69	5748.42	479.62	1138.97	2865.34	115.44	2373.74	511.10	2145.00	2871.98	1526.83	674.88	1108.20	346.71	—	91.42	519.48	—	193.73	301.51	24205.06
Jan.,	873.55	5762.12	92.51	—	2284.72	114.45	3178.82	550.02	—	2102.38	585.17	447.17	360.00	288.81	—	43.15	479.47	—	241.20	79.85	17483.39
Feb.,	995.81	5733.76	373.21	—	848.85	119.46	2881.76	572.24	2200.75	1892.55	1270.47	572.59	253.96	184.88	—	59.60	947.69	—	411.75	118.64	19347.97
Mar.,	899.81	5771.57	573.60	1365.17	390.34	215.40	3055.32	494.59	—	2353.96	903.58	646.21	840.00	173.11	—	72.28	719.20	—	196.15	179.12	18849.41
April,	903.80	5759.96	475.36	52.84	795.16	120.45	1840.27	497.04	1728.38	3496.42	1567.99	1106.96	2228.03	166.76	—	10.57	605.42	—	360.87	187.59	21903.87
May,	1324.63	5765.03	707.96	—	176.33	246.54	2921.10	487.63	450.50	2286.21	2243.47	577.68	2.40	174.55	—	46.60	552.67	—	121.81	144.59	18229.70
June,	1012.14	5881.60	720.27	4559.79	565.52	106.28	2836.50	404.51	1615.00	2850.55	801.46	420.71	827.50	420.86	—	94.29	796.17	—	151.06	349.52	24413.73
July,	1012.14	5930.24	288.57	6563.25	551.99	78.86	2638.16	413.39	825.00	3214.01	1566.80	485.06	—	146.28	—	87.71	876.28	—	207.14	252.71	25137.59
Aug.,	1022.48	5818.09	496.08	9669.05	662.41	195.69	2144.05	278.99	—	3401.45	1357.21	614.77	300.81	61.19	—	195.69	468.16	—	173.72	177.32	27037.16
Sept.,	1020.48	5900.24	555.51	390.02	437.38	125.77	3010.76	303.29	1341.50	2259.96	1024.28	631.95	—	137.15	—	104.84	794.63	—	168.43	72.61	18278.80
Total,	12467.97	69297.54	5147.14	26705.84	12279.16	1707.12	33374.57	5466.43	11008.88	30643.76	16828.97	7169.68	8270.47	2315.05	25.75	880.58	8185.84	—	2722.30	2343.12	256740.17

FARMER'S REPORT.

PRODUCTS.	YEAR ENDING SEPTEMBER 30, 1897.		YEAR ENDING SEPTEMBER 30, 1898.	
	Quantity.	Value.	Quantity.	Value.
Hay, - - - -	280 tons,	$3,640 00	310 tons,	$3,410 00
Ensilage, - - -	200 "	800 00	210 "	735 00
Potatoes, - - -	1,900 bush.,	1,584 00	1,406 bush.,	843 60
Carrots, - - -	352 "	140 00	240 "	80 00
Beets, - - -	2,590 "	1,036 80	1,854 "	741 60
Beet greens, - -	200 "	100 00	210 "	105 00
Onions, - - -	890 "	534 00	615 "	369 00
Turnips, - - -	2,812 "	843 60	1,040 "	312 00
Beans (string, - -	288 "	288 00	270 "	270 00
Beans (shell), - -	208 "	208 00	602 "	602 00
Peas, - - -	450 "	450 00	330 "	330 00
Parsnips, - -	305 "	152 50	156 "	78 00
Sweet corn, - -	1,580 "	790 00	1,130 "	565 00
Cucumbers, - -	305 "	152 50	425 "	212 50
Tomatoes, - -	490 "	336 00	480 "	264 00
Radishes, - -	142 "	142 00	90 "	90 00
Apples, - - -	325 "	195 00	385 "	231 00
Cider, - - -	32 bbls.,	96 00	20 bbls.,	70 00
Lettuce, - - -	5,500 head,	110 00	3,000 head,	60 00
Cabbage, - - -	15,000 "	450 00	16,000 "	480 00
Celery, - - -	14,500 "	435 00	13,700 "	390 00
Squash, - - -	16,200 lbs.,	162 00	18,300 lbs.,	183 00
Veal, - - -	209 "	20 90	—	—
Beef, - - -	5,042 "	327 73	8,480 "	508 80
Pork, - - -	72,557 "	4,353 42	35,520 "	2,131 20
Milk (grass fed), -	90,400 qts.,	3,616 00	85,600 qts.,	2,996 00
Pigs (sold), - -	—	—	—	—
Calves (sold), - -	41	82 00	43	86 00
Total, - - -	—	$21,045 45	—	$16,143 70

The farm live stock consists of 60 cows, 27 young cattle, 18 horses, and 110 hogs.

P. W. SANDERSON, *Farmer*.

GARDEN, LAWN, AND GREENHOUSE.

	YEAR ENDING SEPTEMBER 30, 1897.									YEAR ENDING SEPTEMBER 30, 1898.									
	Jan.	Feb.	March.	April.	May.	June.	July.	Aug., Sept.	Total.	Jan.	Feb.	March.	April.	May.	June.	July.	Aug.	Sept.	Total.
Spinach,	4½	7	71		143¾	12		8	175 bush.	2	7		10	14	89				122 bush.
Lettuce,	10	40		20	312	391			845 doz.	125	40	50	48	110	228	75			676 doz.
Dandelions,																			
Asparagus,				25	306	61			392 lbs.				3	161	170				334 lbs.
Radish,				6	952	100	190		958 doz.				60	896	180	100			1,076 doz.
Rhubarb,									290 lbs.					150	150				460 lbs.
Beet greens,					4			6	4 bush.						8				8 bush.
Beets,									6 "						6	153	137	4	4 "
Peas,						102	132	75	309 doz.						12	7	3½	32	328 doz.
Currants,						16	22½		38½ bush.							1½			22½ bush.
Cucumbers,							6	10	111 "							51	226	9	1½ "
Cucumbers, forced,							596	1965	16							15½	19½	22	
Beans,							17	49¾	2,561 bush.							384	39		286 doz.
Raspberries,							534	18	66½ qts.										57 bush.
Tomatoes,								36½	552 qts.										423 qts.
Grapes,								1,100	36½ bush.									2060	2,060 lbs.
Celery,									1,100 lbs.									1000	1,000 head.
Pears,								10	1,000 head.								46½	27¾	27¾ bush.
Crabapples,								8	10 bbls.								95	16	16 "
Corn,									10 "									17	63½ doz.
Melons,								285	285									558	653
Apples,																		10	10 bush.
Cabbage,								6	6 bbls.								26	97	123

JOS. J. SMITH, *Gardener.*

Sewing Room Report.

Articles.	1896–97.	1897–98.
Aprons,	354	173
Bandages,	552	340
Bed-spreads,	222	201
Bed-ticks,	18	89
Bibs,	74	61
Blankets,	515	982
Bread-cloths,	24	—
Bureau-covers,	6	3
Caps, cut,	318	407
Carpets,	44	22
Chemises,	701	412
Clothes-bags,	54	61
Curtains,	202	163
Dresses,	703	748
Dresses, night,	164	88
Drawers,	307	244
Handkerchiefs,	91	—
Holders,	883	1,076
Mats,	78	74
Mangle-cloths,	30	27
Napkins,	216	250
Pillow-slips,	1,562	1,481
Sacques,	35	21
Sheets,	1,884	1,499
Shirts,	818	605
Skirts,	224	245
Stockings, knit,	116	36
Table-cloths,	128	93
Towels,	1,699	1,577
Underwaists,	7	11

Mending clothing, bedding, etc.

MARGARET DUTTON, *Matron.*

ANNEX WORKSHOP REPORT.

ARTICLES.	1896–97.	1897–98.
Awnings, - - - - - - - - -	—	15
Bandages, - - - - - - - - -	2,091	961
Brooms, - - - - - - - - -	1,449	1,048
Brooms, whisk, - - - - - - - -	253	65
Brooms, barn, - - - - - - - -	—	—
Moleskin shoes (pairs), - - - - - -	—	10
Brushes, horse, - - - - - - - -	—	—
Brushes, painters', - - - - - - -	—	—
Brushes, scrubbing, - - - - - - -	823	266
Burlaps, quilted, - - - - - - -	169	150
Canvas dresses, - - - - - - - -	12	34
Canvas jackets, - - - - - - - -	50	41
Chairs, caned or rattanned, - - - - -	289	380
Combination suits, - - - - - - -	73	50
Cushions, - - - - - - - - -	8	—
Pieces furniture upholstered, - - - - -	68	42
Door mats, - - - - - - - -	—	—
Hassocks, - - - - - - - - -	—	—
Mattresses, - - - - - - - -	313	540
Overalls, - - - - - - - - -	304	429
Pillows, - - - - - - - - -	296	423
Shoes, { Cash, - - - - - -	$181.45 —	$249.58
Shoes, { Patients, - - - - -	577.60—$759.05	627.15
Suspenders, pairs, - - - - - - -	360	80

JAMES L. BALLARD, *Foreman.*

MAIN COTTAGE SHOP REPORT.

Shop opened November 1, 1897.

Fiber mats, - - - - - - - - - - - 137
Rugs, small, including carpet rugs, - - - - - - 67
Rugs, large, - - - - - - - - - - 198
Reclining chairs made, - - - - - - - - 15
Pictures framed, including mirrors, - - - - - - 82
Furniture dressed and polished, - - - - - - - 1
Chairs repaired, - - - - - - - - - - 587
Tables repaired, - - - - - - - - - - 1
Benches and settees repaired, - - - - - - - 40
Chairs bored for caning, - - - - - - - - 27
Patent braces put on chairs, - - - - - - - 240.
Chairs covered, - - - - - - - - - - 3
Shelves for Main Cottage, - - - - - - - - 3
Camp-stool made, - - - - - - - - - 1
Ironing boards covered, - - - - - - - - 6
Flower stands made, - - - - - - - - - 9
Wall dusters fixed, - - - - - - - - - 3
Cots repaired, - - - - - - - - - - 1
Water pails repaired, - - - - - - - - 16
Mops repaired, - - - - - - - - - - 232
Baskets mended, - - - - - - - - - - 15
Crutches repaired, pairs, - - - - - - - - 5
Boxes covered, - - - - - - - - - - 4
Sunshade repaired, - - - - - - - - - 1
Ice-water tank renovated and repaired, - - - - - 1

FREDERICK STEINER, *Foreman.*

BILL OF FARE.

For Patients and Employees.

SUNDAY.

Breakfast.—Roast loin of pork, potatoes, graham bread.
Dinner.—Cold corned beef, potatoes, pickles, apple pie.
Supper.—Apricot sauce or fruit, cake.

MONDAY.

Breakfast.—Beefsteak, potatoes.
Dinner.—Soup with barley, tapioca pudding.
Supper.—Dried beef, sugar cookies.

TUESDAY.

Breakfast.—Corned beef hash.
Dinner.—Roast ham, potatoes, vegetable, boiled rice.
Supper.—Oatmeal, hominy, or cornmeal mush, ginger cookies.

WEDNESDAY.

Breakfast.—Pork sausage, potatoes.
Dinner.—Roast beef, potatoes, vegetable, apple pie.
Supper.—Biscuits, prune sauce.

THURSDAY.

Breakfast.—Hamburger steak, potatoes.
Dinner.—Stewed beef with vegetables, farina pudding.
Supper.—Cold meats or headcheese, crullers.

FRIDAY.

Breakfast.—Boiled salmon, butter sauce, potatoes.
Dinner.—Baked fresh fish, potatoes, vegetable, peach pie.
Supper.—Baked spaghetti, with cheese, and johnny cake or griddle cakes.

SATURDAY.

Breakfast.—Baked beans, brown bread.
Dinner.—Corned beef, cabbage, potatoes, bread pudding.
Supper.—Milk-stewed oysters, crackers.

Bread and butter served with every meal. Coffee with every breakfast. Tea with every supper.

Special diet prescribed for the sick, such as oatmeal or flour gruel, dry or milk toast; eggs, boiled, raw, or on toast; beef-tea and crackers; milk.

ADMISSION OF PATIENTS.

1. Whenever a patient is sent to the Hospital by order of the Probate Court, the order or warrant or a copy thereof, by which the person is sent, shall be lodged with the Superintendent.

2. It is expected that each patient, before admission, shall be made perfectly clean, and be free from vermin, or any contagious or infectious disease.

3. Each male patient should be provided with at least two shirts, one woolen coat, one woolen vest, one pair woolen pantaloons, two pair new socks, one pair new shoes or boots, and one comfortable outside garment.

Each female patient should, in addition to a quantity of underclothing, shoes and stockings corresponding to that required by the male patient, have one flannel petticoat, two good dresses, one cloak or other good outside garment. Extra and better apparel is very desirable for Chapel worship and out-of-door exercise and riding.

4. In all cases the patient's best clothing should be sent; it will be carefully preserved, and only used when deemed necessary, for the purpose above mentioned. Jewelry, and all superfluous articles of dress, knives, etc., should be left at home, as they are liable to be lost, and for them the officers of the Hospital are not responsible.

5. A written history of the case should be sent with the patient, and, if possible, some one acquainted with the individual should accompany him to the Hospital, from whom minute, but often essential, particulars may be learned.

6. Indigent persons, or those partly supported by friends and partly by the State, are admitted under Section 487, General Statutes, 1888, as amended by Public Acts, 1895, Chapter 180.

7. The price of board, including washing, mending, and attendance, for indigent patients is $2.80 per week.

8. Private patients, or those supported by themselves or friends, are admitted to the Hospital when there are vacancies, under Chapter 256, Public Acts, 1895.

9. Pauper patients, or those supported partly by the towns in which they reside, and partly by the State, are admitted agreeably to Section 487, General Statutes, 1888, as amended by Public Acts, 1895, Chapter 180.

10. A bond with satisfactory surety, one or more, will be required with each indigent and private patient for the payment of expenses of board and attendance, quarterly in advance, and for all other expenses whether of damages, removal, or death.

11. Visitors are admitted to the Institution between the hours of 10 A. M. and 12 M., and between 2 and 5 P. M., on Mondays, Wednesdays, and Fridays only, but no visitor shall be admitted to the wards occupied by patients without express permission from the Superintendent, and especial care is to be taken that no amount of visiting is permitted that might prove injurious to the patients.

12. The Connecticut Hospital for the Insane is situated about two miles from the railroad station.   Electric cars run from the station to the Hospital.

Visitors are not admitted on Sunday, but on any other day of the week patients may be seen by their friends, unless in the opinion of the physicians the visit is liable to injure the patients.

Express packages may be addressed to any patient, "in care of the Hospital for the Insane."

The telephone can be used from 11:30 A. M. tò 12:30 P. M., and from 4:30 to 5:30 P. M. daily (except Sundays).   At other times the medical staff are busy.

In every letter about any patient, the full name of the patient and the post office address of the writer should be mentioned.

All letters relating to the patients or the affairs of the Hospital should be addressed to CHARLES W. PAGE, M. D., Superintendent, Middletown, Conn.

COMMITMENT AND SUPPORT OF INSANE PAUPERS AND INDIGENT PERSONS.

PUBLIC ACTS, 1895, CHAPTER 180, SECTION 1.   Section 487 of the General Statutes is hereby amended to read as follows: When any pauper in any town shall be insane, a selectman of such town may apply to the Court of Probate for the district wherein said pauper resides, for his commitment to the State Hospital for the Insane, and said Court shall appoint *two* respectable physicians, who shall fully investigate the facts of the case and report to said Court; and if such physicians shall report that said pauper is insane, the Court may order such selectman forthwith to take such pauper to the Hospital, where he shall be kept and supported so long as may be requisite, and *two dollars per week of the expense of his board shall be paid by the town whose selectman applies for said commitment, and the balance by the State;* and when an indigent person, not a pauper, is insane, application may be made by any person in his behalf to the Court of Probate for the district where he resides, who shall appoint *two* respectable physicians and a selectman of the town where said indigent person resides, who shall fully investigate the facts and report to said Court, which, if satisfied that such person is indigent and insane, shall order him to be taken by the person making the application, or such other person as it may direct, to the Hospital, where he shall be kept and supported as long as may be requisite, and *two dollars per week of the expense of his board shall be paid by the person making the application, and the balance by the State.*   All proceedings in the Court of Probate upon such application shall be in writing, and lodged and kept in the registry of said Court; and whenever a Court shall pass an order for the admission of any pauper or indigent person to the Hospital, it shall record the same and give a certified copy of said order and proceedings to the person by whom such pauper or indigent person is to be taken to the Hospital, as the warrant for such taking and commitment, and shall also forthwith transmit a like copy to the Governor.

SEC. 2. Whenever any insane female shall be committed to the State Hospital for the Insane under the provisions of the preceding section, the Court shall, unless such female is to be accompanied by a member of her own family, direct that at least one adult female shall accompany her, and the expense of such attendant shall be paid by the party making application for such commitment.

COMMITMENT OF PRIVATE PATIENTS.

PUBLIC ACTS, 1895, CHAPTER 256, SEC. 3. Except when otherwise specially provided by law, no person shall be committed or admitted to or detained in an asylum without an order of a Court of Probate, as hereinafter provided; provided, that when a person who has suddenly become clearly and violently insane is brought to an asylum chartered by the laws of this State, such person may be received and detained there for not more than forty-eight hours without special order of a Court of Probate, but in such case the keeper of the asylum shall see that the proper proceedings are forthwith commenced in the Probate Court.

SEC. 4. Upon such complaint being filed in the Probate Court, such Court shall thereupon assign a time, not later than ten days thereafter, and a place for hearing such complaint, and shall cause reasonable notice thereof to be given to the person alleged to be insane, and to such relative or relatives and friends as it may deem proper; such Court may also issue a warrant for the apprehension and bringing before it of the person complained of, and shall see and examine such person, if in its judgment his condition or conduct renders it necessary and proper so to do, or state in its final order why it was not necessary or advisable so to do.

* * * * * * * * *

SEC. 6. In addition to such oral testimony as may be offered at such hearing, the Court shall require the sworn certificates of at least two reputable physicians, whom it shall find to be graduates of legally organized medical institutions and to have been practitioners of medicine at least three years within this State, and not connected with any asylum nor related by blood or marriage to the complainant nor to the person alleged to be insane, and one of whom shall be selected by the Court, to the effect that they have personally examined such person within ten days of such hearing, and that in their opinion such person is insane and a fit subject for confinement in an asylum.

SEC. 7. If on such hearing the Court shall find that the person complained of is insane and a fit subject for treatment in an asylum, or that he ought to be confined, it shall make an order for his commitment to an asylum to be named in such order, there to be confined while such insanity continues or until he shall be discharged in due course of law, and commanding some suitable person to convey him to such asylum, and deliver him, with a copy of such order and of said certificates, to the keeper thereof. In appointing a person to execute such order, Courts shall give preference to a near relative or friend of the insane, so far as they shall deem it practicable and judicious.

*   *   *   *   *   *   *   *   *

Sec. 18.   The foregoing provisions of this act shall not extend to nor affect in any way the cases of persons convicted of or charged with crime as provided for in the following sections of the General Statutes, to wit: Sections 1600, 1601, 1602, 1603, 3385, 3386, 3615, 3617, 3618, 3619, 3620, and 3621, or any amendments thereof; nor shall they be construed as repealing Sections 487, 3683, and 3684 of the General Statutes, or any amendments thereof.

State of Connecticut.

REPORT

OF THE

COMMISSION APPOINTED BY THE GEN-
ERAL ASSEMBLY OF 1897 TO INVES-
TIGATE THE NECESSITY OF ADDI-
TIONAL ACCOMMODATIONS FOR THE
INSANE, ETC.

PRINTED BY ORDER OF THE LEGISLATURE.

HARTFORD PRESS:
THE CASE, LOCKWOOD & BRAINARD COMPANY.
1899.

The following resolution was passed at the last session of the General Assembly : " That Lucius Brown of Norwich, O. Vincent Coffin of Middletown, Amos J. Givens of Stamford, Clifford B. Adams of New Haven, Clinton E. Stark of Norwich, Patrick Cassidy of Norwich, and Edward B. Hooker of Hartford, be, and they are hereby, appointed a commission that shall serve without compensation, and whose duty it shall be to investigate the necessity of additional accommodations for the insane of this State, to consider the expediency of erecting new buildings for this purpose, to inquire into the desirability of the site which the people of Norwich have offered to give to the State for an asylum for the insane, to inquire into the desirability of any other site which any other town may propose to donate, and to report the result of their investigations to the next legislature at the beginning of its session."

The committee have to report the death of one of their number, Dr. C. B. Adams of New Haven, who has never been able to meet with them. They lament his decease and feel deeply the loss of his counsel and advice in reaching their conclusions.

The remaining members of the committee have performed their duties under said resolution, and beg leave to make the following report :

Statistics relating to the subject of the inquiry have been sought of every town in the State, and the committee have had several meetings and hearings which were concluded in December, 1898. They met the officers of the Middletown Hospital and examined that institution, which is a model institution in many respects, and is well conducted and most economically managed, but is overgrown, quite unwieldy, and very much overcrowded, for while in its normal condition it will not properly accommodate over 1,800 inmates, there were then over 1,900. This crowded condition is both unsafe and unsanitary. The directors present, as well as the acting superintendent, frankly admitted that they had 120 more than their full capacity ; they were then, as they of late years have always been, strongly opposed to any further enlargement of the present hospital. It was their unanimous opinion that all further accommodations for the insane should be provided elsewhere, and that immediate provision should be made, not only for the overcrowded ones there, but for the increase which must follow.

Learning, subsequently, that Dr. Page, the newly-elected superintendent, who has been in charge of the hospital since September 1, 1898, had a plan for the enlargement of the hospital, the committee again visited the hospital and conferred with Dr. Page on the subject, about the first of December, and he explained his plan of constructing a large congregate dining-room, where 1,500 or more patients could be massed together for their meals, claiming, thereby, a saving of expense, as well as a benefit to the patients, and that then many of the present ward dining-rooms could be given up for dormitories and additional accommodations furnished. He estimated the first cost of such changes to be one hundred thousand dollars, and might from time to time be further enlarged if desired.

While the hospital has now about $75,000 in the treasury, a portion of which, perhaps, might be used in the construction of such a dining-room, the committee do not feel it their duty to pass upon the question of the wisdom of such a measure. While authorities differ as to the success of congregate dining-rooms, your committee are decidedly of the opinion that a congregate dining-room should not, under any circumstances, be the means of increasing the present number of inmates at the hospital. They feel positive that the best work cannot be done when the number of inmates is so great. There are comparatively few hospitals in the country that are so large as the Middletown Hospital. Massachusetts has several hospitals, but none contain over 1,000 inmates.

The percentage of cures reported in our hospital is probably lower than in most like institutions, and it may be that the greater number of patients in one hospital has some bearing upon this question. Most authorities agree that the results are much more satisfactory where the superintendent can come frequently in contact with his patients; can study their peculiarities, and can cheer them by his presence in looking after each particular case, which is impossible to do with even 1,500.

They have endeavored to ascertain, through communications addressed to the selectmen in every town in the State, the present number of indigent insane not properly cared for, and not in the State Hospital; replies have been received from most towns and 336 cases are reported, which is, undoubtedly, an underestimate rather than the correct number. These reports show, also, that in many cases it has not been possible to get patients admitted to the hospital at Middletown for lack of room, and patients have been compelled to wait their turn before they could be received for treatment. This is unfortunate; for all authorities agree that the greatest hope for the cure of this unfortunate class is treatment in the very inception of the disease; many cases become chronic when neglected, in a few months and frequently in a few weeks, which, if taken in time, might, possibly, be permanently cured.

It is the part of economy, as well as a duty of the State, to furnish early treatment to this class of unfortunate citizens. It is computed the average life of the insane is twelve years; the present cost per week to the public for each inmate at Middletown is $2.80, and at this rate the total estimated expense of each incurable lunatic is $1,747. If they are cured not only is this expense saved the public, but that person becomes a producer again. The committee are, therefore, of the opinion that the present hospital should not be enlarged, either under the plea of economy or for any other reason;

that it is imperative that immediate steps should be taken to provide another institution at some other place. There are at present in the hospital 120 inmates more than can be properly cared for. There are reported to be in the towns at least 336 more. And our annual increase has averaged 64, so that at the end of two years,— the earliest possible date a new hospital could be built,— there would be a demand for accommodations for 600 insane.

Having reached this conclnsion, the committee visited Norwalk and Norwich and examined the sites for the erection of a hospital. Only these two towns have offered to donate⁴ land to the State for the purpose of a hospital. The sites offered each contain about 100 acres, and both are quite desirable locations. The Norwalk site consists of a farm under a high state of cultivation, with buildings on the line of a street railway ; but the land lies on different levels ; water and gas are accessible from the public highway ; spring water to a limited amount can be had by pumping.

It is a pretty and attractive spot, and much can be said in its favor. It would, however, be somewhat expensive to grade, and if more land should be required it would be quite high priced. It is on a hillside, which seems considerably springy, and on this account not so sanitary as a sandy soil.

The Norwich location is, however, in the mind of the comtee, an ideal spot for this purpose, and they would hardly expect to find its equal if they go over the entire State ; it is 2½ miles south of Norwich, on the east bank of the Thames river, and the outlook and view are beautiful. The subsoil is perfect for sanitary purposes ; a sandy, gravel bottom ; situated on the bank of the river, on a level 75 feet above the same, affording perfect drainage in tide water. The main portion of this tract is perfectly level, and no expense for grading would be required. There is a river landing at this point, and it is, also, on the line of the new branch of the N. Y. & N. H. R.R., between Norwich and New London, so that building material can be delivered either by land or water at its very door. There is on the rear of the premises an unlimited supply of the purest spring water, which would be very desirable for both culinary and fire purposes. This is 90 feet above the site for the building and 165 feet above the river. There is, also, quite a stream crossing the premises, which can be ponded for ice purposes, and would possibly furnish power for electric lighting; there is abundant material, also, on the premises for the foundation of buildings. Adjoining land can be obtained if desired in the future for tillage purposes for a moderate sum, probably not exceeding $40 or $50 per acre.

There is every reason for the construction of a hospital at some other point than Middletown. The trustees of this institution have said this a number of times in their former reports to the Legislature. The special committee appointed at the legislative session of 1890 to inquire into the necessity of further accommodations for the insane at Middletown or elsewhere, said—" that for the good of the patients themselves and as a matter of economy in the end to the State, such accommodations should be provided in some other locality."

Your committee, therefore, concludes that there is an immediate necessity that additional accommodations for the insane of the State be provided by the erection of a suitable building to accommodate at least 1,000 patients ; that such hospital should be established at a place other than Middletown, and that the Norwich site above described should be accepted for that purpose, and the construction of the building begun at once under such wise plans as will necessitate no extravagance, but shall give the best results with the least possible expense.

All of which is respectfully submitted.

LUCIUS BROWN,
AMOS J. GIVENS, M.D.
CLINTON E. STARK, M.D.
PATRICK CASSIDY.
EDWARD BEECHER HOOKER, M.D.

Minority Report.

So far as the foregoing report expresses opinions and presents arguments from the standpoint of experts, and so far
as it is claimed to be clear that the proposed changes at Middletown will not fairly meet the needs of the State for at least
five years to come, I find myself obliged, reluctantly and with
the utmost respect for the candor and capacity of the other
members of the commission, to non-concur in the conclusions
they have reached. It is true that I have, in common with
the trustees of the hospital at Middletown, supposed that the
plant there had already exceeded the limits within which the
most desirable results in promoting the welfare of the patients could be secured ; but the scheme of alteration which
has been recently suggested, in behalf of which very forcible,
and, if well founded, apparently conclusive arguments have
been adduced, has led to the conviction that the views hitherto held may require radical revision. The claim is made,
based apparently upon adequate practical observation and
experience, that the welfare of the patients, which is the point
of the first importance, would be promoted to a greater degree
by the proposed arrangement than is possible through the
establishment of another plant. Then it is urged, as a consideration next in importance to that of the welfare and
progress of the patients, that the cost to the State of carrying out the plans for proposed changes would be only a moderate fraction of that involved in the establishment of even
a comparatively small independent plant.

In view, therefore, of the fact that there appears to be a
possibility at least of gaining the ends at present desired to a
more successful extent and at far less cost, by making the
changes suggested, than by the adoption of the recommendations of my associates, it has seemed obligatory, from my
point of view, thus to state one side of the case, and beyond

that simply to commend the large and very important problem to the careful and thorough consideration and wise decision of the General Assembly.

I concur most heartily in all that is stated in the majority report as to the adaptability and beauty of the proposed site at Norwich. In many, perhaps all, important respects, it leaves nothing to be desired.

O. VINCENT COFFIN.

TABLE I.

Showing how much the New England Hospitals for Insane
have received from State treasuries, and their per capita
cost to the State, estimated upon the average number
of patients maintained in each, the last fiscal year. Also
the weekly per capita cost of maintaining State and Town
patients in each hospital.

	Average Number of Patients.	Received from State Treasury to Date.		Weekly Charge Per Capita.
		Amount.	Per Capita.	
Conn. Hospital for Insane,.	1870	$943,043	$504	$2.80
Northampton Hospital,....	546	630,550	.1,153	3.25
Worcester Hospital,........	871	1,211,576	1,391	3.25
Westboro Hospital,........	.564	Old reform school converted into Hospital.		3.25
Taunton Hospital,.........	781	731,519	936	3.25
Medfield Asylum,[1]........	974	1,040,000	1,067	2.99
Danvers Asylum,..........	871	1,979,050	2,272	3.25
Hospital, Concord, N. H.,[2].	413	248,000	600	4.00
Hospital, Waterbury, Vt...	505	377,000	746	3.30

Should the Connecticut Legislature, at its present session,
appropriate $100,000.00 to the Connecticut Hospital for
Insane, gross State appropriations would amount to $1,043,043.
By the time the appropriation could be expended, there
would be 2,000 patients in the Hospital.

	Average Number of Patients.	Received from State Treasury to Date.		Weekly Charge Per Capita.
		Amount.	Per Capita.	
Prospective Connecticut Hospital for Insane,.......	2,000	$1,043,043	$521	$2.80

(1) The Medfield Asylum in Massachusetts accommodates only chronic cases
transferred from the other hospitals. It was erected with a view to economical
construction and management.

(2) The Hospital for Insane at Concord, N. H., has, in addition to the $248,000.00
appropriated from the State Treasury, received large sums from private sources,
and has at present time a permanent fund amounting to about $300,000.00.

TABLE II.

Showing the per capita cost of medical service, of general service, of coal, heat, and lights, the last fiscal year, in the following named institutions — hospitals with which the Connecticut Hospital should be classed.

	Average Number of Patients.	Physicians' Salaries.		All other Salaries and Wages.		Tons of Coal consumed.		
		Amount.	Per Cap.	Amount.	Per Cap	Amount.	Per Cap.	
necticut Hospital r Insane,........	1,870	$10,122	$5.41	$67,407	$36.04	5,216	2.789	$1
imate for next year	1,925	14,300	7.44	Only slight increase expected.				
thampton Hosp.,..	546	5,096	9.33	32,483	59.49	1,762	3.226	1
rcester Hospital,..	871	10,344	11.87	51,248	58.83	2,222	2.556	1
stboro Hospital,..	564	6,000	10.63	43,763	77.59	1,779	3.154	1
nton Hospital,...	781	7,627	9.76	42,955	55.00	1,629	2.085	1
field Asylum,....	974	6,208	6.37	52,599	54.00	3,598	3.694	1
vers Hospital,....	871	7,564	8.69	57,261	65.74	2,350	2.684	1
p.,Concord, N.H.,	413	4,500	10.89	22,925	55.50	1,500	3.631	2
p.,Waterbury,Vt.,	505	6,106	12.09	33,080	66.50	2,870	5.685	2
pital, Utica, N.Y.,	1,014	12,000	10.84	84,773	83.60	4,833	4.766	1
p., Middlet'n,N.Y.	1,218	12,208	10.23	85,426	70.13	6,576	5.399	1
p., Morris Plains, . J., ...	1,058	8,250	7.79	62,075	59.15	5,000	4.725	1
p., Willard, N.Y.,	2,256	21,669	9 60	141,300	62.14	9,621	4.308	
Average,........			$9.35					

Hospitals at Northampton, Medfield, Utica and Willard light with electricity, generated on premises.

TABLE III.

INSTITUTION.	No. Pati-ents.	Meat, all kinds.	Fish, all kinds.	Flour.	Sugar and Mo-lasses.	Tea and Coffee.	Weekly per cap. Charge for main-tenance.
				Yearly per Capita cost of Food Material, 1897-'98.			
Middletown, Conn....	1,870	$16.49	$2.92	$5.88	$3.30	$2.64	$2.80
Northampton,......	546	11.20	2.37	7.59	4.28	1.87	3.25
Worcester, ...	871	15.01	3.49	7.81	4.98	2.35	3.25
Westboro, ...	564	14 85	2.87	8.34	3.57	2.34	3.25
Taunton,...	781	16.88	1.82	9.41	3.02	2.06	3.25
Medfield,..........	974	10.79	0.99	7 21	4.33	2.83	2.99
Danvers,...........	871	15.12	2.83	8.01	4.27	2.08	3.25
Concord, N. H.,....	413	29.78	6.02	6.17	6.27	3.30	4.00
Waterbury, Vt.,....	505	17.80	1.73	7.57	4.11	2.34	3 30
Utica, N. Y.,........	1,014	16.61	2.62	6.53	3.02	2.54	3.55
Middletown, N. Y.,..	1,218	18.04	1.80	5.40	3.36	1.74	3.55
Average,.........		$16.59	$2.67	$7.26	$4.04	$2.37	$3.31

To show conclusively the fact that the economy practiced at the Connecticut Hospital for Insane does not improperly and unwisely abridge the patients' food supply, Prof. Atwater's report, made after a careful, systematic record with necessary analyses of the food actually furnished our patients, is herewith appended.

"C. W. PAGE, M. D.,

"DEAR SIR:—The results of the dietary studies lately made in your institution are of decided interest. Although they were made in only two of the buildings, and continued for but a short time, I see no reason why they should not more or less fairly represent the usage of the establishment as a whole. From a physiological standpoint, the diet in the cases studied was ample in quantity, there was, I should say, an excess rather than deficiency of nutritive ingredients, and the food was every way wholesome and nutritious. The relative waste was considerably larger at the main building with twenty dining rooms than at the middle building with one large and three very small dining rooms. I think the hospital is to be congratulated upon the success in the feeding of its patients. Very truly yours,

"W. O. ATWATER.

"MIDDLETOWN, CONN., January 26, 1899."

13

TABLE IV.

Showing per cent. of patients discharged recovered, on total
number of patients admitted to State hospitals on
original certificates, from year ending September 30,
1889, to year ending September 30, 1897, from the Connecticut Hospital for Insane and the New York hospitals
— the only hospitals publishing this form of statistical
tables.

	Original Admissions.	No. Discharged Recovered.	Per Cent.
Connecticut Hospital for Insane,	2,610	798	30.5
Utica,...........................	2,614	882	33.3
Willard,.........................	2,305	414	18.
Hudson River,...	3,735	942	25 2
Middletown,....	2,510	931	37.1
Buffalo,..........	3,228	940	29.1
Binghamton,........ ....:	1,096	231	21.
St. Lawrence (from Sept. 30, '91).	1,893	456	24.1
Rochester,......	1,187	241	20.3
Long Island,....	4,764	975	20.5
Manhattan.,..................	14,002	1,602	11.4
Average,................			24 6

While the per capita cost for attendants at the Connecticut
Hospital for the Insane is much lower than at the other
hospitals named in Table II, patients requiring special care
and management are not neglected. Strait-jackets, muffs,
straps, etc., are not used here. Of the 1,930 patients in the
hospital at the end of January, 1899, but two were in
seclusion, and none were restrained by mechanical apparatus
applied to the person.

CPSIA information can be obtained
at www.ICGtesting.com
Printed in the USA
BVHW04*1446140918
527538BV00006B/49/P